Ann Lee Morgan works as an independent scholar in Princeton, New Jersey. She has taught art history at the University of Illinois at Chicago and worked in publishing as an editor of art reference books. She specializes in American art, particularly twentieth-century painting.

THE Oxford Dictionary OF American Art AND Artists

Ann Lee Morgan

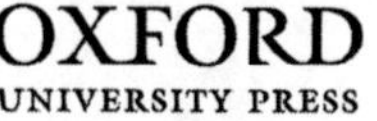

OXFORD
UNIVERSITY PRESS

OXFORD
UNIVERSITY PRESS

Oxford University Press, Inc., publishes works that further Oxford University's objective of excellence in research, scholarship, and education.

Oxford New York
Auckland Cape Town Dar es Salaam Hong Kong Karachi
Kuala Lumpur Madrid Melbourne Mexico City Nairobi
New Delhi Shanghai Taipei Toronto

With offices in
Argentina Austria Brazil Chile Czech Republic France Greece
Guatemala Hungary Italy Japan Poland Portugal Singapore
South Korea Switzerland Thailand Turkey Ukraine Vietnam

Published by Oxford University Press, Inc.
198 Madison Avenue, New York, NY 10016
www.oup.com

First published 2007
First issued as an Oxford University Press paperback 2008

Library of Congress Cataloging in Publication Data

Data available

ISBN 978-0-19-537321-9

Printed in the United States of America
on acid-free paper

For CWG,

light of my life,

and to the memory of JWM,

who showed the way.

Contents

Introduction ix

Entries, A–Z 1

Introduction

This concise guide to selected topics dating from colonial times through the present is intended to provide an up-to-date and informative reference for scholars, students, museumgoers, and others in the general public who take an interest in American art. In combination with the text's factual material, I hope my analytical discussions will enhance readers' appreciation for the nation's cultural history and for the creative accomplishments of its artists and tastemakers.

Most of the entries are biographical, while those that treat movements, terms, artists' associations, museums, and other institutions develop a context for individual achievement. The biographical essays cover painters, sculptors, printmakers, and photographers as well as artists of the contemporary period who work with new and mixed-media techniques. Additional entries treat critics, collectors, curators, art dealers, art historians, and others who have contributed to the evolution of American art. Each biographical entry provides a profile of the individual's life, including such standard information as birthplace, professional training, military service, travel, places of residence, and so forth. Place of death is generally given. When it is not, the essay indicates place of permanent residence, where readers may assume the person remained until the end of his or her life. While contributing to understanding of the subject's achievement, these biographical details may also reveal much about an individual's place in the social history of art.

For each artist, I have tried to characterize the visual nature of his or her work with descriptive and evaluative terminology that may in some cases stimulate readers to form different conclusions. I have also tried to provide some indication of what each has contributed to the ongoing dialogue of American art and/or why he or she has been regarded as an important figure. As appropriate, I have also tried to suggest the nature of professional or social relationships that sustained or otherwise affected careers. Frequently, figures so identified include spouses, children, or other family members. Their names, bold-faced for artists with the same surname or cross-referenced when they were known by a different last name, enlarge the pool of artists included in the book, while also affirming the importance of personal life within artistic practice. Although entries do not include bibliography, I have noted writings by the subjects themselves, as these may offer particularly pointed insights into their creative processes and aesthetic positions. Prizes, awards, honorary degrees and memberships, and other distinctions are not mentioned unless they denote special prestige or markedly affected the recipient's career.

Among nonbiographical subjects, I have included only those styles and movements that are particularly American in origin and/or in their full realization. Thus cubism, futurism, and surrealism do not appear, while abstract expressionism, pop art, and postmodernism do. Most of the technical terms relate to modern or contemporary practice. Since the mid-twentieth century, certain forms of expression have demanded innovative techniques, and many of these processes will be unfamiliar to readers not well versed in recent art. Thus, oil painting, engraving, and bronze-casting do not appear, but assemblage and installation art find a place. In somewhat of an exception, the photography entry describes basic forms of early photography, such as daguerreotype and dry-plate, because the technical development of the medium so strongly conditioned its aesthetic character and also because these processes are not widely understood today. Other nonbiographical entries deal with organizations and institutions active in the United States.

Generally, more prominent figures and topics rate longer entries. However, such factors as complex life histories, varied media, or eccentric careers may call for more discussion than would otherwise appear. Similarly, the art of those who worked outside the boundaries of commonly accepted styles or practices often requires more description and/or contextual evaluation.

Most of the subjects in this volume will be understood as obvious choices, but of course some required hard decisions. Within the publisher's constraints concerning length, it was not possible to accommodate any additional material. In difficult cases, preference went to artists who contributed to an evolving history, as opposed to others whose perhaps esthetically equal achievements were less known or found to be less interesting to contemporaries. I also tried to anticipate topics readers might want to look up. In this respect, even if not central to standard constructions of American art history, artists and movements had an edge if they have been the subjects of recent exhibitions or books, or have otherwise caught the public eye. Finally, I tried to give representative attention to broad-ranging tendencies, media, and movements. Thus, for example, I made a point of including major printmakers, especially those who participated in periods of revived interest in graphic arts, even though they are often less widely known than contemporary painters and sculptors. Likewise, I tried to maintain an evenhanded chronological representation of major currents in American art history.

In these multicultural times, readers may well wonder what constitutes "American" art. Ever in tension with European antecedents, American art finds its identity in emulating, adapting, and challenging Old World traditions and innovations as it variously reflects, sustains, or gives rise to native cultural, intellectual, and social tendencies. For the purposes of this book, anyone who held American citizenship during at least part of his or her life qualified as a candidate for inclusion. Foreigners who distinctly affected the course of American art during periods of residence appear in this volume, as do American-born expatriates whose example remained important at home. On the other hand, I have generally not included the many significant figures who in recent years have maintained studios in the United States, usually in New York, while also practicing in their home countries. Air travel and easy communication have given such artists an American presence, while they still remain widely regarded as representatives of their birth nations. In this overview of mainstream currents, I have not tried to incorporate the traditions of American Indians or of early Spanish influence in the Southwest. However "American," these subjects deserve consideration on their own terms. Trying to shoehorn them into this volume representing a continuously evolving Euro-American aesthetic could not do them justice.

Asterisked words or phrases point to other articles within the dictionary. These are marked at the first mention in each entry. To save space, I have avoided explaining terms or identifying artists that are cross-referenced to other entries. A number of artists who lack entries of their own are subsumed in subject entries. Their names appear as headwords in the alphabetical listing, with directions to see the appropriate topic. The proliferation of "isms" and new tendencies in twentieth-century art particularly recommended this practice. While outstanding minimalists and conceptualists, for example, are accorded individual entries, other leading figures are treated more briefly and with particular attention to the headword in question. For women artists, I have generally noted names of husbands because women have so often been recorded in some contexts under their husband's names. On the other hand, wives of male artists appear only if they, too, were artists or if they played some collaborative role, for example as writers, in their husbands' professional lives.

Illustrations of nearly all works mentioned in these pages may be found online, particularly at individual museum websites. For access to these images, most often the visitor to a museum homepage clicks on "collections" for search instructions. With few and unavoidable exceptions, I have discussed only works in public institutions, nearly all in the United States, in order to facilitate access to reproductions, online or in published form, as well as to the works themselves. The website artcyclopedia .com offers direct links to many works of art mentioned in this volume, as well as to images in other collections and additional useful features. It is searchable by artists' names.

Entries appear alphabetically, with order strictly maintained (regardless of spacing) up to the first punctuation mark. Thus, Chicago, Judy precedes Chicago Imagism; Cole, Thomas precedes Coleman, Glenn O.; and Kent, Rockwell precedes Kent Limner. Names beginning with Mc are alphabetized as if spelled Mac. Numerals in headwords are treated as if spelled out. Uncertain dates for which an established range of possibility exists are rendered with a slash indicating the earliest and latest possible dates, as for instance 1785/88. Dates not securely supported by historical evidence are preceded by c. (*circa*), as, for example, c. 1785. Unknown birth and death dates are represented by question marks.

As a rule, full names and locations of museums or other art repositories appear in parentheses following titles, with the following frequently appearing exceptions: Metropolitan Museum for Metropolitan Museum of Art, Whitney Museum for Whitney Museum of American Art, and Guggenheim Museum for Solomon R. Guggenheim Museum, all in New York; National Gallery for National Gallery of Art, Hirshhorn Museum for Hirshhorn Museum and Sculpture Garden, and Corcoran Gallery for Corcoran Gallery of Art, all in Washington, D.C., and Pennsylvania Academy for Philadelphia's Pennsylvania Academy of the Fine Arts, as well as Philadelphia Museum for Philadelphia Museum of Art. Appearing without their locations are the Museum of Modern Art in New York, the Smithsonian American Art Museum and the Phillips Collection in Washington, D.C., and the Yale University Art Gallery in New Haven, Connecticut. Shortened forms of museum names, as above, as well as the Museum of Modern Art's nickname, MoMA, are used for second and later references within the texts of individual articles.

As in any extended compilation of information, despite all efforts and precautions, errors and omissions may occur. I shall welcome any documentation readers may be able to supply to correct lapses in future editions.

Friends and family—above all, my husband, Bill Gear—have generously indulged my preoccupation with this project over several years. Eleven specialists who anonymously read portions of the manuscript for Oxford University Press contributed to factual correctness, sharpening of aesthetic and historical issues, and clear expression. I am particularly indebted to several who thoughtfully responded line by line to entries they read. Avis Berman, Audrey Lewis, and Daniel Schulman provided assistance with individual details. Without Wanda Corn, this project would probably never have happened. I am grateful as well to the larger Americanist community of art historians whose penetrating recent scholarship has informed so much of this compendium. Independent scholars of the Princeton Research Forum and companions in my Princeton book group have provided invaluable encouragement and friendship. Elda Rotor, who commissioned the book, remained patient with my progress while also providing apt counsel and good cheer. Although she left Oxford University Press shortly before the final manuscript was delivered, her successor, Cybele Tom, proved equally supportive as she offered essential advice on the final manuscript. Production editor Joellyn Ausanka ably supervised publication, while copy editor Mary Sutherland contributed with precision and intelligence to the text's final form. To all, I shall remain deeply appreciative.

Ann Lee Morgan
Princeton, New Jersey
May 2007

The Oxford Dictionary of American Art and Artists

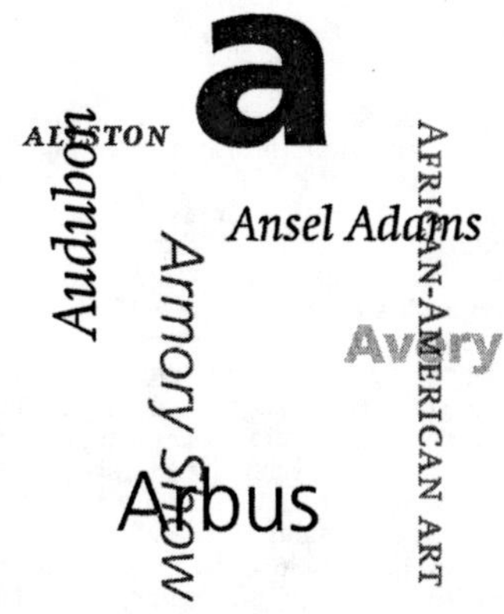

Abbey, Edwin Austin (1852–1911). Painter, illustrator, and printmaker. Known particularly for murals and book illustrations, he lived in England for most of his professional life and usually derived his subjects from British history or literature. His early, exacting realism, appearing mostly in historical *genre scenes, gave way during the 1890s to more symbolic, decorative pageantry with links to art nouveau stylization. Abbey was born in Philadelphia and as a teenager took night classes at the *Pennsylvania Academy of the Fine Arts. For the most part, he developed his professional skills while working as an illustrator in Philadelphia. In 1871, before he was twenty, he moved to New York to join the prestigious publishing enterprise Harper and Brothers. For nearly four decades, he produced drawings for the firm's illustrated books and magazines, while occasionally working for other publishers as well. Already smitten with British art and history, he departed in 1878 for England, ostensibly to verify details for assignments from Harper. However, he permanently made his home there and returned to the United States only for visits. Drawn to *Pre-Raphaelitism, he honed a precise manner suitable to the antiquarian appeal of his art and developed formidable skill in presenting his subjects in large exhibition watercolors. Encouraged by his friend Francis *Millet, he took up oil painting while working during the later 1880s in the Cotswold village of Broadway, Worcestershire, a burgeoning art colony. Around the same time, he embarked on his most ambitious commission from Harper, illustrating all of Shakespeare's plays. Extending over two decades, the heavily researched project encompassed books as well as magazine illustrations. It additionally inspired a number of oil paintings. In 1890 Abbey began work at the new Boston Public Library on his first significant mural project. Fifteen images illustrating the *Quest for the Holy Grail* (1890–1901) catapulted him into the first rank among American muralists and prompted commissions for numerous other decorative schemes. Two awards of 1902 confirmed Abbey's international standing. Although still an American citizen, he was tapped to create the official painting commemorating the coronation of Edward VII (Buckingham Palace, London, 1902–4). For his last important mural project, he was commissioned to embellish Pennsylvania's new state capitol, a vast undertaking completed under the supervision of his friend John Singer *Sargent only after Abbey's death in London.

Abbott, Berenice (1898–1991). Photographer. Besides views of New York and scientific images, she also created distinguished portraits. Born in Springfield, Ohio, Abbott grew up in nearby Columbus and in Cleveland. She enrolled for a semester at Ohio State University in Columbus but left in 1918 for New York, where she studied sculpture. In 1921 she departed for Paris to continue her training, most notably with sculptor Émile-Antoine Bourdelle. After a shorter period of additional study in Berlin, she returned to Paris, where she became an assistant to *Man Ray, a friend from New York. As he taught her photographic processes, she abandoned other artistic pursuits. In 1926 Abbott opened her own portrait studio. Photographing such luminaries as Jean Cocteau, Marcel *Duchamp, James Joyce, and André Maurois, she assembled a visual record of the personalities who created a charged moment in Paris's literary and artistic history. Not long after they became acquainted, she acquired the prints and negatives remaining in Eugène Atget's studio at his death in 1927. After her return to New York in 1929, she and Julien *Levy brought attention to these scenes of Paris and vicinity, rescuing from obscurity, perhaps oblivion, a premier photographic artist. Prompted by Atget's example, Abbott took New York as her subject in a decade-long enterprise that resulted in her most memorable work. As she had in portraits, Abbott aspired to capture not only the physical reality of her subjects but also their spirit. Departing from Atget's poetic nostalgia for his venerable city, Abbott celebrated New York's contemporaneity. Drawing on modern photographic devices, such as fragmentation, unconventional angles, and dramatic light, she produced sharply focused, energetic, often brittle images interpreting the city in terms of its uniquely twentieth-century aspects, ranging from skyscrapers to street life. After 1935 she received *federal art project support, and in 1939 a selection of the photographs appeared in *Changing New York*, with text by friend and art writer Elizabeth McCausland (1899–1965). From 1935 until 1958 Abbott taught at the New School for Social Research (now New School), establishing one of the earliest college-level photography programs. In the 1940s and 1950s she ingeniously photographed events illustrating physical principles. The skill that expedited this work resulted also in two books on photographic technique: *A Guide to Better Photography* (1941) and *The View Camera Made Simple* (1948). In 1966 Abbott moved permanently to rural Monson, Maine, on a lake northwest of Bangor, and two years later published *A Portrait of Maine*. She also wrote *The World of Atget* (1964) and compiled books of her scientific subjects.

Abercrombie, Gertrude. *See* CHICAGO IMAGISM.

Abstract expressionism. A form of art, predominately painting, characterized by large scale, nonrepresentational and nongeometric form, painterly technique, and asymmetrical, relational composition. Originating in New York during the 1940s, it soon became recognized as the leading form of advanced art. Although rooted in earlier European abstraction and surrealism, it represents the first American style to set an international standard of originality and accomplishment. Abstract expressionism initiated New York's replacement of Paris as the world center of contemporary art. The *New York School, which extended and modified abstract expressionism's achievements through the 1950s and beyond, demonstrated the power of the new approach to generate fresh options. Never a formal movement, abstract expressionism coalesced among painters who knew each other and interacted socially as well as aesthetically. The major abstract expressionists developed distinct, individualistic approaches, related less by style than by shared ambition for their art and rejection of existing models, which they found inadequate for expression of their psychic responses to the contemporary situation. Their self-conscious alienation from the provincialism and materialism of American life links their worldview to contemporary Existentialist philosophy. In struggling to locate sources of meaning beyond what they found within themselves, they turned often to myth or to universals thought to be encoded in arts of ancient or tribal people. While rejecting social and political messages, the abstract expressionists nevertheless assumed an ethical basis for their earnest, sometimes anguished, and always irony-free art. Indebted to the history of modern art, including the work of Kandinsky, Matisse, Miró, and Picasso, the abstract expressionists responded also to the presence in New York of a number of European artists who took refuge there during World War II. Max *Ernst, Fernand Léger, André Masson, Roberto *Matta, and Mondrian numbered among the most important. Earlier arrivals John *Graham and Hans *Hofmann also figured significantly in the movement's genesis.

Jackson *Pollock and Willem *de Kooning rank as the movement's most original and influential participants. Adolph *Gottlieb, Mark *Rothko, and Barnett *Newman composed the group's informal manifesto, published in 1943 in the *New York Times*. Most notably, it affirmed, "We favor the simple expression of the complex thought.... We are for flat forms because they destroy illusion and reveal truth.... We assert that the subject is crucial and only that subject-matter is valid which is tragic and timeless." Central figures also included Arshile *Gorky, Philip *Guston, Franz *Kline, Robert *Motherwell, and Clyfford *Still. Others who achieved authoritative personal styles include William *Baziotes, James *Brooks, Lee *Krasner, Conrad *Marca-Relli, Richard *Pousette-Dart, Theodoros *Stamos, Bradley Walker *Tomlin, and Jack *Tworkov. Roughly paralleling the painters' approach, the work of sculptors such as Herbert *Ferber, Ibram *Lassaw, Seymour *Lipton, Louise *Nevelson, and Theodore *Roszak often is considered abstract expressionist. The founding abstract expressionists forged their personal styles during the 1940s while working mostly in obscurity and near poverty. During the 1950s the movement found widespread recognition, not only within the art establishment but also among an interested public, and its leading practitioners began to achieve financial security. By about 1960 new tendencies challenged the movement's creative authority and soon eroded its appeal.

Some of the artists who became abstract expressionists met while working during the Depression on *federal art projects. Others became acquainted upon gravitating to the Greenwich Village area of Manhattan during and after World War II. Among their earliest joint efforts, an informal school called Subjects of the Artist also sponsored important lectures during its single season of operation in 1948–49. Founded by Baziotes, David *Hare, Motherwell, and Rothko on East Eighth Street, it included Newman as well on its faculty. In addition, two gathering places figured importantly in facilitating conversation, exchange of ideas, and camaraderie. Situated in the area where most of the artists worked, the Cedar Street Tavern on University Place between Eighth and Ninth Streets served as a nightly rendezvous until it closed in 1963. Formed late in 1949, an organization known simply as The Club rented an Eighth Street loft where members congregated informally. It also sponsored regular talks and panels that opened the way for vigorous aesthetic and philosophical argumentation. Sculptor Philip Pavia (1912–2005) ran the group until 1955 when John *Ferren took over for a year, followed by Irving *Sandler. It came to an end in 1962.

Although the term "abstract expressionism" had occasionally appeared earlier with respect to modern art, in 1946 *New Yorker* art critic Robert Coates (1897–1973) first applied it to advanced New York painting. Before long, the phrase came into general usage with its current meaning. The name aptly characterizes the desire of its practitioners to produce a nonreferential art of personal expression. Surrealism, however, provided more direct antecedents for abstract expressionism than did the figurative expressionist movement of the earlier twentieth century. In forming their styles, abstract expressionists particularly responded to surrealism's *biomorphic forms and its technique of automatism, which advocated expression of the unconscious directly through the artist's hand, without the mind's rational control. The abstract expressionists' reputation for vigorous, even violent, manipulation of paint gave rise to the term "action painting" to characterize their approach. Coined by Harold *Rosenberg in 1952 and subsequently in common usage, the phrase's usefulness is nevertheless limited to a subset of abstract expressionists whose brushwork suggests forceful and spontaneous movement of the brush across a canvas. The more general term "gesture painting" also is used to characterize abstract expressionists who boldly engage the materiality of paint. Like Rosenberg, Clement *Greenberg became a forceful spokesman for the movement, although the two were at odds over its meaning. Whereas Rosenberg located abstract expressionism's importance within the perceived cultural crisis of postwar civilization, Greenberg saw it primarily as an historically inevitable evolution of form toward realization of painting's material and formal essence.

With increasing momentum during the second half of the 1940s, an institutional infrastructure sympathetic to abstract expressionism developed in New York. Some of the earliest writing devoted to the group appeared in general magazines, including *The Nation* and *Partisan Review*. The first art publication to provide coverage, *Magazine of Art*, edited by Robert *Goldwater, turned its attention to the movement in 1948. *Art News* soon followed. Its editor from 1948, art writer Thomas B. Hess (1920–78), gave abstract expressionism the most enthusiastic coverage of any publication during the 1950s. As well, his book *Abstract Painting* (1951) ranks as the first to focus on abstract expressionists. After 1947 new, small-circulation magazines also spread the word. *Tiger's Eye* (which appeared nine times between 1947 and 1949), published by painter John Stephan (1906–95) and his poet-wife, Ruth, generally reflected the group's interests. The single issue of *Possibilities* (winter 1947–48), put together by such luminaries as Motherwell, Rosenberg, and John *Cage, contained statements by abstract expressionists and illustrations of their work. Although it found little to praise, in October 1948 even *Life* ran a serious article about the "young American extremists." In 1951 its coverage of a dispute between the artists and the *Metropolitan Museum of Art included a now famous photograph of fifteen *Irascibles, as they were dubbed in the picture's caption.

From the mid-1940s, exhibitions also contributed importantly to the movement's self-awareness and self-assurance, as well as to more general public knowledge of recent developments. As early as 1946, Gorky and Motherwell appeared in a group show at the *Museum of Modern Art. The first one-person museum show for an abstract expressionist, Hofmann's 1948 exhibition at the Addison Gallery of American Art, took place in Andover, Massachusetts, but an important catalogue documented the event for New Yorkers who did not attend. Until it closed in 1947, Peggy *Guggenheim's *Art of This Century ranked as a crucial venue for the movement's development. Subsequently, the galleries run by Betty *Parsons, Samuel Kootz (1898–1982), and Charles Egan (c. 1912–93) represented most of the blue-chip abstract expressionists. In 1951 the artists themselves organized the legendary "Ninth Street Show" of more than sixty aesthetically congenial spirits, including most of the movement's major figures. Besides its leaders, numerous other artists contributed to abstract expressionism's strength, variety, and quality. Other notable participants included Fritz *Bultman, Gerome *Kamrowski, Janet *Sobel, and Esteban *Vicente. A second generation of abstract expressionists, coming to maturity in the 1950s, included Grace *Hartigan, Joan *Mitchell, Milton *Resnick, and the Italian-born Angelo Ippolito (1922–2001).

Acconci, Vito (1940–). Performance artist, video artist, conceptual artist, installation artist, photographer, sculptor, and designer. Also a writer. In his best-known work, he used the actions and images of his own body to undermine social conventions and the hypocrisy that often surrounds them. Until the 1980s, most of his work was *performance-based, sometimes presented to a live audience but often recorded in *videos or photographs. His later sculptures, *installations, and other projects emphasize relationships between public and private experience. In 1962 Vito Hannibal Acconci graduated with a major in English from Holy Cross College in Worcester, Massachusetts. In 1964 he received an MFA in creative writing from the Writers' Workshop at the State University of Iowa (now University of Iowa) in Iowa City. Except for his student years, he remains a lifelong New Yorker. His early involvement with poetry, particularly, and other forms of literary endeavor prefigured the interest in language that marks his art. In 1969 he made his first visual works, a series combining photographs and texts. In these he investigated his own body in action, as he performed mundane movements, such as touching his toes. Soon he began to use video (or less often, silent film) to record private performances also centered on his body and sometimes imbued with masochistic overtones. In the early 1970s he gained notoriety for gallery performances, particularly *Seedbed* (1972). While lying in a narrow space beneath a low ramp built on the gallery floor, he projected the sound of his voice uttering sexual fantasies as he masturbated below the feet of visitors. Around 1974 the emphasis of his work shifted from such investigations of the psychological and physical self to his existence as a social being. In the 1980s he turned his attention to sculptures and installations, often inviting visitor participation, and with time he became less confrontational. In 1988 he founded Acconci Studio for collaborative work in community-oriented projects, architecture, and landscape design. *Vito Acconci: Writings, Works, Projects* appeared in 2002.

Action painting. *See* ABSTRACT EXPRESSIONISM.

Adams, Ansel (1902–84). Photographer. In majestic, highly detailed, and dramatic photographs of the American West, Adams created an exalted reality. The splendor of his images resonates with the long-held myth that the landscape, in its power, beauty, and sublimity, symbolizes the nation's greatness. An ardent conservationist, he remained long associated with the Sierra Club and its message of wilderness preservation. Although much of his work records vast spaces, he also sensitively rendered nature's intimate corners and sometimes produced close-ups of vegetation or geological features. On either scale, he masterfully captured transient effects of light, atmosphere, and sky. Adams brought to his photographic medium an exacting craft based on scientific knowledge. The first of several technical books, *Making a Photograph* (1935), anticipated classic manuals that followed. A crusader for unmanipulated photography, he taught and lectured widely. An outgoing personality complemented his knack for forthrightly articulating ideals and procedures. Technically, Adams is particularly known for developing a "zone system" of measuring light in order to capture a range of tones. This provided a precise and logical method of controlling patterns of light and dark. He advocated printing on glossy paper to enhance detail captured in the negative.

A native of San Francisco, as a youngster Ansel Easton Adams began photographing and embraced the Sierra Club's environmentalism but until the late 1920s aspired to become a classical pianist. His first visit to Yosemite, in 1916, presaged annual visits to the locale that provided subjects for his first professionally recognized photographs as well as a continuing source of inspiration. During the 1920s his images gradually evolved from a *pictorialist approach to the more direct method seen in the unfussy, classically composed images taken in 1929 for his first book, *Taos Pueblo* (1930), with text by Mary Austin. In 1930 he met Paul *Strand, who reinforced his continuing development toward lucid, detailed realism. Two years later Adams helped found the *f/64 group of like-minded straight photographers. Although Alfred *Stieglitz in his later years rarely presented new talent, in 1936 he recognized the special nature of Adams's vision with a one-person show at his New York gallery, An American Place. In 1941 the Department of the Interior commissioned a series of photomurals depicting various regions of the country. Public acclaim for these landscapes heralded the popular reputation he enjoyed for the rest of his life. In 1943 he undertook an atypical project, documenting the World War II Japanese internment camp at Manzanar, for the photo-essay *Born Free and Equal* (1944).

Few artists of the modern era have so successfully communicated with a nonspecialist audience while remaining uncompromisingly true to a personal vision and setting professional standards of craftsmanship. His work reached a wide audience in book form after the Sierra Club issued, as the first in its series of distinguished picture-book publications, his collaboration with Nancy *Newhall, *This Is the American Earth* (1960), illustrated mainly with his images. *These We Inherit: The Parklands of America* followed from the Sierra Club in 1962. Among his other books are *Photographs of the Southwest* (1976), *Yosemite and the Range of Light* (1979), *Examples: The Making of 40 Photographs* (1983), and the posthumously published *Ansel Adams: An Autobiography* (1985), left unfinished but completed by Mary Street Alinder. At his death in a Monterey peninsula hospital near his home in Carmel, California, the nation lost the last major artist of the romantic, optimistic, unironic landscape tradition that figured as a central feature of American art for more than a century and a half.

Adams, Clinton. *See* TAMARIND LITHOGRAPHY WORKSHOP.

Adams, Herbert (1858–1945). Sculptor. A major figure in the *American Renaissance, he is known particularly for portraits and allegories in the spirit of fifteenth-century Italian or French precedents. Born in West Concord, Vermont, Herbert Samuel Adams grew up in Fitchburg, not far from Boston, where he studied at the Massachusetts Normal Art School (now Massachusetts College of Art). In Paris he trained at the École des Beaux-Arts with Antonin Mercié. A deftly carved marble bust of his future wife, *Adeline Valentine Pond* (Hispanic Society of America, New York, 1887), demonstrates mastery of contemporaneous French taste for elegant naturalism and the impression of spontaneity. It also prefigures the numerous Renaissance-inspired, idealized likenesses of attractive women that remain his best-known works. Returning in 1890 after five years abroad, he settled permanently in New York. Several years later, he began summering regularly in Cornish, New Hampshire. Reflecting his involvement with ideals of the *aesthetic movement, Adams often innovatively emphasized the decorative aspect of his works, particularly the female busts, by tinting his marble (or choosing colored variants) and adding ornamental elements of wood, metal, or semiprecious stones. While it suggests also the influence of Augustus *Saint-Gaudens, the portrait relief *Singing Boys* (Metropolitan Museum, 1894) directly recalls works by Donatello and Luca della Robbia. Several sets of bronze doors similarly demonstrate his creative allegiance to Renaissance examples. In addition to such work conceived on a relatively small scale, he successfully completed numerous architectural adornments and freestanding monuments, including the bronze William Cullen Bryant (1911) in Bryant Park, behind the New York Public Library. His wife, art writer **Adeline Adams** (1859–1948), is best remembered for *The Spirit of American Sculpture* (1923). She also produced several monographs on individual artists, published numerous articles on art, and wrote short stories and poetry. Born in Boston, she began art studies at the Massachusetts Normal Art School in 1880. Following a brief teaching stint and further study in Paris, she married in 1889. She died in New York.

Adams, Robert (1937–). Photographer. His black-and-white landscapes dispassionately picture the American West but respect its inherent grandeur. Adams's detached aesthetic, concern with formal structure, and disinterest in self-expression or interpretation parallel similar tendencies in *minimal, *conceptual, and *pop art. For a few years beginning in 1976, Leo *Castelli represented his work in New York. Although the practice is common today, Adams numbers among the earliest photographers to be accepted in a major contemporary art gallery. Born in Orange, New Jersey, near Newark, Robert Hickman Adams moved as a child with his family to Madison, Wisconsin, and then to Denver, where he went to high school. After graduating in 1959 from the University of Redlands, he remained in the Los Angeles area to earn a PhD in English at the University of Southern California. By the time he completed the degree in 1965, he was already teaching English at Colorado College in Colorado Springs. He remained there until 1970, when he moved to Longmont, near Boulder, to work professionally as a photographer. In 1997 he settled in Astoria, Oregon, on the Pacific coast. In early work emphasizing the social landscape, he pictured architecture and interiors as well as outdoor suburban views. These photographs first came to national attention with his book *The New West: Landscapes Along the Colorado Front Range* (1974), an implicit indictment of environmentally degrading Denver-area development practices. As he subsequently pulled back to capture less densely populated areas, he frequently included signs of human impact such as telephone poles, roads, or logging operations. With time, inaccessible wilderness and impassive sea have come to dominate his vision. Often accompanied by his own texts, his numerous publications include *Denver* (1977), *Prairie* (1978), *From the Missouri West* (1980), *Our Lives and Our Children* (1983), *West From the Columbia* (1995), and *Turning Back* (2005), stimulated by the bicentennial of the Lewis and Clark expedition. *Beauty in Photography* (1981) and *Why People Photograph* (1994) collect his essays.

An important 1975 exhibition and accompanying catalogue positioned Adams as a leading figure within an emerging photographic tendency de-romanticizing the tradition of Ansel *Adams and others who situated physical and spiritual grandeur in an inviolable nature. Organized by William Jenkins for the International Museum of Photography (now George Eastman House International Museum of Photography and Film) in Rochester, New York, "New Topographics—Photographs of a Man-Altered Landscape" stressed the inseparability of cultural and natural processes in forming the visual environment. Besides German photographers Bernd and Hilla Becher, others identified with the trend included important young Americans, such as Lewis Baltz (1945–), Frank Gohlke (1942–), Nicholas *Nixon, and Stephen Shore (1947–).

Aesthetic movement. Term designating late-nineteenth-century enthusiasm for opulent arts and handcrafts, especially within a domestic context. Advocating beauty as a touchstone for every aspect of life, it grew from the critique of mass production that spawned the related but more socially conscious *Arts and Crafts movement. Instead, the aesthetic movement subscribed to the philosophical aestheticism of art for art's sake. Valuing rich visual and associative effects, its products often found inspiration in exotic or historic cultures. Complex visual spectacle, uninhibited patterning, and luxurious ornamentation stand among characteristic features. Because the movement advocated orchestration of entire interiors, the demand it generated for luxury handcrafts intensified creativity in the design and production of ceramics, metalwork, wallpapers, furniture, and other components of home decor. Many artists turned to such media or provided congenial paintings, sculpture, or prints. Drawing on precedents in Europe, particularly England, the aesthetic movement gained widespread popularity in the wake of Philadelphia's Centennial Exposition of 1876. Many artists regarded decorative arts as progressive alternatives to academically sanctioned forms of art. As well, the movement's goals spurred collaborations among artists intent on fusing varied media into visually coherent wholes. Although sometimes capricious, the aesthetic movement at its best represented an eclectic search through history and nature for unity. Frederic *Church's Olana represents with exceptional clarity such a quest. Other artists who contributed to the aesthetic movement include William Merritt *Chase, Thomas Wilmer *Dewing, John *La Farge, Louis Comfort *Tiffany, Elihu *Vedder, and James Abbott McNeill *Whistler.

Aetatis Suae Painter. *See* PATROON PAINTERS.

African-American art. Term designating art made by Americans of African descent. Compounding the record of neglect that has marked other aspects of American history, the work of black artists has often been excluded from historical accounts. Nevertheless, African-American artists and artisans have been active since colonial days. Until the early twentieth century, African Americans generally worked within and contributed to prevalent styles and themes of their day, despite sensibilities sometimes partially at odds with white culture. Black artists of the nineteenth century include portrait painter Joshua *Johnson and landscape painters Edward M. *Bannister and Robert S. *Duncanson, as well as sculptor Edmonia *Lewis. Painter Henry Ossawa *Tanner, whose career spanned the turn of the century, ranks as the first African-American artist to secure an international reputation. Important social changes around the time of World War I led to a new consciousness of racial identity and, soon, racial pride. In the arts, the *Harlem Renaissance flowered, and for a few years black art interested white as well as black audiences. Black life became for the first time a major subject for the visual arts, and strenuous debate first broke out over the issue of a separate black aesthetic. Alain *Locke served as the leading theorist of the Harlem Renaissance, while Aaron *Douglas played a pivotal role in defining the dimensions of its visual art and James *Van Der Zee provided the principal photographic record. Other major artists who emerged during the 1920s and 1930s include Richmond *Barthé, Romare *Bearden, Selma *Burke, Beauford *Delaney, Palmer *Hayden, W. H. *Johnson, Lois Mailou *Jones, Jacob *Lawrence, Archibald *Motley, Augusta *Savage, and Hale *Woodruff. Employing both African and modern European stylistic devices in interpreting black life, Malvin Gray Johnson (1896–1934) showed great promise as a painter before his early death. San Francisco–based sculptor Sargent Johnson (1887–1967) combined Mexican, Asian, and African influences in work that frequently addressed African-American themes. He drew inspiration at an early age from his aunt, the portrait sculptor May Howard Jackson (1877–1931). Painter and sculptor Charles Alston (1907–77) worked in both figurative and abstract styles while he also pursued an important career as a teacher for the *federal art projects in Harlem, at the *Art Students League (the first black instructor, he taught there for more than twenty years), and as a full professor at City College of New York. James Lesesne Wells (1902–93) produced powerful prints, primarily woodcuts and other reliefs.

Support for Harlem Renaissance artists diminished during the Depression, and World War II largely extinguished the movement. Nevertheless, during the postwar years, a number of important African Americans came to prominence. They included Elizabeth *Catlett, Hughie *Lee-Smith, Alma *Thomas, and James *Weeks. Painter and printmaker Eldzier Cortor (1916–), who brought a romantic sensibility to his depiction of black life, is known for paintings of idealized women, often shown in settings that suggest their circumscribed environments. Norman Lewis (1909–79) left behind his early figurative approach to become the only prominent African-American painter among the first generation of *abstract expressionists. During the civil rights era, black art regained a level of visibility it has not since experienced. The question of a distinctive black sensibility again flared, especially within the Spiral group, which flourished for about two years after its founding in 1963 in Bearden's studio. Other members included Alston, Lewis, Woodruff, and Emma Amos (1938–), known for expressionist paintings and prints on political and feminist themes. Briefly, Spiral operated a gallery, but that enterprise as well as the group itself foundered on implacable issues surrounding the black artist's identity within a white-dominated society. Charles White (1918–79), among the finest draftsmen of his generation in the United States, reached the height of his powers in images related to the 1960s civil rights struggle, which he conceptualized as part of a universalized hunger for freedom and dignity. As idealistic agitation for civil rights evolved into a black power movement in the late 1960s and early 1970s, blacks and whites alike lost interest in sustaining the recently opened dialogue. In recent years, however, more blacks have participated on an individual basis in mainstream art. Robert *Colescott, Faith *Ringgold, silhouette artist Kara Walker (1969–) and photographer Carrie Mae Weems (1953–) have located their African-American heritage at the center of their creative identities, while Sam *Gilliam and abstract painter and collage artist Al Loving (1935–2005) number among those who have not. Many outstanding artists remain committed to their African-American heritage within an American sensibility that engages both white and black audiences. Among these, sculptor and printmaker Melvin Edwards (1937–) is known for abstract welded sculptures, particularly more than two hundred Lynch Fragments, a series initially inspired by the civil rights movement and continued intermittently since 1963. In these wall-mounted pieces, he combines metal objects such as tools, chains, and industrial cast-offs into powerfully composed, abstract metaphors for oppression, resistance, and endurance. Born in Houston, Edwards attended Los Angeles City College and the Los Angeles Art Institute (now Otis College of Art and Design) before earning a BFA at the University of Southern California. Beginning in 1972, he taught for many years at Rutgers University in New Brunswick, New Jersey. As a printmaker, he has worked with etching, lithography, and other processes to address through images as well as abstraction his ongoing exploration of psychological and social identity.

Like Edwards, painter Raymond Saunders (1934–) works primarily with abstract form but achieves more lyrical expression. Often enlivened with collage elements, many Saunders paintings offer elusive, fragmentary images drifting in fields of seductive color, evoking the processes of consciousness. Others seem less introspective, explicitly acknowledging popular culture, urban realities, and black identity while maintaining a perspective rooted in all human experience. Born in Pittsburgh, Raymond Jennings Saunders studied at art schools in the Philadelphia area before earning a BFA degree from Pittsburgh's Carnegie Institute of Technology (now Carnegie-Mellon University). He also received an MFA from Oakland's California College of Arts and Crafts (now California College of the Arts), where he has been on the faculty since 1988. Previously, he taught for twenty years at California State University in nearby Hayward.

Sculptor, *assemblage artist, and printmaker Betye Saar (1926–) draws on autobiographical experience, the passions of the civil rights movement, the survival of her people, and broad appreciation of traditional crafts as well as fine arts. She first came to national attention with such bitingly satirical works as the mixed-media *Liberation of Aunt Jemima* (University of California, Berkeley Art Museum and Pacific Film Archive, 1972), which outfits the African-American mammy with emblems of the black power movement. In the late 1960s, the work of Joseph *Cornell stimulated her adoption of the boxlike framing device for this and many other, often more enigmatic works that address community, continuity, feminism, and the spiritual values encoded in used or discarded objects. The shrinelike aura of the boxes extends as well into freestanding assembled works, which often bear overtones of ritual and commemoration. Born in Los Angeles, Betye Brown at an early age admired Simon *Rodia's Watts Towers near her grandparents' home. She graduated from UCLA in 1949 and three years later married artist, designer, and art conservator Richard W. Saar (1924–2004). They divorced in 1968. Two artist-daughters, both born and raised in Los Angeles, extend their mother's fascination with material culture and its meanings. Both address their experiences as biracial women (their mother is of mixed ancestry, while their father was white) seeking meaning in a contemporary context, as they variously examine popular culture, mythic archetypes, natural phenomena, and other avenues of understanding. Alison Saar (1956–) works mostly as a sculptor and assemblage artist. Since the mid-1980s she has focused on freestanding figures, or parts of bodies, usually carved and then layered and elaborated with other materials to provide visual richness and amplify meaning. In 1978 she graduated from Scripps College in Claremont and three years later received an MFA from the Otis Art Institute (now Otis College of Art and Design). Lezley Saar (1953–) combines mixed-media techniques with painting and collage, often incorporating books or their covers. She graduated in 1978 from California State University at Northridge.

David Hammons (1943–), *installation artist, sculptor, *conceptual artist, and *performance artist, extracts poetry, humor, and irony from the detritus of civilization. Claiming that Harlem is as rich in ruins as Rome, he scavenges, reclaims, builds, and discards in the service of a sly vision. In the early 1960s he left his native Springfield, Illinois, for Los Angeles. After a year at Los Angeles City College, he took classes at the Otis Art Institute and attended the Chouinard Art Institute (now California Institute of the Arts) but developed little regard for conventional art education. Instead, he has drawn on oppositional precedents in dada and outsider creations, Italian Arte Povera, African tribal sculpture, and the improvisatory structure and heartfelt spirit of jazz, as well as the work of Edwards, White, Bruce *Nauman, and Simon Rodia. In the late 1960s and into the 1970s, he produced body prints by taking impressions of his own oiled body, or parts of it, which he pressed against hard surfaces and then dusted with pigment. Among the most politically charged, *Injustice Case* (Los Angeles County Museum of Art, 1973) shows his clothed body in profile, bound to a chair and gagged with a cloth tied across his upturned face. He moved to New York in 1974, after beginning his *junk sculptures from found materials, which have included discarded whiskey bottles, hair, and elephant dung. His performance pieces have included such gestures as selling snowballs on the street in 1983. A visit to Kyoto's Zen gardens, where he has said he observed many kinds of nothingness, inspired an evocative 2002 gallery installation. *Concerto in Black and Blue* comprised several darkened rooms made visible only by tiny blue pinpoint flashlights carried by visitors.

Conceptual artist, sculptor, printmaker, and *video artist Fred Wilson (1954–) specializes in rearranging museum collections to expose previously suppressed biases in institutional display. A lifelong New Yorker (except for grade school days in a Westchester County suburb), he received a BFA from the State University of New York at Purchase in 1976. In 1992 he first gained widespread attention with "Mining the Museum," a temporary exhibition at the Maryland Historical Society in Baltimore. Drawing attention to the effects of presentation on meaning, he rearranged artifacts and introduced new items from storage to highlight the museum's neglect of the city's slave history. By introducing an anthropological point of view, for example labeling as "metalwork" a vitrine containing slave shackles and an ornate silver tea service, he introduced a wry critique of conventional expectations within a museum setting. He has also created public art works, as well as independent installations in galleries and museums. In 1999 he received a MacArthur Foundation "genius" grant, and in 2003 he represented the United States at the Venice Biennale.

Africano, Nicholas. *See* NEW IMAGE PAINTING.

A.I.R. Gallery. *See* SLEIGH, SYLVIA.

Akers, Benjamin Paul. *See* STEBBINS, EMMA.

Albers, Josef (1888–1976). Painter, printmaker, designer, photographer, and color theorist. In more than a thousand paintings titled *Homage to the Square*, luminous, nested squares occupy the larger square of the support. Within this simple format begun in 1950, he achieved great optical and emotional range. His color combinations cause the interior squares of these paintings variously to recede, project, or hover, producing effects of almost mystical intensity. An idealist but also a craftsman at heart, Albers discounted self-expression in art. Among the most important art teachers of the postwar period, he also proved a seminal influence on a wide range of artists who worked with color and/or reductive form during the 1950s and 1960s. Born in Bottrop, in the Ruhr industrial area of Germany, Albers taught school and studied art in Berlin, Essen, and Munich before entering the Bauhaus at Weimar in 1920. From 1923 he served on the teaching staff as it moved to Dessau and Berlin. When the school closed in 1933, he accepted a position at *Black Mountain College, where he taught until 1949. Among the first Bauhaus masters to arrive in the United States, he played an instrumental role in introducing its teaching methods to this country. He became a United States citizen in 1939. During the 1950s he taught at Yale University, serving as head of the art program for the first eight years. He died in a New Haven hospital, not far from his home in Orange, Connecticut, where he had lived since 1970. Besides the paintings and prints for which he is best known, Albers also produced sculpture, murals, photographs, and furniture designs. During his years in Germany, he worked extensively with glass, a practice that honed his sensitivity to light and color. In the early 1920s he mounted irregular pieces of glass on metal sheets to make abstract arrangements with the opulence of early medieval reliquaries. Later, he worked with rectilinear forms in simple color compositions often made by sandblasting areas of opaque flashed glass to produce patterns of transparency and hue. He also designed stained glass windows. Except for rare commissions, he did not work in glass after moving to the United States. Instead, he turned to oil painting, which had not previously interested him. His sustained and methodical investigation of perception and color culminated in his series limited to the square. Yet, sustaining a lyric delicacy, relishing ambiguity, these works address emotions as well as intellect. *Interaction of Color* (1963) remains the most important of his writings, which included a volume of poetry.

His wife, textile artist and printmaker **Anni Albers** (1899–1994), was born in Berlin and first studied art in Hamburg. Anneliese Fleischmann entered the Bauhaus as a student in 1922, married in 1925, and subsequently taught at the school. Along with her husband, she moved to the United States, became a citizen, and joined the Black Mountain faculty. Her weavings reflect a sophisticated understanding of modern abstract design. In the United States, she also incorporated influences from pre-Columbian textiles. Among pioneers who took weaving into the realm of the fine arts, in 1949 she ranked as the first textile artist to have a one-person show at the *Museum of Modern Art. The tapestry *Ancient Writing* (Smithsonian American Art Museum, 1936) vibrates with the formal and coloristic subtlety of a Paul Klee painting. In 1963 she took up printmaking, which by 1970 had gradually supplanted weaving as her primary activity. She died in Orange, where she had continued to reside after her husband's death. She published two books, *Anni Albers: On Designing* (1959) and *Anni Albers: On Weaving* (1965).

Albright, Ivan Le Lorraine (1897–1983). Painter, printmaker, draftsman, and occasional sculptor. Known for obsessively detailed hyperrealism and a grotesque slant on life, he generally focused on individual figures or still lifes, or the two in combination. Most of Albright's paintings describe a world where decrepitude, disintegration, and incomprehension prevail, and where death lingers nearby. In *That Which I Should Have Done I Did Not Do* (Art Institute of Chicago, 1941), a hand rests on the jamb of an ornate but decaying doorway where a somber funeral wreath imparts a tone of regret and melancholy. The artist's use of long, poetic titles suggests his literary inclinations (he also wrote poetry), as do some of his themes. Albright was born near Chicago and spent much of his life in the area. After studying architecture at Northwestern University and the University of Illinois for two years, in 1917 he became a medical illustrator at an army hospital in France, where he recorded soldiers' World War I injuries. After his return, he studied at the School of the Art Institute of Chicago from 1920 to 1923, followed by an additional year at the *Pennsylvania Academy of the Fine Arts and the *National Academy of Design.

With time, Albright's early style of meticulous realism intensified toward exaggerated effects. *Fleeting Time Thou Has Left Me Old* (Metropolitan Museum, 1930), a half-length portrait of a middle-aged, contemplative working man, already emphasizes the ravages of aging. In later work, flesh took on a putrid quality, with every wrinkle and blemish magnified. Lighting became more dramatic, often including violent contrasts of light and dark. Color, expertly manipulated from lurid to garish, enhanced his ghoulish effects. Albright attained wide public acclaim for his *Picture of Dorian Gray* (Art Institute of Chicago), painted for the 1943 Hollywood film based on Oscar Wilde's story of the same name. In this appalling parody of the full-length formal portrait, Dorian Gray appears to be succumbing to rot even as he poses for the artist. Enhancing the sense of disintegration, the figure nearly merges into a surrounding environment of overwrought forms. Critics have sometimes classified Albright's idiosyncratic work within the tendency known as *magic realism. At the same time, while his taste for the bizarre overlaps a similar predilection among some surrealists, his sense of form and drama are more closely related to Baroque painting. Ultimately, Albright's sensibility finds its true community among such expressions as Mathis Grünewald's sixteenth-century religious meditations, Romantic-era horror tales, and early works by an admirer, French artist Jean Dubuffet, as well as in certain more recent works by Edward *Kienholz, Cindy *Sherman, and photographer Joel-Peter Witkin (1939–). At forty-nine, Albright married Chicago newspaper heiress, writer, animal lover, and aviator Josephine Medill Patterson and separated for the first time from his identical twin, painter and sculptor **Malvin Marr Albright** (1897–1983), who never married. The couple traveled widely before settling permanently Woodstock, Vermont, in 1963. The work of his final years includes a memorable series of probing self-portraits. His twin, Malvin (also known as Zsissly), trained at the Art Institute and the Pennsylvania Academy but also studied in France. He died in Warrenville, not far from Chicago. Both brothers received early instruction from their father, **Adam Emory Albright** (1862–1957), who painted portraits, landscapes, and *genre scenes. Born in Monroe, Wisconsin, he studied at the Art Institute, at the Pennsylvania Academy with Thomas *Eakins, and in Paris. He, too, died in Warrenville.

Alexander, Cosmo. *See* STUART, GILBERT.

Alexander, John White (1856–1915). Painter. Remembered for idealized figural works, he also painted portraits, murals, still lifes, and a few landscapes. His best-known painting, *Isabella and the Pot of Basil* (Museum of Fine Arts, Boston, 1897), depicts a languid beauty mourning her dead beloved. With its sinuous art nouveau rhythms, mysterious shadows, and enigmatic mood, it numbers among the artist's most elegant and evocative works. Inspired by a John Keats poem, the theme relates to late-nineteenth-century symbolist interests in death, extreme psychological states, and female suffering. Born in Allegheny City, now part of Pittsburgh, Alexander left in 1875 for New York, where he worked as an illustrator. Two years later he sailed for Europe. While studying at the Royal Academy in Munich he became acquainted with Frank *Duveneck. In 1879 he accompanied the older painter and his student entourage to Italy. In Venice he became a lifelong friend of James Abbott McNeill *Whistler, whose work initiated the redirection of Alexander's painting from a painterly realism characteristic of Munich to a more refined formalism. After returning to New York in 1881, he again worked as an illustrator but also established a reputation for portraits. In conformity with prevailing standards, Alexander normally emphasized a strong likeness for male sitters, but in images of women, whether portraits or ideal figures, stressed decorative aspects such as color harmony, pattern, and ornamental accessories. In addition to visiting the West in 1883, he had again traveled abroad on two occasions before moving in 1891 to Paris for a decade. There, renewed contact with Whistler stimulated the heightened aestheticism of such works as *Isabella and the Pot of Basil*. In the mid-1890s he completed a prestigious commission for six lunettes illustrating the *Evolution of the Book* in Washington, D.C.'s, new Library of Congress. After permanently resettling in New York, while continuing to paint murals and increasingly conventional figure compositions, Alexander also designed sets and costumes for theatrical productions and devoted much energy to activities benefiting the American art community. From 1909 until two months before his death, he served as president of the *National Academy of Design.

All-over painting. Term referring to nongeometric abstract paintings featuring relatively uniform surfaces and no obvious references to directional format or traditional structure. Such compositions generally lack centers of interest and regard for edges. In dripped and poured works of the 1940s, Jackson *Pollock ranked as the earliest major practitioner. Other *abstract expressionists also made such paintings, as did their contemporary Mark *Tobey. More recently, some works by Cy *Twombly and others continue the mode.

Alloway, Lawrence. *See* SLEIGH, SYLVIA.

Allston, Washington (1779–1843). Painter. Also a writer. The first important artist working in the United States to embody a personal, *romantic point of view in his work, he ranks also among the first to acquire a sophisticated understanding of old master technique. The fountainhead of a visionary, meditative strain in American art, Allston through his personal example did much to revise the popular notion of the artist from artisan to creative genius. In addition, his landscapes presaged and helped to inspire the dominant preoccupation of many later American painters. For all that, Allston remains a somewhat isolated figure in American art history. His lyrical, poetic, and fundamentally literary temperament remained singular, while his visual and intellectual understanding of both the European heritage and contemporary romantic theory stood beyond the reach of most American artists. Born into a landowning South Carolina family whose Low Country estates extended along the Waccamaw River near the seaport of Georgetown, he received his earliest education in Charleston. Before he was eight, he was sent to a classical preparatory school in Newport, Rhode Island. In 1800 he graduated with honors from Harvard (where he was class poet). Thereafter he continued to make his home in the area, where his intellectual gifts were appreciated among the educated elite that distinguished Boston. In May 1801 he sailed with Edward Greene *Malbone to London. There he became a student of Benjamin *West at the Royal Academy, absorbed technical know-how, and set his sights on becoming a painter of grand themes in the old master tradition. In the fall of 1803, he traveled to Paris. At the Louvre he was able to study for the first time the painterly style that became his own: the tradition of the Venetians and Rubens, with its rich effects of light and color and its ineffable melding of paint and image. Inspired by the masterpieces at hand as well as his memories of J. M. W. Turner's seascapes, he produced his first major work, *The Rising of a Thunderstorm at Sea* (Museum of Fine Arts, Boston, 1804), also the first dramatic nature painting by an American. In the fall of 1804, Allston continued on to Italy. In four years there, spent mostly in Rome, he gained the respect of the large art community with his landscapes, classical subjects, and portraits. Nicknamed "the American Titian," he established close friendships with the English poet Samuel Taylor Coleridge and American writer Washington Irving.

In the spring of 1808, Allston returned to Boston for three years. During this time, he married the sister of Unitarian theologian and abolitionist William Ellery Channing, painted many of his finest portraits, including one of his new brother-in-law (Museum of Fine Arts, Boston, 1809–11), and wrote most of the poetry for *The Sylphs of the Seasons, with Other Poems* (1813). A reverie from this period, *Coast Scene on the Mediterranean* (Columbia [South Carolina] Museum of Art, 1811) fuses his study of the luminous apparitions of Claude Lorrain with observations of contemporary Italian life. Allston again sailed in 1811 for England, where he remained—except for a six-week excursion to Paris in 1817—until his return to Boston in 1818. Presumably attracted by the richer art life of the English capital and the larger audience for ambitious painting, Allston soon resumed his friendships with British writers and artists and extended his circle of acquaintances to include such prominent figures as Wordsworth and the imaginative painter John Martin. Allston's standing within the English art community was confirmed in 1813 when his monumental, 13 × 11-foot work on a supernatural theme, *The Dead Man Revived by Touching the Bones of the Prophet Elisha* (Pennsylvania Academy, 1811–14), won a major prize, notwithstanding anti-American feeling during the War of 1812. Moreover, the Philadelphia museum's purchase of this work in 1816 for the highest price paid to that date for an American painting underlines Allston's reputation as a history painter among his countrymen. More accessible to later taste are smaller and more personal works of these years. In the finest, *Elijah in the Desert* (Museum of Fine Arts, Boston, 1818), the Old Testament prophet's affecting predicament is amplified by a vast and barren landscape.

In 1817, before his return to Boston, Allston embarked upon an enormous narrative work that he must have hoped would cement his reputation as a history painter in the grand manner. Unfortunately, both circumstances and his own temperament worked against this goal, and the multifigured, 12 × 16-foot *Belshazzar's Feast* (Detroit Institute of Arts) remained unfinished at his death. When Allston brought it home, well-intentioned friends subscribed $10,000 to allow him to finish it, but the artist was never able to bring it to completion. At the same time, he was too conscientious to abandon it. In part, the failure of this project reflects the diminishing interest of both the artist and the American public in the sort of didactic, grand manner painting that West had successfully popularized in the first two decades of the century. Allston's triumphs of his later American years were instead his introspective inventions, such as the mysterious *Moonlit Landscape* (Museum of Fine Arts, Boston, 1819) and the evocative *Italian Shepherd Boy* (Detroit Institute of Arts, 1819). In 1830, some years after the death of his first wife, Allston married the sister of the essayist and poet Richard Henry Dana and settled permanently in Cambridgeport (now part of Cambridge). During these later American years, Allston also continued to write verse, produced a novel, *Monaldi* (1841), and completed his posthumously published *Lectures on Art, and Poems* (1850), arguably the most distinguished consideration of art theory by a nineteenth-century American.

Alston, Charles. *See* AFRICAN-AMERICAN ART.

Ambrotype. *See* PHOTOGRAPHY, AMERICAN.

American Abstract Artists. An organization formed in 1937 to unite abstract artists, as well as promote and exhibit their work. During the 1930s in the United States, abstract art was not widely admired. Most artists were drawn to the *American Scene movement's emphasis on depicting the realities of American life. Critics frequently referred to modernist abstract art as outdated and un-American. Thus, when the American Abstract Artists came together, their point of view represented a minority position. However, within a few years the organization became the rallying point for younger artists of the emerging postwar avant-garde. Most of the original members practiced forms of hard-edged, intellectually rigorous painting in the traditions of synthetic cubism, constructivism, and Mondrian's neoplasticism. They generally rejected both expressionism and surrealism, although before long these styles began to affect some members' work. Preliminary discussions about forming a group began in 1935 and continued, with additional recruits, through 1936. In January 1937 twenty-two artists established a formal organization and elected Balcomb *Greene the first chairman. In April the association, now numbering thirty-nine members, presented its first annual exhibition. At the outset, participants included Josef *Albers, Rosalind *Bengelsdorf, Ilya *Bolotowsky, Byron *Browne, Burgoyne *Diller, Werner *Drewes, Gertrude *Greene, Carl *Holty, Alice Trumbull *Mason, George L. K. *Morris, Ad *Reinhardt, and David *Smith. Within a few years, prominent members included also Willem *de Kooning, Irene Rice *Pereira, and Jackson *Pollock. Although the organization reached its peak of activity and influence in the 1940s, it survives today.

American Academy of the Fine Arts. *See* NATIONAL ACADEMY OF DESIGN.

American Artists' Congress. An activist, left-wing group organized during the Depression to promote artists' interests and to combat war, repression, and fascism. Founded early in 1936, it quickly found widespread support for its agenda but rapidly expired during the early years of World War II. Because the association took no formal position on aesthetic questions, it attracted an eclectic membership. However, reflecting the 1930s' prevailing interests in social realism and other manifestations of the *American Scene movement, representational artists predominated. Nevertheless, the organization's leading light was Stuart *Davis, who headed the organization for several years and assiduously promoted its causes. In the spring of 1935, Davis and about twenty other artists initiated a series of planning meetings aimed at forming an artists' congress. That summer the emergence of the Popular Front lent impetus to the effort, as the international Communist Party abandoned its longstanding aim of worldwide revolution in favor of banding together with democratic forces to prevent the spread of German and Japanese militarism. Artists of varied political allegiances could agree on the advisability of unifying to oppose war and fascism. In addition, collective action attracted artists who were then both economically vulnerable and concerned about repression from the right, in the wake of several incidents of censorship.

About four hundred people attended the first congress in February 1936 and adopted bylaws that called for solidarity among artists, permanent government financing for art, support for freedom of expression, and opposition to war. There was widespread agreement within the Congress that the art community should operate as a progressive cultural force by reaching out to the American public. Within a year the organization had chapters in several cities and political clout in Washington, where it campaigned for matters of interest to its constituency. During the later 1930s it sponsored about twenty exhibitions in New York and some elsewhere, organized symposia, defended artists under attack, and published books. By the end of the decade, opponents increasingly accused the Congress of functioning as a Communist front. Additionally, events in Russia between 1936 and 1939 had the effect of undermining the organization. As Stalin purged the party hierarchy in a series of show trials, outlawed modernism in art, signed a nonaggression treaty with Hitler, and invaded Finland, he destroyed the unity of the American left and undercut any political effort that could be accused of ties to Moscow. By 1940, the Congress was in disarray, and in 1942 it sputtered to an end. By then, a group of Congress dissenters, led by Meyer *Schapiro, had formed the nonpolitical Federation of Modern Painters and Sculptors to support artists' issues.

American Art-Union. A mid-nineteenth-century association of subscribers who supported the production and distribution of American art. Based on European precedents, it was established as the Apollo Association in 1839 but changed its name a few years later. The American Art-Union remained the largest and most successful of several mid-century art unions, and by about 1850 was perhaps the most influential art institution in the country. In return for an annual fee of five dollars, participants received a periodical subscription, an engraving of a painting, and the opportunity to acquire an original work of art through a lottery. Although the bulk of its members lived in the Northeast, the Art-Union attracted a national constituency of middle-class citizens. The Art-Union's purpose was both educational and nationalistic. Its *Bulletin* (before 1848, *Transactions*), the first American art magazine, evolved into an ambitious monthly devoted to inculcating informed taste. Through its articles and illustrations, it acquainted readers with important historical and contemporary art, with techniques and terms of art discourse, and with the literature of art, such as the recent writings of Englishman John Ruskin. The art chosen for distribution to members was exclusively American, reflecting the organization's self-conscious patriotism and desire to foster a native school. As it prospered, the finest American artists became eager to show their work in its New York gallery, in the hope that it would be bought by the organization. Although the Art-Union's first landscape engravings were not issued until 1850, earlier selections included American *genre images and historical scenes, as well as classical subjects and moralizing narratives. Among important artists whose work the Art-Union supported and popularized were George Caleb *Bingham, Thomas *Cole, John *Kensett, William Sidney *Mount, and Richard Caton *Woodville. At the peak of its popularity in 1849, the Art-Union boasted nearly nineteen thousand subscribers. In that year it distributed 460 works of art through the lottery. The organization's swift demise in 1852 followed the New York State Supreme Court's ruling that the lottery, as a form of gambling, was illegal. The organization was directed to liquidate its assets and cease operations. Among similar organizations, Cincinnati's Western Art-Union was founded in 1847; the New England Art-Union organized the following year in Boston; and the Cosmopolitan Art Association, established in Sandusky, Ohio, in 1854, expanded to New York in 1857. There until 1862 it was particularly associated with the highly finished, detailed realism of German painting from Düsseldorf, as it managed to skirt the legal niceties of continuing to run a lottery. It published the monthly *Cosmopolitan Art Journal* from 1856 until 1860.

American Place, An. *See* STIEGLITZ, ALFRED.

American Renaissance. Term applied to a taste in the visual arts and architecture for Renaissance classicism and luxury during the years around 1900. Many at the time believed that the United States had entered a period mirroring the creative, forward-looking, public-spirited character of that earlier age. Typically combining splendor with refined beauty, American Renaissance works often reflect the era's zest for national power and personal wealth. Generally leaving behind the moralizing and didactic qualities common earlier, these works celebrate the value of art as an accompaniment to elite status, a genteel lifestyle, and physical comfort. Cosmopolitan in tone, the art demonstrates an easy familiarity with European precedents. Artists associated in at least some of their work with the American Renaissance include Herbert *Adams, Edwin *Blashfield, Thomas Wilmer *Dewing, Daniel Chester *French, John *La Farge, Henry Siddons *Mowbray, Augustus *Saint-Gaudens, Abbott *Thayer, and Elihu *Vedder. Notably, the term American Renaissance conveys an entirely different meaning with respect to the study of literature. Designating the era from approximately the 1830s through the 1860s, it refers to writers, mostly from New England, who created the first great flowering of American poetry and prose. These include Nathaniel Hawthorne, Henry Wadsworth Longfellow, Herman Melville, Walt Whitman, and Transcendentalists such as Ralph Waldo Emerson and Henry David Thoreau.

American Scene movement. An elastic term describing art that expressly depicts American life, normally with reference to the 1920s and 1930s. In historical terms, the American Scene movement contributed to an extended cultural debate about representation of the American character and experience. The question of what might constitute an authentic American expression arose in the nineteenth century and took on new urgency early in the twentieth century. It continued to intrigue participants and critics in all the arts—modern as well as traditional—until the 1940s. The American Scene movement's most direct predecessors were the New York realists of the first decade of the twentieth century, the *Ashcan painters and their associates. Just as the earlier realists reacted against the mainstream art of the day on the grounds that it had become too aestheticized—too concerned with artistic issues at the expense of connection to lived experience—similarly, and for much the same reason, American Scene painters rejected modernism. They criticized this tendency for its elitism, its emphasis on formal and theoretical issues, and its European (as opposed to native) origins. In wishing to create art that could appeal to ordinary people, American scene artists shared broadly humanistic and democratic goals with their Ashcan predecessors. In addition, American Scene artists often responded to the material suffering and psychic dislocations of the Depression.

Despite enthusiasm for modernism during the 1920s, American life had remained a vital subject for many artists, notably Charles *Burchfield and Edward *Hopper. Toward the end of the decade, Isabel *Bishop, Reginald *Marsh, and Kenneth Hayes *Miller numbered among important leaders in reviving the Ashcan legacy of urban realist painting in New York. Because these artists often drew on the life they observed in the vicinity of Union Square, they are sometimes dubbed the Fourteenth Street School. These and other relatively untheoretical urban realists generally reveled in the bustle of the rapidly modernizing city, where speedy transportation, consumer goods, and cheap public entertainment were transforming ordinary life. During the 1930s two other groups, the regionalists and social realists, with more pointed—and often antagonistic—agendas came to the fore. (In earlier usage, the term "American Scene" was sometimes employed interchangeably with "regionalism.") Emanating from the Midwest, regionalism produced three major practitioners, Thomas Hart *Benton, John Steuart *Curry, and Grant *Wood. Others include Aaron *Bohrod and Joe *Jones. Kansas-born art writer Thomas Craven (1889–1969), a fierce critic of aesthetic modernism, served as the regionalists' primary apologist. Their movement constituted an anti-urban revolt against New York as a symbol of modern life, as well as a repudiation of European modern art. Regionalism sought to portray the virtues of traditional American life associated with farms and small towns. Deeply nostalgic for a way of life that was being destroyed by industrialization and urbanization, it implicitly defined the ideal American citizen as white and Christian, self-reliant and family-oriented, hardworking and anti-intellectual. Some regionalist painting came to be associated with 1930s isolationism and a narrowly conceived set of patriotic values. The social realists, predominately New Yorkers, found the regionalists' glorification of American life simplistic, naive, and even potentially fascistic. Rooted in earlier, leftist critiques of American economic and social inequality, social realists sympathized with the downtrodden and dispossessed, whose personal pain and humiliation they attributed to the iniquities of capitalism and class structure. Cognizant of immigrant experience, they also took a broader view of what constituted American identity. Important artists associated with this point of view during at least part of their careers included William *Gropper, Ben *Shahn, and the *Soyer brothers. As was also the case among the regionalists, social realists shared an attitude and purpose rather than a common style.

For a brief moment, American Scene work fueled the most widespread art movement in American history. Extending far beyond the art galleries, it penetrated the country's museums, schools, civic buildings, and popular press. *Federal art projects bolstered the movement's appeal, as government-supported artists overwhelmingly adopted the American Scene approach in public murals and inexpensive editions of prints. In the 1940s the American Scene movement came to an end, its popularity eroded by World War II, ameliorating economic conditions, internationally oriented politics, the end of federal art sponsorship, and the emergence of a sophisticated but homegrown artistic form, *abstract expressionism.

American Watercolor Society. *See* WATERCOLOR MOVEMENT, AMERICAN.

Ames, Ezra (1768–1836). Painter. Chiefly a portraitist, for many years he ranked as the leading artist in Albany, New York, where he recorded the likenesses of numerous prominent citizens. These included so many of the state capital's politicians that he is sometimes regarded as the semi-official New York State portraitist of the early nineteenth century. Like numerous artists of his time, he supplemented his portrait work by painting signs and carriages, making frames, and accepting other decorative tasks. Following the success of his 1812 portrait of U. S. vice-president and former New York State governor George Clinton (purchased by the Pennsylvania Academy but later destroyed; known also in variants), he was able to concentrate more fully on painting. Born Ezra Emes in Framingham, Massachusetts, he later changed the spelling of his last name. With his family, he moved to nearby East Sudbury (now Wayland), and from around 1790 worked in Worcester before settling permanently in Albany in 1793. Evidently self-taught as an artist, Ames closely studied works by John Singleton *Copley and other eighteenth-century portraitists. His early mature style is particularly indebted to the example of Gilbert *Stuart, whose fluid and imaginative work he simplified. Later works that suggest the styles of John *Vanderlyn or the partnership of Samuel *Waldo and William Jewett demonstrate that Ames continued to absorb elements of contemporary practice. Although somewhat drily factual, Ames's likenesses at their best possess gracious amplitude that enhances the dignity of his sitters. His portrait work includes miniatures on ivory or paper, as well as larger works. He also painted a few landscapes.

Amos, Emma. *See* AFRICAN-AMERICAN ART.

Anderson, Karl. *See* GIVERNY GROUP.

Anderson, Laurie. *See* PERFORMANCE ART.

Andre, Carl (1935–). Sculptor. Also a poet. A major contributor to *minimalism, he remains best known for affectless, horizontal arrangements of identical, contiguous, prefabricated modules not attached to each other. Placed directly on the floor, the sculptures may be disassembled when not on view. In the 1960s he also made scatter pieces that rely on chance for placement of elements. As well, during the same years he initiated a sequence of durable, site-specific, outdoor works. Born in Quincy, near Boston, from 1951 to 1953 he attended the Phillips Academy in Andover, Massachusetts. There he studied with Patrick *Morgan and befriended Frank *Stella, whose early minimalist work later affected his own artistic coming of age. During a 1954 visit to Europe, he admired Stonehenge, initiating a long-standing tie to prehistory. After serving in the U.S. Army, he settled permanently in New York in 1957. While writing concrete poetry, he began to produce large abstract plastic or, more often, wood sculptures indebted at first to Brancusi's example but soon erected from stacked lumber. Four years of railroad work during the early 1960s turned his attention to industrial materials and to the power of functional forms. In the mid-1960s Andre came to national attention by placing bricks in simple rectangular formations on gallery floors. Soon he used other common materials, such as lead or aluminum squares, often in thin sheets inviting foot traffic. These severe constructions drew attention to the weight and mass of materials and to their placement in space, while avoiding allusion, symbols, or other meanings not intrinsic to the work itself. For several years from 1969, Andre promoted leftist politics as a leader in the Art Workers' Coalition. After meeting late in 1979, he and Ana *Mendieta soon became romantically involved. They married early in 1985. The partnership reinvigorated his interest in prehistoric art and opened his thinking to less austere approaches to art making. After Mendieta died in a 1985 fall from a window of their New York apartment, Andre was charged with murder but was acquitted at the conclusion of a highly publicized trial. In recent years, his sculptural work has employed varied materials, including wood blocks, stone, and coiled copper sheeting set on edge, to address issues of scale, monumentality, and the evocative power of stable and timeless structure. Edited by James Meyer, his collected writings appeared as *Cuts: Texts 1959–2004* (2005).

Anshutz, Thomas (1851–1912). Painter. A longtime principal in the Philadelphia art community, he made his reputation with dignified, carefully constructed figural compositions indebted to his mentor Thomas *Eakins. His best-known painting, *The Ironworkers' Noontime* (Fine Arts Museums of San Francisco, 1880) depicts industrial laborers outside a factory during a midday break. Notable for its unromanticized working-class subject, it delineates men in varied poses relaxing in strong sunlight. Although the image reveals shared experience, the workers' apparent isolation from each other suggests also the alienation common to modern industrialism. During the 1890s Anshutz's work took on greater lightness and immediacy, especially in a large number of accomplished watercolors. As a teacher at the *Pennsylvania Academy of the Fine Arts, where he also served as director, he guided numerous younger artists who went on to distinguished careers. Thomas Pollock Anshutz was born in Newport, Kentucky, across the Ohio River from Cincinnati. Throughout his life, he periodically visited the vicinity of Wheeling, West Virginia. He had relatives there and lived in the area before heading to New York to study art. After a year or two in Brooklyn, he began his studies at the *National Academy of Design in 1873. Dissatisfied, he moved to Philadelphia two years later. There he soon began to work with Eakins, who remained among his teachers when he enrolled in the newly reopened Pennsylvania Academy in 1876. Two years later he became Eakins's teaching assistant, initiating a career of more than thirty years on the academy's instructional staff. In 1892 Anshutz left for a year in Europe. While residing most of the time in Paris, he worked at the Académie Julian. Although Adolphe-William Bouguereau numbered among his instructors, impressionism more directly affected his development. Subsequently, working often in watercolor or pastel as well as oil, he rendered many atmospheric landscapes. Around the turn of the century, Anshutz painted a number of bright-hued, stylized watercolors and a few similar oils anticipating modernist developments. As private experiments, these little affected the public reputation he concurrently cultivated with portraits and figure studies, often picturing attractive women at leisure. In 1899 with Philadelphia impressionist Hugh Henry Breckenridge (1870–1937), he founded a summer art school. Located at first in Darby, it later moved to another Philadelphia suburb, Fort

Washington, where Anshutz died. In 1910 ill health had forced him to resign from the academy staff, and the following summer's visit to Europe in search of treatment failed to cure him.

Antin, Eleanor. *See* PERFORMANCE ART.

Antonakos, Stephen. *See* SANDLER, IRVING.

Antoni, Janine. *See* PERFORMANCE ART.

Antreasian, Garo. *See* TAMARIND LITHOGRAPHY WORKSHOP.

Anuszkiewicz, Richard. *See* OP ART.

Aperture. *See* WHITE, MINOR.

Apollo Association. *See* AMERICAN ART-UNION.

Arakawa, Shusaku. *See* CONCEPTUAL ART.

Arbus, Diane (1923–71). Photographer. She specialized in images of people whose inner lives seem rawly exposed, yet ultimately mysterious. While ordinary people sometimes appear outlandish, marginal or disabled figures are shown to share our humanity. Like Garry *Winogrand, Lee *Friedlander, and other social landscape photographers prominent in the 1960s, she drew attention to the boundaries of normal human experience. Her work also notes the instability of representation, social forms, and objective meaning. Diane Nemerov, sister of poet Howard Nemerov, was born in New York and educated at the progressive Ethical Culture and Fieldston Schools, where she demonstrated a talent for painting. At eighteen, she married photographer Allan Arbus, with whom she worked in a successful fashion photography business. (They separated in 1959 and divorced ten years later.) Seeking by the mid-1950s to expand her artistic options, Arbus studied briefly at Alexey *Brodovitch's Design Laboratory before working with Lisette *Model for two years. Soon, following Model's lead, she was photographing eccentric subjects such as nudists, seedy entertainers, transvestites, twins, and deformed individuals. She also became particularly interested in recording people at parades, festivals, and other public rituals. In the 1960s her photo-essays were widely published in *Esquire*, the *New York Times Magazine*, and other leading periodicals. By the early 1960s Arbus had intensified her vision by regularly using a square-format camera in place of her previous 35 mm model. This camera registered more detail and provided a field well suited to her interest in composing around a centrally placed subject. Arbus generally did not capture individuals unaware but rather convinced them to pose for her. Thus, most of them are looking at her (and at the viewer). That they seem, as in family snapshots, to be willingly revealing themselves gives even the oddest of her subjects a strange intimacy. Arbus often took notes about her subjects and sometimes wrote skillfully composed captions to accompany her published photographs. Besides Model, important influences on her work include Richard *Avedon, Robert *Frank, *Weegee, Brassaï, and August Sander. In turn, her idiosyncratic sensibility and its expression in photographs revealing the unexpected have reverberated widely. As a cultural celebrity, she was widely honored after her suicide in New York. The following year, **Aperture* published a monograph commemorating her work, the *Museum of Modern Art mounted a large retrospective (which subsequently traveled the country for three years), and her one-person show at the 1972 Venice Biennale was the first given to an American photographer.

Archipenko, Alexander (1887–1964). Sculptor. The most prominent sculptor of the cubist movement, he is known for semi-abstract, often colorful works. He contributed significantly during his American years to wider knowledge of European modernist ideas and forms. Born Aleksandr Porfirevich Arkhipenko in Kiev, he studied painting and sculpture at the art school there before going to Moscow in 1906. Two years later, he departed for Paris. Except for the war years, 1914–18, which he spent in Nice, Paris remained his home until 1921. He then moved to Berlin for two years before continuing on to New York. In 1929 he became an American citizen and subsequently taught and lectured widely throughout the country. He lived for short periods in several cities, including Chicago, where he taught at the New Bauhaus (now the Illinois Institute of Technology's Institute of Design), as well as Kansas City and West Coast locations. He died in New York. Archipenko reached his creative peak during the Paris years. Emphasizing vigorous, reductive shapes, his approach often incorporated holes or concavities that activate adjacent space. In the bronze *Woman Combing Her Hair* (Museum of Modern Art, 1915), a void cleverly represents the woman's head, which is defined by hair and a raised arm. During the same years, Archipenko also developed an innovative form of constructed relief sculpture in which simplified forms, usually painted, appear against a flat background. Sometimes called sculpto-paintings, these frequently incorporate commonplace, non-art materials. Following his move to the United States, he concentrated on evocations of the standing figure. These sometimes approach pure abstraction, and color often contributes to the variety of novel effects he achieved. A versatile technician, Archipenko produced carved, modeled, and assembled sculpture and occasionally worked with collage. The innovations of his later career include plastic sculptures lit from within.

Archives of American Art. *See* SMITHSONIAN INSTITUTION.

Arensberg, Walter Conrad (1878–1954). Art collector. From 1915 to 1921, Arensberg and his wife regularly hosted a glittering circle of avant-garde artists, writers, and intellectuals in their New York apartment, which served as unofficial headquarters for *New York dada. Marcel *Duchamp set the droll, ironic, iconoclastic tone. Other artists among frequent guests included Charles *Demuth, *Man Ray, and French visitors Francis Picabia and Albert Gleizes. Marsden *Hartley, Morton *Schamberg, Charles *Sheeler, and Florine *Stettheimer often attended, as did an array of other artists on a less frequent basis. Among literary figures, poets William Carlos Williams and Wallace Stevens were familiar faces, as was art critic Henry *McBride. Born in Pittsburgh, Arensberg graduated in 1900 from Harvard University and in 1907 married Mary Louise Stevens (1879–1953). Walter wrote poetry, as well as magazine articles and reviews, and immersed himself in literary pursuits. He developed a lifelong obsession with the idea that Francis Bacon had written Shakespeare's plays and eventually wrote several books promoting this idea. Thunderstruck by the 1913 *Armory Show, Walter decided to move from Boston to New York. He and Louise did so the following year, began to collect modern art, and soon established a role at the city's creative center. The Arensberg evenings had no structure; guests simply dropped in and helped themselves to food and drink into the early morning hours. Above all, they had a good time. In 1921 the Arensbergs decamped for Los Angeles, where they lived a more sedate existence. Eventually they owned about 1,500 works. Comprising African and pre-Columbian as well as modern art, including the finest representation anywhere of Duchamp's work, in 1950 the collection went to the Philadelphia Museum of Art.

Armory Show. An international exhibition that introduced modern art to the American public in 1913. It remains the best known, and perhaps the most influential, art exhibition ever held in the United States. Although only a small fraction of the roughly 1,300 entries in "The International Exhibition of Modern Art" displayed radical styles such as cubism, expressionism, or fauvism, the exhibition stimulated much public interest and indignation. The show is often regarded as the pivotal event in opening American art to avant-garde practice, as well as to new approaches in criticism and collecting. The largest and most sensational of the period's *independent exhibitions, the Armory Show evolved from plans initiated in December 1911 by several artists. They originally had in mind the more modest goal of promoting neglected contemporary work. To this end, they founded the Association of American Painters and Sculptors, which remained dominated by relatively conservative artists, who thought of themselves as progressive but certainly not revolutionary. After Arthur B. *Davies was elected president, the group decided to organize a major invitational show including a review of current European trends. Davies proved the ideal choice to lead. Aesthetically sophisticated, socially well connected, and personally congenial, he quickly threw himself into the project. To select the European work, he sent Walt *Kuhn to Germany before joining him to search out material in Paris and London. Walter *Pach, who was then living in Paris, assisted there.

The show opened on 17 February 1913 at the Sixty-ninth Infantry Regiment Armory, on the corner of New York's Lexington Avenue and Twenty-sixth Street. An edited version of the show traveled to Chicago and Boston in the spring. In an ambitious attempt to recapitulate the growth of modern art for an American audience, the show not only displayed recent, tradition-shattering works, but also reviewed the nineteenth century's major artistic advances. The foreign, predominately French, portion of the exhibition started with work by J.-A.-D. Ingres and Eugène Delacroix, then continued through Gustave Courbet and mid-century realists to strong representation of the impressionists and postimpressionists, including Paul Cézanne and Odilon Redon. Although Italian futurists did not appear in the show, nearly all other advanced artists were represented. These included Brancusi, Georges Braque, Kandinsky, Ernst Ludwig Kirchner, Matisse, Francis Picabia, Picasso, and most notably, Marcel *Duchamp. Vicious ridicule in the public press for Duchamp's *Nude Descending a Staircase, No. 2* (Philadelphia Museum, 1912) brought this work and its maker widespread celebrity. The show's less controversial American section included work by impressionists, Albert Pinkham *Ryder, James McNeill *Whistler, Robert *Henri, and other members of The *Eight, as well as a wide representation of living artists of nearly all but the most academic persuasions. Among the few dozen American modern works were paintings by Marsden *Hartley, John *Marin, Alfred *Maurer, and Joseph *Stella. Despite the overwhelming popular and artistic success of the show, the association responsible for organizing the event did not outlive its triumph.

Arms, John Taylor (1887–1953). Printmaker. Known especially for etchings of picturesque European sites, he was born in Washington, D.C., and studied at Princeton University for two years before transferring in 1907 to the Massachusetts Institute of Technology. In 1911 he received a BS in architecture and the following year, a master's degree. While working as an architect in New York, late in 1913 he began to learn etching. After a stint in the U.S. Navy from 1916 to 1919, he devoted full time to the medium. Although he remained almost entirely self-taught in printmaking, he developed a virtuoso etching technique, sometimes combined with aquatint. He also made a few lithographs. His early prints include American landscapes and cityscapes, but he made his reputation with renderings of historic European architecture, particularly Gothic ecclesiastical buildings. His scenes combine exacting detail and compositional breadth to convey personal affection for the enduring splendor of his subjects. Throughout most of his career, Arms maintained residences near North Pomfret, Vermont, and near Fairfield, Connecticut. He died in New York. He published a *Handbook on Printmaking and Printmakers* (1934) and collaborated with his wife, writer Dorothy Noyes Arms, on several travel volumes, including *Churches of France* (1929) and *Hill Towns and Cities of Northern Italy* (1933).

Arneson, Robert. *See* FUNK ART.

Art Front. *See* DAVIS, STUART.

Artists' colonies. Rural or small-town locations where artists congregate in search of agreeable and stimulating companionship in pleasant surroundings. Often these places have been summer retreats, but some developed into year-round art centers. Originating partly in the appeal of landscape subjects and local color, they were particularly popular at the end of the nineteenth century and during the early twentieth century. Most have been informal, but as their artist populations grew, frequently such communities organized institutions including schools and galleries. The most important artists' colonies include Old Lyme, Connecticut; Woodstock, New York; Provincetown, Massachusetts; and Taos, New Mexico, as well as New Hope and surrounding Bucks County, Pennsylvania. In 1899 Henry Ward *Ranger numbered among the earliest arrivals in Old Lyme, which soon became a center for *Barbizon, *tonalist, and *impressionist painting. It had been preceded by another colony also near the shore of Long Island Sound, in a section of Greenwich known as Cos Cob, which attracted J. Alden *Weir and John *Twachtman. Childe *Hassam had also worked there before his first summer in Old Lyme, in 1903, the same year that Willard *Metcalf initially visited. Other important participants at Old Lyme included Guy *Wiggins and impressionist William Chadwick (1879–1962), as well as the popular teacher Frank Vincent DuMond (1865–1951). For several years, the *Art Students League sponsored summer classes at the Lyme Summer School of Art. The Lyme Art Association, formed in 1914, opened a gallery in 1921.

Woodstock began attracting both summer and year-round residents to the Catskills in 1903, when wealthy, English-born, Oxford-educated reformer Ralph Radcliffe Whitehead (1854–1929), established a utopian community with the assistance of novelist and social worker Hervey White, printmaker Bolton Coit Brown (1865–1936), and other sympathetic artists and teachers. Based on ideals of the *Arts and Crafts movement, Byrdcliffe offered housing and studios for artists as well as a library, a visitors' residence, and other facilities. White subsequently founded a splinter colony, Maverick, which became particularly known for music festivals. In 1906 the Art Students League began conducting summer classes at Woodstock. Founded in 1919 by Konrad *Cramer, Andrew *Dasburg, and Henry Lee *McFee, the Woodstock Artists' Association remains in existence today. Numerous other artists associated with Woodstock include George *Ault, Peggy *Bacon, George *Bellows, Alexander *Brook, Birge *Harrison, Yasuo *Kuniyoshi, and Doris *Lee. Provincetown became a summer outpost of Greenwich Village early in the twentieth century, attracting large numbers of artists and writers, as well as theater people involved in the Provincetown Playhouse, founded in 1915. Charles *Hawthorne established the Cape Cod School of Art there, attracting students for a long period of time. Over the years, many important artists have been associated with the locale, including Hans *Hofmann, who also taught there, and Milton *Avery. Even before 1900 artists had begun congregating in picturesque Taos. The early arrivals generally created vigorously painted, realistic depictions of the landscape and local Indian life. The most important included Oscar Berninghaus (1874–1950), Ernest Blumenschein (1874–1960), Eanger Irving Couse

(1866–1936), Victor Higgins (1884–1949), and Walter Ufer (1876–1936). All actively participated in the Taos Society of Artists, an important organization between 1915 and 1927. From 1917 Mabel Dodge *Luhan held forth in Taos, and her presence attracted a varied retinue including Georgia *O'Keeffe, who eventually settled nearby, and John *Marin. John *Sloan, as well as Raymond *Jonson and other modernists, also numbered among the dozens of important artists who worked in Taos during the 1920s and 1930s. Since then, the area, along with Santa Fe about seventy miles away, has evolved into a major art hub. Edward *Redfield numbered among the first artists to work in the area of New Hope, on the Delaware River north of Philadelphia. Following his lead shortly before 1900, this locale particularly attracted landscape painters favoring a bold, painterly realism with roots in impressionism. As well, during the period notable concentrations of artists could be found elsewhere, including the Gloucester/Cape Ann area of Massachusetts; Carmel on California's Monterey Peninsula; Westport, Connecticut; and Cornish, New Hampshire.

Artists' Equity. *See* KUNIYOSHI, YASUO.

Art of This Century. *See* GUGGENHEIM, PEGGY.

Arts and Crafts movement. A late-nineteenth-century reform movement, primarily in the decorative arts, devoted to countering the spiritually deadening effects of industrialization by introducing simplicity and beauty into all aspects of life. Like the earlier English movement founded by Socialist painter, designer, and poet William Morris, the American tendency also idealized the medieval past and stressed hand production as antidotes to the increasingly mechanized and standardized character of modern products. Aspects of the Arts and Crafts movement overlapped with art nouveau and the *aesthetic movement, but these two lacked Arts and Crafts' morally serious commitments to practical function and social reform. Although the movement on both sides of the Atlantic looked backward in its reverence for the craftsman and for well-made, artistically designed products, it played an important role in the formulation of ideas and attitudes that motivated early modernism. These included dissolution of the barrier between art and lived experience, reverence for the inherent qualities of materials, commitment to utility, an affinity for structure over surface ornament, democratization of art, and interest in nature—as opposed to traditional art, especially officially sanctioned classical or academic art—as a source of formal principles. The German Bauhaus, where founder Walter Gropius tried to assimilate the movement's romantic ideals to machine-based production, may be the best-known modern consequence of Arts and Crafts ideology, but many artists throughout the western world were at least indirectly affected. The American Arts and Crafts movement reached its zenith around 1900, when societies appeared in many cities to promote its principles and sponsor exhibitions of handmade decorative objects. The first of these, Boston's Society of Arts and Crafts, was founded in 1897. Also in the 1890s, the movement found its commercial popularizers in Elbert Hubbard (1856–1915) and Gustav Stickley (1858–1942). Modeling his ambitions on Morris's example, Hubbard opened a workshop known as Roycroft in East Aurora, New York, where he emphasized furniture and printing. Stickley's United Crafts, also in upstate New York, produced the furniture line known as Craftsman (sometimes also called "Mission" for its similarity to furniture made for the Spanish Catholic missions of California), still highly regarded today. His widely read magazine, *The Craftsman*, which first appeared in 1901, promoted Arts and Crafts products and ideals.

Art Students League. A progressive art school opened in 1875 and quickly recognized as a leading force in American art education. Its roster of teachers and pupils comprised many of the most distinguished artists through the early twentieth century. Less influential later, the Art Students League of New York, as it is officially known, nevertheless remains an important institution. At the time it was organized on a studio system, the league's liberal policies contrasted sharply with those of established art academies, including the *National Academy of Design. Practices American artists had encountered during their own training in Europe inspired the league's structure. Abroad, individual schools and ateliers had grown up in opposition to the exclusive national academies, which offered a standard curriculum based on drawing, the classics, and long years of tradition. At the Art Students League, students enroll at will to study with individual instructors. There are no requirements for entrance and no set curriculum. In its early years, the league was allied with the interests of artists trained in the painterly style of Munich and the impressionism of Paris. William Merritt *Chase, who began teaching at the league in 1878, ranked as its leading figure for some years. However, after 1884 Kenyon *Cox offered an important alternative approach, based on classical draftsmanship. After the turn of the century, the league remained identified primarily with figurative imagery and traditional technique. Robert *Henri dominated for a number of years, followed by John *Sloan, Thomas Hart *Benton, and Kenneth Hayes *Miller. Although many modernists received at least part of their training at the league, relatively few taught there before the 1940s.

Ashcan School. A group of realist painters who worked in New York early in the twentieth century. Their subjects, drawn from everyday, mostly working-class urban life, offended prevailing expectations about the purposes of art. In the face of conventional taste for idealized, morally elevating, or pleasurable subjects, their art seemed vulgar and even dangerous. Humanists rather than revolutionaries, the Ashcan artists broke no new stylistic or technical ground in their art, nor did most espouse a radical political program. Their imagery reflected the observational realism that had been the daily practice of several who worked in journalism early in their careers, while their brushwork generally displayed a vigorous and painterly freedom based on old master precedents. The five painters who formed the core of the Ashcan School, William *Glackens, Robert *Henri, George *Luks, Everett *Shinn, and John *Sloan had met in Philadelphia in the 1890s. All had studied at the *Pennsylvania Academy of the Fine Arts, and all but Henri had worked as newspaper illustrators. Henri, a little older than most of the others and better educated as an artist, provided both personal encouragement and theoretical grounding for their art, directing them toward the value of integrating art and life. These five painters gained attention in 1908 when they exhibited, with three others, in the landmark show of The *Eight. The Ashcan epithet did not come into use until the 1930s. Besides the five who exhibited with The Eight, other painters often connected with the Ashcan School include George *Bellows, Jerome *Myers, and Eugene *Higgins. Although not directly associated, certain documentary photographers, such as Lewis *Hine and Jacob *Riis, paralleled Ashcan attitudes and subjects in their work. The orientation of these visual artists can be related to a larger cultural interest in realism, evident in the work of writers such as Theodore Dreiser and in social reform movements.

Ashton, Dore. *See* YUNKERS, ADJA.

Assemblage. Term describing works of art made by combining found or previously existing materials. Also, the process involved in making such objects. Materials may be chosen for their formal properties alone, but they often provide associations or allusions. Although usage is not entirely consistent, assemblage usually refers only to three-dimensional objects or to relief-like constructions. The term *collage* is generally reserved for two-dimensional works created in a parallel manner by pasting papers (and occasionally other flat materials, such as cloth or foil) onto a stiff backing. First popularized by cubists early in the twentieth century, collage provided an essential precedent for the development of assemblage. Additionally, some Picasso sculptures, Marcel *Duchamp's ready-mades, Kurt Schwitters's constructions, Alexander *Calder's circus, and aspects of dada and surrealism fostered the practice of finding art materials outside the studio. French artist Jean Dubuffet is credited with coining the word *assemblage* to describe works he cobbled together from odd scraps. In the United States, Arthur *Dove produced innovative relief assemblages in the 1920s, while Joseph *Cornell specialized in the assemblage technique over many years, beginning in the early 1930s. In the 1950s, increasingly toward the end of the decade, numerous artists found assemblage useful in achieving fresh expression that countered established techniques and styles. They included Bruce *Conner, Mark *di Suvero, Edward *Kienholz, Louise *Nevelson, Robert *Raushchenberg, David *Smith, and Richard *Stankiewicz. "The Art of Assemblage," a landmark 1961 *Museum of Modern Art exhibition examining the new forms and their antecedents, legitimized the process and its name. Since that time, assemblage has lost its controversial nature and found its way into mainstream forms of art.

Association for the Advancement of Truth in Art. *See* PRE-RAPHAELITISM, AMERICAN.

Association of American Painters and Sculptors. *See* ARMORY SHOW.

Atelier 17. Printmaking workshop founded in Paris in 1927, active in New York between 1940 and 1955. Under British abstract surrealist Stanley William Hayter, its founder and guiding spirit, it spurred a print revival based on modern adaptations of traditional intaglio printmaking. Originally identified with European forms of abstraction and surrealism, in New York it served as an important point of contact between European wartime émigrés and experimental American artists, most notably nascent *abstract expressionists. Deriving its name from its street address in Paris, the workshop promoted Hayter's high standards of technical excellence but also encouraged innovation. Hayter had closed the Paris operation in 1939 and returned to England. He arrived in New York the following year and lived there until 1950, when he reopened the Paris branch. His wife, California-born abstract sculptor and printmaker Helen Phillips (1913–95), whom he had met in Paris and married in 1940, returned with him to Paris. After they divorced in 1970, she worked mainly in Paris but later also established a residence in New York, where she died. The New York workshop at first was associated with the New School for Social Research (now New School) but moved into its own quarters in 1945. Karl *Schrag ran Atelier 17 after Hayter left New York. Other participants included major postwar artists, such as Jackson *Pollock, Robert *Motherwell, and Louise *Nevelson. As well, the atelier nurtured leading print specialists, including Mauricio *Lasansky and Gabor *Peterdi.

Audubon, John James (1785–1851). Painter and draftsman. Also a naturalist. The greatest American artist-naturalist, he is best known for an ornithological and aesthetic triumph, the engraved and hand-colored, four-volume *Birds of America* (1827–38), also a landmark in the history of the illustrated book. In addition, he recorded mammals and painted portraits. Jean-Jacques Fougère Audubon was born in Les Cayes, Santo Domingo (now Haiti), but was taken to France when he was four. He grew up in a village near Nantes, attended a naval academy as a youngster, and probably studied art briefly in Paris. Already obsessed with birds, late in 1803 he sailed for the United States and a few months later took possession of family property near Philadelphia. Soon he became acquainted with Mark *Catesby's published work and in his own drawings began to integrate specimens with their natural surroundings. A visit to France extended from the end of 1804 until 1806. In 1807 he departed for the shores of the Ohio River, where he pursued several business ventures, principally in Louisville and Henderson, Kentucky, without much success. The study of birds remained a hobby. A chance encounter in 1810 with Alexander *Wilson, then soliciting subscriptions to his own ornithological publication, may have inspired Audubon's masterpiece. After declaring bankruptcy in 1819 and reassessing his goals, in 1820 he finally determined to produce a comprehensive illustrated survey of American birds and began to travel for the express purpose of observing and recording them. For the next several years he supported himself chiefly with portraiture and instruction in drawing, French, and other polite accomplishments. After 1821, when not traveling, he made his home in the New Orleans area.

Unable to find an American publisher, he sailed abroad in 1826. After a false start with an Edinburgh printmaker, in 1827 Audubon came to agreement with London engraver Robert Havell to produce the 29.5 × 39.5-inch double elephant folio plates for *The Birds of America*. His son, Robert *Havell Jr., soon took over the project. While it was in production, Audubon made two trips to the United States to gather additional specimens and sell subscriptions. The completed *Birds* comprised 435 plates representing 489 species at approximately life size. It was supplemented by Audubon's five-volume text, the *Ornithological Biography* (1831–39), and an index (1839). Shown in lifelike poses within accurate natural habitats, the birds represent an exacting level of scientific knowledge about their characteristic behaviors as well as appearance. In addition, abetted by Havell's masterful technical control of engraving and aquatint, Audubon's illustrations display unparalleled aesthetic distinction. The fine quality of the draftsmanship, the vivacious compositions, and the emotional drama kindled by the birds' struggles for survival guarantee their continuing appeal, even if some details of fact have been found inaccurate. By celebrating nature as a source of beauty and wonder, Audubon also contributed to *romanticism's ascending popularity.

When he returned permanently to the United States in 1839, Audubon settled in New York. From 1842 he made his home on an upper Manhattan estate overlooking the Hudson River. Between 1840 and 1844, he issued an expanded, seven-volume edition of the *Birds*, illustrated with hand-colored lithographs in a smaller format. For his next project, he planned an inventory of American mammals. In preparation (and hoping to find additional bird species as well), he undertook his last extended journey, an expedition of several months up the Missouri River in 1843. The three-volume *Viviparous Quadrupeds of North America* (1845–48), containing 150 hand-colored lithographs, accompanied three descriptive volumes (1846–53). For this publication, Audubon was assisted by his sons, as well as naturalist John Bachman who composed much of the text. In the mid-1840s Audubon's eyesight began to fail, and by 1847 poor health ended his career. He died at his New York home. His sons, artist-naturalists **Victor Gifford Audubon** (1809–60) and **John Woodhouse Audubon** (1812–62), grew up assisting their father. Both also painted portraits and, occasionally, other subjects. Both were born in Kentucky, Victor Gifford in Louisville, and John Woodhouse in Henderson. In the 1830s both lived in London, where they became familiar with current art, and Victor studied at the Royal Academy. The brothers sometimes collaborated on paintings, to which Victor usually contributed landscape backgrounds. After their father's death, both participated in efforts to sustain his legacy by completing and reissuing his work. Both died in New York.

Augur, Hezekiah (1791–1858). Sculptor. A self-taught woodcarver who became a professional sculptor, he was among the first Americans to work in stone and to incorporate elements of *neoclassicism into his designs. A lifelong resident of New Haven, Connecticut, he secured his reputation with the approximately half life-size *Jephthah and His Daughter* (Yale University Art Museum, 1828–32), which toured several cities and has remained his best-known accomplishment. Its two separate figures enact a dramatic moment from the Old Testament with restrained emotion, but their proportions and linearly conceived forms indicate his artistic origins outside the classical tradition, as well as his presumed reliance on engravings as sources. Nevertheless, the boldly intricate cutting, fluid movement, and decorative surfaces derived from woodworking practice provide animation and visual interest. Augur in his youth tried several professions but eventually established a woodworking shop. A friendship with Samuel F. B. *Morse encouraged Augur's switch to marble and his ambition to contribute to the internationally fashionable classical revival. His first success, a marble head (unlocated) based on the antique *Apollo Belvedere* won acclaim when shown in New York during the winter of 1824–25. In several portrait busts, he accommodated realistic physiognomy to the conventions of Roman precedents, including toga-swathed shoulders. Despite praise for his efforts, Augur found few buyers and after 1840 apparently ceased making sculpture. After he received a patent in 1849, however, his marble-carving machine came into wide use.

Ault, George (1891–1948). Painter. Often associated with *precisionism, he extended the disciplined bounds of that style into a more romantic form of expression. Born in Cleveland, as a child he moved with his family to London. There he studied at the Slade School of Fine Arts and St. John's Wood Art School. Visits to France acquainted him with modern movements in art. After settling in New York in 1911, he usually summered in *Provincetown. In the early 1920s, he numbered among the first Americans to adopt machinery as a subject for painting. Besides painting the urban vistas favored by precisionists, he also remained continuously attracted to landscape. *From Brooklyn Heights* (Newark [New Jersey] Museum, 1928) melds several conflicting interests. This view across the river to Manhattan delineates simplified, boxy buildings, tugboats, and railroad cars with precisionist attention to structure and clarity. Yet a passenger liner steaming in from the left implies motion, while steam, smoke, and clouds evoke transient atmospheric conditions. Many other paintings depict night scenes, almost unheard of among other precisionists who favored the neutral, shadow-free light of midday. In 1937 Ault moved permanently to *Woodstock, where his work took on greater poetry but also increased melancholy. Around 1946 his work entered the imaginary territory of surrealism. In an apparent suicide, he drowned in a creek near his home.

Austen, Alice (1866–1952). Photographer. Christened Elizabeth Alice following her birth on Staten Island, she continued to live in that New York borough for most of her life. Although she began to develop her skills with a camera while still a child, photography remained an amateur activity. However, she pursued it with the instincts of a born photojournalist. Her most notable photographs document two categories of social experience at odds with each other in turn-of-the-century New York. Much of her work focuses on the individuals and daily life of her upper-class community, but she also numbered among the first to record the life of lower Manhattan's immigrants and poor. She published a portfolio of these street images in 1896. Austen also took photographs during many trips to Europe. Already slowed by arthritis, then financially ruined by the Depression, she ceased photographing in the 1930s. Overlooking New York Bay and today a National Historic Landmark, the Victorian-style cottage where Austen lived from childhood is today a museum devoted to her work and its context.

Automatism. *See* ABSTRACT EXPRESSIONISM.

Avedon, Richard (1923–2004). Photographer. During the early years of his career, Avedon helped to revolutionize fashion photography, to which he brought new levels of complexity and vitality. Later he amassed a collective portrait of the postwar American experience. This achievement includes arresting large-scale portraits and figure studies that interrogate beauty, power, style, and identity.

A lifelong Manhattanite, Avedon studied at Columbia University for a year before entering the Merchant Marine, where he first worked as a photographer. Upon release in 1944, he attended the Design Laboratory run by graphic designer Alexey Brodovitch (1898–1971) and the following year went to work at *Harper's Bazaar*, where Brodovitch was art director. In one of his most famous fashion shots, *Dovima with Elephants, Paris* (1955), he juxtaposed a celebrated model in a Dior evening gown with a pair of elephants. Their ungainliness contrasts with her perfection, while their restlessness seems to be held in check by the power of her glamour. Such work, at the forefront of a new trend in fashion photography, shifted interest from clothing to attitude. Avedon stayed at *Harper's Bazaar* until 1965, then worked for more than two decades with art director Alexander *Liberman at *Vogue*. In the 1940s, he also photographed street life in New York and in Europe. With time he expanded his range to engage portraiture, advertising, and photojournalism. By 1957 Avedon was so famous that his life inspired the movie *Funny Face*, starring Fred Astaire and Audrey Hepburn. From 1992 until his death he served as the *New Yorker* magazine's first staff photographer. In the 1960s and 1970s, Avedon's ambition drove him ever deeper into the American national character. He recorded pivotal historical events, often by isolating protagonists whose individual psychology he examined in interaction with contemporary culture. He frequently abstracted these subjects against white backgrounds, intensifying their physicality and isolating their psychological uniqueness. In 1963 he recorded the civil rights movement in the South and spent three weeks visiting a mental hospital, shooting an unsparing but sympathetic series. In 1971 he went to Vietnam. Between 1969 and 1973 he produced an extended serial portrait of his father as he died of cancer. From 1979 until 1985 he took on the myth of the frontier West, photographing individual workers whose faces and bodies attest to the region's tensions, disappointments, and fortitude. When the Berlin Wall came down on New Year's Eve 1989, Avedon was there. In characteristic portraits he closed in on sitters with a large-format view camera and wide-angle lens to record every pore and stray hair. He then enlarged these images to life size or greater for exhibition, giving them a compelling presence. In the 1990s he experimented with combinations of negatives in a single image. Most of his work is in black and white. His collections include *Observations* (1959), *Nothing Personal* (1964), *Portraits* (1976), *Avedon: Photographs 1947–1977* (1978), *In the American West* (1985), *An Autobiography* (1993), *Evidence: 1944–1994* (1994), and *Avedon: The Sixties* (1999).

Avery, Milton (1885–1965). Painter and printmaker. His subtle integration of representation and abstraction set him apart from contemporaries but earned admiration from a younger generation. In the 1940s and after, his sophisticated modernism, indebted particularly to the work of Matisse but also to Picasso, provided an important homegrown precedent for certain *abstract expressionists, especially his friends Mark *Rothko and Adolph *Gottlieb, and then for *color field painters. Marked by a personal and poetic tone, his mature figure studies, still lifes, and beach scenes simplify subjects into flat planes of sensitively chosen color. Suiting the contemplative tone of his style, his generally domestic, often whimsical themes offer little in the way of physical action, psychological drama, or narrative meaning. A reticent person who dedicated his otherwise placid life to painting, he left few indications of his motivation or intentions. Born in the upstate New York village of Sand Bank (now Altmar), north of Syracuse, Milton Clark Avery moved with his family in 1898 to the Hartford, Connecticut, area. As an artist, he developed slowly, with only sporadic training. That he remained to a degree self-taught may in part explain his independent aesthetic development and the innocent eye his paintings seem to celebrate. While employed in a succession of factory, shop, and office jobs, from the time he was about twenty he also studied part-time at local art schools. After moving permanently to New York in 1925, he worked intermittently at the *Art Students League until he was over fifty. By the time of his sole visit to Europe in 1952, he had already reached his late sixties. From 1935 he showed his work regularly in New York. In the late 1930s, he worked on a *federal art project. During summer months he usually sojourned at New England beach resorts, especially *Provincetown.

True to its origins in American impressionism, Avery's art featured personal response to nature. In his earliest paintings, he used a heavy impasto to render sun-filled scenes. His characteristic style developed after he moved to New York. In response to a more cosmopolitan milieu and opportunities to see modern art at first hand, he progressively thinned his paint, simplified compositions, eliminated detail, and concentrated on vibrant color relationships. As the paintings became larger in the late 1950s, shimmering hues came to dominate harmonious images so pared down that they sometimes appear purely abstract at first glance. In tandem with his painted subjects, from the 1930s, Avery made intaglio prints, particularly drypoints, and after about 1950 he produced some two hundred monotypes, as well as woodcuts and lithographs. Despite his reputation as a colorist, his graphic work benefited from his habit of sketching constantly, as well as his attention to finished drawings. In 1949 Avery suffered a serious heart attack, requiring long recuperation and leaving him somewhat weakened. For the last several years before his death in New York, poor health limited his activity.

Avery's steady development into a first-rate painter owed much to his wife. He met painter Sally Michel (1902–2003) in Gloucester during the summer of 1924, and it was to be with her that he moved to New York. After they married in 1926, she worked as an illustrator for nearly thirty years, while he never again held a regular job. Nevertheless, she continued to paint and draw in a style so close to his that she likely played a part in formulating their common aesthetic. Born in Brooklyn, she trained at the Art Students League and continued to paint vibrantly colored, intimate scenes into her later years. Their daughter, **March Avery** (1932–), and her son, Sean Avery Cavanaugh (1969–), continue in New York to create variations on the family style of abstracted realism.

Aycock, Alice. *See* LAND ART.

Azara, Nancy. *See* FEMINIST ART.

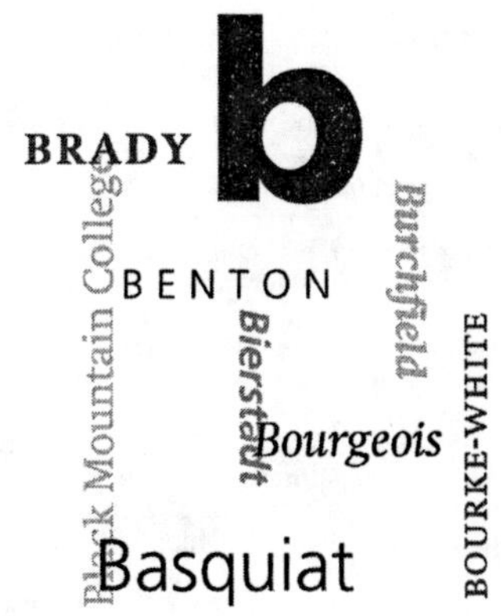

Baca, Judith. *See* FEMINIST ART.

Bacher, Otto Henry (1856–1909). Painter, printmaker, and illustrator. Remembered for scenic prints of Venice, while there in the 1880s he also painted views of the city and its picturesque inhabitants. Later he worked primarily as a portraitist and figure painter, animating solidly constructed forms with impressionist effects of light. He also painted landscapes and still lifes. Born in Cleveland, in 1878–79 he studied at Munich's Royal Academy before entering Frank *Duveneck's classes. Along with convivial young artists dubbed the "Duveneck boys" and their leader, Bacher relocated to Florence in the fall of 1879. The following summer he and others in the circle moved to Venice. Except for a few months in Florence the next winter, he remained for more than two years. While there, Bacher worked closely with James Abbott McNeill *Whistler, perfected his etching technique, and produced about forty prints as well as some paintings. Bacher had taken up etching in his early days in Cleveland, but Whistler provided new impetus to his development. Although, like Duveneck, Bacher favored heavier lines and more solid forms than his new mentor, he followed Whistler's example in picturing commonplace, out-of-the-way scenes in casually organized, sometimes fragmentary compositions. After briefly visiting Whistler in London, at the end of 1882 he returned to Cleveland. During summers, he taught one of the nation's first plein air painting classes at nearby Richfield. He went to Paris for additional study in 1885 and in the summer of the following year moved to Venice for about six months. Again, at the beginning and end of this final sojourn abroad, he visited Whistler in London. Within a few years after returning to Cleveland, he settled in New York. He died in Bronxville, a nearby suburb where he had resided for a number of years. In 1908 he published a memoir, *With Whistler in Venice*.

Bacon, Peggy (1895–1987). Painter and printmaker. A witty satirist, Margaret Frances Bacon was born in Ridgefield, Connecticut. Both parents were artists who encouraged her talent from an early age, exposed their daughter to Europe as a child, and sent her as a teenager to private boarding school. She had already studied privately with Jonas *Lie and Charles *Hawthorne, among others, before she entered the *Art Students League. There, between 1915 and 1920, she worked with Kenneth Hayes *Miller, John *Sloan, George *Bellows, and Andrew *Dasburg. In addition, during summers in *Provincetown, she studied with B. J. O. *Nordfelt. Armed with this formidable artistic education, Bacon found success early. Even before she finished her training, she had exhibited her work and published her first illustrated book. Many more followed, and in addition she illustrated dozens of books written by others. A 1928 solo exhibition at Alfred *Stieglitz's Intimate Gallery indicates the wide appreciation her work enjoyed. In the 1920s, Bacon deployed her penetrating, wiry line and mastery of fine detail in drawings, prints, and watercolors that lacerated snobbery and pretension (usually among the upper class). Less often, her work drew attention to the unfortunate lot of the poor. Later, she lost interest in indicting a social system and more often satirized individuals as types. In the 1950s she gave up printmaking, published a prize-winning mystery novel, and began to paint again in oils, which she had rarely done since her student days. In 1961 she moved to Cape Porpoise, on the coast of southern Maine. She died in nearby Kennebunk. Her satirical 1934 book, *Off With Their Heads*, caricatures artists and others.

In 1920 Bacon married Alexander Brook (1898–1980), who painted still lifes, landscapes, and figural works. Born in Brooklyn, in 1914 he began four years of study at the Art Students League, where Kenneth Hayes Miller ranked as his most important teacher. In his twenties he quickly developed a reputation for sensuous still lifes and posed figures rendered with painterly vigor. Later his work took on a more languid and delicate tone, in emulation of Jules *Pascin. During the socially conscious 1930s, in his choice of subjects Brook sometimes ventured into territory beyond the studio, but he avoided both didacticism and heroics. *Georgia Jungle* (Carnegie Museum of Art, Pittsburgh, 1939) presents a personal response to the impoverished plight of an African-American family and reflects Brook's familiarity with the area around Savannah, where he spent part of each year in this period. Until realist painting fell out of favor in the late 1940s, Brook exhibited widely and won numerous prizes. Inactive as an artist during his last fifteen years, he died in the eastern Long Island village of Sag Harbor, where he had resided since the late 1940s.

Five years after Brook's divorce from Bacon, in 1945 he wed painter Gina Knee (1898–1982), primarily a watercolorist. Born Virginia Schnaufer in Marietta, Ohio, following the end of a ten-year marriage to Goodlow Macdowell, she moved to New Mexico around 1930. In 1933 she married Canadian-born artist Ernest Knee (1907–82), later a photographer known particularly for New Mexico images. They divorced in 1944. Initially inspired by John *Marin's interpretations of the region, in the Santa Fe area during the 1930s she developed a personal and poetic form of modern expression. She died in a Suffolk County hospital, not far from Sag Harbor.

Badger, Joseph (1708–65). Painter. A Boston portraitist, he received little training as he developed an unassuming but distinctive style. Badger did not sign or date his works, but he is credited with more than 150 documented or attributed works. He was born in Charlestown, now part of Boston, where he relocated permanently around 1733. A housepainter and glazier, he probably continued some artisanal tasks after taking up portraiture about 1740. Like other colonial painters, he drew on prints of English paintings for poses and settings but reduced his models' elegance and grandeur. Badger's manner remained hard and literal; his color, drab and somber; and his drawing, weak, while his compositions generally lack atmospheric unity. Nevertheless, at his best Badger's pictured clients possess a forceful dignity, often enhanced by an apparently forthright realism in facial description and by sensitive attention to detail. Including some of the most agreeable, an unusually large proportion of his surviving works, approximately a third, depict children, such as his three-year-old grandson *James Badger* (Metropolitan Museum, 1760). Wearing his best finery (he is still in skirts) and holding a pet bird on one hand, he self-consciously poses before one of the painter's characteristically sketchy landscapes. More delicately painted than many of Badger's subjects, he looks proudly and trustingly at his grandfather. Here the artist's unprepossessing style suits the innocence of his subject.

Baer, Jo (1929–). Painter. She remains known particularly for *hard-edge abstract paintings from the 1960s and early 1970s. Since that time, living in Europe, she has developed a privately coded figuration that has been little exhibited. Born in Seattle, Josephine Gail Kleinberg studied at the University of Washington from 1946 to 1949 and subsequently pursued graduate work at the New School for Social Research (now New School) in New York. In 1953 she moved to Los Angles and married Richard Baer, who worked in television. There she associated with artists of the *Ferus Gallery, while exploring *abstract expressionism. After her divorce in 1958, the following year she married Los Angeles-born painter and printmaker John Wesley (1928–), later known for a personal variation on *pop art, but they divorced in 1969. About two years after moving back to New York in 1960, Baer initiated her wholly original work in a sharply reductivist style. Her most characteristic paintings from this period consist of squarish canvases, painted entirely white (or sometimes pale gray), save for a narrow border, usually black with an inner line of vibrant color. Although in their reduced visual content these works suggest early *minimalism, Baer sustained important painterly concerns abandoned by most adherents to that movement. Her works remain based in intuition rather than systems, and they are informed by traditional concerns for perception, the limits of painting, and the creation of what she has called "poetic objects." In 1969 she began to experiment with color bands that wrapped over the edges of her unframed canvases, and in the early 1970s she produced works that feature organic bands of brilliantly orchestrated color swerving across the surfaces onto wide perpendicular margins. She abandoned abstract art in 1975, the year of her retrospective at the *Whitney Museum of American Art, and left the United States to live in England, Ireland, and most recently Amsterdam.

Baizerman, Saul (1889–1957). Sculptor. Figural works formed from sheets of hammered metal constitute his most characteristic pieces. Born in Vitebsk, Russia (now Belarus), he began his art training as a young teenager in Odessa. In 1909 he traveled through Europe to England before settling permanently in New York in 1910. There he studied at the *National Academy of Design and elsewhere. Gutzon *Borglum numbered among his principal teachers. About 1920 Baizerman abandoned both bronze-casting and the academic tradition in which he had been trained. At this time he turned his attention to a series he called The City and Its People, a thirty-some-year procession of small hammered-metal *genre subjects observed from life in New York. Although modern in their simplified, analytical forms, in their humanitarian subject matter these bridge the concerns earlier inaugurated by the *Ashcan painters and reinvigorated by artists of the *American Scene movement, particularly the social realists, in the 1930s. A 1931 studio fire destroyed many works from the series. By the early 1930s Baizerman had expanded his technique to include a method of hammering large sheets of metal on both sides, giving the material a hand-worked sensuousness. He then formed these into figures or figural fragments, often on a monumental scale. The life-size torso *Slumber* (Whitney Museum, 1948) invokes the classical tradition as it floats lightly above its pedestal, supported only at one point. His wife, painter **Eugenie Silverman Baizerman** (1899–1949), was born in Warsaw but lived as a youngster in Russia. After settling in New York as a teenager, she studied at the National Academy of Design and elsewhere. Her work evolved from its origins in French impressionism to a personal style emphasizing color harmonies.

Baldessari, John (1931–). Conceptual artist, painter, printmaker, collage artist, and photographer. Among artists who have contributed to *conceptual art, he stands out for responsiveness to visual effects. Although he has focused on questions of meaning in visual representation and/or language, he has for the most part avoided the dry, documentary approach that characterizes much conceptual work. Instead, he remains open to the richly allusive powers of optical experience, while also maintaining a sense of humor. A central influence on many younger artists, he has taught in the Los Angeles area since 1970, first at the California Institute of the Arts and more recently, at UCLA. Born in National City, John Anthony Baldessari graduated from nearby San Diego State University in 1953 and received a master's degree there four years later. He also studied in Los Angeles, at the Otis Art Institute (now Otis College of Art and Design) and the Chouinard Art Institute (predecessor to the California Institute of the Arts). At first primarily a painter, in the mid-1960s he began to introduce photographs and/or text to undermine the medium's presuppositions. A witty painting consisting only of lettering (subcontracted to a professional sign-painter) proclaims EVERYTHING IS PURGED FROM THIS PAINTING BUT ART, NO IDEAS HAVE ENTERED THIS WORK (private collection, 1966). In 1970 he ceremonially cremated his paintings and recycled the ashes into other works. Looking to precedents in the work of Marcel *Duchamp, John *Cage, Robert *Rauschenberg, Andy *Warhol, and the *fluxus artists, among others, he subsequently favored open-ended experimental procedures. Using his own photographs or images taken from popular culture, primarily movie stills, he arranges his material in formats that implicitly question the meaning of representation, set up ambiguous narratives, or tease in concert with intriguing texts.

Ball, Thomas (1819–1911). Sculptor and painter. Best known for his *Emancipation Group*, also known as *Lincoln Freeing the Slaves* (Lincoln Park, Washington D.C., 1876; modeled 1865–67), he specialized in portraiture. His straightforwardly realistic style led to many commissions for public memorials honoring prominent Americans. Among the finest, his equestrian bronze *George Washington* (Boston Public Garden, 1869; original model 1858; full-scale model completed 1864) portrays the general with vigor and dignity. He also produced a number of ideal subjects, mostly marble renditions of classical or sentimental themes, including several of children. His small bronzes helped to secure the popularity of sculpture in middle-class interior decor. Born in Charlestown (now part of Boston), before he was twenty he had set up shop in Boston as a portrait and miniature painter, mostly self-taught. In the 1840s he also executed religious and literary subjects. He began modeling in clay around 1850 and soon found success with portrait busts. In 1854 he left for Italy, spending two years in Florence and Rome before returning to Boston. In 1865 he departed once again for Florence, where he made his home until 1897. Moved by Abraham Lincoln's death, which occurred during his trip back to Italy, he soon began work on a tribute depicting a standing Lincoln extending his arm over a black man kneeling in gratitude for his freedom. Ball produced several replicas in marble and bronze of this *Emancipation Group* before 1873, when the Freedman's Memorial Society requested a ten-foot bronze version. Financed by former slaves, it was installed in a Washington, D.C., park three years later. Upon his final return to the United States, Ball settled in Montclair, New Jersey, where he returned to painting before his death there. Ball's autobiography, *My Three Score Years and Ten*, appeared in 1891. The sequel, *My Fourscore Years*, written in 1899 and 1900, was published only in 1993.

Baltz, Lewis. *See* NEW TOPOGRAPHICS.

Bannister, Edward Mitchell (1828–1901). Painter. Known primarily for landscapes, he also painted portraits, historical scenes, and other subjects. Motivated by faith in nature's spiritual harmony, he interpreted undramatic scenery in a moody, painterly style indebted to *Barbizon precedents. Perhaps uniquely among American artists of African descent during the Civil War and Reconstruction periods, he achieved respect within an almost exclusively white art establishment. Garnering the first national art award given to a black, a landscape took a first prize at the 1876 Centennial Exposition in Philadelphia. The mixed-race artist was born in the seaport village of St. Andrews, New Brunswick, near the Maine border. As a young man, he worked as a sailor but settled in Boston by 1850. There he worked as a barber and photographer. Largely self-taught as an artist, in Boston he attended lectures by William *Rimmer and probably came into contact with William Morris *Hunt. About 1870 he moved permanently to Providence, where he became a leading member of its art community. He participated in organizing the Providence Art Club (still in existence), which established the Rhode Island School of Design. He continued to paint into the 1890s, despite poor health in later years and diminishing recognition. Bannister's sensitive *Newspaper Boy* (Smithsonian American Art Museum, 1869) demonstrates familiarity with Hunt's figural works in its attention to contour, flattened volume, and painterly surface. One of his best-known landscapes, *Approaching Storm* (Smithsonian American Art Museum, 1886) responds to impressions of time and place as a small figure scurries into the wind beneath a lowering sky. A free and vigorously impastoed surface suggests rocks and vegetation. Translating emotional response into color and texture, it recalls the period's French-inspired landscapes by such artists as George *Inness and Homer *Martin.

Banvard, John. *See* PANORAMA.

Barbizon, American. Term designating an approach to landscape and rural subjects inspired by the work of the French Barbizon School. American Barbizon paintings, typically moody, intimate views, stress painterly values, formal arrangements, and emotional response. Although these paintings scrutinize natural forms and effects, they generally disregard detailed verisimilitude. William Morris *Hunt was chiefly responsible for introducing the Barbizon style into the United States in the 1850s. In the same decade George *Inness began to draw heavily on Barbizon art in the development of a personal style. The Barbizon School coalesced near Paris in the 1830s in the village of Barbizon and surrounding Forest of Fontainebleau. Its principal figures include Théodore Rousseau, Jean-François Millet, Charles-François Daubigny, and Narcisse-Virgile Diaz, as well as, more peripherally, Jean-Baptiste-Camille Corot and Gustave Courbet. These artists strove to record deeply felt, antiheroic responses to nature, which they regarded as a refuge from modern life and an antidote to academic practice. Their American followers tended to emphasize the emotional and expressive aspects of the Barbizon approach, which provided an alternative to the prevailing *Hudson River School and *Pre-Raphaelite regard for exacting truth to nature. At the same time, the Barbizon ethos continued to revere nature as a source of value. Barbizon painters in both France and the United States generally finished their paintings in the studio, although they made studies outdoors. Following conventional painting technique, they organized their compositions tonally, that is around masses of light and dark. While aspects of their work prefigure impressionism, Barbizon work stops short of the technical and conceptual freedom associated with the later movement. In the late nineteenth century, French Barbizon painting dominated the American art market.

Bard, James (1815–97). Painter. Until around 1850 he collaborated on paintings of ships with his twin, **John Bard** (1815–56), but later continued on his own. They specialized in depicting the new steam-driven vessels of their day on the Hudson River but also portrayed sailboats. Born in New York and self-taught as artists, they found a steady clientele there among ship owners and captains. John seems to have left the partnership a few years before his death, but during the collaboration he apparently added coloring to James's designs. To achieve the specificity admired by their patrons, before embarking on most paintings James is thought to have made measurements and scaled drawings. A prolific worker, he continued to paint until around 1890. He died in White Plains, a New York suburb. Working in an unsophisticated, conceptual style, the Bards employed patterned design, scrupulously observed detail, and fanciful flourishes to achieve lively, even exuberant visions of American technology at work. By sidestepping the traditional European formulas for creating convincing illusionism, their style suggests the independent, nativist spirit that fueled American enterprise and pervaded mid-century political and social life. Exemplifying his customary formula, James Bard's *O. M. Pettit*

(New-York Historical Society, 1857) portrays a side-wheeler, with water in the foreground and hills in the distance. Smoke from its stack streams behind, as do three colorful, outsize flags flapping in the breeze. A few men, also slightly overscaled, are visible on deck. Radiating optimism and delight, the painter's invention floats as confidently as its subject.

Barnard, George Grey (1863–1938). Sculptor. An individualistic romantic inspired particularly by the work of Michelangelo, he employed symbolic figures to explore the human condition. Unlike most sculptors of his day, he rarely accepted portrait commissions and completed only one public monument to an individual, *Abraham Lincoln* (Lytle Park, Cincinnati, 1911–17). Barnard also pioneered an enthusiasm for medieval art before its quality was widely recognized. His extensive collections of Romanesque and Gothic antiquities eventually formed the basis of the Cloisters, an upper Manhattan outpost of the *Metropolitan Museum of Art. He also accumulated an important portion of the Philadelphia Museum of Art's medieval holdings. In his sculpture, he forged an expressive style of somewhat generalized naturalism. His best-known work, the heroic *Struggle of the Two Natures in Man* (Metropolitan Museum, 1892–94; modeled 1888), evokes the immemorial contest between physical and spiritual being. Inspired by Victor Hugo's poetry, this complex interplay of solids and surrounding spaces features two larger than life-size male nudes carved by the artist himself from a single block of marble. This unusual subject avoids the bland allegory of much contemporary sculpture, but its realization fails to equal the formal power and psychological conviction of Rodin's similarly conceived symbolic enterprises of the same period. Born in the central Pennsylvania town of Bellefonte, Barnard lived as a child in several midwestern communities, principally Kankakee, Illinois, for eight years. At the Chicago Academy of Design (now the School of the Art Institute of Chicago), where he began his artistic training in 1880, casts of Michelangelo's work captured his imagination. In 1883 he departed for Paris, where he studied for the first three years at the École des Beaux-Arts. After earning his first public acclaim with *Two Natures* and other works in 1894, he relocated to New York. There, his approach out of step with prevailing taste, he received few of the public commissions that absorbed other major French-trained sculptors of his day. For the most significant undertaking of his career, he was engaged in 1902 to produce a grand ensemble of marble allegorical figures (1902–10; installed 1911) to adorn the Pennsylvania state capitol in Harrisburg. Incorporating his own convictions, the imagery of some thirty over-life-size figures in two groups, *Burden of Life: The Broken Law* and *Love and Labor: The Unbroken Law*, represents complex and exalted notions of personal and social virtue. He departed for France in 1903 to carry out the project while living near Paris. Reflecting his idealism, his liberal and humanitarian political orientation, his penchant for the grandiose, and his growing isolation from mainstream art culture, in the aftermath of World War I Barnard designed a massive sculpture park devoted to peace. However, it failed to attract support. Forced to abandon the plan in 1924, he nevertheless continued for many years to work on its central element. Again employing a figurative vocabulary to explore abstract notions, the colossal *Rainbow Arch* (plaster model, 1933) included more than fifty monumental figures in a Rodinesque ensemble dedicated to the human costs of war and benefits of peace.

Barnard, George N. (1819–1902). Photographer. Among the earliest photographers to record newsworthy events, he contributed importantly to visual documentation of the Civil War. Born in Coventry, Connecticut, he moved as a child to central New York State and later lived in Nashville and Gallatin, Tennessee. In the early 1840s he returned to upstate New York and within a few years operated a *daguerreotype portrait studio in Oswego. When the grain elevators there burned in 1853, Barnard captured the event on full-plate daguerreotypes (George Eastman House International Museum of Photography and Film, Rochester, New York), which number among the earliest existing examples of photojournalism. Soon after, he moved his business to Syracuse, where he diversified his photographic techniques. In 1859 he moved to New York but also traveled in search of subjects for *stereographs. In 1860 he photographed in Cuba, but none of this work is known to survive. The following year Mathew *Brady hired him. After the Civil War broke out, he worked in the field and was present at the important battle of Bull Run. Some of these images appear in Alexander *Gardner's 1866 *Photographic Sketch Book of the War*. From 1863 until the end of the war he worked as an official Union army photographer, producing his most significant contribution to the war's coverage while following troops across South Carolina and Georgia in the well-known 1864 march to the sea. Sixty-one large prints of the trail of desolation and destruction of Atlanta appeared in the portfolio *Photographic Views of Sherman's Campaign* (1866), accompanied by a thirty-page brochure of text and maps. In the later 1860s he worked again in Syracuse, in Charleston, South Carolina, and in Chicago, where his studio was destroyed in the great fire of 1871. Nevertheless, he borrowed a camera to document the conflagration. Later he practiced in several locations, including Rochester, New York, where in the early 1880s he promoted dry-plate technology for George *Eastman. He spent his last decade on a farm outside Cedarvale, not far from Syracuse.

Barnes, Albert C. (1872–1951). Collector and museum founder. Among the world's great collections of modern art when it was formed, the Barnes Foundation focuses on French art. Renoir dominates, but Cézanne and Matisse as well as other impressionists and postimpressionists are well represented. The relatively few Americans represented include Arthur *Carles, Andrew *Dasburg, Charles *Demuth, William *Glackens, and Maurice *Prendergast. The collection also includes sizable holdings in African tribal art and early American crafts. A lifelong resident of the Philadelphia area, Albert Coombs Barnes went to Central High School with Glackens and John *Sloan. After receiving his MD degree in 1892 from the University of Pennsylvania's medical school, he studied and traveled in Europe. He made a fortune from the sale of Argyrol, an antiseptic he and a German acquaintance invented in 1902. Until around 1910 when he became enamored of impressionist and modern art, he for the most part limited his art purchases to conventional nineteenth-century landscapes. As an advisor and buyer for the collection, Glackens may have stimulated this shift in taste. In the 1920s Barnes developed a system (which probably he alone understood) of scientific aesthetics, which he set forth in *Art in Painting* (1925). In 1925 at his new residence in the Philadelphia suburb of Merion, he opened a public gallery intended to function as an educational institution. However, as he feuded constantly with artists, museum personnel, and art lovers, the irritable, discourteous, and dogmatic Barnes restricted visitors so severely that few saw the collection. After Barnes's death in an automobile accident, a court ruling in 1961 forced the foundation to admit a limited number of visitors. Although Barnes's will specified that his collection remain always as he had arranged it, unaltered in any way, a court ruling in 2004 gave permission for the financially beleaguered museum to relocate in downtown Philadelphia.

Barnet, Will (1911–). Painter and printmaker. Although best known for formally refined and slightly enigmatic figural work of recent decades, in the middle years of the twentieth century he pursued abstraction. A devoted printmaker, with technical expertise encompassing lithography, woodcut, and intaglio, Barnet has treated printmaking as a serious undertaking in its own right, not as a sideline to painting. Born in Beverly, on the northern Massachusetts coast, he studied with Philip Leslie *Hale at Boston's School of the Museum of Fine Arts before moving permanently to New York in 1930. There he continued his training at the *Art Students League and became the league's professional lithographer. He also taught there and elsewhere for more than two decades, inspiring many students with his wide knowledge of modern and traditional art history as well as studio practice. During the 1930s, his subjects reflected prevailing interests in the social realism of the *American Scene movement, with particular attention to the children and families that have remained a focus of his representational imagery. He worked primarily in lithography during these years, but in the late 1930s began to make woodcuts. In these, sharper value contrasts, flatter space, and rougher shapes suggest attention to German expressionist precedents. In the 1940s and 1950s, he made few prints as he turned to abstract paintings featuring flat, stylized forms inspired by Northwest Coast and Southwestern Indian art. Bolstered by his enthusiastic and scholarly advocacy for American tribal art, these works figured centrally in the brief flowering of *Indian Space painting. In 1954 he joined the *American Abstract Artists, an organization steeped in the cubism and constructivism that also informed his abstraction. Around the same time, he began spending summers in Maine, the setting for many later paintings. In the early 1960s, as he began to reengage figuration by way of portraiture, his abstract work culminated in relatively large, luminously colored, spare compositions. Since the late 1960s, Barnet has concentrated on stately figurative work combining deliberate composition, patterned form, and shallow space with subtly modulated color. Frequently centering on domestic imagery but also comprising allegorical interests, his subjects project a mood of calm and meditative aloofness. Piero della Francesca, Milton *Avery, Alex *Katz, and Japanese prints variously come to mind.

Barr, Alfred H., Jr. *See* MUSEUM OF MODERN ART.

Barrer, Gertrude. *See* INDIAN SPACE PAINTING.

Barthé, Richmond (1901–89). Sculptor. Remembered for lyric portraits and figure studies of fellow African Americans, he also addressed Christian subjects from a devoutly Catholic perspective. Extending the sculptural mainstream of his youth, Barthé drew on the tradition of such artists as Augustus *Saint-Gaudens and Daniel Chester *French. Little touched by modernism or by the enthusiasm among many black artists of his day for African sources, he gave elegant form and supple movement to his subjects. Nearly all of his work is modeled, rather than carved, and finds its permanent form in bronze. Among the most revered and widely popular African-American artists of the 1930s and 1940s, when he created his best work, he later fell into obscurity as changing critical fashions spurned his romantic sensibility. Born on the Mississippi Gulf coast, in Bay St. Louis, he pursued his study of painting and sculpture at the School of the Art Institute of Chicago from 1924 to 1928. In 1929 he studied at the *Art Students League and soon became a central figure in New York's *Harlem Renaissance. Always interested in performance as well as the expressive capabilities of the human body, in the 1930s he studied modern dance and produced images of its practitioners. One of these, the impassioned bronze *Feral Benga* (Museum of Fine Arts, Houston, 1935), depicts a nude male African. Betokening racial pride, it synthesizes dramatic movement, unselfconscious display of a sensuous body, exoticism, and seeming loss of self in transcendent artistic experience. In 1951 Barthé moved to Jamaica, where he worked until departing for Europe in 1969. The following year he settled in Florence. He died at his home in Pasadena, California, where he had resided since 1977.

Bartlett, Jennifer. *See* NEW IMAGE PAINTING.

Bartlett, Paul Wayland (1865–1925). Sculptor. Known particularly for monumental commemorative and architectural sculpture, he resided for most of his life in Paris. His style reflected late-nineteenth-century French taste for formal elegance, impressionistic surfaces, and spontaneous effects. Born in New Haven, Connecticut, he was schooled in France and received his artistic training at the École des Beaux-Arts. He worked also with animal specialist Emmanuel Frémiet and with Rodin. One of his best-known works, the bronze *Bear Tamer* (Metropolitan Museum, 1887) established his international reputation. Depicting a lithe and nearly nude young man with two cubs, its vivacity, easy naturalism, and complex three-dimensional structure demonstrate the young sculptor's mastery of current French practice. Subsequently, Bartlett specialized in bronze animal subjects before receiving his first important public commission, a pair of bronze historical portrait figures, *Columbus* (1897) and *Michelangelo* (1898), for the reading room of the new Library of Congress in Washington, D.C. These inaugurated a career thereafter devoted primarily to idealizing civic monuments. Among the most important, his equestrian bronze *Lafayette* (1898–1908) for the grounds of the Louvre dramatically presents the Revolutionary War commander astride a vigorous steed with sword raised. This publicly funded American tribute to friendship with France represents as well Bartlett's ongoing aspiration to harmonize his European artistic heritage with American themes. His major public sculptures in the United States include the New York Stock Exchange's pediment decoration, *Integrity Protecting the Works of Man* (1901–4; with John Quincy Adams *Ward), and six allegorical figures on the facade of the New York Public Library (1909–15), as well as the U.S. Capitol's *Apotheosis of Democracy* (1908–16). To facilitate work on this pediment grouping for the House of Representatives wing, late in 1908 he established a studio in Washington. Subsequently he divided his time between the capital and Paris, where he died.

His father, **Truman Bartlett** (1835–1923), was a sculptor of portraits and monuments. A teacher and art historian as well, Truman Howe Bartlett was born in Dorset, Vermont, and, like his son, worked with Frémiet in Paris. He also knew Rodin and in 1889 published an important series of articles about his work. His pioneering *Art Life of William *Rimmer, Sculptor, Painter, and Physician* (1882) remains an important source.

Bartram, William (1739–1823). Painter and draftsman. Also a naturalist. Son of North America's first important botanist, John Bartram, William continued his father's scientific research. He recorded his observations in drawings and watercolors that capture nature's vitality and charm with freshness and precision, while also conveying the interrelatedness of biological life, a view indebted to the published work of Mark *Catesby. Bartram's chief accomplishment, the illustrated *Travels through North and South Carolina, Georgia, etc.* (1791), won acclaim on both sides of the Atlantic for its literary qualities as well as its scientific content. The work's personal tone and appreciation for the grandeur of nature influenced the development of Anglo-American *romanticism. Born in Kingsessing (now part of Philadelphia), where his father had established the first colonial botanical garden on the Schuylkill River, he began drawing specimens as a youngster. He accompanied his father on collecting expeditions, including an ambitious journey in 1765 to Florida, and later worked on his own in Florida and North Carolina. In 1773 Bartram embarked on a journey of some twenty-five hundred miles through Florida and the Southeast, traveling as far west as the Mississippi River. After his return early in 1777, he continued to reside in the house where he was born while assisting a brother in maintaining the family's experimental garden. Remaining engaged with the scientific community of his day, he provided encouragement to younger naturalists, including Charles Willson *Peale and Alexander *Wilson. Bartram died at the family homestead. Today a National Historic Landmark, the house and gardens are open to the public.

Baskin, Leonard (1922–2000). Graphic artist and sculptor. Committed to the expression of moral and tragic themes through figurative imagery, he is remembered especially for expressionistic woodcuts. Although his art reverberates with major themes of twentieth-century art and thought, Baskin maintained a personal course independent of stylistic trends. Male figures and birds provided the major vehicles of his vision of life as a tragic but heroic journey. Although his work is not issue-oriented, he remained motivated by a social mission: sympathetic representation of the human condition. Born in New Brunswick, New Jersey, Baskin moved to New York with his family when he was seven. He spent two years at New York University before transferring to Yale University, where he studied from 1941 to 1943. He then served in the U.S. Navy before continuing his studies in New York at the New School for Social Research (now New School), where he earned a BA in 1949. In 1950 he went to Paris and in the following year to Florence for further study. From 1953 until 1974 he taught at Smith College in Northampton, Massachusetts. After a ten-year interim in England, he returned to teach in nearby Amherst at Hampshire College, remaining on the faculty until 1994. He died in Northampton, where he made his home. Early in his career, he was known primarily as a sculptor, mainly of figures that symbolized man's existential anxiety, poignant suffering, and inevitable demise. Later his prints and drawings extended these themes with even greater psychological subtlety, as in the 1958 woodcut *Tormented Man*, which juxtaposes a man's head with a bird in an image of ambiguous tension. Strong contrasts of light and dark provide drama, while linear elegance suggests ephemeral beauty. Baskin's interests extended not only to the illustration of books but also their total design and fabrication. To serve these ends, in 1942 he founded Gehenna Press, which at the time of his death had published more than a hundred limited edition books of great sumptuousness and sophistication.

Basquiat, Jean-Michel (1960–88). Painter and collage artist. His expressionistic creations packed with personal symbolism drawn from art history, literature, and street life earned widespread acclaim during a meteoric career preceding his death from drugs at twenty-seven. Yet, his deliberate primitivism and frequently clichéd, eclectic allusions drew criticism from those who found his work shallow, derivative, and incompetent. Many also regarded with suspicion his flamboyant lifestyle and inveterate self-promotion. Although such detractors remain, with the passage of time his work has gained respect for its originality, ambition, and expression of a bicultural, bisexual sensibility imbued with the spirit of its historical moment. Born in Brooklyn to a Haitian father and a mother of Puerto Rican descent, Basquiat grew up in a middle-class, cultured atmosphere. Encouraged in his artistic aspirations, he never fit the ghetto-kid stereotype that some tried to apply. Nevertheless, his African-American heritage fueled his creative life as a source of both pride and rage. Around the time he quit school at seventeen, he devised a fictional alter ego, SAMO ("same old"), to sign spray-painted graffiti he and a friend spread around New York in the late 1970s, the peak period of such art vandalism as a form of countercultural expression. In 1980 he appeared for the first time in an art exhibition, the legendary "Times Square Show" that introduced a cohort identified with the nascent punk/new wave East Village, as well as other relatively unknown younger artists. Basquiat's raw, frenetic, unironic paintings seemed to emanate from a fevered consciousness where old masters, advertising, religious imagery, black heroes, childish stick figures, diverse texts, satirical commentary, social protest, and private fantasies mingled in hyperactive delirium. Boundless energy enhanced a talent for painterly brushwork and sophisticated formal invention. He often collaged elements into his canvases and sometimes employed loosely thrown together structures as painting supports. During several years in the mid-1980s, a close friendship with Andy *Warhol produced a number of collaborative paintings. Toward the end of his life, Basquiat's paintings often showed a fresh discipline, suggesting unrealized potentials in the precocious personal style he had already realized. He died in his East Village apartment.

Baur, John I. H. (1909–87). Art writer, curator, and museum director. An early advocate of American art, at a time when scholarly and critical opinion still undervalued native achievement, John Ireland Howe Baur was born in Woodbridge, Connecticut, and educated at Yale University. He graduated with a degree in English in 1932 and two years later received his MA in art history. Afterward, except for U.S. Army service in 1944–45, he worked at the Brooklyn Museum until 1952 and then at the *Whitney Museum of American Art, where he was named director in 1968. He retired in 1974 but remained professionally active. At the time of his death in a New York hospital, he made his home in Katonah, New York. Many of Baur's numerous books incorporating groundbreaking research served also as catalogues of exhibitions he organized. His most important publications include *Revolution and Tradition in Modern American Art* (1951), *Nature in Abstraction* (1958), and monographs on Eastman *Johnson (1942), John *Quidor (1942), Theodore *Robinson (1946), Loren *MacIver and I. Rice *Pereira (1953), Bradley Walker *Tomlin (1957), William *Zorach (1958), Philip *Evergood (1960), Joseph *Stella (1971), and Charles *Burchfield (1982). Working from the artist's manuscript, he edited *The Autobiography of Worthington *Whittredge*, which first appeared in book form in 1969.

Bay Area figurative art. An unprogrammatic late 1950s and early 1960s San Francisco–based tendency featuring representational imagery within a painterly mode conditioned by *abstract expressionism's richly vigorous brushwork. Generalized figurative subjects predominate, landscape holds an important secondary place, humorous or lowbrow elements occasionally crop up, and natural light effects commonly play a leading role. Like the region's *funk artists, the Bay Area figurative group tended to regard as pretentious abstract expressionism's philosophical rhetoric. Organized for the Oakland Art Museum (now Oakland Museum of California) in 1957 by director Richard Mills (1924–2004), the show "Contemporary Bay Area Figurative Painting" crystallized the movement. Richard *Diebenkorn ranks as its most significant participant. David Park (1911–60) set the pace for the Bay Area's revival of figuration. His monumental and simplified figures usually appear individually or arranged in small groups within indeterminate environments. Born in Boston, Park studied at the Otis Art Institute (now Otis College of Art and Design) in Los Angeles before moving to San Francisco in 1928. He painted murals for a *federal art project during the Depression. For several years in the late 1940s and early 1950s he worked in an abstract expressionist style before reverting to figuration, now invested with a strikingly original flavor. He died in Berkeley.

Born in Berkeley, where he lived nearly all his life, subtle colorist Elmer Bischoff (1916–91) achieved warmth and intimacy in his figurative compositions of the 1950s to early 1970s. Earlier, he had worked in a lyric abstract expressionist style, and later he again returned to abstraction. He received a BA from the University of California at Berkeley in 1938 and a master's degree the following year. After his return in 1946 from four years of service in the U.S. Army Air Force, he taught at the California School of Fine Arts (now San Francisco Art Institute). Except for a few years in the early 1950s, he remained there until 1963, when he accepted a position at the University of California at Berkeley. He retired in 1985. Around 1952 he followed Park's example in turning to figuration. Variously inspired by Bonnard, Edvard Munch, and the impressionists, the expressive tenor of his work varied from placid to turbulent, but radiant hues and delectable lighting remained central. About 1974 he switched to an intricate, nongeometric form of abstraction. In 1962 he married painter Adelie Landis, whose work has mixed figuration and painterly abstraction. Born in Brooklyn, she studied at schools in New York and San Francisco before graduating from Berkeley in 1958 and earning a master's degree there the following year. She continues to make her home in Berkeley.

Besides Diebenkorn, Park, and Bischoff, the three central figures, several others contributed importantly to the movement. Painter, printmaker, and sculptor Nathan Oliveira (1928–) maintains ties with old master and modern European art in richly painted canvases and masterful graphic works. Often focused on single figures or animals, his paintings present links to the work of earlier artists, such as Goya, Odilon Redon, and Munch, but also Alberto Giacometti and Francis Bacon. He also draws on landscape and interiors as subjects, and sometimes pushes themes nearly to abstraction. In the 1980s he began making sculptural equivalents of his expressionist figures. Nathan Joseph Oliveira was born in Oakland and studied there at Mills College, where one summer he worked with Max Beckmann. He earned an MFA in 1952 from Oakland's California College of Arts and Crafts (now

California College of the Arts). From 1964 until his retirement in 1992 he taught at Stanford University. In recent years, he has spent much of his time in New Mexico. James Weeks (1922–98) emphasized formal structure in figure studies, including many depicting jazz and classical musicians, as well as landscapes and still lifes. With time, the bright, brushy technique of his early work gave way to softer, more considered application of paint to simplified shapes. Born in Oakland, James Darrell Northrup Weeks trained at the California School of Fine Arts and served in the U.S. military in 1944–45. A teacher throughout most of his career, he remained in the Bay Area until 1967, when he moved to Los Angeles for three years before accepting a position at Boston University. He retired in 1987.

Paul Wonner (1920–) has shifted from the broadly painted figure studies and still lifes of his early career toward a lavish realism stressing minute detail within complex still lifes and interiors. Born in Tucson, Paul John Wonner graduated from the California College of Arts and Crafts in 1941 before spending four years in the U.S. Army. Following a subsequent period in New York, he returned to the Bay Area. In 1953 he received a master's degree from the University of California at Berkeley. His partner since 1952, when they met as graduate students at Berkeley, Theophilus Brown (1919–) continues to paint in a fluid representational manner extending his contribution to the Bay Area figurative movement. Born in Moline, Illinois, William Theophilus Brown graduated from Yale University in 1941. Subsequently, he served in the U.S. military and lived in Paris, where he studied with Amédée Ozenfant and Fernand Léger. In 1950 he relocated for two years to New York, where he worked as an abstract expressionist. Along with Wonner, he has for the most part made his home in San Francisco, although both have at various times accepted teaching posts elsewhere. The sculpture of Manuel Neri (1930–) presents a counterpart to the painted work of other Bay Area figurative artists. Limiting his practice to female figures, he focuses on form and finish rather than individualized characterization. Generally classical in temper, his works usually display an improvisatory execution. He often presents fragments, rather than fully realized figures. He has employed stone as well as bronze and other materials and has sometimes courted abstraction, while at other times responding more directly to his model. Born in Sanger, California, near Fresno, he studied at several Bay Area art schools. In the 1960s he was married to Joan *Brown.

Bayer, Herbert (1900–1985). Painter, photographer, architect, designer, and sculptor. His unspecialized approach to art and design reflected his Bauhaus training emphasizing basic principles of visual communication. He emerged as a veritable one-man band of modernism, able to address problems of form in practically any medium. Born in Haag, in the mountains of Austria, he worked as an apprentice architect and graphic designer in Linz and Darmstadt before arriving at the Bauhaus in 1921. For two years there he studied painting with Kandinsky, as well as typography. From 1925 to 1928 he headed the typography and graphic design studio at the school. For the next ten years he worked on commercial design and personal artistic projects in Berlin. In 1938 he moved to New York and six years later became an American citizen. For twenty years, beginning in 1945, he masterminded Container Corporation of America's innovative design program, including its Great Ideas of Western Man series, which commissioned works from well-known artists. In 1946, Bayer moved to Aspen, Colorado, which he helped to develop as a center for recreation and culture. He served as consultant and architect to the Aspen Institute of Humanistic Studies and founded the International Design Conference held there. He died near Santa Barbara, California, in Montecito, where he had lived in his last years. Ranging from commercial typography to murals, from exhibition design to environmental art, and from buildings to drawings, Bayer's extremely varied output defies simple generalizations. His work as a typographer, graphic designer, and photographer strongly influenced the development of modern advertising. Nevertheless, the fine arts were always at the heart of his enterprise, and he never ceased to think of himself as a painter. Geometric abstractions predominated in his paintings of the 1920s and 1930s, while later he investigated a variety of more personal modes, including coloristic studies and works based on landscape. His photographs, particularly those from his years in Europe, stand among his most vivid contributions to the fine arts. Many reflect the period's avant-garde search for identifiably modern angles of vision in straight photography, while his photomontages surrealistically manipulate reality, often with whimsical irony.

Baziotes, William (1912–63). Painter. An early *abstract expressionist, he created subtly hued, mysterious worlds. Like sea creatures or microscopic life, *biomorphic forms drift across his canvases, suggesting the variety, lyricism, and ineffability of nature and the psychic responses it provokes. Rooted in surrealism, his mature style offers a tranquil alternative to the excited brushwork and tormented tone associated with much abstract expressionism. Still, disquieting undercurrents suggest his longstanding interest in French symbolist poetry, with its romantic attraction to evil and depravity as well as to exaltation and transcendence. Classical myth, too, drew his interest as a source of access to the universal human themes that he, like so many of his abstract expressionist colleagues, found also in the arts of tribal peoples. Born in Pittsburgh, Baziotes grew up in Reading, Pennsylvania. After working for about two years in a stained glass factory, he moved to New York in 1933. There he studied for three years at the *National Academy of Design, where Leon *Kroll numbered among his teachers. From 1936 until 1941 he was employed by a *federal art project as a teacher and easel painter. He soon abandoned his early *social realism to experiment with modern approaches he found in the work of such artists as Picasso and Miró. Persian miniatures also attracted his attention, as did fossils and other aspects of natural history, which he continued for years to study at the American Museum of Natural History. With the outbreak of World War II, Roberto *Matta and other European artists relocating to New York exerted decisive influence on Baziotes's evolution. Along with such recent arrivals as Gordon *Onslow Ford and Jimmy *Ernst, Matta reinforced his interest in surrealism and encouraged use of *automatism to invent forms designed to convey psychological content. Throughout his subsequent career, Baziotes remained closely attached to his surrealist origins, perhaps surpassed in this respect among major abstract expressionists only by Arshile *Gorky.

Soon Baziotes became acquainted with other young Americans who traded ideas in the formation of abstract expressionism. In 1941 he met Robert *Motherwell, who shared his literary interests, as well as Jackson *Pollock and others. The following year he numbered among the handful of Americans invited to exhibit in the "First Papers of Surrealism," organized to showcase exiled Europeans. Baziotes's signature approach began to coalesce around 1946. By simplifying his previously intricate imagery and emphasizing pictorial structure, he achieved the strength evident in *Dwarf* (Museum of Modern Art, 1947), with its allusionistic humanoid, romantic tone, and richly colored, labile surface. During the 1950s he became more introspective and detached from former colleagues. From 1955 he spent summers back in Reading, far from the social centers of New York's art elite. During these years, his work became more deliberate and polished without losing its vital analogies to organic growth, its softly luminous coloration, and the authoritative poetry of the artist's dreamlike imagination. Prevented by illness from working during his final months, he died of lung cancer at his home in New York.

Beach, Emmeline Buckingham. *See* THAYER, ABBOTT.

Beal, Gifford (1879–1956). Painter and printmaker. A lifelong New Yorker, he is remembered particularly for outdoor views and circus scenes, painted in an impressionist style. A 1900 Princeton University graduate, Gifford Reynolds Beal received his training as an artist at the *Art Students League and with William Merritt *Chase. Although he traveled, most of his work depicts scenes of New York or New England. Beal's early work was dark and moody, but by 1910 his seascapes show a lighter, more atmospheric effect. He subsequently continued to develop his skill in capturing radiant light and color. *The Albany Boat* (Metropolitan Museum, 1915) effectively renders a sunny day along the Hudson River. In the foreground, a well-dressed crowd enjoys the pleasant weather; behind and below, docked on the brilliantly blue water, the white paddle-wheel boat receives passengers. Gifford's brother, painter and printmaker **Reynolds Beal** (1867–1951), also a New York native and student of Chase, painted at first in a dark-toned realist manner. Later, he worked in a high-keyed impressionist style, at his most vigorous including touches of nonnaturalistic color in a bright weave of strokes. He traveled widely and was known particularly as a watercolorist. He resided for many years in Rockport, Massachusetts, where he died.

Beall, Joanna. *See* WESTERMANN, H. C.

Beard, James Henry (probably 1811–93). Painter. A specialist in *genre subjects, together with his brother **William Holbrook Beard** (1824–1900), he introduced a form of social satire in which animals stand for human counterparts. James was born in Buffalo, New York, but grew up in Ohio. His brother William was born there, in Painesville. Both remained essentially self-taught as artists. In their own day, they were well regarded and widely popular for their humor, sometimes covertly bawdy, which punctured middle-class pretensions. However, they suffered a decline in reputation when changing tastes came to find much of their art sentimental or shallow. James worked as an itinerant portraitist before settling in Cincinnati by 1830. While residing there most of the time until 1870, when he moved to New York, he painted portraits and anecdotal scenes. Some, such as *The Long Bill* (Cincinnati Art Museum, c. 1840), picturing a. young man in a shop scratching his head in wonderment over the charges on a list in his hand, carried satirical overtones for contemporaries informed about current political debate. For one of his most powerful works, *The Night Before the Battle* (Memorial Art Gallery, University of Rochester [New York], 1865), he drew on his experience as a Civil War soldier. In a Gethsemane-like setting, soldiers sleep as a skeletal Death keeps watch by moonlight at the ramparts. After this time, he turned frequently to animal subjects. These most often anthropomorphize dogs in seemingly human interactions taking place in domestic interiors. He died in the Flushing area of Queens. William traveled to Europe in 1856. He achieved some success in Buffalo before moving permanently to New York about 1860. Although he also painted genre scenes and portraits, he soon specialized in animals. Some are straightforward portrayals, but most cast furry characters in human roles. He particularly favored bears, as in the merry *Bears of Wall Street Celebrating a Drop in the Market* (New-York Historical Society, undated).

Bearden, Romare (1911–88). Painter, printmaker, and collage artist. He started as a realist who anchored his work in his own African-American experience. Soon finding racial definitions of art confining, he sought a more universal view of art's purpose. After the 1960s civil rights movement reignited Bearden's interest in black history and experience, most of his work depicted African Americans, but he avoided propagandistic simplicities, responding instead to the complexity of black life as an aspect of American culture. His keen appreciation of art history, particularly the modern movement, fostered a sophisticated formal language. Bearden was born in Charlotte, North Carolina, but lived also in Pittsburgh and New York as he was growing up. After two years at Boston University, he transferred to New York University. A mathematics major, he graduated in 1935. The following year he enrolled for a year at the *Art Students League, where he studied under George *Grosz. Although inspired by *Harlem Renaissance pride in black creativity, he criticized its tolerance of artistic mediocrity and remained aloof from its institutions. His three-year World War II military service prompted interest in religious and literary sources for universal symbols of human suffering, which he rendered expressionistically. In 1950–51 he studied art history at the Sorbonne in Paris and traveled widely on the Continent and in North Africa. Subsequently he made his home in New York. For a time he explored *abstract expressionism in works that sometimes dispense with figuration altogether. In the 1960s he began to work extensively with collage, using photographic elements in combination with painted areas. In these he mingled allegory and observation to comment on African-American realities, while making effective use of modern techniques such as fragmentation, overlapping, and disjunctions of scale. Hinting in its rhythmic structure at Bearden's love of jazz and demonstrating the artist's grounding in cubist composition, dada collage, Matisse's cutouts, and Stuart *Davis's pre-pop art city scenes, *The Dove* (Museum of Modern Art, 1964) melds local vitality with the spirit of universal humanity within an evocation of black urban life. Later work often reflected his frequent sojourns on the Caribbean island of Saint Martin. He died in New York. Bearden coauthored three books: *The Painter's Mind* (1969), *Six Black Masters of American Art* for young readers (1972), and the posthumously published *History of African-American Artists from 1792 to the Present* (1993).

Beaux, Cecilia (1855–1942). Painter. Known especially for elegant, fluidly rendered portraits, she numbered among the most celebrated American artists of her day and achieved an international reputation. In 1895 she began a twenty-year teaching career in her native Philadelphia at the *Pennsylvania Academy of the Fine Arts, where she ranked as the first woman to receive a full-time appointment. Baptized Eliza Cecilia, Beaux grew up in the care of genteel maternal relatives, following the death of her mother shortly after childbirth. Her early training included art lessons during her teenage years with a distant cousin, Catherine Ann Drinker (later Mrs. Thomas Janvier; 1841–1922), and, between 1876 and 1878, intermittent instruction at the Pennsylvania Academy, where Thomas *Eakins reigned. While working privately in the early 1880s with William *Sartain, she evolved into an accomplished painter conversant with Whistlerian models and *aesthetic movement taste. In 1888 she left for Paris. Abroad for about a year and a half, she studied at the Académie Julian and the Académie Colarossi. During a summer in Brittany, at the Concarneau art colony popular among Americans, including a supportive Alexander *Harrison, she painted landscapes and figural works. Impressionism's impact during her French residency is evident in subsequently looser brushwork, a brighter palette, and increased attention to ephemeral light effects. After returning to Philadelphia, she specialized in portraits, bringing a fresh spirit to the grand manner tradition. In its vivid immediacy, painterly brushwork, and unconventional composition, *Ernesta (Child with Nurse)* (Metropolitan Museum, 1894) demonstrates a grasp of psychological as well as physical experience. A bright-faced toddler smartly attired in white seizes her nurse, whose presence is revealed only by the skirts of her uniform and a hand guiding the child. Beaux's second trip to Europe, a visit to France and England in 1896, confirmed her interest in portraiture, as she responded to the fashionable accomplishments of John Singer *Sargent. From the early 1890s she had often visited New York, and near the end of the decade she relocated there. Her later work sometimes emphasizes opulence and painterly effects at the expense of character and originality, but she remained in constant demand for public and private commissions. She painted little after 1924, when she suffered a crippling hip injury in Paris on one of several later trips to Europe. Her autobiography, *Background with Figures*, appeared in 1930. She died at Gloucester, Massachusetts, on the shore north of Boston, where she had maintained a summer home and studio since 1905.

Bechtle, Robert. *See* PHOTO-REALISM.

Beers, Julie. *See* HART, JAMES.

Bellocq, E. J. *See* FRIEDLANDER, LEE.

Bellows, George (1882–1925). Painter and printmaker. The most important heir to the *Ashcan tradition in American art, he employed vigorous, sensuous brushwork in seascapes, portraits, and scenes of urban life. Although willing to take on a range of artistic challenges, Bellows continues to be particularly known for his few boxing scenes, such as *Both Members of This Club* (National Gallery, 1909). Bellows's death in New York from a ruptured appendix cut short a career still rich with promise. A native of Columbus, Ohio, George Wesley Bellows attended Ohio State University before moving to New York in 1904. There he studied for two years at the New York School of Art (now Parsons, the New School for Design) with Robert *Henri, from whom he absorbed a radical individualism, as well as the belief that good painting demands a passionate involvement with life. Thomas *Eakins, James McNeill *Whistler, and, above all, Winslow *Homer became his personal artistic idols, while at the same time he also benefited from the painterly examples of William Merritt *Chase and James Singer *Sargent. Although he never visited Europe, through these and other influential American artists, he drew on the rich tradition of European realism exemplified by Frans Hals, Goya, and Manet.

Bellows quickly matured into a leading interpreter of contemporary life. *Forty-Two Kids* (Corcoran Gallery, 1907), picturing boys swimming from a dock in the East River, demonstrates acuity as a topical reporter. Although in this and other paintings of the crowded city, the characters he depicts are anonymous types—sometimes stereotypes—Bellows had a talent for portraiture, evident in another painting of 1907, *Little Girl in White* (National Gallery). Responding to his social conscience, he provided drawings for *The *Masses* from 1913 until it ceased publication in 1917. In 1916, he took up lithography, which he used during World War I to produce a notable series on the atrocities of that conflict. Although Bellows's early work showed a natural freshness, he modified his largely intuitive approach in the wake of the 1913 *Armory Show. Like many artists of the period, he became intensely interested in theories of color and composition, especially as put forth in writings by Denman *Ross, Hardesty *Maratta, and Jay *Hambidge. Bellows's fascination with systems occasionally produced a dry artificiality in his paintings, but more often his alignment of major forms within geometric patterns provided structure and monumentality to enhance his fluid painterliness. Some of his most exhilarating later paintings reflect his travels, especially along the Maine coast where he spent many summers. In 1922 he established a seasonal residence at *Woodstock. Portraits, particularly of family, rank among the most tenderly conceived and fully realized paintings of his later career.

Benbridge, Henry (1743–1812). Painter. Chiefly a portraitist, the Philadelphia native received some instruction in 1758 from John *Wollaston. While still a teenager, his encouraging mother and stepfather allowed him to decorate the interior of their house with figural compositions derived from prints of Renaissance and Baroque paintings. Obviously ambitious for his art, in 1765 he arrived in Italy. In Rome he absorbed the same grand manner influences that had recently formed Benjamin *West, whose wife was a relative. Benbridge also evidently admired the paintings of Anton Raffael Mengs, as well as those of Pompeo Batoni, with whom he may have studied. Mingling with the Anglo-American community, he became acquainted with writer James Boswell, who commissioned a portrait of Corsican patriot *Pascal Paoli* (Fine Arts

Museums of San Francisco, 1768). Benbridge traveled to Corsica to execute the likeness, which he sent to London for exhibition before he arrived late in 1769. The Paoli portrait brought him attention (especially since Paoli himself had in the same year fled to London to escape a French invasion), and he worked quite successfully there for about half a year. During this time he became well acquainted with West and absorbed aspects of his style. Benbridge returned to Philadelphia before settling in Charleston, South Carolina, in 1772. In 1780, during the Revolutionary War, he was taken prisoner by the British and exiled to St. Augustine, Florida. Subsequently he spent about a year in Philadelphia before returning in 1784 to Charleston. Following his departure from that city in 1790 or not long after, he lived for some time in Norfolk, Virginia, and may also have resided more briefly in Baltimore. Benbridge apparently painted little during later years, probably because of poor health. He presumably died in Philadelphia, where he was buried. Benbridge's best portraits evidence technical fluency and a clear, smooth, and gracious style. He ranked among the best miniaturists of his day, and following the British vogue for so-called conversation pieces, he often painted small-scale, full-length portraits of individuals or family groups. Among these, his appealing *Enoch Edwards Family* (Philadelphia Museum, probably 1783) includes his own self-portrait seated at left before a casual grouping of his half sister, her husband, and the husband's sister. The figures gather at the edge of a wood, and the composition opens out to the right in a bucolic, feathery landscape. As was often the case, particularly after the 1770s, a slight awkwardness betrays Benbridge's erratic command of anatomy and figural proportion. At the same time, the work displays his reputed facility in rendering luxurious fabrics, his capacity to picture fine detail within a small format, and, with the three standing figures clustered about a gigantic urn on a pedestal, the classical inclinations he had honed in Rome. In Philadelphia, before his 1772 departure for Charleston, Benbridge married Esther (or Letitia, nicknamed Hetty) Sage (d. 1777), a miniature painter trained by Charles Willson *Peale. She joined him in Charleston in 1773. Few works have been attributed to her hand.

Bengelsdorf, Rosalind. *See* BROWNE, BYRON.

Benn, Ben (1884–1983). Painter. An independent modernist, he devoted his long career mostly to colorful, painterly still lifes, landscapes, cityscapes, and portraits. Born Benjamin Rosenberg in Kamenetz Podolski, Russia (now Ukraine), he moved at the age of nine with his family to New York and never afterward strayed far from the city. Between 1904 and 1908 he studied at the *National Academy of Design. Within the next few years, he experimented with cubism but also developed a brightly decorative style related to German expressionism, as in *Mother and Child* (Whitney Museum, 1915). In this depiction of figures in traditional Eastern European garb on a city street, space is compressed to emphasize the composition's decorative patterning, anchored in picturesque clothing. Around the same time, he also tried his hand at the nonobjective color abstraction popular among younger modernists in the 1910s. His stature among these up-and-coming artists was confirmed by his inclusion in the 1916 *Forum Exhibition, which showcased the best of them. By the 1920s, the example of Matisse had come to predominate in his approach, and the rest of Benn's career emphasized pleasurable visual experience. His freely brushed canvases often feature adroitly applied black lines to define contours of objects within lyrical chromatic harmonies. In the 1930s particularly, he sometimes depicted urban scenes. For a time after World War II, he responded to the prevailing enthusiasm for *abstract expressionism by again experimenting with forms of nonrepresentational painting.

Benson, Frank Weston (1862–1951). Painter and printmaker. A leading Boston artist, he is known particularly for summery outdoor scenes featuring attractive young women and children. His somewhat more subdued interiors more closely resemble the work of his good friend Edmund *Tarbell. They met as students at Boston's School of the Museum of Fine Arts, worked and traveled together in Europe, participated as founding members in exhibitions of The *Ten, and served on the museum school's faculty from 1889 until 1913. (From 1914 until 1930 Benson taught there on an occasional basis.) He also painted a number of convincing portraits. Born in Salem, Massachusetts, Benson began his professional training at the museum school in 1880. After three years there, he left for Paris, where he worked with Gustave Boulanger and Jules-Joseph Lefebvre at the Académie Julian. He also summered in Brittany and visited London before resettling in Salem in 1885. He taught for two years in Portland, Maine, before accepting the Boston position, subsequently specializing in representations of upper-class women in quiet domestic settings. He adapted his imagery of gracious young womanhood to allegorical purposes in murals depicting the *Three Graces* and the *Four Seasons* (1896) in Washington, D.C.'s new Library of Congress. Shortly before 1900 he began to work, often outdoors, in a looser and more colorful impressionist technique, although he always retained a preference for the careful draftsmanship of his academic training. During the next decade and a half he painted his best-known images, depicting wholesome and innocent young models (usually his daughters) wearing white or light-colored clothing and often silhouetted against a bright sky. Despite their invigorating surroundings, the subjects generally suggest a reflective psychology. Most of these fresh and vibrant images reflect the clear air of Maine, where he summered from 1901 on North Haven Island in Penobscot Bay. After taking up printmaking in 1912, he turned out more than three hundred etchings and drypoints, preponderantly devoted to hunting scenes and wildlife. In the 1920s outdoor masculine activities came to predominate in his paintings, but he produced lush still lifes, as well. He also exploited a proficiency in watercolor during these years. Active nearly until the end of his life, he maintained a studio in Boston until 1944. He died at his home in Salem.

Benton, Thomas Hart (1889–1975). Painter, printmaker, and muralist. A vigorous style of swirling, interlocking forms energizes his scenes of American life and history. An accomplished nonrepresentational painter early in his career, Benton always remained attentive to the abstract dynamics of composition. However, before 1920 he rejected the individualistic ethos of modernism and sought instead to give expression to the collective American experience. His ideas were not original, but he brought to them a visionary dedication, which had the effect of revitalizing their impact in practice. In the 1930s, along with John Steuart *Curry and Grant *Wood, he attracted much critical and popular attention as a leader of the regionalist variant of the *American Scene movement. Although he personally did not advance a political agenda, his work became caught up in the nativist rhetoric of the pre-World War II decade. To his interpretations of American life, Benton brought a proud and heroic ethos, but he was insensitive to values other than his own, and occasionally allowed coarseness to undermine the merits of his patriotism. He was born in the tiny southwestern Missouri town of Neosho and named for his great-uncle, an eminent U.S. senator before the Civil War. He spent much of his childhood in Washington, D.C., where his populist father served as a congressman. After studying at the School of the Art Institute of Chicago for two years, in 1908 he departed for Paris. He trained briefly at the traditionalist Académie Julian, but spent most of three years in France working on his own, as he absorbed impressionist and modern art. In 1912 Benton settled in New York, where he saw the 1914 *synchromist exhibition organized by Stanton *Macdonald-Wright, a friend from Paris days. Benton began to work with this form of color abstraction, soon took his place among radical young artists of the day, and was represented in the 1916 *Forum Exhibition of modernists. Some paintings of this time, such as *Bubbles* (Baltimore Museum of Art, c. 1914–17), are completely nonrepresentational, but others, abstracted from the figure, led the way into his later style. In these, he used the rhythms of the body as an armature for color patterns. He frequently took Michelangelo's art as a starting point, as he did also in later pictorial work, along with that of El Greco and the great Baroque painters. In 1918–19 he served in the U.S. Navy as an architectural draftsman.

About the time he returned to figural representation in the early 1920s, Benton began to ruminate on the desirability of a uniquely American art, free of foreign influence. Among the most important sources of his thought were the writings of Hippolyte Taine, a nineteenth-century French literary critic and historian who wrote persuasively of the need for expression to be rooted in the artist's environment. Benton's small-town, midwestern background primed his sympathy for the ordinary people that he believed were responsible for the greatness of his country, and he found in their lives or their history the fit subjects of his art. *Boomtown* (Memorial Art Gallery, University of Rochester [New York], 1928) depicts an oil town, *The Lord Is My Shepherd* (Whitney Museum, c. 1926) shows a moment of quiet affection between an elderly couple sharing a meal, and *Threshing Wheat* (Sheldon Swope Art Museum, Terre Haute, Indiana, 1939) presents farmers in vast grain fields, along with their exhaust-belching modern equipment. In the 1920s Benton set out also to translate the American experience into monumental wall painting. His efforts helped to spur the 1930s revival of mural painting, which took place largely under the auspices of the *federal art projects (although Benton himself never participated). Among Benton's numerous murals, the most important include *America Today*, painted for the New School for Social Research (now New School) in 1930 but later installed in New York's Equitable Center, and a 1935–36 cycle for the Missouri state capitol in Jefferson City.

In 1935 Benton departed New York to teach for several years in Kansas City, where he subsequently resided. Even before the end of the 1930s, he presaged the decline of regionalist fervor by engaging other themes, such as stories from mythological or biblical history, often situated in specifically American locales. In the 1938 *Susannah and the Elders* (Fine Arts Museums of San Francisco), a couple of rustics spy on a nude female, while their little country church bears witness in the background. *July Hay* (Metropolitan Museum, 1942–43) continues into the war years his engagement with farm labor, but now the activity takes place in the distance, while foreground elements compose a decorative still life. In later years Benton's style became more sedate, less agitated and emotional, and he produced many unaffected portraits, figural scenes, and landscapes. Active until the end of his life, he died in his Kansas City studio, which, along with his adjacent home, is now a state historic site open to the public on a limited basis. An articulate spokesman for his art and ideas, Benton published two autobiographical volumes, *An Artist in America* (1937) and *An American in Art* (1969).

Berenson, Bernard (1865–1959). Art historian, critic, and art advisor. Through close examination of stylistic and technical qualities in paintings and drawings, he brought discipline and order to the study of the Italian Renaissance, his specialty. In numerous books and articles, he presented the results of painstaking connoisseurship, attributing works to previously poorly understood masters and hypothesizing the artistic identity of anonymous painters. As a consultant and purchasing agent, he assisted the formation and expansion of important American collections. Born in Butrimonys, Russia (now Lithuania), Bernhard Valvrojenski emigrated to Boston with his family in 1875, at that time changing his surname. Upon graduation from Harvard in 1887, he departed for Europe, where he subsequently lived most of the time. Intrigued by Giovanni Morelli's rigorous method for attributing works of art on the basis of morphological similarities, he began an intensive study of Italian art. From the early 1890s American collectors often relied on his expertise. In 1894 he published his first book, *The Venetian Painters of the Renaissance*, and entered into a long-term, fruitful partnership with Isabella Stewart *Gardner. Berenson took a fee from his patrons, individuals as well as dealers, for each purchased work. This practice made him wealthy, but in combination with other possibly self-serving arrangements left him vulnerable to charges of duplicity. From 1906 he was closely associated with the London dealer Joseph Duveen, who in turn sold many important works to American collectors including John Pierpont *Morgan and Andrew *Mellon. Berenson died at Villa I Tatti, his home of some sixty years, near Settignano on the outskirts of Florence. Bequeathed to Harvard University, along with his library, art collection, and gardens, it now serves as a center for Italian Renaissance studies. Berenson's four groundbreaking inventories of Italian painting (1894–1907), organized by region and accompanied by introductory essays, constituted the cornerstone of his scholarship. Later he continued to update, refine, and republish his lists. Among other publications, the two-volume *Drawings of the Florentine Painters* (1903) ranks among the most respected. In addition to book-length studies of individual artists, he also produced theoretical volumes, such as *Aesthetics and History in the Visual Arts* (1948), and autobiographical works, including *Sketch for a Self-Portrait* (1949) and *Rumor and Reflection, 1941–1944* (1952), based on wartime diaries.

Berkowitz, Leon. *See* WASHINGTON COLOR PAINTERS.

Berman, Eugene (1899–1972). Painter and stage designer. Born in St. Petersburg, Russia, he began his art training there. In 1918 he moved to Paris, where he continued his studies and developed a romantic strain of surrealism. After emigrating to New York in 1935, he continued to paint but became known primarily as a designer for ballet and opera productions. During his American years, he resided in New York but also spent time in Los Angeles and sojourned in Mexico. He died in Rome, where he had lived since 1968. Although he also painted portraits, Berman's characteristically melancholy works make use of surrealist incongruities to create illogical, alternative worlds, drenched in despair. The theatrical *Nike* (Hirshhorn Museum, 1943) centers on a nearly life-size woman seen from behind. Loosely dressed in tattered crimson gown and veil, she surveys a foreground space enclosed with the precision of an early Renaissance painting but harboring indecipherable elements as well. Beyond, all is emptiness: a bit of desolate landscape and a vast sky.

Berman, Wallace. *See* FUNK ART.

Bernhard, Ruth (1905–). Photographer. Known particularly for classical studies of nudes and intimate views of shells, she also frequently photographed other subjects from nature, as well as commonplace items seen in unconventional ways. She worked exclusively in black and white, nearly always in the studio. Influenced particularly by Edward *Weston, she pursued a purist approach to form, although her work is sometimes tinged with surrealism. Whatever their subjects, her photographs emphasize mystical and physical qualities of light. She was born in Berlin, the daughter of graphic designer, typographer, and artist **Lucian Bernhard** (1883–1972). Following two years of study at the Berlin Academy of Art, in 1927 she followed her father to New York. After turning to photography, in 1935 on a visit to California she met Weston, whose work so moved her that she relocated there the following year. Not long after returning to New York in 1939, she embarked on her extended seashell series. Examined in close-up views, the shells are at some times isolated; at others, seen in imaginative juxtaposition with other shells or environmental elements. During World War II, she assisted the national effort as a New Jersey farm worker in the Women's Land Army. Following a subsequent period in Los Angeles, in 1953 she moved permanently to San Francisco, where she built an active teaching career. Her concentration on nudes intensified during this period. Sculptural, impersonal, and timeless, these works most clearly embody her insights into the spiritual as well as physical essentials of human experience.

Berninghaus, Oscar. *See* TAOS ARTISTS' COLONY.

Bernstein, Theresa (1890–2002). Painter and printmaker. Known primarily for scenes of urban life, she also painted portraits as well as beach activities observed near her longtime summer home in Gloucester, Massachusetts. Born in Philadelphia, she attended lectures at the *Pennsylvania Academy of the Fine Arts and graduated from the Philadelphia School of Design for Women (now Moore College of Art and Design), where she studied with Elliott *Daingerfield, Daniel *Garber, and Harriet *Sartain. After moving permanently to New York in 1912, she worked briefly at the *Art Students League with William Merritt *Chase. On visits to Europe she encountered expressionist work that influenced her emotionally charged realism. In 1919 she married painter and printmaker William Meyerowitz (1887–1981), who had arrived in New York from Russian Ukraine in 1908 and trained at the *National Academy of Design. His work incorporated both straightforward realism and more modern approaches indebted to Cézanne and cubism. Bernstein's characteristic work continued the vigorous realism promoted by Robert *Henri and the *Ashcan painters. Although committed, as they were, to recording everyday life, in her handling of space she sometimes referred to Cézanne's innovations, and she often introduced unnaturally bright hues. In the 1930s she was active in the *American Artists' Congress, although her work did not directly address social issues. Bernstein's reputation languished during the 1950s and for some time afterward, but she had been rediscovered long before her demise at the age of 111. After Meyerowitz's death, she published a book about his art, followed late in life by three volumes related to her own work. She also wrote poetry.

Biala. *See* TWORKOV, JACK.

Biddle, George (1885–1973). Painter and printmaker. Also a leader in establishing Depression-era *federal art projects. Born in Philadelphia, Biddle graduated from Harvard University in 1908 and received a law degree there three years later. Although admitted to the Pennsylvania bar, he never practiced. Instead, for several years he studied art at the *Pennsylvania Academy of the Fine Arts and in Munich and Paris. In Europe he was drawn to the painterly tradition of the seventeenth century, particularly the work of Rubens and Velázquez, and, later, to the impressionists. Following U.S. Army service in World War I, Biddle continued to travel and paint in Europe, in Latin America, and, for two years, in Tahiti. By 1932, however, he had decided to turn to American subjects, and he returned permanently to the United States. In the following year, he wrote to President Franklin D. Roosevelt, earlier a classmate at Groton preparatory school, urging federal support for artists. Spurred by admiration for the contemporary Mexican mural movement, Biddle urged that American painters be given the opportunity to express "in living monuments the social ideals that you are struggling to achieve."

In the 1930s Biddle was active in the *American Artists' Congress and a vigorous proponent of socially engaged art. His most important murals, painted in the mid-1930s at the Department of Justice in Washington, D.C., illustrate the role of law in promoting an exemplary society. Scenes of sweatshop and tenement contrast with the culminating image of an orderly and pleasant middle-class household. In his later years, Biddle created *genre scenes, sometimes with a satirical flavor. He also painted many portraits. He died in Croton-on-Hudson, New York, where he had maintained a home since the late 1920s. Biddle published his autobiography, *An American Artist's Story*, in 1939. *Artist at War* (1944) recounts his activities while again engaged in military service during

World War II. A collection of critical essays, *The Yes and No of Contemporary Art*, appeared in 1957. *Indian Impressions* (1960) recounts his reactions to a lengthy 1959 stay in India, while *Tahitian Journal* (1968) provides autobiographical material related to his sojourn there.

Biederman, Charles (1906–2004). Painter and relief sculptor. He is known particularly for small, painted reliefs composed of rectilinear elements. Born Karel Joseph Biederman in Cleveland, he studied at the School of the Art Institute of Chicago from 1926 until 1929. He remained in Chicago, working as a painter under the influence of Cézanne and cubism, until moving to New York in 1934. Soon he began to work with pure abstraction, as in *Painting, New York, January 1936* (Whitney Museum). Its hard, shiny *biomorphic forms curve intricately through space as they float before a flat red background. During nine months in Paris in 1936–37, he met many of the modern masters he admired, including Arp, Fernand Léger, and Mondrian, as well as Antoine Pevsner, whose constructivist ideas were important to Biederman's further development. He had begun to make reliefs shortly before going abroad, and subsequently in New York did not return to painting. Working with concepts from constructivism and Mondrian's neoplasticism, he developed an approach he called structurism to analyze structural formations found in nature in terms of abstract arrangements of geometric form. In a characteristic relief, *Work No. 36, Aix* (Museum of Modern Art, 1953–72), small white and colored planes create a buoyant, graceful effect as they float before an arrangement of clustered verticals, painted white in the center, bright yellow on either side. Biederman moved permanently to Red Wing, Minnesota, near Minneapolis, in 1942. During his first three years there, he worked on a U.S. Army medical project. In 1948 he published *Art as the Evolution of Visual Knowledge*, the first of several books on art theory. *Bohm-Biederman Correspondence* (1999), edited by Paavo Pylkkanen, presents letters he exchanged with physicist David Bohm, who shared an interest in philosophical questions. Biederman continued to work into the 1990s, when failing eyesight curtailed his art. He died in the farmhouse where he had lived for half a century.

Bierstadt, Albert (1830–1902). Painter. A specialist in views of the American West, he glorified the region's spectacular scenery in large and detailed canvases, appealing to fascination for untamed wilderness and dreams of national greatness. He also produced occasional historical subjects and other figurative canvases as well as paintings of wild animals. His landscapes frequently include *genre elements, most often portraying Indian life. Bierstadt was born in Solingen, Prussia, but grew up in New Bedford, Massachusetts, where he had moved with his family at the age of two. In 1853 he returned to Germany. During two-and-a-half years in Düsseldorf, under the guidance primarily of Emanuel *Leutze, he mastered a tightly realistic technique. In June 1856, he left with Worthington *Whittredge and William Stanley *Haseltine to pass the summer in Switzerland before continuing on to Italy. Bierstadt spent the following winter in Rome, returning home during the summer of 1857 after a two-month trip as far south as the Amalfi coast with Sanford *Gifford. As he would throughout his career, on his travels Bierstadt recorded his immediate perceptions in clear-eyed oil studies, which modern observers often have found more appealing than many of the finished canvases for which they served as source material.

Back in New Bedford, Bierstadt finished his first enormous landscape, the 6 × 10-foot *Lake Lucerne* (National Gallery, 1858). After exhibiting it to acclaim in New York, he accompanied Frederick Lander's 1859 exploratory expedition to the Rocky Mountains. The first academically trained American artist to record the West, he seized upon its theatrical grandeur to position himself as the region's preeminent interpreter. Upon his return he established a New York studio, where he transferred the representational precision, compositional conventions, and heightened drama of his Alpine subjects to such works as *The Rocky Mountains, Lander's Peak* (Metropolitan Museum, 1863). Characteristically, the painting draws the viewer in through a detailed foreground, this one including an Indian encampment. Beyond the reflective surface of a lake, dramatically lighted, rocky projections lead back to sharp, snow-covered peaks. Although Bierstadt benefited in his rise to celebrity from his audience's familiarity with *Hudson River School landscapes, he shared little of that group's philosophical outlook. Nor did he partake of Frederic *Church's fixation on science. Instead, although genuinely captivated by wilderness and eager to record its botany and wildlife, in his finished paintings Bierstadt usually emphasized breathtaking visual effects. On his second trip west, in 1863 Bierstadt journeyed to California. His traveling companion, writer Fitz Hugh Ludlow, published an account of their adventures as *Heart of the Continent* (1870; serialized in *Atlantic Monthly*, 1864). After a visit to San Francisco and seven weeks in the Yosemite Valley, they progressed north into Oregon before returning home. Able by the mid-1860s to command the highest prices for his paintings, in 1865–66 Bierstadt constructed an enormous residence, Malkasten (destroyed by fire in 1882), overlooking the Hudson River in Irvington, New York. From 1867 to 1869 he expanded his circle of patrons while working in London, Rome, and elsewhere in Europe. There he continued to turn out views of the American West but also recorded the similarly mountainous terrain of Switzerland. From 1871 to 1873 he was again in California, this time focusing on such remote areas as the Hetch Hetchy Valley and the Farallon Islands. From 1877 he traveled often to Nassau, even as he continued also to visit the West. He also made journeys through the Canadian Rockies and to Alaska, and returned quite frequently to Europe. Although public taste had gradually turned away from large-scale landscape dramas, he continued into the 1890s to produce work in much the same vein as his 1860s canvases. Despite their foreground detail, his western scenes had always been composites, but with time he increasingly departed from literal observation to create a mythic land of grandiose splendor. By the time of his death in New York, he was nearly forgotten.

Bierstadt numbered among early enthusiasts for photography as an aid to painting, and his organization of space often shows a debt to the vivid effects seen in *stereographs. He made photographic documents (at least some were stereoscopic views) on his first western trip in 1859. His brothers **Charles Bierstadt** (1819–1903) and **Edward Bierstadt** (1824–1906) entered into a photographic partnership about 1860. They probably published some of the views from the western expedition. By 1867 Charles had opened a studio in Niagara Falls, where he maintained a profitable business for many years, selling scenes from around the world. Edward remained active in New York, where he was involved with publication of photographic books.

Bingham, George Caleb (1811–79). Painter. Known for *genre scenes of the Midwest, he also painted numerous portraits, as well as occasional landscapes and history paintings. As he reported on rural and village life in Missouri, Bingham found poetry, gentle humor, and democratic virtues. Mostly dating to the period between 1845 and 1855, his most compelling works depict trappers, traders, boatmen, and settlers along the Missouri and Mississippi Rivers. His interest in politics provided material for several paintings picturing aspects of the election process. Bingham's later work, following a period of study in Europe, forfeits the fresh immediacy of his best paintings. A native of Augusta County, in western Virginia, in 1819 Bingham moved with his family to Missouri, shortly before the territory gained statehood. They settled in the village of Franklin, near the Missouri River in the central part of the state. The area remained Bingham's permanent base, despite occasionally extended absences. During the summer of 1820, when Bingham was only nine, Chester *Harding worked in Franklin. Bingham apparently assisted in the studio and found his vocational inspiration there. Although essentially self-taught, by the mid-1830s the young man was painting portraits in a simple but clear and forceful style. In 1838 he went to Philadelphia, where he studied for three or four months at the *Pennsylvania Academy of the Fine Arts and painted his earliest genre work. Bingham returned to Missouri with a more sophisticated style but in 1840 moved to Washington, D.C., in search of commissions. Back in Missouri once more in 1844, he soon began to produce the scenes of local life that made his reputation. One of the first of these, the masterful *Fur Traders Descending the Missouri* (Metropolitan Museum, 1845), depicts a grizzled trader and a fresh-faced boy canoeing through an idyllic landscape. Forecasting the most appealing qualities of Bingham's genre work, it combines clear colors, crisply drawn figures set against a hazy summer landscape, glowing light reflecting luminously from unruffled water, and a solidly constructed, classical composition. Countering the more usual contemporary interpretation of the frontier as a place of danger and hardship, in this and other genre paintings Bingham emphasized pleasure, relaxation, and sociability. However, despite its limpid style, pervasive tranquility, balance of man and nature, and intimacy between two people alone in the landscape, *Fur Traders* more prosaically also implies its protagonists' participation in the national economy of goods linking the West with eastern markets. Widely distributed in the form of a print by the *American Art-Union, *Fur Traders* introduced Bingham as the foremost interpreter of what was then the West. He soon followed his initial success with a series of genre views in which boatmen and trappers are major characters. For these he drew on childhood memories to evoke a specifically American way of life that was already disappearing.

Active in Missouri politics from the 1830s, Bingham held several appointed or elected offices during a period of more than two decades. He thus was well positioned to represent and comment upon the political process. Between 1849 and 1854 he produced half a dozen unusual images representing the processes of electioneering and voting. *County Election* (St. Louis Art Museum, 1851–52) incorporates a large cast of recognizable types from varied social and economic groups. Although some engage in questionable or even reprehensible activities, the meticulously constructed ensemble presents a positive view of democracy in action through geometric design, glowing light, and attractive particulars. Bingham's most important history painting, *Boone Escorting Settlers through the Cumberland Gap* (Washington University Gallery of Art, St. Louis, 1851–52) depicts Daniel Boone in a heroic light as he leads his family and others through a threatening landscape into the West. In 1852 Bingham moved to Philadelphia, in part to be near John *Sartain, who engraved some of his works. Four years later he left for Europe. Following a visit to Paris, he settled in Düsseldorf. After he returned permanently to Missouri in 1859, his relatively few subsequent genre works show some of the artificial and sentimental traits common in German painting of that period. He continued to execute portraits and participate in politics. Bingham died in Kansas City, where he had settled in 1870.

Biomorphism. Term used to describe abstract forms derived from or resembling biological organisms. They suggest but do not actually depict living matter. Although they are common in the early-twentieth-century work of such painters as Kandinsky and Arthur *Dove, the term first came into use in the 1930s with respect to surrealist art. Biomorphic forms appear in much *abstract expressionist work, as in the paintings of William *Baziotes and Arshile *Gorky.

Birch, Thomas (1779–1851). Painter and engraver. Known for topographical landscapes and cityscapes, he also introduced into the United States the European traditions of marine painting. Born in Warwickshire, England, he arrived with his family in the United States in 1794 to settle permanently in the Philadelphia area. Many views of specific locales document his adopted city and its surroundings. The light-filled *Delaware River Front, Philadelphia* (Museum of Fine Arts, Boston, c. 1799) precisely delineates waterfront buildings, ships moored along the quay, and characteristic early morning activities. Also exactingly portraying a Philadelphia site, the *Southeast View of "Sedgeley Park," the Country Seat of James Cowles Fisher, Esq.* (Smithsonian American Art Museum, c. 1819) numbers among the artist's many similarly conceived representations of estates situated in the mid-Atlantic states and New England. Correspondingly, on commission Birch also portrayed individual ships. In addition, he often painted the Philadelphia and New York harbors, capturing the vitality of international seafaring trade. His romantic, action-oriented views of the high seas included imaginary scenes of peril and shipwreck, as well as veristic representations, appealing to patriotic sentiment, of American victories in the War of 1812. The marine paintings demonstrate Birch's familiarity with Anglo-Dutch precedents and with works by eighteenth-century French painter Claude-Joseph Vernet. Starting in the 1830s, Birch painted some of the earliest American scenes of rural life in winter, and he also produced portraits.

Birch learned his craft from his father, painter and engraver **William Russell Birch** (1755–1834), who also passed on to his son a grounding in eighteenth-century English landscape and marine conventions. Also born in Warwickshire, during his early years in London William became a leading enamel specialist, in demand for portraits and copies of paintings, including important examples by his friend and mentor Joshua Reynolds. Adept in addition at painted and engraved views, during his residency in the United States he became most widely known for his work on the earliest American color plate book, the ambitious *City of Philadelphia, in the State of Pennsylvania, North America: As It Appeared in the Year 1800* (issued in parts in 1799 and 1800). Undertaken with his son, this publication featured hand-colored engravings based on their paintings, such as Thomas's previously mentioned river-front scene. Another volume of similar format, *The Country Seats of the United States of North America* (1809), heralded a later American vogue for publications devoted to rural scenery. From 1797 until 1828, when he returned permanently to Philadelphia, he lived at a country retreat outside the city, near Bristol. Thomas's sister, Penelope Birch Barnes, was active as a still life painter in Philadelphia, especially between 1812 and 1830.

Birnbaum, Dara. *See* VIDEO ART.

Bischoff, Elmer. *See* BAY AREA FIGURATIVE ART.

Bishop, Isabel (1902–88). Painter and printmaker. Principally interested in urban life, she developed a fluid and delicate technique to convey a lyric potential in her subjects. Like her associates Kenneth Hayes *Miller and Reginald *Marsh, Bishop wished to portray modern experience with traditional means. Less literal than they, she often introduced imaginative elements, as in *Virgil and Dante in Union Square* (Delaware Art Museum, Wilmington, 1932), or reshuffled realistic elements within abstractly organized compositions, as in *Subway Scene* (Whitney Museum, 1957–58). Born in Cincinnati, Bishop grew up primarily in Detroit. In 1918 she moved to New York and soon enrolled at the *Art Students League, where she encountered Miller and Marsh as instructors. A principal influence on her development, Miller encouraged painting the city milieu and may have fostered her special interest in women as subjects. However, Bishop often portrayed office workers or saleswomen, rather than the more passive consumers and spectators that Miller favored. Although dedicated primarily to a nonpolitical form of *American Scene painting, she also painted studio interiors and nudes. Whatever their occupations or activities, her generally pensive women appear to possess private mental lives. Bishop devised a refined and luminous style well suited to her perception of delicacy and beauty in the midst of urban uproar. With time, her delineation of form became looser, giving her work a hazy ambience that suggests the instability of modern life. She also became a proficient printmaker, known especially for etchings of quiet moments in the lives of her subjects. From 1934 until his death in 1962, she was married to neurosurgeon Harold George Wolff. She died at her home in the Riverdale area of the Bronx, where she had resided for some time.

Bisttram, Emil. *See* JONSON, RAYMOND.

Bitter, Karl (1867–1915). Sculptor. Known especially for architectural ornamentation, he also executed independent pieces, including portraits, as well as decorative embellishments for domestic interiors. In later years, he orchestrated architecture, space, and sculpture in urban areas and at temporary expositions. Karl Theodore Francis Bitter was born in Vienna and trained there from 1881 to 1884 at the Austrian Museum of Art and Industry's School of Applied Arts and from 1885 to 1888 at the Imperial Academy of Fine Arts. Simultaneously, he assisted in producing sculptural decorations for major new buildings. After a year of military service, in 1888 he deserted. He arrived in New York near the end of the next year, following an interim in Berlin. Within weeks, preeminent Beaux-Arts architect Richard Morris Hunt recruited him to collaborate on major projects. Besides the Administration Building at the 1893 World's Columbian Exposition in Chicago, these included palatial residences in New York and Newport, Rhode Island, as well as Biltmore (1893–95), a stupendous mansion near Asheville, North Carolina. At the end of 1895, Bitter departed on the first of several return trips to Europe. Already in the planning then, his new home in Weehawken, on the Palisades above the Hudson River, was ready for occupancy in 1896. Although he again lived in Manhattan from 1909, he continued to maintain a workshop at the New Jersey site. In 1906 his style shifted from the naturalistic Baroque mode he had previously practiced to a more severe approach inspired by early Greek sculpture. The first American sculptor to incorporate archaic tendencies, by 1908 he had also adopted elements of the Viennese Secession style, giving much of his later work a modernist tone. His conception of sculpture as a component of public space stimulated Bitter's activism in urban planning, his insistence on integrating memorials into visually coherent settings, and his appointment as director of sculpture for two world's fairs, Buffalo's Pan-American Exposition (1901) and San Francisco's Panama-Pacific Exposition (1915). In mid-Manhattan, Grand Army Plaza (at Fifth Avenue and Sixtieth Street) reflects his vision for a gracious open space. His final sculpture, the bronze figure of *Pomona* (known also as *Abundance;* 1914–16), crowns the Pulitzer Fountain there. He died in an automobile accident in the city.

Blackburn, Joseph (c. 1730–78 or later). Painter. In the 1750s his portraiture introduced to New England rococo fashions denoting a taste for refinement, gentility, and artifice. When he arrived, Blackburn found no competition in Boston or nearby cities for his stylish, even seductive rendering of his sitters' demeanor and attire. Their characteristically cheerful if generalized facial expressions affirm their enjoyment of material prosperity. Nothing is known of Blackburn's origins or training, but his skill suggests experience in London, perhaps as a drapery specialist in a large studio. He painted portraits in Bermuda between mid-1752 and the end of 1753. After approximately a year in Newport, Rhode Island, in 1755 he settled in Boston. Three years later he moved on to Portsmouth, New Hampshire. From there, he made painting excursions to other locales before relocating permanently in 1763 to England, where he painted his last known portrait in 1778. Blackburn's most ambitious American painting, *Isaac Winslow and His Family* (Museum of Fine Arts, Boston, 1755) numbers among the earliest group portraits produced in the colonies. It depicts the couple and their daughters, a baby on her mother's lap and young girl, self-consciously lined up across the canvas. Adapting poses and other conventions of English portraiture to a new social environment, the artist with some success employed gesture and rhythmic patterns to animate the composition and provide a lively, informal tone. Although faces lack individuality, mouths upturned at corners indicate agreeable geniality. Their elaborate, mostly pastel-toned clothing is rendered with great care for the sheen of fabrics and the transparent play of laces. In the right-hand distance, an atmospheric landscape appears behind the young daughter. Her hair adorned with flowers and her raised skirt brimming with abundant fruits, she affects a common eighteenth-century pastoral trope.

Blackburn, Robert. *See* UNIVERSAL LIMITED ART EDITIONS.

Black Mountain College. A tiny North Carolina school that harbored a legendary crucible of artistic creativity during the 1940s and 1950s. Founded in the Blue Ridge Mountains near Asheville in 1933 by John Andrew Rice, a classicist with strongly held and innovative convictions about education, it flowered in the 1940s but survived only until 1957. Within a progressive liberal arts curriculum, the school stressed education in the arts for every student. To foster the experience of community, teachers and students ate together and socialized at evening entertainments, while everyone contributed to the school's upkeep. The faculty owned and ran the college. The school's open-minded ethos encouraged interdisciplinary and multimedia activity, resulting in rich cross-fertilizations just at the time that such activity became particularly critical to experimental tendencies. Josef *Albers, who came directly from the Bauhaus, headed the art program for sixteen years and established its venturesome character. The first American educational institution to adopt the German art school's innovative pedagogy, Black Mountain emphasized individual development and modern forms of knowledge. Albers also was pivotal in recruiting stimulating art faculty, including his wife Anni *Albers, as well as Ilya *Bolotowsky and other European-born artists. In 1944, Albers initiated the practice of inviting supplementary faculty for summer sessions that benefited the creative endeavors of teachers and students alike. Seasonal figures of the next decade included Harry *Callahan, Lyonel *Feininger, Clement *Greenberg, Franz *Kline, Jacob *Lawrence, Robert *Motherwell, Ben *Shahn, Jack *Tworkov, and Peter *Voulkos, as well as British ceramist Bernard Leach. During the fruitful summer of 1948, John *Cage, dancer and choreographer Merce Cunningham, Willem *de Kooning, architect and theorist R. Buckminster Fuller, and Beaumont and Nancy *Newhall, all still relatively unknown, were in residence at the same time, along with students Patricia *Passlof and Kenneth *Snelson. Other Black Mountain students include John *Chamberlain, Raymond *Johnson, Kenneth *Noland, Robert *Rauschenberg, *Dorothea *Rockburne, and Cy *Twombly. Following Albers's departure in 1949, poets became increasingly important in defining the college's identity. Charles Olsen, Robert Creeley, and Robert Duncan attracted other writers and published the signal *Black Mountain Review* from 1954 to 1957. The college at first conducted its programs in rented Blue Ridge Assembly buildings, scenically placed south of the village of Black Mountain. After eight years there, the school moved to its own campus of new and renovated buildings on nearby Lake Eden. In the late 1940s enrollments began to drop as fissures developed within the community, GI bill money for returning World War II military dried up, and a newly conservative social and political climate regarded with disfavor the unconventional college's bohemian atmosphere. The campus today serves as a children's summer camp and the site of the semiannual Lake Eden Arts Festival. The Black Mountain College Museum + Arts Center, founded in 1993 in Asheville, is an exhibition space and resource center devoted to the college's history and legacy.

Bladen, Ronald. *See* MINIMALISM.

Blaine, Nell (1922–96). Painter and printmaker. Known for colorful, painterly still lifes and landscapes, she evolved this approach from a strong start as an abstract painter. Born in Richmond, she began her training in 1939 at the art school of the Richmond Professional Institute (now part of Virginia Commonwealth University). In 1942 she moved to New York, where she studied with Hans *Hofmann until 1944, joined the *American Abstract Artists in that year, around the same time spearheaded the pioneering Jane Street cooperative gallery, pursued etching at *Atelier 17 with Stanley William Hayter in 1945, and took classes at the New School for Social Research (now New School) in 1952–53. Following her first sojourn abroad in 1950, she continued to travel widely. Many of her paintings reflect distant locales in Europe, Mexico, and elsewhere, but familiar places, such as the garden of the Gloucester, Massachusetts, summer residence she purchased in 1975, also provided intimate and visually piquant subjects. At the time of her 1943 marriage (which lasted only six years) to musician Robert Bass, her art reflected a preoccupation with music, especially contemporary jazz, as she painted rhythmic, loosely brushed improvisatory works aligned with *abstract expressionism. In the mid-1940s, her work temporarily became more structural and clean-edged in response to the work of European modernists including Mondrian, Arp, and Fernand Léger. During the 1950 visit to France and Italy, she looked back to such masters of fluid chromaticism as Monet, Pierre Bonnard, and Matisse. By the end of the decade she had defined a personal approach to celebrating visual sensation, while also emphasizing the process of painting. As a printmaker, she worked often with etching and woodcut early in her career but later often turned to lithography. During a visit to Greece in 1959, she contracted polio, which left her partially paralyzed and permanently confined to a wheelchair, but this misfortune had little effect on her vibrant aesthetic. She died in New York.

Blakelock, Ralph Albert (1847–1919). Painter. Remembered especially for evocative, richly painted landscapes, he also painted smaller numbers of figural studies and still lifes. In characteristic, often moonlit images, lambent skies set off darkly silhouetted trees, producing meditative, even otherworldly effects. Often unobtrusively inhabiting the shadows, American Indians rendered without ethnographic specificity imply harmonious coexistence with nature. With its origins in the nature-worshipping *Hudson River School and the painterly intimacy of *Barbizon work, Blakelock's personal style responded as well to contemporary international currents, most notably the psychological subjectivity of symbolism and the general postimpressionist indifference to representational accuracy. In its subdued color harmonies and quietist mood, his work relates also to *tonalism. Like his exact contemporary, the more imaginative and forceful Albert *Ryder, he presents visions of a natural order that subsumes and, in so doing, exalts its human component. Like Ryder, too, he skirted standard technical methods, with the result that many of his paintings have darkened or otherwise deteriorated. Born in New York, in 1866 he left the city's Free Academy (now City College of New York) before graduating. Almost entirely self-taught as a painter, in his early work he emulated the prevailing Hudson River School. In 1869 he departed for the American West, where he sketched the landscape and, occasionally, its native inhabitants. Before he returned home in 1871 he traveled from California through Mexico and Panama to Jamaica. From these experiences, he generalized his introspective and romantic treatment of the wilderness landscape, usually a forest enclosure. Despite his obsessive recapitulation of a single theme, the most completely and carefully realized examples convey a compelling poetry symbolic of larger truths. On occasion he reached beyond his normal range of subjects to achieve singular results, as in the hypnotically radiant marine view, *The Sun, Serene, Sinks into the Slumberous Sea* (Museum of Fine Arts, Springfield, Massachusetts, 1880s). Emptied of incident save drifting clouds, the image centers on a diffused glow just above the horizon of a calm sea, echoing earlier *luminism no less than the reduced aesthetic associated with James Abbott McNeill *Whistler's work. Blakelock's solitary style, puzzling to contemporaries, and his general indifference to marketing his work resulted in chronic poverty for the artist and his family. The psychological stresses of failure contributed in 1891 to the first evidence of the schizophrenia that eventually destroyed him. Hospitalized that year, from 1899 he remained institutionalized almost continuously, while trying intermittently and ineffectually to paint, until his death in the Adirondacks, near Elizabethtown. He won little recognition until his final years. When it was too late for him to benefit, his work snowballed in popularity. In a final irony, his painting shares also with Ryder's the distinction of prompting numerous forgeries to appear on the market. Moreover, his signature was later fraudulently added to some of the landscapes and seascapes painted by his daughter **Marian Blakelock** (1880–1930?). In 1915 she, too, was hospitalized for mental illness.

Blanch, Arnold (1896–1968). Painter and printmaker. Known for portraits, landscapes, and studio scenes, he also painted several murals under the auspices of the *federal art projects. Born in the southeastern Minnesota hamlet of Mantorville, Blanch studied for two years at the Minneapolis School of Fine Arts and served in the U.S. military during World War I before enrolling at the *Art Students League from 1919 to 1921. There, his teachers included John *Sloan, Kenneth Hayes *Miller, and Boardman *Robinson. In 1923 he moved permanently to *Woodstock. A founding member of the *American Artists' Congress, in some paintings from that era he revealed overtly left-wing political attitudes, sometimes creating disturbing, almost surrealist effects to enhance his message. However, among other paintings that suggest social sympathies more indirectly, *Swamp Folk* (Brooklyn Museum, 1939), depicting an African-American couple in a sweeping landscape, acknowledges poverty but sustains a tone of quiet lyricism. In the 1940s he flirted with abstraction but settled on a representational style that from time to time incorporated elements of fantasy.

He collapsed and died on a bus en route from Woodstock to New York.

Blanch's first wife, painter and printmaker **Lucile Blanch** (1895–1981), was born Lucile Linquist in Hawley, Minnesota. Before their marriage in 1922, they studied together in Minneapolis and at the Art Students League. After their divorce in 1935, she traveled frequently but continued to make her home in Woodstock, where she died. Known especially for landscapes, she also painted figurative subjects and turned to abstraction in the 1940s. In 1939 Blanch married Doris *Lee, but that marriage also ended in divorce. He published two books, *Methods and Techniques for Gouache Painting* (1946) and, with Lee, *Painting for Enjoyment* (1947).

Blashfield, Edwin Howland (1848–1936). Painter and illustrator. Probably the most sought-after muralist of his day, he was a major contributor to the *American Renaissance. In numerous decorations for public buildings and private residences, he employed an idealizing classicism to produce effects of dignity and timelessness. Although allegorically conceived, his themes often incorporated American subjects. In his best-known work, the *Evolution of Civilization* (1895–96) in the reading room dome of Washington, D.C.'s Library of Congress, symbolic figures represent the progress of humankind from Egypt to America, suggesting a triumphalism that augments the splendor of the building's architecture. Born in Brooklyn, Blashfield was educated at the Boston Latin School and the Boston (now Massachusetts) Institute of Technology, where he pursued an interest in architecture and engineering. With encouragement from an early mentor, William Morris *Hunt, he departed in 1867 for Paris to study art. There he worked with Léon Bonnat until 1870. Following travel through Europe and eight months in Florence, he settled in New York the following year and took up the career of an easel painter and illustrator. In 1874 he returned to Paris for another six years and subsequently traveled to Europe on a number of occasions. He had painted few murals when he was awarded an important commission for the 1893 World's Columbian Exposition in Chicago. In demand for large-scale projects by the late 1890s, he embellished state capitols, courthouses, churches, and other public venues throughout the East and Midwest. He also designed mosaics and stained glass windows, while continuing as well to produce illustrations for books and magazines. Some of these accompanied his own texts, often written in collaboration with his wife, Evangeline Wilbour Blashfield. Together, they published *Italian Cities* (1902) and, with the assistance of Albert A. Hopkins, in 1896 issued a four-volume set devoted to seventy annotated biographies from Giorgio Vasari's *Lives of the Artists*. In 1913 Blashfield published *Mural Painting in America*, a longtime standard reference on the subject. Although much honored in his later years, he outlived widespread enthusiasm for his high-minded, celebratory, and frequently patriotic traditionalism. In 1933 he retired to Cape Cod, where he had previously summered. He died at his home in South Dennis. His brother, **Albert Dodd Blashfield** (1860–1920) who often signed his work "Blash," worked primarily as a popular illustrator and cartoonist.

Bliss, Lillie P. *See* MUSEUM OF MODERN ART.

Bloch, Albert (1882–1961). Painter. Also a writer. A modernist at an early date, he ranks as the only American to exhibit with the expressionist Blue Rider group in Germany. His work also appeared in its so-called almanac, also titled *Der Blaue Reiter* (1912). A native of St. Louis where he began his study of art, Bloch worked as an illustrator in his hometown and in New York before leaving for Europe in 1908. He lived abroad until 1921, except for several visits home. In Munich, Bloch met Kandinsky, whose work he had already come to admire. Late in 1911, Kandinsky and Franz Marc invited Bloch to join them and eleven others in the Blue Rider's first exhibition, which opened in Munich and then traveled to Berlin and other German cities. Bloch also exhibited in the group's second, and last, larger exhibition the following year in Munich. After he returned to the United States, he taught for a year in Chicago before accepting an offer to head the art department at the University of Kansas. Besides teaching both painting and art history, Bloch remained active as a writer of essays and poetry and a translator of German literature and philosophy. After retirement in 1947, he continued to reside in Lawrence. During his earlier years in Germany, Bloch painted both straightforwardly representational scenes and decorative figural works that evoke the languid mysteries of symbolism. Eventually, he followed Kandinsky's example toward more vigorous composition and expression, but unlike Kandinsky he retained figural elements in his art. *Die Höhen* (Krannert Art Museum and Kinkead Pavilion, University of Illinois, Urbana-Champaign, 1914) envisages weightless figures in a landscape that echoes the rhythms and forms of Kandinsky's work from several years earlier. Later, isolated in Kansas, the idealistic artist nurtured an intense and introverted vision, often suffused with the Christian themes that had inspired him since his days in Germany. Some of Bloch's original and translated poetry appeared as *Ventures in Verse* (1947).

Bloch, Lucienne (1909–99). Muralist, painter, printmaker, sculptor, and photographer. Born in Geneva, Switzerland, the daughter of composer Ernest Bloch, in 1917 she moved with her family to the United States. After the academic year 1924–25 at the Cleveland School (now Institute) of Art, she studied in Paris until 1929 at the École des Beaux Arts and in the studios of painter André Lhote and sculptor Antoine Bourdelle. She also worked in the Netherlands for a year, mastering the technique of glass sculpture. When she moved to New York in 1931, she anticipated a career as a sculptor. The intended course of her life's work changed while she assisted Mexican muralist Diego Rivera between 1932 and 1934 in Detroit and New York. In a small but significant contribution to art history, in May 1933 Bloch made the only photographs of Rivera's controversial Rockefeller Center fresco, *Man at the Crossroads*. The day before it was to be sealed off, and subsequently destroyed because it included a portrait of Lenin, Bloch surreptitiously recorded the work. In 1934 she embarked on an independent career as a muralist, eventually completing dozens of designs across the country, many sponsored by *federal art projects. Although some incorporate semi-abstract elements, others reflect her belief in the social responsibility of the artist. Although only *Childhood* (1935, now demolished) was ever finished, this portion of the projected "Cycle of a Woman's Life" for New York City's women's detention center remains among her best-known designs. This appealing depiction of women and children in a park presented a positive, accessible image intended to inspire inmates to improve their lives. Also a freelance photojournalist, Bloch was known as well for children's book illustrations. In 1936 she married Stephen Dimitroff, Rivera's chief technician, with whom she collaborated for forty years on numerous mural projects. They lived in Flint, Michigan, during World War II and moved to Mill Valley, California, in 1948. They relocated in 1965 to the Pacific coast town of Gualala, where she died.

Bloom, Hyman (1913–). Painter. His expressionistic canvases devoted to psychologically intense themes drenched in allegory and mysticism often address religious, predominately Jewish, subjects. Characteristically, he situates the spiritual within its material expression, as in a notable series of human and animal corpses displaying a morbid fascination with death. Dissected, decaying, or mutilated, these distorted bodies suggest his admiration for Chaim Soutine's work. *Autopsy* (Whitney Museum, 1953) demonstrates his potent combination of disturbing subject matter and ravishing surface effects. In other works of the time, he addressed mythic subjects in compositions approaching *abstract expressionism's formlessness and rich materiality. Born in Brunoviski, Russia (now Lithuania), Bloom emigrated in 1920 with his family to Boston, where he found encouragement from Denman *Ross but otherwise had little training. Nevertheless, he evolved a sensuous, painterly approach based on old masters as well as his admiration for European expressionists, including Georges Rouault as well as Soutine. He also was drawn to William Blake's visionary mode. During the Depression he worked for a *federal art project. He remained in Boston throughout most of his career, pursuing an individualistic vision that has deviated from the mainstream since the 1960s. Attracted also to landscape, he worked as well elsewhere in New England, particularly in Maine. He lives in Nashua, New Hampshire.

Bluemner, Oscar (1867–1938). Painter. Known particularly for semi-abstract interpretations of architectural motifs, he also painted landscapes. In these, a glowing sun or moon often provides visionary overtones. His fondness for bright hues, particularly red, earned him the humorous nickname of "the vermilionaire," but his colors and other formal means reflected a serious engagement with aesthetic questions. Bluemner's personal theory of art drew on currents from romanticism, symbolism, Asian philosophy, and central European metaphysics. Son and grandson of builder-architects, Oscar Julius Bluemner was born in Prenzlau, about fifty miles north of Berlin, where in 1887 he enrolled in the Königliche Technische Hochschule for five years of training in architecture and art. In 1892 he emigrated to the United States, becoming a citizen in 1899. While working as an architect and painting in his free time, he lived mostly in Chicago until moving to New York around 1900. Encouraged by Alfred *Stieglitz, in 1911 he began to paint full time. The following year, he toured Europe and showed paintings in Berlin. He returned to New York early in 1913, in time to participate in the *Armory Show, and Stieglitz exhibited his work in 1915 and again in 1928. Although he remained a peripheral member of the Stieglitz circle, his expressionistic and symbolic goals allied him with others in that group. In 1916 his work appeared in the *Forum Exhibition, a landmark showcase for young modernists. After residing for ten years at various locations in New Jersey, in 1926 he moved permanently to South Braintree, Massachusetts, not far from Boston. There, although he realized some of his most compelling visions, he remained isolated from the New York art world, and sales of his work were few. Finally, ill and losing his sight as his financial situation also deteriorated, he took his own life. In a characteristic work, *Morning Light (Dover Hills, October)* (Hirshhorn Museum, c. 1916), Bluemner deploys simplified shapes and saturated, emotionally charged colors in a rigorous pattern of floating planes. The painting's surface is faceted in a manner derived from cubism, while rectangular houses in the view provide an anchoring grid for the natural elements, including trees and distant purple hills. At the same time, the work fits comfortably into an American tradition of responding to local particulars. Bluemner signed some of his late works Florianus, derived from the Latin form of his name.

Bluhm, Norman. *See* FRANCIS, SAM.

Blum, Robert Frederick (1857–1903). Painter, printmaker, and illustrator. Remembered particularly for picturesque images of Venice and Japan, he also depicted other locales and in the 1890s executed ornamental and allegorical murals. He was born in Cincinnati, where as a young man he worked as an apprentice in a lithography shop, took drawing classes, studied with Frank *Duveneck, and developed an enthusiasm for the work of the recently deceased virtuoso Spaniard Mariano Fortuny. In Philadelphia during 1876–77, he pursued additional instruction at the *Pennsylvania Academy of the Fine Arts and, at the Centennial Exhibition, scrutinized paintings by Fortuny and others, while also deepening an early fascination with Japanese art. Subsequently he worked as an illustrator for New York magazines and earned admiration for light-filled watercolors. During the first of several European sojourns, in 1880 he associated in Venice with the Duveneck circle and encountered James Abbott McNeill *Whistler. Following Whistler's lead, he began to etch suggestive vignettes and produce the pastels for which he became particularly noted. In 1882 in New York, he and William Merritt *Chase founded the Society of Painters in Pastel to promote the medium. In Holland during the summer of 1884 he worked outdoors alongside Chase, a frequent companion. While residing in Venice most of the time between 1885 and 1890, Blum completed the charmingly carefree *Venetian Lace Makers* (Cincinnati Art Museum, 1887), among his best-known works. Characteristically, Blum here concentrated on appearances, little regarding the somber realities of workers' lives. An animated grouping of attractive, appealingly costumed young women, the painting reveals the mature artist's skill in handling light, color, texture, and composition with decorative flourish. Although he drew figures precisely, in outdoor settings particularly, his painterly treatment of other elements yields an impressionist shimmer. In 1890 Blum went to Japan, where he lived for more than two years. Among the first American artists to experience that country at first hand, he recorded his impressions in oils and pastels, as well as published illustrations. After his return to New York, he devoted much of his energy to large mural commissions. He died of pneumonia in New York a month before his forty-sixth birthday.

Blume, Peter (1906–92). Painter. His tightly detailed representational works vary from straightforward description to nightmarish fantasies. Influenced by cubism, his early work was related to *precisionism, but in some later paintings imagination overpowered cool analysis of form. In his best-known works, dating to the 1930s and 1940s, strange and irrational events reflect familiarity with European surrealism. However, Blume usually contrived his imagery rationally, rather than retrieving it from the unconscious mind. His meticulous realism was associated with *magic realism, although it generally offered a grimmer and more pessimistic vision than was common among this group. Blume was born in Smorgon, Russia (now Belarus), moved with his family to Brooklyn in 1911, was naturalized as an American citizen in 1921, and studied at the *Art Students League and elsewhere. Reflecting interest in rural New England, where he lived for part of each year at the time, *Winter, New Hampshire* (Museum of Fine Arts, Boston, 1927) exemplifies Blume's exactingly realistic technique, his precisionist ties, and his penchant for rearranging and condensing architectural and landscape elements into poetic images. By 1930 Blume's crisp, geometric forms had become elements in unsettling dramas. Inspired by two lengthy Italian sojourns during the 1930s, his best-known painting, *Eternal City* (Museum of Modern Art, 1934–37) created a political and aesthetic uproar when first exhibited. In this elaborately staged and vicious satire on Italian fascism, a sickly green Mussolini rises from a jack-in-the-box placed in a setting inspired by the history-drenched decrepitude of Rome. Throughout the painting's deep space, varied figures enact misfortunes or delusions. During the Depression, Blume was employed by *federal art projects. After about 1950 he worked in a more directly realistic manner but continued often to acknowledge the bizarre. A resident for several decades of Sherman, Connecticut, he died after an extended period of ill health in a nursing home in nearby New Milford.

Blumenschein, Ernest L. *See* TAOS ARTISTS' COLONY.

Blunt, John S. (1798–1835). Painter. Known particularly for landscapes and portraits, he also painted marines, ship portraits, and *genre scenes. Like most self-taught artists of his day, he supplemented his income with artisanal services, including furniture and carriage decoration, sign painting, and gilding. Born in Portsmouth, New Hampshire, he worked there until moving to Boston in 1831. He died at sea, on a voyage from New Orleans to Boston. His reputation rests chiefly on sophisticated, original landscapes and exquisitely refined portraits based on conventional models. As he developed his skill in depicting views, Blunt interpreted European traditions with a poetic sensibility perhaps inspired by precedents in the work of Washington *Allston and, later, Robert *Salmon. Blunt's winter view of *Boston Harbor* (Museum of Fine Arts, Boston, 1835) suggests emergent *luminism in its combination of carefully observed detail and atmosphere, perspectivized space, and a softly radiant light. In portraits of beautifully dressed women, expressive, three-dimensionally realized faces dominate flattened, decoratively stylized clothing and accessories to striking effect. At an early stage of research into Blunt's career, many of these were grouped as work of the Borden Limner.

Blythe, David Gilmour (1815–65). Painter. His frequently satirical *genre scenes acknowledge darker realities than were normally apparent in antebellum views of American life. A resident of Pittsburgh during his most productive years, he usually portrayed urban settings and inhabitants, instead of the rural subjects more popular among genre painters. Turning his eye on impoverished losers in an industrializing economy, he often pessimistically rendered them as depraved and irredeemable. His intermittent humor is sardonic and even bitter, far removed from the geniality and optimism of most contemporary art. This bleak outlook may in part have reflected the social and psychological marginality that marked his isolated, alcoholic existence. Blythe's technical skills remained limited, and he often adapted imagery from popular culture. Some of his paintings, while effective as social commentary, rely on caricatural figures and odd mixtures of realistic and symbolic elements. Perhaps only the political cartoons of *Harper's Weekly* illustrator Thomas Nast (1840–1902) more effectively skewered the era's corruption, greed, and stupidity. Yet Blythe's occasional tributes to the humanity of the oppressed bear comparison to paintings by his French contemporary Honoré Daumier. Born in Wellsville, Ohio, Blythe grew up in that rough frontier area on the Ohio River, about forty miles downstream from Pittsburgh. Apprenticed as a teenager to a Pittsburgh woodworker, he learned carpentry and woodcarving. After a period of wandering, in 1837 he enlisted in the U.S. Navy and served in the Caribbean, in the Gulf of Mexico, and along the eastern seaboard. Following discharge in 1840, he became an itinerant portrait painter in eastern Ohio. After about six years, he landed in Uniontown, Pennsylvania, about forty miles south of Pittsburgh. There he continued to paint portraits, started his genre work, carved a monumental wood statue of the Marquis de Lafayette (1847–48) to crown the county courthouse dome, and painted an Allegheny Mountains *panorama (lost; 1850–51), which he took on tour. After 1850 another period of itinerancy followed, but in 1856 he settled permanently in Pittsburgh. Nearly all his significant work dates to the nine years he lived there. Blythe's reputation was entirely local. Only one of his paintings circulated as a print, he apparently had almost no contact with New York or other eastern cultural centers, and after his death he was virtually forgotten for decades. Blythe's artistic education must have come primarily from prints and from illustrations in books and magazines. His paintings suggest familiarity with British graphic artists, including William Hogarth, Thomas Rowlandson, and George Cruikshank, as well as old master painting. Seventeenth-century Dutch and Flemish genre presumably inspired the pictorial construction, closely observed detail, and unified, brownish tonality of *A Match Seller* (North Carolina Museum of Art, Raleigh, c. 1859). Looking at the viewer with sad and frightened eyes as he eats an apple, this young victim of social forces is more sympathetically presented than most of Blythe's numerous street urchins, but there is no suggestion that he will ever transcend squalor and ignorance. Blythe avidly supported Lincoln and the Union cause during the Civil War and in 1861 accompanied a local regiment to Virginia battlefields. The numerous dispirited captives in Richmond's *Libby Prison* (Museum of Fine Arts, Boston, 1863) exhibit the hopelessness of their confinement in this infamously overcrowded former warehouse, but the grandly Rembrandtian space and shafts of supernatural luminosity suggest the valor of their cause.

Bock, Richard. *See* FRASER, JAMES EARLE.

Bodmer, Karl (1809–93). Painter, draftsman, and printmaker. Although he spent only two years in the United States and its territories, Bodmer's depictions of Western Indians and landscape contributed significantly to American art history. Born in Riesbach, near Zurich, he received his early training in Switzerland and then studied in Paris. In 1832 he was engaged by German scientist and explorer Prince Maximilian of Wied-Neuwied as expedition artist to prepare illustrations for a book about the American West. After landing in Boston in July 1832, the party visited East Coast sites before traveling to New Harmony, Indiana, for the winter. From St. Louis, following George *Catlin's route of the previous year, they departed in April 1833 to journey up the Missouri River into territorial Montana, farther than Catlin had gone. Before winter set in, they returned only as far as what is now North Dakota. In 1834 they continued back to St. Louis and then to Europe. Bodmer ranked as the best-trained artist to visit the American West in the early nineteenth century. Precisely detailed, skillfully composed, and beautifully colored, his images reflect the wonder and curiosity with which he and Maximilian saw the land and peoples they studied. Bodmer's drawings and paintings, mostly in watercolor, served as the basis for more than eighty hand-colored aquatints he prepared in Paris for an atlas to supplement Maximilian's two-volume German publication, *Reise in das innere Nord-America in den Jahren 1832 bis 1834* (1839–41). The trilingual atlas also accompanied French and English editions. (The single-volume *Travels in the Interior of North America* appeared in 1843). Maximilian's writings and Bodmer's art together provide a comprehensive and scholarly record of the region they explored. Around 1850, Bodmer settled at *Barbizon to paint and etch landscapes, animals, and other scenes. He returned to Paris a few years before his death there.

Bohrod, Aaron (1907–92). Painter and ceramist. Among regionalists in the *American Scene movement, he generally conveyed an unusually dreary view of small-town and rural life. Later he turned primarily to still life, while concurrently developing an interest in ceramics. Born in Chicago, Bohrod studied at the School of the Art Institute of Chicago between 1927 and 1929. From 1930 to 1932 he worked at the *Art Students League, where he was particularly influenced by John *Sloan. Returning to Chicago, he painted such local scenes as the dispiriting *Landscape near Chicago* (Whitney Museum, 1934), depicting a man working on a car in the midst of an unkempt yard in front of a deteriorating house. *Waiting for the 3:30* (Harry S. Truman Library and Museum, Independence, Missouri, 1941) shows a lone woman with her luggage, waiting beside the railroad tracks in a small town on an overcast winter day. During World War II, Bohrod served as an artist-reporter in the South Pacific and in Europe. From 1948 until 1973 he was artist-in-residence at the University of Wisconsin. Following retirement he remained permanently in Madison and continued to work until his last months. Around the time he moved to Wisconsin, he introduced imaginative elements into some paintings, producing surrealist overtones. By the mid-1950s he had dispensed altogether with his previous subject matter in order to paint highly detailed still lifes, sometimes including symbolic elements. He published *A Pottery Sketchbook* (1959) and *A Decade of Still Life* (1966).

Bolotowsky, Ilya (1907–81). Painter and sculptor. His sensuously colored arrangements of hard-edge, geometric form reflect a search for ideal harmony. Born in St. Petersburg, he spent much of his childhood in Baku, Russia (now Azerbaijan). After the Russian Revolution, the family fled to Istanbul and in 1923 continued on to the United States. Bolotowsky became a citizen in 1929. He enrolled in 1924 at the *National Academy of Design, where he studied for six years. In 1931 he left for nearly a year in Europe. At the outset of his career, he worked as a figurative expressionist, but after returning from abroad he experimented with abstraction. At first, drawn to the work of Kandinsky and Miró as well as Malevich and Mondrian, he incorporated both rectilinear and organic forms in compositions of flat, nonillusionistic shapes. By the early 1940s he had purged his art of *biomorphic elements, and for the rest of his career he worked solely with horizontal and vertical divisions. Although Mondrian's neoplasticism inspired these works, Bolotowsky composed with smaller divisions in more varied colors. From the late 1940s, he often varied the shape of the canvas itself, using diamonds, circles, and ovals. He later also created brightly colored relief constructions and freestanding columnar sculptures. Between 1934 and 1941, while working for *federal art projects, Bolotowsky created some of the relatively few government-sponsored abstract murals, and in 1936 he numbered among founding members of *American Abstract Artists. After serving in World War II, he taught at *Black Mountain College and the University of Wyoming before returning permanently to New York in 1957. He also wrote fiction and plays and made experimental films.

His first wife, versatile painter, sculptor, and illustrator Esphyr Slobodkina (1908–2002), became most widely known for the children's books that she illustrated and sometimes wrote. In her art, she synthesized elements of cubism, constructivism, and abstract surrealism in clever and vigorous works. Born in Chelyabinsk, Siberia, she arrived in New York in 1928 and soon enrolled at the National Academy. In the 1930s she worked for federal art projects and participated from the beginning in the activities of the American Abstract Artists. She and Bolotowsky married in 1933 but divorced after a few years. From 1948 she lived for many years in Great Neck, on Long Island. In 1960 she married longtime companion William Urquhart. She died at her home in Glen Head, Long Island.

Bontecou, Lee (1931–). Sculptor, printmaker, and draftswoman. Best known for abstract relief sculptures from the 1960s, she has continuously given close attention to natural forms and forces. The singular reliefs characteristically present canvas-covered forms that bulge and surge around mysterious, even threatening openings. Protruding hooks and barbs, embedded sawblades or other menacing implements, and roughly stitched, woundlike seams heighten the reliefs' hostile appearance. This work extends surrealist taste for *biomorphic forms, sexual innuendo, and uneasy atmospherics, as well as *abstract expressionist predilections for grand scale and loosely structured, organic composition. At the same time, nontraditional materials and cobbled-together structure contributed to *assemblage and *process art. As a printmaker, she has worked chiefly with lithography, mostly during the 1960s and 1970s. Drawing has remained central to Bontecou's creative experience, as she probes the physical structure, inexhaustible variety, and optical allure of living organisms.

Bontecou was born in Providence, Rhode Island, but grew up in suburban New York and summered on a Nova Scotia island. After graduating in 1952 from Bradford Junior College (later Bradford College, but now closed) in Haverhill, Massachusetts, she studied painting and sculpture for three years at the *Art Students League, where William *Zorach numbered among her teachers. During the summer of 1954 she learned welding at the Skowhegan School of Painting and Sculpture in Maine. In the late 1950s she spent nearly two years in Rome, where she made terracottas based on bird and animal forms. In a technically innovative series of large drawings made with soot, she experimented with velvety black abstract forms organized around roughly circular voids, prefiguring the format of her signature pieces. Following her return in the autumn of 1958 to New York, the idiosyncratic, anxiety-causing reliefs soon appeared, occasioning widespread attention and praise when they were exhibited in a solo show at Leo *Castelli's gallery in 1960. After 1963, instead of welding the structural basis of her sculptures, she worked also with fiberglass to produce smoother and more intricate works. In the late 1960s she turned to vacuum-formed plastics to create stylized, translucent fish and flowers. After exhibiting these works in 1971, in her fourth appearance at Castelli's, she did not again show new work for almost three decades. During this time she commuted to a teaching job at Brooklyn College while living in rural and small-town locations in Pennsylvania, on Long Island, and in Rockland County, north of New York. She returned to clay as a medium toward the end of the 1970s. Within a few years she began fabricating airy constructions of ceramic elements, wire, fabric, and other materials. Hung from above, these floating, fantastic bio-techno visions, often measuring several feet across, materialize a realm of ceaseless generative energy. When she retired from teaching in 1991, she moved to the isolated, central Pennsylvania farm that had been a summer retreat since 1966. In 1965 Bontecou married painter William Giles, who had mounted a show at Castelli's a few months before her own first appearance there. His aggressive work from around 1960 appealed to her, as did the sculpture of their comrades John *Chamberlain and Tom *Doyle. (In 1961 Doyle married Eva *Hesse, who in turn found Bontecou's work stimulating.) A South Carolina native and friend of Jasper *Johns, Giles served in the U.S. military in Korea before arriving in New York. He generated considerable interest in his work in for several years in the 1960s but has subsequently relinquished art making for long periods.

Booth, Cameron. *See* ROSENQUIST, JAMES.

Borden Limner. *See* BLUNT, JOHN.

Border Limner. *See* PHILLIPS, AMMI.

Borglum, Gutzon (1867–1941). Sculptor. Remembered primarily for the colossal presidential portraits he carved from a cliff at

Mount Rushmore in the Black Hills of South Dakota, the prolific artist also created numerous other monuments and sculptural portraits. Trained in the prevailing international Beaux Arts manner of the late nineteenth century and influenced by Rodin during his student years in Paris, he developed a fluid and dynamic approach to naturalistically observed American subjects. Born in rural Idaho Territory, John Gutzon de la Mothe Borglum grew up in Nebraska and Missouri. As a teenager, he worked as an apprentice lithographer in Los Angeles and studied painting. After about a year of additional art training in San Francisco, he left in 1890 for Paris, where he benefited from Rodin's instruction. He returned in 1893 to the Los Angeles area but from 1896 to 1901 lived primarily in London. Following a visit to Paris, he returned to the United States and settled in New York. From 1910 he resided for a decade in Stamford, Connecticut. Borglum's early work focused on themes from western life, including horses, cowboys, and Indians, although he executed some mythological subjects. One of these, the bronze *Mares of Diomedes* (1904), was the first American sculpture bought for the *Metropolitan Museum of Art, in 1906. Borglum's large-scale work commenced in 1905 with statues of the Apostles for New York's Cathedral of St. John the Divine, followed in 1908 by a six-ton marble head of Abraham Lincoln (U.S. Capitol, Washington, D.C.). In 1915, he drew up designs for the world's largest relief sculpture, depicting Robert E. Lee and military associates, at Stone Mountain in Georgia. His initial work there was destroyed after he left the project during a 1925 dispute, long before the present monument was executed. He had already chosen the Rushmore site near Keystone the previous year, and in 1927 his labor commenced. Approximately sixty feet high, the heads of Washington, Jefferson, Lincoln, and Theodore Roosevelt were roughed out with unconventional sculptor's tools—dynamite and pneumatic drills—then finished by hand. Financed primarily by the U. S. Congress, the monument is administered by the National Park Service. Borglum died in Chicago.

His brother, sculptor **Solon Hannibal Borglum** (1868–1922), worked in a similar style. Born in Ogden, Utah Territory, he began painting before joining his brother in California in 1893. In 1895 he entered the Art Academy of Cincinnati, but left after two years for Paris. In three years there he established his career as a specialist in western themes, particularly depictions of animals. After his return, he lived in New York and, from 1906, on a farm in Silvermine, Connecticut, where he died. Portraits supplemented his continued attention to frontier themes. His comparative anatomy textbook, *Sound Construction* (1923), appeared posthumously. After Gutzon's death, his son, sculptor and photographer **Lincoln Borglum** (1912–86), completed final details at Mount Rushmore. Born in Stamford, James Lincoln de la Mothe Borglum trained with his father and in Europe. Gutzon's first wife, painter **Elizabeth Borglum** (1848–1922), known as Lisa, was born Elizabeth Jaynes (or Janes) in Racine, Wisconsin. Following studies in Boston and New York, she specialized in still life subjects, but after moving to San Francisco in 1881, she studied with William *Keith and increasingly turned to landscape. She met Borglum in San Francisco, and they married in 1889 in Los Angeles. Gutzon left her in Paris when he returned permanently to the United States. (They divorced in 1908.) Returning to the Los Angeles area around 1902, she resettled in the home they had purchased in Sierra Madre but spent her last years in Venice, on the coast.

Boughton, Alice. *See* PHOTO-SECESSION.

Bourgeois, Louise (1911–). Sculptor, printmaker, painter, draftswoman, and installation artist. Her celebrated, sexually inflected, autobiographically generated sculptures have proved central in recent decades to debates around representation of gender. Most of her work addresses women's bodily experience, the feelings occasioned by female roles, or the domestic environment. Acclaimed since the 1970s by a feminist movement that broadened her audience, she nevertheless had already enjoyed a career of more than three decades. Steeped in *biomorphic surrealism, her earlier work usually suggests figuration, although forms are not generally descriptive. These works were most often carved in wood, less often in stone, but over the years she has worked in numerous media, including bronze, plaster, latex, and cloth. Since the 1980s *installations have amplified a longtime interest in creating unified environments for groups of sculptures. Some late projects have assumed gargantuan dimensions. Born in Paris, she studied mathematics and philosophy at the Sorbonne, worked with Fernand Léger, and took classes at several art schools. She moved permanently to New York in 1938 and subsequently became a citizen. After her arrival, she studied with Vaclav *Vytlacil at the *Art Students League and remained primarily an abstract painter until the late 1940s. In 1945 she took up printmaking at *Atelier 17. Her early three-dimensional work centered on skinny, totemlike carvings and castings suggesting abstracted human figures. Although she denied any connection, some seem to draw inspiration, if only indirectly, from ethnographic precedents. During the late 1940s, she also produced the startling Femme Maison (Woman House) drawings. Depicting women whose heads or upper bodies have metamorphosed into houses, these surrealistic images comment with wit, economy, and pointed insight on the tendency for the domestic realm to swallow women's identity. During the heyday of *abstract expressionism, *pop art, and *minimalism in the 1950s and 1960s, her art received little attention. Nevertheless, in the work of these years she expanded her vocabulary to encompass organic forms of variously bulbous, stringy, and melting character.

Prefiguring her emergence as a leading 1970s artist, Lucy *Lippard's notable 1966 "Eccentric Abstraction" show reintroduced Bourgeois with work that did not look out of place alongside that of much younger artists, such as Bruce *Nauman and Eva *Hesse. In 1982 the *Museum of Modern Art confirmed her reputation by staging a retrospective exhibition, its first major show ever devoted to a woman. Although she had previously been reticent about her personal life, at this time Bourgeois published a photo-essay revealing the childhood wellsprings of her art. At the age of seventy, she described a lingering trauma caused by her father's treachery in taking for his mistress her girlhood governess while at the same time demanding the compliance of his wife, Bourgeois's mother. Once this narrative was in the open, the artist used room-sized installations (she calls them cells) as well as individual sculptures to conduct an obsessive and presumably cathartic reexamination of her memories and their emotional ramifications. Widely lauded for courage in transforming into artistic expression the psychological difficulties of her otherwise comfortable youth, she became an international art star. In 1993 she was selected as the sole U.S. representative to the Venice Biennale, and in 2000 London's new Tate Modern featured her huge sculptures as the opening display in its multistory atrium. Three of these were large, towerlike, steel assemblages. The fourth was a giant spider, one of a series in bronze and steel, begun in the early 1990s and reaching as much as thirty-five feet in height. These menacing creatures number among the most theatrical manifestations of the fear she has identified as a central outcome of her early ruminations on sexual politics. In 1995 she published *Louise Bourgeois: Drawings & Observations*, with the assistance of Lawrence Rinder. She expanded on her views in *Destruction of the Father, Reconstruction of the Father: Writings and Interviews, 1923–1997* (1998), edited and with texts by Marie-Laure Bernadac and Hans-Ulrich Obrist.

In 1938 she married Robert Goldwater (1907–73), an art historian who specialized in modern and tribal art at a time when these subjects were rarely considered from a scholarly point of view. She met him in Paris while he was doing research for his best-known book, *Primitivism in Modern Art* (1938), a landmark study that remained a standard reference for decades. A lifelong New Yorker, Robert John Goldwater received a bachelor's degree in art history from Columbia University in 1929 and an MA from Harvard two years later. He earned his PhD from New York University in 1937. In 1957 he was appointed the first director of New York's Museum of Primitive Art. When he died, he had nearly completed arrangements for transfer of the museum's holdings in 1974 to the *Metropolitan Museum of Art. He also taught at Queens College from 1939 until 1956 and subsequently at New York University. From 1947 until 1953, as editor of the *Magazine of Art*, he oversaw its pioneering coverage of abstract expressionism. His other publications include monographs on Gauguin, van Gogh, Rufino Tamayo, and Jacques *Lipchitz, as well as studies of African art and other subjects. With Jim M. Jordan, he compiled a critical catalogue of Arshile *Gorky's paintings (1982).

Bourke-White, Margaret (1904–71). Photographer. A leading photojournalist from the late 1920s through the early 1950s, she made her reputation with powerful, glamorous images of American industry. Adventurous, courageous, and ambitious, she also documented poverty in the South, recorded events at numerous foreign destinations, and, as a war correspondent, achieved national celebrity with scenes of combat and its consequences. An originator of the sequenced photo-essay, she took care to relate each image to its context and often provided accompanying texts. Born Margaret White in New York, she grew up in Bound Brook, New Jersey. She studied at several universities before receiving a bachelor's degree in biology from Cornell University in 1927. She also studied photography at Clarence *White's school in New York. In 1926, when a brief marriage ended, she changed her surname to Bourke-White by adding her mother's maiden name to her own. She made her mark with images of the Ohio steel industry and in 1929 was hired as the principal photographer for *Fortune*. Despite the difficult economic times of the 1930s, this lavish new business magazine flourished, reproducing her photographs with serious appreciation for their artistic qualities. In 1930 she photographed German factories and was the first foreign photographer to chronicle Russian industrialization. She described her experiences in the USSR in *Eyes on Russia* (1931), the first of the books that she both wrote and illustrated. When *Life* magazine began publication in 1936, she numbered among four original staff photographers. Her image of Montana's Fort Peck Dam appeared on the cover of the first issue, while the contents included her synthesis of photographs and writing on New Deal dams, perhaps the first such photo-essay in an American periodical.

In the mid-1930s she collaborated with writer Erskine Caldwell on three books. *You Have Seen Their Faces* (1937) documents the lives of impoverished Southern tenant farmers. *North of the Danube* (1939) covers Czechoslovakia during the perilous days before the Nazi takeover, and *Say, Is This the U.S.A.?* (1941) surveys American life. They married in 1939 but divorced three years later. Bourke-White provided extensive World War II coverage for *Life*. In 1941 she was the only foreign photographer present during the German bombing of Moscow, an experience she recounted in *Shooting the Russian War* (1942). As the first woman photographer permitted to accompany the armed forces in action, she sailed to London to cover the Blitz, survived the sinking of a ship in the Mediterranean, and participated in the Italian campaign, the subject of her next book, *They Called It "Purple Heart Valley": A Combat Chronicle of the War in Italy* (1944). As the Allies entered Germany, she photographed the country's devastation and the horrors of the concentration camps for *Dear Fatherland, Rest Quietly: A Report on the Collapse of Hitler's "Thousand Years"* (1946). In the late 1940s, she photographed Gandhi and the division of the subcontinent into India and Pakistan. *Halfway to Freedom: A Report on the New India* (1949) resulted. During the Korean War, she again reported on a ravaged land. In 1952, while still in Korea, she suffered the first symptoms of Parkinson's disease, which increasingly limited her activity. Energetically resisting its toll, she continued working for several years. In 1963 she published an autobiography, *Portrait of Myself*. She died in Stamford, Connecticut.

Brach, Paul. *See* SCHAPIRO, MIRIAM.

Brackett, Edward Augustus (1818–1908). Sculptor. Known for portraits, mostly busts, he also produced imaginative subjects. Only one of these survives. Acclaimed in its day, this melodramatic marble *Shipwrecked Mother and Child* (Worcester [Massachusetts] Art Museum, 1848–51) represents a drowned nude woman clasping her unfortunate baby. Brackett's best-known portrait, a posthumous bust of Washington *Allston (Metropolitan Museum, 1844), sympathetically softens a naturalistic interpretation of the aging painter. Self-taught as an artist, Brackett was born in Vassalborough (now Vassalboro), Maine, near Augusta. He moved as a young man to Cincinnati, where he began to work as a sculptor. Following a stint of about two years in New York, early in the 1840s he moved his studio to the Boston area. From 1843 until his death he made his home in Winchester. After serving for a year in the Civil War, he found few commissions but turned his attention to wildlife conservation and agricultural experimentation. In 1869 he was appointed to a state commission supervising inland fisheries. When he became its head in 1873 he ceased working as an artist. From 1894 until his death he accepted expanded responsibilities as head of the Massachusetts Fish and Game Commission. Brackett published several books, including the poetry collections *Twilight Hours or Leisure Moments of an Artist* (1845) and *My House, Chips the Builder Threw Away* (1904), as well as ruminations on spiritualism. His brother, self-taught painter **Walter M. Brackett** (1823–1919), was known particularly for portraits and for images of game fish. Born also in central Maine, in Unity, he worked for most of his career in Boston, where he died.

Bradford, William (1823–92). Painter. A marine specialist, he is remembered particularly for Arctic views. He also painted landscapes, often depicting the West. A native of Fairhaven, Massachusetts, near the whaling center of New Bedford, by the mid-1850s he was active professionally as a painter of precisely detailed ship portraits. Although mostly self-taught as an artist, he improved his technical skills while working in Fairhaven alongside Rotterdam native Albert van Beest (1820–60), who also imparted an appreciation for Dutch seascape traditions. Fitz Hugh *Lane's shore views stimulated Bradford's affection for the light and clarity associated with *luminism. After passing several winters in Boston, Bradford moved permanently to New York around 1860. (He continued to maintain a residence in Fairhaven, as well.) In 1861 he traveled to Labrador, presumably intrigued by recently published accounts of northern exploration. Undoubtedly spurred in New York by successes of Frederic *Church and Albert *Bierstadt in finding audiences for dramatic and inaccessible landscape subjects, Bradford traveled by boat to frigid latitudes nearly every summer during the 1860s. Consequent works of the

1860s and 1870s convincingly convey the majesty, stupendous scale, and cool resplendence of an undefiled region. A three-month, five-thousand-mile expedition in 1869 crowned and concluded Bradford's Arctic experiences. For this round trip from Newfoundland to Greenland, he chartered a steamer and assembled a party including the noted polar explorer Dr. Isaac Hayes, as well as two Boston photographers. Sketches and photographs from this trip fueled paintings for the rest of his career. In addition, Bradford published a sumptuous, limited-edition book *The Arctic Regions* (1873). His rapturous descriptive text accompanies tipped-in original photographic prints. Although his traveling companions had captured the scenes on glass plates, Bradford likely had a hand in framing them, for many are dramatic and compelling images. While residing during 1872 and 1873 in London, where the book was issued, he delivered his first illustrated lectures on Arctic exploration. While also traveling in the American West and sojourning for extended periods in San Francisco, he successfully continued these in the United States into the last years before his death in New York.

Brady, Mathew B. (1823?–96). Photographer. Known for portraits of illustrious Americans, he also masterminded creation of an extensive visual record of the Civil War, the first military conflict to be comprehensively photographed. An artist, an entrepreneur, and something of a self-promoting showman, he proved instrumental in consolidating photography's role in modern society. Among the earliest photographers to understand and exploit the power of images, he grasped the new medium's potential within a culture that prized information, entertainment, and spectacle. In pursuit of his vision, he eagerly adopted, and often improved, new photographic technologies as they became available. Eventually he served his ambitions by hiring others to do much of the actual photographing in the studio and, more importantly, on the battlefield. Nevertheless, during the Civil War he choreographed their activities and contextualized their images, thus accruing to the Brady name an authenticating power in understandings of the conflict. Born in Warren County, in upstate New York near Lake George, not even he knew the meaning of the middle initial his parents gave him. After working for a short time in Albany with William *Page, in 1841 he accompanied the painter to New York. There Brady learned the new *daguerreotype process from Samuel F. B. *Morse. In 1844 he opened his first studio, the Daguerrean Miniature Gallery, where he made portraits but also displayed likenesses of well-known people. A great success, Brady's establishment drew luminaries from nearly every field, including politics, entertainment, literature, and art, as well as ordinary clients who could relish an association with notables. Following his shrewd instinct for celebrity, in 1850 he published *The Gallery of Illustrious Americans*, with twenty-four lithographic reproductions of his daguerreotypes picturing several U.S. presidents, John James *Audubon, Henry Clay, James Fenimore Cooper, Dolley Madison, and others. Although the volume was widely admired, modest sales quashed Brady's hopes for a series. During the summer of 1851 Brady departed for ten months abroad. He toured the Continent and visited London, where a gold medal for general excellence in the 1851 Crystal Palace international exhibition certified his international prestige.

Although by this time the most famous photographer in the United States, he had been troubled for some time by vision problems. Perhaps because of this deficiency, he had begun to employ assistants to operate the camera. However, Brady retained creative control by continuing to pose, light, and supervise the sittings. He first photographed Abraham Lincoln in February 1860, just before the presidential aspirant delivered his momentous Cooper Union address in New York. The resulting portrait helped to elect Lincoln and established a fruitful relationship that resulted in a number of subsequent likenesses from the Brady studio. By the late 1850s the newer glass-plate technology had supplanted daguerreotypes in Brady's practice. An assistant, Alexander *Gardner, who had arrived highly skilled in the technique from Britain in 1856, facilitated the transition. Reviving a plan that had failed about ten years earlier, in 1858 Brady established a presence in the nation's capital, with Gardner in charge. Extending his zeal to record the history of his time by photographing the country's most important figures, Brady assumed responsibility for documenting the Civil War. He took some early battlefield pictures but for the most part oversaw the operation from his studio. Almost presaging the role of film director, he conceived the plans, directed the working photographers, and maintained editorial control of the undertaking. Among field agents for this unprecedented undertaking, Gardner, George *Barnard, and Timothy *O'Sullivan particularly stand out, although all three left Brady's employ after the first year or two of the war. However, as they continued to photograph the conflict on their own, they contributed to a documentary archive that Brady had done much to conceive. Because photography remained a slow and cumbersome process in the 1860s and because sharply focused clarity appealed to contemporary taste, nearly all Civil War photographs present static compositions. In place of action, we witness camp life, battle preparations, carnage, and ruinous desolation. Instead of heroes, we can usually discern only anonymous fighters. Enduring drudgery or dead on the field, they seem dispensable components of this first mechanized, modern war. Although evidence suggests that Civil War photographers sometimes manipulated subjects in order to heighten the emotional power of their images, the seeming objectivity of the photographic process gave these pictures the aura of unbiased reports. In the aggregate, the mission Brady defined for photography inadvertently demystified military glory and the romance of battle. Assuming there would be a huge market for the images when the conflict ended, he spared little expense in pursuing his epic project. In fact, the public apparently wanted to forget the war once it was over, and Brady went bankrupt within a few years. His appeals to the federal government to preserve for the nation his entire collection of portraits and Civil War images went unheeded. Rather, in 1874 the government purchased his negatives at auction when he could no longer pay for storage. The following year, however, Congress compensated him for title to several thousand images, today in the National Archives. Early neglect of Brady's Civil War achievement has long since been redeemed by acclaim for both the historical value of the images generally and the expressive power of the best. The federal government's payment relieved Brady's debts, but he never regained his financial footing nor his artistic stature. Instead, his postwar years reveal a sad story of depression, alcoholism, illness, and creative stasis. Brady died in lonely obscurity in New York, but he was honored with burial in Arlington National Cemetery.

Brainard, Joe. *See* FLUXUS.

Brecht, George. *See* FLUXUS.

Breck, John Leslie (1860–99). Painter. Among the earliest American impressionists, he painted vibrant, light-filled landscapes indebted to Monet's example. A Bostonian, he frequently depicted the local area, the shore north of the city, or the nearby New Hampshire mountains with careful attention to seasonal effects. Born during a Pacific sea voyage, he spent his early childhood in San Francisco but moved with his family to Boston in 1865. He traveled in 1877 to Munich, where he studied at the Royal Academy until 1880, when he went to Antwerp for an additional year's study. Following his return to Boston, he produced darkly toned, painterly still lifes, often incorporating flowers. In 1886 he sailed for Paris, where he worked at the Académie Julian. The following year in Giverny he became well acquainted with Monet and quickly mastered an impressionist style, although he sometimes worked in a more conservative, *Barbizon-inspired mode. He returned to Boston during the summer of 1890 but subsequently painted again at Giverny in 1891. In notable emulation of his mentor there, he painted a series of fifteen identically composed studies of grainstacks, investigating light effects at different times of day. Soon after, he departed for England, where he painted the countryside of Kent that fall and into the next year. In 1896 he went to Venice, where he remained for more than a year. Breck resided in the Auburndale neighborhood of Newton, a Boston suburb, from the mid-1890s and died in Boston.

Breder, Hans. *See* MENDIETA, ANA.

Brewster, Anna Richards. *See* RICHARDS, WILLIAM TROST.

Bricher, Alfred Thompson (1837–1908). Painter. Specializing almost exclusively in Atlantic coastal views, he created light-filled, horizontal scenes of beaches, cliffs, and sea, usually recording locations along the shores of New England and Grand Manan Island, New Brunswick. Clear and simple spatial organization, meticulously observed rocks and waves, and sharp attention to effects of atmospheric light demonstrate ties to *luminism. Evoking idyllic seaside vacations, Bricher's vistas generally disregard nature's perilous and stupendous aspects. Born in Portsmouth, New Hampshire, but raised in Newburyport, Massachusetts, as a teenager he went to work in Boston. Although largely self-taught as a painter, he found inspiration in an encounter with William Stanley *Haseltine in 1858. Undoubtedly profiting also from precedents in the work of Fitz Hugh *Lane and Martin Johnson *Heade, Bricher may have known them personally. In his early years as an artist, he followed the example of *Hudson River School artists in visiting the Catskills and White Mountains, and in 1866 he journeyed along the Mississippi River into Wisconsin and Minnesota. He moved permanently to New York in the late 1860s. In the 1880s he had a summer home at Southampton and in these years often painted the shores and inlets of Long Island. From 1890 he made his home on Staten Island, in New Dorp, where he died.

Bridges, Charles (1670–1747). Portrait painter. He ranked as the most significant artist working in Virginia between 1735 and the early 1740s, during the moment when the colony's landed families and Williamsburg elite were eager to establish their dignity, sophistication, and taste. Although Bridges supplied images commensurate with his patrons' status-conscious goals, he supplemented his practice, as did most colonial artists, with decorative commissions. Only about thirty attributed Virginia portraits survive, and little documentation of his career has been found. His one extant English commission dates to many years earlier. Besides furthering his career as a portraitist, the elderly Bridges had a secondary motive for traveling to the colonies: founding charity schools for the Society for Promoting Christian Knowledge, which had employed him in London between 1699 and 1713, before he became an artist. Born in Northamptonshire, Bridges was solidly trained in the late Baroque portrait mode dominated by Sir Godfrey Kneller in the decades around 1700. In his formulaic Virginia work, Bridges extended this taste for ponderous dignity, although he was on occasion capable of a lighter touch, especially in images of women. Little individualized in his conventional wig, velvet coat, and ruffled shirt, a three-quarter figure of *Mann Page II* (College of William and Mary, Williamsburg, Virginia, early 1740s) offers an august and imposing presence as he soberly eyes the viewer. Bridges returned to England in 1743 or 1744 and died at Warkton, in the county of his birth.

Bridges, Fidelia. *See* PRE-RAPHAELITISM, AMERICAN.

Bridgman, Frederick Arthur (1847–1928). Painter. An expatriate living in France, he specialized in scenes of North African and Middle Eastern Arab life. Earning renown in the 1870s and 1880s as the leading American orientalist, he also painted the French countryside and its rustic inhabitants, as well as pure landscapes. Born in Tuskegee, he lived as a child in Alabama and Tennessee before moving to Massachusetts in 1860. Initially trained in New York in the technically demanding profession of banknote engraving, while pursuing this profession he attended classes at the *National Academy of Design and elsewhere. After 1866, when he left for Paris, he resided abroad but made occasional visits to the United States. In 1867 he began two years of study with Jean-Léon Gérôme, an academic painter famous for highly finished scenes of oriental life. During the summer of 1866, Bridgman had already visited the village of Pont-Aven, where American artists around Robert *Wylie had recently begun to establish an art colony. He continued to return frequently for several years and first gained recognition with images of Breton life. For several months in 1872/73 Bridgman traveled in North Africa, probably the first American artist to visit many of its fabled sites. Soon known as an interpreter of the region, he produced scenes of contemporary life, as well as archeologically informed reconstructions of the past. Among few Americans to venture into the Sahara, then still little touched by colonialism, he returned on several occasions to North Africa and also journeyed through Egypt and the Near East. His tight, polished style, formed under Gérôme's influence, loosened somewhat during the 1880s as he responded to the period's aesthetic interest in outdoor light, which he often subtly recreated to evoke varied times of day. In 1890 Bridgman published *Winters in Algeria*. During the following decade he began to compose music, some of which was performed publicly after 1900, although by this time his paintings no longer excited much interest. Shortly before World War I, he moved to the picturesque Normandy village of Lyons-la-Forêt, where he again addressed rural subjects. He died in nearby Rouen.

Bridgman, George Brant. *See* SHAHN, BEN.

Brigman, Anne W. (1869–1950). Photographer. The foremost California *pictorialist, she belonged to the *Photo-Secession, exhibited at Alfred *Stieglitz's *291 gallery, and published her photographs in *Camera Work*. She remains especially known for dreamy but emotionally charged nudes and landscapes, commonly combined. Born in Honolulu, at sixteen Anne Wardrope Nott, known as Annie, moved with her family to Los Gatos, California, south of the Bay Area. In 1894 she married Martin Brigman, a sea captain, with whom she traveled in the Pacific. (They separated in 1910.) As a young woman she painted, made copperplate and linoleum prints, and wrote fiction. In 1902 she began exhibiting photographic prints in major exhibitions. In 1910 she visited New York for eight months on her only visit to the East. About 1930 she moved from the San Francisco area to Long Beach and several years later, returned to writing. Her poetry and photographs appeared together in *Songs of a Pagan* (1949). She died in the Eagle Rock neighborhood of Los Angeles. Like other art photographers of her day, Brigman favored a soft focus and often worked on her negatives by hand. Her best-known photographs reflect her apprehension of human life as an extension of nature. The allegorical nudes (sometimes herself) that inhabit her California landscapes suggest nymphs or sylphs. In the 1907 "Soul of a Blasted Pine," a nude woman standing inside a twisted tree stump continues its spiraling lines into an ecstatic pose against the sky, illustrating in an unusually literal way the photographer's appreciation of the unity of existence.

Brinton, Christian. *See* PIPPIN, HORACE.

Brodovitch, Alexey. *See* AVEDON, RICHARD.

Brook, Alexander. *See* BACON, PEGGY.

Brooks, James (1906–92). Painter. A figure painter and accomplished muralist before he turned to *abstract expressionism, Brooks later emphasized nuanced color harmonies in large canvases related to *color field painting. He numbers among the first to experiment with staining unprimed canvas. Throughout, his generally lyric work, often inflected by decorative qualities, balances cogitation with the free play of spontaneous gesture. James Ealand Brooks was born in St. Louis but lived with his family in several western locations as a child. Following high school in Dallas, he studied there for two years at Southern Methodist University and began his formal art training at the Dallas Art Institute. He also studied privately with Martha Simkins (1866–1969), a portrait, landscape, and still life painter who had grown up in Texas but studied at the *Art Students League, where she came under the influence of William Merritt *Chase, before settling permanently some years later in Dallas. In 1926 Brooks moved to New York. He studied at the Grand Central School of Art and the Art Students League, where the well known drawing instructor Kimon Nicolaides (1892–1938) and Boardman *Robinson numbered among his teachers. Subsequently, he supported himself as a commercial artist while painting figurative works indebted to Picasso and Matisse. Under the auspices of *federal art projects, he painted several murals, most notably a 235-foot-long interpretation of the theme of flight (1942) for the Marine Air Terminal rotunda at La Guardia airport. (Painted over in the 1950s, it was restored in 1980.) U.S. Army service took him to wartime Europe and the Middle East from 1942 until 1945. Upon his return to New York, he at first worked in a synthetic cubist manner but soon became interested in early abstract expressionist work, particularly Jackson *Pollock's. Following his example, Brooks experimented with poured paints, while also developing a calligraphic linear element indebted to surrealism. To incorporate chance in the structure of his work, in the late 1940s he began dribbling paint on the back of canvases, then allowing the soaked-through elements to suggest the rhythms and shapes of his compositions. Responding also to the planar relationships in Willem *de Kooning's work, by 1950 he had forged a personal style of carefully considered color areas connected by linear swirls. In the 1960s his works became simpler, more vibrant in color, and compositionally more structured. He resided for some time near the eastern end of Long Island and died after an illness of several years in Brookhaven, not far from his home in Springs. In 1947 Brooks married abstract painter Charlotte Park (1918–). Born in Concord, Massachusetts, she moved to New York in 1945.

Brooks, Romaine (1874–1970). Painter and draftswoman. Remembered particularly for images of women, often portraits, she emphasized melancholy self-absorption, as well as psychological and social isolation. Nevertheless, many subjects radiate inner strength as they defy conventional gender expectations. Born to American parents in Rome, Beatrice Romaine Goddard studied art between 1896 and 1899 at the Scuola Nazionale in Rome and at the Académie Colarossi in Paris. For a time in the early 1900s she lived on Capri, where she met homosexual British pianist and poet John Ellingham Brooks. Their marriage lasted only a year. In England she painted her first mature work, soft and reserved portraits and figure studies inspired by James McNeill *Whistler, whose palette of grays and muted earth tones she continued to favor. In 1905 she moved to Paris, where she became widely acquainted in artistic and literary circles. There her paintings became more stylized, emphasizing line and flat patterning. In *Le Trajet* (The Crossing) (Smithsonian American Art Museum, 1911) an emaciated nude reposes as if in death, her long black hair sweeping beyond the white sheet on which she reclines and into the darkness that surrounds all. In its lugubrious, aestheticized tone and sweeping linear rhythms, it draws on precedents in art nouveau and symbolism, suggesting also the influence of Aubrey Beardsley and Edvard Munch. In a more forthright *Self Portrait* (Smithsonian American Art Museum, 1923), Brooks presents herself as a resolute but somewhat mysterious figure in mannish black riding habit, a black hat shadowing her eyes. After 1930 Brooks rarely painted. However, for another decade she continued to draw hermetic, symbolist reveries, occasionally suggesting contemporary surrealism, in a style emphasizing continuous curving lines. For the half century after 1915, American expatriate writer Natalie Barney was her companion.

Brooks died in Nice, where she had lived since the later 1940s, reclusively in her final years.

Browere, John Henri Isaac (1790–1834). Sculptor and painter. Devoted almost exclusively to portrait sculpture, Browere occupies a distinctive niche in its history. To insure verisimilitude, he made a specialty of taking life masks from his sitters, using a light, quickly hardening plaster. From the resulting molds he made plaster positives, which he refined by hand and set off above generalized shoulders covered with togalike drapery that contributes an air of permanence and distinction. Although his combination of literal realism and *neoclassicism appealed to tastes of his day, he generally failed to be taken seriously as an artist because of the supposedly mechanical nature of his procedure. His hopes to obtain public commissions for bronze replicas of his plaster images of American statesmen and other notables went unfulfilled. Born John Henry Brower in New York, he later gave his name a more stylish flair. He attended Columbia College (now University), took drawing lessons, taught school in Tarrytown (north of the city) for three years, painted portraits and miniatures, and fashioned his first busts before departing to travel and study in Europe for two years. After his return he journeyed around the country accumulating portraits for a gallery of distinguished Americans, which he opened in New York in 1828. His subjects included John Adams, Thomas Jefferson, the visiting Marquis de Lafayette, and other important figures of the Revolutionary generation and Federal era. He also wrote art criticism, signed Middle-Tint the Second. He died at his home in New York.

Painter **Albertus De Orient Browere** (also Alburtis or Albertis) (1814–87), his son, is known primarily for landscapes and *genre scenes, but he also produced still lifes and narrative inventions. Born in Tarrytown, as a young artist in New York he exhibited scenes from history or literature. Particularly attracted to the writings of Washington Irving, he continued to mine these for occasional subjects even late in life. About 1840 he settled permanently in the area of Catskill, New York, and there added landscape subjects to his narrative interests. His work often fails to integrate individual elements into a convincing whole, but rather makes its appeal through attention to particulars delineated with a robust and frequently satirical spirit. Two trips to the West provided subjects for many of his most interesting scenes. In 1852 he sailed around Cape Horn to California, primarily to prospect for gold. After a subsequent period of about two years at home, in 1858 he traveled again to California, this time crossing the Isthmus of Panama, which inspired some tropical scenes. He painted in San Francisco until 1861, often documenting gold mining and other regional activities within his landscapes.

Brown, Bolton. *See* WOODSTOCK ARTISTS' COLONY.

Brown, George Loring (1814–89). Painter and printmaker. A specialist in Italian views, during a long residency abroad he acquired the nickname of "Claude Brown" in response to his affinity for Claude Lorrain's golden vistas enriched with classical architecture and picturesque country life. He also painted American scenes, most often depicting his native Boston or the New England shore. Brown was apprenticed as a teenager to Boston wood-engraver and portrait painter Alonzo Hartwell (1805–73). He also received some instruction in painting from George P. A. *Healy before departing in 1832 for two years in Europe. Following visits to Antwerp and London, he continued on to Paris, where he entered the studio of the romantic landscape and *genre specialist Eugène Isabey. After returning to the United States, he worked in New York, Boston, and other New England locations, producing portraits and narratives as well as landscapes. With Washington *Allston's encouragement, in 1840 he sailed again for Europe and soon settled in Italy. For two decades, he supplied tourists and Boston collectors with paintings and etchings that served as souvenirs of the grand tour. Brown lived in Florence for several years before relocating to Rome. He also traveled widely throughout Italy and occasionally to Switzerland, Paris, or other more northern venues. To meet demand for his scenes, he hired a painting assistant, and many of his works are variants of a single view. Nevertheless his best works display vigorous brushwork, vivid contrasts, sparkling colors, precisely rendered detail, and an atmospheric glow suggesting affinities with *luminism. During the final three decades of his life, Brown lived most of the time in the Boston vicinity. There he produced Italian scenes based on sketches and memories but also successfully adapted his style to the American landscape, as in the shimmering panorama *View of Norwalk Islands, Norwalk, Connecticut* (Addison Gallery of American Art, Phillips Academy, Andover, Massachusetts, 1864). However, his romantic realism soon seemed old-fashioned in the face of newer *Barbizon and impressionist approaches. In 1879–80 he again visited Paris and other European sites. Brown died near Boston, in Malden, where he had resided for some time.

Brown, Henry Kirke (1814–86). Sculptor. Among the earliest Americans to work regularly in bronze, he pioneered in redirecting taste from the widely popular *neoclassicism of the pre–Civil War period toward a greater naturalism of both form and content. Although he also executed invented subjects, he is particularly known for public monuments commemorating notable Americans. The best known, an equestrian *George Washington* (Union Square, New York, 1856), realistically depicts the general, his horse, and his military garb, but its air of classical nobility reaches back to Roman and Renaissance precedents. This large and complex work represents also a technical milestone in American bronze casting. Resisting the practice common among American sculptors to work in Italy, Brown ranks as the first significant American sculptor to choose to make a career in the United States after training abroad. He championed development of an indigenous but sophisticated sculptural practice based on nature and emphasizing American subjects. In 1859–60 he headed a presidentially appointed national arts commission, the first of its kind, to urge recognition of American art, especially in the decoration of the U.S. Capitol. Born and raised on a farm in north central Massachusetts, near Leyden, in 1832 he went to work for painter Chester *Harding in Boston. Four years later he moved to Cincinnati, where he soon turned to sculpture. From 1839 until 1842 he worked in Boston and in Albany and Troy, New York, before sailing to Europe. During two years in Florence and two in Rome, he mastered the prevailing neoclassical approach and completed a number of ideal figures. After settling in New York in the autumn of 1846, he began to emphasize greater realism in his work. About two years later he moved his home and studio to Brooklyn. There he soon also established a foundry, which employed two French artisans, to cast artistic and decorative work, including his own. Largely at Brown's urging, in 1849 the *American Art-Union began distributing small bronzes, such as his classically inflected *Choosing of the Arrow* (Amon Carter Museum, Fort Worth, Texas, 1849). He based this graceful but realistic Indian subject on studies made during an 1848 trip taken for that purpose to Mackinac Island, Michigan. After receiving a commission for a 10.5-foot standing portrait of *De Witt Clinton* (Green-Wood Cemetery, Brooklyn, 1852; model completed 1851), Brown worked with a Massachusetts company to develop the first American facility for casting large-scale sculpture. In 1857 he moved permanently to Newburgh, on the Hudson River north of New York.

Brown and his wife raised her nephew, the sculptor Henry Kirke Bush-Brown (1857–1935). Known particularly for portraits and public memorials, he also executed a number of imaginative subjects. His *Buffalo Hunt* won acclaim at the 1893 Columbian Exposition in Chicago. Bush-Brown was born in Ogdensburg, in northern New York, but grew up in Newburgh after his adoption by the Browns at an early age. Following initial training with Brown, he enrolled at the *National Academy of Design. From 1886 until 1890 he studied and worked in Paris and Florence. He returned to Newburgh but in 1898 moved to New York, where he had maintained a studio for several years. In 1910 he relocated permanently to Washington, D.C. Painter Margaret Lesley Bush-Brown (1857–1944), who also made etchings during the 1880s, became his wife in 1886. She became known especially for portraits but on occasion executed other subjects. Born in Philadelphia, Margaret White Lesley began her training at Philadelphia School of Design for Women (now Moore College of Art and Design) before entering the *Pennsylvania Academy of the Fine Arts in 1876. During four years there, she worked with Thomas *Eakins and Christian *Schussele. In 1880 she departed for Paris to continue her studies. Except for a visit home in 1882, she remained until 1883. She died in Ambler, Pennsylvania, near Philadelphia.

Brown, Joan. *See* FUNK ART.

Brown, John George (1831–1913). Painter. As one of the most popular late-nineteenth-century American artists, he specialized in urban *genre scenes. These usually focus on the lives of impoverished but appealing children, particularly male street urchins and waifs. Newsboys, bootblacks, performers, and sly charmers populate his images. Cute and usually cheerful, innocent although sometimes mischievous, his young entrepreneurs seem to personify the rags-to-riches myth of unbridled capitalism as they hustle pennies. Few contemporaries seem to have considered the adversity and pain that Brown's young subjects conceal. However, in the long run his sentimentally conceived representations of hardship may have contributed to the origins of child welfare reform. Earlier in his career, through the 1860s and 1870s, Brown addressed a wider range of subjects, including country scenes. Even then, however, he favored children, often depicting girls as well as boys in directly observed scenes of daily life. Born in Durham, England, Brown grew up in Newcastle-on-Tyne, where he apprenticed as a glass-cutter and attended evening classes at the local art school. After a year in Edinburgh, in 1853 he emigrated to New York, where he continued his artistic training under Thomas Seir *Cummings. Within two years, he had established his own portrait studio in Brooklyn but subsequently also took classes at the *National Academy of Design. As his interest in genre developed, in 1860 he moved his studio into Manhattan's prestigious Tenth Street Studio Building while continuing to live in Brooklyn and then Fort Lee, New Jersey, until about 1870. Thereafter, he made his home in Manhattan but generally summered in rural locations. With its precisely rendered, clearly illuminated accumulation of detail, *The Music Lesson* (Metropolitan Museum, 1870) inventories features of a middle-class Victorian home. This display of material possessions provides a refined setting for self-improvement. The young man who bends close to his flute pupil is interested in something besides her musical education, yet their relationship remains for the moment free of amatory intentions. In both style and content, the painting reveals Brown's debt to mid-century English *Pre-Raphaelitism, which shaped his enthusiasm for recording the exact appearance of contemporary life, as well as his conviction that art should provide moral instruction. In *Bootblack with a Rose* (Museum of Art, Munson-Williams-Proctor Arts Institute, Utica, New York, 1878), Brown presents a pensive street boy affixing a flower to his jacket. Elevating the moment above the rough-and-tumble world the child inhabits, this gesture of appreciation for beauty implies unsuspected spiritual possibilities.

Brown, Kathan. *See* CROWN POINT PRESS.

Brown, Mather (1761–1831). Painter. A Boston native, he resided in England throughout his adult life. Known chiefly as a portraitist, he also painted ambitious religious and historical subjects. Mather Byles Brown had his first art lessons at twelve from young Gilbert *Stuart. At sixteen he became an itinerant portraitist, painting mostly miniatures. In 1780 he departed for the West Indies before continuing on to Europe. After a stop in Paris, in 1781 he arrived in London, where he entered Benjamin *West's atelier. There he again encountered Stuart, whose style made a strong impression. The next year he began to study at the school of the Royal Academy of Arts. In 1784 Brown established his own portrait studio and soon enjoyed great success in the sophisticated London portrait market. His clients included the British aristocracy as well as numerous prominent American visitors, such as Thomas Jefferson and John Adams. Brown's best portraits recall Stuart's in their painterly technique, stylish air, and evocation of individual personality. In the early 1790s he also gained favorable attention for literary and historical or political subjects. Nevertheless, after the mid-1790s his reputation faltered, and in 1808 he left the capital. During the next two years he worked in Bath, Bristol, and elsewhere. From 1810 until 1824 he taught and painted in Lancashire, primarily in Liverpool and Manchester. He then returned to London, where his now dated style was virtually unmarketable, and spent his last years absorbed in narrative subjects that failed to find an audience. He died in London.

Brown, Milton W. (1911–98). Art historian, educator, and painter. A leader in the study of American art, Milton Wolf Brown was born in Newark, New Jersey, and educated at New York University, where he earned a BA in 1932, an MA three years later, and a PhD in 1949 from the university's Institute of Fine Arts. He also studied painting privately with Louis *Lozowick and at the *National Academy of Design with Leon *Kroll. After returning from World War II service in the U.S. Army, in 1946 he began teaching at Brooklyn College, where he remained for twenty-five years. He then accepted a position at the City University of New York, where he served until 1979 as the first director of a graduate program that achieved considerable success in promoting American art as a field of scholarly endeavor. In addition to his most influential book, the groundbreaking *American Painting from the Armory Show to the Depression* (1955), his publications include *Painting of the French Revolution* (1938), *The Story of the Armory Show* (1963), and *American Art to 1900: Painting, Sculpture, Architecture* (1977). He continued to paint throughout his life, specializing in atmospheric watercolor views done on his travels. He died while on one such sojourn, in Miami Beach, Florida.

Brown, Roger. *See* CHICAGO IMAGISM.

Brown, Theophilus. *See* BAY AREA FIGURATIVE ART.

Brown, William Mason (1828–98). Painter. Early in his career, he produced landscapes in the manner of the *Hudson River School but from the 1860s became one of the nation's best-known still life painters, appreciated for a crisp, almost photographic style that celebrates the textural variety of his subjects. Many of his works feature elaborate tabletop arrangements of fruits, sometimes with other foods and/or flowers, often combined with serving pieces and decorative objects. Revealing ties to *Pre-Raphaelitism, other seemingly artless compositions render botanical specimens informally in natural settings. A native of Troy, New York, Brown lived for a time in Newark, New Jersey, before settling permanently in Brooklyn. His son **Fred C. Brown** painted still lifes in a style similar to his father's before leaving the profession to become a minister.

Browne, Byron (1907–61). Painter. Known chiefly for abstracted still life and figural themes, George Byron Browne was born in suburban Yonkers and lived throughout his career in New York. He trained between 1924 and 1928 at the *National Academy of Design and later studied with Hans *Hofmann. During the 1930s, he produced purely nonobjective arrangements of geometric and *biomorphic forms, as well as works that continued his engagement with the cubist tradition and with the contemporaneous work of Picasso. From these sources, he fashioned the personal style that emerged in the 1940s. Suggesting objects set on a table before a window, *Still Life with City Window* (Whitney Museum, 1945) reveals in the distance a night scene of city buildings below a full moon. Extending the synthetic cubist idiom, the painting presents abstracted and flattened shapes in a pattern of decorative color for an effect that is at once graceful, taut, and sophisticated. During the Depression, Browne completed several *federal art projects commissions, including an abstract mural composed of flat, geometric shapes (1939) for radio station WNYC and a stylized figural mosaic (1937) for the U.S. Passport Office at Rockefeller Center. He also participated from its beginning in the *American Abstract Artists organization.

In 1940 he married abstract painter Rosalind Bengelsdorf (1916–79), who soon relinquished painting for art criticism. A lifelong New Yorker, she studied at the *Art Students League from 1930 to 1934. Her teachers there included George *Bridgman, John Steuart *Curry, and Raphael *Soyer. She continued her training for a year in Germany, and after her return, in 1935–36 she, too, studied with Hofmann. In 1935 she began a five-year association with the federal art projects, which included creation of a major mural (destroyed) at the Central Nurses' Home on Welfare (now Roosevelt) Island, and she participated in establishing the American Abstract Artists. Her mature paintings combine geometric and biomorphic elements, along with occasional representational forms, in rhythmic arrangements within tightly controlled spatial envelopes. Her writing appeared prominently in *Art News*, as well as other publications, and she taught at the New School for Social Research (now New School) for a number of years. In the mid-1930s she evolved a theory she called New Realism, emphasizing the unity of all matter as revealed by science and providing a humanistic rationale for abstract art by connecting it to a fundamental reality beyond appearances.

Bruce, Ailsa Mellon. *See* MELLON, ANDREW.

Bruce, Edward (1879–1943). Painter. Also a New Deal art administrator. Born in Dover Plains, north of New York City, Edward Bright Bruce graduated from Columbia University in 1901 and earned a law degree there three years later. He worked briefly as an attorney in New York before going into business in the Pacific. During the 1920s he studied painting with Maurice *Sterne while living in Italy for six years. At the end of 1933 he was named to head the first of several important *federal art projects, the Public Works of Art Project (PWAP), and the following year he was appointed to direct a longer-lived mural program administered by the Treasury Department. In this position he oversaw commissioning of murals for new public buildings throughout the country. His opposition to both modernism and academicism reflected his preference for the moderation seen in his own work, predominately landscapes and cityscapes related to the *precisionist aesthetic. In these, he responded to particulars with simplified, stable forms, which lend his work dignity and subdued formal elegance. He died in Hollywood, Florida, only months after leaving Washington.

Bruce, Patrick Henry (1881–1936). Painter. Best known for a small group of stunningly original, geometricized still lifes done in the 1920s, he had previously worked in a form of color abstraction related to *synchromism. Born in Long Island, Virginia, he began his artistic training in Richmond, where he grew up. After moving to New York in 1902, he studied with William Merritt *Chase and Robert *Henri at the New York School of Art (now Parsons, the New School for Design). By early 1904 he was in Paris, where in 1906 he met Arthur Burdett *Frost Jr., subsequently a close friend. Along with Frost, from 1908 Bruce studied with Matisse. While working closely between 1912 and 1915 with French painters Robert and Sonia Delaunay, Bruce emulated Robert's use of discs to organize abstract compositions. In 1916 he developed a form of abstract painting that resembled Morgan *Russell's synchromist compositions of muscular, flat color areas, as in *Composition I* (Yale University Art Gallery, 1916). Beginning around 1917, Bruce reintroduced limited representation into his paintings. He assembled still life objects, drastically reduced to simplified volumes, into spatially ambiguous arrangements. Although related to the Purism of French artists Le Corbusier and Amédée Ozenfant, Bruce's paintings achieve more vivacious effects. Playful, decorative, and vividly colored, sometimes dauntingly complex, these sophisticated and original works found little appreciation. In the early 1930s Bruce destroyed many works, moved to Versailles, and nearly ceased painting. In 1936 he returned to the United States for the first time since a visit in 1905. A few months later he committed suicide in New York.

Bruguière, Francis. *See* PHOTO-SECESSION.

Brumidi, Constantino (1805–80). Painter. Trained in Rome, he ranks as the first to work in the United States as a specialist in large-scale public murals. He also produced easel paintings, including a number of portraits. During his European years, he worked also on occasion as a sculptor. He decorated much of the new Capitol in Washington, D.C., including the dome interior, hallways, and several meeting rooms. Working in a classical style based on firsthand knowledge of antique frescoes as well as the paintings of Raphael and his Baroque followers, he enthusiastically adapted his iconography to American circumstances. His work at the Capitol includes major scenes illustrating themes from the nation's history and decorative schemes incorporating native animals, plants, and inventions. Born in Rome, Brumidi studied with leading neoclassicists, including the sculptors Berthel Thorvaldsen and Antonio Canova, as well as painter Vincenzo Camuccini. Leaving a successful career in Rome to avoid imprisonment after being caught up in the political unrest of 1848–49, he lived briefly in Mexico City before arriving in 1852 in New York. About two years later he settled in Washington and soon started work at the Capitol. He was naturalized as a citizen in 1857. In 1865 he frescoed the Capitol's newly completed dome canopy with his best-known work, the resplendent *Apotheosis of George Washington.* Virtually deified, the first president, attended by allegorical figures, sits on a bank of clouds, just below luminous heavens. Earlier, in 1859 Brumidi had designed the illusionistic frieze that circles the rotunda below, but its execution was delayed for nearly twenty years and ultimately finished by others after his death. Painted in grisaille to mimic stone, the life-size figures enact a narrative of the nation's discovery, settlement, and political development. Brumidi also executed decorative commissions for Catholic churches in New York, Baltimore, Washington, Philadelphia, Mexico City, and Havana. He died in Washington. His son, painter **Laurence Brumidi** (1861–1920), a lifelong Washingtonian, trained in Paris. Primarily a portrait specialist, he also assisted his father at the Capitol.

Brush, George de Forest (1855–1941). Painter. He established his career in the 1880s with images of American Indians but later was known for Renaissance-inspired women and children as well as commissioned portraits. Derived from French academic painting, his precise, hard-surfaced, idealizing style equally served his disparate subjects. Born in Shelbyville, Tennessee, Brush grew up in Danbury, Connecticut. He began his professional training at the *National Academy of Design before departing in 1874 for Paris. There he studied with Jean-Léon Gérôme at the École des Beaux-Arts. The year after his return to the United States in 1880, he traveled to the West, where he lived among Indians in Wyoming and Montana for about four years. Following an interlude in New York, in January 1886 he left for rural Quebec. In proximity to First Nations subjects, he again lived in Spartan conditions for almost two years. Although Brush's Indian paintings display exacting ethnographic detail, with time they romantically accentuated tribal peoples' heroism and innate virtue. In autumn 1889 Brush returned to Europe. While living mostly in Paris until 1892, he began to concentrate on tender scenes idealizing innocent childhood and the rewards of maternity, often using his own family as models. After his first sojourn in Italy in 1898, iconographic, stylistic, and technical allusions to High Renaissance art appeared more overtly in his paintings, reinforcing an aura of sanctity in his mother-and-child combinations. As he developed into a major figure of the *American Renaissance, he also became a sought-after portrait painter. Following many summers in New Hampshire, in 1901 he purchased a farm in Dublin, near Mount Monadnock. This subsequently served as his principal residence, although he also maintained a New York studio and traveled frequently to Italy, remaining for periods as long as two years. A 1937 studio fire destroyed many works still in his possession. He died in Hanover, New Hampshire, where he resided during the final few years of his life. Two children became artists. Painter and sculptor **Gerome Brush** (1888–1954), born in New York, was known principally for portraits and murals. He died in Lincoln, Massachusetts, where he had resided for some time. Born in

Paris, painter Nancy Douglas Bowditch (1890–1979) specialized in portraits. She also worked in theater, as a designer and writer. In 1909 she married a student of her father, painter William Robert Pearmain (1888–1912). A few years after his early death, she became the wife of Dr. Harold Bowditch. A longtime New Hampshire resident, she published a biography of her father, *George de Forest Brush: Recollections of a Joyous Painter* (1970).

Brustlein, Janice. *See* BIALA.

Bryson, Bernarda. *See* SHAHN, BEN.

Buehr, Karl. *See* GIVERNY GROUP.

Bufford, John. *See* HOMER, WINSLOW.

Bullock, John G. *See* PHOTO-SECESSION.

Bullock, Wynn (1902–75). Photographer. His technically experimental early work, influenced by László *Moholy-Nagy's example, gave way after he met Edward *Weston in 1948 to a precisely realistic technique, put to the service of metaphors for the mysterious nature of existence. Born in Chicago, Percy Wingfield Bullock grew up in Southern California. In the early 1920s he moved to New York to pursue a career as a tenor. In Paris for two years at the end of the decade, he continued his musical training but, inspired by light-filled impressionist paintings and Moholy-Nagy's images, he also began to photograph. While subsequently working in real estate in Clarksburg, West Virginia, he was particularly attracted to solarization, a process that produces eerie effects through reversal of positive and negative tones. In 1938 he began two years of study at the Art Center School (now Art Center College of Design) in Los Angeles, and in the mid-1940s he relocated to Monterey. There he developed his mature style by adapting Weston's exacting realism to his own romantic quest to reveal the workings of space and time through photography. In 1959 he was appointed head of the photography department at San Francisco State College (now University). Bullock's images convey his mystical feeling for light, which, he believed, vibrates like sound with physiological and psychological effect. When he photographed directly from nature, he framed and lighted selections to produce somewhat otherworldly effects. In more contrived work, he produced surrealistic dream worlds, still sharply detailed. Often, posed and sometimes nude figures inhabit ambiguous settings, such as overgrown natural recesses, which may harbor weather-beaten structures. Although most of his work is in black and white, between 1960 and 1963 Bullock worked almost exclusively in color, making nearly abstract close-ups. He died in Monterey.

Bultman, Fritz (1919–85). Painter and sculptor. Born Anthony Frederick Bultman III in New Orleans, he got his start as an artist under the eye of Morris *Graves, a houseguest of his parents in 1932. As a teenager he studied in Germany but in 1937 enrolled at Chicago's New Bauhaus. Dissatisfied, he stayed only a few months before heading off the next year to begin four years of study with Hans *Hofmann in New York and *Provincetown. By making his home in Provincetown until 1952, Bultman missed much of the early *abstract expressionist ferment in New York. Yet, during the 1940s, his work contributed to the movement with dynamic canvases such as the 1949 *Hunter* (Metropolitan Museum, 1949). Dramatic reds and blacks do fierce battle in homage to the Actaeon myth, demonstrating the artist's links to abstract expressionist interests in archaic and symbolic thought. After he subsequently produced a black-and-white series featuring freer, flatter, rounded forms, in September 1950 he left for Italy to study bronze casting for nine months. Shortly after his return, strong color reappeared in his painting. In 1952 he moved to New York but maintained his connection with Provincetown, where he died at his home after long illness. By the mid-1950s his agitated surfaces began to relax, eventually becoming the sonorous abstract color works that characterized his later career. Many of these, following Matisse's lead, incorporate collage. During the 1960s and 1970s, he also completed a number of bronze sculptures.

Bunker, Dennis Miller (1861–90). Painter. Noted as one of the first Americans to work in an impressionist style, he painted innovative landscapes, as well as highly accomplished figural works in a more conservative mode. Despite a premature death, he affected American taste, particularly in Boston. Born in New York, he grew up in Garden City, on Long Island. He studied at the *National Academy of Design and the *Art Students League, where William Merritt *Chase numbered among his instructors. In 1882 left for Paris to work at the Académie Julian and then at the École des Beaux-Arts with Jean-Léon Gérôme. During summers he painted landscapes in the French countryside. After returning to New York, in the fall of 1885 he accepted a teaching position in Boston. He continued to paint carefully constructed, elegant, and sensitive figural works and portraits, which demonstrated mastery of Gérôme's example, but he also produced moody, *Barbizon-inspired landscapes. Soon well connected in the Boston art community, he benefited particularly from the friendship and patronage of Isabella Stewart *Gardner. After meeting John Singer *Sargent in Boston late in 1887, Bunker traveled to England to paint with him outdoors during the summer of 1888 at Calcot Mill near Reading. Subsequently, especially while painting during the summers of 1889 and 1890 in Medfield, not far from Boston, he applied a sophisticated impressionist technique to brightly lit, usually intimately scaled landscapes. However, sustaining his more traditional approach, figural works of these final years suggest his regard for the work of Abbott *Thayer and Thomas Wilmer *Dewing. In the fall of 1889 Bunker moved to New York. During a Christmas visit to Boston the following year, he died suddenly, probably from meningitis, less than two months after his twenty-ninth birthday.

Burchfield, Charles (1893–1967). Painter. Working primarily in watercolor, he created expressionistic landscapes and small-town scenes informed by a strongly romantic temperament and a searchingly observant eye. In many of his most effective works, powerful, otherworldly forces seem to animate both the natural landscape and its man-made additions, such as barns, Victorian houses, and idled factories. The gnarly pessimism of some works grew from his hatred of modern industrialism and its deleterious effects on village life. In other works, he conveyed a mystical ecstasy before a natural world throbbing with radiant vitality. Born in Ashtabula, Ohio, Charles Ephraim Burchfield grew up in Salem, a small industrial town in the southeastern part of the state. In 1912 he began four years of study at the Cleveland School (now Institute) of Art. Subsequently, except for a few months in New York and half a year in the U.S. Army, Burchfield worked at a Salem metal fabricating plant, while honing an original vision in his spare time. As he drew on childhood memories, buildings became anthropomorphic monsters, trees loomed with menace, and marvelously designed insects threatened. For his characteristic flat patterns, stylized natural forms, and rhythmic movement, he drew on precedents in postimpressionism and art nouveau. During this period, he also attempted to formulate symbols from natural forms to correspond with certain emotional states. In one of the best-known—and most alarming—paintings of this period, *Church Bells Ringing, Rainy Winter Night* (Cleveland Museum of Art, 1917), the bell itself is "fear," while "imbecility," "morbidness," and other symbols also appear. Inspired in part by Sherwood Anderson's *Winesburg, Ohio*, which he read in 1919, around 1920 he turned his sights toward capturing a small-town essence. For two decades, this remained Burchfield's main objective, although industrial subjects also appear.

From 1921 until 1929, when he began painting full time, Burchfield worked in Buffalo, New York, as a skillful designer of wallpaper, ingeniously deriving decorative patterns from plants and flowers. Although the 1920s and 1930s paintings and drawings usually project a subjective bias—a feeling of menace or mystery, for example—these evocations of heartland towns and cities nevertheless represent his most straightforward work. Visible through a window, in *Six O'Clock* (Everson Museum of Art, Syracuse, New York, 1936) a family gathers in a warm interior, while snow and cold shadows pile up against a line of monotonously gabled rowhouses. Other works depict the drab and utilitarian bridges and factories of Buffalo and eastern Ohio. Many of these works fit comfortably within the broad tendency known as the *American Scene movement. From 1925 until the end of his life, Burchfield lived in the same house in Gardenville, a Buffalo suburb. In the early 1940s, inspired by his own work from around 1917 and his memories of the rapture that motivated those paintings, he began once again to emphasize personal, pantheistic feelings. Turning to themes from nature, he achieved powerful, transcendental expression in much larger formats than he had used a quarter century earlier. *Sun and Rocks* (Albright-Knox Art Gallery, Buffalo, New York, 1918–50) reworks an early vision into a dynamic expression of natural forces: flattened, pulsating geological forms push outward from the earth toward an awesome radiance in the sky. Burchfield's health and productivity began to decline in the mid-1950s, but he continued painting almost until the end of his life, moving into more dreamlike territory than he had previously inhabited. While on a brief outing, he died in West Seneca, not far from his Gardenville residence. The Burchfield Homestead Museum in Salem preserves his early home.

Burckhardt, Rudolph (1914–99). Photographer, filmmaker, and painter. Known as Rudy, he became the art magazines' leading photojournalist in the period immediately after World War II. In the 1950s *Art News* in particular published many of his portraits of artists in their studios. In 1935 Burckhardt left his native Basel, Switzerland, where he had received a classical education and taken up photography as a teenager. Settling in New York, he recorded the city's architecture and street life. His informal aesthetic often revealed moments of wry humor or poetic beauty, and he was particularly skilled at capturing the dancelike motion of ordinary people. During the early 1940s he served in the U.S. Army. Also in the 1940s he produced a series of offbeat still life photographs; assured and informal, these studies of scattered objects defy traditional compositional structures. Burckhardt began making films in the 1930s and eventually completed about one hundred. Ranging from documentaries to Hollywood spoofs to lyrical montages, many were collaborative projects with writers, dancers, or other artists. In the 1950s he made four films with Joseph *Cornell. He also worked with Larry *Rivers and Red *Grooms, as well as poet John Ashbery and dancer Paul Taylor. Burckhardt started painting in the 1940s. He studied for a year with French Purist Amédée Ozenfant and also worked at the Brooklyn Museum's school and abroad. Besides notable urban scenes, he also produced subjects from nature and nudes. For the last three decades of his life, he painted intimate views of the forest and other subjects observed on the wooded property of his summer home in rural Searsmont, Maine, where he also occasionally photographed. He drowned in a pond there, an apparent suicide. In 1979 Burckhardt published *Mobile Homes*, a collection of autobiographical essays. Interviews appeared in *Conversations with Rudy Burckhardt about Everything* (1987) and *Talking Pictures: The Photography of Rudy Burckhardt* (1994), with extensive illustration of his work. He also collaborated on *Boulevard Transportation* (1997).

Burckhardt's widow, painter Yvonne Jacquette (1934–), is especially known for night views of New York and other cities, usually observed from a high vantage point. Balancing formal concerns with representation, her adroitly composed scenes vibrate with soft color applied in small strokes. She has also painted the city by day, as well as landscapes and industrial sites. Jacquette was born in Pittsburgh and studied at the Rhode Island School of Design from 1952 to 1956 before moving to New York. She and Burckhardt married in 1964. Their two sons also are artists in New York. **Jacob Burckhardt** (named for an illustrious nineteenth-century historian ancestor) is an independent filmmaker. Painter **Tom Burckhardt** (1964–) combines abstract and representational elements in colorful inventions.

Burden, Chris. *See* PERFORMANCE ART.

Burke, Selma (1900–95). Sculptor. Adapted from her commissioned head, the profile portrait of Franklin D. Roosevelt that has appeared on the dime since 1946 represents her most widely appreciated work. An active participant in the *Harlem Renaissance, she was married at that time to novelist and poet Claude McKay. Known as a portraitist, she also addressed imaginative and symbolic subjects, which often incorporate expressionistic distortions within an overall respect for monumentalized realistic form. Especially in later work, she often addressed universal themes, as in *Mother and Child* (Los Angeles County Museum of Art, 1968). Selma Hortense Burke was born in Mooreshead, North Carolina. After earning a degree in nursing in 1924, she worked in New York while pursuing long-standing artistic interests during her spare time. In 1933–34 she studied ceramic sculpture in Vienna with Secessionist Michael Powolny and in 1936–37, sculpture in Paris with Aristide Maillol, who reinforced her interest in figurative work informed by classicism as well as modernism. After her return to New York, she worked for *federal art projects, studied at Sarah Lawrence College with Neapolitan-born figurative sculptor Oronzio Maldarelli (1892–1963), and earned an MFA degree at Columbia University in 1941. In 1949 she married architect Herman Kobbé (who died in 1955), and they moved to *New Hope. In the late 1960s, she relocated to Pittsburgh, where she continued the educational mission she had previously undertaken at her own Greenwich Village school, as she taught children in an art center renamed in her honor and visited schools. In 1981 she returned to New Hope, where she died.

Burroughs, Bryson. *See* MARSH, REGINALD.

Burroughs, Edith Woodman. *See* MARSH, REGINALD.

Burroughs, Elizabeth (Betty). *See* MARSH, REGINALD.

Busa, Peter. *See* INDIAN SPACE PAINTING.

Bush-Brown, Henry Kirke. *See* BROWN, HENRY KIRKE.

Bush-Brown, Margaret. *See* BROWN, HENRY KIRKE.

Butler, Theodore Earl (1860–1936). Painter. An Ohioan who married into Claude Monet's family, he lived during most of his career within the French painter's circle in Giverny. Although he adopted an impressionist style, he developed expressive possibilities quite different from his renowned father-in-law's. Born in Columbus, he studied from 1876 until 1880 at Marietta (Ohio) College. In 1882 he moved to New York, where he trained at the *Art Students League before continuing on to Paris in 1885. There he studied at several schools and worked in the studio of Émile-August Carolus-Duran. In 1888 he summered in Giverny, where he settled in 1891, following a visit to the United States. There on a sunny day in July 1892 he married Monet's stepdaughter, Suzanne Hoschedé. His friend Theodore *Robinson celebrated the event in *The Wedding March* (Terra Foundation for American Art, 1892), a brisk and joyous memento of the wedding party's promenade through the streets from the city hall to the church. (The year after Suzanne's untimely death in 1899, Butler married her sister, Marthe Hoschedé.) Already an impressionist at the time of his marriage, he produced many of his finest paintings during the following decade. As early as the mid-1890s, however, he demonstrated interests in postimpressionist directions. *The Artist's Children, James and Lili* (Terra Foundation for American Art, 1896) demonstrates his mastery of impressionist broken color and patterned pictorial construction, but its decorative surface and air of warm domesticity suggest the Nabi aesthetic that appears in many of his figural interiors of succeeding years. The strident colors and linear flourishes in some works suggest ties to the work of Gauguin and van Gogh. A series of sketchy landscapes, particularly shore scenes recording summers on the Normandy coast, play on abstraction and emptiness in a mode recalling James Abbott McNeill *Whistler's example. In New York during and just after World War I, Butler produced local views. Generally loosely composed, some demonstrate high-keyed, almost fauve coloration, while others remain muted and suggestive of *tonalism. After his return in 1921 to Giverny, where he died, he produced a series of colorful outdoor views emphasizing ornamental pattern. His son, landscape painter **James Butler** (1893–1976), worked primarily in France but also in the United States.

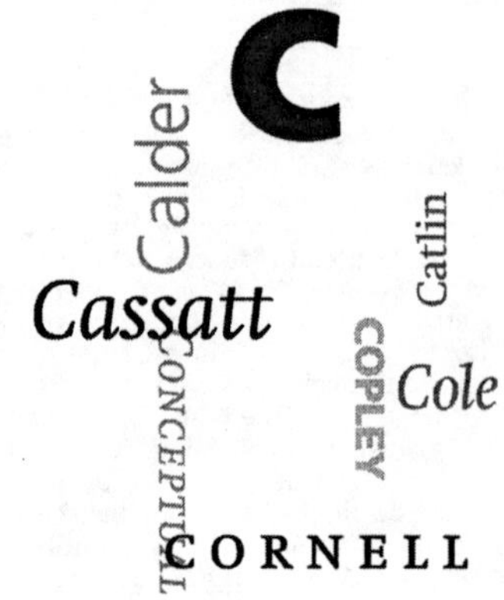

Cadmus, Paul (1904–99). Painter, draftsman, and printmaker. Known for meticulously rendered, often satirical scenes of contemporary life, he derived both his technique and his interest in narrative themes from old master paintings. Much of his work suggests a gay point of view, although he never publicly acknowledged his sexual orientation. Born in New York, Cadmus began his training in 1919 at the *National Academy of Design, where the traditional discipline of drawing from the nude shaped his sensibility. Later Joseph *Pennell numbered among of his teachers at the *Art Students League. With Jared *French, from 1931 to 1933 he traveled in Europe and lived on Majorca. Subsequently employed by *federal art projects, he produced murals as well as easel paintings, including the controversial *The Fleet's In!* (U.S. Navy, on loan to Wolfsonian-Florida International University, Miami Beach, 1934), depicting sailors carousing with young women. The rowdy, undignified atmosphere offended critics, as did revealingly tight garments, the obvious inebriation of some figures, and the depiction of a homosexual pickup. Undeterred, Cadmus continued to contribute to the *American Scene movement with vigorously conceived scenes of urban and suburban life. In the 1940s Cadmus began to work primarily with the painstaking technique of egg tempera, which suited his interest in accumulated detail but also limited the number of paintings he could produce. *Abstract expressionism's domination of the critical discourse in New York marginalized his career, but he continued to attract a small circle of admirers. Some of his work related to the *magic realism of his friend George *Tooker and others. The mysterious *Night in Bologna* (Smithsonian American Art Museum, 1958) typifies Cadmus's frequent themes of human weakness and depravity. Figures dressed in the symbolic colors of lust, avarice, and envy (according to the artist) appear within a complexly ordered and dramatically lit space defined by decaying Renaissance architecture. In 1975 he moved permanently to Weston, Connecticut, where he devoted his final years to drawing. Before his death, as both forms of realism and issues of sexual identity gained increased attention, Cadmus's reputation revived.

Caffin, Charles (1854–1918). Art critic and historian. Although he wrote perceptively on many topics, he demonstrated particularly enlightened sympathy for modern forms of expression and for photography as a fine art. Born in Sittingbourne, Kent, England, Charles Henry Caffin graduated from Oxford University in 1877. In subsequent years he taught and participated in a Shakespearean troupe. In 1892 he came to the United States to assist as a decorator in preparing for the World's Columbian Exposition in Chicago. He also worked in Washington, D.C., before settling permanently in the New York area in 1897. As a critic, he wrote prolifically on both historical and modern art in Europe and the United States. He contributed regularly to several magazines, notably including **Camera Work*, as well as *Harper's Monthly* and *Century*, and served as the art editor for the *New York Sun* between 1901 and 1904 and for the *New York American* between 1913 and his death. His many books include *Photography as a Fine Art* (1901), *American Masters of Painting* (1902), *American Masters of Sculpture* (1903), *The Story of American Painting* (1907), and *Art for Life's Sake* (1913), as well as a monograph on Dwight W. *Tryon (1909).

Cage, John (1912–92). Draftsman and printmaker. Also, and principally, a composer. Although Cage's central contributions lay within musical culture, he deeply influenced the visual arts through his philosophy, personal example, and interactions with artists. He also made drawings and prints of considerable refinement and visual appeal. By rejecting hierarchies of value, he opened the way for artists to abolish distinctions between art and non-art subjects, materials, and processes. In his music, silence and background noise came to serve just as well as conventional musical sounds. He also favored chance and indeterminacy, abhorred notions of great art and fame, rejected personal taste and expression in art, held that elements of the material universe deserve consideration for their own sake, and found interest in the operations of the mind.

Aspects of *process and *conceptual art, as well as *happenings, owed him a strong debt. Born in Los Angeles, John Milton Cage Jr. spent most of his early years there. He began piano lessons as a child, studied for two years at Pomona College in Claremont, and left for Europe in 1930. During a year abroad, he began painting, writing, and composing, while also studying architecture and piano. After his return to the United States, he studied composition and music theory with Richard Buhlig, Adolph Weiss, Henry Cowell, and Arnold Schoenberg. In Seattle during the late 1930s, he befriended Mark *Tobey and first met dancer Merce Cunningham, a longtime collaborator and companion. Cage then lived briefly in the San Francisco area and in Chicago before settling permanently in New York in 1942. A concert of his percussion music the following year at the *Museum of Modern Art established his position as a leading avant-garde composer. In the mid-1940s he undertook an extended study of Asian philosophies, particularly Zen Buddhism, and around the same time became acquainted with Marcel *Duchamp. Cage first taught at *Black Mountain College in 1948 and returned on several later occasions. There, in the summer of 1952, he staged a theatrical event presaging happenings and established a close working friendship with Robert *Rauschenberg, who perhaps more than any other important artist shared Cage's openness to experience. After realizing that shadows and reflections animate the "emptiness" of Rauschenberg's monochrome white paintings, Cage created the celebrated *4'30"*, a silent composition first "performed" in 1962. When Cunningham formed his own dance company in 1953, Cage became musical director and remained permanently involved with the troupe.

In 1969 Cage produced (with the assistance of Calvin Sumsion) his first important visual work, *Not Wanting to Say Anything About Marcel*, consisting of several multipaneled, screen-printed, Plexiglas panes. In 1978 he inaugurated a substantial involvement in printmaking, working primarily with etching. An extended series of delicate Ryoanji Drawings (1983–92) evokes the celebrated Japanese garden in images devised with the assistance of the *I Ching*, a favorite tool in his creative process from about 1950. He also worked in watercolor. Like his musical compositions of the same years, Cage's visual works incorporate random effects or procedures. His first museum exhibition, including prints and elaborated musical scores, opened at the *Whitney Museum of American Art in 1983. *Rolywholyover: A Circus*, an intervention into museum exhibition practices, appeared in several museums posthumously. An accomplished writer whose style became increasingly cryptic with time, he published numerous books. *Silence: Selected Lectures and Writings* (1961) introduces his musical aesthetic. *I–VI* (1990) collects six Harvard lectures that incorporate the original form of poetic text he called "mesostic." Other volumes include *Virgil Thomson: His Life in Music* (with Kathleen Hoover; 1959) and *A Year from Monday: New Lectures and Writings* (1967). *Notations* (with Alison *Knowles; 1969) gathers Cage's selection of significant writings by other composers. Richard Kostelanetz assembled three volumes of Cage texts: *John Cage* (1970), *Conversing with Cage* (1987), and *John Cage, Writer: Previously Uncollected Pieces* (1993). *Musicage: Cage Muses on Words, Art, Music* (1996) transcribes several conversations Cage held with Joan Retallack during the last two years of his life.

Cahill, Holger (1887–1960). Curator, art critic, and New Deal art administrator. Also a fiction writer. A champion of work that challenged the boundaries of conventional good taste, Cahill was born Sveinn Kristjan Bjarnarson in Snifellsnessyslu, Iceland. As a child, he moved with his family to North Dakota. After completing high school, he drifted from job to job for several years in Canada and, later, in the midwestern United States before hopping a freight train to New York to pursue his desire to become a writer. Now known by his chosen name, he frequented bohemian Greenwich Village and studied sporadically at several schools. Around 1918, he began to write on American art and formulated an aesthetic theory that he called "Inje-Inje." Cahill briefly recruited a small number of artists and writers to this movement, which combined aspects of dadaism, primitivism, the search for beauty, and pure silliness. As a movement, Inje-Inje had expired by 1922 when he joined the staff of the progressive Newark (New Jersey) Museum. There, Cahill purchased contemporary American art for the collection and in 1930 and 1931 organized the first major museum exhibitions of American folk art. Hired by the *Museum of Modern Art in 1931, he again made his mark with noteworthy shows, including another of folk art and a pioneering pre-Columbian exhibition. In 1935 Cahill was named director of the Works Progress Administration's Federal Art Project (WPA-FAP), the largest and arguably most significant of the *federal art projects organized to aid Depression-stricken artists. Putting his visionary attitudes to practical good use, he achieved phenomenal, large-scale success. Cahill believed that the agency's purpose was to support creativity throughout the country, not to police standards of quality. "It is not the solitary genius but a sound general movement which maintains art as a vital, functioning part of any cultural scheme," he explained. After the project came to an end in 1943, he diverted his main interest to creative writing. He died at his summer residence in Stockbridge, Massachusetts.

In 1938 he married Dorothy C. Miller (1904–2003), whom he had met while both were associated with the Newark Museum. Born in Hopedale, Massachusetts, Dorothy Canning Miller grew up in Montclair, New Jersey, and graduated in 1925 from Smith College. From 1934, when she joined the staff at MoMA, she held important curatorial positions there for thirty-five years. She organized numerous exhibitions for the museum, including between 1942 and 1963 a legendary series of "Americans" shows that presciently introduced young and under-recognized artists. In addition to exhibition catalogues, in 1983 she coauthored a book on Edward *Hicks. She died at her home in New York.

Calder, Alexander (1898–1976). Sculptor, painter, and printmaker. He also designed jewelry, toys, book illustrations, tapestries and textiles, and decor for dance performances and other theatrical events. A leading American sculptor, he combined high-spirited lyricism and ingenious engineering to delight connoisseurs and public alike. Among the best-known works of American modern art, his lighthearted yet sophisticated mobiles and stabiles distill his experimentation with organic forms and inorganic materials, with physical and expressive balance, and with incorporation of space as a dynamic and essential component of sculptural experience. The mobiles broke new ground in introducing movement as an aesthetic element in serious art. Calder's inventive and inveterate tinkering (he was said to carry pliers in his pocket at all times), his straightforward interest in the mechanics of art, his lack of theoretical pretension, and his good-natured humor seem quintessentially American. On the other hand, his artistic roots are to be found in Paris, where he internalized the constructivist and surrealist precedents that fostered his personal development. The first American modern artist to create a major body of work in a completely unprecedented style, Calder enjoyed an international reputation achieved by few American artists.

Widely known as Sandy, Calder was born into a family of artists in Lawnton, now part of Philadelphia. While growing up in several locations, he demonstrated precocious talent and ingenuity in making small metal animals, toys, and jewelry pieces. Nevertheless, following graduation in 1915 from high school in Berkeley, California, he entered the Stevens Institute of Technology in Hoboken, New Jersey. After he received a bachelor's degree in mechanical engineering in 1919, he drifted through varied jobs until 1923, when he enrolled at the *Art Students League. There he studied with George *Luks, Guy *Pene du Bois, Boardman *Robinson, and most importantly, John *Sloan, whose work inspired paintings of the city. In 1924, while still at the league, he began working as a magazine illustrator, particularly drawing sporting events and the circus that subsequently engaged his imagination. After months of drawing zoo animals, in the spring of 1926 he published *Animal Sketching*. Along with his illustrations, this little book (which went through several editions) included his thoughts about capturing motion. Later that year, he left on his first trip to Paris, where he resided much of the time for the next seven years, with intervals in New York. In Paris he continued to take drawing classes while soon beginning to make the sculptures that prefigured aspects of his mature art. From wire and scraps of wood or other found materials he started fashioning elements of the humorous, hand-manipulated circus (Whitney Museum, 1926–31) that he presented in performance to the delight of artists, among others, in Paris, New York, and elsewhere over a period of many years. From 1927 he also bent lengths of wire into witty sculptures of animals and human figures, capturing the expressive essence of his subjects as well as demonstrating a facility for drawing in space. In the fall of 1928 he met Miró, and thereafter they remained close friends while pursuing many of the same artistic objectives. Calder remembered a visit to Mondrian's Paris studio in October 1930 as a turning point in his career. After experimenting right away with abstract paintings incorporating geometric and organic shapes, he soon adapted these forms to constructions. For his first show of these works, mounted in Paris in the spring of 1931, Fernand Léger wrote the catalogue introduction. A few months later, Calder numbered among few Americans invited to join the newly founded Abstraction-Création organization, an international group of nonrepresentational artists including Jean Arp, Mondrian, Anton Pevsner, and Georges Vantongerloo. In the same year, his latent interest in motion found its first important expression in a group of motorized objects that caused the abstract components to move in relation to each other. These were followed that fall by the first fully realized mobiles, the culmination of earlier experiments with predominately wire constructions. Named by his friend Marcel *Duchamp in 1931 (who at that point had in mind also the mechanized works), the mobiles are structures assembled from weighted elements, usually cut from sheets of metal, hung on armatures balanced to allow the sculpture's component parts to rotate through space with the breeze. (In response, Arp the following year came up with the name stabile to characterize the nonkinetic structures that Calder had begun making a bit earlier, although in more recent usage the term has generally designated only the sheet metal compositions begun later in the 1930s.)

In 1933 Calder purchased a permanent home in Roxbury, Connecticut. There his predominately geometric vocabulary soon accommodated the *biomorphic forms that came to the fore in later works. There, too, over the next few years he began to think in terms of larger works, suitable for placement in outdoor venues. In 1935 he collaborated with dancer Martha Graham to produce his first performance settings. In 1937 he initiated the long series of bolted sheet-metal stabiles in his recognizable individual style. On a monumental scale and usually painted, most often either red or black, these later adorned public places around the world. Calder traveled to Europe only once more before World War II hemmed him in. For the Spanish Pavilion at the 1937 Paris Exposition, he installed a fountain, the first of several inventive water sculptures, in front of Picasso's *Guernica*. When the *Museum of Modern Art's new building opened in 1939, Calder's specially commissioned mobile, *Lobster Trap and Fish Tail*, hung in the main stairwell. With a shortage of metal during the war, he often worked with wood, particularly in a series of Constellations, using wire to connect carved and sometimes painted wood elements. (Coincidentally, although the two artists were out of touch during the war, Miró produced an identically titled series of paintings that share many of the same formal concerns.) MoMA's 1943 retrospective exhibition of his work confirmed Calder's eminence among American artists.

Eager to reestablish himself in Europe at the war's end, in 1946 he traveled to Paris to install a show of recent work. For the catalogue, Jean-Paul Sartre wrote a notable commentary on the mobiles. In 1952 Calder represented the United States at the Venice Biennale, where he was awarded first prize for sculpture. Subsequently, the amazingly prolific artist concentrated on commissions for public venues. The sixty-seven-foot-high *El Sol Rojo* (in front of the Aztec Stadium, Mexico City, 1968), the largest of his works, graced the Olympic Games. A bright orangey-red stabile, *La Grande Vitesse* (Grand Rapids, Michigan, 1969), the first work funded under the Works of Art in Public Places program of the *National Endowment for the Arts, became a rejuvenating symbol of civic pride. Similarly hued and some five stories tall, *Flamingo* (Federal Center Plaza, Chicago, 1972–74) exuberantly plays against the elegant, dark, rectilinear Mies van der Rohe complex behind it. During these years, he also reinvigorated his interest in painting and printmaking, producing numerous colorful abstract images. In 1966 the artist published *Calder: An Autobiography with Pictures*, written in collaboration with Jean Davidson. Almost constantly in motion for the last quarter-century of his life, he traveled the world, visiting acquaintances, showing his work, installing commissions, and accepting honors. From 1953 he retreated periodically to a residence and studio in Saché, in the Loire Valley not far from Tours. Active to the end, he died in New York a few weeks after attending the opening of "Calder's Universe" at the *Whitney Museum of American Art. A major retrospective, it traveled across the country. His seventy-six-foot untitled mobile (installed 1977) for the atrium of the *National Gallery of Art's new East Building in Washington was hung posthumously. Calder's incalculable influence on younger sculptors, who extended, modified, or even challenged accomplishments they could not ignore, remains among his most enduring legacies.

Calder came from a lineage of sculptors. His grandfather, **Alexander Milne Calder** (1846–1923), is known particularly for the sculptural program adorning Philadelphia's city hall, including the thirty-seven-foot bronze statue of William Penn (1894) surmounting its dome. He was born in Aberdeen, Scotland, where his father, another Alexander Calder, also worked as a sculptor. Alexander Milne Calder began his professional training in Edinburgh in 1864. Subsequently, he spent about a year in Paris and London before emigrating to the United States in 1868. (He became a citizen three years later.) He soon settled permanently in Philadelphia, where he pursued additional training at the *Pennsylvania Academy of the Fine Arts. In demand for his knowledge of up-to-date European trends, in 1872 he was selected to create for the elaborate new city hall the interior and exterior decorative sculpture, which combines realistic form with symbolic meanings. For more than twenty years, he labored on this commission, perhaps the most extensive such project undertaken to that time for a single building. He designed some 250 elements and supervised the carving. The bronze equestrian *General George Meade* (Fairmount Park, Philadelphia, 1881–87) numbers among his most important other works.

Alexander Calder's father, **Alexander Stirling Calder** (1870–1945), bridged the sculptural interests from Alexander Milne's generation to his own son's. Initially he worked in a traditional, Beaux-Arts style, but in later life adapted his approach to modern influences. He produced portraits and figure studies, as well as many public monuments. Born in Philadelphia, he began his professional training in 1885 at the Pennsylvania Academy, where Thomas *Eakins and Thomas *Anshutz numbered among his teachers. In 1890 he departed for Paris, where he studied with Henri Chapu and, at the École des Beaux-Arts, with Alexandre Falguière. Two years later he returned to Philadelphia but again was in Paris from 1895 to 1897. Between 1905 and 1910, when he moved his studio to New York for three years, he lived in Arizona and in Pasadena, California. At the height of his career, for San Francisco's 1915 Panama-Pacific Exposition he supervised the sculptural program and created several grandiose works, including the centrally located, prize-winning *Fountain of Energy*. He returned to New York in 1916. Later, although his style did not drastically alter, its newly simplified and slightly abstracted forms demonstrate the impact of modernism, as may be observed in his portrait of George Washington as a statesman, flanked by figures of Wisdom and Justice (1918), positioned on the northern facade of New York's Washington Square Arch. He remained professionally active almost until his death in New York. His wife, Alexander Calder's mother, **Nanette Lederer Calder** (d. 1960), was a painter who studied in Paris and also at the Pennsylvania Academy. After marriage in 1895, she continued to paint, specializing particularly in portraiture.

California decorative style. *See* MATHEWS, ARTHUR.

Callahan, Harry (1912–99). Photographer. Accommodating a broad range of subjects and featuring elegant graphic formalism, his work drew on purist American modernism, as well as European experimentalism. Most of his photographs picture the commonplace circumstances of his own life: the cities where he lived (especially Chicago), the nearby country and shore, and the people closest to him, his wife and daughter. Believing that photographing is an act of inner discovery, he created accessible, unforced, and unpretentious images. An exacting craftsman in exploring expressive possibilities of his medium, he sometimes used multiple exposures, but most of his work is direct, sharply focused, and disarmingly unfussy. In many prints, he made particularly effective use of high contrast, relying on sharp black and white with few gray tones. Although diffident about theory, aesthetics, and interpretive criticism, he nevertheless counted among the most important photography teachers of the postwar period. Harry Morey Callahan studied engineering for two years at Michigan State University in East Lansing. Two years after he left in 1936 to work at varied jobs in the Detroit area, he took up photography as a hobby. Through fellow Detroit native Arthur Siegel (1913–78), who had studied with László *Moholy-Nagy in Chicago, he discovered photographic modernism. A workshop in 1941 with Ansel *Adams redirected Callahan's life. Excited by Adams's technique, his demonstration that a good photograph can picture mundane subject matter, and his exalted view of photography's mission, Callahan experienced a burst of creativity. During the next two or three years, nearly all the themes of his later career appeared. In 1946 he moved to Chicago to teach at Moholy-Nagy's Institute of Design. He became head of its photography department three years later and stayed until 1961. From then until 1973 he served as chairman of the photography department at the Rhode Island School of Design. He retired from teaching in 1977 but continued to live in Providence for a decade before moving permanently to Atlanta.

Callahan pursued an experimental aesthetic but also stressed the role of the artist's subjectivity. For about twenty-five years, his wife, Eleanor, appears nude and clothed, in intimate close-up and as a speck on the horizon, as the subject of near abstractions and in portrait studies. In Chicago, Callahan frequently photographed on the street, recording the movement of people and the stillness of building facades. Many of his most effective multiple exposures amplify the headlong pace of modern city life. The shore also fascinated him. In Chicago he recorded urbanites enjoying Lake Michigan, and during his Providence years he captured the rolling Atlantic, the damp weather, the dunes, and beach life. In retirement, Callahan traveled abroad more frequently than previously, always with camera in hand. Although he used black-and-white film most of the time, he also employed color intermittently throughout his career. However, he did not exhibit this work until the late 1970s, when for several years he worked almost exclusively in color. In 1978, he became the first photographer to represent the United States at the Venice Biennale. Collections of his photographs include *The Multiple Image* (1961), *Photographs: Harry Callahan* (1964), *Callahan* (1976), *Harry Callahan: Color* (1980), *Water's Edge* (1980), and *Eleanor* (1984).

Camera Notes. *See* STIEGLITZ, ALFRED.

Camera Work. Magazine published between 1903 and 1917. Founded and edited by Alfred *Stieglitz, it was conceived as a journal of photography to serve the *Photo-Secession. Before long, as Stieglitz's interests widened and he began to exhibit other art forms at the Photo-Secession's 291 gallery, he also introduced modern art, literature, and critical thought into the magazine. In the crucial years between approximately 1908 and 1915, no other American publication rivaled its presentation of modern art forms and ideas. Designed initially by Edward *Steichen, *Camera Work* numbers among the few most sumptuous magazines ever published. Extraordinary care was lavished on the photographic reproductions, which were usually made from original negatives in painstaking technical processes chosen to suit the nature of individual images. These prints were then tipped into the individual issues by hand, often on pages specially prepared to enhance them. Alvin Langdon *Coburn, Gertrude *Käsebier, Steichen, Paul *Strand, Clarence *White, and Stieglitz himself numbered among photographers whose work was represented. Illustrated works of art in other media included examples by Cézanne, van Gogh, Rodin, Picasso, Matisse, John *Marin, and Abraham *Walkowitz. In its articles, *Camera Work* provided a forum for many, at times contradictory voices. Writers included American critics and theorists such as Charles *Caffin, Marius *de Zayas, and eccentric critic and poet Sadakichi Hartmann (1867?–1944), as well as Europeans including Henri Bergson, Maurice Maeterlinck, and George Bernard Shaw. The publication also provided access to writing not available elsewhere, or very difficult to find. It presented the first American appearance of Gertrude *Stein's prose (plus several later pieces) and the initial English translation of a selection from Kandinsky's *Concerning the Spiritual in Art*. Comments from artists and photographers and reprinted reviews from other periodicals fostered debate. After fifty numbered issues, *Camera Work* ceased publication. Several factors contributed to its demise, including World War I, competing publications, the disaffection of photographers who had initially supported its program, and reverses in Stieglitz's financial situation.

Campoli, Cosmo. *See* CHICAGO IMAGISM.

Capa, Robert (1913–54). Photographer. A photojournalist, he numbers among preeminent war photographers of the twentieth century. He came to international prominence covering the Spanish Civil War, set the standard for close-up photographic reporting during World War II, and was killed in Vietnam. The memorable images he took on D-Day, 6 June 1944, as he landed on Omaha Beach with the American troops, testify to his bravery in working under terrifying conditions. As he advised others, "If your pictures are not good enough, you're not close enough." Born Endre Ernö Friedmann in Budapest, he fled in 1931 after taking part in demonstrations against a repressive government. Interested in becoming a journalist, he studied in Berlin for this career while also beginning to work as a photographer. However, threatened as a Jew by Hitler's rise to power in 1933, he left for Paris. There he redirected his journalistic interests into photography and before long, changed his name. Driven by anti-Fascist sentiments, in August 1936 he took his small, fast camera to Spain in support of the Republican cause. There the distinctive characteristics of his vision quickly coalesced, as is apparent in one of his most widely known pictures, "Death of a Loyalist Soldier" (1936), capturing the instant a bullet brings down a militiaman. Alone in an otherwise empty expanse of hills, he flings his gun outward as he collapses back toward his own long shadow. In addition to combat, Capa recorded the effects of war on ordinary people caught in its orbit. Although he conveyed the heroism of individual fighters, Capa's work rarely glorifies war. Rather, it conveys pain, despair, and desperation endured by soldiers and civilians alike in a context of irrational and incomprehensible strife. He recapitulated his Spanish experiences in *Death in the Making* (1938), adding his captions to his own and others' photographs.

In 1938 Capa went to China to report on the Japanese invasion. In 1939 he emigrated to the United States, but after a year at *Life*, was back in Europe to cover World War II. *The Battle of Waterloo Road* (1941) chronicles wartime life in Britain. He became an American citizen in 1946. The next year he published *Slightly Out of Focus*, a memoir of recent war experiences, with selections from his work, as well as *A Russian Journal*, the collaborative result of a trip through the USSR with John Steinbeck. Also in 1947, he founded the distinguished Magnum cooperative in partnership with others, principally Frenchman Henri Cartier-Bresson, Englishman George Rodger, and American David Seymour (1911–56), born David Szymin in Warsaw and also known as

Chim, an internationally active photojournalist who lost his life during fighting at the Suez Canal. Between 1948 and 1950 Capa covered strife in Israel, but he also took notable peacetime pictures, including some memorable shots of Picasso with friends and family. In 1954 he went to Indochina, intending to cover the war against the French for a few months. Only a short time later, he was killed by a land mine. Ironically, among five wars he professionally witnessed, this was the only one in which he had no passionate involvement in the outcome, and he was not in battle at the time of his fatal accident. *Images of War* (1964) combines Capa's photographs with selections from his writings.

His brother, photojournalist **Cornell Capa** (1918–2008), traveled widely to cover stories in support of social justice. Born Cornell Friedmann in Budapest, he joined his brother in Paris in 1936 and moved to New York a year later. Following service in the U.S. Air Force during World War II, he worked as a *Life* photographer from 1946 until 1954, when he joined Magnum. In 1966 he founded the International Fund for Concerned Photography to support photographers who pursued their calling with a social conscience. Expanding on the success of its activities, in 1974 he established the more ambitious and more formally organized International Center of Photography, which he directed for many years, with an emphasis on humanistic work. Headquartered in Manhattan, it continues a program of exhibitions and classes, as well as lectures and other public events. He presented a selection of his work in *Cornell Capa: Photographs* (1992), assembled with the assistance of Richard Whelan.

Caponigro, Paul (1932–). Photographer. Primarily interested in black-and-white views of nature and landscape, he invests purist imagery with emotional subjectivity. He studied with Minor *White and was influenced by Edward *Weston and Ansel *Adams. Born in Boston, he has lived there much of his life, although he resided for some years in Santa Fe, New Mexico. He trained to become a classical pianist and attended Boston University from 1953 to 1955. Many of Caponigro's images resemble White's close-up abstractions of natural features. In "Rock Wall No. 2, West Hartford, Connecticut" (1959), faceted rocks form a muscular, cubist abstraction. Other photographs take a wider view. The romantic "Stone and Tree, Avebury, England" (1967) contrasts the organic surface of a large tree with a huge and brooding boulder nearby in a bucolic meadow. With time, Caponigro has tended to choose simpler subjects, in which he finds refined formal patterns and poetic mystery. A recent still life series presents disciplined arrangements with tonal perfection. Precisely and tenderly, "October Offering, Cushing, Maine" (1999) pictures grains and fruit composed in a shallow basket. *Paul Caponigro: Masterworks from Forty Years* (1993) surveys his career chronologically, *Meditations in Light* (1996) emphasizes landscape subjects recorded between 1966 and 1995, and *New England Days* (2002) offers more recent images.. He currently lives in coastal Maine, near his son, photographer **John Paul Caponigro** (1965–). Born in Boston and educated at Yale University and the University of California at Santa Cruz, he works extensively with digital processes.

Carles, Arthur B., Jr. (1882–1952). Painter. Among the few Americans who brought French modernism to the United States before the *Armory Show, as well as a significant contributor to a new wave of European-inspired modernism in the later 1930s, he ranks as the only major figure decisively to make that transition. In his fauve-inspired early work, he particularly favored floral still lifes, although he also painted figurative works and landscapes. In the late 1920s he began to fragment objects and rearrange their elements. This technique derived from cubism, but Carles deployed it with vigorous expressionist and decorative effect, as in *Bouquet Abstraction* (Whitney Museum, c. 1930). Visible here, in addition to the bouquet, are parts of a tabletop and other objects, as well as what is probably a view through a window framed by a lace curtain. The strong, almost dissonant colors include red, green, blue, and several variations on his favored eye-assaulting magenta. Soon, some of his still lifes became even more detached from reality, as he transformed visual perceptions into nearly abstract color patches. In the mid-1930s he began to produce strikingly up-to-date studies indebted to Picasso's recent work. Some compositions from this time closely resemble contemporary works of Arshile *Gorky and other future *abstract expressionists. *Composition No. 6* (Pennsylvania Academy, 1936), a vigorous abstraction probably derived from a nude figure, features both geometric and *biomorphic areas of intense color, defined by strong black lines. A lifelong Philadelphian, in 1900 Arthur Beecher Carles began his training at the *Pennsylvania Academy of the Fine Arts, where he studied with Thomas *Anshutz, Cecilia *Beaux, and, most importantly, William Merritt *Chase. From 1907 to 1910 and again for several months in 1912, he lived in Paris and fell under Matisse's spell. In 1912 he mounted his first one-person show at Alfred *Stieglitz's *291 gallery, and the following year he exhibited in the Armory Show. He again lived in France in 1921–22 and from 1929 to 1931. In December 1941 Carles was partially paralyzed in a fall that may have been caused by a stroke. He never painted again.

His daughter, painter Mercedes Matter (1913–2001), a student of Hans *Hofmann and cofounder in 1964 of the New York Studio School, prolonged his chromatic expression. Many of her abstract expressionist paintings suggest logical extensions of his work into gestural, nonobjective color. Born in New York, she numbered among founding members of *American Abstract Artists. In later years, she made her home in East Hampton, New York. In 1939 she married Swiss-born graphic designer and photographer Herbert Matter (1907–84), who emigrated to the United States in 1936. He worked for leading New York magazines and for many years served as professor of photography at Yale University. He died in Southampton, New York.

Carlsen, Emil (1853–1932). Painter. As a leading American still life painter of the 1890s, he specialized in uncluttered, poetic arrangements of humble objects. Later attentive to aspects of impressionism and *tonalism, he produced landscapes and seascapes that extended his interests in decorative form, subtle color harmonies, and lyric effects of light. He also painted portraits and figure compositions. Sören Emil Carlsen studied architecture in his native Copenhagen before emigrating in 1872 to Chicago. There he concentrated on painting for three years before returning to Europe. After a visit to Denmark, he studied for six months in Paris, where he first emulated the kitchen still lifes of eighteenth-century French painter Jean-Baptiste-Siméon Chardin and his seventeenth-century Dutch precursors. After returning to the United States in 1876, Carlsen worked primarily in New York and Boston until 1884, when he headed back to Paris for two-years. Subsequently, following a short period in New York, in 1887 he moved to San Francisco. From 1891 he made his home in New York. After 1905, when he bought a residence at Falls Village in the Berkshire hills of Connecticut, he habitually summered there. Evoking the region, the late *Connecticut Hillside* (Art Institute of Chicago, 1920), with its pastel tones, soft patterning, and dreamy atmosphere, reflects his progression from an early somber realism toward delicacy and abstract form. He also painted elsewhere, particularly in Maine, and returned to Europe at intervals. By incorporating Asian artifacts in his still lifes, Carlsen occasionally contributed to the period's *japonisme, but his son, painter **Dines Carlsen** (1901–66), focused on such works. He also produced landscapes. Born in New York, he studied painting with his father and began to exhibit professionally while still in his teens. He lived for many years at Falls Village but died in New York. He also maintained a residence in Summerville, South Carolina, and painted scenes from numerous locales throughout the Northeast, Southwest, and Mexico.

Carte-de-visite. *See* PHOTOGRAPHY, AMERICAN.

Casilear, John William (1811–93). Painter and engraver. A landscape specialist associated with the *Hudson River School, he created serene, delicately detailed pastoral scenes. Subtle effects of atmosphere and light relate his work to *luminism. Born on Staten Island, he was apprenticed as a teenager to New York printer Peter *Maverick. In 1831 he joined the print shop of Asher B. *Durand, who presumably also encouraged his interest in landscape painting. Later Casilear ranked among the foremost American engravers of banknotes, as well as other documents and works of art. He did not paint full time until the 1850s. In 1840 Casilear departed for England with Durand, John *Kensett, and Thomas P. *Rossiter. During three years abroad, he also toured the Continent, traveling part of the time with Durand. On a second European sojourn, in 1858, he visited Switzerland, which provided alpine motifs for a number of later paintings. He died at Saratoga Springs, New York. Casilear practiced an exquisitely refined form of Hudson River School painting. A shoreline view with several cows wading in the shallows, *Lake George* (Wadsworth Atheneum, Hartford, Connecticut, 1860) exemplifies his unusually fine draftsmanship, as well as his typical bucolic subject matter, shimmering atmosphere, and tranquil mood. Without sacrificing his personal vision, in the last two decades of his life Casilear broadened his touch somewhat to accommodate the newly popular imported methods of *Barbizon painting and even impressionism.

Cassatt, Mary (1844–1926). Painter and printmaker. Admired especially for images of women, often with their children, she counteracted this potentially sentimental subject matter with rigorous design and an expression of introspective gravity. Living in Paris throughout her professional life, she ranked as the only American artist to exhibit in the impressionist group shows. Like her mentor Degas, she concentrated on figural representations of modern life, favored solidly constructed forms over atmospheric veils of color, and often worked in pastel, a medium congenial to her accomplished draftsmanship. Since her own day, she has been acknowledged for the independence of her life and art, unusual for a woman at that time. Despite prolonged absence abroad, she established a considerable reputation at home through contacts with traveling Americans and exhibitions in the United States. She also influenced American taste by advising several important collectors, notably her good friend Louisine *Havemeyer. Born in Allegheny City (now part of Pittsburgh), Mary Stevenson Cassatt lived as a small child on an estate near Lancaster, Pennsylvania, and then in Philadelphia. Between 1851 and their return to the Philadelphia area in 1855, she lived with her family in Paris, Heidelberg, and Darmstadt. In 1860 Cassatt began her professional training at the *Pennsylvania Academy of the Fine Arts. Late in 1865 she commenced upon her sixty-year sojourn abroad, broken by only four visits to the United States. In France she worked with several painters, including Jean-Léon Gérôme and Thomas Couture. Forced home in 1870 by the Franco-Prussian War, the next year she set off to travel and study in Italy and Spain. During this time she developed a dark, rich technique influenced by old masters but showing affinities with the work of Gustave Courbet and Manet. Among these early works, she achieved particular distinction with picturesque Spanish subjects.

Cassatt had missed the opportunity to see the first impressionist exhibition before her return to Paris in mid-1874, but soon acquainted herself with the group's accomplishments. Notably, in 1875 she discovered Degas' work, which by her own admission changed her life. In 1877 he invited her to join the group. She participated in the impressionists' next show, in 1879, and in three of the four subsequent presentations, including the last in 1886. Inspired by their approach, she developed a feathery and caressing brushstroke, lightened her palette, explored pattern as a key compositional element, and experimented with unconventional perspective. Her family and friends often provided subjects, but she also pursued the impressionists' interests in fashionable leisure and entertainment. *On a Balcony* (formerly *Lydia Reading in a Garden*; Art Institute of Chicago, 1878–79), a portrait of her sister perusing a newspaper, and *Women in a Loge* (National Gallery, 1881–82), a rendering of two elegantly dressed young ladies in a theater, demonstrate her mastery of impressionist technique and sensibility. Like other impressionists, after the mid-1880s Cassatt began to accommodate new interests without relinquishing the strengths she had acquired. In the late 1880s she moved toward tighter, more restrained paint surfaces and more grandly proportioned figures, stabilized by strongly drawn contours. Depicting women picking fruit, her mural (destroyed; 1892–93) on the theme of modern woman for the Women's Pavilion at Chicago's World's Columbian Exposition explored the large-scale, decorative possibilities of this mode. Also in the late 1880s, the mother-and-child theme, with its traditional origins and contemporary appeal, became her favorite. Unmarried and childless herself, she nevertheless represented with empathy the affectionate maternal bond. Characteristically tender, *The Child's Bath* (Art Institute of Chicago, 1893) pictures a small girl seated on the lap of her mother, who washes her feet in a basin on the floor. The flattened perspective of this work, with its vantage point above the figures, along with the patterning of the woman's striped dress and the elegant shapes of the bowl and a nearby pitcher, indicate Cassatt's debt to the *japonisme that stimulated impressionists and others of the period. However, Cassatt most clearly revealed her debt to Japanese art in etchings (often combined with aquatint), drypoints, and a few lithographs. From 1879 through the 1890s, printmaking remained a major interest. In atmospheric etchings from the 1880s, figures in intimate interiors often suggest the moody ambiguity of emerging symbolism. Between 1888 and 1890 she turned to the demanding technique of drypoint for a series of simplified and monumentalized figures. After viewing a large 1890 exhibition of Japanese art, including myriad *ukiyo-e* woodblock color prints, she created her most original graphic works, color etchings (enhanced with drypoint) incorporating Japanese design principles. Publicly debuted in 1891, a set of ten pictures women in ordinary activities made fresh through innovative design. In *The Letter* (1890–91), a woman of vaguely Asian appearance holds an envelope to her mouth as she sits before a desk. Seen from slightly above, the intriguing, asymmetrically balanced composition combines such flat, geometric shapes as the envelope, the letter, and the desktop with organically patterned wallpaper and dress material.

Although Cassatt continued to make her home in Paris, she also enjoyed seasonal country sojourns. In 1894 she purchased the seventeenth-century Chateau de Beaufresne at Mesnil-Théribus, where she died. In addition to summering there, about forty miles northwest of Paris, she sometimes went south during the winter. From 1912 to 1924, for half of each year or more, she rented a villa in Grasse. At the end of 1910 she departed for Egypt on a lengthy trip that undermined her health and sapped her ability to work. Productive again only in 1913–14, she was interrupted late that summer by the onset of World War I. Subsequently, cataracts gradually stole her vision, leaving her nearly blind during her last decade.

Castelli, Leo (1907–99). Art dealer. A touchstone of success in the 1960s and 1970s, his New York gallery introduced or promoted most of the period's art stars. From early 1958, when he exhibited recent work by Robert *Rauschenberg and Jasper *Johns, he championed artists who sought alternatives to the prevailing *abstract expressionism. His critical choices proved integral to the subsequent history of American art, as his gallery became the epicenter of *pop art, *minimalism, and *conceptualism. Castelli also reformulated several aspects of the contemporary gallery's role as an institution within the visual arts community. He was born Leo Krauss in Trieste, but the family assumed his mother's maiden name at the time of World War I, when Italy annexed the city, formerly part of Austria. Growing up in this international environment, he learned to speak several languages, earned a law degree at the University of Milan, and as a young man worked in banking and insurance in several locations, including Trieste and Bucharest. In Paris in the late 1930s he and a friend opened a gallery that specialized in surrealism. With the outbreak of World War II, he left for New York, where he resumed his studies at Columbia University before joining the U.S. Army. Following his discharge at the end of the war, he returned to business employment but also became acquainted with abstract expressionists and other advanced artists. After dealing privately, in February 1957 he opened a gallery, which moved into the limelight a year later when he presented Rauschenberg and Johns. Over the following decade and a half, he expanded his stable to include Dan *Flavin, Donald *Judd, Ellsworth *Kelly, Roy *Lichtenstein, Robert *Morris, Bruce *Nauman, Claes *Oldenburg, James *Rosenquist, Ed *Ruscha, Richard *Serra, Frank *Stella, Cy *Twombly, and Andy *Warhol, among others. Most came near the beginning of their careers, few were previously fashionable, and all benefited from the lively and generous atmosphere of the gallery. Under Castelli's management their work sold, and he numbered among the earliest American dealers to offer his artists a stipend, so they could concentrate on their work. Jump-starting the practice of regarding art sales as a national and international business, he looked beyond his own space to establish a network of relationships with galleries in other cities and abroad. In addition, from the late 1960s Castelli Graphics took advantage of the expansion of printmaking as a legitimate sideline for painters and sculptors. In 1971 Castelli moved his gallery from the Upper East Side to SoHo, presaging a shift in the New York art world's center of gravity. (When SoHo's cachet dimmed, he moved back uptown for the final few years of his life.) He never lost interest in promising new artists, but with the enormous expansion of the art market, by the late 1970s he no longer monopolized its cutting edge. He died at his Manhattan apartment. Directed by his widow, Italian art historian Barbara Bertozzi, whom he married in 1995, the gallery remains in business under his name.

After Castelli met the seventeen-year-old Ileana Schapira in Bucharest in 1932, she soon became his first wife. A stimulant to his interest in art, she worked with him on his early ventures in the field. Two years after they divorced on friendly terms in 1960, the remarried Ileana Sonnabend opened a Paris gallery that served for some years as an important conduit to Europe for the Castelli artists. Since 1970, she has also maintained a New York gallery. In 1963 Castelli married French-born Antoinette Fraissex du Bost (d. 1987). Known as **Toiny Castelli**, she ran his graphics outpost.

Castellón, Federico (1914–71). Printmaker, painter, and draftsman. Particularly known for etchings, he specialized in dreamlike scenes inspired by surrealism. Born in Almeria, Spain, Federico Cristencia Castellón y Martinez emigrated with his family to Brooklyn in 1921, was naturalized as a citizen in 1943, and served in the U.S. Army during World War II. He had almost no formal instruction in art but traveled in Europe on several occasions. In the early 1930s he developed a style related to the veristic form of surrealism just coming to be admired in the United States through the work of Salvador Dalí. He died in New York. Castellón's work characteristically features vast, desolate spaces peopled by enigmatic people and objects. In the brightly sunlit but troubling painting, *The Dark Figure* (Whitney Museum, 1938), a menacing individual, garbed and hooded in black, wrings his hands in the foreground. Grouped before a wall behind him is a nightmarish arrangement of people and body parts, along with indecipherable elements and four drooping rings held aloft.

Catesby, Mark (1682–1749). Painter and engraver. Also a naturalist and explorer. Catesby prepared both text and plates for the first illustrated treatise on the flora and fauna of North America, a two-volume masterwork acclaimed for its rigorous scientific observation and aesthetically compelling presentation. *The Natural History of Carolina, Florida, and the Bahama Islands* (1731–43) juxtaposes ecologically related species in 220 hand-colored etchings. The publication's colorful, vigorously conceived compositions gave visual form to a newly emerging notion of nature as a complex realm of interdependent elements, a view that influenced William *Bartram's subsequent botanical endeavors and preceded by a century John James *Audubon's celebrated achievements in picturing native species. Born in Castle Hedingham, Essex, England, Catesby worked for two periods in colonial America. In 1712 he arrived in Virginia, where he recorded data, produced drawings and watercolors, and collected specimens. Before returning to England in 1719, he also traveled to other areas, including the Caribbean and the Appalachian Mountains. Between 1722 and 1726 he resumed his research in the southeastern colonies. Most of the rest of his life was devoted to preparation and serial publication of his books, which went through numerous legitimate and pirated editions. He died in London.

Catlett, Elizabeth (1919–). Sculptor and printmaker. Committed to a social purpose for art, she focuses particularly on the lives of African-American and other minority women. She has lived in Mexico for six decades, but continues to visit New York regularly. A native of Washington, D.C., she was educated there at Howard University, graduating in 1936 with a major in painting. Her teachers included Lois Mailou *Jones, James Lesesne *Wells, and, most importantly, James *Porter. In 1940 she received an MFA in sculpture from the State University of Iowa (now University of Iowa) in Iowa City, where she studied with Grant *Wood. While subsequently studying ceramics at the School of the Art Institute of Chicago, she married Charles *White. (The partnership lasted only a few years.) After they moved to New York, she worked privately with Russian-born, School of Paris sculptor Ossip Zadkine. During the early 1940s, teaching in Harlem increased her sensitivity to the deleterious effects of racial discrimination and to art's potential for ameliorating the lives of disadvantaged peoples. In Mexico, contact with that country's well-known mural painters further stimulated her populist sympathies. She studied with Mexican sculptor Francisco Zuñiga and began making prints at the Taller de Gráfica Popular, where she met Mexican painter and printmaker Francisco Mora. They married in 1947. In 1959 she began teaching at Mexico City's National School of Fine Arts of the National Autonomous University, where she eventually headed the sculpture department. In recent years, she has continued to work in Cuernavaca. Catlett's sculpture in numerous media varies from direct realism to near abstraction but shows consistent attention to surface finish and to humanitarian concerns for social justice. Her bronze half-length of eighteenth-century poet Phillis Wheatley (Jackson [Mississippi] State University, 1973) convincingly evokes an African American whose life story inspires achievement in the arts. On the other hand, in its smoothly abstracted shapes, the black marble *Singing Head* (Smithsonian American Art Museum, 1980; also other versions) displays Catlett's interests in pure form and in the sculptural styles of her African heritage. In her prints, Catlett has characteristically employed vigorously stylized, flattened, high-contrast images, as in the linocut *Sharecropper* (1952). This bust-length, aging woman in a straw hat radiates dignity, fortitude, and inner strength.

Catlin, George (1796–1872). Painter and draftsman. Also a writer. Known for portrayals of individual Indians, tribal life, and western geography, he also amassed the first extensive visual and written record of American Indian customs. In addition, he also painted portraits, some in miniature, and a few historical scenes. Born in Wilkes-Barre, Pennsylvania, Catlin grew up in rural Pennsylvania and New York. As a young man, he studied law in Litchfield, Connecticut, but practiced for only a short time before abandoning this profession. Self-taught as an artist, he gained experience and facility during the 1820s as a professional portrait painter in Philadelphia, Washington, D.C., and New York. Catlin formed the plan of his life's work after encountering an Indian delegation visiting Philadelphia. Inspired by what he saw as their dignified nobility and uncorrupted simplicity, he soon aspired to compile an encyclopedic record of Indian appearance, conduct, and material culture. Catlin's mission was fueled by his fatalistic belief, shared by many contemporaries, that the inevitable expansion of the United States doomed the aboriginal peoples and their way of life to eradication. Through his art, he wished that the Indians might "live again upon canvas" as he preserved individual personalities and tribal ways for the future. To this end, he also chronicled their customs and collected ethnographic artifacts, such as clothing, weapons, and handicrafts. Catlin's technical skills as a painter remained relatively limited, but he compensated for lack of subtlety and finish with a direct, descriptive technique that suited his fresh and perceptive observations. His delicate, ornamental finished drawings register as haunting premonitions of the tragic destiny he foresaw.

In 1830 Catlin departed for St. Louis, which remained his headquarters until 1836. During these years he traveled in the West, most importantly to little known areas of the Upper Missouri and Great Plains, becoming acquainted with nearly fifty tribes. The most extended trip took him in 1832–33 some eighteen hundred miles up the Missouri River to the region now on the border between North Dakota and Montana. In 1837–88 he journeyed to remote areas of the Southeast. While living among indigenous peoples, he observed their modes of existence with previously unparalleled immediacy. Most notably, he sojourned in territorial North Dakota's Mandan villages before these people were decimated by smallpox in 1837. Along with a trader companion, he was the first white person to witness the Mandans' most sacred ceremony, a grueling initiation ritual, which he included among his compelling visual records of the tribe. In all, hundreds of paintings from these years conserved distinctive tribal practices, such as hunting, games, religious dances, and encampments, as well as individualistic likenesses. At half or full length, these portraits included closely observed clothing and personal adornment. However, like other participant-observers, Catlin inevitably failed on occasion to surmount the biases of his culture and audience, and he sometimes sanitized or idealized his human subjects and their activities.

In 1837 Catlin began showing his Indian Gallery, first in the United States and two years later in England and then in France. In addition to his paintings, this exhibition included artifacts he had collected and sometimes featured visiting Indians performing their dances and ceremonies. Although the gallery attracted much praise (Baudelaire numbered among his admirers), reverses and misjudgments eventually drove him into bankruptcy. In 1852 Catlin found an American buyer for the entire collection, which subsequently remained in storage until after the artist's death. Although his activities of the next several years are poorly documented, until 1858 Catlin apparently traveled much of the time in South America, attempting to duplicate his North American accomplishments. However, his visual and written South American records do not bear comparison to his earlier work. Perhaps his age, near deafness, and limited knowledge of the Spanish language inhibited his ability to recapture previous levels of specificity, vigor, and observational accuracy. In any event, combining this material with replicas of works from the original Indian Gallery, he put together a second collection. While again residing in Europe, he showed the new material there before displaying it in the United States. After more than thirty years abroad, he arrived in New York in 1870. He died in nearby Jersey City, New Jersey. More than anyone else at mid-century, he had created in the American mind a mythic ethos for the Indian. His accomplishment drew on complementary personal qualities: romantic devotion to his subject, commitment to accurate documentation, the artistic talent to capture bold design quickly, the human sympathy to produce vivid and stately portraits, the literary skills to write compelling prose, and an instinct for showmanship. Catlin's publications constitute an enduring aspect of his legacy. The two-volume *Letters and Notes on the Manners, Customs and Condition of the North American Indians* (1841), remains the most important. Illustrated with about three hundred engravings, it augmented the didactic purpose of the Gallery by drawing on his own experiences to expand public knowledge of indigenous American life. It was followed three years later by *Catlin's North American Indian Portfolio*, twenty-five hand-colored lithographs, each accompanied by a printed explanatory text. His subsequent publications include *Catlin's Notes of Eight Years' Travels and Residence in Europe* (1848) and *Lifted and Subsided Rocks of America* (1870), a treatise on geology. *Life Amongst the Indians* (1857) and *Last Rambles Amongst the Indians of the Rocky Mountains and the Andes* (1867) are intended for young readers.

Cedar Tavern. *See* ABSTRACT EXPRESSIONISM.

Ceracchi, Giuseppe (1751–1801). Sculptor. Born and trained in Italy, he worked in the United States only briefly but long enough to affect the nation's aesthetic development. His sculptures demonstrated a level of professional skill previously equaled in only a few isolated instances. His example helped to acquaint Americans with up-to-date *neoclassical taste and paved the way for a number of trained Italian workmen who adorned the nation's architecture and urban spaces throughout the next century. In the 1770s and 1780s Ceracchi worked in London and Vienna, as well as Rome. Seized with the idea of producing a great monument to liberty in America, he traveled to Philadelphia in 1791. He remained for more than a year, returned to Europe, and reappeared in mid-1794 to stay for almost another year. During his Philadelphia sojourns he sculpted portrait busts of about thirty prominent citizens and government officials, including Thomas Jefferson and James Madison.

The idealized, neoclassical *George Washington* (Metropolitan Museum, 1791–94), his shoulders draped with a toga, is modeled closely on Roman emperor prototypes. However, *David Rittenhouse* (American Philosophical Society, Philadelphia, 1794) and certain other likenesses suggest forthright realism. After Congress informed the artist in 1795 that funding would not be appropriated for his proposed 100-foot marble monument glorifying liberty within a complex iconographical program of allegorical figures and horses, he soon departed for good to work in Paris. There he achieved considerable success but was caught in a plot against Napoleon and sent to the guillotine.

Chadwick, William. *See* OLD LYME ARTISTS' COLONY.

Chalfant, Jefferson David (1856–1931). Painter. Particularly known for about a dozen trompe-l'oeil still lifes, mostly from the late 1880s, he also painted landscapes, conventional still lifes, *genre scenes, and portraits. Born in Chester County, west of Philadelphia, he attended school in Lancaster and as a young man worked in Philadelphia as a cabinetmaker, specializing in fittings for railway cars. In 1879 he moved to Wilmington, Delaware. Without formal training, he began painting landscapes and still lifes in the early 1880s, becoming a full-time professional artist within a few years. Following the lead of William Michael *Harnett, he perfected a deceptive illusionism in still lifes of refined austerity, depicting groupings of a few familiar articles hung on a vertical surface or reposing on a tabletop. *Violin and Bow* (Metropolitan Museum, 1889), inspired by a Harnett prototype, exhibits Chalfant's usual limited color range and subtle, silvery light in its rendering of only two objects hung against a paneled wall. From 1890 to 1892 Chalfant studied in Paris at the Académie Julian with Adolphe-William Bouguereau and Jules-Joseph Lefebvre. Although this experience only solidified the realistic technique he had honed on his own, it apparently broadened his ambitions, for he returned a figure painter. Subsequently he specialized in genre scenes, notably a series depicting craftsmen at work in their shops, which he depicted in minute detail. After 1900 he turned to portraiture as his main interest. A stroke in 1927 ended his painting career. He died at his home in suburban Wilmington.

Chamberlain, John (1927–). Sculptor, painter, printmaker, and filmmaker. His novel sculptures assembled from multihued automobile body parts draw on *abstract expressionism's large scale, informal composition, and aggressive tenor, while recognizable if damaged pieces of cars emphasize the possibilities of detritus in art. Although the artist's interests remained predominately formal, the central role of the automobile in American life and the material's banged-up condition, suggesting crashes, unavoidably conditioned his effects. Much of this work was conceived as relief sculpture, intended to be mounted on a wall. In freestanding works, he often revealed, or sometimes only implied, a central void that belies massive exteriors. Surfaces, with their "found" colors (in the early days, he did not add paint), seem to extend gestural painting into three dimensions. In later work, he has made inventive use of other non-art materials, including urethane foam, aluminum foil, and Plexiglas. Born in the northern Indiana town of Rochester, John Angus Chamberlain grew up in Chicago. He served in the U.S. Navy before beginning his professional training at the School of the Art Institute of Chicago from 1950 to 1952. He briefly enrolled at the University of Illinois before heading in 1955 to *Black Mountain College for another year of study. Since about 1953, he had been making abstract welded sculpture, which evolved into expansive constructions recalling David *Smith's example. Chamberlain moved to New York in 1957 and within a year began making use of scrapped automobile parts in fabricating the works that quickly made his reputation. For about four years beginning in 1959, he used this material exclusively, becoming a leading proponent of *junk art. Between 1963 and 1965 he sprayed auto lacquer through stencils to create paintings on Masonite or Formica. Subsequently, in addition to automobile parts, he employed all manner of crushed, crumpled, and compacted industrial materials in three-dimensional formats that he freely altered or painted. As a printmaker, he has employed several techniques, including screen print, etching, and monoprint. In the mid-1960s he also began working with film and video. In 1980 he moved to Sarasota, Florida. His recent sculpture emphasizes eye-catching color applied to vivaciously entangled forms.

Chambers, Thomas (1807/08–66 or later). Painter. Known for landscapes and marines, he also painted portraits, but none of these is known today. Mingling observation and imaginative fantasy, while often loosely basing compositions on prints of work by others, he used swooping patterns, repetitive rhythms, and bright, unmodulated color to create unsophisticated but compelling images. He favored themes common to *romanticism, including storms, shipwrecks, and naval battles, as wel as quiet communion with nature. Presumably self-trained as a painter, Chambers was born in London and emigrated to the United States in 1832. He lived in New York at least until 1840. Next recorded in Boston, he left there in 1851 to work in Albany until 1857. The following year, he was back in New York, where he was last documented in an annual directory published in the spring of 1867.

Champney, Benjamin (1817–1907). Painter. Known particularly for views of New Hampshire's White Mountains, he also painted portraits and still lifes, usually depicting flowers. He was born in New Ipswich, New Hampshire, and worked as a teenager in a Boston lithographic shop. He painted portraits before departing in 1841 for Europe, where he spent most of the following seven years. There he worked in Paris, Italy, and Düsseldorf alongside other aspiring American artists, particularly John *Kensett. He came home committed to landscape painting and settled in Woburn, near Boston, where he maintained a studio. About 1850 he began working regularly in the White Mountains. Near North Conway, he soon established the summer home that he visited for half a century. Occasionally he spent winter months there as well. His presence was instrumental in establishing the area as a popular destination for artists. Champney's landscapes of the region depict its scenery with the affection, grandeur, and attention to detail characteristic of the *Hudson River School. Painterly and often intimate, the flower paintings from later years of his career deviate from the hard literalism common in mid-century American still life. Champney's autobiography, *Sixty Years' Memories of Art and Artists* (1900), remains an important source of information about nineteenth-century art life. He died in Woburn.

A distant cousin, **James Wells Champney** (1843–1903), was a painter, printmaker, illustrator, and amateur photographer. Born in Boston, he trained in Europe and specialized in *genre scenes but also painted landscapes and portraits. He made his home for many years in Deerfield, Massachusetts, but died in New York, where he also maintained a studio. Benjamin's nephew **Edwin Graves Champney** (1842–99) also worked as a landscape painter. Born in Boston, he remained a lifelong resident of the area. He served in the Union Army during the Civil War and later studied in Europe.

Chandler, Winthrop (1747–90). Painter. Known primarily for portraits, he also executed still lifes and landscapes, but presumably only on commission to embellish household interiors. In addition, his artisan background provided employment as a house painter and decorator. Often including elaborate settings related to the sitter's occupation or lifestyle, Chandler's ambitious and forceful portraits make their effect through patterned design, vivid color, accurate detail, and sober, unidealized facial description. Chandler was born on a farm near Woodstock, Connecticut, and lived in the area most of his life. As a young man, he may have trained in Boston, perhaps in some branch of the decorative arts. He was back in Woodstock by 1770, when he painted his first known works. In their attempted grandeur, as well as their intense observation of visible facts, these seem to reflect contemporary work by John Singleton *Copley. In 1785 Chandler moved to Worcester, Massachusetts. A few months before his demise at forty-three, he returned—ill, discouraged, widowed, and impoverished—to die at the family farm. Paired, full-length portraits of his brother, *Captain Samuel Chandler*, and brother's wife, *Anna Chandler* (both National Gallery, c. 1780), summarize the artist's characteristic strengths at their best. Samuel appears in his Revolutionary War uniform, grasping his sword, while his hat, trimmed to emphasize exuberant curves, rests on a nearby table. A Revolutionary battle scene is visible within an expansive landscape seen through a window. The simple but solidly constructed composition employs interlocked surface patterns to organize carefully rendered details of costume and personal appearance. Mrs. Chandler sits before well-stocked bookshelves. Like her husband's, her face is convincingly modeled, but her elaborate attire is severely flattened into insistently decorative patterns. A two-dimensional curtain swag arbitrarily framing her space appears to be an imaginative flourish. In its ornamental unreality, it underscores Chandler's inclination to accommodate what appeared before his eyes to a drive for aesthetic force.

Chapman, John Gadsby (1808–89). Painter, printmaker, and illustrator. Known especially for historical and literary subjects, he also produced *genre scenes, landscapes, and portraits. In addition, he wrote the most important drawing manual of the mid-nineteenth century and executed one of eight huge murals that decorate the rotunda of the U.S. Capitol. Born in Alexandria, Virginia, the young Chapman received advice and encouragement from Charles Bird *King and others in the nearby Washington, D.C., area. In 1827 Chapman began working independently in Winchester, Virginia. Following a short period in Philadelphia, in 1828 he left for Europe, where he spent most of three years in Italy. After subsequently working itinerantly as a portraitist in Virginia and Washington, D.C., he moved to New York in 1834. There he soon began to draw for magazines and gift books and in 1836 secured a commission for the Capitol's *Baptism of Pocahontas at Jamestown, Virginia, 1613*, installed in 1840. During the following years, he prepared the designs for most of the 1,400 wood engravings in Harper's *Illuminated Bible* (1846) and published *The American Drawing-Book* (1847), which remained popular as a school text and amateur reference for decades. In 1848 he departed for Europe. After some months in London and a year in Paris, he settled in 1850 in Rome, remaining for more than three decades. There he produced landscape paintings and hand-colored etchings, mostly depicting the Roman Campagna, with its classical ruins and colorful peasant inhabitants. These relaxed and luminous works, studded with closely observed incidental detail, contrast with his earlier figural narratives, which often appear academic and theatrical. After moving to Brooklyn in 1884, he painted little before his death in New Brighton, on Staten Island.

With their father's instruction and encouragement, Chapman's two sons entered his profession. Both were born in Washington and accompanied their parents to Europe in 1848. Landscapist **John Linton Chapman** (1839–1905) remained to paint Italian scenes until 1878. Subsequently, he lived in New York or its environs and died in Westchester County. **Conrad Wise Chapman** (1842–1910) enjoyed a somewhat more eventful and distinctive career. When the Civil War erupted, he sailed to America to fight for the Confederacy and, as it turned out, produce the finest series of paintings to emanate from the Southern point of view. He served in several engagements, was wounded at Shiloh, and in 1863 and 1864 while stationed in Charleston, South Carolina, made studies of its fortifications. From these, he completed twenty-six finished paintings in Rome during an 1864 furlough. When the war concluded, he spent fifteen months in Mexico, becoming the first American painter of any significance to paint its landscape. In 1866 he returned to Rome but went to Paris in 1869 for additional training. He remained there most of the time until 1883, when he moved to Mexico City. After 1889 he lived at various times in Paris, Virginia, New York, and Mexico City before settling in 1909 in Hampton, Virginia, where he died. Despite promising starts, in later years neither brother's career continued to flourish.

Chase, William Merritt (1849–1916). Painter. Cosmopolitan, technically adroit, and attracted solely to subjects drawn from contemporary life, he painted portraits, *genre scenes, landscapes, and still lifes. His bravura technique, incorporating old master and impressionist practices, set the pace among progressive late-nineteenth-century American painters. For some years his carefully constructed artistic personality epitomized the American notion of the aesthetic life. In addition, during a long and influential teaching career, he encouraged such outstanding younger painters as Georgia *O'Keeffe and Charles *Sheeler to develop individual forms of expression. Chase was born in Williamsburg (now Nineveh), about twenty miles south of Indianapolis, where he moved with his family in 1861. There he received his first painting lessons from local artists before going to New York in 1869 to study briefly with Ohio-born portrait, landscape, and genre painter Joseph Oriel Eaton (1829–75) and then at the *National Academy of Design. The next year he rejoined his family, now in St. Louis, where he painted portraits and still lifes. In 1872 he departed for Europe. After visiting London and Paris, in the fall he enrolled at Munich's Royal Academy, where he absorbed the fluid, old master brushwork practiced there. He also admired the vigorous realism of Wilhelm Leibl. In the spring of 1877 he went to Venice, where he worked in company with Frank *Duveneck and John *Twachtman for about nine months. After returning to New York, in the fall of 1878 Chase began teaching at the *Art Students League, initiating a virtually uninterrupted teaching career extending over three and a half decades at that school and others, as well as privately.

As he revisited Europe each year from 1881 to 1885, Chase's familiarity with both traditional and modern art attained a standard unsurpassed among American residents. In Spain and the Netherlands particularly, he deepened his long-standing respect for the art of Velázquez and Frans Hals, but elsewhere he absorbed the latest artistic trends. In Paris he was drawn to impressionism and admired the work of new acquaintances John Singer *Sargent and Belgian painter Alfred Stevens. In London he met James Abbott McNeill *Whistler. Interrelated international currents, including *japonisme, the *aesthetic movement, and interest in photography also affected his emerging personal style. Meanwhile, in New York Chase quickly became a leader in the art community. His exotically furnished quarters in the Tenth Street Studio Building, epicenter of the New York art world, soon became well known as the model of urbane bohemianism among artists, patrons, and others. He also participated eagerly in the activities of progressive art organizations, including the *Society of American Artists (his years as president totaled more than a decade), the *Tile Club, and the Society of Painters in Pastel, which he founded along with his good friend Robert *Blum in 1882. During these transitional years of the early 1880s, he gradually abandoned the dark realism of Munich in favor of Paris's more modern, impressionist aesthetic. Featuring a young woman in old-fashioned dress leafing through an art book so large she has placed it on the floor, *In the Studio* (Brooklyn Museum, c. 1881) pictures the artist's ornate atelier. Its richly painted surface and solid structure recall his earlier work. However, the lightened palette, asymmetrical organization, and patterned composition point to his future. Although he had not studied in Paris, Chase soon played a decisive role in popularizing a French sensibility in the United States.

Particularly during the fifteen years or so after his marriage in 1886, much of his most appealing and innovative work amalgamates stylistic experimentation with fond but somewhat generalized representation of daily life. His wife and children appear often as models but do not usually register as individualized portraits. In the late 1880s while residing in Brooklyn and then in Manhattan, he painted views of nearby parks, balancing landscape and figures in idyllic evocations of sophisticated urban life. Although these reflect impressionist subjects and techniques, Chase's most clearly impressionist works date from the 1890s. Beginning in 1891, twelve consecutive summers teaching on eastern Long Island at his own school in Shinnecock Hills, adjacent to Southampton, presented the opportunity to respond to sunlight, rolling hills, and sea. In addition to numerous landscape views, he created many Shinnecock scenes of his family enjoying outdoor vacation pastimes. Indoor scenes even more pointedly idealize and aestheticize family life, as in the pastel *Hall at Shinnecock* (Terra Foundation for American Art, 1892). Integrating salient thematic and stylistic aspects of his work, it pictures an airy space in his Stanford White–designed residence and offers a meditation on the interplay between illusion and reality. As his wife observes from an easy chair, on the bare wood floor two young daughters in white dresses examine an accordion-pleated folder, displaying sketchily rendered images, presumably Japanese illustrations. Large blue-and-white Chinese vases filled with greenery combine decorative taste with ties to nature, while many framed pictures line the walls. However much Chase had learned about pattern and compressed space from Japanese prints or their reverberations in impressionist methods, his scene pays homage to old master tradition as well. His reflected self-image in a distant armoire recalls his roots in the painterly tradition of Velázquez, while a reproduction of Giovanni da Bologna's sixteenth-century *Mercury* also honors the painter's artistic heritage.

In 1895 Chase closed his Tenth Street studio and resigned his teaching position at the Art Students League. (He again taught there between 1907 and 1911.) After six months in Europe, the following year he opened the Chase School of Art (later the New York School of Art, then the Parsons School of Design, and now a division of the New School), where he taught until 1907. In addition, until 1909 he commuted frequently to Philadelphia to teach at the *Pennsylvania Academy of the Fine Arts and occasionally gave instruction elsewhere as well. Every summer but one from 1903 through 1913, he took students to Europe, and in 1910 he purchased the villa he had previously rented in Florence. The Italian landscape provided light-filled views for his art, and the residence's interior appears in several evocative compositions. However, after about 1900, he turned his attention principally to commissioned portraits and to still lifes, often featuring the glistening fish that showcase his virtuoso technique. Following a year of declining health, Chase died in New York and was honored the following year with a memorial exhibition at the *Metropolitan Museum of Art.

Chicago, Judy (1939–). Painter, sculptor, ceramist, and installation artist. A central participant in 1970s *feminist art, she remains best known for the iconic *Dinner Party* (Brooklyn Museum, 1974–79). Executed with the assistance of hundreds of volunteers (including a few men), the installation features a triangular dinner table, 46.5 feet on each side. This supports thirty-nine place settings for women Chicago admired, including Susan B. Anthony, Emily Dickinson, and Georgia *O'Keeffe. Upon individual needlework runners, each setting comprises a plate, a chalice, and flatware, all decorated to symbolize the individual's accomplishments, with the plates bearing particularly elaborate, often sculptural embellishment. On the floor, names inscribed on white tiles pay homage to an additional 999 women. The piece generated extensive controversy within the art world, as well as among the general public. While some celebrated Chicago's monumental tribute to prominent women in a transhistorical sisterhood, critics found the work conceptually and formally simplistic or, offended by its labial and vaginal imagery, questioned her emphasis on anatomy. A Chicago native, Judith Cohen began her training at the School of the Art Institute of Chicago but transferred to UCLA, where she earned a BA in 1962 and a master's degree two years later. In 1961 she married Jerry Gerowitz, who died in an automobile accident in 1965. Under the name Judy Gerowitz, she established her early reputation with spray-painted, *minimalist paintings and sculptures. With the onset of the women's movement, she questioned the meaning of such work and soon abandoned it. Around 1970 she also changed her surname to reflect her origins. Directing feminist consciousness-raising techniques toward creative endeavor, she pioneered studio programs for women at California's Fresno State College in 1970. With Miriam *Schapiro, the next year she established the landmark Feminist Art Program at the California Institute of the Arts in Valencia. In 1973 she left to co-found the Feminist Studio Workshop in Los Angeles. These institutions contributed to the Los Angeles area's recognition as the most radical center of feminist art production during the early 1970s. Two similarly ambitious collaborative installations followed *The Dinner Party*. The *Birth Project* (now distributed among numerous institutions, 1980–1985) comprises one hundred needlework panels celebrating woman as the source of life. The *Holocaust Project: From Darkness into Light* (Through the Flower Foundation, 1984–1993) employs several media, including tapestry, stained glass, and photography, to meditate on oppression and violence as agents of human suffering, particularly for Jewish women. Besides several volumes chronicling aspects of her art, Chicago has published *My Struggle as a Woman Artist* (1975) and *Beyond the Flower: The Autobiography of a Feminist Artist* (1996). As well, with Edward Lucie-Smith, she co-authored *Women and Art: Contested Territory* (1999). In 1970 Chicago married sculptor and painter Lloyd Hamrol (1937–), known primarily for outdoor public sculptures. After they divorced in 1979, she married photographer and filmmaker Donald Woodman (1945–), who assisted on the *Holocaust Project*. They live in Belen, New Mexico, south of Albuquerque.

Chicago imagism. Term applied to Chicago's varied expressionist and/or surrealist figurative art of the 1950s to 1970s. Like California *funk art, imagism represented an alternative to mainstream modernism, particularly New York abstraction. Many Chicago imagists shared *pop artists' interest in comic books, advertising, and mass-market artifacts, but tribal, folk, and outsider sources exerted even more attraction. The School of the Art Institute of Chicago trained nearly all the imagists and introduced them to each other. The extensive ethnographic collections of the nearby Field Museum of Natural History inspired many. Several other factors also rooted imagism in Chicago. The city already boasted a strong tradition of figural art, including work by painters as varied as Ivan *Albright, Archibald *Motley, and the independent surrealist Gertrude Abercrombie (1908–77). The flourishing photography milieu, centered at László *Moholy-Nagy's Institute of Design, emphasized the interaction of form and representation, as in the work of Harry *Callahan and Aaron *Siskind. Moreover, Chicago's brief exposure to two figures of international stature proved crucial to the aesthetic evolution of imagism's first generation. In 1951 French art brut advocate Jean Dubuffet showed his work and presented a landmark lecture, while in 1954 Roberto *Matta appeared as a visiting professor at the Art Institute.

Although never a formal group, the imagists of the 1950s and early 1960s came to be known as the Monster Roster, thanks to Chicago's premier critic Franz Schulze (1927–), who coined the name in 1959. Like the most prominent, Leon *Golub, these artists generally reflected an existentialist outlook in various forms of expressionist representation. They included sculptor Cosmo Campoli (1922–96), painter and *assemblage artist George M. Cohen (1919–99), and Nancy *Spero, as well as Ellen Lanyon (1926–), a temperamentally surrealistic painter and printmaker drawn to themes of indeterminacy and transformation, and Seymour Rosofsky (1924–81), whose brooding paintings and prints temper realistic imagery with varying degrees of fantasy. Known for painstakingly crafted wood objects, often conjoined with found materials, idiosyncratic sculptor, printmaker, and draftsman H. C. Westermann (1922–81) contributed to the Monster Roster spirit but at an early date also showed an interest in mixing high and low art. Equally indebted to surrealism and to vernacular woodworking, he specialized in obsessively finished, boxlike forms that emphasize enigmatic content over formal invention. His rougher drawings, lithographs, and woodcuts often picture themes of violence and destruction, frequently depicted in cartoonish forms. Born in Los Angeles, Horace Clifford Westermann served in the U.S. Marine Corps for three years during World War II and several years later, again fought in Korea. These formative experiences condition the sinister psychology of many works, particularly a series of Death Ships. In 1947 he began three years of study at the Art Institute. After the second military tour, he returned to Chicago. In 1959 he married painter and sculptor Joanna Beall (1935–97), daughter of graphic designer Lester Beall. In 1961 they settled in rural Brookfield Center, Connecticut. He died in a hospital in nearby Danbury.

A more clearly defined, younger set, which called itself the Hairy Who, showed together three times between 1966 and 1968 but never articulated an aesthetic platform. All alumni of the Art Institute, its six participants produced shamelessly raffish art emphasizing humor, sexuality, popular culture, and the fetishistic vision of the deranged. Their generally patterned compositions usually feature tight, detailed execution. The most widely known of the group, painter and draftsman James Nutt (1928–), known as Jim, came from Pittsfield, Massachusetts. He worked on Plexiglas in the 1960s to achieve a slick surface for vulgar, agitated subjects. Later, in paintings on canvas, his delicate and subtle touch demonstrated a technical debt to old masters. However elegant, his stylized themes nevertheless remained tied to comic strip and movie-land absurdities. In recent years, he has emphasized a calm inner radiance in painstaking, small canvases of slightly zany imaginary women. His wife, Chicago-born Gladys Nilsson (1940–), works primarily in watercolor, achieving a wistful and sensuous fluidity in peculiar figural fantasies, most often relating to women's lives. She also makes prints and collages. Painter and sculptor Karl Wirsum (1939–) specializes in intricately elaborated, brightly colored, often robot-like, flattened figures. Variously ominous and humorous, they draw on multiple sources, including comic books, Japanese prints, Mexican popular art, and tribal sculpture. The Hairy Who also comprised Arthur Nelson (or Art) Green (1941–), Suellen Rocca (1943–), and James (or Jim) Falconer, who later decamped for New York.

Among others who contributed to imagism, Ed Paschke (1939–2004) created lurid imaginary portraits of downtrodden and abnormal individuals, as well as a later series of figures seemingly distorted by television transmission. Acid colors, along with stylized patterns sometimes conflictingly overlaid on modeled forms, intensify frequently masklike visages. Except for brief interruptions a lifelong Chicagoan, Edward Francis Paschke earned a BFA in 1961 at the Art Institute. After serving from 1962 until 1964 in the U.S. Army, he returned to the Art Institute for an MFA degree. Always drawn to street life and subcultures, in the 1960s he lived for a time in New York, where he particularly observed denizens of the Lower East Side and Harlem. He also worked in a psychiatric hospital. From such experiences, he brought to his art a dark and insolent edge that grated against his ties to aspects of pop art, particularly the work of Andy *Warhol. At the time of his death, he had taught at Northwestern University in Evanston for more than twenty-five years.

Roger Brown (1941–97) worked with cartoonlike imagery to construct narratives commenting on contemporary society. Small, silhouetted figures inhabit a world of toylike objects beneath scalloped clouds. His cheery stylizations belie sardonic or even mournful subjects. Born in Hamilton, Alabama, he grew up in nearby Opelika, thinking he would become a preacher. He started toward that goal at Bible school in Nashville before moving to Chicago in 1962. He received a bachelor's degree from the Art Institute in 1968 and a master's degree two years later. His singular style emerged in the early 1970s. Besides paintings, he created prints, sculptural assemblages, murals, and stage sets. In the years before his death in an Atlanta hospital, he maintained homes in New Buffalo on the Michigan lake shore opposite Chicago and in Carpenteria on the Pacific coast in Southern California, as well as in Chicago. Emphasizing individualistic expression and the value of ethnographic and outsider precedents, Art Institute teacher Ray Yoshida (1930–) inspired the Hairy Who and other younger imagists. Born in Hawaii, Ray Kakuo Yoshida graduated from the Art Institute in 1953 and three years later earned an MFA at Syracuse University. His mature paintings and collages disperse quirky representational and abstract forms in formally disciplined arrays. He remains an emeritus professor at the Art Institute.

Chim. *See* SEYMOUR, DAVID.

Christenberry, William (1936–). Photographer, painter, sculptor, and installation artist. Most of his work centers on themes drawn from the traditional rural South, where he grew up. His varied output includes evocative documentary photographs of Southern landscape and architecture; sculptural objects based on architectural forms; assemblages and installations often incorporating timeworn found objects; and an extended project addressing the difficult subject of the Ku Klux Klan. In all media, Christenberry synthesizes the history of modern art with reverence for the vernacular and the small farmer's vanishing way of life. A native of Tuscaloosa, Christenberry spent childhood summers on family farms in nearby Hale County. From 1954 to 1959 he studied at the University of Alabama in Tuscaloosa. While earning a bachelor of fine arts and a master's degree in painting, he developed an *abstract expressionist style. In 1961 he moved to New York. There he observed emerging *pop art and soon befriended Walker *Evans, whose work had strongly attracted him. A year later, he accepted a teaching position at Memphis (Tennessee) State University (now the University of Memphis). Later in 1962 he began his artistic meditation on the Ku Klux Klan with a series of drawings and paintings. This work has continued and diversified into the ongoing Klan Room, which has grown to include several hundred objects and images. After 1964 he rarely painted in the traditional oil-on-canvas technique, turning instead to mixed-media forms and, with time, to greater involvement in photography. In 1968 Christenberry moved to Washington, D.C., where he has since taught at the Corcoran College of Art and Design. However, he has maintained his connection to the South through regular summer visits to central Alabama. Although he had taken snapshots as studies for paintings since the late 1950s, he did not think of his photography as an art form until the early 1970s. In 1977 he began regularly using an 8 × 10-inch view camera to make hushed and stately documents of the South's agrarian environment, focusing on such subjects as abandoned buildings, cemeteries, gas stations, all-engulfing kudzu vines, clotheslines, and Civil War battlefields. Christenberry has always photographed primarily in color, and in the 1970s the persuasive example of his work contributed to the acceptance of color in art photography. *Southern Photographs* appeared in 1983.

Christo (1935–). Environmental sculptor and draftsman. Known worldwide for large-scale temporary fabric installations, he first made his reputation by wrapping objects. These grew in size with time, eventually encompassing entire buildings. In recent years, he has focused primarily on projects based in the landscape. That the artist's youth was spent behind the Iron Curtain may partially explain his commitment to shared beauty free of authority, ulterior purposes, and even personal expression. Disrupting viewers' normal expectations, the works also allude to displacement, echoing from Christo's point of view his own history but also a larger theme in twentieth-century experience. As he has moreover explained, his works' fleeting nature underpins his aesthetic. Impermanence promotes urgency for the work to be seen and appreciated before it shares the mournful fate of all in succumbing to time. Additionally, the insubstantial textiles that form his primary materials enhance the works' transient spirit, while the collaborative nature of their construction fosters communal participation. A native of Gabrovo, Bulgaria, Christo Vladimirov Javacheff studied at the Fine Arts Academy in Sofia from 1953 until 1956. He lived briefly in Prague before going on to Vienna, where he continued his education at the art academy in 1957. In 1958 he settled in Paris, where he supported himself by painting portraits, signed Javacheff, and married his subsequent collaborator Jeanne-Claude. Although all studio work comes from his hand, she is acknowledged as partner on public projects. Born in Casablanca to French parents, Jeanne-Claude Denat de Guillebon (1935–) was educated in France and Switzerland before studying at the University of Tunis. Christo soon began wrapping objects, adapting a surrealist technique to blunt their function and invest them with aesthetic presence. In 1961 on a dockside location in Cologne, he completed his first outdoor piece by covering stacked oil barrels with tarpaulin secured with rope. In the same year he first conceived the idea of wrapping a public building. He moved permanently to New York in 1964 and was naturalized as a citizen in 1973. In the mid-1960s he devised several tantalizing storefront projects that exclude the viewer. In these life-size installations, he concealed lighted interiors by affixing paper or cloth to the inside of display windows. In 1968 he realized the first completely wrapped building, shrouding for a week the Bern Kunsthalle in a light fabric held in place with rope. Despite their reputation, the actual number of additional wrapped structures remains few: Chicago's Museum of Contemporary Art (1969), Paris's Pont-Neuf, a bridge across the Seine River (1985), and Berlin's Reichstag (1995). Landscape projects commenced in 1969 with *Wrapped Coast—One Million Square Feet, Little Bay, Sydney, Australia*, an intervention that extended the idea of wrapping into a natural environment. Subsequent landscape works include Colorado's *Valley Curtain* (1972), an orange veil suspended between hills; *Running Fence* (1976), a white nylon wall traversing the rolling landscape of California's Marin and Sonoma Counties to end in the sea; *Surrounded Islands* (1983), eleven islands in Florida's Biscayne Bay cut off from the water with pink fabric; and *The Gates* (2005) in New York's Central Park, featuring orange curtains hung from seventy-five hundred frames constructed over walkways. Many projects have required years of planning, including engineering studies and regulatory approvals. Christo and Jeanne-Claude finance their work by selling preparatory drawings, collages, and models. In order to preserve complete freedom, they do not accept public money, charitable donations, or corporate sponsorships. Similarly, despite the enormous numbers of assistants and technicians required for the large projects, they do not rely on volunteer labor but rather, pay the construction teams at least minimum wage. Needless to say, the works' aesthetic includes also the creation of splendid effects for the public to enjoy without cost.

Christopher, William. *See* TOOKER, GEORGE.

Chryssa (1933–). Sculptor, painter, and printmaker. Among the first sculptors to work with neon tubing, she also numbered among the earliest artists to exploit commonplace, commercial signage for its formal potential. In paintings and prints, as well as sculptures, she has often employed single letters of the alphabet, Chinese ideographs, or commonly understood symbols, such as arrows, for purely visual effects. Especially in her grid-based paintings, these appear within elegantly austere contexts. Born in Athens, Chryssa Vardea Mavromichaeli began her art training there before leaving for Paris in 1953 to study at the Académie de la Grande Chaumière and absorb the postwar art milieu. In 1954 she enrolled at the California School of Fine Arts (now San Francisco Art Institute) but stayed only a year. Subsequently, in New York, at least partially in reaction to the prevailing enthusiasm for *abstract expressionism, she made undemonstrative paintings and metal reliefs based on simple motifs. Related to the early work of Jasper *Johns in their *pop art acceptance of the commonplace, they also suggest a *minimalist sensibility in their stripped-down clarity. Stimulated by New York's vibrant streetscapes, in 1962 she first put brightly colored neon to use in sculptural constructions, anticipating interest in colored artificial light among other artists, including widely acknowledged master Dan *Flavin. The light sculptures culminated in the mid-1960s in such works as *The Gates to Times Square* (Albright-Knox Art Gallery, Buffalo, New York, 1964–66), a ten-foot cubic volume dominated by an A-shaped Plexiglas structure enclosing neon tubing. While working also in two dimensions, since then she has continued to make sculptures with neon as well as other materials, particularly polished aluminum, in variations and extensions of her early accomplishments.

Church, Frederic Edwin (1826–1900). Painter. A landscape specialist, he numbered among the most celebrated artists of the late 1850s and 1860s. As Thomas *Cole's only student, he worked as a young man within the context of the *Hudson River School. Soon he extended its romantic realism to treat unfamiliar, frequently awesome subjects with grander and more sensuous physical presence. His unusually extensive travels in the Americas, from the Arctic to equatorial South America, provided material for his most notable works, but he also painted views of Europe and the Middle East. At Olana, his Hudson River Valley home of later years, Church fused architecture, ornament, landscape design, objets d'art, and distant views into a dazzling ensemble. Born in New Haven, Connecticut, the artistically precocious teenager studied there with local painters before relocating in 1844 to Catskill, New York, to work with Cole for two years. Before he settled in New York in 1847, he had already exhibited there. Two years later, at twenty-three, he became the youngest person ever to be granted full membership in the *National Academy of Design. Although primarily a landscapist from the outset, like his mentor he also painted some allegorical works in these years. He abandoned overt symbolism in the early 1850s but retained Cole's moral seriousness about the purpose of art. At the same time, Church elevated to a new level of scientific veracity Cole's insistence on the direct study of nature. Like many mid-century American artists, in his formative years Church also heeded English aesthetician John Ruskin's call for truth to nature.

Church's first trip to South America, in 1853, marked a turning point in his career. Inspired by his reading of Alexander von Humboldt's scientific travelogues, he ranked as the first American artist to explore the region. Church roamed in Humboldt's footsteps through Colombia and Ecuador for five months with his friend Cyrus Field (later responsible for laying the first transatlantic cable). The German naturalist and explorer had envisioned nature as an organism that would yield its meaning through scientific investigation. Responding also to the aesthetic qualities of the landscape he explored, Humboldt counseled painters to look to the South American wilderness. Its variety, he believed, summarized nature's creativity. In following Humboldt's lead, Church stressed scientific factuality. But he also glorified the region's geology and botany through compositional strategies designed to emphasize sublimity and transcendence. When exhibited in New York two years later, his visually powerful syntheses of tropical exoticism and scientifically accurate detail drew much praise. Among the most important, *The Andes of Ecuador* (Reynolda House Museum of American Art, Winston-Salem, North Carolina, 1855) crystallizes the panoramic format he often repeated. Close-up foreground detail gives way to a spacious middle ground, enlivened in this instance by dramatic waterfalls and rivers. In the characteristically misty, mountainous distance, the volcano Cotopaxi fumes alongside other peaks. Worshippers before a cross and a tiny, faraway chapel provide Christian overtones. A unifying, glowing atmosphere suggests Church's links with *luminist tendencies and his admiration for the radiant effects achieved by English painter J. M. W. Turner.

Two years later, Church's dramatic, closely studied view of an iconic American site, *Niagara* (Corcoran Gallery, 1857), garnered the artist international art-world celebrity. After a nine-week journey to Ecuador in the same year, Church produced his best-known painting of the tropics, the 5 × 10.5-foot *Heart of the Andes* (Metropolitan Museum, 1859). Again, he organized this idealized summary of the region's topographical and biological variety to be read from detailed foreground to atmospheric distance. Far-off Chimborazo, a snow-capped inactive volcano, towers beyond a middle ground anchored by a huge waterfall. To enhance its optical credibility, Church exhibited the canvas theatrically in a darkened room, within a frame he designed to suggest an embrasured window. More than twelve thousand people lined up to pay twenty-five cents each to view the popular sensation. In 1865 Church went to Jamaica, and he continued until the late 1870s to produce major works based on sketches and memories of his southward travels. Meanwhile, in 1859 he had journeyed by schooner to offshore Newfoundland and Labrador. Church recorded the forbidding resplendence of the north in *The Icebergs* (Dallas Museum of Art, 1861). The same size as *Heart of the Andes*, it similarly recapitulates the emotional and scientific experience of an inaccessible and in this case, treacherous, region. In 1867 Church sailed for Europe. Until 1869 he lingered in London and Rome, traveled through the Near East, and studied classical sites in Greece and Italy. Like other views resulting from this sojourn, *Syria by the Sea* (Detroit Institute of Arts, 1873) exalts antique ruins while remaining attentive to the splendor of the physical world.

Stimulated by his travels, Church returned filled with enthusiasm for building a home on farmland he had owned since 1860 near Hudson, New York. Richard Morris Hunt had designed a residence, and Church had often worked in his studio there during the 1860s. But now Church determined to build a "Persian" hilltop villa overlooking the Hudson River. (In actuality, Church had not visited Persia, now Iran, but the architectural detailing he envisioned offers a generically Islamic flavor.) He engaged Calvert Vaux as architect, but his own contribution to the eclectic design was extensive. Begun in 1870, the house was habitable two years later. For years, however, Church treated the home and its setting as a work in progress, as he tinkered with extensions, decor, and landscape features. Just as Church opened new approaches to landscape painting earlier in his career, so he pioneered in treating his home as a unified work of art. Its richly adorned interior, complemented by carefully arranged furnishings and objets d'art drawn from many civilizations and historical periods, epitomizes the taste of the nascent *aesthetic movement. Like his exactingly detailed, contemporary painting of *The Parthenon* (Metropolitan Museum, 1871), the home offered an homage to culture as an equalizing counterweight to the beauty of nature. A National Historic Landmark owned today by the state of New York, the restored house is open to the public. As he concentrated attention on this architectural gem, Church began to suffer from a form of arthritis that interfered with his ability to paint. Concurrently, after 1870 his highly realistic but rhetorical style began to look old-fashioned. Perhaps in response to both these conditions, as well as his firsthand study in London of Turner's work, his last major works emphasize atmosphere over scientific detail, functioning more nearly as meditations on personal experience than as fact-filled ovations to nature. In any event, he completed relatively few large canvases into the 1880s, and after that limited his painting to brilliant, informal small oils. Although most suggest studies or sketches, some are finished paintings, the last dated 1898. He traveled often in later years to Millinocket Lake in Maine, where he acquired property in 1880, and to Mexico, where he spent fourteen winters beginning in the early 1880s. Many of the small oils reflect those locales. Despite his commanding position in the mid-century art world, the private achievements of his later years, and the honor of a memorial exhibition at the *Metropolitan Museum of Art, by the time of his death in New York Church's art no longer interested a wide audience.

Citron, Minna (1896–1991). Painter and printmaker. After working as an *American Scene realist during the 1920s and 1930s, she later turned to abstraction. Born in Newark, New Jersey, Minna Wright grew up in Brooklyn. She married and had two children before she began her art training. After that, she never hesitated. Her last show of new work took place in a New York gallery in 1990, the year before she died at the age of ninety-five. Citron first studied painting, in 1924–25, with Russian-born painter and printmaker Benjamin Kopman (1887–1965) at the Brooklyn Museum's school.

She enrolled in 1928 at the *Art Students League, where Kenneth Hayes *Miller most influenced her work. In 1934 she divorced her husband in order to devote her life to art. In the early 1930s she painted the urban scene around Union Square, following the lead of Miller and other artists of the *Fourteenth Street School. At this time, spurred by admiration for the nineteenth-century French painter and caricaturist Honoré Daumier, she acutely observed the city's denizens with fond humor. By the later thirties, her art grappled with social problems as she also served as an art teacher and muralist for *federal art projects. In the early 1940s, while studying printmaking at *Atelier 17, she not only learned technical skills but also came to admire the abstract art that predominated there. As she moved away from representation in later work, in both painting and printmaking she made use of textured surfaces and accidental effects. She died in Manhattan.

Clapp, William Henry. *See* SOCIETY OF SIX.

Clark, Larry (1943–). Photographer and filmmaker. His raw approach to social documentary pushes the limits of acceptable subject matter. Born in Tulsa, Oklahoma, he studied photography in Milwaukee at the Layton School of Art and served in 1965–66 in the U.S. Army. His development followed the lead of such photographers as *Weegee and Robert *Frank, who were fascinated by the margins of society, street crime, and rebellious behavior. Clark's combination of straightforward documentation and personal involvement suggests also the approaches of Eugene W. *Smith and Danny *Lyon. Yet, where they found dignity and humanity among their subjects, Clark has observed perversity. For his best-known project, published in 1971 as *Tulsa*, he worked as an insider among unglamorous, self-destructive drug addicts over a period of about eight years. In these intimate and shocking images, he reveals the wasted lives and moral hollowness of his subjects. Clark's other books include *Teenage Lust* (1983) and *Heroin* (2000). In recent years, Clark has been engaged principally in filmmaking. *Kids* (1995), his first feature film, portrays sex and AIDS among New York teenage slackers. A book of the same title (also 1995) presents stills and the screenplay. In the more entertaining *Another Day in Paradise* (1998), two drug junkie couples team up in pursuit of sex, drugs, and low-level crime. *Ken Park* (2002) explores the dysfunctional home lives of several alienated teens. Clark lives in New York.

Claypoole, James. *See* PRATT, MATTHEW.

Claypool, James, Jr. *See* PRATT, MATTHEW.

Clements, Gabrielle de Veaux. *See* HALE, ELLEN DAY.

Clevenger, Shobal Vail (1812–43). Sculptor. Known particularly for unidealized, lifelike portraits, he came from the area of Middletown, Ohio, not far from Cincinnati. A farm boy who received little schooling, as a teenager he began working as a mason. In the late 1820s he moved to Cincinnati, where he worked with a stonecutter and met Hiram *Powers. He had some instruction from Frederick *Eckstein, and in 1836–37 he studied anatomy at the Ohio Medical College. He had achieved considerable skill by the time Henry Clay sat for him in Lexington, Kentucky, late in 1837. Although Clevenger followed standard *neoclassical practice in swathing Clay's shoulders with illusionistic fabric to suggest a toga, the head of this sculpture (Metropolitan Museum, 1841–46; modeled 1837) demonstrates an uncannily natural appearance. In the late 1830s Clevenger traveled several times to the East Coast. In Washington, New York, Boston, and other cities, many eminent persons numbered among his patrons. By the time he departed for Italy in 1840, no other American portrait sculptor was more highly esteemed. He settled in Florence, began translating his portrait busts into marble, and embarked on ideal figures. These included a life-size *Indian Chief* (lost; 1842), then a novel subject and probably the earliest sculpture to treat a distinctly American theme. Suffering from tuberculosis, just three years after his arrival he sailed for home but died at sea. In Florence, Powers arranged for Clevenger's remaining portrait busts and an ideal head to be posthumously carved in marble.

Clonney, James Goodwyn (1812–67). Painter and lithographer. A specialist in *genre subjects, he also executed landscapes and portraits, some in miniature format. Uncluttered compositions, limpid light, and a finely detailed technique characterize his typically small genre paintings. He usually chose outdoor, rural subjects for benign, lightly idealized, and often amusing interpretations of American life. Like other contemporary genre painters, he sometimes employed ostensibly unproblematic themes to carry overtones of political or social commentary, particularly in those images including African Americans. Probably born in Liverpool, by 1830 he was working in the United States as a professional lithographer. During the next several years, he produced both reproductive and original illustrations for major publishers in New York and Philadelphia. By 1833 he had begun studies at the *National Academy of Design. In developing his approach to genre subjects during the 1830s, he must have been aware of precedents in the work of both English and American painters, particularly William Sidney *Mount. Although he showed his work regularly in New York, he apparently took little part in the art life of the city, choosing to reside elsewhere in New York State during most of his career. Before he moved to Cooperstown in 1852, he lived in Peekskill, New Rochelle, and possibly other locations as well. Toward the end of his life, he relocated to Binghamton, where he died.

Close, Chuck (1940–). Painter, printmaker, and photographer. Monumental, close-up heads of the late 1960s brought him to attention as a *photo-realist. As he continued to expand upon this format, vary his means, and shift emphasis to the grids that facilitate transfer of photographic images to canvas, he contributed to aspects of *minimalism, *conceptualism, and *process art. Later, in addition to using photographs as source material, he produced them as independent works of art. Born in Monroe, Washington, near Seattle, Charles Thomas Close spent his youth in Tacoma and Everett. From Everett Junior College, he transferred to the University of Washington. After graduating in 1962, he earned BFA and MFA degrees during the following two years at Yale University. He continued his studies at the Academy of Fine Arts in Vienna for a year before taking a teaching job at the University of Massachusetts in Amherst. There in 1966 he abandoned his previous *abstract expressionist approach and began to paint from photographs, initiating an extended inquiry into representation. In 1967 he moved to New York. The following year he completed *Big Self-Portrait* (Walker Art Center, Minneapolis), the first of the frontal, black-and-white, head-and-shoulders portraits that made his reputation. Approximately 9 × 7 feet, it captures the artist in an offhand moment, with unkempt hair, glasses slightly askew, and a cigarette dangling from his mouth. In these works he made every effort to copy photographs exactly, with no allowances for self-expression, painterly virtuosity, or humanistic content. In 1970 Close added color to portrayals of friends (he refuses to accept commissions), mostly artists. After the late 1970s, he gradually complicated his canvases, giving the gridded armature more prominence and eventually achieving an eye-jarring, expressionistic mediation between the predetermined image and its painted incarnation. Pointillist dots and fingerprints of the 1980s expanded into freely painted lozenges lining up across the grid. Portraits from a distance, the 1990s paintings generally register at close range as bright abstractions. The artist has acknowledged that these exuberant surfaces reflect his relief at regaining partial use of his arms, enabling him to paint, after the nearly fatal collapse of a spinal artery left him almost completely paralyzed in 1988. Since the early 1970s Close has also produced editions in several print media, including mezzotint, etching, woodcut, and screen print, as well as handmade paper pulp. From 1978 he also made large-format Polaroids as studies or finished works and experimented with composite collage portraits. In the late 1990s he began making tiny, exquisite *daguerreotypes that offer a striking counterpoint in scale, facture, and sometimes subject (nude torsos supplement faces) to his paintings. He divides his time between New York and a residence in Bridgehampton, near the eastern end of Long Island.

Club, The. *See* ABSTRACT EXPRESSIONISM.

Coates, Robert. *See* ABSTRACT EXPRESSIONISM.

Coburn, Alvin Langdon (1882–1966). Photographer. His images of the modern city evolved from moody evocations to encounters of a dramatic force rarely encountered among *pictorial photographers. He also made a specialty of portraying writers and artists with sympathy and insight, often seeming to capture the struggles of their inner creative lives. In 1916 and 1917, while associating in London with poet Ezra Pound, painter Wyndham Lewis, and other modernists known as vorticists, he made the first nonobjective art photographs, which he called "Vortographs." Born in Boston, he started taking photographs as a child. After meeting his distant cousin F. Holland *Day in 1898, the two sailed to London together the following year. A few months after his return, in 1902 Coburn established a studio in New York. There he met Alfred *Stieglitz, joined the *Photo-Secession, and published his photographs in **Camera Work*. He also worked in Gertrude *Käsebier's studio, where he absorbed portrait techniques that he soon put to good use on his own. In the summers of 1902 and the following year, he worked with Arthur Wesley *Dow, who increased his appreciation of Japanese design methods. After 1904 Coburn lived mostly in London, where he first gained acclaim for a long portrait series devoted to well-known writers, artists, and other creative luminaries. His subjects included Rodin, George Bernard Shaw, G. K. Chesterton, and H. G. Wells. Coburn visited the United States frequently until 1912 but did not return after that, preferring to remain in the United Kingdom. After World War I, his enthusiasm for photography dwindled as he developed interests in mysticism and the occult. By 1932, when he became a British subject, he had virtually stopped photographing. Following an initial visit in 1916, he built a home in Harlech, on the northwest shore of Wales, and eventually resided there year-round. In 1945 he moved permanently to Rhos-on-Sea, near the town of Colwyn Bay on the north coast of Wales.

Coburn produced his most stunning studies of modern metropolitan life in the years before his final expatriation. Toward the close of this period, he numbered among the first photographers to exploit peculiar camera angles. For "The Octopus" (1912), he found a graphic pattern of light and dark by pointing his camera almost straight down at a park, where paths suggest an "octopus" etched in snow-covered ground. The visual dynamism of such images prefigures the brittle abstractions of unstable forms that he produced as part of the vorticist movement. For these, he photographed through a kaleidoscopic arrangement of mirrors to create fragmented, radically cubistic images. Coburn's printing techniques enhanced the richly expressive quality of his compositions. He often combined the gum bichromate method with platinum and sometimes printed on colored papers. He also demonstrated unusual proficiency in use of the photogravure process. Although he rejected the common pictorialist practice of manipulating negatives, he regularly used a soft-focus lens that obscured detail and contributed to the primacy of broad masses in his images. In addition to more than a dozen literary works illustrated with Coburn's photographs, several publications explicitly showcasing his images often include his own texts. Views prevail in *London* (1909), *New York* (1911), *Moor Park, Rickmansworth* (1915), and *The Book of Harlech* (1920). He collected portraits in *Men of Mark* (1913) and *More Men of Mark* (1922). *Alvin Langdon Coburn, Photographer: An Autobiography*, edited by Helmut and Alison Gernsheim, appeared in 1966.

Cohen, George M. *See* CHICAGO IMAGISM.

Cole, Thomas (1801–48). Painter. A key figure in the development of landscape painting, he also produced many allegories and literary subjects. By merging realistic description and idealism, he inspired the subsequent *Hudson River School. His responses to nature, imagination, literature, and the spiritual imperatives of Christianity reflect a complex and even contradictory mind. Few American artists have achieved such fertile and varied results, and perhaps even fewer have so influenced the course of subsequent developments. Born in Bolton, Lancashire, Cole grew up in the industrialized north of England. In his teens he worked as an artisan, assisting a wood engraver and designing calico patterns. He emigrated to the United States in 1818 and was naturalized as a citizen in 1834. For some months, the young man worked in Philadelphia before traveling briefly to the West Indies early in 1819. He then rejoined his parents in Steubenville, Ohio. After picking up the technical rudiments of painting from an itinerant artist, he worked in the area and in Pittsburgh as a portrait painter. He also began sketching from nature before his return to Philadelphia late in 1823. There he admired the landscapes of Thomas *Birch and Thomas *Doughty.

A pivotal moment in Cole's career occurred within months of his relocation to New York in 1825. In the fall he exhibited three landscapes based on sketches he had made while traveling in the Hudson River Valley that summer. These transformed the twenty-four-year-old painter into a star of the city's tiny artistic community. Departing from the pastoralism of most early American views, Cole's emotionally charged early landscapes usually emphasize dramatic, even fearful aspects of the American wilderness. However, despite acclaim for his original vision of American nature, Cole harbored larger ambitions. He desired to fulfill the aims of traditional history painting, with its emphasis on didactic moralism and spiritual elevation. Paradoxically, Cole's lifelong attraction to European art and theory enabled him to redefine American landscape painting. His ingenious fusion of traditional artistic philosophy with empirical observation transformed topographical study from a literal and unassuming pursuit to a high-minded, virtuous, and edifying enterprise. For the rest of his career, along with pure landscapes he more or less simultaneously produced narrative or literary subjects. Inventively, however, he typically used landscape as an agent of meaning in these works, not just as background.

In 1829 Cole sailed for Europe. He resided in England before continuing on via Paris to Italy, where he spent more than a year. There he found inspiration for arcadian views incorporating picturesque features of Old World culture, such as ancient ruins and colorfully dressed peasants. Perhaps in part responding to the vogue for *panoramas, he also conceived a related series of paintings on the grandiose theme of *The Course of Empire* (New-York Historical Society, 1833–36). With the patronage of Luman *Reed after his return to New York in 1832, Cole realized this subject in five paintings, picturing from its undefiled beginnings to mournful desolation the rise and fall of a civilization. As all five employ the same vantage point, nature provides the enduring constant while human innocence gives way to ostentation, greed, and disrespect for the natural world, leading to mayhem and cultural collapse. A few years later Cole again offered a cyclical interpretation of history and an admonitory tone in the more pointedly personal, four-part *Voyage of Life* (Museum of Art, Munson-Williams-Proctor Arts Institute, Utica, New York, 1839–40; replica, National Gallery, 1841–42). Reflecting the artist's increasingly devout inner life (he became an Episcopalian), this series visualizes the trajectory from infancy to old age, with ambitious dreams and then calamity intervening. Again, nature contributes meaning as the *Voyage* follows its protagonist along a literal river of life. The waterway and nearby landscape, varying from placid to violent, amplify the narrative of each scene. As Cole developed the imaginative aspect of his work, occasionally even indulging in such visionary extravagances as *The Architect's Dream* (Toledo [Ohio] Museum of Art, 1840), he also painted pure landscapes of increasing power. After his first European sojourn, he represented nature in larger, more majestic forms. Moreover, he now painted with a fluidity that enhanced the intensity of visual response intrinsic to his approach. *View from Mount Holyoke, Northampton, Massachusetts, after a Thunderstorm—The Oxbow* (Metropolitan Museum, 1836), an expansive hilltop view of a great curve in the Connecticut River, combines his continuing devotion to wilderness with an appreciation of the pastoral. Alluding to sublime and beautiful categories of aesthetic analysis, the scene juxtaposes an overgrown foreground, anchored by broken but tenacious trees at left, with the graceful river valley tamed by agricultural use.

In 1841–42 Cole again visited Europe, primarily Italy. After his return he often painted subjects related to Christian salvation, including yet another series, *The Cross and the World*, which remained unfinished at the end of his short life. In addition, despite a disillusioned reaction to the materialistic drift of American life, dissatisfaction with the nation's increasingly industrialized character, and pessimism about the future of its democratic experiment, during these same years he also painted some of the loveliest and most persuasive landscapes of his career. In some, charming effects of light and atmosphere, minute detail, and a newfound serenity suggest parallels to emergent *luminism. Cole died of pneumonia at Catskill, New York, where since the mid-1830s he had resided within the Hudson River Valley scenery he treasured and helped to popularize. His home, Cedar Grove, is a National Historic Landmark open to the public on a limited basis. In his funeral oration, the poet, editor, and New York literary lion William Cullen Bryant touchingly averred of his old friend, "The contemplation of his works made men better." Cole was also a gifted poet and prose writer, whose literary bent reflects immersion in *romanticism. His 1835 "Essay on American Scenery" (published in the *American Monthly Magazine*, January 1836) remains a key document for comprehending his art as well as mid-nineteenth-century attitudes in the United States toward nature's roles in spiritual redemption, national progress, and aesthetic taste.

Coleman, Glenn O. (1887–1932). Painter and printmaker. Because he often focused on lower-class life, he is sometimes classified as an *Ashcan School artist. However, a shy lyricism sets his work apart from their typically brasher images. Long after most urban realists had lost interest in the teeming city as a subject, Coleman persevered. Because the New York he painted was disappearing, his scenes seemed increasingly nostalgic. He used a simplified, sometimes even naive, style for sympathetic portrayals of undramatic street life. In his last few years, he rendered architecture in a personal style derived from cubism. Coleman was born in Springfield, Ohio, but grew up in Indianapolis. He worked as a newspaper artist before moving to New York in 1905. There he studied at the New York School of Art (now Parsons, the New School for Design) with Robert *Henri and Everett *Shinn. He died in Long Beach, where he lived near Long Island's Atlantic shore in later years.

Colescott, Robert (1925–). Painter and printmaker. Drawing on the history of art, cartooning, and popular culture, his high-spirited figuration points to African-American experiences. Frenetic, sometimes surrealistic satires include hilarious send-ups of canonical masterpieces. *Les Demoiselles d'Alabama* (Greenville County [South Carolina] Museum of Art, 1985] spoofs Picasso's *Les Demoiselles d'Avignon* (Museum of Modern Art, 1907), which famously mined African sculpture as an aesthetic source for monumental Western painting. Colescott replaces three of the five figures with black female nudes, while reinterpreting as a white woman the Picasso figure who presents an African masklike face. As here, Colescott characteristically employs bright colors, compressed space, intricate patterning, and distorted drawing. Born in Oakland, Robert Hutton Colescott graduated from the nearby University of California at Berkeley in 1949. After additional training with Fernand Léger in Paris, he earned a master's degree from Berkeley in 1952. During the late 1950s and 1960s, he taught in Portland, spent a year in Egypt, and returned to Paris. His early narratives, affected by *pop art and *funk art, moved toward pointed social critique around 1970, after he had returned to California. Since the 1980s, while remaining centered on issues of race, his vision has broadened as he addresses increasingly complex social considerations. His imagery has become less explicit, while his style has moved toward increased fluidity. In the early 1980s he moved permanently to Tucson, where he taught at the University of Arizona until his retirement in 1996. In 1997 he became the first African American to represent the United States at the Venice Biennale.

Primarily a printmaker known particularly for technically accomplished intaglios, his brother **Warrington Colescott** (1921–) employs animated figurative imagery in a more whimsical, less confrontational narrative mode. Although his commentaries on American history and society often originate in a critical point of view, they feature dry wit and imaginative interpretation. Also born in Oakland and preceding his brother to Berkeley, Warrington Wickham Colescott graduated in 1942. After serving in the U.S. Army from 1942 until 1946, he earned a master's degree at Berkeley in 1947, then pursued additional training in Paris and London. In 1949 he joined the faculty of the University of Wisconsin in Madison, where he remained throughout his career. Since retiring in 1986, he has continued to reside in the area. In 1971 he married Frances Myers (1938–), also a printmaker. Born in Racine, she graduated from the University of Wisconsin, where she also earned an MFA degree in 1965 and has taught since 1988.

Collage. *See* ASSEMBLAGE.

Collier, Oscar. *See* INDIAN SPACE PAINTING.

Collins, Jess. *See* JESS.

Collodion process. *See* PHOTOGRAPHY, AMERICAN.

Colman, Samuel, Jr. (1832–1920). Painter, etcher, and designer. Unusually versatile, he painted western scenery and romantically flavored foreign locales, spearheaded the American *watercolor movement, and worked with Louis Comfort *Tiffany on decorative projects. Also an early and knowledgeable enthusiast for Asian culture, he amassed a large collection of Japanese art and decorative objects. A native of Portland, Maine, Colman spent his formative years in New York and probably studied briefly as a young man with Asher B. *Durand. At the outset of his career, he painted landscapes of the Northeast in the style of the *Hudson River School. In 1860 he went abroad for two years, spending most of his time in Paris and Madrid, but also traveling through southern Spain to Morocco. During this time, he developed more fluent brushwork, as well as an increased sensitivity to effects of light. Probably inspired in part by the example of J. M. W. Turner's paintings, these characteristics also may reflect a growing interest in watercolor. After his return to New York, he served as the founding president of the American Society of Painters in Water-Colors (later the American Watercolor Society) from 1866 until 1870 and later remained active in its exhibition program. In 1870 he traveled for the first time to the West, reaching the Rocky Mountains. He may have returned the following summer before departing late in the year for four additional years in Europe and North Africa. Subsequently, his new enthusiasm for printmaking contributed to the *etching revival then under way, and he numbered among the founders of the progressive *Society of American Artists in 1877. In 1879 he joined with Tiffany and two others to form a collaborative interior design firm, Associated Artists. After the group disbanded four years later, Colman continued to work frequently with Tiffany on such sumptuous projects as the decoration of the 1890–91 Henry O. *Havemeyer house in New York, a monument of the *aesthetic movement. From the mid-1880s Colman reinvigorated his fascination with the West, traveling across the continent and visiting Canada and Mexico, as well. The subdued and personal western views of these years often achieve an intimate tone, perhaps reflecting an influence from his own collection of *Barbizon work. After 1900 he increasingly turned his attention from painting to art theory, publishing his thoughts in two books, both written in collaboration with C. Arthur Coan. *Nature's Harmonic Unity* (1912) attempted to provide a mathematical basis for art. A sequel, *Proportional Form* (1920), appeared just before Colman's death in New York.

Color field painting. Term referring to large *New York School paintings that privilege color over form. Deriving from the numinous *abstract expressionist tendency notably exemplified by the work of Mark *Rothko, it developed in the 1950s in the work of such artists as Helen *Frankenthaler, Morris *Louis, and Jules *Olitski. More decorative and less psychologically fervid than most abstract expressionism, color field painting comprised grandly scaled, intensely hued works, often more lyric than anguished.

Columbianum. *See* PENNSYLVANIA ACADEMY OF THE FINE ARTS.

Colyer, Vincent. *See* KENSETT, JOHN.

Conceptual art. A 1960s innovation prioritizing idea over execution. At its extreme, a conceptual art work may consist only of a brief written description or set of instructions for fabrication. However, in practice, conceptual art intermingled freely with other 1960s and 1970s tendencies, such as *minimalism, *earth art, and *performance art, as well as politically oriented art. It has also affected the underlying ethos of later art. Conceptual art repudiated *abstract expressionism's emphasis on process and psychology, *pop art's acceptance of commercial and popular culture, and minimalism's attention to physical presence. Because conceptual art generally undermines craftsmanship, it also offered a rebuff to the art market's growing appetite for saleable products. With his cerebral credentials, Marcel *Duchamp ranks as the grandfather of conceptualism. Sol *LeWitt's 1967 "Paragraphs on Conceptual Art," published in *Artforum*, served to crystallize the movement.

Robert *Morris, Bruce *Nauman, and John *Baldessari number amid prominent artists who have contributed to conceptual art. Among other figures associated with the movement, Hans Haacke (1936–) ranks among the most central. Concerned predominately with systems, his art has proved highly controversial when he brings to light unsavory connections within social or economic relationships. Born in Cologne, Hans Christoph Carl Haacke graduated from the state academy in Kassel in 1960. He spent the following year in Paris, where he worked at *Atelier 17 and became acquainted with Yves Klein and other avant-garde artists. In 1961 he embarked on a year of study at Temple University in Philadelphia. From 1965 he has lived mainly in New York. As he attempted during the 1960s to detach his art from objects, he presented as works of art such real-time physical systems as *Chicks Hatching* (1969) and *Grass Grows* (1969). After turning his attention to social structures around the end of the decade, he achieved widespread notoriety in 1971 when the Solomon R. *Guggenheim Museum canceled an exhibition of his work, which included one particularly grating display. Based on research into ownership of substandard housing, this investigation unmasked ties between slum landlords and powerful public individuals, including museum benefactors. While continuing to pursue such projects, presented with photographs and text, Haacke did not entirely give up the painting that had been at the center of his early endeavors. Since 2002, he has been an emeritus professor at Cooper Union, where he taught for more than thirty years.

Joseph Kosuth (1945–) has staked out an analytical stance that focuses on language and the effects of context on meaning. Initially drawn to the ideas of Ludwig Wittgenstein and A. J. Ayer, he later shifted his interest to theories of Freud and Jacques Derrida, among other ambitious thinkers. Kosuth's early and paradigmatic *One and Three Chairs* (Museum of Modern Art, 1965) juxtaposes an actual chair with a full-scale photograph of a chair and an enlarged photograph of a dictionary definition of the word. A 1969 essay, "Art after Philosophy," published in three parts in *Studio International*, established his credentials as a leading proponent of "idea art." Over the years, Kosuth has gradually elaborated the visual qualities of his work while also remaining engaged with linguistic problems. Born in Toledo, Ohio, Kosuth studied at the Cleveland Institute of Art for a year before heading to Europe in 1964. Upon settling in New York the following year, he trained for two years at the School of Visual Arts (where he later taught for nearly twenty years) and subsequently took classes at the New School for Social Research (now New School). He divides his time between Europe and New York.

Douglas Huebler (1924–97) stopped making objects in 1967, afterward concentrating on ephemeral interventions documented with photographs, maps, charts, and texts, often wryly piquant in tone. Earlier, he was a painter of geometric abstractions before taking up minimalist sculpture in 1962. Born in Ann Arbor, Michigan, Huebler served in the military during World War II before studying painting in Paris and at the Cleveland Institute of Art. In 1955 he earned an MFA at the University of Michigan. His extended teaching career culminated in a stint of more than twenty years at the California Institute of the Arts in Valencia. He died at his home in Truro, Massachusetts, on Cape Cod.

Japanese-born On Kawara (1933–), who has resided primarily in New York since 1965, is best known for an extended series of paintings displaying only the date of their execution. Begun in 1966, this sequence and other works, such as the "I am still alive" telegrams sent to friends in the 1970s, draw attention to the passage of time and its relation to human experience. Also Japanese in origin, Shusaku Arakawa (1936–) generally collaborates with his American wife, poet Madeline Gins (1943–). About two years after settling in New York in 1961, he initiated a decade's concentration on a series of paintings addressing the theme of the Mechanism of Meaning. Later, he gradually extended his explorations of verbal and visual signification into architectural studies. New Yorker Lawrence Weiner (1940–) has since the late 1960s centered his work on language. Most of his dematerialized work appears in the form of wall texts, books, posters, or other means of widespread dissemination, including videotapes and compact discs, but he has also in recent years occasionally produced physical monuments that draw attention to site-specific meanings.

Cone, Claribel (1864–1929) and **Etta** (1870–1949). Collectors. Together, they amassed one of the earliest and best American collections of French modern art. Born in Jonesboro, Tennessee, the independently minded sisters remained unmarried lifelong companions. In 1871 they moved with their family to Baltimore, where they subsequently made their home, although they sojourned frequently in Europe. Claribel earned her MD degree at Women's Medical College of Baltimore in 1890. After additional training, from 1893 she worked as a research pathologist in Baltimore and later, in Europe. The more diffident Etta developed an expertise in art history without formal training. Through a long-standing friendship with Gertrude *Stein (the Cones inspired Stein's "Two Women"), in Paris they met Picasso, as well as their particular favorite, Matisse. They also purchased the work of French precursors to modernism, including Manet, Degas, Gauguin, and Cézanne. Additionally, they amassed a wide range of decorative arts, particularly textiles, but also including oriental rugs, antique jewelry, and furniture. After Claribel's death in Lausanne, Etta continued to expand the collection. Most notably, her regular purchases from Matisse formed a comprehensive survey of the artist's career through those years. Following her death during a visit to Blowing Rock, North Carolina, more than three thousand objects she and her sister had acquired went to the Baltimore Museum of Art. The bequest included more than forty Matisse paintings, as well as nearly twenty sculptures and numerous prints, drawings, and illustrated books.

Conner, Bruce. *See* FUNK ART.

Cook, Clarence (1828–1900). Art writer. The first significant professional art critic in the United States, he wrote prolifically, pointedly, and perceptively about a wide range of topics concerning art and architecture. Born in Dorchester (now part of Boston), Clarence Chatham Cook moved as a child to New York but graduated from Harvard in 1849. His career began to flourish in the 1860s after he helped to found a *Pre-Raphaelite organization, the *Association for the Advancement of Truth in Art, and edited its journal for a year. Beginning in 1864 he wrote regularly for the *New York Daily Tribune* for almost twenty years, while also contributing dozens of articles to leading periodicals. From 1884 until he retired some eight years later, he edited *The Studio*. He also wrote poetry. His most significant books include *The House Beautiful: Essays on Beds and Tables, Stools and Candlesticks* (1878), which supported goals of the *aesthetic movement, and the three-volume *Art and Artists of Our Time* (1888). He died in Fishkill Landing (now part of Beacon), on the Hudson River north of New York, where he had lived in retirement.

Coplans, John. *See* TURRELL, JAMES.

Copley, John Singleton (1738–1815). Painter. Among the greatest American artists, he outshone his colonial contemporaries to create a powerful style that had no exact precedent in Europe. Only the expatriate Benjamin *West preceded him in winning international stature. Copley's career comprised two distinct parts. From the mid-1750s until 1774 he painted intensely realistic portraits, works of stunning visual impact and social significance. In 1774 he left for London, where a second career unfolded. He quickly mastered a more sophisticated technique, which equipped him to compete successfully in the competitive British portrait market. He also embarked on ambitious narrative works that brought fresh energy to contemporary history painting. Copley was born in Boston, where he remained until his departure for London. In 1748 his widowed mother married Peter *Pelham, who lived only another three years—long enough to impart to the youngster the fundamentals of painting and engraving. Perhaps even more important, Pelham's familiarity with the cultivated world of arts and learning sparked Copley's driving ambition, inspiring him to measure his success against the lofty standards of European painting technique and theory. Moreover, Pelham was acquainted with other artists, including John *Smibert, at the time Boston's foremost resident painter. To a neophyte artist, Smibert offered not only the model of his own work, but also a collection of prints, copies, and casts of European art. Among other artists active locally, Robert *Feke provided the most influential example to young Copley.

Copley's longing for greatness surfaced at an early age. While still a teenager, he experimented with mythological scenes derived from engravings. However, in colonial America, these had no market. Copley turned to portraiture, the one form of painting that offered financial success, another mark of achievement that Copley valued. Sufficiently accomplished to work professionally by the time he was fifteen, he at first found little local competition. However, Joseph *Blackburn's arrival in 1755 offered a challenge. Copley quickly updated his style to reflect his British competitor's fashionable rococo. For the most part, what he took from Blackburn was superficial: lighter color harmonies, stylish poses and compositions, and depiction of shimmering fabrics. From the beginning, the illusion of soberly observed verisimilitude remained a constant goal of his American period. To accomplish this, he depended on precisely edged shapes, smoothly modeled three-dimensional forms, and painstakingly polished surfaces. His simple but solidly conceived compositions emphasize richly colored two-dimensional surface pattern to the neglect of atmospheric integration of mass and space. Copley's approach almost uncannily suited his clientele. On the one hand, his unsparing realism signaled their individualism, their suspicion of ostentation, and their respect for common-sense directness. On the other, his compositions and poses adapted from aristocratic prototypes, along with the comfortable luxury that emanated from beautiful surfaces, detailed finery, and fashionable accoutrements, produced an aura of privilege that played well to his sitters' status-conscious appreciation of wealth and good taste. In the 1750s and 1760s Copley strove to perfect his technique by ranging beyond his normal practice of life-size oil portraits. He produced miniatures in both oil and watercolor, and with great success he adapted the fashionable small-scale pastel little seen in the colonies before the second half of the century.

Before he was thirty, Copley ranked as the best painter in the colonies. Moreover, he was producing works that surpassed, in both execution and conception, anything he had ever seen. Aware that he lived in an artistic backwater, he yearned to attain the high standards set in London, where reputations were made. In 1765 he painted *Boy with a Squirrel* (Museum of Fine Arts, Boston) expressly to send to England. Although his half-brother Henry *Pelham modeled for it, the work is less a portrait than an evocation: an attractive adolescent lost in dreamy thought as he plays with his chained pet squirrel. A lustrously reflective table top, a half-filled glass of water, and the contrastingly soft, furry little animal underscore the painter's daunting capacity to mimic both visual and tactile effects. The next year, when it was exhibited, both Benjamin West and leading English painter Joshua Reynolds admired the painting and encouraged its maker to come to London. Well aware that he was already at the top of his profession in Boston but that he could be overwhelmed by British competition, Copley vacillated for eight years. He sent additional works for exhibition in London, but in this interim, life in Boston became increasingly comfortable. The prospering artist married the daughter of a wealthy merchant and purchased a large Beacon Hill property next door to John Hancock's estate. In June 1771 he embarked on his only extended absence from Boston. For a little longer than six months, he painted portraits in New York, with a side trip to Philadelphia. By the time he returned home, the approaching Revolution increasingly consumed Boston's attention. Civil war would obviously ruin Copley's business, and the divided city already tore at his loyalties. His old friends and many clients favored the radicals, whereas his in-laws and many of his recent, more socially prominent customers were Tories. In June 1774 he sailed from Boston and never returned.

In the preceding years, whatever his uncertainties, Copley showed no trace of these in his art. His portraits continued to grow in power, complexity, and psychological discernment. *Paul *Revere* (Museum of Fine Arts, Boston, 1768) exemplifies the strengths of his early maturity. The patriot and silversmith, dressed informally in workman's clothing, holds a silver teapot in one hand as he contemplatively supports his chin with the other, linking art and thought through gesture. The strong lighting, clear outlines, minuscule detail, and pyramidal composition enhance the sitter's personal nobility. In its greater intricacy and subtlety, a late work of Copley's American period, *Mr. and Mrs. Thomas Mifflin* (Philadelphia Museum, 1773) represents the consummation of his colonial style. Here he masterfully engaged the problems of integrating two figures of equal importance in a unified composition. Thomas Mifflin pauses in reading to glance at his wife, who in turn looks out at the spectator as she continues to work on a small loom set on the table before her. Their hands animate the space between them and aid in visually uniting the two figures. Otherwise, silhouetted against a dark background, the Mifflins enjoy an uncluttered ambience, free of distractions. A single classical column, visible to the right where the architectural setting gives way to sky, testifies to their classical learning. In its clarity, geniality, monumentality, understated luxury, and emphasis on the sitters' individuality, the painting summarizes the features that so attracted colonists to Copley's art. As well, the rigorous spirit of the Mifflin portrait presages the *neoclassical ideal soon practiced by French painter Jacques Louis David and his followers in France.

Copley spent only a few weeks in London before setting out for a yearlong study tour of Italy. During this time, he painted only one commission, a double portrait of the visiting Americans *Mr. and Mrs. Ralph Izard* (Museum of Fine Arts, Boston, 1775). In this painting, Copley gave expression to enhanced ambitions and demonstrated an astonishingly rapid alteration of his style. The result forms a striking contrast to the Mifflin double portrait. Stylistically, the Izard portrait is softer and more atmospheric. Although faces are individualized, an elaborate composition diminishes their impact. The Izards are nearly overwhelmed by evidence of their wealth and taste, including specific works of antique art and a view of the Coliseum in the distance. The couple seems less concerned with character than with an aristocratic elegance distant from the Mifflins' forthright graciousness and intellectual probity. Shortly after he returned permanently to London, Copley developed a more convincing version of the fluent British portrait manner, and the best of his later likenesses ravishingly combine his hard-won feel for structure, color, and line with painterly technique and atmospheric unity.

Soon the new ambitions signaled in the Izard portrait found expression also in history painting. In his first significant work of this type, *Watson and the Shark* (National Gallery, 1778; replica by the artist, Museum of Fine Arts, Boston), Copley followed West's lead of a few years earlier in realistically representing a recent event. However, Copley amplified West's novelty by selecting an incident of personal rather than public significance. Here the nude Brooke Watson (whose pose derives from a classical sculpture) is threatened by a shark as his companions in a small boat attempt to kill the predator and pull the victim from harm. Anticipating the concerns of *romanticism, the painting portrays a dramatic, emotionally compelling moment in which individual heroism is conceived in terms of conflict between man and nature. In other works depicting contemporary history, Copley tackled events of political significance and included portraits of individual participants, again anticipating certain works of the French Revolutionary period. In their immediacy, Copley's contemporary narratives provided his most significant legacy to the international history of painting, although his colonial portrait style continued to influence some younger American painters after the American Revolution. Because of personal and professional setbacks, Copley's career was in decline after the mid-1780s, and few later paintings approached the standard set by his best work. After 1800 his output became increasingly feeble, and he no longer exerted significant influence on either side of the Atlantic. Despite Copley's superior achievements during his last decade in Boston and first decade in London, in the long run West held greater sway among up-and-coming American artists, who began to travel abroad regularly in the late eighteenth century. Presumably more intuitive as an artist, less articulate, and surely less amiable than his competitor, Copley possessed little of West's aptitude for engaging the political and social aspects of London's art life. Thus Copley missed the opportunity that West embraced to nurture, through instruction and encouragement, the major artists of the new republic's early years.

Coram, Thomas *See* FRASER, CHARLES.

Corcoran, William Wilson (1798–1888). Collector and museum founder. Also a banker and philanthropist. An early enthusiast for American art, the lifelong Washington, D.C., resident studied for a year at Georgetown College (now University) before entering business and financial services. In 1840 he and a partner founded the highly successful Corcoran and Riggs Bank (later Riggs National Bank, now merged with PNC Bank). In the mid-1840s Corcoran began acquiring significant works of art, which soon included Hiram *Powers's *Greek Slave* (1846; modeled 1840–43) and many works by *Hudson River School landscapists. Five years after retiring from business in 1854, Corcoran commissioned architect James Renwick to design a public gallery for his collection. Corcoran spent the Civil War years in France, while construction was halted. Finally opened to the public in 1874, the Corcoran Gallery of Art remained for decades the only important art museum in Washington. The original building now serves as the Renwick Gallery of the *Smithsonian American Art Museum, while the Corcoran Gallery occupies a nearby building, its home since 1897. Ernest Flagg designed the larger quarters, and Charles Platt added a new wing in 1928. Corcoran's collection remains the core of much expanded holdings that position the museum among the nation's most important repositories of American art, particularly with respect to the nineteenth century. It also retains a smaller selection of European art, mostly from the eighteenth and nineteenth centuries. From 1878, in conjunction with his museum Corcoran supported the art school that continues today. In 1879 he published an autobiography, *A Grandfather's Legacy*.

Cornell, Joseph (1903–72). Sculptor, collage artist, and filmmaker. A homegrown surrealist, he filled shallow, glass-fronted boxes with all manner of found, scavenged, and collected items that together create an iconography of wistful nostalgia. Astronomy, movie stars, birds, old masters, dancers, botany, toys, and games number among the recurrent subjects woven into dreamy *assemblages. He also produced collages and experimental films. Despite a quiet, even reclusive life, his unassuming but powerfully evocative work earned admiration from major art-world figures, such as longtime friend Marcel *Duchamp. In the early 1940s André Breton thought his work the most genuinely surrealist being done in the United States. Since Cornell's death, his reputation has only expanded, attracting sustained attention among scholars and critics, emulation from younger artists, and the admiration of a museum-going public. Completely self-taught as an artist, he never traveled. Exhibitions, books, movies, and Manhattan's rich mixture of vernacular and high culture sufficed to fuel his romantic imagination. His huge collections of raw materials for art making included all sorts of books and prints, postcards, toys, trinkets, and bric-a-brac. Appreciating the intrinsic beauty and affective value of these fragments from the recent or distant past, he allowed them to speak within the context of his constructions as messengers from another era. Seasoned, frayed, even abused by time, they invite inspection as individual items and contemplation as parts of uncanny systems.

Joseph I. Cornell Jr. was born in Nyack, on the Hudson River north of New York. After four years at Phillips Academy in Andover, Massachusetts, he left in 1921 without earning a diploma. While he was there, his family moved to Bayside, Queens. Joining them, he took a job as a textile salesman. While making the rounds of garment manufacturers in Manhattan for ten years, he used his free moments to visit bookstores, antique shops, and art galleries. He was drawn particularly to modern forms of expression he encountered at Alfred *Stieglitz's showrooms and elsewhere. He also read widely, with particular attention to French symbolists and other European writers. With his mother and disabled brother, Robert, in 1927 he moved into the modest, two-story frame house where he lived for the rest of his life, on Utopia Parkway in the Flushing area of Queens. During the Depression, Cornell became unemployed for about three years before finding a job designing textiles. After leaving that position in 1940, he worked intermittently until 1957 on freelance magazine illustration and layout assignments. Cornell may already have started tentative experiments with collage when he discovered Julien *Levy's newly opened gallery, shortly after he lost his first job in 1931. In any case, the Max *Ernst collaged images he saw there proved critical to Cornell's early days as a practicing artist. In January 1932 Levy included Cornell's collages (along with a lost assembled object) in New York's first public presentation of surrealism. Soon Cornell had the idea of composing three-dimensional "collages" within empty boxes, and by November he had enough of these ready to mount his first one-person show at Levy's gallery. For the early shadowboxes, he employed found containers, but after a short time he learned to fabricate his own.

In 1936 an untitled work from the Soap Bubble series (Wadsworth Atheneum, Hartford, Connecticut, 1936) appeared in Alfred *Barr's landmark "Fantastic Art, Dada, Surrealism" at the *Museum of Modern Art. Among the earliest fully realized works in his personal style, it brings together objects related only by conceptual association or visual form. An egg in a cordial glass, a small plaster child's head, an antiquated French map of the moon, a white clay pipe, three glass discs, and four wood cylinders, two decorated with reproductions, engage among themselves in a dialogue of shapes and unstable meanings regarding human destiny within the passage of cosmic time. Despite Cornell's pioneering position among American artists in embracing the essence of the surrealist project, he remained at arm's length from surrealist orthodoxy. He shared its literary tastes, its admiration for Odilon Redon and other creators of fantastic imagery, its delight in dreams, and its worship of the marvelous wherever it might be encountered. Nevertheless, he disavowed the movement's interests in psychoanalysis, eroticism, intellectual theorizing, and *automatism. Late that year he completed his first film, a scrambled remake of a 1931 Hollywood potboiler. Extending his penchant for finding and assembling, he cut apart a commercial film and rearranged it to achieve new and unexpected expressive ends.

For nearly two decades, Cornell focused on boxed reliquaries of the imagination. The objects they hold adduce contemplation of beauty, the passage of time, the loneliness of the soul, and the innocence of childhood, among other themes. Never sentimental and not entirely retrospective, they accept modern fragmentation—of space, of time, of meaning—as an element of feeling. Cornell often worked in series, including the Soap Bubble set; a Pharmacy group, built around drug store paraphernalia; and a Medici unit, in which members of the Florentine family make ghostly appearances through reproductions of painted portraits. Besides the boxes, he engaged also in other creative activities. During the 1940s he gave considerable attention to writing, publishing articles in distinguished small-circulation magazines, notably *View* and *Dance Index*. He continued to make collages, especially from the 1950s on. Between 1954 and 1958 he produced several additional short movies. (A final one followed in 1965.) Unlike his earlier experimentation with found films, for these he directed cameramen who included Rudy *Burckhardt and Stan Brakhage. During the 1950s, although pleased to receive visitors, he became increasingly reluctant to leave the residence that served also as storehouse and workshop. In declining health during the 1960s, he made increasingly fewer boxes but continued to produce collages. After the deaths of his brother, Robert, in 1965 and his mother in 1966, he suffered an incapacitating and extended grief. He died in the home they had shared.

Corson, Helen. *See* HOVENDEN, THOMAS.

Cortissoz, Royal (1869–1948). Art critic. An influential spokesman for art during more than half a century, he remained loyal to the aesthetic principles of his youth, maintaining a high regard for tradition, masterful technique, and idealistic expression. Although intrigued by aspects of experimental art in early decades of the twentieth century, by the 1920s he had become an implacable foe of modernism. Born in Brooklyn, he remained a lifelong New Yorker. In his youth he apprenticed at the architectural firm of McKim, Mead and White. At twenty he became a full-time writer for the *New York Commercial Advertiser*. After two years there he was appointed to the influential post of art editor at the *New York Tribune* (later *Herald Tribune*). In 1944, fifty-three years later, he retired because of ill health. He also wrote magazine articles and published several collections of essays on art, including *Art and Common Sense* (1913), *American Artists* (1923), and *Personalities in Art* (1925). In addition, he wrote monographs on Augustus *Saint-Gaudens, John *La Farge, and others, as well as a few volumes devoted to non-art subjects.

Cortor, Eldzier. *See* AFRICAN-AMERICAN ART.

Cos Cob, Connecticut. *See* ARTISTS' COLONIES.

Cosmopolitan Art Association. *See* AMERICAN ART-UNION.

Cottingham, Robert. *See* PHOTO-REALISM.

Couse, Irving. *See* TAOS ARTISTS' COLONY.

Covert, John (1882–1960). Painter. Active primarily between 1915 and 1923, he contributed to the *New York dada spirit that flourished in the circle of Walter *Arensberg, his cousin. In his paintings, Covert may have been the first American artist to incorporate non-art materials, such as the string glued to the surface of *Brass Band* (Yale University Art Gallery, 1919) to distinguish forms in its abstract design. Born in Pittsburgh, Covert began art studies there before leaving for Munich in 1908. After four years there, he continued to work in Paris until 1914. He renounced academic painting only after his return to the United States in 1915. Apparently introduced to modern art by Arensberg, he soon embarked on an experimental course influenced particularly by the example of Marcel *Duchamp. *Time* (Yale University Art Gallery, 1919), among his strongest works, engages the viewer both visually and intellectually. Its casually disposed elements include numerous tack heads, as well as cryptic notations that refer to compass directions, geometry, and mathematical formulas. *Water Babies* (Seattle Art Museum) of the same year could hardly be more different. Presenting two dolls, one submerged in a container of water, the startling and unsettling image plays on Covert's interest, derived from Duchamp and Francis Picabia, in the equivalence of human and inanimate forms. Despite his originality, Covert found little support for his work. In 1923 he closed his studio and entered the family steel-related business. Although he did not subsequently exhibit his work or otherwise actively participate in the art life of his day, he painted a number of figurative works, as well as some landscapes. He also took photographs, mostly of studio models, and kept cryptic daybooks that include sketches and marginal decorations. He died in Pittsburgh.

Cox, Kenyon (1856–1919). Painter. Remembered as a vigorous defender of classicism in its waning days, he numbered among major figures of the *American Renaissance. French academic standards inform his allegorical or literary murals and easel paintings, which present idealized, nearly always female figures as embodiments of ennobling concepts. An important teacher at the *Art Students League for twenty-five years, he also wrote and lectured extensively, in time becoming noted as the preeminent voice of reactionary traditionalism during a period of increasing artistic experimentalism. Not completely immune to progressive tendencies, however, he painted broadly conceived, lyric landscapes and a few unassuming *genre scenes. He also appreciated the work of such friends as William Merritt *Chase and Augustus *Saint-Gaudens. Both appear in his best-known portrait (Metropolitan Museum, 1908), which shows Saint-Gaudens in his studio, at work on a relief depicting Chase. A native of Warren, Ohio, Cox enrolled at the *Pennsylvania Academy of the Fine Arts following preliminary training in Cincinnati, where he studied for a time with Frank *Duveneck. After a year in Philadelphia, he arrived in Paris in the fall of 1877. There he studied with Émile-Auguste Carolus-Duran for about a year and a half before entering the École des Beaux-Arts, where Jean-Léon Gérôme became his principal teacher. He returned to Ohio in 1882 but settled permanently in New York the following year. The 1893 World's Columbian Exposition in Chicago provided his first major opportunity to work as a muralist. Subsequently, he numbered among those who embellished the new Library of Congress (1896), and he remained in demand until the final years of his life for decorations in numerous public buildings, including the state capitols of Minnesota (1904), Iowa (1906), and Wisconsin (1912–15). Motivated by a humanistic belief in the social utility of art, Cox sought in his murals to symbolize universal ideas in beautiful form accessible to the general public. He revered antique and Renaissance precedents, but strong draftsmanship, slightly flattened forms, and pale tonal harmonies reveal his admiration for contemporary French decorative painting, particularly the work of Pierre Puvis de Chavannes. From the late 1890s, Cox generally summered in the vicinity of Cornish, New Hampshire, a popular artists' destination. Among his publications, *The Classic Point of View* (1911) presents the most systematic statement of his ideas, with examples drawn from the history of painting since the Renaissance. His other books include *Old Masters and New* (1905), *Painters and Sculptors* (1907), *Artist and Public* (1914), and *Concerning Painting* (1917).

Painter **Louise Cox** (1865–1945) became his wife in 1892. Born in San Francisco, Louise Howland King enrolled at the *National Academy of Design in 1881 and two years later transferred to the Art Students League, where she studied with Thomas *Dewing and her future husband. She painted still lifes, ideal figures, and portraits, becoming especially known for her likenesses of children. After her husband's death she lived in Italy and Hawaii, as well as in north suburban New York. She died in Windham, Connecticut. Their son, painter **Allyn Cox** (1896–1982), specialized in murals. Born in New York, he trained at the National Academy and the Art Students League before spending several years in Rome on a fellowship at the American Academy. His murals generally present historical themes, rather than allegorical abstractions. At the U.S. Capitol, he completed Constantino *Brumidi's rotunda frieze in the early 1950s and spent much of the next thirty years adorning additional areas of the building. He died in Washington.

Craftsman, The. *See* ARTS AND CRAFTS MOVEMENT.

Cramer, Konrad (1888–1963). Painter. Among the first Americans to paint abstract works, he lost his radical edge by about 1920. Subsequently, Cramer painted landscapes and still lifes that continue a modern preference for simplified and sometimes faceted forms. He also created whimsical collages and several views of gas stations, at that time infrequent subjects. In the 1930s, with the encouragement of Alfred *Stieglitz, he turned largely to photography. Born in Würzburg, Germany, he trained at the Academy of Fine Arts in Karlsruhe before moving to Munich in 1910. There he knew Franz Marc and may have been acquainted with Kandinsky during the period just before the Blue Rider group coalesced. In 1911 he emigrated to the United States. At that time he favored compositions combining enigmatic symbols. Within a year or two, he had turned to abstractions suggesting Kandinsky's turbulence and chromatic intensity but without his elegance or complexity. Shooting linear elements and unbounded color areas characterize *Strife* (Hirshhorn Museum, c. 1912). Others of Cramer's abstractions demonstrate an interest in cubism. An early resident and active participant in the *Woodstock art colony, he died there. His wife, **Florence Ballin Cramer** (1884–1962), painted sensitively drawn figurative works indebted to modernist simplification of form. She also created landscapes and still lifes. A native New Yorker, she met her husband in Munich.

Crane, Bruce (1857–1937). Painter. A *tonalist landscape specialist, he concentrated on intimate, informally composed scenes. Restrained color harmonies, often silvery or golden, support quiet, contemplative moods. Many of his works describe late autumn views tinged with melancholy. With its nearly bare trees, diffused light, overcast sky, and warmly brownish tonality, *Autumn Hills* (Heckscher Museum of Art, Huntington, New York, 1901) characteristically combines observation and memory into a retrospective elegy for the passing of a particular moment. A screenlike arrangement of forms limits depth and reinforces the composition's decorative appeal. Robert Bruce Crane was born in New York and grew up there. While working as a young man in an architectural office, he painted in his leisure hours. Upon his return from a brief sojourn in Europe, in 1878 he turned to painting full time and soon relinquished the literalism of his early work for more evocative goals. In 1879 he studied with Alexander *Wyant. From June 1880 until late in the following year, he worked in Paris and the nearby countryside. After returning to New York, he traveled often to rural areas of the Northeast in search of scenery. From 1904 the area around *Old Lyme provided subjects for some of his most admired paintings. He resided in the New York suburb of Bronxville for more than two decades before his death there. His wife, landscape painter **Ann Brainerd Crane** (1881–1948), was born in New York and studied there with John *Twachtman. She continued her training in Paris before marriage in 1904. After her husband's death, she continued to live in Bronxville.

Craven, Thomas. *See* AMERICAN SCENE MOVEMENT.

Crawford, Ralston (1906–78). Painter, printmaker, and photographer. Architectural subjects rendered in a style related to *precisionism made his reputation in the 1930s. On assignment for *Fortune* magazine in 1946, Crawford witnessed an atomic explosion in the Pacific. This experience fostered abstract works that reflect the energy of the bomb and its destructive potential. Subsequently, his work emphasized dynamic structural patterns, while deriving from a somewhat wider range of subjects than earlier. In these later works, sleek, flat planes of cool color relate to similar aspects of 1960s *hard-edge painting, while vernacular American subjects parallel those of *pop art. Born in St. Catherines, Ontario, George Ralston Crawford moved with his family in 1910 to nearby Buffalo, New York. During a year in Los Angeles, he worked at the Walt Disney studio and studied at the Otis Art Institute (now Otis College of Art and Design). In 1927, he enrolled for three years at the *Pennsylvania Academy of the Fine Arts, and in 1932–33 he studied for some months in Paris. Upon his return he settled more or less permanently in New York. (An avid traveler, he often worked elsewhere for short periods.) He soon devised his characteristic, sharply simplified style for American urban, industrial, or vernacular architecture and related subjects. Reflecting Crawford's paramount interest in abstract structure, the dramatic *Buffalo Grain Elevators* (Smithsonian American Art Museum, 1937) depicts faintly rounded cylinders held in tense balance with nearby rectangular elements and the flat blue sky. Although his paintings never resemble photographs, in the late 1930s he began using a camera to record the urban environment with an eye for the formal qualities seen in his paintings. Later he also captured transient incidents including human subjects. During World War II, Crawford served in the U.S. Air Force. In Europe for a year in 1951–52, he devoted much time in Paris to lithography, which he subsequently employed extensively. He died during a visit to Houston.

Crawford, Thomas (c. 1813–57). Sculptor. Known particularly for sculptures embellishing the U.S. Capitol, together with Horatio *Greenough and Hiram *Powers he established *neoclassicism as the prevailing style in American sculpture before the Civil War. He also designed many ideal figures and portraits as well as *genre subjects, mostly picturing children. Expanding upon an undercurrent of idealized naturalness in his work, several late sculptures move away from neoclassical restraint to indulge decorative effects, a fluid sense of movement, and tender expression. A New York native, Crawford learned woodcarving before going to work in John *Frazee's shop. In 1835 he sailed to Europe, where he remained except for occasional visits to the United States. The first American sculptor of consequence to settle in Rome, he studied there with Danish neoclassicist Berthel Thorvaldsen. Within a few years, Crawford made his mark with a full-length ideal figure, *Orpheus* (Museum of Fine Arts, Boston, 1843; modeled 1839), an ambitious life-size marble of the mythological figure accompanied by his three-headed dog Cerberus. Upon its arrival in Boston, the work formed the centerpiece of an exhibition of Crawford's work at the Boston Athenaeum, the first one-person sculpture show held in the United States. In 1850 Crawford won a competition for a monument to George Washington (1850–69) on the grounds of the state capitol in Richmond, Virginia. Crowned by the general's equestrian portrait, Crawford's first bronze, the large ensemble includes six subsidiary figures (he lived to complete only three) as well as allegories and decorative motifs. With this well-received commission, Crawford became the country's leading public artist and soon contracted to provide several works to decorate the U.S. Capitol. Designed in 1853–54, fourteen over-life-size marble figures represent the *Progress of Civilization* (completed 1863) in the pediment of the Senate wing. In 1855 he began work on bronze doors for the Senate (completed 1868), followed by a pair for the House of Representatives (completed 1905). Loosely inspired in their format by Lorenzo Ghiberti's celebrated "Gates of Paradise" for the Florence Baptistery, the individual panels on both represent events from the Revolutionary War and subsequent peacetime. Crawford's most conspicuous contribution to the Capitol's appearance, the posthumously installed allegorical bronze *Statue of Freedom* (also known as *Armed Liberty*; 1855–63), extends nearly twenty feet above the top of the dome. While so much engaged during the 1850s with the sober neoclassicism appropriate to public discourse, in some of his more private work Crawford edged toward a newer sensibility. With motion captured in her billowing drapery, undercut shadows enlivening complex surfaces, and profusion of ornamental detail, the graceful *Flora* (Newark [New Jersey] Museum, 1853) prefigures aspects of late-nineteenth-century taste. He died in London, following surgery for a cancerous brain tumor. Randolph *Rogers and William Henry *Rinehart, friends and colleagues in Rome, and Clark *Mills in Washington brought his unfinished commissions to completion.

Crayon, The. Art magazine published from 1855 until 1861. Founded in New York by William James Stillman (1828–1901), a painter and art critic who later became a journalist, diplomat, and photographer, it soon became the preeminent American voice of the visual arts. John Durand, son of Asher B. *Durand, served as co-editor before taking charge in 1856. The magazine popularized the writings of British aesthetician and art critic John Ruskin, as well as the *Pre-Raphaelite painting he favored. It also supported the *Hudson River School, and by reporting on their activities, fostered a sense of community among American artists. In its final issues, the periodical gave readers a foretaste of the later nineteenth century's subjective and imaginative aesthetic.

Cresson, Margaret French. *See* FRENCH, DANIEL CHESTER.

Cropsey, Jasper Francis (1823–1900). Painter. Also an architect. Remembered chiefly for landscapes, he also painted literary and allegorical works, still lifes, and a few other subjects. Associated with the *Hudson River School, he specialized in dramatic autumn scenes filled with colorful foliage. Cropsey was born on a farm in Rossville, on Staten Island, and apprenticed in 1837 to New York architect Joseph Trench. In addition to becoming an expert draftsman, he started painting before he left the firm in 1842 to open his own practice. Although art soon displaced architecture as his primary pursuit, he continued to practice design at intervals throughout his career. Thomas *Cole's ardent appreciation of nature and vigorous brushwork particularly inspired Cropsey's early efforts. In 1847 he departed for Europe, where he traveled in England and Scotland before settling in Rome, where he painted many views including detailed renderings of antique ruins and other architectural monuments. After his return to New York in 1849, he produced varied American landscapes, Italian scenes based on his sketches, and allegorical works reminiscent of Cole's moralizing narratives, using landscape to support thematic content. While living in London from 1856 until 1863, Cropsey painted his most ambitious and splendid account of American scenery, *Autumn—on the Hudson River* (National Gallery, 1860), an eleven-foot-wide panorama infused with patriotic and spiritual fervor. His characteristically meticulous detailing of every natural feature recalls also his admiration for *Pre-Raphaelitism and his friendship with critic John Ruskin, proponent of truth to nature. At the same time, the sky's unifying radiance reflects his acquaintance with J. M. W. Turner's work and suggests Cropsey's growing sympathy for *luminist poetics. Along the valley of a winding stream leading to the distant river, Cropsey placed hunters languidly contemplating the view from the foreground, children at play, farm animals, a log cabin, and other suggestions of human presence. Reverential attention to particularities and numinous light enhance the painting's celebration of harmony between mankind and benevolent nature. In 1866 Cropsey bought forty-five acres a few miles from the New Jersey border in Warwick, New York, where in the next three years he built a Gothic revival mansion, Alladin, his home for nearly twenty years. In 1885 he remodeled and extended an 1835 cottage, Ever Rest, overlooking the Hudson River in Hastings-on-Hudson. By this time his work sometimes showed the influence of *Barbizon taste. Slowed by a stroke in 1893, he nevertheless continued painting, often in watercolor, which had provided a longtime interest. Listed on the National Register of Historic Places, the restored house, where he died, is open to the public under the auspices of the Newington-Cropsey Foundation, which also maintains a collection of Cropsey's paintings.

Crown Point Press. *See* TAMARIND LITHOGRAPHY WORKSHOP.

Cummings, Thomas Seir (1804–94). Painter. Known especially for miniatures, he also executed larger oil portraits. He played a significant role in the early history of the *National Academy of Design, which he helped to establish and served in official and unofficial capacities during a period of several decades. In 1865 he published the important *Historic Annals of the National Academy of Design*, which details events in the organization's founding and development. Born in Bath, England, he arrived in New York as a child. He studied with Henry *Inman before the two artists formed a partnership in 1824. During its three years in business, Cummings principally handled miniature commissions. The vogue for these finely detailed little likenesses went into decline before mid-century, and Cummings became largely inactive as an artist after 1851. In 1866 he moved to Mansfield, Connecticut, although he returned to New York during winters. He relocated again in 1889, to Hackensack, New Jersey, where he died.

Cunningham, Imogen (1883–1976). Photographer. Known especially for portraits, nude studies, and botanical subjects, in her most striking work she stressed clarity, simplicity, and formal elegance. Born in Portland, Oregon, she grew up on a farm near Seattle and majored in chemistry at the University of Washington. Inspired in 1901 by Gertrude *Käsebier's published work, she enrolled in a correspondence course to learn photographic technique. Cunningham worked in Edward *Curtis's Seattle studio before studying photographic chemistry at the Technische Hochschule in Dresden for a year. Upon her return to Seattle in 1910, she opened her own portrait studio. Two years after her marriage in 1915 to Roi Partridge (1888–1984), they moved to San Francisco. An etcher, born in Centralia, Washington Territory, and trained at the *National Academy of Design and in Munich, he was hired to teach at Mills College in 1920, and they moved across the Bay to Oakland. (He taught at Mills until 1954 and died in Walnut Creek, not far from Oakland.). Before long, impressed with Edward *Weston's example, Cunningham abandoned the soft, dreamy *pictorialism she had pursued for more than twenty years. In such works as "Magnolia Blossom" (1925), she demonstrated the power of sharp focus to create dramatic images. Here, light-bathed, sculptural petals, which push beyond the edges of the picture, surround a highly magnified pistil. Luxurious in effect, the close-up view also reveals more of the flower's reality than the unaided eye can see. In the early 1930s, she also photographed movie stars for *Vanity Fair*, simultaneously probing their personalities and endowing them with the glamour of her flowers. Also in the 1920s and 1930s, in studies of vegetation, the nude, or mundane objects, she sometimes emphasized abstract patterns. In 1932 she numbered among founding members of the *f/64 group. Following her divorce in 1934, she lived permanently in San Francisco. In the 1940s she tested more often than previously the possibilities of double exposures and other experimental techniques. From about 1950, she specialized in portraits relating sitters to their environments. Her 1958 photograph of Morris *Graves in an outdoor setting evokes the ethereal atmosphere of his paintings. A year before her death in San Francisco, she embarked on a final project: photographing others who had also reached the age of ninety. These appeared in the posthumous *After Ninety* (1977). She published two earlier collections: *Imogen Cunningham: Photographs* (1970) and *Imogen! Imogen Cunningham Photographs, 1910–1973* (1973).

Currier, Joseph Frank (1843–1909). Painter. A Boston native, he lived abroad during most of his career. In 1869 he went to England but soon left for Antwerp, where he studied at the Royal Academy. He continued on to Paris in 1870, but within a few months the Franco-Prussian War precipitated his departure for Munich. There he studied at the Academy of Fine Arts from the beginning of 1871 until some time in 1872. He also associated with artists of the city's American community, including Frank *Duveneck and William Merritt *Chase. Like other young Americans, Currier developed a personal style based on the painterly realism associated with Munich, but he pushed its possibilities to unusually vigorous and expressionistic conclusions. Currier remained for nearly three decades in Munich and the nearby Bavarian countryside. Following his return to Boston in 1898, he abandoned painting but continued to show his work. He committed suicide in Waverley, a Boston suburb. An individualistic and experimental artist, Currier produced landscapes rooted in the tradition of *Barbizon painting, as well as portraits, figure studies, and still lifes. He also tried his hand at photography. Although generally dark in tone, his paintings often achieve a visionary intensity. Some landscape watercolors astonished contemporaries with audacious use of the medium, even incorporating accidental effects. His figure studies sometimes extend the flashy brushwork he admired in the work of Frans Hals toward a modern engagement with medium and process.

Currier & Ives. Lithographic firm that dominated the market for inexpensive prints from the mid-nineteenth century into the early years of the twentieth. Its unpretentious products decorated households throughout the country. Although the range of subjects was large, attractive landscapes and cheerful *genre scenes predominated. Sporting and hunting scenes, portraits, historical and religious narratives, political cartoons, railroad views, clipper ships, and children's subjects numbered among other well-received types. Today the name Currier & Ives evokes a rosy view of American life in a supposedly less complicated time. But to the original buyers, the prints offered numerous forms of access to knowledge and vicarious experience. Individual scenes variously stimulated excitement, nostalgia, contemplation, imaginative flight, and new understandings of the nation's expansion, industrialization, and social development. Importantly, the images also expanded the nation's taste for visual art. Born in Roxbury (now part of Boston), Nathaniel Currier (1813–88) worked for lithographers in Boston and Philadelphia before moving permanently to New York in 1834. He founded his own company the following year. His earliest successes pictured newsworthy events of the day, particularly disasters. In one such scene, which appeared only days after the incident, numerous passengers flounder in the water as a passenger steamer goes up in flames. The print bears the caption "Awful Conflagration of the Steamboat 'Lexington' in Long Island Sound on Monday Evening, January 13, 1840, by which Melancholy Occurrence over 100 Persons Perished." James Merritt Ives (1824–95) joined the firm in 1852. When he became a partner five years later, the firm was renamed Currier & Ives. Born in New York and trained as a lithographer, he initially worked for Currier as a bookkeeper. His business acumen probably underpinned the company's subsequent prominence. He died in suburban Rye, New York, where he had made his home for some time.

Currier & Ives flourished through effective marketing within a national distribution system and through shrewd intuition for what would attract the public. During the half century between formation of the partnership and its demise, the firm issued more than seven thousand images, many of which had print runs in the thousands. Both house artists and freelancers furnished designs, which were customarily printed in black and white, and then usually hand colored. This work normally was performed in the shop by about a dozen young women, who applied a single watercolor hue each as a print was passed along. However, by the 1860s the firm had begun to experiment with chromolithography, using colored inks in the printing process. Most often these images were only partly printed in color and finished by hand. With few exceptions, Currier & Ives did not produce true chromolithographs until after Currier retired in 1880. Fanny *Palmer was the most important staff artist, while Arthur *Tait, George *Durrie, and Eastman *Johnson numbered among painters who also contributed designs. After the deaths of the partners, the business continued in the hands of their sons until 1907.

Curry, John Steuart (1897–1946). Painter and printmaker. Along with Thomas Hart *Benton and Grant *Wood, Curry led the regionalist thrust of the *American Scene movement. Like them, he believed that art should be rooted in the lives of ordinary people, although he had a taste for violence and melodrama. Because he strove for immediacy and artlessness, his work is formally and theoretically less sophisticated than theirs. Yet, it evidences a truer sense of identity with common people and a more heartfelt concern for social justice. Born into a farming family near Dunavent in eastern Kansas, Curry studied briefly at the Kansas City Art Institute before enrolling in 1916 for two years at the School of the Art Institute of Chicago. He spent the academic year 1918–19 at Geneva College in the southwestern Pennsylvania town of Beaver Falls, then went to New York where he worked as an illustrator until 1926. From 1924, he lived mostly in Westport, Connecticut. During a year in Paris, he was most impressed by the spacious and dramatic art of seventeenth-century Flemish painter Peter Paul Rubens. Curry returned in 1927 determined to create an art independent of European precedents. Turning to the world he had known in childhood, he soon exhibited his first major work, *Baptism in Kansas* (Whitney Museum, 1928). Still among his best-known paintings, it depicts a farmyard immersion ceremony attended by a crowd of faithful in their Sunday best. This painting gained him critical attention, confirmed his new mission, and nurtured nascent critical and popular interest in midwestern regionalism. Suggesting Curry's particularly acute feeling for the relationship between man and the landscape, *Tornado over Kansas* (Muskegon [Michigan] Museum of Art, 1935) shows a farm family rushing for their storm cellar as a tornado advances across the prairie. Among few regionalists to take particular note of African Americans, Curry painted a number of works that depict blacks in contemporary or historical situations. He also engaged the life of abolitionist John Brown, notably in *The Tragic Prelude*, a mural of 1938–39 in the Kansas state capitol in Topeka. Other mural commissions came to Curry through the *federal art projects. In 1936 he moved permanently to Madison, Wisconsin, to serve as artist-in-residence at the state university. In this rural setting, he often turned to pure landscape, as in the expansive *Wisconsin Landscape* (Metropolitan Museum, 1938–39), with scudding clouds adding atmospheric drama.

Curtis, Edward Sheriff (1868–1952). Photographer. Dedicating his life's work to a detailed and impassioned record of American Indians, Curtis complemented his ethnographic impulse with refined artistry. Working within the *pictorialist aesthetic of his day, he produced sensuous, luxurious photographs that convey the Indians' spirituality and their tragic plight as a supposedly vanishing people. Born in Whitewater, Wisconsin, Curtis lived as a youngster in Cordova, Minnesota, learned the essentials of his craft from published manuals, and entered the photographic profession in a St. Paul studio. In 1887 he moved with his family to Sidney (now Port Orchard) on Puget Sound and four years later settled in Seattle. While practicing as a portrait and landscape photographer, he nurtured an interest in Indians by accompanying expeditions to Alaska in 1899 and to Montana in 1900. Soon he had conceived a vast project to record indigenous peoples, their customs, and ceremonies. Like earlier nineteenth-century documentarians, such as painter George *Catlin and photographers who accompanied western exploratory expeditions, Curtis was sincerely motivated by the desire to document the imperiled Indian way of life. But his concerns were by no means purely anthropological. He also sought commercial success in a market already saturated with tribal images, for by the turn of the century the American public was broadly enthralled by the West's landscape, its cowboys, and its Indians. Curtis succeeded in this market by creating aesthetically superior images that emphasize the Indians' heroism, psychic integrity, unity with nature, and tragic fate, qualities that the public had already widely come to accept. He consistently presented his Indians as living representatives of a mythic past untouched by European contact, although in fact many of the Indians he photographed were partly assimilated. To bolster his vision, he often cropped and manipulated his negatives and even posed Indians in borrowed costumes. Nevertheless, Curtis created an artistically coherent vision, which appealed to the period's nostalgia for pre-modern cultures. Between 1907 and 1930 Curtis doggedly labored on his masterwork, *The North American Indian*, covering about eighty tribes. Its illustrations include portraits, usually soft-focus close-ups, and views of traditional activities. President Theodore Roosevelt gave his encouragement and wrote the introduction. J. P. *Morgan provided early financing. Curtis himself supported the endeavor by producing sumptuous individual prints for sale to the public. These included many produced by his "orotone" process, which used gold to provide luminous richness to photographs printed on glass. When the *Indian* project was completed, he had published twenty volumes of text, which included 1,500 small gravure illustrations, as well as more than seven hundred large gravures in twenty accompanying portfolio volumes. Curtis also made a film, *In the Land of the Headhunters* (1914), depicting a staged Northwest Coast whale hunt. He died in Los Angeles, where he had lived for some years. His brother, photographer **Asahel Curtis** (1874–1941), enjoyed a successful career in Seattle, where he recorded individuals, local events, and, most notably, the region's majestic scenery.

Dabo, Leon (1865–1960). Painter. Known for delicately toned, often misty landscapes indebted to the art of James Abbott McNeill *Whistler, Dabo also painted floral compositions. As well, he adorned ecclesiastical interiors with decorative, figurative murals and stained glass windows. Possibly born in Paris before his parents moved to Detroit, Leon Scott Dabo worked in New York in the mid-1880s with John *La Farge before sailing to Europe. He studied for three years in Paris, then lived in Italy until 1892, when he settled in New York. In the characteristically *tonalist *Sun and Mist* (Montclair [New Jersey] Art Museum, 1909), vaguely defined forms of low hills appear before an expanse of silvery water. Sunlight plays on its surface from behind clouds in the sky beyond. In 1913 Dabo exhibited in the *Armory Show. During World War I, he served in the U.S. Army and between the wars lived for some time in Paris before returning permanently to New York. His brother, painter **Theodore Scott Dabo** (1877–1928), also studied in Paris and worked in a similar style.

Dada, New York. *See* NEW YORK DADA.

Daguerreotype. *See* PHOTOGRAPHY, AMERICAN.

Daingerfield, Elliott (1859–1932). Painter. Also a poet and art writer. Dedicated to revealing spiritual truths through art, he aspired to this goal in disparate subjects, including landscapes, mysterious figural allegories, and still lifes. Stylistically, too, his work shows considerable variety, ranging from relatively straightforward, romantically tinged description to imaginative fantasy. Particularly in his late, memory-laden landscapes, he achieved richly expressive brushwork, often heavily scumbled and luxuriantly hued. A leading spokesman for contemporary *tonalist and romantic painting, Daingerfield published monographs on George *Inness (1911) and Ralph *Blakelock (1914), as well as many articles. Born in Harper's Ferry, Virginia (now West Virginia), he grew up in Fayetteville, North Carolina. After preliminary art studies in the South, in 1880 he arrived in New York. He worked with figure painter Walter Satterlee (1844–1908), studied intermittently at the *Art Students League, and became acquainted with Inness. He did not pursue rigorous formal training, however, and until 1897 did not visit Europe. Grounded in admiration for the *Barbizon approach and for Inness's work, his painting of the 1880s focused on rural *genre, which elicited comparisons with Jean-François Millet's French peasant subjects, along with landscape, a preoccupation throughout his career. From 1886 many views

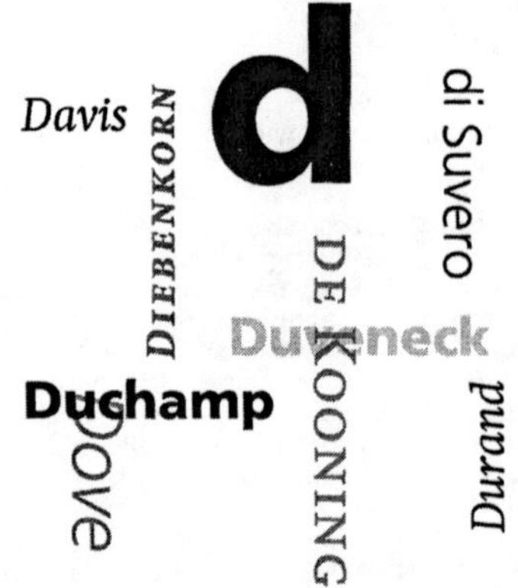

reflect the topography of North Carolina's scenic Blue Ridge Mountains around Blowing Rock, where he subsequently maintained a home. During the 1890s he painted religious subjects and began to create mysterious visions, suggesting the appeal of symbolism. In late 1910 the first of several visits to the Grand Canyon initiated a series of expressive interpretations of the area's dramatic scenery, as well as symbolic inventions incorporating figural elements. Also in the 1910s and into the early 1920s, he continued to paint intimate views, such as the glowingly poetic *Sunset Glory* (also known as *Carolina Sunlight*; Morris Museum of Art, Augusta, Georgia, c. 1915). In its free brushwork, ornamental patterning, and luminous glow, it intensifies the mystical power of Inness's late landscapes. A second trip abroad, in 1924, produced a number of scenes inspired by Venetian motifs. The following year, his health began to fail, curtailing his ability to paint. He died in his New York studio. Figurative sculptor **Marjorie Daingerfield** (1900–1977), his daughter, worked in marble and bronze. Born in New York, she trained there at Solon *Borglum's school and the Grand Central School of Art. She became the wife of J. Louis Lundean.

Dallin, Cyrus (1861–1944). Sculptor. Known particularly for depictions of American Indians, he also portrayed historical figures and other subjects. Born in Springville, near Provo, Utah, Cyrus Edwin Dallin as a boy was already familiar with local Indians. In 1880 he went to Boston, where he worked in Truman *Bartlett's studio for two years before establishing his own. He had already found some success with Indian themes before 1888, when he departed for two years of additional training in

Paris. After his return to the United States, Dallin lived in Utah and Philadelphia. In 1896 he once again headed for Paris to study at the École des Beaux-Arts. Four years later he settled permanently in suburban Boston. During his initial Paris sojourn, Dallin created his first widely acclaimed work, *A Signal of Peace* (Lincoln Park, Chicago, 1889–90), one of several monumental equestrian Indian subjects. Appealing to the period's fascination with the "Noble Savage," often thought to be doomed by fate to vanish, it displays Dallin's characteristically dignified and sympathetic approach to aboriginal Americans, as well as his careful attention to ethnographic detail. Another warrior on horseback, *Appeal to the Great Spirit* (Huntington Avenue entrance, Museum of Fine Arts, Boston, 1909), remains his best-known work. This emotionally affecting figure arches backward to face the sky, his hands extended to either side in a gesture of supplication. His posture implies the vulnerability of a spiritually intact but overwhelmed people.

Darger, Henry (1892–1973). Painter. A troubled recluse, he is best known for large, scroll-like watercolors (sometimes double-sided) that feature little girls in scenes of peril. These narratives elaborate scenes from the artist's fifteen-volume fiction manuscript, "The Realms of the Unreal." Intended meanings of individual works remain uncertain, but the naked or prettily dressed girls seem to function as emblems of vulnerability in a threat-filled world. Darger's storybook style underscores their innocence and provides a counterpoint of fantasy to the menace, real or implied, that drives the action. In addition to these works, Darger also created individual paintings of other subjects and wrote extensively: journals, fiction, and a highly imaginative autobiography. Collage, pencil drawing, and tracings of appropriated elements often supplement his luminous, pastel washes. Darger's art and writings emanated from a strange, lonely life. Probably born in Chicago, he lived there nearly all his life. His mother died when he was four. At eight, when his father's health began to fail (he died five years later), the boy was placed in a Catholic children's home where he continued to perform well academically. However, because his behavior was odd and perhaps disruptive, Darger was transferred to a home for retarded children in Lincoln, Illinois. When he was seventeen, he made his way back to Chicago where he worked at menial jobs, attended daily Mass, and lived alone for the rest of his life. From 1932 until his final months in a charitable nursing home, Darger rented a room from photographer, painter, and designer Nathan Lerner (1913–97). During his final illness, Lerner recognized the special nature of his tenant's efforts and initiated arrangements to preserve a legacy that might otherwise have been lost.

Darley, Felix Octavius Carr (1822–88). Draftsman and watercolor painter. The foremost American illustrator of the mid-nineteenth century, he was as popular as he was prolific. With his attractive compositions, vivid narratives, and pungent character portrayals, he almost single-handedly established illustration as a legitimate branch of art. He is known particularly for book illustrations, which accompanied texts by many of the period's best-known authors, including Washington Irving, James Fenimore Cooper, Harriet Beecher Stowe, Edgar Allen Poe, and Henry Wadsworth Longfellow, as well as Shakespeare and Charles Dickens. He also contributed to important American periodicals and designed bank notes. Born in Philadelphia, he worked there as an illustrator by the time he was twenty. In 1848 he moved to New York, where his versatility and productivity quickly established his preeminence. In 1859, by now well established, he relocated permanently to a country estate in Claymont, Delaware. Darley's most distinctive and appealing drawings rely on linear contours, which so effectively create form and space that he used almost no shading. Although this style was indebted to the example of English draftsman John Flaxman, Darley's exhibits greater fluidity and lyrical feeling. The flat patterning inherent in this approach made it particularly suitable for the printed page. However, Darley also produced highly finished but more conventional drawings, which demonstrate his mastery of old master chiaroscuro techniques for creating volume and perspective.

Darley, Jane Cooper Sully. *See* SULLY, THOMAS.

Dasburg, Andrew (1887–1979). Painter and draftsman. A contributor to adventurous color abstraction of the 1910s, he built his mature reputation on landscapes, still lifes, and portraits combining acute observation with structural techniques learned from the work of Cézanne and the cubists. Born in Paris, Andrew Michael Dasburg lived for three years in Germany before he arrived in New York in 1892. He was later naturalized as a U.S. citizen. In 1902 he began his formal studies at the *Art Students League, where Kenyon *Cox numbered among his teachers. He also studied with Robert *Henri. During the several years following a 1909–10 sojourn in France, he pushed cubism close to pure abstraction in a few particularly daring works. He also made a brief detour into a form of color abstraction related to *synchromism. In 1916 Dasburg abandoned his colorful expressionistic modernism to begin forging a personal style reinvigorating the classical tradition as received through Cézanne. Typically, warmth of tone and a deft touch animate the rigorously structured, pared down *New Mexican Village* (Museum of Fine Arts, Santa Fe, 1926). In spare landscape drawings of the 1950s and 1960s, he pushed rigorously toward formal essentials and expressive marking, approaching aspects of contemporary *abstract expressionism. Between 1906 and the late 1920s, Dasburg regularly worked at *Woodstock. After extended visits to the Southwest beginning in 1918, he settled permanently in *Taos in 1930. With a discerning eye for unconventional expression, Dasburg figured importantly in popularizing American Indian art and instrumentally in bringing attention to John *Kane. At his death, he was thought to be the last surviving exhibitor in the *Armory Show. His first wife, a financially independent, freethinking "New Woman," sculptor Grace Mott Johnson (1882–1967), born in New York, studied at the Art Students League primarily with Gutzon *Borglum, but worked also with Hermon *MacNeil and James Earle *Fraser. She and Dasburg married in London in 1909, on a side trip from France, but divorced in 1922. A specialist in animal subjects, she, too, exhibited in the Armory Show and participated in Woodstock activities. Although she visited Dasburg in New Mexico, she never resided there. Later among the earliest agitators for the civil rights of African Americans, she became relatively inactive as an artist during the final two decades of her life. From 1922 until 1928, Dasburg lived with sculptor, painter, and theater professional Ida Rauh (1877–1970), another feminist, who had been married from 1911 until 1922 to Max Eastman, crusading editor of *The *Masses* and, subsequently, *The Liberator*.

Daum, Howard. *See* INDIAN SPACE PAINTING.

Davidge, Clara Potter. *See* TAYLOR, HENRY FITCH.

Davidson, Bruce (1933–). Photographer and filmmaker. Specializing in documentary work, he often records socially marginalized people, frequently offering, as have Robert *Frank and Danny *Lyon, a darker and more complex view of American life than is customarily acknowledged. Born in the Chicago suburb of Oak Park, he began to work in photography as a teenager. He earned a degree in photography at the Rochester Institute of Technology and then continued for a year of graduate study at Yale University, where he worked with Joseph *Albers, Herbert *Matter, and Alexey *Brodovitch. Following his discharge in 1957 from service in the U.S. Army, the next year he joined *Magnum and worked as a freelance photographer based in New York and Paris. A teenage gang in Brooklyn, Welsh miners, and New York's Verrazano Narrows Bridge under construction numbered among early subjects. Between 1961 and 1965 he documented southern poverty and the struggle for civil rights. In the late 1960s he worked for two years with a large-format camera and a tape recorder in Spanish Harlem on one of his finest achievements. His selection of images from this project, *East 100th Street* (1970), comprises rich and detailed black-and-white prints that record with dignity and sensitivity local residents and their slum homes. For the 1986 book *Subway*, he photographed in color on New York's underground trains. In the 1990s he returned to black and white for the images published in *Central Park* (1995), examining the park and its diverse visitors through all seasons. In a departure from more usual interests, his *Portraits* (1999) brings together studies of celebrities ranging from Samuel Beckett to Newt Gingrich. Davidson's other books include *Bruce Davidson: Photographs* (1978) and *Brooklyn Gang: Summer 1959* (1998). Becoming interested in filmmaking in the late 1960s, he made *Living Off the Land* (1970) and *Zoo Doctor* (1971) before dramatizing two Isaac Bashevis Singer stories in the prize-winning *Isaac Singer's Nightmare and Mrs. Pupko's Beard* (1973). He lives in New York.

Davidson, Jo (1883–1952). Sculptor. The vigorous naturalism of his portraits suited his interest in individual personality. Adept at both carving and modeling, in either technique Davidson captured facial verisimilitude with great sensitivity to flesh as well as bone structure, while also suggesting individual character through facial expression. He portrayed world leaders of his time, including Woodrow Wilson (1916), Mahatma Gandhi (1931), and on several occasions, Franklin D. Roosevelt. Ignace Paderewski (1920), Joseph Conrad (1916), and André Gide (1931) numbered among numerous creative luminaries who sat for him. He lived much of his adult life in France, although he frequently visited the United States and resided during World War II in Bucks County, Pennsylvania. A New York native, Joseph Davidson studied at the *Art Students League and for a few months attended classes at Yale University. In 1903 he became a studio assistant for Hermon *MacNeil. Four years later, he departed for Paris, where he pursued formal training only briefly, imbibed the spirit of Rodin's work, and socialized with the community of progressive American artists. Although his art remained relatively untouched by avant-garde movements, it was considered modern in its day because it deviated from academic practice. His early work includes allegorical figures, which later recurred occasionally. A lively early portrait of John *Marin (1908) suggests why portraiture became his mainstay. Davidson exhibited in the *Armory Show and by the end of World War I had acquired an international reputation. In his desire to leave a historical record of his time, he sought out many of his sitters. Between 1918 and 1920, he executed the fourteen likenesses of his Peace Conference series taken from major participants in the World War I treaty negotiations, including Georges Clemenceau (1920) and General John J. Pershing (1919). At the height of his fame, Davidson portrayed a vast range of celebrities, ranging from Will Rogers (1938) to Albert Einstein (1934) and Frank Sinatra (1946). Among his most famous works is a life-size, seated rendition of a Buddhalike Gertrude *Stein (1922). Because they could be editioned from rapidly produced clay models, most of his portraits are bronze casts. He also frequently made variants of a specific image, such as the Gertrude Stein, in more than one size. He died near Tours, at the estate that had been his primary residence since 1926. In 1951 he published a memoir, *Between Sittings: An Informal Autobiography*. His second wife, painter and sculptor Florence Gertrude Lucius (1887/88–1962), studied at the Art Students League and with Émile-Antoine Bourdelle in Paris. She married Davidson in 1941 and died in New York.

Davies, Arthur Bowen (1862–1928). Painter and printmaker. Although best known for dreamy landscapes inhabited by nude figures, Davies was always interested in new ideas and in a wide range of historic and contemporary styles. In 1908 he exhibited with The *Eight. As president of the *Association of American Painters and Sculptors, he spearheaded the organization's effort to mount a major exhibition of contemporary art, the 1913 *Armory Show, which included six of his own works. Along with Walt *Kuhn, he selected most of the European entries and was therefore largely responsible for the particular scope and variety of modern art that first confronted the American public. Davies was born in Utica, New York. He moved with his family in 1878 to Chicago, where he began his art studies at the Academy of Design. During a two-year hiatus, he worked as a draftsman in Mexico before resuming his studies in 1883 at the new Art Institute. In 1886 he moved to New York, where he continued his training at the Gotham Art School and the *Art Students League and worked as an illustrator before making his first trip to Europe in 1893. Indebted to symbolism, tradition, and the decorative style of French painter Puvis de Chavannes, his softly romantic art evokes at its best an innocent arcadia. In the mysterious *Unicorns* (Metropolitan Museum, 1906), three mythical beasts tenderly confront two draped maidens on the shore of a luminous lake. After the Armory Show, he briefly experimented with cubist form, which he superficially applied in bright colors to human figures. From 1924 he painted landscapes for part of each year in Europe. He died in Florence. Later, it became known that the inconsistencies in his life as an artist paralleled contradictions in his private life: for more than twenty years, he secretly headed two households, with wife on their Hudson River Valley farm, mistress in New York, and offspring in both locations.

Davis, Charles Harold (1856–1933). Painter. A landscape specialist, he is known especially for views of the Connecticut countryside. He also painted French scenes and early in his career produced figure paintings. His landscapes demonstrate particular attention to skies and cloud formations. Born in Amesbury, Massachusetts, north of Boston, he painted in his free time after leaving school at fifteen to work for a carriage maker. He attended drawing classes in Boston before beginning his professional training there in 1877 at the School of the Museum of Fine Arts. Subsequently he resided for nearly a decade in France. He worked at the Académie Julian in Paris during his first year but afterward painted scenes of Normandy and the *Barbizon area. Upon his return to the United States in 1890, he settled permanently in Mystic, on the Connecticut shore. Until the mid-1890s, his intimate, softly lit, Barbizon-inspired views contributed to the vogue for *tonalism. Later, this meditative and subtle approach gave way to impressionist interests, as his brushwork became more vigorous and his colors brightened.

Davis, Gene. *See* WASHINGTON COLOR SCHOOL.

Davis, Stuart (1892–1964). Painter and printmaker. The most important American painter to emerge between the world wars, he invented a cosmopolitan and strikingly modern idiom attuned to American life. Although

Davis's bright, semi-abstract compositions derive from cubism, the rhythms of these syncopated ensembles echo with his enthusiasm for jazz. Their iconography reflects the vernacular landscape, ranging from urban commercial culture to traditional New England villages. Davis also played a major role in the art life of New York for many years. He actively participated in 1930s politics, taught for a decade at the New School for Social Research (now New School), and wrote broadmindedly about art. He reacted appreciatively to the work of artists as different as Glenn O. *Coleman and surrealist Salvador Dalí. With respect to his own paintings, he articulated a clearheaded purpose: to give a spiritually authentic response to the experience of living in the America of his day. His work, he believed, extended the realism of his youthful art and translated the concerns of the *American Scene movement into a language more appropriate to the modern era. He emphasized that paintings possess their own reality and should not be expected to mirror the physical world.

Born in Philadelphia, as a child he moved with his family to East Orange, New Jersey, not far from Newark. Davis left high school there in 1910 to study for three years in New York with Robert *Henri, who imbued Davis with an anti-academic viewpoint and a belief in the artist's social responsibility. In 1913 Davis showed five watercolors in the *Armory Show, which kindled his interest in modernism and initiated his thinking about the autonomy of art. Already working as a magazine illustrator, in the same year he joined the staff of *The* **Masses*, where John *Sloan served as art editor. After two summers in *Provincetown, on Cape Cod, where he became an "addict of the New England coast," as he put it, in 1915 he went to Gloucester, Massachusetts, which seasonally drew him back most years until 1934. In 1918–19 he served in the U.S. Army. After he left *The Masses* in 1916, Davis's early *Ashcan style gradually gave way to modern impulses, as he experimented with unnaturalistic color, odd viewpoints, and painterly textures. A vigorously executed 1919 *Self-Portrait* (Amon Carter Museum, Fort Worth, Texas) demonstrates a debt to van Gogh's work in its thickly applied paint and striking compression of volume. In the early 1920s Davis began an apprenticeship to cubism, starting with a series of highly original still life paintings. These forecast his mature style in their combination of flattened, fragmented design and mundane subjects. Within the abstracted formal arrangement of *Lucky Strike* (Museum of Modern Art, 1921), he emblazoned the name of the cigarette, along with other words and numbers adapted from its packaging. Although the image is painted, it resembles a cubist collage. The imitation of advertising typography here is an innovation that Davis developed as an essential aspect of his career repertoire. Additionally, the playful exuberance of this piece suggests an American brashness that exceeds the boundaries of the artist's starting point in cubist taste for witty play with unexpected materials. Resolving in 1927 to paint only an electric fan, a rubber glove, and an eggbeater, in the disciplined Eggbeater series produced during the following year, he achieved a personal analysis of cubist form and space. In 1928 he left for fourteen months in Paris, where he delighted in interpreting the city with a formal and expressive range that forecasts his later, more intricate individual style. There he also completed his first extended engagement with printmaking, producing twelve lithographs. Subsequently, he intermittently produced about a dozen additional prints, mostly also lithographs

Indicating the depth of his commitment to social issues, after his permanent return to New York he soon focused on art-related political work. In 1934 he was elected president of the Artists' Union, and in 1935–36 he edited its journal, *Art Front*. For many months in 1935 he worked with a few other artists toward the establishment the following year of the *American Artists' Congress, which he led as national secretary and chairman until his resignation over policy issues in 1940. Davis completed relatively little new work during this activist period, except for two murals he painted under the auspices of the *federal art projects, which employed him from the end of 1933 until 1939. The 1938 *Swing Landscape* (Indiana University Art Museum, Bloomington; executed for New York's Williamsburg Housing Project) numbers among few nonrepresentational government-sponsored murals. Representing Davis's most exhilarating work of the 1930s, this riotous conglomeration of posterlike shapes, both abstract and representational, celebrates American life. Shapes and vivid colors lifted from both commercial culture and the natural landscape combine in a rambunctious, visually stimulating frenzy. After this, Davis never looked back, building on the strengths of this composition in a coherent and consistent body of work that varied little in its stylistic devices or expressive reach. No other American's work so vividly and directly represented a living link from the early days of American modernism to postwar interests in large-scale abstraction and in imagery originating in popular culture. Nevertheless, although artists as different as Arshile *Gorky and Donald *Judd admired his paintings

Davis's easily recognizable individual style inspired little imitation. Perhaps the very qualities that make Davis's accomplishment so appealing worked against it after World War II. His sureness, optimism, elegance, lack of irony, uncritical acceptance of American life, and disregard for psychological self-revelation no longer interested many artists. A relatively brief autobiography, *Stuart Davis*, appeared in 1945.

Dawson, Manierre (1887–1969). Painter and sculptor. An early contributor to abstraction, he flourished as an artist for only a few years. Born in Chicago, he trained there as a civil engineer. Upon graduation in 1909 from the Armour Institute of Technology (now Illinois Institute of Technology), he joined the architectural firm of Holabird and Roche. On his own, he already had been painting for several years, trying out varied stylistic approaches. Early Whistlerian landscapes preceded compositions featuring insubstantial nudes in outdoor settings. Evidence of Cézanne's influence soon followed. Independently, he formulated the idea that art, like music, could be separated from representation. He apparently began to paint abstractly in the spring of 1910, even before departing later that year for a five-month tour of Europe. *Prognostic* (Milwaukee Art Center, 1910) suggests Kandinsky's contemporaneous abstractions from landscape, which Dawson could not have known. Subsequent rhythmic compositions suggest knowledge of cubism and sometimes anticipate aspects of futurism. In 1911–12 he produced notable semi-abstract figural studies, such as *Lucrece* (John and Mable Ringling Museum of Art, Sarasota, Florida, 1911). During these years, he exhibited in several progressive art shows, including the Chicago installation of the 1913 *Armory Show. In the spring of 1914, the twenty-six-year-old artist moved to a farm in Ludington, Michigan. There, living in isolation, he often could not afford to buy art supplies. He continued to paint sporadically, as well as to experiment with sculpture, but his career as a potentially significant artist had ended. He later moved to Sarasota, Florida, where he died.

Day, F. Holland (1864–1933). Photographer. A major figure in the *pictorialist movement, he notably starred as Jesus in striking interpretations of the life of Christ. His romantic, often softly focused images also include landscapes, portraits, and dreamy figural compositions. Day's control over effects of natural light, his delicately balanced compositional harmonies, and the originality of his vision complement his dedication to beauty. In the late 1890s Day audaciously turned to Christian subjects popular in late nineteenth-century painting, devoting in particular the summer of 1898 to producing more than two hundred religious photographs. The images include scenes such as the Crucifixion, the Descent from the Cross, and the Resurrection, along with seven images illustrating the last words of Christ. These close-ups display his own bony, bearded face, surmounted by long hair and a crown of thorns, in a variety of attitudes suggesting suffering and resignation. In portraits, Day particularly pictured exotic individuals, including American Indians, African Americans, and a protégé, the photogenic Lebanese-American poet and artist Kahlil Gibran (1883–1931). Especially after 1900, Day composed many classical idylls featuring young men, often nude, in natural settings. Born in Norwood, Massachusetts, Fred Holland Day grew up there and in nearby Boston and was for the most part privately educated. He began to photograph in the late 1880s as an adjunct to his literary interests, particularly a devotion to John Keats. On frequent trips to England, he assembled a vast collection of Keats material, promoted establishment of a memorial, and photographed sites associated with his life. In Boston during the 1890s he attracted a circle of aesthetes: artists, writers, and musicians attuned to the international fashion of art for art's sake and to rarified psychic and occult pursuits. Between 1893 and 1899, as a partner in Copeland and Day, he published nearly a hundred finely designed books in the spirit of the *Arts and Crafts movement. In 1900 he arranged a huge London exhibition of recent American art photography, which for the first time brought together the leaders of the movement in a high-profile venue and successfully challenged British preeminence. Alfred *Stieglitz's refusal to send his work signaled the rivalry already distancing art photography's two leaders, whose personalities and aesthetic goals were incompatible. Later, spurning Stieglitz's invitation, Day remained the most prominent pictorial photographer outside the *Photo-Secession. For about twenty years until 1917, Day usually summered in Maine, where he eventually built a large house on Georgetown Island. In 1904 his Boston studio burned, destroying nearly all work still in his possession as well as his collection of Japanese artifacts. In subsequent years, the pace of his photographic work diminished. He rarely photographed after 1917, when he retired into seclusion at his family home in Norwood. Adopting the lifestyle of an invalid, he died there sixteen years later.

Dearth, Henry Golden (1864–1918). Painter. Born in Bristol, Rhode Island, as a young man he worked with a local painter in Waterbury, Connecticut. After about four years in Paris, where he studied at the École des Beaux-Arts, he settled in New York in 1887. However, he maintained a summer outpost near Boulogne, in Montreuil-sur-Mer, where in many years he spent several months. Often his moody, richly worked landscapes depict sites nearby in Normandy. Reflecting *Barbizon precedents, they suggest as well his aesthetic affinity with *tonalism. *An Old Church at Montreuil* (Smithsonian American Art Museum, c. 1906–7) characteristically displays intimate scale, gentle harmony of tone, and romantic appreciation of nature. In the last years of his life, Dearth responded to impressionist and even postimpressionist fashions with high-keyed color, heavy impasto, and compressed space. He continued to paint landscapes, some including figures, but also produced decorative still lifes that often incorporate the medieval and Asian art objects he avidly collected. He died in New York.

Deas, Charles (1818–67). Painter. Known primarily for dramatic scenes of western life, he often pictured danger or conflict, as in *The Death Struggle* (Shelburne [Vermont] Museum, 1845), perhaps his best-known painting. Here a frontiersman and an Indian grapple in combat, even as their horses plunge from a cliff, taking both to certain death. Violent movement and the sensation of deep space below the plunging steeds reinforce the terror of the moment. Deas helped to define the independent, action-oriented western male as a mythic American type. Born in Philadelphia, he grew up there and in New York State. With little formal instruction, as a young man he nevertheless gained recognition in New York for *genre and literary scenes. Probably inspired by the example of George *Catlin, in 1840 he traveled west. For the next seven years, he made his headquarters in St. Louis, while also traveling to record his impressions of Indians, trappers, hunters, and other frontiersmen. These descriptive drawings and watercolors generally document his observations with factual directness that contrasts with the exaggerated emotionalism of his romanticized studio narratives. Shortly after Deas returned permanently to New York, he suffered a breakdown that effectively ended his artistic career. For most of the next twenty years, he remained hospitalized for mental illness.

DeCamp, Joseph Rodefer (1858–1923). Painter. Known mainly for figural compositions, he also painted landscapes. Born in Cincinnati, he resided during most of his professional life in Boston. There he achieved popularity with elegant, polished portraits and figure studies picturing upper-class women at leisure. As in *The Guitar Player* (Museum of Fine Arts, Boston, 1908), spare compositions, attentively rendered details, alluring light, and psychological inwardness combine in an austere aestheticism. Like many Boston artists of his day, he responded to Vermeer's example in the formation of his mature style. His relatively fewer landscapes reflect a looser, more impressionist approach. Most of his extant works postdate a 1904 studio fire that destroyed almost everything still in his possession. An influential teacher at Boston's School of the Museum of Fine Arts and elsewhere, he also numbered among the founding members of The *Ten. Following early studies in Cincinnati, in 1878 DeCamp began his training at the Royal Academy in Munich, where he soon came under Frank *Duveneck's spell. The following year DeCamp numbered among several high-spirited "Duveneck boys" who accompanied their mentor to Italy. After working in Florence and Venice until 1881, he lived in Cincinnati and Cleveland before settling in the Boston area in 1884. There Edmund *Tarbell's work affected his developing style. In 1909 he traveled in Europe and North Africa, and from 1911 he regularly summered in Vinalhaven, Maine. Following illness and two surgeries in a Boston hospital during the fall of 1922, he died after a few weeks in Boca Grande, Florida, where his daughter **Sally DeCamp** (1892/93–?) (Mrs. Donald Moffat) resided. Born in suburban Boston, she was a portrait painter.

DeCarava, Roy (1919–). Photographer. Drawing subjects from his African-American community in Harlem, he has extracted a deeply felt and poetic vision. His work typically displays rich tonalities emphasizing velvety blacks and grays, luminous moments shimmering in mysterious shadows, and empathetic responses to individuals, always treated with seriousness and dignity. Although he believes that the black artist has a responsibility to speak for his people, DeCarava rarely emphasizes oppression. Rather, he focuses on his subjects' innate worth as human beings whose complex psychology responds to their social position in white-dominated society. He has also photographed urban life more generally, as well as landscapes. A lifelong New Yorker, DeCarava studied painting at Cooper Union from 1938 to 1940. During the following two years, he pursued printmaking at the Harlem Community Art Center, where Augusta *Savage provided encouragement. During World War II he served in the U.S. Army. He first used photography as an aid to painting, but turned seriously to the medium in 1947. Supported by Edward *Steichen, in 1952 he became the first black photographer to win a Guggenheim fellowship. For two years in the mid-1950s, he served as the founding director of A Photographer's Gallery, one of few galleries then showing fine art photography. Around the same time he came to wider public attention upon publication of *Sweet Flypaper of Youth* (1955), with text by Langston Hughes. In 1956 he embarked on a long-term series of jazz portraits. "Coltrane No. 24" (1963) pictures the musician's body emerging from deep shadow to fill the picture's surface. Light falls primarily on his face, hands, and saxophone, where it glints with a slight blur to suggest the soulful resonance of his music. In the 1960s DeCarava recorded the period's momentous agitation for civil rights with a more objective and less moody attitude than was previously common in his work. This less inward and symbolic approach continued in some later photographs, such as "Asphalt Workers" (1975), a masterfully composed frieze of black laborers. A formally sophisticated, objective record of street activity, it also confirms the implicit value of the workers' physical effort and their moral integrity. DeCarava has taught at New York's Hunter College since 1978.

Decker, Joseph (1853–1924). Painter. Admired primarily for still lifes, he also painted *genre scenes, landscapes, and occasional portraits (including several of his pet squirrel). Decker's life is not well documented, and his career as an artist seems to have followed a bumpy trajectory, as he switched styles and subjects. Success in his lifetime eluded him, and even before his death in a hospital charity ward, his work had been forgotten. Yet, he is admired today for idiosyncratic still life paintings in two different styles. Born in Württemberg, Decker arrived in the United States with his family in 1867. Soon they settled in Brooklyn, where the artist thereafter resided, although he later made several extended visits to his native Germany. As a young man, Decker worked as a housepainter and sign painter while taking evening classes for about three years at the *National Academy of Design. In 1879 he enrolled for a year's study at the Munich academy, where he mastered a hard, closely observed realism. The most distinctive of his subsequent still lifes depict unnaturally abundant fruits still attached to tree boughs. Intensely observed individual fruits and leaves disquietingly crowd together in shallow, compressed, and seemingly discontinuous spaces, while compositions seem, as in cropped photographs, to spill beyond the frame. He probably knew the still lifes of William Michael *Harnett and fellow Brooklynite William Mason *Brown, as well as those of Levi Wells Prentice (1851–1935), who also lived in that borough and painted fruit in a photographically detailed style. However, Decker's works of this time remain singular, perhaps as much indebted to commercial horticultural illustrations as to the accomplishments of his fellow artists. In the 1890s he completely altered his style, adopting a soft, impressionist-influenced brushstroke and a preference for the generalized atmosphere he admired in the work of George *Inness. Still lifes remained his most noteworthy contributions, with characteristic examples clustering a few softly glowing fruits on a white tablecloth. They suggest the period's renewed appreciation for still lifes by French eighteenth-century painter Jean-Baptiste-Siméon Chardin. The most original, such as *Twelve Plums* (Yale University Art Gallery, 1896), also invoke the spare concentration of Chinese or Japanese art, with which Decker is known to have had some familiarity. His poetic landscapes of these years vaporize form in misty atmospheres. Decker ceased exhibiting his work in the 1890s and apparently did not paint for more than a decade before his death.

De Creeft, José (1884–1982). Sculptor. Known particularly for amply proportioned figural works carved from wood and stone, in developing his formal vocabulary he drew on pre-Columbian, African, and other non-Western sources, as well as modern tendencies. He also worked in other media, notably hammered metal, but shunned indirect methods of casting from modeled clay. With its elegant stylization, rounded forms, and varied surface textures, the black granite *Maya* (Wichita [Kansas] Art Museum, 1937) demonstrates the artist's gracious adaptation of indigenous Mesoamerican precedents to contemporary expression. Born in Guadalajara, de Creeft moved with his family to Barcelona in 1888. As a teenager he modeled figurines and apprenticed in a bronze foundry before entering the Madrid workshop of the government's official sculptor in 1900. He also studied with the internationally known painter Ignacio Zuloaga. In 1905 de Creeft left for additional training in Paris, where he became acquainted with Picasso and other modern artists. In 1915 he redirected his interests toward direct carving emphasizing the innate beauty of materials. Subsequently, through the 1920s he also experimented with other methods, even including assemblages of found objects. After working on a commission for two years on Majorca (where he returned frequently until 1937), in 1929 de Creeft emigrated to the United States. (He became a citizen in 1940.) Within months, he settled in New York, where he quickly found recognition for his accomplishments. In 1936 he numbered among founding members of the *American Artists' Congress and in 1940, of the *Federation of Modern Painters and Sculptors. He taught regularly almost until the end of his life. The mature aesthetic he had evolved through considerable experimentation remained stable during his American years, as he concentrated on single figures or heads, usually presenting women as examples of ideal and timeless beauty, characteristically informed by non-European physiognomy. At the time of his death in Manhattan, he also maintained a home and studio in Hoosick Falls, New York, near the Vermont border west of Bennington.

Sculptor **Alice de Creeft** (1899–1996), born Alice Robertson Carr in Seattle, served as his assistant on Majorca before they married in London in 1929. After they divorced in 1939, she lived in Santa Barbara. She was known especially for animal subjects. In 1944 he married sculptor and printmaker Lorrie Goulet (1925–), who carves stone and wood in a simplified figural style related to de Creeft's. A New York native, she studied in a pottery studio there and, in 1943–44, at *Black Mountain College, where she worked with de Creeft during the summer of 1944. Sculptor Nina de Creeft Ward (1933–), a child of his first marriage, was born in New York, grew up in California, graduated in 1956 from Scripps College in Claremont, and earned an MFA in 1964 from Claremont Graduate College. She lived and taught in Iowa for more than two decades before returning to California. Her sculpture, in several media, focuses particularly on animals.

De Feo, Jay. *See* FUNK ART.

De Forest, Roy. *See* FUNK ART.

Dehn, Adolf (1895–1968). Painter and printmaker. Originally a satirical realist, he later produced benign landscapes and industrial scenes. A farm boy from Waterville, Minnesota, Adolf Arthur Dehn began his professional training at the Minneapolis School of Art (now Minneapolis College of Art and Design) between 1914 and 1917. Attracted by the radical politics of *The *Masses*, he arrived in New York shortly before the magazine ceased publication in 1918. However, he soon contributed to the newly founded *Liberator*, where his satirical drawings fit comfortably with the magazine's left-wing social philosophy. He also worked at the *Art Students League with Boardman *Robinson and Kenneth Hayes *Miller and was jailed as a conscientious objector during World War I. Throughout the twenties, he produced amusing drawings and watercolors poking fun at the foibles of contemporary society. Oddly, as social realism became a major force within the *American Scene movement in the 1930s, Dehn gradually turned away from such commentary. His lithograph *Central Park*, done in the 1930s for a *federal art project, presents a pleasantly romantic view, while the watercolor *Hay Meadows* (Terra Foundation for American Art, 1938) straightforwardly depicts a rural scene. Among numerous commercial commissions, in 1943 he painted Standard Oil's Baton Rouge refinery with noncommittal realism. Occasionally, he incorporated surrealist effects. Dehn lived in Europe, mostly in Vienna, through much of the 1920s and later continued extensive travels abroad. He died in New York. He published *Water Color Painting* (1945), *How To Draw and Print Lithographs* (1950), and *Water Color, Gouache, and Casein Painting* (1955). His widow, painter and printmaker **Virginia Engleman Dehn** (1922–2005), moved permanently to Santa Fe, New Mexico, in 1985. Born in Nevada, Missouri, she grew up in Hamden, Connecticut, near New Haven. After graduating from Stephens College in Columbia, Missouri, she trained at the *Art Students League. She interpreted natural themes in nearly abstract forms.

Dehner, Dorothy. *See* SMITH, DAVID.

De Kooning, Willem (1904–97). Painter, sculptor, and printmaker. A preeminent *abstract expressionist, he created a thoroughly contemporary form of expression, filled with raw energy, anxiety, brazen transgressions of good taste, and delight in the process of painting, while at the same time extending traditional European painting's spatial, structural, chromatic, and technical principles. Forward-looking yet infused with the history of art, this work exerted greater influence over subsequent painters than any other mid twentieth-century artist's. Rich, fresh, and indeterminate, it offered myriad pathways to artists interested in figurative painting as well as abstraction. A charismatic, handsome, and eloquent art star, he also came to personify the romantic myth of the artistic life through commitment to his craft through years of poverty. Born in Rotterdam, de Kooning left school at twelve to work for a decorating and commercial design firm. After four years there, in 1920 he found employment in a department store's art division. Concurrently, for eight years he took evening classes at the Rotterdam

Academy (now the Willem de Kooning Academy of the University of Rotterdam). There he was exposed to a broad range of fine art and decorative techniques, as well as the history of art. In 1924 he left Rotterdam to work as a commercial artist in Brussels and Antwerp. Two years later, de Kooning arrived in the United States as an illegal stowaway. After his ship docked at Newport News, Virginia, he made his way to Hoboken, New Jersey. Some months later he took a studio in Manhattan, where he continued to support himself as a house painter, carpenter, and commercial artist. Within two or three years, he had established friendships with John *Graham, Stuart *Davis, and, most significantly, Arshile *Gorky, who proved essential to de Kooning's artistic maturation. He shared de Kooning's admiration for Picasso, instilled a belief in art as an exalted calling, and demonstrated that abstraction and representation need not be incompatible. In 1935 de Kooning began working for a *federal art project but had to leave the following year because he was not a citizen. (He was naturalized in 1962.) At this point, de Kooning for the first time began to conceive of a future as a full-time painter. His work of the late 1930s and early 1940s encompassed both figure studies (at first they were men, but by 1940 he preferred women) and abstractions loosely based on still lifes or interiors. Drawings from these years demonstrate virtuoso technique, but the paintings look more tentative, as he intentionally undermined his facility in search of individual expression. In its assurance and stylistic coherence, the abstracted figuration of *Pink Angels* (Frederick Weisman Art Foundation, Los Angeles, 1945) announced his personal approach. The model is rearranged into flesh-colored biomorphic forms indebted to surrealism. Contour line moves with great velocity, while spontaneous brushwork and abstract lines enliven the painting's surface. The tension evident here between order and disorder, between the studio and the world, between classicism and romanticism pervades his subsequent work.

De Kooning's career as an artist never proceeded by clearly identifiable stages. Rather, he alternated between abstraction and figuration, while frequently also backtracking or experimenting unsystematically. Nonetheless, certain key groups of paintings can be identified. Between 1946 and 1949 he painted a series of black-and-white works that made his public reputation when they appeared in his first one-person show in April 1948. Just months earlier Jackson *Pollock had introduced his signature *all-over drip paintings. Despite an inevitable rivalry between these two giants of *action painting, they respected each other's work. De Kooning's comment that Jackson had "broken the ice" acknowledged that Pollock had made a new kind of painting feasible in New York. In his 1948 show Pollock both introduced and summarized a form of painting that left little room for further development, but de Kooning's retained many loose ends. Executed in commercial enamel, sometimes textured with additives, de Kooning's seething black-and-white canvases achieve an invigorating interchange between the activated surface of the canvas and intimations of three-dimensional volume. As would continue to be the case, even though much of his gestural work appears to be totally nonrepresentational, hints of the figure or of landscape generally can be discerned. As de Kooning pursued the implications of his breakthrough, he produced many of his most forceful and inventive works, such as *Excavation* (Art Institute of Chicago, 1950). Here, employing vividly hued accents within a neutral-toned expanse, he employed interlocking shapes reminiscent of body parts to comment on cubist space. As usual, lines activating the surface inextricably entwine his painting with drawing, typically with a generously loaded brush. No sooner had de Kooning established his credentials as an abstract painter than he returned to figure painting. In 1950 he started on *Woman I* (Museum of Modern Art, 1950–52), the most terrifying of the startling paintings and drawings of women he showed in 1953. At once repulsive and fascinating, the wild-eyed, corpulent *Woman I*, baring fanglike teeth in a grotesque smile, seems to emerge and disintegrate simultaneously within a field of violent brushstrokes. The product of eighteen months of painting, repainting, rubbing out, and over-painting, *Woman I* presents a surface equal to its monstrous subject: vicious, outrageous, and yet touched with vulnerabilities. Attacked for their misogynism, for their betrayal of abstract art, and for their low-life vulgarity, the Woman paintings fuse rage, fear, erotic desire, and even ironic humor in a contradictory mix. Subsequently, in the late 1950s and into the 1960s, de Kooning produced abstract works that gradually moved toward simplification. In *Easter Monday* (Metropolitan Museum, 1956), springlike greens, yellows, and pinks give a lyrical note to a vigorous and complex composition. Completed four years later, *Door to the River* (Whitney Museum, 1960) relies on a relatively few broad brushstrokes in subdued colors to create an almost architectonic image, somewhat in the spirit of the work of his good friend Franz *Kline.

In 1963 de Kooning moved permanently to Springs, a district of the eastern Long Island town of East Hampton, where he had intermittently sojourned since 1948. Here, as art world fashions turned toward *pop art and then *minimalism, he was no longer the center of attention (and object of criticism) he had been in New York. In the peaceful surroundings of his relative isolation, de Kooning's art gradually relaxed. Through the 1960s and 1970s, he continued to produce figural and abstract works, as well as direct responses to landscape. Masterfully expanding and refining his vision within a pastoral mood, he loosened compositional structure and gave free rein to color, achieving on occasion a rococo delicacy and sensuality. In 1969 he began to model small, expressionistic clay figures (later to be cast into bronze) bearing the imprint of his fingers. Around the same time, he also returned to printmaking, which he had only occasionally tried previously, to create a series of lithographs. De Kooning continued to paint into the late 1980s. During that final decade, he produced nearly 350 paintings of an entirely new character before the ravages of Alzheimer's disease overwhelmed him. (In 1989 a court declared him incompetent to manage his affairs and appointed guardians.) As the art world became aware of his declining mental capacity, questions about the authenticity of the 1980s paintings erupted. Detractors accused studio assistants of being overly helpful. The consistency of the late works suggests, however, that the aging painter remained in control, distilling to their essence in one last series the fundamentals of his art. In these luxuriant, serene paintings, ribbons of color traverse white fields in graceful strips, recapitulating a lifetime of experience with painted line, sonorous color, and cubist space.

His wife, painter, printmaker, and sculptor **Elaine de Kooning** (1918–89), is remembered particularly for expressionist portraits. In addition, she published art criticism, particularly in *Art News* during the late 1940s and 1950s. Although she also wrote about other forms of art, her articles proved instrumental in interpreting abstract expressionism to a contemporary audience. She and Willem met around 1938, were living together by the following year, and married in 1943. Before the end of the 1940s, the marriage was in trouble. They separated for good (or so they thought) in 1956 but never divorced. Following their reconciliation in 1975, she moved to a house near his in Springs. As he declined, she assisted with his care and management of the studio. Born in Brooklyn, Elaine Fried enrolled briefly at Hunter College before switching in 1937 to the Leonardo da Vinci Art School and then, the following year, to the American Artists School. Her early work reveals an interest in social realism, but after she met Willem, she was drawn to abstraction. Her strongest paintings, as in a notable series of portraits, generally combine figuration with agitated brushwork. In the mid-1960s, she created a group of bronze sculptures. She died in a Southampton hospital, not far from her home. A selection of her criticism appeared in 1994 as *The Spirit of Abstract Expressionism.*

Delaney, Beauford (1901–79). Painter. Although he mostly relinquished the expressionist figurative style that made his reputation to work subsequently in an *abstract expressionist mode, he remained interested in portraiture. Both his art and his life betray tensions between his intelligence and creativity on the one hand and, on the other, his social position as African American, poor, and homosexual. Perhaps partially because of relatively limited artistic instruction, he developed a personal vision that somewhat distanced his work from clearly recognizable critical categories, further adding to his alienation. Intermittently, these contradictions affected his stability and eventually—in combination with age and, possibly, congenital psychological problems, alcoholism, or disease—triggered career-ending mental illness. Born in Knoxville, Tennessee, he graduated with honors from a segregated high school there. In 1923 he moved to Boston, where he studied art in museums, pursued intermittent instruction, and charmed his way into both black and white art circles. Moving on to New York in 1929, he found encouragement in the flourishing *Harlem Renaissance. Soon he settled in Greenwich Village, relishing its bohemian culture. Delaney's scene of homeless figures gathered for warmth, *Can Fire in the Park* (Smithsonian American Art Museum, 1946) set within a limited and ambiguous space relies for vivid effect primarily on painterly facture and patterns of color set off by characteristic black outlines. He had gained some attention for such scenes of life in and around Washington Square, as well as for portraits and landscapes, before he became a celebrity upon publication of his friend Henry Miller's laudatory, romanticized 1945 tribute. While still in New York, Delaney experimented with nonrepresentational painting prefiguring the colorful linear tangles he produced after moving to Paris in 1953. He settled on the Left Bank near his close friend James Baldwin. However, he never entirely abandoned recognizable imagery, which he used to particular effect in acute but stylized portraits. After 1970 the artist's mental deterioration became increasingly obvious, and in 1976 he was permanently hospitalized in Paris, where he died.

His brother **Joseph Delaney** (1904–91), a painter of portraits and New York scenes, worked in a vivacious, figurative style. He studied in the early 1930s at the *Art Students League with Thomas Hart *Benton and Alexander *Brook. Later in the decade he was employed for several years by *federal art projects. He remained in New York until 1986, when he accepted a position as artist-in-residence at the University of Tennessee in Knoxville, the city of his birth, where he also died.

Delano, Jack. *See* FARM SECURITY ADMINISTRATION (FSA) PHOTOGRAPHS.

Delanoy, Abraham, Jr. *See* DUNLAP, WILLIAM.

De Maria, Walter. *See* EARTH ART.

De Meyer, Baron Adolf. *See* STETTHEIMER, FLORINE.

De Montebello, Philippe. *See* METROPOLITAN MUSEUM OF ART.

Demuth, Charles (1883–1935). Painter. A key participant in the early development of modernism in the United States, he produced sophisticated still lifes, architectural abstractions, and figural subjects marked by elegant refinement, ironic wit, and vibrant sensuousness. In his highly varied output, Demuth invented aspects of *precisionism, but his work also bears important affinities with the art produced in the groups allied to Alfred *Stieglitz and Walter *Arensberg. Charles Henry Buckius Demuth came from Lancaster, Pennsylvania, which remained his primary residence all his life. His detached sensibility probably developed early. In childhood, a rare disease of the hip joint made him an invalid for two years and left him frail and limping. Before he was forty, he contracted the diabetes that often made him ill, as it slowly ended his life. His homosexuality further distanced his outlook. In 1903 he began his professional art studies at Drexel Institute of Art, Science, and Industry (now Drexel University) in Philadelphia, where he studied illustration before transferring in 1905 to the *Pennsylvania Academy of the Fine Arts. There, Thomas *Anshutz ranked as his most influential teacher, and Demuth remained a relatively traditional realist painter for several years. Although he visited Paris for five months in 1907–8, it was only after a second European sojourn between late 1912 and spring 1914 that his slowly maturing style became personal, original, and modern. Besides the work of such disparate turn-of-the-century innovators as James Abbott McNeill *Whistler, Cézanne, Odilon Redon, and Aubrey Beardsley, the European early modern styles then came to his attention. Other formative influences include Japanese prints and Rodin's drawings.

While spending much of his time in New York between 1914 and 1921, Demuth synthesized these sources in brilliant, opulent watercolors. Subjects included flowers, literary themes, vaudeville, and nightlife, as well as incidents of homoerotic desire. In these years, Demuth became involved with Stieglitz's circle, although the photographer did not show his work until 1925. In addition, Demuth soon became widely acquainted within other circles of artists, writers, and social revolutionaries. Notably, at the Arensbergs' gatherings, he came into contact with Marcel *Duchamp and *New York dada. In the summer of 1916, while working with Marsden *Hartley in *Provincetown, Demuth began to paint in the precisionist mode that dominates his major works in oil and tempera. Starting usually with an inherently geometric architectural subject (most often a Lancaster motif), Demuth dissected and sometimes rearranged elements, using cubist fragmentation and, often, raylike lines probably adapted from futurism. In these works, he anticipated the precisionists' taste for clarity, hard edges, and planar forms. Like them, he was clearly attracted to modern industry and technology, but his paintings' ironic or even playful tone often undercuts respectful qualities typically emphasized by other precisionists. Portraying grain elevators in Lancaster, the slyly titled *My Egypt* (Whitney Museum, 1927) suggests that such utilitarian structures provide an American equivalent for the timeless, sacred edifices of ancient times. Among Demuth's most singular accomplishments is a set of "poster portraits," as he called them, from the late 1920s. In these, Demuth cleverly symbolized several colleagues, including Georgia *O'Keeffe, Arthur *Dove, and John *Marin. Best known, *The Figure 5 in Gold* (Metropolitan Museum, 1928) honors poet William Carlos Williams, a longtime friend. The painting symbolically represents a phrase from a Williams poem, which describes the number seen on a rapidly passing fire engine. Of all Demuth's works, this may best suggest his relevance to a younger generation emerging in the 1950s and 1960s. *Pop artists, too, were interested in clean and impersonal forms, in letters and numbers that function doubly as elements of design and meaning, in conceptual approaches, and, most importantly, in imagery appropriated from mass culture. After a final visit to Paris in the fall of 1921, illness kept Demuth mostly in the care of his mother in Lancaster, where he died. His home there serves today as a museum that focuses on his life, work, and artistic context.

De Peyster Painter. *See* PATROON PAINTERS.

De Rivera, José (1904–85). Sculptor. In characteristic works, a single narrow tubular form flows in a closed, irregular loop through the space it inhabits and defines. Fabricated from gleaming metal, each seemingly weightless sculpture rests on a single point. De Rivera sometimes provided mechanized rotating bases to enhance the interplay of light, space, and reflection with his undulating curves. While not unprecedented, his interest in movement, both implied and actual, was previously shared by few Americans. He also numbers among early proponents of a mathematical and technological aesthetic. Born in West Baton Rouge, José A. Ruiz spent most of his childhood in New Orleans. Following high school graduation in 1922, for two years he gained experience as a machinist and blacksmith before moving to Chicago. There he attended art classes in the evenings and around 1930 began making sculpture. His early figurative work reflected dedication to precise craftsmanship and interest in the art of such streamlined modernists as Alexander *Archipenko and Brancusi. After traveling for most of 1932 in Europe and North Africa, he settled permanently in New York to pursue a serious, full-time commitment to sculpture. Around this time, he began using his mother's surname as his own. Although he experimented broadly for several years with varied materials and methods, he was drawn primarily to a constructivist approach emphasizing the interaction of space with sculptural form. From the late 1930s until the early 1950s, he worked primarily with sheet metal, which he shaped, curved, and sometimes painted. In *Black, Yellow, Red* (National Gallery, 1942), thin aluminum *biomorphic shapes painted in those colors dance separately, with swirling abandon, above the base. He was employed by a *federal art project in 1937–38 and served in the U.S. military from 1942 until 1946. Several years later, he began to work almost exclusively with the metal rods that define his signature style.

Dewing, Thomas Wilmer (1851–1938). Painter. A figurative specialist, he is known particularly for evocative depictions of languorous, introspective women, depicted singly or in small groups. Inhabiting spare but atmospheric interiors or nebulous gardens, they nearly always dress in long, graceful gowns. These cultured, upper-class beings shun the competitive, activist spirit of industrial and commercial modernity, yet they nevertheless represent contemporary types. Usually no longer young, rarely conventionally pretty, and often cerebral, they involuntarily reveal the pressure of the exterior world they avoid. Building on indirection, internal tension, and paradox, the meaning of such images lingers in uncertainty. Dewing also painted portraits and a few outright allegories, as well as interior decorations. A major figure in establishing *tonalism's popularity, he responded to aspects of impressionism and symbolism, as well as to the *aesthetic movement, the *American Renaissance, and *japonisme in forming his distinctive approach. The old masters, particularly Vermeer, and James Abbott McNeill *Whistler's example also informed his development.

Born in Boston, Wilmer Dewing chose as a young man to be known as Thomas. He learned lithography and achieved some success with portrait drawings before departing in July 1876 for Paris. There he studied at the Académie Julian under Gustave Boulanger and Jules-Joseph Lefebvre. He returned to Boston in October of the following year but moved to New York in the autumn of 1880. While executing portraits and murals there, he continued to paint enigmatic works demonstrating mastery of academic figure construction but also an increasingly refined aestheticism. Securing his early reputation, *The Days* (Wadsworth Atheneum, Hartford, Connecticut, 1887), inspired by a Ralph Waldo Emerson poem of the same name, depicts in pale tonalities a decorative frieze of idealized young women in an outdoor setting. Suggesting the spirit of late *Pre-Raphaelitism, which Dewing had encountered in England while traveling abroad in 1883, the image also prefigures his later use of amorphous landscape environments for figural works. These evolved while he summered from the mid-1880s in the art colony of Cornish, New Hampshire. During the 1890s, as he refined his mature subject matter and style, he also worked in pastel and silverpoint, demonstrating a technical facility that marked also his increasingly distinguished handling of oil. From October 1894 until July of the following year Dewing sojourned abroad for the last time. In London, he met Whistler and intermittently worked alongside him for several months. He then moved to Paris and subsequently rented a house in the impressionist stronghold of Giverny. In 1898 he joined other leading progressives in founding The *Ten. From 1905 he summered in a backwoods area of the White Mountains along the state border between Conway, New Hampshire and Fryeburg, Maine. After the earliest years of the twentieth century, he focused almost exclusively on small-scale, contemplative interiors such as *The Necklace* (Smithsonian American Art Museum, 1907). Within an austere, asymmetrically balanced space, a well-bred if slightly awkward woman lifts a necklace while staring fixedly at a mirror visible only as a frame cut by the edge of the painting. A shimmering, golden aura and exquisite, luxuriant brushwork counterbalance the painting's compositional and psychological edginess. Dewing's productivity declined during the 1920s, as the appeal of his quietist vision succumbed to the clamor of modern styles in art. For several years before his death in New York, poor health precluded painting.

Painter **Maria Oakey Dewing** (1845–1927), his wife, is remembered particularly for floral subjects, including a notable series set outdoors. In addition, she painted other forms of still life, as well as figural works, including portraits. Also a poet and art writer, she published articles and books on topics related to the aesthetic movement. Born in New York, Maria (she pronounced the name Ma-RYE-ah) Richards Oakey acquired more thorough art training than her husband. She enrolled in 1866 at Cooper Union, where her teachers included William *Rimmer, as well as painter and etcher Robert Swain Gifford (1840–1905), who specialized in landscapes. She continued to study at the *National Academy of Design from 1871 until 1875, when she numbered among the founders of the *Art Students League. She also worked with John *La Farge in Newport and in Boston with William Morris *Hunt before traveling to Paris in 1876 to study with their teacher, Thomas Couture. At the time of her marriage to Dewing in April 1881, she was better known as an artist than he and more widely connected in progressive New York art circles. Publication of *Beauty in Dress* (1881) and *Beauty in the Household* (1882) signaled her expertise in the decorative pursuits of the day. After marriage, she concentrated on still life painting, drawing particular inspiration from La Farge's flower paintings and from Asian approaches to ornamental depiction of nature. The appeal of the East is apparent, too, in the appearance of Japanese items within some of her tabletop still lifes. It is generally thought that she contributed to the gardenlike settings for some of her husband's figure paintings, including *The Days*. Summers in Cornish fostered innovative outdoor flower scenes marked by limited depth, informal composition, even lighting, and decorative surfaces. Their botanical credibility benefited from her serious interest in horticulture. Probably begun during the early summer in Giverny but completed in Cornish, the luxuriant *Garden in May* (Smithsonian American Art Museum, 1895), a profusion of softly painted pink and white blooms against verdant foliage, immerses the viewer an exaltation of nature and beauty. She died in her New York studio.

De Zayas, Marius (1880–1961). Caricaturist, illustrator, and art dealer. In abstract caricatures produced between 1913 and about 1916 and in writings for Alfred *Stieglitz's **Camera Work*, he anticipated *New York dada's nihilism, wacky humor, and fascination with machines as metaphors for human beings. Born in Veracruz, Mexico, de Zayas studied art in Europe and worked as a newspaper caricaturist in Mexico before moving to New York in 1907. Continuing to work for the press, he soon met Stieglitz, who showed his caricatures at the *291 gallery in 1909, 1910, and 1913. In the final show, de Zayas introduced abstract portraiture, in which lines, geometric forms, and mathematical formulas represent individuals' personalities. Between 1911 and 1914 he contributed several provocative articles to *Camera Work*. In 1915 de Zayas led a cautious movement to reinvigorate the spirit that Stieglitz had fostered at 291. With Stieglitz's blessing and the help of a few other 291 supporters, in that year he started a monthly magazine called 291 and opened the Modern Gallery, intended to be a more commercially oriented extension of the 291 gallery. Perhaps inevitably, given his uncompromising temperament, Stieglitz's cooperation soon diminished. At the same time, de Zayas grew closer to the group that gathered at Walter *Arensberg's apartment. He also renewed a friendship with French visitor Francis Picabia and forged ties with other dada-oriented artists in Europe. Early in 1916, the magazine folded at the end of its first year. The Modern Gallery survived until 1918. The gallery de Zayas opened the next year under his own name closed in 1921. After that, he no longer played a significant role in the New York art world. He died in Greenwich, Connecticut. De Zayas published *A Study of the Modern Evolution of Plastic Form* (with Paul Haviland, 1913) and *African Negro Art: Its Influence on Modern Art* (1916). Assembled in the late 1940s, *How, When, and Why Modern Art Came to New York*, edited by Francis Naumann, appeared posthumously in 1996.

Dickinson, Edwin (1891–1978). Painter and draftsman. His romantic figural works sometimes recall *magic realism or aspects of surrealism, but generally they remain inward and private, dedicated to personal experience, aloof from trends. These painterly, evocative images fuse memory and direct perception, as well as abstraction and realism. Born in Seneca Falls, Edwin Walter Dickinson spent his early years in New York's upstate Finger Lakes region. In 1910 he entered Brooklyn's Pratt Institute before enrolling the following year at the *Art Students League, where William Merritt *Chase numbered among his teachers. From 1913 he worked with Charles *Hawthorne in *Provincetown, and following service in the U.S. Navy between 1917 and 1919, he studied in Paris. At that time, he also traveled through Europe, responding particularly to the richly painted works of the Spanish visionary El Greco. Upon his return, he settled once again on Cape Cod. From 1944 until 1958 he taught in New York. In 1959 he left for a year in Greece, later a frequent destination, where he made refined drawings of ancient ruins. He died in Orleans, on Cape Cod. Dickinson's most impressive achievements comprise large, moody paintings, filled with incoherent imagery, discontinuous spaces, and lights flickering through deep shadows. These dreamlike scenes cannot be rationally deciphered, although their strongly constructed compositions and authoritative brushwork insure their pictorial power. The enigmatic *Fossil Hunters* (Whitney Museum, 1926–28), centering on a sleeping figure surrounded by a tumult of drapery, alludes in its title to the artist's interest in searching geological remains for embedded traces of the distant past. He is known also for softly rendered landscapes and for a long series of self-portraits, which often convey disquieting psychological effects.

Dickinson, Preston (1891–1930). Painter. Painterly touch, exceptional formal complexity, and muted, often pastel color harmonies distinguish his contribution to *precisionism. *Industry* (Whitney Museum, c. 1923) compresses a number of factory buildings into an intricate arrangement, further complicated by the presence of shadows, smokestacks, water towers, and other extraneous elements. On occasion, he also experimented with dynamic fragmentation of forms derived from cubism. Born in New York, he studied at the *Art Students League from 1906 to 1910. George *Bellows, William Merritt *Chase, and Ernest *Lawson numbered among his teachers. In 1910 he left for several years in Europe. There he absorbed a wide range of artistic influences, including Cézanne's example, fauvism, and cubism. However, he was also drawn to the structural integrity of Giotto's fourteenth-century frescoes and to the decorative surfaces of Japanese prints. Upon his return, he gradually simplified his style toward precisionist essentials. During the last years of Dickinson's short life, visits to Quebec provided subjects of many paintings. He died of pneumonia in Bilbao during a visit to Spain.

Diebenkorn, Richard (1922–93). Painter and printmaker. A principal contributor to *Bay Area figurative art, he later developed a personal abstract approach indebted to Cézanne, Matisse, *abstract expressionism, and the sunny California coast. Begun in 1967, his extensive nonfigurative Ocean Park series features radiant color, often suggesting sun-filled oceanfront sky and sand, in large-scale, formally harmonious arrangements. Born in Portland, Oregon, Richard Clifford Diebenkorn Jr. grew up in San Francisco. He entered Stanford University in 1940 but left in 1943 to serve in the U.S. Marine Corps. While stationed near Washington, D.C., he often visited Duncan *Phillips's museum, where he particularly admired the work of Matisse and gained familiarity with other modern European and American painters. Upon discharge in 1945, he enrolled at the California School of Fine Arts (now San Francisco Art Institute). His teacher David *Park almost immediately became a friend and mentor, while the work of other faculty, including particularly Clyfford *Still and Mark *Rothko, also caught his attention. During this time, he began to move away from his early work, which suggests admiration for Edward *Hopper, to develop an abstract expressionist approach. After completing his degree at Stanford in 1949, he left the following year for Albuquerque, where he earned a master's degree from the University of New Mexico in 1952. He then taught for a year at the University of Illinois at Urbana-Champaign and spent a few months becoming familiar at first hand with abstract expressionism in New York before settling in Berkeley. There in the mid-1950s in frequent contact with Park and Elmer *Bischoff, he followed their lead in returning to figure studies, landscapes, and still lifes while maintaining the vibrant, sensuous surfaces of his abstract paintings. In 1966 Diebenkorn accepted a teaching appointment at UCLA and moved into a studio in Santa Monica. Within months, overt representation abruptly disappeared from his work, as he initiated the Ocean Park sequence of more than 140 examples. Composed primarily of color planes parallel to the picture surface, many of these suggest architecturally framed landscape spaces, sometimes in tension with implied interiors, while others carry only the faintest hints of the light-filled local environment that inspired him. His sumptuous palette, characteristically rich in blues and greens, enlivened by bright whites and yellows, defines orderly structures that characteristically balance large, flat areas of pigment against smaller, more highly worked detail. In several print media, including etching and woodcut, he explored concerns related to his paintings but also addressed purely graphic problems. Without abandoning a California sensibility, Diebenkorn contributed intelligently to the language of late-twentieth-century art, occasioning widespread praise in New York and internationally. In 1988 he moved to Healdsburg, north of San Francisco. Poor health limited his practice to small works in the last years before he died at his Berkeley pied-a-terre.

Diller, Burgoyne (1906–65). Painter and sculptor. Among the foremost American creators of geometric abstractions, Burgoyne Andrew Diller was born in New York but moved with his family in 1919 to Battle Creek, Michigan. He attended Michigan State College (now University) in East Lansing before returning to New York in 1929. There he studied until 1933 at the *Art Students League, where his teachers included Jan *Matulka and George *Grosz. He also worked with Hans *Hofmann. The Cézannesque still lifes of his student years initiated an extended inquiry into the forms of modernism, including cubism, Kandinsky's abstraction, constructivism, and other European models. His mature, purely geometric style evolved in the mid-1930s in response to the neoplasticism of Mondrian and Theo van Doesburg, positioning Diller as perhaps the first significant American to realize the possibilities of this approach. He limited form to rectangles defined by verticals and horizontals and color, to the primary hues, plus black and white, but nevertheless achieved considerable variety. An untitled painting of 1944 (Museum of Modern Art) consists solely of three tall rectangles of unmodulated red, yellow, and black asymmetrically arranged on a square canvas. On the other hand, the intricate *Third Theme* (Whitney Museum, 1946–48) presents a vivacious arrangement of red, blue, and yellow rectangles interrupting black verticals of varying widths. Later Diller also made relief sculptures and columnar structures that translated his principles into three dimensions. As an administrator from 1935 to 1941 of the New York mural division of the Works Progress Administration *federal art project, Diller was single-handedly responsible for most of the Depression-era, government-sponsored abstract wall decorations. Ilya *Bolotowsky, Byron *Browne, Stuart *Davis, Arshile *Gorky, and Balcomb *Greene numbered among the beneficiaries. In the mid-1930s Diller assisted in the formation of the *American Abstract Artists group, from 1943 to 1945 he served in the U.S. Navy, and from 1946 until his death he served on the faculty at Brooklyn College. In his later years he maintained his home and studio near the shore in Atlantic Highlands, New Jersey. He died at a New York hospital.

Dine, Jim (1935–). Painter, printmaker, sculptor, and photographer. Also a poet. An early participant in *happenings, he soon contributed obliquely to the birth of *pop art by including in his work commonplace objects, both literal and represented. However, his art generally maintains a personal quality at odds with pop's emphasis on mass-media imagery. Generally allusive and pensive, his work often draws on autobiographical subjects and retains evidence of the artist's hand in its sensuous materiality. Dine has worked prolifically in varied media, often transferring a single theme from one to another while investigating the expressive possibilities of each technique. He has been particularly active as a printmaker, generally preferring the etching process to a more limited involvement in lithography, screen printing, and woodcut. He has also illustrated a number of books. Born in Cincinnati, James Dine studied at the University of Cincinnati and at Boston's School of the Museum of Fine Arts before enrolling at Ohio University in Athens. After receiving his BFA, he stayed on for a year of graduate work but then moved to New York in 1958. There he quickly became involved with the experimental milieu of happenings along with Allan *Kaprow, Claes *Oldenburg, and Robert *Whitman, among others. He also created his first *assemblages, often slathered with paint in a manner recalling his origins in *abstract expressionism, as well as walk-in environments, and he began to devise an iconography of domestic items, handyman tools, and studio-related objects that he reworked for years. Suggesting his sympathy for recent art by Jasper *Johns and Robert *Rauschenberg, in the early 1960s he began to attach real objects to canvases, sometimes accompanying them with their painted shadows or lettered names. From the mid-1960s several images became particularly associated with his name through extensive repetition. Besides a necktie and a heart, these included, most notably, an empty bathrobe, sleeves akimbo, since 1962 a surrogate for the artist himself. In various forms, Dine has also addressed other subjects, particularly classical sculpture and icons of popular culture, with the Venus de Milo seeming to combine the two. In the late 1960s Dine moved to London, where he befriended the American-born figurative painter R. B. Kitaj

(1923–). During this period his art lost its rough edges, as he refined his drawing and nurtured his romanticism. Upon his return in 1971 he settled in Putney, Vermont. Since 1986 he has divided his time between New York and Washington, Connecticut. In recent years he has photographed set-up tableaux. Printed on canvas or aluminum, these slightly melancholy scenes rework themes from his personal and aesthetic history. Dine's writings appear in *Welcome Home Lovebirds: Poems and Drawings* (1969) and *Diary of a Non-Deflector: Selected Poems* (1987).

Di Suvero, Mark (1933–). Sculptor. Known for abstract work on an enormous scale, he ranks among the finest and most influential sculptors of the late twentieth century. In developing his personal approach during the late 1950s, he combined *abstract expressionism's gestural exuberance, constructivism's structural probity, and the attraction to commonplace materials that characterized *junk sculpture. After the mid-1960s he worked most often with clean, industrial building materials, such as steel beams and plates, although he has continued to incorporate varied media and found objects. By engineering his works to appear at first glance unstable and decentered, he creates startling and complex visual effects. Moving parts in numerous works add to their animated presence. Many of di Suvero's works are so large they can be shown only outdoors. Believing in a democratic role for art, he has devoted much of his career to such sculpture commissioned for public places. With their all-American iconography of industrial strength, urban grit, optimistic ambition, and untrammeled individuality, these intensely physical works enter into spirited dialogues with their surroundings. Many even invite the passerby to sit, swing, or clamber on them. The fervor that animates di Suvero's art comprehends a moral dimension, as well. Especially during the 1960s and 1970s, he numbered among major activists in the New York art community. In addition to participating in early efforts to provide noncommercial exhibition opportunities, he led opposition to the Vietnam War. In 1966 he spearheaded construction of a Peace Tower (dismantled after a few months) in Los Angeles, and in 1971 left the country for four years to register his dissatisfaction with the United States government. Later he initiated a community effort to establish the Socrates Sculpture Park at a waterside location in the Long Island City section of Queens. Then an abandoned landfill and now a city park, it provides a graceful setting for large works.

Born to Italian parents in Shanghai, Marco Polo di Suvero arrived with his family in San Francisco in 1941 and graduated with a major in philosophy from the University of California at Berkeley in 1956. Subsequently, in New York he supported himself with skills he had already developed in carpentry, house painting, and other handyman tasks. Concurrently, he made expressionistic bronze and wood pieces, but as he became more familiar with abstract expressionist painting and David *Smith's sculpture, he soon introduced an original approach making use of weathered beams, cast-off lumber, architectural timber, disintegrating barrels, and other raw and splintered wood components. The ponderous elements generally angle outward in precarious compositions finding equilibrium among real physical forces. Often compared to the paintings of Franz *Kline, the sculptures realize in three dimensions those paintings' restless and heroic tenor. Along with wood, di Suvero also frequently incorporated chains, ropes, tires, or other junk items that intensify the works' origins in the detritus of an urban civilization. This innovative work debuted to acclaim in a one-person show during the autumn of 1960. Several months earlier, di Suvero was paralyzed in an elevator shaft accident while working for a repair company. Permanently affecting his back and legs, this nearly fatal injury confined him to a wheelchair for two years. During this period he learned to weld, so he could make "laptop" sculptures, while continuing also to work with wood on a small scale. Although he did not substantially recover until 1964, against all odds in 1963 he began to design the monumental pieces that constitute his best-known accomplishments. Nevertheless, he has continued throughout his career to fashion smaller and more intimate works. With their handmade fabrication, these generally display more intricate form and a more lyric sensibility than the huge sculptures.

The Peace Tower he designed displayed more than four hundred uniformly sized paintings by artists who shared his antiwar stance. By this time, he had begun working primarily with steel beams, which he bolted together in vigorous yet elegant works. In the late 1960s he acquired his own crane and learned the construction techniques needed to put together his architecturally scaled pieces. An early example, the forty-foot *Are Years What? (for Marianne Moore)* (Hirshhorn Museum, 1967), is composed entirely of I-beams, except for the cable that suspends one V-shaped element to swing in the breeze. Although di Suvero left the surfaces of many outdoor sculptures to weather naturally, others are painted. Here, a bright orange-red complements the work's structural drama. During his antiwar exile, he lived and worked in the Netherlands and Germany before settling in 1973 in the Burgundian region of France, at Chalon-sur-Saône, where he has subsequently retained a studio. He also has maintained contact with his roots in California, where he established a studio in Petaluma, north of San Francisco.

Dixon, Maynard. *See* LANGE, DOROTHEA.

Dodge, Mabel. *See* LUHAN, MABEL DODGE.

Doolittle, Amos. *See* EARL, RALPH.

Doughty, Thomas (1793–1856). Painter and printmaker. Probably the first American artist to make a living specializing in imaginative landscapes, he anticipated achievements of the *Hudson River School and influenced its early development. Born in Philadelphia and self-taught as a painter, he was apparently painting full time before 1820. In Philadelphia in 1830, with his brother John, he established a periodical, *The Cabinet of Natural History and American Rural Sports*, which published his lithographs. This enterprise occupied him fully for two years. Subsequently, he moved to Boston, where he had previously lived for nearly two years in the late 1820s. In 1837–38 he spent several months in England. After his return, he did not remain rooted for long in any location. He traveled, intermittently lived in New York, and resided at times elsewhere throughout the Northeast, as well as in Washington, D.C., and New Orleans. In 1845 he again left for Europe, this time visiting Paris as well as England during two years abroad. He died in New York. His wandering years probably reflected difficulty selling his work in the face of ever increasing competition from more accomplished landscape painters. Although Doughty attentively drew from nature, his paintings fall short of mature Hudson River School accomplishments. His views remain generalized, lacking both fidelity to given locales and accuracy in portraying plants, rocks, and other specific features. Compositionally, they generally mimic earlier conventions of landscape design, inherited primarily from eighteenth-century England. Nevertheless, his poetic, meditative scenes reverberate with feeling for the beauty of the natural world. With its rapturous treatment of a lone observer's contemplation before a plenteous landscape and light-filled sky, *In Nature's Wonderland* (Detroit Institute of Arts, 1835), epitomizes his strengths.

Douglas, Aaron (1899–1979). Painter. A leader of the *Harlem Renaissance, he led the way for African-American artists to employ explicitly black themes, fostering a resurgence of racial pride in black art. Born in Topeka, Kansas, he held several blue-collar jobs and served in the military during World War I before earning a BFA in 1922 from the University of Nebraska in Lincoln. After additional study at the University of Kansas, he taught in a Kansas City high school until 1925, when he moved to New York. There he soon established himself as the Harlem Renaissance's leading graphic artist with book and magazine illustrations for the movement's literature. His boldly stylized, black-and-white compositions benefited from private instruction between 1925 and 1927 with German-born painter and graphic artist Winold Reiss (1886–1953). In 1927–28 Douglas worked for a year at the *Barnes Foundation, and in 1931 he left for a year of study in Paris. After his return, Douglas painted murals under the sponsorship of the *federal art projects and was active as an organizer of the *American Artists' Congress. At its first national meeting in February 1936, he delivered a paper on "The Negro in American Culture," calling for an end to racial discrimination as a means of resisting fascism's spread. From 1940 he was employed intermittently at Fisk University, where he joined the full-time faculty upon receiving a master's degree from Columbia University in 1944. After retirement in 1966 he continued to live in Nashville, where he died. Douglas's easel paintings, generally rather straightforwardly realistic portraits or *genre scenes, include such characteristic works as *The Composer* (Carl Van Vechten Gallery, Fisk University, Nashville, Tennessee, 1967), a sensitive and dignified likeness of classical musician William Hurt, and *Triborough Bridge* (Amistad Research Center, Tulane University, 1935), depicting the idle unemployed in a snowy park. However, Douglas's reputation depends largely on his more stylized graphic work and murals. In both media, he made effective use of energetic flat patterns reflecting the fragmentations and reductions of post-cubist art, as well as African, Egyptian, and early Greek design. Installed in 1934 in the New York Public Library's 135th Street branch (now the Schomburg Center for Research in Black Culture), his best-known achievement comprises four murals collectively titled *Aspects of Negro Life*. Flattened silhouettes, sometimes partially transparent, enact a decorative, dreamlike pageant of the African-American journey from Africa through slavery and emancipation. In the final panel, a jazz musician triumphantly brandishes his saxophone to symbolize liberation of the race. Although Douglas's narrative skirts stereotype, exoticism, and primitivism, his elegant and balanced forms materialize within a restricted palette to convey spiritual reverence for the distant origin and difficult history of his people.

Dove, Arthur (1880–1946). Painter and assemblage/collage artist. Known particularly as an interpreter of nature, he ranks as the first American to exhibit abstractions and the only American to work continuously as an abstract artist from before the *Armory Show into the *abstract expressionist period. The stylistically varied course of his career reflects two lifelong interests. Besides contributing to the ongoing dialogue of modern art, he wished to open a pathway to essential reality through authentic and original responses to personal sensations, particularly responses to nature. A native of New York's upstate Finger Lakes region, Arthur Garfield Dove was born in Canandaigua but grew up in nearby Geneva. After two years at Hobart College (now a constituent of Hobart and William Smith Colleges) there, he transferred to Cornell University. Upon graduation in 1903, he moved to New York to work as an illustrator. After five years, he departed for France to paint for a little more than a year. During this time, he abandoned his soft impressionist manner for a brightly colored fauve approach influenced by Matisse. Soon after his return he met Alfred *Stieglitz, who became his champion as well as a close friend. In 1912 Stieglitz mounted Dove's first one-person exhibition in New York, at the *291 gallery, and subsequently continued to arrange all shows of new work.

Toward the end of 1910 or early the next year, Dove tested his evolving ideas by painting six entirely abstract little oils. Revolutionary for their day, when pure abstraction did not yet exist as an art form, they were never exhibited during the artist's lifetime. (He may have considered them informal studies, not finished works.) Dove then produced ten large semi-abstract pastels featuring natural motifs within abstract contexts influenced by cubism. Energetic, organic commalike forms suggesting stylizations of germinating seeds dominate *Nature Symbolized No. 2* (Art Institute of Chicago). Rhythmically patterned flat shapes overlap each other in a manner that suggests cubism's faceted planes but not their transparency. Exhibited at 291 in 1912, this and the other pastels constituted the first public display of nonillusionistic art by an American. Although this show confirmed Dove's place in the vanguard of international modernism, his progress remained hesitant for a number of years afterward, and he did not exhibit a substantial body of new work for another thirteen years. Meanwhile, Dove had by 1910 moved to Westport, Connecticut, where he hoped to be able to support his art through farming and fishing. This was only the first of several unconventional lifestyle choices. He never again lived in New York full time (although he spent two Westport-era winters there, pursuing illustration jobs). In 1921 he moved to a houseboat, moored off upper Manhattan, for about a year. Then he bought a sailboat, which was his residence for several years, mostly on Long Island Sound. From the late 1920s he lived and/or worked intermittently on shore. He found winter quarters he particularly liked in Halesite, Long Island, at a yacht club, where he lived rent-free as caretaker. In 1933, almost penniless during the Depression, he moved back to Geneva and lived successively in two farmhouses on family property before he moved into an office block's loftlike top floor, previously used as a roller-skating rink. In 1938 he purchased his final home, a tiny former post office hugging the water in Centerport, on the north shore of Long Island.

Dove's meager output in the 1910s included a handful of strong paintings and drawings, some startlingly abstract. In the summer of 1921 Dove renewed his commitment to art and never again faltered. During the early 1920s, he experimented with varied forms of partial abstraction, including some pieces, such as *Lantern* (Art Institute of Chicago, 1922), based on mechanical subjects. In 1924 he began making variously witty or poetic collage-like *assemblages, nearly all completed in the next two years. Incorporating found objects and non-art materials, as well as painted areas, they exemplify a technique that was not yet widely accepted as art. *Goin' Fishin'* (Phillips Collection, 1925) evokes a lazy afternoon at the river through an abstract arrangement of bamboo, denim shirtsleeves, bark, and pieces of wood. Later in the 1920s, some of his pure abstractions, often interlaced with fast-moving lines, interpret musical themes, while the rich and sonorous *Alfie's Delight* (Herbert F. Johnson Museum of Art, Cornell University, Ithaca, New York, 1929) presents a freely painted abstraction based on circular forms. (The title refers to Alfred *Maurer, who had been a close friend since Paris days.) After Dove moved upstate, his art took on the visual characteristics of the area's rolling farmland. Occasionally his work became more directly representational, but other paintings demonstrate masterful organic abstraction. A composition of ample bovine forms interpenetrating and overlapping within a pasturelike space, *Cows in Pasture* (Phillips Collection, 1935) displays *biomorphic form related to surrealism. Because he lived in provincial circumstances for most of his life and because his art so clearly responded to the natural world, some observers have thought of the artist as an unworldly nature poet. However, he kept up with the latest developments through art magazines, exhibition catalogues, and visits to New York galleries and museums. Arp, Kandinsky, Paul Klee, Mondrian, and other leading modernists stimulated his thinking. Despite poor health after 1938, in his final years Dove produced some of the most dramatic nonrepresentational paintings of his career. Organic abstractions such as *Rose and Locust Stump* (Phillips Collection, 1943) suggest the rhythms and mythic overtones found in aspects of contemporary abstract expressionism. Featuring saturated colors, a number of totally or partially geometric abstractions, such as *That Red One* (Museum of Fine Arts, Boston, 1944), leapfrogged current practice to anticipate, if on a smaller scale, color field painting of the 1960s. Dove died in a hospital at Huntington, not far from his Centerport home.

His second wife, painter Helen Torr (1886–1967), nicknamed Reds for the color of her hair, worked in a related but usually more realistic manner. They lived together from 1921 and married in 1932. A Philadelphian, Helen Spangler Torr began her training there in 1902 at the Drexel Institute (now University) and three years later entered the *Pennsylvania Academy of the Fine Arts, where William Merritt *Chase numbered among her instructors. In 1913 she married fellow art student Clive Weed (1884–1936), later an editorial cartoonist. They lived in New York and Philadelphia until moving to Westport around 1920. Although with Dove's encouragement she became an accomplished artist, she often deferred painting to the strenuous demands of their life together and to her self-sacrificing devotion to his career. After his death, she remained in the Centerport house but no longer worked as an artist. Following her final few months in a nursing home in Bayshore, Long Island, she died in a hospital in nearby West Islip. Today owned and administered by the Heckscher Museum of Art in Huntington, the Centerport residence numbers among Historic Artists' Homes and Studios of the National Trust for Historic Preservation. Born in New York, where she continues to reside, Dove's granddaughter **Toni Dove** (1946–), a graduate of the Rhode Island School of Design, works primarily with *video and other electronic media.

Dow, Arthur Wesley (1857–1922). Painter, printmaker, photographer, and educator. Through his book *Composition* (1899) and his systematic teaching methods, he encouraged individual expression within an aesthetic of simplicity, harmony, and reverence for natural form. In the process, he significantly enlarged the scope of decorative sources available to artists and artisans in the United States. He particularly drew on Japanese principles of design in formulating his emphasis on line, color, and equilibrium between light and dark masses. While contributing to the *Arts and Crafts movement, his efforts also spurred development of modernist ideas about the priority of abstract form and pictorial structure. An idealist, he believed that beauty, the mark of art's spiritual value, could be realized in any medium and should become part of everyday life within reach of a wide public. Born in Ipswich, Dow grew up there, on the Massachusetts coast north of Boston. Upon completing high school, he became a teacher, while continuing his studies informally and developing an antiquarian interest in local craft traditions. Around 1880 he took up painting. Inspired in part by an acquaintance with Frank *Duveneck, in the fall of 1884 Dow departed for Paris, where he studied at the Académie Julian. During his years abroad, interrupted by a trip home in 1887, he spent periods of time working at the artists' colony of Pont Aven in Brittany but seems not to have been susceptible at this point to the art of Gauguin and other postimpressionists there. He returned to Ipswich in 1889 but a year later took a studio in Boston. There he focused on landscapes in a style reflecting *Barbizon scenes but also explored the arts of non-Western cultures. Although the vogue for *japonisme had been under way in both France and the United States for some years, until 1891 Dow did not respond enthusiastically to the Japanese prints that became the touchstone of his mature aesthetic. Soon after, he became acquainted with the Museum of Fine Art's Ernest *Fenollosa, whose views on Asian art he adopted as his own. From 1893 Dow, too, held curatorial positions at the museum for several years.

In the decisive year of 1891 Dow also established the Ipswich Summer School of Art, which he continued to direct (except for one season) until 1907. Putting into practice his innovative teaching methods, he encouraged students to explore crafts media as well as the traditional fine arts. In 1895 he took a position at Brooklyn's Pratt Institute and three years later began teaching at the *Art Students League as well. When *Composition* was published, his impact on the education of artists, photographers, and designers expanded beyond his personal sphere. Following a trip around the world through Asia to Europe in 1903 and 1904, he consolidated his reputation as the country's leading art educator while serving as art department head at the influential Teachers College of Columbia University. Later in life he traveled to the West on several occasions, finding subjects for his art and photography in California and especially at the Grand Canyon. He died in New York. Although Dow's principles and educational methods exerted a decisive influence on the development of American art (Georgia *O'Keeffe and Max *Weber numbered among admirers), Dow's personal expression did not present radical innovations. In the context of the period's impressionist and postimpressionist tendencies, his gentle and romantic landscape paintings remained relatively conservative. However, Dow's prints and photographs contributed to more progressive currents. The notable color woodcuts he began producing in the early 1890s masterfully exploit flat pattern, asymmetrical balance, and subtle tonalities in the depiction of landscape or other natural motifs. Dow first took up photography in the 1880s, but his most active use of this medium dates from the years between about 1890 and 1912. Combining abstract composition with particular features of landscapes or picturesque sites, his photographic work contributed to the flowering of *pictorialism. He directly influenced a number of its well-known practitioners, especially Alvin Langdon *Coburn.

Downing, Thomas. *See* WASHINGTON COLOR SCHOOL.

Doyle, Tom. *See* HESSE, EVA.

Dreier, Katherine (1877–1952). Painter, collector, and crusader for modern art. Attracted to modern art as a source of both spiritual renewal and social improvement, she tirelessly campaigned for the most advanced international art of her day. After exhibiting in the 1913 *Armory Show, she took on the mission of educating the public about modern art. In 1920, along with Marcel *Duchamp and *Man Ray, she founded the *Société Anonyme, Inc. The organization was Dreier's idea, and her energy fueled its accomplishments. Born in Brooklyn, as a young woman Katherine Sophie Dreier participated in social reform movements. After early art studies in Brooklyn, she spent a year in Europe and then studied for five years with Walter *Shirlaw. While living in London between 1909 and 1911, she painted impressionist works often recalling James Abbott McNeill *Whistler's example. In 1912 during European travels she developed an interest in more modern forms of expression, with particular enthusiasm for van Gogh's work. After meeting Marcel *Duchamp in 1917, she soon commissioned for her library *Tu m'* (Yale University Art Gallery, 1918), his last painting. Also in 1918, she began to paint nonobjectively, in a mode indebted primarily to Kandinsky, whose work and theoretical writings she by then particularly admired and whose belief in Theosophy she shared. A characteristic work, *The Garden* (Newark [New Jersey] Museum, 1918), combines circular shapes (perhaps intended to evoke flowers) within a dynamic arrangement of angular lines and high-contrast colors. While frequently traveling over the years to Europe, from the 1930s she made her home primarily in Connecticut, first in West Redding and after 1946 in Milford, where she died. As an executor of her will, Duchamp apportioned her personal collection of modern art between Yale University and other institutions. *Five Months in the Argentine from a Woman's Point of View* (1920) recounts a 1918 South American journey to survey social reforms. *Western Art and the New Era: An Introduction to Modern Art* (1923) presents her philosophy of art.

Drewes, Werner (1899–1985). Painter, printmaker, and occasional sculptor. Born in Canig, Germany, he served in the German army during World War I and began his professional training in Berlin and Stuttgart before studying at the Bauhaus. In 1921–22, when the school was in Weimar, he worked with Johannes Itten and Paul Klee. For the next several years, Drewes traveled around the world and visited the United States. After the Bauhaus had moved to Dessau, he returned in 1927–28 to work with Kandinsky and Lyonel *Feininger. He moved permanently to the United States in 1930. During the Depression years, he was employed by *federal art projects, and in 1936, the year he became a citizen, he participated in establishing the *American Abstract Artists. He also worked at *Atelier 17 before moving in the mid-1940s to St. Louis, where he taught at Washington University until 1965. As one of Kandinsky's closest followers in the United States, Drewes maintained an extensive correspondence with him while developing a painting style reflecting the hard-edge abstraction of Kandinsky's Bauhaus years. Drewes also shared his teacher's philosophy of art, believing that art could express spiritual universals. In characteristic paintings of the 1930s and 1940s, geometric and *biomorphic forms float in ambiguous spaces. As an active printmaker who specialized in woodcuts, often in color, he made many abstract prints before the mid-1940s. Later, working in a vigorous and expressionistic descriptive style, he specialized in landscapes but also produced strong self-portraits. Printed in cool blue, lavender, and green relieved with touches of orange-red, *Cliffs on Monhegan Island* (1969) offers a semi-abstract treatment of rocks and pine trees forcefully jutting into a sky filled with angular indications of clouds. Infrequently, Drewes also produced sculpture, including a prize-winning Plexiglas abstraction of 1939. He died in Reston, Virginia, where he had lived for nearly twenty years.

Driggs, Elsie (1898–1992). Painter and assemblage artist. Although noted in the late 1920s as a rising young artist and contributor to *precisionism, following her one-person show in 1930 she did not have another for fifty years. Nevertheless, she remained creative into her nineties, over the years producing art in a range of styles and techniques. Born in Hartford, Connecticut, Driggs moved with her family in 1908 to the New York suburb of New Rochelle. In 1918 she began her training at the *Art Students League, where her teachers included George *Luks, John *Sloan, and Maurice *Sterne. Late in 1922 she departed for more than a year of study and travel in Italy. A 1926 visit to Pittsburgh, where the steel mills fired her imagination, led to the work upon which her reputation primarily rests. *Pittsburgh* (Whitney Museum, 1927), perhaps her most celebrated work, depicts hard-edged smokestacks, pipes, and other industrial forms riding triumphantly above billows of smoke. Compared to the staid tone of most precisionist work, this painting offers a more emotional, romantic response to subject, as well as a more vigorous and less buttoned-down composition. Her attraction to classical, orderly forms remained in tension with her fondness for animated, inventive elements. During the Depression, Driggs worked for a *federal art project. In 1935, she married painter Lee *Gatch, and they moved to a small rural residence in Lambertville, New Jersey, where she had to make do without her own studio. After his death in 1968, Driggs returned permanently to New York, where her art remained in touch with the moment. In the 1970s she made *assemblages enclosed in Lucite boxes, while her 1980s paintings interpreted the contemporary urban environment.

Dry-plate process. *See* PHOTOGRAPHY, AMERICAN.

Du Bois, Guy Pène. *See* PÈNE DU BOIS, GUY.

Duchamp, Marcel (1887–1968). Painter, sculptor, and experimental artist. Among the most influential artists of the twentieth century, he provoked a media frenzy when his celebrated *Nude Descending a Staircase, No. 2* (Philadelphia Museum, 1912) appeared in the 1913 *Armory Show. Dismissive of art that appeals only to the eye, or what he called "retinal" art, Duchamp believed that art emanates from the mind. He raised many significant questions about the boundaries between art and non-art, and between art and life. Continuing to echo in the creation and criticism of art, these conundrums affected not only the advent of *conceptual art but also key aspects of such major movements as *minimalism and *pop art. His continuing appeal through the twentieth century also has much to do with his commitment to freedom as a major principle of both life and art. Duchamp communicated his theories about art largely through his work, for he mistrusted language. His views are known mainly through the reports of what he said to others on either public or private occasions, and he was not always consistent. Personally, he was urbane, charming, and serene. He cared almost nothing for fame or wealth. Because he often seemed as enigmatic as his work, both his personality and his art have been the subjects of intense critical and art historical scrutiny and speculation.

Born in Blainville, a Normandy village, Henri-Robert-Marcel Duchamp began as a painter in the impressionist style. In 1904 he moved to Paris, where he enrolled at the Académie Julian for a year's study. It was clear from the beginning of his artistic career, however, that he had little interest in technique or in the normal routes to success. In 1911 he started to incorporate cubist practices into his work and very quickly arrived at an original approach featuring fragmented planes. Completed early the following year, *Nude Descending a Staircase, No. 2* visualizes the passage of time, implying flux and metamorphosis. While the method of segmenting the nude's body derives from cubism, photographic multiple exposures undertaken for scientific analysis of action inspired the figure's "movement" across the canvas. The Armory Show momentarily transformed Duchamp into the most famous artist in America, although he was not well known in Europe. For the public, *Nude Descending a Staircase, No. 2* symbolized the incomprehensibility of modern art, and many reacted with scorn or humor. For his part, Duchamp apparently saw no point in further work along these lines, and before long he gave up painting except on an occasional basis. After moving to New York in 1915, he soon was the main attraction at Walter *Arensberg's informal salon. Along with Man *Ray and French visitor Francis Picabia, he figured at the center of *New York dada. Epitomizing this group's high spirits, Duchamp's rejected entry to the 1917 *Society of Independent Artists' exhibition again provoked public controversy. Titled *Fountain*, and signed "R. Mutt," this work entailed only a commercial urinal mounted upside down. (The original is now lost, but in 1964 Duchamp made eight replicas.) *Fountain* numbers among a number of "ready-mades" that Duchamp produced, beginning in 1913, in each case claiming the status of art for a found object, usually a commercially made product. (Some recent research has suggested that Duchamp may have done more alteration to these objects than he let on.) His approach raised disturbing questions about the nature and value of artistic effort, as well as about the nature of art itself. In the ready-mades, Duchamp proposed an aesthetic of indifference, but paradoxically, many draw attention to the inherent formal beauty of objects not originally produced as art, as was the case with respect to *Fountain*'s elegant contours. Its resemblance to the reductive, organic abstraction of Brancusi's recent sculpture would not have been lost on knowledgeable observers. In 1915 Duchamp embarked on the construction of a singular work, which had begun to engage his thinking around 1912, and which took eight more years to complete. On two glass panels, which together measure nearly 9 × 5.5 feet, he painted and glued a combination of representational and indecipherable elements. When the glass accidentally shattered after the piece was first exhibited in 1926, the work's nonplussed creator carefully glued it back together, cracks and all. He claimed he liked it better that way, and indeed, the fissures add to the work's visual and intellectual complexity. The work's title, *The Bride Stripped Bare by Her Bachelors, Even* (sometimes also known as *The Large Glass*; Philadelphia Museum), divulges that the subject is sexual attraction, although the imagery is mechanical. No entirely satisfactory explanation of the piece has been advanced, although it remains among the most analyzed art objects of the twentieth century. Despite his usual distaste for interpretation, Duchamp contributed a detailed written commentary, which is integral to the meaning and experience of *The Large Glass*. Nevertheless, even here he writes playfully and poetically, employing analogy, metaphor, hyperbole, and—possibly—farce. The reader remains uncertain not only about meaning but about the writer's intentions. In the end, the satiric and melancholy *Large Glass* remains an object of contemplation and endless unfulfillment.

In 1918–19, Duchamp spent nine months in Buenos Aires, mostly playing chess, which had become an obsession while he was in New York. After a visit home, he returned to New York in 1920. That year, he joined Katherine *Dreier and *Man Ray in founding the *Société Anonyme, Inc. In 1923 Duchamp settled in France for nearly twenty years, although he visited New York from time to time. In 1942 he reversed that arrangement, now living in New York but often visiting Europe. In 1955 he became an American citizen. For the last two decades of his life, he told people that he had given up making art. Chess appeared to be his main interest. But he had one final surprise. After he died during a visit to France, it was revealed that he had been building an elaborate installation that again enigmatically proposed a sexual theme. Usually known by its French name, *Étant donnés* (or, "given," as in a mathematical proof), the work has two subtitles: 1. *The Waterfall*, 2. *The Illuminating Gas*. (The work includes the illusion of a small waterfall, as well as a gas lamp). As installed in the Philadelphia Museum of Art according to the artist's directions, peepholes in a massive wood door provide a glimpse. The viewer encounters a partial but surprisingly frank view of a nude female woman, who raises a gas lamp in one hand as she reclines in a lushly detailed landscape. The work's dense, inscrutable meanings recall those of *The Large Glass*, but this undeniably retinal work moderates the intellectual rigor of his career. Enigmatic to the last, Duchamp wrote his own epitaph for his gravestone in Rouen, making light even of the end. Translated, it reads, "Besides, it's always others who die."

DuMond, Frank Vincent. *See* OLD LYME ARTISTS' COLONY.

Duncan, David Douglas (1916–). Photographer. Known especially for combat reporting during the Korean War and for an extended pictorial record of Picasso's life and work, he was born in Kansas City and graduated from the University of Miami in 1938. As a Marine during World War II, he took his camera into battle in the South Pacific and accompanied dangerous aerial missions, including many over Okinawa. In 1946 he joined the staff of *Life* magazine, which sent him to Korea in 1950. Duncan became the preeminent photographer of the conflict there, as he compiled an intimate record of the lives of individual soldiers fighting a brutal and not entirely comprehensible war. In 1951 he published *This Is War!*, which combines images and text. The photographs themselves constitute not so much a record of events as a philosophical rumination on the nature and human costs of modern warfare. What he saw in Vietnam in 1967 so discouraged him that he published an angry book, *I Protest!, Khe Sanh, Vietnam* in 1968. His collected Vietnamese War photographs appeared in *War Without Heroes* (1970). In the mid-1950s, around the time Duncan left *Life* to work independently, he became acquainted with Picasso. This fruitful relationship eventually resulted in seven books, including *The Private World of Pablo Picasso* (1958), the first; *Picasso's Picassos* (1961), a color record of the artist's collection of his own work; and *The Silent Studio* (1976), a posthumous tribute. Among numerous other works of photojournalism, *The Kremlin* (1960) followed a trip to Russia. In the 1970s he produced books of experimental work, *Prismatics: Exploring a New World* (1972) and *Magic Worlds of Fantasy* (1978). Duncan has also published two autobiographical volumes, *Yankee Nomad: A Photographic Odyssey* (1966) and *Photo Nomad* (2004). He lives at Mouans-Sartoux, in the south of France near Cannes.

Duncanson, Robert S. (c. 1821–72). Painter. A landscape specialist, he also painted literary subjects, portraits, still lifes, and *genre scenes. Of mixed-white and African-American parentage, he ranks as the first black artist to establish a national and even international reputation. Born in Fayette, in the Finger Lakes region of New York State, he worked as a young man as a housepainter in Monroe, Michigan, where he had moved as a youngster with his family. Self-taught as an artist, by 1841 he was painting clients while also employed as a *daguerreotypist in Cincinnati. In search of portrait commissions, he subsequently worked for several years itinerantly, moving between Cincinnati, Monroe, and Detroit. At the end of the decade, on commission from wealthy Cincinnati businessman and art patron Nicholas Longworth (1782–1863), Duncanson undertook his first major project, a series of murals in the foyer of Longworth's mansion, Belmont (now the Taft Museum of Art, where the paintings remain). Eight landscapes with trompe-l'oeil frames demonstrate Duncanson's familiarity with English and French traditions of decoration. Painted about a year later, *Blue Hole, Little Miami River* (Cincinnati Art Museum, 1851) more pointedly responds to a specific site, today located in John Bryan State Park. With its closely observed detail and romantic interpretation of nature, it follows the *Hudson River School approach established by Thomas *Cole, whose work Duncanson admired. The placidly reflective water, orderly space, and delicate light also suggest links to *luminism. Possibly Duncanson had already traveled to Europe, but in 1853 he departed on his first extended visit, a tour ranging from Italy to London. Returning to Cincinnati in 1854, he found success with both local views and European scenes. The first of several ambitious landscapes inspired by British romantic literature, *Land of the Lotus Eaters* (Swedish Royal Collections, Stockholm, 1861), brought renown at home, in Canada, and in Europe. Responding to an 1832 Tennyson poem, he imagined an exotic landscape surrounding small figures who illustrate its theme, but also respond obliquely to contemporary racial issues. At approximately 4 × 7 feet, the painting rivals the dimensions of contemporary heroic travelogues then in vogue, such as Frederic *Church's *Heart of the Andes* (Metropolitan Museum, 1859), which it clearly emulates. Previously active for some time in the abolitionist movement, Duncanson left the country for four years in 1863 as the Civil War raged. After two years in Montreal, he moved on to Dublin, Scotland, and England, where his accomplishments were highly praised. During his last several years in Cincinnati, he painted some of his most satisfyingly integrated works, while also showing symptoms of a psychotic condition that often interfered with his ability to paint. On a visit to Detroit in 1872, he suffered a breakdown and died there a few months later.

Dunlap, William (1766–1839). Painter and first historian of American art. Also a writer and theater professional. A versatile contributor to the cultural life of the new nation, Dunlap intermittently tried his hand at portraiture, landscape, and history painting. Sometimes dubbed "the American Vasari," he is best remembered for his *History of the Rise and Progress of the Arts of Design in the United States* (1834). Emphasizing painters but encompassing artists from all fields, including sculpture, printmaking, and architecture, this pioneering survey remains a valuable primary source for the colonial and federal eras. For the most part biographically organized, the publication is especially useful for artists of Dunlap's own day because he knew most of them personally and brought a discerning eye to their work. While compiling the two volumes, he sought information directly from his subjects. Dunlap also wrote an important *History of the American Theatre* (1832). Born in Perth Amboy, New Jersey, he moved with his family in 1777 to New York, where he studied briefly in the early 1780s with portrait painter Abraham

Delanoy Jr. (1742–95), a pupil in London of Benjamin *West. At sixteen, Dunlap was practicing professionally as a portraitist. In England between 1784 and 1787, he worked rather offhandedly with West while also acquainting himself with the London theater. His best known painting, *Portrait of the Artist Showing the Picture of Hamlet to His Parents* (New-York Historical Society, 1788) documents his dual interests in painting and theater. Palette in hand, Dunlap displays a canvas depicting a scene from Shakespeare. Informally grouped in a simple domestic interior, the small family gathering records Dunlap's competence in constructing an engaging conversation piece and in rendering individual likenesses and attire.

Dunlap devoted himself primarily to the theater during much of his life. He wrote more than thirty plays and translated or adapted numerous others. From 1798 until 1805, he served as director and manager of the Park Theatre in New York. When the company went bankrupt, he traveled to Philadelphia, Baltimore, and Washington in search of portrait commissions. From 1806 to 1811, he returned to the reorganized theater company. He then resumed his portrait career along the eastern seaboard, venturing from Virginia to Montreal. Nevertheless, for the most prestigious commissions, he could not compete with more expert portraitists active in the early nineteenth century. His sitters remained people of modest means, and Dunlap never escaped financial insecurity. During the 1820s he helped to found the *National Academy of Design and painted several large dramatic works, which he took on tour. By about 1830 he had turned principally to writing newspaper reviews and working on his histories. He died in New York. His writings include also the two-volume *Life of Charles Brockden Brown* (1815) and other biographical and historical works, as well as a temperance novel, *Memoirs of a Water Drinker* (1836). The three-volume *Diary of William Dunlap (1766–1839)*, based on his writings and edited by D. C. Barck, was published in 1930.

Durand, Asher Brown (1796–1886). Painter and engraver. A key figure in the *Hudson River School, he was generally acknowledged as the leading American landscape painter for about two decades following Thomas *Cole's death in 1848. During these years he also served as an important spokesman for the Hudson River School aesthetic and for the moral values that sustained it. Durand's detailed but poetic views of nature reverberate with the spiritual intensity he brought to painting. Early in his career, Durand numbered among the finest American engravers. When he turned to painting in the 1830s, he produced narratives, *genre scenes, and portraits. His concentration on landscape began in the 1840s. His best-known work, *Kindred Spirits* (Walton Family Foundation, 1849), painted as a memorial to Cole, depicts the painter together with poet William Cullen Bryant in a woodland setting. Born in Jefferson Village (now Maplewood), west of Newark, New Jersey, Durand was apprenticed in 1812 to metropolitan New York's premier engraver, Peter Maverick (1780–1871), whose print shop at that time was in Newark. As Maverick's partner, from 1817 until 1820 Durand ran the New York branch of the firm. Subsequently his own shop produced banknotes, certificates, and other items, as well as reproductions of art works. In 1823 Durand's version of John *Trumbull's *Declaration of Independence* made his reputation as a leading American engraver, while his notable 1835 print of John *Vanderlyn's *Ariadne* numbered among his last works in this medium.

Increasingly committed to painting and becoming particularly interested in landscape, Durand departed on his only trip to Europe in 1840. After an initial sojourn in London, he made the conventional grand tour of the Continent, all the while studying the art of museums and galleries, copying old masters, and working from studio models as well as nature. Already in his mid-forties when he returned to New York a year later, Durand then rapidly built on his European experience. When his mentor Cole died, Durand was perceived as his successor, but not just because of the quality of his painting. His status rested also on his earlier preeminence as an engraver and his active participation in the New York art world. Previously sponsored and befriended by major art patrons, such as Luman *Reed and his business partner Jonathan Sturges (1802–74), he had in addition been president since 1845 of the *National Academy of Design. A founding member, he continued to head the organization until 1861. He augmented his leadership in the New York art community by publishing nine gracious and persuasive "Letters on Landscape Painting" in *The *Crayon* in 1855 and early 1856. Conceived as advice to a young painter, these essays provide salient insights into the methods and purposes of mid-nineteenth-century landscape art. They particularly stress the artist's need to work toward technical proficiency in an attitude of humility before nature. To see nature "truly," Durand thought, "long practice is necessary." Adhering to the traditional neo-Platonic belief that "the true and the beautiful are inseparably connected," he conflated landscape and theology. Nature, he wrote, is "fraught with lessons of high and holy meaning, only surpassed by the light of Revelation." While his spiritual yearnings recall contemporary Transcendentalism, Durand's emphasis on truth to nature parallels a position advanced in the writings of English aesthetician and critic John Ruskin. An early advocate of painting in oil as well as sketching outdoors, Durand usually spent his summers in scenic areas of the Northeast. In 1869 he moved back to the village of his birth, where he completed his last painting in 1878. Poor health prevented further accomplishment before his death in Maplewood.

Reflecting his early involvement with the black-and-white process of engraving, Durand's painting generally features meticulous drawing, pearly tonalities, and subordinated but nuanced color. His interest in glowing atmospheric effects allies some of his work with *luminism. For all his talk about exactitude to nature, most of Durand's paintings are actually idealizations, pleasing compositions combining individually observed motifs. Moreover, influences from European masters continued to pervade his art long after his trip abroad. Aspects of work by Claude Lorrain, John Constable, and Dutch painters including Paulus Potter and Aelbert Cuyp echo frequently. Correspondences with *Barbizon art also appear, although he could have become acquainted with such work only after his return from Europe. Durand's quite varied landscape practice comprises three predominant types. His most ambitious undertakings consist of large compositions embellished with symbolic or literary meanings. Widely admired during the artist's lifetime, these acknowledge the moralizing aspirations of grand Salon paintings. *Landscape—Scene from "Thanatopsis"* (Metropolitan Museum, 1850) encompasses references to Bryant's poem within its spacious scope. Much more numerous in Durand's output are idyllic pastorals that echo the golden amplitude of Claude and his followers. Some of these also incorporate elements, such as farm animals, that descend from earlier Dutch work and may also have been partly inspired by such Barbizon painters as Jean-François Millet. Finally, and most original to the modern eye, intensively visual and unsentimental views avoid associational elements, traditional motifs, and standard compositional formulas. Particularly notable among these, a group of forest interiors have few precedents in earlier painting. Durand's are more tightly executed than Gustave Courbet's woodland studies, but some call to mind the French painter's radical realism and brooding tone.

Durand, John (active 1765–82). Painter. Known for portraits, he harbored aspirations to other forms, especially grand manner history painting. Probably of French ancestry, he may have been born in France but almost certainly did not train there. He was first recorded in Virginia in 1765. Although he apparently spent much of his career in that state, he traveled often. During the years immediately following his first appearance in New York in 1766, he numbered among the most actively engaged portraitists there, and in 1767 he advertised a drawing school. He also worked in Connecticut and in Bermuda. After 1775 he is not known to have left Virginia. Despite his acquaintance with the conventions and theoretical underpinnings of fashionable European art, Durand possessed only limited technical skills. Yet he combined boldly designed, strongly outlined, flattened forms into lively compositions heightened by an acute sense of color. His only known group portrait, *The Rapalje Children* (New-York Historical Society, c. 1768) presents four cheerful, naturally posed figures in an informal arrangement of overlapping shapes. Although the faces show little individuality, clothing is attentively rendered to suggest the family's social position. A teenage boy wears a striped waistcoat with his blue suit, while each younger sibling is attired in a different color. The pattern of these vivid hues, set off by white accouterments, provides a fresh and animated air. Some of Durand's later work shows a more volumetric approach to form, perhaps stimulated by contact with the work of John Singleton *Copley.

Durrie, George Henry (1820–63). Painter. Best known for winter scenes romanticizing cozy seasonal pleasures in the country, he also painted summer landscapes, portraits, still lifes, and a few narratives. A lifelong resident of New Haven, Connecticut, he was mostly self-taught as an artist, although from 1839 to 1841 he intermittently worked with New Haven portrait painter and engraver Nathaniel Jocelyn (1796–1881). In the early 1840s he traveled itinerantly in search of portrait commissions but around the middle of the decade began to concentrate on the Connecticut landscape. Influenced by Thomas *Cole's paintings, he shared many interests with *Hudson River School painters. Yet Durrie put more emphasis on *genre elements than they commonly did. His compositions were less sophisticated, and his concentration on detail worked against their more unified effects. Yet, although his works rarely display the metaphysical grandeur of the finest Hudson River School paintings, they compensate with charming domestic contentment. The characteristic *Returning to the Farm* (New-York

Historical Society, 1861) depicts a farmer bringing to his homestead a sled-load of logs. Snow-covered ground and thick cloud cover provide the dominant grayish tonality, against which bare trees and farmyard details stand out insistently. A heavy atmosphere obscures the clarity of distant hills. Although snowfall seems imminent, the treatment implies pleasures of the fireside, rather than danger or privation. Issued in the 1860s as *Currier & Ives prints, ten of Durrie's winter scenes found particularly widespread popularity and inspired imitation. His brother **John Durrie Jr.** (1818–98), who also studied with Jocelyn, painted portraits and still lifes in New Haven. **George Boice Durrie** (1842–1907), a son, painted as well, although in addition he became a physician. He left New Haven in the mid-1860s to live in the New York area. He occasionally signed his name George H. Durrie, creating the possibility (perhaps intentionally) of confusion with his father's work.

Duveneck, Frank (1848–1919). Painter, printmaker, and sculptor. As a young painter, he made his reputation with dark, vigorously executed portraits and *genre scenes. During the 1880s, as he responded to Italy's landscape and picturesque inhabitants, his work became more subdued and elegant, closer to the style popular at the Paris Salon, with a tighter technique and more delicate colors. From the 1890s on, he painted nudes and other subjects but achieved his strongest results in outdoor views often indebted to impressionist light and color. Active as a printmaker only during the early 1880s, he concentrated on scenes of Venice. His first sculpture, a bronze portrait memorial for his wife's grave (Allori Cemetery, Florence, 1892; modeled 1889–91), remains the most important of the few he completed. As a teacher and mentor, he displayed a gift that attracted many students and earned their affection. Born Francis Decker in Covington, Kentucky, he grew up using the surname of his stepfather. As a young man he worked for several years in the Cincinnati area and elsewhere as an assistant to a German studio specializing in church decoration. In 1869 he departed for Munich, where in January of the following year he began his studies at the Royal Academy. There he quickly developed an energetic, nonacademic realism indebted to the example of Wilhelm Leibl and, through him, to Gustave Courbet. Early, Munich-style works such as the vigorously brushed *Whistling Boy* (Cincinnati Art Museum, 1872) remain among his most admired creations. After an interlude in Cincinnati from late 1873 until 1875, he shared a Munich studio with William Merritt *Chase. In the spring of 1877 Duveneck traveled with him and John *Twachtman to Venice, where he remained for nine months. Once again in Munich, early the next year Duveneck began conducting his own classes for American students. When summer came, he moved the enterprise to Polling, in the Bavarian countryside, where he painted some of his earliest landscapes. In 1879 Duveneck and about a dozen of his students, jocularly known as the "Duveneck boys," relocated to Italy to work in Florence and Venice. The following year, while in Venice, Duveneck began making etchings influenced by the style and subjects of his new acquaintance James Abbott McNeill *Whistler. In 1881–82 Duveneck worked for about a year in the United States, largely in Boston, and then resided in Italy and Paris until 1888. Subsequently, after a short time in Boston, he settled permanently in Cincinnati, where he taught for many years at the Art Academy. During summers in Gloucester, Massachusetts, he conducted classes, painted landscapes, and enjoyed the companionship of some of the erstwhile "boys." In these later years, he also visited Europe on a number of occasions.

His wife, Boston-born **Elizabeth Otis Lyman Boott Duveneck** (1846–88), painted landscapes, genre scenes, and still lifes in oil and watercolor. From the time she was about eighteen months old, she lived mostly in Florence and Rome. In the late 1860s, during her first extended sojourn in her native city, she studied with William Morris *Hunt and several years later worked in France with Thomas Couture. Her style remained indebted to both. During the summer of 1879 she traveled to Munich to study with Duveneck and was instrumental in persuading him to relocate to Florence that fall. After a working visit to Spain, in 1881 she resettled once again in Boston. With her paintings increasingly well received at American exhibitions, in 1885 she decided to advance her career in Paris. She and Duveneck married there the following year. The couple then worked in Florence for about a year and a half before once again taking up residence in Paris. A few months later she died there of pneumonia.

Duyckinck family. *See* PATROON PAINTERS.

Dwight, Mabel (1876–1955). Printmaker and painter. Best known as a lithographer of subjects from contemporary life, she believed that the artist must function as an agent of social justice. While some scenes carry a satirical edge, others empathize with the difficult lives of ordinary workers. Born in Cincinnati, in 1921 Mabel Jacque Williamson took the name of

Dwight. She grew up mostly in New Orleans. In San Francisco in the 1890s, she studied at the Hopkins School of Art, where Arthur *Mathews ranked as her most important teacher. After moving to New York in 1903, she was married to Eugene *Higgins from 1906 until 1917. Following additional study in Paris, as well as travel in Europe and Asia, in her fifties she took up lithography. Her first major work in this medium comprised a set of picturesque views of Paris, done before her return to the United States in 1928. Known by the mid-1930s as a leading printmaker, she participated actively from 1935 until 1939 in the WPA's *federal art project in New York. Among lithographs produced under its auspices, *Silence* (undated) gives an affectionate view of a library reading room crowded with assorted studious types absorbed in their books. Depicting heavily burdened dockworkers, *Banana Men* (1936) treats the hardworking poor with dignity, betokening the conscience that had attracted her to socialism as a young woman. In later years, she lived in Bucks County, Pennsylvania, where she died in Sellersville.

Dynaton movement. *See* MULLICAN, LEE.

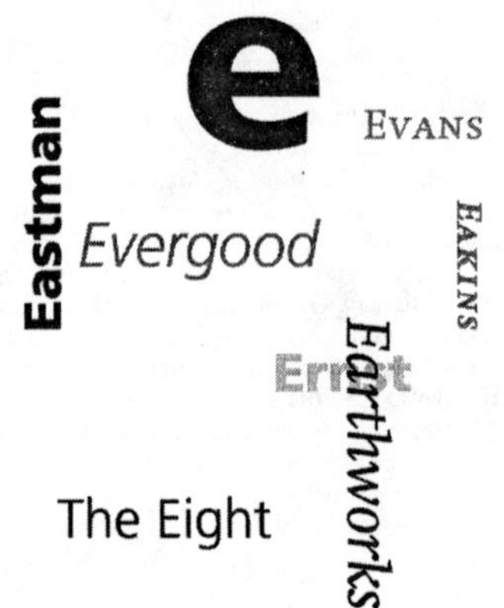

Eakins, Thomas (1844–1916). Painter, sculptor, and photographer. Principally a painter of portraits and *genre scenes, Eakins employed old master techniques to depict his modern world. Devoted to science as a tool of understanding, he nevertheless remained at heart a romantic, committed to beauty and the perplexities of human existence. In striving to understand the structure of the reality he depicted, Eakins methodically pursued studies in perspective and human anatomy. His convincing and affecting images show little regard for the period's progressive artistic tendencies, such as impressionism. His most famous canvas, *The Gross Clinic* (Pennsylvania Academy and Philadelphia Museum, 1875), depicts a surgeon at work. Shockingly frank for its time, the painting exalts its subject as a hero of science but also acknowledges suffering and human frailty. Eakins remained too independent to pursue popular success, although later observers have admired his individualism and stubborn probity. His complex and sometimes contradictory nature perhaps accounts for the depth of human feeling encountered in his work. A Philadelphian, Thomas Cowperthwaite Eakins resided elsewhere only during his student days in Europe. Mechanical drawing and perspective numbered among the subjects the youngster encountered while excelling at Central High School, Philadelphia's finest secondary institution. He graduated in 1861, before his seventeenth birthday, and a year later began his professional training at the *Pennsylvania Academy of the Fine Arts, where he studied with Alsatian-born figurative painter Christian Schussele (1824–79). In 1864 and 1865 he also studied anatomy at Jefferson Medical College. In the fall of 1866 he departed for Europe, where he remained for four years except for a three-month visit at home. Until 1869 he studied in Paris at the École des Beaux-Arts, where Jean-Léon Gérôme ranked as his principal teacher. He also received some instruction at the École from sculptor August-Alexandre Dumont and, independently, from painter Léon Bonnat. Near the end of 1869 Eakins briefly visited Madrid before settling for nearly six months in Seville. During this critical Spanish interlude, he absorbed the conceptual directness and painterly brushwork of Baroque naturalism, particularly as seen in the work of Velázquez. He also admired paintings by Rembrandt and José de Ribera.

Upon his return home in 1870, he painted portraits and images of family life, but scenes of outdoor leisure, generally depicting people he knew engaged in sports or hunting, constitute his most original early works. Executed between 1870 and 1874, a number of these depict rowing on the Schuylkill River, then a popular competitive male pastime. The series includes Eakins's first masterpiece, *The Champion Single Sculls (Max Schmitt in a Single Scull)* (Metropolitan Museum, 1871), a complex but precisely calculated work picturing his friend Schmitt, a racing ace, looking at the viewer as he rests his oars. Eakins himself rows in the middle distance. Intersected by two precisely drawn, identifiable bridges, the river setting offers an intimate slice of nature within an urban setting. In its stillness and attention to light, the painting recalls *luminist precedents, while its highly finished technique suggests Eakins's debt to Gérôme. The underlying geometry of the composition imparts classical stability and supports the meditative poetry of a moment in the passage of time. Technically and conceptually a very different work but also centered on a portrait, *The Gross Clinic* shares with *Max Schmitt* its analytical foundations. Dr. Samuel Gross pauses during an operation to speak to the audience gathered in a teaching theater, recalling earlier paintings of anatomy lessons, particularly Rembrandt's. Here the placid harmony of the sculling picture is replaced by towering drama, reinforced by more painterly, less detailed technique. Dark and subdued colors predominate, but brilliant red accents invigorate the scene and reinforce its charged meaning. The compositional structure relies on a solid figural pyramid, befitting the power of scientific thought. Exalting the role of intellect, a shaft of light bathes the surgeon's head, creating an effect resonating with the divine overtones of Baroque painting. Light isolates also his bloodied, scalpel-wielding right hand, drawing attention to the potentially lifesaving work he performs, but at the time repelling many observers.

Despite his powerful achievement in this painting, for Eakins it led principally to disappointment. Deemed too tasteless to be exhibited with the art at Philadelphia's 1876 Centennial Exposition, as he had hoped, it was instead relegated to a medical section.

Like the Schmitt and Gross paintings, most of Eakins's paintings directly confront the circumstances and individuals he observed in Philadelphia. However, the fictional exceptions, appearing to be as acutely observed as those derived from real life, serve to underscore the fluid interchange between literal fact and imaginative invention that animates all his work. In preparation for *William *Rush Carving His Allegorical Figure of the Schuylkill River* (Philadelphia Museum, 1876–77), Eakins engaged in art historical research paralleling his more usual methodical scientific study. Honoring Rush as a kindred Philadelphian, the painting (like several variants and later versions of the same subject) serves as a meditation on the creative life. It also pays homage to American history, a subject of widespread appeal in the years around the nation's centennial. After teaching during this time, mostly on a volunteer basis, at the Pennsylvania Academy and elsewhere for about four years, in the fall of 1878 Eakins accepted a regular position at the academy. Later he also commuted to New York to teach there. Appointed the academy's director in 1882, he instituted a rigorous program of professional training that included anatomical study and drawing from the nude model. These demanding methods, along with his general unwillingness to defer to the school's board of trustees, set the stage for his ouster in 1886. Ostensibly, he was asked to resign for removing the loincloth from a nude male model, while lecturing on musculature, before a drawing class that included women. Eakins continued to teach elsewhere for several more years, but he never again wielded his previous influence. Wounded by the academy's rejection and depressed by lack of interest in his images of modern life, he remained unable to work productively for about a year and a half. Restored in 1887 by a few months among cowboys in territorial North Dakota, he subsequently limited his practice principally to exploring the human condition through portraiture. *Professor Benjamin Howard Rand* (Thomas Jefferson University, Philadelphia, 1874), a chemist lost in thought as he absently pets a cat stalking across his study table, and *The Artist's Wife and His Setter Dog* (Metropolitan Museum, 1885, with later reworkings) number among his finest paintings. Because few commissions came his way, the late portraits continue to depict family, friends, or accomplished individuals invited to pose. Personal rather than social statements, these render sitters unsparingly, usually in sober moods of disengagement, pessimism, or even defeat. They nevertheless radiate an inner life of intelligence and feeling, which finds expression through the artist's mastery of painterly brushwork, commanding composition, and absorbing light effects. Eakins's portraits reflect the era's intellectual fascination with issues related to the nature of consciousness, the processes of human psychology, and the deleterious effects of social repression on the individual mind. The portrayal of his brother-in-law as an isolated standing figure in *The Thinker: Louis N. Kenton* (Metropolitan Museum, 1900) captures the essence of reflection. Although most of his likenesses portray men, the *Portrait of Mrs. William D. Frishmuth* (originally, *Antiquated Music;* Philadelphia Museum, 1900) and *Actress (Portrait of Suzanne Santje)* (Philadelphia Museum, 1903) number among his most compelling. Surrounded by her collection of musical instruments, the majestic and solemn Frishmuth matron stares into space. A single finger abstractedly depressing a piano key underscores her psychological distance from the physical environment. The languid actress slouching in a rigid chair suggests dejected enervation. Her fiery crimson gown, a devastating caress of paint, offers a poignant counterpoint.

Sculpture and photography initially attracted Eakins's interest as tools for achieving accurate representation in his paintings, but each took on a life of its own within his practice. His interest in sculpture grew from making occasional anatomical models of people or animals, as he did for the figures depicted in Rush's studio. In the 1880s and early 1890s he produced a number of independent bronzes. Excepting two horses for equestrian monuments, all of his finished sculptures are reliefs and most depict subjects related to his two-dimensional work. The role of photography in Eakins's creative life was less straightforward. Although he had previously made occasional use of photography as an aid to realistic representation, Eakins became seriously involved with the medium early in the 1880s. Subsequently, his photographic endeavors encompassed both artistically composed images and anatomical studies of movement. The number and quality of his contrived photographs suggests that the medium's expressive possibilities equaled the appeal of its objectivity. Although he conceived and arranged these subtle and poetic scenes with great care, he never exhibited them, did not leave a record of his intentions, and may not have regarded them as works of art. Recalling the *pictorialism of his day, they sometimes served as studies for paintings. Recent research has demonstrated that in a few instances during the early 1880s Eakins apparently projected images onto a canvas to trace outlines, sometimes combining several photographs into one composition. This was almost certainly his method in compiling *Mending the Net* (Philadelphia Museum, 1881), picturing Delaware River fishermen bound together in shared endeavor, along with two children, a passerby, and a man reading. Yet the factuality of the image yields to mood. Its tender realism and attention to community provoke evocative, meditative, and even allegorical responses. The anatomical studies served more analytical purposes, although to the modern eye some may seem aesthetically charged. Early stopped-motion studies by Eadweard *Muybridge and others who examined the gaits of horses had informed Eakins's image of *The Fairman Rogers Four-in-Hand* (originally, *A May Morning in the Park*; Philadelphia Museum, 1879–80). It depicts an academy board member's new coach pulled by four horses through verdant surroundings. (Preparations for this painting also advanced the artist's interest in sculpture. As studies, he made wax models for the horses.) Eakins played a role in bringing Muybridge to Philadelphia in 1883, worked along with him, and made parallel experiments on his own. These included stopped-motion sequences of the nude figure, including himself. The sexual implications of such photographs might be disregarded as a byproduct of his scientific goals were it not for this highly unusual appearance in the nude, along with his unclothed wife and friends, in many of the staged photographs. (Questions remain in the attribution of some photographs, but the works from his circle share a common sensibility.) Perhaps because they were not meant for public inspection, in such photographs Eakins inadvertently divulged the unacknowledged eroticism that sharpens the impact of many paintings.

Still underappreciated in his hometown, Eakins received scattered national recognition after 1900. Poor health ended his painting career by 1910. The year after his death, memorial exhibitions in New York and Philadelphia brought to light his accomplishment and inaugurated his modern reputation. It soon came to be recognized that his achievement exemplifies a goal he set for the nation's painters in a 1914 interview: "to peer deeper into the heart of American life." His wife, painter **Susan Eakins** (1851–1938), specialized in portraits and indoor genre groups. Her interest in photography may have preceded his. Also a lifelong Philadelphian, Susan Hannah Macdowell studied at the Pennsylvania Academy, where Eakins numbered among her teachers. After they married in 1884, she continued to paint in a style resembling his but devoted much time to the household and her husband's career. Following his death, she worked actively almost until the end of her life. With its characteristically rich brushwork, dark tonality, and dramatic lighting, the haunting portrait of her husband in his studio (Philadelphia Museum, c. 1920–25), thought to be a posthumous likeness, indicates her interest, paralleling his, in probing inner life.

Earl, Ralph (1751–1801). Painter. A leading portraitist, he also pursued a notable interest in landscape. In addition to independent views, he pictured bucolic scenery behind many sitters. Born near Worcester, Massachusetts, by 1774 Earl was painting portraits in New Haven, Connecticut, where he had the opportunity to see examples of John Singleton *Copley's work. The following year, after the opening battles of the American Revolution, he journeyed to Lexington and Concord, Massachusetts. His friend and traveling companion, New Haven printmaker and political cartoonist Amos Doolittle (1754–1832), issued four engravings based on Earl's representations of the military encounters there. These unique images of Revolutionary War battles number among the earliest attempts to depict contemporary American historical events. Earl's first masterwork, the austere and concentrated *Roger Sherman* (Yale University Art Gallery, 1776–77), shows the Connecticut patriot seated in a simple Windsor chair. Only an unobtrusive swag of curtain relieves the otherwise spare interior. The painting follows Copley's precedents in its detailed verisimilitude, emphatic volumes, airless ambience, and smooth finish. However, Earl's intensified side lighting abstracts form with a harshness unknown in Copley's work, while the painting's nearly monochrome, reddish-brown tonality contrasts markedly with Copley's rich combinations of hue. In addition, Earl's Sherman reflects little of the aristocratic ease to which Copley's sitters appear to aspire. By emphasizing his sitter's taut demeanor and ascetic surroundings, Earl underscored the impression of a forceful and uncompromising personality for whom pleasure was secondary to rectitude.

Earl's interest in the war of independence did not stem from patriotic American sentiments. To the contrary, he cooperated with the British and in 1778 fled to England. During his seven years there, he studied with

Benjamin *West in London, carefully observed the sophistications of such leading portraitists as Joshua Reynolds and Thomas Gainsborough, and successfully served clients in London and elsewhere. His work so assimilated fashionable English practice that it has passed in modern times for the work of an unidentified local artist. Late in 1785 Earl set up a portrait business in New York. Although he attracted important customers, in September 1786 he went to debtors' prison for about sixteen months. He earned the money for his release by painting portraits of a number of prominent and sympathetic sitters. Subsequently, he worked in numerous Connecticut localities and in the 1790s also traveled to Long Island and sometimes worked in New York. After settling in 1798 in Northampton, Massachusetts, the following year he visited Niagara Falls. As the first significant artist to undertake this journey, he anticipated a standard pilgrimage for nineteenth-century landscapists. Earl subsequently evoked the iconic vista in a *panorama that toured American cities and eventually appeared in London. After returning near the end of his life to the area of his birth, he died in Bolton, Connecticut, near Hartford.

In post-Revolutionary portraits, Earl adjusted the worldliness of contemporary English work to American clients' more down-to-earth, less elitist attitudes. He retained a painterly touch, as well as a facility for suggesting his sitters' gracious amiability, but he often simplified his brushwork and played down elegant effects. Many of his portraits emulate the English preference in this period for placing the sitter before a landscape, and like other Americans, Earl also frequently adapted the popular British device of including attributes of the sitter's profession or lifestyle. Imposingly scaled, the full-length, life-size *Elijah Boardman* (Metropolitan Museum, 1789) stands before his writing desk in an unusually complex space that includes a view into another room. There, bolts of cloth represent the source of the client's wealth as a dry goods merchant in New Milford, Connecticut. Yet Boardman's aspirations were apparently not only material, for names of both classical and modern authors visible on the spines of leather-bound books behind him testify to his interests in the life of the mind. Self-assured, graceful, stylishly attired, forthright and benevolent in expression, he represents the ideal gentleman-entrepreneur of the early republic.

Trained by his father, as a young man **Ralph Eleazer Whiteside Earl** (1785/88–1838) painted portraits the Connecticut River Valley and in Troy, New York. In 1809 he went to London, where West and John *Trumbull supported his efforts and interested him in history painting. After working as a portraitist in Norwich for four years, in 1814 he proceeded to Paris. Following his return to the United States at the end of 1815, he traveled through the South making likenesses in preparation for a representation of the Battle of New Orleans. While pursuing this project, he befriended the battle's hero, General Andrew Jackson, in Nashville. Earl soon settled there, becoming that city's leading portraitist. He also operated a Museum of Natural and Artificial Curiosities. From 1829 to 1837, while Jackson was president, Earl resided in Washington, where he portrayed Jackson many times, as well as other dignitaries. He died in Nashville.

James Earl (1761–96), Ralph's brother, enjoyed a successful portrait career in England. He, too, was born in the vicinity of Worcester and probably also left America in 1778. First documented in London in 1787, he was by then an accomplished painter familiar with recent English work. His portraits effectively combine the breezy conventions of contemporary British portraiture with strikingly individualized likenesses. He spent the final two years of his life in Charleston, South Carolina. James's daughter **Phoebe Earl** (1790–1863), a painter who became known for still lifes, had a successful career in London. She exhibited as Mrs. Dennis Dighton after her marriage to a well-known painter of battle scenes. After 1838, when she remarried, she was known as Mrs. Peter MacIntyre. Her brother, painter **Augustus Earle** (1793–1838), who preferred an alternate spelling of his surname, was especially recognized for travel watercolors.

Earth art/earthworks. Large-scale interventions in the landscape, made with the intention of incorporating the features and/or meanings of the site's natural and/or historical conditions. Earth art emerged in the 1960s and peaked in popularity during the 1970s, reflecting the period's critique of commercialism, embrace of nonsectarian spirituality, and newborn enthusiasm for ecological issues. Because of the works' characteristically remote locations, photographic documentation provided access for most viewers. Much earth art thus shared with *conceptual art a similar attitude about the role of photography as an intermediary in the aesthetic experience. Earth art also overlapped with *process art in those instances that incorporated an intentional role for natural forces. Virginia Dwan's New York gallery introduced the tendency in an "Earth Works" show of October 1968, underwrote a number of the most compelling monuments, and generally served as the movement's headquarters. (After the gallery closed in 1971, Dwan intermittently continued her patronage.)

Robert *Smithson ranks as earth art's most visionary practitioner. Among others significant to the movement, only sculptor, painter, and printmaker Michael Heizer (1944–) has remained almost continuously focused on earth art as a primary interest. Born in Berkeley, California, in the early 1960s Heizer studied painting for a year at the San Francisco Art Institute. After moving to New York in 1966, the next year he turned from *minimalist canvases to pursue projects in the desert West. For the notable *Double Negative* (Museum of Contemporary Art, Los Angeles, 1969–70) near Overton, Nevada, he blasted and bulldozed tons of rock and earth to form two ramps facing each other across a fifty-foot-deep canyon. Although he returned to conventionally scaled art in the early 1970s, he also continued outsize projects, such as the *Effigy Tumuli* (1983–85) in a strip-mined area that is now a state park near Ottawa, Illinois. Here he "sculpted" abstracted representations of five indigenous creatures, including a frog, a turtle, and a snake, each several hundred feet in length. Meanwhile, in the early 1970s he began *City*, a series of massive structures inspired by pre-Columbian architecture and still under construction at an isolated desert site in the middle of Nevada, where he spends most of his time.

Among other major contributors to earth art, Walter De Maria (1935–) participated in varied avant-garde activities of the 1960s and 1970s. He graduated in 1957 from the University of California at Berkeley, not far from his birthplace in Albany. He stayed on to earn an MFA in painting two years later and moved permanently to New York in 1960. He took part in *happenings and before long began creating minimal sculpture. In addition to earth art, he also devised varied conceptual works. However, his single best-known creation remains the *Lightning Field* (Dia Foundation, 1977) in the high desert near Quemado, New Mexico. Here, he installed four hundred slender, pointed, stainless steel poles, evenly distributed across a square kilometer. Visitors to the remote site must agree to remain for nearly twenty-four hours in order fully to appreciate the juxtaposition of art and nature encoded in the work and its site. In a cheeky inversion of the earthwork idea, for a 1968 exhibition in Munich, De Maria filled a room with 1,600 cubic feet of dirt. Repeating the format, the *New York Earth Room* (Dia Foundation, 1977) covers thirty-six hundred square feet of Soho floor space to a depth of twenty-two inches.

Dennis Oppenheim (1938–) worked early in his career as an earth artist but has since gone on to other forms of expression. Born in a hospital in Mason City, Washington, near his parents' home in Electric City, Dennis Allen Oppenheim grew up in the San Francisco Bay Area. He graduated from Oakland's California College of Arts and Crafts (now California College of the Arts) in 1964 and received an MFA degree from Stanford University two years later. For *Directed Seeding—Cancelled Crop* (1969), near Finsterwolde, Holland, he planted a field of wheat, then had an enormous X-shape harvested from its midst. A number of his earth art projects relied on strenuous bodily activity, a form of *performance art, to make their point. In *Reading Position for Second Degree Burn* (1970), he shifted toward a more conceptual mode. For this work, he stretched out in the sun for five hours, allowing his skin to burn except where it was protected by an open book on his chest. Subsequently, he became particularly interested in all sorts of mechanical constructions and installations, but he also continues to produce sculptural objects that generally maintain a zany edge. He lives in New York.

Although earth-moving and related large-scale activities have been infrequently pursued as art in recent years, James *Turrell and Charles Ross (1937–) have explored the possibilities of burrowing into the earth to affirm a place in the universe. Following five years of planning, Ross started construction in 1976 on a huge architectural reconfiguration of the Chupinas Mesa, eighty-five miles southeast of Santa Fe. When completed, *Star Axis* will allow the visitor to traverse the mesa through chambers connected by a tunnel and then ascend into a pyramid along an axis paralleling the earth's. The heavenward view will reveal patterns of movement as the earth spins once a day, rotates about the sun each year, and over millennia reorients its axis. A native of Philadelphia, Ross completed a bachelor's degree in mathematics in 1960 and a master's degree in sculpture two years later, both at the University of California at Berkeley. While also investigating other ways of using the sun's energy, in 1965 he began working with large-scale prisms, which he has since employed to create meditative spaces filled with fluctuating colored light. He generally spends winters in his New York studio and summers at the New Mexico site.

A form of art closely related to earth art more appropriately may be termed land art. Such sculptures or installations are intimately related to their particular placement in the landscape and may interact with or draw attention to features of their sites, but they alter the environment very little, if at all. *Christo's temporary interventions suggest one approach, but more frequently artists such as Nancy *Holt have sought permanence. Among others who contributed to land art, in the early 1970s Alice Aycock (1946–) constructed architecturally scaled, metaphorical structures related to their settings. In the 1980s she incorporated metaphysical overtones in more complicated, machinelike endeavors, which she sometimes elaborated with long titles or accompanying texts incorporating playful and irrational elements. More recently, she has worked internationally on commissions for numerous public sculptures that characteristically draw attention to natural phenomena. Born in Harrisburg, Pennsylvania, she graduated from Douglass College in New Brunswick, New Jersey, in 1968. Three years later, she received a master's degree from New York's Hunter College, where she worked with Robert *Morris. Others who contributed to land art in the 1970s and whose work continues to reflect that early experience include Mary Miss (1944–), Jody Pinto (1942–), and Michele Stuart (1938–).

Eastman, George. *See* PHOTOGRAPHY, AMERICAN.

Eastman, Seth (1808–75). Painter and draftsman. A career army officer, he specialized in painting American Indian life but also produced many landscapes. He accomplished much of his finest work in territorial Minnesota, where he was stationed during the 1840s. Later he served as principal illustrator for Henry Rowe Schoolcraft's government-sponsored, six-volume *Historical and Statistical Information Respecting the History, Condition and Prospects of the Indian Tribes of the United States* (1851–57), a landmark of early anthropology. Eastman was born in Brunswick, Maine. In 1824 he entered the United States Military Academy at West Point, New York. Trained there as a topographical draftsman, following graduation he was assigned to work in this specialty, mostly in the upper Midwest. After he returned in 1833 to teach drawing at West Point, Robert W. *Weir aided his development as an artist. From 1841 until 1848 Eastman served at Fort Snelling, in what is now Minnesota. There he undertook a sustained inquiry into indigenous peoples' culture, customs, and language. In addition to painting many direct studies of Indian life, he also recorded the landscape of the upper Mississippi region and, later, other areas of the country where he was stationed. His numerous small drawings and watercolors, many apparently done directly from nature, convey specific landscape features, atmosphere, and light with appealing freshness. Suggesting human harmony with nature, these often include Indians or frontiersmen in characteristic activities. Some of his more ambitious oils, such as the carefully composed *Lacrosse Playing Among the Sioux Indians* (Corcoran Gallery, 1851) include informative details about tribal life, but they lack the immediacy of his directly observed studies and sometimes employ violence or sentimentality to accentuate the American Indians' exoticism. After he left Minnesota, Eastman served in Texas for a year before arriving in Washington, D.C., to work on the Schoolcraft project. Washington remained his permanent residence, although between 1855 and 1867 he served for relatively brief periods in many locations throughout the country. Subsequently he painted many western scenes on commission from Congress to adorn committee rooms in the U.S. Capitol. While he was at West Point, the academy published his *Treatise on Topographical Drawing* (1837). Later, Eastman provided illustrations for several books by his wife, Mary Henderson Eastman, a writer of fiction and poetry as well as nonfiction. These include *Dahcotah; or, Life and Legends of the Sioux Around Fort Snelling* (1849), *The American Aboriginal Portfolio* (1853), and *Chicora and Other Regions of the Conquerors and the Conquered* (1854).

E.A.T. *See* EXPERIMENTS IN ART AND TECHNOLOGY.

Eaton, Joseph Oriel. *See* CHASE, WILLIAM MERRITT.

Eberle, Abastenia St. Leger (1878–1942). Sculptor. Humanitarian concerns inspired her characteristic small bronzes naturalistically depicting lower-class children and women. Influenced by reformer Jane Addams and the turn-of-the-century Progressive movement, Eberle admired what she perceived as the vitality and uninhibited zest for life in New York's tenement culture. Like contemporary *Ashcan School painters, she employed a vigorous, anti-academic style suitable to her *genre subjects. *Girls Dancing* (Corcoran Gallery, 1907) exemplifies the spirited animation of her best works. Two girls holding hands swirl in movement, their hair and dresses flying. In the energetic *Windy Doorstep* (Peabody Art Collection, State of Maryland, 1910), wind tosses the long skirt of a woman wielding a broom. Born in Webster City, Iowa, Mary Abastenia St. Leger Eberle spent her childhood primarily in Canton, Ohio. After a year with her family in Puerto Rico, in 1899 she entered the *Art Students League for three years of study. George Gray *Barnard and

Kenyon *Cox numbered among her teachers. Between 1904 and 1906 she collaborated on several sculptural groups with studio-mate Anna Hyatt *Huntington. She visited Italy in 1907 and again in 1908 and Paris in 1913. From 1907 she lived and worked much of the time on New York's Lower East Side, where she acted on her belief in the artist's social responsibility by devoting her art to themes derived from the lives of the unfortunate. Although art professionals admired her achievements, her social radicalism positioned her work outside public taste. From 1909 she summered at *Woodstock, and in 1913 she exhibited in the *Armory Show. Although she completed a few later pieces, increasingly severe heart problems effectively ended her career by 1920. In later years, she spent most of her time in Westport, Connecticut. She died in New York.

Eby, Kerr (1889–1946). Printmaker. Known particularly for etchings of New England, he numbered among few artists to produce eyewitness scenes of the world wars. Born in Tokyo, the son of Canadian missionaries, Harold Kerr Eby returned to Canada as a child. Upon moving to New York in 1907, he trained at the Pratt Institute and the *Art Students League. From 1913 until he entered the U.S. Army during World War I, he worked in *Cos Cob, Connecticut, while afterward he resided in Westport. In 1943 and 1944, he served as an artist-war correspondent in the Pacific. Although more explicitly detailed, Eby's prints, which include lithographs in addition to his more numerous intaglios, reflect the lingering influence of James Abbott McNeill *Whistler's example in their simple compositions, empty spaces, and quiet mood. Exemplifying Eby's debt, the etching and aquatint of a ship in harbor by moonlight, *Night Loading* (1930), achieves its effect through moody tone, inexplicit subject matter, and a broad expanse of still water across an empty foreground. Even many of Eby's war scenes display aesthetic detachment. Also combining etching and aquatint, *September 13, 1918—St. Mihiel* (1934) portrays an army on the move, seen from a distance before a sky that dwarfs human significance. Although some records, such as the drawing *D-Day, Tarawa* (1944), get close to military action, their horrors are offset by refined composition and delicate draftsmanship. Felled by a tropical disease contracted in the South Pacific, he died in a Norwalk hospital, not far from Westport. Eby's antiwar *War*, an illustrated response to his military experiences, appeared in 1936.

Eckstein, Frederick. *See* POWERS, HIRAM.

Edgerton, Harold Eugene (1903–90). Photographer. After perfecting strobe lighting, he used high-speed photography to reveal previously unseen events, creating dramatic images that often enlarge their scientific interest with the disclosure of unanticipated beauty. Born in Fremont, Nebraska, he earned a degree in electrical engineering from the University of Nebraska in 1925 and a PhD in that subject at the Massachusetts Institute of Technology in 1931. He remained at MIT for the rest of his career and died in Cambridge, Massachusetts. His experiments with bursts of intense illumination enabled him to photograph motion that eludes normal human perception. One extended series, for example, captures crown-like splashes of milk. He also photographed such instantaneous phenomena as bullets tearing through varied materials and tennis racquets hitting balls, as well as the stop-action motion of birds, animals, and people. Later Edgerton worked with Jacques Cousteau in developing methods for deep-water photography. The novelty of his approach drew particular attention to *Flash! Seeing the Unseen by Ultra High-Speed Photography* (1939), the first of several books. He coauthored *Moments of Vision: The Stroboscopic Revolution in Photography* (1979).

Edmonds, Francis William (1806–63). Painter. Known for *genre scenes, he also painted literary subjects, portraits, and landscapes. Born and raised in Hudson, south of Albany, in 1823 he went to work at a New York bank. When the *National Academy of Design began offering classes three years later, he enrolled. In 1829 he exhibited his first painting, but the following year he took a position at a Hudson bank for two years and during this period neglected his art. After resettling in New York, he pursued dual careers in finance and painting for more than twenty years, eventually becoming a leader in both the business community and the city's cultural life. He resumed exhibiting in 1836, at first under the pseudonym E. F. Williams. Late in 1840 Edmonds sailed for Europe to spend eight months traveling from London to Rome and back. He left banking in 1855 but soon founded a banknote-engraving firm. He died in the New York suburb of Bronxville, where he had maintained a home since his retirement from finance. The subjects of most of Edmonds's paintings derive from American life, although in some cases literary sources inspired narrative concepts. Most represent domestic interiors as the setting for dramas of everyday middle-class existence. Like other antebellum genre painters, he sometimes commented indirectly on contemporary social or political issues. His images generally display the optimistic good cheer that Americans of this period preferred, and many include humorous touches. Although figures often exhibit a sentimental cast, meticulously rendered still life items ground the works in observable reality and provide appealing visual richness. In developing his style, Edmonds drew on the work of William Sidney *Mount, the internationally popular Scotsman David Wilkie, and seventeenth-century Dutch masters. He devoted much of his tour of Europe to searching out paintings by Gabriel Metsu, Pieter de Hooch, Adriaen van Ostade, and their contemporaries, and to collecting prints of such work. His scene of winsome seduction, *The Bashful Cousin* (National Gallery, c. 1842) displays characteristic features, including easily readable emotional states among the stock characters, a sweetly humorous domestic theme, tolerantly observed human foibles, precisely detailed accessories and furnishings, interest in the play of light, and views into partially revealed subsidiary spaces beyond a corner interior where the action occurs.

Edwards, John Paul. *See* F/64 GROUP.

Edwards, Melvin. *See* AFRICAN-AMERICAN ART.

Egan, Charles. *See* ABSTRACT EXPRESSIONISM.

Eggleston, William (1939–). Photographer. Best known for color photographs recording small-town and rural life in the South, he has also worked in locations around the world. In his most distinctive work, people appear infrequently, but ordinary objects, variously treasured, abandoned, or disregarded, bear witness to human activity. Eggleston's controversial 1976 show at the *Museum of Modern Art, the first solo exhibition of color photography there, did much to stimulate interest in color among photographers in that decade. In addition, the deceptive casualness of his highly controlled style helped to develop appreciation for the snapshot aesthetic. Born in Memphis, Tennessee, he continues to make his home there, although he spent much of his early life in northern Mississippi. He studied at Vanderbilt University in Nashville, Delta State College (now University) in Cleveland, Mississippi, and the University of Mississippi in Oxford. The discovery of Henri Cartier-Bresson's photography in the early 1960s fueled his passion for the medium. Soon, work by Robert *Frank and other young street photographers came to his attention. Following their lead in concentrating on anti-heroic aspects of his native region, in the mid-1960s he began to employ resplendent color. By treating unromantic subjects such as pick-up trucks and humble dwellings with aesthetic seriousness and flawless technique, he produced a powerful tension between expectation and visual impact. "I am at war with the obvious," an often-quoted remark, gets to the heart of his purpose. In conjunction with his 1976 MoMA show, he assembled the photographs in *William Eggleston's Guide*, a smaller and more focused selection of images. His other publications include *The Democratic Forest* (1989), *Faulkner's Mississippi* (1990), and *Ancient and Modern* (1992).

Ehninger, John Whetten (1827–89). Painter and illustrator. He is remembered particularly for *genre and historical scenes of New England and, less frequently, the South. Born in New York, he graduated in 1847 from Columbia College (now University). In Europe during the next six years he studied in Paris with Thomas Couture and in Düsseldorf, where Emanuel *Leutze numbered among his teachers. He also traveled, particularly in Italy. Returning to New York, he adapted his European training to self-consciously American subject matter. Rendered with punctilious and sometimes crowded detail, his subjects appear to provide accurate glimpses of rural or middle-class experience. However, these views often idealize and sentimentalize a way of life already disappearing as the country industrialized and urbanized. Ehninger's illustrations frequently appeared in best-selling books and leading periodicals. He also introduced to the United States an early photographic process that facilitated distribution of drawings and prints. Employing this *cliché-verre* technique, in 1859 he edited *Autograph Etchings by American Artists Produced by a New Application of Photographic Art*, which included his own work as well as examples by other leading artists. In the 1870s he moved permanently to Saratoga Springs, New York.

Eichholtz, Jacob (1776–1842). Painter. Known primarily for portraits, he also painted a few landscapes and narrative scenes. Born in Lancaster, Pennsylvania, he became a metalsmith there and remained mostly self-taught as an artist. During an 1808 visit, Thomas *Sully provided some instruction, and a few years later Eichholtz traveled to Boston to seek out Gilbert *Stuart. By around 1820 he was painting full time for a middle-class clientele. Although he never mastered the fluid painterliness of his mentors, his unpretentious, carefully observed realism and deft suggestion of character secured for him the status of a leading portrait painter in Philadelphia and Baltimore. His approach relied generally on sharply defined form, clear colors, and simple compositions.

A relatively ambitious work, and more ingratiating than most, the full-length *Ragan Sisters* (National Gallery, c. 1820), portrays two endearing little girls in white within a classically inflected setting. In the early 1820s Eichholtz moved to Philadelphia for nearly a decade, and he may have resided there again between 1838 and 1841, but otherwise he remained a Lancaster resident.

Eight, The. A group of anti-academic painters who banded together to show their art in 1908. Although their aims and styles varied, most depicted subjects from contemporary American life, rendered in a relatively loose and painterly technique. Much of their work offended genteel taste because of its lack of finish and its unidealized subject matter. The Eight's single exhibition stands as a landmark in the development of a modern American art that responded to new conditions of life in the twentieth century. It also foreshadowed the rise of the *independent exhibitions that speeded the early twentieth century's liberalization of art institutions. Five of the group, under the leadership of Robert *Henri, sometimes are known as the *Ashcan School because of their interest in painting scenes from everyday urban life among the working and impoverished classes. William *Glackens, George *Luks, Everett *Shinn, and John *Sloan shared Henri's Ashcan approach, while the remaining three, Arthur B. *Davies, Ernest *Lawson, and Maurice *Prendergast, seldom addressed prevailing social realities.

The Eight came together in a spirit of protest in 1907 after a number of progressive painters were rejected by that year's exhibition jury of the *National Academy of Design, at the time the most powerful artists' institution in New York. Henri was a member, who had hoped to bring reform from within. Infuriated by the jury's action, one of several intense disagreements between him and the conservative body, Henri soon began to make plans with his associates for a show that they themselves would assemble. The forward-looking William Macbeth (1851–1917) agreed to turn over his New York gallery to the artists for two weeks in February. The show drew a large audience and energetic press coverage, succeeded commercially, and went on tour to nine other cities.

Eilshemius, Louis (1864–1941). Painter. Although he was a well-trained and widely traveled artist, his characteristic landscapes and dreamy figurative compositions display a seemingly naive and sometimes roughly sketched style. Born near Newark, New Jersey, Louis Michel Eilshemius moved with his family to Germany in 1875. In 1882 he entered Cornell University but left after two years to study at the *National Academy of Design and the *Art Students League. In 1886 he went to Paris for a year of study at the Académie Julian with the painter Adolphe-William Bouguereau. Subsequently, he lived in New York, but for the next two decades traveled often, visiting Europe, North Africa, Hawaii, and the South Seas. Eilshemius's relatively progressive early work indicated his interest in the French *Barbizon painters, impressionism, and *tonalism. In *Approaching Storm* (Phillips Collection, 1890) sun drenches a deftly brushed, colorful landscape before gathering storm clouds. By the later 1890s, he turned more frequently to fantasies of wispy nude females in outdoor settings, as in *Afternoon Wind* (Museum of Modern Art, 1899). Later his themes became less innocent, as disturbing narratives of fear and tragedy appear. Simultaneously, his technique became looser and less refined. Although Eilshemius admired Albert Pinkham *Ryder and is often regarded as a representative of the same visionary strain in American culture, his paintings display little of the formal power and psychic tension that make Ryder's work so compelling. In 1920 Eilshemius had his first one-person show, arranged by the *Société Anonyme, but this step toward recognition came too late. Within about year the embittered, eccentric, and increasingly unstable artist ceased painting. Paralyzed in an automobile accident in 1932, he spent his remaining years as an invalid, while paradoxically his art found greater appreciation.

Eisenstaedt, Alfred (1898–1995). Photographer. A pioneering photojournalist, he was born in Dirschau, West Prussia (now Tczew, Poland), but moved with his family to the Berlin area in 1906. As a teenager, he took up photography as a hobby. Drafted into the German army in 1916, he was severely wounded in 1918 and returned to Berlin. While gradually developing photojournalistic skills, he continued working as an amateur in a soft *pictorialist mode before becoming a full-time professional in 1929. An early enthusiast for the small handheld camera, he made use of its potential for speed and adaptability in covering news events and capturing candid moments of human interest. After settling in New York late in 1935, he subsequently was naturalized as a citizen. In 1936 he joined the new *Life* magazine as one of its original staff of four photographers. There he became a mainstay, publishing some twenty-five hundred photo-essays on widely ranging topics. A famous 1945 cover photograph depicts a soldier and a nurse embracing in Times Square to celebrate the end of World War II.

For a period in the 1970s he worked for *Time*. Continuing to photograph well into his nineties, he still had an office at *Life* at the time of his death on vacation in Oak Bluffs, Massachusetts, on Martha's Vineyard. Eisenstaedt discussed his life and work in *The Eye of Eisenstaedt* (1969). His other publications include *Witness to Our Time* (1966), *People* (1973), *Eisenstaedt's Album: Fifty Years of Friends and Acquaintances* (1976), *Eisenstaedt's Guide to Photography* (1978), *Eisenstaedt: Germany* (1981), and *Eisenstaedt on Eisenstaedt; A Self-Portrait: Photos and Text* (1985).

Elliott, Charles Loring (1812–68). Painter. New York's leading portraitist after Henry *Inman's death in 1846, he occasionally also painted imaginative subjects. His popular portrait style combined *romantic stress on individual spirit with contemporary photographic literalism in exactingly detailed, unidealized faces. In later years he actually based some of his less inspired works on *daguerreotypes. Although much of his large output repeated poses, compositions, and color tonalities, his best portraits convey lifelike alertness and physical presence. Elliott's male sitters particularly exude the vitality and optimism admired as character traits in mid-century. Fleeting expressions enhance his portraits' immediacy. Rendered with respect but not flattery, *Mrs. Thomas Goulding* (National Academy Museum, New York, 1858) peers at the viewer with forceful, unsmiling gaze. The eyeglasses she has apparently just removed appear in one hand, providing an enlivening momentary gesture. The artist's unrelenting precision details every item of clothing, as well as the flesh of her middle-aged face. A frilly, beribboned bonnet does little to soften the impression of this dowager's willful personality. Born in Scipio, in the Finger Lakes region of New York State, in 1827 Elliott moved with his family to Syracuse and soon began training as an architect at a nearby academy. Although he became a proficient draftsman, in 1829 he left for New York to study painting. For several months he worked at the *American Academy of the Fine Arts, where he had some contact with John *Trumbull, and then sought instruction from John *Quidor. After about a year in the city, he wandered as an itinerant portraitist upstate. During this period, he acquired a Gilbert *Stuart portrait, which he so admired that he kept it with him on his travels. Even in his highly factual, mature technique, Elliot's method of building up layers of paint retained vestiges of Stuart's approach, and he usually followed Stuart's practice of placing sitters against blank backgrounds. In 1839 Elliott returned to New York. From 1853 he lived in Hoboken, New Jersey, while maintaining a New York studio. He moved to Albany not long before his death there.

Engel, Morris. *See* ORKIN, RUTH.

Enneking, John Joseph (1841–1916). Painter. Known primarily for New England landscapes, he also painted still lifes, figure studies, and European views. His early work reflected *Hudson River School realism, but exposure to contemporary French work reoriented his interests toward form, color, and the expression of mood. Reflecting *Barbizon painters' intimate pastoralism, by the 1880s he had achieved a painterly, unrhetorical approach to spatially limited views. He became known for slightly melancholy autumnal sunsets alight with nuanced color. Some works, particularly among those dating late in his career, demonstrate an impressionist dissolution of form into small strokes of color, often in lustrous hues. A native of the western Ohio village of Minster, he grew up on a farm. He received some instruction in drawing in Cincinnati after moving there in 1856. In 1861 he joined the Union Army. Wounded in the Civil War, he returned to Cincinnati to recuperate. In 1864 he walked to New York before continuing on to Boston. There he studied lithography and industrial drawing but did not work full time as an artist until the late 1860s. In 1872 he departed for Europe, where he traveled widely during four years abroad. He studied at the academy in Munich for six months and spent three months painting in Venice before taking up residence in Paris for three years. There he studied with the academic realist Léon Bonnat, but his contacts with Barbizon artists had more lasting effect. He sought criticism from Charles-Francois Daubigny and became acquainted with Jean-Baptiste-Camille Corot and Jean-François Millet. After two years at home, in 1878 he again returned to Europe to revisit Paris and spend six months in the Netherlands. In 1880 he purchased a summer home in North Newry, Maine. Many subsequent paintings depict the nearby White Mountains across the New Hampshire border or Maine locations ranging to the Atlantic shore. In 1903 he made a final visit to Paris. He died in the Boston suburb of Hyde Park, where he had made his home since the 1860s.

Epstein, Jacob (1880–1959). Sculptor. His vigorously expressionist figurative works, chiefly dedicated to themes of human struggle and aspiration, often suggest his close study of ancient and tribal art. He worked primarily in bronze, but on occasion carved directly in stone. The distortions and frank sexuality of his early monuments created controversy, but after World War II his work was much honored. He also modeled spirited bronze portrait busts, notable for their psychological intensity and fluid, impressionistic surfaces indebted to Rodin's example. His sitters included many celebrated individuals of the early- and mid-twentieth century. Born in New York, he intermittently studied drawing at the *Art Students League between 1894 and 1902. In 1900 he began working in a bronze foundry while attending evening classes taught by George Gray *Barnard at the league. He also worked as an illustrator before going to Paris in 1902 for further study. He returned to the United States on only two subsequent occasions. In 1905 he settled permanently in England and several years later became a British citizen. On a 1912 sojourn in Paris, he was impressed by the work of avant-garde artists he met there, including Picasso and Brancusi. On his return to Britain he helped to found the modernist London Group in 1913. After they came together in 1914, Epstein associated with the radical vorticists, among whom his supporter Ezra Pound was a leader. (Epstein was never an official member.) After World War II, when his art no longer offended public taste, he received many commissions for large-scale works, often related to architectural settings. *St. Michael and the Devil* (1956–58) at Coventry Cathedral numbers among the most prominent. In 1954 Epstein was knighted. He died in London. In 1940 he published an autobiography *Let There Be Sculpture* (revised in 1955 and retitled *An Autobiography*). His conversations on art were collected as *The Sculptor Speaks* (1931).

Ernst, Max (1891–1976). Painter, sculptor, collage artist, and printmaker. A participant in the German dada movement, he numbers also among leading surrealists. In addition, he contributed substantially to avant-garde ferment in New York during the years immediately after his arrival in 1941. Most importantly, his fertile experimentation with several "automatic" techniques, giving chance a free rein in the creative process, resonated with younger American artists such as Jackson *Pollock. Born in Brühl, Germany, near Cologne, Maximilian Ernst became an American citizen in 1948, although he spent most of his life in Europe and became a French citizen in 1958. Before he returned permanently to Europe in the early 1950s, Ernst had married two of the most interesting American women associated with surrealism: Peggy *Guggenheim and Dorothea *Tanning. (Just before World War II, he had lived in France for three years with an equally fascinating English-born painter, Leonora Carrington, who later emigrated to Mexico.)

Ernst studied philosophy and psychology at the University of Bonn for two years but left in 1911 to become a painter. He never attended art school. After serving in the German artillery from 1914 to 1918, he lived briefly in Munich before settling in Cologne. There, he and Jean Arp soon led the local dada movement. While indulging in bitterly nihilist hijinks, he began to paint works that anticipate surrealism. He moved to Paris in 1922 and two years later numbered among charter members of the surrealist group. In the same year, he traveled to Southeast Asia, where he visited Angkor Wat, among other exotic sights. Although it did not affect the course of his work, Ernst broke with official surrealism in 1938 during a disagreement with its leader, André Breton. Ernst was interned as an enemy alien in 1939, but after a hair-raising two years of narrow escapes, he managed to find passage to New York. There he soon joined in the activities of the surrealist exile community and married Guggenheim before the end of 1941. Only months later, the unstable, conflict-ridden marriage was doomed when he met Tanning. Their 1946 marriage proved a lasting match. During the late 1940s and early 1950s, he and Tanning lived much of the time near Sedona, Arizona, where he was particularly attracted to the spectacular natural rock formations that resembled those he had earlier painted from imagination. For the last twenty-three years before his death in Paris, Ernst lived there and in the south of France. Ernst's attraction to irrational, startling, and often hallucinatory imagery unified the varied course of his art. At times dryly sardonic, whimsical at others, most of his work deftly manipulates dreamlike states, often veering toward psychological torment. In its unexpected amalgamation of painted and three-dimensional elements, *2 Children Threatened by a Nightingale* (Museum of Modern Art, 1924) underscores the uncomfortable psychic dislocation communicated by both the strange poetry of the title and the enigmatic image. Ernst also possessed an uncanny ability to scour the culture for potent images, and by reassembling them, reassemble meaning. In the five-volume collage-novel *Une Semaine de Bonté*, published in 1934, he combined printed nineteenth-century illustrations, his principal source, with cutouts from contemporary journals and scientific treatises. Infused with sexual overtones, the disconcerting results configure unsettling interpretive collisions. In one of the era's most pointed responses to World War II, a painting titled *Europe after the Rain* (Wadsworth Atheneum

Hartford, Connecticut, 1940–42), Ernst presented a microscopically focused phantasmagoria of human existence amid vegetal and geological forms, an allegory of degraded civilization on the brink of ruin. In his final years, Ernst's work tended to be more affirmative and abstract than previously.

His son, painter and printmaker **Jimmy Ernst** (1920–84), was the child of his first wife, writer and art historian Louise Straus. Born in Cologne, Hans-Ulrich Ernst studied typography and worked in the printing business but received no formal art training. In 1938 he preceded his father to New York, soon took up painting, began teaching at Brooklyn College in 1951, and in 1952 became an American citizen. His early surrealist-influenced, automatist abstraction, particularly indebted to the work of Roberto *Matta, earned him a place in 1950 among the *Irascibles. In paintings of the 1950s and 1960s, webs of crisscrossing lines and airy geometric structures commonly occur. A late Sea Grass series of semi-abstract marsh themes reflects the surroundings of his studios in East Hampton, where he moved in 1969, and in the Florida Keys, where he maintained a second home from 1980. His autobiography, *A Not-So-Still Life*, appeared in 1984.

Estes, Richard (1936–). *See* PHOTO-REALISM.

Etching revival. Term describing the heightened popularity of etching in the United States during the late 1870s and 1880s, when many painters took up the medium. The movement represented renewed interest in the creative possibilities of intaglio printmaking, which earlier in the nineteenth century had been regarded predominantly as a method for reproducing works of art. Stimulated by a similar enthusiasm in England and France, American artists and their public looked to precedents in the work of James A. M. *Whistler and his circle in London and to the *Barbizon painter-etchers of France. The New York Etching Club, formed in 1877, drew many of the leading practitioners together and sponsored exhibitions, while the short-lived *American Art Review* (1879–81), edited by graphics specialist Sylvester Rosa Koehler (1837–1900), fueled the medium's popularity. Along with biographical and critical essays, it published original etchings. The expanding audience for art in the later nineteenth century provided a middle-class market for these relatively inexpensive products. Generally not tightly descriptive, prints associated with this movement commonly depict outdoor scenes. Typically they offer informal compositions, spontaneous execution, impressionistic imagery, appealing effects of light and atmosphere, and a poetic mood, often suggesting the restful pleasure of solitude. William Merritt *Chase, Samuel *Colman, Thomas *Moran, John *Twachtman, and Julian Alden *Weir number among the period's leading painters who were also drawn to etching. Not surprisingly, the taste and objectives of the etching revival overlapped those of other late-nineteenth-century anti-academic tendencies, particularly American *impressionism, the *aesthetic movement, and *tonalism.

Eugene, Frank. *See* PHOTO-SECESSION.

Evans, Walker (1903–75). Photographer. Known particularly for images of Depression-era poverty and American commercial culture, he remains the country's preeminent and most influential documentary photographer. The artless look of his pictures is only an effect of his consciously forged documentary style, a plainspoken visual rhetoric of clear detail and delicate tonal range. Few artists or writers have so precisely located a personal poetry in the unadorned facts of American experience. Evans's interest in mundane contemporary life belongs to a widespread impulse in the United States during the 1920s and 1930s, as can be seen also in the art of the *American Scene movement. The period's related rediscovery of Americana also found echoes in the subjects of many of Evans's photographs, for he rarely photographed new or modern material, preferring instead the tangled emotional resonance of timeworn objects. At the same time, his appreciation for unexpected imagery links his work to contemporary surrealist attention to the bizarre, paradoxical, and ironic in everyday life. However, his uninflected objectivity also prefigured the draining of personal feeling from aspects of art and photography in the 1950s and 1960s. Born in St. Louis, Evans moved with his family in 1908 to the Chicago suburb of Kenilworth. In 1914 they relocated to Toledo, Ohio, and five years later, to New York. Evans spent most of the next three years at three boarding schools. Initially drawn to literature, in 1922 he enrolled at Williams College in Williamstown, Massachusetts, but left after a year. He worked at the New York Public Library for about a year and a half in the interim before his departure for Paris in 1926. There, he spent a year absorbing French culture and working on his writing. For several years, Evans had occasionally taken amateur pictures, but he began to photograph seriously only after returning to New York. Affinities with writers, intellectuals, and artists, rather than other photographers, formed his sensibility. In 1930 he provided illustrations for the publication of Hart Crane's epic poem *The Bridge*. Frenchman Eugène Atget provided the most direct model for his development, but he also came to admire work by Mathew *Brady, Ralph *Steiner, and August Sander. For a couple of years in the early 1930s, he had a studio in the basement of the Greenwich Village house where Ben *Shahn lived and worked.

When he was hired in 1935 by the photography program of the Resettlement Administration, later known as the *Farm Security Administration, his photographs of Victorian houses had already been shown at the *Museum of Modern Art in 1933. Working for the federal initiative primarily in the South, he took hundreds of pictures, including studies of houses, stores, small-town commercial culture, and agricultural activities as well as portraits. Although other FSA photographers generally used handheld cameras, Evans continued to work most of the time with a view camera and tripod. During a leave, he collaborated with his friend James Agee, then a staff writer for *Fortune* magazine, on an article about tenant farmers. Together they traveled to Hale County, Alabama, where they worked for about a month in 1936, although rarely together. *Fortune* turned down their submission, but it was later published as *Let Us Now Praise Famous Men* (1941). Text and illustrations parallel each other but function independently. In the late 1930s and 1940s, Evans turned his attention to urban settings. In a well-known 1938–41 series, he caught New York subway riders with a small, concealed camera. Although Evans had finished his purest, most intense work by the time he turned forty, until almost the end of his life he continued to mine the complexities, contradictions, and layered meanings of American civilization. Beginning in 1943, he worked as a writer of movie and art reviews for *Time* magazine. In 1945 he accepted a position as staff photographer at *Fortune* and two years later became its photography director. During the next two decades, while also commissioning work from others, he created numerous photo-essays, usually accompanied by his own writing. From 1965 until shortly before his death, he taught at Yale University. Although he sometimes worked in color during the *Fortune* period, in the early 1970s Evans for the first time fully embraced color photography. He particularly enjoyed the point-and-shoot Polaroid camera. He died in New Haven. *American Photographs* (1938), based on a MoMA exhibition, documents the museum's first full-scale show devoted to a single photographer. In 1966 he published *Many Are Called*, a selection of the subway photographs, and *Message from the Interior*, images of unpeopled architectural spaces.

Evergood, Philip (1901–73). Painter and printmaker. Interested in both imaginative reveries and social criticism, Evergood produced his most trenchant social commentary in the 1930s. Even then, however, his work often featured fanciful elements. Later, when his art emphasized more personal themes, he nevertheless continued to include frequent allusions to societal and moral dilemmas. Born in New York as Philip Blashki (in 1914 the family adopted the anglicized surname of his paternal grandparents), he received an unusually rich education. As a child in England, he studied at Eton before matriculating at Cambridge University. Without finishing his degree in English literature, he went to London in 1921 for two years of study at the Slade School of Art. In 1923 he enrolled for a year at the *Art Students League, where George *Luks numbered among his instructors. Returning abroad, he lived for two years in Paris, where he worked at first at the Académie Julian with André Lhote and Jean Paul Laurens. After another period in New York, between 1929 and 1931 he traveled in France and Spain, absorbing such disparate influences as the work of El Greco and Cézanne while painting biblical and imaginative subjects. By the time he returned, he had begun to forge a distinctive style of fast-moving line, loosely defined form, and insubstantial figures barely anchored in ambiguous spaces. Evergood's art directly engaged political and social themes after he settled in New York and became active in left-wing politics. In the 1930s he worked for the *federal art projects, painted socially conscious murals, played a conspicuous role in the *American Artists' Congress, and served as president of the Artists' Union. Many paintings of this period contribute to the social realism of the *American Scene movement, sometimes optimistically but at other times emphasizing darker forces. Reflecting the period's labor unrest, *An American Tragedy* (Whitney Museum, 1937) recreates the violence of a recent confrontation between Chicago steelworkers and police. Intermittently in the 1930s and more consistently in later years, Evergood engaged other approaches extending from straightforward description to allegory. While some paintings evoke states of bliss, others exhibit a grotesque and even repellent quality that borders on surrealism. The unsettling *Lily and the Sparrows* (Whitney Museum, 1939), perhaps his best-known work, suggests moral and spiritual decay. In a complex symbolic image, *The New Lazarus* (Whitney Museum, 1954), suffering, civil strife, destruction, and redemption combine in a provocative anti-war statement. From 1946 he lived primarily in Connecticut, where he died in a fire at his home in Bridgewater. Also in 1946 he published *Twenty Years of Evergood.*

Experiments in Art and Technology (E.A.T). Organization founded in the fall of 1966 to facilitate interactions between artists and scientists. Initially, interest was keen on both sides as E.A.T. promised to expedite collaborative works incorporating advanced technologies, particularly new electronic and computer-controlled processes. Within a year and a half, the organization sponsored some forty chapters across the United States and abroad. It soon claimed six thousand members. Corporations offered handsome financial support, and a number of innovative exhibitions appeared. Still, the organization foundered and then disintegrated in the early 1970s, its idealistic and humanistic vision too difficult to achieve in practice. Few artists or scientists, not to mention corporations, felt committed to a sustained research partnership of the sort originally envisioned. Nevertheless, the group's legacy echoes through performance events, multimedia creations, and the continued attempts of academic and corporate institutions to integrate art and science. Robert *Rauschenberg and electrical engineer Billy Kluver (1927–2004) mobilized E.A.T.'s formation. After meeting in 1960, the two had worked together informally before spearheading the celebrated "9 Evenings: Theater and Engineering" at New York's Sixty-ninth Regiment Armory in the fall of 1966. For this series of performances, artists worked with Kluver's professional acquaintances, mostly colleagues from Bell Telephone Laboratories in Murray Hill, New Jersey. The success of these evenings prompted establishment of E.A.T. to pursue similar ends. Swedish by birth, although born in Monaco, Johan Wilhelm Kluver graduated in electrical engineering from the Royal Institute of Technology in Stockholm. While still a student, Kluver became enamored with film. After earning a PhD from the University of California in Berkeley, in 1958 he moved to New Jersey and subsequently often attended, and soon participated in, avant-garde art events in New York. He left Bell Labs in 1968 to devote full time to E.A.T. and until the final months of his life continued to arrange matches between artists and scientists. Active also as a writer, he and his wife, Julie Martin, wrote *Kiki's Paris* (1989), and in 1997 he published *A Day with Picasso.* Engineer Fred Waldhauer and New York-born artist Robert Whitman (1935–) also assisted in founding E.A.T. Known for poetic multimedia installations and performances incorporating film, Whitman ranked among leading activists in the early days of *happenings and multimedia experimentation. He graduated in 1957 from New Jersey's Rutgers University in New Brunswick, where he studied literature and play writing, took art courses, and became acquainted with Allan *Kaprow. Subsequently, he studied art history at Columbia University for a year. He lives in Warwick, New York, in the Hudson River Valley near the New Jersey border.

FEKE

f

Federal art projects

Feininger

Frank

Fluxus

Frankenthaler

f/64 group. An informal association of California photographers dedicated to sharp-focus imagery printed with technical perfection. Founded in 1932, the group rejected the lingering *pictorialist aesthetic that remained popular among art photographers. Members particularly favored nature subjects, often seen in extremely close views that emphasize abstract form. Coalescing around Edward *Weston as its leading spirit, the group's founders included also Ansel *Adams, who came up with the group's name, Imogen *Cunningham, John Paul Edwards (1883–1958), and Henry Swift (1891–1960), as well as Sonya Noskowiak (1900–1975), a Weston student and his companion at the time, and Willard Van Dyke (1906–86), also a Weston student, later known as a documentary filmmaker. Although the group disbanded after three years, its influence continued in an important strain of American straight photography. The group's most important show, at San Francisco's de Young Museum in 1932, included the work of the seven charter members, along with invited photographers Preston Holder (1907–80), Consuelo Kanaga (1894–1978), Alma Lavenson (1897–1989), and Brett *Weston. The organization's name indicates the smallest aperture possible on the 8 × 10-inch view cameras that its members preferred. This setting produced sharp detail in large negatives that were printed, usually on glossy paper, without enlargement. The group generally took a purist approach to their medium, disdaining any influence from other visual arts as interfering with honest photographic vision.

Farm Security Administration (FSA) photographs. Many thousands of black-and-white photographs produced between 1935 and 1943 to document and promote New Deal programs and policies, particularly those benefiting agriculture. Most report on life in rural and small town America. Under the Resettlement Administration (RA) until 1937 when that agency became the Department of Agriculture's Farm Security Administration, the program that commissioned the work numbers among the *federal art projects that aided visual artists during the Depression of the 1930s. Altogether, about twenty photographers worked for the RA/FSA. The resounding success of the photography program must in large part be credited to its director, Roy Emerson Stryker (1893–1975). He hired many of the country's most able photographers, sent them on assignment, and recognized the aesthetic component of their work. Although Stryker was an economist, even before he became a government administrator he had understood the importance of visual documents in making persuasive arguments for economic or social policies. He knew that President Franklin D. Roosevelt's allies could better support their case for government relief with photographs that revealed the needs of the country's rural citizens. In a larger context, the agency hoped that its photography project would help to unify the country by promoting awareness of its citizens' varied circumstances. The program's earliest photographers included Walker *Evans, Dorothea *Lange, Arthur *Rothstein, and Ben *Shahn. Jack Delano (1914–97), Russell Lee (1903–86), Gordon *Parks, John Vachon (1914–75), and Marion Post *Wolcott numbered among later recruits. Except for Evans, who for the most part continued to use an 8 × 10-inch view camera on a tripod, the program's photographers generally embraced the recently introduced handheld camera, which permitted flexibility and speed. To a large extent, FSA images still epitomize the Depression era. Perhaps the best known is Lange's "Migrant Mother, Nipomo, California" (1936), depicting a despairing woman with her three needy and joyless little children. This and hundreds of other iconic representations of American life across the continent remain a salient historical record of these years, providing evidence of hardship, hard-won successes, human dignity, and the endurance of grace among the nation's struggling populace.

Farny, Henry Francis (1847–1916). Painter and illustrator. Specializing in the Indian inhabitants of the American West, he offered accurately detailed, sympathetic renditions of their life emphasizing domesticity and harmony with nature. Although he did not sentimentalize his subjects, he generally sidestepped contemporary realities of warfare, disease, and poverty. Sometimes he included clues that point to white intrusion into their territory. Such paintings particularly fed the common late-nineteenth-century perception that Euro-American expansion was destined to extinguish a noble way of life. Farny was born in Ribeauville, in the Alsace region of France. He moved with his family to northwestern Pennsylvania, near Warren, in 1853 and six years later to Cincinnati, which remained his permanent home. There he learned lithography and began working as an illustrator. After a brief stint in New York, he left in 1867 for Europe. For three years he traveled and studied in Rome and Düsseldorf. He returned twice to Europe in the 1870s, on the second occasion traveling with Frank *Duveneck to Munich, where he worked for a year. Coming home to Cincinnati in 1876, he resumed his successful career as an illustrator, honing the skills that combined with his European training in a clear, structurally sound, and painterly style. He journeyed west for the first time in 1881 and subsequently traveled there often until 1894. About 1890 he relinquished illustration to paint full time. On trips west, he not only made sketches and notes but also collected Indian artifacts and photographs to facilitate the verisimilitude of his studio creations.

Farrer, Henry. *See* PRE-RAPHAELITISM, AMERICAN.

Farrer, Thomas Charles. *See* PRE-RAPHAELITISM, AMERICAN.

Fasanella, Ralph (1914–97). Painter. Self-taught, he specialized in large, detailed scenes of quintessential New York subjects: Coney Island to Yankee Stadium, subway throngs to street festivals. Some of his works treat politically charged subjects such as labor strikes, the Julius and Ethel Rosenberg spy case, and President John F. Kennedy's assassination. Born in the Bronx, Fasanella grew up in Greenwich Village. He fought in the Spanish Civil War with the Abraham Lincoln Brigade before becoming a union organizer in 1940. Blacklisted for his left-wing views during the McCarthy era, he was often unable to find work during the 1950s. Later he pumped gas at a station in the Bronx. He had started painting in the mid-1940s, but widespread recognition came only after the *New York Times Magazine* ran a feature in 1972. A scene from a late 1970s historical series on a mill town labor dispute, the 5 × 10-foot *Lawrence, 1912—The Great Strike*, hung in the Capitol Hill hearing room of a House labor and education subcommittee for some years. Indicative of Fasanella's ambitions for his art and donated by fifteen unions, it was returned early in 1995 to the AFL-CIO shortly after the Republican party took control of the House. Fasanella died in a Yonkers hospital, not far from his longtime home in suburban Ardsley.

Federal art projects. Several programs supporting artists during the economic depression of the 1930s and early 1940s. The most important of these was the Federal Art Project (FAP) of the Works Progress Administration (later, the Works Projects Administration, both abbreviated to WPA). The federal art projects represent the only sustained support ever offered to artists by the U.S. government. While the financial assistance proved decisive to many individual artists, the programs also had a pronounced cultural effect. Even as paychecks gave artists dignity as workers in society, the projects' communal aspects brought them together, resulting in cross-fertilization of ideas and enhanced creativity. There were major exceptions—artists who did not need or refused to accept government aid—but most of the period's major artists participated, as did thousands of lesser names and the majority of younger artists later prominent as *abstract expressionists.

The federal art projects operated within a massive federal government relief program for unemployed workers. Programs for visual artists paralleled those for other creative people, especially in literature, theater, and music. In May 1933 George *Biddle proposed a mural-painting program to his friend President Franklin D. Roosevelt, who responded favorably. Activation of the program may also be credited in part to the director of the Federal Emergency Relief Administration, Harry Hopkins, who had been petitioned by organized artists to do something on their behalf. In December 1933 the Public Works of Art Project (PWAP) was set up to provide assistance over the next six months by employing artists to work on public projects. Directed from Washington by Edward *Bruce, this program benefited more than 3,700 artists before it went out of business at the end of June 1934. The success of PWAP made evident the desirability of continuing federal support. In October 1934 the Section of Painting and Sculpture within the Treasury Department was set up, with Bruce once again in charge, for the purpose of commissioning works of art for new public buildings. This was not a broad-based relief program: only those artists whose designs were selected in competition received payment. Nevertheless, it provided much needed employment for those who were chosen, and before the program expired in 1943 it sponsored more than fourteen hundred works (mostly murals) for government buildings. (In 1938 the name of this program was changed to Treasury Section of Fine Arts. The following year it moved out of the Treasury Department and was again rechristened as the Section of Fine Arts of the Public Buildings Administration of the Federal Works Agency.) The Treasury Department also administered a smaller and less prestigious program, known as the Treasury Relief Art Project (which was actually sponsored by the Works Progress Administration). Under the direction of Olin Dows, it mostly hired artists from relief rolls. These artists, too, were assigned decorative projects in government buildings, usually small post offices or previously built government edifices.

Administered by Holger *Cahill, the WPA's Federal Art Project, established in the fall of 1935, survived until the summer of 1943. This ambitious undertaking eventually employed more than five thousand artists within numerous subdivisions: easel painting, sculpture, posters, graphics, murals, photographs, and others. It also sponsored the Design Laboratory, the Art Teaching Division, and the celebrated Index of American Design, which employed about a thousand artists to record examples of eighteenth- and nineteenth-century crafts and decorative arts. More than eighteen thousand Index illustrations, today archived at the *National Gallery of Art, document furniture, fabrics, utensils, folk art, and many other types of objects. Compared with the Index and programs restricted to public art commissions, artists on the payroll of most programs within the FAP had considerably more freedom to follow their own stylistic inclinations and choices of subject. What they produced, however, belonged to the government. The breadth of WPA-FAP programs reflected Cahill's goals. He wished not only to provide steady paychecks to artists but also provide instruction for art students, introduce art into rural areas and underserved communities, and document the country's artistic heritage. (The WPA-FAP also underwent changes of name and administration. In a 1939 administrative reorganization that weakened the program, it became the Art Program of the Works Projects Administration of the Federal Works Agency. In 1942, it was handed over to the Graphic Section of the War Services Division.) Finally, a smaller program under the Resettlement Administration was set up in 1935 to benefit painters and photographers. The photographic element was soon transferred into the Historical Section of the *Farm Security Administration. Here, until 1943, under the visionary leadership of Roy Stryker, who hired many of the nation's most talented photographers, an invaluable record of life in rural America was assembled. Like other relief efforts, the federal art projects ended in the early 1940s as the economy strengthened and the nation turned its attention to World War II. In addition, accusations of subversive, un-American sympathies within the federal art projects during their last few years caused political acrimony that weakened their stature. The bureaucratic intricacies of the federal art projects' history should not obscure the value of the enterprise. Collectively, the federal art projects decisively affected the course of modern American creativity, and their memory remains alive in every debate over public funding for the arts.

Federation of Modern Painters and Sculptors. *See* AMERICAN ARTISTS' CONGRESS.

Feeley, Paul (1910–66). Painter and sculptor. Disavowing *abstract expressionism in favor of clarity, structure, and composure, he fostered the growth of *color-field and *hard-edge tendencies. Signature works feature fluid, clean-edged, organic shapes that respond to each other in intricate rhythms within a systemic approach to design. Additionally, his interest in non-Western decorative arts, such as fabrics and Islamic tiles, opened the way for *pattern-and-decoration painters and others interested in ornamental effects. Born in Des Moines, Feeley grew up in Palo Alto, California. In 1931 he moved to New York. Already an accomplished portrait painter, he worked privately with Cecelia *Beaux, while studying also at the *Art Students League with Thomas Hart *Benton, among others. He painted several murals during the 1930s and also worked as a commercial artist. Except for military service during World War II, from 1939 until his death he taught at Vermont's Bennington College, where he built a distinguished art program. His singular style emerged in the early 1960s, as he developed a formal vocabulary capable of great subtlety and refinement. A shape reminiscent of children's toy jacks recurs most often, while other common forms suggest bowling pins, barbells, vases, or butterflies. Usually, all pattern elements, each in a single, unmodulated hue, float independently on the canvas, without touching. He often worked in series, repeating a single composition in several intuitively chosen color combinations for variant effects. During the final year or so of his life, he also made painted wood sculptures that extrapolate his two-dimensional forms into space.

Feininger, Lyonel (1871–1956). Painter and printmaker. Generally based on architectural or maritime subjects, his lyrical, even mystical compositions feature fragmented, overlapping, and often translucent planes derived from cubism. Glowing color abets transcendental aspirations to achieve a soaring, idiosyncratic expression in the tradition of romantic painters such as Caspar David Friedrich. Born in New York, Léonell Charles Adrian Feininger spent most of his adult life abroad. After training as a violinist, between 1887 and 1893 he studied art in Hamburg, Berlin, and Paris, and spent a year at a college in Liège, Belgium. Developing an aptitude for caricature, by the mid-1890s he was a leading political cartoonist in Germany. A contract in 1906 from the *Chicago Tribune* to draw for the Sunday comics section allowed him to move to Paris for two years. There, he seriously began to paint, soon doing so full time. His early paintings make use of previous experience in imagining expressive, exaggerated figures. *Street in Paris* (University of Iowa Museum of Art, Iowa City, 1909) employs energetic contours, brightly colored patterns, and caricatural human forms to capture the animation of urban life.

Having returned to Berlin, he saw cubist work for the first time on a visit to Paris in 1911. He also met Robert Delaunay, whose lyrical, coloristic orphism, a variant of cubism, influenced the development of his personal style, as did Delaunay's interest in working from architectural motifs. Although he remained stylistically independent of German expressionists, Feininger was in touch with many of the major artists of Die Brücke and Der Blaue Reiter, including Alfred Kubin and Franz Marc. By 1913 he had developed his own variant of cubism, using its angularity and fragmentation to create dynamic, often nearly abstract works. Associated with the Bauhaus from its inception in 1919, Feininger designed the woodcut illustrating the school's manifesto and remained at the school throughout its existence. (He was the only artist continuously on the Bauhaus staff, first in Weimar, later in Dessau and Berlin, as well as the only American-born teacher.) In the school's early years, Feininger headed the print workshop, where he shared his enthusiasm for the direct and dramatic effects of woodcuts, although he also worked in etching and lithography. In the years following its formation in 1924, he exhibited widely with the Blue Four, which comprised also Kandinsky, Paul Klee, and Alexei von Jawlensky. By the early 1920s his style had become serene and luminous, using cubist-derived planes to dematerialize his subjects. Inspired by a favorite Gothic church, *Gelmeroda IX* (Folkwang Museum, Essen, Germany, 1926) depicts the church spire soaring above tiny figures, as architectural forms and atmosphere merge in a crystalline evocation of spiritual desire. Made uneasy by the increasingly ominous political climate of 1930s Germany, especially after the Nazis shut down the Bauhaus in 1933, Feininger visited the United States in the mid-1930s but did not depart for good until they tagged his own art as "degenerate" in 1937. He then settled permanently in New York, fifty years after he had left. Stimulated by its skyscrapers, he often pictured them in his art, which became freer and often more abstract in his final years. In *Lunar Web* (Brooklyn Museum, 1951), a diffuse and glowing orb floats above indistinctly rendered darker shapes suggesting mountains or waves. Spare tracery of delicate golden lines floats against warm brown and gray tones, unifying the surface of this contemplative vision.

Two sons also became artists. Photographer **Andreas Feininger** (1906–99), born in Paris, grew up in Germany. Andreas Bernhard Lyonel Feininger studied at the Bauhaus from 1922 to 1925, before earning an architectural degree in 1928 from the Bauschule in Zerbst. After moving in 1933 to Stockholm, he became a full-time photographer in 1936 and emigrated to the United States in 1939. Evidencing an architect's sensitivity to space and structure, his analytic, visually nuanced photographs often pinpoint unexpected eloquence in the material world. He traveled widely as a photojournalist but became particularly known, during two decades as a *Life* magazine photographer, for evocative and dramatic New York scenes that often rely on unusually effective use of a telephoto lens. He was the author of more than thirty books, including collections of his photographs such as *The Face of New York* (1954), *Changing America* (1955), *The World Through My Eyes: 30 Years of Photography* (1963), *Forms of Nature and Life* (1966), and *Nature in Miniature* (1989). Technical works reflecting his expertise include *Feininger on Photography* (1949), *Photographic Seeing* (1973), and *Andreas Feininger: Experimental Work* (1978). His autobiography, *Andreas Feininger: Photographer*, appeared in 1986. He died in New York.

Photographer and painter **Theodore Lux Feininger** (1910–), whose middle name (from the Latin, for "light") reflects his father's fascination with the forms and meaning of illumination, has sometimes exhibited under the names Theodore Lux or Theodore Lukas. Born in Berlin, he graduated from the Bauhaus in 1929 and worked in Germany as a photographer until 1932. While subsequently living in Paris, he began painting full time. In 1936 he emigrated to the United States and served in the U.S. Army during World War II. For more than twenty years before his retirement in 1975, he taught at Harvard University and then the School of the Museum of Fine Arts in Boston. His painting typically focused on trains and ships, which he depicted with dreamlike nostalgia, as in *Ghosts of Engines* (Museum of Modern Art, 1946). He lives in Cambridge, Massachusetts.

Feitelson, Lorser (1898–1978). Painter and printmaker. Between early and late abstract work, he turned to neoclassical and surrealist representation. Born in Savannah, Georgia, he grew up in New York and saw the *Armory Show as a teenager. Before he first went to Paris in 1919, he had already evolved an animated abstract style influenced by cubism and futurism, but he subsequently followed Matisse's example. After a 1922 trip to Europe, he switched to a neoclassical approach, inspired by Renaissance and Mannerist painting. In 1927 Feitelson moved to Los Angeles, where he contributed importantly over the years to local appreciation for modern art. Soon he was attracted to surrealism, which formed the basis of his work for about twenty years. In the 1930s, together with his wife, painter and printmaker Helen Lundeberg (1908–99), he developed a variant called post-surrealism or subjective classicism. The movement claimed to supersede surrealist *automatism and taste for the bizarre by substituting rational control of aesthetic order and subjects from the "normal" mind. Nevertheless, Feitelson's imagery generally surpasses common-sense understanding. Both partners participated during the Depression on murals for *federal art projects. By about 1950, he had moved on to a final phase of his career, focused on large works anticipating 1960s *hard-edge abstraction.

Born in Chicago, Lundeberg grew up in Pasadena, where she studied literature at Pasadena City College before enrolling at the Stickney School of Art, where Feitelson numbered among her instructors. Although some of her paintings from the 1930s incorporate disorienting *biomorphic imagery, her best-known work, *Double Portrait of the Artist in Time* (Smithsonian American Art Museum, 1935), displays a refined and controlled use of surrealist techniques, in a spirit suggesting *magic realism. In this crisply delineated representation, she adapted a photograph to portray herself as a two-year-old who mysteriously casts the shadow of her adult self on the wall behind. In turn, the shadow intersects the edge of a recently painted self-portrait hung on the wall. Other works reiterate the unthreatening charm, contemplative ambiguity, and classic restraint evident in this painting. While remaining interested in the unconscious and in dreams, in the 1950s she began to work more abstractly, often creating complex and mysterious spaces. Both she and Feitelson died in Los Angeles.

Feke, Robert (c. 1707–51 or later). Painter. Among colonial artists, only John Singleton *Copley surpassed his accomplishments as a portraitist. Sumptuously rendered fashion, graceful poses, and atmospheric settings reflect his clients' success and refinement. Although anatomical stiffness, linear definition of form, and a tendency to generalize faces linger in even in his most integrated works, Feke struck a new note in colonial art: pleasure as a key ingredient in his work. No other native-born painter of his time possessed his feel for the sensuous quality of paint, his ability to deploy rich color harmonies, nor his indulgence in tactile experience. His light palette, emphasizing pastels and silvery tones, and his discrimination among the surfaces of expensive textiles, such as satin and velvet, appealed to younger, style-conscious colonists. Rejecting the pompous seriousness of late Baroque taste, his sitters appear at ease with themselves and their prosperity. Many of Feke's portraits are set against feathery landscape backgrounds that contribute idyllic notes and suggest the landed wealth of sitters. How Feke developed into an artist of such sensitivity and distinction remains obscure. Made plausible by a family tradition that held he was a mariner, the conjecture that Feke traveled abroad at some point in his early career has been offered, but no substantiating evidence has been found. He was born in Oyster Bay, on Long Island, and apparently began painting in New York during the 1730s. His substantive career began in 1741, when his first important painting revealed a previously unheralded major talent at work in Boston. *Isaac Royall and His Family* (Harvard University), his only group portrait, suggests awareness of John *Smibert's *Bermuda Group*. Since this work was still in Smibert's possession, Feke probably had made his acquaintance and may have sought instruction from the older painter. Feke's presence is documented in Newport, Rhode Island, in 1742 but not again until 1744. For some months in 1746–47 he worked in Philadelphia, where he completed the first known portrait of Benjamin Franklin (Harvard University). His career reached its height in 1748, the year he returned to Boston to paint several of his most imposing three-quarter figures, all clients from leading families. In 1749 and 1750 he was again in Philadelphia, where, as in Boston just previously, his level of accomplishment put him beyond the range of local competitors. Feke probably visited Virginia in 1750 before returning to Newport, where the last evidence of his existence dates to 1751. Again according to tradition, he sailed for Bermuda or Barbados, where he might reasonably have expected to find a portrait market, but no corroboration of this hypothesis has been found. Whatever the case, presumably he died late in 1751 or soon after, at home, at sea, or at his destination.

Fellig, Arthur. *See* WEEGEE.

Feminist art. Art intentionally stressing women's concerns. As an identifiable tendency, it emerged shortly before 1970, along with the women's liberation movement. It quickly coalesced into a major force in the art world but began to diminish before the end of the decade. However, during these years, feminist art made significant contributions not only to the role and status of women in the arts but also to the replacement of *minimalism and *conceptualism with more personally inflected aesthetic directions that subsequently entered the mainstream. Exemplifying the range of possible approaches, Louise *Bourgeois, Judy *Chicago, Joyce *Kozloff, Ana *Mendieta, Faith *Ringgold, Martha *Rosler, Miriam *Schapiro, Sylvia *Sleigh, and Nancy *Spero number among scores of women who vitalized the movement during its heyday in the 1970s. Stylistically diverse and from the beginning fraught with contradictions, feminist art centered on attempts to represent women's experience and aspirations with a positive and authentic voice. At the outset there was considerable enthusiasm for the "essentialist" belief in women's distinctive nature. On a creative level, feminist artists felt empowered to infuse into their art their own histories and their feelings about sexuality, motherhood, and the gendered body. Narrative, ritual, and autobiography, which had been neglected in recent art, numbered among powerful options identified by feminist artists. They also frequently rejected as inventions of patriarchy the conventional media of painting and sculpture, turning instead to craft traditions, *performance art, *installation art, *video art, and other fresh means of expression. On a political level, the movement also worked to counter entrenched sexism by improving women's access to exhibitions, teaching, and other mechanisms of professional success. Feminist artists also broke new ground in researching neglected women artists of the past, in the process turning up suppressed material that generated increased interest among art historians and other scholars.

Among early signs of a feminist resistance, in 1969 New York women participating in the politically oriented Art Workers Coalition spun off a subgroup, Women Artists in Revolution, to protest women's lack of exhibition opportunities. The following year, Judy Chicago began teaching the first college-level feminist art course at California's Fresno State College. In January 1971 art historian Linda Nochlin (1931–) galvanized women with a landmark essay in *Art News*. "Why Have There Been No Great Women Artists?" located their relative lack of historical accomplishment in social exclusion, not absence of talent. Later that year, Chicago and Schapiro inaugurated a Feminist Art Program at the California Institute of the Arts in Valencia, near Los Angeles. For several years, this functioned as the epicenter of the feminist insurrection in art, but shortly new organizations, publications, and educational opportunities sprang up nationwide. Other writers soon followed Nochlin, with essays and books addressing theoretical and critical issues. A notable contributor to the dialogue, art historian and critic Lucy Lippard (1937–), once an advocate for minimal and conceptual art, gathered her views in *From the Center: Feminist Essays on Women's Art* (1976). As a tongue-in-cheek homage to feminist artists' success, in October 1980 *Art News* ran a cover photograph of twenty prominent women artists under the headline "Where Are the Great Men Artists?" Since then, although feminist art has lost intensity, it still motivates artists of widely different sensibility and intention. The Guerrilla Girls, founded in the mid-1980s, continue to stage protest actions in gorilla suits that preserve participants' anonymity. In strident, sloganeering photo-works, Barbara Kruger (1945–) takes aim at stereotypes that mask male privilege, while Nancy Azara (1940–) invokes feminist spirituality in roughhewn, painted and gilded wood relief sculptures frequently featuring a handprint motif. Los Angeles muralist Judith Baca (1946–) prominently features women's concerns within a context of advocacy for ethnic and racial justice. While younger women continue to incorporate gendered experience into their work, feminist art in general, however meaningful, no longer carries the political charge it once did. The movement's legacy now permits men to adapt the techniques and themes of earlier women's art, and many do.

Fenollosa, Ernest (1853–1908). Art historian and scholar of East Asian civilization. Also a poet. Instrumental in shaping American perceptions of East Asia, he lived for many years in Japan, immersing himself in art, religion, and philosophy. His work fostered appreciation of Asian art and culture in the United States, initiated new areas of research, and indirectly influenced early modern developments in American art and design. Born in Salem, Massachusetts, in 1874 Ernest Francisco Fenollosa graduated from Harvard College, where Charles Eliot *Norton stimulated his interests. He subsequently enrolled in the Harvard Divinity School but left to enter Boston's School of the Museum of Fine Arts in 1877. The following year he left for Japan, where he taught philosophy and other subjects at Tokyo University until 1886. Concurrently, he became fascinated with Japanese culture and traveled throughout the country. Named commissioner of fine arts by the Japanese government in recognition of his service to preservation, art education, and encouragement of pride in the nation's history, he also tutored touring American collectors and intellectuals in the intricacies of Japanese art. There or later in the United States, Bernard *Berenson, Arthur Wesley *Dow, Charles Lang *Freer, Isabella Stewart *Gardner, and John *La Farge numbered among tastemakers who valued his expertise. Upon his return to Boston in 1890, he served as the first curator of Asian art at the Museum of Fine Arts, where he oversaw the initial stages in building the foremost collection of Japanese art in the United States. During these years, Fenollosa also maintained his interest in education, lectured often to public audiences, traveled in Europe, and organized the Japanese display at the 1893 World's Columbian Exposition in Chicago. From 1896 until 1900 he again lived in Japan. Later he resided in New York, working primarily on a sweeping two-volume history, *Epochs of Chinese and Japanese Art* (1912), which he did not live to complete. (Assembled by his widow and marred by factual errors, the published work nevertheless broke new ground in Western understanding of Asian culture.) He died while visiting London. Fenollosa's other publications include *East and West: The Discovery of America and Other Poems* (1893) and several Japanese art catalogues, such as *The Masters of Ukioye* (1896). Working from Fenollosa's notes, after his death Ezra Pound edited *Cathay* (1915), *Certain Noble Plays of Japan* (1916), and *The Chinese Written Character as a Medium for Poetry* (1936).

Ferber, Herbert (1906–91). Sculptor and painter. Also a dentist. Among the earliest artists to produce an *abstract expressionist form of sculpture, from the late 1940s he drew on constructivist and surrealist precedents to achieve vigorous, almost gestural welded abstractions. In time, his work evolved toward environmental sculpture, culminating during the 1960s in room-size *installations of abstract form. Later he devoted much of his time to painting. A lifelong New Yorker, Herbert Ferber Silvers worked as an artist under his middle name to avoid being thought of as a dentist who made art as a hobby. He studied at City College of New York and Columbia University, where he graduated from dental school in 1930. For many years, he continued to practice and teach dentistry part-time. He took drawing classes at the academic Beaux Art Institute of Design, but was mainly self-taught as a sculptor. Encouraged by William *Zorach, whose work he admired, he carved stylized wood and stone figures early in his career. These also demonstrate his fondness for the work of Ernst Barlach and other German expressionists, as well as his attraction to African and pre-Columbian sculpture. His first visit to Europe in 1938 opened his eyes particularly to Romanesque sculpture. Thematically, some of his work from the 1930s reveals the social consciousness of the period. Henry Moore's work strongly affected Ferber for a short period in the mid-1940s, just before he began to work with welded metal to achieve open, abstract compositions stressing the interaction of space with solid form. Relating to mythic and symbolic themes, these free compositions of primarily *biomorphic shapes evolved in the mid-1950s toward "roofed" and "caged" sculptures, which contain their forms within defined spaces. Combined with experience during the same years in making large-scale architectural and public sculpture, these achievements in turn led, around 1960, to sculptural ensembles that activated interior spaces. An observer venturing into such a room in effect entered the sculpture. A longstanding interest in painting culminated during the 1970s in reliefs and painted sculptures that combine three-dimensional form with color. He died at his summer home at North Egremont, in western Massachusetts.

Ferren, John (1905–70). Painter and sculptor. An abstract painter remembered for exquisite chromatic effects, he was born in Pendleton, Oregon, grew up in California, and worked first as a sculptor. During a year in Europe in 1929, he began to paint, inspired by the example of Matisse and encouraged by Hans *Hofmann. After a return to California, he lived in Paris between 1931 and 1939 (except for a year in 1932–33 on Majorca). There his mature work evolved as Ferren became personally acquainted with many of the leading modernists whose work he admired, including Picasso, Miró, and Kandinsky. In Kandinsky's writings, he found confirmation of his own beliefs in the expressive power of abstract form, in the psychological effects of color, and in the spiritual mission of art. In the early 1930s, Ferren painted lusciously colored, cubist-derived arrangements of abstract shapes and lines. Soon he developed a poetic response to Kandinsky's work in paintings featuring a vocabulary of floating arcs, planes, and lines but treated with a lightness and freedom not generally associated with Kandinsky's severe contemporaneous work. Shortly, Ferren developed a more original approach, deploying warped planes in complex and colorful arrangements, as in *Composition on Green* (Whitney Museum, 1936). Between 1935 and 1938, he also produced more than fifty colored plaster reliefs, made by pouring plaster onto a metal intaglio plate, then working the surface of this "print" after the plaster had hardened. The series grew out of an experimental printmaking technique he encountered at *Atelier 17. After Ferren's return to New York, he exhibited with the *American Abstract Artists and soon developed a looser form of colorful abstraction, related to *abstract expressionism. During World War II he served in the publications office of a military psychological operation. From the late 1950s into the early 1960s, in particularly engaging, freshly sparkling large paintings, he applied extemporaneous gestural passages on top of geometrically organized hues. He died at a hospital in Southampton, not far from his home in East Hampton, on Long Island. His widow, **Rae Ferren** (1929–), paints vivid landscapes and flowers, sometimes in semi-abstract arrangements, with colorful, painterly flair. Staying on in East Hampton after his death, she served as a curator at the Guild Hall Museum there for some years. Born in Brooklyn, Rae Tonkel studied before marriage in 1949 at the Brooklyn Museum's school.

Ferris, Stephen James. *See* PENNELL, JOSEPH.

Ferus Gallery. *See* KIENHOLZ, EDWARD.

Field, Erastus Salisbury (1805–1900). Painter. After first concentrating on portraits, in the 1840s he began to picture religious and historical subjects, which became his specialty in the mid-1860s. His masterpiece, the 9 × 13-foot *Historical Monument of the American Republic* (Museum of Fine Arts, Springfield, Massachusetts, 1867–88) presents a synoptic view of the nation's history from its founding through the post–Civil War years. More than 130 simulated reliefs adorning ten fanciful towers recount American history from its earliest times as a colony through the Philadelphia Centennial Exposition of 1876. Conceived in mystical, rather than documentary terms, the work treats the American experience as a struggle between iniquity and redemption, reflecting the beliefs of Field's Calvinist upbringing. Born in the central Massachusetts town of Leverett, Field grew up on a farm. In 1824 he went to New York, where he studied for a few months with Samuel F. B. *Morse. After returning to Leverett the following year, he became an itinerant portrait painter, traveling throughout western Massachusetts, as well as into Connecticut and New York State. Despite contact with sophisticated models in Morse's studio, Field practiced a style closer to that of country painters such as Ammi *Phillips, whose working territory overlapped his own. Emphasizing simplified, flattened shapes and bold, patterned design, he nevertheless observed his clients with a sharp eye as he recorded their individual features. One of his finest portraits, *Joseph Moore and His Family* (Museum of Fine Arts, Boston, 1839) presents parents and four children in an interior setting enlivened by a boldly patterned carpet. Stately, yet decorative, its arresting qualities overpower deficiencies in academic drawing and perspective. While in New York from 1841 until 1848, Field first tried his hand at literary subjects. There he also encountered the new technique of photography. When he returned to his native region, he added *daguerreotypes to his repertoire as he moved from one small town to another. Usually he based his painted portraits on them, giving a somewhat photographic cast to these likenesses that rarely match the quality of his portraits from the 1830s. After 1859 he resided most of the time in the Leverett area. There, as the Civil War raged, the abolitionist Field turned inward, painting idiosyncratic works usually inspired by literary texts and illustrations. Among the considerable variety of topics he tackled, Old Testament subjects particularly revealed his obsessive fervor. Following the example of spectacular epics by English romantic artists such as John Martin, he filled his scenes with great crowds who enact historical destiny. The *Historical Monument* realizes a grandeur, complexity, and philosophical integration unparalleled among American nonacademic painters. Undertaken to celebrate the impending centennial of the nation, it was finished in 1876. However, in 1888, shortly before retiring from painting, Field added the towers near either edge. He died in Leverett.

Field, Hamilton Easter. *See* LAURENT, ROBERT.

Fiene, Ernest (1894–1965). Painter and printmaker. Varied in subject and approach, Fiene's mildly expressionistic, stylized realism ranges from intimate figure studies and emotionally charged landscapes to *precisionist-related architectural compositions. Born in Elberfeld,

Germany, in 1912 he arrived in New York and was naturalized as a citizen in 1927. He began his training in 1914 at the *National Academy of Design and later studied at the *Art Students League, where he subsequently taught for many years. From the early 1920s he maintained a residence in *Woodstock, while from 1933 until 1957 he owned a retreat in Southbury, Connecticut. During the Depression he found work with *federal art projects. Besides oil paintings, murals, and book illustrations, he produced many prints, mainly lithographs such as *Empire State Building* (1930), which frames the soaring new building with jutting, partially abstracted forms. Fiene died in a Paris atelier, while editioning color lithographs. He was the author of *Complete Guide to Oil Painting* (1964). In 1945 he married painter and muralist Alicia Wiencek (1918–61). His brother, sculptor **Paul Fiene** (1899–1949), also arrived from Germany in 1912. Particularly known for animal sculptures, both carved and cast, he, too, worked at Woodstock.

Finley, Karen. *See* PERFORMANCE ART.

Finster, Rev. Howard (1916–2001). Painter and sculptor. Frustrated that his words as a Baptist preacher often were quickly forgotten, he concluded that he might exert a more lasting effect by casting his thoughts in permanent form. Remaining self-taught as an artist, he directed much of his religious devotion into the creation of an idiosyncratic "paradise garden." In the early 1960s he began to construct what amounted to an ever-changing environmental sculpture in Pennville, Georgia. Defined by concrete walls painted white, the garden is embellished by all manner of found and ornamented objects. Mirror fragments, hubcaps, photographs under plastic, and other objects are set into the walls, producing opulent effects that respond to changing conditions of light. While also creating independent works of art, in the mid-1970s Finster began to incorporate paintings into the garden. For these, he generally used discarded materials or plywood, which he painted with enamel, automobile paint, or other weather-resistant media. After purchasing a lot adjacent to his garden in 1981, he remodeled an abandoned church into the World's Folk Art Church, crowned with an enormous decorative cupola. By this time, his offbeat art and gregarious, quirky personality had brought national attention. Although Finster's drawing remained resolutely unrefined, his paintings achieve considerable vivacity through bright color, anecdotal detail, and dense compositions. *Vision of a Great Gulf on Planet Hell* (Smithsonian American Art Museum, 1980) warns against the sinful life by combining numerous texts with imagery of hideous creatures, all set against a crimson background. A little less than two feet high, his tower of discarded television parts and other materials, *The Model of Super Power Plaint* (Smithsonian American Art Museum, 1979), offers gaily painted imagery and religious exhortations to suggest, as does his garden, Finster's faith in visual experience as a path to God and righteousness. Born in Valley Head, Alabama, Finster resided all his life in small towns along the Alabama-Georgia border, about ninety miles northwest of Atlanta, although he also traveled in the region to lead revivals and otherwise pursue his religious vocation. He left school after the sixth grade and became a preacher while still in his teens. In 1941 he settled in Trion, Georgia, where he experimented with an earlier garden before starting on the nearby Pennville example. He died in a hospital in Rome, Georgia, not far from his final home in Summerville.

Fisher, Alvan (1792–1863). Painter. An early enthusiast for landscape, he also painted *genre subjects, often depicting farm life, and portraits, not only human but animal. Like others associated with the *Hudson River School, he traveled widely in search of appealing scenery, although he tended to generalize rather than highlight the particular. Among the first artists to appreciate the Maine coast, he traveled also throughout New England and to Niagara Falls. *Souvenir of Bear Island* (Shelburne [Vermont] Museum, 1851) characteristically presents recognizable but not highly individualized natural features within a pleasingly pastoral composition. Two observers and a dog on one side and cows on the other anchor a cove opposite the island. Rhythmically rounded shapes, nearly still waters, high clouds, and a light sky, along with distant sailboats and a beached rowboat, contribute to a tranquil mood. Fisher also painted storms and other scenes of peril, such as *Mishap at the Ford* (Corcoran Gallery, 1818), depicting a runaway horse carriage. A resident of the Boston area nearly all his life, as an adult Alvin Fisher changed the spelling of his first name. He was born in Needham but grew up in Dedham, where he again lived for some years before his death there. He trained between 1811 and 1814 with John Ritto Penniman (1782–1841), a versatile Boston painter known for portraits and landscapes. Even before he departed in 1825 on his sole journey abroad, Fisher's fluid style and chosen subjects reveal familiarity with British precedents. In addition to visiting England, he toured the Continent. He returned the following year to Boston to take his place among the city's most prolific and well-respected artists.

Fitler, William Crothers. *See* HIRST, CLAUDE RAGUET.

Flannagan, John Bernard (1895–1942). Sculptor. Known particularly for animal imagery, he preferred direct carving, although he also cast works in bronze. Often, he made only minimal alterations to selected fieldstones, so their original shapes and textures contribute to compact final effects. This respect for natural stone enhanced the pantheistic spirit he wished to express. Believing in the relatedness of all life forms, he frequently invoked the cycle from birth to death, and perhaps to rebirth. Yet, he also relished humorous touches. Born in Fargo, North Dakota, Flannagan took painting classes at the Minneapolis Institute of Arts from 1914 to 1917. After service in the merchant marine and a brief period in New York, in 1922 he went to work as a farmhand on Arthur B. *Davies's Hudson River Valley acreage. With the older artist's encouragement, he returned to painting and began to carve in wood and, a few years later, in stone. Following two extended sojourns in Ireland between 1930 and 1933, in the mid-1930s he suffered a mental breakdown, exacerbated by alcoholism. Nevertheless, most of his finest works date from the 1930s, as he developed toward greater abstraction. For *Jonah and the Whale: Rebirth Motif* (Brooklyn Museum, 1937), he incised a smoothed bluestone boulder with the barest exterior features of a whale and the visualization of a nude Jonah curled up inside. In 1939 Flannagan suffered severe injuries when hit by a car. Although he eventually returned to his art, he remained impaired by his injuries and committed suicide in his New York studio.

Flavin, Dan (1933–96). Sculptor and *installation artist. A leading artist associated with *minimalism, he specialized in spare arrangements of colored fluorescent lights, achieving subtle yet magisterial meditations on visual experience. Because his works illuminate surrounding space and often require specific conditions of display, his example fostered development of *installation art and other site-specific forms. Born in New York, Daniel Nicholas Flavin Jr. studied for the priesthood for several years before entering military service in 1954. After returning to New York, in 1956 he embarked on studies in art history at the New School for Social Research (now New School) and, the following year, at Columbia University. He remained mostly self-taught as an artist, for several years experimenting with variants of prevailing *abstract expressionism until an encounter with Russian constructivism clarified his thinking. Undertaken in late 1961, the breakthrough *icon I* (estate of the artist), a square, painted wood relief surmounted with a fluorescent light along the top edge, prefigured his mature approach. In 1963 he began to explore the use of colored tubes on their own. Most of his works activate a spatial envelope through reflections on adjacent surfaces, often the corner of a room. He generally chose mellow hues of yellow, pink, blue, and green, along with white, rather than the brighter, more strident colors associated with advertising and other utilitarian uses. However, by employing only commercially available fixtures, he cast his lot with those twentieth-century artists interested in the aesthetic potential of non-art materials. In arrangements of only a few steadily glowing "lines," Flavin achieved a wholly original form of expression combining the three-dimensionality of sculpture, the color sensations of painting, and the volumetric discriminations of architecture. His transcendent effects belie their clear and logically ordered structural arrangements. However, despite his Catholic youth and the inherently ecstatic appeal of his luminous effects, he spurned overtly spiritual interpretations of his art. At the time of his death in a Riverhead hospital, he resided in nearby Wainscott, on eastern Long Island, and in Garrison, on the Hudson River north of New York.

Fluxus. An unstructured, international movement dedicated to a loosely defined cluster of attitudes favoring change, chance, conceptual gestures, and anti-institutional initiatives. Fluxus artists generally supported dematerialized or at least impermanent forms of art, but they worked in numerous styles, techniques, and materials, often in unconventional mixtures. Mail art, concrete poetry, and various forms of *performance are particularly associated with the movement. Fluxus performance events in several respects paralleled *happenings but deviated in their general preference for shorter, less scripted, less elaborately staged, and more "lifelike" works. They also usually strove for a more impersonal tone, less inflected by individual artistic ego. Generally hoping to subvert bourgeois order, many fluxus artists supported social rather than aesthetic goals. Although founded in Germany in 1962, fluxus soon became a New York phenomenon. Its popularity waned after the 1970s, but vestiges of the movement remain alive. Like *pop art, happenings, and *assemblage, fluxus belonged to a constellation of initiatives and movements in the same historical moment, all seeking to expand the artist's expressive possibilities and to abolish the division between art and life.

Their roots lay in precedents set by dadaists, Marcel *Duchamp, and John *Cage.

In the 1960s, as fluxus festivals flourished in Europe and New York, numerous Americans made important contributions to the movement. In 1961 Lithuanian-born writer, designer, composer, and performance artist George Maciunas (1931–78) coined the name, connoting flow or change in several languages indebted to Latin. In Wiesbaden, along with German artist Wolf Vostell and Nam June *Paik, he soon established fluxus as a movement. Joseph Beuys became its most celebrated practitioner, but Maciunas remained its godfather, publishing collections of fluxus material and unlimited editions of inexpensive multiples democratically intended for distribution to a mass audience. He also wrote a series of "Fluxmanifestos" attempting to define the movement. A native of Kaunas, Yurgis Maciunas (he changed his first name around 1960) moved with his family to Germany in 1944 and then to the United States in 1948. After training from 1949 to 1952 at Cooper Union, in 1954 he received a bachelor of architecture degree from the Carnegie Institute of Technology (now Carnegie Mellon University) in Pittsburgh. Subsequently, he studied art history at New York University's Institute of Fine Arts and came into contact with John Cage at the New School for Social Research (now New School). After closing a New York gallery he ran, Maciunas left for Germany in 1961 but returned in 1963. In 1976 he moved to New Marlborough, in western Massachusetts. He died of cancer in a Boston hospital.

Dick Higgins (1938–98), an "intermedia" artist (he introduced the term), painter, composer, writer, and filmmaker, founded Something Else Press, the movement's principal publisher and distributor from 1964 until the mid-1970s. He subsequently directed Unpublished Editions (later Printed Editions) in West Glover, Vermont, and New York until 1986. Born in Cambridge, England, Richard Carter Higgins moved with his family to the United States as a small child. He enrolled at Yale University in 1955 but left after two years. In 1960 he earned a degree in English from Columbia University and in 1977 received a master's degree from New York University. He also studied with Cage in the 1950s. He published more than forty volumes encompassing poetry, art theory, literary criticism, and other matters. In later years he divided his time between New York and Barrytown, in the Hudson River Valley. He died in Quebec while attending an experimental art festival. His wife, Alison Knowles (1933–), a painter, printmaker, performance artist, and writer, participated in early fluxus events and worked with her husband on fluxus publishing projects. They married in 1960, divorced in 1970, and remarried in 1984. Born in New York, she attended Vermont's Middlebury College for two years before earning a BFA in 1956 from Pratt Institute in Brooklyn. Her writing appears in a number of published volumes. She continues to reside in Barrytown. Their daughter Jessica Higgins also is an artist, while Hannah Higgins, her twin, is an art historian.

Yoko Ono (1933–), widely known to a popular audience after her marriage to John Lennon in 1969, had previously established herself as a versatile New York–based *conceptual artist, assemblage artist, painter, sculptor, *installation artist, musician, performer, and filmmaker. Born in Tokyo, as a child she lived with her family for periods of time in the United States. She studied philosophy at Tokyo's Gakushuin University for two semesters before entering Sarah Lawrence College in Bronxville, a New York suburb. Two early marriages, in 1957 to Juilliard-educated pianist and composer Toshi Ichiyanagi (today a leading presence in Japanese musical life) and in 1964 to filmmaker and art promoter Tony Cox, ended in divorce. By the late 1950s (along with Ichiyanagi) she belonged to the circle of experimental artists that included Cage and dancer-choreographer Merce Cunningham. In 1961 Maciunas mounted her first one-person show in his gallery, and soon she numbered among the central early participants in fluxus. Important to the interchange of aesthetic and philosophical ideas between East and West, she worked between 1962 and 1964 in Tokyo with avant-garde Japanese artists, as well as Paik, who happened to be there at the time. Later Ono and Lennon worked as creative partners on film projects. Since his death in 1980, she has also made music videos that have extended her influence into the work of a younger generation. Underlying the multiplicity of her approaches to art lies a deceptively simple quest for peace and love. She lives in New York.

Raymond (or Ray) Johnson (1927–95), the originator of mail art (also known as correspondence art), used the United States postal service to deliver his subversive, understated, witty, and sometimes bizarre art around the world. Circumventing the gallery system, he made the point that art should be free of commercial entanglements. At the same time, he carefully selected his audience from a roster of friends and art world insiders. He also produced collages related to pop art but generally more poetic in tone. In addition, especially in the early part of his career, he painted abstract geometric compositions and participated in the *American Abstract Artists organization. Born in Detroit, Raymond Edward Johnson studied from 1945 to 1948 at *Black Mountain College, where Josef *Albers, John *Cage, and Richard *Lippold numbered among his teachers. From 1968 he circulated collages, drawings, photocopies, and other works, all characteristically combining visual and verbal components, under the rubric of the New York Correspondence School (or, from 1975, sometimes Buddha University). Also in 1968 he moved from New York to Locust Valley on Long Island, not far from the city. Living there in relative seclusion, perhaps he was emulating Joseph *Cornell, whose work he greatly admired and whose home, not much more than ten miles away, he visited on a number of occasions. Johnson drowned, an apparent suicide, after jumping from a bridge at Sag Harbor, on eastern Long Island. Others who contributed significantly to the fluxus moment include Joe Brainard (1942–94), George Brecht (1926–), Al Hansen (1927–95), Geoffrey Hendricks (1931–), Robert Watts (1923–88), and Emmett Williams (1925–2007).

Force, Juliana. *See* WHITNEY, GERTRUDE VANDERBILT.

Ford, Charles Henri. *See* TCHELITCHEW, PAVEL.

Forum Exhibition. *See* INDEPENDENT EXHIBITIONS.

Foster, John (1648–81). Printmaker and painter. Important also as the first printer-publisher in Boston, he numbers among the earliest native-born painters, although no certain attributions to his hand survive. His most significant extant work and the first known example of the medium in the colonies, his woodcut likeness of Richard Mather (c. 1670) provides an auspicious beginning for the history of American graphic arts. Despite its naive qualities, in its bold design and ornamental finesse the elderly Dorchester minister's portrait felicitously engages the problems of composing in black and white. This print also numbers among the earliest surviving portraits in any medium by an artist native to English-speaking America. Born in Dorchester (now part of Boston), Foster graduated from Harvard College in 1667. He taught school until 1675, when he established his own printing press, from which he issued books, pamphlets, broadsides, almanacs, and other materials. The map of New England that he drew and published in 1677 ranks as the first American printed map from the eastern seaboard colonies. Foster is known to have been involved as well in astronomy, music, medicine, mathematics, and other pursuits. Upon his death at thirty-three in Dorchester, he was buried there beneath a tombstone (on loan to the Museum of Fine Arts, Boston, from the Boston Parks and Recreation Commission) that resembles other designs he is known to have drawn. Ranking among the most important to have survived from the era, although typical of the period in its general characteristics, the monument features a Latin inscription composed by Richard Mather's son, Foster's friend and Puritan clergyman Increase Mather, below an unusually complex scene incorporating a range of symbolic elements. The central representation portrays Time attempting to stay the hand of a skeletal death, who snuffs out the candle of Foster's life. Although the modeling is crudely two-dimensional, the work's intellectual and emotional aspirations sustain complex medieval and Renaissance traditions of thought.

Fourteenth Street School. *See* AMERICAN SCENE MOVEMENT.

Francis, John F. (1808–86). Painter. A leading mid-nineteenth-century still life specialist, he favored sumptuous arrangements of food and tableware chosen to suggest a luncheon or dessert. Often these are large and complex compositions, including fruits, nuts, cheeses, and baked goods in combination with wine bottles, serving dishes, pitchers, and crystal stemware. Backgrounds sometimes open out into landscape. Francis also painted more concentrated and intimate groupings of fruit, frequently spilling from baskets. He clearly reveled in particularity, treating every item with full attention to its unique visual and textural qualities. Yet stable compositions, harmonious colors, and painterly brushwork unify his visions of abundance and gastronomic pleasure. Born in Philadelphia, he began as a portrait painter there and in the nearby countryside, working in a romantic style related to Thomas *Sully's, before turning almost exclusively to still life around 1850. Building on the achievements of still life painters in Charles Willson *Peale's family, he addressed his subjects with breadth and ambition seldom rivaled in his day. Although he maintained ties with Philadelphia throughout his career, Francis lived in a number of localities in Pennsylvania, Delaware, and Kentucky. Eventually he settled not far from Philadelphia, in Jeffersonville, where he lived for about two decades before his death.

Francis, Sam (1923–94). Painter, printmaker, and occasional sculptor. His brilliantly hued, asymmetrical abstract compositions feature fluid, irregular patches of color, often accompanied by gestural drips and splashes. Generally, these appear against white grounds. Allied to *abstract expressionism in their improvisational and painterly character, these lyrical and sensuous works relate also to *color field painting. A native of San Mateo, California, Samuel Lewis Francis started painting in 1944 while recuperating from an injury sustained in the Army during World War II. After the war, he resumed his interrupted studies at the University of California at Berkeley, where he earned bachelor's and master's degrees in 1949 and 1950. During additional studies at the California School of Fine Arts (now San Francisco Art Institute), he developed an expressionistic style under the guidance of David *Park. In 1950 he moved to Paris, where he worked briefly at Fernand Léger's school. Demonstrating an understanding of contemporary New York abstract expressionism, including the work of Jackson *Pollock and Mark *Rothko, Francis's maturing style also suggested the appeal of chromatically oriented work being done in Paris by such artists as Canadian Jean-Paul Riopelle and a circle of young Americans including Joan *Mitchell, Norman Bluhm (1920–99), and Shirley Jaffe (1923–). He also closely observed the uses of saturated color in earlier work by such masters as Monet and Matisse. Soon the leading expatriate American in Paris, during his days there he established an international reputation. His luminous, vivacious, and decorative work remained widely admired abroad, over decades outdistancing his critical reputation in the United States. On an initial trip around the world in 1957, Francis made the first of numerous visits to Japan, where he found an enthusiastic audience for his art. Responding to the aesthetic he encountered there, his compositions became more open, frequently making use of a white "void," and more daringly asymmetrical. This tendency reached its ultimate expression in the 1960s "edge paintings," which restrain color only to the periphery of the canvas. Between 1958 and 1961 he lived in New York and Bern, Switzerland. Subsequently he resided in the Los Angeles area but continued also to travel and work elsewhere. As lithography became an increasing interest, in 1970 he established the Litho Studio in Santa Monica to publish his work. In addition, his Lapis Press produced books of interest to the art community, often featuring philosophical or poetic writing. From the late 1950s, he executed a number of murals, and some of his later canvases approach the dimensions of wall paintings. At his death in Santa Monica, he also maintained residences in Point Reyes Station, north of San Francisco, and in Paris.

Frank, Robert (1924–). Photographer and filmmaker. His controversial 1959 book *The Americans* crystallized an alienated sensibility and set the pace for a generation of photographers. With its introduction by Jack Kerouac, it probably exerted more influence than any other photographic book of its era, although many abhorred its seemingly casual style and gritty content. The volume's contemporary iconography of disaffection and pessimism gave the nation an unsettling look at postwar American society. It also revealed the power of a subjective, uncondescending, and unaestheticized approach to unexceptional subjects. The book first appeared in France, as *Les Américains* (1958), after publishers in the United States rejected it. Frank was born in Zurich, where he learned the rudiments of photography and became acquainted with the medium's modernist achievements. In Paris he achieved success as a fashion photographer before coming to the United States in 1947. In New York he continued fashion and freelance work, while also photographing the streets with a small, 35 mm camera. Until 1953 he spent much time abroad, traveling in South America and Europe. In 1955 and 1956 his mature vision coalesced while he traveled the country on Guggenheim grants. He exposed about eight hundred rolls of film, from which he selected the eighty-three images of *The Americans*. What Frank found was neither picturesque nor inspiring, but rather, commercialized, spiritually empty, and inherently inexpressive. The anxious and lonely individuals he observed undercut the period's bedrock beliefs about the virtues of religion and democracy. However, the freshly seen content of Frank's photographs could also accommodate lyricism, irony, and low-key astonishment. Although powerfully original, Frank's images nevertheless resonated with intellectual and cultural currents of the 1950s. Walker *Evans, who offered personal encouragement, provided the most important photographic model. Frank expanded on Evans's fondness for popular culture and advertising, his deadpan, nonjudgmental attitude, and his taste for absurdity. Other observers of modern life, such as André *Kertész and German-born British photographer Bill Brandt, also influenced Frank's direction. In addition, the independent spirit of the *abstract expressionist painters attracted his notice, as did their dedication to art and their rhetoric of personal authenticity.

In 1959 Frank made his first film, the prize-winning *Pull My Daisy*. Co-directed with Alfred *Leslie and narrated by Kerouac, this improvisatory lark exemplified the beat generation's antibourgeois temperament. Other participants included Allen Ginsberg, Gregory Corso, Alice *Neel, and Larry *Rivers. During the following decade Frank devoted most of his time to filmmaking. Around the time he moved to the tiny community of Mabou, Nova Scotia, in 1970, he began to work again with still photography. In 1972 he published a retrospective survey of his work, *The Lines of My Hand*. He has continued since then to produce individual photographs, including a 1991 documentary series shot in Beirut. However, in general more involved with relationships between images and the interaction of pictures with words, he has crafted complex art works comprising two or more photographs, often in combination with lettering or painting. He also makes videos. All of this work explores the inner self, often invoking themes of mourning (particularly in relation to the deaths of two children), the passage of time, and the ambiguities of experience.

His first wife, sculptor, painter, printmaker, and draftsman **Mary Frank** (1933-) was born Mary Lockspeiser in London. Her mother, American abstract painter Eleanore Lockspeiser (1900–86), who had studied with Max *Weber and later became active at *Woodstock, sometimes incorporated representational motifs into painterly works emphasizing light and color. When Mary was seven, they moved to New York. As a teenager she studied dance, principally with Martha Graham but also with José Limon and others, married at seventeen, and studied with Max Beckmann and Hans *Hofmann. She and Frank separated in 1969 and subsequently divorced. She has worked primarily as a sculptor, principally interested in the human form, although she is also drawn to animal imagery. Much of her work since the 1970s has been in clay. She abstracts and rearranges elements of her figures to create evocative, sometimes mythic metaphors enriched by the sensuous, earthy material. In the 1990s she turned more to painting, producing works in which figures appear in visionary contexts. In 1997 she married musicologist Leo Treitler, her companion of more than a decade. They generally spend several months a year at their home near Woodstock.

Painter and sculptor June Leaf (1929-) moved with Frank to Nova Scotia in 1970, and they married in 1975. Born in Chicago, she studied for a few months at the Institute of Design (now part of the Illinois Institute of Technology) before leaving in 1948 for Paris. Following her return four months later, she became acquainted with the *Chicago imagists. In 1954 she received a BA in art education from Roosevelt University. She left Chicago in 1958 to work again in Paris. The following year she settled in New York and married saxophonist Joel Press. Although principally a painter, she has made sculpture in varied media since the 1960s. She addresses human and animal subjects with expressive effects ranging from painterly force to quirky or monumental impressions. In the 1990s she combined painting and sculpture into melancholy, gray-toned figural reliefs suggesting isolation and inwardness.

Frankenstein, Alfred V. *See* HARNETT, WILLIAM MICHAEL.

Frankenthaler, Helen (1928-). Painter, printmaker, and occasional sculptor. A leading painter of chromatic abstractions for more than fifty years, in 1952 she augmented the practice of *abstract expressionism by staining unprimed canvas, an innovation that proved central to the development of *color field painting. Since then she has sensitively but boldly used color to construct ever varied, sumptuous, and often very large compositions investigating the expressive possibilities of depth, scale, atmosphere, and illusions of light. Composed without premeditation from imagination, her paintings nevertheless often indirectly suggest landscape. As an active printmaker, Frankenthaler has employed several media, including lithography, intaglio, and screen print, but has established particular eminence in the color woodcut technique. Born in New York, she studied at a private secondary school with Mexican painter and printmaker Rufino Tamayo. She worked in 1947 at the *Art Students League with Vaclav *Vytlacil. Paul *Feeley numbered among her teachers at Vermont's Bennington College, where she earned a BA degree in 1949. The following year she studied for a short time with Hans *Hofmann. Around the same time, she became acquainted with Clement *Greenberg and leading abstract expressionists, including Jackson *Pollock. Adopting his technique of pouring and splattering paint onto unstretched canvas spread on the floor, she thinned her medium to soak into the surface, producing a watercolor-like effect that allowed the weave of the material to remain visible. (Although Pollock had previously made limited use of raw canvas, he did not exploit the potential of color staining.) First fully realized in *Mountains and Sea* (on loan from the artist to the National Galley, 1952), this approach negated the distinction between image and support. Among artists who responded to her novel effect, Morris *Louis and Kenneth *Noland spurred the development of color field and related modes of painting. Subsequently, Frankenthaler has varied her technique to suit the needs of formal inquiry and her romantic temperament, but she has continuously remained fond of abstract expressionism's gestural painterliness. Although stained canvas appears in many works, she has used paints of varying viscosity, opacity, and saturation. In the 1960s she began using an acrylic medium that fostered articulation of more definite shapes. While married from 1958 until 1971 to Robert *Motherwell, she summered in *Provincetown. In the mid-1970s she acquired a residence on the Connecticut shore. In 1994 she married investment banker Stephen DuBrul.

Frasconi, Antonio (1919–). Printmaker and painter. A woodcut specialist, he has addressed subjects from literary works, as well as images of everyday American life, landscapes, and themes related to social justice. He has designed and illustrated scores of books. He often uses color to enhance bold and expressive drawing influenced by German expressionist and Japanese prints, among other sources. Born to Italian parents in Buenos Aires, he grew up in Montevideo, Uruguay, where he began his artistic training. Originally a painter, as a young man he worked also as a political cartoonist. He had already shifted his focus to printmaking before he arrived in New York in 1945. There he continued his studies at the *Art Students League and the New School for Social Research (now New School). Interpreting Walt Whitman's *Leaves of Grass*, Frasconi's *The Neighboring Shore*, based on more than one hundred of his own woodcuts, won the 1960 grand prize at the Venice Film Festival. Since 1957 he has lived in Norwalk, Connecticut. He remains an emeritus professor at the State University of New York in Purchase, where he began teaching in 1973. In 1951 he married printmaker Leona Pierce (1921–2002), also known for color woodcuts. Born in Santa Barbara and educated in the Los Angeles area, Pierce enrolled in 1940 at Scripps College in Claremont for two years before transferring to the Chouinard Art Institute (now California Institute of the Arts). She subsequently studied also at the Art Students League and the New School for Social Research.

Fraser, Charles (1782–1860). Painter. A lifelong resident of Charleston, South Carolina, he numbered among leading miniaturists of the nineteenth century, when the format was nearing the end of its popularity. On occasion, he traveled to northern cities to execute commissions. He also painted landscapes, still lifes, and other subjects, as well as oil portraits on canvas. Fraser's early work displays decorative charm, but in his mature approach he rendered sitters more realistically, yet still with grace and dignity. Fraser began painting miniatures around 1800, after brief early training with painter and engraver Thomas Coram (1757–1811). Born in Bristol, England, Coram had arrived in Charleston in 1769. In the 1790s his interest in picturesque landscape spurred Fraser to produce detailed topographical watercolors of the nearby Low Country. Like Coram's more conventionalized views from the same decade, these rank among the earliest independent American landscapes, and Fraser later continued to sketch and paint scenes of nature. His early portrait miniatures show the influence of Edward Greene *Malbone, who worked intermittently in Charleston, and he knew Washington *Allston, as well as Thomas *Sully, a lifelong friend. Following intermittent study of the law, in 1807 Fraser was admitted to the bar but practiced only until 1818, when he returned to painting full time. He was known also as a writer and orator.

Fraser, James Earle (1876–1953). Sculptor. Widely known for his design of the Indian Head/Buffalo nickel, he also achieved success as a portraitist and created many public monuments. Born in Winona, Minnesota, he lived as a child on a ranch in the Dakota Territory before moving with his family briefly to Minneapolis and then to Chicago. There he worked with German-born sculptor Richard Bock (1865–1949) and took classes at the School of the Art Institute of Chicago. At seventeen, he modeled *The End of the Trail* (Cowboy Hall of Fame, Oklahoma City, 1894), a romantic evocation of American Indian plight. Depicting a weary brave on an equally exhausted pony, it became not only Fraser's best-known creation, but for a period of many years probably the most popular sculptural image in the United States. The following year Fraser left for Paris, where he studied at the École des Beaux-Arts with J.-A.-J. Falguière, as well as at the Julian and Colarossi academies. After assisting Augustus *Saint-Gaudens for about three years in Paris, he continued to work for him in Cornish, New Hampshire. In 1902 Fraser settled in New York. In 1911 he designed the western imagery of the long-lived five-cent piece first issued two years later. In 1913 he purchased a Westport, Connecticut, summer home, which became his year-round residence in 1935. His wife, sculptor **Laura Gardin Fraser** (1889–1966), specialized in animal subjects and achieved distinction for the design of commemorative medallions. In addition, she executed a number of fountains and often assisted with her husband's monumental commissions. Born in Chicago, she trained for four years at the *Art Students League, where her future husband numbered among her instructors. They married in 1913. Both died in Westport.

Frazee, John (1790–1852). Sculptor. An early portrait sculptor, he combined realism and *neoclassicism in gaining the patronage of a New York audience newly interested in commissioning sculpture. His 1824 memorial for John Wells (St. Paul's Chapel, New York) may have been the first marble portrait carved by a native-born artist. Indicating the spread of his reputation, in 1831 Congress ordered a marble bust of first chief justice John Jay (U.S. Capitol, Washington, D.C.), thought to be the first federal award to an American-born sculptor. Born in Rahway, New Jersey, Frazee grew up on his grandparents' farm. With little formal schooling, he picked up basic stone-carving skills when apprenticed at fourteen to a mason and builder. On his own from 1811, he worked as a stonecutter, while also producing cemetery monuments, fireplace mantels, and other embellishments. In 1818 he moved from New Brunswick, where he had resided for about four years, to New York. Within a few years and without professional training, he had remade himself as a fine artist and begun to receive important commissions. Nevertheless, he did not relinquish the marble-cutting business, which he operated from 1831 until 1837 with a partner, sculptor Robert Launitz (1806–70), a recent immigrant who had worked in Rome with neoclassicist Berthel Thorvaldsen. Born in Riga, Russia (now Latvia), Launitz later became known particularly for the design of public monuments. In 1835 Frazee accepted a time-consuming but salaried position. As supervising architect for construction of Wall Street's new Custom House (today the Federal Hall National Memorial), designed by Ithiel Town and Alexander Jackson Davis, he devoted most of his energy to this project, to which he contributed significant design modifications, until the building was completed in 1842. Subsequently, he received few sculpture commissions. In 1851 he collapsed while working on a marble version of his ruggedly naturalistic 1834 plaster head of Andrew Jackson (Princeton [New Jersey] University Art Museum). This misfortune ended his artistic career, and he never regained full health. He died in Compton Mills, Rhode Island. A boastful account of his career, "The Autobiography of Frazee, the Sculptor," appeared in two consecutive 1835 issues of the *North American Quarterly Magazine*.

Freake Painter. Painter. Known solely as a portraitist, North America's first major artist remains anonymous. Active in Boston during the 1670s, he takes his name from a pair of portraits depicting Mr. and Mrs. John Freake (Worcester [Massachusetts] Art Museum, about 1671; reworked about 1674). Trained in England or by someone familiar with Elizabethan art forms, the artist balances simple design, shallow space, and delicate drawing with linear elegance, rich color accents, and luxuriant embellishments. His masterpiece, the portrait of Elizabeth Freake with her baby, tenderly and respectfully evokes the sitter's dignified presence and maternal affection. Although scholars disagree about attributions, altogether as many as eight or nine extant portraits from the 1670s may be the work of the Freake Painter or his shop. All depict sitters at slightly less than life size in oil on canvas. Representing the most sophisticated artistic expression known in the colonies during the seventeenth century, they demonstrate the artist's uncommon sensitivity to design and color, as well as his training in an established decorative style that was by then old-fashioned in England. In their attention to economic and social status, the Freake portraits demonstrate that from the beginning, American portraiture incorporated goals other than capturing likeness. Prosperous John Freake represents the emerging mercantile class, eager to differentiate himself from an older generation's austere Puritanism. His ambition to be recognized as a gentleman is evident in his choices of clothing and hairstyle. Although the air of reserve and decorum that characterizes both Freakes testifies to their distaste for ostentation, the couple lays claim to the finest material goods available, as is evident especially in the wife's representation. Her jewelry, laces, and sumptuous apparel fabrics, her baby's ornamental attire, her expensive chair covered with colorful turkey-work upholstery, and the curtain pulled back to one side bespeak a taste for sensory pleasures and the financial power to import them. The artist is alternatively known as the Freake *Limner. Scholars have suggested that he might be identified with Samuel Clement (1635–c. 1678), known to have been working in Boston during the period of the Freake Painter's activity. Clement was the son of an artist who arrived in Massachusetts in 1635, after training in England.

Freer, Charles Lang (1854–1919). Collector and museum founder. Also a railroad-car magnate. A pioneer in connoisseurship of Asian and Near Eastern art, he collected also the work of American contemporaries but limited his purchases almost exclusively to the work of four *tonalists he knew personally: Thomas *Dewing, Abbott *Thayer, Dwight *Tryon, and James Abbott McNeill *Whistler. Possessed of a faith in the universality of beauty, Freer valued aesthetic refinement above all, but in his non-Western acquisitions demanded also historical significance within a major tradition and a superior condition of preservation. At fourteen Freer left school in his native Kingston, New York. There, he worked in a cement factory before entering the railroad business as a clerk. After four years in Logansport, Indiana, in 1880 he moved to Detroit where he made a fortune in the manufacture of rolling stock. Soon he began collecting European prints, followed by Whistler etchings in 1887 and then paintings by Dewing, Tryon, and Thayer. After establishing a friendship with Whistler in 1890, Freer eventually amassed more than nine hundred Whistler prints, along with another three hundred paintings and pastels, as well as Whistler's celebrated Peacock Room. While assembling the foremost representation of Whistler's work, Freer concurrently absorbed the artist's interest in Eastern art. With time, this became a near obsession, especially during the collector's last two decades, following retirement from business. He first traveled to Asia in 1894, but his most significant acquisitions from the region postdated his acquaintance in 1901 with Ernest *Fenollosa, whose scholarly knowledge guided Freer's development as an internationally respected connoisseur of non-Western art. Formally accepted in 1906 as the *Smithsonian Institution's first art collection, Freer's gift to the nation, including large holdings in Japanese and Chinese art, as well as Korean, South Asian, and Near Eastern work, comprised the most comprehensive and finest collection of Asian art then in private American hands. Freer also financed construction of the museum building on Washington's Mall. Involved in every detail of its design, from 1912 he worked with architect Charles Adams Platt on plans for the Freer Gallery of Art, which opened to the public in 1923. Until his death in New York, where he had moved in 1916, Freer retained control of the collection, which he continued to augment and refine. His will stipulates that objects in the collection cannot be de-accessioned or loaned, but he provided for future Asian acquisitions. Today the museum inventory numbers more than three times the approximately nine thousand objects Freer donated. Additions have maintained his preference for exceptional specimens, without regard for encyclopedic completeness. The American collection remains as he shaped it. In 1987 the museum was linked underground to the Smithsonian's new Arthur M. Sackler Gallery of Asian art, providing an extended context for the Freer holdings and creating a comprehensive center for the study of Asian art.

Freilicher, Jane (1924–). Painter and printmaker. Her landscapes, cityscapes, and still lifes respond emotionally to visual motifs while also emphasizing color, sensual pleasure in paint, and respect for constraints of the pictorial surface. Born Jane Niederhoffer in Brooklyn, she graduated from Brooklyn College in 1947 and earned a master's degree from Columbia University the following year. As well, she studied in New York and *Provincetown with Hans *Hofmann, who guided development of her early *abstract expressionist work. A large 1948 *Museum of Modern Art retrospective of Pierre Bonnard's work stimulated much in her work during the next few years as it evolved toward a softly brushed, meditative lyric. Married at seventeen to jazz pianist Jack Freilicher, she parted ways with him after about five years, but through him she met Larry *Rivers, who became her companion into the early 1950s. During these formative years she also established lasting friendships with John Ashbery, Frank O'Hara, and other important literary figures with whom she later occasionally collaborated. From 1952 she maintained a close and, in artistic terms, mutually beneficial friendship with Fairfield *Porter. In 1957 she married her partner of the previous several years, Joseph Hazan, previously a dancer, then a businessman, and later a painter. That summer she began dividing her time between New York and Water Mill, on eastern Long Island. Both localities figure prominently among subsequent subjects. Ever aware of the tension between perceived image and artistic process, she has practiced a sharp-eyed and fluent style balancing the intensity of the moment against a sober assessment of its transitory nature. A number of her most appealing images juxtapose a foreground floral still life against marshy vistas near her Long Island home or the urban geometry observed from her high-rise residence on lower Fifth Avenue. Embracing intaglio processes, as well as woodcut and lithography, her print work also indulges her feeling for color.

Frelinghuysen, Suzy. *See* MORRIS, GEORGE L. K.

French, Daniel Chester (1850–1931). Sculptor. Among the most prominent artists of his day, he specialized in figural compositions honoring notable individuals or portraying allegorical concepts. In his best work, a fluent and dignified realism rooted in the *neoclassicism of his youth gives expression to memorial or patriotic sentiments. Often designed to complement Beaux-Arts architecture, his work contributed to the prestige of the *American Renaissance. Besides his masterwork, the seated *Abraham Lincoln* (1911–22) in the Lincoln Memorial on the Mall in Washington, D.C., other important public sculptures include *The Minuteman* (Old North Bridge, Concord, Massachusetts, 1875; modeled 1873–74), the *Thomas Gallaudet Memorial* (Gallaudet College, Washington, D.C., 1885–89), and Columbia University's *Alma Mater*

(1900–1903). His gilded, sixty-foot, robed female *Republic* (destroyed) dominated the central axis of the 1893 World's Columbian Exposition in Chicago. A native of Exeter, New Hampshire, at the age of six French moved with his family to Cambridge, Massachusetts. As a teenager he lived for about two years in Amherst, Massachusetts, before the family moved to Concord, near Boston. Achieving only academic disgrace during a year at MIT, he decided to pursue a career in sculpture. His irregular but varied artistic education commenced in John Quincy Adams *Ward's New York studio for about a month in the early spring of 1870. Soon emulating the success of John *Rogers's statuettes, French began producing for commercial distribution small *genre and literary subjects. While continuing to model these for approximately the next four years, he studied intermittently with William *Rimmer and William Morris *Hunt. French's first important commission, for *The Minuteman*, made his reputation and has remained among his most popular works. Commemorating the one hundredth anniversary of the American Revolution, the young citizen-soldier, posing in a stance based loosely on the antique *Apollo Belvedere*, memorably embodies patriotic readiness.

In 1874 French departed for Florence, where he worked with Preston *Powers, while studying also with Thomas *Ball. After two years there, he resided in Washington, D.C., and in the Boston area, executing commissions for portraits and architectural embellishments. A ten-month sojourn in Paris, in 1886–87, provided the final ingredient in his mature style. Working there with Augustus *Saint-Gaudens and others, he assimilated current French taste for graceful immediacy and vibrant modeling, as can be seen in the *Gallaudet* monument. This depiction of the pioneer in education for the deaf as he introduces language to a little girl achieves an easy and tender naturalism. Incorporating three-dimensional vigor and surface variety within a stable composition, it suggests also the psychological significance of the moment for both participants. Upon his return to the United States, French settled permanently in New York. Only occasionally traveling abroad, he remained constantly occupied with major public sculptures, culminating in the iconic *Lincoln* for the Washington memorial. Placed in a classical shrine designed by a friend and frequent collaborator, architect Henry Bacon, the marble figure rises about eighteen feet from an eleven-foot pedestal. It majestically projects the slain president's steadfastness, intelligence, and humility. Among his more private works, two funerary monuments rank among French's most affecting accomplishments. Honoring Martin *Milmore and his lesser-known sculptor-brother, the Milmore Memorial (Forest Hills Cemetery, Boston, 1893; modeled 1889–91) features a bronze representation of *Death Staying the Hand of the Sculptor*, showing a large and solemn angel gently impeding the chisel of an active young artist. Realized almost completely in the round, the two figures stand before a low-relief sphinx that alludes to a Civil War memorial among the Milmores' most significant achievements. The marble Melvin Memorial (Sleepy Hollow Cemetery, Concord, Massachusetts, 1906–8) centers on a *Mourning Victory*, one of the period's most poignant tributes to grief. She emerges in strong relief from a vertical shaft set within an elegant classical setting designed by Bacon.

Entering the twentieth century at the height of his career, French was showered with honors and remained in demand as both an artist and advisor. He helped to found and financially supported the American Academy in Rome, influenced the appearance of the nation's capital through many commissions as well as his assistance in overseeing the city's beautification program, and as a trustee of the *Metropolitan Museum of Art for nearly three decades promoted development of its sculpture collection. French died at Chesterwood, his retreat near Stockbridge, Massachusetts, where he had spent the warm months of nearly every year since 1897. With its large house and studio surrounded by extensive gardens, the estate today serves as a memorial and museum under the aegis of the National Trust for Historic Preservation. His daughter, Margaret French Cresson (1889–1973), also a sculptor, chiefly produced portrait busts in a style resembling his. She was born in Concord and grew up in New York, with summers at Chesterwood. After studying in 1912 at the New York School of Applied Design for Women, she subsequently worked with Abastenia St. Leger *Eberle in New York and George Demetrios (1896–1974) in Boston. From 1921 she lived in Washington, D.C., but continued to spend summers at Chesterwood. Most active as a sculptor in the 1920s, after her father's death she devoted herself largely to tasks associated with preserving his creative legacy. In later years she lived at Chesterwood, where she died, after arranging in 1969 for its permanent preservation. In 1947 she published *Journey into Fame: The Life of Daniel Chester French*.

French, Jared (1905–88). Painter. Dislocation, irrational behavior, and inscrutability prevail in his enigmatic figurative works. Enacted by individuals who generally fail to connect with each other psychologically, his scenes emphasize loneliness and alienation. As an artist who combined minute detail with incomprehensible narratives, he is often identified as a significant practitioner of *magic realism. Born in Ossining, New York, he grew up in New Jersey and graduated in 1925 from Amherst (Massachusetts) College, where he studied poetry with Robert Frost. Until 1929 he worked in New York while taking evening classes at the *Art Students League. For the following two years, he trained there full time, with Boardman *Robinson as his most influential teacher. Following an initial visit to Europe in 1927–28, between 1931 and 1933 he traveled there and lived in Majorca with Paul *Cadmus. After returning to New York, he was employed by *federal art projects. During the 1930s, French simplified and smoothed the surfaces he depicted and began to emphasize pattern over spatial depth. In 1940 he switched from oil paint to the more painstaking medium of tempera, producing enamel-like surfaces with the highly calculated quality of early Renaissance altarpieces. These techniques enhanced the increasingly automaton-like nature of his static and self-absorbed figures and emphasized the ritualized, iconic quality of his compositions. In the unsettling *State Park* (Whitney Museum, 1946), five figures on a seaside boardwalk seem isolated not only from each other but from an otherwise deserted vacation spot in which they apparently find no pleasure. In the foreground, a stiffly profiled lifeguard (who might have walked out of an Assyrian relief sculpture) stares into the distance as three immobilized figures, perhaps a family group, escape the sun's glare under a large umbrella. Behind them, a skinny, tattooed boxer flexes his muscles against an imaginary opponent. Particularly in such beach scenes, French drew upon photographs he had taken since 1937, mostly at the shore on Fire Island, where he vacationed regularly for several years, but also at *Provincetown and elsewhere. Painter and etcher **Margaret French** (?–1998), his wife, and Cadmus also participated in staging and taking these artfully composed, psychologically charged scenes of each other and their social circle. Born in Hoboken, New Jersey, Margaret Hoening graduated from Smith College in Northampton, Massachusetts, and studied at the Art Students League before marriage in 1937. During the 1960s French embarked on a new direction in his art, as he combined dismembered human and animal parts into unsettling combinations of abstracted form. He died in Rome, where he had made his home for nearly two decades, although he maintained a residence in Hartland, Vermont.

Frick, Henry Clay (1849–1919). Art collector and museum founder. Also an industrialist, associated with the steel industry, and philanthropist. Widely regarded among the finest small museums anywhere, New York's Frick Collection houses his selection of old masters, European and American nineteenth-century paintings, prints, drawings, and decorative arts. Born into a farming family in West Overton (now Scottdale), Pennsylvania, about forty miles southeast of Pittsburgh, Frick briefly attended Westmoreland College in nearby Mount Pleasant and Otterbein College, near Columbus, Ohio. Uninterested in academic learning, he left to pursue profitable opportunities and in his early twenties entered the coke business. A millionaire by the time he was thirty, he soon entered a lucrative partnership of nearly twenty years with Andrew Carnegie. Influential in the formation of the United States Steel Corporation in 1901, he also maintained interests in mining, finance, and related enterprises. Frick lived in Pittsburgh until 1904, when he moved permanently to New York. Before the turn of the century, he had limited his purchases primarily to French *Barbizon and Salon work. As his interests later broadened, he sold many of these works. With the intention of eventually transforming it into a museum, in 1913–14 he constructed a Fifth Avenue residence designed by architect Thomas Hastings in emulation of eighteenth-century Parisian townhouses. Upon the death of his widow, the City of New York inherited the house and collection, along with an endowment for upkeep and future purchases. The museum opened to the public in 1935. Among its treasures are paintings by Giovanni Bellini, Rembrandt, Vermeer, Gainsborough, Joshua Reynolds, J. M. W. Turner, French impressionists, and James Abbott McNeill *Whistler. His daughter **Helen Clay Frick** (1888–1984) remained involved with the museum's administration for some years. In 1920 she founded the Frick Art Reference Library, an important resource for art historians, and served as its director until 1983. Since 1935 it has been located adjacent to the museum in a Renaissance-style building designed by architect John Russell Pope. She died in her native Pittsburgh, where among other benefactions in that city, she built the Frick Art Museum in 1969 to house her art collection.

Friedlander, Lee (1934–). Photographer. Cool and witty, working almost exclusively in black and white, he numbers among the premier artists of his generation. His intricate, precise, and visually sophisticated work generally pictures American vernacular experience or landscape. Friedlander grew up in his native Aberdeen, Washington, and studied at the Art Center School (now Art Center College of Design) in Los Angeles from 1953 to 1955. After moving to New York the next year, he specialized in portraits of New York and New Orleans jazz musicians. Soon, indebted to the examples of Eugène Atget, Walker *Evans, and Robert *Frank, he worked primarily as a street photographer and became known, along with Garry *Winogrand and Diane *Arbus, for social landscape photographs. In these he observed street life with a dispassionate eye but also appreciation for ironic or ambiguous juxtapositions. In the early 1960s he also produced a peculiar and unsettling series picturing television sets glowing in domestic settings. Delighting in intellectual play with form and content, he has more recently often turned to nature for subjects, or has combined the natural with the manmade in psychologically layered compositions. To heighten both spatial and interpretive ambiguity, he often incorporates reflective, transparent, or translucent surfaces, or he complicates perception by including screening elements such as tree branches. Transience and his own fleeting participation inform numerous images including his shadow or reflection within the frame. In 1958 he rediscovered brothel portraits from around 1912 by E. J. Bellocq (1873–1949), a New Orleans photographer whose life inspired Louis Malle's 1978 film *Pretty Baby*. After acquiring Bellocq's surviving glass plates, in 1966 Friedlander employed appropriately old-fashioned methods to produce prints for an exhibition at the *Museum of Modern Art and an accompanying publication, *E. J. Bellocq: Storyville Portraits* (1970). Friedlander's published collections include *Self Portrait* (1970), *The American Monument* (1976), *Lee Friedlander: Photographs* (1978), *Like a One-Eyed Cat: Photographs by Lee Friedlander, 1956–1987* (1989), *Nudes* (1991), *The Desert Seen* (1996), and *American Musicians* (1998).

Friedman, Arnold (1874–1946). Painter. A lifelong New Yorker, Arnold Aaron Friedman began working for the postal service at the age of seventeen and remained in that employment for more than forty years. As a young man he attended night classes at City College of New York, and between 1905 and 1908 he worked at the *Art Students League, where Robert *Henri ranked as his most influential teacher. In 1908 he left for six months in Paris, where the work of Georges Seurat and Camille Pissarro particularly caught his attention. It was not until he saw the *Armory Show in 1913 that he became aware of cubism. For the next few years, in paintings related to *synchromism, he combined glowing colors with planar forms derived from that style. By 1920 Friedman had returned to representation without rejecting modernism. Simplified form and compressed space continued. Isolated at the post office by day and painting at night, he produced intentionally naive work that bears little resemblance to major currents of the day. Even after he retired in 1933 and was able to paint full time, his art remained at arm's length from the mainstream. He developed a method of stippling to produce gentle color gradations in compositions that suggest Pierre Bonnard's work. These richly luminous and densely textured still lifes and landscapes combine modernist interest in structure with color drawn from his first love, late impressionism.

Frieseke, Frederick Carl (1874–1939). Painter. His decorative images of composed and pleasant women or languorous nude models earned an international reputation, as well as immense popularity in the United States. Rendered in a modified impressionist style, most picture attractive, middle-class women in flower-filled gardens or richly furnished homes. Usually posed outdoors, the nudes typically enjoy a dappled play of sunlight caressing their bodies. An expatriate throughout his professional life, Frieseke produced most of these signature canvases at Giverny, his principal residence at the height of his career. Born in the central Michigan city of Owosso, Frieseke began his professional training at the School of the Art Institute of Chicago and the *Art Students League. From 1898 on, France remained his home, although he visited the United States on a number of occasions. In Paris he studied at the Académie Julian, but James Abbott McNeill *Whistler provided the most important stimulus to his early development. Following his example, for several years Frieseke focused on delicate figural works set in spare interiors. During this time, he began to visit Giverny during summers. After 1906, when he began spending most of each year there, his painting style featured impressionism's bright colors, strong illumination, and vigorous brushwork as epitomized in the work of Monet, the village's most prominent artist-resident. Although the two lived in close proximity, Frieske had only limited personal contact with the French master. While he learned from Monet's style, Frieseke's individual approach owes more to Renoir's ample nudes and to aspects of postimpressionism, particularly the ornamental domesticity evident in the work of Pierre Bonnard and Édouard Vuillard. In *The Garden Parasol* (North

Carolina Museum of Art, Raleigh, 1910), a huge umbrella, set aslant over an outdoor tea table, provides a warm-toned foil to the greens of the background hedge and the cool whites delineating a surface pattern of furniture, tablecloth, silver tea set, and the frocks of its two models. The parasol's Japanese design of stylized birds and flowers emphasizes the painting's central concern with the beauties of nature and artifice, melded by the play of sunlight. The summer of 1919 proved Frieseke's last in Giverny. Subsequently, he resided in rural Normandy east of Rouen, at Le Mesnil-sur-Blangy, where he died. There, his work became simpler and less decorative, usually confined to interior scenes. Like many European artists between the world wars, he often engaged a more ordered and classically inflected form of expression. This work did not sustain his popular reputation, however, and it remains relatively little known.

In Giverny, Frieseke ranked as the most accomplished exponent of a late-impressionist mode practiced among like-minded Americans who lived there for varying lengths of time during the same years. Identified as the Giverny group as early as 1910, Frieseke and his circle concentrated on comfortable scenes of family life at home and in the garden, rendered in a style indebted primarily to impressionism but also accommodating postimpressionist stylization. The subjects they preferred almost exclusively reflected their expatriate lifestyle. Unlike the first American impressionists who had arrived there in the late 1880s, the Giverny group virtually ignored the village, its French inhabitants, and the local landscape, the very features that had charmed such artists as John Leslie *Breck, Lila Cabot *Perry, and Theodore *Robinson. Like Frieske, most of the Giverny group came from the Midwest, and several studied at the School of the Art Institute of Chicago. Richard Miller (1875–1943) came closest to rivaling Frieseke's accomplishment, although Miller's execution generally displayed a harder edge. Born in St. Louis, where he began his training, he studied at the Art Institute before meeting Frieseke at the Académie Julian. After some twenty years abroad, he returned to the United States following the outbreak of World War I and in 1918 settled permanently in *Provincetown. To a greater extent than others in the group, Frieseke's particularly good friend Lawton Parker (1868–1954) shared his interest in painting the nude. A Chicagoan, he studied at the Art Institute. He, too, departed for the United States when World War I erupted but returned to France about ten years later. He remained through World War II, losing many of his paintings, but thereafter resided in Santa Monica, California, where he died. Born in Lithuania and taken by his family to Chicago around 1900, Louis Ritman (1889–1963) spent nearly every summer from 1910 until 1928 at Giverny, probably more seasons than any other artist in the informal community. Later, he taught for many years in Chicago at the Art Institute, where he had begun his studies. Among others associated with the group, the most accomplished include Karl Anderson (1874–1956), George *Biddle, Karl Albert Buehr (1866–1952), Edmund W. Greacen (1877–1949), and Guy Rose (1867–1925).

Frishmuth, Harriet (1880–1980). Sculptor. During the 1920s and 1930s, her lighthearted bronze nudes achieved great popularity, particularly as garden and fountain decorations. A Philadelphian, Harriet Whitney Frishmuth spent much of her childhood in Europe. As a young woman she studied art in Paris, where contact with Rodin was formative, and in Berlin before settling in New York. There, after working at the *Art Students League under Gutzon *Borglum and Hermon *MacNeil, she served as an assistant to Karl *Bitter. Among the first of her works to gain wide popularity and still the best known, *The Vine* (1922) displays the animated joy and playful sensuousness typical of her sculpture. Caught in motion, a lithe young woman on tiptoe arches backward, for balance extending one arm from which a vine loops back to the torso. Like many of her successful images, which exist in large editions and more than one size, this tabletop piece was cast in an edition of 350. Later the artist enlarged it to more than six feet in height. After the 1920s, she produced little new work but continued to edition and sell earlier pieces. Frishmuth occasionally worked in stone, and her output includes memorials and a few portraits. In 1937 she moved to the outskirts of Philadelphia where she lived in semiretirement for thirty years before relocating to Southbury, Connecticut. She died in a nursing home in nearby Waterbury some months before her one hundredth birthday.

Frost, Arthur Burdett, Jr. (1887–1917). Painter. His color abstractions number among the earliest American examples. Born in Philadelphia, he was a son of the important turn-of-the-century book and magazine illustrator **A. B. Frost** (1851–1928), who also painted popular outdoor sporting scenes. In 1890 the family moved to an estate near Morristown, New Jersey. Frost's formal artistic education began at the *Pennsylvania Academy of the Fine Arts. In 1905 he went to New York to study with

William Merritt *Chase and Robert *Henri. The following year, his family moved briefly to London before settling in Paris, where Frost studied at the Académie Julian and soon met Patrick Henry *Bruce, who became a close friend. From 1908 they attended Matisse's class, and by 1912 both were working with French abstract color painters Robert and Sonia Delaunay. Frost returned permanently to New York early in 1915. Although not officially a *synchromist, he pursued similar interests and was instrumental in spreading ideas about chromatic abstraction to Americans. As the synchromists had, Frost often used the figure (sometimes adapted from photographs) as the basis for color organization. He also produced completely nonobjective work even before his return to the United States. Tuberculosis took Frost's life four days before his thirtieth birthday. Almost none of his mature work survives, although some lost paintings are known in black-and-white photographs.

Fuller, George (1822–84). Painter. An independent and somewhat isolated figure, he is remembered for soft and painterly images, primarily figural works set outdoors. Extending Washington *Allston's poetic romanticism, they suggest as well aspects of *Barbizon practice, *tonalism, and late-nineteenth-century symbolism. He also painted landscapes and portraits. Associated through much of his life with Deerfield, Massachusetts, where he was born, he grew up there on a farm. His training as an artist was erratic, and he did not define a personal style until he had reached middle age. Recognition arrived only during the productive final eight years of his life, when he completed many of his finest works. Active in his youth as an itinerant portraitist alongside a half brother, in 1842 he studied drawing in Albany with Henry Kirke *Brown. Later that year he moved to Boston, where he benefited from a friendship with Thomas *Ball and admired Allston's work. In 1847 he relocated to New York, where he studied briefly at the *National Academy of Design. While making his home there for twelve years, he continued to travel, most notably sojourning during three winters in the South. On the last of these visits, in 1857–58, he recorded slave life in Montgomery, Alabama, but these subjects appear in finished paintings only much later, as poetic evocations. During the first half of 1860 he made his only trip abroad, studying the art of museums in England as well as on the Continent, and acquainting himself with recent Barbizon and *Pre-Raphaelite achievements. Upon his return, he settled in Deerfield to run the family farm. Although he continued to paint, he rarely exhibited and for the most part remained apart from the art world. In these circumstances, he more or less abandoned the portraits that had previously offered the mainstay of his career, turning instead to landscapes and imaginative subjects. After financial pressure induced him to exhibit in Boston in 1876, he soon reaped critical acclaim for the evocative and idealist approach he had developed in near seclusion. He subsequently wintered in Boston and returned to Deerfield during the warmer months. He died in the Boston suburb of Brookline. With their dusky tonalities, simplified forms, and richly worked paint surfaces, Fuller's signature works relinquish close description of reality to indulge a private aesthetic vision. Although he refrained from illustrating texts directly, many of these characteristic works make reference to literary themes. He also painted numerous ideal heads or figures, usually picturing attractive, dreamy women, as well as generalized pastoral scenes, some peopled by African Americans.

Augustus Fuller (1812–73), who provided his younger half brother's earliest instruction, remained an itinerant portrait painter working in a simplified, nonacademic style. Born deaf, he studied art at what is now the American School for the Deaf in West Hartford, Connecticut, before working in 1833 with Chester *Harding. Among several younger members of the Fuller family who became artists, George's eldest son, **George Spencer Fuller** (1863–1911), combined painting with farming in Deerfield, where he was born. Many of his landscapes picture winter vistas near his home. George Spencer's daughter **Elizabeth Brooks Fuller** (1896–1979) studied with Abbott Handerson *Thayer at his studio in Dublin, New Hampshire, and graduated in 1916 from Boston's School of the Museum of Fine Arts, where she worked with Philip Leslie *Hale. Later she continued her training at the Corcoran School of Art (now Corcoran College of Art and Design) in Washington, D.C., and in 1924 departed for two additional years of study in Europe. She produced vibrant scenes of the Maine coast, as well as refined portrait drawings. While maintaining ties with Deerfield, in later years she lived chiefly in Arizona. Another of George's sons, **Henry Brown Fuller** (1867–1934), painted ideal subjects, landscapes, and portraits. Born in Deerfield, he studied at Boston's Cowles School of Art, where Dennis Miller *Bunker ranked as his most important instructor, at the *Art Students League, and in Paris. He died in New Orleans. His wife, **Lucia Fairchild Fuller** (1872–1924), achieved considerable success with portrait miniatures. Born in Boston, she too studied at the Cowles School with Bunker and at the Art Students League, where William Merritt *Chase numbered among her instructors. The couple married in 1893 and from 1897 numbered among active participants in the art colony at Cornish, New Hampshire. After separating from her husband, she resided for some years in Madison, Wisconsin, where she died.

Fuller, Meta Vaux Warrick (1877–1968). Sculptor. Her pioneering interest in black themes helped to stimulate the *Harlem Renaissance. Exemplifying African Americans' nascent racial pride and interest in origins, her best-known work, the bronze *Ethiopia Awakening* (Schomburg Center for Research in Black Culture, New York Public Library, 1914), symbolizes the rebirth of Afrocentric consciousness, as the personification rouses herself from sleep. Although based on widely admired Egyptian funerary precedents, the groundbreaking treatment incorporates Negroid facial features. The empathetic humanism of Fuller's work typically embeds race in profound human experience. Eloquently speaking to the African-American situation while more generally particularizing mortality, the poignant *Talking Skull* (Museum of Afro-American History, Boston, 1937) depicts a young man of African descent, subtly modeled, kneeling before a skull on the ground. His gentle demeanor and absorption in the memento mori before him suggest universal connotations, as well as African-American familiarity with suffering and death. In addition to other literary subjects, Fuller also produced many sensitive portraits and fluidly modeled *genre figures, including workers and mothers with their children. Born in Philadelphia, Meta Warrick graduated in 1899 from the Pennsylvania School of Industrial Art (now University of the Arts). During subsequent study abroad, in Paris Rodin provided encouragement and informal criticism, and her supple realism owes much to his example. Returning to Philadelphia, she enrolled at the *Pennsylvania Academy of the Fine Arts for four additional years of training. In 1909 she married Solomon Fuller, a Liberian-born neurologist known as the first African-American psychiatrist, and moved permanently to Framingham, Massachusetts, not far from Boston.

Fuller, Sue (1914–2006). Sculptor and printmaker. Remembered especially for constructions made of string, she was born in Pittsburgh. After graduating from the Carnegie Institute of Technology (now Carnegie-Mellon University) there in 1936, she earned an MA from Columbia University three years later. She also studied with Hans *Hofmann and briefly with Josef *Albers. Between 1943 and 1945 she worked as a studio assistant to Stanley William Hayter at *Atelier 17. Incorporating both abstract and representational elements, her soft-ground etchings make inventive use of varied materials. For a popular prize-winner, *Hen* (1945), she formed her whimsical chicken by impressing a lace collar into the etching ground before adding engraved details. For the nonrepresentational *Sailor's Dream* (1944), fabric, ribbon, and string produce a vigorous composition of lines and textured shapes. During the 1950s she gradually gave up printmaking to concentrate entirely on the weblike string creations she had been making for some time under the influence of constructivism. She also studied glassmaking in England and Italy and calligraphy in Japan, as well as lacemaking. In 1969 she patented her method of embedding string in plastic, giving permanence to her complex sculptural inventions. She eventually settled permanently in Southampton, near the eastern end of Long Island.

Fulton, Robert (1765–1815). Painter. Although his name is linked chiefly with development of the steamboat, Fulton first pursued a career in art. After the mid-1790s, when he turned to science and engineering, he painted only occasional portraits. With the fortune he accumulated, he formed a collection of paintings that contributed to development of American interest in the fine arts. Born on a farm, Fulton grew up in nearby Lancaster, Pennsylvania. As a young man in Philadelphia, he found success painting portraits and miniatures. In late 1786 or 1787 he departed for Europe, where he lived for nearly two decades. He studied with Benjamin *West in London and exhibited portraits and history paintings at the Royal Academy in the early 1790s. While in London he also became interested in water transport and in 1796 published a treatise on canal navigation. From 1797 until 1804 he lived in France. He was involved in introducing the idea of *panoramas to Paris, but never completed the painting he had projected. Instead, he pursued inventions related to mechanically powered travel on, and under, water. (He designed an early form of the submarine.) Following another period in England, he returned to the United States late in 1806. His intensive mechanical investigations came to commercial fruition in August 1807 when his steamboat, the *Clermont*, made a successful voyage up the Hudson River. He died in New York.

Funk art. A visual equivalent to California's 1950s and 1960s beat culture of free expression, contempt for social and aesthetic conventions, and experimental lifestyles. Peaking in 1960s

San Francisco, but also in enclaves around Los Angeles, funk art contributed to the countercultural social and political upheavals of that decade. The sensuous, earthy, transgressive qualities of funk inspired varied approaches, including a particularly uninhibited form of *junk art. In 1967 Berkeley's University of California art museum (now Berkeley Art Museum and Pacific Film Archive) presented "Funk," which formalized the tendency's nomenclature and defined what the museum's director, German-born art historian and critic Peter Selz (1919–), called its "go-to-hell attitude." The spirit of funk art parallels Robert *Rauschenberg's all-inclusive combines, but funk's vulgarity, bumptious humor, and raucous energy often exceed the expressive demeanor of generally more style-conscious East Coast work. Drawing on popular culture sources that also fueled *pop art, funk looked back, as well, to surrealism's weird juxtapositions and dadaism's anti-art gestures.

Many works by Edward *Kienholz and *Jess exemplify a funk attitude. Among central members of the Bay Area funk community, sculptor Robert Arneson (1930–92) extended its premises into ceramic work, demonstrating funk's disregard for the traditional hierarchy of art materials. Born in Benecia, where he also died, Arneson spent most of his life in the Bay Area or nearby. In 1954 he graduated from the California College of Arts and Crafts (now California College of the Arts) in Oakland and four years later received an MFA from Mills College, also in Oakland. In 1962 he embarked on an influential teaching career of nearly thirty years at the University of California at Davis. Also in the early 1960s he broke with conventional pottery traditions to produce amusingly satirical and sometimes provocative ceramic transformations of ordinary objects. Many self-portraits from the 1970s and subsequent decades address questions of identity with wry humor. His later work often engaged more serious social and political issues, such as nuclear war. He also cast some work in bronze.

Bruce Conner (1933–), *assemblage and collage artist, draftsman, printmaker, and filmmaker, has worked in San Francisco since 1957. Born in McPherson, Kansas, the versatile and mercurial Bruce Guldner Conner grew up in Wichita. He earned a BFA in 1955 from the University of Nebraska in Lincoln and pursued additional training at the Brooklyn Museum's school and at the University of Colorado. His early work generally combined detritus and other degraded materials in disenchanted statements of alienation, eroticism, and fearsomely distasteful abjection. Yet, these also incorporated lyrical touches. From the late 1950s he contributed to the underground film movement with experimental works that often reflected his unease with contemporary consumer culture. In the same period, he began to produce intricate drawings evoking hallucinogenic states and spiritual longings. A series of collages begun in the 1980s combine drawing with antique prints, recalling Max *Ernst's technically similar surrealistic mélanges but often infused with a more intensely personal romanticism.

Painter, sculptor, and photographer Jay De Feo (1931–89) numbered among friends in Conner's San Francisco circle. Born in Hanover, New Hampshire, Mary Jane De Feo grew up in California and Colorado. She earned BA and MA degrees at the University of California in Berkeley. Combining elements of abstraction and representation in her work, she particularly emphasized the role of materials. From 1958 until 1966 she worked almost exclusively on a single canvas measuring more than ten feet high and nearly eight feet wide. By dint of slow accretion, *The Rose* (Whitney Museum) grew into a relief some eight inches thick and weighing a ton or more. Its heavily worked surface centers on a geometric starburst form. Her subsequent paintings, drawings, and photographs generally expand upon an earlier interest in transforming ordinary objects into mysterious presences. In 1954 she married painter and assemblage artist Wally Hedrick (1928–2003), but they later divorced. His richly layered works also incorporate both abstract and representational approaches. Born in Pasadena, he was drafted into Korean War military service in 1951. Upon his release the following year, he moved to San Francisco to study at the California School of Fine Arts (now San Francisco Art Institute), where he earned a BFA in 1955. In 1958 he received a master's degree from San Francisco State College (now University). Often addressing antiwar and other politically fraught themes, his irreverent work also encompassed allusions to popular culture. He taught at the College of Marin, north of the city, from 1974 until his retirement in 1993 and died at his home in Sonoma County.

Painter and sculptor Joan Brown (1938–90), also an active participant in the small funk circle of the 1960s, came from a background in *abstract expressionism and admiration for *Bay Area figurative art, particularly the work of her teacher Elmer *Bischoff. A San Francisco native, she earned a BFA at the California School of Fine Arts in 1959 and a master's degree the following year. Until 1965 she painted thickly impastoed figurative compositions and arrangements of commonplace objects, often with comic overtones, while also occasionally trying her hand at bizarre assemblages. During this period, she was married to Manuel *Neri. In the late 1960s Brown worked out a personal, vivaciously decorative, thinly painted figurative style of flattened shapes. Her subjects often explored questions of identity through autobiographical imagery, including numerous self-portraits and likenesses of family members, as well as animals endowed with enigmatic inner lives. From the late 1970s, she also investigated varied avenues of spiritual experience. She died in an accident during installation of an obelisk (the last of almost a dozen similarly shaped, ornamentally tiled public monuments from the previous decade) at an ashram in Puttaparthi, India.

Bay Area painter, printmaker, and sculptor William T. Wiley (1937–) is best known for loopy paintings integrating words and images into eccentric, pun-laden, faux-naif, faux-Zen mixtures. From 1960s detailed watercolors, these have grown into large canvases. In those earlier years, he also made assemblages and tableaux, largely from found objects. In addition, he has created steel sculptures, as well as numerous lithographs and etchings. A native of Bedford, in southern Indiana, he moved with his family to Richland, Washington. In 1956 he began his professional training at the California School of Fine Arts, where he received a BFA in 1960 and an MFA two years later. He lives in Marin County, north of San Francisco.

Other notable contributors to funk art include Los Angeles-based collage and photoreproduction artist and poet Wallace Berman (1926–76), a New York native who often infused his art with Hebrew mysticism, and two additional participants in the San Francisco milieu: Nebraska-born Roy De Forest (1930–), known for bright, busy animal paintings suggesting equal appreciation for folk art and surrealism, and Salt Lake City native Robert Hudson (1938–), a sculptor whose frenzied, sometimes fetishistic assemblages gave way to colorful, formally complex fabricated works.

Gabo, Naum (1890–1977). Sculptor. His visionary abstract works dematerialize mass and, by incorporating voids, introduce space as a dynamic element. By fabricating his sculptures from such transparent or translucent materials as plastic or glass, he permitted light to function as an internal element, supplementing its more traditional function as illumination of surface. Linear elements within transparent solids or across spaces often guide the observer's eye. Gabo's lyrical effects grace such works as the nylon string and Lucite *Linear Construction, Variation* (Phillips Collection, 1942–43), which builds ambiguous, shifting volumes around a central emptiness. He also experimented at an early date with kinetic art, but soon abandoned movement as a distraction to the purity of his aims. While living in Moscow in 1920, Gabo drew up the Realist Manifesto, a statement of basic principles for the future of modern art. Co-signed by his older brother Antoine Pevsner, this ringingly idealistic document held that the new sculpture should be grounded in scientific principles derived from analysis of space and time. This work was to be constructed of fundamental formal elements, together with space, using the new industrial materials appropriate to the modern age. In upholding the desirability of nonutilitarian, spiritually oriented art, Gabo departed from Russian constructivism's materialism, but his ideas and example proved crucial to the spread and reinterpretation of constructivist ideas in western Europe and the United States. Born Naum Neemia Borisovich Pevsner in Klimovichi, Russia (now Belarus), he grew up in Briansk, Russia. Between 1910 and 1914 he studied medicine, engineering, philosophy, and art history in Munich. As an artist, he remained self-taught. He changed his name to avoid confusion with his artist-brother in 1915, the year he began to make cubist-derived sculptural constructions while living in Oslo. Along with his brother, in 1917 he moved to Moscow, where they participated in the constructivist-dominated avant-garde for several years. Gabo left for Berlin in 1922. Ten years later, he moved to Paris for three years and then went to England. He lived in London from 1935 to 1939 and in Cornwall until he left for the United States in 1946. Naturalized as a U.S. citizen in 1952, he resided in Connecticut—in Woodbury until 1953, then in Middlebury—and died in a hospital in Waterbury. In 1962 Gabo published *Of Divers Arts*.

Gág, Wanda (1893–1946). Printmaker, illustrator, and painter. A native of New Ulm, Minnesota, Wanda Hazel Gág studied from 1914 to 1917 at the Minneapolis School of Art (now

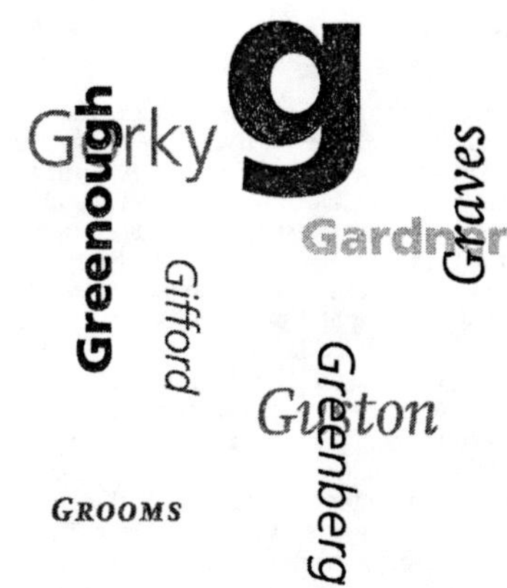

Minneapolis College of Art and Design) and subsequently at the *Art Students League, where John *Sloan numbered among her teachers. From the 1920s, she achieved considerable success with inventive prints, chiefly lithographs. These interiors, landscapes, and architectural scenes feature strong compositions of simplified form. Exemplifying the moody drama of many, the 1929 lithograph *Lamplight* depicts an uninhabited room filled with mysterious shadows. Several children's books followed the success of Gág's illustrated tale *Millions of Cats* (1928). She also prepared drawings for other works, including four volumes of Grimm's fairy tales. After a year in Connecticut, in 1924 she moved to the northern New Jersey town of Glen Gardner. In 1930 she married an intermittent companion of many years, Earle Humphrey, and moved to a Delaware Valley farm near Milford, New Jersey. She died in New York. Although she regretted her limited time for painting and printmaking, Gág's commercially successful illustrated books freed her from economic insecurity and permitted an independent life consciously modeled on the image of the sexually liberated and professionally accomplished "New Woman" of the 1920s. "A Hotbed of Feminists," which appeared in *The Nation* in 1927, included her opinion that "the aesthetic value of sin is not to be sneezed at." In 1940, she published a memoir, *Growing Pains: Diaries and Drawings for the Years 1908–1917*, based on her journals.

Gallatin, Albert Eugene (1881–1952). Collector, painter, and art writer. In 1927 he founded the Gallery of Living Art (from 1936, Museum of Living Art) to exhibit his collection of European and American modern art. Installed at New York University, the gallery then numbered among few places where abstract art could be regularly seen. After the showcase closed late in 1942, some months later Gallatin gave most of his collection to the Philadelphia Museum of Art. Born in Villanova, Pennsylvania, he was named for his illustrious great-grandfather, the early secretary of the treasury and diplomat Albert Gallatin. He briefly studied law but otherwise did not pursue higher education. In his early collecting and writing, he focused on impressionists and *Ashcan School painters, along with such turn-of-the-century favorites as Aubrey Beardsley and James Abbott McNeill *Whistler. In the late 1910s he turned his attention to modern art and soon started to assemble a survey ranging from Cézanne through Picasso and Georges Braque to Miró. Challenged by the opening of the *Museum of Modern Art in 1929 and the *Whitney Museum of American Art two years later, in 1932 he began to redefine his collection more narrowly. With the advice of French painter Jean Hélion, he eliminated nearly everything that failed to contribute to what he saw as the logical unfolding of modern art from cubism to contemporary forms of abstraction. In 1933 he named George L. K. *Morris a curator of the Gallery of Living Art, and the two worked closely in further developing the collection. Besides such Europeans as Mondrian, Fernand Léger, and Jean Arp, the gallery purchased the work of young American abstractionists, including Morris, Alexander *Calder, and John *Ferren. Gallatin did not seriously work as a painter until the 1930s, when he developed a simplified geometric style related to work in his collection. From 1937 he participated in the *American Abstract Artists organization. He died in New York. Gallatin's numerous publications include books on John *Sloan, Charles *Demuth, and American watercolor painters, as well as several about Whistler. *Art and the Great War* appeared in 1919.

Gansevoort Painter. *See* PATROON PAINTERS.

Ganso, Emil (1895–1941). Printmaker and painter. Born in Halberstadt, Germany, Ganso was working as a dishwasher on a transatlantic steamer when he jumped ship in Hoboken, New Jersey, in 1912. After working at odd jobs in several locations, in 1914 he began taking classes at the *National Academy of Design. He had little formal training as an artist and did not work full time at his craft until 1925. Between 1922 and 1934 he made three lengthy visits to Europe. Some of his early work was indebted to the example of his friend Jules *Pascin, but concurrently he also produced bold expressionist relief cuts. From 1926 on, he spent every summer at *Woodstock. Between 1935 and 1937 he worked for a *federal art project. He taught for a year at Lawrence College (now University) in Appleton, Wisconsin, before accepting a position in 1940 at the State University of Iowa (now University of Iowa) in Iowa City. He died of a heart attack at his home there the following spring. Ganso's subjects included studio scenes, mostly still lifes and figural studies, as well as landscapes and views of rural settings. His style varied from one of dramatic force, achieved with strong contrasts and distorted forms, to a somber realism. Better known as a printmaker than painter, he worked in many graphic media, including wood engraving, lithography, aquatint, and etching.

Garber, Daniel (1880–1958). Painter and printmaker. Primarily a landscape artist, he also painted figural scenes, sometimes set indoors. Particularly interested in the visual and emotional effects of light, he developed a personal variant of impressionism emphasizing bold and sometimes unnaturalistic color harmonies that suggest postimpressionist and even fauve precedents. Born on a farm near North Manchester, Indiana, he began his training at Cincinnati's Art Academy. In Philadelphia he studied for five years at the *Pennsylvania Academy of the Fine Arts, where Thomas *Anshutz ranked as his most important teacher, while working also as an illustrator and portrait painter. Upon return in 1907 from a two-year visit to Europe, he acquired a country residence near Lumberville, Pennsylvania, a Bucks County village on the Delaware River not far from *New Hope. In the mid-1920 he relinquished his Philadelphia home to live there permanently. Regarded as a leading New Hope artist, he also taught for many years at the Pennsylvania Academy. Although some landscapes display carefully rendered detail in combination with glowing but naturalistic light, his most striking and individual work combines rich and febrile brushwork, intense coloration, and carefully regulated spatial recession in a highly charged and decorative style. At once mysterious and dynamic, *Tohickon* (Smithsonian American Art Museum, 1920) depicts a darkened tree and other sinuous vegetation sprawling across the foreground and impeding a view of the sunlit hillside across the Tohickon River. The image's patterned surface displays the artist's characteristic palette of purple-blue shadows, greens from grayed to acidic, and highlights in warmer tones.

Gardner, Alexander (1821–82). Photographer. Known especially for images of the Civil War and its aftermath, he also documented the

West and created notable portraits. Born in Paisley, Scotland, as a young man he worked as a jeweler in Glasgow. Drawn to literature and issues of social welfare, he became a follower of utopian socialist Robert Owen; in 1850 he traveled to Iowa with his brother **James Gardner** (1829–?), later also a photographer, to purchase land for a cooperative community. Subsequently in Glasgow he worked as a reporter and editor, while also becoming interested in photography. Intending to settle in Iowa, he traveled there in 1856 but soon left for New York. There he found employment in Mathew B. *Brady's studio, where his technical skill with the new glass negative technology proved particularly valuable. In 1858 Brady put him in charge of his Washington operation, which prospered under Gardner's artistic direction and canny management. When the Civil War broke out, Gardner worked on Brady's project to document the conflict. After they quarreled over Brady's practice of issuing his reporters' work under his own name, in 1863 Gardner opened a rival Washington studio in partnership with his brother. Among Alexander's subsequent portraits, several important images of Abraham Lincoln included the last, taken only days before his death. He also compiled his own record of the ongoing war. As official photographer for the Army of the Potomac, he enjoyed access to major events and military staff. As Brady did, he hired other photographers to contribute to his Civil War archive but always scrupulously credited their work. His own contributions include many of the strongest and most affecting images of the war. After the surrender, he continued to pursue newsworthy events. His moving series portraying the conspirators in Lincoln's assassination and their public execution ranks among photojournalism's earliest pictorial essays. In 1866 he published a lavish, two-volume *Photographic Sketch Book of the War*, illustrated with one hundred tipped-in original photographs by Gardner and others. Each was accompanied by a text presumably composed by Gardner. In 1867 Gardner traveled west for the Union Pacific Railroad, and in this capacity recorded landscapes, townscapes, and local features, as well as rail construction. He also photographed the West's Indian inhabitants, particularly those attending an 1868 peace conference in Laramie, Wyoming. He died in Washington.

Gardner, Isabella Stewart (1840–1924). Collector and museum founder. Fenway Court, her opulent Boston residence reminiscent of a Venetian palazzo, houses the museum that bears her name. Noted particularly for its Renaissance paintings, her collection comprises also sculpture, prints, books and manuscripts, and decorative arts dating from antiquity through the nineteenth century. Gardner's motto, *C'est mon plaisir*, characterizes the museum's spirit as well as her own freewheeling style. Born in New York, Isabella Stewart was educated in private schools there and in Paris. Following marriage in 1860 to wealthy Bostonian John Lowell ("Jack") Gardner Jr., she resided in Boston but regularly traveled the world. During the 1870s, as she seriously began to collect books, manuscripts, and prints, Charles Eliot *Norton often served as her advisor. Later her interest shifted to painting, and Bernard *Berenson directed her taste toward the Renaissance. Her collection eventually encompassed examples by Giotto, Botticelli, Titian, Vermeer, Rembrandt, Rubens, and other old masters. She also acquired work from contemporary artists she knew, including John Singer *Sargent, James Abbott McNeill *Whistler, and cosmopolitan Swedish-born painter Anders Zorn. Construction of Fenway Court began in 1899, and the collection opened to the public in 1903. Although most of her major pieces were in hand by then, she made additions to the collection until about 1916. Partially paralyzed by a stroke at the end of 1919, she no longer managed the museum on her own but nevertheless continued to reside in Fenway Court's private quarters. In her will, Gardner stipulated that the museum remain permanently as she left it, in an arrangement she considered an integrated aesthetic ensemble. Comfortably complemented in the galleries by antique furniture and decorative arts, her paintings and other treasures surround a lushly planted interior court evoking the richness of Italy.

Garman, Ed. *See* TRANSCENDENTAL PAINTING GROUP.

Gatch, Lee (1902–68). Painter and collage artist. Attracted primarily to landscape motifs, he also painted still lifes and figurative canvases, as well as *federal art project murals. His evocative, richly colored works reconcile motifs from nature with sensuous design. During his career he moved toward increasing abstraction, as he sought to express a spiritual response to visible reality. Certain late works incorporate flagstone fragments. A slow and meticulous worker, he finished relatively few works, but these earned a major reputation in the 1950s. He was born in Benton Heights, near Baltimore, where he studied at the Maryland Institute of Fine Arts (now the Maryland Institute College of Art) with John *Sloan and Leon *Kroll. During a year in Paris, he worked with modernists André Lhote and Moïse Kisling before moving to New York in 1925. He was married briefly in the 1920s to Jack *Tworkov's sister, known professionally as *Biala. After Elsie *Driggs became his wife in 1935, Gatch settled in Lambertville, New Jersey, on the Delaware River. He died in a hospital in nearby Trenton.

Gaugengigl, Ignaz Marcel. *See* HASSAM, CHILDE.

Gay, August François. *See* SOCIETY OF SIX.

Gay, Walter (1856–1937). Painter. Remembered particularly for the elegant interior scenes he began painting in the 1890s, at earlier stages of his career he painted still lifes, historical costume pieces, and bleak depictions of workers, particularly French peasants, as well as occasional portraits. He made his home in France during his adult life. Also a collector of antique decorative arts and old master drawings, for the last three decades of his life he maintained a large chateau on vast acreage at the edge of the Forest of Fontainebleau. Born in Hingham, not far from Boston, he lived as a youth in Dorchester (now part of Boston). While still in his teens, he worked professionally as a still life painter, specializing in depictions of flowers. In 1876 he departed for Europe. After visiting London, he continued on to Paris and in the nearby countryside became familiar with *Barbizon painting. For about three years he studied with Léon Bonnat, absorbing his academic technique. Before the end of the decade, Gay was turning out eighteenth-century anecdotes of the sort popularized by Jean Louis Ernest Meissonier and Mariano Fortuny. These generally small, precisely delineated works gave way in the mid-1880s to somewhat larger, simpler and darker, more somber renderings of contemporary urban labor and Breton peasant life. By the mid-1890s he had virtually abandoned other subjects to concentrate on interior views, usually unpopulated. Furnishings and decor signify human presence in these accurately delineated, yet atmospheric evocations of a cultivated lifestyle. Most depict the light, rococo rooms he particularly favored, but some are devoted to other styles of decoration. Among favorite subjects was his own eighteenth-century Château du Bréau in Dammarie-les-Lys, where he died. *Memoirs of Walter Gay* appeared in 1930.

Gay's formative experiences included contact with an uncle, **Winckworth Allan Gay** (1821–1910), a widely traveled landscape painter. Born in West Hingham, he studied at West Point with Robert W. *Weir. His early efforts included portraiture, but he specialized in landscape from the time of his arrival in Europe in 1847. Perhaps the first American to study with an artist identified with the Barbizon school, he worked in Paris with Constant Tryon. After his return to the United States in 1850, he combined elements of that style with the *Hudson River School approach. He made his home in the Boston area but also painted regularly in the White Mountains of New Hampshire. In the mid-1870s he again visited Europe and spent several months in Egypt. In 1877 he departed on a five-year trip around the world. After a lengthy stay in Japan, as well as sojourns in China and India, he returned to Paris for another two years. In 1894 he resettled permanently in West Hingham.

Geller, Todros. *See* SIPORIN, MITCHELL.

Gemini G. E. L. *See* TAMARIND LITHOGRAPHY WORKSHOP.

Genre. Term referring to art that depicts everyday activities of ordinary people. In its more general sense, not necessarily limited to discussions of art, the word is used also to refer to a specified branch or category. Still life, for example, is a genre of painting, while the symphony is a genre of music. With respect to its more limited meaning, in the United States a distinctive form of genre painting flourished between about 1830 and 1860. Along with *landscape painting, it was thought to represent a genuinely American form of expression. In this period, genre painting most frequently depicted rural subjects and rarely acknowledged problematic, painful, or vulgar aspects of life. It thus presented an idealized interpretation of the preindustrial, vernacular origins of American experience. By the time of the Civil War, interest in such scenes had begun to decline, as their view of life came to be seen as simplistic. William Sidney *Mount ranks as the first important American genre specialist. Others include George Caleb *Bingham and Richard Caton *Woodville. After the Civil War, the subjects of genre painting broadened, often to reflect the nation's urbanization and material prosperity. Moreover, as painters increasingly looked to European precedents and more cosmopolitan and varied taste took hold in the United States, painters often combined the observation of mundane experience with other interests, such as elements of Victorian sentimental moralizing or literary narrative. In other works, technical or stylistic concerns subordinate the genre content. John George *Brown and Thomas *Hovenden numbered among the most popular genre specialists of the later nineteenth century, and genre subjects persisted among the works of such major artists as Thomas *Eakins, Eastman *Johnson and Winslow *Homer. Much *Ashcan School painting extended interest in genre into the early 1900s, while Edward *Hopper continued its subjects through mid-century even as documentary photography largely subsumed the concerns of genre painting. Duane *Hanson provided a form of genre sculpture into the 1990s. Historical precedents for American genre date back at least to seventeenth-century Holland, which produced the first market for scenes of everyday life. Many American artists knew these works, either at first hand or through intermediary copies or prints, but the example of early nineteenth-century British art proved generally more influential. In particular, the internationally popular work of Charles Wilkie impressed many Americans, including Mount. From the mid-nineteenth-century, many genre subjects found mass appeal through printed reproductions, especially those of the *Currier & Ives firm.

Genthe, Arnold (1869–1942). Photographer. Best known for the only surviving images of the San Francisco Chinatown destroyed by the 1906 earthquake, Genthe was born in Berlin and lived as a child in Frankfurt. In 1894 he earned a doctorate in classical philology at the University of Jena. He continued his studies at the Sorbonne in Paris before emigrating the following year to the United States. While living in San Francisco, he began photographing the still unassimilated Chinese community there. His unposed but carefully organized street photographs rank among the first to seize transient moments, by their nature casual, modern, and emblematic. In 1897 he became a professional portrait photographer. Although he lost his studio in the earthquake, his Chinatown negatives, stored in a vault, survived. He had to borrow a camera to record the disaster's destruction and ensuing fire. In 1907 he numbered among the earliest photographers to experiment with the Autochrome color process, and he remained interested in color photography. Genthe moved to New York in 1911 and was naturalized as a citizen in 1918. His portrait studio drew many celebrities, and in the 1920s he developed a specialty of photographing dancers and other entertainers. He died on a visit to New Milford, Connecticut. In 1936 Genthe published an illustrated autobiography, *As I Remember*. In addition, he collected his photographs in several books, including *Pictures of Old Chinatown* (1908; revised as *Old Chinatown*, 1913), *Impressions of Old New Orleans* (1926), and *Isadora Duncan* (1929).

Gentle, Esther. *See* RATTNER, ABRAHAM.

Gesture painting. *See* ABSTRACT EXPRESSIONISM.

Gibran, Kahlil. *See* DAY, F. HOLLAND.

Gifford, Robert Swain. *See* DEWING, MARIA OAKEY.

Gifford, Sanford Robinson (1823–80). Painter. A landscape specialist, he took particular interest in effects of light and atmosphere. *A Gorge in the Mountains (Kauterskill Clove)* (Metropolitan Museum, 1862) summons to mind a valley in the Catskill Mountains, as Haines Falls glints in the far distance under a late afternoon sky. This extensive autumnal vista combines meticulous description of natural features with hazy golden light that unifies the scene without dissolving it. Offering an escape into nature's timeless perfection, the painting may have seemed a balm to its first viewers during the Civil War. Born in upstate Greenfield, Saratoga County, New York, Gifford moved as a small child with his family to Hudson, on the Hudson River south of Albany. In 1842 he enrolled at Brown University in Providence, Rhode Island, but left after three semesters to pursue an artistic career. In 1845 he settled permanently in New York, where he studied chiefly with London-born painter-printmaker John Rubens Smith (1775–1849), known for descriptively oriented topographical views as well as figural works. That summer Gifford set off on a sketching tour that took him all the way to Canada, setting a lifelong pattern of devoted nature study at firsthand. An admirer of Thomas *Cole's work, Gifford gained recognition for *Hudson River School paintings before departing in 1855 for Europe. During more than two years abroad, while following an extended circuit from London to Naples, he was on the move much of the time. A particularly indefatigable and attentive traveler, he studied the art of museums, sought out contemporary landscape paintings, and incessantly made sketches and notes that often informed subsequent paintings. His exposure to the work of English painter J. M. W. Turner decisively influenced the appearance of glowing atmospherics in his own work. However, American mid-century *luminism provided homegrown support for this poetic aspect of Gifford's style. Like other New York landscapists, Gifford usually spent the summer months working in scenic Northeast locations. Even during intermittent National Guard duty in the Civil War, he made use of opportunities for sketching. In 1868 Gifford again sailed to Europe and remained abroad for more than a year, including five months in Egypt, the Middle East, and Greece. Through the following decade, this excursion provided material for numerous paintings, including a group devoted to the picturesque lagoons of Venice and his last important work, *The Ruins of the Parthenon* (Corcoran Gallery, 1880). With Worthington *Whittredge and John *Kensett, he traveled to the Rocky Mountains in 1870. From there he accompanied a survey expedition through Wyoming and Utah. Four years later, he again journeyed west, continuing on through British Columbia to Alaska. Weakened by an illness during a trip to Lake Superior, he died shortly after returning to New York. Personally and professionally esteemed by the New York art community, Gifford was honored the year after his death by the *Metropolitan Museum of Art. The first event of its kind there, his huge retrospective exhibition, accompanied by a detailed catalogue, set a precedent for such New York art world milestones.

Gignoux, Régis François (1816–82). Painter. A landscape specialist, he favored winter scenes fusing meticulous detail with expressive effects. Born in Lyon, he trained in Paris, most notably with the romantic academic Paul Delaroche, before moving to New York about 1840. The *Hudson River School provided a sympathetic context for his work as he turned to American subjects. Although his approach remained rooted in European technical and conceptual conventions, he gained considerable success around mid-century. Characteristically, he enlivened *Winter Scene* (Corcoran Gallery, 1850) with appealing *genre touches that recall popular seventeenth-century Dutch precedents. On a frozen river, skaters and others enjoy the pleasures of snow-dusted surroundings. Pearly tonality, spatial plenitude, and delicately rendered, precise detail typify his best works. Some compositions are stitched together from fragments, however, and effects often skirt sentimentality. He returned to France in 1870 and died in Paris.

Gikow, Ruth. *See* LEVINE, JACK.

Gile, Selden Connor (1877–1947). Painter. The leading spirit of the San Francisco Bay Area's Society of Six, he specialized in colorful, boldly patterned landscapes. Impressionist and fauve precedents underpinned his modernist interest in abstract structure. In the undated *Boat and Yellow Hills* (Oakland Museum of California), interlocking shapes represent unnaturally golden hills rising beyond a placid, predominately cool-toned cove, only to terminate in a dark blue sky. Born in Stow, Maine, near the New Hampshire border, in 1901 he made his way to California, where he studied in Oakland at the California College of Arts and Crafts (now California College of the Arts) and painted impressionist-influenced landscapes. His more personal style began to coalesce around 1915. In 1927 he moved across the bay from Oakland to Marin County and soon settled for a number of years on a houseboat in Belvedere. He died in San Rafael.

An informal and somewhat rambunctious association of progressive landscape painters, the Society of Six came together in the wake of San Francisco's 1915 Panama-Pacific Exposition, which provided the area's first large-scale introduction to recent trends in European art. Reacting against the moody gentility and somber tonalities of San Francisco's leading artists, Arthur *Mathews and the recently deceased William *Keith, the group self-consciously sought modern forms of expression. The society peaked during the mid-1920s, as its members vigorously traded ideas, worked frequently outdoors together, and exhibited annually at the Oakland Art Gallery (now the art division of the Oakland Museum of California). Economic hard times during the 1930s undermined the society, although members continued to meet upon occasion through the decade. Canadian-born William Henry Clapp (1879–1954), the only participant who had studied abroad and the least adventurous as a painter, served also as the curator of the Oakland Art Gallery. The other four were native Californians who had grown up in the Bay Area. Bernard James von Eichman (1899–1970) produced some of the group's most radical works, sometimes nearing abstraction, before he moved to New York during the 1930s. Louis Bassi Siegriest (1899–1989) after World War II went on to paint poetic abstractions based on the California desert. The best of August François Gay's (1890–1948) fluid, light-drenched scenes portend achievements of Richard *Diebenkorn and other post–World War II Bay Area painters. Maurice George Logan (1886–1971) later continued to paint oils, as well as more numerous illustrational watercolors, while achieving considerable success as a commercial artist in San Francisco.

Gilliam, Sam. *See* WASHINGTON COLOR SCHOOL.

Gilmor, Robert, Jr. (1774–1848). Collector and patron. He is credited with assembling the premier art collection in the United States during the first half of the nineteenth century. It included the work of numerous American artists, as well as paintings by or attributed to important old masters and contemporary Europeans. Because Dutch and Flemish works of the seventeenth century were particularly well represented, Gilmor's patronage may have encouraged American artists' interest in *genre, but he also sponsored landscape and portraiture. Cultivated and well traveled, he was born on Maryland's eastern shore. In 1778 he moved with his family to Baltimore, which remained his permanent home, except for the period from 1782 to 1784 when the family lived in Amsterdam. Subsequent travels took him along the eastern seaboard from Charleston to Boston and, between 1799 and 1801, on a grand tour of Europe. He also traveled to Europe in 1817–18. Privately educated, he supplemented his art acquisitions with a large and wide-ranging library, as well as collections of scientific and antiquarian interest. He may have owned as many as five hundred paintings and twenty-five hundred works on paper, but probably possessed only three or four hundred paintings at any one time. The collection included examples of work by most of the period's leading American painters, including Washington *Allston, Thomas *Cole, William Sidney *Mount, Charles Willson *Peale, Gilbert *Stuart, and Thomas *Sully. He also commissioned sculptures from Horatio *Greenough and others. Hoping that his collections would remain intact, Gilmor offered them near the end of his life to the nascent *Smithsonian Institution, which turned him down. Ultimately, his holdings were dispersed at auction after his death.

Gilpin, Laura (1891–1979). Photographer. Born in Colorado Springs, she remained primarily an interpreter of the American West. Already photographing before she was in her teens, between 1916 and 1918 she studied in New York at Clarence *White's school. There she absorbed her mentor's commitment to impeccable print technique, his interest in design, and his affinity for poetic effects. Even her most documentary works feature these qualities. Following her return to Colorado, she produced portraits, landscapes, and architectural studies, with particular emphasis after 1930 on Navajo life. In 1945 she moved permanently to Santa Fe, New Mexico. There she continued documenting and researching native southwestern cultures and the archeological remains of their histories. The result of nearly two decades of work, her most important book, *The Enduring Navajo* (1968), for which she provided both text and illustrations, probes the tribe's traditions, culture, and geography. In addition, Gilpin published *The Pueblos: A Camera Chronicle* (1941), *Temples in Yucatán: A Camera Chronicle of Chichén Itzá* (1948) and *The Rio Grande, River of Destiny: An Interpretation of the River, the Land, and the People* (1949).

Giverny group. *See* FRIESEKE, FREDERICK.

Glackens, William (1870–1938). Painter and illustrator. While his drawings contributed to the *Ashcan School's boisterous account of contemporary urban life, his canvases generally relate the metropolitan experience of middle and upper classes, reflecting French impressionist precedents. In later years, he specialized in studio subjects, especially nudes. A Philadelphia native, in the early 1890s William James Glackens attended classes at the *Pennsylvania Academy of the Fine Arts while working as a newspaper illustrator. During these years, he associated with Robert *Henri, as well as fellow news artists John *Sloan, George *Luks, and Everett *Shinn. After a fifteen-month sojourn in Paris, with side trips to other art centers, in 1896 Glackens returned only briefly to Philadelphia before moving to New York. There, he furnished newspapers and magazines with animated drawings, deftly evoking the crowds that congregated in tenement streets, beaches, and city parks. In his paintings, the young artist evolved from a fluid, painterly technique indebted to Henri and old masters toward an impressionist approach. Included among his works in the 1908 exhibition of The *Eight, Glackens's best known painting, *Chez Mouquin* (Art Institute of Chicago, 1905), reveals a debt to Manet and Degas in technique, composition, and choice of subject—fashionable diners at a popular restaurant. Subsequently, Glackens adopted a more purely impressionist manner, inspired especially by Renoir's late, florid palette. With time, as he produced fewer illustrations, he also retreated from the street to the studio for the subjects of his paintings, as in the early example *Nude with Apple* (Brooklyn Museum, 1910). Although he served as an organizer for the *Armory Show and bought postimpressionist art in Paris for Dr. Albert C. *Barnes (a high school classmate), his art remained attached to the ideals of an older generation of artistic innovators. During later years he summered at Bellport, on the south shore of Long Island, and traveled often to Europe. He died during a visit to Westport, Connecticut. Painter and illustrator **Edith Dimock Glackens** (1876–1955), born in Hartford, Connecticut, and married to Glackens in 1904, studied with William Merritt *Chase and exhibited in the Armory Show. She died at her home in Hartford. Writer **Ira Glackens** (1907–90), their son, published *William Glackens and the Ashcan Group: The Emergence of Realism in American Art* (1957) and *William Glackens and the Eight: The Artists Who Freed American Art* (1984).

Glarner, Fritz (1899–1972). Painter and printmaker. From the mid-1940s, he focused on Relational Paintings composed of rectangular or nearly rectangular shapes in simple color combinations. Although inspired by the example of Mondrian's neoplasticism, Glarner's works are less rigid, less doctrinaire, and visually more fluid. As well, he often employed circular formats. In the characteristic *Relational Painting* (Whitney Museum, 1949–51), color is limited to his usual red, blue, and yellow, along with black, white, and two shades of gray. Most of the flat, geometric elements deviate slightly from pure rectangles, suggesting subtle adjustments to compositional pressure across the surface. While reduced in means, the composition is intuitively structured, producing a dynamic interplay between discipline and freedom. Although born in Zurich, Glarner spent most of his early years in Naples, where he studied at the Royal Institute of Fine Arts from 1914 to 1920. After moving to Paris in 1923, he absorbed the influence of Cézanne, Robert Delaunay, and other leading modernists as he gradually developed a semi-abstract style. For nine months in 1930–31 he lived in New York but then returned to Paris. In 1935 he relocated to Zurich for a year before heading back to New York, where he soon began to exhibit with the *American Abstract Artists as he purified his style. He was naturalized as a United States citizen in 1944. From 1957 he lived in Huntington, on Long Island, but toward the end of his life returned to Switzerland. He died in Locarno.

Gohlke, Frank. *See* NEW TOPOGRAPHICS.

Goings, Ralph. *See* PHOTO-REALISM.

Goldin, Amy. *See* PATTERN AND DECORATION.

Goldin, Nan (1953–). Photographer. Autobiographical experience fuels most of her raw and refractory expression. Loneliness, alienation, despair, and, ultimately, the search for meaning through human relationships provide her major themes. She is best known for an evolving slide show, *The Ballad of Sexual Dependency* (1981 and later). Also presented in book form (1986), the searing images document, sometimes with provocative intimacy, her freewheeling immersion in a subculture of sex, drugs, degradation, and nihilism. Goldin provided an important precedent for many recent artists who use their own histories as the basis of art making in varied media. Born in Washington, D.C., she grew up in Boston, where as a teenager she began photographing her off-limits clique. While studying at the School of the Museum of Fine Arts, she first presented the slide show, often shown in clubs to accompaniment of a musical soundtrack, as well as in galleries. Continuing to augment *The Ballad*, she subsequently lived in New York, but also worked frequently in European cities, particularly Berlin. The AIDS crisis also colored her work, as she photographed ill and dying friends. Travel in Asia in the 1990s documented forays into the alternative scene there. In 1994 she collaborated with Japanese photographer Nobuyoshi Araki on an exhibition and book, both titled *Tokyo Love: Spring Fever*. By the later 1990s, her newly introspective work occasioned a somewhat less strident tone. Less often picturing antisocial behavior, her images, now including landscapes and still lifes, show the greater formal refinement and probing psychology seen in her 2003 book, *The Devil's Playground*.

Goldwater, Robert. *See* BOURGEOIS, LOUISE.

Golub, Leon (1922–2004). Painter. His figurative paintings explore the existential condition of the modern self and expose vile cruelties human beings inflict on each other. Few late-twentieth-century artists possessed the sophisticated technical skills and humanistic insights he applied in meshing metaphysical, political, and psychological concerns. A Chicago native, Leon Albert Golub received a BA in art history from the University of Chicago in 1942. After service from 1943 to 1946 in the U.S. Army, he earned a BFA from the School of the Art Institute of Chicago in 1949 and an MFA the following year. Along with other local artists who sought alternatives to prevailing postwar abstraction, he helped to originate *Chicago imagism. In early paintings indebted to Picasso's *Guernica* and the work of Jean Dubuffet, as well as to primitive and outsider arts, figural distortions convey human frailty and vulnerability. Particularly after a residence in Italy in 1956–57, he brutalized classical prototypes by scraping and reworking paint surfaces to suggest the distance separating contemporary man from the heroic ideal. As he developed this approach, he taught for a year in Bloomington, Indiana, then left for Paris in 1959. Upon his return to the United States, he settled permanently in New York in 1964. There the early work culminated in fatalistic Gigantomachies, huge battling gods derived from the Hellenistic Altar of Zeus at Pergamon. Constituting his initial response to the Vietnam War, these archetypal images came to seem inadequate as the war dragged on and protests intensified. Wishing to address contemporary reality more directly, in 1972 he began a series picturing uniformed men and their weapons in generalized combat scenes loosely based on news photographs. To increase the works' immediacy, he often draped unstretched paintings directly on the wall and sometimes cut into the canvases as if to mutilate his own images. In the late 1970s he produced unflattering portraits of world leaders. The

Mercenaries series, begun in 1975, and Interrogations, begun in 1981, drew attention to atrocities committed in the name of politics, generally in the shadows of conflict. In these psychologically chilling works, Golub focused powerfully on participants' consciousness of their roles and on social relationships revealed in body language and facial expressions. Disturbingly contemporary, some directly prefigure the sadistic 2003 Abu Ghraib photographs from the war in Iraq. Altering his approach around 1990, Golub embarked on more personally inflected mélanges of symbolic fragments, sometimes accompanied by texts, but always sustaining his fist-shaking resistance to easy answers.

His wife, painter and draftsman Nancy Spero (1926–), has been an equally distinctive voice in late-twentieth-century art of social responsibility. As suits the era, she has specialized in feminist issues. Often incorporating text along with images, her modestly scaled, idiosyncratic works unsparingly interrogate social and psychological realities. Born in Cleveland, she met Golub as a student at the Art Institute, where she, too, earned a BFA in 1949. She soon left for Paris to study for a year at the École des Beaux-Arts and the Atelier André Lhote. She and Golub married in 1951. During their years mostly abroad between 1956 and 1964, she produced a series of "black paintings," dark canvases exploring women's erotic and maternal roles in a male-dominated society. After they moved to New York, she abandoned canvas to work almost entirely on paper. Her drawn, collaged, and hand-stamped works direct anger primarily at socially imposed restrictions on women's lives and at the Vietnam War. In the striking Codex Artaud series (1971–73) she juxtaposed typed quotations from defiant French surrealist Antonin Artaud with schematic figural imagery deployed in a scroll-like format. Her attack on the violence of war and female subjugation continued in the 1980s, as she also introduced more transcendent themes, often based on myth, history, or literature. These works employ an idiosyncratic vocabulary of recurrent motifs derived from wide-ranging sources, including Egyptian hieroglyphs, the classical tradition, and contemporary popular culture. In later years, she has also worked directly on the wall to produce mural installations.

Goodrich, Lloyd (1897–1987). Museum director, curator, and art writer. His discerning support for American art of the late nineteenth and twentieth centuries was exceptional in a period when European art was more highly regarded. Born in Nutley, New Jersey, at fifteen he paid several visits to the 1913 *Armory Show. The next year he began three years of study at the *Art Students League, where he worked with Kenneth Hayes *Miller. After subsequently continuing his training for a year at the *National Academy of Design, in 1918 he gave up painting and entered business. However, in 1924 he began writing for *The Arts* and the following year took a full-time editorial job there. Late in 1929, he accepted a staff position at the nascent *Whitney Museum of American Art, where he remained for the rest of his career, rising through curatorial and administrative positions to become director in 1958. After stepping down from that post in 1968, he continued to serve in an advisory capacity until 1971 when he retired. The most visible achievement of his tenure as director was construction of the Whitney Museum's present Madison Avenue building, which opened in 1966. Intellectually, he was instrumental in establishing American art as a field of scholarly inquiry, while also identifying a solid usable heritage of achievement for artists of his day. Goodrich's *Thomas Eakins: His Life and Work* (1933; revised and expanded, 1982) ranks as the first significant study of this preeminent American artist. Other major works among his numerous publications (many served also as exhibition catalogues) include *Pioneers of Modern Art* (1963) and monographs on Winslow *Homer (1944), Ralph *Blakelock (1947), Max *Weber (1949), John *Sloan (1952), Albert P. *Ryder (1959), Edwin *Dickinson (1966), Georgia *O'Keeffe (1970), and Edward *Hopper (1971). As an advocate for artists, he served the art community in many capacities, including an important post for a *federal art project in the 1930s. He also contributed to the founding of the *National Endowment for the Arts. He died at his New York residence.

Goodwin, Richard La Barre (1840–1910). Painter. A trompe-l'oeil still life specialist, he favored large arrangements of hanging game, usually displayed against a rustic support. An undated *Cabin Door Still Life* (Smithsonian American Art Museum) exemplifies a type he repeated in many variants. In this clear and harmonious composition, several birds accompany a fringed game bag and powder horn against a paneled door. Born in Albany, the son of portrait painter **Edwin Weyburn Goodwin** (1800–45), he was wounded as a young man in the Civil War. Subsequently he painted portraits in western New York State before turning to still life while living in Syracuse in the mid-1880s. Dating to 1889, the earliest of his characteristic game paintings was inspired by William *Harnett's *After the Hunt* (Fine Arts

Museums of San Francisco, 1885), which had been on display in New York since 1886. Goodwin resided in Washington, D.C., from 1890 to 1893 and then in Chicago for seven years. He was in Colorado Springs from 1900 to 1902 and later worked in several locations on the West Coast, including San Francisco, where he lost recent paintings in the earthquake and fire of 1906. In addition to his many game compositions, Goodwin produced refined tabletop arrangements of fruit, as well as kitchen paintings that show foodstuffs in combination with utensils and furnishings. He died in Orange, New Jersey, near Newark.

Gorky, Arshile (c. 1904–48). Painter. A leading *abstract expressionist, he ranks as the movement's most accomplished draftsman. Edged with sinuous, elegant line, the *biomorphic forms of his mature works hover in tension with vivid, sometimes jarring swathes of color, creating complex spatial interactions between the picture plane and shallow implied space behind it. Among his best-known works, the nonsensically titled *The Liver Is the Cock's Comb* (Albright-Knox Art Gallery, Buffalo, New York, 1944) demonstrates his transformation of surrealist precedents into a singular style of great emotional resonance. The assurance of his art during the middle 1940s, when most first-generation abstract expressionists were still formulating their signature styles, provided an influential precedent and heralded the movement's power. Gorky's unshakable attachment to the romance of art fueled his ambition and the urgency of his work but also sustained the artist through hardship and loneliness. Like many aspects of the embroidered past he later recounted, the date of his birth is uncertain, probably earlier than the 1904 he claimed. He was born Vosdanig (or Vosdanik, and sometimes known as Manoug) Adoian in Khorkom, a village in the mountains of western Armenia, then part of the Ottoman Empire. After Turkish massacres of Armenians when he was a small boy, his father departed for the United States but his family never was able to join him. Gorky, his mother, and sisters lived for a time in Van but fled in 1915 to escape further persecution, becoming for several years destitute refugees, sometimes enduring grim circumstances. In Yerevan, Gorky's mother died in 1919 of illness and starvation. She is memorialized in the finest of the artist's early paintings, the stylized *Portrait of the Artist and His Mother* (Whitney Museum, c. 1926–36; variant, National Gallery, c. 1926–c. 1942; both unfinished), based on a 1912 photograph. In this tender record, the somber boy (resembling perhaps not by chance the young Picasso) stands beside his seated, iconic mother in Armenian attire. Dressed rather formally, he holds flowers, like a suitor or a mourner. In its autobiographical and elegiac mood, it forecasts the emotional tenor of his mature style.

After their mother's death, in 1920 the teenager and a sister made their way to the United States. He became a citizen in 1939. At first he lived with relatives in Watertown, Massachusetts, where he found factory work. Drawn to the practice of art since early childhood, in 1922 he moved to Boston, where he took classes at the New England School of Design. About three years later he left for New York, assuming a new identity as Arshile Gorky. (The Armenian name of Arshile refers to Achilles. The artist followed the Russian writer Maxim Gorky in adopting a surname meaning "bitter" in Russian.) In New York he studied at the *National Academy of Design and the Grand Central School of Art, where he remained as an instructor from 1926 into the early 1940s. Despite relatively little professional training, on his own he transformed himself into one of the most knowledgeable artists in the United States. For some twenty years he immersed himself in the culture of art, looking to the old masters but also absorbing modern developments. After working in an impressionist manner, by the mid-1920s he emulated Cézanne in a series of still lifes. During the same period, in figurative works, such as the rendering of himself with his mother and other portraits, he refined his facility with line, sometimes disclosing an admiration for Matisse. Especially in drawings, he sometimes achieved an incisive grace reminiscent of J.-A.-D. Ingres's masterful example, which he deeply admired. Although often bleak and fearsome, his childhood provided material to imagine a frequently invoked idyllic dreamland. Lyric memories of landscape, decorative items in his home, and the art of churches inform some works from this and subsequent periods. In the late 1920s, he established close friendships with John *Graham and Stuart *Davis, who encouraged his interest in experimental art. (He broke with Davis in the mid-1930s over the issue of art's social responsibility. As Davis became active in left-wing politics, Gorky remained committed to a non-utilitarian art of personal expression.) Toward the end of the 1920s, he also began an intensive exploration of cubism, inflected somewhat by an interest in the surrealism of Miró, André Masson, and even Paul Klee. However, he became increasingly attracted to Picasso, whose influence pervades Gorky's work of the 1930s. Like the Spaniard, Gorky often combined cubist space with ambiguous surrealist forms suggesting biological elements. These simplified natural forms anticipate the subtler, allusionistic method that underlay the great paintings of the mid-1940s.

Intermittently from 1933 until 1944, Gorky found employment with *federal art projects, for which he completed two notable abstract murals: *Aviation* (two panels, Newark [New Jersey] Museum; eight panels, destroyed; 1937), placed in the Newark Airport administration building, and *Man's Conquest of Air* (1939; destroyed) for the Aviation Building at the New York World's Fair. Around 1940 Gorky began to produce distinctly original works. In the Garden in Sochi series (c. 1940–43), he demonstrated increasing agility in deploying biomorphic forms with a freedom that recalls his longstanding admiration for Kandinsky's early abstractions. Gorky's artistic evolution was accelerated at this point by the presence in New York of European artists, particularly surrealists, fleeing World War II. After they met in 1940, Roberto *Matta became a good friend. From the surrealist example, Gorky learned to incorporate in his work elements of memory and fantasy. Moreover, his personal acquaintance with exiles from the School of Paris he idolized gave him confidence to synthesize eclectic leanings into a fresh vision.

During the summer of 1942 in Connecticut, Gorky drew extensively from nature for the first time in many years. This experience led to the realization of his mature style, in which line and color operate independently and nondescriptively to suggest psychic states. Nature served to release Gorky's creativity into a liminal arena of suggestion and psychic process, as vegetal and animal shapes took on metaphorical, often erotic impact. Rooted in drawing from nature, the subsequent, culminating works of his career emphasize instability, transience, metamorphosis, and possibility. However, they display a range of moods, from rending psychic distress to sentimental yearning. No matter how free they may appear, his paintings remained carefully planned, never spontaneous. With its searing colors and grievously extruded shapes, *Agony* (Museum of Modern Art, 1947) suggests unbearable physical and psychic pain. On the other hand, their oriental decorativeness harking back to the artist's Armenian childhood, the several versions of the *Plow and the Song* (e.g., Allen Memorial Art Museum, Oberlin [Ohio] College, 1947) present pale-toned, lyric evocations of joy in rural life. For several years, Gorky productively turned out major and original works of great beauty and passion, admired not only by such up-and-coming artists as Willem *de Kooning and Mark *Rothko but also by Miró and Fernand Léger. In March 1945, when Julian *Levy presented Gorky's first solo show, surrealism's high priest André Breton wrote a laudatory catalogue introduction. Paintings sold, for the first time bringing the artist a measure of financial security. He moved in September to Sherman, Connecticut, while also retaining his Union Square studio. At the height of his powers and seemingly poised for greatness, Gorky experienced a series of calamities. In January 1946 many recent paintings and drawings, as well as the artist's collection of books, burned in a fire in his Connecticut studio. That February he had colon cancer surgery that necessitated a colostomy. Marital discord followed as he became increasingly demanding, but he was devastated in June 1948 when his beloved wife, whose patient attention since 1941 had been at least partly responsible for the flowering of his talent, began a brief affair with Matta. Later that month, a broken neck and other injuries suffered in an automobile accident required painful traction and disabled his painting arm. In July, less than a month afterward, his wife left with the two young children he adored, following one of his violent rages. Five days later, the artist hanged himself at his Connecticut residence. He died on the verge of abstract expressionism's triumphal moment, too soon to know the acclaim his work has since enjoyed.

Painter **Maro Gorly** (1943–), his daughter, was born in New York and graduated from the Slade School of Art in London in 1965. She has exhibited regularly in Europe but did not have a New York gallery show until 2006. Her colorful style of abstracted representation has most recently featured landscape motifs. The life she has shared in Italy since the late 1960s with her British husband, sculptor Matthew Spender, served as an inspiration for Bernardo Bertolucci's 1996 film *Stealing Beauty*.

Gottlieb, Adolph (1903–74). Painter, sculptor, and printmaker. A leading *abstract expressionist, he is noted for three extended series. The Pictographs of the 1940s comprise compartmented fields containing enigmatic emblems, such as body parts, animals, and abstract forms. The large-scale Imaginary Landscapes of the following decade contrast horizontal areas of "land" and "sky," without creating an illusion of depth. Below a "horizon," the lower part of each canvas is filled with dense, rough brushwork. Above, celestial masses hover in quivering skies. Around 1957, Gottlieb simplified this approach into Bursts, vertically oriented works balancing two contrasting forms in tension. Never directly narrative or allegorical, Gottlieb's allusive paintings invoke psychic processes and mythic consciousness to comment on alienation, transcendence, and the search for meaning. A lifelong New Yorker, Gottlieb acquired a more thorough professional education than most of his abstract expressionist colleagues. He began his training in 1919 at the *Art Students League, where he studied with John *Sloan and attended Robert *Henri's lectures. At seventeen he left for three years in Europe, where he traveled but worked primarily in Paris at the Académie de la Grand Chaumière. Following his return, he continued his studies at several schools. His early representational expressionist style gave way to Milton *Avery's influence in the 1930s. In 1935 Gottlieb participated in founding *The Ten. He worked for a *federal art project in 1936 before moving in 1937 to the desert near Tucson, Arizona. During a year there, as he absorbed the spatial grandeur of the Southwest, his painting moved toward surrealistically tinged evocation of landscape.

Although some works of the period are more freely composed, around 1941 he began painting the Pictographs, combining the rectilinear grid familiar from the work of Mondrian and his followers with a repertoire of symbolic forms that draw on precedents in the work of Picasso, Miró, and Paul Klee. The work of Uruguayan modernist Joaquín Torres-García may have suggested the general format, while the art of the archaic and primitive cultures that Gottlieb deeply admired inspired the signs. His development in the early 1940s also depended on a newly enriched involvement with surrealism, as many of the movement's European exponents fled to New York during World War II. Under their influence, he became more attuned to the uses of *automatism and the significance of the unconscious, which he claimed underlay his ambiguous symbols. Evidencing his desire to formulate a universal form of communication, *Voyager's Return* (Museum of Modern Art, 1946) combines recognizable signs, including a snake and two disparate human heads, with other *biomorphic or geometric elements suggesting representational origins. In the Imaginary Landscapes, Gottlieb moved toward the combination of gestural and *color field approaches that finds its ultimate expression in the Bursts. In *Frozen Sounds* (Albright-Knox Art Gallery, Buffalo, New York, 1952) four irregular shapes, two red and two black, hover in a richly painted, mostly white area above vigorous, swirling forms contained below a horizontal "horizon." In the more reduced and hieratic Bursts, agitated brushwork in the lower of two forms continues to suggest movement and energy, while a clearly defined, monochromatic disk floats serenely above. These polar forms imply duality held in equilibrium: earth and sky, matter and spirit, confusion and enlightenment, tribulation and transcendence. In addition to producing occasional sculptures and prints, he also carried out decorative commissions, most notably stained glass and other embellishments for synagogues. Partially paralyzed and confined to a wheelchair following a stroke in March 1971, Gottlieb nevertheless not only continued to paint but produced several of his largest, most unrestrained, and most compelling variations on recent themes. For some years before his death he maintained a second residence in East Hampton, near the eastern end of Long Island.

Goulet, Lorrie. *See* DE CREEFT, JOSE.

Gowin, Emmet (1941–). Photographer. Known especially for landscapes, including many taken from the air, he combines representation of particular localities with environmental and formal concerns. He has also produced a long series intimately chronicling his family life. Although he generally crafts fastidious, rich, and precise black-and-white prints, he has also worked with color. Born in Danville, Virginia, he discovered photography as a fine arts student at the Richmond Professional Institute (now part of Virginia Commonwealth University). There he came to believe that photography could integrate imagination and reality more powerfully than painting. From 1965 to 1967 he continued as a graduate student at Providence's Rhode Island School of Design, where he worked with Harry *Callahan. Gowin has also identified the work of Alfred *Stieglitz, Robert *Frank, and Frederick *Sommer as influences on his development. He has taught at Princeton University since 1973 and lives in nearby Newtown, Pennsylvania. Gowin has been photographing regularly from the air since 1980, when he used the technique to record the devastation of the Mount Saint Helens volcanic eruption. Much of his subsequent aerial work treats the landscape in relation to large-scale human transformation or desecration, often of a military or industrial nature. However, his images avoid both irony and overt moralizing. Rather, in the seriousness and formal coherence of his compositions, he conveys an inherent message of respect for the earth. His publications include *Emmet Gowin: Photographs* (1976), *Petra: In the Hashemite Kingdom of Jordan* (1986), and *Emmet Gowin: Aerial Photographs* (1997). His son, photographer **Elijah Gowin** (1967–), born in Dayton, Ohio, graduated from Davidson (North Carolina) College and received his MFA from the University of New Mexico in Albuquerque. He teaches at the University of Missouri-Kansas City.

Grafly, Charles (1862–1929). Sculptor. A lifelong Philadelphian, he is remembered for portrait busts and for civic monuments featuring figural allegories. He also created a number of ideal works, sometimes employing arcane symbolism. After working as a stonecutter and assisting in carving Alexander Milne *Calder's sculptural embellishments for the Philadelphia city hall, Grafly enrolled in 1882 at the *Pennsylvania Academy of the Fine Arts. There he worked with Thomas *Eakins and Thomas *Anshutz before departing four years later to study in Paris. From 1892, the year after his return to Philadelphia, he taught at the academy. In 1895 he again traveled to Paris for a year, his final sojourn abroad. Subsequently, his mastery of the period's naturalistic and graceful French style assured his preeminence among Philadelphia sculptors for many years. After purchasing property in Lanesville, Massachusetts, in 1905, he became a regular participant in the summer colony that gathered on Cape Ann each year. Among his many portraits, more than a dozen likenesses of artist-friends rank among the finest in their vivacity and psychological acuity. The first, created in Paris, represents Henry O. *Tanner (Metropolitan Museum, 1896) with characteristically vigorous but subtle modeling of carefully delineated features. The painter's gently bemused, transient expression gives an impression of his interior individuality. Others in the series include Thomas *Anshutz (Pennsylvania Academy, 1912), Frank *Duveneck (Cincinnati Art Museum, 1915), and Childe *Hassam (Philadelphia Museum, 1918). Grafly's most important public sculpture, the marble *Meade Memorial* (in front of the E. Barrett Prettyman Federal Courthouse, Washington, D.C., 1915–27), portrays the standing Civil War general before a dramatic ensemble of allegorical figures.

Graham, John (c. 1886–1961). Painter. Although he served as a fountainhead of ideas for *abstract expressionism, his own painting did not directly contribute to the movement. His best-known works, strangely mannered paintings of women, combine admiration for the classical tradition, especially its nineteenth-century French master, J.-A.-D. Ingres, with the abstracting and expressionist tendencies of modern art. An unusually tender example, less stylized than many, the bust-length *Portrait of Elinor Gibson* (Phillips Collection, 1930) depicts his third wife (they were married from 1924 to 1934), also a painter. Here, interests in line and harmony descend from Ingres through Picasso's neoclassical work of the 1920s. Influence of Picasso's more abstract work is suggested by the patterning caused by strong side lighting and the conceptual reshaping of facial features. Suffused with feeling, this realization of an enigmatic, melancholy large-eyed woman also prefigures some early works by Graham's friend Arshile *Gorky. Incorporating varying degrees of abstraction, Graham also painted still lifes, landscapes, and a few other subjects. Born Ivan Gratianovich Dombrowski (or Dombrovsky) in Kiev, as a young man he associated with the Russian avant-garde and apparently served in the Russian cavalry during World War I. Much about his life before he arrived in New York around 1920 remains obscure. He studied during the early 1920s at the *Art Students League, where he worked with John *Sloan. After a short residency in Baltimore, he lived again in New York but traveled frequently to Paris. Through the early 1940s he acted as an important conduit for the transmission of European modernism to receptive ears in New York. He held Picasso in particularly high regard. Among others, Willem *de Kooning, Jackson *Pollock, and David *Smith, as well as Gorky, benefited from Graham's knowledge, ideas, and extravagant dedication to art. His 1937 book, *System and Dialectics of Art*, proved widely influential among adventurous New York artists, who were attracted by its cosmopolitan discussions of the unconscious, primitivism, process, and expression. Before the 1940s ended, Graham had lost interest in modern art, turning instead to meditation and study of the occult. He spent his later years in Paris and in London, where he died.

Graves, Morris (1910–2001). Painter and occasional sculptor. An independent West Coast spirit, he painted somewhat abstracted images from nature, birds especially, emphasizing the fragility, mystery, and lyricism of creation. He developed this personal symbolic vocabulary in response to East Asian philosophical traditions, particularly Zen Buddhism. He also drew on aspects of surrealism and homegrown transcendentalism. An admirer of Mark *Tobey's work, he remained almost entirely self-taught as an artist. He accomplished his most sensitive and singular work during the 1940s and 1950s. Later, he painted still lifes of a more decorative and less spiritually compelling nature. A native of Fox Valley in rural Oregon, south of Portland, Morris Cole Graves moved as a child with his family to the Seattle area. He left high school after his second year to become a seaman. Three voyages to the Far East sparked his interest in Asia. While living with an aunt and her family in Beaumont, Texas, in 1932 he graduated from high school, where art classes provided rudimentary professional training. Returning to Seattle, he painted heavily impastoed, somewhat expressionistic interpretations of birds and other motifs drawn from the natural environment of the Northwest coast. Following a stint with a *federal art project, he visited New York for several months in 1937. Upon his return to Seattle, he struck up a friendship with John *Cage, whose unorthodox ideas he found stimulating, and a short time later became acquainted also with Tobey. During this period, he began working mostly with water-based paints on paper. In 1939 he took up residence on an island in Puget Sound, where he lived in seclusion in a cliff-top cabin he built himself. There, he reached a mature realization of his aesthetic aims in a series of visionary works that generally incorporate abstracted birds, sometimes blinded or wounded, within painterly fields. When these were shown in 1942 at his first one-person New York gallery show and in an important *Museum of Modern Art group exhibition, he quickly became an art-world celebrity. In 1947 he left his isolated home and built another near Seattle. Subsequently, he incessantly traveled the world. From the mid-1950s to the mid-1960s he sojourned at length in Ireland, where for several years he maintained a residence. From 1964 he made his home near Loleta, on twenty-five acres of redwood forest close to Humboldt Bay on the northern California coast. There, while continuing to paint, he indulged a longtime love of gardening. By this time, his work had become less mystical and passionate in tone, as he turned his attention largely to effects of color and light in restrained still lifes of flowers, vegetables, and Chinese bronzes. In the early 1960s he also produced tabletop sculptures, collectively known as Instruments for a New Navigation, constructed primarily from metal, stone, and glass elements. He died at his Loleta estate, The Lake. His will created a foundation to maintain and administer the buildings and grounds as a retreat for artists and scholars.

Graves, Nancy (1940–95). Sculptor, painter, printmaker, and filmmaker. In 1968 she created a stir with furry, life-size camels that seemed at the time perilously close to the limits of art. Spurred by long-standing interests in natural history and archeology, through the 1970s she drew on such sources as animal anatomy, paleontology, prehistoric artifacts, and scientific documents while working in several media. Later she combined constructivist methods with allusive, even surrealistic imagery taken from natural and man-made sources to create colorful, idiosyncratic sculptures. Born in Pittsfield, Massachusetts, Nancy Stevenson Graves studied English literature at Vassar College in Poughkeepsie, New York. After receiving a BA in 1961, she earned an MFA from Yale University in 1964. For the next two years she lived in Europe, first in Paris and then in Florence, but also traveled in North Africa and the Near East. From 1965 until 1970 she was married to Richard *Serra. Her fascination with the camel as a subject for art began abroad and continued after she settled in New York in 1966. Challenging the literalism of current *minimalism and the intellectualism of *conceptual art, her ungainly animals seem to essentialize "camelness," drawing into play questions of illusion, perception, and the purity of art. After 1972, for several years she worked primarily on two-dimensional projects and on films before mastering the lost wax process that facilitated production of her later sculptures. For these, she cast all manner of perishable natural and artificial objects, such as leaves, fish, seedpods, potato chips, and rope, producing replicas that she combined into welded assemblages, along with kitchen tools, farm implements, and other metal items. She generally painted parts of these works in bright, unnaturalistic colors, and toward the end of her life incorporated glass elements. Indebted to David *Smith's precedents, her sculptures nevertheless achieved an entirely personal flavor. In 1991 she married Dr. Avery Smith. At the time of her death in Manhattan, she also maintained a home in Kingston, in the Hudson River Valley.

Gray, Henry Peters (1819–77). Painter. Besides allegorical and literary works, he also painted about five hundred portraits. A lifelong New Yorker, he studied for a year with near contemporary Daniel *Huntington, subsequently a longtime friend, before they departed together for Europe in 1839. He spent most of two years in Italy studying the old masters, especially the work of Titian, whose painterly fluency however eluded him. After another sojourn in Italy, in 1845–46, he established a reputation for paintings of ideal figural subjects. Hailed as a masterpiece, *The Wages of War* (Metropolitan Museum, 1848) was purchased by the *American Art-Union for $1500, a strikingly large sum at the time. Appealing to mid-century taste with classical references and a moralizing theme, it depicts a muscular, seminude warrior straining to rise from the ground before a sarcophagus of antique inspiration. Adapted from Renaissance precedents, figures on either side mourn his plight with tasteful decorum. Still admired in 1872, *The Wages of War* became the first American painting to enter the *Metropolitan Museum of Art. Again traveling with Huntington, Gray visited England for a few months in 1851. In 1871 he departed for a four-year sojourn in Florence. Artist Susan Clark, whom Gray married in 1843, later served as president of the New York Association of Women Painters.

Greacen, Edmund W. *See* GIVERNY GROUP.

Greatorex, Eliza (1819–97). Painter, printmaker, and illustrator. A specialist in landscapes and city views, she published many travel scenes, often with her own descriptions. Born in Manor Hamilton, County Leitrim, Eliza Pratt emigrated with her family from Ireland in 1840. They settled in New York, where she married the prominent English-born musician Henry Wellington Greatorex in 1849. Although she and her husband traveled often as he fulfilled professional engagements, she began to exhibit in New York during the 1850s. After his death in 1858, she soon astutely produced saleable drawings, prints, and illustrations for a middle-class market, as well as more expensive oil paintings. To augment earlier assistance from New York landscapists (including her friends James *Hart and his brother William), in the early 1860s she journeyed to Paris for further instruction. Subsequently, she traveled in Europe and in the early 1870s worked in Colorado. Especially around the time of the nation's centennial, she promoted interest in Americana. A series of etchings, for example, appeared in book form as *Old New York, from the Battery to Bloomingdale* (1875), with text by her sister Matilda Pratt Despard. While abroad from 1878 to 1881, she returned to Paris in 1879 for additional training in etching. At this time, her style became more attuned to *Barbizon poetics and less straightforwardly descriptive. After 1886 she lived in France but continued to travel widely, while exhibiting in the United States as well as Europe. Illustrated with her graphic work, Greatorex's publications include also *The Homes of Oberammergau* (1872) and *Summer Etchings in Colorado* (1873). From the time they were small children, Greatorex raised her daughters to become self-sufficient artists. They trained at the *National Academy of Design and the *Art Students League, as well as in Munich, Rome, and Paris. As adults they continued regularly to travel and work with their mother. Versatile, they pursued decorative arts such as china painting, along with painting, printmaking, and illustration. **Kathleen Honora Greatorex** (1851–1913), born in Hoboken, New Jersey, and **Eleanor Elizabeth Greatorex** (1854–97), born in New York, spent much of their childhood with their mother in Cornwall-on-Hudson, about fifty miles north of New York. Later they all summered at the art colony of Cragsmoor in New York's Shawangunk Mountains. Along with their mother, they relocated to Europe in 1886. After her mother and sister died in Paris during the same year, Kathleen continued to live abroad. She died not far from Paris.

Greenberg, Clement (1909–94). Art critic. A forceful supporter of mid-twentieth-century American abstraction, he championed such artists as Jackson *Pollock, David *Smith, Helen *Frankenthaler, Barnett *Newman, and Kenneth *Noland. His voice drew attention to *abstract expressionism, *color field painting, and other aspects of the *New York School, particularly the *hard-edge work that he christened "post-painterly abstraction." In the 1940s and early 1950s he secured his reputation by presciently and courageously identifying and defending the abstract expressionists before they were widely recognized as the leading painters of the immediate postwar era. Advocating art for art's sake, the centrality of formal concerns, the irrelevance of literary or representational subject matter, and historically determined progress in artistic production (reflecting an early interest in Marxism), he dominated critical writing for more than two decades. His theory that modern art advanced by gradually purifying the means intrinsic to each medium became the keystone of his influence. As *pop art, *minimalism, and other movements introduced fresh ideas and gained an audience, by the late 1960s Greenberg's views had begun to lose much of their authority. Although his aesthetic stance was not so simpleminded as many detractors claimed, his position soon came under intense criticism. This censure extended before long to his personal reputation as well. Greenberg's arrogant, dogmatic, pugnacious manner, the proportions of his influence in the art market, and some ethically questionable transactions in his dealings with artists and galleries incited a certain enthusiasm for vilifying everything he stood for. Greenberg wrote little in the last quarter-century of his life but remained a tastemaker behind the scenes. Later critics and theorists have generally pursued richer, more intellectually nuanced explanations of art's genesis and meanings, rejecting Greenberg's fondness, especially in the 1960s, for unproved, intuitive value judgments based on taste. Despite the formalism of his aesthetic, his writing generally remained oddly deficient in formal analysis of the sort that explains how and why certain colors, shapes, and other material considerations create successful and meaningful works of art.

A New York native, he briefly attended the *Art Students League before earning a BA in languages and literature from Syracuse University in 1930. From 1936 until 1942 he held civil service jobs and translated books, while beginning to publish articles on art. Two of his most important essays, "Avant-Garde and Kitsch" (1939) and "'American Type' Painting" (1955) appeared in *Partisan Review*, where he worked as an editor from 1940 until 1942. After leaving that magazine, he served as the art critic for *The Nation* until 1949. In 1944 he also took on the position of managing editor for *Contemporary Jewish Record*, which merged the following year into *Commentary*. Greenberg remained as associate editor until 1957. Besides freelance articles for a number of journals, he published monographs on Joan Miró (1948), Matisse (1953), and Hans *Hofmann (1961), as well as a critical anthology, *Art and Culture* (1961). Greenberg supplemented the influence of his writings by curating exhibitions featuring the work of artists he admired, jurying shows internationally, conducting seminars, and teaching intermittently at several leading colleges. Edited by John O'Brian, his *Collected Essays and Criticism* appeared in four volumes between 1986 and 1993. After his death, essays and seminar transcripts appeared as *Homemade Esthetics: Observations on Art and Taste* (1999).

Greene, Balcomb (1904–90). Painter. After working nonobjectively in the 1930s and early 1940s, he gradually turned to painterly, romantically charged imagery. Born in Niagara Falls, he grew up in Iowa, South Dakota, and Colorado. Following graduation in 1926 from Syracuse (New York) University with a major in philosophy, he departed for Vienna, where he studied psychology with Sigmund Freud and others. Upon returning to the United States in 1927, he studied English for a year at Columbia University before accepting a teaching position at Dartmouth College in Hanover, New Hampshire. While living in Paris between 1931 and 1933, he had his first one-person show, despite almost complete lack of formal training. Subsequently back in New York, in 1934 he found employment in the *federal art projects, for which he painted murals and designed a stained glass window. Active in 1936 in organizing the *American Abstract Artists, he was elected the group's first chairman in 1937. In 1943 he earned a master's degree in art history at New York University. From 1942 until 1959 he taught at the Carnegie Institute of Technology (now Carnegie Mellon University) in Pittsburgh, although he maintained a New York residence. By 1935 Greene had evolved a style marked by hard-edge, planar geometries, occasionally relieved by the inclusion of *biomorphic shapes. Beginning in the early 1940s, figures sometimes appeared in his work, which became amorphous and atmospheric, more in tune with the fluent styles of emerging *abstract expressionism. The loosely painted *Composition: The Storm* (Whitney Museum, 1953–54) suggests clouds and turbulence. In certain works of his later career, sometimes based on photographic images, exaggerated lights and darks veil representation and create patterns of movement. *Place Pigalle* (Blanton Museum of Art, University of Texas, Austin, 1964) portrays numerous blurred people traverşing a city square, suggesting the anonymous, unstable, and sometimes unintelligible character of contemporary life. Other works reflect the rugged seashore near the summer residence he maintained from the late 1940s near Long Island's Montauk Point. He died there, following two years in poor health.

His wife, painter and sculptor **Gertrude Greene** (1904–56), is noted for painted relief sculptures deftly combining two- and three-dimensional forms in skillful manipulation of reality and illusion. Born in Brooklyn, in 1924 Gertrude Glass began two years of study at the tradition-oriented Leonardo da Vinci School of Art. She married Greene in 1926. Exposure to varied forms of abstract art in Paris during their sojourn in the early 1930s enriched her development. Particularly struck by the work of Brancusi, Mondrian, and Naum *Gabo, by the mid-1930s she had begun to produce her characteristic reliefs. In addition, in partnership with Ibram *Lassaw, she experimented with sheet metal as a sculptural material. She, too, numbered among the founding members of the American Abstract Artists. Also affected by abstract expressionism in the 1940s, she incorporated spontaneous effects into reliefs, while also producing vigorous, gestural paintings. In later years, she constructed three-dimensional canvas pieces as well. She died in New York after a long illness.

Greene, Stephen. *See* STELLA, FRANK.

Greenough, Horatio (1805–52). Sculptor. Besides generating nineteenth-century enthusiasm for *neoclassical sculpture, he wrote memorable essays on art theory and launched the vogue among American sculptors for living in Italy. His best-known work, a colossal *George Washington* (National Museum of American History, Washington, D.C., 1832–41) demonstrates fervid allegiance to the antique. But the seated, semi-nude figure suggests as well the triumph of an abstract idea over common sense. Despite the evidence of this sculpture, Greenough championed "Greek principles, not Greek things." This viewpoint, buttressed by the forward-looking Transcendental idealism of his time, underlay writings prefiguring a modern, functionalist credo. Greenough was born in Boston, where he received early instruction from local sculptors and artisans. Upon his graduation from Harvard in 1825, he followed the advice of a mentor, Washington *Allston, to travel to Italy. He ranks as the first major American sculptor to pursue the life of an artist through European study instead of emerging from a craft tradition. In Rome, where he numbered among the first Americans to work regularly in marble, he imbibed the fashionable neoclassical aesthetic congenial to his classical education and received encouragement from its principal local exponent, Bertel Thorvaldsen. Forced home by illness in 1827, Greenough concentrated for about a year on portraiture, which remained a mainstay of his practice. In 1828 he settled in Florence, where he at first studied with Lorenzo Bartolini, a neoclassicist nevertheless attracted to nature as a source of beauty. On commission from his friend James Fenimore Cooper, Greenough soon executed his first ideal subject, *Chanting Cherubs* (unlocated, 1828–29), a pair of putti adapted from a Raphael painting. Suggesting the challenge facing an artist who wished, as Greenough did, to encourage appreciation of sophisticated art in his young nation, the childish figures' nudity repelled many American viewers when the piece was first exhibited in 1831. Apparently undeterred, Greenough continued to produce unclothed subjects such as the *Venus Victrix* (Boston Atheneum, 1837–c. 1841). This life-size standing female figure anticipated a long series of nineteenth-century idealized nudes, nearly always invested with some narrative or symbolic meaning.

Controversy over nudity also marred reception of the imperious *George Washington* when it was unveiled in 1841, but some observers also ridiculed its stiffness and artificiality. To symbolize Washington's heroic stature, Greenough adapted the pose from Phidias's fifth-century BC Zeus for Olympia. For the sake of historical accuracy, he modeled the face after portraits taken from life, particularly those by Gilbert *Stuart and French sculptor Jean-Antoine Houdon. Although the work fell short of the sculptor's aspiration to fashion a unifying and inspiring emblem of the popular leader, it was initially placed in the Capitol rotunda, as planned by Congress. The first major sculpture ordered for the Capitol, it ranked also as the federal government's first monumental commission awarded to an American sculptor. Even before *Washington* was installed, Greenough was at work on another commission for the Capitol. His most complex ensemble, *The Rescue*, (U.S. Capitol, in storage, 1837–51), a grouping of over-life-size figures originally placed alongside the east stairway, highlights violence between Indians and settlers. As here, Greenough frequently applied his neoclassical style to nonclassical subjects, revealing the romantic tendency within American neoclassicism almost from the start. Other subjects often came from literature or the Bible. The first American sculptor to develop an international reputation, Greenough stood at the height of his fame when he returned to the United States in 1851. About a year later he fell ill and died in Somerville, near Boston. During the last decade or so of his life, Greenough devoted considerable attention to writing. Published under the pseudonym Horace Bender, *The Travels, Observations, and Experience of a Yankee Stonecutter* (1852) comprises essays, some previously published, along with fragments and miscellaneous thoughts. Much of this book, along with a few additional pieces, appeared as *Form and Function: Remarks on Art, Design, and Architecture* (1947), edited by Harold Small. Although his art respected retrospective principles, his thinking advanced boldly into the future, advocating an organic, utilitarian, and liberated approach to design.

Two brothers also were artists. Known particularly for arcadian views of Italy, painter **John Greenough** (1801–52) also produced portraits. Born in Boston, he left Harvard to study art in London. Remaining abroad from the mid-1820s until 1841, he worked primarily in London and Florence before returning to Boston. In 1850 he sailed for Italy and soon resettled in Florence. He died in Paris. The more successful **Richard Saltonstall Greenough** (1819–1904), a sculptor, extended Horatio's neoclassical style to include more elaborate and decorative effects, but also increased naturalism, a combination that suited Victorian taste. Born in Jamaica Plain, near Boston, he studied in Florence with his brother. After returning home he worked primarily as a portraitist, developing the dignified realism evident in one of his best-known works, the bronze *Benjamin Franklin* (1855) commissioned for the grounds of Boston's city hall. After 1848, except for extended visits to the United States in the 1850s and 1860s, he worked abroad, mostly in Rome. However, he ranks as the first American sculptor of any importance to spend significant periods in Paris, where he resided much of the time from the mid-1850s until the mid-1870s. He died in Rome.

Greenwood, John (1727–92). Painter and printmaker. Besides portraits, he is known for early attempts to broaden the range of acceptable subjects in colonial art. He is credited with the first major North American *genre painting, *Sea Captains Carousing in Surinam* (Saint Louis Art Museum, 1757–58). Although the uninhibited subjects of this Hogarthian tavern scene are Anglo-Americans (many are identifiable), the locale is the South American colony (once known as Dutch Guiana), where Greenwood lived for six and a half years. Born in Boston, in 1742 he was apprenticed to Thomas Johnston (1708–1767), a sometime portrait painter and prolific engraver of maps, city views, bookplates, and other items. In addition, Johnston's all-purpose shop made signs and did varied decorative work. (His sons William [1732–1772] and John [1753–1818] developed into creditable portraitists, and John also painted still lifes.) By 1747 Greenwood was undertaking portraits professionally. He soon achieved some success, although his rather stiff images show a colonial painter's typical compositional dependence on imported engravings, as well as technical limitations in drawing and paint application. They also reveal a venturesome artist whose unevenness suggests a willingness to take risks. His best-known painting, the ambitious *Greenwood-Lee Family* (Museum of Fine Arts, Boston, c. 1747) emulates John *Smibert's *Bermuda Group* and Robert *Feke's portrait of the Isaac Royall family. Unprecedented in the colonies as the subject of an independent work of art, the mezzotint *Jersey Nanny* (known in only a single impression, Museum of Fine Arts, Boston, 1748) presents a working-class woman, whose uncouth, buxom image is accompanied by a light-hearted poem. Greenwood left in 1752 for Paramaibo, the capital of Surinam, where he became a successful portraitist. In 1758 he went to Amsterdam to pursue mezzotint engraving. By 1763 he had settled permanently in London. Abroad, his work became more adroit, but in England he worked primarily as an art dealer. He died in Margate, Kent. As the first native-born artistic talent to leave the New World in search of better training and opportunities, he initiated a pattern that prevailed for the next two centuries. Unlike many who followed, however, Greenwood exerted negligible influence on the course of American art.

Greenwood, Marion (1909–70). Painter and printmaker. Remembered especially for socially conscious, Depression-era murals, she was born in Brooklyn and began her training at the *Art Students League at the age of fifteen. There she worked with George *Bridgman, Frank Vincent *Dumond, and John *Sloan until 1928. She continued her studies at the Académie Colarossi in Paris as well as in *Woodstock with Emil *Ganso and Alexander *Archipenko. In 1931 she traveled to the Southwest to paint Pueblo and Navajo Indians. The following year, attracted by the work of Diego Rivera and José Clemente Orozco, she went to Mexico. There, she completed two large mural commissions while absorbing the artistry and left-wing politics of the flourishing Mexican mural movement. In 1936 she returned to the United States and, until 1940, painted murals for *federal art projects. Her fresco *Blueprint for Living* (1940), executed for the government-sponsored Red Hook Houses in Brooklyn, presented monumentalized figures constructing a better future for themselves. During World War II she served as an accredited artist-correspondent. Subsequently she traveled in China with her British husband, writer and adventurer Charles Fenn, and visited other foreign locales. In later years, living in *Woodstock as well as New York and married to writer Robert Plate, she produced figurative easel paintings and prints, as well as two final murals. She died in an infirmary at Kingston, New York, following a long illness. Her sister, painter **Grace Greenwood** (1905–79), also born in Brooklyn, accompanied her to Mexico, painted murals there, and later also was employed on federal art projects. As Grace Crampton, she, too, subsequently resided in Woodstock.

Grooms, Red (1937–). Sculptor, painter, installation artist, filmmaker, and printmaker. An eager participant in late 1950s *happenings, in the 1960s he developed high-spirited, mixed-media environmental sculpture on an enormous scale. In these "sculpto-pictoramas," as he has called them, multiple, life-size, cartoonish figures inhabit sharply observed localities, usually areas of New York. Related to *pop art, his zany work often carries a sarcastic edge but not at the expense of good-natured hilarity. It also plays on nostalgia that stems from the artist's evident affection for his acutely rendered subjects, as befits an admirer of Edward *Hopper's paintings. Born in Nashville, Charles Roger Grooms left Peabody College there to enroll in the School of the Art Institute of Chicago for a year. He then decamped for New York to continue his studies at the New School for Social Research (now New School). He also attended Hans *Hofmann's summer school in *Provincetown. In the late 1950s, along with Allan *Kaprow, Jim *Dine, Claes *Oldenburg, and others, he pioneered the creation of happenings. The experience he gained with sets, costumes, characterization, and theatrical effects opened the way to subsequent paintings, constructions, mixed-media works, and eventually the characteristic *installations. In 1962 he made the first of a dozen experimental films, some in collaboration with Rudy *Burckhardt. In the mid-1960s he first realized large-scale constructed assemblages in his idiosyncratic, detailed, comic-book style. He intended his best-known installation, *Ruckus Manhattan* (1975–76), as a novelistic survey of the teeming island. A huge conglomeration of New York City landmarks, peopled with characteristic types, its World Trade Center stood some thirty feet tall. In the production of this and other large installations, he acknowledged his assistants and technicians under the rubric of the Ruckus Construction Company. Throughout his career, Grooms's graphic work has sustained the high-energy, expressionistic style of his sculptures in prolific numbers of color lithographs, drawings, and watercolors. Grooms was married to a significant Ruckus collaborator, Mimi *Gross, in the 1960s and 1970s.

Gropper, William (1897–1977). Painter, printmaker, illustrator, and cartoonist. In the 1920s and early 1930s, at the height of his powers as a graphic artist, he numbered among the most powerful satirists in American art. His drawings fused bold design, pointed characterization of social types, sympathy for the oppressed, and clear-headed anger at a political and economic system responsible for suffering. In the mid-1930s, he turned chiefly to painting but continued to use his art in the service of social issues, primarily by poking fun at incompetence, greed, and pretension but also by treating laborers with heroic dignity. Born in New York, Gropper studied at the Ferrer School with Robert *Henri and George *Bellows, as well as at the *National Academy of Design and New York School of Fine and Applied Art (now Parsons, the New School for Design). In his twenties, he worked chiefly for newspapers and magazines, including the politically radical journals, *Liberator* and *New Masses*, as well as the more stylish *Vanity Fair*. In 1927 he made an extended visit to the USSR. Often accused of being a communist (an allegation he denied), he was widely blacklisted after taking the Fifth Amendment when called to testify before Senator Joseph McCarthy's infamous investigative subcommittee in 1953. Among *American Scene painters, as well as other contemporary realists, Gropper demonstrated an unusual interest in modern styles. His early expressionistic manner particularly evidences a debt to George *Grosz's example. In the 1930s his work became more amusing and less abrasive in both style and content. His painting of *The Senate* (Museum of Modern Art, 1935) mocks its stereotypically overfed, blathering denizens. For a *federal art project, Gropper produced murals that honor the common man, as in *Construction of a Dam* (Department of the Interior, Washington, D.C., 1939). In later years, Gropper turned to themes of more generalized human experience than he had previously pursued. After residing for many years in Croton-on-Hudson, north of New York, he moved near the end of his life to Great Neck, on Long Island. Active as an artist until his final months, he died in a hospital in nearby Manhasset.

Grosman, Tatyana. *See* UNIVERSAL LIMITED ART EDITIONS.

Gross, Chaim (1904–91). Sculptor, printmaker, and painter. He is best known for figurative, expressionist sculptures, characteristically carved by hand from wood to exploit the inherent qualities of the medium. Their blocky forms reflect the artist's desire to remove as little as possible from his chosen timbers, while surfaces, usually polished and always sensuous, demonstrate his affection for the patterns and irregularities discovered in the wood grain. Generally playful in tone, the works often feature generalized acrobats, dancers, or other active subjects, whose spiraling movements lead the eye around three-dimensional compositions. Other subjects generally relate to women and/or children. Gross also worked in stone and, from the 1950s, cast in bronze airy, less constrained pieces with impressionistically rendered surfaces. Born in Wolow (now Poland), in Galicia, a zone of the Austro-Hungarian Empire, he came from a region of woodworkers, including his father. The family moved to the Galician town of Kolomiya (now Ukraine) in 1911, and from 1919 Gross studied art in Budapest and Vienna. After settling permanently in New York in 1921, he studied at the Educational Alliance Art School (from 1927 he taught there for more than sixty years) and at the Beaux-Arts Institute of Design, where Elie *Nadelman briefly numbered among his teachers. After deciding to become a sculptor, he enrolled in 1927 at the *Art Students League to study carving for a short time with Robert *Laurent. During the 1930s he worked for a *federal art project, which resulted in commissions for sculptural embellishments to buildings in Washington, D.C., and New York. After World War II, he traveled frequently to Europe and Israel. Gross's ancestral ties to woodcarving meshed comfortably with modern fervor for truth to materials. The formal vocabulary of his carvings was indebted to cubism and the work of Brancusi and Henry Moore, as well as to ancient and tribal sculpture. His bronze work acknowledges the subtle fluidity of Rodin and his successors. His lithographs and woodcuts often illustrate themes seen also in his sculpture, but in addition they include landscapes and fanciful scenes, as do his numerous watercolors. In addition, particularly after World War II, his two-dimensional work frequently reflected Jewish life and traditions. Gross published *A Sculptor's Progress* (1938), an autobiographical look back at his early years, and *The Technique of Wood Sculpture* (1957), an instructional manual. Under the auspices of a foundation established by the artist and his wife, the Chaim Gross Studio Museum preserves his legacy. Housed in his former Greenwich Village residence, it maintains his studio as it was during his lifetime and presents rotating exhibitions of his work. His daughter, New York–born painter, sculptor, printmaker, and theater designer **Mimi Gross** (1940–) studied for two years at Bard College in Annandale-on-Hudson, New York, before continuing professional training as an artist. She married Red *Grooms in 1961 and participated in the creation of many of his sculptures and films before they parted sixteen years later. She lives in New York and paints mostly expressionistic landscapes and figural works.

Grosz, George (1893–1959). Painter and draftsman. Among the most trenchant satirists in twentieth-century art, he attacked complacency, stupidity, greed, and gluttony, unmasking the faces of evil in Western civilization. Born Georg Ehrenfried Groß in Berlin, he altered the spelling of his name in 1917 to protest German militarism and reactionary nationalism. Following training in the art academies of Dresden, Berlin, and Paris, he served during World War I in the German army, an experience that solidified for all time his loathing for the military. After the war, he participated in the Berlin dada group and a few years later, in partnership with Otto Dix, led the movement known as Neue Sachlichkeit (New Objectivity). In 1932 he accepted an unexpected invitation to teach at the *Art Students League and soon settled on Long Island, at first in Queens and from 1952 in Huntington. In 1936 he began summering on Cape Cod. Although in 1938 he became an American citizen, he moved back to Berlin only a few weeks before his death there. Even before the end of World War I, Grosz had earned an international reputation for vicious satirical drawings and watercolors denouncing an irrational and meaningless world. For sheer outrage, he rarely surpassed an early drawing, *Fit for Active Service* (Museum of Modern Art, 1918), showing a corpulent doctor approving a skeleton for military duty. In his earliest American work, New Yorkers fared little better in his estimation. *Couple* (Whitney Museum, 1934) brutally caricatures the inner depravity of an upper-class pair. With time, democracy mellowed his bite somewhat, as he turned to romantic landscapes and still lifes. However, an anxious pessimism continued to surface from time to time. World War II reignited his anger, fueling a number of cataclysmic scenes that address the human condition more generally than the topical satires for which he had been known. His oil painting *The Pit* (Wichita [Kansas] Art Museum, 1946), a swirling nightmare, inventories the destruction and suffering of military conflict. In 1946 he published an autobiography, *A Little Yes and a Big No*.

Guerrilla Girls. *See* FEMINIST ART.

Guggenheim, Peggy (1898–1979). Gallery owner, collector, and museum founder. An enthusiast for modern art, Guggenheim showed some of the most adventurous and important art of the early 1940s at her New York gallery, Art of This Century. This significant venue promoted contact between European modernists and their American successors, while helping also to legitimize the nascent *abstract expressionist movement. Later, she lived in Venice, where she established a museum of twentieth-century art. Born in New York, Marguerite Guggenheim was the niece of Solomon R. *Guggenheim. Her father went down with the *Titanic* in 1912, leaving her with an independent but not unlimited income. In 1919 she moved to Paris and three years later married Paris-born, Cambridge-educated, American artist and writer Laurence Vail (1891–1968). The couple separated in 1929 and later divorced. In 1938 she opened a London gallery, Guggenheim Jeune, to show surrealist and abstract art. Following the inaugural show of work by Jean Cocteau, artists whose work appeared there included Kandinsky (his first solo appearance in London), Arp, Brancusi, Alexander *Calder, Max *Ernst, and Henry Moore. As World War II erupted, she returned to France in September 1939. There, as a gesture of support for artists, she bought their work in quantity. In July 1941 she fled to New York with her art, as well as Ernst, whom she soon married. Art of This Century created an art world sensation at its opening in October 1942. Its controversial exhibitions appeared in a futuristic interior designed by Frederick *Kiesler. This setting featured curved walls, *biomorphic furniture, and art works suspended in space. After she and Ernst separated in 1943, she increasingly refocused her attention from prominent Europeans to little known but up-and-coming American artists. Besides Jackson *Pollock, artists who had their first one-person shows at her gallery included Adolph *Gottlieb,

Robert *Motherwell, Richard *Pousette-Dart, Ad *Reinhardt, Mark *Rothko, and Clyfford *Still. In 1947 Guggenheim moved to Venice, thereafter her principal residence, and continued to acquire art. When she opened her Grand Canal *palazzo* to the public in 1951, her collection stood as the most comprehensive survey of modern art on display in Europe. Before she died in Padua, she had ceded permanent administrative control of her museum to the Solomon R. Guggenheim Foundation. In 1942 Guggenheim published *Art of This Century*, a carefully compiled catalogue of her collection. An autobiography, *Out of This Century*, appeared in 1946, followed in 1960 by a second volume of memoirs, *Confessions of an Art Addict*.

Guggenheim, Solomon R. (1861–1949). Art collector and museum founder. Also a mining magnate and financier. Noted for its singular architecture and its collection of modern European art, New York's Solomon R. Guggenheim Museum opened to the public in its present quarters in 1959. Designed by Frank Lloyd Wright, the unique Fifth Avenue whorl was challenged as an audacious art museum only in 1997 by another Guggenheim-operated facility, Frank Gehry's showcase in Bilbao, Spain. Born in Philadelphia, Solomon Robert Guggenheim worked in family business enterprises until 1919, when he retired. A collector of traditional work, he turned his attention to modern art in the late 1920s after he met painter and collage artist Baroness Hilla Rebay (1890–1967). He died at his Long Island estate in Sands Point. In 1939 Guggenheim's collection opened to the public as the Museum of Non-Objective Painting. Despite an eccentric atmosphere maintained by its director, the mystical Rebay, and her sometimes questionable acquisitions, this museum remained important to New York artists for some years as the only venue where first-rate abstract art was continuously on display. Hildegard Anna Augusta Elisabeth Rebay von Ehrenweisen was a native of Strasbourg, raised in Freiburg, and trained in Cologne, Paris, and Munich. She emigrated to the United States in 1927 and became a citizen in 1947. Devoted particularly to Kandinsky's work, she tirelessly promoted completely nonrepresentational art, interpreting this extreme form of abstraction in spiritual terms. In 1952 the museum took its present name, reflecting the widening of the collection's scope to include more varied forms of modernism, and the museum's board replaced Rebay with James Johnson Sweeney (1900–1986), a writer and museum administrator known as a spokesman for modern art. Rebay died at her home in Greens Farms, Connecticut. Today the museum offers a broadly representative collection of European and American art from the late nineteenth century to the present. Its holdings include the largest number of Kandinsky works anywhere. The umbrella Solomon R. Guggenheim Foundation, set up in 1937, supervises not only the original New York museum and the celebrated Bilbao venue but also Peggy *Guggenheim's former palazzo in Venice and smaller outposts elsewhere. The John Simon Guggenheim Foundation, which awards grants to artists as well as scholars, was established in 1925 by Solomon R. Guggenheim's brother Simon, in memory of his son John.

Guglielmi, O. Louis (1906–56). Painter. Accenting individual isolation and the irrationality of social institutions, his bizarre visions of the 1930s achieve an unusual American synthesis of surrealism and left-wing politics. Indebted also to *precisionism and the social realist faction of the *American Scene movement, his best-known works also exemplify important aspects of *magic realism. Born in Cairo to Italian parents, Osvaldo Louis Guglielmi lived also in Milan and Geneva as a child. In 1914 his family settled in Manhattan, and in 1927 he was naturalized as a United States citizen. While in high school, in 1920 Guglielmi started attending classes at the *National Academy of Design, where he studied full time between 1923 and 1926. After working at several jobs in the intervening years, in 1932 he began serious pursuit of a painting career. Later in the 1930s, he worked for *federal art projects. Following service in the U.S. Army during World War II, he began to emphasize the formal aspects of painting, often fragmenting and rearranging his still clearly delineated forms. Eventually, he adopted a completely abstract form of painting related to nonrepresentational forms of surrealism and *abstract expressionism. He died at his home in Amagansett, on eastern Long Island. Some of Guglielmi's socially oriented paintings, such as *Relief Blues* (Smithsonian American Art Museum, c. 1938), depicting four dejected adults whiling away their time in an impoverished apartment, use only distortion and exaggeration to convey the psychological costs of societal dislocation. Others employ unsettling imagery to dramatize similarly bleak messages. *Terror in Brooklyn* (Whitney Museum, 1941) depicts three women in mourning, trapped within a bell jar incongruously located on a desolate street. The nineteenth-century commercial architecture is embellished with odd details, such as a beribboned pelvis suspended high on the side of a building. The women's anguished faces suggest pain and loss, the glass enclosure prevents contact with others, and the ominous setting suggests that little comfort would reward their escape.

Guston, Philip (1913–80). Painter and printmaker. Arguably the most perplexing major artist of his generation, Guston first established his reputation as a figure painter. After 1950 he ranked among major *abstract expressionists. In a second reinvention of his artistic persona, in the late 1960s he abruptly sloughed off that movement's visual and aesthetic premises, abandoning the signature style that had brought him critical and financial success. What came next was unprecedented. Retaining the large format common in abstract expressionist work, he veered into aesthetic territory that offended nearly everyone's taste. His enigmatic and brooding, awkwardly rendered images feature cartoonish characters or the detritus of everyday life. These works speak of personal obsessions, social dysfunction, the nature of evil, and the fear of death, although on occasion they evoke tenderness and intimacy. Guston's daring reorientation to a radically different form of expression stands as a rare deviation from the normal course of individual artistic development in middle age and a unique occurrence among major abstract expressionists. Guston's late style provided a fertile precedent to many younger painters, who took up the challenges posed by his raw self-appraisal, his openness to social and political concerns, his particularly overt dismay over the Vietnam War and his revulsion toward Richard Nixon, his responses to popular and demotic culture, the instability of meaning in his disturbing images, his tacit recognition that *pop art had shifted the ground for contemporary art, his sardonic humor, the bold unconventionality of his pictorial construction, and his deliberate violations of what remained a masterful painting technique.

Born Philip Goldstein in Montreal, he moved with his family to Los Angeles in 1919. At Manual Arts High School there, he and Jackson *Pollock became such close friends that they were expelled together for disruptive behavior. Later Guston studied briefly at the Otis Art Institute (now Otis College of Art and Design). An acquaintance with Lorser *Feitelson roused his interest in both modern and Renaissance painting, and his work briefly engaged Feitelson's post-surrealism. Subsequently, Guston's early figurative style blended the idealism and spatial construction he admired in the work of such fifteenth-century masters as Ucello and Piero della Francesca, the current taste for socially relevant art, and the lessons of modernism, particularly as gleaned from the work of Picasso and Giorgio de Chirico. Guston first became known as a muralist. He worked for about a year in Los Angeles on a *federal art project before moving in 1936, at Pollock's urging, to New York, where he continued to paint government-sponsored murals. In 1937 he adopted Guston as his surname. During the following decade, he focused on easel painting while teaching from 1941 until 1945 at the State University of Iowa (now University of Iowa) in Iowa City and for the next two years at Washington University in St. Louis. During these years he moved from the generalized social subjects of his 1930s murals to a more private iconography, as in the cryptic *If This Be Not I* (Washington University, St. Louis, 1945), depicting costumed figures in a surreal setting. These paintings drew both critical and popular acclaim, augmented in 1946 by a *Life* magazine feature about him. In 1948–49 during a visit to Italy, he veered toward abstraction while working at the American Academy in Rome.

Back in New York, Guston soon developed a lush personal variant of abstract expressionism. In the 1950s, small strokes of color coalesced loosely in shimmering, lyrical fields. In the characteristic *Dial* (Whitney Museum, 1956), painterly marks gather in a multihued cloud of great sensuous appeal in the middle of the canvas. Around 1960 the poetic hues began to drain from his works, as he increasingly favored tonal gradations of gray. In these somber works, brushstrokes often gelled into masses that seem to veil ineffable objects they cannot actually reveal, suggesting Guston's dissatisfaction with his recent practice and straining impulse to engage the world. In 1967 Guston gave up his New York studio and moved permanently to *Woodstock, where he had resided part-time for some years. There he rebuilt his art by concentrating at first on drawings of simple objects, such as shoes and light bulbs, which fed the vocabulary of his subsequent paintings. Many such items had appeared in his earlier representational work, as had the Ku Klux Klan figures that soon also reemerged. However, the reused elements took on entirely new expressive powers, as he yanked them into oppressive and disorienting contexts.

When Guston first exhibited the new work in October 1970, critics reacted with contempt, howls of betrayal, and accusations of insincerity. The work failed to sell. Guston retreated to Rome to accept a position as artist-in-residence at the American Academy. When he returned two years later, renewed by the cultural grandeur of Italy, he continued to elaborate the premises of his new style, proceeding into territory where it became increasingly difficult to assign meaning to individual works, although he seemed consistently to revile the refinement that he apparently had come to regard as inauthentic. In many of the most puzzling, yet powerful of these works, a large-eyed, lima-bean head serves presumably as the artist's alter ego. In the disquieting *Painting, Smoking, Eating* (Stedelijk Museum, Amsterdam, 1973), painted mostly in sugary pinks and bloody reds, the persona, lying in bed, confronts his weaknesses. During these years, Guston taught at Boston University but continued to maintain a residence and studio in Woodstock. By the end of the decade, his recent work had found an audience. In 1979 Guston suffered a heart attack. Slowed by illness, in the final year before his death in Woodstock, he relinquished his taste for monumental scale as he produced a number of elegiac meditations on familiar appurtenances of domestic life. Few artists have worked successfully in three such different modes as Guston did. Yet his life and work show no deviation from unsparing commitment to art, its continuity, and its renewal.

Guston met his wife, Pennsylvania-born painter Musa McKim (1908–92), at the Otis Art Institute. They married in 1937. She, too, painted government-sponsored murals in the period before they moved to Iowa City. Later she became better known as a writer of poetry, fiction, and essays. Like several friends, including Bill Berkson and Stanley Kunitz, she provided springboards for Guston's 1970s "poem pictures" (as he called them), combining short texts with drawings. She died in a hospital at Kingston, not far from her home in Woodstock. A posthumous collection, *Alone with the Moon: Selected Writings*, appeared in 1994.

Guy, Francis (1760–1820). Painter. Numbering among the earliest to specialize in American views, he was born in England's Lake District. He worked in London as a silk-dyer before emigrating to the United States about 1795. Continuing to practice his craft, he added other skills as well and evidently taught himself to paint. He lived first in Brooklyn, but about 1798 moved to Baltimore. There his views of the city and "portraits" of individual country estates in the surrounding area were apparently quite popular, but relatively few have survived. These generally suggest that his strength lay in his observational skills rather than any grasp of the English picturesque. Contemporaries described his novel working methods, including sketching scenes on black gauze suspended between the artist and his subject. His paintings generally offer sharply edged, descriptive forms recorded with limited technical skill and little sense of atmospheric integration. Nevertheless, despite their lack of academic finish, these effectively composed works convey lively and frequently appealing impressions. He also worked in the Philadelphia area and recorded marine battles during the War of 1812. In 1817 or the next year he returned permanently to Brooklyn, where he produced his best-known painting, *Winter Scene in Brooklyn* (Brooklyn Museum, c. 1817–20). Incorporating more than two dozen figures going about their daily affairs in a snow-covered street, the skillfully constructed, yet informal vista records the untidy vitality of urban life during the early years of the republic.

Gwathmey, Robert (1903–88). Painter and printmaker. Combining representation with attention to abstract form, he mostly portrayed scenes of Southern life, particularly among African Americans. These sometimes engage economic and social justice issues that he actively supported in private life, but most focus straightforwardly on the dignity and inherent worth of his subjects. As well, some paintings caricature white southerners, while a few include allegorical elements. In the 1950s Gwathmey added still lifes to his repertoire of subjects. Born near Richmond, Virginia, he studied for the 1922–23 academic year at North Carolina State College (now University) in Raleigh and in 1925–26 at Baltimore's Maryland Institute (now Maryland Institute College of Art) before enrolling at the *Pennsylvania Academy of the Fine Arts, where he remained until 1930. He taught near Philadelphia for several years, then in Pittsburgh before moving to New York, where he served on the Cooper Union faculty from 1942 until 1968. In 1938 he destroyed nearly all of his previous work as he embarked on his distinctive style featuring carefully related, flatly painted shapes. The most significant Caucasian artist to give African-American life a central place among his subjects, he naturally responded as a socially conscious artist coming of age in the 1930s to the work of politically motivated artists within the *American scene movement. Like Ben *Shahn and Jacob *Lawrence, he effectively extended its concerns long after that movement had been submerged by a new wave of interest in abstraction. With his aesthetically sophisticated style and humanistic approach to subject, Gwathmey gained widespread respect. His democratic impulses found affirmation in a form of silkscreen printing known as serigraphy, which made possible relatively inexpensive works of art. Parkinson's disease slowed his hand in later years, then stopped it altogether in 1984. He died on Long Island, in a Southampton nursing home not far from his celebrated Amagansett house and studio built in 1966 to the designs of his son, the architect Charles Gwathmey.

His wife, **Rosalie Gwathmey** (1908–2001), a painter who turned to photography, often provided photographic "sketches" for her husband's paintings during the 1940s. They came across many of these subjects while summering for years at Wrightsville Beach on the shore near Wilmington, North Carolina, her home state. Rosalie Dean Hook grew up in Charlotte and met her husband while studying at the Pennsylvania Academy. They married in 1935, and she took up photography toward the end of the decade. After they moved to New York, she numbered among central figures in the politically liberal Photo League but abandoned socially conscious documentary work in the years after anti-Communist hysteria forced dissolution of the organization in 1951. She later designed textiles. She died at her Amagansett home.

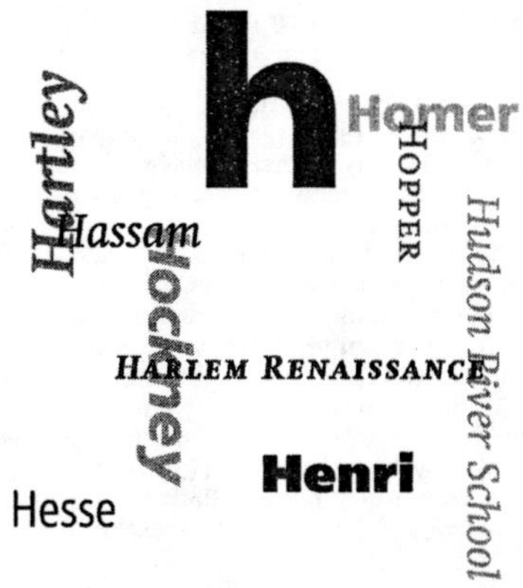

Haacke, Hans. *See* CONCEPTUAL ART.

Haberle, John (1856–1933). Painter. A still life specialist, he numbered among the most skilled and original trompe-l'oeil practitioners of the late nineteenth century. He addressed numerous subjects, often with a wry humor that complements the inherent jest of deceptive illusionism. Many of these paintings include commercially produced everyday objects, suggesting an interest in popular culture quite at odds with the sensibility apparent in most contemporary still life. Often, a barely controlled disorder in his compositions underscores the insouciance of this unruly subject matter. Born in New Haven, Connecticut, he was trained and then employed there as a lithographer. He worked at this profession in New York and elsewhere before returning to New Haven in 1880. There he also worked with paleontological materials as a preparator, designer, and occasional illustrator for Yale University's Peabody Museum of Natural History. After studying in 1884–85 at the *National Academy of Design, he settled permanently in the New Haven area to concentrate on the trickery that sustains his reputation. His best-known trompe-l'oeil subjects include paper money, blackboards with chalk attached by a string, and assortments of flat odds and ends, such as playing cards, readable clippings, photographs, and envelopes. His extraordinarily precise technique fooled viewers into insisting that he had "cheated" in his deceptions by pasting in stamps, currency, or other intricately detailed items. His three versions of one subject, *Torn in Transit*, pose particularly sophisticated and amusing questions about representation. In these, a landscape painting seems to have been wrapped and tied for shipment, but the paper has been torn back to reveal the painting itself. The simulated painting, however, displays a broad, almost impressionistic style. Haberle thus presents the conundrum of precisely replicating a painting that represents nature imprecisely. Apparently because of difficulty with his eyesight, after 1894 Haberle switched to painting fruit and flower still lifes in a soft and painterly but accomplished style. He also tried his hand at undistinguished animal paintings, as well as modeling in clay.

Haidt, John Valentine. *See* WEST, BENJAMIN.

Hairy Who. *See* CHICAGO IMAGISM.

Hale, Philip Leslie (1865–1931). Painter, critic, and art historian. A Bostonian conversant with advanced currents in Paris, he introduced aspects of impressionism, postimpressionism, and symbolism to the United States. In addition, he wrote criticism for periodicals and for a Boston newspaper and spurred the American revival of Vermeer's reputation. Within the Boston art community, his enthusiasm for the Dutch artist affected other artists even before publication of *Jan Vermeer of Delft* in 1913. Born in Boston, Hale came from a distinguished family known for intellectual, literary, and political accomplishments. Following a year at Boston's School of the Museum of Fine Arts, he trained at the *Art Students League with J. Alden *Weir and Kenyon *Cox before departing for Europe early in 1887. In Paris he studied at the École des Beaux-Arts and the Académie Julian. In the summer of 1888 he worked in Giverny, where he returned each year but one through 1893. Among the earliest Americans to visit there, he became acquainted with Monet and adopted an impressionist technique. During the same years, he traveled in Europe and returned home several times. In 1893 he embarked on a teaching career of more than thirty years at Boston's museum school and, later, elsewhere. In the 1890s he developed a method sympathetic to the postimpressionism of Georges Seurat and other pointillists. Characteristic images picture women nearly dissolved in veils of color in golden outdoor settings. These works have a dreamy, nonnaturalistic quality that presages his later symbolist mode. Around 1900 he returned to firmer drawing, along with brightly colored impressionist brushwork. A sparkling scene, *The Crimson Rambler* (Pennsylvania Academy, c. 1908–9) couples the appeal of a pretty girl with luxuriant red climbing roses in a freely brushed evocation of summer. Soon Hale also began a series of interior scenes that suggest the impact of his Vermeer studies, while also pursuing a taste for mysterious and suggestive symbolist allegory. In the early 1920s he returned to figural impressionism, often conveying sweetness of tone of within relatively simple compositions. In addition to his Vermeer monograph, he published several other books on art topics. He died in Boston.

His wife, **Lilian Westcott Hale** (1880–1963), primarily a figurative painter, ranked among the period's leading Boston artists, more successful as a painter than her husband. She concentrated on domestic interiors and portraits, but also painted landscapes and still lifes. A distinguished draftsman, she produced exquisitely finished charcoal drawings, as well as accomplished pastels. Born in Hartford, Connecticut, Lilian Clarke Westcott trained at the art school there and in William Merritt *Chase's summer school before entering Boston's museum school in 1900. Principally Edmund *Tarbell's student there, she married in 1902 and graduated in 1904. From 1908 on, she and her husband lived in suburban Dedham. She worked at their residence, a circumstance that perhaps encouraged her partiality to themes of children and domesticity. In paintings such as *Home Lessons* (Phillips Collection, 1919), depicting a studious little girl surrounded by artifacts of high culture, she combined the compositional rigor, firm drawing, and quietude of Vermeer's example with an impressionist interest in the play of light. From the mid-1950s she lived in Virginia but continued, as she had for some time, to summer in Rockport, on the Massachusetts shore. Only months before she died on her eighty-third birthday during a visit to St. Paul, Minnesota, she won her last award for painting and visited Italy for the first time.

Painter and printmaker **Ellen Day Hale** (1855–1940), Philip's sister, also numbered among prominent Boston artists. Known for portraits, landscapes, and domestic *genre scenes, she practiced photography as well. Around 1900 she also painted idealized or allegorical themes. Born in Worcester, Massachusetts, she studied in Boston with William *Rimmer in 1873 and the following year began her training with William Morris *Hunt. On visits to Philadelphia later in the 1870s, she studied at the *Pennsylvania Academy of the Fine Arts with Thomas *Eakins. In 1881 she first traveled abroad, initiating an extended sequence of visits to Europe and, eventually, North Africa and the Middle East. In Paris between 1881 and 1883 and again in 1885, she studied at the Académie Julian and independently with several artists, including Émile-Auguste Carolus-Duran, as she developed a fluent technique indebted to impressionism. While in France, in 1885 she took up etching and by the late 1880s counted among the earliest Americans to introduce color into the process. From 1887 Hale regularly summered in Rockport. She spent many winters in Charleston, South Carolina, and between 1904 and 1909, lived in Washington, D.C. Occasionally she sojourned at some length elsewhere. In the 1880s she wrote art criticism and in 1888 published a study of several old masters. She died in Brookline, a Boston suburb. Her companion from the mid-1880s, Philadelphia-born painter and printmaker Gabrielle DeVaux Clements (1858–1948), who shared Hale's progressive approach to etching, also became known for murals. After graduating from Cornell University in 1880, she studied for three years at the Pennsylvania Academy, where Eakins numbered among her instructors. She continued her training in Paris in 1884–85. From 1895 until 1908 she taught at a private school in Baltimore. During vacations she and Hale traveled or sojourned at the Massachusetts shore. She died in Rockport. Painter **Susan Hale** (1833–1910) provided early instruction to her niece and nephew, Ellen and Philip. A lifelong Bostonian, she was known particularly for watercolors, often landscapes. She studied in Munich and Paris for a year in 1872–73, taught art in Boston, and traveled extensively. She also was a writer on nonfiction subjects, including history, travel, and literature. Her books include several on travel, some in collaboration with her brother Edward Everett Hale, and a technical manual on painting. She died at Matunuck, Rhode Island, where she had regularly summered for many years.

Hall, George Henry (1825–1913). Painter. Popular in his day as a leading still life specialist, he nevertheless devoted much of his career to figurative work. He often painted picturesque *genre scenes inspired by extensive travels in Europe and the Mediterranean. As a still life painter, he is known particularly for elaborate fruit and flower arrangements set on shiny table tops, but in the 1860s particularly, he sometimes placed his subjects in informal outdoor settings, reflecting a *Pre-Raphaelite approach. Hall was probably born in Manchester, New Hampshire, although it is possible that he was a native of Boston, where he began to paint as a teenager. In 1849 he traveled to Düsseldorf with Eastman *Johnson. There he studied at the academy for a year before proceeding to Paris and then to Rome, living in each city for approximately a year. He returned in 1852 to settle permanently in New York, although he sojourned frequently in Europe for another four decades. The polished technique he had mastered abroad emphasized descriptive detail, warm and harmonious tonalities, and rigorously organized compositions unified by light and atmosphere. In still lifes he commonly deployed these skills to render textural variety within complex arrangements of varied natural specimens, played off against the harder surfaces of furniture, serving dishes, and decorative objects.

Halpert, Samuel (1884–1930). Painter. Stylistically indebted to the examples of Cézanne and Matisse, Halpert's cityscapes, still lifes, portraits, and interiors demonstrate solid pictorial composition, technical proficiency, and expressive warmth. Born in Bialystok, Russia, he moved with his family in 1889 to New York. In 1899 he began three years of training at the *National Academy of Design. Subsequently he lived in Paris for several years before returning to New York. Abroad, following a year of study at the École des Beaux-Arts, he became intrigued with modern art. At first influenced by the fauves, he soon developed a lifelong admiration for the work of Cézanne and became acquainted with Matisse. Combining their strengths, he generalized form in an approach that varied relatively little throughout his career. He died in Detroit, where he had resided for about three years. His wife, gallery owner and collector **Edith Gregor Halpert** (1900–1970), played a major role in promoting American early modern art and folk art. Born in Odessa, Russia (now Ukraine), Ginda Gregoryevna Fivoosiovich arrived with her family in New York in 1906 and studied in 1914–15 at the National Academy of Design. She married Halpert in 1918, but they separated when he accepted a teaching position in Detroit in 1927. In 1926 she established the Downtown Gallery (known for the first year as Our Gallery) in partnership with Berthe Kroll Goldsmith, sister of the Halperts' close friend Leon *Kroll. (Halpert bought her share in 1935.) Isabel *Bishop, Stuart *Davis, Arthur *Dove, Ben *Shahn, Charles *Sheeler, and William *Zorach numbered among major early-twentieth-century artists whose careers or estates the gallery represented. She died in New York.

Halsman, Philippe (1906–79). Photographer. Witty, ingenious, and technically accomplished, he specialized in celebrity portraits that probe the psychology of his sitters. For a celebrated series, he photographed subjects as they jumped into the air, letting down their guard with this playful act. Born in Riga, Russia (now Latvia), Halsman began taking pictures before enrolling in 1924 at the Technische Hochschule in Dresden to study electrical engineering until 1928. In 1930 he moved to Paris, where he became a successful portrait photographer. In surrealism he found keys to his artistic development, including the aesthetic value of surprise and the importance of psychology. "Dalí Atomicus" (1948) pictures Salvador Dalí aloft, along with his easel, a chair, three wet cats, and the arc of a bucket of water, all caught in split-second mid-trajectory. As the German army approached in 1940, Halsman fled to the United States and was later naturalized as a citizen. He settled permanently in New York, where he soon found success in advertising, fashion, and magazine photography. His 101 covers for *Life* magazine outnumber those of any other photographer. Halsman's publications include *Dalí's Mustache* (1954), pictures of his friend and frequent collaborator; *Philippe Halsman's Jump Book* (1959), images from the series begun in 1950; *Philippe Halsman on the Creation of Photographic Ideas* (1961); and *Sight and Insight* (1972).

Hambidge, Jay. *See* ROSS, DENMAN.

Hamblin, Sturtevant J. *See* PRIOR, WILLIAM MATHEW.

Hamilton, James (1819–78). Painter, printmaker, and illustrator. Chiefly a painter of marine views, he also produced landscapes and narratives. His taste for romantic tumult and his startlingly free, painterly style earned him the sobriquet, "the American Turner." Born in Ireland, at Entrien, near Belfast, in 1834 he arrived with his family in Philadelphia. The city remained his home base, although he later traveled in the mid-Atlantic and New England areas and, once, to England. As a young man in Philadelphia he received some instruction in painting, studied manuals on the subject, and found encouragement from John *Sartain, John *Neagle, and Thomas *Birch. Studying the work of J. M. W. Turner, John Constable, and other English romantics at firsthand in 1854 enabled Hamilton to consolidate an individual style. Many of his most impressive and audacious works convey nature's power at sea. Paint itself contributes to the frenzy, dissolving form into abstract color. Based on an 1830 poem of the same title by Oliver Wendell Holmes, *Old Ironsides* (Pennsylvania Academy, 1863) depicts the imagined break-up of the USS *Constitution* in surging waves before a stormy sky. (In actuality, rebuilt in 1833, the ship remains docked in Boston harbor and open to the public.) Light streams through a single opening in the clouds, perhaps alluding to divine providence. Metaphorically, the painting may also refer to the written Constitution, in some peril as the Civil War raged. Hamilton also painted more tranquil images, including shore views suggesting affinities with *luminism. Working also as a book illustrator from the 1840s, he achieved his greatest success with images for Elisha Kent Kane's *Arctic Explorations* (1856). In 1876 Hamilton arrived in San Francisco, heading west on a projected trip around the world, but he was still there at the time of his death.

Hammons, David. *See* AFRICAN-AMERICAN ART.

Hampton, James (1909–64). Assemblage artist. An untrained African-American religious visionary, his only known work is an installation painstakingly assembled in a Washington, D.C., garage. *The Throne of the Third Heaven of the Nations' Millennium General Assembly* (Smithsonian American Art Museum, 1950–64) represents a vast and splendid summary of the artist's spiritual beliefs. Constructed from old furniture, as well as other humble and cast-off materials, the work nevertheless shimmers with divine fervor. Although the general outline of its meaning has been deciphered, elements of the work's complex iconography remain elusive. It is likely that Hampton considered the work unfinished when he died. The altarlike work features a central, elevated throne, prepared for the Second Coming of Jesus Christ. This is flanked by intricately elaborated, symmetrically paired objects. Although the artist used a variety of materials to introduce color, aluminum and gold foil predominate, providing transcendent luster. His symbolic program refers to the Old Testament on the throne's left and New Testament on the right. Crowned with the words "Fear Not," the work includes inscriptions that identify some elements, but others are labeled in a secret handwriting that has not been decoded. The ensemble comprises about 180 pieces in a configuration that measures approximately twenty-seven feet wide. A native of Elloree, South Carolina, Hampton moved to Washington around 1928. Following military service between 1942 and 1945, he worked as a janitor for the General Services Administration. Although he had probably begun fabricating the work elsewhere, about 1950 he arranged to rent the garage where he worked in solitude for the rest of his life. Almost no one knew of his spare-time obsession until after his death.

Hamrol, Lloyd. *See* CHICAGO, JUDY.

Hanks, Nancy. *See* NATIONAL ENDOWMENT FOR THE ARTS.

Hansen, Al. *See* FLUXUS.

Hanson, Duane (1925–96). Sculptor. Fooling even sophisticated museumgoers, his lifelike sculptures of ordinary people, outfitted with real clothing and accessories, delineate an iconography of late-twentieth-century American life. Although highly individualized, through body language and apparel nearly all also suggest social types. Like Norman *Rockwell's seemingly truthful renditions of human appearance, Hanson's sculptures provoke amused delight as viewers recognize familiar characters. But Hanson shared little of Rockwell's cheery sentiment. Instead, he cast a sympathetic eye on the dilapidating effects of time and experience on the human body, registering a bleak fatalism beneath his subjects' stoic dignity. Related to *pop art's acceptance of the vernacular and mass culture, his works also suggest the veristic aims of *photo-realism. Because they are so specific to moments between the 1970s and the turn-of-the-century years, nostalgic overtones are bound to increase as the sculptures themselves age. Duane Elwood Hanson was born in Alexandria, Minnesota, about halfway between Minneapolis and Fargo but only a short distance from Sinclair Lewis's Sauk Centre, the fictional Gopher Prairie of *Main Street*. For writer and artist alike, the small-town Midwest sharpened sensitivities to the outward expression of distinctive personality types among ordinary people. Hanson studied at Luther College in Decorah, Iowa, and at the University of Washington in Seattle before enrolling at Macalaster College in St. Paul. After graduating in 1946, he continued his training at the University of Minnesota in Minneapolis and then at the Cranbrook Academy of Art, near Detroit. Two years after receiving his MFA there in 1951, he departed for Germany. During seven years in Munich and Bremerhaven, he developed technical knowledge of the fiberglass and polyester resin processes that allowed him to make casts from living models. His highly realistic figural work emerged in the mid-1960s, about the time he moved from Atlanta to Miami. The trompe-l'oeil figures at first appeared in emotionally charged scenarios presenting such difficult subjects as highway fatalities, abortion deaths, race riots, and the Vietnam war. Around 1970 he relinquished drama to specialize in unguarded moments. Tourists, shoppers, waitresses, construction workers, maintenance men, and retirees invite reflection on habits that disclose the national unconscious. From 1969 to 1973 Hanson lived in New York but otherwise remained in Florida. At the time of his death in a Boca Raton hospital, he made his home in the Fort Lauderdale area.

Happening. Term designating free-form performance events of the late 1950s and early 1960s. Intentionally multifarious, fleeting, and ambiguous, they remain difficult to characterize precisely. Happenings belonged to an extended lineage of artist-initiated performances, with a particular debt to dadaism. They emphasized improvisation, audience participation, and the mixing of visual art with practices and techniques associated with theatrical performance, including music, light effects, and sometimes film. Although freewheeling by nature, happenings generally were carefully planned and even to some degree, rehearsed. Their meanings and purposes were closely tied to their historical circumstances. Like *pop art, *junk art, *assemblage, and other experimental forms of the same time, they originated in young artists' desire to break free of the strictures of high art in order to achieve more valid forms of expression through closer relationships to lived experience. They sought to energize art by absorbing non-art materials, as well as "real" dimensions of space and time. While conceptually self-aware as an art form, happenings were nevertheless rarely somber events. High spirits, comedy, and whimsical absurdity prevailed, although mythic and ritualistic overtones were not uncommon. A fountainhead of ideas for the genesis of happenings, John *Cage staged an anticipatory event at *Black Mountain College during the summer of 1952. In 1958 Allan *Kaprow organized the first true happening at George *Segal's chicken farm near New Brunswick, New Jersey. The following year, Kaprow gave the form its name and offered a more formal presentation for a larger audience of his first major example, *18 Happenings in 6 Parts*. It ran for a week at New York's Reuben Gallery, the principal sponsor of happenings until it closed in 1961. Other artists who contributed creatively to happenings include Jim *Dine, Red *Grooms, Claes *Oldenburg, and Robert *Whitman. Happenings opened the way among visual artists for extensive experimentation with multimedia and theatrical forms of expression. However, even before the mid-1960s the originators had lost interest, and within a short time happenings as such had run their course. While news coverage and popular attention destroyed the form's subversive edge, many artists tired of ephemeral projects, as others began to prefer more orderly and often austerely minimalist forms of *performance art.

Hard-edge painting. Term referring to abstract painting emphasizing clean, clear shapes executed in flat colors. Occasionally employed to describe the art of other periods, the phrase came into general use with reference to large, intensely hued works produced in the late 1950s and 1960s. The hard-edge painters of this era generally retained the heroic scale and ambition of *abstract expressionism but dispensed with its ambiguities and with the personal element registered through painterly touch. Sometimes known also as post-painterly abstraction, hard-edge painting generally shares its capacious size and coloristic emphasis with *color field painting, but produces a more disciplined and "cooler" impact. Barnett *Newman and Ad *Reinhardt provided important precedents. In 1959 Los Angeles critic Jules Langsner first used the term in this specific sense, but the artists he had in mind represented a less advanced aesthetic than the New York painters generally grouped under the rubric. Innovative hard-edge painters include Ellsworth *Kelly, Kenneth *Noland, and Frank *Stella.

Among others who made important contributions, two particularly shared Kelly's interest in basing invented shapes on visual experiences. Often circular or irregular in format and typically limited to two or three colors, characteristic works by Leon Polk Smith (1906–96) present extremely simplified, interlocking organic forms that resist figure-ground distinctions. Smith grew up on a central Oklahoma farm. In 1934 he earned a BA from Oklahoma State University (now East Central University) in nearby Ada, and four years later, an MA from Teachers College, Columbia University, in New York. His early expressionistic realism gave way to surrealistic impulses around 1940. A few years later, he turned to lively arrangements of gridded, unmodulated rectangular elements, dependent on Mondrian's example, but soon gravitated toward complex patterning associated with his part-Indian heritage. His fluid, personal style emerged in the mid-1950s and, with time, gained in complexity, scale, and power. He also returned on occasion to geometric compositions and during his final decade often relied on black lines alone to activate pictorial space. He worked in Delaware as an art teacher for about twenty years before returning permanently to New York in the late 1950s.

Myron Stout (1908–87), a quiet poet of the movement, departed from its usual preoccupations with intense hue and large size. Instead, he focused on small black-and-white compositions featuring very few shapes, often only a single organic form, obsessively reworked toward some personal ideal of perfection. From Denton, Texas, not much more than a hundred miles south of Ada, Myron Stedman Stout Jr. not only shared Smith's geographical origins but also earned a master's degree in 1938 from Teachers College, Columbia University. Previously, after graduating in 1930 from North

Texas State University in Denton, he had taken art classes in Mexico City in 1933. In the 1940s he taught in Honolulu, served in the U.S. military, pursued additional training at Columbia, and studied intermittently for several years with Hans *Hofmann in New York and at his summer school in *Provincetown. After he left his Honolulu job in 1949, Stout traveled in Europe, admired Matisse's work, and, like Smith, painted vibrant geometric abstractions indebted to Mondrian. In 1952, drawn to the Cape Cod landscape, he settled permanently in Provincetown. A couple of years later, he formulated his individual form of *biomorphic abstraction, distilling the natural forms he encountered in the area. Diminished eyesight prevented painting after 1980. He died in Chatham, not far from his Cape Cod home. *The Journals of Myron Stout*, edited by Tina Dickey, appeared in 2005.

Harding, Chester (1792–1866). Painter. Specializing almost exclusively in portraiture, he established himself among its most popular mid-nineteenth-century practitioners. Born in the west-central Massachusetts town of Conway, he moved with his family in 1806 to central New York State. As a young man with little formal education, he knocked about in backwoods America, plying a variety of crafts and trades. In 1816 while working as a house and sign painter in Pittsburgh, Harding first tried his hand at portraiture. The result made him "frantic with delight." Already in his mid-twenties, he optimistically embarked upon an artistic career. On his own, he succeeded surprisingly quickly through hard work, practice, enthusiasm, and imitation. Despite limited technical competence, he worked professionally in the Lexington, Kentucky, area. During a short visit to Philadelphia in the winter of 1819–20, he first saw the work of well-trained artists such as Thomas *Sully. Drawing lessons at the *Pennsylvania Academy of the Fine Arts provided his only professional training. Harding moved on to St. Louis later in 1820 and to Washington, D.C., the following year. After a trip to Boston to seek out Gilbert *Stuart, who provided helpful advice, he relocated there early in 1823. By this time his skills, abetted by his personal charm, were sufficiently developed to draw numerous clients. After about six months, he sailed for England. In London he emulated the work of Thomas Lawrence, broadening his own technique while finding abundant patronage among prominent clients, including members of the nobility. After a few months in Glasgow in 1825–26, he returned to Boston. From 1830 the artist made his home in Springfield, Massachusetts, although he continued to maintain a Boston studio and participate in the art life of the city. He also traveled extensively, visiting Washington and New Orleans several times, as well as Montreal, St. Louis, and other cities. In 1847 he made a return visit to England. He died in Boston. The honest directness with which he presented sitters, combined with an ability to suggest their character, brought him wide patronage. Among many dignitaries, he painted top federal officials, including several presidents. In one of his most ambitious and admired works, textile manufacturer *Amos Lawrence* (National Gallery, c. 1845), luxuriously costumed as a gentleman at home, relaxes in a grandiose interior furnished with a classical column and red drapery, status signals familiar from traditional aristocratic images. Although the painting numbers among his virtuoso performances in coordination of space, color, light, and textures, Harding's homespun, factual account of the client's features chafes against the patrician setting and costume. The painter summed up his rags-to-riches life story in "My Egotistography," published as *A Sketch of Chester Harding, Artist* (1866).

Hare, David (1917–92). Sculptor, photographer, painter, and occasional printmaker. Known primarily for surrealist-oriented, mostly metal sculpture combining abstract and representational elements, his work explores the inner life of thought and feeling. He played a central role in New York's artistic community during World War II as editor of *VVV*, a short-lived avant-garde publication intended to promote "imaginative works of universal interest." Although he associated with *abstract expressionists and shared many of their interests, as an artist he remained tethered in the long run to surrealism. Born in New York, in his youth Hare lived with his family in Santa Fe, New Mexico, and Colorado Springs, Colorado. He never pursued formal training in art, going to work instead as a commercial photographer. In the late 1930s he was hired by New York's American Museum of Natural History to document American Indians of the Southwest. By the time he published a 1941 portfolio of works from this expedition, he was investigating a surrealist technique to distort photographic images by using heat to cause the emulsion to flow. He showed these works at Julien *Levy's gallery in New York late in 1940 and soon entered the circle of European émigrés waiting out World War II. As managing editor of *VVV*, he worked with surrealist leader André Breton (the magazine's founding and controlling spirit), Marcel *Duchamp, Max *Ernst, and Robert *Motherwell, among others.

(In 1943 Breton's wife, painter Jacqueline Lamba, left him for Hare. They married the following year but separated about ten years later.) Although the magazine appeared only three times between 1942 and 1944, it provided an influential focus of thought among surrealist-oriented New Yorkers and abetted the interchange of aesthetic notions and artistic forms between Americans and Europeans.

Hare quickly showed promise after taking up sculpture in 1942. He used varied materials to assemble figural inventions indebted to Alberto Giacometti and Alexander *Calder, as well as to tribal sculpture. Later that year, he numbered among few Americans admitted to the "First Papers of Surrealism" show, and his work soon appeared at Peggy *Guggenheim's gallery. In 1948 he helped to found the *Subjects of the Artist school, along with Motherwell, Mark *Rothko, and other abstract expressionists. Later that year, he departed for Paris, where he lived for about five years. (He also summered there before and after this sojourn.) Around 1951 he began to work with welded metal, later also using poured methods and innovative techniques of creating textured surfaces. His *biomorphic and symbolic vocabulary suggests similar concerns in the contemporary work of such sculptors as Herbert *Ferber and Theodore *Roszak, but Hare's work remained generally smaller, less aggressive in tone, and more attuned to surrealist fantasy. The bronze and steel rods and cutout shapes of *Sunrise* (Albright-Knox Art Gallery, Buffalo, New York, 1954–55) vaguely evoke the French Riviera landscape that inspired the work. Yet, the work's spiky forms speak of menace and psychological disquiet, familiar themes within surrealism, to create a tense and vibrant composition. In the late 1950s Hare took up painting, which for a time in the 1960s absorbed his full attention and subsequently remained an interest equivalent to sculpture. In their organic forms, sometimes incorporating representation, the paintings extend his mythic and symbolic purposes into another medium. During the 1940s Hare had a country home in Connecticut's popular northwest corner, which drew many artists and writers of the period, including a large contingent of Europeans. Later, when eastern Long Island attracted the summer art crowd, he maintained a residence there. In 1985 he moved to Victor, Idaho, not far from Jackson Hole, Wyoming, where he died in a hospital.

Haring, Keith. *See* POSTMODERNISM.

Harlem Renaissance. A period of African-American cultural renewal that peaked in the 1920s before gradually diminishing during the Depression years of the 1930s. Like the *American Scene movement, the Harlem Renaissance grew in part from the period's fascination with American identity. In its drive to fashion a distinctly contemporary African-American point of view, the movement self-consciously engaged modern styles of expression. Sometimes alternatively known as the New Negro movement, the Harlem Renaissance also reflected a black nationalism that found its most fervent expression in Marcus Garvey's back-to-Africa movement. Its sociological and political roots may be traced to early twentieth-century solidarity movements, soon followed by large-scale black migration to the industrialized North. Although centered on Harlem, the northern part of New York's Manhattan Island, the Renaissance flourished nationwide as Americans of African descent engaged the arts with a cosmopolitan verve that appealed as well to fashionable white audiences. Innovative performers such as Louis Armstrong, Count Basie, Duke Ellington, Ella Fitzgerald, Billie Holiday, and Bessie Smith permanently altered the course of American music. Langston Hughes, Zora Neale Hurston, James Weldon Johnson, Claude McKay, and Jean Toomer number among leading contributors to a flourishing African-American literature. Through scholarship and advocacy, philosopher Alain *Locke guided the movement. He encouraged explicitly modern but distinctively African-American achievement and interpreted the results to a wider public. In the visual arts, the Harlem Renaissance encompassed a wide range of styles and subjects. Most artists celebrated African-American life or their African heritage, while also drawing on mainstream art traditions derived from European models. Among the participants, major painters include Aaron *Douglas, Palmer *Hayden, William H. *Johnson, Jacob *Lawrence, and Archibald *Motley. Richmond *Barthé and Augusta *Savage number among important sculptors. James *Van Der Zee ranks as the most widely known photographer. Many of the issues they addressed continue to resonate. These include the appropriateness of ancestral African art as a model for the African-American artist, the nature of a black aesthetic, and the racial dimensions of the African-American artist's intended audience.

Harnett, William Michael (1848–92). Painter. The leading American practitioner of trompe-l'oeil still life, he inspired a school of followers. His best-known painting, *After the Hunt* (Fine Arts Museums of San Francisco, 1885) offers an elegant and sonorous arrangement of meticulously rendered items. An old door with elaborate metal fittings serves as backdrop for emblems of pursuit, including dead game, a rifle, antlers, a hunting horn, a flask, and a Tyrolean hat. Besides three earlier variants of this work and other groupings of hanging objects, he also painted many tabletop compositions, as well as at least two rack pictures depicting envelopes, announcements, clippings, and other scraps of paper stuck behind tapes on a vertical surface. Although Harnett today numbers among highly regarded nineteenth-century painters, his deceptive illusionism found little sympathy within the art establishment of his own time. His work rarely appeared in accepted high art venues and was not popular among major collectors. Instead, the patrons responsible for his financial success and public recognition were generally prosperous but relatively unsophisticated businessmen and merchants. The masterful *After the Hunt* hung in a New York saloon. After his death, Harnett's reputation languished for decades. When his work was resurrected, modern viewers appreciated his skillful manipulation of abstract form and shallow space. His cool exactitude seemed to anticipate *precisionism, while the intensity of his gaze appealed to viewers familiar with certain forms of representational surrealism. Born in Clonakilty, County Cork, as an infant Harnett left Ireland with his family to settle in Philadelphia. There he learned the exacting craft of engraving silver and studied at the *Pennsylvania Academy of the Fine Arts. In 1869 he moved to New York, where he continued to work as an engraver until the mid-1870s. He also studied at the *National Academy of Design and at Cooper Union. In 1876 he returned to Philadelphia. There he again attended classes at the academy while solidifying his personal trompe-l'oeil style featuring sharply delineated life-size objects, illusionistic textures, and dark-toned, rich coloration suggestive of old masters. His early fruits and vegetables yielded by about 1877 to more original combinations of manmade items, ranging from the humble furnishings of a bachelor existence to expensive decorative objects denoting cosmopolitan society. He painted three memento mori, juxtaposing skulls with symbols of worldly experience, and in 1879 produced the first of his two known rack pictures, drawing on a device with European roots. Although several of Harnett's thematic types had previously appeared rarely if at all in American art, in this case it is likely that the earliest rack picture by his friend John *Peto stimulated Harnett's endeavor.

In 1880 Harnett departed for Europe, where he worked in London and Frankfurt before settling in Munich early in 1881. Apparently impervious to the painterly style eagerly appropriated by other Americans working in this popular art center, he refined but did not substantially alter his approach. Items of European manufacture joined his repertoire of subjects, as his work became more fully realized and sophisticated. He began painting reduced-scale still lifes (some are nearly miniaturistic), in addition to large arrangements featuring timeworn objects. Among these, the four hunt themes, possibly inspired by Alsatian photographer Adolph Braun's still lifes, demonstrate familiarity with seventeenth-century Dutch and Flemish game pieces. The magisterial 1885 example was executed in Paris, where he spent the final year or so of his sojourn abroad before settling permanently in New York. Although by 1888 failing health limited his output, during his last years he completed some of his most convincing and satisfying works. Among these are several that appear to be particularly rich in associative meanings. Since the late 1870s, Harnett had on occasion assembled objects to recapitulate aspects of the lives of those who commissioned them. Many other paintings employ items of material culture to symbolize notions of transience, solitude, and the consolations of music, objets d'art, or literature. In contrast to the exuberant well-being generally associated with earlier American still life, Harnett's works characteristically stress solemnity, retrospection, and even melancholy.

Harnett's twentieth-century rediscovery involved one of the great detective stories in American art history. When his work first came on the market in the mid-1930s, the astute dealer Edith *Halpert took note and by 1939 was avidly promoting his art. However, not until San Francisco critic Alfred V. Frankenstein (1906–81) began his research in the 1940s did the true dimensions of Harnett's accomplishment become disentangled from misattributions and forgeries. Presented in an article in 1949 and in the landmark 1953 book *After the Hunt: William Harnett and Other Still Life Painters, 1870–1900* (revised in 1969), Frankenstein's sleuthing established the basis for subsequent appreciation and analysis of late-nineteenth-century illusionistic still life. Besides Peto, other figures include Jefferson David *Chalfant, Richard La Barre *Goodwin, John *Haberle, Claude Raguet *Hirst, and Alexander *Pope.

Harrison, Birge (1854–1929). Painter. Known especially for subtle evocations of nature's tranquil moments, he deployed a limited range of hues to create poetic, *tonalist views. Particularly fond of effects produced by muted illumination, as at twilight or under cloudy conditions, he often exploited the reflective qualities of large expanses of water or snow to create alluring although relatively featureless compositions. Tempered by the example of James Abbott McNeill *Whistler's elegantly spare visions, Harrison's mature work sustains a romantic attachment to long-established belief in nature as a source of beauty. An influential teacher in *Woodstock, where he persuaded the *Art Students League to relocate its summer outpost in 1906, he also produced articulate and theoretically informed writings, including *Landscape Painting* (1909). Born in Philadelphia, Lowell Birge Harrison studied at the *Pennsylvania Academy of the Fine Arts before leaving for Paris in 1875. There he studied with figure painters Alexandre Cabanel and Émile-Auguste Carolus-Duran. Remaining in France for several years, he worked at the art colonies of Pont-Aven and Concarneau in Brittany and Grèz-sur-Loing, near the Forest of Fontainebleau. The precisely drawn human forms and atmospheric sensitivity of his early work suggest an attraction to the paintings of Jules Bastien-Lepage. As figural compositions gave way to pure landscape, in the 1880s Harrison began to travel the globe, recording in his work many locales. He lived for five years in Santa Barbara, California, before relocating to the New York region. He eventually settled permanently at Woodstock. His brother, painter **Alexander Harrison** (1853–1930), lived in Paris throughout his professional life and died there. Also interested first in figural subjects, he, too, turned his attention primarily to landscapes during the 1880s. He became known especially for marine views, particularly as seen by moonlight. Also born in Philadelphia, Thomas Alexander Harrison worked for several years for the United States Coast and Geodetic Survey before studying art in San Francisco. He returned to Philadelphia to train at the Pennsylvania Academy before heading to Paris in 1879. There he studied with academic realist Jean-Léon Gérôme. Subsequently, while frequenting the same art colonies as his brother, he and Bastien-Lepage became good friends. By the mid-1880s he was recognized on both sides of the Atlantic as a leading American artist in Paris. Exemplifying his newfound enthusiasm for pure landscape, *The Wave* (Pennsylvania Academy, c. 1885), an elongated view along the shore of a quiet sea, combines exquisite detail with expansive space sheltered under a pearly sky. Later he generally emphasized mood and tonal subtlety over exacting description.

Hart, George Overbury "Pop" (1868–1933). Painter and printmaker. An irreverent, bohemian personality who spent much of his life recording extensive travels in informal sketches and watercolors, he often included humorous or satirical touches. Executed in his characteristically fluid, illustrative watercolor technique, *The Bahamas* (Whitney Museum, c. 1918) depicts black inhabitants along a shore. As usual, Hart's grasp of gesture, picturesque detail, and amusing incident lends charm and visual interest to a simply but effectively composed scene. After taking up printmaking in his fifties, he often used earlier drawings as the basis for drypoints, etchings, and lithographs. Born in Cairo, Illinois, Hart briefly attended the School of the Art Institute of Chicago. He worked as an illustrator for a Chicago newspaper before 1900, when he began wandering through Europe, Central America, and the Pacific islands. Between 1907 and 1912 he worked as a sign painter in the New York City area, and for the following eight years he painted movie sets in Fort Lee, New Jersey. He spent much of the 1920s traveling again, in the West Indies, Europe, Mexico, and North Africa. He died near Fort Lee, in Coytesville, where he had lived in poor health during his final years.

Hart, James MacDougal (or McDougal) (1828–1901). Painter. A *Hudson River School landscape specialist, he was born in Kilmarnock, Scotland, and emigrated to the United States with his family in 1831. They settled in Albany, where he was later apprenticed to a coach and sign painter and briefly tried his hand at portraiture. In Europe from 1850 until 1853, he studied primarily in Düsseldorf. Although he left Albany for New York in 1857, the bucolic upstate New York landscape remained his chief subject. His pastoral scenes often include cattle, and he was recognized as a leading painter of farm animals. Carefully recorded details enrich his romanticized if often somewhat formulaic views, which found an appreciative audience among nostalgic urbanites. He died in Brooklyn, where he had resided for some time. His brother, **William MacDougal Hart** (1823–94), painted similar landscapes and enjoyed a comparable reputation. Born in Paisley, he too emigrated from Scotland to Albany with the family and there also received an artisan's training in painting. Working as a portrait painter by the early 1840s, he traveled as far as Michigan in search of commissions. After returning to Albany about 1845, he turned to landscape subjects. From 1849 until 1852 he worked in Great Britain, primarily Scotland. About two years later he settled in New York. In addition to bucolic landscapes, he painted Adirondack mountain views and atmospheric, sometimes stormy shore scenes based on observations of the New England

and Canadian coasts. He died in the New York suburb of Mount Vernon, his home in later years. Born in Pittsfield, Massachusetts, their sister Julia Hart Beers Kempson (1835–1913), as an artist generally known as Julie Beers, numbered among few professional women landscape painters of the nineteenth century. She also exhibited still lifes. With her first husband, painter Marion R. Beers (?–1876), she settled in New York in the mid-1850s but later lived in Metuchen, New Jersey. She remarried in 1877, to Peter Kempson, and died in Trenton. Born in Lakeville, Connecticut, James's wife, **Marie Theresa Gorsuch Hart** (1829–1921), studied at the *National Academy of Design and painted watercolor flower studies. Their children, **William Howard Hart** (1863–1937), **Letitia Bonnet Hart** (1867–1953), and **Mary Theresa Hart** (1872–?), became artists as well. A painter of landscapes and figurative works, William Howard, born in Fishkill-on-Hudson, New York, worked under J. Alden *Weir, studied in Paris, and remained in France for some years, often painting at Giverny, before returning in the mid-1890s. Later he lived in Plainfield, New Hampshire, and participated in activities of the nearby Cornish art colony. Letitia, who was born in New York and studied at the National Academy, became a popular figure and portrait painter, influenced by impressionism. She died in Eau Gallie, on Florida's east coast. Mary, born in Brooklyn, also studied at the National Academy and worked as a figurative painter and illustrator.

Hart, Joel Tanner (1810–77). Sculptor. A portrait specialist, he is particularly associated with likenesses of Henry Clay, whose features he reproduced in life-size and reduced versions made of marble, bronze, or plaster. Born on a farm near Winchester, Kentucky, as a teenager Hart worked as a stonemason. About 1835 he moved to Lexington, where he met Shobal Vail *Clevenger who aided his development and inspired his efforts to become a full-time portrait sculptor. A sculpture of Andrew Jackson (Kentucky Historical Society, Frankfort, 1838) did much to establish his local reputation. His first model of Clay's visage (plaster cast, Maryland Historical Society, Baltimore, early 1840s) secured an 1845 commission from the Ladies Clay Association in Richmond, Virginia, for a full-length statue. After making additional studies of his subject, in 1849 Hart departed for Italy, where he established a studio in Florence. Various difficulties and distractions delayed the project until 1859, when the finished marble (state capitol, Richmond, Virginia) was shipped. Rather literal in its treatment of the standing figure, it nevertheless conveys quiet dignity. In 1860 Hart made his only return visit to the United States. Subsequently in Florence, he continued to turn out Clay memorabilia and maintained a steady business in portrait busts. He also tried his hand at a few ideal works, most notably a life-size nude, *Woman Triumphant* (also known as *The Triumph of Chastity*; 1864–77). Several years after his death, a group of Lexington women arranged for a marble version to be carved. Installed in the rotunda of the Fayette County courthouse, it was destroyed in an 1897 fire.

Hartigan, Grace (1922–). Painter and printmaker. Grounded in *abstract expressionism, she has employed colorful, gestural brushwork to create purely abstract paintings, as well as a greater number of works that incorporate representational fragments. Inspired principally by Willem *de Kooning, she has generally emphasized improvisatory surface, vigorously applied paint, shallow space, and tension-filled composition. Thick, dark lines often separate forms while also weaving them into a unified whole. Commonplace subjects align some work with *pop art, although she has disparaged the detached emotional tenor of that movement. As a printmaker, she has created lithographs and screen prints related to her paintings. Born in Newark, New Jersey, she grew up in the area. As a young child she lived in Bayonne but at the age of seven moved with her family to Millburn, where she graduated from high school in 1940. Married the following year to Robert Jachens (they divorced in 1948), she moved to Los Angeles, where she began drawing and working with watercolor. After her husband was called to military service, in 1942 she returned east to work as a mechanical draftsman for several years until she was able to begin painting full time. Stunned by the first exhibition of Jackson *Pollock's signature drip paintings early in 1948, she soon became acquainted with him and then with de Kooning and others in the their circle. While briefly married to Cody, Wyoming, sculptor and painter Harry Andrew Jackson (1924–), a Chicago native best known for western themes, in 1949 she worked for several months in San Miguel de Allende, Mexico. In 1951 she showed abstract expressionist paintings in her first one-person gallery show. Mostly self-taught as a painter, late in 1952 she began to investigate the foundations of her craft in freely painted reinterpretations of old master paintings. In the spring of 1954 she embarked on a series of works based on urban imagery, such as *Grand Street Brides* (Whitney Museum, 1954), loosely depicting the "brides" in the display window of a wedding apparel shop. Although such paintings reaped considerable acclaim, she turned to landscape-inspired abstractions while working on Long Island during the summer of 1957. In 1958 she visited Europe and the following year, bought a house on eastern Long Island, in Bridgehampton, where she lived for only a short time. A yearlong marriage to Long Island gallery owner Robert Keene ended in 1960. She then married Johns Hopkins University medical researcher Winston Price, moved to suburban Baltimore, established a studio downtown, and began summering in Maine. She has directed the graduate painting program at the Maryland Institute College of Art since the mid-1960s. Around that time, she returned to vernacular subject matter, including dolls, children's books, and a few years later, once again street life. Memorable groups of later works have addressed great women in history, entertainment icons, and well-known works of art from the past. With time, her paint has often been applied in thinner washes, and she has continued to work productively in watercolor.

Hartley, Marsden (1877–1943). Painter and printmaker. Also a poet and essayist. After painting some of the early twentieth century's most impressive abstractions, in 1917 he adopted an expressive, bold, and sensuous approach to landscape, still life, and figurative subjects. A wanderer who never established a home, he spent much of his adult life in Europe, but in later years he became particularly identified with subjects from Maine, the state of his birth. A Lewiston native, Edmund Hartley lived as a youth in nearby Auburn and left school at fifteen. After moving to Cleveland in 1893, he entered the Cleveland School (now Institute) of Art. While learning the rudiments of his craft, he discovered the writings of Transcendentalist philosopher and poet Ralph Waldo Emerson, who ignited romantic aspirations. After moving to New York in 1899, he studied with William Merritt *Chase before embarking on four years of training at the *National Academy of Design. He subsequently toured for a year with a theater company before returning in 1906 to Maine. In the same year, adopting his stepmother's maiden name, he began to call himself Edmund Marsden Hartley, and two years later he dropped the first name altogether. In Maine, Hartley developed a postimpressionist approach stimulated by illustrations of work by Italian divisionist painter Giovanni Segantini. By 1908 he had achieved a distinctive landscape style of colors applied in minute, parallel lines. A mountain landscape featuring bright autumnal colors and stylized forms, *Cosmos* (Columbus [Ohio] Museum of Art, 1908–9) announces the impetus of Hartley's mature art: a desire to push beyond optical description to disclose spiritual meaning. The simplified shapes, particularly the stylized clouds, may derive from Japanese prints, but they also suggest Hartley's reverence for an older soul mate, Albert Pinkham *Ryder.

In April 1909 Hartley met Alfred *Stieglitz, who almost immediately staged the young artist's first New York exhibition at his *291 gallery and for nearly thirty years afterward provided indispensable psychological and financial support. Working from memory and imagination, in the summer of 1909 Hartley began a group of Dark Landscapes directly indebted to Ryder, whom he personally sought out. His subsequent paintings reflect the art he saw at 291, including work by Cézanne, Matisse, and Picasso, as well as other young American modernists. At thirty-five, Hartley at last sailed across the Atlantic. Within months of his 1912 arrival in Paris, he had forged a style he sometimes called Cosmic Cubism. Formally, these compositions derive from the angular planes of cubism, but emotionally they reflect a German point of view. Kandinsky, the *Blue Rider Almanac*, and an intensified dose of the romantic primitivism he had already encountered in New York fueled his mystical, exploding shapes. The paintings of his Paris year marked him as a sophisticated innovator whose work integrated numerous eclectic sources. In the spring of 1913 he moved to Berlin, where he remained for two and a half years, interrupted by a visit to New York in the winter of 1913–14. Comfortably at home within Berlin's homosexual subculture, he soon produced startlingly original paintings. Bold and colorful, continuing to reflect aspects of both German expressionism and French cubism, they incorporate varied symbols and emblems, some representational and some abstract. In their references to popular culture and their assertive, frontal organization, these vigorous, flattened compositions remained unique in their time. Paying homage to his lover, a younger officer killed early in World War I, the best known of the Berlin paintings prominently feature militaristic and patriotic references, as in *Portrait of a German Officer* (Metropolitan Museum, 1914). Another important group centers on American Indian motifs.

At the end of 1915, Hartley returned to the United States for five and a half years (except for several months in Bermuda), his only sustained period of residence in his homeland during the middle years of his life. Hartley spent the summer of 1916 in *Provincetown and reoriented his style to a controlled form of synthetic cubism, sometimes verging on abstraction. He spent the last few weeks of the season with Charles *Demuth, whom he had met in Europe and who joined him for a time in Bermuda the next winter. There, Hartley experimented productively with approaches to representation purged of his previous emotionalism. In the satisfyingly decorative *Bermuda Window in a Semi-Tropic Character* (Fine Arts Museums of San Francisco, 1917), a tabletop still life appears before a shore scene visible through a window. The format derives from Matisse, but the flattened yet heavy forms herald Hartley's subsequent personal development. Several months in New Mexico in 1918 resulted in landscapes of the region, as well as images based on artifacts of its Hispanic culture. Except for two visits home, from 1921 until 1930 Hartley remained in Europe, living in Germany, Paris, and the south of France, where he repeatedly painted Cézanne's iconic Mont Sainte-Victoire. In 1932 he went to Mexico for year, then directly to Europe again before returning permanently to the United States early in 1934. Reflecting his psychological isolation, his search for personal and artistic meaning, and his ambition, his travels produced uneven results. The work of these years generally was not well received in New York, partly because its largely foreign subject matter conflicted with the period's growing cultural nationalism. In the mid-1930s Hartley achieved aesthetic consistency and eventually found renewed respect. Summer visits to Nova Scotia in 1935 and 1936 proved decisive. There, living with a pious fishing family, he was sexually attracted to one of its sons. After this young man drowned, along with a brother and a cousin, Hartley poured his grief into some of the most compelling paintings of his career, including many imaginary portraits of acquaintances from the simple, isolated community. *Christ Held by Half-Naked Men* (Hirshhorn Museum, 1940–41), presenting a "drowned" Jesus mourned by stolid, muscular men, evokes in raw, symbolic terms those events he had witnessed.

In the late 1930s Hartley consciously undertook to achieve renown as a regional painter of New England, particularly Maine. There he painted the seacoast with a forcefulness equaled only by Winslow *Homer's renditions of its rocks and waves, while also recapturing Ryder's mystic intensity. *Evening Storm, Schoodic, Maine* (Museum of Modern Art, 1942) presents a single, side-lit wave about to crash on heavy rocks, as Homer's do. Yet, in the darkened sky beyond float Ryderesque clouds that recall those of Hartley's neo-impressionist landscapes from thirty-five years earlier. Inland, Maine's Mount Katahdin became Hartley's homegrown Mont Sainte-Victoire, a spiritually charged motif encompassing both stability and flux within the majesty of nature. In his final three years, failing health diminished Hartley's productivity just as he began to find the critical attention and financial success he had long sought. He died in Ellsworth, Maine. Hartley published a collection of essays, *Adventures in the Arts* (1921), and three small books of poems, from which the posthumous *Selected Poems* (1945) was assembled. His autobiographical writings have been collected in *Somehow a Past: The Autobiography of Marsden Hartley* (1996), edited by Susan Elizabeth Ryan.

Hartmann, Sadakichi. *See* CAMERA WORK.

Hartwell, Alonzo. *See* BROWN, GEORGE LORING.

Haseltine, William Stanley (1835–1900). Painter. A landscape specialist, he is remembered for crisp views of the New England shore and for Italian scenes. An expatriate during most of his professional life, he earned an international reputation. Born in Philadelphia, he studied at the University of Pennsylvania while also working with the recently arrived, German-born landscapist and portrait painter Paul Weber (1823–1916). He transferred to Harvard for his final two years of college, returning after his graduation in 1854 to Philadelphia. The next year he departed for Düsseldorf where he studied with Andreas Achenbach and became friendly with Americans in Emanuel *Leutze's circle. In the spring of 1856 he headed off with Worthington *Whittredge and Albert *Bierstadt through Switzerland to Italy, reaching Rome in the fall. While he also sketched widely in the Italian countryside, the city remained his headquarters until the summer of 1858, when he moved to New York. His popular coastal views from subsequent years continued the *Hudson River School's realistically detailed reverence for nature. In their preoccupation with effects of natural light these works demonstrate links with *luminism as well. In 1866 he departed, more or less permanently, for Europe. In Paris he admired *Barbizon painting and proto-impressionist plein air experiments. Three years later he settled in Rome but continued to travel within Europe and frequently visited the United States. After 1874, when he took up residence in the stately Villa Altieri, his home functioned as a gathering spot for American artists, writers, and travelers. Haseltine spent much of the 1890s in the United States and at his death had only recently returned to Rome from a trip to the American West and Alaska

Characteristic of his American shore scenes, *Castle Rock, Nahant* (Corcoran Gallery, 1865) offers sparkling summer sun playing across blue water and warmly toned rocks. Tiny vacationers scramble on the stony seaside or scan the ocean, serving to humanize the sharply recorded, otherwise austere terrain. Haseltine's European views include many additional shore scenes, such as *Capri* (Cleveland Museum of Art, 1869), which counterpoises a huge and ungainly rock outcropping against a gentle sea. The softer light here reveals the more atmospheric approach he adopted after his return to Europe. Subtly variegated tones, rendered in delicate, feathery brushwork, suffuse distant clouds, as well as the water's surface.

Sculptor **Herbert Haseltine** (1877–1962), the painter's son, specialized in animal subjects, both life-size and in tabletop reductions. Born in Rome and educated at Harvard, he studied art in Munich, Rome, and Paris, where he spent most of his adult life. His early, fluent realism conveys his subjects' fleet energies, but after World War I he drew on Egyptian precedents to stylize and simplify forms in a more modern conceptualization of animal vitality. During World War II, he resided in the United States but returned abroad in 1947. He died in Paris. William Stanley's brother, sculptor **James Henry Haseltine** (1833–1907), also born in Philadelphia, interrupted his European training to serve in the Union military during the Civil War. Known for ideal subjects, as well as portraits, he resided in Paris, Nice, and Rome, where he died. A third brother, **Charles Field Haseltine** (1840–1915), painted landscapes and worked as an art dealer in Philadelphia.

Hassam, Childe (1859–1935). Painter and printmaker. Often regarded as the premier American impressionist, he numbered among early proponents of the style in the United States. Bright hues, vigorous brushwork, and uncomplicated subjects yield joyous, light-filled scenes. New York, Boston, and the picturesque summer retreats of New England and Long Island provided most of his subjects. He also painted indoor scenes, nudes, still lifes, and portraits. He never relinquished the zest for descriptive detail he acquired during early experience as an illustrator, and more explicitly than any other American impressionist he relished scenes of distinctly modern life. Drawn to printmaking in 1915, he eventually produced about 375 etchings or drypoints, as well as approximately forty-five lithographs, nearly all dating to 1917 or 1918. A founding member of The *Ten, he enjoyed professional esteem, popular success, and countless honors. Born in Dorchester (now part of Boston), Frederick Childe Hassam preferred as an adult to be known by his middle name. His formal education ended during his second year of high school, and his training as an artist remained unsystematic. From 1876 until 1881 he worked in a Boston wood-engraving shop. During these years, he also began to provide drawings for several major periodicals. (Later he also illustrated books.) As well, he painted watercolors, took evening art classes, and received advice or instruction from Boston artists including William *Rimmer and German-born painter-etcher Ignaz Gaugengigl (1859–1932), who specialized in historical *genre scenes. In 1883 Hassam toured Europe, painting watercolors all the way. After his return, he worked more often in oil, producing *Barbizon-inflected landscapes benefiting from his acquaintance with William Morris *Hunt and George *Fuller, as well as more original depictions of Boston street life. Although executed with careful draftsmanship and a darkened palette, the urban subjects, atmospheric effects, and unconventional compositions of these city views parallel French impressionists' interests. In 1886 he settled for three years in Paris. Thinking he needed instruction in academic drawing, he enrolled at the Académie Julian but soon realized that methods taught there held little interest. Instead, although he never acknowledged a debt to their example, he absorbed impressionist broken brushwork and light, bright colors. Although these later distinguished his art, firm traditional structure continued throughout nearly all his work.

After his return to the United States in October 1889, Hassam resided in New York but usually worked elsewhere during warmer months. Favorite sites included Appledore Island, in the Isles of Shoals off the coast of New Hampshire, and the Connecticut shore sites of *Cos Cob and *Old Lyme. However, he often wandered greater distances. He visited Havana in 1895 and the following year sailed for Europe, where he wintered in Italy before visiting Paris, Pont-Aven, and England on his way home in 1897. After 1900 he visited the West Coast on several occasions. In 1910 and again in 1911 he worked in Paris. Around this time he began regularly visiting eastern Long Island. From 1920 he spent about half of each year there, at a summer residence in East Hampton, where he died after nearly a year in poor health. In an expression of support for native artists, Hassam bequeathed nearly 450 oils, prints, and pastels to the American Academy of Arts and Letters in New York. Income from their sale was directed toward the purchase of works by artists from the United States and Canada for museums in those countries.

For some four decades, Hassam captured modern experience in colorful, fluent, eye-catching images, although after 1900 he also produced more meditative and sometimes experimental work. Some of his most convincing paintings date to the years immediately following the return from Europe in 1889, when he first gloried in impressionism's exhilarating effects. Depicting a riotous screen of flowers abutting the rock-strewn but placid sea at a friend's estate, *Celia Thaxter's Garden, Isles of Shoals, Maine* (Metropolitan Museum, 1890) captures a clear and carefree summer day at a classic vacation spot. By the late 1890s his work began to show hints of the decorative and less insistently naturalistic tendencies that appeared more often later, as he intermittently responded to aspects of postimpressionism, Nabism, *tonalism, and the example of James Abbott McNeill *Whistler. However, although he exhibited in the *Armory Show, he deplored the more extreme aspects of modern art. Nearly thirty celebratory flag paintings constitute the greatest achievement of later years. Dating from 1916 to 1919, they document the patriotic spirit evident in New York during the World War I years, as parades and banners encouraged public support for the conflict. In *Allies Day, May 1917* (National Gallery, 1917), the red, white, and blue flags of the United States, France, and Great Britain, suspended from buildings along Fifth Avenue, flatten the painting's space into a decorative burst of enthusiasm for the allied effort, disregarding war's darker realities. During the 1920s, as his interest in printmaking prevailed, Hassam's paintings often show looser brushwork, while their subjects, drawn from studio and village, display a reticent tone, disengaged from urban commotion.

Hathaway, Rufus (1770–1822). Painter. Also a medical doctor. Chiefly a portraitist, he also painted landscapes and other views, primarily as elements of interior design, and made wood carvings and frames. Born in Freetown, Massachusetts, he moved with his family several times before they settled in Bristol, Rhode Island, in the mid-1780s. Hathaway may have worked as an apprentice ship-carver or decorative specialist but was otherwise presumably self-taught as an artist. In the 1790s he worked as a painter in several Massachusetts localities before taking up the study of medicine in 1796. The previous year he had settled at Duxbury, Massachusetts, where he lived for the rest of his life. As the town's only physician, he apparently painted infrequently. Best-known among Hathaway's portraits, the imaginatively conceived *Lady with Her Pets* (Metropolitan Museum, 1790) combines naively rendered but acutely observed detail, exuberant pattern, flattened space, and immobilized forms. The seated client, tentatively identified as Molly Wales Fobes (later Mrs. Elijah Leonard), poses with her cat and two perched birds, while a pair of large, mothlike insects animates the empty space beside her head. Her high-style finery culminates in two huge, eye-catching feathers that sprout from her coiffure, converting recent French fashion into provincial whimsy. In other portraits as well, Hathaway translated into a personal idiom his contact with eighteenth-century portrait conventions, probably known from European prints and from work of more sophisticated American artists such as John Singleton *Copley.

Havell, Robert, Jr. (1793–1878). Painter and printmaker. Most widely known as the engraver of John James *Audubon's masterpiece, *The Birds of America* (1827–38), Havell actually enhanced Audubon's originals. His hand-colored, engraved *Birds* surpass Audubon's watercolors in precision, clarity, and visual dynamism. Shortly after completing that project, in 1839 Havell emigrated to the United States. At first he specialized in engravings of his own topographical views, often depicting New York City or the Hudson River Valley, although he also traveled throughout the Northeast. After 1850 he apparently abandoned printmaking to devote himself to landscapes in watercolor and oil. Extending English and Dutch formulas as he contributed to the *Hudson River School, his poetic American prospects combine closely observed detail and atmosphere with expansive space. Born in Reading, as a young man Havell worked in the busy London engraving shop owned by his father and grandfather, as well as at another establishment, while in his spare time pursuing his lifelong interest in making watercolor sketches of the countryside. After arriving in New York, he lived in Brooklyn until 1842, when he moved to Sing Sing, (now Ossining), on the Hudson River. In 1857 he moved several miles south, to Tarrytown, where he died.

Havemeyer, Louisine (1855–1929). Art collector and patron. Also a suffragist. With her husband, **Henry O. Havemeyer** (1847–1907), also a collector and patron as well as a businessman, she amassed a stellar collection of old master and nineteenth-century paintings, particularly notable for its representation of modern French artists. Through donation and bequest, many of these numbered among the more than two thousand Havemeyer art objects given to the *Metropolitan Museum of

Art. A native New Yorker, Louisine Waldron Elder began making adventurous art purchases as a young woman in Paris. Guided by the expertise of her friend Mary *Cassatt, in 1875 she bought her initial contemporary works—a Degas pastel and the first Monet painting to enter an American collection. After marriage in 1883, she took the lead in acquiring the finest collection in the United States of contemporary French painting, including work by Gustave Courbet, Jean-Baptiste-Camille Corot, Jean-François Millet, Manet, Cassatt, and Cézanne. The Havemeyers also owned choice examples of work by Rembrandt, Goya, and other masters, including El Greco, then an underappreciated artist. Particularly after about 1910, she campaigned ardently for women's right to vote. She died in New York. Written around 1917, *Sixteen to Sixty: Memoirs of a Collector* was published in 1961. Also born in New York, her wealthy husband (familiarly known as Harry) worked in his family's sugar business. As a collector, he was drawn particularly to old masters and to Japanese and Chinese decorative arts, but through his wife he developed an appreciation for impressionism. They agreed jointly on all purchases, which they displayed throughout the home they completed in 1892. Louis Comfort *Tiffany and Samuel *Colman designed its sumptuous and sophisticated interiors. (Colman also masterminded the interior decor of their Connecticut country house, finished in 1890.) By the time Henry died in New York, his refineries produced nearly half the sugar used in the United States.

Their daughter, art collector Electra Havemeyer Webb (1888–1960), in 1947 founded Vermont's Shelburne Museum, which opened to the public five years later. A leading repository of American material culture, the eclectic assemblage reflects her passion for American crafts, vernacular art, and architecture. Born in Babylon, New York, on Long Island, before she turned twenty she was collecting Americana, exercising an independent taste that her parents did not understand. After marriage in 1910 to insurance executive and sportsman James Watson Webb, the couple traveled often and shuttled between several residences, including a huge Webb family estate on Lake Champlain at Shelburne. She also interested herself in civic causes. She died in a hospital in Burlington, not far from Shelburne. Situated on forty acres, the museum includes among its unconventional exhibits a covered bridge, a steamboat, a lighthouse, and more than twenty other nineteenth-century American structures, as well as significant collections of utilitarian objects such as sleighs and carriages, toys, weathervanes and whirligigs, quilts, trade signs, and cigar store figures. The Shelburne's collection includes also hundreds of paintings and sculptures by artists who worked outside the fine art mainstream. In addition, a large gallery devoted primarily to her family inheritance displays old master, American, and French impressionist paintings, along with European and Asian decorative arts.

Electra Webb's grandson, art historian and collector John Wilmerding (1938–), numbers among leading scholars of American art. Born in Boston, he was educated at Harvard University, where he completed his PhD degree in 1965. Since 1988 a professor at Princeton University, he formerly served as a curator and administrator at the *National Gallery of Art. His numerous books on American subjects include monographs on Fitz Hugh *Lane, Robert *Salmon, Winslow *Homer, and Andrew *Wyeth, as well as investigations of marine and still life painting. *American Art* (1976; 1984), a volume in the Pelican History of Art series, ranks among other important contributions. In 2004 he donated to the National Gallery about fifty items from his collection of nineteenth-century American paintings and works on paper.

Hawes, Josiah. *See* SOUTHWORTH, ALBERT SANDS.

Hawthorne, Charles Webster (1872–1930). Painter. A figure painter who straddled old and new currents in the art of his time, his work eludes narrow characterization. Like the impressionists, he generally favored scenes of leisure and domestic life. At times, especially early in his career, he employed a rugged approach more allied with the *Ashcan painters' robust examination of low-life topics. Hawthorne's technique pays homage to the painterly tradition of Frans Hals (whom he particularly admired), Velázquez, and Manet. He also appreciated the work of James Abbott McNeill *Whistler and William Merritt *Chase, his most influential teacher. Thoughtful and dignified, his mature portraits and *genre scenes combine solid structure with adroit brushwork. Born in the Midwest (while his mother visited relatives), Hawthorne grew up in Richmond, on Maine's Kennebec River. After moving to New York in 1890, he studied with George de Forest *Brush and H. Siddons *Mowbray, as well as Chase. His first trip abroad, in 1898, took him to Holland. Later, he made extended visits to Italy and Paris, and traveled widely to other locations. Hawthorne taught for many years in New York and in *Provincetown, where he founded the Cape Cod School of Art in 1899. Although his art remained untouched by modernist styles, he remained widely respected among artists for his masterful technique and the integrity of his vision. He died in a Baltimore hospital. His wife, painter **Marion Campbell Hawthorne** (1870–1945), worked chiefly in watercolor. Born in Lacon, southwest of Chicago, Ethel Marion Campbell studied at the School of the Art Institute of Chicago and with Chase before marriage in 1903. In 1938 she published *Hawthorne on Painting*, a compilation of his teaching methods. She died in New York.

Hayden, Palmer (1890–1973). Painter. An African American who depicted contemporary black life and folklore, he also painted cityscapes, seascapes, and other subjects. His best-known work, *The Janitor Who Paints* (Smithsonian American Art Museum, c. 1937), poignantly honors African-American struggles to earn creative legitimacy. In a cramped space further crowded by a prominent foreground garbage can, the artist-janitor, equipped with palette and beret, paints a mother with her child, a snoozing cat at her feet. Twelve paintings relating the legendary life of railroad-worker folk hero John Henry (California African American Museum, Los Angeles, 1944–47) constitute a major statement on the dignity of black workers and their contribution to the life of the nation. Born Peyton Cole Hedgeman in Wide Water, Virginia, he worked as a young man at numerous, mostly back-breaking jobs and served in the U.S. Army. At the age of thirty he settled in New York, determined to become an illustrator, but soon realized his true interest lay in painting. Early in 1927 he departed for five years of study and work in Paris. There he met Alain *Locke and made his earliest paintings of blacks, later the central focus of his work. After his return, he participated in *federal art projects between 1934 and 1940. He died in New York. Given the academically conventional control evident in other works, he presumably chose to favor the naive stylistic qualities often seen in his animated and sympathetic depictions of blacks. Perhaps he regarded deviations from European tradition particularly suited to African-American subjects. Although Hayden rejected the accusation that he sometimes perpetuated negative racial images, some works incorporate what appear to be pejorative stereotypes derived from white caricature. The black arts community of the time roundly condemned these images, which may have been sardonically conceived, but his intent remains unclear.

Heade, Martin Johnson (1819–1904). Painter. Known for landscapes as well as depictions of hummingbirds and flowers, early in his career he also painted portraits and a few other subjects. An idiosyncratic and aloof personality, he deviated from common lifestyle patterns of contemporaries, as he restlessly resisted acquiring a permanent address and seems not to have courted conventional routes to success. His diverse, original, and psychologically unsettling body of work obsessively treats a few themes, sometimes pursued for decades. These include marsh landscapes, hummingbirds paired with tropical flowers, and tabletop flower arrangements, usually focused on a few lush blossoms painted about natural size. He also painted numerous views across the sea from shore vantages, including several striking views of approaching storms. In addition, he published a few poems and, after 1880, more than a hundred pseudonymous articles and letters on nature and environmental subjects in *Forest and Stream*. Born with the surname Heed, he later adopted a variant spelling. He grew up in his birthplace, Lumberville, Pennsylvania, on the Delaware River, and trained in the late 1830s with Edward *Hicks in nearby Newtown. Subsequently he worked primarily as a portraitist as he adopted a nomadic existence that persisted for more than forty years. Gradually he progressed toward a more academically fluent style and undertook more varied subjects. He may have traveled in Europe in the early 1840s, and his presence is documented in Italy in 1848. After meeting Frederic *Church in New York, he turned his full attention to landscape. Among the earliest convincing expressions of his personal vision, *The Coming Storm* (Metropolitan Museum, 1859) exemplifies salient qualities of *luminism in its combination of sharp detail, measured space, reductive composition of abstracted forms, close attention to light effects, and glossy surface. Yet its foreboding tone is exceptional. Two small boats offshore on the darkened water, along with a foreground man observing the threatening conditions with his dog, symbolize vulnerability to potentially shattering forces.

Heade soon undertook a long series examining meadows, particularly the Massachusetts salt marshes. In these, under closely observed meteorological conditions, haystacks provide the measure of a flat landscape devoid of picturesque features. Late in 1863 on a visit to Brazil, Heade first painted hummingbirds. At first isolated in pairs, after 1870 he combined them with passion flowers or orchids, seen close-up against misty tropical backdrops. Subsequently he returned to South America on two occasions and also visited Central American and Caribbean sites. In addition, he traveled to London in 1865. In 1883 he first painted the Florida landscape. After briefly returning to New York, in the fall he settled permanently in St. Augustine. Much of his attention in later years was given to flower paintings, nearly all showing Cherokee roses or, more notably, magnolias, theatrically lighted as they languish in claustrophobic spaces. With their erotic overtones, intimations of transience and death, and hallucinatory hyperrealism, they remain among the most peculiar and enigmatic products of nineteenth-century American painting.

Healy, George Peter Alexander (1813–94). Painter. Internationally acclaimed for portraits, he also painted historical and documentary subjects (some including likenesses of public figures), as well as a few landscapes. He regularly crossed the Atlantic for nearly fifty years and made his home in Europe during extended periods. Although his mature style emphasized intense realism, his glittering career hinged on the cosmopolitan glamour he imparted to European royalty, American politicians, and the rich and powerful from both continents. Ambitious and industrious, in later years he fulfilled so many commissions that his painting often seemed formulaic and much influenced by the prevailing taste for the literalism of photographs, which he sometimes employed as models. Healy was born in Boston where he set up a studio while still in his teens. With encouragement from the visiting Thomas *Sully, he determined to study abroad. In 1834 he went to Paris, where some months in the studio of Antoine-Jean Gros provided his only sustained artistic education. There he met the slightly younger Thomas Couture, whose friendship and stylistic example continued to be important to Healy's development. Healy left for Italy late in 1835 and the following year settled in London, where he built a successful portrait practice. After returning to Paris in 1839, he soon gained the opportunity to paint the French king. Impressed with Healy's skills, Louis-Philippe sent him back to London and then to the United States to paint national leaders for his gallery at Versailles. Healy lost his patron in 1848 when Louis-Philippe was forced from power. In the aftermath of political upheaval, French and even English commissions were fewer, so in 1855 Healy settled in Chicago. There he reigned as the leading artist in the Midwest but also traveled widely to execute commissions. In 1867 he returned to Europe, residing in Rome from 1868 until 1872 and then in Paris for another twenty years. During this period, he continued to travel throughout Europe and frequently to the United States. In 1892 Healy returned permanently to Chicago. *Reminiscences of a Portrait Painter* was published in 1894.

Much of Healy's finest work dates to the Parisian period of the 1840s and early 1850s. Among the most alluring female likenesses of his career, the three-quarter image of visiting American *Euphemia White Van Rensselaer* (Metropolitan Museum, 1843) exemplifies his strengths. Direct and unostentatious but self-possessed and worldly, the beautifully attired young woman regards the viewer with a coquettish glance and the hint of a smile. Dramatic accents of color set off her black dress, while a hazy landscape background refers to her recent travels in Italy. By striking contrast, in 1864 Healy sketched one of the best-known images of Lincoln, who numbered among several United States presidents he painted. Healy's seated *Abraham Lincoln* (National Portrait Gallery, Washington, D.C., 1887, and other versions) is a character study showing the troubled leader resting his chin on his hand in the classic pose of meditation. Lincoln's awkwardly crossed legs and off-balance torso signify that this is no ordinary official portrait but the record of a man whose greatness transcended cultivation of a public image. A few years later, Healy reproduced this pose in *The Peacemakers* (White House Historical Association, Washington, D.C., 1868), a major historical canvas. With factual accuracy abetted by portrait photographs from Matthew *Brady's Washington studio, it depicts an important conference between Lincoln and three military leaders just before the Civil War's end. A large collaborative testimonial to the nineteenth-century American romance with Italy, *Arch of Titus* (Newark [New Jersey] Museum, 1868–71) shows the Roman monument with the Coliseum beyond, while in the foreground Frederick *Church sketches the scene as Jervis *McEntee and Healy himself observe. At middle distance, framed in the arch, stand Henry Wadsworth Longfellow and his daughter Edith. (Because the poet had already departed Rome, the Longfellow vignette was directly lifted from a photograph.) The tribute to his artist-friends was more than nominal, for Healy persuaded McEntee to paint the arch and Church, the Coliseum and sky above.

Hedrick, Wally. *See* FUNK ART.

Heizer, Michael. *See* EARTH ART.

Held, Al (1928–2005). Painter and printmaker. Known for monumental abstract paintings, Brooklyn-born Alvin Jacob Held left school at sixteen and the next year enlisted for two years in the U.S. Navy. He then studied at the *Art Students League for about a year before sailing at the end of 1949 for Paris to continue his training at the Académie de la Grande Chaumière. Abroad until 1953, he abandoned an early figurative style for abstraction that attempted to combine Mondrian's example with aspects of Jackson *Pollock's work. After his return to New York, he worked in an aggressive, gestural style indebted to Willem *de Kooning's paintings as well as Pollock's. Becoming dissatisfied in 1959 with the structural laxity of *abstract expressionism, he introduced simpler forms that dominated through the mid-1960s, as he gradually smoothed out his brushwork. Although these canvases verge upon *hard-edge painting, Held's continuing emphasis on the materiality of paint and his ready accommodation of awkward formal conjunctions produced a tenor somewhat different from the authoritative crispness of most contemporary hard-edge work. Along with close friend George *Sugarman, he emphasized structure without abandoning abstract expressionism's punch. In a major break with New York taste at that time, in 1967 Held banished color in favor of black and white, and resuscitated three-dimensional geometric volumes delineated in Renaissance perspective. From 1969, he interwove these shapes to produce complex, exhilarating spatial effects, enhanced by the enormous dimensions of his canvases. In the late 1970s color reappeared, providing epic dazzle to his visionary quest for a humanistic, heroic, even utopian form of expression. Later, skirting retinal overstimulation, he often added stripes or checkerboard patterns to the surfaces of the mathematical solids that fill his theatrical "landscape" spaces. Held also worked in several print media, including woodcut and intaglio processes. In 1956 he married avant-garde choreographer and, later, filmmaker Yvonne Rainer (1934–), who moved to New York with him from San Francisco, where he had lived during the previous year. They divorced in 1957. In 1969 he wed Toronto-born sculptor Sylvia Stone (1928–), known for large-scale Plexiglas abstractions. This relationship also ended in divorce. From 1962 until 1980 he taught at Yale University. In 1965 he bought a farm in the Catskill Mountains village of Boiceville, New York, for use as a summer retreat, and in 1988 he restored a farmhouse in the central Italian town of Todi. In the mid-1990s he left New York to divide his time between these two residences. He died in the swimming pool at his Todi home.

Heliker, John (1909–2000). Painter and draftsman. His supple, painterly landscapes, interiors, still lifes, and portraits balance representational elements with abstract design. Difficult to place among twentieth-century artists, he approached his craft with profound understanding of traditional as well as modern painting. Widely acquainted and respected among major New York painters, he also served as an important teacher. Heliker was born in Yonkers, just north of New York City, but grew up on a farm. He left high school in 1923 to spend much of his time copying old master paintings in the *Metropolitan Museum of Art. Between 1927 and 1929 he studied at the *Art Students League, where Kenneth Hayes *Miller and Thomas Hart *Benton numbered among his teachers. In subsequent years he painted landscapes chiefly, in a somewhat expressionistic style indebted also to the example of Cézanne. He departed in 1948 for an extended sojourn in Italy, the first of several visits. Drawn to light, color, and structure by the visual qualities of that country, for the next several years he emphasized abstract form in reinterpretations of Italian landscape and architecture. In the mid-1950s he developed the soft, suggestive representational approach that thereafter characterized most of his work. Characteristically, he suggested the allure of transient moments by focusing closely on a few compositional elements, while deftly implying the rest. Heliker's masterful drawings represent his sensibility in its purest form. While teaching from 1950 until 1977 at Columbia University, in 1965 he helped to found the New York Studio School, where he later also taught. For many years a summer resident of Maine, he died in a Bar Harbor health center, not far from his Cranberry Island home. Painter Robert Lewis LaHotan (1927–2002), his companion of nearly five decades, favored a delicately nuanced representational style. Born in Cleveland Heights, Ohio, he graduated from Columbia University and taught for more than thirty-five years at the Dalton School in New York. He died in Bangor, Maine.

Hendricks, Geoffrey. *See* FLUXUS.

Henri, Robert (1865–1929). Painter. A leading progressive in early twentieth-century American art, he championed the vigorous realism associated with the *Ashcan School. Henri's insistence on the unity of art and life challenged turn-of-the-century aestheticism and redirected attention to modern experience. In 1923 he published an influential collection of theories and exhortations concerning both art and life. Compiled by his student Margery Ryerson, *The Art Spirit* announces a broadly humanistic approach in the opening words: "Art when really understood is the province of every human being." Henri's idealism about individual potential and his philosophical zest for life derived largely from the American literary tradition of Emerson, Thoreau, and Whitman. Nevertheless, except for the work of Thomas *Eakins, he looked primarily to Europe for artistic models. Manet, Velázquez, and Frans Hals provided the technical basis of his mature paintings, featuring straightforward, nonsymbolic subjects depicted with energetic, sometimes flashy brushwork.

Born in Cincinnati, as a child Robert Henry Cozad moved with his family to Cozad, Nebraska, founded by his father, a real estate promoter and erstwhile riverboat gambler. Although young Henri's education was not neglected (he returned several winters to Cincinnati for schooling), his impressionable years on the frontier did much to shape his character. In 1881 the family moved to Denver. After his father killed a man during a fight on a visit to Cozad the following year, the family hurriedly departed for Atlantic City. To avoid suspicions about the Cozad surname, Robert decided to emphasize his French ancestry by adopting the name Henri, but insisted on an American pronunciation: HEN-rye. In 1886 Henri enrolled at the *Pennsylvania Academy of the Fine Arts, where he studied with Thomas *Anshutz and Thomas *Hovenden. Between 1888 and 1891 he studied for a year in Paris at the Académie Julian and the École des Beaux-Arts, traveled in Europe, and acquired an impressionist technique. Returning to Philadelphia for four years, he enrolled for further study at the academy with Robert *Vonnoh, initiated his own long teaching career, and befriended a circle of artists who met regularly in his studio. They included William *Glackens, George *Luks, Everett *Shinn, and John *Sloan. Between 1895 and 1900, Henri again worked mostly in Paris. During these years, he renounced impressionism and began to develop a darker, painterly realism.

In 1900 Henri moved permanently to New York, although he frequently traveled abroad in later years and eventually acquired a summer home in County Mayo, Ireland. Soon a presence on the city's art scene, first as a teacher and then as a crusader against the conservative art establishment, he taught almost continuously from 1902 nearly until his death, most notably for many years at the *Art Students League. His students form an illustrious roster, including, among dozens of others, George *Bellows, Stuart *Davis, and Edward *Hopper. Although critical of its conservative stance, Henri accepted membership in the *National Academy of Design in 1905. Disgruntled with the institution's policies, Henri responded by organizing an important exhibition of forward-looking artists, known as The *Eight, in 1908. Subsequently, he continued to support *independent exhibitions, including the *Armory Show. Perhaps more than any other single individual, he advanced the early twentieth century's changing climate of art discourse by opening exhibition opportunities to a wide range of viewpoints.

Henri's art from the earliest years of the twentieth century includes dark but vigorous cityscapes, such as *Street Scene with Snow* (Yale University Art Gallery, 1902), as well as somewhat brighter landscapes. Portraits and figure studies increasingly dominated from 1904. While some offer trenchant portraits, as in his likeness of *George Luks* (National Gallery of Canada, Ottawa, 1904), many present representative types or costume studies. Their chief appeal lies in a fresh and lively spirit embedded in spontaneous and energetic brushwork, which became more colorful during the 1910s. However, the art public's interest in the formal inquiries of modernism soon overtook Henri's brand of artistic radicalism. Although the new styles had little impact on his finished work, even Henri for a time experimented with small abstract studies. These reflect methods devised by Hardesty *Maratta and Jay *Hambidge for systematically achieving chromatic and compositional harmony. Although the canvases he completed after the Armory Show seemed to belong more to the past than to the future, his idealistic faith in individual expression remains a cornerstone of art practice to this day.

In 1908 Henri married graphic artist and watercolor painter Marjorie Organ (1886–1931). Born in Ireland, she moved with her family to New York in 1899 and while still a teenager launched a successful career as New York's first woman newspaper cartoonist. Along with her husband, she, too, exhibited in the Armory Show.

Henry, Edward Lamson (1841–1919). Painter. A *genre specialist, he is remembered particularly for examples set in the past. Idealizing traditional values, he recreated particular events, as well as typical experiences. His sensitivity to light, space, and atmosphere complements a meticulously detailed technique and devotion to observational accuracy. Something of an antiquarian at heart, Henry led architectural preservation efforts and collected old-fashioned artifacts, including paintings, furniture, clothing, and carriages. In his quest to preserve the past and to achieve convincing illusions in his paintings, Henry made photographic studies of buildings, objects, and people. Although his exacting realism seemed dated before the end of the nineteenth century, his paintings and the reproductive prints they generated remained popular. Both scholarly and freshly imagined, the images contributed to the era's enthusiasm for American history, particularly the colonial and federal periods. Born in Charleston, South Carolina, Henry was orphaned as a young child. He lived with relatives in New York from 1848 and entered the *Pennsylvania Academy of the Fine Arts in 1858. Two years later, he left for Europe, where he studied in Paris with Charles Gleyre and Gustave Courbet but also traveled widely. After his return in 1862, he lived in New York. He made three later trips abroad. While spending several months with the Union Army in Virginia during 1864, he completed many sketches documenting military activities. Among resulting paintings, *Westover Mansion* (Corcoran Gallery, 1869) presents a poignant record of the well-known eighteenth-century residence occupied by northern troops. From the early 1870s he summered in Cragsmoor, an artists' colony he helped to found in New York's Shawangunk Mountains. After building a house in 1883, he often remained most of the year, and died there. Many of Henry's paintings provide documentary records of buildings in New York and Philadelphia. Signaling the artist's fascination with modes of transportation, these views vibrate with carriages, streetcars, and horses, as well as pedestrians. This interest came to fruition in a series of paintings of trains and stations. Despite their technological slant, many are historical scenes, depicting particular railroading events of some fifty or sixty years earlier. Henry's warm appreciation for the nation's past also animates such nostalgic scenes as the ambitious *Colonial Wedding* (Warner Collection, Gulf States Paper Corporation, Tuscaloosa, Alabama, 1911), with its jewel-like surface, lively crowd in period costume, and incidental details of architecture, farm implements, and boats.

Herter, Albert. *See* OSSORIO, ALFONSO.

Herter, Adele McGinnis. *See* OSSORIO, ALFONSO.

Hess, Thomas B. *See* ABSTRACT EXPRESSIONISM.

Hesse, Eva (1936–70). Sculptor and painter. Among the most innovative and influential artists of the late 1960s, she infused *minimalism with expressive and allusive powers while maintaining its formal and conceptual rigor and its unsentimental probity of spirit. Her unorthodox sculptural materials featured soft and malleable substances. In themselves, these posed a challenge to traditional assumptions about the rigid nature of sculpture, even as they also suggested metaphors for the body or for the unstable nature of inner life. Embracing contradictions, Hesse's offbeat sculptures variously evoke order, confusion, sexual desire, loneliness, tenderness, and rage. Hesse was born in Hamburg. Fearing Nazi persecution, her parents sent her as a toddler to an orphanage in Amsterdam, but the family reunited and left for New York in 1939. She was naturalized as a citizen in 1945. Hesse's uneasy beginnings were compounded in childhood. When she was nine, her parents divorced, and the following year her mother committed suicide. The introspective artist wrestled all her life with anxieties about her own history, her personal identity, and the expression of her individuality. She studied at the Pratt Institute in Brooklyn, the *Art Students League, and Cooper Union before entering Yale University in 1957. During the following two years, she completed a BFA in painting. After moving back to New York, in 1961 she married Ohio-born sculptor Tom Doyle (1928–   ), who had earned BFA and MFA degrees from Ohio State University. Known especially for large-scale abstract works, he remains an emeritus professor at Queens College where he taught for more than twenty years prior to his retirement in 1992.

In the early 1960s Hesse struggled in paintings and drawings with the conflicts between representation and abstraction, as she also explored the possibilities of her craft with attention to formal and technical issues. When Doyle received an offer of working space in the vicinity of Düsseldorf in 1964, Hesse accompanied him to Germany. While residing there, they also traveled in Europe, and Hesse began work as a sculptor, starting with a sequence of reliefs. After she and Doyle returned in the summer of 1965, they lived almost separate lives, but her sculpture quickly advanced. She also resumed a friendship with Sol *LeWitt, who remained a great source of encouragement and introduced her to many of the important younger artists active in New York. Early in 1966 she completed *Hang Up* (Art Institute of Chicago), which she later regarded as her first mature sculpture, approvingly citing its "absurdity." The ungainly *Hang Up* foretells many salient qualities of the work from Hesse's remaining four years. Combining the rectangularity of a wall-mounted square with flaccid tubing that loops out from it, the sculpture acknowledges the minimalist embrace of form while at the same time reacting against it. Further confounding straightforward readings, the square, framelike element is covered with cloth, which softens its impact, while the tube is simultaneously organic, industrial, medical, and sexual. In subsequent work, Hesse often employed minimalist devices such as gridded compositions and modular forms but characteristically subverted them with soft edges, evident handwork, and other contrasting elements. She incorporated a wide variety of idiosyncratic, often synthetic, and sometimes impermanent materials, such as swags of string, prickly wire webs, latex, molded fiberglass, and rubber. These highlighted her drive for an individual form of expression, promoted the period's interest in overturning traditions, played on the tension between art and non-art, and contributed a sensuous materiality. Symptoms of the brain tumor that caused her death appeared as early as 1968, just as her career reached fruition. In 1969 two surgeries, radiation, and chemotherapy failed to produce a cure, but despite illness she continued to work productively. While deflecting physical and emotional pain into her art, she avoided confessional, or even directly autobiographical content. More or less an invalid after a third brain operation in March 1970, she died two months later. Although Hesse deferred explicitly feminist intentions to an ambition for excellence, she nevertheless soon served as a beacon for a generation of female artists seeking in the 1970s to incorporate into their work, as she had, their physical and psychological experiences as women.

Hesselius, Gustavus (1682–1755). Painter. The leading artist in the mid-Atlantic colonies during the first half of the eighteenth century, in 1712 he arrived in Philadelphia as a trained artist. For several years after 1719 or 1720, he lived in Maryland but then returned permanently to Philadelphia. In addition to portraits, his chief subjects, he is known to have painted religious scenes, which number among the earliest colonial examples. Similarly, his two surviving mythological subjects may have been the earliest classical works executed in North America. As was the custom among painters of the period, he also accepted varied decorative tasks. Born in Falun, Sweden, Hesselius lived in also Folkarna and Uppsala before spending several months in London on his way to America. Like other colonial portraitists, he derived poses and settings from imported engravings, but his familiarity with late Baroque tradition enabled him to integrate such borrowings more seamlessly than did less technically skilled contemporaries. Although he sometimes drew awkwardly, he convincingly rendered texture, atmosphere, and three-dimensional form. Quite remarkably for their time, his best portraits transcend physical description to capture the individual personalities of his sitters. In 1735 he painted bust-length images of the careworn Delaware Indian chiefs *Tishcohan* and *Lapowinsa* (both Historical Society of Pennsylvania, Philadelphia), who had come to Philadelphia to negotiate a land dispute. Thought to be the first objective renderings of America's indigenous peoples, these dignified portrayals capture an inner life as well as respectfully observed details of physiognomy and costume. About five years later, Hesselius painted unostentatious half-length pendants of himself and his wife, Lydia (both Historical Society of Pennsylvania, Philadelphia), in middle age. His thoughtful visage reflects the character of a man known to have been devoutly religious, as well as interested in science and music. As she alertly appraises the viewer, his visibly intelligent and warmhearted spouse gives a hint of a mischievous smile. Probably no other painter in the colonies at this time could so effectively have rendered a fleeting expression. Hesselius was apparently inactive as a painter after about 1750, perhaps entering retirement so his son could take over the business.

John Hesselius (1728–78), also a portrait painter, worked in the mid-Atlantic colonies and Virginia. Probably born in Philadelphia, he presumably trained with his father but was attracted to the up-to-date styles of Robert *Feke and John *Wollaston. John Hesselius's mature work displays smooth surfaces, clear colors, decorative embellishments, and sprightly animation, but his figures often seem woodenly posed, and he rarely approached Gustavus's ability to suggest the psychology of his sitters. Nevertheless, he attracted a stylish clientele, and more than a hundred of his portraits survive. Sometime around 1760 he moved to Maryland, where he subsequently resided in the vicinity of Annapolis. In 1763 he married a wealthy widow and settled on a large estate but continued occasionally to travel to paint portraits. *Charles Calvert and His Servant* (Baltimore Museum of Art, 1761) characterizes his strengths, although the juxtaposition of a five-year-old subject with a subserviently positioned, young black slave may jar contemporary sensibilities. Posed in the grand manner before an atmospheric landscape, young Calvert is a pretty child in van Dyck–style finery, including adroitly rendered feather plumes, laces, ribbons, and sumptuous fabrics. John Hesselius's late work sometimes shows increased realism in his approach to appearance and character.

Hicks, Edward (1780–1849). Painter. Known particularly for more than sixty versions of *The Peaceable Kingdom*, he devoted much of his art to his Quaker faith. He also produced historical subjects, landscapes, and farm scenes. Born in Attleborough (now Langhorne), Pennsylvania, he continued to reside in Bucks County throughout most of his life. Orphaned as a toddler, Hicks was brought up by the Quaker Twining family, whose farm numbered among several he later pictured. Upon completion of a seven-year apprenticeship to a coach maker, in 1801 he moved to Milford, near the state's northeastern corner, where he soon branched out from carriage painting into ornamental and sign painting. About 1810 he returned to Bucks County, established a shop in Newtown, and two years later became a Quaker preacher. Although successful, he nevertheless turned to farming for a living between 1814 and 1820 in an attempt to resolve the contradiction between his worldly, aesthetic impulses and his religious convictions. After failing at agriculture, he expanded his career as a utilitarian painter to include easel painting as well. During the following three decades, he executed dozens of *Peaceable Kingdoms*. Based on a passage in Isaiah, the theme of man and animals living in harmony appealed to his Quaker pacifism. The *Kingdoms* vary in detail, but all present a visionary ensemble of wild and domestic animals gathered together in peace with human infants. The serious, wide-eyed gaze of ferocious beasts adds to the charm of these technically unsophisticated, yet compelling scenes. Many versions include a background vignette of William Penn negotiating with Indians, suggesting Hicks's belief in Penn's Quaker realm as a parallel fulfillment of the biblical prophecy. For the composition of this subsidiary scene, Hicks relied on a print of Benjamin *West's *William Penn's Treaty with the Indians* (Pennsylvania Academy, 1771–72), but this instance of borrowing was not unusual. Nearly all Hicks's imaginary subjects, including the conception of his signature theme, rely on prints or illustrations for inspiration. Until his final years, his style and technique continued to evolve toward a more proficient, conventionally academic standard. He died at his home in Newtown, the day after completing a final *Peaceable Kingdom*. His *Memoirs of the Life and Religious Labours of Edward Hicks* (1851) appeared posthumously.

He provided early training for painter **Thomas Hicks** (1823–90), a cousin, but Thomas moved on from his artisanal origins to become a well-patronized New York portraitist. He also painted landscapes, *genre scenes, and, infrequently, still lifes. Born in Newtown, he studied at the *Pennsylvania Academy of the Fine Arts and the *National Academy of Design. Between 1845 and 1849 he lived in Europe, spending most of three years in Italy before studying for a year in Paris with Thomas Couture. Subsequently his successful New York studio attracted many prominent clients. His full-length official portrait of *Hamilton Fish* (City of New York, 1852) exemplifies the direct realism and attention to material surroundings that appealed to mid-nineteenth-century patrons. He died at his country home near Trenton Falls in upstate New York.

Higgins, Dick. *See* FLUXUS.

Higgins, Eugene (1874–1958). Painter and printmaker. Known especially for depictions of poor and laboring city dwellers, Higgins studied in Kansas City, his birthplace, before traveling to Paris for additional training at the Académie Julian and the École des Beaux-Arts. Abroad, he adapted the tradition of Daumier, Millet, and other French social commentators in depictions of the outcast and downtrodden. As he found recognition for his grim pessimism, in 1904 the well-known satirical magazine *Assiette au beurre* devoted an entire issue to his drawings. Returning to the United States later in that year, Higgins soon settled permanently in New York, where he turned his sympathetic gaze on its less fortunate inhabitants. His lower-class subject matter paralleled interests of the *Ashcan School. However, in contrast to their characteristically vivacious and even optimistic attitude, Higgins's work typically suggests hopelessness and helplessness. Rarely depicting specific individuals, his paintings generalize and symbolize social conditions. He exhibited his work in the *Armory Show and during the Depression, painted two murals for *federal art projects. For some years he maintained a second studio in *Old Lyme, Connecticut. From 1906 until 1917 he was married to Mabel *Dwight.

Higgins, Victor. *See* TAOS ARTISTS' COLONY

Hill, Gary. *See* VIDEO ART.

Hill, John William (1812–79). Painter and printmaker. Along with his father and son, also artists, he did much to popularize and sustain American interest in landscape art. Chiefly a watercolorist, he also recorded urban scenes, rural pursuits, and still lifes. Born in London, Hill emigrated as a child to Philadelphia. In 1822 the family moved to New York, where he became a capable engraver while working in his father's shop. Most of his early work records city views or rural activity, such as scenes along the Erie Canal. In 1833 Hill visited London, and later he traveled widely in the United States. From 1836 he made his home in the area of the Hudson River town of Nyack. Between 1836 and 1841 he worked as a topographical artist for the New York State Geological Survey, and in the 1840s he visited many American cities to produce views for publication. After developing an interest around 1850 in the writings of English aesthetician John Ruskin, he more often turned to pure landscape or to still life. Subsequent vibrantly detailed, delicately stippled watercolors exemplify the skill, sensitivity, and reverence for nature associated with American *Pre-Raphaelitism. Hill's most innovative works blur the categories of landscape and still life by presenting in natural surroundings flowers, fruits, or other subjects normally associated with still life.

His father, **John Hill** (1770–1850), was an expert engraver whose aquatints enhance two of the earliest compilations of landscape views: Joshua *Shaw's *Picturesque Views of American Scenery* (1819–21) and William Guy *Wall's *Hudson River Portfolio* (1821–25). Born in London, he enjoyed a successful career as a printmaker there before settling in Philadelphia in 1816. After moving to New York, he continued to collaborate as a printmaker with important painters, while also producing drawings and watercolors. Following his retirement, he lived for the last decade or so of his life in the vicinity of Nyack, where he died. John William Hill's son, painter and etcher **John Henry Hill** (1839–1922), extended his father's interests in landscape and in watercolor. From his earliest work, he shared his father's interest in tightly detailed Pre-Raphaelitism, although he later softened his technique somewhat. His many seemingly artless works effect a lively freshness as they also serve his empirical bent. Born in the Nyack area, John Henry Hill died there as well. Trained as an artist by his father, he made three trips to Europe, to London in 1864–65 and 1878 and to the Continent in 1879. In 1868 he painted scenes of the West while on a government expedition led by Clarence King, but most of his works depict locations in New England or New York State, particularly Lake George. His 1867 etching portfolio, *Sketches from Nature*, advanced firsthand observation of nature as the basis of art. In 1888 he published a brief biography, *John William Hill: An Artist's Memorial*, illustrated with etchings of his father's work.

Hill, Thomas (1829–1908). Painter. Known particularly for grandiose landscapes of the American West, particularly the Yosemite area, he also painted more intimate forest scenes. In addition, he produced New England scenes, portraits, *genre works, and still lifes. His light-filled, freshly observed oil studies, which he often sold as finished works, helped to popularize outdoor painting in California. Hill was born in Birmingham, England. In 1844 he emigrated to Taunton, Massachusetts, with his family, including his brother, **Edward Hill** (1843–1923), who later specialized in painting New Hampshire's White Mountain scenery. (He died in Hood River, Oregon, after moving west in later years.) Both brothers initially trained as artisans, painting coaches, furniture, and interiors. As a young man in Boston, Thomas came to admire *Hudson River School painting. In 1853 he moved to Philadelphia, where he studied at the *Pennsylvania Academy of the Fine Arts and achieved some recognition as a portrait and still life painter. After two years, he returned to Massachusetts but left in 1861 for San Francisco. Recent views by Carleton *Watkins and Albert *Bierstadt probably motivated his subsequent visits to the Yosemite Valley. In 1866 Hill departed for Paris, where he encountered *Barbizon landscape painting. Returning the following year with a richer and more painterly technique, he settled in Boston. There he generated regional views but also used earlier sketches to paint ambitious depictions of the West. *Great Canyon of the Sierras—Yosemite* (Crocker Art Museum, Sacramento, California, 1871), a 6 × 10-foot panoramic vista features detailed rocks and vegetation leading into an imposing vastness bathed in warm, slightly hazy light. Following another California sojourn of some months, in the fall of 1872 he moved there permanently. He later journeyed east several times to paint in New England and also ranged through other areas of the western United States, as well as to Alaska and Mexico. In the 1870s he numbered among leading figures in San Francisco's art community. Later he often worked for extended periods in the southern part of the state, while also maintaining ties to Yosemite. In the mid-1880s he established a summer studio at Wawona, near what became the southern entrance to the park when the area was put under federal protection in 1890. There he turned out somewhat formulaic views of Yosemite's rugged rock formations and waterfalls, varied by shifts in point of view and in the activities of diminutive figures that typically enliven his landscapes. Consistently true to the majestic features of the area, these paintings employ a loosening brushstroke but remain grounded in observation of light, atmosphere, and foreground detail. He often wintered in the San Joaquin Valley town of Raymond, where he died after a decade of reduced activity caused by ill health. His sons **Edward Rufus Hill** (1852–1908) and **Thomas Virgil Troyon Hill** (1871–1922) also worked as painters.

Hine, Lewis Wickes (1874–1940). Photographer. A documentarian, he is known for themes of labor and immigration. His touching photographs of young factory workers influenced passage of laws regulating child labor. Born in Oshkosh, Wisconsin, Hine studied at a local college before enrolling in 1900 for a year at the University of Chicago. He then moved to New York, where he taught at the progressive Ethical Culture School. He also earned an education degree from New York University in 1905 and subsequently pursued graduate work in sociology at Columbia University. Hine initially turned to photography as a teaching tool, but his interest in social issues soon led him beyond the classroom. Although Hine had no training in the visual arts, he achieved aesthetically informed results by consciously emulating the compositional principles of traditional painting. Hine's principal subject—indeed, very nearly his only subject—remained the life of the individual in relation to the forces of modern industrialism. Although fundamentally optimistic about the future of machines in improving human life, Hine fumed at abuses the industrial system inflicted on the powerless. His photographs generally achieve more forthright and less romanticized effects than contemporaneous *Ashcan School paintings that similarly portray the poor with sympathy. Widely published as illustrations in newspapers, magazines, books, and pamphlets, Hine's images numbered among the most efficacious of the Progressive era.

Hine's early photography included a notable series on immigrants, taken at Ellis Island and in the New York neighborhoods where they settled. After he left teaching in 1908, he worked for the National Child Labor Committee, traveling widely to record the lives of children, primarily in their work environments. In these, he portrayed his young subjects as dignified but vulnerable individuals wasting their lives in dehumanizing work routines. In 1918 he went to Europe with the Red Cross. There, in the last months of World War I and the early months of the peace that followed, he recorded damage and misery in the wake of war across France, Belgium, and southeastern Europe. During the 1920s he focused on workers in relation to industrial production in the United States. In 1930–31 this topic culminated in a notable series documenting construction of the Empire State Building. Often exalting the individual, Hine's worker subjects appeared in an extended photo-essay, *Men at Work: Photographic Studies of Modern Men and Machines* (1932). During the Depression, he worked for the Tennessee Valley Authority and other government agencies, accomplishing his most compelling work of these years in rural and small-town Tennessee, Kentucky, and Arkansas. Like the *Farm Security Administration photographers and the regionalists among the *American Scene painters, Hine found solace in the endurance of ordinary people. He died in a Dobbs Ferry hospital, not far from his longtime home in Hastings-on-Hudson, north of New York.

Hirsch, Joseph (1910–81). Painter, printmaker, and draftsman. Like other social realists associated with the *American Scene movement, he affirmed the value of the individual beset by social and economic stresses. *The Prisoner* (Whitney Museum, 1942) sympathetically depicts a German prisoner of war under interrogation. Authority is represented only by the hands of a questioner, writing on a clipboard in the foreground. Facing him, the defeated soldier in uniform bleakly responds without making eye contact. In other works, Hirsch sometimes satirized self-important elites, such as businessmen, implicitly condemning their soulnessness. Born in Philadelphia, Hirsch studied at the Philadelphia Museum School (now University of the Arts) before going to New York where he worked with George *Luks in 1932. Soon afterward, he was employed by *federal art projects, for which he completed three mural commissions in Philadelphia. In 1943–44, he served as a World War II artist-correspondent in Italy, Africa, and the South Pacific. Hirsch's later work combines realistic observation and colorful patterning to examine varied experiences. *Invocation* (Butler Institute of American Art, Youngstown, Ohio, 1966–69) focuses on the individuals playing official roles in a college graduation ceremony. He died at his home in New York.

Hirsch, Stefan (1899–1964). Painter and draftsman. Known for poetic, detailed realism, he was born in Nuremberg to American parents, grew up in Europe, and enrolled at the University of Zurich in 1917. There he knew the dada painters and writers before he moved to New York in 1919. Dreamily interpreting the ideas of *precisionism, *Mill Town* (Phillips Collection, c. 1924–25) displays the standard features of that approach: an urban and industrial theme, simplified forms, hard edges, smooth surfaces. But with a pale red sun hanging in a brownish (perhaps polluted) sky and a black river sweeping past, the view takes on an otherworldly tone foreign to the central achievements of precisionism. Other paintings more clearly demonstrate interests in surrealism and in naive painting. A fine draftsman, Hirsch produced delicate and animated flowers and other subjects. Sponsored by a *federal art project, his mural for the courthouse in Aiken, South Carolina, initiated one of the bitterest controversies of the federal programs. Because of its modernist characteristics, townspeople reviled *Justice as Protector and Avenger* (1938). Eventually, the work was covered with a velvet drape and shown only upon request. For his trouble, Hirsch was rewarded in 1943 with another commission in yet another small southern town, Boonville, Mississippi. This time he painted a central panel showing pieces of mail wafting through the air above a stack of packages. On either side of this postal conceit, World War II soldiers and their loved ones at home read or write letters. No one protested this imagery. Hirsch taught for nearly two decades before his retirement in 1961 at Bard College in Annandale-on Hudson, New York. He died in New York after a protracted illness.

Hirshfield, Morris (1872–1946). Painter. Untrained as an artist, he turned to painting in 1937, upon retirement from the garment industry, and produced only seventy-seven known works. However, his imaginative visions almost immediately found favor in the New York art world. Surrealist leader André Breton spoke admiringly of his work, and in 1943 the *Museum of Modern Art honored his achievement with a solo exhibition. Although he labored over realistic detail, a spirit of fantasy pervades his patterned compositions. His most popular works offer naively rendered nude females in stylized settings. *Inseparable Friends* (Museum of Modern Art, 1941) depicts two paper-doll women holding hands as they approach a decoratively edged mirror that reflects one of them. A stylized potted plant and two pairs of fancy high-heeled shoes complete the foreground, while a flattened swag of drapery fills the upper part of the canvas. Among other subjects, Hirshfield particularly favored animals, which he often adapted from children's book illustrations. Born in the Polish sector of Russia, he moved permanently to New York in 1890.

Hirshhorn, Joseph H. (1899–1981). Collector and museum founder. Also a financier. In 1966 he donated some six thousand works to the nation, establishing Washington, D.C.'s Hirshhorn Museum and Sculpture Garden, a unit of the *Smithsonian Institution. Focused primarily on twentieth-century art, the collection boasts particular distinction in its holdings of sculpture, which include also examples of nineteenth-century work. Artists represented in particular depth include Thomas *Eakins, David *Smith, and Willem *de Kooning, as well as British sculptor Henry Moore. Designed by architect Gordon Bunshaft of Skidmore, Owings and Merrill, the circular museum building on the Mall opened in 1974. Hirshhorn contributed a million dollars to its federally financed construction. Born in the village of Jukst, near Mitau (now Jelgava), Russia (now Latvia), Joseph Herman Choneh Hirshhorn arrived in New York in 1907. He grew up in poverty in Brooklyn, left school at twelve or thirteen, and began to amass his fortune through shrewd stock investments before he was twenty. Later he expanded his interests into gold and uranium mining in Canada. In the 1930s he started collecting seriously, beginning with living American artists (concern for their welfare heightened his passion for their work), mostly those associated with the *American Scene movement, along with impressionist and other European paintings. From 1947 until 1955 he was married to painter and printmaker Lily Harmon (1912–1998), known primarily for figural works, especially portraits. In 1948 he sold his European paintings to concentrate on subsequent interests: recent art, American art of the early twentieth century, and sculpture from the mid-nineteenth century on. Hirshhorn maintained an estate in Greenwich, Connecticut, and later lived in Naples, Florida, as well as in Washington, where he died. Including a final bequest, he eventually nearly doubled the number of works of art in his original gift. He left the museum free to acquire or de-accession works. His widow, **Olga Hirshhorn** (1920–), an enthusiastic participant in her husband's collecting activities after they married in 1964, maintains a small art collection and an active interest in the Washington art community. She continues to reside also in Naples, while summering on Martha's Vineyard.

Hirst, Claude Raguet (1855–1942). Painter. The only woman among significant late-nineteenth-century trompe-l'oeil still life specialists, she sensitively adapted William *Harnett's tabletop groupings of books, objets d'art, antiques, and other costly bric-a-brac. Interestingly, she often included items such as pipes, tobacco, and matches, which at that time signified a masculine realm. Although most of her works are small, as suits the watercolor medium she preferred, she overcame its challenges to achieve astonishing verisimilitude. Born in Cincinnati and named Claudine, she grew up in the suburb of Clayton, Ohio. In the 1870s she studied at the University of Cincinnati's art school (now the Art Academy of Cincinnati) before moving to New York, where she worked privately with several artists. In early work, she concentrated on fruit and flower compositions. Soon after Harnett returned from Europe in 1886, Hirst abruptly switched to arrangements of man-made artifacts. No doubt his influence was direct and personal, as he occupied a neighboring studio on Fourteenth Street. Although she exhibited regularly for several decades, at the time of her death in New York she lived in obscure poverty. In 1901 Hirst married landscape painter William Crothers Fitler (1857–1915), a *tonalist known for poetic interpretations of nature, primarily in watercolor and monotype. Born in Philadelphia, he studied at the *Pennsylvania Academy of the Fine Arts before settling permanently in New York around 1880.

Hitchcock, George (1850–1913). Painter. Living abroad during most of his career, he became known for Dutch landscapes and peasant scenes, some with religious overtones. Despite his Netherlandish subjects, he worked to satisfy the interests and tastes of Paris, where he regularly and successfully exhibited. With time, his realist style veered toward the bright colors and brilliant sunlight of impressionism. Born in Providence, Rhode Island, he graduated from Brown University in 1872 and received a law degree from Harvard two years later. While subsequently in practice in Providence and New York, he painted watercolors. In 1879 he left for Europe, where he studied in London, Paris, Düsseldorf, and The Hague. The first of many American painters attracted to the picturesque village of Egmond-aan-Zee, on the North Sea about twenty-five miles from Amsterdam, he began working there in the early 1880s. Although he often spent winters in Paris and occasionally visited the United States, he maintained a studio in Egmond for the rest of his life and died not far away at Marken. Between the mid-1880s and mid-1890s, an aura of religious devotion often suffused his images of peasants, relating these works to the period's romantic attribution of piety and virtue to unsophisticated people. *Blessed Mother* (Cleveland Museum of Art, 1892) conflates a Dutch maid and her infant with the Virgin in an ambiguous yet moving conception of female purity. Hieratically "enthroned" on a heavy wood chair idiosyncratically placed in a sunlit, flower-filled meadow, the young Madonna gazes solemnly but expectantly ahead. Only an unobtrusive, translucent halo, rising just above her lacy head covering, refers overtly to spiritual content. Later he abandoned such subjects to concentrate on straightforward views of the colorful, flower-filled fields of Holland.

Hockney, David (1937–). Painter, printmaker, draftsman, photographer, and theatrical designer. First known for a personal variant of *pop art, he later produced inventive photographic collages and high-spirited, expressionistic landscapes. Since the mid-1970s he has also designed acclaimed theatrical productions. Responsive to currents of his time, his multifarious and unpredictable practice nevertheless maintains a dialogue with masters of the modern tradition, principally Picasso, but also Matisse and others. Born in Bradford, England, Hockney began his training at the Bradford School of Art in 1953. Upon leaving in 1957 he worked for two years in hospitals to fulfill his national service requirement as a conscientious objector. In 1959 he began three years of study at the Royal College of Art in London. There he continued to refine his facility as a draftsman, but also experimented with abstraction before turning to a more individual form of expression allied to British pop art. He quickly established his singular artistic identity with paintings on the theme of homosexual love, rendered in a pseudo-naive style, often with graffiti-like inscriptions. Sixteen etchings collectively titled *A Rake's Progress* (1961–63) announced his arrival as a major printmaker. Inspired by William Hogarth's well-known eighteenth-century set of the same name, they comprise an autobiographical reinterpretation of the theme. He also has worked with lithography and has illustrated a number of books.

Hockney visited New York during the summer of 1961. The Los Angeles area has been his home most of the time since his first sojourn there late in 1963. For nearly three decades he has resided in the hills above Hollywood, although he continues to travel widely and frequently. California's glamour, sunshine, brilliant colors, and unaffected hedonism stimulated a new phase in his art. Switching from oil to acrylic, he create large, flatly painted, emotionally cool paeans to the sybaritic life amid palm trees and swimming pools. Often based on snapshot photographs, these include particularly successful portraits that connect a way of life with individual character. His stage work allowed full reign to his penchant for stylistic frolics, as he fancifully reimagined settings and costumes, particularly for opera. A serious interest in photography and the possibilities of varied processes dates from the 1970s. This activity culminated in several hundred scintillating cubistic collages fabricated from instant color prints. His analysis in these of landscape space, as well as the synthesis of memory and optical experience, led in turn to a number of enormous, panoramic, painted landscapes that immerse the viewer in brilliantly hued, sometimes vertiginous reconstituted environments. Hockney has published a number of books concerning aspects of his work. *David Hockney by David Hockney* (1976) and *That's the Way I See It* (1993) rank as the most substantive. Claiming that great artists of the past used mechanical aids to capture accurate likenesses, *Secret Knowledge: Rediscovering the Lost Techniques of the Old Masters* (2001) instigated an art historical uproar.

Hoffman, Malvina (1885–1966). Sculptor. A specialist in portraits and ballet subjects, she is particularly remembered for a series of ethnographic studies. Born in New York, Malvina Cornell Hoffman studied painting and sculpture with John White *Alexander, Herbert *Adams, Gutzon *Borglum, and George Grey *Barnard before first traveling to Europe in 1910. In Paris she worked as Janet *Scudder's assistant and studied with Rodin before returning to New York the following year. Traveling again to Paris in 1914, she made the acquaintance of ballerina Anna Pavlova and other Russian dancers, who inspired many pieces. A tinted wax head of Pavlova (Metropolitan Museum, 1924) combines naturalistic and decorative elements in a sensuous and lifelike icon, while in numerous other works she depicted this dancer and others in motion. In 1930 Chicago's Field Museum of Natural History commissioned Hoffman to produce more than one hundred representations (most are in bronze) of the world's peoples. In preparation for this task, Hoffman traveled widely, but she produced most of the pieces in Paris, where she maintained a studio for many years. Although this project inadvertently reinforces racial stereotypes, the series was enthusiastically received when installed in the Hall of Man between 1933 and 1935. Casts were widely exhibited, along with related figures and ensembles based on her research. She died in her New York studio. Autobiographical reflections appear in *Heads and Tales* (1936), *A Sculptor's Odyssey* (1937), and *Yesterday Is Tomorrow: A Personal History* (1965). A technical work, *Sculpture Inside and Out* (1939), foregrounds her competence in sculptural processes.

Hofmann, Hans (1880–1966). Painter. A renowned teacher who influenced the development of many mid-twentieth-century abstract artists, he produced stylistically varied paintings, typically emphasizing brilliant color, painterly technique, and vigorous composition. His example contributed substantially to the genesis and reputation of *abstract expressionism. As the most important Paris-trained European to live and work in the United States at length during the modern era, he represented to Americans the aesthetic sophistication of Continental culture. Dating mostly to the 1950s, his most distinctive paintings feature monochrome rectangles floating amid gestural brushwork. Born Johann Georg Albert Hofmann in the Bavarian town of Weissenberg, he moved with his family to Munich in 1886. At sixteen he was employed by the Bavarian public works director. During the following two years he contributed inventions to engineering and architectural projects, but in 1898 he abandoned science to begin art studies in Munich. While working with several teachers, he adopted impressionist and then postimpressionist styles for his early work. From 1904 until 1914 he studied and worked in Paris, where he made the acquaintance of leading artists, including Picasso, Matisse, and most importantly, Robert Delaunay. During this period he maintained contact with progressive artists in Germany, as he continued to visit and exhibit in his native country. Although he never met Kandinsky, Hofmann held his work and theories in high regard. The exact nature of Hofmann's achievement during his decade of immersion in fauvism, cubism, and expressionism remains obscure because nearly all of his work from this time disappeared during World War I. When the conflict broke out, he happened to be in Germany and was prevented from returning to Paris; health problems allowed him to avoid military service. Instead, in Munich he opened a school, which became well-known internationally in the 1920s, even attracting Americans such as Carl *Holty, Alfred *Jensen, and Louise *Nevelson. The demands of teaching prevented much painting during these years, although he continued to draw. Through visits to Paris, he also remained informed about continuing developments there.

Hofmann first visited the United States during the summer of 1930, when he taught at the University of California at Berkeley. After another visit to California the following year, in 1932 he accepted a position at the *Art Students League and moved permanently to New York, becoming an American citizen in 1941. In 1933 he opened the Hans Hofmann School of Fine Arts and two years later began regularly conducting summer classes in *Provincetown, on Cape Cod. He counted among his students numerous prominent artists, including Helen *Frankenthaler, *Lee Krasner, and Larry *Rivers, as well as many members of *American Abstract Artists, such as Burgoyne *Diller. Hofmann's teaching stressed the interaction of nature, theory, and paint on a two-dimensional surface, their relationships determined by intuitive rather than logical means. He believed in the spiritual content of painting but also insisted on drawing from observation. With time, he assigned an increasing role to color as the primary element of structure. His formulation of "push-pull" as the means of realizing plasticity on a flat surface became the most widely known aspect of his teaching. This approach to a painting's internal dynamic, independent of representation, gave direction to students who grappled with the problem of creating modern art that maintained the optical authority invested in traditional painting, as passed down through Cézanne and his successors.

During the 1930s, despite continued immersion in teaching, Hofmann also returned actively to painting. At first, he favored stylized representation in portraits, still lifes, and landscapes indebted to Matisse. By the early 1940s the abstracting impulse predominated, as he was drawn toward the *automatism associated with surrealism. In some works he employed a drip technique that prefigured a method associated with Jackson *Pollock's breakthrough *all-over compositions. Through Krasner, the two became acquainted, and during the early 1940s mutual influences can be traced in their approaches to form and interests in mythic subjects. By the end of the 1940s Hofmann had begun to formulate his characteristic variation on abstract expressionist practice. Marked by rigorous concern for structure and lyric feeling for color, these works contrast the severity of geometric shape with magisterial, emotionally resonant hues and sensuous materiality. During the final few years of his career, the paintings tended toward looser organization. Never formulaic, his work of every period demonstrated stylistic variety born of the artist's desire to achieve visual equivalents of the intuitive inner life. After relinquishing teaching in 1958, as he neared eighty, Hofmann painted prolifically nearly until his death. In *Creation in Form and Color*, begun in 1904 but not completed (and translated into English by Glenn Wessels) until 1931, Hofmann set forth basic principles. *The Search for the Real, and Other Essays* appeared in 1948.

Hogue, Alexandre (1898–1994). Painter. Known especially for desolate Depression-era landscapes, he later responded to the inhabitants, environmental concerns, and spiritual dimensions of the Southwest. Hogue's hard, unforgiving stylization well suited the bleak vision of his Dust Bowl scenes. In *Drouth Stricken Area* (Dallas Museum of Art, 1934), vultures await as a pathetically skinny cow poses inertly by an empty water tank while sand dunes engulf a nearby farmhouse. Although not motivated by a political ideology, Hogue's unrelenting, often exaggerated scenes of despair ally him with the social realists of the *American Scene movement. Hogue often suggests the misery visited on ordinary people through no fault of their own, but he blamed human carelessness for the land's destruction. Occasionally, Hogue made use of symbolic elements, as in *Erosion No. 2—Mother Earth Laid Bare* (Philbrook Art Center, Tulsa, 1936). At a glance another ravaged landscape, set off by an abandoned plow in the foreground and unused farm buildings in the distance, the image's eroded gullies and mounds form the body of a prostrate nude woman. Born in the northern Missouri town of Memphis, Hogue spent his childhood in Denton, Texas, and graduated from high school in nearby Dallas. He studied for a year at the Minneapolis School of Art (now Minneapolis College of Art and Design) and worked as a Dallas newspaper illustrator before moving to New York in 1921. During four years there, he painted in Texas during summers, and eventually he moved to Dallas. From 1926 until 1942 he often sojourned in *Taos. During the Depression, he painted murals for a *federal art project, and from the 1950s, he sometimes experimented with abstracted and even nonobjective form. Also active as a lithographer, Hogue taught at the University of Tulsa from 1945 until he retired in 1968. Subsequently, he divided his time between Tulsa, where he died, and an Oklahoma farm.

Holder, Preston. *See* F/64 GROUP.

Holt, Nancy. *See* SMITHSON, ROBERT.

Holty, Carl (1900–1973). Painter. Devoted throughout his career to abstraction, Carl Robert Holty arrived with his family in Milwaukee only months after his birth in Freiburg, Germany. In 1919 he began his training at the School of the Art Institute of Chicago, but the following year he moved to New York to work at the *National Academy of Design until 1921. In 1926 he studied at Hans *Hofmann's school in Munich and afterward remained abroad for a decade, traveling widely in Europe and North Africa. In the early 1930s, he worked in Paris, incorporating into his art influences from the *biomorphic abstraction of Kandinsky, Miró, and Jean Arp, as well as Mondrian's geometric discipline. Settling permanently in New York upon his return, he numbered among the founding members of the *American Abstract Artists. He taught at Brooklyn College from 1956 until three years before his death. In the late 1930s and early 1940s, Holty worked primarily with flat, precisely delineated geometric and organic shapes arranged in dynamic compositions based on cubist structure. Notably, these paintings employ lines as independent compositional elements as well as edges, and they offer unusual and sophisticated color combinations, which often feature warm oranges, reds, and pinks against white backgrounds. In *Orange and Gold* (Whitney Museum, 1942), vigorous, hard lines whip across the surface, suggesting gestural motions and knitting together the composition's spatial ambiguities. Sometimes Holty's titles suggest the subject matter in which his abstractions originated, while at other times representational elements themselves appear in an abstract context, as in the still life *Flowers* (Butler Institute of American Art, Youngstown, Ohio, 1947). In the 1950s Holty's work evolved through a more geometric phase toward the style of his later career. In these works of about the last fifteen years of his life, fluid washes intermingle with more disciplined forms in paintings that continued to reflect his expertise as a colorist. With Romare *Bearden, Holty wrote *The Painter's Mind* (1969).

Homer, Winslow (1836–1910). Painter, printmaker, and illustrator. Known especially for scenes of contemporary life and for seascapes, he also painted landscapes, wildlife, a few Civil War subjects, and a small but notable group devoted to African-American life in Virginia. Careful observation, a sensuous response to light and color, and strong yet often decorative design distinguish his evocative but unsentimental work. A leading illustrator before he redirected his ambition to painting, Homer achieved his finest early magazine work as a Civil War reporter. After the conflict, in both paintings and illustrations he concentrated on commonplace moments in American life. An 1881–82 sojourn in England turned his attention to new subjects and darkened the mood of his art. After settling in Maine soon afterward, he depicted the sea and its mariners in a tone of fatalistic gravity. A watercolorist of unsurpassed distinction among artists working in the United States, he produced brilliant outdoor views. Homer's etchings date to the years between 1884 and 1889. All but one of his eight plates reinterpreted previous oils or watercolors picturing people in engaged in activities related to the sea. Homer was born in Boston. From the age of six, he grew up in nearby Cambridge, then a village that fostered his lifelong affection for nature and outdoor activities. By the time he was ten, he drew with a skill considerably beyond expectations for his years. In 1854 he began an apprenticeship in the shop of John Bufford (1810–70), Boston's leading lithographer. On his twenty-first birthday, he opened his own studio. Within months, his drawings of contemporary life began regularly to appear as wood engravings in major magazines, including *Ballou's* and *Harper's Weekly*. After two and a half years, he moved to New York, the epicenter of American publishing and already the heart of the American art world. Homer enrolled right away for part-time study at the *National Academy of Design, where he continued to work in two subsequent seasons. Except for these life drawing classes at the academy and a few painting lessons from French-born *genre and landscape artist Frédéric Rondel (1826–92), he remained otherwise self-taught as an artist. In the fall of 1861, the spring of 1862, and again in the fall of 1864, he traveled south to observe the Civil War. The resulting vivid but dispassionate illustrations for *Harper's* center on soldiers' daily routines behind the lines, implying but generally not picturing violent conflict. Similar subjects appear in his earliest paintings, based on material from the 1862 trip, his longest.

Although his career as an exhibiting artist began in 1863, Homer continued regularly illustrating for magazines and books for more than a decade. His first ambitious painting, the sharply observed, psychologically acute *Prisoners from the Front* (Metropolitan Museum, 1866) secured his reputation as an artist. Representing a Union officer confronting a defeated rebel leader and his small band, it drew accolades at the National Academy exhibition that year and at Paris's 1867 Exposition Universelle. Homer visited the fair during a stay in France. He departed in December 1866, worked in a Montmartre studio, and traveled in the countryside, particularly to the nearby village of Cernay-la-Ville. His subsequent paintings suggest admiration for *Barbizon work and for paintings of other progressive artists whose interests coalesced a few years later around impressionism. His palette grew brighter, light began to sparkle, his brushwork became more spontaneous, and he grew partial to transient moments. Vision itself became a principal theme. Homer may also have encountered Japanese prints in Paris, where their popularity preceded the pervasive *japonisme soon seen as well in the United States. The patterning and asymmetrical balance of some paintings and illustrations suggest these Asian precedents. Yet Japanese models proved no more decisive to his long-term development than classical ones, which presumably inspired the friezelike disposition of figures in many paintings. Similarly, English *Pre-Raphaelitism later encountered in London may have affected his choice of unassertive, large-boned women as ideal types. In general, however, he remained an unusually independent artistic personality. After resettling in New York in the fall of 1867, Homer traveled during summers in search of material for drawings and paintings. Although his illustrations occasionally depicted New York scenes, he concurred with many fellow landscape and genre specialists in dismissing the city as a subject for painting. Instead, his canvases of these years generally document attractive young women or children at leisure in the country, often enjoying vacation spots along the shore or in the mountains. *Breezing Up (A Fair Wind)* (National Gallery, 1873–76), picturing a listing sailing dinghy, and *Crack the Whip* (Butler Institute of American Art, Youngstown, Ohio, 1872), a vigorous rendition of rough-and-tumble play, capture lively, unproblematic views of American life. Homer emphasized his subjects' well being with pleasurable, even ornamental color and design, while easily grasped, though increasingly sophisticated compositions provide structure and coherence. During the summer of 1873 in Gloucester, Massachusetts, he first worked intensively with watercolor, initiating a sustained engagement with a medium suited to his interest in purely visual phenomena. Stimulated no doubt by the burgeoning American *watercolor movement, he shrewdly capitalized thereafter on a market for the medium.

Watercolor dominated his practice during his residency in England. For several years before departing in March 1881, Homer had sporadically painted images that indicate an interest in more profound subjects than his normally lighthearted ones. Leaving behind the self-indulgent subjects that had dominated his work since the Civil War, he now engaged lives dominated by unremitting labor. During most of his time in Britain, he lived near Tynemouth, at Cullercoats, a North Sea fishing village that attracted artists in summer months. A large proportion of his English works depict women left on shore rather than the men whose perilous labor supported the community. As Homer's months there passed, these figures evolved from picturesque peasants to tragic protagonists of an existence dominated by human struggle with nature. After his return to New York in November 1882, Homer interpreted American subjects with the new seriousness and monumentality he had achieved abroad. Picturing the dramatic transfer from one ship to another of a listless woman suspended in the embrace of her rescuer above a stormy sea, *The Life Line* (Philadelphia Museum, 1884) boosted his reputation to new heights when it appeared in the National Academy's 1884 spring show.

After spending the previous summer at Prout's Neck, a spit jutting into the Atlantic about ten miles south of Portland, Maine, in the summer of 1884 he moved into a studio residence (today a National Historic Landmark) on family property perched above the seashore. He traveled often, especially during many winters when he headed south, usually to Florida but twice to the Bahamas and, on one occasion each, to Cuba and Bermuda. On his way home in the spring, he customarily stopped in New York. Most years, during warmer months he visited the Adirondacks or Quebec's Saguenay River region, where he and his brother owned a cabin. He also traveled in 1884 as far as the Grand Banks with a fishing fleet and, in 1893, to Chicago to see the World's Columbian Exposition. Watercolors from these later years generally depict his travel destinations in liquid strokes of pure color, vibrantly simulating outdoor color and light. The ocean dominates his Prout's Neck oils. At first he concentrated on the age-old standoff between the sea and those who live in daily contact with it. In *Eight Bells* (Addison Gallery of American Art, Phillips Academy, Andover, Massachusetts, 1886), two men in oilskins take navigational readings from the deck of their ship. *The Fog Warning* (Museum of Fine Arts, Boston, 1885) depicts a lone fisherman rowing his catch while looking over his shoulder at ominous distant clouds. Admirable for their industriousness and courage, Homer's impassive actors generally lack individuality nor do they represent identifiable social types. Homer painted only a handful of portraits, early in his career, and generally his art shows little interest in questions that intrigued many of his contemporaries concerning consciousness, psychology, or emotion.

Begun in 1890, a long series of stunning marine oils, usually devoid of human presence, conjure ceaseless coastal energies under varying conditions of weather and light along the rugged shore. Increasingly preoccupied through the following years by these meditations on the ocean's force and beauty, when he turned to other subjects he produced exceptions that include a few of his best-known paintings. In *The Fox Hunt* (Pennsylvania Academy, 1893), a solitary animal silhouetted against deep snow attempts to evade crows, black against the sky, in one of Homer's most spare, elegant, and "Japanese" compositions. Taking as its subject a current that seamen considered treacherous, *The Gulf Stream*, (Metropolitan Museum, 1899) features a black man adrift on an incapacitated boat as sharks circle in the waves. A distant waterspout and a passing ship on the far horizon intensify the pathos of his situation, exposing a tinge of romantic horror rare in Homer's work. In such pure seascapes as *Northeaster* (Metropolitan Museum, 1895), with its foamy arabesques representing waves crashing against a rocky coastline, he rendered with artful grace nature's awesome power. Homer's late subjects suggesting nature's amoral ferocity have given rise to grim and pessimistic constructions of their meaning. Yet, aesthetic pleasure tempers his subjects' naturalism, and he is not known to have held philosophically despairing views. In May 1908 Homer suffered a temporarily incapacitating stroke. Subsequently in declining health, he nevertheless within months resumed normal activities. He completed his final oil near the end of the next year. For the previous decade or so, artists and public alike had generally regarded him as the nation's greatest living painter. He died in his Prout's Neck studio home.

Hopper, Edward (1882–1967). Painter and printmaker. His plain style and sharp observation offer quintessential images of ordinary Americans going about routine lives in mundane cities and small towns. Yet, Hopper's attentiveness implies an unarticulated meaning within their commonplace existence. An alluring, sometimes dramatic, flow of light often intensifies a mysterious aura of significance. There is no explicit narrative, although many paintings suggest a hidden story. Viewers may more often wonder what his typically immobilized protagonists are thinking than what they are doing. This evocation of each individual's inscrutable inner nature, in combination with rigorously planned and stable compositions, bestows on the best of Hopper's work uncommon amplitude and monumentality. The most personal of the *American Scene painters, Hopper did not hold an ideological attitude toward subject matter, he was not interested in analyzing class structure nor in reforming society, and he did not wish to reveal "America" as an abstraction. "My aim in painting has always been the most exact transcription possible of my most intimate impressions of nature," he succinctly stated around 1930. Consciously avoiding beauty of surface for its own sake, he achieved a stylistic austerity that underscores a generally bleak psychology. A contemporary of the generation that invented modern art, Hopper exhibited in the *Armory Show. Although he had no interest in a modern style of painting, he understood the psychology of the modern era: introspective, isolated, resigned. His persuasive version of the reality of American life entered popular culture almost immediately, as illustrators and filmmakers, particularly the makers of *noir* movies, adapted what he had taught them to see. His empty streets, desolate cafeterias, lonely roadsides, run-down hotels, and gaudy entertainment venues continue to reverberate in notions of an earlier day.

A native of Nyack, New York, on the Hudson River, Hopper studied from 1900 to 1906 at the New York School of Art (now Parsons, the New School for Design), where his teachers included William Merritt *Chase, Kenneth Hayes *Miller, and his favorite, Robert *Henri. For nearly two decades after leaving school he made his living as an illustrator. He spent most of a year, in 1906–7, in Europe, primarily in Paris. Again in 1909 and 1910, he went abroad, both times returning to Paris. There, he may have witnessed early developments in modern art, but it was to French culture, Manet, and then to the impressionists that he was drawn. He also developed a special fondness for Rembrandt. Hopper did not return to Europe, but he visited Mexico and traveled widely in the United States. From 1930 he spent nearly every summer on Cape Cod, where in 1934 he built a house in South Truro. In 1915 he took up etching, and it was in this medium rather than painting that his signature style emerged. Although he abandoned it in 1923, on the basis of his accomplishments during those eight years, he numbers among outstanding printmakers of the twentieth century. In *Evening Wind* (1921) a nude woman climbs into bed, but turns her face away toward a window where a curtain billows in the breeze. The city corner, seen from above, in *Night Shadows* (1921), reveals a solitary man making his way through a patch of light. In such etchings, Hopper realized the essentials of his mature vision: contemporary subject matter, carefully structured form, and existential tone.

In 1924 Hopper relinquished commercial work to paint full time. His distinctive art had taken a long time to mature (he turned forty-two that year), but thereafter it changed hardly at all as an extended series of iconic American works emerged from his studio. Seen from a low, dramatizing viewpoint, *House by the Railroad* (Museum of Modern Art, 1925) depicts light playing across a mansarded Victorian mansion and along a railroad track that abruptly crops the edifice's foundations. *Early Sunday Morning* (Whitney Museum, 1930) shows a deserted city street in early light, unpopulated, watched over by a barber pole and a fire hydrant. In *Nighthawks* (Art Institute of Chicago, 1942)—arguably his most famous work—the viewer looks from the darkened city through the window of a lunch counter populated by four people: a white-uniformed worker, an isolated man, and a couple. *Gas* (Museum of Modern Art, 1940) reveals a lone attendant and red filling station pumps beside a deserted stretch of road. In such characteristic works, Hopper's deadpan reality bears the imprint of significance and the weight of emotion.

His wife, landscape, still life, and portrait painter **Jo Nivison Hopper** (1883–1968), also served as his favorite model. They married in 1924. Born in New York, Josephine Verstille Nivison graduated in 1905 from the Normal College of the City of New York (now Hunter College) and studied during the following academic year at the New York School of Art with Henri, her most important artistic mentor. She toured Europe during the summer of 1907 and in 1918 worked in France at a U.S. Army hospital. Following marriage, household responsibilities and her husband's career absorbed much of her time, but she never abandoned painting, which became tighter and less brightly colorful under his influence. Both artists died in New York, only ten months apart.

Hopps, Walter. *See* KIENHOLZ, EDWARD.

Hosmer, Harriet (1830–1908). Sculptor. The most prominent of a sizable contingent of expatriate American women sculptors in mid-nineteenth-century Rome—Henry James famously dubbed them "the white, marmorean flock"—she was the first to arrive and remained there throughout her professional life. Her sculpture satisfied the prevailing taste for *neoclassicism, but like many Victorian contemporaries she relished ornamental and narrative detail. Unlike most sculptors of her day, she undertook few portrait commissions, concentrating instead on imaginative subjects, often drawn from literature. Her boldness and eccentricity as a woman enhanced her fame as a sculptor. A tomboy in childhood, she dressed in men's clothing and lived independently. Yet, she charmed patrons and other visitors with her sociability, high spirits, and enthusiasm for her work. Besides other American women, such as Emma *Stebbins and Vinnie Ream *Hoxie, her friends included Robert and Elizabeth Barrett Browning, Nathaniel Hawthorne, William Wetmore *Story, and other prominent artistic and literary figures in the city's fluid Anglo-American community. Born near Boston, in Watertown, Harriet Goodhue Hosmer decided to become a professional sculptor while studying for three years at a progressive girls' school in Lenox, Massachusetts. Returning home in 1849, she worked with Peter Stephenson (1823–61), an English-born neoclassicist active in Boston, before departing the following year for St. Louis. Because no Boston-area medical school would allow a woman to study anatomy, she enrolled instead at Missouri Medical College (now Washington University School of Medicine). After returning home, in 1852 she carved her first marble, a female bust depicting *Hesper, the Evening Star* (Watertown Public Library) before sailing later that year for Europe. In Rome she studied with the English neoclassicist John Gibson and soon began to produce the pieces that within a few years made her international reputation.

Hosmer accomplished most of her finest work between the mid-1850s and mid-1860s. The first work she created in Rome, a restrained but tender bust of *Daphne* (Metropolitan Museum, 1853), anticipates her numerous sculptures of literary or historical women. Embodying sensitivity to women's experience, these often stress such qualities as intellect, power, or resistance to authority. Among them, the vulnerable grace of mistreated *Beatrice Cenci* (Mercantile Library of St. Louis, 1856; modeled 1853–55) contrasts with the regal nobility of a colossal *Zenobia in Chains* (lost, 1858–59; reduced version, Wadsworth Atheneum, Hartford, Connecticut, after 1859). Yet Hosmer's softly sensuous *Sleeping Faun* (Museum of Fine Arts, Boston, 1865) stands as one of the mid-century's most affecting male nudes. Her several public monuments include the over-life-size senator *Thomas Hart Benton* (Lafayette Park, St. Louis, 1860–68), one of few works she realized in bronze. Hosmer also produced a number of playful fancies, which ranked as her most commercially successful creations. The most popular, the childlike 1856 *Puck* (Smithsonian American Art Museum), a subject from Shakespeare's *A Midsummer Night's Dream*, is known in more than thirty marble replicas. Hosmer outlived the vogue for neoclassical sculpture and devoted much of her later life to scientific study and tinkering with mechanical inventions. During these years, she frequently sojourned in England, where her many friendships elicited commissions for fountains, gates, and domestic decorations. She ceased making sculpture in the 1890s and returned permanently to Watertown in 1900.

Hovenden, Thomas (1840–95). Painter and printmaker. A versatile and accomplished artist, he is best known for *genre scenes. He also painted narrative subjects inspired by history and literature, portraits, and other figure studies. Late in life, he turned to landscape. On occasion he made etchings. Hugely popular when it was first exhibited, his most famous painting, *Breaking Home Ties* (Philadelphia Museum, 1890), depicts a young man taking leave of family and rural home. Appealing with tender sentiment to a common experience of bittersweet farewell, the image reflects the pattern of young Americans leaving home for metropolitan opportunities in an urbanizing nation. At the same time, the painting's carefully constructed composition, clear modeling, and naturalistically rendered detail demonstrate strengths of the artist's cosmopolitan training in European traditions. As here, Hovenden's major paintings often probe psychological responses to themes of loss, separation, illness, or death. The serious tone of these works conveys respect and admiration for the dignity and courage of his typically unassuming protagonists. Born in Dunmanway, Ireland, and orphaned as a small child, Hovenden studied at an art school in nearby Cork while apprenticed to a frame maker. In 1863 he emigrated to New York, where he attended classes at the *National Academy of Design. He had mastered a polished, tightly detailed style indebted to mid-century English *Pre-Raphaelitism by the time he relocated to Baltimore in 1868. There his work attracted the attention of William T. *Walters and others whose patronage enabled him to leave for France in 1874. After a year in Paris, where he studied with Jules Breton and Alexandre Cabanel, Hovenden spent most of the next five years in Brittany, residing at the Pont-Aven art colony founded by Robert *Wylie. There he drew on local peasant life and history for the paintings that first made his reputation. Hovenden returned to New York in 1880. The following year, he married a painter of genre and animals, Helen Corson (1846–1935), whom he had met at Pont-Aven. They soon settled permanently at her family homestead at Plymouth Meeting, Pennsylvania, near Philadelphia. Their daughter, **Martha Hovenden** (1884–1941), worked as a sculptor.

Soon after his move, he initiated a lengthy engagement, unusual for the time, with themes drawn from African-American life and history. The large, carefully staged rendition of *The Last Moments of John Brown* (Metropolitan Museum, 1884) ranks as the most ambitious of these. Equally notable are numerous smaller, low-key homages to black individuals and family life. These fit comfortably into the specialty he developed in the 1880s, domestic scenes that embody what he and his audience could identify as bedrock American virtues. He presented such values with appreciative sincerity at a time when they were threatened by destablizing currents of modern social life. In 1891 Hovenden sailed to England, where he spent a year and a half living among artists who gathered in Cranbrook, Kent. In the few years remaining after his return, he completed a group of impressionist landscapes. In addition, one of his last major works, the moody, loosely painted *Jerusalem the Golden* (Metropolitan Museum, 1894), reveals an interest in the shallow, asymmetrical compositions and indeterminate narratives of the *aesthetic movement. Hovenden died heroically, trying to save a child who had darted in front of a train.

Hoving, Thomas. *See* METROPOLITAN MUSEUM OF ART.

Howald, Ferdinand (1856–1934). Collector. Also a businessman. An early and discriminating buyer of progressive and modern American work, he bequeathed the cream of his collection to the Columbus (Ohio) Museum of Art. When he was an infant, Howald's parents left his birthplace, Wangen-am-Aar, Switzerland, to settle on a farm near Columbus. Later, they moved into Columbus, where Howald graduated with Ohio State University's first class. In 1881 he earned a second degree in mining engineering and went to work in the West Virginia coal industry, where he made a fortune sufficient to retire in 1906 and move to New York. Excepting a few etchings, Howald apparently did not buy art before 1913. The few pieces he acquired that year included commissioned family portraits by Leon *Kroll and Eugene *Speicher. He also purchased examples of European art, as he continued to do on an occasional basis. During the following year, he purchased his first modernist American work, a painting by the decorative symbolist Edward Middleton Manigault (1887–1922). In 1915 he bought paintings by Ernest *Lawson and Maurice *Prendergast, who subsequently became favorites well represented in the collection. He began to collect in earnest in 1916. Eventually his unprecedented collection included important groups by Charles *Demuth, Preston *Dickinson, Marsden *Hartley, John *Marin, *Man Ray, and Charles *Sheeler. It also represented the work of Arthur *Dove and other artists from the Alfred *Stieglitz circle, William *Glackens and George *Luks of The *Eight, independent modernists such as Samuel *Halpert and William *Zorach, and progressive realists, including Charles *Burchfield, Rockwell *Kent, and Raphael *Soyer. Howald contributed substantially to the costs of building the Columbus Museum of Art, which opened as the Columbus Gallery of Fine Arts in 1931 with a show of his collection. He died in Columbus, once again his home in later years.

Howard, Charles (1899–1978). Painter. In characteristic compositions, geometric and *biomorphic, often vibrantly colored, hard-edged, and predominately planar forms appear within luminous spaces. In their precision and delicacy, Howard's works reiterate the spirit of Alexander *Calder's contemporary mobiles and recall aspects of work by Kandinsky, Ilya *Bolotowsky, and early Ad *Reinhardt. Within an unusually subdued scheme of desertlike colors, *Hare Corner* (Whitney Museum, 1939), a bipartite image of shapes floating across an indeterminate space, anticipates Howard's drift in the 1940s toward a less rigid, more intuitive approach. Born in Montclair, New Jersey, Charles Houghton Howard moved with his family to the San Francisco Bay Area. After graduating from the University of California in Berkeley, he pursued additional study at Harvard and Columbia. As an artist, he remained mainly self-taught. Before World War II and again for some years afterward, he lived in London, where he associated with Ben Nicholson, Barbara Hepworth, Henry Moore, and others of the Unit One group. Later he lived in San Francisco. In 1970 he moved permanently to Italy, where he died at Bagni di Lucca.

A brother, sculptor and painter **Robert Boardman Howard** (1896–1983), born in New York, studied at the California College of Arts and Crafts (now California College of the Arts) in Oakland and at the *Art Students League. His sculptural work embellished a number of architectural venues and outdoor locations, mainly in San Francisco. A third brother, painter **John Langley Howard** (1902–99), born in Montclair, graduated from the University of California in Berkeley before following Robert to the same art schools. Both participated in the decoration of San Francisco's Coit Tower. In Depression-era paintings detailing the plight of economically disadvantaged citizens, John contributed to the social realist strain of the *American Scene movement. He also painted many scenes of the area around Monterey, California, while residing there for some years before returning to San Francisco.

Howland, Alfred Cornelius. *See* MOWBRAY, HENRY SIDDONS.

Hoxie, Vinnie Ream (1847–1914). Sculptor. Best known for a life-size marble *Abraham Lincoln* (1870; modeled 1866–68) in the U.S. Capitol, she produced many other portraits as well as ideal subjects reflecting the prevailing taste for *neoclassicism. Nearly all her significant work dates before 1878, when she married Richard Leveridge Hoxie. Born in Madison, Wisconsin, before the territory became a state, Vinnie Ream grew up in several midwestern localities. In 1861 she moved with her family to Washington, D.C., where she studied with Clark *Mills. During 1864–65 she modeled Lincoln from life while he worked at the White House. This experience subsequently gave her an edge in the stiff competition for a standing figure of the assassinated president to be placed in the Capitol rotunda. In the summer of 1866, she had not yet turned nineteen when she became the first woman to receive a sculptural commission from the federal government. After completing the plaster model of *Lincoln* in 1868, she departed for Europe to supervise the carving. Abroad, she briefly studied drawing in Paris and visited other art capitals before arriving in Rome. There she produced also several other portraits and imaginative subjects. Shortly after her return, the unveiling of *Lincoln* in January 1871 brought her fame and numerous commissions. Congress also mandated the most important of these, *Admiral David Farragut* (1881; modeled 1875–80). Cast in bronze from the melted-down propeller of his flagship, it stands in Washington's downtown Farragut Square. Hoxie did not again work professionally until 1906, when she accepted the first of two additional major portrait commissions. Although she lived in several other locations during her marriage, she resided much of the time in Washington, where she died.

Hubard, William James (1807–62). Painter, silhouette artist, and sculptor. Chiefly a portrait painter, he also undertook historical and literary subjects. His distinctive, miniaturistic paintings portray full-length subjects within crisply detailed settings. Cabinet-size works also include a few imaginative themes, such as the haunting *Dream of Columbus* (Valentine Richmond [Virginia] History Center, early 1850s), which pictures the dozing explorer seated in his study, while in a visionary apparition, ships approach an alpine-flavored new world in the background. The diminutive portraits, such as *Charles Carroll of Carrollton* (Metropolitan Museum, c. 1830), forcefully evoke individual character despite their size. Born in Whitechurch, Shropshire, while still a child Hubard gained renown for his ability to cut portrait silhouettes. He toured Great Britain with a traveling showman, who brought him to the United States in 1824. While making silhouettes in New York and Boston, he became interested in portrait painting and in 1826 began working professionally. In changing specialties, he apparently received advice and encouragement from Robert W. *Weir, Gilbert *Stuart, and Thomas *Sully. He worked in New York, the mid-Atlantic states, and Virginia before traveling to Italy and France for about three years. There his style became more academically polished but less individual, and afterward he less often worked in the small format he had so effectively exploited. Soon after his return in 1841 he settled in Richmond, Virginia. There in 1853, newly interested in sculpture, he opened a bronze foundry, where he most notably produced six bronze casts of Jean Antoine Houdon's standing *George Washington* (state capitol, Richmond, 1785–88). During the Civil War, the plant was converted to the manufacture of war munitions. Hubard died from injuries sustained in an accidental explosion there.

Hudson, Robert. *See* FUNK ART.

Hudson River School. Designation applied to the earliest distinctively American landscape specialists. Their work combined meticulous, factual description with romantic feeling for the beauty, grandeur, and nobility of American scenery. Active from the 1820s, nearly all were native-born, although most studied and traveled in Europe. There they absorbed traditional skills and theories, but their attention to American subjects gave their work an indigenous flavor and helped to crystallize an optimistic national consciousness. The style peaked from the 1840s through early 1860s. By about 1880 it had gone out of fashion. Although centered in New York and bound by friendships, the Hudson River School painters never formally organized. Originally a derogatory tag, the name came later, when the style was seen as naive, finicky, and provincial. Usage of the term has been inconsistent. Some observers have employed it to embrace all realistic nineteenth-century landscapes, but art historians today generally limit its applicability to a smaller group of painters whose work most consistently exemplifies the School's salient characteristics. Thomas *Cole's landscapes proved pivotal to the birth of the School. Such earlier landscapists as Alvan *Fisher and Thomas *Doughty are variously considered precursors or early adherents. Core members of the School include Asher B. *Durand, John *Kensett, Worthington *Whittredge, and Jasper *Cropsey. Although some writers include them, Albert *Bierstadt, Frederick *Church, and Martin Johnson *Heade, among other major landscapists, are often now seen as related figures whose interests diverged from those of the central group. Typical Hudson River School landscapes picture undefiled scenery of the northeastern United States, chiefly New England and New York State. The Hudson River Valley, including the Catskill Mountains, served as the earliest and most frequent locus of activity. Views may be intimate or sweeping, but vegetation, rocks, clouds, and other features are acutely observed, often painted with tiny brushes for maximum detail. Light is carefully rendered, but also controlled to contribute to harmonious or even transcendental effects. Typically, the mood of the paintings is pastoral and poetic, although some convey the awesome impassivity of untouched nature. Painters and contemporary observers frequently read patriotic meanings into the views, which were seen as evidence of the young country's inherent greatness and possible superiority to the Old World. Moreover, interpreting the landscapes as evidence of God's handiwork, many also read moral and spiritual messages there. Hudson River School painting paralleled contemporaneous literary responses to landscape, as in James Fenimore Cooper's novels, the poetry of William Cullen Bryant, and the philosophical ruminations of Ralph Waldo Emerson and Henry David Thoreau. The period's responsiveness to nature benefited from familiarity with English romantic art and literature, as well as by an urbanizing population's nostalgia for the country.

Huebler, Douglas. *See* CONCEPTUAL ART.

Hunt, William Morris (1824–79). Painter and occasional sculptor. Important also as a teacher and tastemaker, he created landscapes, *genre scenes, portraits, and ideal subjects. Reflecting his immersion in progressive French painting, his broadly conceived, painterly works helped to redirect American painting from the tightly detailed realism of mid-century toward more personal and more aesthetically oriented approaches favored later. A great admirer of his friend Jean-Francois Millet, Hunt triggered the popularity of *Barbizon painting among American collectors, particularly in New England. His brother, Richard Morris Hunt, ranked among preeminent American architects of the late nineteenth century. Born in Brattleboro, Vermont, as a youngster he lived in Washington, D.C., and New Haven, Connecticut, before moving in 1838 to Cambridge, Massachusetts. There he entered Harvard College in 1840. At the same time, initially drawn to sculpture, in Boston he studied with Scots-born, self-taught portraitist John Crookshanks King (1806–82). In 1843 he departed with his family for Paris, but they soon resettled in Rome, where Hunt worked for about six months under Henry Kirke *Brown. In 1845 he enrolled at the art academy in Düsseldorf; dissatisfied with its rigid pedagogy, he left after nine months. He went to Paris still intending to become a sculptor, but instead in 1847 entered Thomas Couture's painting studio, where he remained for five years. Drawn to the feeling for humanity expressed in Millet's work, in 1853 he moved to Barbizon, where he pictured dignified but sweetly appealing rustics, usually shown outdoors in harmony with landscape. Before he returned to Boston in 1855, Hunt bought *The Sower* (Museum of Fine Arts, Boston, 1850), Millet's iconic image of a heroically conceived peasant striding across a field. An adventurous purchase, it was the first significant painting by a Barbizon artist to be acquired by an American. After a year in Brattleboro,

Hunt moved to Newport, Rhode Island, where he offered art instruction in his studio, while also establishing himself professionally. His majestic rendering of *Judge Lemuel Shaw* (Essex County Bar Association, Salem, Massachusetts, 1859) exemplifies the strengths of his French training in its easy naturalism, bold contours, painterly finesse, and balance between description and abstract pattern. With its stylistic challenge to the literalism of contemporary American portrait practice, the Shaw likeness positioned Hunt as New England's leading portrait painter.

In 1862 he moved to Boston, where he soon came to be regarded as a cultural leader. Four years later he departed on his only repeat visit to Europe. For two years he lived in Paris and Rome while also traveling widely. On his return to Boston, in 1868 he established an art school, where for seven years he provided up-to-date training, notably open to women. Hunt's unsystematic but invigorating *Talks on Art* (1875; revised and enlarged edition 1883), compiled by a friend and student, the painter Helen Mary Knowlton (1832–1918), recapitulates his innovative teaching methods, which had their foundation in Couture's studio practice. In 1872 a fire that ravaged Boston's center destroyed his studio and many items from his collection of contemporary French work. Burdened also by difficulties in his personal life around the same time, he took refuge in painting landscapes. Stimulated by trips to Florida, Cuba, and Mexico, as well as the Massachusetts countryside and shore, he produced freely painted, fresh, and intimate responses. Despite this introspective turn, in 1878 he accepted a major civic commission, the most prestigious recognition of his career, comprising two enormous allegorical murals for the ornate New York state capitol just being completed in Albany. *The Discoverer* depicted Columbus with allegorical figures, while the more imaginative and powerful *Flight of Night* portrayed Anahita, the Persian goddess of the night. Reprising a theme that had interested him for years, he presented the allegorical figure in a chariot drawn by horses that seem to plunge through the skies. Some months after the paintings' debut in January 1879, he died on a visit to Appledore Island, in the Isles of Shoals off the coast near Portsmouth, New Hampshire. His drowning may have been a suicide brought on by the strain of completing his first murals, well received though they were, while already haunted by other cares.

Huntington, Anna Hyatt (1876–1973). Sculptor and collector. Known for bronze animals and monumental equestrian statues, she fused detailed naturalism with lively motion. In *Reaching Jaguar* (Metropolitan Museum, 1906), a life-size animal perches on the edge of a boulder, endangering its balance with a paw extended downward. Born in Cambridge, Massachusetts, Anna Vaughn Hyatt received her earliest training as a sculptor from her sister Harriet and exhibited forty animal sculptures in her first one-person exhibition, in Boston, before moving to New York in 1902. There she studied for about two years at the *Art Students League with George Gray *Barnard, Gutzon *Borglum, and Hermon *MacNeil. From 1903, while sharing a studio, she collaborated with Abastenia St. Leger *Eberle on several works. In 1907 she sailed for Europe, where she lived in France and Italy for three years. In Paris in 1910 she modeled her first equestrian statue, the *Joan of Arc* that she revised and enlarged in 1915 for a site on New York's Riverside Drive. The over-life-size young martyr strikes a defiant pose, standing in her stirrups to raise her sword as her massive horse drives forward. After 1914 she worked mainly in a studio on family property at Annisquam, on the Massachusetts shore, before returning to New York in 1920.

In 1923, on her forty-seventh birthday, she married **Archer M. Huntington** (1870–1955), heir to a vast railroad fortune, scholar and poet, founder of the Hispanic Society of America, art collector, and philanthropist. After she was diagnosed with tuberculosis four years later, they lived in several salubrious locations as she cured her disease while continuing to work with little interruption. Planning to build a winter home, in 1930 they purchased four South Carolina plantations near Myrtle Beach and the following year, converted much of their nine-thousand-acre parcel into a nature refuge and public sculpture park. Offering, as the couple intended, a representative survey of American figurative sculpture and today a National Historic Landmark, Brookgreen Gardens holds some nine hundred works, displayed in a 350-acre garden as well as indoor galleries. After settling in 1939 on a large farm near Redding, Connecticut, the following year the Huntingtons gave their Manhattan townhouse to the *National Academy of Design for use as the organization's headquarters. Having continued to work well into her eighties, she died at the Connecticut estate, now the Collis P. Huntington State Park (named for her father-in-law) where some of her sculptures may be seen. A nephew, widely published art historian A(lpheus) Hyatt Mayor (1901–80), son of her sculptor-sister, Harriet Hyatt Mayor (1868–1960), served as curator of prints at the *Metropolitan Museum of Art for twenty years, beginning in 1946. Born in Salem, Massachusetts, his mother produced portrait busts, reliefs, and commemorative medals. She died in Bethel, Connecticut.

Huntington, Daniel (1816–1906). Painter. Remembered particularly for mid-century allegorical, literary, and historical works, he also painted about a thousand portraits, as well as landscapes and *genre scenes. Active for many years in the art life of his native New York, he served as president of the *National Academy of Design for all but seven years of the period between 1862 and 1891 and as a founding vice president of the *Metropolitan Museum of Art from 1871 until 1903, except for two years. An organizer of the prestigious Century Club in 1847, he headed the group from 1879 until 1895. Huntington studied for a semester at Yale before transferring in 1833 to Hamilton College in upstate Clinton, New York. While studying there, he met Charles Loring *Elliott, who offered instruction and encouragement. Without graduating, in 1835 he returned to New York to study with Samuel F. B. *Morse and later with Henry *Inman. He traveled in Europe with Henry Peters *Gray in 1839–40, and between 1843 and 1845 he lived mostly in Rome. He again visited Europe on four subsequent occasions between 1851 and 1883. Between the first two trips abroad, he established his reputation with his most popular work, *Mercy's Dream* (Pennsylvania Academy, 1841; replicas in Corcoran Gallery, 1850, and Metropolitan Museum, 1858), illustrating an episode from John Bunyan's *Pilgrim's Progress*. Widely distributed as an engraving, this image of an angel appearing to a swooning and alluringly pretty young woman appealed to contemporary taste with its sentimental Christian moralism, old master veneer, and romantic sweetness. As the public lost interest in pious themes after the Civil War, Huntington became a premier New York society portraitist. Although realistically detailed, his likenesses characteristically generalize and soften to create impressions of delicacy, virtue, and good taste. Although major changes of style and subject altered American painting before the end of the century, Huntington remained a revered personality until his death in New York.

Hurd, Peter (1904–84). Painter and printmaker. Known for depictions of life in the Southwest and for portraits, he shared with other regionalists in the *American Scene movement an interest in recording the experience of ordinary people. Harold Hurd Jr. was born in Roswell, New Mexico, and made his home in the area most of his life. After two years at the United States Military Academy at West Point, he transferred in 1923 to Haverford College near Philadelphia for a year. Subsequently, he studied at the *Pennsylvania Academy of the Fine Arts and for several years with artist-illustrator N. C. *Wyeth, whose daughter Henriette *Wyeth he married in 1929. Drawn back to his native region, he made its spacious landscapes and unsophisticated inhabitants his main subjects. In *The Dry River* (Roswell [New Mexico] Museum and Art Center, 1938), a diminutive rancher on horseback crosses the foreground of a steeply rolling landscape thrown into relief by low shafts of sunlight. A woman in the middle distance waits before a humble dwelling, but the narrative of their lives is subordinate to the vast and empty landscape caught at a poetic moment. Hurd also worked in Texas and New Mexico as a *federal art project muralist and served from 1942 to 1945 as a war correspondent for *Life* magazine. His official portrait of President Lyndon B. Johnson (National Portrait Gallery, Washington, D.C., 1967) occasioned a public controversy when Johnson rejected it as "the ugliest thing I ever saw." After an incapacitating illness of several years, Hurd died in Roswell. *Sketch Book* (1971) includes autobiographical notes. His letters and journals appeared as *My Land Is the Southwest* (1983), edited by Robert Metzger.

Immaculates. *See* PRECISIONISM.

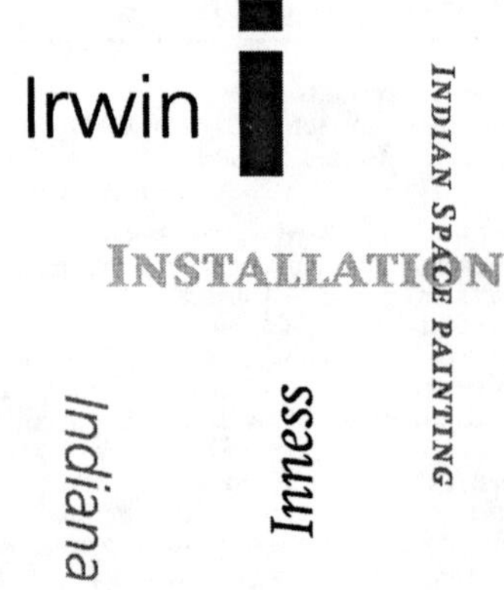

Impressionism, American. Late-nineteenth- and early-twentieth-century movement centered on optical experience, with particular attention to fixing contemporary subjects in momentary perceptions of light and color. Inspired by the French tendency, the American movement nevertheless took on a distinctive character. Most notably, American artists generally refrained from dissolving solid objects into sensations of light. In place of the French artists' screenlike arrangements of small, individually colored paint strokes, American artists typically clung to the academic training most of them had sought, as they superimposed brilliant effects on compositions constructed tonally, in terms of light and dark. This more intellectual approach promoted intelligible representation within three-dimensional pictorial space, while French delight in surface favored perception at the expense of knowledge. Consequently, the French style seemed unpleasantly extreme to American artists, critics, and patrons alike. Similarly, sustaining an interest in the figure as a carrier of meaning, Americans characteristically shied away from French impressionists' depersonalized treatment of individuals. Although less radical in such respects than its French counterpart, the American movement nevertheless often accommodated up-to-date expressive ends by incorporating aspects of other progressive currents, such as symbolist reverie or postimpressionist interests in order, stability, and decorative design.

In France, originating in the late 1860s, impressionism culminated in the 1870s and early 1880s. During those years, with the exception of Mary *Cassatt, the only American to exhibit in the canonical impressionist exhibitions in Paris, and her friend, Louisine *Havemeyer, an early collector of impressionist work, Americans almost entirely ignored the French movement. The first significant exhibition of French impressionist painting in the United States dates to 1886, the year of the impressionists' final group show in Paris. Although such sophisticated internationalists as James Abbott McNeill *Whistler, John Singer *Sargent, and William Merritt *Chase had already responded to aspects of impressionism, American artists more generally did not admire the practice until later in the decade. By then, demonstrating that impressionism's classic moment had passed, most of its French adherents had begun to pursue interests in formal structure or in symbolic meanings. Thus, if they studied the most recent examples, American artists encountered French impressionist art when it had arrived at a new stage in its own history. Despite Americans' initial hesitancy, during the 1890s no other country surpassed the enthusiasm seen in the United States for impressionism. Moreover, remaining viable for at least another quarter of a century, the American version's popularity forced nearly all significant younger painters, along with many of their elders, to reckon with its aesthetic and methods. American painters who embraced impressionism, during at least part of their careers, include Frank Weston *Benson, John Leslie *Breck, Dennis Miller *Bunker, William *Glackens, Philip Leslie *Hale, Childe *Hassam, Ernest *Lawson, Lila Cabot *Perry, John *Twachtman, Robert *Vonnoh, and J. Alden *Weir. Many artists associated with *tonalism accommodated aspects of impressionism to poetic, intuitive ends.

Independent exhibitions. Art shows arranged by artists and their supporters, usually outside the institutional framework provided by museums, art schools, and commercial galleries. Such exhibitions served a particularly important purpose in the early decades of the twentieth century. Because the conservative establishment controlled most venues during that period, anti-academic artists often had difficulty presenting their achievements. Following European precedents, they organized their own exhibitions to show and sell their work. In unjuried shows, the most radical of these events, anyone who paid the entrance fee could show work of his or her own choice. The history of independent exhibitions in Europe goes back at least to 1863, when artists in Paris staged a Salon des Refusés in order to exhibit work rejected that year by the all-powerful, government-sponsored Salon

The eight Impressionist shows between 1874 and 1886 together provide an important early example of artists joining to draw attention to stylistically compatible work. In 1884 Paris artists formed the Société des Artistes Indépendants, which thereafter held annual exhibitions open to anyone who paid a nominal fee. Similar groups sprang up in other European countries, including Belgium and Germany.

In the United States, Robert *Henri first made significant use of the independent exhibition as a vehicle for enlarging aesthetic debate. Following two smaller shows in previous years, he provided the impetus for The *Eight's 1908 exhibition. In 1910, along with Walt *Kuhn and John *Sloan, he instigated the "Exhibition of Independent Artists." Presenting about five hundred stylistically varied works in rented space on West Thirty-fifth Street, this event followed the policy of "no jury, no prizes," which remained a cornerstone of subsequent independent efforts. Although sales were disappointing, the show drew a huge crowd and provoked controversy, proving that large, inclusive, anti-academic shows could be successful without institutional support. The following year, Rockwell *Kent organized a smaller show that numbered among the first restricted to modern art. The *Armory Show of 1913 ranks as the greatest American independent exhibition. Three years later, along with a committee of notables, *Forum* magazine art critic Willard Huntington *Wright organized the "Forum Exhibition of Modern American Painters" at the Anderson Galleries. This invitational display of about two hundred works by seventeen artists consolidated claims for the importance of current modern work. It included Thomas Hart *Benton, Arthur *Dove, Marsden *Hartley, Stanton *Macdonald-Wright, *Man Ray, John *Marin, Alfred *Maurer, Charles *Sheeler, and William *Zorach.

The notion of the independent exhibition was itself institutionalized in 1917 with the formation of the Society of Independent Artists, modeled on the French example. The first of its annual shows, opening in April 1917 at the Grand Central Palace exhibition hall, presented about twenty-five hundred works by more than eleven hundred American and European artists. Although it surpassed in size any previous New York exhibition (and perhaps all subsequent ones), this show remains particularly noteworthy for a single entry's memorable attack on good taste. Ever alert to a mischievous opportunity, founder-member Marcel *Duchamp managed to subvert the open exhibition policy by entering a piece so outrageous that it was rejected. Using the pseudonym "R. Mutt," he submitted *Fountain*, simply an inverted porcelain urinal mounted as a sculpture. The following year, John Sloan was elected president of the Society and remained in that post throughout the organization's existence. Through the 1920s its exhibitions were important if uneven events, which gave regular visibility to many experimentalists as well as public exposure to young, untested artists. By the 1930s the exhibitions became less significant, and they were discontinued during World War II. Since then, artists have from time to time organized independent exhibitions, but they no longer serve the key purpose of earlier decades.

Indiana, Robert (1928–). Painter, printmaker, and sculptor. An important contributor to *pop art, he is known for bright, sharp compositions featuring brief exhortations, such as *eat*, *hug*, and *die*. These adapt the imperative diction of advertising to noncommercial themes with humor, irony, and no little regret for the purity of the American dream. *LOVE*, since 1966 his most popular image in paintings, prints, and sculptures, has appeared also on postage stamps and unauthorized merchandise. Born Robert Clark in New Castle, Indiana, in 1958 he took the name of his home state. In addition to fulfilling military service in the U.S. Army Air Force, he studied at the Herron School of Art (now Herron School of Art and Design of Indiana University-Purdue University at Indianapolis) and the school of the Munson-Williams-Proctor Institute in Utica, New York, before enrolling at the School of the Art Institute of Chicago, where he received a BFA in 1953. Following the subsequent academic year studying in Edinburgh, he settled in New York. Partly under the influence of his friend Ellsworth *Kelly, he soon evolved a personal, eye-catching style. Indiana's ties to Americana go beyond a romantic fascination with the country's commercial signage, road culture, and urban iconography to include also more philosophical allusions to eminent American authors and artists. Closer in approach than other pop artists to *precisionism, he paid homage to Charles *Demuth in several works that quote the earlier artist's famous regressing numbers from *The Figure 5 in Gold*. Indiana's paintings have also commented pointedly on social questions, politics, and peace issues. His best-known sculptures form smoothly finished words or numbers on a mammoth scale, but he has also made rough-hewn, vertical "herms" (as he calls them) that maintain a longtime interest in *assemblage. Since 1978 he has lived year round in his former summer residence in the village of Vinalhaven, located on the island of the same name in Maine's Penobscot Bay.

Indian Space painting. A form of abstraction practiced mainly in the 1940s and early 1950s. Aiming to produce a distinctive national style, the Indian Space painters fruitfully melded American tribal motifs, most often taken from Northwest Coast examples, with the European modern tradition. Picasso, Miró, Paul Klee, late Kandinsky, and Hans *Hofmann informed these artists' ambitions. Indian Space paintings and occasional prints generally display vigorous flat patterns of bright, unmodulated colors. Symbolic elements sometimes occur, but nonobjective forms predominate. Shapes are more often organic than geometric, and surface is emphasized at the expense of figure-ground relationships. Tantalizing overlaps with the goals of contemporary *abstract expressionism suggest the sophistication of Indian Space ideas. Announcing themselves as "8 and a Totem Pole," the informal Indian Space group appeared together only once, in a 1946 gallery show. Peter Busa (1914–85), Howard Daum (1918–88), and Gertrude Barrer (1921–97) rank as the best known of the exhibition's participants (perhaps not counting the totem pole). Will *Barnet and Steve Wheeler (1912–92), who shared the group's aesthetic but did not participate in the 1946 show, are commonly included in considerations of Indian Space achievement, and others also experimented with Indian Space principles.

Originally from Pittsburgh, Busa began his training at Carnegie Institute of Technology (now Carnegie Mellon University). After arriving in New York in 1933, he studied at the *Art Students League (where he was in Thomas Hart *Benton's class with Jackson *Pollock) and with Hofmann. Friendships with Arshile *Gorky and Stuart *Davis also influenced his early development. A veteran of the late 1930s *federal art projects, Busa participated eagerly in the heady atmosphere of experimentation fostered in the early 1940s by exile surrealists and soon-to-be abstract expressionists, including Pollock, Gorky, Robert *Motherwell, and Roberto *Matta. Throughout his career, while pursuing both the Indian Space approach and a looser abstract expressionism, he sometimes incorporated suggestions of representational subjects in his work. He also produced geometric abstractions during the 1960s and 1970s. From 1962 he taught for a number of years at the University of Minnesota, while also maintaining a residence in *Provincetown, on Cape Cod. He died in Minneapolis.

Although he proposed it, Daum later believed that the Indian Space label failed to do justice to the broader aims of the approach. In any event, he remained always committed to brightly patterned, flat abstraction. Born in Poland, he arrived in New York only a few years before the Indian Space debut. He studied with Hofmann. Despite the striking verve and considerable originality of his work, he died in obscurity in New York. Barrer, born in New York, studied at the State University of Iowa (now University of Iowa) when Philip *Guston taught there and at the *Art Students League, where Barnet ranked as her most influential teacher. In Iowa City she married fellow art student, Texas-born Oscar Collier (1924–98), who also studied with Barnet and showed with the Indian Space group in 1946. (He later abandoned painting, worked in publishing, and eventually moved to Ohio.) Following a second marriage to artist Frank Russell (1921–88), she moved permanently to Roxbury, Connecticut, in 1959. By the end of the 1940s she worked in a looser, abstract expressionist mode, often incorporating the wandering lines and amorphous spaces of surrealism. In later years she also worked on decorative projects, sometimes in collaboration with Russell, and illustrated a number of children's books.

Although he refused to allow his work to appear in Indian Space exhibitions or publications, Wheeler exploited the style more single-mindedly and perhaps for a longer time than any of the others. Born Stephen Brosnatch in Slovakia, he changed his surname in 1939. As a toddler he relocated with his family to New Salem in the Pennsylvania coalfields south of Pittsburgh. After a year at the School of the Art Institute of Chicago, in 1932 he moved to New York, where he studied for three years at the Art Students League with Vaclav *Vytlacil and George *Grosz, and then at Hofmann's school until 1937. During the late 1930s he socialized with Busa and the circle of future abstract expressionists. By 1940, inspired by Klee particularly, as well as Miró, Kandinsky, and pre-Columbian precedents, he had developed a lively and original approach to distributing flattened pictorial elements across a field. His work quickly developed toward frantic intricacy that often incorporated allusions to representational or even narrative subjects. By the mid-1940s he numbered among New York's most admired young artists, but his last one-person show took place in 1951. Lost in the enthusiasm for abstract expressionism's larger scale and more informal approach to composition, his subsequent work almost never appeared publicly during his lifetime. Wheeler continued working productively through the 1950s but later finished fewer paintings. In the mid-1970s, discouraged and eventually embittered, he virtually quit. After withdrawing into seclusion in his last years, he died in his New York studio.

Ingham, Charles Cromwell (1796–1863). Painter. A portrait specialist, he also produced *genre scenes and occasional landscapes. Much admired for the delicacy of his highly finished surfaces, for the sensuous luster he imparted to skin tones, and for colorful articulation of decorative accessories, particularly flowers, he was in great demand for portraits of women. Contemporaries often found competitor Henry *Inman's somewhat broader and more insightful approach more satisfying for male subjects. Rarely including much consideration of individual character, Ingham's virtuoso performances suggest sweetness beyond reproach. An ambitious work, *Amelia Palmer* (Metropolitan Museum, 1830) offers a poetic idyll. Situating its full-length pre-adolescent subject within a landscape, it pictures a gracefully posed, delicate girl who carries a broad-brimmed hat spilling with flowers as she pauses within a lush natural setting. Ingham's best known painting, the sentimental but sexually charged *Flower Girl* (Metropolitan Museum, 1846) prettifies a lower-class subject, while ambiguously entertaining questions about her psychology, her social role, and the reactions she might have provoked from her viewers. Born and trained as an artist in Dublin, Ingham moved permanently to New York in 1816, already in command of a securely professional technique that hints at firsthand knowledge of the contemporary, more decorative phase of French *neoclassical portraiture. An active participant in New York's art life, Ingham numbered among founders and active participants in the *National Academy of Design and the Sketch Club, precursor to the prestigious Century Club. In 1837, while accompanying the New York State geologist on a survey trip, he produced some of the earliest landscape images of the Adirondack area.

Inman, Henry (1801–46). Painter. A leading portraitist, he also produced popular *genre scenes, as well as occasional literary subjects and landscapes. In the mid-1830s he supplanted his teacher, John Wesley *Jarvis, as the preeminent New York portrait specialist. Although speed sometimes compromised the quality of his prolific output, nevertheless his work demonstrates an easy versatility. His characteristically glossy, fluently executed, and highly realistic portraits typically emphasize glamour over character as they give form to the taste and aspirations of his subjects. For female clients, he generally emphasized beauty and sweetness, but his genial male sitters radiate dignified vigor. At his best, as in *The Reverend Dr. James Melancthon Mathews* (Metropolitan Museum, 1838), Inman achieved a compelling and lifelike sense of individuality. With his face partly shaded for dramatic effect, the moodier, quickly executed *Self-Portrait* (Pennsylvania Academy, 1834) demonstrates his ability to work in a more painterly and expressive mode than was usual in his commissioned work. Mostly dating from the 1840s and relatively few in number, Inman's widely admired major genre scenes typically romanticize his subjects, often drawn from lower-class or rural life and frequently focusing on the innocence of children. Born in upstate Utica, Inman moved with his family to New York in 1812 and two years later became Jarvis's apprentice. The gifted youngster soon became Jarvis's collaborator on what virtually amounted to a portrait assembly line. Around 1822 Inman opened his own studio, and between 1824 and 1827 he and Thomas Seir *Cummings worked in a partnership. Although Inman had developed a facility with miniature painting during his years with Jarvis, he handed over to Cummings most of that part of the practice. In 1826 Inman helped to organize the *National Academy of Design and was elected its initial vice president. From 1831 to 1834 he lived in or near Philadelphia, where he entered into a short-lived partnership in an early lithographic firm. After another decade in New York, he sailed for England to work there for almost a year. Returning to New York in failing health in 1845, he painted little before his death. Soon after, to benefit his family, Inman's friends and fellow artists staged the first full-scale retrospective exhibition for an American artist. His son, painter **John O'Brien Inman** (1828–96) produced genre scenes, still lifes, and portraits. His watercolor *Studio Interior* (Brooklyn Museum, 1872) records an artist's chamber, probably his own, in Paris, where he resided for a number of years. During this time, he started painting tightly detailed, historical costume pieces.

Inness, George (1825–94). Painter. A landscape specialist, he created harmonious, broadly painted views of domesticated scenery. His work fostered the shift in taste from the detailed realism of the mid-nineteenth-century *Hudson River School to a more ambiguous, subjective, and aesthetically oriented form preferred later. Inness's art combines devotion to art as a spiritual quest, respect for old master tradition, and scrutiny of natural appearances. His paintings correlate also with important artistic and intellectual tendencies of his age, including *Barbizon painting, impressionism, symbolism, *tonalism, and philosophical rumination on the psychological relationship between material existence and inner experience. His mystically tinged final works presage the formal experimentation and emotional intensity of modernist tendencies. Born in the Hudson River Valley near Newburgh, New York, Inness grew up in the rural surroundings of Newark, New Jersey. A frail epileptic little interested in conventional education, he left schooling in Newark at fourteen or fifteen. Mostly self-taught as an artist, he developed slowly and with hesitations, absorbing into his personal idiom ideas and influences from varied sources that are not always clearly identifiable. After brief early instruction from a local painter, he left home probably in 1841 to work for a year or two in New York for an engraving firm. Régis *Gignoux provided some technical assistance to the aspiring painter and probably advanced Inness's knowledge of traditional European models through prints he owned. Combining elements of such prototypes, particularly the work of Claude Lorrain, with the currently popular Hudson River School approach, Inness achieved modest success in the later 1840s with landscapes that already reveal greater interest in the moods of nature than in its beguiling details.

In 1851 Inness left on the first of several trips to Europe, marking the onset of the restlessness that characterized his subsequent lifestyle. He lived in Florence at first, moved to Rome in 1852, and stopped in Paris on his way home in the spring of that year. In 1853 he again headed for Europe, this time to work in France, where his development advanced sharply as he absorbed Barbizon techniques. Shortly after his return to New York in 1855, he produced his best-known early work, *The Lackawanna Valley* (National Gallery, 1855). In this commission from the president of a railroad, Inness embedded several trains and a distant roundhouse in his evocation of a scene near Scranton, Pennsylvania. An early example of the intrusion of industrial progress into the pastoral landscape, the painting nevertheless conveys a peaceful and harmonious mood. Although glowing light, luxurious vegetation, and a relaxed observer reclining in the foreground celebrate nature's sovereignty, Inness must have been aware of the subject matter's inherent challenge to his view of nature's sanctity. He never again allowed modern life to disrupt his essentially romantic and retrogressive vision of nature and man's place within it. During the late 1850s Inness worked in the Delaware Valley, broadening and integrating elements of his maturing style. In the summer of 1860 he moved to Medford, Massachusetts, not far from Boston. There in relative isolation he achieved quite regularly the expressive equilibrium of real and ideal that culminated in *Peace and Plenty* (Metropolitan Museum, 1865). Its Edenic tenor seeming to promise fulfillment of life on earth at the Civil War's end, it was painted after he moved late in 1863 or early the following year to Eagleswood, an estate overlooking the mouth of the Raritan River in what is now Perth Amboy, New Jersey. This community, founded in the 1850s as a utopian experiment, retained an idealistic flavor and welcomed artists. Here William *Page, whom he had previously met in Italy, transmitted to Inness his enthusiasm for Swedenborgianism, a religious philosophy initiated in the eighteenth century by scientist and theologian Emanuel Swedenborg. Emphasizing correspondences between nature and the divine, it provided a theoretical and inspirational basis for Inness's flowering as an original artist. In the middle of the nineteenth century, the idea that spiritual meaning could be found in nature's physical attributes had already become commonplace, but Inness modified this quest by shifting emphasis from multifarious details to mood, structure, and inner unity as manifestations of divine presence.

After a residence of about three years in Brooklyn, in 1870 Inness again sailed to Europe, stopping in London and Paris before settling in Rome. Bringing his previous experience to bear on the Italian landscape, he completed a number of particularly original paintings. Unprecedented in its daringly abstracted forms and colors and its darkly ambiguous impact, *The Monk* (Addison Gallery of American Art, Phillips Academy, Andover, Massachusetts, 1873) presents its subject as a tiny, hooded figure meditatively wandering at sunset through a compressed, vertically layered space below towering trees flattened to decorative patterns. Inness returned to France for about nine months before sailing home in 1875. He then lived in Boston but resettled the following year in New York. From 1878 he made his permanent home in Montclair, New Jersey, but continued to travel often. During the 1880s he responded, often rather indirectly, to the topography of many locations in New England and the mid-Atlantic states, while Florida, California, and Mexico lured him in the early 1890s. In 1887 he visited England. While on a tour of Europe, he died in Bridge of Allan, Scotland. In paintings of his final decade, Inness entered the realm of poetic mystery, dissolving nature's details into symphonic harmonies of glowing color. Evoking rather than recording woodland interiors or other spaces of limited depth, dematerialized and flattened shapes create patterns of rich hues. Inness vehemently rebuffed any attempt to connect his work with impressionism, he showed no interest in scientific theories of vision, and he rejected the broken color characteristic of the movement. Yet, his tremulous late works capture transient effects of light and of atmospheric density with impressionist precision. As well, he shared that movement's interest in seemingly spontaneous brushwork and in oddly cropped, asymmetrical, and casual compositions. His paintings also suggest symbolism's fascination with introspection and enigma. Widely recognized in later years as the leading American landscape painter, he exerted an influence on contemporaries that did not cease with his death.

George Inness Jr. (1854–1926) followed his father into landscape painting. Born in Paris, he studied with his father and in Paris with Léon Bonnat in 1874. After his family's return to the United States the following year, he began to achieve success on his own while working frequently alongside his father. He remained in New York when the family moved to Montclair, but following his father's death he resided in Paris for a few years. After 1900 he divided his time between Tarpon Springs, Florida, and the Shawangunk Mountains art colony of Cragsmoor, New York, where he died. In his art, he attempted to differentiate himself from his father by featuring figures or, more often, farm animals within rustic settings. He also painted some religious themes and worked as an illustrator. In 1917 he published *Life, Art, and Letters of George Inness*.

Installation art. Art designed and made for a particular space, generally indoors. Usually temporary, or at least capable of being disassembled, installation art originated in the late 1960s. In its early days, installation art was associated with countercultural forces interested in eliminating barriers between art media, extending the sphere of art into the participatory space of real life, exploring relationships instead of creating permanent monuments, and producing art work that resisted commercialization. While those concerns often still pertain, by the 1990s installation art had also evolved into a conventional art form much favored in high-profile, big-budget international art fairs, transitory by their very nature but generally aimed at art-world insiders and hardly lacking in mercantile aspirations. *Assemblages, *happenings, and environmental sculptures by such artists as Red *Grooms, Claes *Oldenburg, and Edward *Kienholz provided precedents for installation art. Hans *Haacke's ensembles helped to fuel a taste for installations directed at social or political issues, while *performance art contributed to its interactive spirit.

International Center of Photography. *See* CAPA, CORNELL.

Intimate Gallery, The. *See* STIEGLITZ, ALFRED.

Ipcar, Dahlov. *See* ZORACH, WILLIAM.

Ippolito, Angelo. *See* ABSTRACT EXPRESSIONISM.

Irascibles, The. Fifteen painters, mostly leading *abstract expressionists, who appeared together in a *Life* photograph taken by Russian-born staff photographer Nina Leen (c. 1909–95). Published in the magazine's issue of January 15, 1951, with the caption, "Irascible Group of Advanced Artists Led Fight against Show," the image accompanied a report on the *Metropolitan Museum of Art's recently opened "American Painting Today 1950." The selection process for this exhibition, which included modernist work but ignored abstract expressionism, initiated a confrontation between avant-garde artists and the museum. Drawn from among eighteen painters who had signed an open letter decrying the museum's policies concerning contemporary art, those pictured were William *Baziotes, James *Brooks, Willem *de Kooning, Jimmy *Ernst, Adolph *Gottlieb, Robert *Motherwell, Barnett *Newman, Jackson *Pollock, Richard *Pousette-Dart, Ad *Reinhardt, Mark *Rothko, Theodoros *Stamos, Hedda *Sterne, Clyfford *Still, and Bradley Walker *Tomlin. Since its initial appearance, the image has assumed iconic status as the most significant photograph of the cadre that redefined postwar New York painting. However, several key contributors to abstract expressionism, notably Philip *Guston, Franz *Kline, and Jack *Tworkov, were associated with neither the letter nor the photograph. The letter, which had appeared on the front page of the *New York Times* on May 22, 1950, precipitated a small art-world uproar. Taken on November 24 at the magazine's headquarters, the photograph countered the popular image of artists as antisocial bohemians. Neatly dressed, as if for a business occasion, the men wear jackets and ties (Pollock, turned to the side, may have been so posed to conceal his probable lack of a tie), while the lone woman is fashionably attired. The three letter-signers who were out of town and thus did not make the photo shoot were Hans *Hofmann, Fritz *Bultman, and Weldon Kees (1914–55), a Nebraska native known primarily as a poet but also as an abstract expressionist painter from 1944 until he moved to San Francisco in 1950 to devote his energies primarily to film and photography. In a gesture of support, ten sculptors had also signed the original letter.

Irwin, Robert (1928–). Installation artist, sculptor, painter, and landscape designer. Best known for *installations that combine scrims and illumination to create perceptually puzzling, dematerialized visual experiences, he claims the process of seeing as his subject. Since about 1980, he has also worked on large public art projects, with special attention to gardens. Born in Long Beach, California, Robert Walter Irwin began his professional training in 1948 at the Otis Art Institute (now Otis College of Art and Design) in Los Angeles. Two years later, he continued at the now defunct Jepson Art Institute but eventually completed his education at the Chouinard Art Institute (now California Institute of the Arts) in 1954. After painting in an *abstract expressionist style, in the early 1960s he engaged in increasingly *minimalist experiments. A few years later, he abandoned painting to concentrate on a series of Discs, shown under precise illumination in order to activate highlighted and shadowed surrounding spaces as part of each work. In the late 1960s he did away with physical objects altogether, concentrating instead on singular installations that focused attention on mysterious visual effects. During this period, he worked on problems of visual perception in the Los Angeles County Museum of Art's Art & Technology Program with physiological psychologist Edward Wortz (who remained a collaborator for years afterward) and, for about a year and a half, James *Turrell. In recent years, he has devoted much attention to public sites, relishing the opportunity to shape environments and enhance viewers' comprehension of their visual and spatial qualities. Between 1992 and 1997 he designed the new Getty Center's outdoor environment in Los Angeles, creating a lush spill of foliage, flowers, and walkways down its adjacent hillside. For the Dia Foundation exhibition space (opened 2003) in Beacon, New York, overlooking the Hudson River, he devised a master plan to enrich every facet of the visitor's experience of the building and grounds, in addition to designing its formal gardens. Upon leaving Los Angeles, Irwin lived for a time in Las Vegas before settling permanently in San Diego in the early 1980s. *Being and Circumstance: Notes Toward a Conditional Art* (1985) introduces his theoretical notions.

Ives, Chauncey Bradley (1810–94). Sculptor. Known for ideal marble creations conforming to the prevailing *neoclassicism of his day, he also produced many portraits, including public monuments. Ives grew up on the Hamden Township farm where he was born, not far from New Haven, Connecticut. He was apprenticed as a teenager to a woodcarver in New Haven. There he probably also received some instruction from Hezekiah *Augur. Subsequently, he worked as a portrait sculptor in New Haven, Boston, and elsewhere in New England before tackling the New York market in 1840. Four years later, he departed for Italy. Thereafter, he occasionally visited the United States but made his home abroad. He resided in Florence until 1851, when he moved permanently to Rome. There he produced a steady stream of well-received imaginative subjects, beginning with the life-size nude *Pandora* (Virginia Museum of Fine Arts, Richmond, 1854; modeled 1851; revised 1863). A biblical subject, *Rebecca at the Well* (Metropolitan Museum, 1866; modeled 1854), proved his most popular, with twenty-five copies sold. Besides classical and religious subjects, he produced realistically detailed genre pieces, often depicting children, as well as literary subjects. Illustrating a popular nineteenth-century tale, *Undine Receiving Her Soul* (Yale University Art Gallery, 1859; revised 1880) renders in stone with great technical finesse the moist drapery fluidly enclosing a gracefully posed woman whose upward regard suggests spiritual rapport. In 1872 Ives's full-length portraits of Connecticut noteworthies Jonathan Trumbull (1869) and Roger Sherman (1870) were unveiled in Statuary Hall of the U.S. Capitol, but by this time the neoclassicism he favored was losing popularity. After about 1880 he was relatively inactive.

Ives, James Merritt. *See* CURRIER & IVES.

J

JACKSON Japonisme Judd JOHNSON *Jasper Johns*

Jackson, Harry Andrew. *See* HARTIGAN, GRACE.

Jackson, May Howard. *See* AFRICAN-AMERICAN ART.

Jackson, William Henry (1843–1942). Photographer and painter. Known chiefly for photographs of the American West and its native inhabitants, he numbered among the first to record many of its scenic wonders. The dramatic power of his thousands of western photographs crystallized ideas about wilderness and its conquest in the American mind. He hauled into remote areas a huge camera that accommodated 20″ × 24″ glass plates, the largest ever used in field photography. Jackson sketched and painted early in his career, but also produced panoramic western scenes in the 1930s. He was born in Keeseville, near Lake Champlain in northern New York State. He learned photography as a teenager, while working in studios in Troy, New York, and in Vermont. Following military service in the Civil War, he returned in 1863 to work again in Vermont. Three years later he headed west. After traveling in the region for some months, he opened a studio in Omaha, in partnership with his brother Edward. For the next several years he photographed the region's landscape, its Indian inhabitants, and the progress of the Union Pacific railroad. In 1870 he accompanied Ferdinand V. Hayden's U.S. government-sponsored expedition along the Oregon Trail. Their association continued through the 1878 season, as they explored varied western regions, including the Wyoming territory, the Rocky and Teton Mountains, and the Southwest. Painters who also sometimes traveled with the group enriched Jackson's aesthetic sensibility. During the first summer Sanford *Gifford was his companion, while Thomas *Moran accompanied later travels. Working alongside Moran in 1871, Jackson produced a series of revelatory photographs that, together with Moran's paintings, proved instrumental to Congress's designation of Yellowstone as a national park in 1872. Jackson settled in Denver in 1879 but traveled widely throughout the United States and into Canada and Latin America. Often his journeys were sponsored by railroads, which found his views useful in stimulating tourism. In 1893 he showed his work at the World's Columbian Exposition in Chicago and served there as an official photographer. The following year, on commission from *Harper's Weekly* magazine, he departed with the World's Transportation Commission on a global tour, which resulted in many effective studies of India and other far-flung locales. In 1898 he became a partner and chief photographer for the Detroit Photographic Company (later, the Detroit Publishing Company). Among other accomplishments there, he spearheaded important developments in the color postcard industry, but administrative duties increasingly displaced photography. Following the firm's dissolution in 1924, he worked independently as a photographer, painter, and lecturer, almost until the end of his ninety-nine years. He died in New York. Jackson issued a number of portfolios and bound volumes of his views (some sponsored by the federal government), as well as *Time Exposure: An Autobiography* (1940). *The Diaries of William Henry Jackson, Frontier Photographer* (1959), edited by LeRoy R. Hafen and Ann W. Hafen, covers the years 1866 through 1874.

Jacquette, Yvonne. *See* BURCKHARDT, RUDY.

Jaffe, Shirley. *See* FRANCIS, SAM.

Japonisme. Term, originally French, referring to the European and American vogue for Japanese art and culture during the late nineteenth century. Collectors and artists alike responded to Japan's exotic and refined products shortly after the country opened trade links in 1853. Displays at London's 1862 international exhibition and subsequent world's fairs widened interest in its decorative arts. Among painters and printmakers, the French generally first grasped the potential of Japanese precedents. Setting the pattern for the American response, they initially incorporated Japanese objects into Western scenes but soon adapted features of Japanese style, particularly the asymmetrical harmonies, patterned shapes, and compressed space seen in Japanese prints. By providing a sophisticated alternative to academic art, the Japanese aesthetic proved crucial to the development of impressionism, post-impressionism, art nouveau, and subsequent modern styles. In the United States, Japanese displays at the 1876 Centennial Exposition in Philadelphia initiated a wave of enthusiasm. As early as the mid-1860s James Abbott McNeill *Whistler had spearheaded a Japanese-influenced sensibility, while John *La Farge, who traveled to Japan, numbers among the artists most deeply involved with that country. Japanese art played an important part in defining the taste of the *aesthetic movement, while *tonalists and *pictorialist photographers numbered among fine artists who particularly responded to it. As teachers and authors, Ernest *Fenollosa and Arthur Wesley *Dow proselytized effectively for Japanese aesthetics. Charles Lang *Freer stands out among the many collectors enamored of Japanese decorative arts. His taste exemplifies also the period's parallel interest in other East Asian countries, particularly China. Although connoisseurs had already admired its art for nearly two centuries, Chinese exports had not structurally affected Western practice, but only provided occasional decorative motifs.

Jarves, James Jackson (1818–88). Writer, critic, and collector. Although he lived abroad for much of his life, *The Art-Idea: Sculpture, Painting, and Architecture in America* (1864) remains a major document in the development of American art criticism. His collection of Italian paintings, glass, and textiles enriched American art museums. As a critic, Jarves boldly dismissed the prevailing emphasis on realism in mid-century American painting. Instead, he championed the more poetic and painterly approach of such artists as George *Inness and William Morris *Hunt, who represented the emerging aesthetic of the late nineteenth century. Similarly, in his approach to art of the past, Jarves preferred those forms that emphasize concepts and spiritual values. Steeped in French and Italian taste, he also appreciated Japanese art at an early date. Born in Boston and privately educated, between 1840 and 1848 Jarves intermittently edited the first newspaper published in Hawaii. After returning to the United States, he acted on behalf of Hawaii in negotiating an 1849 treaty that governed Hawaiian-American relations for half a century. In 1851 he departed for Europe, where he soon established a permanent residence in Florence. There he began to collect art, discerningly favoring the so-called "primitives" who predated the High Renaissance. The core of his painting collection eventually went to the Yale University Art Gallery. From 1880 to 1882 he served as the U.S. vice consul in Florence. He died while on vacation in Switzerland. Jarves's other books include *History of the Hawaiian or Sandwich Islands* (1843), *Art Hints* (1855), *Art Studies; The "Old Masters" of Italy* (1861), *Art Thoughts, the Experiences and Observations of an American Amateur in Europe* (1870), *A Glimpse of the Art of Japan* (1876), and *Italian Rambles* (1883).

Jarvis, John Wesley (1781–1840). Painter. A leading New York portrait painter and miniaturist, in his best likenesses he offered fresh and vivacious impressions of individual personality. His most famous painting, the dramatic if somewhat stagy *Oliver Hazard Perry* (City of New York, 1816), gave visual form to the romantic hero as a cultural ideal and appealed to the nationalistic enthusiasm encouraged by the War of 1812. The courageous and glamorous American naval commander appears in his moment of victory over the British fleet. Three subordinate figures in his small boat intensify the sense of action, while behind Perry a vigorously waving flag bears his motto "Don't Give Up the Ship." Born in South Shields, Durham, near Newcastle-upon-Tyne, to an English mother and American father, from 1786 Jarvis spent his boyhood in Philadelphia. There, in the mid-1790s he was apprenticed to Edward *Savage and moved with him to New York in 1801. Soon working on his own, he also studied miniature painting with Edward Greene *Malbone. A partnership formed in 1802 with portrait painter and miniaturist Joseph Wood (c. 1778–1830), who later worked in Philadelphia and Washington, D.C., came to an end in 1810 when Jarvis left on the first of numerous winter trips to the South. He spent most of that season in Charleston, South Carolina, where he sometimes returned in future years, while at other times he sojourned in New Orleans and Mobile. On occasion during his career, he also journeyed to Boston, Washington, and other cities. In 1811 he moved to Baltimore but two years later was back in New York, which remained his permanent home. In 1814 New York commissioned for city hall six full-length likenesses of heroes from the War of 1812, including the Perry portrait. This prestigious recognition cemented Jarvis's reputation. For most of the ensuing two decades, he remained the city's most sought-after portrait painter. In 1834 a stroke ended his career. His son **Charles Wesley Jarvis** (1812–68) also became a successful portrait painter, although his competent work did not attain the eloquence of his father's. Born in New York, he grew up with his mother's family on Long Island following her death when he was an infant. Between 1828 and 1834 in New York and then in Philadelphia, he was trained by

Henry *Inman, who had been his father's assistant. In 1835 he opened his own New York studio. Although he continued to work in New York, by 1854 he had moved to Newark, New Jersey, where he died.

Jaudon, Valerie. *See* PATTERN AND DECORATION.

Jennys, William (1774–1858). Painter. A portrait specialist, he is known for crisp, insistently realistic, and psychologically acute likenesses. His forcefully rendered, unidealized clients seem intensely alert as they gaze sharply at the viewer. Most of his works present the sitter at waist length, turned at an angle to the picture plane, and placed against a plain background. Probably born in Boston, Jennys is first documented in New London, Connecticut, in 1793. He worked in several Connecticut towns until 1797, when he went to New York for two or three years. There his style became somewhat more painterly, colorful, and three-dimensional. After 1800 he worked primarily in Massachusetts but also in New Hampshire and Vermont. While residing for some years after 1804 in Newburyport, Massachusetts, he painted some of his finest and most complex works. Subsequently, he turned to various business ventures in New York, the Bahamas, and elsewhere. No paintings are known from the last half century before he died in New York. Several portraits are jointly signed by his father, painter and engraver **Richard Jennys** (c. 1734–c. 1809). Probably born in Boston, though possibly in England, Richard entered the historical record as an artist about 1766, when he issued a memorial mezzotint portrait of Boston cleric Jonathan Mayhew. Based on his own painted likeness of Mayhew, it extends the technique, format, and late Baroque style of Peter *Pelham's earlier prints of clergymen. Documents indicate that he later visited the West Indies and worked in South Carolina and Savannah, Georgia, although he seems to have been relatively inactive as an artist for some years. In 1792 he arrived in New Haven, Connecticut, where he restarted his career. By this time, his manner resembled the simpler approach his son was then forming. After completing several portraits in New Milford, Connecticut, during the mid-1790s, he subsequently traveled throughout New England in search of commissions. After his son moved to Newburyport, Richard joined him there. Both painters at times supplemented their portrait careers with ornamental work and art instruction.

Jensen, Alfred (1903–81). Painter and occasional sculptor. An idiosyncratic spirit, he devised a personal style of geometric, often diagrammatic compilations of small, brightly colored shapes, usually rectangles or diamonds, sometimes inscribed with letters, numbers, or tiny symbols. He frequently worked on a huge scale, enhancing the visual power of his obsessive patterns realized in luscious, opaque color. Jensen organized his paintings with the aid of theoretical systems so complex they defied explanation. In this visionary work, optical boldness, intricacy, and evocative allusion stand on their own terms. Almost fifty when he had his first one-person New York show and a few years older by the time he crystallized his mature approach, Jensen led an oddball existence before settling in New York during the 1950s to work full time at painting. Born in Guatemala City to a Danish father and Polish-German mother, Alfred Julio Jensen had a Mayan nurse as a youngster. After his mother died in 1910, he was sent to Denmark, where he started school. From 1917 he worked as a seaman and farmer until 1924 when he moved to San Diego. There, he attended night school for a year to complete his high school education. He then enrolled in art school for a year before heading to Munich in 1926 to work with Hans *Hofmann. He left the following year after meeting Saidie Adler May, a wealthy would-be painter who for years facilitated his intense absorption in a vertiginous panoply of scientific and speculative subjects, including among other interests, mathematics and geometry, color theory, Mayan and Incan culture (particularly architectural and astronomical achievements), electromagnetics, Chinese philosophy (notably the *I Ching*), Christian theology, and the writings of Leonardo da Vinci. The two traveled in Europe and North Africa, all the while painting and collecting art for her collection (mostly bequeathed at her death to the Baltimore Museum of Art). During sojourns in Paris, Jensen studied with or met a number of prominent artists. Contact with Naum *Gabo in the 1940s inspired experiments in sculpture. In 1934 he established a residence in New York, but it was not until after May's death in 1951 that he began to work seriously as a painter. By the time of his first show in 1952, he had inflected his vigorous *abstract expressionist paintings with notions derived from Goethe's color theories. The inimitable signature style he soon developed made an important contribution to wide-ranging 1960s and 1970s interests in color, geometry, surface, seriality, conceptualism, and mysticism. He died in a nursing home in Livingston, near the northern New Jersey suburb of Glen Ridge, where he had resided since 1972. In 1963 he married abstract painter, sculptor, and photographer Regina

Bogat. Born in Brooklyn, she earned a BA at New Jersey's Rutgers University and also studied at the *Art Students League. She continues to live in New Jersey.

Jess (1923–2004). Collage artist, painter, and sculptor. Drawing on symbolist and surrealist traditions, he created imaginative, evocative works independent of mainstream concerns. His most striking pieces, which he called "paste-ups," combine cutouts from magazines, advertisements, and other sources into opulently layered mélanges. Particularly in early examples incorporating comic strips, Jess's work often suggests *pop art's fascination with mass culture, but it deviates from pop's sardonic worldliness. His frequent use of cast-off and found materials in *assemblages as well as collages relates his approach to the practices of San Francisco *funk art colleagues. However, Jess's work shows greater formal discipline, as well as more romantic intentions. Born in Long Beach, California, Burgess Collins intended to become a scientist. He studied at the junior college in his hometown before transferring to the California Institute of Technology in Pasadena. As a chemist for the Army Corps of Engineers after he was drafted in 1943, he worked for the Manhattan Project in Oak Ridge, Tennessee. In 1946 he returned to Cal Tech, where he earned a degree in chemistry during the next two years. After taking a job at the Hanford Atomic Energy Project in Richland, Washington, he began to harbor reservations about the value of scientific progress. He discarded his surname around the time he moved permanently to San Francisco in 1949. There he studied at the California School of Fine Arts (now the San Francisco Art Institute), where his teachers included Elmer *Bischoff, David *Park, and Clyfford *Still. About the time he began to make his distinctive collages in the early 1950s, he met poet Robert Duncan, whose objectives paralleled his own. Duncan often used collagelike methods of composition, he cultivated a lyric and spiritually charged form of expression, and he resisted societal norms while acknowledging the power of tradition and its symbols. They became partners and sometime collaborators until Duncan's death in 1988. Jess's paintings, which he continued to produce concurrently with the pasteups, often parallel the allusive concerns of his collages. Some copy preexisting images, while others offer atmospheric abstractions.

Jewett, William. *See* WALDO, SAMUEL LOVETT.

Jocelyn, Nathaniel. *See* DURRIE, GEORGE HENRY.

Johns, Jasper (1930–). Painter, printmaker, and sculptor. Resisting easy interpretation at every stage, his art chiefly addresses the nature of art itself—how it is made, what it means, and how we know. Beginning in 1954, his most influential work challenged prevailing *abstract expressionism. He turned away from personal expression to focus on mundane objects as sources of visual interest and aesthetic form. Essential to the development of *pop art, this work also foreshadowed aspects of *minimal, *process, and *conceptual art. As he continued to respond into the 1960s to commonplace subjects, his work examined the play of art, reality, and enigma in a more complex fashion than was generally true of most pop art. In the 1970s he focused on abstraction in paintings featuring intricate patterns of parallel brush marks. Usually concealing more than they elucidate, surrealistic mélanges dominate his later work. Born in Augusta, Georgia, he spent a ramshackle childhood in Allendale and other small South Carolina towns. After graduating from high school in Sumter, he attended the University of South Carolina for three semesters but left in 1949 for New York. He remained mostly self-taught as an artist and self-educated in subjects that interested him, including art history, philosophy, and poetry. Drafted in 1951 into the U.S. Army, he returned to New York in 1953 after a tour of duty that included six months in Japan. From early 1954 Robert *Rauschenberg remained a close companion, friendly rival, and sometime lover for about six years. At first, the two also worked together as designers of department store window displays.

In Johns's breakthrough paintings of the mid-1950s, he rendered flags, targets, and other two-dimensional objects as if they were coextensive with the picture surface. Although the design of these painted "objects" was predetermined, the artist's sensuous, tradition-laden handling of materials countered any impression of mere replication. Rather, his visible touch emphasized the process that brought the painting into being. These works neither "representing" nor symbolizing the originals confound the potential relationships between art and commonsense reality but generally do so with tact and even elegance. *Gray Alphabets* (Menil Collection, Houston, 1956) subsumes small, regularly aligned letters into a poetic aestheticism of extreme refinement and subtlety. Johns sometimes further complicated painted emblems by combining them with three-dimensional objects. In *Target with Four Faces* (Museum of Modern Art, 1955), four casts of the same face seem wedged into boxes that permit only the mouth and lower part of the nose to be seen. These mysterious and lifelike representations surmount a painted square featuring a blue and yellow circular target against a red background. A hinged flap, which may be let down to hide the faces, adds to the work's cryptic chill. Johns also made freestanding sculptures that share the paradoxes of his paintings. Seemingly replicating beer cans, light bulbs, and other ordinary items, these are not castings from the originals but complex constructions, often with painted surfaces. Despite the transgressive, ironic, and sometimes humorous nature of the early work, its expressive demeanor revealed the maker to be at heart, as he has remained, a slightly melancholy, somewhat evasive intimist. As he originated this new form of expression, Johns responded to the ideas of John *Cage, a personal friend, and Marcel *Duchamp, with whom he became acquainted toward the end of the 1950s. Readings in the work of philosopher Ludwig Wittgenstein also stimulated his thinking about relationships between art, language, and reality. Johns's first one-person show, mounted at Leo *Castelli's gallery in January 1958, nearly sold out (the *Museum of Modern Art bought three pieces) and transformed the artist from an unknown into an art star.

For a few years beginning about 1959, Johns often combined the rich, painterly surfaces of abstract expressionism with his deadpan imagery. Letters, numbers, and maps appear frequently in contexts that challenge their reality. The extroverted *False Start* (private collection, 1959) resembles at first glance a brightly hued gestural painting. Where brush marks of a single primary color gather together, the artist superimposed stenciled names that generally identify other colors. Thus, a red "red" appears over one yellow area and a blue "blue," over a red one, but a blue "yellow" appears on top of another yellow swatch. In the mid-1960s, Johns worked on an increasingly large scale, often combining aspects of earlier work into synthetic units. With time, these tended toward increased abstraction, which became his main concern during the 1970s. Using hatching as a leitmotif, he explored questions of perception and compositional structure. In the early 1980s, Johns entered into a new and more self-referential phase of his career. Since then, he has combined all manner of clearly and dimly perceived imagery into abstractly structured compositions. His own earlier work, masterworks of other artists, the furnishings of his home and studio, and psychic detritus sucked into the vortex of his imagination serve his hermetic devotion to painting. Despite a tendency to mystification, over the long haul his effort asserts the inviolability and independence of private life as an element within social experience, while also continuing his unrelenting probe into pictorial meaning.

After taking up printmaking in 1960, Johns soon achieved masterful results with this inherently repetitive, layered, and craftsman-like practice. He has particularly stressed interaction between image and medium in some four hundred prints, mainly lithographs. His activity as a designer and artistic advisor for the dance company of his friend Merce Cunningham culminated in an ethereal set for *Walkaround Time* (Walker Art Center, 1968), inspired by Duchamp's *The Bride Stripped Bare by her Bachelors, Even (The Large Glass)*. Johns maintains secluded residences in the northwest Connecticut town of Sharon and on the Caribbean island of St. Martin. Since the late 1990s, he has simplified his work, sometimes radically so. A recent group of paintings features catenary curves of attached strings and similarly shaped painted lines. Some include subsidiary imagery drawn from his grand repertoire.

Johnson, David (1827–1908). Painter. A landscape specialist, he responded at different times and in varying combinations to the major mid-century currents, including the *Hudson River School, *luminism, *Pre-Raphaelitism, and the *Barbizon approach. His compositions often drew on standard Hudson River School formulas, but many works achieve a fresh veracity by dispensing with common picturesque devices, such as foreground or framing elements. His most characteristic landscapes feature finely drawn detail and expansive vistas, but he also produced a number of closely observed woodland interiors, often featuring rocks. In these, he attained a surprisingly effective naturalism by ostensibly recording nature with few aesthetic adjustments, as in *Brook Study at Warwick* (Museum of Art, Munson-Williams-Proctor Arts Institute, Utica, New York, 1873), which brings together his interests in the poetic empiricism of the Hudson River School, Pre-Raphaelite crispness of detail, and luminist sensitivity to light. In response to Barbizon influence, beginning in the 1870s some works experiment with softer painterly effects but most preserve clear detail even when indulging Barbizon's lush version of the pastoral. Born in New York, Johnson resided there until his last years. In 1845 he began two years of study at the *National Academy of Design. He worked in 1850 with Jasper *Cropsey and was also acquainted with John *Kensett and John *Casilear. His brother, **Joseph Hoffman Johnson** (1821–90), a New York portrait painter, may also have contributed to his artistic education. Johnson's subjects demonstrate that he traveled extensively throughout the northeastern United States and at least once, around 1860, as far south as Virginia. Evidence suggests that he may also have journeyed to Europe and the Rocky Mountains during the 1860s. In 1904 he moved permanently to Walden in the Hudson River Valley. Johnson also produced portraits (oddly, most of these are copies of photographs or other paintings) and a few still lifes.

Johnson, Eastman (1824–1906). Painter and occasional lithographer. Known for *genre scenes and portraits, he employed old master skills to depict contemporary American life. Some notable portrait groups set in individualized interiors take on the tone of genre paintings, while other subjects include memorable views of rural activity in Maine and Nantucket. Born in Lovell, Maine, Jonathan Eastman Johnson later lived also as a child in nearby Fryeburg on the Maine-New Hampshire border and in Augusta. In 1840 he began training in a Boston lithography shop but after two years returned to Maine. There and later in Washington, D.C., and Boston, he concentrated on portraits, working mainly in pencil or charcoal. In 1849 he departed for Europe. During two years in Düsseldorf, he studied at the art academy and worked in Emanuel *Leutze's studio. Subsequently based in The Hague, he closely scrutinized seventeenth-century Dutch and Flemish painting, particularly Rembrandt's work. In 1855 he worked for some months under Thomas Couture in Paris. That fall, he moved to Washington. In 1856 and 1857 he made extended visits to Superior, Wisconsin, near Duluth. There he painted studies of local Ojibwa life as well distinguished portraits of Indians. After a brief period in Cincinnati, in 1858 Johnson settled permanently in New York. The following year he completed *Negro Life at the South* (later nicknamed *Old Kentucky Home*; New York Public Library, on permanent loan to the New-York Historical Society), which made his reputation. An unproblematic, even sentimental view of life among urban slaves he had observed in Washington, it depicts African-American adults and children enjoying leisure time outdoors in their disorderly quarters. Unusual in portraying African Americans in a family context, it reveals the painter's sympathetic attitude toward blacks, who provided subjects for several other works during the Civil War period. Only the arrival of a young white woman at one side suggests more complicated realities that this painting otherwise skirts.

Technically skilled and versatile, Johnson sometimes worked in a relatively tight and detailed manner, while on other occasions he used a painterly approach emphasizing broad masses of form. Among several precisely rendered domestic interiors, *The Hatch Family* (Metropolitan Museum, 1871) depicts more than a dozen individuals belonging to three generations, arranged within the richly appointed, fashionable library of the family home. At once informal and dignified, it documents a way of life among wealthy New Yorkers. More loosely painted and more richly suggestive, *The Funding Bill* (Metropolitan Museum, 1881), an interior with two men in discussion of financial matters, employs light streaming from an unseen window to inject Rembrandtian drama and nobility. After his arrival in New York, Johnson's genre subjects included urban street life, war-related subjects, and country experiences, including maple sugaring in Maine. From 1870 he regularly summered on Nantucket. Here and sometimes elsewhere in New England, he continued to find rural and often somewhat old-fashioned activities that he presented to his urban audience with a hint of nostalgia for a vanishing era. *Cranberry Harvest* (Timken Museum of Art, San Diego, California, 1880) integrates numerous figures into a broad Nantucket landscape caught in slanting sunlight. As others search for berries, the scene pivots around a central standing woman. Motionless, she contributes to a timeless grandeur offset by enigmatic strangeness. Despite acclaim for his genre work, during the 1880s Johnson gradually relinquished these subjects to specialize almost exclusively in portraits, nearly all picturing successful men. He visited Europe in 1885, 1891, and 1897 but seems to have taken little notice of recent developments in painting there.

Johnson, Grace Mott. *See* DASBURG, ANDREW.

Johnson (or Johnston), Joshua (active c. 1795–1824). Painter. The first documented African-American professional artist, he worked as a portrait painter for a well-to-do Baltimore clientele. Only two representations of black subjects are known. Employing limited technical skills within current Anglo-American conventions, Johnson often achieved charming effects, particularly in rendering women and children. Their prim demeanor and doll-like immobility suit his attention to decorative detail and pattern. Johnson's sitters reveal little character, but their social aspirations and his artistic ambitions are evident in his attempts to emulate sophisticated contemporary standards. Among the more than eighty surviving paintings attributed to his hand, an unusually high percentage depict children, and a number tackle the difficulties of showing a family group. Evidence about almost every aspect of Johnson's life remains open to question. Contradictions even undermine the prevailing view that he was black; he might have been a mulatto whose light skin created confusion about his racial ancestry. In any event, Johnson probably came from the West Indies, possibly Haiti. Following his liberation from slavery, he lived as a free black in Baltimore, where he was listed as a painter in the city directory between 1796 and 1824. Stylistic affinities with the work of Charles Willson *Peale suggest that Johnson may have studied with him or with some member of that extended artistic clan. In any event, he must have been familiar with examples of their work commissioned by families of the Baltimore area.

Johnson, Malvin Gray. *See* AFRICAN-AMERICAN ART.

Johnson, Raymond. *See* FLUXUS.

Johnson, Sargent. *See* AFRICAN-AMERICAN ART.

Johnson, William H. (1901–70). Painter. During his early maturity, he worked as a sophisticated and passionate expressionist, influenced particularly by Chaim Soutine's example. In paintings of this period, agitated lines enclose flattened forms rendered with rich and spontaneous brushwork. He also produced forceful woodcuts, usually hand-colored, that recall German expressionist precedents. In a distinct stylistic turn, after 1938 he focused on his African-American heritage in narrative paintings and serigraphs executed in a colorful, patterned, less painterly approach based on precedents in naive, untrained work, although bearing some stylistic ties to the earlier relief prints. His new direction reflected the *Harlem Renaissance's pride in black life and recent successes of Jacob *Lawrence and Horace *Pippin, who used simplified styles to treat similar subject matter. Johnson's devotion to characterizing an aspect of national life also paralleled the objectives of contemporaries in the *American Scene movement. Some observers have thought his change of style resulted from a long-standing search for authenticity in folk culture, while others emphasize calculated careerism. Born in Florence, South Carolina, in 1918 William Henry Johnson moved to New York, where he trained at the *National Academy of Design. There, Charles *Hawthorne offered particular encouragement as he developed an accomplished form of realism. Johnson worked also with George *Luks before heading for Paris in the fall of 1926. After returning to the United States for some months in 1929–30, he married a Danish ceramist and weaver, and settled with her in the fishing village of Kerteminde. They traveled extensively in Europe and North Africa, and lived for a time in Norway, before returning to New York in 1938. Between 1939 and 1943, Johnson received support from *federal art projects. By the mid-1940s, the quality of his art was in decline as he showed increasing symptoms of mental deterioration. During an impulsive return to Scandinavia in 1946–47, he suffered a breakdown and upon his return was committed permanently to a state hospital on Long Island. He did not resume painting. The turbulent, spiritually charged *Sun Setting, Denmark* (Smithsonian American Art Museum, 1930–32) reveals the emotional fervor and knowledgeable grasp of European models that characterize Johnson's earlier style. During these years, he generally focused on nonliterary subjects such as figure studies, landscape, and still life. Colorfully depicting a barefoot farmer with his produce-laden donkey, *Going to Market* (Smithsonian American Art Museum, c. 1940) features stylistic and thematic characteristics of his later paintings. In addition to memories of the rural South, major subjects of these years include contemporary life in Harlem, African-American history, and the World War II experience of blacks in the military and on the home front. In addition, Johnson broke new ground in his renderings of Christian motifs enacted by black figures.

Johnston, David Claypoole (1798–1865). Printmaker, draftsman, and painter. The first important satirical draftsman in the United States, he became the nation's earliest commercially successful lithographer. He also produced wood engravings, etchings, and numerous book illustrations. For *genre scenes and landscapes, he occasionally painted in oils but generally preferred watercolor. Although he poked fun at many aspects of American life, he is remembered particularly for anti-slavery cartoons. Born in Philadelphia, between 1815 and 1819 he trained there as an engraver in the shop of Francis Kearney (1785–1837), who sometimes published his own drawings and cartoons. Before settling permanently in 1825 in the abolitionist stronghold of Boston, Johnston toured for several years as an actor. His earliest notable prints were portraits of American and British stage celebrities. Informed by an unusually extensive knowledge of art history and literature, including precedents in the work of Englishmen George Cruikshank and Thomas Rowlandson, his satirical works demonstrate lively interest in contemporary political and social issues. Between 1828 and 1849 he issued a series of *Scraps*, pictorial pamphlets featuring humorous vignettes concerning topics of the day. In 1831 he designed the first pictorial banner for William Lloyd Garrison's *The Liberator*, mouthpiece of the abolitionist movement. Despite unsophisticated technique and farcical humor, Johnston put his vigorous and unacademic style to unparalleled use in reaching a broad audience with comic and egalitarian themes. His five children all had artistic inclinations, and three remained active in the Boston art community, working in the orbit of William Morris *Hunt. **Thomas Murphy Johnston** (1836–69) was known for portrait drawings as well as landscape paintings, while **John B. Johnston** (1848–86), made a particular specialty of painting animals posed before landscape settings. **Sarah J. F. Johnston** (1850–1925), among Hunt's most accomplished and admired students, specialized in large-scale charcoal drawings, often depicting children or domestic subjects.

Johnston, Frances Benjamin (1864–1952). Photographer. An early photojournalist, she also worked as an art photographer. Her best-known achievement, a series of photographs taken in the winter of 1899–1900 at the Hampton (Virginia) Normal and Agricultural Institute, fuses documentary and aesthetic concerns. Portraying the African-American and American Indian students of the school in daily activities, the classically composed, sensitively lit tableaux honor the school and its mission of providing dignity and opportunity to socially marginalized young people. Born in Grafton, West Virginia, Johnston lived as a child in Rochester, New York, and Washington, D.C. She studied art in Paris between 1883 and 1885 and then in Washington, where she also learned photography. After opening her own studio, she quickly became the capital's leading portrait photographer. Her subjects included several U.S. presidents and their wives, government officials, and visiting notables. She also accepted wide-ranging assignments for newspapers and magazines, investigating subjects as varied as bleak Pennsylvania coal fields and Chicago's World's Columbian Exposition of 1893. An active member of the turn-of-the-century photographic community, she exhibited in several important national shows. Alfred *Stieglitz published her work in *Camera Notes*, and she later joined the *Photo-Secession. An 1899 series on the schools of Washington led to an invitation to photograph at Hampton. Subsequently, she undertook similar projects at the African-American Tuskegee (Alabama) Institute and at the Carlisle Indian School in Pennsylvania. Beginning in 1909, Johnston added architectural and interior design photography to her pursuits. Besides working for such powerhouse clients as Cass Gilbert and the McKim, Mead and White firm, she later recorded much of the South's historic and vernacular architecture. She died in New Orleans, her home in later years.

Johnston, Henrietta (c. 1674–1729). Painter. Working almost exclusively in pastel, she produced portraits in Charleston, South Carolina, as well as a few in New York during a 1725 visit. She is thought to have been the first professional woman artist working in the colonies, as well as the first professional artist active in the South and the first to specialize in pastel. Most of Johnston's American portraits concentrate on faces and do not extend much below the shoulders. Despite weaknesses in delineating anatomy, she created delicate images of softly sensuous charm, particularly suited to renderings of women or children. Her use of pastel reflected an international vogue for the medium during the late seventeenth and eighteenth centuries. Henrietta de Beaulieu came from French lineage, although she may have been born in England or Ireland. In London in 1694 she married into an important Anglo-Irish family and soon moved to Dublin, where her husband, Sir Edward Dering, died a few years later. Although her training, if any, remains unknown, by about 1704 she was producing pastel portraits in Ireland. In 1705 she married Gideon Johnston, an Anglican clergyman, and three years later moved permanently to Charleston. She returned to England only once, in 1711–12. Widowed again in 1716, she continued her portrait career until 1726.

Johnston, Joshua. *See* JOHNSON, JOSHUA.

Johnston, Thomas. *See* GREENWOOD, JOHN.

Jonas, Joan. *See* PERFORMANCE ART.

Jones, Joe (1909–63). Painter and printmaker. His uncompromising depictions of subjects from America's heartland contributed to both regionalist and social realist currents of the *American Scene movement. Born in St. Louis, Joseph John Jones remained essentially self-taught as an artist. His left-wing social views inform the lithograph *A Poor Heritage* (c. 1940), juxtaposing a small child and a garbage can within a derelict environment. *American Farm* (Whitney Museum, 1936) presents farm buildings perched in a ravaged, eroded landscape. A poignant tribute to the American farmer's persistence, it also suggests the precariousness of that way of life. Many of Jones's scenes are less politically loaded, describing agricultural activities such as harvesting and threshing with simple directness. He also painted cityscapes, usually emphasizing architecture, as in *View of St. Louis* (St. Louis Art Museum, c. 1939). After moving to New York in 1935, Jones participated in the *American Artists' Congress and painted *federal art project murals. From the late 1940s he focused on benign shore and harbor views, mostly of Bermuda and New Jersey. He died in Morristown, in the New Jersey area where he had resided for more than twenty years.

Jones, Lois Mailou (1905–98). Painter. Adept in several styles varying from direct realism to stylized near abstraction, she is known particularly for such paintings as *Les Fétiches* (Smithsonian American Art Museum, 1938), a dynamic, cubistic arrangement of five African masks, combining modernist expression with subjects from her racial heritage. From 1930 until she retired in 1977, she taught at Howard University in Washington, D.C. A native of Boston, she studied for four years there at the School of the Museum of Fine Arts. While spending the summer of 1934 in New York to study at Columbia University, she increased her involvement with the *Harlem Renaissance and with African art. During the academic year 1937–38, she studied in Paris and traveled through Italy. In the early years of her career, she worked in an accomplished impressionist style, which gave way to interest in cubism and other forms of modernism. During the 1940s she concentrated on scenes of African-American life. Following marriage in 1953 to Haitian artist Louis Vergniaud Pierre-Noel, she frequently employed colorful, flattened patterns to depict blacks in his homeland, as well as in Africa following a 1969 visit of several months. Jones often returned to France to depict picturesque vistas, and in her last years she renewed an early interest in idyllic nature subjects. She died at her Washington home.

Jonson, Raymond (1891–1982). Painter. Among the first progressive artists to settle in New Mexico, he worked in relative obscurity throughout most of his career while producing accomplished abstractions inspired by Kandinsky. He also created powerful, idiosyncratic interpretations of the New Mexico landscape. Born near Chariton, Iowa, Carl Raymond Johnson moved several times with his family before they settled in 1902 in Portland, Oregon. In 1909–10 at the Portland Museum Art School he worked with a teacher who had been a student of Arthur Wesley *Dow. In 1910 he moved to Chicago, where he studied with Swedish-born painter and printmaker B. J. O. (Bror Julius Olsson) Nordfeldt (1878–1955), the city's foremost postimpressionist, and at the School of the Art Institute of Chicago. During his Chicago years, while also doing innovative design work for the theater, he painted works indebted to the emotionally and spiritually charged work of Albert *Bloch and Russian artist Nikolai Roerich, who arrived for an extended visit to the city in 1920. After reading *Concerning the Spiritual in Art* in 1921, he adopted Kandinsky as his guiding light. Following a visit in 1922, he moved to Santa Fe two years later. At this time, he altered the spelling of his surname. For his subsequent Earth Rhythms series, he incessantly drew the hard, arid forms of New Mexico's landscape, as he sought to comprehend the forces of nature. From these studies, he composed paintings that use cubist angularity and fragmentation as tools to construct expressive, at times almost violent, evocations of natural forms and processes. Some landscapes include allegorical figures. From about 1929, he worked mostly nonobjectively, combining geometric and organic forms in intricate compositions. Hard-edge boundaries suggest discipline and control, while vigorous, sometimes whiplash, lines often energize surfaces. At their best, his paintings communicate mystical inner visions, independent of the material world and realized through imagination.

In 1934 Jonson joined the faculty at the University of New Mexico in Albuquerque, where he also painted murals for the university library under auspices of a *federal art project. In 1938, with Kandinsky follower and influential *Taos teacher Emil Bisttram (1895–1976), Jonson organized the Transcendental Painting Group, which existed for about three years. This loose association of ten spiritually oriented abstract painters also included Ed Garman (1914–2004), William Lumpkins (1909–2000), Agnes *Pelton, Florence Miller Pierce (1918–), Horace Towner Pierce (1916–58), and Canadian Lawren Harris. With a gift of his own works along with others from his collection, in 1950 he founded the university's Jonson Gallery, which showcases this material along with the work of emerging or underrepresented artists. Jonson retired from teaching in 1954 but continued to promote the exchange of ideas that underlay New Mexico's development in recent decades as a vital center for contemporary art. He died in Albuquerque.

Jouett, Matthew Harris (1788–1827). Painter. A portrait and miniature specialist, he occasionally painted landscapes. Born on a farm near Harrodsburg, Kentucky, and a resident of that state all his life, he ranks as the first notable painter of what was then the American West. About 1804 he arrived in Lexington, which remained his home. He graduated from Transylvania College there and subsequently practiced law. Although mostly self-taught as an amateur painter, after returning in 1815 from service in the War of 1812, he decided to become a professional. The following year he traveled to Philadelphia and then to Boston, where he spent about four months in Gilbert *Stuart's studio. His earnest record of Stuart's advice remains the most important documentary source about the master's technique and theories. Following his return to Lexington, he often sought commissions during winters in New Orleans and other southern cities along the Mississippi River. Jouett generally practiced a workmanlike approximation of Stuart's approach, but his development suggests also admiration for the work of John Wesley *Jarvis, whom he met in New Orleans, and Thomas *Sully, with whom he became acquainted on subsequent visits to Philadelphia. In his most appealing likenesses, he normally employed a bust-length format and plain background in order to concentrate on the face. His undated *John Grimes* (Metropolitan Museum) renders a convincing likeness, while moody shadows add romantic flair. Jouett died of yellow fever at his home near Lexington.

Judd, Donald (1928–94). Sculptor, printmaker, and art critic. As a leading *minimalist, he created precisely fabricated, boxlike serial arrangements, usually set directly on the floor or suspended from a wall in carefully calibrated, stacked compositions. Softening reflections from tinted Plexiglas sheets, typically inserted on the underside of forms, sometimes ameliorate the cold, uncompromising effects of characteristically sleek but unadorned metallic surfaces. A principal spokesman for minimalism, he set forth his views particularly cogently in a 1965 article "Specific Objects," published in *Arts Yearbook*. Here, he proposed a new form of autonomous three-dimensional art that straddled—or transcended—conventional definitions of painting and sculpture by eluding both illusionism and literal space. To insure proper presentation of his art, he established the Chinati Foundation in Marfa, Texas, for the permanent display of his own work, along with examples by like-minded artists. Born in Excelsior Springs, Missouri, not far from Kansas City, Donald Clarence Judd moved frequently during childhood. He entered the U.S. Army's Corps of Engineers in 1946, shortly after graduating from high school. Late the following year, he left military service and moved to New York to study at the *Art Students League. He also studied at the College of William and Mary in Williamsburg, Virginia, in 1948–49 and after returning to New York to continue at the league, earned a bachelor's degree in philosophy at Columbia University in 1953. Several years later, Meyer *Schapiro numbered among his teachers as he pursued graduate training there in art history. While working as an abstract painter, in 1959 he began to write art criticism regularly for *Arts Magazine*, soon making a reputation for hard-headed support of younger artists intent on replacing prevailing *New York School conventions. By the time he relinquished this activity in 1965, he had also established his signature method of art making and, to eliminate all evidence of the artist's hand, transferred production to industrial fabricators. In the mid-1970s he bought the Marfa property. With the support of the Dia Foundation, in 1986 he opened the independent, nonprofit museum, which showcases his work along with examples by such friends as Dan *Flavin and John *Chamberlain. He remodeled buildings there to his own designs and, for his home and studio, began making furniture, which developed into a commercial sideline in the mid-1980s. As a printmaker, he used several media, including woodcut, etching, and silkscreen to explore aesthetic issues related to his sculptures. He died in New York. At that time, in addition to homes in Manhattan and Marfa, he also maintained a residence in Switzerland, where he was working on commissions. His collected writings appear in *Complete Writings, 1959–1975* (1975) and *Complete Writings, 1975–1986* (1987).

Junk art. Term describing art assembled at least partly from detritus. The junk elements may be selected for formal or associational properties. Ironically commenting on the transformation of valueless materials into saleable and aesthetically significant art objects, junk art suggests the profligate nature of a throw-away society. Although precedents may be detected in the early decades of the twentieth century, junk art rose in popularity during the late 1950s, as *assemblage in general became a prominent method of art making. Richard *Stankiewicz's pioneering sculptures constructed from industrial cast-offs provided an important precedent, soon amplified by Robert *Rauschenberg's delight in all manner of debris, including tires, rags, and other household rubbish. Critic Lawrence *Alloway named the tendency in 1961.

K

Kertész Krasner Kent Kline KENSETT Kelly

Kadish, Reuben. *See* POLLOCK, JACKSON.

Kahn, Wolf (1927–). Painter and printmaker. Primarily a landscape painter, he renders impressions of nature in ravishing colors. His flattened space and painterly brushwork reflect the *abstract expressionist context of his youth. A screen of trees or bushes seen against the sky or distant hills often provides a patterned foil for ornamental effects that recall, on a greatly magnified scale and with Matisse's chromatic accomplishments in mind, the *tonalist work of Dwight William *Tryon a century earlier. Born in Stuttgart, Kahn left Germany in 1939. After an interlude in England, he settled in New York the following year. There he studied with Hans *Hofmann, who imbued in the young artist the desire to construct works of art balancing nature and abstract form. After more than two years with Hofmann, he enrolled at the University of Chicago, where he earned a bachelor's degree in 1951. His characteristic style has grown richer but deviated little from its basic objectives since it came together after his return to New York. He has for many years also worked at a residence in Vermont. Kahn's extensive work in pastel is reflected in the subject matter of two books, *Pastel Light* (1983) and *Wolf Kahn Pastels* (2000), which share his working methods and aesthetic goals. In *Wolf Kahn's America* (2003), reproductions of his paintings from locales across the United States accompany his reminiscences and observations. He has also worked with lithography, usually in color, as well as intaglio processes. In Italy in 1957 he married Emily *Mason. Their daughter **Cecily Kahn** also is a painter. A lifelong New Yorker with a second residence in Friendship, Maine, near Rockland, in 1981 she received a BFA degree from the Rhode Island School of Design in Providence. A member of *American Abstract Artists, she paints bright and vigorous abstractions that combine constructivist geometry with *biomorphic or irregularly formed elements. Wolf Kahn's brother **Peter Kahn** (1921–97) was a painter and graphic artist, as well as a typographer, book designer, and art historian. Also born in Germany, he taught at Louisiana State University in Baton Rouge before moving permanently in 1969 to Ithaca, New York, where he served on the faculty of Cornell University.

Kainen, Jacob (1909–2001). Painter, printmaker, and curator. Born in Waterbury, Connecticut, he moved with his family to New York in 1918. He received his artistic training at the *Art Students League and Pratt Institute, from which he graduated in 1930. For more than a decade, he then eagerly participated in the art life of the city. In 1935 he joined the graphics workshop sponsored by a *federal art project, and by about 1940 he was active among the artists who initiated the *abstract expressionist movement. These formative influences defined his interests as an artist, although he left for Washington, D.C., in the early 1940s. There he worked until 1970 in the *Smithsonian Institution's graphic arts collections, serving during the last four years as curator of prints at the National Collection of Fine Arts (now the Smithsonian American Art Museum). During his long career as an artist, Kainen worked in varied styles and media. In the 1930s, he was drawn to the predominant *American Scene movement and often depicted the ordinary realities of life during the Depression. The lithograph *Drought* (c. 1935), for example, underlines the precariousness of farming. His less detailed color lithograph *Cafeteria* (1936) suggests in its emphasis on structure Kainen's evolving interest in abstract form. From the 1940s abstraction predominated, although he sometimes returned to representation. His abstract work included both geometric and freely painted inventions. However, he consistently pursued unified compositions featuring painterly facture and resonant color, as in the lushly painted *Only in Darkness* (Phillips Collection, 1955). An advocate for printmaking, he worked in many techniques and wrote widely on the medium and its historical masters. He died at his home in the Washington suburb of Chevy Chase, Maryland.

Kalina, Richard. *See* JAUDON, VALERIE.

Kamrowski, Gerome (1914–2004). Painter. An *abstract expressionist, he numbered among the first Americans to explore the abstract potential of surrealism. Intricately detailed, organic forms in predominately acidic hues writhe, seeming to separate and merge, across the surface of *Emotional Seasons* (Whitney Museum, 1942). He also made evocative shadow boxes in this period. Born in Warren, Minnesota, in 1932 he began his training at the St. Paul School of Art, where he adopted a cubist-inflected modernism. In the mid-1930s he worked for a *federal art project before moving in 1937 to Chicago. There he studied with László *Moholy-Nagy and Alexander *Archipenko at the New Bauhaus (now the Illinois Institute of Technology's Institute of Design) and joined the *American Abstract Artists. After working during the following summer with Hans *Hofmann in *Provincetown, he moved to New York. He became particularly friendly with William *Baziotes and associated with the group that formed in the early 1940s around Roberto *Matta. In 1946 he settled permanently in Ann Arbor, where he taught at the University of Michigan for many years. Although his New York reputation suffered from his geographical remove, he continued to paint strong abstract work.

Kanaga, Consuelo. *See* F/64 GROUP.

Kane, John (1860–1934). Painter. Self-taught, he is remembered mostly for carefully observed, stylized cityscapes, interior views, and industrial scenes of Pittsburgh. He also painted portraits and, from memory, scenes of his native Scotland. In his best-known work, *Self-Portrait* (Museum of Modern Art, 1929), he depicted his half-length nude body in a dramatic frontal pose. Strongly side lit to enhance three-dimensional form, his torso reveals physical power that complements strength of character suggested in his serious demeanor. A black backdrop intensifies the contours of his body and sets off the flesh tones, while three abstract white arches above his head intensify the design and contribute to an iconic effect. Born in West Calder, near Edinburgh, John Cain left school at nine and worked in coal mines and factories before he arrived in the United States in 1879. He continued to toil as a miner and laborer in several locations until 1891, when loss of a leg in an accident necessitated less physically demanding employment. Among his subsequent varied jobs, painting houses and freight cars and coloring photographs extended his growing interest in sketching and, later, painting in his leisure time. His early work reveals much stumbling, but perseverance improved his skill at composition and representation. Sometime before he settled permanently in Pittsburgh during the World War I era, he changed the spelling of his surname. He apparently did not endeavor to exhibit his work until the mid-1920s, but he achieved sudden fame when one of his paintings appeared in Pittsburgh's Carnegie International Exhibition in 1927. Most of his best work dates to subsequent years, when he affectionately recorded complex, fact-based Pittsburgh views, sometimes filtered through imagination or memory. The subjects of these works relate to the contemporary *American Scene movement. An autobiography, *Sky Hooks* (written in collaboration with newspaper reporter Marie McSwigan), appeared posthumously in 1938.

Kantor, Morris (1896–1974). Painter. An independent, he employed both representational and nonobjective elements, often to gently bemused effect. Originally from Minsk, Russia (now Belarus), he came with his family to New York in 1911. With little training as an artist, in 1919 he began to paint energetic abstractions. Some of these incorporate elements of fantasy, producing visionary effects. After subsequently practicing a rather hard realism for three years, in 1927 he departed for Paris. This yearlong sojourn stimulated his most personal and original works as he enriched representation with shifting, layered, or transparent planes to suggest instability and dreamlike, surrealistic states. Among his most effective paintings from this period, *Haunted House* (Art Institute of Chicago, 1930) details an old New England interior, but around its edges the room becomes transparent to admit intruding views of other houses and a mysterious human silhouette. Kantor also painted views of Union Square from his Fourteenth Street studio, as well as scenes inspired by the New England countryside and shore. From 1936 until illness compelled retirement in 1972, he taught at the *Art Students League. He died in a Nyack hospital, not far from his Hudson River Valley home in New City.

His wife, painter Martha Ryther (1896–1981), experimented imaginatively with modern styles during the early part of her career. In the 1940s she began to specialize in delicately composed, introspective interiors painted on glass, although she essayed other subjects as well. Born in Boston, she worked with Maurice *Prendergast before moving in 1917 to New York, where she continued her studies with William *Zorach and Hugo *Robus at the Modern Art School. She later traveled and worked in Europe. After a divorce from Jock Fulton, she and Kantor married in 1928. In her final years, prevented from painting by illness, she worked with collage almost until her death at her New City home.

Kaprow, Allan (1927–2006). Assemblage artist, painter, art critic, and theorist. Also a writer and teacher. He remains best known as the originator of *happenings. Born in Atlantic City, New Jersey, he graduated from New York University in 1949. He also studied painting with Hans *Hofmann during his undergraduate years. Between 1950 and 1952 he studied with Meyer *Schapiro while earning a master's degree in art history from Columbia University. His vigorously constructed, gestural paintings, collages, and *assemblages of the 1950s revealed at first admiration for *abstract expressionism, particularly the work of Jackson *Pollock, but gradually moved closer to the spirit of mixed-media work by his friend Robert *Rauschenberg. Between 1956 and 1958 he took courses from John *Cage at the New School for Social Research (now New School). By then he was already teaching at Rutgers University in New Brunswick, New Jersey, where he held an appointment from 1953 until 1961. During those years, he figured centrally in making Rutgers a center of innovation, as he drew together artists attracted to popular culture, performance-based forms of art, and obliteration of the divide between art and life. They included George *Brecht, Geoffrey *Hendricks, Roy *Lichtenstein, Claes *Oldenburg, Lucas *Samaras, George *Segal, Robert *Watts, and Robert *Whitman. In 1958 at Segal's nearby chicken farm, Kaprow staged what is generally considered the first happening. In the same year *Art News* published his influential article calling for a lifelike art of chance operations, perishable materials, unconfined spatial dimensions, and methods uninhibited by craftsmanship. Subsequently, he ceased making art objects to concentrate on performance-based events, temporary environments, and theoretical speculation. After 1968 he substituted less theatrical Activities for happenings, bringing a private tone, more in the spirit of *fluxus, to low-key participatory events. Kaprow moved in the 1960s to California. From 1974 until 1993 he taught at the University of California at San Diego. He died at his home in nearby Encinitas. His numerous published writings include *Assemblage, Environments & Happenings* (1966) and *Essays on the Blurring of Art and Life* (1993).

Karfiol, Bernard (1886–1952). Painter. His figurative work indebted to French modernism gradually became less stylized. Karfiol was born in Budapest but grew up in New York and subsequently resided in the city or nearby. In 1900 he began his training at the *National Academy of Design, but left the following year, at fifteen, for Paris. There he studied at the Académie Julian and the École des Beaux-Arts, while also absorbing much from art currents of the day. André Derain provided an important example, while Renoir, Cézanne, and early Picasso also contributed to Karfiol's formation as an artist. After returning to New York in 1906, he exhibited in the 1913 *Armory Show and the following year first visited Ogunquit, Maine, where he thereafter summered. From French sources, along with an admiration for early Greek art, he developed a personal manner of elongating the human form, which he flattened somewhat and described with graceful contours. His psychologically inward figures usually appear within a shallow space, spread across the canvas to emphasize pattern rather than volume or depth, as in *Summer* (Corcoran Gallery, 1927). Karfiol's characteristic sense of unhurried repose prevails in this depiction of his wife and two teenage children at a table before the shore view from their summer home. Later he specialized in more monumentally rendered studio figures, nude or clothed, achieving in these works simple, unified effects. He died at his home in suburban Irvington-on-Hudson.

Käsebier, Gertrude (1852–1934). Photographer. Widely acknowledged as the leading American portrait photographer at the turn of the twentieth century, she also ranked as the most important woman associated with *pictorialism. Born in Fort Des Moines (now Des Moines), Iowa, Gertrude Stanton moved with her family to the Colorado Territory in 1860 and then to Brooklyn in 1864. From 1868 until 1870 she studied at the Moravian Seminary for Women in Bethlehem, Pennsylvania. In 1874 she married Eduard Käsebier, a German immigrant businessman. After fifteen years as a wife and mother in Brooklyn and rural New Jersey, in 1889 she entered the Pratt Institute in Brooklyn to study painting. She graduated in 1893 but stayed on for further instruction for two additional years, which bracketed the year of 1894–95 in France and Germany. There she traveled, continued to study painting, and sought technical instruction in photography. After opening a Manhattan portrait studio about 1897, she soon achieved success with artistry derived from the poses and lighting of old master paintings. Banishing the era's standard paraphernalia, such as backdrops and furniture, she made her mark with dignified and broadly composed renditions of human character. Her subjects included such notables as Mark Twain, Booker T. Washington, Stanford White, and his celebrity paramour, Evelyn Nesbitt. Her many particularly sensitive likenesses of other photographers and artists included portraits of Alvin Langdon *Coburn, Robert *Henri, and Rodin (who sat for her in

Paris during one of several trips abroad). She also sought out and photographed American Indians, fondly recalling their companionship during her Colorado years in childhood. Unlike most other turn-of-the-century photographers of Indians, she pursued neither ethnographic nor sentimental aims but revealed her sitters' essential humanity in elegant, deeply respectful portrayals.

By the late 1890s Käsebier had also found recognition as an art photographer. She soon participated actively in the *Photo-Secession, and her prints were featured in **Camera Work*. She specialized in photographs of women and children together. A small number of these, including several that brought her fame at the time, are literary, staged compositions that to a later age seem inauthentic and mawkish. In most, however, Käsebier represented unaffected tenderness among her subjects. Many of these images incorporated the period's progressive ideas about the interaction of mothers with their children. In their formal integrity and luxurious printing, the photographs also validate the inherent worth of the early years of life. Despite straightforward effects, her process was in fact often complex, including retouching and re-photographing of negatives. About 1907–8 she began to withdraw from the Photo-Secession, and in 1916 she numbered among founders of the *Pictorial Photographers of America. By this time she had accomplished nearly all of her best work. Her eyesight failing, she ceased photographing in the late 1920s. She died at her home in New York.

Katz, Alex (1927–). Painter, printmaker, sculptor, and collage artist. A leader in the return to figuration in the early 1960s, he is known for very large, blandly unemotional, flattened images. In their smooth, simplified, and formal stylization, his works bear a tangential relationship to *pop art. His subjects also include interiors, landscapes, and magnified flowers. Although many works picture individuals known to the artist, particularly his wife and son, generalized facial features foster an impersonal air. A lifelong New Yorker, in 1949 he graduated from Cooper Union, where Robert *Gwathmey influenced his thinking. That summer Katz first visited Maine to study at the Skowhegan School of Painting and Sculpture. Since 1954 he has maintained a seasonal residence in Lincolnville, on Penobscot Bay. During the 1950s he painted *abstract expressionist works that gradually incorporated representation as he also simplified his forms and brushwork. Between 1954 and 1960 he made collages, and in the late 1950s he first experimented with distinctive cut-outs, wood or metal silhouettes of painted figures. His personal style of representation coalesced in the early 1960s, contributing to the clean, literal aesthetic of the period as well as to the continuing taste for monumental painting among *color field painters and others. Unlike *photorealist artists, he remains committed to visual perception as the basis of his work. Cropping, huge scale, and eye-catching, decorative pattern align his work with the distinctly contemporary styles of fashion advertising, mass media, and wide-screen movies. Active as a printmaker throughout his career, he has skillfully extended the imagery of his paintings into several media, including silkscreen, lithography, and woodcut.

Kawara, On. *See* CONCEPTUAL ART.

Kearney, Francis. *See* JOHNSTON, DAVID CLAYPOOLE.

Kees, Weldon. *See* IRASCIBLES, THE.

Keith, William (1838–1911). Painter. A longtime San Francisco resident, he specialized in California scenes but also painted views of other western locales, as well as some New England subjects and a few portraits. His mature work featured broad, painterly interpretations of nature's spiritual content. Born in Oldmeldrum, not far from Aberdeen, Scotland, Keith arrived in New York in 1850. There, as a teenager, he learned wood engraving. While employed by Harper and Brothers publishers, he first visited California on assignment in 1858. Following a subsequent trip to England and Scotland, in 1859 he returned to San Francisco, where he at first continued his craft as an engraver but increasingly turned to painting. In 1869 he headed east to sail for Europe. There he studied in Düsseldorf but also visited Paris, where he was attracted to contemporary *Barbizon landscapes. Subsequently, after some months during the winter of 1871–72 in Boston, he returned to San Francisco. Soon he established a close friendship with a Scots contemporary, the conservationist John Muir, who championed his friend's work as the visual equivalent of his own ideas about the inspirational value of wilderness. Keith's work of this time combined closely observed realism with painterly values in solidly constructed compositions. Most of these depicted the region's spectacular, mountainous scenery, sometimes on grandiose canvases, but others anticipate his later intimate responses to unprepossessing sites. Keith again resided in Europe from 1883 to 1885. During this sojourn he studied in Munich and traveled widely but also returned to Paris. The increasingly atmospheric tendency of his subsequent paintings reflected his high regard for the work of Jean-Baptiste-Camille Corot. George *Inness reinforced this direction in his friend's work during an extended San Francisco visit in 1891. Inness also reanimated Keith's interest in the writings of the Swedish scientist and theologian Emanuel Swedenborg, whose beliefs about the spiritual reality behind nature's exterior appearance encouraged Keith's subsequent emphasis on subjective responses to the poetry of landscape. Concomitantly, influenced by Inness's rich technique, he developed a painterly style related to contemporary *tonalism. In 1893 and 1899 he again visited Europe, on the latter trip devoting most of his time to scrutiny of Rembrandt's work. The San Francisco earthquake and fire of 1906 destroyed Keith's studio, as well as some two thousand paintings. He nevertheless continued a productive career until the last months of his life. A luminary in San Francisco's turn-of-the-century cultural life, he died in Berkeley, where he had resided for some years.

Kelly, Ellsworth (1923–). Painter, sculptor, and printmaker. A wizard of color relationships, a master of formal subtlety, he celebrates purely optical experience. Pared-down, precise, and grandly scaled, his untheoretical, entirely nonrepresentational art affirms a personal sensibility through his practice of basing chromatic and formal choices on observation of visual phenomena. A leading mid-twentieth-century innovator, Kelly ranks as the most prominent pioneer of *hard-edge painting. As well, his work spurred *minimalist interest in modular organization, reductive composition, and preference for object over illusion. His intermittent use of high-contrast colors engages the visual paradoxes of *op art. He also employed nonrectangular supports at an early date, contributing to the 1960s and 1970s interest in shaped canvases. His three-dimensional constructions of intensely hued planar forms broke ground in unifying the concerns of painting and sculpture.

Born in Newburgh, about fifty miles up the Hudson River from New York, Kelly began his training at Brooklyn's Pratt Institute in 1941. From 1943 until 1945 he served in a U.S. Army Air Force camouflage unit. Following additional study at Boston's School of the Museum of Fine Arts, where Karl *Zerbe numbered among his teachers, he left for Paris in October 1948. There he became better acquainted with traditional and contemporary European art, studied desultorily for about two years at the École des Beaux-Arts, fell in love with the city's architectural fabric and its light effects, tried to rid himself of preconceived ideas by sampling *automatism and techniques based on chance, and met important artists, including Brancusi, Arp, and Mondrian's follower Georges Vantongerloo. After losing interest in an early figurative style in 1949, Kelly experimented with gridded compositions, as well as monochrome paintings, and soon hit upon his individual approach to deriving painted shapes from the outlines of objects, shadows, or negative spaces. Little attracted to cubist space, he exaggerates Matisse's technique of flattening illusionistic elements by emphasizing contour and reducing internal modeling, while promoting color as the primary expressive agent. Neither geometric nor *biomorphic, Kelly's idiosyncratic, slightly irregular, frontal forms are nearly always so stripped down as to conceal their sources. His process produces a personal aesthetic of refined perception, sensuous delicacy, and intuitive sentiment nearly as distant from the ideal geometries of Mondrian, Malevich, and their disciples as it is from abstract expressionism's subjective passions.

Kelly also traveled in France and painted at Sanary, on the Mediterranean coast. After settling in New York in 1954, he limited his palette to black and white before adding color, often restricted to primary hues, around 1957. Generally built around one or two elegantly simplified, cleanly defined shapes, these works masterfully resolve figure-ground ambiguities. His pioneering contribution to hard-edge painting was a only a byproduct of his concentration on shape, as he denied any interest in edges for their own sake. Kelly's preoccupation with form soon led him toward sculpture, and by the end of the 1950s he was producing polychromed metal objects suggesting freestanding versions of his painted elements. During the same years Kelly also began to work regularly with purely geometric compositions and to create multipanel works comprising two or more separate but adjacent monochrome canvases. In 1970 Kelly moved to upstate Columbia County, New York, where he continues to reside at Spencertown, while working in a studio in nearby Chatham. In subsequent paintings, he extended earlier interests, while uncrowded, rural surroundings reinvigorated his sculpture. He soon began producing large-scale outdoor aluminum, stainless steel, or bronze works sometimes suggesting his admiration for David *Smith's example. Unpainted, emphasizing shape and metallic surface, these works embellish numerous public venues. Throughout his career, Kelly has continued to draw, producing stylish and graceful linear interpretations of flowers, plants, and the human figure. More than seventy botanical subjects also appear as lithographs, contributing to his considerable activity as a graphic artist since 1964.

Kelpe, Paul (1902–85). Painter, printmaker, and sculptor. A native of Minden, Germany, he studied art in Hannover. After coming to the United States in 1925, he worked for *federal art projects during the Depression. A government-sponsored painting, *Abstract #2* (Smithsonian American Art Museum, c. 1934), suggests the power of industry by representing a single worker amid semi-abstracted machine and factory forms, such as gears, wheels, a gauge, smokestacks, and a water tower. Also during the 1930s, responding to constructivism, cubism, and other forms of modern expression, Kelpe refined a purely abstract style. An untitled work from about 1938 (Brooklyn Museum, on loan from the New York City Housing Authority) presents hard-edge geometric forms in a simple but dynamic arrangement that advantageously shows Kelpe's sensitivity to color. Pinks ranging from salmon to lavender, along with a creamy yellow, dominate the middle of the canvas, against backdrop planes of black, brown, and gray. Other works include organic forms, sometimes carrying surrealistic overtones. His abstract constructed reliefs from the 1920s pioneered works of this type created in the United States. He numbered among the founding members of the *American Abstract Artists. In the 1950s Kelpe earned a PhD in art history at the University of Chicago. He taught at several schools, including the University of Texas in Austin, where he died.

Kemeys, Edward (1843–1907). Sculptor. The first significant American sculptor to specialize in animals, he especially favored large species native to the West. His example contributed to widespread popularity of animal subjects during the late nineteenth century and into the early years of the twentieth. Desiring particularly to record those threatened by encroaching civilization, Kemeys traveled extensively to observe animals in their native habitats. His broadly realistic treatment of them precisely registers characteristic demeanor and temperament. Born in Savannah, Georgia, he grew up in the Hudson River Valley near Ossining, and then in New York. Visits during his teenage years with Illinois relatives in Dwight, southwest of Chicago, stimulated his interest in frontier experience. After serving in the Union army during the Civil War, he farmed in Illinois for two years. In 1868 he found work in New York's Central Park, where zoo animals attracted his interest, and he soon developed proficiency at modeling them. Apparently without any professional training, in 1872 he completed his first public commission, a life-size bronze *Hudson Bay Wolves Quarreling over the Carcass of a Deer* for Philadelphia's Fairmount Park (later moved to the zoo). In 1877 he sailed for a year abroad, first in London and then in Paris. He successfully exhibited his work in both cities and was able observe the recent French practice of vibrant animal sculpture. Reestablishing his studio once again to New York, he produced much of his finest work before leaving for Chicago in 1892. There he created a number of pieces for the World's Columbian Exposition of 1893. He remained in the area during the 1890s, completing several important commissions, including the pair of bronze lions at the entrance to the Art Institute of Chicago (1894). After two years in the Southwest, Kemeys relocated in 1902 to Washington, D.C., where he died.

Kensett, John Frederick (1816–72). Painter and engraver. His refined yet powerful landscapes incorporate closely observed particulars of geology, vegetation, sky, and atmosphere, rendered with miniaturistic but painterly touch. Although masterfully organized, serene compositions appear natural and unforced, with sparse, simplified shapes often asymmetrically counterpoising eloquent voids. In the representative *Beacon Rock, Newport Harbor* (National Gallery, 1857), a large, rocky outcropping at right dominates a delicately naturalistic, slightly hazy summer afternoon. A few foreground rocks and distant headland measure distance at left. Near the middle, far-off sailboats punctuate the sovereign space. Born in Cheshire, Connecticut, Kensett embarked on his mastery of engraving under the tutelage of his English-born father **Thomas Kensett** (1786–1829). As a young man, Kensett worked in engraving shops in New Haven, New York, and Albany while beginning to paint on his own. In 1840 he left for Europe in the company of John *Casilear, Thomas *Rossiter, and Asher B. *Durand. After visiting relatives near London that summer, he settled in Paris where he continued to support himself with engraving jobs for American firms but also attended drawing classes and copied paintings at the Louvre. In 1843 he returned to England to attend to family affairs, but while there he studied both the English landscape and the work of painters who depicted it. His paintings from this time are broadly executed, with rich impasto. Although his mature technique was much smoother and less aggressive, more closely related to his training as an engraver, this artistic evolution provided a basis for the technical facility apparent in later years. In 1845

Kensett again visited Paris before setting off on the standard grand tour of the Continent. For much of the following two years, he resided in Rome.

When Kensett returned to New York after seven years abroad, his reputation preceded him, for he had forwarded paintings, some bought by the *American Art-Union. He quickly became active in the art life of the city, established relationships with major collectors who sometimes fought over his popular work, and eventually ranked among arbiters of American cultural life. Like fellow *Hudson River School landscapists, he soon established a lifelong pattern of summer travel to sketch scenes that provided the basis of finished views produced in his New York studio. He visited the major scenic areas of New England and upper New York State, but he also returned to Europe and went west on several occasions, including one journey as far as Colorado. By the early 1850s Kensett had solidified his personal combination of detailed realism and the lambent light that allies his work with *luminism and in certain late works prefigures *tonalist effects. In his most radical and abstract last paintings, Kensett treated emptiness as an almost uninterrupted delicate, pearly ambience. Although he concentrated on the scenery of the Northeast, with particular attention to the resort locations of his day along the Atlantic shore or fronting inland lakes, his travels produced views of other locales, as well. He addressed a variety of landscape types, but even when painting remote mountain locations, he moderated nature's wildness toward a serenity that seemed to offer spiritual benediction. In 1867 Kensett began regular working visits to Contentment Island, connected by a causeway to the shore at Darien, Connecticut. He purchased land there and built a studio but stayed in the home of his friend Vincent Colyer (1825–88), known for crayon portraits and, later, topographical watercolors of the American West, as well as studio oils taken from these subjects. In November 1872 Kensett contracted pneumonia after unsuccessfully attempting to rescue Colyer's drowning wife near their home. He subsequently returned to New York but died in his studio within a few weeks.

Kent, Rockwell (1882–1971). Painter and printmaker. Known principally for crisp, mystically tinged landscapes, he frequently depicted rugged northern terrain, usually in winter and often incorporating generalized figures signifying heroic individualism. His romance of nature's harshness came in part from his admiration for Winslow *Homer's work, whereas from William Blake he learned much about the expression of spiritual yearning. A committed socialist, he showed no interest in urban underclasses as subjects for painting, but he sometimes pictured the arduous life of ordinary laboring people who courageously resist the implacable power of an awesome nature. Born in Tarrytown Heights, north of New York, Kent began his training as an artist while studying architecture at Columbia University. Under his principal teachers, William Merritt *Chase, Robert *Henri, Kenneth Hayes *Miller, and Abbott *Thayer, he quickly developed a vigorous realist style. In 1905 Kent settled on Monhegan Island, Maine. There he secluded himself while developing a personal approach, as in the snowy *Maine Coast* (Cleveland Museum of Art, 1907). After his first one-person exhibition in New York in 1907, Kent lived in several locations in Maine, Connecticut, and New York City, while soon also beginning his extensive travels to such far-flung locations as Newfoundland, Alaska, and Tierra del Fuego. These and other travels to distant and usually inhospitable locales provided material for both his visual art and his writings, which appeared in several illustrated books. Around 1920 Kent took up wood engraving, his primary printmaking medium, and soon became renowned for his graphic art. His stylized black-and-white works appeared as illustrations to his own works and to numerous classic texts issued in both limited-edition and mass-market form. From 1927 he lived principally on a farm, until 1948 a working dairy operation, near Au Sable Forks in New York's Adirondack Mountains.

In the final two decades of his life, Kent fell into disfavor aesthetically and politically. As abstract art came to dominate postwar discourse, his art was no longer taken seriously. Simultaneously, Kent's radical views provoked bitter anti-Communist censure in the Cold War environment. Hauled before Senator Joseph R. McCarthy's infamous investigations subcommittee in 1953, he invoked the Fifth Amendment rather than respond to the question of his allegiance to Communism. (Outside the courtroom, he denied membership in the party.) As an ironic side effect of his politics, however, Kent's paintings outnumber the works of any other American in Russian national collections, notably St. Petersburg's State Hermitage Museum. Emblematic of both his defiant individualism and his flawed judgment of totalitarianism, in 1967 he accepted the Lenin Peace Prize in Moscow. He died at his upstate New York farm. His first book, *Wilderness: A Journal of Quiet Adventure in Alaska*, appeared in 1920. Other publications include *Voyaging: Southward from the Strait of Magellan*

(1924) and three books dealing with trips to Greenland: *N by E* (1930), *Salamina* (1935), and *Greenland Journal* (1962). He also issued two volumes of autobiography, *This Is My Own* (1940) and *It's Me, O Lord* (1955).

Kent Limner. *See* PHILLIPS, AMMI.

Kepes, György (1906–2001). Photographer, designer, filmmaker, and painter. Prolific in several media, Kepes devoted his career to general questions of perception and expression, with particular attention to light and color. Much of his work is abstract or imaginative, although some of his straight photographs capture the material as well as emotional reality of their time. Convinced that visual communication has a role to play in promoting human values, in 1967 he founded MIT's Center for Advanced Visual Studies to foster interdisciplinary cooperation and mutual research among artists, designers, architects, scientists, and theorists. Born in Selyp, Hungary, he studied painting at the Academy of Art in Budapest from 1924 to 1928. Before leaving for Berlin in 1930, he became interested in experimental photography and produced cameraless images, or photograms. Soon, he also took up filmmaking. In Berlin he was close to László *Moholy-Nagy and, through him, to the Bauhaus circle. Although never formally affiliated with the school, in his later teaching and writing Kepes became instrumental in disseminating its principles. His Berlin work ranged from film to stage designs to commercial exhibitions. After working for about a year with Moholy-Nagy in London, Kepes followed him in 1937 to Chicago, where he taught photography and other subjects at the New Bauhaus. The year after he published the precepts of his teaching in the influential *Language of Vision* (1944), he joined the faculty of MIT in Cambridge. In 1956 he became a United States citizen. Kepes's American work extended the wide range of his earlier production. Among other activities, he designed exhibitions and collaborated with numerous architects. For the new St. Mary's Cathedral in San Francisco, he created faceted glass windows in 1965. He came up with novel ways to incorporate new technologies into artistic expression, as in an unrealized 1964–65 project for a mile-long wall in Boston harbor, with programmed lighting to interact with mirrored buoys. His abstract paintings of the period, which sometimes incorporate non-art materials, generally evoke natural forms and processes. He died at his home in Cambridge. His other books include *The New Landscape in Art and Science* (1956) and exhibition catalogues for *Light as a Creative Medium* (1965) and *The MIT Years, 1945–1977* (1978). He edited *The Visual Arts Today* (1960) and a seven-volume Vision and Value series (1965–72), exploring the nature of the creative act and its social functions.

Kertész, André (1894–1985). Photographer. His eye for design and relish for the lyricism of everyday life distinguish a great variety of subjects and approaches. An early master of the 35 mm camera, he intuitively understood that it could capture fleeting, delicate moments to which his feelings responded. Born in Budapest, where he grew up and graduated from business school, Andor Kertész remained self-taught in photography, which he took up as a hobby around 1912. From 1914 to 1918 he served in the Austro-Hungarian army, although he was gravely wounded in 1915. Subsequently, photography gradually became his principal interest as he tenderly recorded evanescent impressions of the Hungarian capital, the surrounding countryside, and his friends. In 1925 he moved to Paris, with the intent of becoming a professional photographer. There Kertész quickly absorbed photography's up-to-the-minute stylistic interests, such as unconventional angles of vision and abstract formal patterns. The insouciant "Satiric Dancer, Paris" (1926) reveals his affinity for modern art, suggests his pleasure in its freedoms, and exemplifies his courtly humanism. Beside an old couch pushed into the corner of a room, a modern sculpture of a fragmentary, striding man hovers commandingly over a woman who parodies the traditional odalisque. All angles in her short, strapless dress, she grins as she vamps for the camera with arms and legs bent into improbable positions. Few photographs suggest how much fun it could be to live as a modern artist. While mingling with the legendary artistic community in interwar Paris, Kertész often photographed other creative leaders, such as Brancusi and Chagall, or their environments. In 1926 he photographed the studio of his good friend Mondrian, capturing in the sensitively lighted space the austere grace of its dweller's vision. Kertész's fresh and gentle-spirited photojournalism quickly brought him success in European newspapers and magazines. In 1936 he arrived in New York, planning to stay for a year or two. As a Jew, he was afraid to return to Europe, which was then under the threat of Fascism. He remained permanently and became a U.S. citizen in 1944. As he trained his camera on American subjects, he found little sympathy for his modest and artful form of photojournalism. Until 1962 he made his living with relatively routine photography, while continuing his more personal work privately. Subsequently his international reputation revived. His later vision developed a sharper edge but never lost its sympathetic resonance. His books include *Day of Paris* (1945), *On Reading* (1971), *André Kertész: Sixty Years of Photography* (1972), *Washington Square* (1975), *Of New York* (1976), and *Kertész on Kertész: A Self-Portrait* (1985), as well as *Distortions* (1976), featuring a 1933 series of surrealist-influenced nudes deformed by parabolic mirrors.

Kienholz, Edward (1927–94). Sculptor. Combining found and fabricated elements, his life-size figural tableaux reflect contemporary society through the lens of a surrealistic imagination. Themes of violence, decay, hypocrisy, illness, and death recur in grotesque imagery related to the spirit of *funk art. Born in Fairfield, Washington, south of Spokane, Edward Ralph Kienholz grew up on a farm. He aimlessly attended several colleges but never finished a degree and remained self-taught as an artist. In 1953 he moved to Los Angeles, where he began making painted wood reliefs and three years later opened a short-lived avant-garde gallery. In 1957, in partnership with curator, critic, and, later, museum director Walter Hopps (1932–2005), he established the legendary Ferus Gallery, which served as a rallying point for adventurous young Southern California artists. In the late 1950s Kienholz made detritus-rich *assemblages commenting on social and political issues. His first room-size work, *Roxy's* (1961), evokes a 1940s brothel. Characteristically, the period-piece realism of the setting heightens inhabitants' deficiencies, enhanced by substituting objects for body parts, as in the madam's head replaced by a skull. In one of his best-known works, *The Beanery* (Stedelijk Museum, Amsterdam, 1965), stopped clocks stand in for mannequins' faces. Within this railroad-car-sized, greasy-spoon diner, sound and odor enhance its verisimilitude. Despite their humiliating content, many of Kienholz's works elicit empathetic responses. Particularly tender, *Sollie 17* (Smithsonian American Art Museum, 1979–80) shows a dingy hotel room harboring an elderly man dressed only in underpants. His visage replaced by a framed photograph of a face, he appears in three poses as he listlessly waits out his days. Recorded sound once again contributes authenticity. After their marriage in 1972, Kienholz credited Los Angeles-born photojournalist **Nancy Reddin Kienholz** (1943–) as a collaborator on all his works. The couple divided their time between Berlin and an isolated cabin near Hope in northern Idaho. They later also maintained a home and studio in Houston. Their experience abroad led to a number of works addressing Nazism and other manifestations of German culture. Kienholz died in a hospital in Sandpoint, not far from his Idaho home.

Kiesler, Frederick (1890–1965). Sculptor and architect. A visionary in treating form and space, he sought continuous, organic, and fluid relationships emblematic of human consciousness. Born in the Austro-Hungarian city of Czernowitz (now Chernivtsi in western Ukraine), he received his professional training in Vienna. Before moving to the United States in 1926, he devoted his architectural practice principally to theatrical projects and exhibition designs. From 1924 he was associated with the avant-garde Dutch art and design movement De Stijl. During these years, he also began to develop ideas for what he called the "endless theater," followed by the "endless house." Anticipating artists' and architects' later interests in unimpeded space, he proposed innovative curved concrete shells enclosing flexible interiors. During the 1930s and 1940s his imaginative exhibition installations and environmental sculptures contributed to international surrealism. He was responsible for the dramatic and unique interior of Peggy *Guggenheim's *Art of This Century gallery, which opened in 1942. Along with his friend Marcel *Duchamp, he designed the flamboyant setting of the 1947 "International Surrealist Exhibition" in Paris. Working as a sculptor from the late 1940s, he ranked among the first to pursue integration of sculptural objects with viewers' space, an approach he dubbed "endless sculpture." As stage director and designer from 1933 until 1957 of the Juilliard Opera Theater at the Juilliard School of Music, he was responsible for more than fifty productions. He also directed an architectural design laboratory at Columbia University from 1936 to 1942. Near the end of his life, he designed (with architectural partner Armand Bartos) Jerusalem's celebrated Shrine of the Book (1959–65), which houses the Dead Sea Scrolls. Naturalized as an American citizen in 1936, he died in New York. His *Inside the Endless House; Art, People, and Architecture: A Journal* (1966) appeared posthumously, as did *Selected Writings* (1997). Austrian-born **Stefi Kiesler** (?–1963), born Stefanie (sometimes shortened to Steffi) Frischer, graduated from the University of Vienna in 1920 and married Kiesler that year in Vienna. Beginning in 1925, she produced more than one hundred inventive "typo-plastics," compositions created on an ordinary typewriter by arranging letters and symbols into black and red abstract patterns. (Early examples appeared under the pseudonym Pietro de Saga in the magazine *De Stijl*.)

While working at the New York Public Library for more than thirty years, she also served as a bibliographer and researcher for the *Société Anonyme. She died in New York. **Lillian Kiesler** (1909/10–2001), his second wife, was a painter, sculptor, and actress, who had studied with Hans *Hofmann and subsequently assisted at his school. Lillian Olinsey met Kiesler in 1934, but they did not marry until 1964, six months after Stefi's death.

King, Charles Bird (1785–1862). Painter. Although chiefly a portraitist, he is remembered especially for a few innovative still lifes that incorporate thematically related objects in unsettling combinations. He also compiled an important early record of American Indians and painted imaginative subjects and *genre scenes. King was born in Newport, Rhode Island, and it is thought he received his earliest professional instruction from Samuel King (1749–1819), an unrelated Newport painter and nautical-instrument maker. He apprenticed in New York with Edward *Savage, returned to Newport in 1805, and headed for London in 1806 to study with Benjamin *West and at the Royal Academy. After returning to the United States in 1812, he painted portraits in several cities before settling permanently near the end of 1818 in Washington, D.C. There, he maintained a steady portrait business, numbering among his clients many prominent federal officials. On commission from the U.S. government, between 1822 and 1842 he also documented the appearance and costumes of nearly 150 visiting Indians. The first large body of American Indian likenesses, these include the first portraits of tribal representatives from the far West. Although nearly all of these paintings were destroyed in a fire at the *Smithsonian Institution in 1865, many of the images survive as widely distributed hand-colored lithographs in the landmark McKenney and Hall serial publication, *History of the Indian Tribes of North America* (1836–44). Without precedent in American painting, King's most interesting still lifes consist of trompe-l'oeil arrangements in shallow niches. His combinations of intense illusionism, oddly chosen items, and formal complexity carry surrealistic overtones. With sardonic wit, *The Vanity of the Artist's Dream* (Fogg Art Museum, Harvard University, Cambridge, Massachusetts, 1830) comments indirectly on the financial and psychological insecurities of an artist's life.

King, John Crookshanks. *See* HUNT, WILLIAM MORRIS.

King, Samuel. *See* KING, CHARLES BIRD.

Kingsley, Elbridge (1841/42–1918). Printmaker and painter. Known almost exclusively for wood engravings, he ranked among the finest technicians of his day. Along with a few others, he expanded the expressive possibilities of what had been predominately a reproductive technology. Late nineteenth-century American specialists in this skill outranked their European counterparts in achieving fine detail and subtle effects. Paralleling the aims and interests of the *etching revival, Kingsley and others sought to imbue their medium with a creative spirit. To promote their work, the Society of American Wood-Engravers was founded in 1881. Kingsley's original compositions, mostly landscapes, often were adapted as magazine or book illustrations. Kingsley was born near Cincinnati, in Carthage, Ohio, but grew up on a farm in Hatfield, Massachusetts, near Northfield. As a young man, he moved to New York and studied at Cooper Union. He later worked in Massachusetts and California, as well as New York, where he died. Conceived to accompany a Henry Wadsworth Longfellow text, the undated *Winter* exemplifies the artist's ability to render with poetry and precision the atmospheric subtleties of a snowy landscape.

Kitson, Henry Hudson. *See* LACHAISE, GASTON.

Klein, William (1928–). Photographer and filmmaker. More widely appreciated in Europe than in the United States, he remains best known for innovative work of the 1950s. In these startling and subjective photographs, he introduced a raw, high-impact aesthetic into art photography. Often Klein's camera revealed unexpected absurdities within the mundane texture of everyday experience. He used stylistic devices such as brutal cropping, awkward poses and gestures, and strong patterns to capture the immediacy of candid moments. Previously, such techniques had usually been tolerated only as unanticipated side effects in journalistic photography-on-the-run. A native New Yorker, he attended City College of New York before serving for two years in postwar Europe with the U.S. Army. Since his 1948 discharge in Paris, he has made his home there. He took classes at the Sorbonne, studied painting with Fernand Léger before turning to photography, and subsequently experimented with mural-sized abstract photograms. On a 1954–55 visit of several months in New York, he captured the images for *Life Is Good and Good for You in New York: Trance Witness Revels* (1956; expanded and reissued in 1995 as *New York 1954–55*), which established his early reputation upon publication in Paris. Although not widely known in the United States for many years, in both style and subject the book anticipated Robert *Frank's landmark *The Americans* (1959). Like Frank, Klein injected sarcasm, social criticism, and tastelessness into a photographic aesthetic that could still accommodate lyricism. From the mid-1950s to the mid-1960s, Klein also brought a new dramatic edge to fashion photography in highly successful, elegant work for *Vogue*. In 1958 he made his first film, *Broadway by Light*, and from 1965 until 1980 worked principally as an experimental filmmaker. Klein's other publications include *Rome* (1958), *Tokyo* (1964), *Moscow* (1965), *Close Up* (1990), *In and Out of Fashion* (1994), *Portfolio* (1999), and *Paris + Klein* (2002).

Kline, Franz (1910–62). Painter. An *abstract expressionist, he made his mark with large black-and-white paintings featuring architectonic forms constructed from broad, slashing lines. Swaths of black paint, sometimes applied with a housepainter's brush, are held in tension with intervening white areas, also vigorously brushed, so that his compositions avoid figure-ground relationships in favor of a flat surface. Decentralized compositions suggest space continuing beyond the edge of the canvas, creating with very different means the effect of boundlessness seen also in Jackson *Pollock's *all-over paintings. The bleakness and raw power of Kline's paintings suggest the eastern Pennsylvania industrial landscape that framed his early life. A number of titles alluding to the region confirm the emotional and visual power it held for him. Born in Wilkes-Barre, Franz Rowe Kline was educated after his father's death in 1917 at Philadelphia's Girard College, a residential free school for orphan boys. From 1925 he lived with his remarried mother in Lehighton until 1931, when he began four years of study at Boston University, followed in 1937–38 by additional training in London. Upon his return he settled permanently in New York. Through most of the 1940s he painted representational works, mostly figure studies and landscapes, which generally feature simplified massing of forms and distinct value contrasts. Stimulated by the early development of abstract expressionism and particularly by his friendship with Willem *de Kooning, in the late 1940s Kline pushed his images toward abstraction. While viewing slides of his own sketches, he suddenly grasped the abstract potential of greatly magnified line. Introduced to the public in 1950 at his first New York gallery show, his signature style won Kline a distinctive place among the best known *action painters. Although many observers noted that his graphic images resemble overblown ideograms from Asian calligraphy, the artist always denied any connection. In the late 1950s he sometimes introduced sumptuous hues into his works, providing lyrical overtones to his art's aggressive tenor. Presumably, he felt the need to enlarge his scope after nearly a decade of concentrated focus, but before he was able to explore the full potential of color, he died of heart failure.

Kluver, Billy. *See* EXPERIMENTS IN ART AND TECHNOLOGY.

Knaths, Karl (1891–1971). Painter and printmaker. His poetic, semi-abstract landscapes and still lifes feature compositional structures drawn from cubism, along with brushy, suggestive drawing and painterly, refined, and muted color. Knaths skillfully adapted European modernism to American subjects and feelings, while also nourishing a faith in nature's spiritual values. Somewhat of a loner, personally as well as artistically, from 1919 he lived year-round in *Provincetown, on Cape Cod, a setting that informs most of his mature paintings. Born in Eau Claire, Wisconsin, Otto G. Knaths (the initial K is pronounced) grew up in Portage, north of Madison, and in Milwaukee. Following preliminary training in Milwaukee, he studied until for several years at the School of the Art Institute of Chicago before settling in Provincetown. During the Depression he painted murals for *federal art projects and served on the national executive committee of the *American Artists' Congress. He also participated from its founding in exhibitions of the *American Abstract Artists. He died in a Cape Cod hospital, in Hyannis. Knaths's early, impressionist work indicated Cézanne's appeal even before he met the modernist artists who summered in Provincetown. By about 1930 he had worked out systems of composition and color based largely on theories of Kandinsky and Mondrian. His concern for measured relationships between elements of form and within color combinations produced controlled and harmonious paintings, which at the same time showcase lush, painterly passages. *Duck Flight* (Whitney Museum, 1948) combines a cubist tabletop still life with a window view onto a landscape. A V-shaped flock of birds is visible in the distance, while a single duck (possibly a decoy) perches on the table, the bright touches in its plumage providing color accents echoed in more subdued tones elsewhere. The arrangement masterfully negotiates the tension between two-dimensional pattern and the space of three dimensions. Not all forms are legible as representation, but the charm of the subject is as clear as the satisfying and unaffected probity of the work's artistry.

Knee, Gina. *See* BROOK, ALEXANDER.

Knight, Daniel Ridgeway (1839–1924). Painter. A resident of France during most of his career, he is known especially for images of peasant life. Calm and charmingly picturesque, his rural actors generally neither labor nor suffer, although they may perform undemanding chores. Typically they populate ample, poetic landscapes bathed in soft, unifying light. Born in Philadelphia, Knight studied at the *Pennsylvania Academy of the Fine Arts from 1858 until 1861, when he departed for Paris. There he studied with Charles Gleyre and Alexandre Cabanel. In 1863 he returned to Philadelphia and enlisted to fight in the Civil War, which provided subjects for later paintings. He worked in Philadelphia until late 1871 or 1872, when he left permanently for France. He soon purchased a spacious sixteenth-century chateau in Poissy, on the Seine west of Paris. This remained his permanent primary residence, although he also maintained a Paris pied-a-terre and in 1896, to use as a painting retreat, bought an ancient dwelling in the isolated village of Rolleboise, farther down the Seine. He died in Paris. *Hailing the Ferry* (Pennsylvania Academy, 1888) depicts attractive female rustics beckoning an unseen ferry from river's edge in a silvery landscape. Clearly drawn and modeled, the two figures and their carefully detailed costumes are brought to a high finish, reflecting Knight's academic training. Their atmospheric, pastoral environment, less emphatically detailed, sustains the spirit of *Barbizon quietism. Some of his late work, often combining appealing young women with flower gardens, reflects a debt to impressionism in looser handling of paint and brighter colors. Impressionism also informed the feathery, prettified landscapes and garden scenes of his son, painter **Louis Aston Knight** (1873–1948). Born in Paris and trained there, he remained in France most of his life. For many years he lived in a Normandy country house at Beaumont-le-Roger. He also visited the United States, on occasion for lengthy periods. In 1940 he moved to New York. A stroke curtailed his career a few years before he died there.

Knight, Gwendolyn. *See* LAWRENCE, JACOB.

Knowles, Alison. *See* FLUXUS.

Knowlton, Helen. *See* HUNT, WILLIAM MORRIS.

Koehler, Sylvester Rosa. *See* ETCHING REVIVAL.

Kohn, Misch (1916–2002). Printmaker. A versatile technician, he worked in a wide variety of print media, both intaglio and relief, and often employed color. Similarly, his style ranged from representational to abstract, although most of his mature work inhabited a middle ground where design and imagery freely interact. While some works reflect a light-hearted delight in life, during the Cold War and Vietnam War periods particularly, he created many ominous evocations of existential torment and calamity. By the late 1970s, his work had became more frequently abstract, or nearly so, and he often incorporated lettering and found objects into brightly patterned compositions, sometimes presented on handmade paper. Harris Kohn adopted a new first name while studying at the Herron School of Art (now Herron School of Art and Design of Indiana University-Purdue University at Indianapolis), about fifty miles south of his birthplace in Kokomo. After receiving a BFA in 1939, he moved to New York for a few months before signing on with a *federal art project in Chicago. In the mid-1940s, a sojourn in Mexico—where he made the acquaintance of its muralists and popular printmakers—pushed his development toward new levels of energy and monumentality. Virtuosic wood engravings first made his reputation in the early 1950s, but by the end of the decade he had come to prefer etching and aquatint techniques. In 1961 he numbered among the first artists invited to work at the *Tamarind Lithography Workshop, which renewed his interest in working on stone. He taught at the Illinois Institute of Technology for more than two decades before moving in 1972 to the San Francisco Bay Area to teach at California State University in Hayward. He retired to emeritus status in 1986 and died at his home in nearby Castro Valley.

Konti, Isidore. *See* MANSHIP, PAUL.

Koons, Jeff. *See* POSTMODERNISM.

Kootz, Samuel. *See* ABSTRACT EXPRESSIONISM.

Kopman, Benjamin D. *See* CITRON, MINNA.

Kosuth, Joseph. *See* CONCEPTUAL ART.

Kozloff, Joyce. *See* PATTERN AND DECORATION.

Kozloff, Max. *See* KOZLOFF, JOYCE.

Krasner, Lee (1908–84). Painter and printmaker. The only woman among originators of *abstract expressionism, she nevertheless found relatively little recognition until some years after the 1956 death of her husband, Jackson *Pollock. Born Lena (called Lenore)

Krassner in Brooklyn, she changed her first name in childhood and revised the spelling of her family name around 1943. She entered Cooper Union in 1926 and two years later transferred to the *National Academy of Design. She also haunted the *Museum of Modern Art from its opening in 1929. Her early, directly realistic paintings display vigorous brushwork and strong compositions. After leaving the academy in 1932, at the height of the Depression, she remained somewhat adrift for several years as she worked at odd jobs, took evening classes in education, and continued to draw. In 1937 she began studying with Hans *Hofmann, who enlarged her understanding of European modernism during her three years at his school. While there she began exhibiting with the *American Abstract Artists and gained employment with a *federal art project that provided support until 1942.

Late in 1941 Krasner and Pollock became acquainted (they may have met in passing at an earlier date) after John *Graham invited both to participate in an important gallery show. They began living together about six months later. Krasner had benefited from a thorough artistic education and had acquired considerable sophistication about modern art, while Pollock, after hitching his wagon to the descending star of *American Scene regionalism, had been marking time through most of the 1930s. Nevertheless, she realized that he possessed an extraordinary talent. Despite her own ambition, she devoted much of her time through the rest of his life to helping him achieve his potential and to assuring recognition for his accomplishments. In the early years of their relationship, she produced little work of consequence while trying to come to terms with the surrealist *automatism that was crucial to Pollock's formation as an artist. After their marriage in October 1945 and immediately subsequent move to a small house in the Long Island village of Springs, a hamlet within the town of East Hampton, limited working space restricted the size of her work, while Pollock's took on a grand scale after he converted a barn into his studio. Nevertheless, about the time he embarked on his huge poured and dripped paintings in 1947, she found her footing with a Little Image series. These small-scale, *allover abstractions featuring dense linear layers, often poured, sometimes recall Mark *Tobey's work more than her husband's. Often they incorporate hieroglyphic symbols indebted to the Hebrew writing she learned in childhood and to her admiration for Celtic manuscripts. In the variations among these paintings, as she alternated between the freedom of the drawn line and the discipline of a gridded structure, she demonstrated a tension in her practice that played out through much of her later work. In the early 1950s, she produced a series of strong collages incorporating fragments of her own and Pollock's discarded paintings and suggesting admiration for Matisse.

In the late 1950s Krasner took over her deceased husband's studio and began regularly producing larger, sometimes enormous works. At first she used umber and white paints in vigorous, emotionally charged paintings. In the 1960s her works often made reference once again to calligraphic forms, now embedded in expansive spaces. In the 1970s she recapitulated another aspect of her own history in a collage series that incorporated torn charcoal drawings from her student years with Hofmann. Unlike the more prominent first-generation abstract expressionists, Krasner did not crystallize a signature style. Instead, her continuously evolving work reflected her sense that art is a quest, rather than the expression of an essential self. Unwell in her final years, she nevertheless continued painting nearly until her death in New York. The Pollock-Krasner Foundation established by her will helps painters, sculptors, and printmakers who demonstrate achievement and financial need. In addition, the foundation gives unsolicited Lee Krasner Awards for lifetime accomplishment.

Krimmel, John Lewis (1786–1821). Painter. The earliest significant American artist to specialize in scenes of everyday life, he is known particularly for lively representations of specific events and locations in Philadelphia. He also painted portraits. Johann Ludwig Krimmel was born in Ebingen, Würtemberg, and had some art training before leaving Germany. He anglicized his given names upon arriving in Philadelphia, his home after 1809, except for a return visit to Europe between 1817 and 1819. He died in an accidental drowning. Krimmel drew on precedents in the topographical cityscapes of William and Thomas *Birch, as well as prints of anecdotal subjects by William Hogarth, David Wilkie, and other European painters. His Philadelphia scenes, such as *Fourth of July in Centre Square* (Pennsylvania Academy, c. 1810–12), typically depict public events that attracted crowds to clearly identifiable locales. In this case, he anchored the celebratory scene with newly acquired emblems of civic pride, Benjamin Henry Latrobe's neoclassical water pumping station and William *Rush's nearby *Water Nymph and Bittern*, a fountain centerpiece. He also created more general *genre scenes, such as *A Quilting Frolic* (Winterthur [Delaware] Museum, 1813). Although poses of his characters characteristically remain somewhat artificial, their interrelated gestures combine with a wealth of minute detail in skillfully organized, animated compositions. Always, the gentle good humor of Krimmel's observant eye conveys delight in registering the activities, clothing, and mannerisms of varied social types.

Kroll, Leon (1884–1975). Painter and printmaker. Primarily a figure painter, he also produced landscapes, cityscapes, and still lifes. Admired for his mildly romantic temperament, sensuous taste, and suave technique, he numbered among the most respected artists of the 1920s and 1930s. Born in New York, Abraham Leon Kroll studied at the *Art Students League, where John *Twachtman ranked as his most important teacher, and at the *National Academy of Design before going to Paris in 1908 for two years of additional training. After his return, he exhibited in the *Armory Show, and between 1925 and 1929 he again lived in France. After painting Depression-era murals for a *federal art project, he received several other commissions to decorate public spaces. He summered for many years in the area of Gloucester, Massachusetts, where he died at his home. In the early years of his career, Kroll painted views of New York, celebrating its growth and vitality with vigorous brushwork. Later, the female figure, clothed or nude, became his usual subject as he built on classicism filtered through his knowledge of impressionism and the work of Poussin, Renoir, and Cézanne. Painted with verve and directness, *In the Country* (Detroit Institute of Arts, 1916) shows figures in a landscape setting. A later studio scene combining a female nude with two clothed women, *Summer—New York* (Smithsonian American Art Museum, 1931) reflects the more generalized form and languid mood of his mature career at its best. Visual intensity and unresolved, ambiguous meaning rescue this painting from the conceptual banality and circumspect artistry of his lesser efforts.

Kruger, Barbara. *See* FEMINIST ART.

Kubota, Shigeko. *See* PAIK, NAM JUNE.

Kühn, Justus Englehardt (d. 1717). Painter. Born in Germany and presumably trained there as an artist, he numbered among the earliest painters working in the colonies south of New York. In 1708 he applied for naturalization in Annapolis, Maryland. His surviving works are portraits commissioned by three major landowning Maryland families, although his estate inventory suggests he occasionally undertook other subjects. He died in Anne Arundel County, near Annapolis. Kühn's known works are limited to several conventional, usually three-quarter-figure adults and three or four lavishly conceived representations of doll-like children. Clothed in finery, the youngsters pose in expansive, fictionalized settings that owe more to internationally fashionable late Baroque conventions than to anything that then existed in the colonies. *Henry Darnall III as a Child* (Maryland Historical Society, Baltimore, c. 1710) includes a second child, Darnall's liveried slave, notable as the first representation in American painting of an African-American subject. As in the portrait of his sister *Eleanor Darnall* (Maryland Historical Society, Baltimore, c. 1710), who poses in a companion portrait with her dog, the young master idles on a terrace before an elaborate balustrade. In the backgrounds of both paintings, vast formal gardens lead to grandiose palaces. Faces and clothing are meticulously rendered, lending an air of plausibility to these decorative documents of family aspiration.

Kuhn, Walt (1877–1949). Painter. Primarily a figure painter, he is known especially for images of performers from the circus and other popular entertainments. He also played an essential role in introducing European modernism into the United States. Born in Brooklyn, William Kuhn worked as a young man as an illustrator and cartoonist. In 1899 he moved from New York to San Francisco, where he changed his first name. Two years later he went to Europe to study, primarily in Munich. After returning to New York in 1903, he again found employment as a commercial artist but also painted impressionist landscapes. With three other progressive artists, he founded the association that planned the *Armory Show. Abroad, he and Arthur B. *Davies chose most of the European entries for the show. He recorded these experiences in *Twenty-five Years After: The Story of the Armory Show* (1938). He also brought much advanced art to the United States through his activity as advisor to important collectors, including John *Quinn and Lillie P. *Bliss. For many years, he summered in Ogunquit, Maine. Following nearly a year of deteriorating health, he died in White Plains, New York, where he had been hospitalized. For more than a decade after the Armory Show, Kuhn worked through a succession of modern styles. Following many years of self-critical labor, his individual style finally emerged only after he returned to Europe in 1925–26 to engage a close study of old master and ancient art. Subsequently, he pursued an individual approach to single-figure compositions featuring strongly modeled sitters against blank backgrounds. An early example of his mature approach, *The White Clown* (National Gallery, 1929), presaged many dignified, introspective men and women dressed in the costumes of their professional work. Realized with strong colors and bold volumes, they invoke the human condition in their contrast of psychological inwardness with frivolous masquerade. He also painted similarly intense still lifes, such as the luscious little *Bread and Knife* (Phillips Collection, 1934).

Kuniyoshi, Yasuo (1893–1953). Painter and printmaker. Best known for imaginative themes and studio scenes, he typically combined precise observation with elements of fantasy. Deft draftsmanship, refined and earthy color harmonies, decorative pattern, and a wry, sometimes wide-eyed angle on life remained constants in his work. Born in Okayama, Japan, Kuniyoshi arrived in the United States in 1906. He lived in Seattle and Los Angeles before moving permanently to New York in 1910. Following preliminary studies elsewhere, he enrolled in 1916 at the *Art Students League, where he studied for four years, notably with Kenneth Hayes *Miller. He traveled to Europe in 1925 and again in 1928 and made his only return voyage to Japan in 1931–32. During the Depression he found employment with the *federal art projects. For the last twenty years of his life, he taught at the Art Students League, and in 1947 he was named the first president of Artists' Equity, an association that protects artists' rights and economic interests. During the 1920s he summered in Ogunquit, Maine, but after 1929 he regularly sojourned at *Woodstock. In the 1920s Kuniyoshi combined elements drawn from expressionism and cubism into sophisticated, pseudo-naive images, often gently humorous, of the studio, daily life, and landscape. Like many artists and collectors of the period, he responded to American folk art, which colored the spirit of this work. He acknowledged the darker climate of the 1930s with greater realism but remained more interested in problems of painting than social issues. Jules *Pascin and André Derain served as important exemplars during this part of his career. With the coming of World War II, Kuniyoshi's art became more troubled and sometimes evidenced a surrealist approach, as in the enigmatic *Headless Horse Who Wants to Jump* (Cranbrook Academy of Art, Bloomfield Hills, Michigan, 1945). After the war, Kuniyoshi's color brightened along with his mood. His best works of the late period, such as *Amazing Juggler* (Des Moines [Iowa] Art Center, 1952) make complex use of fantasy, along with brilliant chromatic effects, in suggesting more ambiguous and richer meanings than had been seen in his earlier work. Although critical response to Kuniyoshi has customarily credited his art with combining East and West—a position the artist himself encouraged because he felt emotionally tied to his native country—his work evidences little influence of traditional Japanese art.

In 1919 he married painter and draftswoman Katherine Schmidt (1898–1978). Born in Xenia, Ohio, as a child she moved with her family to New York. She met Kuniyoshi while studying at the Art Students League. She produced landscapes, still lifes, and figural studies until the late 1930s when, dissatisfied with her art, she virtually ceased working. In 1961 she returned to a meticulous descriptive realism, concentrating on ephemeral motifs such as crumpled paper and disintegrating leaves. After her divorce in 1932, she married Irvine J. Shubert. She died in Sarasota, Florida, where they resided, while also maintaining a home in Little Compton, on the Rhode Island shore.

Kusama, Yayoi (1929–). Painter, sculptor, installation artist, and performance artist. A Japanese native who achieved prominence among the New York avant-garde during the 1960s, she is known particularly for large *all-over paintings, sculptures of common objects upholstered with phallic forms, installations in mirrored rooms, and nude performances. After returning to Japan in 1973, she built a following there while her name faded from the history of contemporary art in the United States. In the 1990s a new generation of American artists and critics reassessed her work, finding it once more relevant in relation to postmodern interests, including autobiography, feminism, performance, and exploration of the body as both subject and material for art. Born in Matsumoto, as a child Kusama began to experience the hallucinations and obsessions of a form of mental illness. Her drawings from these years already reveal an affinity for the dots and skeins that later characterized much of her art. After World War II she went to Kyoto for a year and a half to study at the Municipal School of Arts and Crafts. Subsequently she worked at home and showed small paintings (of which the most compelling were *biomorphic abstractions) in Matsumoto and Tokyo. Late in 1957 she left for six months in Seattle before moving on to New York. In the fall of 1959, her first solo show in New York brought instant acclaim for what she called Infinity Net paintings. Demonstrating her sophisticated understanding of advanced painting in New York at that time, the white-on-white paintings feature lacelike surfaces so dense they nearly obscure the backgrounds. Their flatness, ambitious size, and all-over compositions related these works to other forms of field painting growing out of *abstract expressionism, whereas their lack of incident attracted the younger artists associated with *minimalism. The next year, Kusama introduced color into the series.

The Infinity Net paintings demonstrate as well the uncomfortably obsessive nature of her creativity. Repetition also marks the large 1962 collage *Airmail Stickers* (Whitney Museum), which elegantly combines these mundane items into a gridded abstract arrangement suggesting aspects of both *pop art and minimalism. In the early 1960s, she also began to make stuffed sculptures of everyday objects (armchairs and rowboats were favorites) entirely covered with cloth penile forms. Despite their surrealistic flavor, these Accumulations, as she called them, were shown in the company of work by the emerging pop artists and understood at the time in that critical context, at least partly because they share pop's irreverent and frolicsome spirit. She worked at a frantic pace throughout the decade, often inventively anticipating the better known work of other artists, such as Andy *Warhol in the use of repeated images and Lucas *Samaras in mirrored rooms. Kusama often had professional photographs taken of herself with (sometimes in or on) her sculptures, thus producing secondary art objects that included her presence. In the mid-1960s she enlarged this performative tendency by staging events akin to *happenings. In one of the most famous of these, in 1969 she directed a small group of nude performers in an unsanctioned event in the sculpture garden of the *Museum of Modern Art. As the sixties drew to a close, Kusama's desire for public acclaim interfered with her reputation as a serious artist. Moreover, she was often physically unwell, and money was always a problem, partly because no gallery would take her on. After her close friend Joseph *Cornell died in 1972, she soon returned to Japan. She voluntarily entered a private psychiatric facility in Tokyo in 1977 and has lived there ever since, while elaborating in her nearby studio on the achievements of the New York years and expanding her creative range into writing. She has published poetry in addition to twelve books of fiction. *Manhattan Suicide Addict* (1978) is an autobiographical novel about her life in New York.

Kushner, Robert. *See* PATTERN AND DECORATION.

Lichtenstein La Farge LeWitt LAWRENCE Luminism LACHAISE LANGE

Lachaise, Gaston (1882–1935). Sculptor. He specialized in graceful but heroic interpretations of the female body, exaggerated for dramatic effect. The voluptuous torsos of his intensely sexualized, mythic women soar above long, slender legs. These works reflect his affection for classical precedents, as well as scrutiny of non-Western exemplars, such as Indian temple sculptures. Also an effective portraitist, he caught slightly stylized likenesses, mostly of friends and associates. Born in Paris, Lachaise acquired a lasting sense of craftsmanship from his father, a master cabinetmaker. At thirteen, he began formal art training and in 1898 entered the École des Beaux-Arts. Following brief military service in 1904–5, he went to work for the jeweler and glassmaker René Lalique. At the end of 1905 he left France, never to return, arriving in January 1906 in Boston, where he worked for English-born Beaux-Arts sculptor Henry Hudson Kitson (1863–1941). Lachaise moved to New York in 1912 and several years later became a citizen. From 1913 to 1921 he worked as an assistant to Paul *Manship, while formulating a personal vision for his own art. Like Manship and his own exact contemporary Elie *Nadelman, Lachaise saw the problem of modern sculpture as one of subordinating naturalism to structure and form within a taste for elegant line and finish. However, Lachaise's work was generally less decorative, more expressionistic, and, at the extreme, more daring than theirs.

Among the finest expressions of his ideal type, the monumental *Standing Woman* (Albright-Knox Art Gallery, Buffalo, New York), was begun in 1912 but cast in bronze only in 1927. Commanding, yet feminine, the amply proportioned figure rises on tiptoe. Her arms and hands move fluidly through space, while her face remains an impassive mask. A semi-reclining woman, metaphorically titled *The Mountain*, is known in six powerful variations. The original was begun in 1913, the year he exhibited in the *Armory Show, but not cast until 1930 (Arizona State University Art Museum, Tempe). An intermediate carved version (Worcester [Massachusetts] Art Museum) served as the source of a reworked golden bronze (Metropolitan Museum). As in this case, Lachaise often creatively reworked a single idea, sometimes in varied media. Eventually, Lachaise further emphasized the symbolic nature of his earth mother-woman by fragmenting the body and often greatly enlarging breasts and genitalia. Recalling some of Rodin's audacious evocations of the female principle, these achieve an expressive eroticism tempered by formal sophistication. Even in truncated subjects that bear little intrinsic sexuality, such as knees, he achieved great sensuality through sensitivity to the feel and weight of flesh. Lachaise supported his more adventurous work largely through sales of less controversial animal sculptures, such as the lively bronze *Dolphin Fountain* (Whitney Museum, 1924). Only months before his death, the *Museum of Modern Art honored Lachaise with a retrospective exhibition, the first ever granted to an American sculptor. Besides his residence in New York, where he died, he maintained a summer home at Georgetown, in coastal Maine.

La Farge, John (1835–1910). Painter, sculptor, illustrator, and stained glass artist. Versatile, worldly, and intellectually sophisticated, he numbered among the late nineteenth century's most respected American artists. A leading figure in the *aesthetic movement, an important contributor to the *American Renaissance, and an instigator of *japonisme, as a painter he is admired particularly for introspective flower paintings and landscapes. He produced figural subjects as well, including portraits. His varied decorative projects included some of the period's finest and most original stained-glass windows. He also executed murals, most notably for Boston's Trinity Church. Innovative yet grounded in the tradition of old masters, he shared interests with American and European impressionists and symbolists. An early advocate of painting outdoors, he intently scrutinized light and color but remained unsatisfied with purely visual effect. Rather, he attempted to register the interaction of sensation with thought, aspiring to evoke the reality known to human consciousness but transcending scientific observation. Among his eloquent and well-informed writings, the theoretical *Considerations on Painting* (1895) remains an important pathway into the period's progressive ideas about aesthetics informed by current psychology and philosophy.

Born into a French-speaking family in New York, John Frederick Lewis Joseph La Farge received his earliest artistic instruction from his French-born maternal grandfather, Louis Binsse de Saint-Victor (1773–1844), who painted portraits and miniatures. Later he had some lessons from Régis François *Gignoux. He enrolled in St. John's College (now part of Fordham University) in New York but completed his academic training at Mount St. Mary's College in Emmitsburg, Maryland. Returning to New York, he entered a law firm to prepare for a legal career but continued to pursue an interest in art in his free time. In the spring of 1856 he traveled to Paris, where his omnivorous and mostly self-directed artistic education began in earnest. Cultivated and well-connected family members introduced him to leading French artists, writers, and intellectuals. He also made the acquaintance of the American community and haunted the Louvre. He studied with Thomas Couture, but only for a few weeks, and began to investigate the color theories of Eugène Chevreul. Already familiar with the *Barbizon artists, whose graphics he had bought in New York, he started to collect Japanese prints, perhaps the first artist in the West to do so. Before his return home in the fall of 1857, he traveled widely on the Continent and visited England, where he was impressed by *Pre-Raphaelitism. In New York he worked again in the legal profession but abandoned that endeavor permanently in 1859 when he left for Newport to study with William Morris *Hunt. He resided there until the mid-1870s, while traveling often to Boston and New York. Later he lived primarily in New York but remained at least tenuously connected to Newport, where his wife and children remained. Besides assisting him technically, Hunt reinforced his attraction to the intimacy and naturalism of Barbizon painting. While still connected to Hunt's circle, as he developed a personal and delicately expressive style La Farge deviated from the older painter's tutelage. Notably, La Farge was more interested in color than Hunt, and he relished plein air painting, whereas Hunt preferred the studio. Through Hunt he became acquainted with fellow art student William James, who later achieved eminence in philosophy and psychology, and with his brother, the novelist Henry James. Several years older and more intellectually cultivated, La Farge must have been instrumental in formulating a central concern in the careers of all three: representing a material world that can be known only equivocally, in terms of its impact on mind. La Farge soon denoted this radical subjectivity most clearly in unassuming floral still lifes. Here brushwork, light, and shifting focus combine to suggest the fluidity of consciousness and the absence of clear demarcation between the material world and personal experience. These same elements at work in 1860s landscapes from nature give these works also a modern tenor that parallels and even anticipates French impressionists' handling of light and color.

During the 1870s La Farge's painting became tighter and more decorative as he considered figural subjects related to literary or ideal themes. Developing concurrently with his investigations of optical reality and spurred in part by commissions received since the mid-1860s for book and magazine illustrations, this stylistic approach melded the appeal of Pre-Raphaelitism, knowledge of Japanese graphic conventions, and his great admiration for the work of his longtime friend Pierre Puvis de Chavannes, the outstanding French muralist of his day. La Farge's own interest in mural painting unfolded after a second trip to Europe in 1872–73 renewed his admiration for English Pre-Raphaelites and intensified his appreciation of medieval French architecture. Shortly after his return he began to discuss with architect Henry Hobson Richardson plans for embellishing the architecture of Boston's Trinity Church (1874–77). Eventually La Farge assumed responsibility for the entire decorative ensemble. Subsequently, his easel painting languished for a decade as he committed his talents to murals, stained glass, and other forms of decoration for public and private spaces. At Trinity, he not only painted murals but also supervised a team of artists who produced an interior of splendor and unity unprecedented in the United States. This success led to other important ecclesiastical mural commissions, as at New York's Church of the Incarnation (1885) and Church of the Ascension (1886–88). However, among decorative media, he made his most original and lasting contribution with stained-glass windows. La Farge initiated the popularity of floral designs, patented "opalescent" glass in 1879, and revolutionized standards of craftsmanship in fabrication. Along with his younger colleague, the more commercially successful Louis Comfort *Tiffany, he shares credit for establishing stained glass as a legitimate art form in the United States. His stained glass often adorned sumptuous domestic spaces and private clubs he designed for multimillionaire clients in New York and Newport, usually in collaboration with other leading artists, such as Augustus *Saint-Gaudens.

While continuing to accept decorative commissions, after the mid-1880s La Farge painted more regularly, specializing in the watercolor medium that had aroused his enthusiasm in the late 1870s. He also traveled, wrote, and lectured. With Henry Adams, in 1886 he sojourned for three months in Japan (where they were met by Ernest *Fenollosa) and in 1890–91 spent a year and a half in the South Seas. In declining health toward the end of his life, La Farge suffered a nervous collapse in the spring of 1910. He withdrew to Newport but before long had to be hospitalized in Providence. He died there a few months later. Among his many articles, "An Essay on Japanese Art" (1870) numbers among pioneering studies of that subject in the United States. His books include *An Artist's Letters from Japan* (1897), *Great Masters* (1903), and *The Higher Life in Art* (1908), devoted to French Barbizon painting. *Reminiscences of the South Seas* (1912) and *One Hundred Masterpieces of Painting* (1912) appeared posthumously, as did *The Gospel Story in Art* (1913), left unfinished at his death but completed by his executrix. His son, painter **Bancel La Farge** (1865–1938), born in Newport, was also known for decorative work, particularly murals and mosaics. He collaborated with his father on projects in the 1890s.

LaHotan, Robert. *See* HELIKER, JOHN.

Lambdin, George Cochran (1830–96). Painter. The outstanding flower painter of his day, he also painted *genre scenes, portraits, and other types of still life. Born in Pittsburgh, in 1838 Lambdin moved with his family to Philadelphia, where he remained, except for brief periods, all his life. His father, **James Reid Lambdin** (1807–89), a Pittsburgh-born portraitist who later headed the *Pennsylvania Academy of the Fine Arts for nearly twenty years, provided his son's early training. In the mid-1850s Lambdin studied abroad for two years, in Munich and Paris. He made his early reputation as a genre painter, specializing in unrhetorical, finely executed childhood scenes and Civil War episodes at the home front or behind the lines. At the end of the 1860s Lambdin lived in New York for about two years. During this period he probably admired the early flower paintings of John *La Farge, and in 1870 he may have seen the floral still lifes of French painter Henri Fantin-Latour during a second trip to Europe. Upon his return, Lambdin settled permanently in the Germantown neighborhood of Philadelphia. There he turned to roses as a specialty, both as a subject for his art and as a passionately pursued hobby. Many subsequent flower paintings picture mixed bouquets featuring variety in texture, shape, and color, but the roses he adored offered opportunities for greater originality. Although he sometimes portrayed conventional tabletop groupings of luxuriant blooms, his more distinctive paintings fall into two types. In his garden, he often painted roses as they grew, creating informal studies that incorporate greater attention to light and atmosphere than is common in traditional still life work. Alternatively, he placed meticulously rendered, sumptuous blossoms before shiny black backgrounds, creating decorative displays that probably owe their inspiration to the Japanese lacquer ware exhibited, and much admired, at Philadelphia's 1876 Centennial Exposition.

Land Art. *See* EARTH ART.

Landis, Adelie. *See* BISCHOFF, ELMER.

Landscape art. For two centuries, landscape has remained a central preoccupation of American art and its public. Throughout the colonial period and the early years of the Republic, landscape rarely figured as a subject of serious art, although it sometimes appeared in conjunction with portraits or in the less common history paintings of the period. Descriptive views had some currency, and decorative interior schemes often included scenes of nature. With the development of *romanticism, early nineteenth-century artists and their patrons took a greater interest in landscape for its own sake. The work of pioneer landscape painters, such as Thomas *Birch, Francis *Guy, Joshua *Shaw, and William Guy *Wall, remained largely topographical, although they often adjusted what they saw to accommodate traditional European formulas. During this early period, only Washington *Allston created imaginative landscapes, but these nearly always embrace historical or literary themes. By the 1820s such artists as Thomas *Doughty, Alvan *Fisher, and Robert *Salmon had begun to explore landscape as an expressive subject. The meteoric rise of Thomas *Cole after 1825 brought new awareness of landscape's potential for conveying symbolic and allegorical meanings. *Hudson River School painters combined exacting description of particular locations with idealism suggesting nationalistic or religious content. As epitomized in the work of Fitz Hugh *Lane, *luminism provided a particularly intense variation on the Hudson River formula, stressing measure, order, and tranquillity in combination with radiant effects of light. Around mid-century *Pre-Raphaelitism fostered a taste for rendering even the tiniest natural details with deliberate scrupulousness. By the 1860s American landscape artists traveled to the far West and to exotic foreign locations in search of new material, often incorporating their observations into canvases of grandiose dimensions. The work of Albert *Bierstadt, Frederic *Church, and Thomas *Moran exemplifies this taste. During these same years, photographers such as Carleton *Watkins and William Henry *Jackson first documented the western landscape as a major subject. Anticipated at mid-century by William Morris *Hunt and others intrigued by *Barbizon painting, such painters as Ralph *Blakelock, George *Inness, Dwight *Tryon, and James Abbott McNeill *Whistler later spurned descriptive realism to treat landscape in painterly and introspective terms. Others in the late nineteenth century followed the lead of French impressionist painters in creating informal, colorful views of nature. Among these, Childe *Hassam achieved the most widely admired American approach, while Winslow *Homer and Maurice *Prendergast developed personal variants of the French style.

Many modernists of the early twentieth century in the United States portrayed landscape motifs in abstracted or stylized form. Among artists associated with Alfred *Stieglitz, this tendency was particularly notable, as seen in work by Arthur *Dove, Marsden *Hartley, John *Marin, and Georgia *O'Keeffe. During the 1930s, artists of the *American Scene movement, such as Thomas Hart *Benton and Grant *Wood, regularly used landscape to provide context for figural subjects, although they produced pure landscapes as well. In this period also, Ansel *Adams initiated his long engagement with landscape photography, primarily in the American West. Jackson *Pollock's *abstract expressionist work evolved from a style based on Benton's to a nonrepresentational mode that continued to suggest the rhythms and spaces of landscape. Similarly, works of Helen *Frankenthaler, Franz *Kline, and Mark *Rothko, among others, suggest responses to landscape, while Joan *Mitchell made a specialty of working from outdoor motifs. During the 1960s and 1970s, interest in the landscape was made literal in the work of Robert *Smithson, Michael *Heizer, and others who produced *earth art. Today many artists continue to engage landscape, directly or obliquely, for its own sake or to comment on related environmental issues. James *Turrell labors to transform an extinct volcano into a work of art, while Jane *Freilicher numbers among artists who continue scenic imagery in paint on canvases. Calling into question Americans' traditionally positive engagements with landscape, such photographers as Richard *Misrach and *Robert Adams present disquieting views, often revealing the negative impact of human activity.

Lane, Fitz H. (1804–65). Painter and lithographer. Known for coastal and harbor scenes, chiefly in the earlier years of his career he also produced city views, ship portraits, narratives, and other subjects. His most typical work, dating from the 1850s and 1860s, epitomizes the salient features of *luminism. Its attention to detail and esteem for nature also parallel contemporaneous work of the *Hudson River School. In his characteristic paintings, time seems suspended in order to reveal the design and structure of space, the most infinitesimal details of natural matter, and the sundry manifestations of light. Lane recorded topography and marine vessels with utmost fidelity, but the compositional adjustments he employed in representing his subjects indicate that he consciously pursued an aesthetic of serenity and stability. Whether he also brought a philosophical or religious purpose to his work remains unclear. He led a relatively solitary life and left almost no written records. Lane was at least casually familiar with Transcendentalism, and he may also have been attracted to spiritualism. Whether intentionally or not, many of Lane's paintings seem to parallel Ralph Waldo Emerson's optimistic, mystically tinged rhetoric. Accordingly, some historians have interpreted his paintings as reflections of faith in the clarity and order of the universe. Yet, in stressing stasis, emptiness, and impersonality, especially in his late, radically stripped-down images, his work sometimes hints at a bleaker and more disquieting metaphysics.

Nathaniel Rogers Lane was born in coastal Gloucester, Massachusetts. According to a document discovered in 2005, he petitioned the state to change his name to Fitz Henry Lane. Although the request was granted in 1832 and he subsequently signed at least two paintings by that name, for unknown but apparently mistaken reasons he has been known in modern times as Fitz Hugh. Crippled by an early childhood disease (probably polio), he traveled relatively little, generally only to places he could reach by ship. While employed at a print shop in Boston, where he lived from the early 1830s until 1848, he gained prowess as a draftsman. By 1835 he was making lithographs on his own or, later, with a partner, and about 1840 he began painting. He probably became acquainted with Robert *Salmon, whose work clearly inspired him. He must have also become at least passingly acquainted with prints after the work of J. M. W. Turner, as well as English and Dutch seascape traditions. Before the end of the 1840s he had defined a recognizably individual approach. Working full time as a painter after he returned permanently to his hometown, he continued over time to refine his style. By eliminating nonessentials, eradicating picturesque compositional strategies, abstracting forms, and disciplining brushstroke to a vitreous and impersonal surface, he achieved a uniquely powerful reductive style. Many of his subjects are taken from the Gloucester area, but he also painted other points along the Atlantic coast, most particularly Boston harbor and the Maine shore. On summer trips he had opportunities to trade ideas with other artists exploring the scenery. By about 1860, his work demonstrates awareness of work by Martin Johnson *Heade, for example. Lane's patrons remained largely in Boston and Gloucester, although he occasionally exhibited paintings in New York. The *American Art-Union distributed several as prints. Nevertheless, his work was generally considered peripheral to mainstream art history until the mid-twentieth century. Like other studies of marine activity, *New York Harbor* (Museum of Fine Arts, Boston, 1850) describes ships with an accuracy that seafarers found convincing and appealing. Two rowboats near the foreground and some tiny figures on more distant vessels record human activity. The placement of boats clearly measures the visible space receding over tranquil water, and the sky glows with a luminous haze. A spare work of his final years, *Brace's Rock, Brace's Cove* (Museum of Fine Arts, Boston, c. 1864) exemplifies the stark power he later achieved by eliminating people, organizing shapes into elemental forms parallel to the picture plane, presenting detail with preternatural clarity, and featuring absolutely still reflective waters. The sole indication of human experience, a beached sailboat wreck, hints at alienating currents beneath Lane's characteristic poetry of optical experience.

Lange, Dorothea (1895–1965). Photographer. Her simply composed but affecting Depression-era documentary photographs reveal human despair and suffering, but also dignity and strength. Facial expressions, gestures, and body language of individual subjects illustrate the effects of large-scale social forces. In "Migrant Mother, Nipomo, California" (1936), a careworn farm worker holds a sleeping infant on her lap, as two other children bury their faces on her shoulders. Perhaps the most famous of all *Farm Security Administration photographs, this arresting image compels the viewer's sympathy, fulfilling Lange's intent to use her medium to promote social change. Born in Hoboken, New Jersey, Dorothea Margretta Nutzhorn assumed her mother's maiden name in 1918. Polio, contracted at age seven, left her with a limp and conditioned her responsiveness to human distress. From the age of twelve she lived in New York, where she worked between 1912 and 1917 in several portrait studios, including Arnold *Genthe's. During these years, she mastered a softly flattering *pictorialist approach to portraiture, studied briefly with Clarence *White, and set her sights on working her way around the world. She got as far as San Francisco. In 1918 she took a job there and in 1919 opened a successful portrait studio. Her artistic development slowed after marriage in 1920 to Maynard Dixon (1875–1946), a painter of western landscapes and American Indians, followed by the birth of children and travels with her husband in the Southwest. However, in 1932, as she observed effects of the Depression in San Francisco, she dedicated herself to documenting socially induced suffering. One of her earliest works in this vein, "White Angel Bread Line" (1932/33), centers on a man in shabby dress, as he turns away from others in a charity queue to lean heavily on a barrier, his battered tin cup resting between his arms. Seen from slightly above, his face is obscured by his hat brim, giving him the anonymity of a symbol. His bearing reveals failure, alienation, and sadness, representing the plight of millions.

After meeting economics professor Paul Taylor in 1934, Lange soon started to work with him documenting migrant workers for a government program. Following her divorce, she and Taylor were married in 1935, forming a thirty-year personal and professional partnership. Also in 1935, she began a four-year association with the Farm Security Association (known until 1937 as the Resettlement Administration). Taylor, a labor expert, continued to work for another government agency, so they often traveled together, sharing a dedication to social justice as they roamed the West and South, witnessing the devastation of the Depression and Dust Bowl. In 1939 their work culminated in *American Exodus: A Record of Human Erosion*. Among the finest documentary publications of the period, it includes not only Lange's photographs and Taylor's scholarly analysis but also the words of her subjects. Although her strongest work dates to the 1930s, Lange completed a forceful series on the internment of Japanese Americans during World War II. Also in the early 1940s she photographed utopian religious communities. In the 1950s she pursued a variety of projects, including a number of magazine assignments, as she sustained her interests in rural communities and in transformations brought by industrialization. From the late 1950s until her death, she accompanied her husband to rural Third World locations where he served as an international consultant on agrarian problems. On these expeditions, she continued to photograph but did not rival earlier accomplishments, partly because of failing health. She died in San Francisco.

Lanyon, Ellen. *See* CHICAGO IMAGISM.

Lasansky, Mauricio (1914–). Printmaker and draftsman. Known for technically virtuosic, figural intaglio prints, he also drew much attention for his sequence of monumental Nazi Drawings (1961–66, 1971) related to the Holocaust. Following in the tradition of Goya and Picasso in lamenting the brutality of war, the thirty individual drawings and one triptych portray individual life-size and larger figures suggestive of perpetrators, victims, and the personification of death. Born in Buenos Aires, where he trained in fine arts, Lasansky arrived in the United States in 1943 and became an American citizen in 1952. He worked at *Atelier 17 in New York before moving in 1945 to Iowa City. There he established the print workshop at the State University of Iowa (now University of Iowa), soon a leading center for the medium. Since his retirement in 1984, he has continued to work in Iowa City. Lasansky's imagery has centered on the enigma of the human condition, especially as revealed through suffering and brutality. During the 1940s and 1950s, he favored complex compositions, often tinged with surrealism, in rich tones of black and white. Later he preferred simpler depictions of individuals, singly or in small groups, on a larger scale, while his technique broadened to include complex color printing. Three sons who became artists earned MFA degrees at the University of Iowa. **William Lasansky** (1938–), a sculptor, was born in Argentina. He taught from 1968 until his retirement in 2006 at Bucknell University in Lewisburg, Pennsylvania. He also maintains a home and studio in Vinalhaven, Maine. He has produced cast and welded, as well as carved stone sculptures in both figurative and abstract styles. **Leonardo Lasansky** (1946–), born in Iowa City, has followed his father as an intaglio printmaker and draftsman working with figurative imagery. Since 1972 he has served on the faculty of Hamline University in St. Paul. Also born in Iowa City, where he continues to reside, painter **Tomas Lasansky** (1957–) specializes in images related to the Indians of the American Southwest and their culture.

Lassaw, Ibram (1913–2003). Sculptor. An abstract artist from the outset of his career in the early 1930s, he was known for asymmetrical, latticelike, three-dimensional metal structures with sensuous and irregular surfaces. He originated these "drawings in space" (as he and others called them) around 1950 in response to the work of Jackson *Pollock and other *abstract expressionists whose work he admired. Like many of them, he sought to infuse his work with symbolic and transcendental meanings. Although his wide-ranging intellectual interests and familiarity with Zen Buddhist philosophy supported his aspiration to universal energy and order, he steadfastly maintained that each sculpture should be "only itself," free of associative images. Born to Russian parents in Alexandria, he spent his early childhood in Egypt, where he attended a French school, but moved with his family to New York in 1921. He was naturalized as a citizen in 1928, the year after he began his professional training at the Clay Club (now Sculpture Center), where he worked until 1932. Concurrently, in 1930–31 he studied at the Beaux-Arts Institute of Design. He also was enrolled for a short time at City College of New York. While employed from the mid-1930s until 1942 by a *federal art project, in 1936 he joined the *American Abstract Artists as a charter member. Although Lassaw at first investigated *biomorphic forms in clay and plaster, he soon was attracted to a constructivist approach using metal, sometimes in combination with other materials. While serving for two years in the U.S. Army during World War II, he learned welding, later his preferred artistic technique. For a time in the 1940s, under Mondrian's influence, he produced strictly composed geometric compositions, sometimes incorporating organic details. He often employed unconventional materials, such as steel and plastic, in idiosyncratic combinations. Later, Lassaw worked with a wide range of substances to lend color, texture, and organic luster to surfaces, while also engaging the problems of scale in works that range in size from tabletop pieces to monumental architectural embellishments. After previously summering there, in 1962 he moved to the eastern Long Island hamlet of Springs, where he died at his home.

Laughlin, Clarence John (1905–85). Photographer. Known for romantic, sometimes surrealistic images that intimate a reality beyond appearances, he freely employed double exposures, staged scenes, montage, and other stratagems to realize his fantasies

In unmanipulated photographs, he masterfully captured unstable moments of great delicacy and poetic implication. Although he shared the South's fascination with its own grandeur and decay, his ambitions transcended regional concerns. Spurred by imagination and love of literature, he dreamed of devising visual equivalents for psychological states and inventing a mythology of the modern world, uniting subjective and objective realities. In his creative process, memory and desire served as constant companions. Born in Lake Charles, Louisiana, he grew up in New Orleans. He wrote poetry inspired by French symbolism before turning to photography in the mid-1930s. His early work, devoted primarily to architectural photography, culminated in *Ghosts Along the Mississippi* (1948), a study of plantation houses. Indicating overtly more surrealistic interests, in 1939 he initiated a sustained series of theatrical images titled Poems of the Interior World, in which he attempted to symbolize the psychological tensions of war-torn Western civilization. Until younger photographers revalidated his nonpurist approach in the 1960s, Laughlin remained the most important American link to the fictional forms of photography that had, for the most part, vanished with *pictorialism. He died in New Orleans. Laughlin also published *New Orleans and Its Living Past* (1941), *Photographs of Victorian Chicago* (1968), and *Clarence John Laughlin: The Personal Eye* (1973).

Launitz, Robert. *See* FRAZEE, JOHN.

Laurent, Robert (1890–1970). Sculptor. Among early modern exponents of direct carving, truth to materials, and nonacademic form, he was born in Concarneau, in the Brittany region of France. At twelve, he arrived in the United States as the protégé of painter, editor, and art enthusiast Hamilton Easter Field (1873–1922). Working first as a painter, in 1905 he went to Paris, where became acquainted with modern and non-Western art. Two years later he continued on to Rome. There he learned woodcarving and studied with Maurice *Sterne. After his return to New York in 1910, directly carved wood reliefs depicting stylized natural forms placed him among the most progressive sculptors of the day. Within a few years, he began to carve in the round, as in his lithe, curving, nearly abstract wood sculpture *The Flame* (Whitney Museum, c. 1917). From 1921 he worked also in stone, as he increasingly focused on the female figure. Between the late 1920s and the late 1930s he produced bronze pieces, as well. In characteristic mature work, he carved ample, idealized figures, such as *Seated Nude* (Pennsylvania Academy, 1940), related to similar subjects by Gaston *Lachaise and French sculptor Aristide Maillol. In 1942 he accepted a faculty position at Indiana University in Bloomington, but continued during summers to direct the Ogunquit, Maine, art school he had inherited from Field. Upon his retirement from Indiana in 1960, he settled in the Ogunquit area. He died at his home in nearby Cape Neddick.

Lavenson, Alma. *See* F/64 GROUP.

Lawrence, Jacob (1917–2000). Painter. Best known for narratives of African-American life and history, he nevertheless often thoughtfully responded to contemporary issues without regard to race. His interest in recording the lived experience of his era relates his artistic origins to the *American Scene movement. Independent in his form of expression as well as his politics, he devised a personal style of patterning, bright colors, and jazzy rhythms. Born in Atlantic City, New Jersey, Jacob Armstead Lawrence spent his early years in Easton and Philadelphia, Pennsylvania. In 1930 he moved to New York, where his education ended after two years of high school. Charles *Alston, whom he first met in an after-school arts-and-crafts class, had already kindled his interest in art. In his later teenage years, Lawrence gained an appreciation of African-American culture and history through a continuing relationship with Alston, acquaintance with other figures of the *Harlem Renaissance, free classes at the Harlem Community Art Center (directed by Augusta *Savage, who encouraged him), and his own extensive reading. He also learned from both African and European artistic traditions, eventually devising his own distinctive style from disparate influences, including African masks, works of the Mexican muralists, Picasso's synthetic cubism, and early Renaissance painting, as well as contemporary work by Ben *Shahn and Stuart *Davis.

When he was old enough to enroll, at twenty-one, in a *federal art project, he was able for the first time to think of art as something more than a hobby. Attracted to abstract pattern since his earliest efforts, he quickly developed a posterlike style. For his first major project, he produced forty-one paintings recounting the life of Toussaint L'Ouverture (Amistad Research Center, New Orleans. 1938), the black slave who founded the Republic of Haiti. When this affecting series appeared in the initial major museum exhibition of African-American art, at the Baltimore Museum of Art in 1939, Lawrence, not quite twenty-two years old, became one of the first black artists to win acclaim from the white art public. The series format suited his interest in telling African-American stories, and several others followed. *The Migration of the Negro* (equally divided between the Museum of Modern Art and the Phillips Collection, 1940–41) comprises sixty scenes tracing the movement of African Americans to the North, while the John Brown series of twenty-two paintings (Detroit Institute of Arts, 1941) relates the history of the radical abolitionist. Lawrence served in the U.S. Coast Guard during World War II. Afterward, he painted many works dignifying ordinary African-American workers, as in *The Cabinetmaker* (Hirshhorn Museum, 1957). He also broadened his subjects to include whites, as for example in a 1955–56 series of thirty paintings devoted to events in American history. Stylistically, his work became more complex, more analytical, and less reliant on flat color areas. In the postwar years, Lawrence also embarked on an extended teaching career, first at *Black Mountain College, later at the Pratt Institute, the *Art Students League, and elsewhere. Although the classroom absorbed much of his time by the 1960s, he nevertheless responded in paintings to the civil rights struggle and to his experience of an extended visit to Nigeria. In 1970 he moved to Seattle, where a professorship at the University of Washington afforded him more time to paint. He stayed on in retirement and died there. While remaining a socially conscious observer, he tended in later years to work with more universal subjects than he had earlier and to use a subtler, more modulated, and often more decorative palette. In 1941 he married portrait and still life painter Gwendolyn Knight (1913–   ). Born in Barbados, she studied at Howard University in Washington, D.C., and elsewhere.

Lawrie, Lee (1877–1963). Sculptor. Known especially for public monuments and architectural embellishments, he employed a simplified and stylized form of representation. Born in Rixdorf, Germany, Lee Oscar Lawrie grew up in Chicago. In 1891 he began working for neoclassical sculptor Richard Henry Park (1832–1902), preparing decorations for the World's Columbian Exposition of 1893. Subsequently, he worked for sculptors in Chicago, Massachusetts, and New York, where he assisted Augustus *Saint-Gaudens. In 1910 he earned a BFA from Yale University and remained to teach until 1918. Later, for many years he maintained a studio near Easton, Maryland, where he died. Lawrie developed a style of broadly conceived volumes, often flattened in the case of his architectural decorations, appropriate to the large scale of much of his work. He provided stylistically congruent sculptures for numerous Gothic revival and art deco buildings designed by Ralph Adams Cram or Bertram Goodhue. These include the monumental reredos and other decorative elements (1916–13) for St. Thomas Church in New York and embellishments for the early 1920s Nebraska state capitol in Lincoln. Lawrie served as director of sculptural programs at the 1933 Century of Progress Exposition in Chicago and also made significant contributions to the sculpture of the 1939 World's Fair in New York. His most widely known work, the huge bronze *Atlas* in New York's Rockefeller Center, dates to 1937.

Lawson, Alexander. *See* WILSON, ALEXANDER.

Lawson, Ernest (1873–1939). Painter. Dedicated principally to landscape, he developed a personal, highly impastoed impressionist style. Critic James Hunecker memorably compared his opulent and intricate surfaces to "crushed jewels." Although Lawson was more interested in beautiful effects than in capturing the rough vitalism of contemporary American life, he often included aspects of urban infrastructure in his compositions, and in 1908 he exhibited with the *Ashcan School–dominated *Eight. Probably born in Halifax, Nova Scotia (he sometimes claimed he was a native of San Francisco), he lived in Canada until 1888, when he moved to Kansas City. He began his art training there and in Mexico City before moving in 1891 to New York, where he worked at the *Art Students League with J. Alden *Weir and John *Twachtman, his most important mentor. In 1893 he went to Paris, where he studied at the Académie Julian and gained a firsthand knowledge of impressionism. He lived in Toronto and Columbus, Georgia, during the three years before he settled in Washington Heights in 1898. There, the Hudson River and the wooded reaches of upper Manhattan provided characteristic subjects for some time. Completed in 1913, the year he exhibited in the *Armory Show, *Spring Night, Harlem River* (Phillips Collection) uses the strong forms of a bridge to stabilize a composition anchored in ample, interlocking two- and three-dimensional shapes. Bright touches of warm yellows and reds enliven the moody blue-and-green tonality. Although Lawson's style remained rooted in impressionism, Cézanne influenced his conception of form, while the heavy paint—often laid on with a palette knife—can function independently as the medium of purely visual experience. With their bright colors and edgy shapes, some later paintings evince an expressionistic intensity. Lawson also painted in Spain, Canada, and numerous locations in the United States. In failing health, he moved in 1936 to Florida, where he died in the surf at Miami Beach.

Lazzell, Blanche (1878–1956). Printmaker and painter. Known especially for color woodcuts, she usually composed with simplified and stylized representational forms but also produced abstract works. Born near Maidsville, West Virginia, Nettie Blanche Lazzell graduated in 1905 from West Virginia University in Morgantown. Three years later, she enrolled at the *Art Students League, where she worked with William Merritt *Chase. Following a return to West Virginia in 1908, from 1912 to 1914 she continued her studies in Paris. Subsequently, she studied with Charles W. *Hawthorne, took up cutting and printing wood blocks, and settled into a longtime habit of spending summers (and occasional winters) on Cape Cod, in *Provincetown. In Paris again in the early 1920s, she enriched her training by working with Fernand Léger, Albert Gleizes, and André L'Hôte. In this environment, her work became more abstract. In 1933 she returned to Morgantown to work for a *federal art project. She continued to maintain ties in that city, where she died. Lazzell's technical mastery of the woodcut medium is already evident in the tightly designed 1919 *Monongahela*, an abstracted landscape. Lunging branches of a foreground leafless tree balance a sweeping river curve that recedes to geometric rhythms of a bridge and distant, rounded hills. Although forms are flattened and simplified, soft and painterly color provides a delicate atmosphere. More directly indebted to her experience of cubism, the 1926 *Non-Objective (B)*, also a color woodcut, abstracts a tabletop still life. Tiny patterning, recalling effects seen in certain French collages, enlivens some of the interlocking, harmoniously colored shapes.

Leaf, June. *See* FRANK, ROBERT.

Lebrun, Rico (1900–1964). Painter, draftsman, printmaker, and sculptor. Lebrun's expressionistic humanism treated themes of suffering, death, inhumanity, and redemption. Among few artists to dwell productively on the horrors of World War II, he also drew on the art of such past masters such as Grünewald and Goya to create modern variations of their emotionally searing images. Born in Naples, Federico Lebrun trained as an artist there and in Florence. After working as a designer in a stained glass factory for two years, he first came to the United States in 1924, when the business opened a branch in Springfield, Illinois. The following year he moved to New York, where he became a successful advertising artist, but during frequent visits continued to steep his sensibility in the historical art of his homeland. In 1938 he moved permanently to the Los Angeles area, where he taught and worked as a Disney animator. He died at his home in Malibu. Lebrun's characteristic approach appeared in the late 1930s in paintings of socially marginal types, such as beggars, cripples, and performers. After World War II he increasingly addressed ponderous and tragic subjects. Lebrun's Crucifixion series, begun in 1947 and comprising more than two hundred paintings and drawings, culminated in a huge triptych (Syracuse [New York] University, 1950). In the mid-1950s, concentration camp photographs served as the impetus for a series on Buchenwald and Dachau, in which piles of corpses bear timeless witness to the stupidity of war and the transience of life. Yet, even here formal coherence and elegantly conceived drawing leaven despair with intimations of spiritual transcendence. Whatever his subject, Lebrun brought to it masterful resources: first-rate draftsmanship, bold and glowing color, and internalized command of Renaissance, Baroque, and modern traditions. As a result he could range with seeming effortlessness from realistic detail to abstract form, fluidly addressing his central subject, the human body, and creating mood and atmosphere appropriate to particular subjects. Lebrun extended his practice to a serious engagement with sculpture in the last two years of his life.

Lee, Doris (1905–83). Painter and printmaker. Among her droll contributions to *American Scene painting, the well-known *Thanksgiving* (Art Institute of Chicago, 1935), a bustling dinner preparation scene filled with homely details, presents an amusing but affectionate look at the labor behind a uniquely American ritual. If the content is calculatedly naive, the painting also demonstrates Lee's sophisticated control of color, drawing, and composition. Doris Emrick was born in Aledo, Illinois. Upon graduation in 1927 from Rockford (Illinois) College, she married Russell *Lee. During the next four years, she studied at the Kansas City Art Institute with Ernest *Lawson, in Paris with André Lhote, and at the California School of Fine Arts (now San Francisco Art Institute), where Arnold *Blanch redirected her interest from abstraction to nature. After moving in 1931 to *Woodstock, where she remained active in the art community for many years, in 1939 she married Blanch. Like her first, this marriage also ended in divorce. Although Lee became known for scenes of homespun Americana, she also depicted urban life in such paintings as *April Storm, Washington*

Square, New York City (Rhode Island School of Design, c. 1932). In this sweeping view, leafless trees bend to the wind as dozens of people respond in varying ways to the changing weather. Lee's eye for detail and for humorous characterization led to a number of magazine commissions for illustrations, in some cases based on travel experiences. She also painted murals for *federal art projects in the 1930s and, with Blanch, wrote *It's Fun To Paint* (1947). Lee died in Clearwater, Florida.

Lee, Russell. *See* FARM SECURITY ADMINISTRATION (FSA) PHOTOGRAPHS.

Leen, Nina. *See* IRASCIBLES, THE.

Lee-Smith, Hughie (1915–99). Painter and printmaker. Born in Eustis, Florida, he lived in Atlanta as a small child but moved to Cleveland when he was ten. He studied at the Cleveland School (now Institute) of Art, performed with a dance company, designed sets for a theatrical group, and worked for a *federal art project. After graduating in 1938, he taught in North Carolina before moving to Detroit in 1940. In 1944 he joined the war effort as an artist for the U.S. Navy, and in 1953 he earned a bachelor's degree from Wayne State University. Five years later, Lee-Smith moved to New York and became in 1963 only the second African American elected to membership in the *National Academy of Design. He taught at the *Art Students League for fifteen years, beginning in 1972, and later lived near Princeton, New Jersey. He died in Albuquerque. During his career, Lee-Smith moved from socially oriented themes related to the *American Scene movement to more personal statements. These generally portray psychological and symbolic themes suggesting loneliness or alienation. In the painterly and haunting image of *The Stranger* (Smithsonian American Art Museum, c. 1957–58), a lone figure stands in a field that has been partially bulldozed or otherwise ravished. Behind, and separated from him, a cluster of simple houses and barns catches the slanting light that illuminates the face of the man, as he turns toward it. At once beautiful and menacing, the moment's enigmatic air suggests the melancholy undertow seen also in Edward *Hopper's characteristic works. Later works incorporated surrealistic elements, as in *Two Girls* (New Jersey State Museum, Trenton, 1966). Here, isolated figures pose within puzzling environments, in which more tightly rendered but now incomprehensible elements contribute to an uncanny atmosphere. Lee-Smith was known also for portraits.

Lemet, Louis. *See* SAINT-MEMIN, CHARLES B. J. F. DE.

Le Moyne de Morgues, Jacques. *See* WHITE, JOHN.

Lerner, Nathan. *See* DARGER, HENRY.

Leslie, Alfred (1927–). Painter, printmaker, and filmmaker. An *abstract expressionist in the 1950s, during the following decade he played an important role in the revival of figurative painting. As a filmmaker, he is particularly known for his central role in making *Pull My Daisy* (1959). Born in New York, he served in the U.S. Coast Guard before entering New York University, where Tony *Smith numbered among his teachers. He left without a degree in 1949. Quickly recognized as a leading second-generation abstract expressionist, he painted large works filled with violent brushwork. An underlying structural grid became more prominent toward the end of the 1950s, and soon geometric forms emerged, sometimes accompanied by collage. In 1964 he adopted a forthright, unidealized, large-scale figural realism, as in *Self-Portrait* (Whitney Museum, 1967). Like a deadpan Caravaggio, he harshly scrutinizes himself, sloppily dressed in work clothes with unbuttoned shirt. Strong value contrasts, rigid surfaces, and a dark surrounding void intensify his confrontational visage. Later, he added to his series of similarly conceived portraits staged *genre scenes of contemporary subjects and narrative or historical inventions. He has also made lithographs and landscape monoprints. Leslie began experimenting with film in the 1940s. He directed the beat classic *Pull My Daisy* in partnership with Robert *Frank. Written and narrated by Jack Kerouac, it featured as "actors" Larry *Rivers, Alice *Neel, French actress Delphine Seyrig (then Jack *Youngerman's wife), and poets Allen Ginsberg and Gregory Corso, among others. More or less plotless, the film provides a wry, oblique glimpse into a high-spirited moment in countercultural history. Based on Leslie's memories of an abstract expressionist institution, *The Cedar Bar* (2001) explores the meaning and purposes of art while reimagining an alcoholically charged evening of conversation between artists, other denizens of the art world, and a critic based on Clement *Greenberg. Intercut often bizarrely unrelated film clips interrupt Leslie's script, adding an anarchic note.

Leutze, Emanuel Gottlieb (1816–68). Painter. Among the best known art works in the United States, his *Washington Crossing the Delaware* (Metropolitan Museum, 1851) remains an icon of American culture. Primarily a painter of historical and literary narratives

Leutze also produced portraits and occasional landscapes. Abroad for much of his professional life, he became an esteemed member of the art community in Düsseldorf, where he originally sojourned as a student. As a popular teacher and genial friend, he attracted many American students and visitors. His passionate devotion to personal and political liberty, which fueled his most convincing work, appealed to patriotic sentiment in both the United States and Germany. Born in Schwäbisch Gmünd, about thirty miles east of Stuttgart, in 1825 he emigrated with his family to the United States and soon settled in Philadelphia. There as a teenager he received instruction in drawing from John Rubens *Smith before working as a portraitist in Philadelphia and elsewhere. In 1841 he went to Düsseldorf. He studied at the art academy there and worked with romantic realist Karl Friedrich Lessing, whose artistically anti-academic and politically progressive ideas appealed to the son of a dissident. From the outset Leutze worked primarily for an American market, adapting his technical prowess to the expression of themes from or related to American history. After traveling in Germany and Italy for two years, in 1845 he returned to settle in Düsseldorf. Advocating democracy and German unification, he soon became a leader of the liberal artists' faction. Already internationally known for historical scenes from the life of Columbus and other subjects, at this time he embarked on an extended series of paintings devoted to incidents in the progress of freedom. Reflecting prevailing taste in Düsseldorf, his style featured emphatic realism, smoothly finished surfaces, rich coloration, accurate historical detail, and emotionally charged narratives. However, he avoided Düsseldorf's fondness for finicky detail and for sentimental anecdote. His conviction that the subjects of paintings should be chosen in the service of ideas underpinned the power of his best paintings, although some by today's standards seem theatrical.

Then, as now, *Washington Crossing the Delaware* was his most popular painting. Depicting a critical moment in the Revolution, the detailed rendering of Washington's Christmas night river crossing heroicizes the commanding general. A personification of resolute courage, impervious to danger and personal discomfort, he intently faces into the wind, focusing on the New Jersey shore ahead, as his boatmen ferry him across waters strewn with ice floes. Victory at the Battle of Trenton, a turning point in the war, awaited him the next day. After completing the painting in Düsseldorf, Leutze showed it to instant acclaim in New York during the fall of 1851 and, several months later, in Washington, D.C., where it was honored with a place in the U.S. Capitol rotunda. After 1853, when a prestigious European firm issued a modestly scaled engraving of the grandiose original (more than 12 × 21 feet), the image appeared on the walls of homes throughout the nation. Leutze returned to Düsseldorf in 1852 but after 1859 worked in New York and Washington, where he died. His 1862 mural, *Westward the Course of Empire Takes Its Way* in the U.S. Capitol ranks as the most important commission of his later years. Epitomizing mid-century American enthusiasm for westward expansion, it also provided reassuring promise of greatness to a country then mired in civil war.

Levine, Jack (1915–). Painter and printmaker. Typically sympathizing with the poor or satirizing the powerful, his expressionistic works contributed in the 1930s to the social realist tendency within the *American Scene movement. He has also painted portraits, scenes of Jewish life, and religious themes. Born in Boston, he studied there at the School of the Museum of Fine Arts and, from 1929 to 1931, with Denman *Ross, who encouraged his interest in old master painting. Levine developed his own rich variation on traditional techniques he admired in the emotionally charged works of such painters as Rembrandt, Goya, and Daumier, as well as modern expressionists including Chaim Soutine and Georges Rouault. His indistinctly defined forms and flickering, painterly surfaces suggest indeterminacy and mutability, providing a generalizing tone that suggests larger meanings inherent to the specific situations he depicts. In 1935 Levine joined a *federal art project, through which he came to national attention for his morally informed social protest. Between 1942 and 1945, he served in the U.S. Army. Levine's best-known work, the derisive *Gangster Funeral* (Whitney Museum, 1952–53), portrays political and law enforcement bigwigs gathered respectfully beside an underworld leader's coffin. Levine has lived in New York for many years. His wife, figurative painter and printmaker Ruth Gikow (1915–82), was born in Ukrainian Russia, emigrated to New York as a child, studied art at Cooper Union, and worked for a federal art project. She painted humanistic themes, often incorporating social criticism. She died in New York.

Levine, Sherrie. *See* POSTMODERNISM.

Levitt, Helen (1913–). Photographer and filmmaker. Known especially for candid, poetic views of neighborhood life in her native

New York, she worked often in lower-class areas, where she observed personality, charm, humor, and sociability on the streets. Her lively and appealing children at play often enact dramas that seem to portend the larger themes of adult life. An unusual series is devoted to children's street drawings and graffiti. Except for photographs made while living in Mexico City in 1941, nearly all of Levitt's work depicts Manhattan. She began photographing in the mid-1930s, influenced at first by Walker *Evans, Ben *Shahn, and Henri Cartier-Bresson. Through the late 1940s, she roamed Spanish Harlem, the Lower East Side, and other poor neighborhoods, where she photographed unobtrusively with a small handheld camera, sometimes fitted with a right-angle lens. Levitt's motivation was only partly documentary. Spontaneity, unconstrained expression, and the poetry of experience carried equal weight in the determination of her subjects. In the early 1940s, she began working as a film editor and soon extended her photographic practice into this medium. Writer James Agee collaborated on both her films, *In the Street* (1945–46) and *The Quiet One* (1946–47). She numbered among the first to use color in fine art photography, an interest she began to pursue in 1959, and to show her work in a museum by means of automated continuous slide projection, as she did in 1974 at the *Museum of Modern Art. In 1965, nearly twenty years after it had been assembled, she published *A Way of Seeing*, with text by Agee. *Crosstown*, with an introduction by Francine Prose, appeared in 2001. *Slide Show* (2005) presents earlier color work.

Levy, Julien (1906–81). Art dealer. Between 1931 and 1949, his provocative New York showplace promoted surrealism and photography at a time when few galleries were interested in either. Levy also occasionally showed mass-media work, such as posters and Disney studio drawings, then not widely regarded as art, and he brought to public attention the work of Joseph *Cornell. Born in New York, Levy studied fine arts at Harvard. In 1927, he sailed for Paris in the company of Marcel *Duchamp, whom he had earlier contrived to meet. Filled with dreams of becoming a filmmaker, within the year he married Joella Loy (they divorced in 1942), daughter of British-American poet and artist Mina Loy (1882–1966), who later acted informally as his agent in Paris. Succumbing to practical considerations, he soon returned to New York to enter his father's real estate business. Four years afterward, he opened his gallery with an American photography retrospective. A few months later, early in 1932, he staged the first American gallery show of surrealism, comprising work by Cornell, Duchamp, Max *Ernst, *Man *Ray, Salvador Dalí, and others. This exhibition, which galvanized the New York art world, followed by only a little more than two months the first museum show of surrealism, at the Wadsworth Atheneum in Hartford, Connecticut. It had included, on loan, virtually the entire European component of Levy's show, including Dalí's celebrated *Persistence of Memory* (Museum of Modern Art, 1931). In succeeding years, Levy mounted one-person shows of work by these and numerous other significant artists, most of whom were at least loosely associated with surrealism. They included Eugene *Berman, Peter *Blume, Jared *French, David *Hare, Roberto *Matta, Kay *Sage, Yves *Tanguy, Dorothea *Tanning, Pavel *Tchelitchew, Paul Delvaux, Alberto Giacometti, and Rene Magritte, as well as photographers Berenice *Abbott, George Platt *Lynes, Brett *Weston, Eugene Atget, and Henri Cartier-Bresson. In 1936 he published *Surrealism*, the first American book on the subject, and in 1966, a monograph on Arshile *Gorky, whose worked he had shown. The autobiographical *Memoir of an Art Gallery* followed in 1977. Levy died in New Haven.

Lewis, Edmonia (c. 1840–after 1909). Sculptor. Of African-American and American Indian ancestry, she ranks as the first important American sculptor of color. Her work tempered *neoclassicism with realistic observation. Nearly all her ideal creations interpret themes relating to her racial heritage or her experience as a woman, while many portraits picture leaders in the struggle for Emancipation. She lived in Rome throughout her professional life, although she visited the United States on a number of occasions. Mary Edmonia Lewis was born to a black West Indian father and a Chippewa (Ojibwa) mother (probably half African American), most likely near Albany, New York. The family resided in Newark, New Jersey, at the time she was orphaned in 1847. Subsequently, she may have lived for a time with her mother's people in western New York. She attended Oberlin (Ohio) College but did not complete a degree. In 1863 she left for Boston, epicenter of abolitionism. There she received some instruction in sculpture from Edward *Brackett and Anne *Whitney, but as an artist she was mostly self-taught. In 1865 she departed for Europe. In Florence, Hiram *Powers and Thomas *Ball offered assistance and encouragement before she arrived in Rome the following year. Soon she completed her best-known work, *Forever Free* (Howard University Gallery of Art,

Washington, D.C., 1867), celebrating the 1863 abolition of slavery. His chains broken, a black man raises one arm in exultation as he offers with the other protection to the woman who crouches prayerfully beside him. One of her finest pieces, *Hagar* (Smithsonian American Art Museum, 1875; modeled 1868–69), tenderly evokes the lonely suffering of biblical exile, a symbol of alienation and abused womanhood. Shown to great acclaim at the Philadelphia Centennial Exhibition, Lewis's last major work, *The Death of Cleopatra* (Smithsonian American Art Museum, 1876; modeled 1872–73), interprets the expiring Egyptian queen with nobility and restrained pathos. By this time neoclassical marbles were quickly going out of fashion, and records of her later life are few. Last documented in Rome in 1909, she presumably died there.

Lewis, Martin (1881–1962). Printmaker and painter. Capturing the era's emerging modernity, his characteristic prints depict the urban America that interested the *American Scene movement. Although Lewis's work rarely achieves his friend Edward *Hopper's nuanced evocation of mood, he vividly combined sharp observation and dramatic light effects to convey the restless energy of modern city life as well as its occasional menace. In the many night scenes for which he is particularly known, long shadows provide both mysterious overtones and intriguing compositional effects, as in *Relics* (1928). Lewis was born in Castlemain, Victoria, Australia, and briefly studied art in Sydney. After arriving in San Francisco in 1900, he soon moved permanently to New York. In the aftermath of the *Armory Show, he experimented for a short time in his paintings with modernist color effects. About 1915 he turned to etching and drypoint as his preferred media.

Lewis, Norman. *See* AFRICAN-AMERICAN ART.

LeWitt, Sol (1928–2007). Sculptor, draftsman, printmaker, and installation artist. After rising to prominence during the 1960s and 1970s with austere, serial, *minimalist constructions and wall drawings, in later decades he elaborated his original premises with more visually beguiling, even playful elements. Exemplifying as well a *conceptual bent, his works came into being through rigidly predetermined schemes fabricated by assistants. Some pieces, however, incorporate chance into the rules for their execution. LeWitt's invention of a formal vocabulary capable of accommodating variation according to syntactical rules paralleled 1960s fascination with linguistics. His late-1960s writings on art rank among the most clear-headed and effective statements related to the enthusiasm of that time for rationally ordered, literalist affronts to style and sensibility. Born in Hartford, Connecticut, LeWitt received a BFA from Syracuse (New York) University in 1949. While serving in the U.S. Army in 1951–52, he was posted in Japan. In 1953 he moved to New York, where he painted while supporting himself as a graphic designer. A decade later, he began to concentrate on reliefs and other constructions. His development had benefited from encounters with Jasper *Johns's early work, Eadweard *Muybridge's sequential photographs, and Russian constructivism before he met other artists who would become known as minimalists. In the early 1960s Dan *Flavin particularly urged increasingly radical simplification. In 1965 LeWitt first showed the reductive three-dimensional forms that made his reputation. For some years he continued to focus on latticelike constructions displaying permutations of rectangular, often cubic elements. Slender, impeccably finished strips of white wood and, later, metal defined only the edges of his forms, leaving voids at the interior of each. In 1968 he first showed wall drawings, predetermined patterns of delicately rendered, straight lines limited to red, yellow, blue, and black. In the 1980s, with a nod to Matisse and Victor Vasarely, LeWitt began to realize wall pieces in colored inks or, later, in bright acrylic paints, presenting exuberant, monumental variations on geometric regularity. In the 1990s curved shapes entered his two-dimensional repertoire and by the mid-2000s dominated a set of brilliantly hued sculptures reminiscent of stalagmites. After living for some years during the 1980s in Spoleto, Italy, LeWitt settled in Chester, Connecticut, where he died.

Liberator, The. *See* MASSES, THE.

Liberman, Alexander (1912–99). Painter, sculptor, photographer, graphic designer, and editor. For decades, his creative flair was widely, if anonymously, known to millions through Condé Nast publications, as he guided the company's prestigious magazines with taste, intelligence, and imagination. Born in Kiev, Alexander Semeonovich Liberman lived as a child in Moscow. He spent the years from 1921 to 1924 in English boarding schools and completed his education in Paris. There he studied at the Sorbonne and the École des Beaux-Arts, worked for two years with painter André Lhote and then as an assistant to the poster designer Cassandre, and served from 1933 to 1936 as an assistant art director for the magazine *Vu*. After painting in the south of France for several years, in 1941 he decamped for New York, where he was hired at *Vogue*. He was naturalized as an American citizen in 1946. From 1960, as editorial director of the entire Condé Nast operation, he guided the design and content of such magazines as *Glamour*, *House and Garden*, and *Gourmet*, among other publications. After retiring in 1994 he maintained residences in New York and Florida. He died in a hospital in Miami Beach. As a painter and sculptor, he worked independently and inventively with abstract form. In the 1950s and 1960s, when *abstract expressionism predominated, he adopted a geometric manner, producing simple, forceful canvases that presaged the taste for *hard-edge painting. The reduced pictorial content of *Continuous on Red* (Museum of Modern Art, 1960) provokes afterimages of the sort soon popularized by *op art. By the late 1960s, when *minimalist reduction was in favor, Liberman had turned to expressionist forms in his paintings, while continuing to pursue geometric abstraction in sculpture. He favored welded pieces of large, painted shapes, although he also assembled junk elements. As a photographer, he became known especially for his images of artists and their workplaces. Accompanied by his own text, *The Artist in His Studio* (1960; revised and expanded 1988) surveys notable artists working in France. He also published two photographic memoirs, *Marlene* (1992), devoted to his friendship with Marlene Dietrich, and *Then* (1995), drawing on his experiences through seventy years. *Prayers in Stone* (1997) surveys connections between religion and architecture.

Lichtenstein, Roy (1923–97). Painter, printmaker, and sculptor. A central figure in *pop art, he came to public attention in the early 1960s with provocative paintings ostensibly replicating comic-strip images. He later applied this personal style of pure colors and flat, clear shapes (generally bounded by black lines) to disparate subjects, including interiors, landscapes, architectural elevations, confounding representations of mirrors, and well-known old master and modern paintings. Although generally whimsical, often amusing, and occasionally hilarious in tone, his work serves the larger purposes of examining the conventions of representation, the mechanisms of vision, and the psychology of form. Lichtenstein spent his early years on the Upper West Side of Manhattan, where he was born. Following a summer studying painting with Reginald *Marsh at the *Art Students League, in the fall of 1940 he enrolled at Ohio State University. Drafted early in 1943, he served in the U.S. Army for three years before returning to Columbus to resume his education. He received a BFA degree in 1946 and an MFA three years later. He remained on the teaching staff at Ohio State until 1951, when he moved to Cleveland. Subsequently, while variously employed, he traveled often to New York, where he showed expressionist figurative work. In 1957 he accepted a teaching position at the State University of New York at Oswego, north of Syracuse. Three years later he moved to New Jersey to teach, again for a three-year stint, at Douglass College of Rutgers University in New Brunswick. There he met Allan *Kaprow, other faculty members, and their friends interested in *happenings, *fluxus, and other unconventional forms of creativity. Stimulated by these encounters, as well as by the work of Jasper *Johns and other early contributors to the pop sensibility, he abandoned a recent excursion into *abstract expressionism to adopt cartoons, including dialogue, as subjects for paintings. To enhance the illusion of verisimilitude, he replicated in paint the commercial printing process employing dots to mix primary colors and adjust tonal values. These works created a sensation when first shown in 1962, at Leo *Castelli's gallery. Although Lichtenstein's work gave the impression of mindless copying, in fact he revised the originals to strengthen their formal impact. A close student of modern art, he particularly revered Picasso but also admired Fernand Léger's monumentality and structural clarity. Lichtenstein's care in choosing scenes related to American obsessions, such as romantic love and the violence of war, augmented their power. A mix of cliché, melodrama, pathos, and absurdity, *Drowning Girl* (Museum of Modern Art, 1963) presents a close-up of the composed but tearful face, chic dark-blue hair, and elegantly gesturing hand of a young woman foundering in stylishly drawn waves. Her thoughts appear in a balloon: "I don't care! I'd rather sink—than call Brad for help." Even as he produced such works in the early 1960s, Lichtenstein simultaneously branched into other subjects, and within a few years comics disappeared entirely from his repertoire. As his subjects changed, so too his method of rendering them evolved to include other textures, richer coloration, and more intricate compositions.

Active as a printmaker even before he became a pop artist, Lichtenstein continued throughout his career to engage varied media for subjects related to the interests of his painting. In the early 1960s he employed the commercial technique of offset lithography and a couple of years later began to make screen prints, some printed on synthetic materials. His interest in sculpture evolved from *assemblages through several media, including ceramics, enameled steel, and painted bronze. In 1967 he introduced a series based on art deco motifs, such as *Modern Sculpture with Velvet Rope* (Whitney Museum, 1968), made from brass and velvet-covered cord reminiscent of theater lobbies. Occasionally earlier but more often from the late 1970s, he produced large-scale sculptures, notably several free-standing brushstrokes (extending a motif that appears in paintings as early as 1965), and murals for public places, including a fifty-three-foot-long, tongue-in-cheek, futuristic travel fantasy in the spirit of the 1950s (1994; installed 2002) in New York's Times Square subway station. From 1967 he spent at least part of each year in Southampton, on eastern Long Island. He died in New York.

Lie, Jonas (1880–1940). Painter. Born in Moss, Norway, he lived as a child in Oslo. In 1893 he arrived with his family in New York. After they settled in nearby Plainfield, New Jersey, as a young man he designed textiles there while pursuing training at Cooper Union, the *National Academy of Design, and the *Art Students League. He had already achieved some success as a painter before he returned in 1906 for the first of numerous visits to Norway. From there, he continued on to Paris, where he admired Monet's work. Lie helped to organize the *Armory Show in 1913, and became known as a voice for liberalization within the National Academy, which he served as president from 1934 to 1939. At the time of his death in New York, he was so widely revered that honorary pallbearers at his funeral included Mayor Fiorello La Guardia, the Norwegian ambassador to the United States, and the president of Columbia University, among other notables. Primarily interested in landscapes, seascapes, and broad urban views, Lie achieved fresh and vigorous effects. Expanding upon impressionism, he applied his colorful approach to views of New York, the New England coast, and various locales abroad. Following a visit to Panama in 1910, he completed a celebrated series of paintings depicting construction of the canal. In *The Conquerors: Culebra Cut, Panama Canal* (Metropolitan Museum, 1913), his brushy impressionism vividly captures activity of men and machines at work in the deep gash that would become the waterway.

Limner. An imprecise term sometimes used to describe the anonymous colonial- and federal-era painters who worked in predominately linear styles. These included artists who extended the Elizabethan tradition, such as the *Freake Painter, as well as those who simplified the volumetric Baroque manner, such as the Gansevoort Limner, a *Patroon painter. The word derives from an English corruption of "illuminator," or manuscript illustrator. Beginning in the sixteenth century, it designated painters of miniatures, but came to be applied to artists who undertook larger works in a similar style.

Lin, Maya (1959–). Sculptor. Also an architect, landscape designer, and furniture designer. Although she had not yet graduated from college, in 1981 her design was selected from among more than fourteen hundred entries in a competition for the Vietnam Veterans Memorial on the Mall in Washington, D.C. Completed in 1982, the unprecedented monument comprises two tapering black granite walls, more than ten feet high where they abut. Partially set into the earth at a wide angle to each other, each measures nearly 250 feet long. Arranged without hierarchy according to the dates of their deaths, the names of all U.S. military personnel killed in the war (more than fifty-eight thousand) are engraved on their polished, slightly reflective, black granite surfaces. Although criticized by some observers for its austerity and abstraction, the monument has found widespread acceptance as a suitable commemoration for the victims of a war that remains an unresolved affliction in the American psyche. With its acknowledgement of each individual death, its restrained rhetoric, and its openness to varied observer responses, her design has also proved highly influential on subsequent notions of public memorials. The first major public monument in the United States to adopt the *minimalist vocabulary of the late twentieth century, Lin's memorial also suggests connections with aspects of the period's *earth art. (Later added nearby to satisfy malcontents, two figurative sculptures officially completed the memorial. Lin's central creation is now designated as the Vietnam Veterans Memorial Wall.) Lin has gone on to design other public monuments, as well as gallery sculptures, while also pursuing a career as an architect and designer of interiors, landscapes, and furniture. Born in Athens, Ohio, Maya Ying Lin studied architecture at Yale University. Upon completion of her bachelor's degree in 1981, she supervised construction of the Vietnam monument and then went back to Yale to earn a master's degree in 1986. Among other projects, she has also designed a Civil Rights Memorial (1989) for Montgomery, Alabama, and the *Women's Table* (1993), celebrating women students, at her alma mater in New Haven, Connecticut. Throughout, her multidisciplinary work displays simplicity, harmony, and sensitivity to natural environments. Married to art and photography dealer Daniel Wolf, she lives in Manhattan and summers in Colorado. She shares insights into her work in *Boundaries* (2000).

Lindner, Richard (1901–78). Painter and printmaker. Best known for 1960s paintings of stylized and eroticized female figures related to aspects of *pop art, his art remained rooted in European history and literature, as well as traditions of expressionism, cubism, and, especially, surrealism. Attracted to the art of Fernand Léger and Oskar Schlemmer, he also collected toys and admired the work of obsessive mental patients. Born in Hamburg, he grew up in Nuremberg and studied at art schools there and in Munich. From 1927 he worked as a graphic designer in Berlin and Munich before moving to Paris in 1933. After arriving in New York in 1941, he worked for about twenty years as a successful illustrator for prestigious magazines and was naturalized as a citizen in 1948. In 1954 he mounted his first one-person show at Betty *Parsons's gallery. Among his most ambitious efforts of this period, *The Meeting* (Museum of Modern Art, 1953) presents an imaginary group portrait of family and friends. Part allegory, part fantasy, it centers on the back of a tightly corseted woman who faces seven other figures and an oversized cat. Its precisely drawn, flattened forms, decorative surface pattern, and ambiguous, discontinuous space create a dreamlike juxtaposition of elements from memory and observation. The naively rendered, wide-eyed cat separates mad Bavarian King Ludwig from a portrait of the artist's friend Saul *Steinberg, while the artist's own sailor-suited self-portrait as a child appears among other family members. In the 1960s Lindner drew more directly on his observations of New York street life to give his hallucinatory works a satirical edge that meshed with pop art's fascination with urban and mass-market culture. Although his crisply mechanistic representations of alienated modernity found an audience, after 1968, as he spent part of each year in Paris, he once again admitted more personally symbolic elements into his iconography. As a printmaker, he worked mostly with color lithography. He also made small numbers of collages and *assemblages. He died in his New York studio.

Lipchitz, Jacques (1891–1973). Sculptor. After gaining prominence as one of the earliest cubist sculptors, while working in Paris alongside Picasso and other modern artists, he later specialized in expressionistic treatments of mythical and Old Testament themes passionately reimagined in dynamic, baroque forms. Primarily after World War II, he fulfilled numerous commissions for monumental public works. The largest and one of the most powerful, *Bellerophon Taming Pegasus* (Columbia University, New York, 1964), intended as an allegory of man's mastery of nature, portrays the conflict between man and horse in bulbous forms swirling dynamically in space. Like most of his sculptures, this was cast in bronze, although he also worked in stone and very occasionally in wood. Born in Druskieniki, Russia (now Lithuania), Chaim Jacob Lipchitz studied engineering at a high school in Vilnius. In 1909 he moved to Paris to study art. There he also familiarized himself with classical and non-Western sculpture, particularly African work, which he collected. Spurred particularly by Picasso's cubism, around 1913 he began to formulate a personal variant of the style. He also responded to the work of other modern artists, including Brancusi and, a bit later, Alexander *Archipenko and Juan Gris. By the middle of the decade, he had achieved a highly abstracted figuration, generally interpreting the human form as an assemblage of planar geometries.

Around the time he became a French citizen in 1924, Lipchitz began experimenting with less massive forms, often spun around voids integral to the work's formal definition. These inventive works incorporating space intimate awareness of constructivism and advance a continuing preoccupation of twentieth-century sculpture. At the same time, many indicate Lipchitz's interest in a newly personal and more psychologically engaged form of expression, often addressing themes of anguish, resistance, and the triumph of the human spirit. During the 1930s, at least partly in response to the period's political horrors, his forms grew unruly, their agitated surfaces recalling precedents in the work of Rodin and animal sculptor Antoine-Louis Barye. When Germany invaded France in 1940, Lipchitz decamped for Toulouse. He continued on to New York the following year, leaving behind his art collection and most of his own work. Nevertheless, after this move his art took on a generally affirmative tone, as he concentrated for the rest of his career on benevolent themes related to regeneration, renewal, joy, and affection. His expressionistic and fundamentally romantic art soon impacted the development of sculptors allied with *abstract expressionism, including Herbert *Ferber and Seymour *Lipton. At the end of World War II, Lipchitz returned briefly to Paris before settling permanently in the United States. From around 1950 he made his home in Hastings-on-Hudson and in 1958 became a U.S. citizen. Following a visit to Italy in 1961, he began to spend the summer months there. He died on the island of Capri. His autobiography, *My Life in Sculpture*, written with H. H. Arneson, appeared in 1972. He also wrote the text for a monograph on his friend Amadeo Modigliani (1952; republished in varied formats).

Lippard, Lucy. *See* FEMINIST ART.

Lippold, Richard (1915–2002). Sculptor. Admired by connoisseurs and public alike, his elegant hanging sculptures float like geometric gossamer in the spaces to which they are tethered. Fabricated from metallic wire and/or thin rods, they orchestrate large volumes with a minimum of physical bulk. Most of his signature installations are coated with shiny metallic substances, even gold, to provide alluring shimmer. He sometimes arranged for his works to be displayed against black or dark backgrounds to enhance the glamour of their weblike patterns. Lippold's unique variation on constructivist practice emerged in the late 1940s and later won many commissions from public and commercial institutions as well as museums. Born in Milwaukee, he attended the University of Chicago before transferring to the School of the Art Institute of Chicago. After earning a BFA in industrial design in 1937, he worked in that field in Chicago and Milwaukee. In 1941 he moved to Ann Arbor to teach at the University of Michigan. There he began to make sculptures from wire and found metal. In 1944 he relocated to New York and, three years later, produced the first of his characteristic lyrical hanging sculptures. His reputation was secured in 1950, when the *Museum of Modern Art purchased the ten-foot-tall *Variation Number 7: Full Moon* (1949–50), featuring pyramidal and cubic forms interpenetrating as their edges pass through implied volumes. The first of many works of art commissioned for the new Lincoln Center, *Orpheus and Apollo* (1961–62), a 190-foot tumble of shimmering blades above the Grand Promenade at Philharmonic (now Avery Fisher) Hall, and *Flight* (1963) for the Pan Am (now MetLife) Building, both in New York, number among numerous pieces designed for specific interiors. His fewer outdoor sculptures include *Ad Astra* (1976), a 115-foot-tall double spire in front of the National Air and Space Museum in Washington, D.C. At the end of his life, he was designing a memorial to victims of the 2001 World Trade Center calamity. He died in a hospital in Roslyn, not far from his north-shore Long Island residence in Lattingtown, where he had lived since 1955.

Lipton, Seymour (1903–86). Sculptor. Also a dentist. His welded sculptures of the late 1940s number among the earliest allied with *abstract expressionism. Evolving from surrealist and constructivist precedents, they present vigorous, often menacing arrangements of generally *biomorphic forms suggesting turmoil and psychological distress. In characteristic later works, he employed welded sheet metal to probe tensions between expansion and compression, solid and void, volume and line, weight and delicacy, and passion and serenity. His work often engages mythic themes, sometimes on a monumental scale. Born in New York, Lipton studied for a year at City College of New York before entering Columbia University. He graduated from its dental school in 1927 and continued to practice dentistry after he became committed to sculpture around 1932. Self-taught as an artist, at first he made expressionistic woodcarvings, often allied with the socially conscious sensibility of the period. This figurative approach yielded to increasingly abstract forms in the 1940s, and by the middle of the decade representation had almost entirely disappeared. Around 1950 he forged a personal style featuring fluid, generally organic forms fabricated from curving sheet-metal elements and textured with brazing and hammering. His innovative techniques for joining sheets of metal and for activating surface alloys facilitated original and varied effects of considerable power, seen at their best in such works as *Ancestor* (Phillips Collection, 1958). Intended by its maker to allude indirectly to a human figure, the bulky piece stands more than seven feet tall. Yet it suggests surprising lightness, as it balances on "tiptoe" above its four contact points with the base. Gracefully curved, yet strong shapes gather in dynamic interaction, loosely suggesting living form and exposing a mysterious core. At the time of his death in a hospital in Glen Cove, a New York suburb on the north shore of Long Island, he resided in nearby Locust Valley and in Manhattan.

Little Galleries of the Photo-Secession. *See* PHOTO-SECESSION.

Locke, Alain (1886–1954). Philosopher, writer, and principal theorist of the *Harlem Renaissance. Born in Philadelphia, Alain LeRoy Locke graduated magna cum laude from Harvard in 1907. That year, he was the first African American to be awarded a Rhodes scholarship. After studying in England at Oxford University until 1910, he continued at the University of Berlin for an additional year. Except for a two-year hiatus to complete a PhD at Harvard in 1918, he taught philosophy at Howard University in Washington, D.C., from 1912 until he retired in 1953. He then moved to New York, where he died. Although he believed race to be socially constructed, Locke urged artists to rediscover their roots in African culture as a source of racial pride. At the same time, he recommended study of recent European art, for he held that the black artist could respond to his racial identity without compromising the quality of his work as a modern artist working in the United States. He thought that artistic and intellectual achievement mattered more to the advancement of African Americans than economic or political action. Locke's views gained wide attention with the publication of his anthology of black writing and art, *The New Negro* (1925), which included also his vision for African-American cultural renewal. In numerous later books and articles, Locke continued to present black literary and artistic achievement to the public, and he was instrumental in organizing important exhibitions of African-American art. Material he gathered in hopes of establishing a Harlem museum for African art belongs today to the New York Public Library's Schomburg Center for Research in Black Culture.

Lockspeiser, Eleanore. *See* FRANK, MARY.

Logan, Maurice George. *See* SOCIETY OF SIX.

Longo, Robert. *See* POSTMODERNISM.

Longworth, Nicholas. *See* DUNCANSON, ROBERT.

Louis, Morris (1912–62). Painter. A leading exponent of *color field painting, he is known for enormous abstractions featuring fluid, glowing color areas stained into the canvas by allowing acrylic paint to flow or puddle. Often the chromatic effects contrast with large swaths of unprimed canvas. Accentuating pure hues that are not so much *on* the canvas as *in* the canvas, his method fused figure and ground, negated the painter's touch, minimized the illusion of depth, and produced exhilarating optical effects. While Helen *Frankenthaler's work directly stimulated the direction he chose, he drew also on Jackson *Pollock's unpremeditated and informal compositions, as well as the vast frontal abstractions of Barnett *Newman and Clyfford *Still. Along with his close friend Kenneth *Noland, Louis ranks as a leader of the *Washington Color School. Morris Louis Bernstein legally changed his name in the 1930s. Born in Baltimore, where he studied at the Maryland Institute of Fine Arts (now Maryland Institute College of Art), he moved to New York in 1936. There he received support from *federal art projects for both easel and mural painting and attended an experimental workshop organized by Mexican muralist David Alfaro Siqueiros. Painting in a figurative style attuned to Max Beckmann's work, he returned to Baltimore in 1943. Four years later he moved to the Washington area, where he met Noland in 1952. In New York together the next year, they saw recent *abstract expressionist works as well as Frankenthaler's pathbreaking *Mountains and Sea*, which stimulated both to new directions in their painting. In addition to experiments with staining, Louis also tried gestural brushwork during the next several years. He later destroyed most of this work, for the most part retaining only those paintings that prefigure the signature approach that crystallized in 1957. Appearing to acclaim in his solo show of 1959 in New York, these works belong to the first of four distinct groups that comprise most of his mature works. The paintings in this initial cluster generally are known as Veils, although Louis titled neither the groups nor individual works. Suggesting billowing draperies, these paintings in predominately muted but lustrous hues feature superimposed layers of thinned paint spread with the aid of gravity. The brighter and more decorative Florals of 1959–60 present individually colored, petal-like flows congregating around a center, where they overlap. In the audacious Unfurled series of 1960–61, Louis left most of the white canvas untouched, playing against the center void with irregular stripes that run diagonally across two corners. In a final Stripes series (sometimes called Pillars) of 1961–62, contiguous vertical bands of color seem to rise through the middle of vertical canvases. Exactly what studio procedures Louis employed in producing his novel paintings has not been ascertained, and no other artist achieved quite the same effects. He died at his home in Washington.

Loving, Al. *See* AFRICAN-AMERICAN ART.

Low, Mary Louise Fairchild MacMonnies. *See* MACMONNIES, MARY.

Low, Will Hicok (1853–1932). Painter. An important figure in the *American Renaissance, he is remembered for classicizing allegorical and mythological subjects, particularly murals. Early in his career he produced *genre paintings and tried his hand at literary themes. He also wrote art criticism for major New York magazines and published two memoirs, *A Chronicle of Friendships: 1873–1900* (1908) and *A Painter's Progress* (1910). Born in Albany, he was introduced to art by Erastus Dow *Palmer, father of school friend Walter Launt *Palmer. In 1871 he moved to New York to work as an illustrator but the following year departed for five years in Paris. There he studied relatively briefly with Jean-Léon Gérôme and, for a longer period, with Émile-Auguste Carolus-Duran. During four summers he worked at *Barbizon, where he benefited from Jean-François Millet's example and advice. After returning to New York late in 1877, he participated in the *aesthetic movement decorative projects that attracted many progressive young artists, designed stained glass windows and book illustrations, and numbered among the earliest members of the *Society of American Artists. Emphasizing sentiment and decorative embellishment, his small, domestic genre scenes of these years display precise but atmospheric treatment of undramatic moments. In the summer of 1886 he sailed a second time for Europe, where he visited Paris and Barbizon, then traveled in Italy and England for several months. In later years, he again returned to Europe, sometimes for extended sojourns. For nearly three decades after 1892, when he secured his first major commission, he counted among the nation's foremost muralists. After completing the reception rooms (destroyed) that year in New York's old Waldorf-Astoria hotel, he was called upon to decorate numerous public and private spaces, culminating in a cycle of thirty-two scenes for the New York State Education Building in Albany (1913–18). However, even as he worked on this series, he lamented that his devotion to a tradition of ideal beauty now seemed old-fashioned. From 1896 he lived in a New York suburb frequented by artists, the newly established community of Bronxville, where he died. He spent many summers in Milton, near Boston. In 1909 he married Mary *MacMonnies.

Lowe, Jean (1960–). *See* MACCONNEL, KIM.

Loy, Mina. *See* LEVY, JULIEN.

Lozowick, Louis (1892–1973). Printmaker and painter. Known especially for lithographs, he embraced both *precisionism and the humanistic concerns of the *American Scene movement. Lozowick's firsthand experience of contemporary art in Germany and the Soviet Union, unusual among American artists of his day, opened his eyes to some of the period's most radical ideas about artistic form and the relation of art to the public. Born in Ludvinovka, Russia (now Ukraine), Leib Lozowick received his early training in Kiev before moving to the United States in 1906. He studied from 1912 to 1915 at the *National Academy of Design, where Leon *Kroll ranked as his most important teacher. In 1918 he graduated from Ohio State University in Columbus. Following military service, he toured the United States before departing in 1920 for Europe. After a stay in Paris, he continued on to Berlin, where he joined the Novembergruppe, a stylistically varied group of radical left-wing artists who sought to heal and rebuild Germany in the post-World War I years by promoting a closer relationship between artists and public. He also traveled to the Soviet Union, where he associated with constructivists and other advanced artists. Following his return to New York in 1924, he published *Modern Russian Art* (1925) and contributed drawings to the socialist periodical *New Masses*. During the 1930s he helped to found the *American Artists' Congress and participated in the *federal art projects. He died in South Orange, New Jersey, where he had resided since 1944. Lozowick's work ranged over varied subjects, from machine abstractions to political protest to photographically realistic still lifes, but strong, restless forms generally dominate. During the 1920s he drew on travel impressions for a series of drawings, lithographs, and paintings inspired by the cities he visited. In these triumphant evocations of the urban and technological features of American life, he combined futurist and cubist techniques with a precisionist interest in geometric form, plain surfaces, hard edges, and depopulated spaces. *Butte* (Hirshhorn Museum, 1926–27) interprets the mining town in a dynamic scramble of architectonic forms. Later depictions of city life were characteristically more realistic and less austere. Following a trip to the Soviet Union in 1932, he responded to the Depression in many subsequent works exemplifying the interests of social realism. Lozowick also designed theater sets. In 1947 he published documentation on *100 Contemporary American Jewish Painters and Sculptors*, an early investigation of the subject, for which he also wrote an introduction. His recollections appeared posthumously as *Survivor from a Dead Age: The Memoirs of Louis Lozowick* (1996), edited by Virginia Hagelstein-Marquardt.

Lucier, Mary. *See* VIDEO ART.

Lucius, Florence Gertrude. *See* DAVIDSON, JO.

Luhan, Mabel Dodge (1879–1962). Writer and bohemian salon hostess. Willful and flamboyant, inspired by philosophers Henri Bergson and Friedrich Nietzsche, she epitomized the liberated New Woman of the early twentieth century. In unrestrained pursuit of freedom and creativity, she sought the company of forward-looking artists, writers, social reformers, and intellectuals. They gathered from 1913 at her New York apartment and, after 1917, at her legendary compound,

Los Gallos, on the outskirts of *Taos. Mabel Ganson was born in Buffalo, New York. Married to Karl Evans in 1900 and widowed three years later, she sailed for Europe in 1904. On shipboard, she met architect Edwin Dodge, whom she married in Paris. From 1905 they lived in Florence, where at their manorial Villa Curonia, she honed her aptitude for attracting celebrities. After returning to New York in November 1912, she decided, according to a later account, that "Edwin blocked my growth." They separated and divorced in 1916. In 1913 she entered into an intense but ill-fated year-long affair with leftist journalist and political activist John Reed. Meanwhile, her apartment at 23 Fifth Avenue, on the edge of Greenwich Village, served as a meeting place for radicals of all stripes. Visitors included practically everyone interested in revolutionizing politics or the arts. Most of the principals associated with *The *Masses* showed up, as did Andrew *Dasburg, Emma Goldman, Hutchins Hapgood, Marsden *Hartley, Walter Lippman, Lincoln Steffens, Carl *Van Vechten, and, on occasion, even Alfred *Stieglitz. In 1917 Dodge married painter Maurice *Sterne. He almost immediately preceded her to New Mexico, where she arrived at the end of that year. Sterne was soon dismissed, and following their divorce, in 1923 she married an unlettered, dignified, and taciturn Taos pueblo dweller, Antonio (known as Tony) Luhan. The union with Luhan signaled Dodge's recently developed passion for American Indian culture. Promoting their social, aesthetic, and spiritual values and their relationship to the fabulous southwestern landscape, she now aspired to facilitate nothing less than the renewal of western culture. She also spent much of her time during succeeding years aiding local Indians. Concurrently, her insistent hospitality benefited numerous artists and writers, among them Ansel *Adams, D. H. Lawrence, John *Marin, and Georgia *O'Keeffe. She died in Taos. Her house is now marketed as an "historic inn and conference center." She published a book about Lawrence, *Lorenzo in Taos* (1932), as well as *Winter in Taos* (1935) and *Taos and Its Artists* (1947). A four-volume autobiography collectively titled *Intimate Memories* comprises *Background* (1933), *European Experiences* (1935), *Movers and Shakers* (1936), and *Edge of Taos Desert: An Escape to Reality* (1937).

Luks, George (1866–1933). Painter. Associated with the *Ashcan School, he remains best known for vivid scenes of immigrant and lower class New York from the first decade of the twentieth century. Later, his palette lightened, he drew on impressionist styles, and his newly carefree subjects included landscapes and leisure scenes. He also painted numerous portraits. A native of the central Pennsylvania mining town of Williamsport, Luks commenced his spotty art training in 1884 with a stint at the *Pennsylvania Academy of the Fine Arts. After sailing for Europe the following year, he continued intermittently in Düsseldorf, Munich, and Paris. More importantly, independent study of the old masters in European museums during most of a decade abroad and the later practice of news illustration shaped his sensibility. While working for Philadelphia newspapers, in the mid-1890s he met Robert *Henri, as well as fellow illustrators including John *Sloan, William *Glackens, and Everett *Shinn. In 1896 he moved permanently to New York, where he continued with newspaper work until 1905, but soon turned his attention more seriously to painting. In 1902–3 he worked in Paris, where he focused on street scenes. After his return, he joined his transplanted Philadelphia friends in exhibiting opportunities, most importantly the 1908 show of The *Eight. His characteristic work of this time, such as *Hester Street* (Brooklyn Museum, 1908) empathetically depicted the street life of working class, immigrant neighborhoods, seen with the observant eye of his newspaper years and rendered with loose, sketchy brushwork. After 1912, when he moved to upper Manhattan, he for the most part left behind proletarian subjects, except for a series depicting coal miners. In 1913 he exhibited in the *Armory Show and subsequently continued to grow artistically as he moderated his heavy, dark brushwork derived from Frans Hals and Manet. In later years he often worked in watercolor with verve and freshness suitable to his sunlit views. Irascible and impetuous, given to frequent inebriation, he left an uneven legacy of artistic quality when found on a doorstep, dead of undetermined causes.

Luminism. Term used to describe mid-nineteenth-century American landscape painting emphasizing light and its effects. Less a style than a sensibility, luminism anticipated *impressionism's responsiveness to light but otherwise shared little with that style. Luminist paintings emphasize precisely drawn detail, virtually invisible brushwork, and lucidly measured space. Effects of light and atmosphere are achieved through elegantly nuanced gradation of tone, which often produces a hushed radiance. Reflections and carefully observed renderings of the effects of light on variously textured surfaces often contribute to a delicate and unrhetorical stillness. Typically lyrical and meditative in mood, luminist painting evokes spiritual mysteries embodied in nature. *Hudson River School painters often worked in a luminist mode, particularly in the 1850s and 1860s when the approach was most popular. By about 1880 most artists had lost interest in luminism.

First given currency in a 1954 article by John *Baur, the name meant nothing to the artists whose work is called luminist. The tendency originated spontaneously in the 1830s, never became an organized movement, and had no leader. In its international context, luminism can be seen as an American manifestation of tendencies associated with romanticism. Luminism's possible sources include the landscapes of Claude Lorrain and Caspar David Friedrich, seventeenth-century Dutch seascapes, the Transcendentalism of such writers as Ralph Waldo Emerson and Henry David Thoreau, and, after about 1840, the vogue for crystalline *daguerreotype images. Baur named Fitz Hugh *Lane and Martin Johnson *Heade as central figures. Many of John *Kensett's paintings epitomize the adaptation of Hudson River School principles to luminist poetics. Others whose work is often included under the luminist rubric include Alfred Thompson *Bricher, Frederick *Church, Sanford *Gifford, and Robert *Salmon. The historical and critical literature has used the term inconsistently. Some writers restrict its application to a small core of views that summarize luminism's central features, while others use it more loosely to refer to nearly any preimpressionist painting that stresses analysis of light.

Lumpkins, William. *See* TRANSCENDENTAL PAINTING GROUP.

Lundeberg, Helen. *See* FEITELSON, LORSER.

Lynes, George Platt (1907–55). Photographer. Known for dance, fashion, and portrait photographs, he also treated the male nude with romantic sensuality and frankness. Surrealism conditioned much of his work, and he often openly acknowledged, or even featured, the artifice in his staged subjects. Born near Newark, in East Orange, New Jersey, Lynes as a young man was interested in literature and spent periods of time in Paris. In 1926 he enrolled at Yale University but left after a year to pursue a serious interest in photography. He returned to Europe in 1928. For the next decade, he lived in a complex triangular relationship with novelist Glenway Wescott and writer, editor, and publisher Monroe Wheeler (1908–88), an amateur of the arts, later a *Museum of Modern Art staff member for more than thirty years. From the 1930s, Lynes's commissioned work appeared frequently in *Harper's Bazaar*, *Vogue*, and other high-end magazines, while his more personal, creative photographs, first exhibited by his friend Julien *Levy, tantalized the art world. He photographed many writers and artists in studio settings that he enlivened in unusual ways. Around Paul *Cadmus, he hung half a dozen naked light bulbs that bear no obvious relation to the subject but nevertheless activate the space and, by contrast, amplify the sitter's inward mood. In addition to homoerotic nudes, he photographed staged scenes of unclothed young men enacting dreamily conceived scenes from ancient Greek mythology. Almost none of his most sexually provocative work was exhibited publicly during his lifetime. From 1946 to 1948 he worked in Hollywood for *Vogue*. Unproductive and in ill health during his last years, he died in New York.

Lyon, Danny (1942–). Photographer and filmmaker. His socially conscious documentary photographs recording misfits, outcasts, and counterculture figures speak for recognition of their humanity, for justice, and for reform. Born in New York, Daniel J. Lyon began taking pictures at twelve. After receiving his BA in history from the University of Chicago in 1963, Lyon signed on with the Student Nonviolent Coordinating Committee as its first staff photographer. During the next two years, he traveled to many scenes of dramatic events at the height of the civil rights movement. His photographs illustrate *The Movement* (1964), with text by Lorraine Hansberry. Later in the 1960s Lyon turned his quasi-anthropological attention to motorcycle riders, with whom he socialized and traveled for several years. Among marginalized individuals in an outlaw club, he saw admirable resistance to mainstream values. *The Bikeriders* (1968) combines his photographs with his subjects' reminiscences. For his next book, Lyon collaborated with Texas prison inmates. *Conversations with the Dead* (1971) implicitly advocates more humane standards of sentencing and incarceration. Lyon had traveled to Colombia in 1966, and in the early 1970s he again photographed there as well as in Mexico. By this time, he frequently used color film. After living briefly in New Mexico, he worked in New York in the 1980s. In the 1990s Lyon exhibited collages created from photographs related to his family life. He lives on a farm in the Hudson River Valley. His other books include *Memories of the Southern Civil Rights Movement* (1992) and *Knave of Hearts* (1999), a photographic memoir. He has also made a number of films.

Macbeth, William. *See* EIGHT, THE.

McBride, Henry (1867–1962). Art critic. Remembered for broad-minded interests, he offered insightful appraisals of modern art in a time when its validity remained controversial. Born in the Philadelphia suburb of West Chester, he arrived in New York in 1889 to train as a painter at the *Art Students League and elsewhere. In 1894 he made the first of many trips to Europe. As an art teacher, he worked in New York and Trenton, New Jersey, while continuing to travel, educate himself about all the arts, and write occasionally. At forty-six, he was hired as a critic by the New York *Sun*, just in time to appraise the 1913 *Armory Show. He continued to publish regularly there until 1950, when it merged with another newspaper. From 1920 until its ceased publication in 1929, he also wrote a monthly column for the modernist magazine *The Dial*. From 1930 to 1932 he served as editor of *Creative Art*. In his eighties, between 1950 and 1955, he wrote regularly for *Art News*. From Thomas *Eakins and Cézanne through Arp and Jackson *Pollock, McBride remained attentive to the best in recent art. He was an advocate for American art and interested in art's social context. Debonair and personable, he mixed easily with artists, patrons, and writers. Reflecting his wit and charm, his style of writing remained conversational rather than theoretical or polemical. Yet his casual manner could not obscure his sophistication, his informed understanding, nor the fresh responses of his eye. In later years he divided his time between New York, where he died, and a residence in Pennsylvania. A selection of his writings appeared as *The Flow of Art: Essays and Criticisms of Henry McBride* (1975), edited by Daniel Catton Rich.

McCausland, Elizabeth. *See* ABBOTT, BERENICE.

MacConnel, Kim. *See* PATTERN AND DECORATION.

McCoy, Sanford. *See* POLLOCK, JACKSON.

McCracken, John. *See* MINIMALISM.

Macdonald-Wright, Stanton (1890–1973). Painter and experimental artist. An early proponent of abstraction, he co-founded *synchromism. His expansive, chromatically drenched canvases of the later 1910s had no equal in American painting until the 1960s. Born in Charlottesville, Virginia, Macdonald-Wright moved with his family to Santa Monica, California, when he was ten. His art studies began in 1905 at the Los Angeles Art Students League. There he mastered a dark, painterly realism,

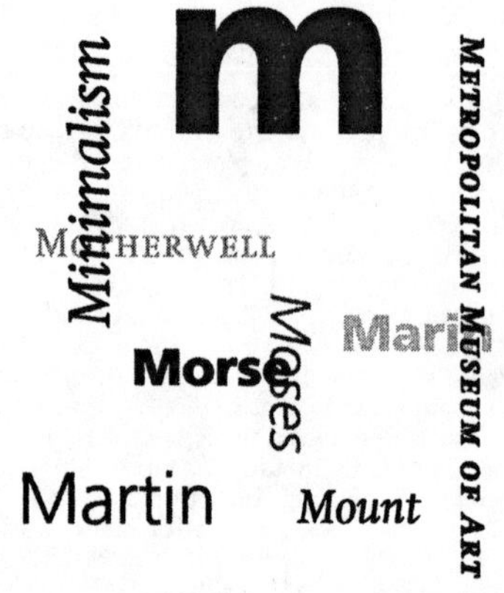

but after two years left for Paris, where he studied at several schools and became familiar with the work of Cézanne and the early modern artists. Drawn to the scientific analysis of color, he entered the color theory class of Canadian painter Ernest Percyval Tudor-Hart, where he met Morgan *Russell in 1911. Together, they formulated the basic principles of synchromism in 1912 and went public with their paintings and supporting statements the following year. Following a 1914 visit to assist in staging the only New York synchromist exhibition, Macdonald-Wright worked independently in Paris and London toward a personal form of totally nonobjective abstraction based on rhythmic color planes. However, after a short time he reverted to his earlier practice of using representational motifs for underlying structure. Between 1916 and the end of the decade, while living in New York, he created his most distinguished and original work. In these paintings featuring diaphanous veils of color, as in *Oriental Synchromy in Blue-Green* (Whitney Museum, 1918), fragmentary figural elements may sometimes be discerned, but graceful chromatic harmonies predominate. Despite growing power in these sophisticated works, Macdonald-Wright became discouraged and in 1919 moved back to the Los Angeles area, where he turned his creative energies to varied projects. He experimented with color films and built the kinetic light machine he had been thinking about for decades. Becoming involved with theater in the late 1920s, he wrote and directed plays and designed sets. In the 1930s he supervised a *federal art project, for which he also painted murals and developed a mosaic technique to be used in architectural decoration. He taught at UCLA and elsewhere from the 1920s through the early 1950s. In later years, his longtime attraction to Asia intensified, and he spent part of each year in Japan. At the same time, he returned to an abstract style of painting close to his earlier synchromist work. He died at his home in Pacific Palisades.

His brother, Willard Huntington Wright (1888–1939), reflected Macdonald-Wright's thinking in three significant books championing modern art: *Modern Painting: Its Tendency and Meaning* (1915), *The Creative Will: Studies in the Philosophy and the Syntax of Aesthetics* (1916), and *The Future of Painting* (1923). Also born in Charlottesville and transplanted to California, he attended several colleges and worked as a writer in Los Angeles before moving to New York. There, from January 1913 until the following December he edited the high-octane literary magazine *Smart Set*. During a year abroad in 1914–15, under his brother's influence he took up a serious interest in art. After returning to New York, while serving as the art critic for *Forum* magazine, Wright organized the 1916 "Forum Exhibition of Modern American Painters," among the most significant *independent exhibitions of the early modern era. From 1926, under the pseudonym S. S. Van Dine, he published popular detective novels. Earlier, he had also written *What Nietzsche Taught* (1915), as well as several other literary and analytical works. He died at his home in New York.

McEntee, Jervis (1828–91). Painter. Known chiefly for landscapes, he occasionally painted works with narrative content. He had little interest in the dramatic panoramas popularized by fellow *Hudson River School landscapists, preferring instead intimate impressions of nature seen in subdued light. His numerous realistic but suggestive autumn and winter scenes emphasize the bittersweet melancholy of nature's transience. Born in the Hudson River Valley village of Rondout (now part of Kingston), he studied in New York during the winter of 1850–51 with Frederic *Church but then entered a business career in Rondout. Before the end of the decade, however, he returned to New York to devote himself full time to painting. He served in the Civil War, which inspired a few metaphorical images commenting on its tragic meanings for the country. In 1868 he departed for Europe, where he spent about half of his year abroad in Rome. He died in Rondout, where he had continued to maintain a summer home. Deviating from the optimism of much mid-century American painting, the somber tone of his work appealed to the introspective mood of the later nineteenth century. Although the spirit of his work in the 1870s and 1880s often recalls *Barbizon feeling for rural life, McEntee's continuing attention to nature's specifics seemed old-fashioned as the Hudson River School abated. For nearly the final two decades of his life, McEntee kept a detailed diary (now owned by the *Archives of American Art) that records his life and thoughts within the context of New York art life. Although never published in its entirety, it remains an important resource for scholars.

McFee, Henry Lee (1886–1953). Painter. Primarily interested in still life, in the later years of his career he also occasionally essayed landscape and figure subjects. McFee's work evolved from an adventurous engagement with cubism to a form of realism dependent on Cézanne's analysis of structure. Born in St. Louis, McFee studied at the *Art Students League and in Paris. When he participated in the important *Forum Exhibition of 1916, he took his place among sixteen leading American modernists. At this time, he worked in a handsome cubist-derived style, as in the 1916 *Still Life* (Columbus [Ohio] Museum of Art), evoking a glass compote with fruit, along with books on a table top. Like most Americans who experimented with cubism, McFee gave his painted objects greater solidity than the French, and he used brighter colors than they commonly did. During the 1920s McFee moved gradually away from the faceted planes of cubism but remained attentive to composition. Formal order and rich color harmonies remained linchpins of his art. An early arrival at *Woodstock, he made his home there for many years, but by the 1930s was spending much of his time in the Los Angeles area. From 1942 on, he taught at Scripps College in Claremont. He died in a hospital in nearby Altadena.

Maciunas, George. *See* FLUXUS.

MacIver, Loren (1909–98). Painter. In lyrical semi-abstractions, particularly sensitive to light and color, she skillfully reinterpreted precedents in the work of Matisse, Paul Klee, perhaps Lyonel *Feininger, and others. However, the spirit of her work owes more to the many poets with whom she maintained long-term friendships, including Elizabeth Bishop, Marianne Moore, and most notably, Lloyd Frankenberg, whom she married in 1929. Hoping to make something permanent from what is transitory, she drew her subjects from the studio, the street, or, after 1948, her extensive European travels, imbuing everyday imagery with warmth and pleasure but also ambiguity.

A lifelong New Yorker, MacIver briefly took art classes as a child but otherwise remained self-taught as an artist. Adopting a nontheoretical, eclectic attitude, she worked out an unforced, independent vision. During the late 1930s, she worked for *federal art projects. In *Venice* (Whitney Museum, 1949), the city shimmers on a distant, watery horizon, balanced in space by a single abstracted sail cutting across the foreground. A shimmering veil of color binds the image to the picture plane and unobtrusively demonstrates her sure understanding of sophisticated modern design. Her treatment of a humbler subject, *Window Shade* (Phillips Collection, 1948) approaches the mysterious poetry of a Mark *Rothko abstraction.

McKim, Musa. *See* GUSTON, PHILIP.

MacMonnies, Frederick (1863–1937). Sculptor and painter. Although remembered for high-spirited, decorative, technically adroit sculpture, in the years around 1900 he worked regularly as a painter of portraits and landscapes. He produced his most compelling work during three decades spent almost entirely in or near Paris. Thoroughly French in taste, his sculptures generally treat classical, allegorical, or historical themes, but they also encompass portraiture. His fountains helped to spark a turn-of-the-century vogue in public and private gardens. Born in Brooklyn, Frederick William MacMonnies entered Augustus *Saint-Gaudens's studio in 1880. While progressing from menial tasks to the rank of assistant, he studied part-time at the *National Academy of Design, Cooper Union, and the *Art Students League. In 1884 he departed for a year in Europe. He studied in Paris and Munich, traveled, and then returned to New York to assist Saint-Gaudens. In 1886 he again sailed for Paris, where he studied at the École des Beaux-Arts under Alexandre Falguière and worked also with Antonin Mercié before establishing his own studio. The exuberant early bronze *Young Faun with Heron* (Naumkeag, Stockbridge, Massachusetts, 1889–90) depicts a gleeful preadolescent male wrestling with a bird about his own size. Its spiraling forms, impressionistic surfaces, varied textures, and naturalistic observation demonstrate MacMonnies's mastery of the Beaux-Arts approach. Two works from the year he turned thirty made him a celebrity, paving the way to a lifetime of commissions and financial security. For the main court of the 1893 World's Columbian Exposition in Chicago, he designed the neo-Baroque Columbian Fountain (destroyed), including nearly forty figures. Its central feature, *The Barge of State*, an enormous allegorical confection, offered an enthroned Columbia borne atop a vessel steered by Father Time, propelled by eight oar-wielding female Arts and Industries, and guided at the prow by Fame. Soon after visiting the Chicago fair, MacMonnies began a more intimate work, the mirthful bronze *Bacchante and Infant Faun* (Metropolitan Museum, 1893–94). This over-life-size nude dancer lightly holds a baby in one arm, a bunch of grapes raised temptingly in the other as she prances on tiptoe with carefree abandon. The work found acclaim in Paris, but when it was installed in the courtyard of the new Boston Public Library in 1896, outrage over its nudity and frivolity was so great that it was permanently removed.

At the height of his fame and enormous productivity, MacMonnies began to take a serious interest in painting, and about 1900 he temporarily renounced sculpture. For the preceding several years he had summered in Giverny, where a renovated priory (soon waggishly nicknamed the MacMonastery) became his year-round home. There he taught, entertained, and painted portraits and garden scenes in a style reflecting the interests of his friends James Abbott McNeill *Whistler and John Singer *Sargent, as well as his admiration for the paintings of Velázquez. After a few years MacMonnies turned his attention once again primarily to sculpture. In this later period, his work rarely attained the vivacious elegance of his best work. At the same time, taste for modern styles further hindered recovery of his former preeminence. Nevertheless, he continued to win prestigious commissions for public sculptures, including Denver's bronze *Pioneer Fountain* (1906–11), a large ensemble of frontier types below an elevated equestrian statue of Kit Carson, and the *Princeton Battle Monument* (Princeton, New Jersey, 1908–22), a grandiose limestone memorial depicting General George Washington inciting troops to victory. His last important sculpture, the immense *Battle of the Marne Memorial* (near Meaux, France, 1924–32; modeled c. 1920–24) pays tribute to French military valor. World War I, which prompted this remembrance, had motivated MacMonnies's repatriation in 1915. After the war he visited France frequently while living in New York, where he died.

His wife, painter **Mary MacMonnies** (1858–1946), produced portraits, impressionist garden scenes, and decorative murals. Notably, for the Women's Building at the 1893 World's Columbian Exposition, she created a large mural, *Primitive Woman* (destroyed), which complemented Mary *Cassatt's *Modern Woman* (destroyed) across the central hall. Born in New Haven, Connecticut, Mary Louise Fairchild lived as a child in New Orleans and St. Louis, where she enrolled at the new St. Louis School of Fine Arts after teaching school for several years. In 1885 she began her studies in Paris, where she married MacMonnies three years later. Following their divorce early in 1909, she soon married Will Hicok *Low, whose surname she subsequently used professionally. With her new husband, in 1910 she settled permanently in the New York suburb of Bronxville, where she continued to work until her last years.

McNay, Marion Koogler (1883–1950). Collector and museum founder. Trained as a painter at the School of the Art Institute of Chicago, McNay moved permanently to San Antonio after her first husband died in 1918. There she built a Spanish-style mansion, which became the Marion Koogler McNay Art Institute (now Marion Koogler McNay Art Museum) after her death. During the 1930s she spent much time in *Taos, where she painted watercolors and bought the work of local artists. One of them, Victor *Higgins, became her husband in 1937, but after their divorce in 1940 she ceased to collect Taos art. Instead, she concentrated on building the holdings of late-nineteenth- and twentieth-century American and European art for which the museum is particularly known today. Opened to the public in 1954 as the first modern art museum in Texas, it has since expanded beyond its original building and enlarged the collection.

MacNeil, Hermon Atkins (1866–1947). Sculptor. Known especially for works illustrating American Indian subjects, he also addressed historical or allegorical themes in civic monuments and architectural embellishments. In his most famous piece, the bronze *Sun Vow* (Metropolitan Museum, 1898), an aging seated warrior transmits his heritage to a lithe nude youth, who extends his bow skyward in a gesture followed in the glance of both figures. Born near Boston, MacNeil studied there at the Massachusetts Normal Art School (now Massachusetts College of Art) before taking a teaching position at Cornell University in Ithaca, New York. In 1888 he departed for three years of training in Paris, including study at the École des Beaux-Arts under Alexandre Falguière. Upon his return, he went to Chicago to assist on preparations for the 1893 World's Columbian Exposition. American Indians performing at the fair stimulated his interest in their experience and prompted a trip to the Southwest. He left Chicago in 1896 to return to Europe, where he worked for three years in Rome and another in Paris. In 1900 he settled permanently in College Point, Queens. After about 1910, he turned his attention from Indian subjects to large-scale treatments of idealized themes appropriate to public commissions. His wife, sculptor **Carol Brooks MacNeil** (1871–1944), specialized in small bronzes, typically portraying children and *genre subjects. She also made decorative tableware and other utilitarian objects. Born in Chicago, she studied at the School of the Art Institute of Chicago and worked as an assistant to Lorado *Taft. Subsequently she studied with Frederick *MacMonnies in Paris. Married in 1895, she devoted much of her time to domestic responsibilities following their return from Europe in 1900.

Magic realism. A mid-twentieth-century form of sharp-focus representation featuring fantasy, paradox, or irrationality. Its practitioners never thought of themselves as a group, and the concept has not had much theoretical precision. The term had been coined by German critic Franz Roh in 1925 to describe work in which exaggeratedly sharp detail lent eerie overtones to otherwise realistic work. Some American magic realists similarly achieved hallucinatory effects from intensely realistic techniques alone, but the style is more often associated with those who introduced frankly imaginary elements. Rooted in the precise realism much favored in the American nineteenth-century, magic realism also derives from a visionary strain in American *romanticism. Its hard-edge approach recalls *precisionism, while the interest of many magic realists in everyday life parallels a similar fixation among contemporary artists of the *American Scene movement. Although some magic realists drew on European surrealism, they generally avoided its pessimism and nihilism, accenting instead gentle mystery or astonishment.

In the United States, the term was popularized in 1943 by the *Museum of Modern Art's "American Realists and Magic Realists," organized to examine an interest among younger artists in representational exactitude. Lincoln Kirstein's introduction to the catalogue generalizes that in the work of these artists, "our eyes are deceived into believing in the reality of what is rendered, whether factual or imaginary" and specifies their means: "crisp hard edges, tightly indicated forms, and the counterfeiting of material surfaces." The exhibition surveyed the work of such figures as Peter *Blume and Louis *Guglielmi, who clearly made use of fantasy in their work, as well as Peter *Hurd and Andrew *Wyeth, who did not. However, most of the painters in the show, including Ivan *Albright and Paul *Cadmus, worked in more ambiguous territory, and the catalogue does not specifically assign the artists to one camp or the other.

Magnum. *See* CAPA, ROBERT.

Malbone, Edward Greene (1777–1807). Painter. His reputation rests almost entirely on portrait miniatures, unrivaled by any other American artist's work in this genre. He occasionally painted larger works in oil. A native of Newport, Rhode Island, he may have received encouragement from Samuel *King, but was apparently for the most part self-taught. In 1794 the young artist moved for two years to Providence where he found success with his miniatures. Later he worked in Boston, New York, Philadelphia, and Charleston, South Carolina. In the spring of 1801 he sailed for London, where he sought advice from Benjamin *West. A miniature portrait of his friend and traveling companion Washington *Allston (Museum of Fine Arts, Boston, c. 1801) exemplifies Malbone's finely detailed and delicate technique, his characteristically sensitive rendering of both features and personality, and his taste for decorative charm. After about six months abroad, Malbone returned to Charleston. For the next few years, he again traveled on the eastern seaboard, enjoying abundant patronage wherever he visited. Following an extended 1804–5 sojourn in Boston, he moved back to Charleston, already suffering from tuberculosis. By the early months of 1806 he was able to work very little. In search of a cure, he left for the warmer climate of Jamaica in December 1806 but remained there only briefly. In January 1807 he arrived at Savannah, Georgia, where he died a few months later.

Maldarelli, Oronzio. *See* BURKE, SELMA.

Mangold, Robert. *See* MINIMALISM.

Mangold, Sylvia Plimack. *See* MANGOLD, ROBERT.

Manigault, Edward Middleton *See* HOWALD, FERDINAND.

Man Ray (1890–1976). Painter, sculptor, photographer, and filmmaker. A major contributor to the early twentieth century's international avant-garde as well as surrealism's most eminent photographer, he numbered among leaders of *New York dada. In 1921 he emigrated to France, where his wit and unaffected iconoclasm enabled him to move easily into the sophisticated ambience of dadaism and surrealism. Born Emmanuel Radnitsky in Philadelphia, he grew up in Brooklyn. His name as an artist derived from the nickname Manny and a shortening of his surname, adopted when he was a young man by his entire family. Before 1912 he trained only sporadically but then enrolled at the Ferrer School, where Robert *Henri ranked as his most important teacher. From 1913 to 1915, he lived in a small rural artists' colony near Ridgefield, New Jersey, across the Hudson River from Manhattan. There, often working alongside Samuel *Halpert, he worked out responses to the cubist and other modern art he had seen in the *Armory Show. In 1915 he met Marcel *Duchamp, subsequently a lifelong friend. Soon, along with French visitor Francis Picabia, they became leaders of the lighthearted anti-art movement known as New York dada. Liberated by Duchamp's example, Man Ray soon surpassed his own recent experiments with cubist collage. In *The Rope Dancer Accompanies Herself with Her Shadows* (Museum of Modern Art, 1916), flat color planes sustain a small, abstracted, starlike "dancer" who flourishes six sinuous stringlike forms, suggesting the rope's movement through time and space. After completing this painting in the traditional oil-on-canvas technique, Man Ray turned his attention primarily to newer forms. Notably, from 1917 he used a spray gun to execute paintings with stencils, and, following Duchamp, began to make assisted "ready-mades" (altered found objects), most famously *Cadeau* (Gift) (1921, original lost; replica in the Museum of Modern Art), an ordinary iron embellished with a menacing row of tacks affixed to its flat surface. In 1920 he participated in the founding of the *Société Anonyme, for which he designed a logo.

After moving to Paris, he enjoyed a major reputation for portrait and fashion photography. His likenesses of artists and writers preserve the individuals who gave the French capital its intellectual and creative cachet in the 1920s. At the same time, more experimental works placed him in the front ranks of surrealism. In New York he had already invented the "rayograph" or cameraless photograph, made by placing objects on or in front of a film subsequently exposed to light. (While the technique actually dates to the earliest years of photography and other modernists revived it as well, Man Ray gave the approach a distinctive name and a new expressive function.) In Paris he maximized its potential, as in a 1922 example featuring two barely kissing profiles, along with handprints and abstract shapes, in a compelling image marked by ambiguity, transparency, and formal tension. He also experimented with solarization (reversal of tones) to give some portraits an unearthly radiance. Between 1923 and 1929, he made several experimental films that incorporate abstract and surrealist elements. In the early 1930s he produced his best-known painting, *Observatory Time—The Lovers* (private collection). This icon of surrealism envisions a woman's lips floating mysteriously in the sky above a landscape. After moving to Los Angles in 1940, Man Ray concentrated on painting. In 1951 he returned to Paris and again engaged other media. He died there in his studio. In 1963 he published an autobiography, *Self Portrait.*

Manship, Paul (1885–1966). Sculptor. Known for lithe, decorative figurative works, he numbered among the most celebrated American artists of the 1920s and 1930s. His gilded 1934 *Prometheus* overlooking New York's Rockefeller Center skating rink remains among the best-known sculptures in the United States. Lending a modern veneer to traditional subjects and compositions, his stylized and idealized forms contributed also to the art deco sensibility that emerged in the 1920s. He worked primarily in bronze but also created marble pieces. Born in St. Paul, Minnesota, Paul Howard Manship left high school to work as a commercial designer and illustrator, while pursuing an interest in fine art. After arriving in 1905 in New York, he studied only briefly at the *Art Students League before beginning as an assistant to Solon *Borglum. In 1906 he moved for a year to Philadelphia, where he studied with Charles *Grafly at the *Pennsylvania Academy of the Fine Arts. After a summer trip to Spain, he returned to New York to work as an assistant to Vienna-trained Beaux-Arts sculptor Isidore Konti (1862–1938). In 1909 he won a fellowship to spend three years at the American Academy in Rome. In Italy and on travels around the Mediterranean, he assiduously absorbed the heritage of that region. *Centaur and Dryad* (Metropolitan Museum, 1913), a tabletop bronze, illustrates his mastery of these precedents, particularly Renaissance and archaic Greek art. When this work and others were shown in New York in 1913, Manship was acclaimed for his revitalization of tradition and his technical virtuosity. He quickly was in demand for architectural sculptures and garden decorations. *Dancer and Gazelles* (Corcoran Gallery, 1916), a frontally composed bronze, demonstrates the lyrical and lively manner that accounts for much of the appeal of his work. In both subject and style, this graceful depiction of delicate animals flanking a semi-nude woman mediates between modernism and the classical tradition, even as it also hints at his appreciation of South Asian sculpture. In 1921 Manship went to London before continuing on to Paris, where he lived until 1926, while also traveling extensively and renewing his ties to the American Academy. He maintained a studio in Paris until 1937. By the end of the 1930s, Manship had completed the bulk of his most original and admirable work. As abstract art came to dominate taste in the 1940s, the new climate diminished his opportunities for critical and commercial success. Nevertheless, he continued to receive important commissions, including one for the John F. Kennedy inaugural medal in 1960. He died in New York. Painter and sculptor **John Paul Manship** (1927–2000), his son, was known especially for religious subjects. Born in New York, he was educated at Harvard University. His biography *Paul Manship* appeared in 1989. He died in Gloucester, Massachusetts.

Mapplethorpe, Robert (1946–89). Photographer, sculptor, and collage artist. Most widely remembered for homoerotic photographs that prompted firestorms of public criticism, he contributed to the broadening dialogue about gay identity and culture while also perfecting an elegant, classicizing approach to form. Besides figural works, he also specialized in similarly ravishing flower studies. A lifelong New Yorker, he was born in the Floral Park section of Queens and trained as an artist between 1963 and 1969 at Brooklyn's Pratt Institute, although he did not graduate. He had no intention of becoming a photographer and to the end, wished to be evaluated as an artist. Nevertheless, while making use of photographic reproductions in early 1970s collages and *assemblages, he began taking black-and-white Polaroids, which he incorporated in such combinations or mounted in sequences. By the middle of the decade, he had turned to the large-format cameras that he subsequently employed to produce highly detailed, immaculate images. In the overtly homosexual works, emphasis on ideal form contrasts startlingly with subject matter that seemed at the time highly controversial, even distasteful. In the 1980s, as he refined his technique of sharp focus, dramatic lighting, and masterful control over tonal gradation, he broadened his interests to include flowers, as well as portraits and a series devoted to bodybuilder Lisa Lyon. During that decade, he also experimented with color in a series of dye transfer prints, mostly devoted to still lifes. Concurrently, he continued to produce wall-mounted sculptural assemblages, some incorporating photographs. While undergoing treatment for AIDS, he confronted his demise in an anguishing progression of self-portraits.

At the time of his death while undergoing medical treatment in Boston, a major exhibition of his work was touring the country. When it arrived in Cincinnati the next spring, public uproar led to an unprecedented obscenity trial that eventually cleared the director of the Contemporary Arts Center. Mapplethorpe's published collections include *Lady: Lisa Lyon* (1983) and *Black Book* (1986), photographs of African-American men.

Maratta, Hardesty. *See* ROSS, DENMAN.

Marca-Relli, Conrad (1913–2000). Collage artist, painter, sculptor, and printmaker. Best known for vigorously conceived, richly textured canvas collages collectively constituting a singular contribution to *abstract expressionism, he nurtured an underlying classicism in works frequently marked by great lyrical breadth. From the 1960s, he often employed novel materials, such as vinyl or sheet metal. He also worked as a painter throughout most of his career and for a time produced sculptures stylistically related to the collages, which sometimes allude to the figure or to landscape. Born Corrado Marcarelli to Italian parents in Boston, he spent much of his childhood in Italy, where he began his study of art. As an adult, he continued to maintain ties there. His aesthetic owed much to the traditions of that country, as well as to its modern masters such as Giorgio de Chirico and, later, Alberto Burri. After studying briefly at Cooper Union, by the time he was eighteen he had begun working independently in New York. While employed as a painter and muralist for a *federal art project during the later 1930s, he became acquainted with Willem *de Kooning, John *Graham, and Franz *Kline. During World War II he served in the U.S. Army. By the end of the 1940s, he had abandoned his early surrealistic approach to embrace gestural abstraction. In 1953 he embarked on the signature collages, formed from irregular pieces of canvas or other fabric fixed to a canvas support and then painted. Around the same time, he moved to the eastern Long Island town East Hampton and became friendly with Jackson *Pollock, who lived nearby. During the 1960s, while experimenting with other collage materials, he turned as well to sculpture, usually combining spare aluminum shapes to form suave reliefs and free-standing works. In the 1970s he began focusing once again on painting, although he never lost interest in the collage technique, and his characteristically muted palette expanded to include, on occasion, brighter tones. In later years, he lived at times in the northern New Jersey town of Wayne and in Sarasota, Florida, as well as several European locations, including Ibiza, Spain. Four years before his death he settled permanently in Parma, Italy.

Marden, Brice (1938–). Painter and printmaker. He made his mark in the 1960s with geometric compositions combining *abstract expressionism's touch, scale, and heroic aura with *minimalism's reduced effects and attention to the work of art as an independent object. Since the later 1980s, linear elements have activated his pictorial surfaces. At first appearing in scrawled webs, they soon looped and crisscrossed in languorous tangles ambiguously related to figuration and to the previous history of abstract art. In recent years, his work has displayed startlingly intense hues, building on the central role that his color has always enjoyed. Born in Bronxville, he grew up in the more distant New York suburb of Briarcliff Manor and received a BFA degree from Boston University in 1961. After earning an MFA at Yale University two years later, he settled in New York, where he became an assistant to Robert *Rauschenberg in 1966. Following a sojourn in Paris during the spring and summer of 1964, he began to paint monochrome canvases that emphasize personal expression through subtleties of color and surface. By leaving narrow, irregular, unpainted strips around the edges of each canvas thickly coated with paint (in the early work, usually encaustic, which does not soak into the support), he emphasized the art object's materiality. In the late 1960s he began juxtaposing contiguous canvases into stately rectangles. From the mid-1970s, perhaps in consequence of regular summer visits to Greece (he has maintained a residence on the island of Hydra since 1973), his color took on more radiant qualities that reflect his admiration for the work of Mark *Rothko. From 1977 until 1985, he worked on stained-glass windows for Basel Cathedral, an experience that further affected his notions of chromatic relationships. Evolving from landscape and botanical drawings, the linear works first came to fruition in the acclaimed Cold Mountain series (1989–91), revealing an important interest in Chinese culture and its ideograms. An active printmaker throughout his career, Marden has explored territory related to his paintings in etchings primarily, but including occasional forays into other media. Besides properties in New York and Hydra, he has owned a home and studio in Eagles Mere, Pennsylvania, since 1991 and another, overlooking the Hudson River, in Tivoli, New York, since 2002. In 2006 he purchased land on the island of Nevis, in the Caribbean, with plans to build a fifth residence. His wife, abstract painter and printmaker **Helen Marden** (1941–), born Helen Harrington in Pittsburgh, was educated at Pennsylvania State University. They met in New York and married in he late 1960s.

Margo, Boris (1902–95). Painter, printmaker, and sculptor. Associated with a theatrical form of surrealism during the 1930s, he later contributed to *abstract expressionism. Born in Volochisk, Russia (now Ukraine), he studied art in Odessa, Moscow, and Leningrad (now St. Petersburg). He lived in Montreal for a little more than a year before arriving in New York in 1930 and subsequently becoming a United States citizen. Exemplifying his 1930s taste for fantasy, *Performance* (Hirshhorn Museum, 1934) suggests a magician on stage, conjuring horrible apparitions below curtainlike forms. In this creepy mélange of *biomorphic elements in unpleasant colors, everything appears to be in flux, decaying or emerging. In the mid-1930s Margo invented a process known as decalcomania (transferring wet paint directly from one surface laid upon another, in order to take advantage of chance effects), which was soon taken up by other surrealist-oriented artists, most notably Max *Ernst. By 1940, Margo's images often verged on abstraction, with partially transparent organic forms floating through indeterminate and shifting spaces. His interests in painterly effects determined by chance and in the canvas as a painterly arena for metamorphic effects undoubtedly interested Arshile *Gorky. In addition to working together on a *federal art project, in the late 1930s they shared a studio, as did Margo and Mark *Rothko in 1943–44, when both were working in a similar vein of semi-abstraction. An active and experimental printmaker, Margo developed a technique known as cellocut (made by dissolving celluloid with acetone), a forerunner of the collograph process. In *The Sea* (1949), a color cellocut on wood support, the wood grain suggests clouds in a sky as a crescent moon floats above abstract organisms seeming to rise from the waters. In the 1950s and 1960s, he also produced reliefs and sculptural *assemblages. A stroke in 1968 curtailed his productivity. A longtime summer visitor to *Provincetown on Cape Cod, he died at a hospital in Hyannis, not far away.

Marin, John (1870–1953). Painter and printmaker. A watercolor enthusiast, Marin painted landscapes, seascapes, and city views in a fresh and vigorous semi-abstract style. His work combines impressionist sensitivity to visual effects, expressionist emotional intensity, and cubist fragmentation of forms. His earliest notable works, etchings that extended James Abbott McNeill *Whistler's aesthetic through the first decade of the twentieth century, demonstrated technical expertise and pictorial nuance but little awareness of modernist upheavals already attracting other young Americans. From 1911, however, his work developed rapidly toward a personal modern style. With the possible exception of Georgia *O'Keeffe during the 1920s and 1930s, Marin remained the most popular of the early modernists during his lifetime. Respected by the art community, his work spoke as well to a larger audience that admired his expressive individualism and enthusiasm for nature. In mid-century, as he entered his eighties painting as strongly as ever, he was widely esteemed as a living old master. He represented the United States in the Venice Biennale of 1950 and was held in high repute among many supporters of *abstract expressionism.

A New Jersey resident most of his life, John Cheri Marin was born in Rutherford, grew up in Weehawken, and later lived in Cliffside Park. He started painting on his own at an early age, but artistically he matured slowly. In 1886 he enrolled at the Stevens Institute of Technology in Hoboken but left after a year and a half. Employed for several years as a draftsman and then in private architectural practice, the young artist developed a permanent appreciation for structure, balance, and weight. In 1899, already nearly thirty, he began serious study of art at the *Pennsylvania Academy of the Fine Arts, where Thomas *Anshutz and William Merritt *Chase numbered among his teachers. Between 1901 and 1903, he worked at the *Art Students League in New York. From 1905 until early 1911 he lived in Europe, except for a few months in 1909–10. Although he visited Amsterdam, Venice, and other locales, Paris served as his base. Upon arrival there, he immediately took up etching, and before his European sojourn ended, he had completed more than one hundred plates. His urban and architectural subjects responded to an established market for mementos of monuments and historic or picturesque sites. Among many delicate yet powerful images, *Notre Dame, Paris* (1908) represents the cathedral's ornamental facade as a hulking form, slightly angled and cut off on the right edge. Along with his printmaking, Marin simultaneously continued to paint watercolors in a soft, late-impressionist style, as he had for about twenty years. A particularly strong group of these date from a 1910 trip to the Austrian Alps. Through contacts in Paris with young American acquaintances of Alfred *Stieglitz, he arranged to show his watercolors in a 1909 joint display with Alfred *Maurer's work at Stieglitz's *291 gallery. The following year, after the two had met in Paris, Stieglitz presented his first one-person exhibition, initiating the strong bond and professional relationship that remained until Stieglitz's death in 1946. After his return home, Marin never again visited Europe. As he now entered his forties, he began to develop the linear energy that characterized his mature work. Soon he interpreted the New York cityscape with brio sometimes approaching delirium. After the *Armory Show, in which he exhibited, he integrated devices from cubism, futurism, and expressionism to picture a metropolis exploding with rhapsodic energies. A number of these works, depicting the Brooklyn Bridge, the Woolworth Building, and other modern structures, bend and twist with an abandon similar to French painter Robert Delaunay's interpretations of the Eiffel Tower. Writing memorably, as he often did, about his portrayal of New York, Marin stated, "Buildings, people, all are alive; and the more they move me the more I feel them to be alive. It is this 'moving of me' that I try to express." When Marin soon turned to nature for characteristic motifs, his real subject remained inner emotional response, usually joyous, to the great forces he perceived.

In 1914 Marin first visited Maine, where he painted regularly thereafter. The seacoast fostered development of his personal blend of calligraphic line and fluid color, but it was not his only subject. Other rural areas inspired him, and the city also remained important. On visits to New Mexico in 1929 and 1930, he responded with newly spacious views, devoid of the eastern landscape's dominant greens and blues. About this time, he began to work more frequently in oil, as he subsequently continued to do. He also made occasional prints, but most of his significant work in this medium had been accomplished by 1915. In the late 1940s, Marin's work often displayed increased abstraction and linear intensity, perhaps encouraged by the abstract expressionist interest in process that his work had presaged for a long time. However, Marin's art and his writing about it remained untheoretical, optimistic, and affirmative, rooted more in Transcendentalism and Walt Whitman than in abstract expressionism's twentieth-century preoccupations with tragedy, psychoanalysis, and existential philosophy. Marin died near Addison, Maine, at the Cape Split summer home he had purchased in 1933. His writings appear in two volumes: *Letters of John Marin* (1931), edited by H. J. Seligmann, and *The Selected Writings of John Marin* (1949), edited by Dorothy Norman.

Marisol (1930–). Sculptor, printmaker, and installation artist. Her amusing sculptures gently satirizing modern life drew widespread attention during the heyday of *pop art in the 1960s. To generally blocklike approximations of the human figure, she adds carved or cast body parts, then paints the surfaces, completely or in part, to suggest clothing, accessories, facial expression, and other signifiers of identity. Often she also adds real accessories, such as jewelry and handbags, sometimes achieving a material richness bordering on *assemblage. Thematically related figures frequently appear in groups, or *installations. Notable for their decorative panache, her works display as well sophisticated interplay between two- and three-dimensional elements and between illusion and materiality. Most of her sculptured individuals are anonymous types, often graphically skewered for their foibles, but she sometimes portrayed celebrities, including prominent artists. She has also worked in other media, notably bronze, and much of her later work privileges whimsy over irony. In a memorable departure from more characteristic imagery, in the 1970s she produced mythically charged fusions of the human form with aspects of undersea creatures. In lithographs, screen prints, and intaglio works, she has often further evoked surrealistic fantasy with references to anatomical and biological forms. Born in Paris to Venezuelan parents, in the mid-1950s Marisol Escobar dropped her surname professionally. She spent much of her childhood in Caracas and Los Angles. In 1949 she returned to Paris to study for a year at the École des Beaux-Arts before settling in New York. There she studied at the *Art Students League, where Yasuo *Kuniyoshi numbered among her teachers, and subsequently at Hans *Hofmann's school and the New School for Social Research (now New School). She became an American citizen in 1963. While New York has remained her base, she travels widely. Although nearly all of her training focused on two-dimensional media, in the early 1950s she began to experiment with sculptural form in small terra cottas influenced by pre-Columbian and American folk art. These appeared in a first solo show, mounted in 1958 at Leo *Castelli's gallery. Positioned to enter the limelight, she lived in Italy for a year before introducing her signature work in New York.

Mark, Mary Ellen (1940–). Photographer. A leading photojournalist, she has worked internationally, capturing images of life in varied cultures. She concentrates on distinctive but commonplace moments to record a panoply of human experience. Although much of her work documents harsh realities, her stated goal is to "discover the common human element that connects people all over the world." A notable body of work resulted from repeated visits to India. Closer to home, while traveling the United States she has photographed homeless people, mental patients, prostitutes, drug addicts, attitudinizing adolescents, retirees, circus performers, and celebrities. She works mostly in black and white, but has also produced highly effective color series, particularly while working in India. Born in Philadelphia, Mark studied painting and art history at the University of Pennsylvania. After graduation in 1962, she continued at the university's Annenberg School of Communication to earn a master's degree in photojournalism two years later. She is married to filmmaker Martin Bell. Her photographs have appeared in leading magazines and in some fifteen books devoted to aspects of her work. These include her first published collection, *Passport* (1974), a selection of work from the previous decade; *Falkland Road: Prostitutes of Bombay* (1981), a series shot in color; *Streetwise* (1988), picturing Seattle teenagers on the margins of society; *Indian Circus* (1993), scenes of eighteen troupes; *American Odyssey* (1999), a selection of work from thirty-five years; *Twins* (2003), a collection of large-format Polaroids taken at the Twins Days Festival in Twinsburg, Ohio; and *Exposure* (2005), a retrospective survey of forty years' work.

Marsh, Reginald (1898–1954). Painter and printmaker. His lively, often dramatic, portrayals of modern city life number among the most vivid such subjects produced by *American Scene painters. Marsh communicated the physical energy of crowds, the brash behavior of masses of people enjoying themselves, the seedy underside of nightlife, and the unceasing movement of life in a modern metropolis. Less often, but equally effectively, he represented the isolated condition of individuals in the midst of urban activity, as in *Why Not Use the "L"?* (Whitney Museum, 1930) focusing on a rider who sleeps as others obliviously keep to themselves. Whether caught up in the frenzy or lost in solitude, his actors are rarely individualized psychologically. Rather, black or white, rich or poor, male or female, they remain subordinated to the spectacle of modern life. Marsh followed his mentor Kenneth Hayes *Miller in delineating modern, uniquely American themes with styles and techniques appropriated from the old masters. Neither had any use for modern art nor much interest in critiquing social conditions. Particularly valuing draftsmanship, Marsh painted mostly in the demanding media of watercolor and tempera. From Michelangelo and Rubens he learned much about displaying the human form in space and suggesting movement. His compositions typically feature a fluid array of interlocking forms across the pictorial surface. With no visual center, these accommodate a wealth of incident. Because the undulating forms prevent the eye from resting, they emphasize his subjects' dynamic character. Marsh was born in Paris to American parents, but grew up in Nutley, New Jersey, with summers at Sakonnet, Rhode Island, on Narragansett Bay. His family moved to New Rochelle, New York, two years before Marsh entered Yale University in 1916. After graduation in 1920, he settled in New York, where he worked for a year with John *Sloan and quickly established a reputation as a leading illustrator. In 1922 he began taking classes at *Art Students League, and following a European sojourn in 1925–26, returned to study there with Miller, as well as George *Luks, among others. In the 1930s he painted murals in Washington, D.C., and New York for a *federal art project. Marsh also produced more than 250 prints, primarily etchings and engravings. In 1945 he published *Anatomy for Artists*. He died in Dorset, Vermont. In 1923 Marsh married sculptor Elizabeth Burroughs (1899–1988), known as Betty, the daughter of Paris-trained figurative painter Bryson Burroughs (1869–1934), also an important curator at the *Metropolitan Museum of Art for more than twenty-five years before his death. Her mother, sculptor Edith Woodman Burroughs (1871–1916), reflected progressive French taste in bronze allegories and portraits. Betty studied at the Art Students League and in Paris. Divorced in 1933, she later became Betty Burroughs Woodhouse. Marsh's second wife, painter Felicia Meyer (1913–76), studied at the Art Students League with Miller and Guy *Pène du Bois before marriage in 1934.

Marshall, William Edgar. *See* RYDER, ALBERT PINKHAM.

Martin, Agnes (1912–2004). Painter. Her reductive, spiritually charged, grid-based abstract work achieves expressive power with the most delicate means. Martin's signature art superficially resembles *minimalism's nonreferential, nonsymbolic, unemotional, pared-down approach. Yet, her handcrafted method, open to irregularity on a minute scale, her *all-over compositions, her preference for optical effects over literal objects, her ties to nature as a source of inspiration, and her subjective ethos tie the work to core values of *abstract expressionism. In extensive writings, she affirmed an art of humility, contemplation, detachment, and idealism. Born in the western Saskatchewan town of Macklin, Agnes Bernice Martin moved in 1932 to the United States and became a citizen in 1950. She enrolled at the New Whatcom Normal School (soon Western Washington College of Education, now Western Washington University) in Bellingham but moved to New York to complete a bachelor's degree in art education at Columbia University in 1942 and, ten years later, an MFA. She taught in several places before moving to *Taos, where Betty *Parsons saw her work and urged her to relocate to New York. After doing so in 1957, Martin lived in the Coenties Slip area of lower Manhattan. She associated with the area's like-minded younger painters, including Robert *Indiana, Jasper *Johns, Ellsworth *Kelly, and Jack *Youngerman, but also admired the work of friends Barnett *Newman and, particularly, Ad *Reinhardt. In this milieu of resistance to abstract expressionist theatrics, Martin quickly abandoned her previous *biomorphic abstraction and by 1960 had established a fully nonobjective approach featuring repeated geometric forms tethered to a grid. She soon almost exclusively limited her practice to 6 × 6-foot canvases until her elder years, when she reduced the dimensions to five-foot squares.

Although her work drew recognition, in the spring of 1967 she abruptly left the city to wander through the Canadian and American West alone. More than a year later, she settled in New Mexico but did not resume painting. Instead, she built herself an adobe house on an isolated site near the town of Cuba, about sixty miles north of Albuquerque, and devoted much of her time to writing, refining the purposes and objectives of the art making she resumed in the mid-1970s. Subsequently, she generally inscribed her canvases with barely visible pencil lines and pale bands of color. Their surfaces foster the veil-like effects she achieved. With few deviations, for the next thirty years she pursued this spare purity reverberating with the West's ineffable effects of space and light. However, for her final New York show, only months before her death, she revived the circles, triangles, and other geometric shapes that had appeared in paintings of some forty years earlier. In 1978 she moved to Galisteo, south of Santa Fe, and then, in 1989, to Taos, where she died. In 1992 she published *Writings*, a compilation of ruminations on art and life. Illuminating her paintings, although from a point of view more ethical than aesthetic, the essays and epigrams draw from Zen Buddhism, Taoism, Emersonian transcendentalism, her Scottish heritage of self-reliance, the quest for ideal beauty, and long experience of life.

Martin, Fletcher (1904–79). Painter and printmaker. Known for vigorous scenes of American life, particularly western subjects, he was born in the western Colorado town of Palisade, grew up in several locations in the West, and did not finish high school. Following his 1926 discharge from the U.S. Navy, he moved to the Los Angeles area, where he assisted Mexican artist David Alfaro Siqueiros in painting a 1933 mural. Otherwise largely self-taught, Martin came to artistic maturity during the years dominated by the *American Scene movement. Much of his early work reflected the social concerns of the time. Particularly powerful, his *Mine Rescue* (University of Maryland, 1939), designed for a *federal art project mural in the Kellogg, Idaho, post office, offended local industrialists, who objected to the somber theme drawing attention to the danger of mine labor. As executed, Martin's revised mural depicts an uncontroversial event in local history: the arrival of the prospector for whom the town was named. Other Martin paintings of about the same time portray labor themes without overt social commentary. The best known of these, *Trouble in Frisco* (Museum of Modern Art, 1938) depicts a pair of brawling dockworkers, seen through a ship's open porthole. With interest in the American Scene waning from about 1940, Martin intensified the abstraction of form already seen in his work of the late 1930s. He often enhanced such energetic subjects as sport or cowboy life with simplified forms and animated compositions. He also painted landscapes. A war correspondent for *Life* during World War II, in 1947 Martin built a permanent residence and studio in *Woodstock, but subsequently maintained his restless lifestyle as he accepted numerous teaching stints, usually lasting no more than a year or two, at schools around the country. He also produced illustrations, lithographs, and woodcuts. In later years he divided his time between Mexico and Sarasota, Florida. He died at his home in Guanajuato.

Martin, Homer Dodge (1836–97). Painter. Almost exclusively interested in landscape, he first worked within the *Hudson River School aesthetic but later responded to the examples of John *La Farge and James Abbott McNeill *Whistler. His career culminated in a personal style indebted to *Barbizon precedents and, eventually, impressionism. His best-known painting, *View on the Seine: Harp of the Winds* (Metropolitan Museum, 1893–95), recalls rural France. Memorable for its distinctive, harp-shaped frieze of graceful poplars, it combines poetic retrospection with impressionist-influenced brushwork in the subdued harmonies of *tonalism. Born in Albany, New York, and mostly self-taught, Martin received early encouragement from Erastus Dow *Palmer and briefly studied with James MacDougal *Hart before moving to New York in the early 1860s. Favoring wilderness scenery, he generally undertook summer sketching expeditions, from 1864 frequently visiting the Adirondack Mountains. The panoramic *Lake Sanford* (Century Association, New York, 1870) combines detailed observation of selected, unidealized foreground features with an overcast sky and indistinct distance, producing a brooding, even melancholy effect quite distinct from Hudson River School optimism. A growing interest in La Farge's poetic subjectivity and decorative form found reinforcement during his first trip to Europe in 1876. Besides visiting France, where he particularly admired Jean-Baptiste-Camille Corot's work, in London he befriended Whistler, who apparently stimulated his subsequently frequent use of watercolor. By the early 1880s, when he resided in Normandy for several years, he had largely abandoned his interest in documenting natural detail, in favor of concentrating on the aesthetic issues of form, color, and expressive brushwork that interested progressive American artists of the day. After returning to the United States in 1886, in 1893 he settled permanently in St. Paul, Minnesota. As his eyesight and then his general health deteriorated during his final decade, he regularly based his work on sketches and memories, sometimes dating from years before, as his art addressed the reverie of nature, rather than its reality.

Mason, Alice Trumbull (1904–71). Painter and printmaker. Her refined but varied abstract work includes both rectilinear and organic approaches. Born in Litchfield, Connecticut, Alice Bradford Trumbull spent much of her youth in Europe, where she first pursued training in art. After returning to the United States, she studied at the *National Academy of Design with Charles *Hawthorne and later worked with Arshile *Gorky. In 1930 she married Warwood E. Mason. Widely conversant with the forms of modernist abstraction, she developed the belief that abstract art provided the best opportunity for the artist to work on a universally effective level. In 1936 she participated in the formation of the *Abstract American Artists and remained a leader in the association for some three decades. By 1929 she had developed a completely nonobjective style, based on precedents in the work of Kandinsky and Miró. In the early 1930s, Mason often painted loosely defined color areas in counterpoint with gestural lines and other markings, but her characteristic mature works demonstrate greater control. *Brown Shapes White* (Philadelphia Museum, 1941) features three smoothly painted and sharply edged organic brown forms floating beneath an overlay of elegant black lines that bind the image together. Through a personal friendship with Mondrian while he resided in New York during the 1940s, she was inspired to create a number of compositions based solely on verticals and horizontals. However, idiosyncratic color combinations and irregular distributions of rectangular shapes distinguish her approach from his. After embarking in the mid-1940s on printmaking at *Atelier 17, she produced numerous etchings, often incorporating softground and aquatint, demonstrating a wide range of coloristic effects achieved through texture. In the later years of Mason's life, her work showed a simplification of form. She died at her home in New York. Her daughter **Emily Mason** (1932–), also a painter, is known for chromatic abstractions. She studied for two years at Bennington (Vermont) College before transferring to Cooper Union, where she earned a BFA degree in 1955. She continued her study of painting in Venice and in 1957 married Wolf *Kahn.

Masses, The. Socialist literary and political magazine dedicated to freedom, justice, and progressive culture. Flourishing in the bohemian atmosphere of Greenwich Village in the pre-World War I years, *The Masses* welcomed both utopian and practical forms of socialism. The magazine championed individualism and fostered the belief that political reform and the revolution of consciousness went hand in hand. However, despite the publication's political radicalism, it showed no interest in experimental modernism in the arts. Founded in 1911 as an organ of cooperative socialism, the magazine came into its own after 1912 when it was reorganized and Max Eastman was appointed editor. He remade it into a lively publication of ideas, humor, social conscience, and artistic quality. Between 1912 and 1916, its art editor John *Sloan published the work of numerous anti-academic realists, including George *Bellows, Glenn O. *Coleman, Stuart *Davis, and Boardman *Robinson. With satire and drama, they attacked social injustice and supported the magazine's commitment to broad-based reform. Sloan and most of the important artists withdrew from the magazine in 1916 in disputes over editorial content, and the magazine folded the next year when it was suppressed by the government for opposing the war. Between 1918 and 1924, Eastman edited a successor, *The Liberator*. In 1926 Michael Gold and Joseph Freeman started *The New Masses*. Both of these journals published work by some of the same artists, but as they drifted toward a more doctrinaire leftism, neither was able to replicate the creative sparkle of *The Masses* in its finest years.

Mather, Frank Jewett, Jr. (1868–1953). Art critic, historian, and museum director. Conservative by temperament, he saw little merit in modern art, judging it to reflect excessive individualism. However, his critical writing usually maintained a scholarly and judicious tone, a byproduct of his academic training. Born in Deep River, Connecticut, he earned a BA degree in 1889 at Williams College in Williamstown, Massachusetts, and a PhD in English at Baltimore's Johns Hopkins University three years later. After teaching languages at Williams from 1893 until 1900, he spent the following decade as a journalist, in New York until 1906 and subsequently in Italy. He then returned to teaching but in addition wrote art criticism, especially for *The Nation*, where he served as a regular contributor from 1907 until 1917. From 1910 until 1933, he taught at Princeton University, where he also directed the school's art museum from 1922 to 1946. Besides several books on Italian art, his numerous publications include an examination of modern painting, a monograph on Homer *Martin, a study of aesthetics, and collected essays, which included clear-eyed estimates of recent American artists such as Thomas *Eakins and Winslow *Homer. In his final years, he resided on a farm in Bucks County, Pennsylvania. He died in Princeton.

Mather, Margrethe. *See* WESTON, EDWARD.

Mathews, Arthur Francis (1860–1945). Painter and designer. A leading figure in the San Francisco art community, in the years around the turn of the twentieth century he ranged nimbly across several media while promoting progressive aesthetic ideas. As a painter, he preferred poetic views of the California landscape and dreamy allegories in the classical mode of the *American Renaissance. Among his many murals for private and public spaces, the most ambitious depicts *The Story of California* (1913–14) in twelve panels at the state capitol in Sacramento. He also spearheaded the region's elegant conflation of the *Arts and Crafts movement, the *aesthetic movement, art nouveau, and indigenous motifs in what is sometimes designated the California decorative style. As well, he was an influential teacher at the California School of Design (now San Francisco Art Institute), where he also served as director for sixteen years. Usually known as Frank, Mathews was born in the central Wisconsin town of Markesan, but in 1867 settled with his family in Oakland, California. As a young man, he trained as an architect in his father's office and worked in San Francisco as a designer and illustrator. In 1885 he left for Europe, where he studied in Paris at the Académie Julian and spent a summer painting in the Netherlands. In 1889 he resettled permanently in San Francisco. The following year he assumed direction of the art school, where he revamped the curriculum to reflect the standards of his French experience. Indebted also to his Parisian training, his solidly constructed narrative and *genre paintings of these years sometimes demonstrate an interest in impressionist brushwork. Mathews's mature style coalesced during a second European sojourn of nearly two years in 1898 and 1899. Demonstrating appreciation of work by James Abbott McNeill *Whistler, French painter Pierre Puvis de Chavannes, Japanese printmakers, and art nouveau designers, his subsequent, less naturalistic paintings emphasize flat patterns, limited color range, and idealized subjects. Although he continued to paint, the need for rebuilding after the 1906 San Francisco earthquake and fire redirected Mathews's interests toward design for both domestic and public spaces. He left the art school to publish *Philopolis*, a monthly magazine issued through 1916, covering city planning and decoration; found a press, active through 1918, devoted to fine editions of California subjects; and establish the Furniture Shop, which until 1920 sold his designs for furniture and household accessories. His wife, painter **Lucia Mathews** (1870–1955), participated extensively in the design and production of her husband's decorative projects. Born and raised in San Francisco, Lucia Kleinhans numbered among his students before they married in 1894. During their 1898–99 sojourn abroad, she studied with Whistler. Her paintings generally demonstrate a more delicate touch and less emphatic stylization than her husband's. She moved to Los Angeles several years before her death there.

Matta Echaurren, Roberto Sebastian Antonio (1911/12–2002). Painter and sculptor. Of all the European surrealists, Matta exerted the most direct influence on the emergence of *abstract expressionism in New York during the early 1940s. Although he was about the same age as the young Americans, the authority and originality of his work provided a powerful stimulus, as did his idealism, ambition, erudition, visionary purpose, and forceful personality. Born in Santiago, Chile, he trained there as an architect but also studied drawing at the Academia de Bellas Artes. After his arrival in Paris in 1934, he worked for the architect Le Corbusier (also a painter, under the name Charles-Édouard Jeanneret). By 1937 he had decided to devote himself entirely to art, and he joined the surrealist group that year. His early development was particularly indebted to the work of Yves *Tanguy. Before he departed for New York in 1939, he had established an original style of *biomorphic abstraction, emphasizing flux, discontinuity, and impermanence. He initiated these works with the chance effects of *automatism, then elaborated on forms that emerged, motivated by the desire to find metaphors for psychological experience and by his interest in the occult. In the early 1940s he reached the full realization of this approach, in large, spatially complex landscapes bursting with amorphous organic forms. In succeeding years, his spaces became vaster, almost galactic, and the floating forms frequently took on sharper definition, sometimes suggesting mechanical origins. Matta's soaring paintings of the 1940s provided emerging abstract expressionists with the example of very large, nonillusionistic paintings that hinged on the tension between conscious control and unconscious impulses. Matta imparted his methods and aims directly to a number of young Americans, most particularly to a group that met in his studio in the fall and winter of 1942. Regular participants were William *Baziotes, Peter *Busa, Gerome *Kamrowski, Robert *Motherwell, and Jackson *Pollock. The following year, Matta also worked with Arshile *Gorky. Matta left New York in 1948, partly because the political climate in the United States was inhospitable to his left-wing views. Later he lived for some years in Chile, but for the most part he resided in London, Paris, and Italy, while expanding on his early accomplishments and initiating an involvement with sculpture. He died in a hospital near his home at Tarquinia, Italy.

*Installation artist, draftsman, photographer, filmmaker, and *performance artist Gordon Matta-Clark (1943–78) was a son of Matta and his American first wife, Anne Clark. Born in New York and named for Gordon *Onslow Ford, he lived as a child also in Paris and Chile. After training in architecture at Cornell University in Ithaca, New York, from 1963 to 1968, he resettled permanently in New York. As an artist, he is best known for literally deconstructing derelict buildings by partially dismantling them, making alterations, and leaving the ruptures exposed. His photographs documenting such temporary installations constitute final elements of the art works. These images often reappear as the material of cubistic collages, in which the artist slashed and cut the photographs as he had the buildings. He died of cancer.

Matter, Herbert. *See* CARLES, ARTHUR.

Matter, Mercedes. *See* CARLES, ARTHUR.

Matteson, Tompkins Harrison. *See* VEDDER, ELIHU.

Matulka, Jan (1890–1972). Painter and printmaker. Adept in a number of modern styles, he functioned as an important intermediary in transmitting European modernism to his American students and colleagues. Originally from Vlachovo Brezi, Bohemia (now Czech Republic), near Prague, he arrived in the United States in 1907. He soon began his art studies at the *National Academy of Design and in 1917–18 used a fellowship to travel widely, particularly through the Southwest. He numbered among the earliest modernists to appreciate that region's landscape and its Indian and Hispanic cultures. Upon his return, he began to work toward abstraction. At first, he fractured motifs, often figures, into brightly colored planes, related to *synchromist color abstraction. By about 1920, some of his work was completely abstract, consisting of precisely drawn forms interlocking in dynamic two-dimensional patterns. In the 1920s, Matulka spent considerable time in Paris, where he kept a studio until 1934. He also returned many times to paint the landscape in the region of his birth. In these years, he began to incorporate realistic elements into compositions that continue to emphasize abstract structure. Often these depict urban environments in hard-edge, patterned compositions that compress depth to a shallow space. Although these resemble contemporary *precisionism in their subjects and clean construction, Matulka generally placed greater emphasis on abstract pictorial energies. The work of Fernand Léger provided an important model. In the same period, Matulka also painted landscapes, which depend structurally on Cézanne's method but often aim for more dramatic, expressionistic effects, as in the watercolor *White Oak* (Hirshhorn Museum, c. 1923). In the 1930s, as much of his work responded to surrealism, he also worked for a *federal art project. Matulka strongly influenced many students through his teaching at the *Art Students League and in his studio. As interest mounted in a renewal of abstract art in the late 1930s, he aided the full assimilation of earlier European painting necessary to the emergence of *abstract expressionism. Perhaps because he did not suppress his wide-ranging interests in favor of a recognizable signature style, his work failed to attract much critical or financial support. Nevertheless, at his death in New York, he remained highly esteemed among leading artists.

Maurer, Alfred (1868–1932). Painter. Known primarily for semi-abstract landscapes and still lifes, he also produced a sizeable number of figure studies, most notably bust-length women seen alone or in pairs. A lifelong New Yorker, Alfred Henry Maurer had the misfortune to be the son of a successful lithographer and *Currier & Ives artist. **Louis Maurer** (1832–1932) hated his son's work. Nevertheless the two men lived uneasily together under the same roof until their deaths less than a month apart. Maurer left school at sixteen to work as a commercial artist before beginning his studies at the *National Academy of Design. In 1897 he departed for Paris, where he lived (except for two visits home) until 1914. His *Self-Portrait* (Frederick R. Weisman Art Museum, University of Minnesota, Minneapolis, 1897) from the time of his expatriation shows a handsome, confident man. Bravura brushwork and dramatic lighting demonstrate the young artist's mastery of the turn-of-the-century's cosmopolitan manner. In Paris, he perfected a fluid, dark, Whistlerian figure style, seen in *An Arrangement* (Whitney Museum, 1901). This painting of a young woman in an interior decorated with Japanese objects won first prize in the prestigious Carnegie International Exhibition of 1901. However, within a few years, Maurer became a follower of Cézanne and Matisse. By about 1905, in advance of any other American, he had adopted the bright colors of fauvism. In 1909 at his *291 gallery, Alfred *Stieglitz presented Maurer's first show, a double bill with John *Marin, and he included Maurer's work in a 1910 group show. However, although they remained friendly, Stieglitz did not again display Maurer's work.

Maurer's work appeared in the *Armory Show before his permanent return from Europe. Subsequently, he worked in a brushy, often brightly colored expressionist style, occasionally approaching complete abstraction. From 1915 he regularly summered at Marlboro-on-Hudson, north of the city. Around 1920 he began to add to his repertoire of landscapes and still lifes a series of long-faced, large-eyed women's heads. Their rigid expressions may be intended to suggest masks concealing inner unease, but they never found many admirers among puzzled observers. By about 1930, Maurer developed renewed interest in cubism, which had provided an occasional alternative approach to his color-based work. In the ensuing sophisticated still life compositions, such as *Still Life with Doily* (Phillips Collection, c. 1930), fragmentation and spatial compression contribute to decorative effects. During the same years, he sometimes distorted his figures, almost beyond recognition, with shattering cubist techniques. When two heads appear together they often merge strangely, suggesting some enigmatic spiritual intent. One of the more realistic figure studies from about the same time, his *Self-Portrait with Hat* (Walker Art Center, Minneapolis, c. 1927), contrasts starkly with its counterpart of thirty years earlier. Here the energy of his brush has dissipated, and the surface of the painting has little vitality. An aging man presents himself as the mournful soul that sometimes got the better of his normally convivial personality. The source of the apparent despondency that caused him to take his own life has been variously attributed to remorse about the strained relationship with his recently deceased father, concerns about his health, and disappointment in his own accomplishments.

Maverick, Peter. *See* DURAND, ASHER BROWN.

Mayor, A. Hyatt. *See* HUNTINGTON, ANNA HYATT.

Mayor, Harriet Hyatt. *See* HUNTINGTON, ANNA HYATT.

Mead, Larkin Goldsmith (1835–1910). Sculptor. Although he executed imaginative subjects as well, he remains known particularly for portraits and public monuments, particularly Lincoln's Tomb in Springfield, Illinois. A lingering fondness for *neoclassicism flavors his realistic, sometimes literal works. Born in Chesterfield, New Hampshire, and raised in Brattleboro, Vermont, he trained as a sculptor in the New York studio of Henry Kirke *Brown. After two years there, he returned in 1855 to Vermont, where he soon was awarded a commission for a monumental *Ceres* (1857), symbolizing the state, to crown the capitol dome in Montpelier. During the first year of the Civil War he worked for *Harper's Weekly* as an illustrator at the front. In 1862 he sailed for Europe with his sister to attend her wedding in Paris to writer William Dean Howells. Mead then settled permanently in Florence but often visited the couple in Venice and occasionally served as acting United States consul there in his brother-in-law's absence. His popular marble *Venezia* (New Hampshire Historical Society, Concord, c. 1865), an ideal bust, realizes an unusual subject, for few American sculptors took an interest in that city. In 1866, on the first of several return visits to the United States, Mead brought with him the model for his colossal memorial to Abraham Lincoln. The 117-foot-tall ensemble features a standing image of Lincoln below a towering obelisk, with ancillary figures at a lower level. Although it was dedicated in 1874, the finishing touches were not put in place until 1883. For the 1893 World's Columbian Exposition in Chicago, Mead designed *The Triumph of Ceres* (destroyed) for the pediment of the Agricultural Building designed by the firm of McKim, Mead and White, which numbered his brother William Rutherford Mead among founding partners. By this time, however, his style seemed old-fashioned, supplanted by taste for the livelier French mode of the late nineteenth century. He subsequently completed few major pieces, and by 1900 his artistic career had essentially come to an end. Elinor Mead Howells (1837–1910) was a painter and illustrator. Her subjects included portraits and scenes of Venice. She served in addition as her husband's acknowledged (if behind-the-scenes) collaborator in literary matters. Also born in Chesterfield, New Hampshire, and raised in Brattleboro, after returning from Venice in 1865 she lived mostly in the Boston area and in New York, where she died.

Meatyard, Ralph Eugene (1925–72). Photographer. Known for visionary fictions, he created a body of challenging, experimental, and emotionally resonant work while remaining independent of mainstream currents. He was born in Normal, Illinois, and served in the U.S. Navy before settling permanently in Lexington, Kentucky. There he worked as an optician and took up photography as a sideline around 1950. The development of his personal approach benefited from interests in philosophy and literature, as well as the examples of Minor *White and Aaron *Siskind, among others. In countering prevailing currents of formalist and documentary photography, his work presaged the nonpurist tendencies of later decades. Often he used such techniques as out-of-focus effects or double exposures to suggest the instability of reality. For his most notable series, Romances, he employed a straight photographic technique to record staged or posed scenes of ambiguous or bizarre character. Often his actors were children. Halloween masks, a favorite device for drawing attention to artifice, frequently blurred distinctions between fantasy and commonplace experience. In a final major project, posthumously published as *The Family Album of Lucybelle Crater* (1974), he subverted the family snapshot with an atmosphere of foreboding. Showing his own family wearing masks of aged faces, the collection speaks to his longstanding preoccupation with the inevitable progress of life toward death.

Mehring, Howard. *See* WASHINGTON COLOR PAINTERS.

Melchers, Gari (1860–1932). Painter. Known for portraits, figure studies, and *genre scenes, he also painted religious subjects, as well as murals attuned to the prevailing taste for ideal themes. Versatile and cosmopolitan, he lived in Europe during much of his career and achieved an international reputation. Born in Detroit, Julius Garibaldi Melchers mastered the essentials of the academic tradition at the Royal Academy in Düsseldorf, which he entered shortly after his seventeenth birthday. Four years later, in 1881, he moved to Paris, where he studied at the Académie Julian. Although impressionism intrigued him, his work demonstrates a stronger attraction to the example of such painters as Jules Bastien-Lepage, who combined careful figure construction with more painterly, atmospheric settings. Choosing to remain in Europe when he completed his training, in 1884 he settled in the Dutch art colony of Egmond, on the North Sea about twenty-five miles from Amsterdam. There he painted picturesque local subjects, typically unsophisticated peasant life treated with appreciation for simplicity and piety. Sojourning often in Paris during the 1890s, he became attuned to symbolist currents there and to postimpressionist styles of painting, which generated a decorative tendency in his work. The example of his friend Pierre Puvis de Chavannes particularly influenced the flattened design and subdued colors of Melchers's mural commissions for Chicago's World's Columbian Exposition (1893) and for Washington, D.C.'s new Library of Congress (1896). Around the turn of the century he painted a number of biblical subjects, overtly extending the implied religious content of some earlier peasant works. A substantial number of mother-and-child images to varying degrees invoke the Christian Madonna theme. After marriage in 1903, he painted domestic interiors and garden scenes in a brighter, more loosely brushed impressionist manner. Concurrently, he developed an active portrait practice, generally retaining a more conservative, disciplined approach for these commissions. Melchers lived in New York from 1905 until 1909, when he accepted an invitation to teach at the art academy in Weimar. When World War I erupted in 1914, he left Germany, returning permanently a few months later to the United States. While retaining a studio in New York, from 1916 he made his home at Belmont, a late-eighteenth-century property overlooking the Rappahannock River in Stafford County, near Fredericksburg, Virginia. This locality and the nearby countryside inspired many later works. In the 1920s he also completed murals for the Detroit Public Library and the Missouri state capitol. Melchers remained active and much honored until his death at Belmont. A National Historic Landmark administered by Fredericksburg's University of Mary Washington, the home, studio, and gardens today comprise a public memorial, featuring a large collection of the artist's work. An early mentor, his father **Julius Melchers** (1829–1909), was a leading Detroit sculptor. Before arriving there in the 1850s, he trained as an apprentice in his native Prussia and later studied at the École des Beaux-Arts in Paris. Among his best-known works, four over-life-size figures of the area's French founders (1874; now installed on the campus of Wayne State University) graced the city hall facade. He was also known for wood sculptures and other items, including elaborately carved furniture and such functional emblems as shop figures.

Mellon, Andrew William (1855–1937). Art collector and philanthropist. Also a financier and public official. The *National Gallery of Art in Washington, D.C., was his gift to the nation. Born in Pittsburgh, he left Western University (now the University of Pittsburgh) before graduation to enter business. He soon went into banking and became one of the wealthiest men in the country through investments in coal, oil, and aluminum. Secretary of the Treasury under three presidents between 1921 and 1932, he served as ambassador to Great Britain in 1932–33. Only months before his death, he gave his extensive art collection, rich in old master paintings, to the United States government, along with $15,000,000 to build the National Gallery. The original building opened to the public in 1941. He died on eastern Long Island, at Southampton, where he regularly summered.

His son, **Paul Mellon** (1907–99), a collector and philanthropist, further enriched the National Gallery with more than nine hundred European and American works, notably from the impressionist and early modern periods. He also served as a trustee of the museum for many years, as well as its president from 1963 to 1979. Along with his sister, philanthropist Ailsa Mellon Bruce (1901–69), he underwrote construction of the East Building when the National Gallery expanded in the 1970s. Born in Pittsburgh, he graduated from Yale University in 1929 and for the next two years pursued additional study of English literature at Cambridge University. He served in the U.S. military during World War II. He had spent his childhood partly in England, and affection for that country fostered his passion for its art. Eventually he amassed a representation second in scope and quality only to that of London's Tate Gallery (now Tate Britain). This collection provided the core holdings of the Yale Center for British Art, which he founded in 1966. His gift included funding of its Louis Kahn–designed museum and research facility, which opened in 1977, as well as an endowment. Paul Mellon also established the Bollingen Foundation and contributed hundreds of millions of dollars to educational, cultural, and environmental causes. From the mid-1930s he made his home on an immense estate in Upperville, Virginia, where he died. His autobiography, *Reflections in a Silver Spoon*, appeared in 1992.

Mendieta, Ana (1948–85). Performance artist, sculptor, painter, printmaker, photographer, and filmmaker. In notable work featuring her own body as substance and metaphor, she employed a variety of techniques related to *performance art, but also encompassing aspects of *process art, *conceptual art, and even *earth art. Much of her art is known through photographic or filmed documentation, although she also produced paintings and drawings and, in her final years, a sequence of large-scale sculptures. She achieved only limited recognition during her lifetime, but since her premature death has come to be recognized as a leading contributor to *feminist art. Born in Havana, at twelve she numbered among thousands of Operation Peter Pan children airlifted from Cuba after Fidel Castro came to power. She spent her teenage years in orphanages and foster homes in Iowa, engendering permanent feelings of insecurity and exile. After graduating from the University of Iowa in Iowa City, she stayed on to earn an MFA degree in the new intermedia program headed by German-born painter, photographer, and sculptor Hans Breder (1935–) who became her partner as well as her mentor. Concentrating primarily on ephemeral creations during the 1970s Medieta centered her work on female identity. Although some performance events, such as those employing blood or nudity, employed grotesque or provocative effects, others achieve poetic distinction with no loss of drama. In the extensive Silhueta series begun in 1973 and staged mostly around Iowa City or Oaxaca, she employed her body or an imprint of its shape (made visible by painting, burning, or otherwise setting off its contours) to produce interventions in the landscape, conveying hunger to connect with the spirit of specific places and materials. She created the Mexican Silhuetas during several summer visits there with Breder. (Suggesting a collaborative aspect to their relationship, many of the 1970s works photographed by Breder number among the strongest works either of them ever accomplished.) In Mexico, she reconnected with Latin culture and made a point of investigating archetypal forms of art and architecture, particularly those related to the goddess myth, an interest she later also pursued in other travels abroad.

In 1978 she moved to New York and in 1980 made the first of seven return visits to Cuba, where she sought connections with Afro-Cuban and Santeria culture. Reprising the Silhueta series, the Rupestrian Sculptures (begun 1981) comprise figural allusions carved into the rock in a park near Havana. Around this time, Mendieta began to reorient her creative life to studio practice, producing drawings, often on bark or other natural substances, and sculptures made from such materials as clay, mud, and wood. Carl *Andre may in part have spurred this interest in more permanent form. After he and Medieta met late in 1979, they soon formed a romantic relationship intensified by their mutual interest in prehistoric art, as well as aesthetic issues more generally. In 1983 while working in Rome, Mendieta began working in earnest on monumental sculptural pieces gouged and burned from tree trunks. Mendieta and Andre married there early in 1985 and visited Egypt's ancient monuments on their honeymoon. However, later that year, she died in a fall from the window of their New York apartment. Andre was charged with murder, but was later acquitted in the face of evidence that her death was an accident or suicide.

Merrild, Knud (1894–1954). Painter, sculptor, and printmaker. His varied work responded to cubism, constructivism, surrealism, and Kandinsky's nonobjective painting. In 1921 he arrived in New York after studying at the Royal Academy in Copenhagen. Following a winter in *Taos, in 1923 he settled in Los Angeles, where he became a leading figure in the area's small avant-garde. Through the 1930s, he worked mostly with abstract form, demonstrating a sure hand in composing with geometric elements arranged in interpenetrating or overlapping relationships. Some of these works are shallow relief sculptures, formed by affixing three-dimensional elements to a flat background. He also experimented with surrealist-induced *biomorphic forms and with collage, often including representational photographic fragments. In the mid-1930s, he exhibited with the post-surrealist group founded by Lorser *Feitelson and Helen Lundeberg. In the 1940s he incorporated chance in freely poured and splashed paint of Flux abstractions that prefigure Jackson *Pollock's grander achievements. He returned permanently to his native Denmark in 1952. In 1938 he published *A Poet and Two Painters: A Memoir of D. H. Lawrence*, whom he had met in Taos.

Metcalf, Willard Leroy (1858–1925). Painter and illustrator. Remembered particularly for New England landscapes, he worked in an impressionist style tempered by the atmospheric poetry of *tonalism. Generally he depicted the hilly scenery of the region in pleasant weather, but he also painted numerous winter views of the same terrain, as well as several unusual but widely praised nighttime images. He forged the personal combination of feathery brushwork and precise observation that secured his reputation after withdrawing late in 1903 for nearly a year of relative isolation in Maine, at his parents' farmhouse home near the Damariscotta River. Born in Lowell, Massachusetts, he spent much of his childhood in Maine before 1871 when the family moved to the Boston suburb of Cambridge. At sixteen he began working in a Boston wood engraving shop while also attending classes at the Massachusetts Normal Art School (now Massachusetts College of Art). In 1875 he began a year's instruction with George Loring *Brown, and in 1877 he entered the School of the Museum of Fine Arts. From the early 1880s he worked intermittently as a magazine illustrator until the mid-1890s. Notably, he depicted the Zuni peoples, observed during many months in the Southwest, before departing for Europe in September 1883. In Paris he enrolled at the Académie Julian, where he studied with Gustave Boulanger and Jules-Joseph Lefebvre. While abroad he traveled widely, working during vacation periods in England, Italy, North Africa, and several French locations, including Pont-Aven in Brittany. At Grez-sur-Loing, near Fontainebleau, he completed *Sunset at Grez* (Hirshhorn Museum, 1885), a masterwork of his early period. Depicting a slender peasant girl carrying water from the river behind her, it suggests the artist's admiration for Jules Bastien-Lepage's popular synthesis of academic figure construction and atmospheric surroundings. Although Metcalf aspired to become figure painter, the sensitive rendition here of the setting's light and color point to interests that later chiefly absorbed his attention. In the year he completed this work, Metcalf made the first of several visits to Giverny. He may have been the first American artist to arrive there, anticipating the appearance of numerous Americans drawn by Monet's reputation. Although Metcalf's landscapes of the late 1880s demonstrate increasing skill in rendering effects of light with painterly brushwork, he remained partial to a *Barbizon sensibility and did not at this time emulate Monet's impressionist technique.

Metcalf returned to the Boston area in December 1888 but before long moved on to Philadelphia and then to New York in search of portrait commissions. During the productive summer of 1895 in Gloucester, Massachusetts, he mastered a bright approach to sun-filled outdoor scenes. In 1898 he joined with others to form The *Ten. A 1902 visit to Cuba again produced vivid responses to an optically stimulating environment. After consolidating his progress during the 1903–4 interlude in Maine, Metcalf entered a decade of particularly productive and creative accomplishment. On one of his intermittent visits to *Old Lyme, he painted *May Night* (Corcoran Gallery, 1906), a moonlit scene of a woman in flowing dress on the lawn of a porticoed house. Immediately acclaimed, more mysterious and moody than most of his work, it suggests appreciation for symbolist currents and for the example of James Abbott McNeill *Whistler. From 1909 until 1920 he often worked around Cornish, New Hampshire, but primarily during the winter months, after the summer art crowd had departed. Among snow scenes painted there, *White Veil* (Detroit Institute of Arts, 1909) pictures whitened fields and bare trees during a storm. Its decorative arrangement of flattened forms, enhanced by the square format he came to favor, together with its delicate, grayed tonality create an idyll of solitude and aesthetic contemplation. He continued to produce compelling images of nature in its seasonal phases almost until his death at his New York home.

Metropolitan Museum of Art. A New York institution ranking among the great art museums of the world, it is the largest and most comprehensive art museum in the western hemisphere. No other museum surpasses its encyclopedic representation of art traditions from around the globe during more than five thousand years of human history. Many of its seventeen curatorial departments boast collections that number among the finest anywhere in their individual fields. In 1870 the Metropolitan obtained its state charter. Among American art museums, only Boston's Museum of Fine Arts and Washington's *Corcoran Gallery of Art, both founded the same year, equal its age. In 1872 works of art went on display in temporary quarters. Eight years later, a museum building opened at the museum's present location in Central Park. Designed by Calvert Vaux and Jacob Wrey Mould in the fashionable Victorian polychrome Gothic style, the brick structure soon proved too small for the museum's ambitions and was swallowed by the central portion of today's building. Designed in 1895 by Richard Morris Hunt, this opulent Beaux-Arts edifice provided the museum with an imposing Fifth Avenue facade and stately entrance hall. Within a few years of its completion in 1902, McKim, Mead and White began to extend the museum's neoclassical grandeur to the north and south, completing the present appearance along Fifth Avenue in 1926. As the museum again sought more space, in 1971 Kevin Roche completed a master plan, fulfilled twenty years later, for alterations to the west side of the building, facing the park, and also burrowing below ground.

By the late 1880s, the Metropolitan already possessed the country's finest collection, consisting mostly of old master paintings. However, two important paintings by Manet (the first of his works to enter any museum), a trove of Cypriot antiquities, and a sizable group of Chinese ceramics signaled the museum's all-inclusive intentions. As president of the museum between 1904 and his death in 1913, John Pierpont *Morgan raised the museum's ambitions to new heights. Caring little for the moralistic idealism of the museum's founders, he determined to acquire in quantity the finest art that money could buy. He filled the board with acquaintances who could assist in that quest and, to implement his vision, professionalized the staff by hiring stellar and experienced museum men (and a lone woman, Gisela Richter [1882–1972], whose distinguished career in the department of Greek and Roman art extended from 1906 until 1948). After Morgan's death, much of his personal collection, more than six thousand objects, came to the museum. The 1929 *Havemeyer bequest of nearly two thousand items numbered among several large gifts that substantially enriched the museum in subsequent years.

In the early twentieth century, the Metropolitan led the way among museums in attending to American art, particularly from the colonial and federal periods. In 1924 it inaugurated an American wing that featured period settings. In a related attempt to contextualize the art it shows, in 1938 the museum opened a separate medieval outpost, the Cloisters. Its architectural fabric was assembled from fragments acquired in France by George Gray *Barnard and purchased from him for the museum by John D. *Rockefeller Jr., who also donated the site above the Hudson River in upper Manhattan and provided an endowment for enrichment and upkeep. The Cloisters numbered among few major enhancements during the 1930s and 1940s, when the Depression and World War II slowed museum activities. Spectacular growth followed, along with new forms of public outreach. Although not alone in this pursuit, the Metropolitan played a leading role in democratizing the image of American museums by attracting large numbers of nonscholarly visitors. During his tenure as director from 1967 to 1977, New York-born, Princeton University–educated Thomas Hoving (1931–) particularly encouraged populist innovations. During these years, the so-called blockbuster exhibition entered museum practice, and the Metropolitan's character took on aspects of leisure-industry entertainment, with a distinctly commercial aspect. Still, many of the special exhibitions proved rich in scholarly content. Moreover, during Hoving's administration the museum doubled its space, abandoned its previous conservatism with respect to the twentieth century by instituting an aggressive acquisition program in contemporary art, and dramatically expanded its other holdings, especially in the areas of East Asian and tribal or "primitive" art. At Hoving's departure, the reins passed to Philippe de Montebello (1936–). Born in Paris, Philippe Lannes de Montebello graduated from Harvard University in 1958 and received a master's degree from New York University's Institute of Fine Arts in 1963. He served as the director of the Museum of Fine Arts in Houston from 1969 to 1974, but otherwise held positions at the Metropolitan until his retirement. A steady hand during sometimes turbulent times, he maintained the museum's balance and burnished its reputation while continuing incremental expansion of the museum's holdings and enhancement of its capacious quarters.

Metzker, Ray K. (1931–). Photographer. Known especially for the innovative practice of printing intricate compositions from multiple negatives, usually sections of contact sheets, he has also combined partially overlapping images and on occasion, has started with double exposures made in the camera. His composites stress formal values, but through repetition and variation they also enlarge the individual images' significance. His single-negative images are often somewhat more complex than those he chooses to combine, but they too demonstrate his interest in black-and-white form as a vehicle for exploring relationships across time and space. Born in Milwaukee, Metzker graduated in 1953 from Beloit (Wisconsin) College. In 1959 he earned a master's degree from the Institute of Design (now part of the Illinois Institute of Technology), where he worked with Harry *Callahan and Aaron *Siskind. During this period he photographed the streets of downtown Chicago. He taught at the Philadelphia College of Art (now University of the Arts) from 1962 until 1981, when he returned for several years to Chicago. In the 1960s he began printing sizable contact sheets, creating image grids that at first glance resemble abstract patterns of light and dark. A closer look reveals small-scale human activity. These complex and fluid works emphasize transparency, simultaneity, and the poetry of everyday experience. In the 1980s Metzker began a landscape series of single frame prints, usually selected from intimate, undramatic corners of nature. In these he often exploited the camera's capacity to register selective focus, so that sharply defined elements contrast with vaguer forms. Although he had sometimes used this technique as early as the late 1950s, in the landscapes he achieved shimmering equivalents of nature's unity. A Philadelphia resident, he spends part of each year in Moab, Utah.

Meyer, Felicia (1913–74). *See* MARSH, REGINALD.

Meyerowitz, Joel (1938–). Photographer and filmmaker. An early proponent of color in art photography, he is known for atmospheric views combining finely detailed naturalism with classical formal construction. A lifelong New Yorker, in 1959 Meyerowitz received a BFA from Ohio State University in Columbus. While subsequently working in advertising design, he was inspired by a chance meeting with Robert *Frank in 1962 to take up photography. By the late 1960s he had made a reputation as a black-and-white street photographer. His distinctive style emerged in 1976 as he worked in color with an 8 × 10-inch camera and long exposures to capture evanescent effects of light and color around his Cape Cod summer home in *Provincetown. A selection of images from that summer and the next appeared as *Cape Light* (1978). Reflecting the photographer's admiration for Edward *Hopper's compositions, these contemplative views usually include evidence of human presence. Any subject can suffice in the construction of a satisfying formal arrangement, and he often includes banalities, ranging from clotheslines to roadside eateries. Interested in conveying the emotional textures of experience through light, space, and hue, Meyerowitz also intensifies the process of vision itself. For *St. Louis and the Arch* (1980), he examined the gleaming Eero Saarinen structure from numerous perspectives. Modifications in scale, weather, and context vary perceptions of the arch, its mathematical perfection, its contrast with urban disorder, and its symbolic possibilities. The only photographer granted unimpeded access to Ground Zero, almost immediately after 9/11 Meyerowitz began photographing at the World Trade Center site, accumulating an archive of several thousand photographs. A series of these appears in *Aftermath* (2006). Meyerowitz's other books include *Wild Flowers* (1983), *A Summer's Day* (1987), *Bay/Sky* (1993), and *George Balanchine's "The Nutcracker"* (1999). He also made a prize-winning documentary film, *Pop* (1998), which chronicles a drive to Florida with his son and his ailing eighty-seven-year-old father.

Michals, Duane (1932–). Photographer. Suggesting frames from black-and-white films, his innovative serial fictions allude to the passage of time through enigmatic, symbolic action. Personal, evocative, even metaphysical, his unconventional format enlarged photography's expressive range in the 1970s. Born in McKeesport, not far from Pittsburgh, he studied art education at the University of Denver. Following graduation in 1953, he served in the U.S. Army for two years before settling in New York. There he studied for a year at the Parsons School of Design (now Parsons, the New School for Design) and began commercial work in photography. Eugène Atget's views of Paris inspired Michals's 1964 New York photographs in the same spirit. *Sequences* (1970) introduced his early staged work, inspired in part by Balthus's erotically charged, mysterious paintings. Later he wrote or painted on photographs or joined them with drawings. Many other works present witty parodies or engage a playful *conceptualism, combining punning titles with quirky images. On occasion, he works quite straightforwardly, as in an early-twenty-first-century project comparing everyday lives of German families with their Kurdish guest-worker counterparts. He has published numerous selections of images, usually accompanied by texts, in extended essays such as *Take One and See Mount Fujiyama* (1976), *The Nature of Desire* (1986), *Eros and Thanatos* (1993), and *Questions without Answers* (2001).

Michel, Sally. *See* AVERY, MILTON.

Mignot, Louis Rémy (1831–70). Painter. A versatile landscapist, he is particularly remembered for winter scenes and for views of the South American tropics. Born in Charleston, South Carolina, he went abroad while still in his teens, probably late in 1848. In 1849 he began his training in The Hague, where he remained for about five years. While studying with landscape painter Andreas Schelfhout, he developed technical facility and understanding of Dutch landscape traditions, including winter views. Upon his return to the United States, he settled in New York and found success with scenes in keeping with the prevailing *Hudson River School aesthetic. In 1857 he accompanied Frederic *Church on an ambitious four-month expedition to Ecuador. They traveled from the lowland rain forest into the interior to view the snow-capped Andes. Like Church's South American prospects, Mignot's similarly exotic views combine closely studied detail, vast spaces, and resplendent light. After visiting Niagara Falls to prepare studies for a large painting, in 1862 Mignot departed for England. There he found a ready market for his views of North and South American locales, as well as British and Alpine scenes. During the years he resided in London, he traveled on a number of occasions to the Continent and was in Paris when the Franco-Prussian war broke out. Shortly after fleeing to England, he died of smallpox at Brighton.

Miller, Alfred Jacob (1810–74). Painter. Known chiefly for early scenes of the West, he also painted portraits, historical narratives, and occasional *genre subjects. Born in Baltimore, he probably studied for a time with Thomas *Sully in Philadelphia before leaving in 1833 for Europe. There he studied at the École des Beaux-Arts in Paris, admired the work of Eugène Delacroix, and traveled through Italy to Rome. When he returned to Baltimore late in 1834, he wished to become a history painter, but found himself, as most artists with such ambitions then did, for the most part restricted to portraits. Two years later, he relocated to New Orleans, where he met Captain William Drummond Stewart, a wandering Scottish aristocrat with a taste for big game. At Stewart's invitation, Miller joined an expedition of several months, leaving in May 1837, for what is now Wyoming. On this trip, he became the first American artist to travel along the Oregon Trail, to view the Rocky Mountains, and to record the fur trade. He made about two hundred watercolors of landscape, Indians, settlers, and mountain men. Unlike George *Catlin and Karl *Bodmer, who preceded him into the West by a few years, Miller was less interested in scientific and ethnographic information than in the purely visual spectacle of western life. Although he often romanticized his subjects, at their best Miller's detailed but atmospheric scenes evoke the drama of open spaces, the charm of secluded spots, and the natural interplay between the region and its human inhabitants. Following his return to New Orleans, he created oils based on the watercolors, which he used as source material for the rest of his life. In 1838 he moved back to Baltimore and two years later traveled to Great Britain. There he produced enormous western scenes for Stewart, fulfilled commissions for others in his patron's circle, and visited London. He returned permanently to Baltimore in 1842 to resume his portrait career while also producing additional western scenes, as well as other subjects.

Miller, Dorothy C. *See* CAHILL, HOLGER.

Miller, Kenneth Hayes (1876–1952). Painter and printmaker. The leader of the *Fourteenth Street School, Miller chronicled modern life, particularly the experience of middle-class, urban women. Many of his works picture the shoppers or salesgirls whose consumer-oriented aspirations seemed to exemplify an up-to-the-minute lifestyle. Born in the upstate religious colony of Oneida, Miller moved permanently to New York in 1888. Trained at the New York School of Art (now Parsons, the New School for Design) and the *Art Students League, he augmented his knowledge in the museums of Europe. Although William Merritt *Chase and Kenyon *Cox numbered among his teachers, his early art reflected an attachment to Albert Pinkham *Ryder. He began a lifelong teaching career in 1899 at the New York School of Art. In 1911 he moved to the Art Students League, where he remained an influential instructor for forty years. After exhibiting four dreamy early works in the *Armory Show, Miller strove for a more disciplined approach. From Renaissance paintings, he learned both traditional techniques and an intellectualized method of composition. From Renoir's expansive late nudes, he gleaned an appreciation of the monumentalized female figure. After 1923, when he moved into a studio on Union Square, he specialized in subjects observed in his Fourteenth Street neighborhood. Immobilized within a classically constructed design and psychologically disengaged, the hefty, fashionably attired *Shopper* (Whitney Museum, 1928) pauses outside a millinery store. In such paintings, Miller attempted to reconcile yearning for ideal beauty and appreciation for the modern woman. Although this conjunction of competing interests coexists uneasily, his work found a wide audience in his own time.

Miller, Lee (1907–77). Photographer. Following an early involvement with surrealism, she turned to fashion photography and photojournalism. As a leading World War II correspondent, she numbered among the first to photograph German concentration camps when they were liberated in 1945. A native of Poughkeepsie, New York, Elizabeth Miller initially desired a career in theatrical design and lighting. In pursuit of training, at eighteen she went to Paris for a year. Subsequently she studied at the *Art Students League for three years, while also modeling for top photographers of the day, including Edward *Steichen, who taught her the rudiments of his craft. In 1929 she traveled in Italy before returning to Paris. There she began her serious work in photography, played a leading role in Jean Cocteau's surrealist film *Blood of a Poet*, and became *Man Ray's assistant, model, and lover. Back in New York in 1932, she continued the success she had achieved in the Paris fashion industry with elegantly striking images. After marrying an Egyptian businessman, Aziz Eloui Bey, in 1934, she lived mostly in Cairo but did not abandon her madcap ways. Her photographs of Egyptian landscapes and ancient monuments demonstrate more interest in surrealist poetics than factual documentation. In 1939 she left her husband and moved to England to live with surrealist artist, Picasso biographer, and art collector Roland Penrose, later a central figure in the founding and promotion of London's Institute of Contemporary Art. She again worked as a fashion photographer, but with the onset of German bombing in 1940 began to document the war's effects in England. As an accredited correspondent accompanying Allied troops, she departed for the Continent early in 1944 and remained through 1945 to photograph and write about some of World War II's major events. Present for the liberation of Paris, she then witnessed the fall of Germany and the war's turbulent aftermath in eastern Europe. Somewhat unhinged by the brutalities she witnessed, she subsequently photographed relatively little. After marriage to Penrose in 1947, she participated with her husband in advancing the cause of modern art in England while turning her imaginative spirit to cooking and entertaining at their artistically decorated home, Farley Farm. She died there, in the hamlet of Muddles Green, Chiddingly, East Sussex, near Lewes in southern England.

Miller, Richard. *See* GIVERNY GROUP.

Milles, Carl (1875–1955). Sculptor. His characteristically lithe, elongated figures caught in movement combine classical idealism with modern simplification. Born Carl Wilhelm Andersson in Lagga, near Uppsala, Sweden, he later adapted a family name for his surname. He attended art school in Stockholm before moving in 1897 to Paris, where he worked for a time at the Academy Colarossi and was in contact with Rodin. In 1904 he moved to Munich and then lived in Italy before returning to Stockholm in 1908. There he made his reputation with outdoor sculptures, mostly fountains, for several cities. He also established a studio (today Millesgården, an open-air museum of his work) at Lidingö, an island in Stockholm harbor, where he produced a large number of monumental works. He first visited the United States in 1929. Two years later he accepted an appointment at the Cranbrook Academy of Art in Bloomfield Hills, near Detroit. He taught there until 1945, the year he was naturalized as a United States citizen. From 1951 he spent winters in Rome and summered at Lidingö, where he died. During his American years, he completed numerous sculptures for public spaces, often outdoors. Many of these are fountains, demonstrating his continuing fascination with the interplay between water and sculptural form. Symbolizing the confluence of the Mississippi and Missouri Rivers, *The Meeting of the Waters* (1936–40), an enormous fountain in front of St. Louis's Union Station, exemplifies the idiosyncratic classicism of his mature style, his ability to infuse allegorical statement with imaginative vitality, and his penchant for heroic scale.

Millet, Francis Davis (1846–1912). Painter. Also a writer. Best known for detailed *genre scenes, often set in the historical past, he also painted murals and portraits and designed stained glass windows. As well, he intermittently worked professionally as a journalist, illustrator, and fiction writer. An inveterate traveler, he earned an international reputation and participated actively in the art affairs of Europe as well as the United States. Known informally as Frank, Millet was born in Mattapoisett, Massachusetts, near New Bedford. As a toddler he moved with his family to East Bridgewater, about twenty-five miles south of Boston. He graduated from Harvard in 1869. During the next three years he earned a master's degree there in modern languages and literature, while also working for Boston newspapers and studying lithography. In the fall of 1871 he began two years of study at Antwerp's Royal Academy, where he earned impressive distinctions, and during the following winter he worked in Rome. He had traveled extensively in Europe by the time he returned home in 1875. After working as a journalist at Philadelphia's 1876 Centennial Exhibition, he assisted John *La Farge in painting murals for Boston's Trinity Church. He departed in January 1877 for Paris but soon left to work as a war correspondent and illustrator during the Russo-Turkish conflict of 1877–78. Following another sojourn in Paris and a visit to London, he returned in 1879 to the Boston area. Subsequently he worked in New York for Louis Comfort *Tiffany on decorative projects before heading again for Europe in 1881 to resume his peripatetic ways and varied activities. Three years later he first visited Broadway, Worcestershire, a Cotswold village where he was before long at the hub of an expatriate art colony that included Edwin Austin *Abbey and John Singer *Sargent. However Millet often wintered in New York, where until 1892 he maintained a residence. He never ceased traveling, ranging widely in Europe, North America, North Africa, and eventually, Asia. Between 1892 and about 1908 he completed a number of ambitious mural commissions in the United States. These became his chief interest after about 1900, when he virtually abandoned easel painting. He had recently been appointed director of the American Academy in Rome when he perished at sea in his evening clothes after the *Titanic* sank. Millet's characteristic genre scenes emphasize period decor over dramatic narrative. A close student of fashions and furnishings, he exploited the play of light to highlight picturesque details and unify his scenes, usually interiors. In historical pieces, he depicted early American, British, and classical subjects. Millet published several books and numerous articles, often illustrated with his own drawings. An eleven-week canoe trip down the Danube River in 1891 resulted in *The Danube from the Black Forest to the Black Sea* (1892). *The Capillary Crime and Other Stories* (1892) collects fictional pieces. After organizing artistic aspects of Chicago's 1893 world's fair, where he also painted several murals, he published *Some Artists at the Fair* (1893). He also coauthored, with the exhibition's architectural chief Daniel Burnham, *World's Columbian Exposition* (1894), a chronicle of the spectacle's inception and realization. Following an 1898 sojourn in Manila as a newspaper and magazine correspondent during the Spanish-American War, he published *The Expedition to the Philippines* (1899). As well, in 1887 he issued an English rendition of Tolstoy's *Sebastopol*, taken from a French translation.

Mills, Clark (1810–83). Sculptor. His best-known work, a bronze equestrian statue of Andrew Jackson (modeled 1847–48), demonstrates the conceptual boldness and technical ingenuity that sustain his reputation. As the centerpiece of Lafayette Park in Washington, D.C., facing the White House, it remains among the most prominent monuments in the capital city. Although it was the nation's first equestrian statue, Mills devised a daring and technically challenging pose, with the horse rearing on its hind legs. One of the earliest monumental bronzes cast in the United States, it was unveiled in 1853 to great acclaim for its novel design and dynamic effect, despite its stubby proportions and contrived simulation of movement. After learning the technique from books and experiencing several failures, Mills successfully cast the work himself in a foundry he built. Mills was born in or near Syracuse, New York, orphaned early, and indifferently educated. In 1830 or the following year he settled in Charleston, South Carolina. There he worked as a house plasterer until taking an interest in sculpture around 1835. By the early 1840s he was finding some success with portrait busts, first in plaster and then in local stone. While planning for study in Italy, he visited Washington, D.C. There in 1847, although he had never seen an equestrian statue, he was commissioned to prepare a life-size model for the Jackson memorial. After completing this in Charleston, in 1848 he won the contract for the statue and moved to the nation's capital. Following its successful completion, Mills purchased land just north of Washington, where he erected more substantial studio and foundry facilities. Soon he received a congressional commission for an equestrian *George Washington*, placed in Washington Circle in 1860. Because of his technical expertise, in that year also he was commissioned to cast the deceased Thomas *Crawford's enormous *Statue of Freedom*, placed atop the U.S. Capitol dome in 1863. During the rest of his career, Mills specialized in portrait busts. He died in Washington.

Milmore, Martin (1844–83). Sculptor. Known particularly for Civil War monuments, he also produced straightforwardly realistic portraits and a few ideal subjects. Born in Sligo, Ireland, he arrived with his family in Boston in 1851. He received his earliest instruction in carving from his brother, **Joseph Milmore** (1842–86). After working in Thomas *Ball's studio between 1858 and 1862, he opened his own Boston establishment and remained in that city permanently except for the years from 1870 until 1876, when he worked in Rome. Commissioned in 1867, Milmore's Civil War remembrance in Roxbury, Massachusetts, glorified the common soldier in an over-life-size bronze image. It provided an important model for numerous later sculptures acknowledging the role of ordinary men in the conflict. His more elaborate *Soldiers' and Sailors' Monument* (1877), commissioned in 1874 for the Boston Common, similarly influenced subsequent endeavors to honor the war's sacrifices. A bronze personification of Liberty stands atop a granite column, while realistic images of a sailor and a soldier, as well as supplementary allegorical figures, appear at lower levels. Reliefs depicting aspects of Boston's involvement in the Civil War further enrich the ensemble's meaning. Also born in Sligo, Joseph established a successful stone-cutting business in Boston and sometimes worked alongside his more talented brother. In a notable collaboration, the two produced a monumental granite sphinx to serve as a unique Civil War memorial (1872) for Mount Auburn Cemetery in Cambridge, Massachusetts. After Joseph's demise in Geneva, Switzerland, the family commissioned Daniel Chester *French to create a tribute honoring the brothers' early deaths.

Minimalism. A reductive form of art associated particularly with the late 1960s and 1970s. It emphasized highly simplified, usually geometric form, clear composition, clean execution, and impersonal appearance. Minimal art made use of grids, serial or modular organization, and machined fabrication to reduce or eliminate evidence of the artist's role in producing the work or making decisions about its appearance. Like *pop art, minimalism emerged in reaction to *abstract expressionism's commitments to spontaneous brushwork, psychological authenticity, and philosophical content. With its high regard for aesthetic purity, minimalism concentrated exclusively on physical existence and perceptual experience. Minimalism offered no consistent theoretical framework, and its dimensions, meaning, and origins remain open to interpretation. Constructivist and other early-twentieth-century achievements in geometric abstraction provided precedents. Josef *Albers, Barnett *Newman, Ad *Reinhardt, and Tony *Smith offered more immediately generative examples, as did Ellsworth *Kelly, Kenneth *Noland, and other *hard-edge painters. Frank *Stella's nonrelational stripe paintings of the late 1950s particularly heralded the new sensibility. An emphasis among minimalist artists on the work of art as a physical object encouraged three-dimensional approaches, while aspects of minimalism shared reciprocal relationships with *conceptual art and *process art. The earliest major museum exhibition to define a coherent minimalist viewpoint, "Primary Structures," organized in 1966 by curator Kynaston McShine (1935–) for New York's Jewish Museum, lent its name to an alternative designation for minimal sculpture. A few months later "Systemic Paintings," curated by Lawrence *Alloway at the Solomon R. *Guggenheim Museum, clarified recent painted work. Principal minimalists include Carl *Andre, Dan *Flavin, Donald *Judd, Sol *Lewitt, and Robert *Morris.

Among others who contributed significantly to the minimalist aesthetic, sculptor and painter Ronald Bladen (1918–88) is remembered especially for 1960s grandly scaled, black sculptures defining simple volumes. Born in Vancouver, he trained there and at the California School of Fine Arts (now San Francisco Art Institute). He worked as an abstract expressionist painter until several years after moving permanently to New York in 1957. His sculpture retains a sense of romantic aspiration despite its reductive formalism. Painter and sculptor John McCracken (1934–) remains best known for simple "planks," monolithic, affectless boards that lean against a wall. Like a number of other Californians drawn to minimalist form, he prefers highly finished, immaculate surfaces that contribute ethereal overtones to highly simplified objects. Born in Berkeley, John Harvey McCracken served in the U.S. Navy before studying at Oakland's California College of Arts and Crafts (now California College of the Arts) from 1957 to 1965. The signature planks first appeared the following year. His more varied recent work remains concerned with meticulous execution and impeccable surface. He has lived in New Mexico since the mid-1990s.

Painter Robert Mangold (1937–) made his mark in the mid-1960s with bulky, monochrome relief paintings that reflected minimalist taste for literal, nonallusive work. Within a few years, he had established his more refined signature approach, relying on flatly painted, reduced form, relieved by linear elements dividing the painted surface. Since about 1970 he has frequently employed shaped canvases. Like Brice *Marden and some other painters of their generation, he has sought to preserve abstract expressionism's heroic demeanor while responding to minimalism's reduced expectations. Robert Peter Mangold was born in North Tonawanda, New York, and grew up in nearby Buffalo. He studied at the Cleveland Institute of Art before transferring to Yale University, where he earned BFA and MFA degrees. He subsequently lived in New York until the early 1970s. Since then he has lived in rural environs west of the Hudson River. His wife since 1961, painter and printmaker Sylvia Plimack Mangold (1938–), works in a representational mode, with close attention to the abstract values of her subjects. Born in New York, Sylvia Plimack trained at Cooper Union for three years before enrolling at Yale University, where she received a BFA in 1961.

Fred Sandback (1943–2003), *installation artist, sculptor, and printmaker, achieved a distinctive, nearly evanescent variation on the minimalist aesthetic. Generally working solely with string, wire, or, most frequently, colored yarn, he limned transparent volumes that interpenetrate their environments. Frederick Lane Sandback was born in the New York suburb of Bronxville, moved with his family several times as a child, and was educated at Yale University. After earning a bachelor's degree in philosophy and sculpture in 1966, he received an MFA three years later. By then, he had already established his singular approach. Sandback maintained a home for many years in the southern New Hampshire town of Rindge. He committed suicide in his New York studio. His widow, Amy Baker Sandback, an art historian and curator who specializes in prints and artists' books, serves as director of collection research for the Dia Art Foundation.

Coined in 1971 by critic Robert Pincus-Witten (1935–), the term "postminimalism" refers to a visually richer and more personally inflected offshoot of minimalism, as seen in the work of Eva *Hesse and Richard *Tuttle, among others. This modification first came into view in the "Eccentric Abstraction" show curated by Lucy *Lippard for New York's Fischbach Gallery in 1966.

Misrach, Richard (1949–). Photographer. Best known for large-format color photographs of the American West, since about 1980 he has produced Desert Cantos lamenting ecological desecration. Some specifically indict the military or other human agents for abuse of the land, while others contemplate sky or sand in elegiac, formally *minimalist terms. Born in Los Angeles, Richard Laurence Misrach received a bachelor's degree in psychology from the University of California at Berkeley in 1971. An early interest in street photography soon gave way to landscapes, including magisterial images from Europe and Hawaii. In the

1970s he numbered among pioneers of serious photography in color. The ample scale, luminous hues, and simplified monumentality of his work recall aspects of contemporary painting. In a recent diversion from his usual subjects, he photographed details of well-known art works to illuminate their cultural values. He lives near San Francisco. Misrach has published his work in a number of collections, including *Telegraph 3 A.M.: The Street People of Telegraph Avenue, Berkeley, California* (1974), *Bravo 20: The Bombing of the American West* (1990), *Crimes and Splendors: The Desert Photographs of Richard Misrach* (1996), *The Sky Book* (2000), *Golden Gate* (2001), and *Pictures of Paintings* (2002).

Miss, Mary. *See* LAND ART.

Mitchell, Joan (1926–92). Painter and printmaker. A skillful and passionate abstract painter, from the 1950s onward she resolutely sustained *abstract expressionism's gestural energy in the face of changing taste. Her brilliantly colored, sensuous, and often grandly scaled works feature tangled brushstrokes in variously lyrical, elegiac, stormy, or even desolate moods. The artist's response to the light and colors observed in landscape inspired much of her work. While living in France during most of her career, she remained connected with the living tradition of chromatic expression embodied in the work of such artists as Monet, Matisse, and Hans *Hofmann. Born in Chicago, Mitchell studied at Smith College in Northampton, Massachusetts, for two years before transferring in 1944 to the School of the Art Institute of Chicago. After earning her BFA in 1947, she went to New York with fellow Chicagoan Barnett Lee (known as Barney) Rosset Jr., from 1951 the visionary force behind Grove Press and, later, the *Evergreen Review*. In 1948 she left to work in Paris and the south of France, where she married Rosset. (They separated in 1951 and divorced the following year.) After returning to New York in 1949, she studied art history at Columbia University and New York University before receiving an MFA in 1950 from the Art Institute. During these first years back in New York, she turned away from the representational and then cubist styles she had previously embraced to work toward abstract expressionism. Although affected by the work of Kandinsky, Mondrian, Arshile *Gorky, Philip *Guston, and Jackson *Pollock, she most admired the paintings of her friends Willem de *Kooning and Franz *Kline. Still, Cézanne and van Gogh remained ever close to her heart. By the time of her first one-person New York show in 1952, she had established her fundamental approach featuring exuberant, linear brushwork. Mitchell returned often to France and by the end of the 1950s had effectively become an expatriate. Although she continued to maintain a New York apartment, she did nearly all of her painting in France. From 1955 until 1979 Canadian abstract painter Jean-Paul Riopelle was her companion. In 1967 Mitchell bought a house, soon her year-round residence, northwest of Paris, in Vétheuil. Overlooking the Seine, the two-acre property provided privacy, the visual allure of a garden, and a tangible connection to Monet, who had once lived nearby. Although in declining health during her last years, she continued almost to the end to paint with undiminished power and elegance. She died in a Paris hospital.

Model, Lisette (1901–83). Photographer. Known for images that reveal the psychology of modern social experience by unmasking its pretenses and anxieties, she often captured indignity, aberration, and self-delusion in candid documentary portraits. Born in Vienna and privately educated, Lisette Seybert found in Arnold Schönberg a mentor for her early ambition to become a professional musician. In 1926 she left for Paris to study music. Essentially self-taught as a photographer, she began her camera work in 1933, not long after turning to the study of art in Paris. Her first major project, from the following year, summarizes her central interests and remains among her most admired accomplishments. On the Promenade des Anglais along the beach in Nice, she surreptitiously photographed vacationers of the haute bourgeoisie, capturing in their body language, facial expressions, and clothing a rich commentary on social class and its effects. In 1937 she married Russian-born painter Evsa (or Yevsa) Model. When they settled permanently in New York the following year, she turned her sardonic camera on local street life. She worked for *Harper's Bazaar* and other magazines in the 1940s and taught at the New School for Social Research (now New School) from 1951 until her death. Her students included many accomplished photographers of the next generation, most notably Diane *Arbus, who extended Model's sensibility to new levels of intensity.

Modotti, Tina (1896–1942). Photographer. As she learned the craft of photography under the guidance of her lover Edward *Weston, she often made images that resemble his in their simplicity and formal elegance. However, her interests in people and politics ultimately led her to subjects that have no counterpart among his. Born in Udine, Italy, Assunta

Adelaide Luigia Modotti arrived in the United States at sixteen and soon joined relatives in San Francisco. In 1917, with her new husband, poet and painter Robaix de l'Abrie "Robo" Richey, she moved to Los Angeles, where they became acquainted with local artists and intellectuals, including Weston. Her great beauty soon led to small Hollywood movie roles. In 1922, while they were visiting Mexico, her husband died of smallpox. The following year, Modotti settled in Mexico City with Weston. When he left Mexico for good in 1926, Modotti stayed behind. They continued to correspond but never saw each other again. Modotti's early photographic work includes many carefully composed studies of ordinary objects, usually bathed in natural light. Before long, however, she began to see her camera as a tool of revolutionary purpose, examining the lives of ordinary people, especially women and children. In 1927 she joined the Mexican communist party and three years later was expelled from the country for political reasons. That event effectively ended her photographic career. Returning to Europe, she did humanitarian work and participated in leftist political operations in several countries, most notably Spain during its Civil War. In 1939 she returned to Mexico. She died in Mexico City.

Moholy-Nagy, László (1895–1946). Photographer, painter, sculptor, filmmaker, and designer. A pioneer in the uses of abstract forms and modern materials, he also numbered among the most important art teachers of the twentieth century. His crisp, unsentimental work, with its logical approach to problem solving, reflects a utopian reach for a fully modern form of visualization. Moholy-Nagy repudiated a spiritual dimension in art, rejected the traditional fine arts as outmoded forms of personal indulgence, and believed that art should contribute to improving society. Born László Weisz in the southern Hungarian village of Bácsborsod, he adopted the surname Nagy from an uncle while living with him in Szeged during his teenage years. Later, apparently wishing to make his name more distinctive, he hyphenated it with the name of a village, Mohol, where he had lived for a time as a child. In 1913 he enrolled in law school in Budapest but interrupted his studies to serve in the Austro-Hungarian army from 1915 to 1918. As an artist, he remained almost completely self-taught. He worked in Vienna before moving on in 1920 to Berlin, where he came into contact with dadaist and, more importantly, constructivist artists. By the early 1920s he was producing abstract paintings, collages, photomontages, and innovative photograms (cameraless photographs made by placing objects directly on light-sensitive paper). From 1923 until 1928 Moholy-Nagy taught at the Bauhaus in Weimar and then in Dessau. There he was responsible for the metal workshop and taught the basic course that exposed all students to fundamental design principles. Subsequently in Berlin until 1934, he turned principally to stage design and filmmaking. After a brief period in Amsterdam followed by two years in London, he moved in 1937 to Chicago to head the New Bauhaus. When it closed after a year, he opened his own school, which became the Institute of Design (since 1949 part of the Illinois Institute of Technology). Naturalized as an American citizen, he taught until his death in Chicago.

Moholy-Nagy's fascination with light and with vision, the means of perceiving light, provides a unifying theme for his varied work in numerous media and gives emotional resonance to what might otherwise seem cold or didactic. Much of his art draws attention to light itself or to its effects, such as transparency, as can be seen in his abstract sculptures made of plastic. Many works manifest his conscious intention to subvert habits of visual perception. His photographs and graphic designs consistently employ unexpected points of view, unforeseen juxtapositions, or disorienting abstractions. Moholy-Nagy put forth a dynamic view of the transformative powers of photography in *Painting Photography Film* (1969; originally published as *Malerei Fotografie Film* in 1925). *The New Vision: From Material to Architecture* (1932; originally published as *Von Material zu Architektur* in 1929) explained the fundamentals of his artistic vision, as promulgated at the Bauhaus. He amplified his views in the posthumously published *Vision in Motion* (1947). In 1921 he married Czechoslovakian photographer and writer Lucia Schulz, who collaborated on many of his early experimental works before they separated in 1929. As Lucia Moholy, she worked in England after their divorce. **Sibyl Moholy-Nagy** (1903–71), born Sibyl Pietzsch in Dresden, married Moholy-Nagy in 1932. A writer and architectural historian, she extended her husband's intellectual legacy after his death.

Monster Roster. *See* CHICAGO IMAGISM.

Moore, Charles Herbert (1840–1930). Painter and printmaker. Also an architectural historian, educator, and museum administrator. Associated with *Pre-Raphaelitism, he produced highly detailed landscapes and nature studies. A sensitive and exacting draftsman, he often worked in watercolor and also made etchings. Born in New York, as a young teenager he took drawing lessons but remained otherwise mostly self-taught as an artist. Exhibiting professionally before he was twenty, Moore was attracted by the writings of English art critic and historian John Ruskin, who promoted truth to nature as an aesthetic standard. In 1863 he numbered among the small coterie that founded the *Association for the Advancement of Truth in Art to foster Pre-Raphaelite ideas. He moved to the Hudson River Valley village of Catskill in 1865. In 1871, his career as a practicing artist more or less came to a close when he secured a position teaching drawing and watercolor painting at Harvard's Lawrence Scientific School in Cambridge, Massachusetts. At the invitation of Charles Eliot *Norton, whom he had known since the mid-1860s, he joined Harvard University's new fine arts department three years later. Together they pioneered in integrating the study of fine arts into the liberal arts curriculum. Additionally, in 1895 Moore was appointed curator at Harvard's Fogg Art Museum and the following year became director, a position he held until retirement in 1909. Granted a leave to prepare for his teaching assignment, in 1876 Moore left for two years in Europe, where he traveled in Italy with Ruskin. His 1877 watercolor *Venetian Doorway* (Fogg Art Museum, Harvard University, Cambridge, Massachusetts, 1877), later a gift to Norton, replicates in characteristically microscopic detail an architectural feature of a sort that attracted Ruskin's interest. On a second sojourn abroad, in 1885, he explored France, and when he left Harvard he settled in England. He died there, in Hartley Wintney, Hampshire. In addition to other books and articles on varied topics, in his scholarly specialty he published *The Development and Character of Gothic Architecture* (1890), *The Character of Renaissance Architecture* (1905), and *The Mediaeval Church Architecture of England* (1912).

Moran, Thomas (1837–1926). Painter and printmaker. Best known for grandiose vistas of the American West, he also painted other landscapes, literary themes, marines, and Venetian scenes. An accomplished watercolorist, he produced etchings and lithographs as well. Although his western views celebrate a landscape of untouched majesty, modernization had already intruded on the region in Moran's heyday. In fact, although he visited a number of inaccessibly remote locations, he usually took the train at least part of the way to the seemingly isolated areas he depicted. Moreover, throughout his career as an interpreter of distinctive and spectacular natural phenomena, Moran benefited from the patronage and support of railroad companies, which recognized the utility of his romantic images in promoting tourism. Born in Bolton, Lancashire, as a child Moran settled with his family in Philadelphia. He worked as a teenager in a wood-engraving shop before turning to painting with the assistance and encouragement of James *Hamilton and other local artists. His early landscapes reflect *Hudson River School and *Pre-Raphaelite precedents. In 1861 he departed for a year in England, where he sketched in the country and studied at first hand the paintings of J. M. W. Turner, whose atmospheric and dramatic effects soon enlivened Moran's work. In 1866 he ventured again to Europe. During a year abroad, he resided chiefly in Paris, made the acquaintance of Jean-Baptiste-Camille Corot, and traveled through Italy to Rome. Upon his return, he signaled his ambitions by adapting Turner's surging forms and mysterious atmospheres to an authentically American myth in a sequence of three paintings (not finished for ten years) based on Longfellow's *Song of Hiawatha*. From a visit to Lake Superior in 1860, he knew something of the region, but his narratives take place in a realm of powerfully visualized fantasy. In 1871 Moran's technical mastery, romantic temperament, and sharp eye for particulars fused in his response to Yellowstone's bizarre and majestic scenery. That summer, he and photographer William *Jackson accompanied Ferdinand Hayden's survey expedition to the region. During sixteen days there he made hundreds of watercolor sketches of the marvels that he and Jackson customarily explored together. Largely on the basis of Moran's watercolors and Jackson's photographs, Congress was persuaded to set aside the area as the nation's first national park in 1872. Not long after his return from California, Moran moved from Philadelphia to the New York area. (Until 1881 he made his home in Newark, New Jersey.) There he soon completed a 7 × 12-foot view of the *Grand Canyon of the Yellowstone* (Smithsonian American Art Museum, on loan from the U.S. Department of the Interior, 1872), which Congress quickly purchased for the substantial sum of $10,000 to adorn the Capitol. As is generally the case with Moran's landscapes, the view down the canyon assembles carefully observed features into an essentially fictional epic intended to convey the locale's spirit and impact. Moran traveled to Yosemite in 1872 and the following year, to the Grand Canyon with John Wesley Powell's survey group. Soon he produced an equally large pendant canvas, *Chasm of the Colorado* (Smithsonian American Art Museum, on loan from the U.S. Department of the Interior,

1873–74), which Congress also purchased. In contrast to the Yellowstone painting, which acknowledges traditional landscape formulas in its spatial construction and inclusion of two tiny witnesses, *Chasm of the Colorado*, devoid of human presence, combines forbidding rock formations and seething atmospheric effects into a grandiose but startlingly alien vision. Geology and climate seem almost equally insubstantial, suggesting a realm of flux and endless creation. Subsequently, Moran rarely created such otherworldly effects, but he continued to interpret topography and atmosphere as equal partners in his scenic dramas. Moran continued throughout his life to travel widely and frequently. Besides journeying to Europe on several later occasions, he toured the West repeatedly until the year before this death, interpreting its stupendous sights in large and small canvases, watercolors, prints, and magazine illustrations. However, other subjects also interested him. He depicted Florida and Mexico, as well as many sites in Great Britain. Based on sketches from 1886 and 1890, he produced numerous shimmering evocations of Venice, a subject congenial to his interests in atmosphere and light. Following previous visits to East Hampton, near the eastern end of Long Island, in 1884 he built a summer home. There he painted many seascapes but also produced views of the area's unprepossessing marshes and gentle farmland. He continued annual stays there until 1922. In 1916 he began spending winters in Southern California, and during his last four years he lived year round in Santa Barbara, where he died.

Together with his wife **Mary Nimmo Moran** (1842–99), the artist played a leading role in popularizing printmaking during the *etching revival that peaked in the 1880s. Primarily a landscapist, Mary Moran also painted but after 1879 specialized in printmaking, quickly becoming the country's most prominent woman etcher. Born in Strathaven, Lanarkshire, Scotland, she settled with her family in the Philadelphia area in 1847 and married early in 1863. A characteristic etching, *The Old Homestead* (1880), recalls *Barbizon precedents in its humble subject, focus on nature, vigorous draftsmanship, and strong massing of contrasting tones. She often worked outdoors, directly on the plate. She died of typhoid fever in East Hampton. Moran had three artist-brothers, who shared his birthplace and emigrated along with him to Philadelphia. **Edward Moran** (1829–1901), a painter and printmaker, studied with Hamilton and eventually became a leading marine specialist, although he also painted landscapes, *genre scenes, and other subjects. In 1861 he accompanied Thomas to London, where he, too, admired Turner's work and the local countryside before his return home that fall. His early marines demonstrate his regard for the English artist's romantic, lashing seas, but he never relinquished precise drawing to follow Turner's lead in dissolving form into color. After he moved permanently to New York in 1872, Edward Moran's marines became quieter and more contemplative, suggesting an interest in contemporary *luminism. In 1877 he departed for France, where his attention turned to Barbizon painting during a sojourn of about a year and a half. In the 1890s he added historical marines to his repertoire of watery scenes. **Annette Parmentier Moran** (1835–1904), whom he married in 1869, painted landscape and figure subjects. A second brother, painter and etcher **Peter Moran** (1841–1914), who remained in Philadelphia throughout his career, received his principal instruction in painting from his older brothers. He visited England in 1863, took up etching in the 1870s, and became one of Philadelphia's most prominent printmakers. He also tried his hand at theater design. In his art, he specialized in animals, farm scenes, and ethnographic studies of the Indians of the Southwest, but on occasion also rendered trompe l'oeils and other subjects. His wife, Dublin-born painter and etcher **Emily Kelley Moran** (c. 1850–1900), whom he married in 1867, favored Barbizon-inflected landscapes. Another brother, photographer **John Moran** (1831–1903), pioneered during the 1860s in promoting photography as a fine art. His best-known works, mostly from the 1860s, are quiet, finely composed, and sharply detailed views of Philadelphia architecture and the nearby countryside. In 1871 he served as photographer for a government expedition to Panama, where he recorded the tropical landscape. In 1874 he went to the South Seas with a scientific mission to photograph a rare astronomical event known as the transit of Venus. He also painted. Born in Philadelphia, **Paul Nimmo Moran** (1864–1907), son of Thomas and Mary, learned painting from his father before studying in Paris. Primarily a portrait and landscape painter, he lived in Los Angeles for about a decade before his death there. Edward's Philadelphia-born sons, **Edward Percy Moran** (1862–1935) and **John Leon Moran** (1864–1941), commonly known as Leon, followed the familiar family career path as painter-etchers. The older worked at the *Pennsylvania Academy of the Fine Arts, and both studied at the *National Academy of Design and in London and Paris before settling in New York. Both brothers painted landscapes but remained better known for figurative narratives and genre scenes. Edward Percy specialized in colonial and other historical themes but also painted portraits. He died in New York. In later life, Leon lived in the suburb of Plainfield, New Jersey. He died in nearby Watchung.

Morgan, Barbara (1900–1992). Photographer. Known especially for images of dancers, she often employed complex methods of shooting and printing. Yet, she remained less interested in clever compositions than in human experience or psychology. She also made light drawings, photographs of children, and close-ups, most often of nature subjects. Born in the southeastern Kansas town of Buffalo, Barbara Brooks grew up in Southern California. She graduated in 1923 from UCLA, with a major in art. She continued painting after marriage two years later to photographer **Willard Detering Morgan** (1900–1967), later the first photo editor for *Life* magazine and an author of books on photographic technique. Moving in 1930 to New York, they made their home in suburban Westchester county, and she turned seriously to photography about five years later. To evoke the vital rhythms of city life, she often combined negatives into composites, or photomontages. Although this technique had been popular among serious European photographers since the early 1920s, it hardly interested Americans of the period. For "In Spring on Madison" (1938), she superimposed two oversized flower silhouettes on a profile of dancer Erick Hawkins, then overlaid this double image on a picture of New Yorkers trudging through late winter snow and slush. Hawkins was then a member of Martha Graham's troupe, the focus of Morgan's dance work, although she also photographed many others. Particularly between 1935 and 1941, she worked closely with Graham on a long series of unsurpassed studies. Morgan sometimes combined and superimposed dance images to suggest action, but she also developed the capacity to freeze essential transitional moments to imply movement. Her best-known dance image, from 1940, pictures Graham bending forward so that her body is horizontal as her floor-length skirt swings momentarily into an arc over her back. Morgan collected the Graham photographs in *Martha Graham: Sixteen Dances in Photographs* (1941), a landmark in establishing both their reputations. She also published *Summer's Children: A Photographer's Cycle of Life at Camp* (1951) and *Barbara Morgan: Monograph* (1972). She died in a hospital in North Tarrytown, not far from suburban Scarsdale, her home of more than fifty years.

Morgan, John Pierpont (1837–1913). Art collector. Also a book collector, financier, industrialist, and philanthropist. While dominating Wall Street for many years, he amassed the largest and most formidable private art collection of his time, perhaps of any time. Of superb quality throughout, it encompassed Western fine and decorative arts from ancient times through the eighteenth century, as well as Asian porcelains. This collection greatly enriched the *Metropolitan Museum of Art, while the Wadsworth Atheneum in Hartford, Connecticut, also received a major donation. New York's Morgan Library and Museum, a scholarly research institution and gallery much enlarged since his death, houses his books, manuscripts, works of art on paper, and medieval objects, as well as some paintings and sculpture. Born in Hartford, Morgan attended Boston's English High School before his family moved to London in 1854, and he was then sent for a year to a private school in Switzerland. He spent the following two years at Göttingen University in Germany. In 1857 the cosmopolitan young man returned to New York to work in investment banking and soon established a powerful presence in international finance. Later he was instrumental in reorganizing American railroads and central to the formation of several dominant corporations, including United States Steel, General Electric, and International Harvester. Drawn to beautiful things since childhood, he turned to serious collecting of books and manuscripts during the 1890s. Between 1902 and 1906 Morgan built as a repository and personal office the Renaissance-style Library designed by architect Charles Follen McKim. During the same years he began to purchase works of art on a grand scale, aggressively seeking the most desirable items available rather than pursuing a representative or encyclopedic strategy. Relying on the advice of experts, as he had earlier with books, he sometimes bought entire collections previously amassed with painstaking scholarship. Although he remained undecided about the precise disposition of his holdings, he intended to donate at least a substantial portion of his staggering compendium to the Metropolitan Museum, which he had supported with increasing largesse from 1871, as a donor of both funds and art, as a trustee, and, from 1904 until his death, as president. After Morgan died on a visit to Rome, his son and heir sold about half the art, while the Metropolitan received the bulk of what remained. In 1924 he endowed the Library as a public institution in memory of his father. Although touching as well on other interests, the Library focuses on the West's literary, artistic, and musical heritage, with particular emphasis on the medieval and Renaissance periods.

Morgan, Patrick. *See* STELLA, FRANK.

Morris, George L. K. (1905–75). Painter and critic. A devoted admirer of abstract art, he fostered its development over a period of several decades. Born in New York, George Lovett Kingsland Morris graduated from Yale University in 1928. He then studied at the *Art Students League with John *Sloan, Kenneth Hayes *Miller, and Jan *Matulka and under Fernand Léger and Amédée Ozenfant at the Académie Moderne in Paris. There he also met a number of leading European abstract artists, including Mondrian and Arp. By the mid-1930s Morris had developed an eclectic, nonrepresentational approach indebted to a wide range of European modernists. He assisted in formation of the *American Abstract Artists organization, often represented the group as its informal spokesman, and served as president between 1948 and 1950. Extending his advocacy of modern art into print, between 1937 and 1939 he served as an editor of the multilingual *Plastique*, which he had helped to found. From 1937 to 1943 he was a contributing editor for *Partisan Review*, which he also supported financially and where his art criticism frequently appeared. Reflecting his admiration for the many varieties of modernism exemplified by the School of Paris, Morris's art echoes at different times nearly all the modern masters. Yet, his interpretation, emphasizing order, clarity, and pure form, is never entirely derivative. His strongest work, completed for the most part in the late 1930s and early 1940s, depends on cubist structure, usually realized in hard-edge, unmodulated shapes, which are dynamically organized, often swirling around a central element. Although representational motifs occurred occasionally in this period, in the 1950s and 1960s they appeared regularly. *Santo Spirito* (Smithsonian American Art Museum, 1951–55), suggests a church interior by picturing within intersecting cubist planes certain architectural features, including a stained glass window, vaulting, and a patterned floor, as well as candles and the statue of an angel. Over a period of twenty years late in his career, Morris produced a number of paintings consisting of small, uncomplicated geometric shapes arranged in whirling patterns and producing effects that presage *op art, as in *Recessional* (Honolulu Academy of Arts, 1950). Morris also occasionally tried his hand at sculpture and collage. He died in an automobile accident near Stockbridge, Massachusetts.

In 1935 he married Suzy Frelinghuysen (1911–88), whose accomplishments as a painter and collage artist belied her lack of professional training. Born in Newark, New Jersey, Estelle Condit Frelinghuysen received painting as well as music lessons during her childhood in Elberon and Princeton. Later, following Morris's example, she painted in a cubist style. Although these works tend to be more directly derivative of Synthetic cubism than his, they are also more personal, wittier, less intellectualized, and more ingratiating. She exhibited with the *American Abstract Artists from 1938 until two years before her death. Throughout her career, she also painted in a realistic style, although she did not exhibit this work. Even more attracted to music than to art, as Suzy Morris she debuted at the New York City Opera in 1947 and performed there during several subsequent seasons. She died in Pittsfield, Massachusetts. Together, during 1944–45 in Lenox, Massachusetts, the couple decorated an International Style home Morris had helped to design. Their abstract frescoes contributed to the comfortable but strikingly modern elegance of the home's ambience, enhanced by their distinguished collection of European and American abstract art. Adjacent to Tanglewood, the residence is now a museum seasonally open to the public.

Morris, Robert (1931–). Sculptor, painter, printmaker, experimental artist, and writer. A protean innovator of the 1960s, he ranks as a central contributor to *minimalism but also broke new ground related to *conceptual art, *process art, *performance art, *installation art, and *earth art. His theoretical and critical writings rank among the most provocative and influential of the 1960s and early 1970s. If any factor unified his work during these polymorphous decades, it was a focus on questions related to viewers' perceptions, rather than on works of art as objects. Born in Kansas City, Morris took classes for two years at colleges and art schools there before enrolling at the California School of Fine Arts (now San Francisco Art Institute) for a short time. He entered the U.S. Army in 1951. After his discharge the following year, he studied at Reed College in Portland, Oregon. In 1955 he returned to San Francisco, where, for the rest of the decade, he painted in an *abstract expressionist style while also working extensively with dance and theater companies on experimental projects. After moving permanently to New York, he continued this involvement as a choreographer, designer, and performer, primarily with the avant-garde Judson Dance Theater. A few years later, he exhibited roughly made performance props as a form of minimalist sculpture. Certain concurrent, enigmatic works suggest

Marcel *Duchamp's intellectual gamesmanship while anticipating aspects of conceptual and process art. *Box with the Sound of Its Own Making* (Seattle Art Museum, 1961), an elegantly crafted wood cube, houses a tape recording playing the banging that went into its construction. In 1966 Morris earned a master's degree in art history from Hunter College, where he has subsequently taught for four decades.

From the mid-1960s into the 1970s, Morris exhibited spare, minimal "unitary objects," usually fabricated from common plywood or industrial materials. At the same time, from the late 1960s he spurred interest in process art with works made from soft materials, particularly felt but also such peculiar substances as industrial threadwaste. In contrast to the uncompromising immutability of the generally rigid, geometric minimal sculptures, these limp, contingent works evoked impermanence, transition, and decay. At the extreme, several works of the late 1960s utilized steam as a medium, leaving photographic documentation as their only trace. A related group of late 1960s "scatter pieces" consisted of materials strewn randomly across the floor of a room. From the mid-1960s, Morris also tried his hand at earthworks and videotaped performance art pieces. In the 1980s he moderated his cerebral approach to art making, turning for a time to large-scale drawing and painting. His expressionistic Firestorm pieces of the mid-1980s featured apocalyptic landscapes set in heavy, molded frames displaying body parts and other intimations of disaster. Other projects since the 1980s have varied from drawings done while blindfolded to polychromed metal sculptures. He maintains a second home in Gardiner, New York, in the Shawangunk Mountains west of the Hudson River. *Continuous Project Altered Daily: The Writings of Robert Morris* (1993) serves as a compendium of his most significant writings, including the four-part "Notes on Sculpture" (1966–67 and 1969), "Anti Form" (1968), "Some Notes on the Phenomenology of Making: The Search for the Motivated" (1970), and "Aligned with Nazca" (1975), which presents his views on earth art. All originally appeared in *Artforum*.

Morse, Samuel F. B. (1791–1872). Painter and photographer. Also an inventor. Although best known today for the telegraph and the Morse code, he devoted nearly thirty years to art before turning almost exclusively to science and technology. He excelled at portraiture but also painted imaginative compositions and landscapes. His best-known works, *Old House of Representatives* (Corcoran Gallery, 1822) and *Grand Gallery of the Louvre* (Terra Foundation for American Art, 1832–33), testify to his ambitions. Arguably his finest and most original artistic achievements, they accommodate the principles of grand manner painting to a democratic audience lacking interest in traditional historical and mythological themes. Indicating with particular clarity Morse's interest in purely pictorial effects, they demonstrate his sophisticated fusion of style and representational description, as well as the problem-solving temperament he brought to his art. Born in Charlestown (now part of Boston), Samuel Finley Breese Morse was educated from the age of eight at Phillips Academy in Andover, Massachusetts, and then at Yale University. The young man started painting miniature portraits before he graduated in 1810. The following year he departed for England in the company of his mentor Washington *Allston. During four years in London he imbibed the tradition-based, academic theories of the day while working with Allston and studying with Benjamin *West at the Royal Academy. He also executed portrait commissions. Finding no market for other subjects after his return, he painted portraits in New England and Charleston, South Carolina. Many of these suggest familiarity with the works of Gilbert *Stuart and Thomas *Sully, as well as his close attention in London to the works of Thomas Lawrence and the Baroque masters. However, Morse continued to aspire to a more exalted form of painting, with which he hoped to appeal to American viewers and elevate their taste. With these aims in mind, he embarked on his documentary *Old House of Representatives*, depicting more than eighty individual congressmen and other political figures. As they gather for a night session, chandeliers cast a luminous glow over Benjamin Henry Latrobe's recently refurbished chamber. Despite its combination of factual reporting, poetic effect, and patriotic sentiment, the painting failed to find a popular audience when it was exhibited in New York and other cities, dashing the painter's hopes for fame and financial security. In 1823 Morse settled in New York and for a few years worked as a leading portraitist. His most important likeness, a full-length official portrait of the *Marquis de Lafayette* (City of New York, 1825–26), captures the mythic stature as well as the appearance of the celebrated Frenchman, who toured the United States on the occasion of the fiftieth anniversary of his support for the American Revolution. Concurrently, during the winter of 1825–26 Morse also spearheaded the *National Academy of Design's organization. He served as its first president until 1845 and again for a year considerably later. In 1829 Morse departed for a three-year sojourn in Europe. Except for relatively brief visits to London at the beginning and end of his trip, he remained on the Continent. Between February 1830 and late summer of the following year, he visited the major centers of Italy. While subsequently based in Paris, he began his imaginative reconstruction of the Louvre's Salon Carré, creating a veritable mini-history of Renaissance and Baroque painting. Like the *Old House of Representatives*, it features painstakingly achieved realistic detail, in this case tiny "portraits" of individual paintings belonging to the museum, although not in fact clustered in the room represented. As was also the case with the earlier masterwork, a unified visual experience of space and light provides the salient impression. In once again appealing to Americans' desire for self-improvement, Morse was disillusioned for a second time when he exhibited the work in New York in 1833. Like Allston, John *Trumbull, and John *Vanderlyn, Morse ultimately failed to transplant the idealistic aims of his European training to the new nation for which they all harbored high expectations.

During his 1832 return voyage to New York, Morse began to conceptualize the telegraph. During the next several years, scientific work gradually crowded out aesthetic interests. Nevertheless, he completed major paintings and in 1834 accepted the responsibilities of an unpaid appointment from the recently founded New York University as the first professor of art in an American college. In 1837 he completed his last ambitious exhibition piece, an idealized, full-length portrait of his teenage daughter Susan Walker Morse (Metropolitan Museum), seated in a richly appointed loggia before lambent clouds. Although the painting has been informally titled *The Muse*, Morse more likely intended the image as a tribute to his profession. Represented in the act of drawing and accompanied by symbolic references to artistic endeavor, his subject remains absorbed in the processes of her own mind, suggesting the painter's exalted view of his calling. While traveling during the winter of 1838–39 to England and France in search of support for his telegraph, in Paris he met the inventor of the brand-new *daguerreotype process. Morse seized enthusiastically upon this early photographic method, was among the first to experiment with it in New York later that year, and within months pioneered in meeting the difficult challenge of producing portraits. During the final three decades of his life, Morse virtually abandoned the practice of art. However, the fame and wealth that had so long eluded him finally arrived after 1844, when he conclusively demonstrated the telegraph's practicality. In 1847 he built a mansion overlooking the Hudson River near Poughkeepsie but continued to maintain also a residence in New York, where he died.

Moses, Grandma (1860–1961). Painter. Untrained as an artist but celebrated in old age for her scenes of rural life, she began painting in her seventies, had her first New York gallery show at the age of eighty, and achieved widespread fame as she approached one hundred. Her affectionate views of old-fashioned ways, filled with engaging anecdotal detail, were widely hailed as authentic memories of a cherished but nearly vanished way of life. Known to most through reproductions, her homespun work found great commercial success in the mid-twentieth-century mass-market economy. Born near the northern New York hamlet of Greenwich, Anna Mary Robertson grew up on a farm and received little formal education. After marrying farmer Thomas Salmon Moses in 1887, she bore ten children (five survived to adulthood) while living on a Staunton, Virginia, farm for nearly two decades. The family then moved to a dairy farm at Eagle Bridge, near the Vermont border not far from her birthplace. Although she had produced embroidered and other decorative items, she did not begin painting in earnest until widowed and hindered by age from farm chores. She continued to paint at her home in Eagle Bridge until a few months before her death when she was hospitalized in nearby Hoosick Falls, where she died. Moses's interest in recording American life paralleled the *American Scene movement popular when she started painting. She also occasionally painted historical subjects, notably Revolutionary War events. Drawing on memories of her long experience in the country, her works at first generally focused on a few figures, but with time she opened up her spaces to encompass wide areas in which numerous people often can be seen attending to varied activities. In the best of these, such as *The McDonell Farm* (Phillips Collection, 1943), deftly designed color and pattern provide structure. Here, the color patches of field crops move the eye through the composition, while green areas establish unifying connections. Interspersed throughout as unmodeled shapes, are five pairs of work horses, a couple of cows, at least eight adults engaged in farm activities, and a cluster of children, along with several farm buildings. In hundreds of similarly charming scenes, she presented an unproblematic version of the country's mythic origins in rural virtues and pleasures. In 1952 she published an autobiography, *My Life's History*.

Moskowitz, Robert. *See* NEW IMAGE PAINTING.

Motherwell, Robert (1915–91). Painter, printmaker, and collage artist. A leading *abstract expressionist, he produced elegant yet powerful works. As the most articulate of the major abstract expressionists, he often was regarded as the movement's spokesman. In his youth, he acquired a rich intellectual foundation, forming the basis of lifelong interests in literature, aesthetic theory, and psychology. A vigorous participant in the formative milieu of abstract expressionism, he served as an important conduit to European culture. His best-known paintings belong to a series of more than 150 works known as the Elegy to the Spanish Republic, begun in 1949 and extended intermittently for many years. These grandly scaled arrangements of simple ovoid shapes and vertical bars in muted hues, mostly black and white, form a dignified and stirring memorial to the fascist defeat of democracy and a tribute to the many heroic deaths incurred in the Spanish Civil War. As the series progressed, it took on more general resonance as a meditation on the interrelation of life and death.

Born in Aberdeen, Washington, Motherwell spent many summers as a youngster along the Pacific shore in that area, although his family no longer lived there year round. They moved to San Francisco when he was three and during his childhood lived for a total of about five years in Salt Lake City and Los Angeles before returning to San Francisco. He began his studies at Los Angeles's Otis Art Institute (now Otis College of Art and Design) in 1926, when he was only eleven. Nevertheless, he did not fully commit himself to working as a full-time artist for another fifteen years. In the interim, although he continued to make art sporadically, he developed a cosmopolitan grasp of related fields of inquiry. In 1932, he entered Stanford University, where he majored in philosophy, but also developed strong interests in French literature and psychoanalytic theory. In 1935 he made his first visit to Europe. In 1937 he began graduate work in philosophy at Harvard University. After spending the 1938–39 academic year in Europe, he joined the art department at the University of Oregon in Eugene as an assistant. Following a final summer on the Aberdeen coast in 1940, he moved to New York to study art history at Columbia University with Meyer *Schapiro. Unexpectedly, by introducing his student to a number of artists, most importantly European surrealists, Schapiro proved instrumental to his choice of career as an artist. Yet, Motherwell never relinquished his scholarly interests, remaining always active as a teacher, writer, and editor.

Already an admirer of Picasso and Matisse, now he met a number of wartime exiles, including Marc Chagall, Fernand Léger, and Mondrian, who enlarged his understanding of European modernism. But it was his acquaintance with surrealists, especially Roberto *Matta and André Masson, that he found most stimulating. Surrealist theory meshed with his interest in psychoanalysis and prompted him in 1941 to follow the inclination he had harbored since his year in Europe, to commit himself to the life of a professional artist. After studying briefly with Kurt *Seligmann, in the summer of 1941 he traveled to Mexico with Matta and stayed on to work with the Austrian-born surrealist Wolfgang Paalen. Back in New York, he soon met William *Baziotes and then other Americans interested in surrealism, including Jackson *Pollock and Willem *de Kooning. In 1942, Motherwell's accomplishments as an artist were sufficiently advanced to win him a spot among a handful of Americans in the "First Papers of Surrealism" exhibition, organized by André Breton and Marcel *Duchamp to showcase European visitors. In 1944 he had his first one-person show in New York, at Peggy *Guggenheim's *Art of This Century. Included in this exhibition, *Pancho Villa, Dead and Alive* (Museum of Modern Art, 1943), a painting with collage elements, brings together the fundamental qualities of his personal style. On the one hand, it demonstrates the controlled composition and sensuous color, pattern, and texture he had observed in the work of Matisse, Picasso, and Mondrian. On the other, its handling of line and paint embraces the freedom of *automatism.

While making progress with his painting, he continued his interests in theory and writing. In 1942, along with Breton, Max *Ernst, Matta, and poet William Carlos Williams, he was a moving force in conceiving an ultimately short-lived new magazine, **VVV*. (Although Motherwell had been named as editor in the prospectus, he appeared only as a contributor, while David *Hare was listed as editor.) In a more lasting contribution to contemporary art, Motherwell agreed in 1944 to act as series editor of the Documents of Modern Art (later titled Documents of Twentieth-Century Art) published by George Wittenborn to make available to American audiences classic texts of European modernism. Mondrian, Kandinsky, and László *Moholy-Nagy numbered among authors selected. Motherwell provided several introductory essays, including one for the first to appear, Guillaume Apollinaire's *The Cubist Painters* (1944). He also selected and introduced the material in a landmark of this series, *The Dada Painters and Poets: An Anthology* (1951), which became an influential standard reference. In addition, Motherwell edited, along with John *Cage, Harold *Rosenberg, and French architect Pierre Chareau, yet another celebrated periodical, *Possibilities* (Winter 1947–48), which appeared in only a single issue, and in partnership with Ad *Reinhardt, he compiled *Modern Artists in America* (1952), also a significant volume from the era.

By the end of the 1940s, Motherwell's art had achieved a power that lifted him to the front ranks of the movement. Combining collage and paint, *The Voyage* (Museum of Modern Art, 1949) combines symbolic references to sun and moon with a measured cadence of irregular black, white, sandy, and golden verticals (a single horizontal green area offers respite at lower right) to imply the space and time of a journey. Its large size (nearly eight feet wide), unerring design, evocative but controlled colors, serious theme, and amplitude of feeling announce the maturity of his art. The title, echoing a poem by Charles Baudelaire, recalls the painter's long-standing fondness for French symbolist literature. Formally and emotionally, the extensive Elegy for the Spanish Republic series that soon followed builds directly on this work. Motherwell often worked on more than one series at a time, or alternated between media and approaches, but distinct groups appeared. Mid-1950s canvases organized around the French words *je t'aime* (I love you) incorporate the text as a calligraphic element within fervent designs. For the Lyric Suite series of 1965, he exploited automatism as a working method, combining it with the accidental effects that occurred as ink or paint absorbed into the Japanese paper he used. These small and delicate works were accomplished very quickly, sometimes in a matter of minutes, but they persuasively record the interaction of artist and material, the effects of time, and the interaction of intent and accident. The Open series, begun in 1967 and continuing for several years, portray three sides of a rectangle, inscribed on large monochrome canvases. His most reductive works, they demonstrate his response to contemporary *color field painting and *minimalism, while at the same time retaining the essentials of his abstract expressionist approach. Concurrently with his painting, Motherwell continued throughout his career to make collages and prints. The poetic, modestly scaled collages, incorporating bits of varied papers and often combined with drawing or painting, address the viewer more intimately than the paintings. As a printmaker working with intaglio processes, as well as lithography, he was more active than any other abstract expressionist, producing more than four hundred images.

From 1958 until 1971 Motherwell was married to Helen *Frankenthaler. In 1972 he married German-born photographer Renate Ponsold. He resided in New York or nearby throughout most of his career. In 1947 he built a Chareau-designed house and studio on eastern Long Island, in East Hampton, where he lived for several years. From 1970 he made his home in Greenwich, Connecticut, a New York suburb. In the mid-1950s he started regularly summering in *Provincetown, where he died. *The Collected Writings of Robert Motherwell*, edited by Stephanie Terenzio, appeared in 1992. His daughter, painter **Jeannie Motherwell** (1953–), frequently also incorporates collage elements in mostly semi-abstract work. Born in New York, she earned a BA in painting from Bard College in 1974 before studying at the *Art Students League. She has summered in Provincetown much of her life and currently lives in Cambridge, Massachusetts.

Motley, Archibald John, Jr. (1891–1981). Painter. He numbered among the first African-Americans to portray blacks as sophisticated, fashionable, and confident urbanites who energetically partake of the city's pleasures. Although his paintings confirm the *Harlem Renaissance's racial pride, the artist remained somewhat aloof from the movement, believing that its emphasis on blacks' distinctive origins in Africa and the rural South encouraged a retrograde mythology. Born in New Orleans, Motley grew up in Chicago and lived there most of his life. He graduated from the School of the Art Institute of Chicago in 1918 but returned the next year to attend a course of lectures given by George *Bellows. His early proficiency is evident in *Mending Socks* (Ackland Art Museum, University of North Carolina at Chapel Hill, 1924), a detailed portrait of his grandmother. In 1928 he was the second African American (only Henry Ossawa *Tanner preceded him) to hold a one-person show at a New York gallery, and the following year he won a Guggenheim fellowship that sent him to Paris for year. During the Depression he found support in the *federal art projects. Depressed after his wife's death in 1945 he painted little until 1953, when he made an extended visit to the Cuernavaca, Mexico, home of a nephew, the novelist Willard Motley. However, he suffered critical neglect when his integrationist beliefs became unpopular in the 1960s and beyond. From the late 1920s, Motley's mature style featured color patterns and simplified surfaces emphasizing light effects, often giving his figures a chic sleekness within vigorous but tightly constructed compositions. In *Black Belt* (Hampton [Virginia] University Museum, 1934), a nighttime frieze of passersby on a city street, multiple light sources define jostling figures. Across the street behind them, a street light and windows illuminate additional sidewalk activity and the advertising signs of a bustling neighborhood. Colors echo around the canvas, anchored by the design's strong verticals and horizontals.

Moulthrop, Reuben (1763–1814). Painter and wax modeler. Remembered for portrait paintings, he was born in East Haven, worked in Connecticut all his life, and died in his native town. His training, if any, remains unknown, and his work displays unevenness in execution and conception. At their best, his portraits offer convincing images, often attentive to his sitters' psychology. Although none of his wax figures is known today, modeling may have been his main occupation. Like Patience *Wright, he put together traveling exhibitions of wax figures from history and contemporary life. In developing his career as a painter, he probably benefited from Winthrop *Chandler's example. In addition, he presumably observed paintings by more thoroughly trained artists who worked in Connecticut, most notably Ralph *Earl, who may have been the source of Moulthrop's knowledge of English prototypes. Moulthrop's earliest known portraits date from the late 1780s. By 1790 he was capable of joining pattern, realistic detail, and appealing likeness into such effective images as the paired portraits of *Job Perit* and *Sarah Stanford Perit* (both Metropolitan Museum). Although Moulthrop's works often betray his lack of training in foreshortening and anatomy, these portraits effectively combine decorative embellishment, nuanced color, and evocation of character. A portrait of the *Reverend Thomas Robbins* (Connecticut Historical Society, Hartford, 1801) exemplifies a more detailed and more carefully modeled style, still linear but closer to standard academic practice. Although the decade separating the works might be taken to indicate artistic development, over time his work seems to have fluctuated widely, if current attributions are correct.

Mount, William Sidney (1807–68). Painter. A leading *genre painter, he also produced many portraits, as well as examples of history painting, still life, and, more rarely, landscape. The first American painter successfully to specialize in genre, Mount created undramatic moments in rural life. Executed in a direct, lucid, and realistic style, his scenes radiate optimism, good humor, and affection for a familiar way of life, although disquieting undertones may sometimes be discerned. He intentionally cultivated a popular response to his art, and in the form of prints many of his works reached a wide audience. Mount spent most of his life on Long Island. He was born at Setauket, about fifty miles from New York, and died there, although from the age of six he grew up in nearby Stony Brook and in New York. In 1824 he went to work in New York for his brother **Henry Smith Mount** (1802–41). A commercial artist who produced signs and ornamental designs, from the late 1820s Henry also exhibited still life, landscape, and genre paintings. In 1826 William enrolled at the *National Academy of Design and soon began to paint portraits and historical subjects. He moved back to the Stony Brook area in 1827, but subsequently resided intermittently in New York. In 1830 he exhibited *Rustic Dance after a Sleigh Ride* (Museum of Fine Arts, Boston, 1830), his first significant genre subject, which drew an enthusiastic response. Depicting dancers and other revelers crowded into a boxlike room, this scene of lighthearted merriment suggests Mount's interest in the work of David Wilkie. Distributed as prints, the Scotsman's anecdotal scenes had already been internationally popular for two decades. Although prior American genre paintings had been few, Mount presumably also knew the work of John Lewis *Krimmel, an earlier admirer of Wilkie. David Claypoole *Johnston's published caricatures probably assisted Mount's understanding of the potential for comedy in mundane activities. As Mount's work matured in the 1830s, he profited from close observation of old master composition and from studies in geometry and perspective. He progressed by degrees toward the structural clarity and rigor that endow his scenes with dignity, stability, and even grandeur. Depicting two men and a horse in a sunlit barnyard, *Bargaining for a Horse* (New-York Historical Society, 1835) at first glance seems disarmingly simple. Yet its visual features are locked into place within a carefully contrived geometric scheme. Moreover, as is the case with some other images, its seemingly unproblematic content may disguise comment on social or political issues of the day, in this case rampant political "horse trading." Whatever his precise intentions, however, Mount never sacrificed his close scrutiny of life and landscape to moralizing, social commentary, or literary allusion. Throughout his career, he remained committed to drawing and to sketching in oil outdoors. In 1861 he even outfitted a wagon as a horse-drawn studio.

Mount's first notable genre scene, the *Rustic Dance*, introduced two recurrent themes, music-making and black engagement in American life. In *Rustic Dance*, a prominently placed African-American violinist numbers among key participants, while two additional black men appear in the crowd. *The Power of Music* (Cleveland Museum of Art, 1847) depicts a middle-aged black workman leaning against a barn wall, beguiled by the music of a white violinist who plays inside for two other men. Perhaps the most humanly realized black person in antebellum painting, he expresses an interior life rare for any of Mount's characters. His apparent sympathy for this black listener reflects Mount's own passion for music. He played the violin and in 1852 patented an improved model that he called the Cradle of Harmony. In other settings, Mount's blacks are sometimes treated with less dignity, as in *Farmers' Nooning* (Long Island Museum of American Art, History and Carriages, Stony Brook, 1836), showing a youngster teasing a snoozing African-American during a midday break from labor. Although the amusing veneer of this painting masks complex and contradictory northern attitudes toward blacks, the sensuous African-American figure is neither caricatured nor maligned. Mount's masterwork, *Eel Spearing at Setauket* (New York State Historical Association, Cooperstown, 1845) includes his most heroically conceived black person, a middle-aged, monumentalized woman, grandly poised to thrust her spear into the water. Behind her in their skiff, a white boy watches. Linked visually at the corners of a compositional triangle, the two figures share a moment of communion, as they float serenely on undisturbed water, described with *luminist precision. Behind them, a soft summer landscape completes the pastoral idyll. As his health declined during the 1860s, Mount painted few works except portraits, although he continued to sketch numerous compositions. However, in 1862–63 he produced his finest pure landscape, the luminous *Long Island Farmhouses* (Metropolitan Museum), depicting bare trees and scattered buildings in delicate spring sunlight. Despite its lack of program, this work too may have implied deeper meaning. Painted during the Civil War, which deeply troubled Mount, its idealized plainness may attest to the democratic realization, in the lives of ordinary citizens, of the nation's cornerstone values.

A third Mount brother, painter **Shepard Alonzo Mount** (1804–68), found success in portraiture. He painted occasional still lifes and genre subjects, as well, and, after an 1847 sketching tour in Pennsylvania, took up landscape painting. Born, like his brothers, in Setauket, he joined them in New York in 1827, after six years as a carriage maker's apprentice in New Haven, Connecticut. The three brothers studied and sketched together, and by the next year, Shepard had followed William to the National Academy. In the early 1830s he mastered a portrait style suggesting close attention to the work of Henry *Inman. Subsequently he readily found clients in New York and on Long Island, where he resided during most of his adulthood. He died in Stony Brook. A sister, **Ruth Hawkins Mount** (1808–88), also a painter, worked primarily in watercolor, often illustrating the sentimental themes popular in mid-century. She married Charles Saltonstall Seabury. Henry's daughter **Evelina Mount** (1837–1920) also painted, particularly floral subjects.

Mowbray, Henry Siddons (1858–1928). Painter. A major figure in the *American Renaissance, he executed numerous classicizing murals for public and private spaces. In easel paintings, he specialized in idealized figural compositions depicting attractive women in situations with historical or exotic, often orientalist, overtones. Their recondite air can suggest affinities with symbolist interests in the unknowable and in female sexual allure. He also painted portraits and worked as a magazine illustrator. Born Henry Siddons to an English couple in Alexandria, Egypt, he was soon orphaned. Adopted by an aunt and her husband, whose surname he then assumed, he was widely known as Harry. He lived in Titusville, Pennsylvania, until 1869, when the family moved to North Adams, Massachusetts. Unhappy at the United States Military Academy at West Point, he returned home within a few months to work in nearby Williamstown with landscape and *genre painter Alfred Cornelius Howland (1838–1909), who had trained in Düsseldorf and Paris. Mowbray departed in the fall of 1878 for the French capital, where he studied with Léon Bonnat and absorbed the principles of French academic painting before gradually establishing himself as an independent painter. In 1885 he settled in New York and for a decade concentrated on the precisely drawn, delicately colored, romantic scenes that had already proved successful in Paris. The decorative sensibility promoted by the *aesthetic movement informed his style, as did the oriental fantasies of Jean-Léon Gérôme and the fictions of contemporary English painters, including Edward Burne-Jones and Lawrence Alma-Tadema. A few years before he first visited Italy in 1896, he had begun painting murals in a decorative French style. Overwhelmed by Pintoricchio's late-fifteenth-century decorative ensembles in the Vatican, he subsequently concentrated on allegorical mural painting based, often quite closely, on Renaissance precedents. His most imposing ornamental schemes include the library of New York's University Club (installed 1904), painted in Rome while Mowbray served from 1902 until 1904 as director of the American Academy, and interior areas of J. P. *Morgan's library (1905–7), also in New York. From 1907 he made his home in Washington, Connecticut, where he died. There he embellished a ceiling in the Gunn Memorial Library (1914). His accomplishments during subsequent, less active years include a series of stylized easel paintings treating the life of Christ with devotional simplicity.

Mullican, Lee (1919–98). Painter and sculptor. Best known for an aberrant, loosely geometric, abstract style derived from sources in surrealism and indigenous art, he continued throughout his life to experiment with varied forms reflecting transcendent philosophies. Born in Chickasha, Oklahoma, he studied at Abilene (Texas) Christian College (now University) and at the University of Oklahoma at Norman before enrolling at the Kansas City Art Institute in 1941. A year later, he was drafted into the U.S. Army to serve as a topographical draftsman in the Corps of Engineers. Following his release in 1946, he moved to San Francisco. There he soon collaborated with Wolfgang Paalen, an Austrian abstract painter and surrealist, and Gordon *Onslow Ford in founding the Dynaton movement. (The name derives from the Greek for "the possible."). Paalen generated the coalition's operative ideas, which he had begun to formulate in the pages of his magazine *Dyn*, an important international avant-garde publication between 1942 and 1944. The movement ambitiously aimed to synthesize surrealism with pre-Columbian styles and current concepts from physics. After the Dynaton movement culminated in a radical 1951 exhibition at the San Francisco Museum of Art (now San Francisco Museum of Modern Art), the founders drifted apart. Although not the driving force of the group, Mullican produced some of the most important art to emanate from it. In 1952 he moved permanently to the Los Angeles area, where he taught at UCLA for nearly thirty years before he retired in 1990. In glowing, vibrating compositions generally constructed from linear striations of paint applied with a knife edge, at mid-century he drew particularly on his understanding of Indian art, especially Navajo weavings and sand paintings, to create elastic patterns denoting spiritual energy. While extending surrealist interests in *automatism and the unconscious, these works also sustain the period's avant-guard concern for preserving the integrity of the flat picture plane. Yet, Mullican's paintings shun the rhetoric of inner revelation prevalent among contemporary *abstract expressionists. While expanding upon early interests, his later work incorporated also a range of stimuli from Eastern religions, tribal and modern art, and other sources. He also produced surrealistically tinged sculptures, often *assemblages suggesting roots in tribal precedents.

Matt Mullican (1951–), painter, sculptor, draftsman, collagist, and performance artist, extends his father's universalizing aspirations into the art of a distinctly different present. Born in Santa Monica, in the mid-1970s he moved to New York after graduating from the California Institute of the Arts in Valencia. Like many of his contemporaries who became known as appropriationists in the 1980s, he often culls imagery directly from the popular culture, although his purpose is not to critique the social construction of meaning. Rather, in enormous, encyclopedic grids of representational and abstract forms, he symbolizes the endless flow in all human experience between the conscious, the unconscious, and the external environment.

Mural painting. Wall painting, generally integral to its architectural setting, particularly in spacious public or institutional venues. Although important examples date throughout the period since the early nineteenth century, two eras dominate the history of its popularity in the United States. Initiated in the late 1870s, the first instance contributed to the *aesthetic movement and the *American Renaissance. It flowered with the decoration of exhibition buildings at Chicago's 1893 World's Columbian Exposition and the new Library of Congress in 1896, as well as construction of numerous state capitol buildings and other civic venues. World War I ended the period as commissions became few and modern styles of art disrupted taste for the allegorical classicism that dominated the practice. A second wave of mural production appeared during the 1930s, as funds for such projects became available through the *federal art projects, while a renewed social consciousness among artists encouraged efforts to reach a broad public. These murals generally portrayed subjects related to the lives of ordinary people, in representational styles often affected by modernist simplification or by precedents in the work of several outstanding Mexican muralists. World War II and yet another wave of modernism curtailed this period. During the 1960s and 1970s, an important if more limited enthusiasm for mural painting appeared, mostly in outdoor locations, to serve political interests, community involvement, and such countercultural themes as opposition to war and racism. Compared to the two earlier mural eras, fewer of the period's best-known artists participated.

Installed between 1826 and 1855, eight large-scale paintings in the U.S. Capitol rotunda rank as the first notable decorative ensemble for a public space. John *Trumbull painted the first four to be installed. These were followed, successively, by contributions from John Gadsby *Chapman, Robert *Weir, John *Vanderlyn, and New York portrait and history painter William Henry Powell (1823–79). Constantino *Brumidi subsequently expanded the Capitol's mural program with numerous decorative elements executed over a period of some twenty-five years. Concurrently, he also led the way in embellishing church interiors. However, mural commissions remained uncommon before the success of John *La Farge's decorative ensemble at Boston's Trinity Church (1876–77). Subsequently, many painters became mural specialists, during at least part of their careers. These included Edwin Austin *Abbey, Edwin *Blashfield, Kenyon *Cox, and Henry Siddons *Mowbray. Among important muralists of the 1930s were Thomas Hart *Benton, Marion *Greenwood, Reginald *Marsh, Anton *Refregier, Boardman *Robinson, and Mitchell *Siporin. Like most, they painted representational imagery, but the period also saw a small number of distinguished abstract murals by such artists as Stuart *Davis and Arshile *Gorky.

Murch, Walter Tandy (1907–67). Painter. A still life specialist, he assembled objects in odd combinations, giving surreal overtones to atmospheric, moody compositions. Although his technique extended the golden patina of old master traditions, Murch's frequent inclusion of machines and other paraphernalia unmistakably of the twentieth century and his interest in purely formal arrangement mark his work as modern. In the 1950s and 1960s, some of his images took on an otherworldly quality, as he concentrated more intensely on the abstract qualities of form and light and sometimes incorporated undecipherable, perhaps imaginary geometric elements. Born in Toronto, he studied between 1925 and 1927 at the Ontario College of Art before moving permanently to New York. There he worked briefly at the *Art Students League and studied with Arshile *Gorky. During the 1930s and 1940s, he worked as a fashion illustrator and painted a number of murals in apartment houses and in public places, such as restaurants and department stores. A friendship with Joseph *Cornell spurred the development of his mature style in the late 1930s.

Murphy, Gerald (1888–1964). Painter. Also a businessman. Reflecting their creator's stylish, playful, and generous character, his innovative 1920s paintings reflect the cosmopolitan jazz age in spirit but find few similarities with art styles of the period. Incorporating depictions of everyday objects into large abstract designs, these works prefigure important aspects of *pop art. Widely known during those same years among artists and writers in Paris and the south of France, Murphy personified the era's glamorous chic, as chronicled in Calvin Tomkins's vignette, *Living Well Is the Best Revenge* (1962). Murphy and his wife also inspired the central couple in F. Scott Fitzgerald's *Tender Is the Night*. Gerald Cleary Murphy was born in Boston but grew up in New York. After graduating in 1912 from Yale University, he studied landscape architecture at Harvard for two years before relocating to Paris in 1921. There he soon settled comfortably into the clever and creative society idealized in the historical romance of that era. Perhaps to his own surprise, Murphy was so overwhelmed by the experience of seeing work by Picasso, Georges Braque, and Juan Gris that he decided to become a painter. He studied briefly with Russian emigré painter Natalia Goncharova before setting his own course. Between 1922 and the end of the decade, Murphy completed his entire life's work as an artist: ten major canvases, of which seven survive. (Two of the lost paintings are known in photographs.) An extremely slow and meticulous worker, he astonished Paris with his detailed renditions of ordinary objects set within abstracted, cubist compositions. *Razor* (Dallas Museum of Art, 1924) features a safety razor, a fountain pen, and a matchbox, all enormously enlarged and painted in a hard-edge technique. The audacious *Boatdeck, Cunarder* (1923, now lost) depicted smokestacks and air vents in a manner related to *precisionism. However, at 18 × 12 feet, this painting addressed problems of scale that were to beguile pop artists. Later, Murphy's work inched toward more complex and unsettling effects. *Wasp and Pear* (Museum of Modern Art, 1927) presents a flat assemblage of elements including exterior and interior views of a pear, along with a grotesquely enlarged wasp. Parts of the insect are simplified while others are blown up in textbook-style detail. Murphy's artistic career ended along with the twenties, when family problems claimed his attention. Following three years in Switzerland, he returned to New York. Murphy worked in his family's Mark Cross luxury leather goods business until he retired in 1956. Before his death on eastern Long Island, at his vacation home in Southampton, he lived to see the beginning of a revival of interest in his small but piquant contribution to the history of art.

Murphy, John Francis (1853–1921). Painter. A landscape specialist, he offered undramatic woodland and farm views representing nature in its quiet moments. The season is often autumnal. Rooted in the popular *Barbizon mode, his work increasingly approached *tonalism in its subdued coloration, contemplative mood, and Whistlerian aestheticism. Born in upstate Oswego, New York, Murphy never pursued systematic training as an artist and did not visit Europe until he had achieved success. As a young man he worked as a sign painter in Chicago and persevered on his own as an artist in Orange, New Jersey, before moving the short distance to New York in 1875. Gradually, his detailed, topographical early work in the spirit of the *Hudson River School gave way to the richer brushwork of Barbizon-inspired painting. From 1887 he lived for a substantial part of each year in the Catskills, at Arkville, where Alexander *Wyant lived also from 1889 until his death three years later. Murphy's continuing development away from observed motifs toward a more generalized and evocative approach signals admiration for Wyant's work, as well as for George *Inness's broadly executed and poetic late style. Murphy's work culminated after 1900 in pensive reconstructions of local scenery, typically marked by subtle color harmonies, atmospheric unity, and expressive brushwork indebted to impressionist light effects. During the final two years of his life, failing health diminished his output. He died in New York. **Adah Clifford Murphy** (1859–1949), also known as Ada, painted portraits, as well as landscapes in a style related to her husband's. Born in upstate Saratoga, she studied in New York at Cooper Union and with Paris-trained Douglas Volk (1856–1935), a painter of portraits and romantic figural scenes. After marriage in 1893, she continued to exhibit actively for many years.

Museum of Modern Art. The leading American museum devoted to the modern tradition in the visual arts. At its founding in 1929, New York's MoMA represented an original concept in the notion of a "museum," since almost none then collected modern art. Only the Washington, D.C., establishment founded by Duncan *Phillips preceded MoMA in specializing in the recent past. However, the Phillips Collection (as it is now known) includes a small old master collection as well as significant representation of impressionism and other nineteenth-century tendencies. By contrast, from the beginning MoMA focused exclusively on the work of postimpressionists, particularly Cézanne, and their artistic descendants. (To this day, however, the Phillips Collection boasts a much finer representation of early American modernism.) MoMA also led the way in presenting photography, film, and design within an art museum context.

MoMA owes its genesis to art patrons and friends Abby Aldrich *Rockefeller, Lillie P. Bliss (1864–1931), whose discerning gifts and bequests number among the museum's key treasures, and Mary Quinn Sullivan (1877–1939), a former art educator and the wife of Cornelius J. Sullivan, the new museum's first legal counsel. Founding director Alfred H. Barr Jr. (1902–81), proved central to MoMA's realization, growth, and, ultimately, phenomenal success, an accomplishment that helped to reconceptualize the purposes of American museums and their relationship to the public. He also articulated an intellectual viewpoint and narrative structure that together informed American understanding of modern art. Born in Detroit, Alfred Hamilton Barr studied art history at Princeton University, where he received a BA in 1922 and an MA the following year. Subsequently, he taught at several colleges and pursued additional professional training at Harvard University, where he received a PhD in 1946. Appointed director of the museum a few months before it opened in November 1929, he brought to the job a disciplined commitment to visual quality in works of art and a devotion to the museum's educational role, as well as detailed knowledge of European modern movements. During extensive travels abroad, he had visited the Bauhaus, gained first-hand knowledge of avant-garde art in Russia, and recognized the importance of such artists as the cubists and Matisse. Barr's understanding of modern art as an expression of modern civilization informed his vision of the museum's mission and guided its development and influence. He organized or supervised pioneering exhibitions that introduced to the American public new forms of art, architecture, and industrial design, while also acquiring an impeccable core collection. A diffident administrator whose accomplishments at the museum owed much to supportive staff, board members, and donors, Barr stepped down as director in 1943. However, he continued to shepherd the museum's fortunes from other posts until he retired in 1967. Barr's exhibitions produced lucid, well-informed catalogues that remain landmarks in the study of their subjects. Among numerous examples, these include *Cubism and Abstract Art* (1936), *Fantastic Art, Dada and Surrealism* (1936), and retrospectives of the work of Picasso and Matisse. He also wrote the popular guide *What Is Modern Painting?* (1943, and numerous revised editions). Incapacitated in his final years, he died in Salisbury, Connecticut.

In 1932 MoMA moved from its original premises on Fifth Avenue to a town house at 11 West Fifty-third Street, its address to the present time. These domestically scaled quarters were demolished to accommodate construction of Philip Goodwin and Edward Durrell Stone's elegant modern structure, which opened in 1939. During the 1950s and 1960s, Philip Johnson designed extensions and gave the sculpture garden its present form. In 1984 the museum inaugurated Cesar Pelli's substantial enlargement, followed by Yoshio Taniguchi's enormous expansion and redesign of the premises, which opened in 2004. In 2000 MoMA and the P.S.1 Center for Contemporary Art, a cutting-edge showcase in Queens, entered into a partnership that heightens MoMA's involvement with art of the present moment.

Muybridge, Eadweard (1830–1904). Photographer. Best known for his studies of human and animal locomotion, he originally made his reputation as a San Francisco–based landscape photographer. He also invented a device known as a zoopraxiscope to project closely spaced, stop-action images in sequence, anticipating later development of motion pictures. His other subjects included the city of San Francisco, interior and exterior views of area mansions, winemaking activities, and the scenery and Indian inhabitants of the larger western region and Latin America. Born Edward James Muggeridge in Kingston-on-Thames, near London, in adulthood he adopted a variant spelling of his name, claiming its more authentic Anglo-Saxon origins. He emigrated about 1852 to the United States to work in publishing and bookselling, at first in the East but later in San Francisco. In 1860 he returned to England, where he learned photographic techniques. He made his way back to San Francisco in 1867, with the ambition of photographing the American West. He started that spring in the Yosemite Valley. Acclaimed internationally when they were made public the following year, these romantically conceived views included many vistas not previously photographed. Contemporary painters, including Albert *Bierstadt, particularly admired his original and artfully constructed landscapes capturing atmospheric effects in delicate gradations of tone. In 1872 Leland Stanford, railroad tycoon, former state governor, and horse fancier, recruited Muybridge to help settle a bet on whether a racehorse in motion ever took all four feet off the ground simultaneously. Muybridge set up a series of cameras activated by tripwires to photograph Stanford's prize horse. In his earliest investigations, limitations of the wet-plate medium prevented a definitive answer to Stanford's query, but by 1873 Muybridge's photographs seemed to indicate that horses do lose contact with the ground. In more refined experiments in 1877, Muybridge proved the point conclusively. In the meantime, in 1874 Muybridge found it expedient to leave San Francisco after murdering his wife's lover, even though a jury exonerated him. In early 1875 he embarked on a yearlong journey to Mexico and Central America, where he turned his discriminating eye on landscapes, architecture, and native inhabitants.

In 1878 he put together the zoopraxiscope, combining the rotating element of a children's toy, the zoetrope, and a "magic lantern" projector. His public demonstration of the invention in San Francisco in 1880 might be considered the first motion picture show. After an extended visit to Paris and London, in 1883 he moved to Philadelphia to begin preparations for his most extensive and significant motion studies, sponsored by the University of Pennsylvania. Now employing the faster dry-plate process, in 1884 and 1885 Muybridge investigated hundreds of human and animal subjects, including clothed and nude figures carrying out varied actions. These studies opened new understandings of processes that had previously been inaccessible to the human eye and mind. In 1887 he published the multivolume *Animal Locomotion: A Electro-Photographic Investigation of Consecutive Phases of Animal Movements, 1872–1885*. Its 781 plates include thousands of photographs. These sequential images of motion, sometimes recorded simultaneously from more than one vantage point, initiated a history of scientific studies using ever more sophisticated technology. But their visual impact had equivalent repercussions. At the time, many artists, such as Thomas *Eakins (who had been partially responsible for bringing Muybridge to Philadelphia), consulted Muybridge's work to increase the realism of their work. Others soon drew on the evocative images for more imaginative purposes. Among them, Marcel *Duchamp took his point of departure from results achieved by Muybridge and subsequent experimentalists for the revolutionary *Nude Descending a Staircase, No. 2*. The Muybridge images also constitute an early form of *conceptual art, in their application of a rigorous intellectual system for producing images that have no expressive intent but nevertheless stir the mind. Muybridge spent much of the late 1880s and 1890s traveling the world to lecture about his methods and demonstrate his results. Shown by invitation at Chicago's World's Columbian Exposition of 1893 in a specially constructed Zoopraxographical Hall, which might be considered the first movie theater, his work became widely known among the public. He spent the final decade of his life in England. There he put together two books, *Animals in Motion* (1899) and *The Human Figure in Motion* (1901), based on his earlier work. He passed his final years quietly in the town where he had been born.

Myers, Jerome (1867–1940). Painter and printmaker. Although sometimes included among *Ashcan painters because of his interest in the lower classes, he remained more romantic than they generally were. In the life of New York's poor, Myers found qualities of beauty and joy that he translated into a decorative exoticism. His compositions typically feature somewhat flattened, patterned forms enlivened with touches of glowing color. Oddly, although he had himself experienced an impoverished youth, social reform was not among his concerns, and although he knew slum life at first hand, better than nearly all the Ashcan painters, he provided only distanced, poetic views in his art. His actors in fantasy spectacles rarely demonstrate individual psychology. Born in Petersburg, Virginia, Myers first became a sign painter in Baltimore. After he moved permanently to New York in 1886, he painted theater sets and attended art school, first at Cooper Union, then at the *Art Students League where George de Forest *Brush ranked as his most important teacher. In the 1890s he worked as a newspaper artist before traveling to Paris in 1896. After 1900 he began to paint full time, exhibited regularly while associating with realist painters, and served as an organizer of the 1913 *Armory Show. In later years, he maintained a vacation home in Carmel, New York, north of the city, but claimed he visited rarely because of his fascination with the urban panorama. His autobiography, *Artist in Manhattan*, appeared the year he died. His wife **Ethel Myers** (1881–1960) was known primarily for small bronze figurative works. She exhibited nine in the Armory Show and continued to specialize in realistic, or sometimes caricatural, studies of New Yorkers. She also painted, particularly in watercolor. Born in Brooklyn, Ethel Mae Klinck studied at the New York School of Art (now Parsons, the New School for Design) with Robert *Henri and Kenneth Hayes *Miller before marriage in 1905. She died in Cornwall, on the Hudson River above New York.

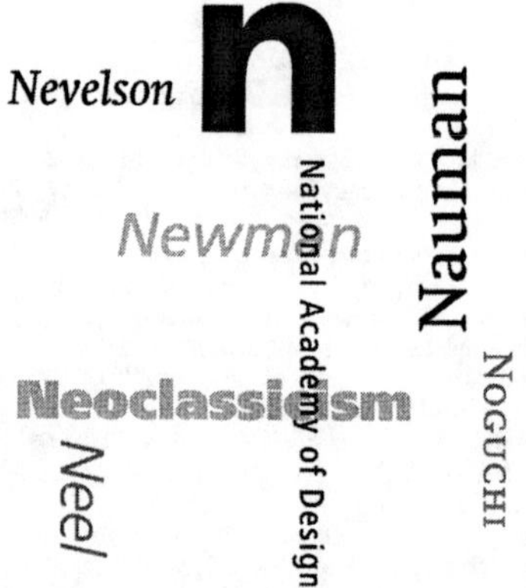

Nadelman, Elie (1882–1946). Sculptor, draftsman, and collector. His sleek, stylish figurative works draw on modern and classical traditions, while also displaying a droll humor based on sharp-eyed observation of social conventions. An early collector of American folk art, he sometimes incorporated his admiration for untutored expression into his own work. The modern veneer and sophisticated charm of his sculpture suited 1920s taste, but during the more socially conscious 1930s, his reputation declined. Born in Warsaw, Nadelman studied art there and served for a year in the Imperial Russian Army before moving to Munich and then on to in Paris in 1904. Initially drawn to Rodin's work, he soon turned to more modern expression, as he became acquainted with Brancusi, Picasso, and other leading figures. At the same time, he also closely studied the ancient sculpture on view at the Louvre, as well as African masks in the ethnographic museum. In the Paris years, he experimented with considerable originality across styles and media. Drawings from about 1905 anticipated aspects of cubist fragmentation, but he never pursued broken forms in his three-dimensional work. By 1906 some of his sculpture rivaled Brancusi's in radical simplification. Nadelman's work appeared in the *Armory Show before he left Paris in 1914. He went first to London before continuing later that year to New York. His first American one-person show at Alfred *Stieglitz's *291 gallery initiated his success in 1915. The exhibition included a plaster version of the genial bronze *Man in the Open Air* (Museum of Modern Art, 1915), which exemplifies the characteristics that brought Nadelman fame. The sculpture's svelte, sensuously smoothed forms suggest modernist simplification, but they also reveal the artist's preference for decorative, curved shapes. The pose derived from classical sculpture ties the work to tradition, while the bowler hat and string tie add witty contemporary touches. Appealing as this work may be, it foreshadows a loss of ambition in the later work of an artist whose early career promised leadership in the development of sculptural modernism.

From the late 1910s through the 1920s, when he numbered among the most prominent New York artists, Nadelman received numerous portrait commissions. Their polished surfaces and refined, slightly simplified forms glamorized sitters. An early patron, the Polish-born cosmetics baroness Helena Rubinstein, placed his idealized marble busts in her beauty salons. Simultaneously, through about 1924, inspired by newfound enthusiasm for American folk art, he often worked in wood, which he sometimes painted, as in *Woman at the Piano* (Museum of Modern Art, c. 1917). With gentle mockery, many of these pieces depict entertainers or high society. In 1926 he opened to the public his enormous folk art collection, displayed in a building on the grounds of his home in the Riverdale neighborhood of the Bronx. (He also had a town house in Manhattan until forced to sell it during the Depression). Nadelman became an American citizen in 1927. After the 1929 stock market crash, which decimated his fortune and precipitated a decline in the popularity of his work, he became reclusive. Following his last one-person exhibition, mounted in Paris in 1930, he accepted a few commissions, such as the limestone decoration for New York's Fuller Building (1930–32), but for the most part withdrew to his studio. In 1937 he sold his entire folk art collection to the New-York Historical Society. Leaving no clue to his intentions, during his last sixteen years he produced more than four hundred odd little figurines in a variety of materials. He committed suicide at his Riverdale home.

Nakian, Reuben (1897–1986). Sculptor and printmaker. Often reminiscent of human figuration yet not directly representational, the roughly finished, expressive forms of characteristic works parallel the grandeur, ambition, and emotional charge of *abstract expressionist paintings. These pieces often refer to mythological themes or to literary subjects with universal overtones. Erotic elements appear frequently, suggesting the regenerative powers of sex. Much of his work achieves a monumental scale appropriate to display in public interiors or outdoors. As a printmaker, he worked with etching and lithography, mostly during the 1960s. Born in New York, as a youngster Nakian moved with his family from Queens into Manhattan, and then to the city's New Jersey suburbs. He took drawing lessons in Jersey City but left formal schooling in 1912, without attending high school. He briefly studied at the *Art Students League, but for most of the next four years he worked in advertising and magazine design. After taking evening art classes in 1915, the next year he became an apprentice to Paul *Manship. During three years in Manship's studio, he befriended the chief assistant, Gaston *Lachaise, and they shared a studio in the early 1920s. Nakian's early work demonstrates smooth modeling and fluid design derived from Manship and Lachaise, but suggests also his admiration for the work of acquaintances William *Zorach and Brancusi. Nakian specialized for a time in animal sculptures and also became known for portraits. In 1931 he visited Italy and France. Around the time he found employment with a *federal art project in the mid-1930s, he moved to Staten Island. There, for ten years, he made little sculpture but worked out his ideas in drawings. After becoming acquainted with Arshile *Gorky and then Stuart *Davis and Willem *de Kooning, he reevaluated his artistic goals. Moving away from representation, by the early 1940s he was working in a semi-abstract and more expressionistic mode. He found his way back into consistent sculptural production through two series of appealing terra cottas, plaques incised with drawings and three-dimensional pieces, both featuring female nudes. Usually in the guise of mythological characters, they recall Picasso's playful eroticism, as well as de Kooning's Woman series. In the 1950s Nakian hit his stride with larger and more abstract works that he typically fabricated with plaster and cloth over metal armatures and then cast in bronze, as in *Birth of Venus* (Sheldon Memorial Art Gallery and Sculpture Garden, University of Nebraska, Lincoln, 1963–66; cast 1970). Eight feet tall and nearly eleven feet long, loosely assembled from craggy but majestic organic elements, the work suggests the energy of a figure rising from the sea but only indirectly alludes to body parts. Nakian died in Stamford, Connecticut, where he had made his home since 1948.

Namuth, Hans. *See* POLLOCK, JACKSON.

Nast, Thomas. *See* BLYTHE, DAVID GILMOUR.

National Academy of Design. New York's oldest professional artists' association, art school, and museum, inspired by the academies that once dominated European art production and instruction. It superseded an earlier attempt to support such an organization, the American Academy of the Fine Arts founded in 1802. The National Academy of the Arts of Design, which two years later shortened its name, came into being under the leadership of Samuel F. B. *Morse in 1826. Serving as its first president until 1845, Morse shaped an institution quite distinct from the American Academy. He loosely modeled the National Academy on London's Royal Academy, with which he was familiar. In a significant reform, the National Academy was run by its artist-members, rather than by businessmen and amateurs such as those who dominated American Academy policy. As it still does, the National Academy offered instruction and lectures, mounted an annual juried exhibition of original contemporary work, and continually augmented its collection. Like the Royal Academy and other European academies, the National Academy invites artists to membership, with the intent of validating artistic quality and honoring those who qualify. Members include painters, sculptors, printmakers, and architects.

The American Academy of the Fine Arts was known before 1816 as the New York Academy of Arts and then as the American Academy of Arts. It was devoted primarily to exhibiting and collecting classical and old master work (often represented by copies) and European contemporary art. John *Trumbull had been its autocratic president for almost a decade when a group of dissident, mostly younger artists met late in 1825 to organize an association focused on professional development and instruction. When the American Academy was dissolved in 1842, the National Academy acquired its sculpture casts. By the 1870s, progressive artists viewed the National Academy itself as rigid and unresponsive to their interests. In 1875 the *Art Students League began to offer more informally structured art training. After its establishment in 1877, the *Society of American Artists challenged the National Academy's exhibition policies by sponsoring more democratically chosen shows. By the time of the *Armory Show in 1913, the National Academy was viewed, by conservatives and experimentalists alike, as an institutional bulwark against modern art. Subsequently, although many prominent artists have been associated with the organization or its school, the National Academy has not for the last century exerted the influence it once did. Today officially known simply as the National Academy, it survives as a school, as well as a museum of American art headquartered nearby in a renovated and enlarged Fifth Avenue townhouse donated in 1940 by its former owners, Anna Hyatt *Huntington and her husband.

National Collection of Fine Arts. *See* SMITHSONIAN INSTITUTION.

National Endowment for the Arts. A federal agency that provides financial support for creation, presentation, documentation, and transmission of the arts in the United States. A sister agency, the National Endowment for the Humanities, supports parallel scholarly and public endeavors related to nonscientific fields of inquiry, such as literature, philosophy, languages, and history, including art history. Founded together with the NEH in 1965, the NEA represents the national government's commitment to the arts as integral to American civilization. Over the course of its history, patterns of funding have varied, but in general the NEA makes allocations to state arts councils in support of their activities while also giving grants to individuals and nonprofit organizations. Besides the visual arts, the NEA has supported programs in literature, music, dance, and theater, as well as arts education and arts reporting and criticism. Under the leadership of Nancy Hanks (1927–83), the NEA's second and most effective head, between 1969 and 1977 the agency skyrocketed into an important force for arts support across the country. Born in Miami Beach, Hanks graduated from Duke University in 1949. She worked in Washington for a federal agency for two years before becoming Nelson *Rockefeller's personal assistant in 1953. Subsequently, in Washington and New York she gained administrative experience while in the employ of Rockefeller family public policy programs. Although she had no specialized training in the arts, she advocated adroitly on the NEA's behalf within official Washington's political and institutional circles. Her success enabled the fledgling agency to expand its original outreach, introduce new programs, innovate effective arts financing, and gain nationwide respect. After she left the NEA, she returned to Rockefeller and other projects in New York, where she died following a period of failing health. In more recent times, the NEA has on several occasions become embroiled in controversies over such volatile questions as artistic merit of funded projects and distribution of resources among the states. Nevertheless, despite repeated congressional threats to its continued existence, the NEA has prevailed as a mainstay in the cultural life of the United States.

National Gallery of Art. A federal art museum in Washington, D.C. The collection comprises European and American painting, sculpture, and works on paper from the late middle ages until the present. Initially a gift to the nation from Andrew *Mellon, it opened to the public in 1941, four years after Congress accepted his donation of $15,000,000 for its construction, along with 115 old master paintings. John Russell Pope designed the original neoclassical building on the Mall. Now known as the West Building, it continues to house most of the collection's older art. Connected underground, the East Building, designed by I. M. Pei and completed in 1978, exhibits primarily modern and contemporary art. In 1999 a six-acre sculpture garden opened just west of the original building. Two administrators, each associated with the museum for some three decades, led the institution to its present eminence. John Walker (1906–95), born in Pittsburgh and educated at Harvard, started as the museum's chief curator two years before the building opened. During the years after he became director in 1956, the museum began planning for the East Building and acquired Leonardo da Vinci's *Ginevra de' Benci*, as well as Chester Dale's important collection focusing on impressionist and postimpressionist French paintings. Walker's numerous publications include *Self-Portrait with Donors: Confessions of an Art Collector* (1974). He died in Amberly, England. Upon his retirement from the museum in 1969, J. Carter Brown (1934–2002) became director. Born in Providence and also educated at Harvard, John Carter Brown earned an MBA there in 1958 before pursuing additional art history training in Europe. After earning a master's degree at New York University's Institute of Fine Arts in 1961, he served as Walker's assistant. During his tenure as director, the museum increased its efforts to attract a general audience. The East Building opened to the public, and the museum presented large exhibitions of international note, including "Treasures of Tutankhamun" (1976) and "Treasure Houses of Britain" (1985). Brown retired in 1992 and died in Boston. His replacement, current director Earl Alexander Powell III (1943–), was born in Spartanburg, South Carolina. After graduating in 1966 from Williams College in Williamstown, Massachusetts, he entered Harvard to earn an MA in 1970 and a PhD four years later. He served as director of the Los Angeles County Museum of Art for twelve years before moving to the National Gallery.

National Museum of American Art. *See* SMITHSONIAN INSTITUTION.

National Portrait Gallery. *See* SMITHSONIAN INSTITUTION.

Nauman, Bruce (1941–). Sculptor, video artist, printmaker, conceptual artist, installation artist, performance artist, and photographer. Among the most mercurial, innovative, and controversial artists of recent decades, he has sustained a freewheeling investigation into the limits of art and the role of the artist. His witty, disturbing, and profound challenges often interrogate art's relationship to language, politics, technology, and human communication. Repetitive, crass, emotionally draining effects force viewers to confront the superabundance of such qualities in contemporary American life. His art offers a series of propositions showing little sequential development. There is no Nauman visual style, nor much sense of technical progress, although more recent projects have tended toward greater physical and emotional amplitude. Born in Fort Wayne, Indiana, he first studied mathematics but then turned to art at the University of Wisconsin in Madison, where he earned a BFA in 1964. His teachers included the Italian-born Italo Scanga (1932–2001), whose high-spirited sculpture and painting combined modern and folk art tendencies in diversified media, often with the addition of found objects. At the University of California at Davis, where Nauman earned an MFA during the following two years, he worked with Robert *Arneson, Wayne *Thiebaud, and William *Wiley. He lived in the San Francisco area until 1969, when he moved to Pasadena. In 1979 he relocated to Pecos, New Mexico, in the Santa Fe vicinity. Since 1989, when he married Susan *Rothenberg, he has resided on a ranch in nearby Galisteo.

Even as a graduate student, Nauman anticipated the work that distinguished a widely noticed New York debut at Leo *Castelli's gallery in 1968. Much of this early work dealt with the implications of literalism. *A Cast of the Space Under My Chair* (private collection, 1965–68), offers a blocky chunk of concrete replicating the open area beneath a chair. *Hand to Mouth* (Hirshhorn Museum, 1967) presents a veristic cast of an arm, extending from fingertips to chin. This sort of humorous wordplay paralleled initial investigations into less obvious questions about language. In 1966 Nauman began to work with common words or short statements formed from neon tubing, pointing to a troubling intrusion of commercial advertising into the unconscious. Soon, he addressed interactions of perception and awareness in increasingly more complicated ways. Beginning in 1968, several corridor installations allowed a single viewer at a time to walk along a narrow hallway fitted with surveillance cameras and one or more television screens. These showed the corridor itself, as well as the viewer's progress from behind, producing disorientation within the claustrophobic space. With time, the interest in representing mental processes took on sinister implications. In the video installation *Clown Torture* (1987), two conventionally costumed clowns, stand-ins for the contemporary artist, are subjected to humiliation, while *Carousel* (Gementemuseum, The Hague, 1988) presents simulated wild animal bodies hung from a whirling metal structure, invoking the life of suffering and incomprehension we share with animals. Recent works offer a more relaxed but no less thorny worldview. Accompanied by an equal number of soundtracks, the seven-screen *Mapping the Studio* (2001) in its original form presented a nearly six-hour, infrared view of the artist's "empty" studio at night. (Alternative and edited versions followed.) Cats, mice, and insects provide animation that reminds us how little human presence matters. For *Raw Materials*, a 2004 installation at the Tate Modern in London, Nauman relied on sound alone. Twenty-two speakers arranged the length of the museum's enormous atrium offered spoken texts of varying audibility and intelligibility. These blended with visitors' conversations to create an acoustic collage mirroring the world's buzz. Janet Kraynak edited *Please Pay Attention Please: Bruce Nauman's Words; Writings and Interviews* (2003).

Neagle, John (1796–1865). Painter. His most innovative and celebrated work, *Pat Lyon at the Forge* (Museum of Fine Arts, Boston, 1826; replica, Pennsylvania Academy, 1829), notably adapts the formulas of grand manner portraiture to a working-class subject, suggesting for a democratic audience the nobility of labor and the irrelevance of aristocratic birth. Born in Boston, Neagle grew up in Philadelphia and remained a resident of that city nearly all his life. As a portrait specialist, from time to time he traveled to paint clients elsewhere. He began producing likenesses while apprenticed to a coach painter. Soon he developed a painterly style indebted primarily to his mentor Thomas *Sully and, to a smaller extent, Gilbert *Stuart, who offered advice when Neagle visited Boston in 1825. He also received instruction from Bass *Otis and others. As a young man, he worked briefly in Lexington, Kentucky, and in New Orleans. In the mid-1820s Patrick Lyon commissioned the painting that established Neagle's reputation. In a composition pulsing with energy, the heroicized blacksmith pauses at his labor within his shop. In the distance, signifying his defiant attitude toward authority, can be seen the prison where once he had been wrongly held. *Pat Lyon* exemplifies the strengths of Neagle's mature style in its fluent application of paint, strong colors and textural effects, control of space and light, and air of optimistic confidence. Second only to Sully by the late 1820s, Neagle flourished in Philadelphia's portrait market through the 1840s. With time, Neagle's handling of paint became somewhat tighter, as he became more attentive to detail. Later, his productivity waned, and a stroke in the late 1850s ended his career.

Neel, Alice (1900–1984). Painter and occasional printmaker. Known for vivid, expressionistic, and unsentimental portraits, particularly early in her career she also painted subjects that engage social or psychological issues. On occasion, she also painted landscapes and still lifes. Recording an array of mostly unconventional friends and acquaintances, her self-reliant contribution stands outside main currents of contemporary art practice. She often delineated effects on her subjects of illness, social injustice, psychological suffering, or aging. This powerful but uningratiating art found little recognition until the artist reached her seventies. Born in the Philadelphia suburb of Merion Square, Alice Hartley Neel grew up in nearby Colwyn. In 1925 she graduated from the Philadelphia School of Design for Women (now Moore College of Art and Design) and married Cuban painter Carlos Enriquez. She moved with him to Havana in 1926. A few months after they resettled in New York the next year, their infant daughter died. A second daughter was taken from her in the spring of 1930, when Neel's husband left with the toddler for Havana. In the wake of these difficulties, she had a nervous breakdown and moved back to Philadelphia for treatment. After her permanent return to New York in the fall of 1932, for about a decade she received support from *federal art projects. In 1935 she moved from Greenwich Village to Spanish Harlem. With two different men, she had sons in 1939 and 1941 but never remarried; she raised her children alone while enduring many hardships. Like other 1930s *social realists, Neel responded to economic and political conditions in works that engage the effects of poverty and discrimination, although portraits already claimed her primary attention. Among her most affecting works, *T.B. Harlem* (National Museum of Women in the Arts, Washington, D.C., 1940) depicts a Puerto Rican man hospitalized after surgery for tuberculosis. Displaying the characteristic expressive distortion of her personal style, it presents the young victim with compassion and dignity. He weakly gestures toward a bandage on his chest as he gazes in the viewer's direction with Christlike melancholy. Typically, strong, dark outlines and flattened space draw attention to character and meaning at the expense of representational exactitude and ideal beauty.

With abstract art ascendant during the late 1940s and 1950s, Neel worked in obscurity, known to few except other artists. In 1959 she appeared in the classic beat film *Pull My Daisy*, directed by Robert *Frank and Alfred *Leslie. As interest in representation reappeared, the art community rewarded her with opportunities to paint numerous artists, critics, and their associates. Emphasizing his vulnerability, *Andy *Warhol* (Whitney Museum, 1970) dwells on torso scars from an attack on his life. Other prominent subjects included the elderly brothers Isaac and Raphael *Soyer (Whitney Museum, 1973), poet Frank O'Hara (National Portrait Gallery, Washington, D.C., 1960), art historian Linda Nochlin with her daughter (Museum of Fine Arts, Boston, 1973), composer Virgil Thompson (National Portrait Gallery, 1971), and *Village Voice* critic John Perreault (Whitney Museum, 1972), reclining in full frontal nudity. As always, however, she continued to focus primarily on family members and acquaintances whose appearance or character interested her. The 1970s feminist movement brought Neel her first sustained public exposure. Although sales continued to be meager, her work appeared in museums and she found herself in demand as a speaker, a role she evidently relished. Despite improved circumstances, she continued to live in the small West Side apartment she had inhabited since 1962, although she also was able to enjoy an unassuming summer house in Spring Lake, New Jersey. In failing health near the end of her life, she nevertheless continued to paint until a few months before her death at her New York home.

Neoclassicism. Term referring to enthusiasm for Greek and Roman forms and ideals. Although the classically oriented art of other post-antique eras can be described as neoclassical, the word usually refers to work from the late eighteenth and early nineteenth centuries. At that time, interest in the reinterpretation of antiquity swept Europe and continued on to the United States. Signaling a rejection of Baroque and rococo styles, the more disciplined and morally didactic neoclassicism often approached the antique with a fresh appreciation for correctness, stimulated by Enlightenment rationalism as well as recent archeological discoveries. The links between democracy and ancient Greece, as well as between republicanism and Rome, enhanced the resonance of neoclassical art in the United States. Imitation of classical prototypes was most direct in architecture, sculpture, and the decorative arts, but related concerns emerged in painting. To suggest the classical qualities of restraint, harmony, rational order, and noble grandeur, neoclassical painting emphasized clarity, intelligibility, firm modeling of generalized three-dimensional forms, cool coloration, and polished paint surfaces devoid of visible brushstrokes. Narrative paintings in the neoclassical style often take subjects from classical literature. Benjamin *West played an important role in popularizing neoclassical themes and forms. The style reached its culmination in the paintings of French artist Jacques Louis David.

In America, John Singleton *Copley's mature paintings anticipated the taste for neoclassical principles. Many American painters who studied abroad after the Revolution brought home aspects of the new style. In portraiture, it began to gain ascendancy in the 1790s and by the early nineteenth century dominated current practice. In some of his likenesses, Rembrandt *Peale displays a knowledgeable version of the French style. In narrative painting, John *Vanderlyn ranks among the first to base figures on classical examples. Among sculptors, Horatio *Greenough led the way in adapting ancient forms and subjects to contemporary uses. Thomas *Crawford and Hiram *Powers soon joined the trend. Erastus Dow *Palmer, William Henry *Rinehart, Randolph *Rogers, and William Wetmore *Story held sway after mid-century. Working almost exclusively in marble, these and other neoclassical sculptors typically valued exaggeratedly smooth surfaces that contribute to the idealized and universalized intent of their work. Although increasingly tinged with *romanticism, neoclassical style dominated American sculpture long after it had become unfashionable in other arts. Proximity to antique models, as well as availability of high-quality marble and inexpensive stonecutter-assistants, drew most neoclassical sculptors to Italy.

Neo-expressionism. *See* POSTMODERNISM.

Neri, Manuel. *See* BAY AREA FIGURATIVE ART.

Nevelson, Louise (1899–1988). Sculptor, printmaker, and painter. A leading twentieth-century sculptor, she is best known for massive and theatrical wall-size pieces, usually comprising modular, boxlike units that enclose small abstract compositions. Appearing first in the late 1950s, these works feature allusive found objects and fragments that appear to derive from architecture or furniture. Poetic and mysterious, they reveal the potential grandeur of commonplace objects. While producing these characteristic works, she continued also to experiment with other approaches, as she had through previous years. Cubist, surrealist, and constructivist methods, as well as pre-Columbian and tribal sculpture, informed her development. The personal synthesis she achieved during the 1950s contributed to the *abstract expressionist aesthetic, although she did not associate personally with those painters. Besides wood, Nevelson on occasion worked also with a wide range of other materials, including plastics, Formica, and metal. Outdoor pieces are generally fabricated from steel or aluminum. When she became famous, the flamboyant Nevelson relished the role as one for which she had long prepared. Exotic fashions, dramatic makeup (including enormously long fake eyelashes), and outspoken opinions enhanced her imperious demeanor. Despite the public hauteur, she lived simply and participated actively in the art community, often with generosity. She freely opened her home to gatherings, joined (and sometime led) organizational efforts on behalf of artists, and collected the work of artists she knew or admired.

Born near Kiev, Leah Berliawsky moved with her family in 1905 to Rockland, Maine. There she developed a familiarity with wood and its properties while playing with scraps from her father's lumberyard. She later recalled that even as a child she had decided to become a sculptor, but this professional dream was for the most part deferred until after she turned forty. She achieved prominence only as she approached sixty. She graduated in 1918 from high school and two years later married Charles Nevelson, a well-to-do ship owner from New York, where she subsequently made her home. Although she took drawing and painting lessons from Theresa *Bernstein and her husband William Meyerowitz, Nevelson also studied acting, dance, and singing. Not until 1929 did she enter the *Art Students League to pursue serious professional training with Kenneth Hayes *Miller, among others. In 1931 she separated from her husband (they were divorced ten years later) and left for Europe. Besides traveling, she studied briefly with Hans *Hofmann in Munich. Back in New York the following year, she again studied with Hofmann. In 1933 she worked for Mexican muralist Diego Rivera on a project in New York. While continuing also to paint in a loose, expressionistic style, around this time she began making small sculptures of wood, plaster, or terra cotta. Chaim *Gross assisted this endeavor by providing her only instruction in sculpture, at the Educational Alliance Art School. Between 1934 and 1939 she found employment with a *federal art project. In 1941 she had her first one-person gallery show, and the following year began to incorporate found objects into surrealist assemblages. After two shows in 1943, she destroyed large numbers of earlier paintings and sculptures. In 1947 she initiated her activity as a serious printmaker while working at *Atelier 17. Later that year, she left on a European trip that extended until 1949. Subsequently, she twice traveled in Central America, particularly to view Mayan sites.

By the early 1950s, along with her friend Louise *Bourgeois, she was making totemlike wood sculptures featuring *biomorphic components. A 1958 gallery exhibition announced her signature style and prepared the way for public success. By painting the wall constructions a uniform matte black, she emphasized the enigmatic character of the found and manufactured artifacts nestled in boxes, while at the same time submerging details into an integrated whole. Patterns of highlights and inky shadows enhanced the works' occult tone. These sculptures ranked as her first definitively to share abstract expressionism's grand scale, diffused focus, limited depth, symbolic atmospherics, and ambition to transcend history while retaining its humanistic values. Nevelson's attention to installation design for her own exhibits made clear her interest in creating environments. The black sculptures generated an all-white series the following year and then a number of elegant works in gold. During the 1960s, her work became more geometric and precisely crafted. She also experimented with varied materials on large and small scales. On her way to becoming a major figure in printmaking, in 1963 she first worked at the *Tamarind Lithography Workshop, where she produced a number of editions, supplementing her similarly extensive involvement in etching. Many of her multiples incorporate collage, cast-paper, or other unusual techniques. Nevelson's first commission for a monumental public sculpture came in 1969 from Princeton University. *Atmosphere and Environment X*, in Cor-Ten steel, prefigures a lengthy succession of works in durable materials for outdoor spaces. Her interest in integrating sculpture into total environments culminated in architectural commissions, notably The Chapel of the Good Shepherd (1977) at Saint Peter's Church in New York. The first chapel to be designed in its entirety by an American artist, this Lutheran place of worship and meditation features white walls animated by low reliefs. Besides all the room's fittings, Nevelson also designed liturgical vestments for use there. She worked productively nearly until her death. The autobiographical *Dawns Plus Dusks: Taped Conversations with Diana MacKown* appeared in 1976.

Her son, **Mike Nevelson** (1922–), born Myron, is a sculptor of partially abstract work. Born in New York, he has worked mainly in metals and lives in Danbury, Connecticut. His oldest child, **Neith Nevelson** (1946–), who lives in the West Coconut Grove area of Miami, spent most of her formative years in Florence. She paints colorful semi-abstract works. A second daughter, **Maria Nevelson**, makes abstract wood sculpture in the tradition of her grandmother. Also an interior designer and the founder of the Louise Nevelson Foundation, she lives in Philadelphia. She majored in art history at George Washington University in Washington, D.C.

New Deal art projects. *See* FEDERAL ART PROJECTS.

New England Art-Union. *See* AMERICAN ART-UNION.

Newhall, Beaumont (1908–93). Photographic historian, curator, and photographer. He served as the *Museum of Modern Art's first curator of photography and later headed the George *Eastman House Museum of Photography (now George Eastman House International Museum of Photography and Film), a leading museum and archive. As the first scholar to treat the history of photography from the point of view of art history, he wrote a landmark history of the medium, which remained essential for decades. His carefully composed, black-and-white photographs most notably record architectural subjects and portraits. Born in Lynn, Massachusetts, Newhall studied art history at Harvard, where he earned bachelor's and master's degrees in 1930 and 1931. He continued his studies in Paris and London before becoming MoMA's librarian in 1935. There in 1937 he organized an unprecedented and wide-ranging exhibition surveying the history of photography. The show's catalogue, revised and expanded, became the classic *History of Photography from 1839 to the Present Day* (1949). In 1940 he was appointed head of the newly created department of photography. During World War II he served for three years in U.S. Air Force photographic intelligence in Europe and North Africa. He taught at *Black Mountain College for two years before joining Eastman House in Rochester, New York, in 1948. There, as curator, he shaped its collection before becoming director in 1958. From 1971 until his retirement in 1984 he taught at the University of New Mexico in Albuquerque. Subsequently, he lived in Santa Fe, where he died. His other books include *The *Daguerreotype in America* (1961), *Latent Image: The Discovery of*

Photography (1967), and *Focus: Memoirs of a Life in Photography* (1993).

His wife, **Nancy Newhall** (1908–74), a writer on photographic and environmental subjects, created photographs as well. Also born in Lynn, Massachusetts, Nancy Wynne studied at the *Art Students League after graduating in 1930 from Smith College in Northampton, Massachusetts. She married Newhall in 1936. In 1942, when her husband departed for the war effort, she was appointed his substitute as MoMA's curator of photography. Her numerous publications include *Time in New England* (1950), a collaboration with Paul *Strand; the Sierra Club's *This Is the American Earth* (1960), with photographs mostly by Ansel *Adams; and *P. H. Emerson: The Fight for Photography as a Fine Art* (1975). *Ansel Adams: The Eloquent Light* (1963) accompanied an exhibition she organized. She died in Jackson, Wyoming, of injuries sustained in a boating accident.

New Hope, Pennsylvania. *See* ARTISTS' COLONIES.

New Image painting. *See* ROTHENBERG, SUSAN.

Newman, Arnold (1918–2006). Photographer. Interested in the psychology of individual lives, he was known especially for portraits of major figures in the arts, usually posed in environments that evoke their creative achievements. He also portrayed political leaders, scientists, entertainers, other celebrities, and ordinary people. His subjects participate self-consciously in the photographic act, which Newman controlled through careful lighting, composition, and timing. Born in New York, Arnold Abner Newman grew up in Atlantic City and Miami Beach. Intending to become an artist, he studied at the University of Miami in Coral Gables for two years but left to work in a Philadelphia portrait studio from 1938 until the end of 1939. There he picked up the fundamentals of his craft, while studying on his own the work of Walker *Evans and other leading photographers. His early street photographs reveal interest in pure form and sensitivity to personality, prefiguring the fundamentals of the mature approach that emerged during the winter of 1941–42, when he began photographing New York artists in their quarters. Finding success with these works, he left Florida to settle permanently in New York in 1946. In a dramatic and unusually spare example of his method, composer Igor Stravinsky (1946) sits sideways at a keyboard, leaning on his elbow as he contemplates the camera. Only his head and shoulders are visible below the dark, Brancusian form of the raised piano lid, an analogue to the purity and clarity of Stravinsky's methods. Also metaphorically embodying musical tradition, the piano dwarfs and challenges even so creative a figure as the sitter. Newman usually employed a large view camera and black-and-white film, but on occasion worked in color. He also photographed urban views, landscapes, and still lifes. Although identified with a straightforward approach, he at times responded to cubism and other modern movements in experiments with collage and manipulated prints. Newman's work appears in several collections, including *One Mind's Eye: The Portraits and Other Photographs of Arnold Newman* (1974), *Artists: Portraits from Four Decades* (1980), and *Arnold Newman: Five Decades* (1986).

Newman, Barnett (1905–70). Painter, sculptor, and printmaker. An *abstract expressionist who set precedents for *color field painting, he is known for enormous solid-color canvases broken only by one or more stripes or "zips," as he preferred to call them. Like other abstract expressionists, he accepted art as a calling of high seriousness, inherently concerned with existential truths and mystical insights. Nevertheless, the work appealed to younger artists who generally relinquished metaphysics in favor of the reduced expectations of *minimalism. Although active in abstract expressionist circles as a theorist and writer during the 1940s, Newman did not have his first one-person show until 1950 and did not attract much interest in his work, even among artists, until the 1960s. A lifelong New Yorker, Newman was given the first name of Baruch, which his parents later Americanized. Everybody called him Barney. Although he began his art studies at the *Art Students League in 1922, during his final year of high school, he did not launch a professional art career until more than two decades later. He continued taking drawing classes while attending the City College of New York, where he earned a bachelor's degree in philosophy in 1927. He then joined a family business, expecting to leave after two or three years to follow his interest in art. However, the Depression dashed those plans, and Newman remained with the firm until 1937. From 1931 until 1947 he also worked as a substitute art teacher in the public schools. In the 1930s, he dabbled in politics, revealing an anarchistic passion for social justice that he never relinquished. He painted off and on in his spare time but later destroyed virtually everything he had done. In the early 1940s he became so interested in botany and ornithology that he studied during the summers of 1940 and 1941 at an Audubon Society camp in Maine and at Cornell University, respectively.

Eventually it was writing, not painting, that made him known among the nascent abstract expressionists. Even when he had temporarily abandoned his own art around 1939–40, he continued to produce unpublished theoretical essays. In 1943 he joined Mark *Rothko and Adolph *Gottlieb in formulating for publication in the *New York Times* a classic statement of abstract expressionist intentions, stressing the centrality of "tragic and timeless" subjects. He organized and composed catalogue essays for revealing exhibitions of little known pre-Columbian sculpture in 1944 and Northwest Coast Indian painting in 1946. He also wrote for *The *Tiger's Eye*. Around 1944 Newman returned purposefully to art making. His first surviving work on canvas dates to 1945, when he was already forty. Like Gottlieb, Rothko, and others in his circle, he was drawn to *biomorphic surrealism, in his case enhanced by familiarity with the biological sciences. After joining the Betty *Parsons stable in 1946, he took part in several group exhibitions, including "The Ideographic Picture," which he organized in 1947 to showcase selections by such artists as Rothko and Clyfford *Still, along with his own work.

In early 1948 Newman achieved a breakthrough that defined the course of his subsequent art. *Onement I* (private collection), a dark red field with a lighter, rough-edged, saturated red zip, crystallized the format that he made his own. Energized by his success, he entered the most productive period of his career, completing more than twenty large paintings before his first one-person show in January 1950. Also reflecting his ebullient mood, in December 1948 he published in *The Tiger's Eye* an essay titled "The Sublime Is Now," asserting that American painting had finally shed its European origins to achieve in concrete images an exhilaration surpassing classical beauty. However, the exhibition was poorly received, and the only buyer was a friend of his wife's. Undeterred, Newman readied for a second show in April 1951 by painting even more audacious works, including one of his best known, the eighteen-foot-wide *Vir Heroicus Sublimis* (Museum of Modern Art, 1950–51), a red expanse with five zips. *The Wild* (Museum of Modern Art, 1950), resembling a sculpture hung on the wall, posed even more of a challenge to what a painting might be. Eight feet tall but only one-and-one-half inches wide and deep, it features a centered cadmium red zip, applied with a palette knife, with just barely visible gray-blue at either side. In this exhibition, he also exhibited the plaster of his first sculpture *Here I* (1950; bronze, 1962), two uprights with a zip of space between. Again, at this show critical reaction proved negative, and nothing sold. Newman withdrew from the Parsons Gallery and generally refrained from showing his work for about seven years. In 1955, despite support from Clement *Greenberg in an important article published that spring, after finishing one large painting Newman quit for more than two years. Following a heart attack at the end of November 1957 and a long period of recuperation, in 1958 he returned to work, just as his earlier paintings began to find an appreciative audience. The 1960s saw a complete turnaround in his fortunes, as his work sold for increasingly high prices and he came to be regarded as a leading figure in the New York art world. In 1964 and 1968 he finally had opportunities to travel in Europe. In 1965 he journeyed to Brazil when he and a handful of younger Americans represented the United States in the São Paulo Bienal.

In his final decade, Newman refined and elaborated his zip approach to painting, continued to expand his interest in sculpture, experimented on a limited basis with shaped canvases, and produced lithographed and etched groups of prints. Among the first paintings completed when he returned to painting in 1958 were two of the fourteen related works he collectively titled *The Stations of the Cross: Lema Sabachthani* (National Gallery, 1958–66). The sensitive manipulation of black and white paint on these austere 6.5 × 5-foot raw canvases provides an aesthetic experience of considerable power. However, even among observers who find in the series emotionally resonant metaphors for human suffering and redemption, some feel that the artist overreached by invoking Christ's ordeal. While working on this series, Newman also produced his most successful sculpture, the monumental Cor-Ten steel *Broken Obelisk* (Museum of Modern Art, 1963–67), a memorial to Martin Luther King Jr. A tall, upside-down obelisk balances, as if weightless, on the point of a pyramid. At the upper extremity, the tall shaft reaches poignant termination in an irregular break. At the time of his death, Newman was the most widely admired artist of his generation. Younger artists found in aspects of his work the means to escape the hold of abstract expressionism. They responded also to his erudition, verbal prowess, and theoretical sophistication. Ironically, his dictum "Aesthetics is for the artist as ornithology is for the birds" remains a well-remembered epigram. In respect to this claim, however, it is worth recalling Newman's fondness for the study of birds. Edited by John P. O'Neill, *Barnett Newman: Selected Writings and Interviews* appeared in 1990.

Newman, Henry Roderick. *See* PRE-RAPHAELITISM, AMERICAN.

Newman, Robert Loftin (1827–1912). Painter. His freely painted, suggestive figure compositions evoke mysterious and romantic content, usually drawn from literature or religion. Born in Richmond, Virginia, he lived there or nearby until 1838, when his family moved to Clarksville, Tennessee. Mostly self-taught as an artist, in 1850 he went to Paris, where he studied for a few months with Thomas Couture. In France again in 1854, he met Jean-François Millet through William Morris *Hunt, painted at *Barbizon for a few months, and copied works by Eugène Delacroix, whose expressive style and masterful use of color attracted his admiration. Newman worked as a portrait painter and drawing teacher in Clarksville before serving for a short time in the Confederate army during the Civil War. Subsequently, after visiting Baltimore and New York, he worked in Nashville. In the early 1870s he moved permanently to New York. He traveled to Europe in 1882, 1908, and 1909. Although supported by other artists and a few discerning collectors, he died in obscurity and poverty, perhaps a suicide. Newman normally worked on a small scale, emphasizing rich color and brushwork in dark and moody depictions of few figures in limited space. His introspective, emotionally potent paintings bear similarities to the work of his friend Alfred Pinkham *Ryder and to the work of contemporary symbolists more generally. Disregarding careful finish, he often distorted figures or left them vaguely defined, enhancing his works' urgency. Like many of his religious subjects, *Virgin and Child* (Brooklyn Museum, 1897) reinterprets a traditional image with a poetic flavor that emphasizes human tenderness over divine presence.

New Masses. *See* MASSES, THE.

New Path, The. *See* PRE-RAPHAELITISM, AMERICAN.

New Topographics. *See* ADAMS, ROBERT.

New York dada. The independent American branch of an international nihilistic movement reflecting the malaise and disillusionment occasioned by World War I. Led by Marcel *Duchamp, *Man Ray, and French visitor Francis Picabia, New York dada flourished between approximately 1915 and 1921. The movement's epicenter, Walter *Arensberg's avant-garde salon, was indeed very nearly the only center. Although some dada activity occurred among peripheral members of Alfred *Stieglitz's circle, New York dada directly touched relatively few Americans. Nevertheless, numerous artists occasionally reflected its spirit of irony and world-weary disrespect for traditions and established values. Aspects of New York dada preceded the formal establishment of the European dada movement in Zurich in 1916. Inherent in a pessimistic strain of modern thought, it had occasionally surfaced in New York as early as 1913 in work by Picabia (who left the United States permanently in 1917), Marius *de Zayas, writer Benjamin de Casseres, and a few others. It was not until 1921, when the American movement was about to dissolve, that the dada name was directly appropriated in New York. In that year, Duchamp and Man Ray published the sole issue of *New York Dada*. Several other magazines in the same spirit, including *The Blind Man* and *291*, which were nearly as short-lived, had anticipated this publication. When Man Ray and Arensberg left the city later in 1921, the movement deflated. Duchamp's departure in 1923 signaled its demise.

In general, American dada remained jauntier than its European counterpart. Abroad, artists such as George *Grosz and John Heartfield produced art of extreme bitterness and cynicism. In New York, the dada artists valued a light touch, which may have reflected Duchamp's sensibility as much as it did the greater distance from the killing grounds of war. Like their European counterparts, the participants in New York dada used non-art materials to distance their work from traditional fine art, explored the metaphorical similarities between human beings and machines, de-emphasized emotional expression in art, made use of chance as a creative tool, and willfully provoked outrage. They also remained firmly committed to having a good time. These characteristics have enjoyed a long if intermittent afterlife in the history of later American art.

New-York Gallery of the Fine Arts. *See* REED, LUMAN.

New York School. An imprecise term, most usefully limited to self-consciously avant-garde work of the 1950s, a period characterized by *abstract expressionism's hold over the creative imaginations of New York artists. Sometimes the phrase is intended to embrace abstract expressionist work of the 1940s, as well. On occasion and rather too broadly to be meaningful, it is employed to designate all innovative New York artists and styles since World War II, much as School of Paris covers heterogeneous accomplishments of the interwar period. Even narrowed to the 1950s, the New York School includes varied styles and aims. During this decade, as the original abstract expressionists continued to amplify accomplishments of the 1940s, they were joined by an emerging second generation, including Grace *Hartigan and Joan *Mitchell. At the same time, many New York School artists deviated from central aspects of the movement while nevertheless building on its example. *Color field painting emerged in the work of such artists as Helen *Frankenthaler and Morris *Louis. Toward the end of the 1950s painters such as Ellsworth *Kelly and Kenneth *Noland emphasized structure in *hard-edge painting, which came to be known also as post-painterly abstraction. Other artists, such as Larry *Rivers and Nell *Blaine, continued the abstract expressionists' gestural approach while accommodating representation. Another line of development extended the spontaneity and material richness of abstract expressionism into *assemblages, as in the sculpture of Mark *di Suvero and Richard *Stankiewicz. Robert *Rauschenberg and Jasper *Johns reached even farther in blurring art and life, while Allan *Kaprow and others substituted *happenings for physical works of art. Although the New York School range might at a glance seem too broad to constitute a meaningful category, it gains coherence in contrast to the new sensibility emerging in the early 1960s. This new point of view rejected the assumption held by abstract expressionists and most 1950s successors that individual expression and ethical content composed art's essential bedrock. The new "cool" approach rejected emotion, autobiography, and "meaning," instead embracing the work of art as an object free of its creator's inner life and of its context's social values. Irony and detachment took center stage. *Pop art and *minimalism provided the two most significant avenues of art making in this environment.

Ney, Elisabet (1833–1907). Sculptor. Known primarily for portraits, she combined realism with the *neoclassicism of her early training. Internationally successful in Europe before settling in Texas, she portrayed leading citizens of that state and stimulated support for the arts. Ney's unsettled life saw success but also hardship, disappointment, and impediments to sustained artistic growth. Born Franzisca (or Francizca) Bernardina Wilhelmina Elisabeth Ney in the Westphalian town of Münster, she studied for two years at the Munich Academy. In 1854 she was the first woman to receive a diploma in sculpture from that institution. She then worked in Berlin under the leading German neoclassicist Christian Daniel Rauch and at the Berlin academy. Soon the most accomplished woman sculptor in Germany, she worked throughout Europe during the 1860s, fulfilling numerous commissions for likenesses of distinguished Europeans. These included Jacob Grimm (Elisabet Ney Museum, Austin, Texas, 1858), Arthur Schopenhauer (Elisabet Ney Museum, 1859), Giuseppe Garibaldi (Fort Worth Art Museum, 1866; modeled 1865), Otto von Bismarck (Elisabet Ney Museum, 1867), and the eccentric Bavarian monarch Ludwig II (Elisabet Ney Museum, 1868). In 1863 she had wed Edmund Montgomery, a Scottish physician, scientist, and philosopher, but she continued to work under her own name and did not publicly acknowledge the marriage. Early in 1871 the couple sailed for the United States. Failing to find in Thomasville, Georgia, the arcadian life they had envisioned, in 1873 Ney and her husband bought Liendo Plantation, a large cotton-and-cattle ranch near Hempstead, Texas. Consumed by other responsibilities, Ney put her artistic career on hold for nearly twenty years. After attracting the governor's interest with a portrait bust, in 1892 she built a studio in Austin, about a hundred miles to the west. Her workplace served also as a gathering place for discussion of intellectual and aesthetic questions. Trips to Germany in 1895, 1902, and 1903 allowed her to bring to Austin many of the works she had executed twenty-five or more years earlier. Her most visible new commissions included standing figures of Sam Houston (1903, modeled 1892) and Stephen Austin (1903, modeled 1893) for the Texas state capitol. Among few imagined subjects, her last important work, a life-size *Lady Macbeth* (Smithsonian American Art Museum, 1903) notable for its psychological insight, ranks among her finest accomplishments. She died in Austin. Her studio there remains as the Elisabet Ney Museum.

Nicolaides, Kimon. *See* BROOKS, JAMES.

Nilsson, Gladys. *See* CHICAGO IMAGISM.

"Ninth Street Show." *See* ABSTRACT EXPRESSIONISM.

Nixon, Nicholas (1947–). Photographer. His stately, yet intimate glimpses into individual lives suggest psychologically and socially determined readings. Over time, his work has become increasingly contemplative, as he has been drawn ever closer to his immediate circumstances. Born in Detroit, in 1969 Nixon received a BA in English from the University of Michigan and in 1974 an MFA from the University of New Mexico. Selections from an early 1970s series of city views appeared in the landmark 1975 *"New Topographics" exhibition. Although he has subsequently concentrated on studies of people, he returns on occasion to considerations of the urban fabric. Nixon often works in series, slowly surveying a single topic for a range of visual and emotional possibilities. The best known of these ruminative sequences portrays his wife and her three sisters, who have posed as a group, arranged in the same order, each year since 1975, tracing their passage into adulthood and on to middle age. In addition to other photographs of his immediate family, he has portrayed young people at three schools (his son's fifth-grade class, Boston Latin School, and the Perkins School for the Blind), the mentally ill, people with AIDS, and the elderly in nursing homes. Nixon normally uses a large-format view camera, which forces him to work slowly, usually in collaboration with his subjects, as he registers the fine detail and delicately nuanced range of tones that suit his compassionate form of documentation. He lives in the Boston area. Nixon has published his work in a number of collections. These include *Photographs from One Year* (1983), *Pictures of People* (1988), *Family Pictures* (1991), *People with AIDS* (1991), *School* (1998), and *The Brown Sisters* (1999).

Nochlin, Linda. *See* FEMINIST ART.

Noguchi, Isamu (1904–88). Sculptor. Also a designer of home and office furnishings, performance settings and costumes, playgrounds, gardens, and environments. A leading twentieth-century sculptor, he synthesized European modernism and his Japanese heritage into an internationally acclaimed form of personal expression. A versatile manipulator of numerous media and an innovator in the articulation of public spaces, he thought as profoundly as anyone of his generation about art's communicative role and its place in creating and sustaining human relationships. Noguchi's development drew particularly on Brancusi's example, along with aspects of surrealism, constructivism, and Japanese predilections for elegant simplification, decorative surfaces, and integration of art into everyday life. His characteristic abstract sculptures generally emphasize intrinsic qualities of materials, the interaction of solid and void, and the transcendent dimension of artistic form. Aspects of his aesthetic parallel tendencies as different as *abstract expressionism and *minimalism, yet he remained independent of movements. Although best known for simplified stone carvings, often highly polished but sometimes featuring roughly textured surfaces, he experimented fruitfully with many substances, including metals, clay, and even humble materials, such as paper, string, and found objects. Although most of his independent sculpture seems to be directed primarily toward aesthetic effects, from his earliest days as a mature artist Noguchi sought to affect people's lives through socially oriented statements or ameliorative projects, such as playgrounds and urban gardens. Particularly in later years, he expressed his creative responsibility to the public in large-scale design projects that manifest a vision of art as an essential adjunct to life.

Noguchi was born in Los Angeles to an Irish-American mother and a Japanese father. As a small child, he was taken to Japan, where he grew up in Tokyo, Chigasaki, and Yokohama. At thirteen, he returned alone to Indiana to continue his education. Following graduation in 1922 from La Porte High School, he traveled to Connecticut to work for the summer in Gutzon *Borglum's studio, where his artistic ambitions received little encouragement. That fall Noguchi entered the premedical program at New York's Columbia University, but in 1924 he began to take evening classes in sculpture at the Leonardo da Vinci Art School. He soon left Columbia to work on his own as an artist until 1927, when he went to Paris. There he took drawing classes while, more importantly, serving for several months as Brancusi's assistant. Before long, Noguchi abandoned his earlier academically determined practice in favor of abstract sculpture reflecting his mentor's attachment to purity of form and respect for materials and tools. Before returning to New York at the end of 1928, he made numerous abstract drawings and experimented with stone, wood, and metal. (He even created a model, now lost, for a sculpture to be fabricated from neon tubing.) His formal vocabulary at this time drew on both organic and geometric shapes, reflecting the strong influence of Brancusi but also interest in constructivism. Back in New York, until the early 1940s Noguchi supported himself with a successful portrait practice marked by sleek and simplified classicism, while also experimenting with more adventurous ideas.

In 1930 Noguchi traveled to Paris for two months before continuing on to Beijing. Remaining there for seven months, he studied ink-brush painting with a Chinese master. In March 1931 he arrived in Japan for his first visit as an adult. There he studied pottery and admired the gardens of Kyoto. After returning to New York in October, he soon contributed to the socially conscious ethos of American art during the 1930s. Although none was realized at the time, in 1933 he designed his first large-scale public spaces, including the elegantly conceived children's park *Play Mountain* (plaster model, Isamu Noguchi Garden Museum,

Long Island City, New York), which forecasts his future development as a playground and garden designer. The following year, he produced his most overt work of social criticism, the shocking *Death* (Isamu Noguchi Garden Museum, 1934). In this protest against contemporary lynchings, a slightly abstracted, grotesquely distorted human figure cast from metal alloy hangs by the neck from a real rope supported from a wood frame. In 1935 he designed the set for dancer and choreographer Martha Graham's *Frontier*. Although his earliest involvement with performance dated to the mid-1920s, this important collaboration heralded a significant aspect of his work for the next forty years. Noguchi declined to design backdrops for ballet and other staged works but instead created sculptural objects that enlivened the performance space and supported dramatic intentions. His subsequent collaborators included Erick Hawkins, John *Cage and Merce Cunningham, Georges Ballanchine, and the Royal Shakespeare Company. Later in 1935, he worked in California before continuing on to Mexico City, where the following year he completed for the Abelardo Rodriguez Market his first monumental public work, a seventy-two-foot-long, low-relief, brick and colored-concrete mural addressing peasants' triumph over political oppression.

Shortly after returning to New York in 1937, he found his first successes in designing objects for mass production, such as lamps and furniture. The elegant, surrealistic, glass-topped coffee table, balanced on paired *biomorphic wood supports (1944; manufactured by Hermann Miller Company, 1947) and the numerous Akari lamps (1951 and later), sheathed in mulberry paper, rank among the most widely known and admired of these designs. Forecasting many later fountains, his first realized example, designed in 1938, was installed at the 1939–40 New York World's Fair. During the summer of 1941, Noguchi relocated to California. When the Japanese attacked Pearl Harbor some months later, he quickly sensed the potential repercussions of this event for Japanese Americans and became active in attempting to mitigate the impact of their forced internment. To this end, in May 1942 he voluntarily entered the camp in Poston, Arizona, where he had agreed to oversee an arts program. Frustrated almost from the beginning with the situation there, he left in disillusionment six months later. Noguchi immediately resettled in New York and there embarked upon his most surrealistic work. Reflecting despair about the war, this direction acknowledged also heightened interest in surrealism among the New York art community, as many European practitioners arrived to escape the military conflict. Arshile *Gorky had already been a close friend for several years. In 1944 he began a stunning series of works that occupied much of his attention for several years. Consisting of almost flat, interlocking shapes, they call to mind similar biomorphic constructions seen in surrealist painting, particularly the work of Yves *Tanguy. Perfectly stable when assembled, the sculptures can be taken apart for transport. Besides denoting enormous skill in carving and exquisitely finishing the component parts, this approach emphasizes fragility and temporality, metaphorically encoding the World War II period's widely held anxieties about the future. One of the most magisterial, the pink marble *Kouros* (Metropolitan Museum, 1945), stands nearly ten feet tall. Its title reveals the artist's clear intention to reinterpret a type of early Greek sculpture in terms of modern needs. *Monument to Heroes* (Isamu Noguchi Garden Museum, 1943) provides another surrealist-inflected commentary on contingency. A hollow black cardboard column, pierced with openings, features bones and slender, ominously shaped wood elements suspended with string to interlace through the column. Between 1943 and 1948 Noguchi also produced Lunars, a highly original series of abstract relief and freestanding sculptures incorporating hidden electric lights that produce glowing effects through openings and interstices in the organic shapes.

In May 1949 Noguchi departed on a round-the-world tour, financed by a Bollingen Foundation fellowship. His grant application spoke of studying the "relationship between the emotional stability of a community and its physical appearance" through an investigation of "environments of leisure." For him, these comprised spiritually nourishing communal spaces, with special attention to sites of contemplation and play. His goal to write a book on the subject never came to fruition (although Bollingen extended his travel financing over a period of several years). However, he accumulated a large trove of photographs and drawings and, stimulated by his findings, subsequently put this experience to good purpose in numerous gardens, plazas, and other environmental spaces. These include his first major landscape project, a *jardin japonais* (1956–58) for UNESCO headquarters in Paris, as well as a white marble "garden" (1960–64) in the courtyard of the Beineke Rare Book and Manuscript Library at Yale University. Noguchi concluded his initial Bollingen trip in 1950 with five months in Japan (his first visit there since 1931). During this period, he worked for a short time at Seto, a traditional pottery center. Here he produced unprecedented works that combine tendencies from such surrealist practitioners as Miró with a Japanese sensibility. In 1952 he lived for several months near Tokyo, in Kita-Kamakura, where he immersed himself in ceramic work, interacted with Japanese potters, and sparked new dimensions in their work. Subsequently, he divided his time between Japan and the United States.

During the 1960s, as the surrealist vocabulary fell out of use in New York, Noguchi simplified and enlarged his independent sculptures to create commanding variations on mostly geometric form. From 1966 Japanese master stone carver Masatoshi Izumi assisted Noguchi on such large projects, starting with *Black Sun* (Seattle Art Museum, 1966–69), a dark granite ring articulated with bulging protuberances. A few years later, they established a studio complex, where Izumi supervised a team of assistants, in the Shikoku island village of Mure. Also in the 1960s Noguchi traveled frequently to Italy to work near the stone quarries there. A series of banded marble sculptures numbers among the striking results. During the 1970s and 1980s, he created another memorable group from huge Japanese boulders left in their natural state except for cavelike excavations treated with contrastingly smooth interiors. In 1985 in Long Island City, the artist opened the Isamu Noguchi Garden Museum across the street from the studio he had maintained in this area of Queens since 1961. Administered by the Noguchi Foundation, today it remains devoted to his legacy. He died in New York. His autobiography, *A Sculptor's World*, appeared in 1968, with a foreword by visionary architect and longtime friend R. Buckminster Fuller, who had encouraged Noguchi's expansive notions of art and its place in the world.

Noland, Kenneth (1924–). Painter and occasional printmaker and sculptor. Known particularly for series featuring targets, chevrons, or stripes, he has also experimented with nonrectangular canvases that permit numerous variations on the relationship between color and shape. Crisp, simplified compositional geometry enhances chromatic effects. He generally accentuates the flatness of the picture plane by manipulating color to negate any appearance of recession or depth. The artist has noted that he thinks of "painting without subject matter as music without words." Matisse has been his artistic beacon. A leading pioneer of *hard-edge painting, he also shared with his close friend Morris *Louis a central role within the *Washington Color School. Born in Asheville, North Carolina, Kenneth Clifton Noland served in the military during World War II. Between 1946 and 1948 at *Black Mountain College, Josef *Albers and Ilya *Bolotowsky numbered among his teachers. In 1948 he left for a year in Paris, where he studied sculpture with Ossip Zadkine, while also continuing to paint. Upon his return, he settled in Washington, D.C., but returned for the 1950 summer session at Black Mountain. There he met Clement *Greenberg and others who put him in touch with the latest developments in *abstract expressionism. To this point, Noland's painting had responded particularly to the work of Paul Klee, but it soon demonstrated his interest as well in Jackson *Pollock and other gestural painters. Accompanied by Louis, whom he had met the previous year, in 1953 Noland visited Helen *Frankenthaler's New York studio, where he saw her *Mountains and Sea*. Responding immediately to the stained color she had employed in this work, he initiated a personal course of experimentation with thin washes of paint. Before long he worked almost exclusively with acrylic paint on unsized canvas, promoting a fusion of color and support. In the mid-1950s he worked toward centered arrangements of the concentric circles that first appeared publicly in his 1959 New York show. At first, edges remained roughly delineated, but by 1961 they took on the precision that characterizes his best-known work. In 1963 the targets gave way to chevrons, or V-shaped arrangements of nested stripes, often asymmetrically placed for dynamic effect. From the mid-1960s, he frequently worked with diamond- or lozenge-shaped canvases, and late in the decade he added horizontal stripes to his repertoire. For a time in the early 1970s Noland interlaced stripes into plaids, reinterpreting Mondrian's grids. Since then, working mainly within the restricted formal vocabulary established previously, he has achieved great variety of effect while investigating the expressive and visual properties of color. On occasion, particularly in the 1970s and 1980s, he used oddly shaped, eccentric canvases or reintroduced painterly surface texture. In addition to creating a new series of horizontally banded paintings in recent years, he has returned to a sustained investigation of the concentric circle motif. Noland moved to New York for about two years before departing in 1963 for more tranquil surroundings. He resided for some years in South Shaftesbury, Vermont, near Bennington. In 1979 he moved to South Salem in Westchester County, north of New York City. In recent years, he has made his home in Port Clyde, on the shore not far from Rockland, Maine. In 1994 he married longtime *Architectural Digest* editor Paige Rense.

Nordfeldt, B. J. O. *See* JONSON, RAYMOND.

Norton, Charles Eliot (1828–1908). Art historian. Also a literary scholar, writer, editor, political activist, and teacher. Seemingly omnipresent in American cultural life during the second half of the nineteenth-century, he numbered among the most important and influential intellectuals of his day. Norton made his lifelong home in Cambridge, Massachusetts. After graduating in 1846 from Harvard, he was employed for about five years by an East India trading company. In 1849 he left to travel for two years in India and Europe. Subsequently, he worked as a social reformer in Boston before departing in 1856 for nearly two years in Europe. From 1864 he summered regularly in the small western Massachusetts town of Ashfield. He was again in Europe between 1868 and 1873. Shortly after his return, he was appointed Harvard University's first professor of fine arts. During almost twenty-five years there before his retirement, he was instrumental in establishing art history as a field of academic study. Regarding art as an index of civilization, he promoted education in the humanities as a counterweight to contemporary vulgarity and materialism. Although he eventually espoused broader views, Norton often echoed English aesthetician and moral idealist John Ruskin, a friend whose writings he helped popularize in the United States. A political liberal, Norton argued the Union cause during the Civil War and participated in founding *The Nation* magazine in 1865. Among other wide-ranging accomplishments, from 1864 to 1868 he served with James Russell Lowell as co-editor of the newly founded *North American Review*. A founder in 1879 of the Archaeological Institute of America (he served as its first president), he also assisted in organizing the Dante Society in 1881. A prolific editor and writer, he published dozens of books. Among numerous compilations, he devoted volumes to Lowell, Thomas Carlyle, Rudyard Kipling, Ralph Waldo Emerson, Henry Wadsworth Longfellow, Anne Bradstreet, and John Donne. His other books include *Considerations on Some Recent Social Theories* (1853), *Notes of Travel and Study in Italy* (1860), *Historical Studies of Church-Building in the Middle Ages: Venice, Siena, Florence* (1880), *History of Ancient Art* (1891), and a notable prose translation of Dante's *Divine Comedy* (1891–92).

Noskowiak, Sonya. *See* F/64 GROUP.

Nourse, Elizabeth (1859–1938). Painter. Remembered primarily for sympathetic studies of peasant life, often centering on women and children, she also painted still lifes and landscapes. She worked in Paris throughout her professional life. Her direct realism and painterly touch allied her work of the late 1880s and 1890s with progressive taste mediating between academic tradition and impressionist innovation. After 1900, her brushwork showed greater interest in the light and transience of impressionism. Born in Mount Healthy, Ohio, Nourse studied for several years in nearby Cincinnati at the McMicken School of Design (now Art Academy of Cincinnati). In 1882 she started some months of study at the *Art Students League, but then returned for additional training at McMicken. In Cincinnati she also participated in the city's enthusiasm for the *aesthetic movement, trying her hand at decorative arts media. (Her artistically inclined twin sister, **Adelaide Nourse** [1859–93], married one of the city's leaders in the movement, Benn Pittman [1822–1910], and remained involved with decorative projects.) In 1887 Nourse left for Paris, where she subsequently made her home. With years of artistic experience behind her, she studied for only a short time in Paris before establishing herself as an independent professional. She sometimes painted outdoors, in search of the tonal unity seen in the paintings of such artists as Jules Bastien-Lepage, who particularly influenced her treatment of peasant subjects. She visited the United States only once, in 1893, but abroad she traveled widely, from Russia to North Africa, often depicting local scenes in her work. She continued to exhibit regularly until 1924 and died in Paris.

Nutt, Jim. *See* CHICAGO IMAGISM.

Nutting, Wallace (1861–1941). Antiquarian, collector, photographer, and tastemaker. Also an author, Congregational minister, and entrepreneur. A popularizer of the colonial revival, he produced hand-tinted photographs of quaintly retrospective subjects, which sold millions of copies. He also published a steady stream of books and articles idealizing the American past and manufactured reproduction furnishings, making available copies of pieces from his own first-rate antiques collection. To the burgeoning consumer society of a modernizing era, he promoted a comforting lifestyle of simplicity and traditional values. By using modern sales and marketing techniques to promote his interconnected activities, he successfully capitalized on his vision of the old-fashioned virtue and taste embedded in New England history. A native of Marlborough, Massachusetts, west of Boston, Nutting spent his early years in Maine. Educated at Harvard, Hartford Theological Seminary, and

New York's Union Theological Seminary, he was ordained in 1888 prior to serving as a clergyman in several locations. Even before physical and psychological ailments drove him from the ministry in 1904, he had taken a serious interest in photography. When this became his primary occupation, he focused on New England landscapes and interiors of colonial homes, sometimes including costumed inhabitants, and soon recruited a staff to color his platinotypes for sale. In 1905 he bought a vintage house in Southbury, Connecticut, and began educating himself about antique furnishings, which he bought at first to provide decor for his photographs. Before long, he had become an authority on then underappreciated colonial furniture. In 1912 he moved permanently to Framingham, Massachusetts, not far from his birthplace, and the following year began issuing books combining photographs with his own texts. His many publications include travel guides for historically minded motorists and authoritative manuals on antiques, as well as *Wallace Nutting's Biography* (1936). Eventually he owned five restored New England residences, the Wallace Nutting Chain of Colonial Houses, furnished with antiques and open to the fee-paying public. In 1917 he established a workshop for production of handcrafted reproduction furniture, which he sold by mail order. After restoring an eighteenth-century forge in Saugus, Massachusetts, he added colonial-style hardware to his product line.

O

O'SULLIVAN

Okada

Op art

Oldenburg

O'Keeffe

Okada, Kenzo (1902–82). Painter. His abstractions from the 1950s and later temper *abstract expressionism's scale, richly worked surfaces, and accidental effects with the sensibility of his native Japan. He is known particularly for poetic, delicately colored compositions that often suggest landscapes or refer indirectly to the natural world. He generally left much of the canvas free of pictorial incident, while clustering simple forms asymmetrically to create intriguing, serene effects. Born in Yokohama, he studied at the Tokyo Fine Arts University (now Tokyo University of Arts) from 1922 to 1924. For the next three years he lived in Paris, where he worked briefly with his countryman Tsugouharu Foujita, met a number of leading artists, and painted views of city life. After returning to Japan, he painted figurative works and landscapes in an impressionist style based on western tradition. In 1950 he settled in New York and ten years later became an American citizen. He at first felt nearly overwhelmed by unaccustomed personal and creative freedom as well as the city's raw energy. Through Betty *Parsons, who mounted his first New York show in 1953, he became familiar with leading abstract expressionists and their work. Like many of them, he was drawn to *automatism as a means of revealing the unconscious, a practice that meshed with familiar Zen Buddhist meditative techniques. He called the process "doing without knowing." Explaining the marked shift in his approach after moving to the United States, he remarked that when living in Japan he thought all the time about the West, while in New York he dreamed only of Japan. *Memories* (Whitney Museum, 1957), conceived on the large scale of abstract expressionism, engages totally abstract, floating forms in a decorative yet restrained evocation of his aesthetically rich Japanese heritage. Okada made his first return trip to Japan in 1958, by the late 1960s traveled there often, and eventually established a second residence in Tokyo. In 1963 he purchased a home in Rensselaerville, New York, not far from Albany. He died in Tokyo while on a visit coinciding with his first retrospective organized by a Japanese museum.

O'Keeffe, Georgia (1887–1986). Painter. Few twentieth-century artists so convincingly registered the transcendental American attraction to physical fact as a manifestation of some unknowable reality. During a long career, she painted abstractions, flowers, landscapes, still lifes, cityscapes, and New Mexican vistas. Her controlled technique typically contrasts sharp edges with sweeping color areas. Although many works include dramatic spatial recession, she remained particularly attentive to the decorative design of painted surfaces. After Alfred *Stieglitz introduced her art in a 1916 group exhibition at his 291 gallery, their lives remained entwined until his death thirty years later. In 1918 he left an unrewarding marriage to live with O'Keeffe, and they wed in 1924. Professionally, he supervised her career: exhibiting her work, publicizing it, and acting as her agent. In return, she served as a favorite subject of his photographs, particularly in their early years together. At the end of the 1920s, O'Keeffe established an independent life in New Mexico, where she found her own friends, an enthralling landscape, and, soon, her own residence in Abiquiu. Nevertheless, she spent part of every year with Stieglitz, and after his death she devoted much time to preserving his legacy. During her remaining forty years, O'Keeffe became something of a national icon, representing to many women an exemplar of freedom, integrity, and creative vision.

Although she had been a figure of celebrity in the 1920s and 1930s, between the 1940s and the 1960s, O'Keeffe's work was not held in high esteem. In the early 1970s she was rediscovered by a new wave of feminist artists and activists keen to discover accomplished role models and women artists whose work had been unfairly neglected. Responding also to a heightened interest during the same period in earlier American art generally, in 1970 the *Whitney Museum of American Art held a major retrospective of her work, providing exposure she had not recently enjoyed. Among the public at large, O'Keeffe's great popularity rode on her attachment to widely understood American subject matter, her impeccably crafted and appealingly hued surfaces, the erotic charge fueling many compositions, and the aura of spiritual rapture her work provoked. With time, many observers wrapped her in mystique, fusing her character with her imperturbable style to regard her as austere and ethereal. Few bothered to point out that she was funny, passionate, kind, and adventurous, and that she cultivated a public persona largely to protect her privacy (and perhaps, slyly, to heighten her art's marketability). By the time of her death at ninety-eight, she ranked among the most widely appreciated and honored artists in the United States. In 1997 a museum dedicated to her work opened in Santa Fe, and the following year her Abiquiu home, about fifty miles north, was designated a National Historic Landmark.

Georgia Totto O'Keeffe's origins lay in Sun Prairie, Wisconsin, near Madison, where she was born and grew up on the family farm. At fifteen, she moved with her family to Williamsburg, Virginia. Following graduation from high school, during a bumpy formative period of more than a decade, O'Keeffe studied art in Chicago, in New York, and at the University of Virginia summer school. She worked as a commercial artist and taught. At one point, she even renounced painting. Her professional training began during the 1905–6 academic year at the School of the Art Institute of Chicago. In 1907 she moved to New York and worked at the *Art Students League, where William Merritt *Chase ranked as her most important teacher. During this period she visited Stieglitz's gallery and saw exhibitions of work by Rodin and Matisse, but was not yet impressed by the gallery's proprietor nor the work he showed. Dissatisfied with her progress, the following autumn she moved back to Chicago, where she worked as a commercial artist until 1910. Following a return to Virginia, she taught in the public schools of Amarillo, Texas, for two years before enrolling, in the fall of 1914, at Teachers' College, Columbia University. There, she studied with Arthur Wesley *Dow, who exerted immeasurable influence on her artistic development. He opened her eyes to Japanese art, taught her to emphasize the two-dimensional design of a painting, and insisted on originality, deriding imitation of both nature and the works of other artists. Near the end of her life, O'Keeffe commented that for her, art meant "filling a space in a beautiful way," a succinct summation of Dow's most important teaching. O'Keeffe taught at Columbia (South Carolina) College from autumn 1915 until March 1916, when she resumed study with Dow. In the fall of that year, she moved to Canyon, near Lubbock, to head the art department at West Texas State Normal College (now West Texas A&M University).

Meanwhile, early in 1916, a friend had shown some of O'Keeffe's drawings to Stieglitz, supposedly eliciting his famous comment, "Finally, a woman on paper!" He mounted her first one-person show in the spring of 1917, while she was in Texas. The work that so captivated Stieglitz consisted of dramatically simplified charcoal, ink, or watercolor abstractions, mostly suggesting natural organic forms. Occasionally, they were completely nonrepresentational, as in the startlingly reduced watercolor *Blue Lines X* (Metropolitan Museum, 1916), which shows two vertical lines of varying breadth, one broken in the middle, "standing" in a pool of ink. It is noteworthy that O'Keeffe's journey to abstraction took a quite different path from those of other young modernists. Although she read widely in modern literature, political thought, and art theory (including Kandinsky's early defense of abstract art), uniquely among important early modernists she did not visit Europe. (Her first excursion there occurred nearly forty years later.) The usual models for the other young modernists—Cézanne, cubism, and Matisse—meant relatively little to her development. Rather, her familiarity with the abstracting tendencies within art nouveau design and the principles she had learned from Dow sufficed to free her creativity while she remained isolated in South Carolina.

When she left her job in Texas in June 1918 to return at Stieglitz's urging to New York, their romance immediately flourished. Subsequently, she painted a number of abstract oils. *Blue and Green Music* (Metropolitan Museum, 1919), a flowing evocation of melody, sharply constrained by geometric shafts, demonstrates her familiarity with the period's popular analogy between abstract art and music. By this time she also knew the work of Arthur *Dove and others in the Stieglitz circle who experimented along these lines. In the 1920s O'Keeffe's work became more representational. However, abstract or nearly abstract works occurred throughout her career, and she consistently stressed the formal qualities of objects she depicted. To some degree, her work in the 1920s reflects the seasonal nature of her life with Stieglitz. Normally, they spent the warm months in upstate New York, at Lake George, where she painted the verdant landscape. During winters, she painted still lifes and views from her city windows. In such works as *East River from the Thirtieth Story of the Shelton Hotel, New York* (New Britain [Connecticut] Museum of American Art, 1928), she contributed to *precisionist interest in formalized depictions of modern architectural subjects. In her celebrated close-up flowers from the middle years of the 1920s, she demonstrated close attention to the era's sharp-focus photography that zeroed in on objects for dramatic effect, precisely O'Keeffe's procedure in these richly sensuous works. Elegant and sexually charged, *Black Iris III* (Metropolitan Museum, 1926) takes viewers to the heart of a flower as its curving lines and filmy forms push against the edges of the canvas. On her first visit to New Mexico, she stayed from April until August 1929 as a guest of Mabel Dodge *Luhan in *Taos. Exhilarated by the landscape and by her freedom there, she returned the next two summers and for at least part of nearly every year from 1934. Besides landscapes, O'Keeffe's New Mexican subjects included emblematic motifs, such as bones and rocks, which also appealed to her sense of form. *Cow's Skull: Red, White, and Blue* (Metropolitan Museum, 1931) depicts a white, horned skull suspended against a blue backdrop bordered by red stripes, but it suggests a crucifixion in its formal relationships. O'Keeffe remained characteristically reticent about its meaning, but like many others the painting gains strength from its enigmatic character.

Stieglitz died in the summer of 1946, while O'Keeffe's retrospective, the first ever given to a woman artist, was on view at the *Museum of Modern Art. Until 1949, she painted little while remaining mostly in New York to disperse Stieglitz's art collection and papers to appropriate institutions and to organize exhibitions of his work. Subsequently she generally lived at her house in Abiquiu during winters, while spending summers in her residence near Ghost Ranch, outside of town. In the 1950s she began to travel more widely than previously, visiting Mexico and Europe and enjoying the experience of flying. In the early 1970s, macular degeneration diminished her vision, curtailing her ability to paint. She continued intermittently, however, and also tried her hand at ceramics. In 1984 she moved to Santa Fe, where she died. In 1976, the artist published *Georgia O'Keeffe*, an autobiographical statement and commentary on its many color plates of her work. Two years later, for the *Metropolitan Museum of Art she assembled an exhibition of Stieglitz's photographs of her and for its catalogue produced a brief memoir. O'Keeffe wrote little else for publication, but many of her surviving letters have appeared in print. Spare and suggestive, like her painting, her writing vividly evokes her cleverness, curiosity, and wry serenity. A sister, **Ida Ten Eyck O'Keeffe** (1889–1961), studied art intermittently, but became a nurse by profession. In New York and elsewhere during the 1930s and later, she exhibited flower paintings often somewhat reminiscent of Georgia's.

Oldenburg, Claes (1929–). Sculptor, printmaker, and draftsman. A pioneering creator of *happenings, in the early 1960s he contributed to *pop art with witty soft sculptures of common objects, such as typewriters and hamburgers. Since the mid-1970s, he has specialized in monuments for public places. These, too, generally invoke the iconography of everyday life, but their gigantic size frees their subjects from normal associations, producing effects ranging from whimsy to menace. Many drawings for unrealized projects present fantastic visions that amplify the surrealist underpinnings of his sculpture. Since the late 1960s, he has also produced prints and sculptural multiples. Born in Stockholm, as a small child Claes Thure Oldenburg lived in New York and Oslo before his family settled in Chicago in 1936. After earning a BA degree from Yale University in 1950, he worked as a journalist and took classes between 1952 and 1954 at the School of the Art Institute of Chicago. In 1953 he became an American citizen. In 1956 he moved to New York, where he soon became acquainted with Jim *Dine, Allan *Kaprow, George *Segal, and others who invented happenings. An eager participant in these high jinks, around 1960 he began creating environments, such as *The Street* (1960) and *The Store* (1961), transitioning toward more permanent forms of art. In conjunction with these, he made roughly modeled, painted plaster representations of ordinary objects. Negating the normal barrier between art and life, such works for sale filled *The Store's* Lower East Side shop. Soft sculptures soon followed. Made of stuffed cloth, vinyl, or other pliable material and generally much larger than life-size, they present good-humored challenges to viewers' preconceptions about the mass-produced furnishings of everyday life. Often so loosely constructed that they assume variant "poses" when moved, they interrogate notions of sculptural integrity. From the mid-1960s, he also made hard versions of such sculptures, as well as soft and colorless "ghost" variations. In addition, he initiated a series of drawings and collages projecting imaginary monuments and forecasting his first actualization of a large-scale work, *Lipstick (Ascending) on Caterpillar Tracks* (1969; later removed) at Yale. Made of painted Cor-Ten steel, it presented a startling conjunction of tanklike tracks, politically resonant in the period of the Vietnam War, with a vertically positioned retractable red lipstick that reached more than twenty feet into the air, suggesting both phallic energy and conventional femininity. His public monuments since the mid-1970s include simplified representations of such items as a baseball bat, a flashlight, a rubber stamp, a trowel, and binoculars. When sometimes partially buried or intersecting with nearby architectural structures, fragmentation heightens their mysterious nature.

From 1960 to 1970 Oldenburg was married to artist Patty Mucha (born Patricia Joan Muschinski, and in those days generally known as Pat Oldenburg), who participated with him in happenings and in the construction of soft sculptures. She lives in northern Vermont, where she is associated with the Catamount Art Center in St. Johnsbury. Since the mid-1970s, Oldenburg has worked in partnership with Dutch art historian and critic Coosje van Bruggen (1942–), his wife since 1977. Born in Groningen, she holds a master's degree in art history from the university there. Her publications include monographs on Bruce *Nauman, John *Baldessari, and Hanne Darboven. The artist's brother **Richard Oldenburg** (1933–) served as director of the *Museum of Modern Art from 1972 until 1994. Also born in Stockholm, Richard Erik Oldenburg graduated from Harvard University in 1954, served in the U.S. Army from 1956 to 1958, became an American citizen in 1959, and worked in publishing before taking a position at the museum in 1969. Chairman for Sotheby's American operations from 1995 until 2000, he remains in New York.

Old Lyme, Connecticut. *See* ARTISTS' COLONIES.

Olds, Elizabeth (1896–1991). Printmaker and painter. Known particularly for prints representing contemporary American life, often from a leftist, worker-oriented viewpoint, she also produced satirical and nonpolitical subjects. In her early years, she also painted portraits and later, worked with watercolor and collage. Born in Minneapolis, she studied architecture at the University of Minnesota before transferring to the Minneapolis School of Art (now Minneapolis College of Art and Design). In the early 1920s George *Luks became a mentor at the *Art Students League. In 1925 she left for Europe to study and travel. After returning to the United States in 1929, she lived in New Hampshire before moving to Omaha in 1932. There she took up lithography and, convinced that American artists should confront the realities of American life, produced a series of ten lithographs picturing subjects observed in the Omaha stockyards. Between 1933 and 1940 she worked for *federal art projects in Omaha and, from 1935, in New York. Reflecting her interest in egalitarian causes, she became a leader in advocating large editions of prints that could be made available to the general public at an affordable cost. In 1936 she participated in founding the *American Artists' Congress. Stylistically, her work varied, according to its purpose, from straightforward realism to forcefully patterned, emotionally charged interpretation. Her color lithograph *Steel Mills* (1938) falls somewhere in between: a sketchy cluster of workers' houses cowers before strong, overpowering mill forms. Olds also contributed illustrations to several publications, including **The Masses*, and after World War II she wrote and illustrated six notable children's books. She died in Sarasota, Florida, where she had resided since 1972.

Olitski, Jules (1922–2007). Painter, sculptor, and printmaker. Known primarily as a *color field painter, about 1960 he renounced his drab, heavily textured style of the 1950s, turning instead to large stained canvases featuring intense color planes, often contrasting with black, generally in roughly circular arrangements. In the mid-1960s he switched to spray-painting soaked canvases to create an opulent personal style of vast, amorphous mists, often accented with brushwork, particularly along the edges. During the 1970s he moved away from sprayed paint toward nearly monochromatic impastos. Expressionistic works begun in the 1990s display heavily textured, intensely colored, writhing paint surfaces. Some seem to reverberate with the power of natural phenomena, as observed from his summer home on New Hampshire's Lake Winnipesaukee, his winter retreat in the Florida Keys, and elsewhere. Late in 1968, during a visit to Anthony Caro in England, Olitski took up a serious interest in sculpture. His subsequent, typically large-scale abstract works, usually constructed from sheet steel, featured colored surfaces at first, but later he preferred the unadorned sheen or weathered surface of metal. Born in Snovsk, Russia (now Shchors, Ukraine), Jevel (or Yevel) Demikovsky officially took his stepfather's surname, Olitsky, when he became an American citizen in 1943. (He later altered the spelling.) Olitski was brought to New York the year after his birth. He trained mainly at the *National Academy of Design before entering the U.S. Army in 1942. In 1949 he went to Paris, where he studied sculpture with Ossip Zadkine but also continued to paint. After returning to New York in 1951, he studied art education at New York University, earning a BA in 1952 and an MA two years later. He died in New York.

Oliveira, Nathan. *See* BAY AREA FIGURATIVE ART.

Ono, Yoko. *See* FLUXUS.

Onslow Ford, Gordon (1912–2003). Painter. Born in Wendover, not far from London, he attended the Royal Naval College at Dartmouth before serving for several years as a naval officer. In 1937 he resigned his commission and moved to Paris to become an artist, despite lack of formal training. There he worked briefly with André L'Hote and Fernand Léger but soon befriended surrealists, particularly Roberto *Matta. Developing their early work together with admiration for the paintings of Yves *Tanguy, they attempted to incorporate visionary impulses into their art. In 1940 Onslow Ford traveled to New York, where early the next year his articulate lectures on surrealism at the New School for Social Research (now New School) thrilled some of the future *abstract expressionists and other young Americans. Later in 1941 he moved to Mexico, where he met Austrian visionary abstractionist Wolfgang Paalen. In 1947 he preceded his associate to San Francisco, where the two artists, together with Lee *Mullican, founded the *Dynaton movement. Onslow Ford became an American citizen and in the 1950s settled in Inverness, California, within a coastal nature preserve near Point Reyes. At the time of his death at his home there, he numbered among the last of the Parisian surrealist group, which he joined in 1938. While still in Paris before World War II, Onslow Ford devised a technique called coulage (pouring), anticipating the method made famous by Jackson *Pollock. By letting enamel paint flow freely onto a canvas, he took advantage of chance effects so admired by surrealists in their quest for automatic procedures that could tap into the unconscious. Sometimes he superimposed geometric lines and shapes over the fluid, indeterminate forms to bring order and stability to the canvas. During the same years, he also produced landscapes teeming with *biomorphic forms. Finely elaborated paintings of this type, often incorporating cryptic symbols, continued to evolve for some time thereafter. In California, he continued his quest to represent an inner world in harmony with nature by picturing ineffable ethers sustaining hovering abstract forms and points of light.

Op art. A 1960s phenomenon exploiting retinal effects, such as afterimages, reversible perspective, chromatic vibration, and other forms of physiological and psychological visual ambiguity. In response to recently popularized, subject-oriented *pop art, abstract op art offered pure form in the service of perception. The catchy name, a shortened form of optical art, first appeared in print in *Time* magazine in 1964. A 1965 touring exhibition, "The Responsive Eye," organized by painter and critic William C. Seitz (1914–74), then a curator at the *Museum of Modern Art, crystallized the tendency's dimensions and represented the high water mark of its reputation. Widespread public enthusiasm briefly greeted the tendency's confounding visual dazzle and nontheoretical accessibility. An international movement, op art drew on a legacy of modernist investigation into the expressive possibilities of pure form. In the United States, Josef *Albers's work provided cogent precedents. Painter, printmaker, and sculptor Richard Anuszkiewicz (1930–) has made the most enduring contribution to the American strand of op art. Born in Erie, Pennsylvania, he earned a BFA at the Cleveland Institute of Art in 1953 and two years later, an MFA from Yale University, where he studied with Albers. Before moving to New York, he also earned an education degree from Kent (Ohio) State University in 1956. In the mid-1950s he relinquished his earlier representational approach to initiate the investigation that has subsequently remained at the heart of his work: considering structural properties of abstract form combined with intuitive color. Around 1960 he developed the rectilinear, symmetric, hard-edged discipline that soon made his reputation within the op art context. Over the years, he has enriched his practice by experimenting with varied approaches that generally rely on line as his basic compositional element, while also presenting fresh and often opulent color effects. In addition, he has created painted reliefs and sculptures of linear openwork. He lives in the suburb of Englewood, New Jersey. Among other important contributors to op art, Larry Poons (1937–) painted large fields containing regular arrays of small ellipses in color combinations that cause a flickering effect upon extended observation. By the end of the 1960s, he had moved on to other forms of large-scale abstract painting. Another Albers student, Polish-born Julian Stanczak (1928–) made his name in the mid-1960s with perceptually unstable, bright canvases featuring wavering lines in contrasting colors. The lines tended to straighten in the late 1960s, and he has continued to deploy them as principal elements in later undulant and diaphanous images.

Oppenheim, Dennis. *See* EARTH ART.

Organ, Marjorie. *See* HENRI, ROBERT.

Orkin, Ruth (1921–85). Photographer and filmmaker. Born in Boston, she was the daughter of silent film actress Mary Ruby and grew up in Hollywood. She began taking photographs as a child and was developing her own film by the time she was twelve. She served briefly in the Women's Auxiliary Army Corps in 1943. In 1944 she moved permanently to New York and soon worked as a freelance photographer for many magazines, including *Life*, *Look*, and *Ladies' Home Journal*. In 1952 she married New York–born photographer Morris Engel (1918–2005), who shared her interest in recording everyday life. Together they co-directed *Little Fugitive* (with Ray Ashley; 1953), a prize-winning predecessor of New Wave cinema, and *Lovers and Lollipops* (1955). Orkin's most celebrated image, "An American Girl in Italy" (1951) shows a young woman confidently striding past the stares and taunts of a dozen men in Florence. Otherwise, Orkin remains particularly noted for lyrical photographs of New York and its inhabitants, observed with sympathy and wit. She particularly enjoyed photographing from windows of her apartments, especially the one where she lived from 1955, facing Central Park. In later years she frequently used color for her views. A 1977 photograph of a hot-air balloon floating in the mist above the park exemplifies her control of subtle chromatic effects. *A Photo Journal: Ruth Orkin* (1981) documents her career. She also published *A World Through My Window* (1978) and *More Pictures from My Window* (1983).

Ossorio, Alfonso (1916–90). Painter, assemblage artist, printmaker, and collector. An idiosyncratic artist with roots in surrealism, he contributed to *abstract expressionism in the 1950s. Later, he concentrated on richly inventive *assemblages that constitute his most original work. These gradually became more overtly sculptural over time. Wealthy and cosmopolitan, openly gay in a tough-guy era, responsive to Catholic themes in a secularized creative milieu, Eurasian in a virtually all-white art world, he made his luxurious East Hampton estate a central venue in the social life of the New York avant-garde who frequented eastern Long Island. Born in Manila, he was educated in Catholic boarding schools, first in England and from 1930 in Providence, Rhode Island. In 1933 he became a U.S. citizen. During summers between his four years at Harvard, he worked in England with sculptor and engraver Eric Gill. Following graduation in 1938, he studied at the Rhode Island School of Design in Providence for a year before moving to *Taos. There he encountered Betty *Parsons, who first showed his surrealist-oriented work in New York in 1941. From 1943 until 1946 he served in the U.S. Army as a medical illustrator, posted in Illinois. Subsequently attracted to abstract expressionism, he embedded unconventional imagery in spontaneous and gestural brushwork before altogether doing away with representation, albeit temporarily. After buying his first Jackson *Pollock painting in 1949, Ossorio established a supportive and admiring relationship with him. His purchases included the masterful *Number 1, 1950 (Lavender Mist)* (National Gallery, 1950), as well as works by Pollock's wife, Lee *Krasner. Eventually he built a first-rate contemporary collection, including works by his close friend Jean Dubuffet, as well as important abstract expressionists such as Willem *de Kooning and Clyfford *Still.

In 1950 Ossorio returned for the first time since childhood to the Philippines to execute a religious mural commission. While there, he also produced a notable group of small, mostly abstract paintings stylistically attuned to the work of Pollock and other abstract expressionists. After spending most of 1951 in Paris with Dubuffet, in January 1952 he took possession of the sixty-acre East Hampton property, known as The Creeks, where he lived most of the time for the rest of his life. (Built shortly before the turn of the twentieth century by Paris-trained painters and decorative arts enthusiasts Albert Herter [1871–1950] and his wife, Adele McGinnis Herter [1869–1946], the establishment passed after Ossorio's death to billionaire entrepreneur Ronald Perelman.) Here Ossorio restored the mansion to elegance, transformed the gardens into a horicultural wonderland, exhibited his distinguished art acquisitions, and in the decade before 1962 housed Dubuffet's unprecedented art brut collection. Stimulated by this outsider art, in the late 1950s he began adding miscellaneous trinkets and other found items to his paintings, forming hybrid objects he dubbed "congregations." Eventually, as the accumulative impulse overwhelmed his interest in painting, the richly ornamental mixed-media pieces took on a thoroughly three-dimensional nature. Reflecting untrammeled imaginative play and a fascination with the bizarre, they demonstrate also the power of objects to encode thoughts, desires, and emotional states. Ossorio died in a New York hospital.

O'Sullivan, Timothy H. (1840–82). Photographer. Known for Civil War scenes and western landscapes, he overcame the harsh working conditions of wartime and rugged terrain to produce some of the nineteenth century's most technically and aesthetically compelling images. Born to Irish immigrant parents shortly before or possibly soon after they took up residence on Staten Island, he began his professional career as an apprentice in Mathew B. *Brady's New York studio. Soon he moved to Washington, D.C., subsequently his home base, to work under Alexander *Gardner in

Brady's outpost. Upon the outbreak of the Civil War, he became a field reporter for Brady, but when Gardner established his own photographic enterprise, O'Sullivan went with him. Traveling for three years with the Union army, he was present at some of the war's most significant moments, including battles at Manassas, Petersburg, Antietam, Bull Run, Fredericksburg, Appomattox, and, importantly, Gettysburg. There O'Sullivan made a particularly memorable series, including one of his best-known images, "A Harvest of Death, Gettysburg, Pennsylvania," which numbered among forty-five of his views that appeared in Gardner's 1866 *Photographic Sketch Book of the War*. In this poignant image, military corpses lie strewn in an abstract progression into the distance, as a distant lone horseman and another figure on foot bear witness. Although it presents a horrifying spectacle, with mangled bodies clearly visible in the foreground, the evocative, pale light and heavy July atmosphere soften harsh factuality, suggesting consolation and redemption. After the war, as attention turned to the nation's expansion, O'Sullivan turned his sights westward. Except for a relatively unproductive excursion to Panama with an 1870 survey, O'Sullivan spent most of his time from 1867 through the summer of 1874 roaming the West, usually in the company of federally sponsored expeditions. From time to time, generally during winter months, he returned to Washington to sort and print negatives. Convincingly conveying the drama and vastness of the region's natural features, he composed sharply focused landscapes with a modern eye for the large abstract masses of its grandeur. In one of the best known, the 1873 "Ancient Ruins in the Cañon de Chelle," a forbidding cliff face soars beyond the top of the photograph, looming powerfully above remains of an ancient Indian pueblo. He also photographed contemporary Indians of the Southwest, creating dignified and unsentimental documents. During the late 1870s few opportunities opened, and he spent much of this time printing his backlog. In November 1880 he became chief photographer at the Treasury Department, but ill health forced him to resign after only five months. He died of tuberculosis at his father's home on Staten Island.

Otis, Bass (1784–1861). Painter and printmaker. Chiefly a portraitist, he also painted a few landscapes and at least one *genre scene, the first significant depiction in American painting of an industrial subject. He issued engravings and mezzotints reproducing his own and others' work, and he made the first lithographs known to have been produced in the United States. Born in Bridgewater (now East Bridgewater), Massachusetts, Otis was apprenticed to a scythe maker in his youth and may also have worked with a coach painter. Like many artists of his day, he continued throughout much of his life to supplement his fine art career with artisanal jobs. Upon finishing his apprenticeship in 1805, he probably started to paint portraits professionally while working itinerantly. He may have received some instruction from Gilbert *Stuart in Boston before he arrived in 1808 in New York. There he worked with John Wesley *Jarvis. In 1812 Otis moved to Philadelphia, which remained his primary base of operations, although he traveled extensively. At various times, he worked in Baltimore, rural Virginia, Washington, Boston, and Wilmington, Delaware. For about a decade after 1845, he made his home in Boston, while traveling often in New England, before returning again to Philadelphia, where he died. Although Otis's portraits show influences from Stuart, Jarvis, and Thomas *Sully, all more stylish painters than he, his plain-spoken approach apparently attracted clients, for he numbered among the most prolific portraitists of the time. Typically, his straightforward likenesses, usually in bust or half-length, focus on the sitter's face. On occasion, he undertook more elaborate compositions, such as the winsome *Portrait of a Seated Boy* (Westmoreland Museum of American Art, Greensburg, Pennsylvania, c. 1825). Like several other works, this adapts grand manner portraiture to the intimate scale of the conversation piece. In this case, the diminutive full-length figure appears before a majestic red curtain within an ample interior, beyond which at one side sky and landscape are visible. Dramatic light effects pervade Otis's single anecdotal subject, the intriguing *Interior of a Smithy* (Pennsylvania Academy, c. 1815), a pragmatically detailed workplace. His first known attempt at lithography, an author portrait, embellished a collection of sermons published in 1818. A more widely circulated magazine illustration of a landscape appeared the following year.

Outerbridge, Paul (1896–1958). Photographer. During the early 1920s, analytical yet poetic studies of form and tone first embodied his perfectionist approach. These distilled, aestheticized platinum prints occasionally approach pure abstraction. Among them, closeup views of mechanical objects demonstrate Outerbridge's regard for Paul *Strand's pioneering photographs of similar subjects. Later he produced notable color photographs. Born in New York and possessed of a restless, artistic temperament, Paul Everard Outerbridge Jr. never single-mindedly followed any pursuit for long. He began his training at the *Art Student

League in 1915 and took his first photographs while serving in the military during World War I. In 1921 he entered Clarence *White's photography school and the following year began to study sculpture with Alexander *Archipenko. In 1925 Outerbridge left for four years in Europe. In Paris he made contact with *Man Ray, Marcel *Duchamp, and others in the surrealist orbit. After moving on to Berlin, he went to London to take a second stab at a career in film, which he had briefly sampled in Hollywood a few years earlier. In the 1930s in New York he worked mainly as a color photographer on commercial assignments after mastering the fiendishly difficult carbro process, then the best means of making high-quality color prints. In 1940 he published *Photographing in Color*. A series of disturbing, surrealistic nude studies in naturalistic hues may have hastened his departure for Southern California in the early 1940s. There and in Mexico he employed the color process for casual but strikingly composed, sharply focused street scenes, anticipating the achievements of William *Eggleston and others who established color photography as an artistic medium during the 1970s. He died in a hospital in Newport Beach, not far from his home in Laguna Beach.

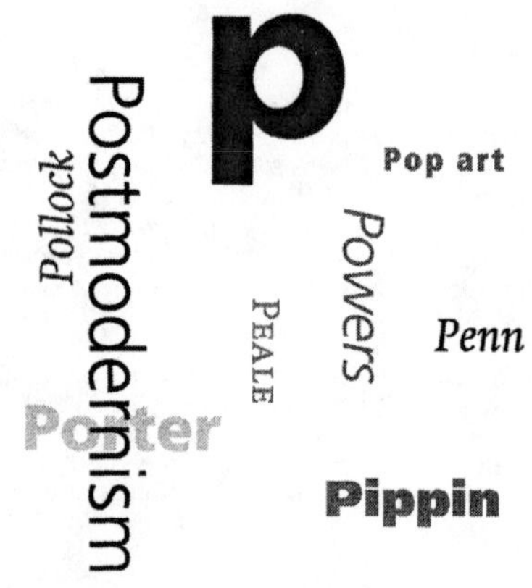

Pach, Walter (1883–1958). Painter, printmaker, and art writer. He played an important role in the selection of European art for the 1913 *Armory Show and remained instrumental in educating Americans about the modern movement and its sources. A lifelong New Yorker, except for periods abroad, Pach graduated from City College of New York in 1903. He also studied painting with William Merritt *Chase and Robert *Henri. By 1912, when the Armory Show's principal organizers arrived in Paris in search of new art, Pach had already lived there during most of the previous eight years and was well equipped to guide them through galleries and studios. He later selected additional work for the show, including Marcel *Duchamp's *Nude Descending a Staircase, No. 2* (1912), before returning to assist in mounting the exhibition (which included his work) and then to travel with it to Chicago and Boston. He again lived in Paris from 1929 to 1932, while in 1922 and 1942–43 he sojourned in Mexico City. Pach's art ranged from realism to abstraction. His early, rather dreamy work showed relatively little impact of the advanced art he so discerningly appreciated. After the Armory show he generally incorporated representational elements into compositions influenced by cubism and futurism. In the 1930s, as his work became more straightforwardly representational, he specialized in still lifes and portraits. Also known as a lecturer and teacher, he published numerous articles and books, including a memoir, *Queer Thing, Painting: Forty Years in the Art World* (1938), as well as *The Art Museum in America* (1948) and the posthumously published *Classical Tradition in Modern Art* (1959). His 1908 *Scribner's* article on Cézanne figured as the first by an American on this artist, and he translated several volumes from French, including *The Journal of Eugène Delacroix* (1937) and Elie Faure's five-volume *History of Art* (1921–30). In addition, he published monographs on Odilon Redon (1913), Georges Seurat (1923), Raymond Duchamp-Villon (1924), van Gogh (1936), and J.-A.-D. Ingres (1939). His wife, painter and printmaker **Magda Pach** (1884–1950), produced portraits, landscapes, and still lifes. Born in Dresden, Magdalene Frohberg studied in Paris. Married in 1914, she died in New York.

Page, William (1811–85). Painter. His poetic, introspective portraits and figure studies stand somewhat at odds with mid-nineteenth-century taste for genial, fact-based images. Page's command of painterly technique, his sensitivity to light and texture, and his feeling for dignified, monumental design derive from wholehearted immersion in old master painting, particularly the work of Titian and other Venetians. Despite the balanced grandeur of his mature work, Page's life and his artistic development suggest a mercurial personality. Erratic, inconsistent, fond of elaborate theories, and spiritually hungry, he experimented extensively with styles and techniques but completed relatively few paintings. His known output is further diminished by irreversible deterioration of some works, in part a result of unorthodox methods. Page was born in Albany, New York, but moved with his family to New York City in 1819. As a teenager, he studied for about a year with Samuel F. B. *Morse, who directed his attention to the work of Washington *Allston. He then enrolled at Phillips Academy in Andover, Massachusetts, with the intention of studying for the ministry but two years later returned to art full time. Painting portraits, miniatures, and subjects from literature and history, he worked in Massachusetts and upstate New York, as well as in New York City. In 1843 he settled in Boston, where he mingled with Transcendentalists and other members of the intellectual elite. In 1847 he returned to New York for three years before sailing to Europe. After two years in Florence, he settled in Rome. There he rose to prominence as a favorite of the Anglo-American community, numbering among his friends many artistic and literary figures, notably Robert and Elizabeth Barrett Browning. Despite distinguished supporters, financial success eluded him. In Florence, Hiram *Powers had introduced to him the visionary philosophy of Swedenborgianism. Soon an eager advocate, Page also pursued spiritualist practices, such as communing with the dead at séances. Spurred by these quasi-religious interests, he developed a complex theory of art, embracing the modern notion that the quality of a painting depends on its interior vitality, independent of visual reality. Abetted by his enthusiasm for Titian, this belief encouraged his concentration on the purely painterly aspects of his art, resulting in richly glazed surfaces, jewel-like color, sensuous treatment of the human body, and complex interplay of light, shade, and texture. At the conclusion of his stay in Rome, Page started his best-known portraits, pendant images of himself and his third wife (both Detroit Institute of Arts, 1860–61). (Earlier spouses had deserted him.) Both he and Mrs. Page stand before references to the antique, he in the studio before a sculpture cast, she outdoors in front of the Coliseum. Each evokes a timeless gravity, enhanced by subtle, muted coloration, as well as compositional equilibrium between representation and abstract elements. Spatial compression slightly flattens all forms and creates a vitalizing tension by pushing the figures against the picture plane. By the time Page returned to New York in 1860, most of his best work had been accomplished. From the late 1870s, ill health limited his activity. He died at his home of some years on Staten Island.

Paik, Nam June (1932–2006). Multimedia artist, known especially for works incorporating electronic elements, principally televisions. Also painter, sculptor, filmmaker, performance artist, and composer. Entertaining, futuristic, and psychologically resonant, his television works introduce into late twentieth-century art the era's most distinctive and significant communications medium. In a characteristic format developed in the late 1960s, the sets appear in groups, showing preprogrammed video loops. Paik is credited with coining the phrase "electronic superhighway" in 1974. Born in Seoul, at seventeen he left Korea with his family to settle in Japan. In 1952 he entered the University of Tokyo to study philosophy and music. In 1956 he departed for Munich to continue university training in music for two years. He studied as well with composer Karlheinz Stockhausen in Darmstadt, where he also met John *Cage, and in the late 1950s worked with an electronic music studio in Cologne. In addition, he participated in activities reminiscent of dadism and tried his hand at experimental filmmaking. In 1959 he began toying with television sets, at first distorting broadcast signals with magnets. In Wiesbaden in 1962 he participated in founding the *fluxus movement and the following year in Wuppertal, he mounted a gallery exhibition of his television works, thought to be the first display of art incorporating the new technology. In 1964 he arrived in New York. On a legendary day in October 1965, he acquired one of the first Sony portable video recorders available to the public, filmed his first video, and showed it to friends that night, thereby establishing *video art as a new expressive medium. Around the same time, he initiated a longtime working partnership with classically trained cellist and inveterate avant-gardist Charlotte Moorman (1933–91), who appeared in numerous *performance events. In the late 1960s she earned notoriety (and was even arrested) for playing his music with her upper body nude or concealed only by Paik's video bra, a device strapping two tiny televisions to her breasts. Subsequently, among other projects, Paik produced robots, sculptures, and the well-known wall-sized banks of televisions, typically orchestrating relentless on-screen movement for visually dynamic effects. For a number of years from the late 1970s, he divided his time between New York and Germany, where he taught at the Düsseldorf art academy. Partially paralyzed by a stroke in 1996, in his New York studio he continued to dream up new projects, realized by associates. Among the most resonant, *32 Cars for the 20th Century: Play Mozart's Requiem Quietly* (1997) deploys thirty-two silvered vintage cars with their radios programmed to play Mozart's last major work. He died at his winter residence in Miami Beach.

His wife, Shigeko Kubota (1937–), also works with video, frequently in combination with sculptural *assemblage or *installations. Born in Niigata, Japan, she earned a degree in sculpture from the University of Tokyo in 1960. She arrived in New York in 1964 to continue her education and soon also participated in the fluxus movement. Some of her initial video works, realized in the early 1970s, pay homage to Marcel *Duchamp, while others engage a diaristic format, setting precedents for her gradually more autobiographical later work, often incorporating themes of loss and desire. Still, she shares with her husband a sly humor and belief in an art of the moment.

Palmer, Erastus Dow (1817–1904). Sculptor. Among the most prominent American sculptors of the mid-nineteenth century, Palmer specialized in classical and literary subjects but also executed portraits. Shaped as an artist by contemporary taste for *neoclassicism during the pre–Civil War period, the self-taught artist nevertheless championed study of nature as the source of the ideal. He remained the only important neoclassical sculptor who never studied abroad, and many observers in his day thought his work displayed a peculiarly American spirit. Despite success in the New York art world, he never lived there, preferring to remain in his native upstate region. Born in Pompey, not far from Syracuse, at the age of nine he moved with his family to Utica. As a young man he worked as a carpenter but in 1846 turned to making cameos. Quickly achieving success with these tiny images, he soon began to model larger reliefs, which remained a specialty throughout his career, and, about 1850, figures in the round. After moving permanently to Albany in 1849, he consolidated his reputation in 1856 by exhibiting to great acclaim a dozen works, including his first full-length figure, *Indian Girl* or *The Dawn of Christianity* (Metropolitan Museum, 1853–56). This semi-nude woman contemplates a small cross held in one hand, while dangling in the other feathers symbolic of her abandoned way of life. Playing on the period's enthusiasm for Christian morality and its anxieties about the country's aboriginal population, the work prefigures in form and thematic content *The White Captive* (Metropolitan Museum, 1858–59; modeled 1857–58). His best-known work and the first important fully nude female sculpture produced in the United States, the *Captive* demonstrates Palmer's characteristic deviation from classical norms toward fleshier and more individualized treatment of bodily form. Providing an American twist to the precedent of Hiram Powers's sensationally popular *Greek Slave*, first exhibited about a decade earlier, this melancholy figure, tied to a tree stump and armed only with her virtue, resolutely contemplates her predicament at the hands of unseen Indians. Palmer's marble relief *Peace in Bondage* (Albany [New York] Institute of History and Art, 1863), depicting a restrained half-length angel, numbers among particularly poignant artistic responses to the Civil War. By the late 1860s, fervor for neoclassical sculpture had abated, and Palmer's commissions diminished. In 1873 he sailed for the first time to Europe. After touring the Continent, he settled for some months in Paris in order to take advantage of expert bronze-casting facilities for his *Robert R. Livingston* (Statuary Hall, U.S. Capitol, 1874). Palmer's later years were devoted primarily to portraiture, including a number in bronze. He traveled briefly to England in 1886.

A son, painter **Walter Launt Palmer** (1854–1932), specialized in landscapes, notably views of Venice and snowy scenes. He numbered among the first American artists to travel to China and Japan. Born in Albany, he studied as a young man with Charles Loring *Elliott and Frederic *Church. In 1873 he accompanied his family to Europe. Except for a short visit home, he then studied in Paris until 1876. Subsequently, he lived in New York but returned permanently to Albany in 1882. In later years, he summered often at Gloucester, Massachusetts.

Palmer, Frances (1812–76). Painter and lithographer. Known as Fanny, she produced more images than any other artist for *Currier & Ives. Her widely varied characteristic American scenes include landscapes, cityscapes, farm life, hunters, river boats, trains, stylish estates, and covered-wagon caravans. During a prolific career, she also produced architectural renderings, flower pieces, sheet music covers, and scenes of recent events with historical significance. Born Frances Flora Bond in Leicester, England, she had arrived in New York by early 1844 with her husband, Edmund Seymour Palmer, a lithographer. As they had in Leicester, the pair worked together in Brooklyn, with Fanny usually providing the designs for her husband to print. Currier & Ives first published her work in 1849, and when the partnership with her husband failed in 1851, she joined the staff as a house artist. There she was the only woman to create images or to work on the lithographic stones themselves, as she sometimes did. Combined with experience and technical skills, her ability to create decorative and well-constructed scenes that appealed to a large audience insured her important place within the firm. Her subjects characteristically celebrate American life and optimistically portray the growth and development of the nation. She died in Brooklyn.

Panorama. A type of enormous painting, sometimes hundreds of feet long, displayed on a curved or circular background or, later, mounted on rollers to be scrolled past an audience. Installed panoramas strove to create illusions of reality by surrounding the viewer with exotic or imagined locales, whereas moving panoramas also suggested the passage of time and space, as in a theatrical performance. A spoken narrative, music, dramatic lighting, and other special effects often accompanied showings of both types. During their heyday, in the decades before the Civil War, panoramas provided amusement and instruction. Many presented landscape themes, while others took their subjects from historical events, literary subjects, or the Bible. Because they were not widely regarded as fine art, nearly all have perished. One of the finest American panoramas, John *Vanderlyn's cylindrical *Palace and Gardens of Versailles* (Metropolitan Museum, 1818–19) remains also the best preserved complete, large-scale survivor by an American artist. The first known panorama was exhibited in Edinburgh in 1787. The format arrived in the United States in 1795, when two panoramas depicting London appeared. New York hosted one by William Winstanley (active 1793–1806), an English-born landscapist, whereas in Philadelphia Edward *Savage exhibited his own rendition. Many of the most popular moving panoramas represented journeys. In an early instance, William *Dunlap used a panorama as the backdrop for his play *A Trip to Niagara*, staged in 1828. In 1840 the most successful American panoramist, John Banvard (1815–91), first exploited a popular theme for moving panoramas: travel along the Mississippi River. Among other subjects, moralizing literature often offered a springboard. Designs by Frederick *Church, Jasper *Cropsey, and Daniel *Huntington provided the basis for an interpretation of John Bunyan's *Pilgrim's Progress* (York Institute Museum, Saco, Maine, 1851) in more than fifty scenes. The execution of panoramas generally followed the technical practices of stage-set production, which required designs readable at a distance. Their popularity presumably contributed to nineteenth-century artists' interests in serial imagery and in landscape painting on a large scale. The form has persisted as entertainment to the present day in a few instances, including Civil War cycloramas in Atlanta and Gettysburg, Pennsylvania.

Park, David. *See* BAY AREA FIGURATIVE ART.

Park, Richard Henry. *See* LAWRIE, LEE.

Parker, Lawton. *See* GIVERNY GROUP.

Parks, Gordon (1912–2006). Photographer and filmmaker. Also a writer and composer. Self-educated and multitalented, as a photojournalist Parks addressed a wide variety of subjects with empathy, elegance, and ingenuity. A special sensitivity to the experience of fellow black Americans particularly distinguishes his work. Born in Fort Scott, Kansas, as a teenager Gordon Alexander Buchanan Parks lived briefly with an older sister in St. Paul, Minnesota, before taking varied jobs there and elsewhere. He never finished high school. In 1937 he bought his first camera and soon began working as a freelance photographer, primarily shooting fashion advertisements. While living in Chicago, he also documented slum life there, and in 1942 he joined the *Farm Security Administration for a year. With this opportunity to respond directly and personally to social conditions, he matured artistically. Satirically titled "American Gothic" (1942) in reference to the widely known Grant *Wood painting of the same name, his most memorable FSA image shows an African-American cleaning woman, stalwartly brandishing her mop and broom as she poses in front of an enormous American flag. During World War II Parks was employed by the federal Office of War Information. Subsequently he worked for *Vogue*, and in 1948 he published his first photo-essay, on Harlem gangs, in *Life*, where his stories on a wide range of subjects appeared for nearly twenty-five years. In the 1950s, based in Paris for several years, he covered haute couture, celebrities, and events throughout Europe. In the 1960s his strong and insightful images provided notable coverage of the civil rights movement, its leaders, and moments of crisis. A celebrated 1961 *Life* series told the story of a Rio de Janeiro youngster and his impoverished family. (*Flavio*, a 1978 book illustrated with his photographs, provided a sequel.) Concurrently with his documentary work, from the late 1950s Park created expressive prints using experimental techniques such as multiple exposures and collage to incorporate elements of both realism and abstraction. He brought this tendency to fruition in the 1990s with a romantic series of color fantasies based on landscapes and studio arrangements of flowers and decorative objects.

As Parks expanded into to filmmaking in the late 1960s, he became the first black to direct a mainstream movie. *The Learning Tree* (1969), which he also wrote and scored, was based on an autobiographical memoir of his youth, published in 1963. Subsequently, he wrote and directed several films, including the hit movie *Shaft* (1971), which is often credited with changing the way African Americans are portrayed in entertainment media. He also wrote additional film scores, popular and blues songs, and orchestral works. Among his numerous books are four additional autobiographical works, *A Choice of Weapons* (1966), *To Smile in Autumn* (1979), *Voices in the Mirror* (1990), and *A Hungry Heart* (2005). *A Poet and His Camera* (1968), *Whispers of Intimate Things* (1971), and *Moments without Proper Names* (1975) number among several volumes of poetry illustrated with his photographs. In addition, he published a collection of essays, *Born Black* (1971), and the novel *Shannon* (1981). *Half Past Autumn* (1997) provides a retrospective survey of his photographs, along with an autobiographical text. Combining poetry with photographs of women, *A Star for Noon* (2000) includes also a compact disk carrying his own piano rendition of his suite of the same name for piano and cello. He died at his home in Manhattan.

Parrish, Maxfield (1870–1966). Painter and illustrator. Sharp draftsmanship, closely observed detail, dramatic color harmonies, luminous light effects, and decorative compositions characterize his widely appreciated treatments of playful themes. He drew many subjects from literature, particularly nursery rhymes and children's stories, but also invented pastoral idylls combining figures, often nude, with landscape. These romantic images combine nostalgia for human innocence with an exalted view of nature. His work received wide exposure through book and magazine illustrations, advertisements, public murals, and color reproductions that sold by the millions. Despite the popular acclaim these earned, during the 1930s he turned away from commercial ventures to concentrate on landscape painting. Born in Philadelphia, Frederick Parrish later adopted the family name of Maxfield. As a youngster he traveled extensively in Europe with his family. Having decided to study architecture, he entered Haverford (Pennsylvania) College in 1888 but left after three years without a degree. From 1892 until 1894 he studied at the *Pennsylvania Academy of the Fine Arts, where Thomas *Anshutz and Robert *Vonnoh numbered among his teachers. He worked informally as well with illustrator Howard *Pyle. His distinctive style grew also from admiration for the *Pre-Raphaelite painters and for the great art nouveau-era poster designers, such as Czech-born Alphonse Mucha. He revisited Europe during the summer of 1893 and again for three months in 1903. The brilliant hues and clear atmosphere he observed during several months in the Southwest in 1901–2 encouraged development of his singular color schemes and otherworldly light effects. The New England terrain he knew best provided most settings, however. In 1898 he moved permanently to Plainfield, New Hampshire, in the vicinity of Cornish, a popular artists' summer retreat. In the final years before his death there, he witnessed a revival of interest in his work, following a mid-century period of neglect attributable to changing aesthetic taste. Parrish's father, landscape painter **Stephen Parrish** (1846–1938), numbered also among important contributors to the *etching revival. Born in Philadelphia and mostly self-taught as an artist, he was nearly forty before he left business to devote himself full time to the profession. Partial to shore scenes, he generally depicted sites in New England, maritime Canada, or Europe. He died in Cornish, New Hampshire, where he had resided since 1895. His brother, **Thomas Parrish** (1837–99), painted landscapes, portraits, and other subjects.

Parsons, Betty (1900–1982). Art dealer, sculptor, painter, printmaker, and collector. Best known for welcoming *abstract expressionists to her gallery at an early date, she also exhibited the work of many other leading American artists, often providing their first New York exposure. Throughout her years in business, she continued to create and exhibit her own sculpture and painting. At twenty, New York–born Elizabeth Bierne Pierson married socialite Schuyler Livingston Parsons. They divorced in Paris in 1923, but she stayed on for a decade, studying with sculptors Émile-Antoine Bourdelle and Ossip Zadkine. After living in Southern California for three years, in 1936 she resettled permanently in New York. Over the next ten years she apprenticed in the art trade by working in several art galleries. From 1940 until 1944 she managed a small but important contemporary venue within the Wakefield Bookshop, where she exhibited such talented newcomers as Adolph *Gottlieb, Alfonso *Ossorio, Theodoros *Stamos, and Hedda *Sterne. During the next two years, she ran the contemporary department at Mortimer Brandt's gallery. Hans *Hofmann, Ad *Reinhardt, and Mark *Rothko numbered among the artists she presented there. In September 1946 she opened her own space, which became the prime venue for abstract expressionism after Peggy *Guggenheim closed her gallery the next year. Between early 1948 and the end of 1951, Jackson *Pollock showed with Parsons five times. Herbert *Ferber, Seymour *Lipton, Barnett *Newman, Ossorio, Richard *Pousette-Dart, Reinhardt, Rothko, Clyfford *Still, and Bradley Walker *Tomlin also appeared during these years. However, Pollock departed when his contract expired early in 1952, others followed, and the gallery soon ceased to function as the premier showplace for abstract expressionism. Among the defectors, Parsons was regarded as insufficiently commercial and too open-minded because she refused to limit her support to abstract expressionism. In continuing to discover new artists, she presented the first one-person New York shows of such major figures as Ellsworth *Kelly, Lee *Krasner, Alexander *Liberman, Kenzo *Okada, Robert *Rauschenberg, Richard *Tuttle, and Jack *Youngerman. Particularly alert to the contributions of women, she exhibited the work of Agnes *Martin and Anne *Ryan, among others. Best known among her own works are constructions, usually painted and often incorporating found materials, such as driftwood. Her early, representational painting shifted toward abstraction during the mid-1950s. Her large collection of contemporary art centered on the works of painters and sculptors she had exhibited. She died in the studio at her home in Southold, on the North Fork of eastern Long Island.

Partridge, Nehemiah. *See* PATROON PAINTERS.

Partridge, Roi. *See* CUNNINGHAM, IMOGEN.

Paschke, Ed. *See* CHICAGO IMAGISM.

Pascin, Jules (1885–1930). Painter, draftsman, and printmaker. Born in Vidin, Bulgaria, as a child Julius Mordecai Pincas moved with his family to Bucharest, Romania, and later resided in Vienna, Prague, and Berlin. He changed his surname in 1905, after arriving in Paris, where he spent much of his subsequent life. There he belonged to the Montmartre circle that included Chagall, Modigliani, and Chaïm Soutine. In the United States, his art was highly regarded for its sophisticated French tone, and he influenced a number of American figure painters who sought a cosmopolitan alternative to straightforward realism. In his earlier years, Pascin portrayed the low life of European centers—entertainers, prostitutes, circus people—often with hints of wickedness and depravity. Later, although he also painted still lifes and portraits, he focused on the female figure, usually nude or semidraped, and at its best, combining tenderness with unsparing observation. Described in a delicate but precise linear style, Pascin's insubstantial women emit a low-keyed, provocative sexuality (which on occasion veers into explicit description). Although less interested in volume and structure, in his patchy handling of paint Pascin learned much from Cézanne, but his line derived largely from the examples of Degas and Toulouse-Lautrec. Pascin moved to New York the year after his work was shown in the 1913 *Armory Show. During the next few years he experimented briefly with cubism but also made numerous drawings and watercolors on travels in the South, Southwest, and Cuba. He became an American citizen in 1920 but soon returned to France. After a visit of nearly a year in 1927–28, he permanently left the United States. He committed suicide in Paris.

Passlof, Patricia. *See* RESNICK, MILTON.

Patroon painters. A group of painters, active in New York and the Hudson River Valley from about 1690 until about 1750. Portraiture accounted for nearly all their artistic output, although religious subjects also survive. Working in related styles, they served a small clientele of merchants and landowners, many descended from the Dutch settlers of the region. (Huge chartered manors granted to so-called patroons in seventeenth-century New Netherlands survived into the era of English colonialism.) Patroon painters drew inspiration from internationally fashionable late Baroque models, which they knew primarily from engravings. Although they often individualized faces, they usually drew on European prints for the elegant costumes, accessories, and backgrounds they and their patrons preferred. Typically, these artists flattened and simplified forms to emphasize line and pattern over modeling and atmosphere. After the mid-eighteenth century, more academically trained artists gradually supplanted them. While some patroon painters remain anonymous or little understood, a small number of clear artistic identities has emerged.

Nehemiah Partridge (1683–1737 or earlier) has been identified as the creator of a group of Hudson Valley paintings previously grouped together as the work of the anonymous Aetatis Suae Painter. (The name derives from the Latin words for "at the age of," a phrase taken from precedents in European art and often appearing on this artist's paintings, along with the sitter's age.) Born in Portsmouth, New Hampshire, Partridge was almost certainly in Boston by 1699, if not earlier. There as a young man he practiced several decorative arts and began painting portraits. Partridge was in New York in 1718, and it is likely that he worked also in Newport, as well as in Virginia in 1722–23. About fifty of approximately eighty known Partridge works depict members of an elite class living in and around Albany, New York. He was active in that area from 1718 to 1721 and again in 1724 and 1725. Partridge's full-length portrait of wealthy, independent *Ariantje Coeymans* (later Mrs. David Ver Planck; Albany [New York] Institute of History and Art, c. 1718) epitomizes his characteristic combination of credible facial description with high-style fantasy in costume and setting. His artistic practice seems to have been curtailed after 1725. Evidence suggests that he was still alive in the late 1720s but had died by 1737.

Netherlands-born Pieter Vanderlyn (c. 1687–1778) arrived in New York in 1718, probably by way of Curaçao. From the early 1720s he lived in Kingston, eighty miles north of New York on the Hudson River, or in Albany. He may have been inactive as an artist for many years before he died in Shawangunk, New York, for no work from his hand can be dated even as late as 1750. Vanderlyn has plausibly been credited with the body of work formerly attributed to the Gansevoort Limner (so-called for his portraits of that family), who was active around Albany and Kingston between the 1720s and about 1745. He developed a distinctive style based on flat patterns, rhythmic contours, and appealing color. His portrait of the young *Pau de Wandelaer* (Albany Institute of History and Art, c. 1730), who stands with a small bird perched on one hand before a Hudson River landscape, exemplifies Vanderlyn's ability to summon a coherent, idyllic vision.

Among New York City's four-generation Duyckinck dynasty, no individual seems to have achieved eminence, but the lineage of the Duyckinck family documents the power of a family workshop in this era to sustain economic viability through the practice of fine art and related artisanal activities. Because positive attributions to the Duyckinck painters are few, their artistic personalities are not well defined. Evert Duyckinck I (1621–c. 1703), born in Borcken, Holland, settled in New Amsterdam (now New York) in the late 1630s. A craftsman as well as painter, he worked as a glazier, stained glass maker, and decorator of utilitarian objects. His son Gerrit Duyckinck (1660–1710) worked with his father on varied projects. Presumably from his hand, three-quarter figures identified as Gerrit and his wife (New-York Historical Society, c. 1691) display a reduced version of grand-manner Baroque painting. As was so often also the case among his artistic peers, facial features seem to be delineated with greater realism than costume and setting. Gerrit's son Gerardus Duyckinck I (1695–c. 1745) better grasped the rudiments of the European painting tradition than perhaps any other native-born artist of the early eighteenth-century. Notably, in 1713 he painted one of the earliest definitely attributable religious subjects in the colonies. Although solid evidence has not yet been found, it is possible that Gerardus I was responsible for the fetching, delicately painted *De Peyster Boy with Deer* (New-York Historical Society, c. 1730) and related works by the anonymous De Peyster Painter. Gerardus I's much older cousin, Evert Duyckinck III (1677–1727) was born in Holland but came to New York as a small child, in 1680. His father died in that year, so Evert III presumably worked in his youth alongside his uncle Gerrit, his grandfather Evert I, or both. Gerardus I's son Gerardus Duyckinck II (1723–97), born some eighty-five years after his great-grandfather's arrival in the New World, extended the family legacy beyond the colonial period. He was known especially for paintings on glass, but specific examples of his work have not been identified. He also sold paints and other supplies, taught drawing, and continued to offer the decorative arts services (including varnishing, gilding, and japanning) that had long sustained the family.

Pattern and decoration. A tendency in late 1970s painting, emphasizing ornamental or visually luxuriant two-dimensional design. Quickly nicknamed "P & D," its adherents found inspiration in fabrics, Islamic architectural embellishment, Japanese kimonos and fans, folk traditions, ceramics, theatrical design, Persian and Celtic manuscripts, and other forms of colorful, eye-catching artistry. They also looked to certain forms of high art, including work by Matisse, George *Sugarman, and Frank *Stella. Although interested artists came together in a loosely organized movement, they maintained individually distinctive styles. Some pattern and decoration work incorporated representational elements, but abstract compositions prevailed. By promoting the value of visual pleasure, pattern and decoration artists countered the austere appearance and intellectual aesthetic of prevailing *minimalism and *conceptual art. Yet their work generally sustained the period's preoccupations with compositional grids and with serial or modular forms. Within a few years, pattern and decoration faded as a distinct tendency, but its legacy entered the mainstream. By reinvigorating painting after a period of neglect, it facilitated the medium's large-scale 1980s revival. In drawing on decorative approaches from around the globe, casting a discerning eye on craft traditions, and elevating folk or vernacular forms, it helped to legitimize a multiethnic and pluralistic aesthetic outlook. What was then seen as its transgressive mixing of media, a tendency to draw from anything at hand, has since become commonplace practice. Pattern and decoration's earliest stirrings originated among *feminist artists such as Miriam *Schapiro. Admiring traditional domestic needlework and other crafts, they sought to find acceptance for such expression within the purview of high art. Much of the early interest in pattern and decoration appeared in Southern California. However, as a movement, a theoretical discourse, and a commercially viable enterprise, it coalesced in New York. Key artists began meeting there early in 1975. The first large pattern and decoration exhibition, "Ten Approaches to the Decorative" took place at the Alessandra Gallery in 1976. Individual pattern and decoration artists had already exhibited during the previous year at the Holly Solomon Gallery, which soon became identified as the movement's headquarters.

Along with Schapiro, painter and printmaker Robert Rahway Zakanitch (1935–) helped to organize like-minded painters into a movement. His New York studio hosted early informal gatherings of invited artists. An Elizabeth, New Jersey, native who later took the name of his nearby boyhood hometown for a middle name, Zakanitch studied at Cooper Union and the Newark School of Fine and Industrial Art. His early work in an *abstract expressionist style preceded a period of more disciplined abstract paintings. In the early 1970s, he became increasingly dissatisfied with art's drift toward intellectualization. After meeting Schapiro and others interested in purely visual art in 1974 while teaching for a year in California, he adopted a lush visual style incorporating middlebrow representational elements. Drawn to such precedents as wallpaper and linoleum, he repeated individual, relatively flat elements within a painterly context. His early pattern and decoration paintings most often featured flowers, but later works have incorporated varied, usually domestic subjects, including household furnishings and pets. Despite the casual and homey tone of his imagery, he frequently works on a monumental scale, sometimes heading for the sublime.

Among other important pattern and decoration artists, Valerie Jaudon (1945–) has consistently offered a personal version of great purity. Born in Greenville, Mississippi, she attended Mississippi State College for Women (now Mississippi University for Women) in Columbus before studying art for a year in Mexico City and another in London. By the early 1970s, she had developed a colorful form of geometric abstraction. At its outset in 1975, her signature pattern and decoration approach showed much greater restraint. She now concentrated on square, monochrome works featuring systematic interlace patterns of repeated elements separated by narrow strips of bare canvas that read as the edges of forms. She countered their intellectual severity with rich single hues (sometimes given a metallic sheen), painterly brushwork, and the exotic Middle Eastern flavor of her formal inventions. Jaudon has systematically built on this early work by gradually admitting greater variation. By the 1990s, she often pursued less tightly organized forms of composition, giving a freer tenor to her work, despite continuing attention to symmetry and repetition. Since the late 1970s, she has also completed numerous decorative commissions for public spaces. In 1979 she married painter and art critic Richard Kalina (1946–). Born in New York, he graduated from the University of Pennsylvania in 1966 and has taught at New York's Fordham University for some years.

Painter and printmaker Joyce Kozloff (1942–) also has focused on patterned abstraction but prefers more informal, less static compositions. Born in Somerville, New Jersey, Joyce Blumberg earned a BFA degree at Pittsburgh's Carnegie Institute of Technology (now Carnegie Mellon University) in 1964 and an MFA at Columbia University three years later. Struck by art and architecture she saw on travels in Europe, Mexico, and Morocco, she became increasingly convinced of the cultural significance of ornament and its humanizing potential. Following a sequence of 1970s paintings that combined motifs from varied sources, she began to paint also on ceramic tiles. In the years around 1980, she created large *installations, sometimes filling entire rooms, combining her tiles with other media, such as collage, lithography, and silk hangings. Subsequently, she has specialized in decorating public spaces with tiles that she designs with the specific characteristics of each location in mind, but she remains engaged also with other projects. Recently, she has produced collages and tiny frescoes freely commenting on antique maps. In 1967 she married art critic and photographer Max Kozloff (1933–). Since the mid-1970s he has written mostly about photography, which he also began to practice around the same time. Born in Chicago, he earned a BA from the University of Chicago in 1953 and an MA five years later. He also later studied at New York University's Institute of Fine Arts. His publications include *Renderings: Critical Essays on a Century of Modern Art* (1969) and *Photography and Fascination* (1979).

Two other painters central to pattern and decoration met as students at the University of California at San Diego. Visiting art history professor Amy Goldin (1926–78), later a principal spokesperson for the movement, encouraged their interest in decoration and provided an intellectual foundation. Painter, printmaker, and sculptor Robert Kushner (1949–) made his mark in the mid-1970s with fabric pieces that grew out of performance costumes. Pinned loosely to the wall, they subverted the usual notions of painting. Open to both abstract decorative motifs and representational elements, he has since refined his work through sophisticated understanding of historical precedents. Although Islamic ornament provided an initial inspiration, his first trip to Japan in the mid-1980s reoriented his interest toward the traditions of that land. Through it all, he remains indebted to Matisse. In recent decades, he has worked in numerous formats, ranging from mosaics in public spaces to delicately opulent Japanese screens. Born in Pasadena, Robert Ellis Kushner moved to New York the year after he graduated from UC San Diego in 1971. A 1974 journey with Goldin through Turkey, Iran, and Afghanistan deeply affected his early development.

In the mid-1970s, his friend Kim MacConnel (1946–) also made unframed hangings, which he generally fabricated from strips of clashing cotton fabrics. Often he overpainted these with his own designs, *pop art motifs, or appropriated representations. He also showed a distinctive interest in furniture. Generally recycling out-of-date cast-offs, he reupholstered and painted to garish effect. Later, he visited Africa, Japan, and other exotic destinations, apparently gleaning motifs at every halt.

In recent years, his most notable works have included constructed wall works and huge murals incorporating enlarged snapshots and/or kitschy souvenirs from his travels. His general aversion to tastefulness remains strong. Born in Oklahoma City, he earned BA and MFA degrees in 1969 and 1972 at UC San Diego, where he has served on the faculty since 1977. He is married to painter and installation artist Jean Lowe (1960–), who specializes in room-size send-ups of historical interiors. Born in Eureka, California, she graduated in 1983 from the University of California at Berkeley and five years later received an MFA from UC San Diego.

Pavia, Philip. *See* ABSTRACT EXPRESSIONISM.

Paxton, William McGregor (1869–1941). Painter. A leading Boston artist, he favored exquisitely finished figural compositions, usually depicting leisured women in tastefully furnished, upper-class interiors. On occasion, attractive young female servants appear, generally as ornaments rather than laborers. Successful as well as a portraitist, Paxton also painted more freely brushed landscapes and outdoor *genre scenes indebted to impressionism, as well as a few still lifes and nudes. Born in Baltimore while his parents were visiting from Boston, he grew up in Newton, a Boston suburb. In 1887 he began his professional training at the Cowles School of Art with Dennis Miller *Bunker. On the first of a number of visits to Europe, in June 1889 he departed for Paris to study with Jean-Léon Gérôme. He returned in 1893 with sound knowledge of academic draftsmanship. A studio fire in 1904 destroyed much of his early work. Partly in response to the Vermeer craze gripping Boston during the first decade of the century, his mature style features carefully staged, placid interiors where subtle effects of light play across porcelains and porcelain complexions alike. *The New Necklace* (Museum of Fine Arts, Boston, 1910), picturing two idealized women amid decorative objects, characteristically evokes a nostalgic fantasy of cool languor and sumptuous wealth. During most of his career, Paxton lived in Newton and then in Newton Centre, where he died. He generally summered at the seashore, usually on Cape Cod. His wife, painter **Elizabeth Vaughan Okie Paxton** (1877–1971) specialized in domestic genre scenes and soft, unostentatious still lifes, recalling those of eighteenth-century French artist Jean-Baptiste-Siméon Chardin. Like her husband, she favored carefully constructed compositions, controlled light, and studied color harmonies. Born in Providence, Rhode Island, she trained in Boston with Joseph *DeCamp, Edmund *Tarbell, and Philip Leslie *Hale, as well as Paxton. They married in January 1899. Following her husband's death, she lived in Boston, where she died.

Peale, Charles Willson (1741–1827). Painter and printmaker. Also a museum proprietor, naturalist, and inventor. No other major American artist has so richly combined the practice of art with distinction in other areas of endeavor. An active participant in the political and intellectual life of his time, Peale mingled with Philadelphia's cultured, learned elite and numbered among his acquaintances such eminent contemporaries as Benjamin Franklin and Thomas Jefferson. A fervent patriot, he interrupted a thriving artistic career to serve as an officer during the Revolutionary War. During this time, on several occasions he painted from life the war's commander, George Washington, providing the earliest monumental icons of the nation's first leader. In his art as in other pursuits, Peale exemplified the common sense, amiability, and idealism of the founding generation of Americans. A product of the Enlightenment, he shared his era's confidence in the unity of knowledge encompassing both art and science, in republican government based on and contributing to the virtue of its citizenry, and in the power of reason to fathom the harmony of creation and to nourish human happiness. His belief in public education motivated the design of the museum he founded. Aware of the need for institutional support of the visual arts, he played a leading role in mobilizing Philadelphia's efforts on their behalf. His devotion to a large family reflected not only personal preference but also his awareness of progressive European thinkers' interests in children, sentiment and affection, and the importance of family ties. By training and encouraging younger members of his clan, Peale founded a painting dynasty that kept his name alive in American art history throughout the nineteenth century.

Peale's multiple and varied accomplishments owed much to his boundless energy and inquisitive mind. Self-made in many respects, he had a limited artistic education, even less formal schooling, and no scientific training. Born in Queen Anne's County, Maryland, as a young man Charles Wilson Peale altered the spelling of his middle name. After his father's death when he was nine, Peale moved to Annapolis with his mother and four younger siblings. There in 1754 he was apprenticed to a saddle maker. At the end of 1761 he opened his own shop, where he expanded his practice into other crafts, including watch making and silversmithing. As was the case for most colonial artists, his entry into the fine arts came by way of artisanal experience. This background conditioned his temperament, persisting in his versatility, his knack for tinkering, his craft-related manual skills, and his interest in practical solutions to aesthetic as well as technical problems. In this spirit, and on his own, he first tried his hand at painting. In his early twenties, on a visit to Philadelphia he took the first steps toward artistic professionalism. There he purchased an English instructional manual, obtained artists' colors at a shop where he solicited advice, and visited two or three painters' studios. Soon after, he arranged with John *Hesselius, then living near Annapolis, to trade a saddle and fittings for instruction in painting. During the winter of 1764–65 he lived in Boston, where he saw John *Smibert's collection and received encouraging instruction from John Singleton *Copley. Although Copley was less than three years older than Peale, he was already the most proficient painter in the colonies, and Peale was clearly fascinated by his work. After he returned to Annapolis, he so impressed local patrons that in 1767 they funded a two-year sojourn in London. There he studied with Benjamin *West (only two and a half years older than Peale), who was beginning to make an impression as a history painter. Peale also became acquainted with major British portraitists and their work, advanced his technical skills (although, like West, he remained unmoved by the sensuous painterliness favored in England), and widened his proficiency to include miniature painting, mezzotint engraving, and sculpture. As well, he furthered his knowledge of art theory, picking up the prevailing academic ideas of the day, including enthusiasm for history painting and reverence for classical art. By the time he sailed for home in 1769, his experience abroad had secured a foundation for artistic accomplishment.

In Annapolis his knowledge of fashionable British practice enabled Peale to establish himself as a leading portrait painter. *Margaret Strachan (Mrs. Thomas Harwood)* (Metropolitan Museum, c. 1771), shown against a shadowed background, rests one arm on a foreground ledge. Her steady gaze directed at the viewer, she combines youthful beauty with charm and intelligence. Her elegant costume, her pearl choker, and the flowers in her hair, all rendered with veracity and taste, contribute to a compositionally and psychologically satisfying evocation of individual personality. Within twenty years of completing this work, the darkening of some of its pigments distressed the artist. Such deterioration is not uncommon in Peale's work and may account for the harshness that mars some paintings today. Caused largely by the artist's experimental habits, such defects may also reflect his relatively limited training in studio practice. In this period, he also popularized the British fondness for informally posed, outdoor family gatherings. Although Copley's work of the same time demonstrated superior technique, a more potent illusionism, and a finer ability to suggest the psychology of his sitters, Peale stood unrivaled in the colonies after Copley left for England in 1774. Shortly before he enlisted in the Pennsylvania militia in 1776, Peale moved permanently to Philadelphia. During his period of military service, he continued to paint portraits, particularly miniatures that were prized in those uncertain times. In 1772 Peale had painted the earliest known portrait of Washington (Lee Chapel Museum, Washington and Lee University, Lexington, Virginia), and between 1776 and 1779 he completed six additional likenesses. For his monumental 1779 full-length portrait of the general at the Battle of Princeton (Pennsylvania Academy), he drew on traditional grand manner practice for the figure's pose and military accoutrements. Both realistic and symbolic, the cannon, flags, and sword give the image historical weight and amplify particulars of the portrait with universalizing overtones of heroism and moral valor.

As he had since the early 1760s, Peale continued to play an active role in radical Whig affairs. He also served from 1779 to 1781 in the state's General Assembly. By 1782 when he opened a small art gallery at his home, mainly to show portraits of war heroes, his attention was increasingly shifting toward science. As his involvement in political matters gradually ebbed, he began seriously to collect natural history specimens. His interests in science, in art, and in display and installation for didactic ends came together in the mid-1780s, as he organized a museum to put on public view a general display of human knowledge. In addition to birds, fish, animals, minerals, other natural specimens, and American Indian artifacts, he showed portraits of exemplary individuals. As a Deist, he wished to impress upon his audience the notion that all of creation belongs within an orderly scheme, which man can apprehend through intellect and observation. Peale also pioneered in museum display, with such innovations as taxidermy imitating movement and naturalistically painted habitats. For many years, the museum was a semiofficial Philadelphia attraction, housed in Philosophical Hall from 1794 to 1802 and later in the old statehouse (now Independence Hall). By about 1790, Peale was devoting nearly all his energy to natural history and museum administration. Until he ceded day-to-day supervision of the museum to one of his sons in 1810, he painted relatively little. Complementing his work on a museum devoted to scientifically organized knowledge, Peale also led efforts to promote the arts. Addressing the lack of exhibition opportunities in Philadelphia, at the end of 1794 he joined with about thirty artists to found an artists' society, the short-lived *Columbianum. In 1805 he assisted the effort to organize the *Pennsylvania Academy of the Fine Arts. For the academy's initial acquisition of antique sculpture casts, Peale drew up the list of desirable items. At the Columbianum's first exhibition, Peale showed one of his most enduringly appealing works. *The Staircase Group* (Philadelphia Museum, 1795) shows two sons looking at the painter from the entrance to a stair. To enhance its illusionism, Peale placed a doorframe around the work and a real stair on the floor below it, confounding the boundary between art and reality and drawing attention to the painting's artifice. According to a famous but undoubtedly apocryphal anecdote, George Washington was so deceived by the trompe-l'oeil effect that he bowed in greeting to the painted youngsters.

Among later works, two of the most interesting and challenging relate directly to Peale's scientific interests. *The Exhumation of the Mastodon* (Maryland Historical Society, Baltimore, 1806–8) commemorates an important event of 1801, discovery of gigantic bones near Newburgh, New York. Peale mounted a recovery effort that yielded the nearly complete skeleton of a mastodon from the marl pit that he depicted in his painting. Nearby he also unearthed another nearly intact skeleton, as well as other fragments. Peale's results affected vigorous contemporary scientific and theological debates over the extinction of species. Dominating the composition, the triangular frame of a huge mechanical contrivance Peale devised to drain the cavity towers above numerous active workers. Peale positioned himself with his family (although in reality only one son had accompanied him to the site) at the right. Indicating his position as both scientist and artist and his role as mediator between the physical and intellectual aspects of the project, with one hand he gestures to the work in progress, as the other holds one end of a large drawing of bones. With its complex iconography and didactic meaning, the painting extends the notion of history painting into new territory, raising science to the level of an heroic, morally instructive enterprise. In his museum Peale exhibited the *Exhumation* painting along with a reconstructed skeleton, which appears in the summarizing masterwork of his old age. Completed when he was eighty-one, *The Artist in His Museum* (Pennsylvania Academy, 1822), a full-length self-portrait, shows the artist raising a curtain on his "world in miniature." Commissioned in 1822 by the museum's trustees (the institution had been incorporated the previous year), the work honors Peale's resumption of direct control over the museum the previous year, when he came out of retirement in the country to live again in the city. In this painting, Peale's dual interests in art and science merge in a unified statement about the importance of both in his philosophy. The artist literally and symbolically unveils a system of rationally organized knowledge, the basis for both self-fulfillment and human progress. Peale's peripheral accomplishments remained numerous and varied. He conceived and built ephemeral settings for civic celebrations in Philadelphia and promoted a form of moving pictures. A new type of eyeglasses and an improved heating system numbered among his inventions, and he received a patent for a bridge design. At Belfield, from 1810 his home in Germantown (now part of Philadelphia), he conducted agricultural experiments. At this estate also, in his sixties he reinvigorated a previously dormant interest in landscape painting. At eighty-five he wrote his memoirs, published as *The Autobiography of Charles Willson Peale* (2000; vol. 5 of *The Selected Papers of Charles Willson Peale and His Family*, edited by Lillian B. Miller). Less than a year before his death, he went into business making false teeth, and during his last months he was actively seeking a wife to replace the three he had outlived. Peale fathered seventeen children (several promisingly named for artists, two for scientists), of whom ten survived to adulthood. The achievements of five of his six sons suggest that despite some conflicts along the way, he provided a stimulating and nourishing environment, especially for the four with artistic inclinations. (Although they, too, drew and painted in their early years, the four daughters married and raised families. Their numerous offspring included Philadelphia landscape and still life painter Anna Sellers [1824–1905].) Peale also raised and trained an orphaned nephew, portrait painter Charles Peale Polk (1767–1822), born in Annapolis. During the 1790s, when he was most productive as an artist, Polk painted primarily in Maryland and Virginia. Despite his early immersion in the sophisticated Peale household, Polk's characteristic portraits seem naively stylized, achieving their success through decorative pattern, bright colors, and sharply rendered detail. From 1801 he resided in Washington, where the following year he took a government job. During the last few years before his death in Warsaw, Virginia, he lived in a rural area of that state.

One of Peale's most intimate and touching paintings suggests his pleasure in the achievements of other family painters. The warm-toned, lamplight portrait of his brother **James Peale** (1749–1831) (Detroit Institute of Arts, 1822) offers a meditation on art-making. With painting equipment on the table beside him, James examines his daughter Anna's miniature of Charles Willson's granddaughter Rosalba, then a budding artist herself. James was particularly noted as a miniaturist, but the range of his oil paintings included nearly every genre known in his day. Mostly dating to the 1820s, his still lifes are especially satisfying, with crisp detail, painterly textures, and soft lighting enhancing quiet arrangements of fruits or vegetables. James was born in Chestertown, Maryland, and trained by his older brother. He served in the Continental Army from 1776 until 1779, when he settled permanently in Philadelphia. Until 1782, when he married a daughter of painter James *Claypoole and established his own household and studio, he worked in his brother's shadow, assisting him first as a craftsman and then as a painter. Later he also worked at his brother's museum.

Under his guidance, five of James's six children who survived infancy became painters. **Maria Peale** (1787–1866) painted still lifes, and **James Peale Jr.** (1789–1876), a banker, in his leisure turned out some still lifes and creditable landscape watercolors. However, three younger sisters outdistanced these siblings' artistic attainments. All were born in Philadelphia and died there. **Anna Claypoole Peale** (1791–1878) achieved great success as a miniaturist, portraying many prominent individuals of her day. Before about 1817 she also did occasional still lifes in oil. Philadelphia remained her lifelong home, but she traveled to other cities, including Washington, New York, Boston, and, particularly, Baltimore, where she ranked as the city's most popular portrait miniaturist in the 1820s. After her marriage in 1841 to William Duncan, she was inactive until 1864, when she was widowed for a second time. (Her first husband, the Rev. William Staughton, died in 1829, only a few months after they wed.) Like her sister Anna, **Sarah Miriam Peale** (1800–1885) also enjoyed a flourishing career as a portraitist, although she preferred full-size oils. She, too, painted still lifes. She received instruction in portraiture from her cousin Rembrandt, then living in Baltimore, and eventually became a leading portraitist in that city. In 1847 she departed for St. Louis, where she lived for thirty-one years before returning to Philadelphia. In 1824 she and Anna were the first women elected to membership in the Pennsylvania Academy, and they share the distinction of being the first American women to establish successful long-term, independent careers as artists. Their sister, **Margaretta Angelica Peale** (1795–1882), following the example of her cousin Raphaelle, showed particular affinity for still life painting and became an accomplished specialist in this field even before her father seriously turned his attention to it. Like Raphaelle's, her simple yet dramatic works often achieve a nearly uncanny intensity. She also enjoyed the trompe-l'oeil effects that delighted Raphaelle, and on rare occasions she painted portraits.

Together with his uncle James, Charles Willson's son **Raphaelle Peale** (1774–1825) established the popularity of still life painting in the United States. He began to specialize in the subject around 1812. Apparently free of literary or philosophical pretensions, Raphaelle's illusionistic compositions reveal a hushed poetry within the materiality of nature. His uncommonly acute observational skills and sensitive, restrained handling of paint enhance unaffected, normally uncomplicated, yet formally adroit arrangements. His best-known painting, the trompe-l'oeil *Venus Rising from the Sea—A Deception* (sometimes known as *After the Bath*; Nelson-Atkins Museum of Art, Kansas City, c. 1822) exemplifies his fondness for trickery. It depicts a starchy napkin pinned over a painting of a female nude. Only the woman's gracefully upraised arm, her long hair, and her bare feet are visible behind the "curtain." With sophisticated skill, the artist differentiates between his illusion of the real (the cloth) and his rendering of an illusion (the "painting"), which is based on an engraving after an English work. Raphaelle moved with his family to Philadelphia soon after his birth in Annapolis. The city remained his home, although he frequently was away on working trips for as long as a year or more. Like his three artist-brothers, he was trained by his father, whose versatility he emulated. Raphaelle painted portraits in oil and miniature, made silhouettes with the assistance of a mechanical device known as a physiognotrace, worked on inventions, assisted in the family museum (in 1793 he traveled to South America to collect specimens), and with his brother Rembrandt attempted unsuccessfully in the mid-1790s to establish a branch museum in Baltimore. However, sustained artistic success and financial security always eluded him. From the time he was about thirty, he suffered health problems, depression, and alcoholism. Like his artist-brothers, he died in Philadelphia.

Rembrandt Peale (1778–1860), a painter and printmaker known primarily for portraits and history paintings, also painted still lifes and landscapes. Although he participated in family activities related to the museum and its scientific mission, he pursued an artistic career more single-mindedly than any other of Charles Willson's children. Several trips to Europe suggest his ambition to participate in the mainstream of art, and he alone of his siblings established a major reputation in his own day. As a portraitist, he became one of the finest and most inventive practitioners of the early nineteenth century, although his reputation in this field has suffered from his production late in life of many pedestrian replicas of his likeness of George Washington. He emphasized the authenticity of these portraits with the claim that he was the only living painter to have painted the great man from life, an event that took place when he was seventeen. Rembrandt's best-known history painting, a theatrical, twenty-four-foot-wide moralizing allegory, toured the country to great acclaim. In a pamphlet that accompanied *The Court of Death* (Detroit Institute of Arts, 1819–20), the artist explained that the painting's intent was to "render useful the rational contemplation of death." He also painted scenes from mythology, the Bible, and recent history. Rembrandt was born near Philadelphia, in Bucks County, where the family lived temporarily to avoid Revolutionary War dangers in the city. He lived in Philadelphia most of his life, although he was absent from the city for prolonged periods. After accompanying his father on the 1801 expedition to recover the mastodon, the following year Rembrandt and his brother Rubens took one of the completed skeletons to Europe. During 1802 and 1803, while Rubens toured with their scientific oddity, Rembrandt used the opportunity to study in London at the Royal Academy and informally with West. He was in Paris in 1808 and again in 1809–10. There he admired the prevailing *neoclassical fashion, set his sights beyond portrait painting by studying the old masters, and enriched his knowledge of techniques, including a system of glazing that he imparted to his enthusiastic seventy-year-old father. In 1814 he established Baltimore's Peale Museum, which consumed much of his time until 1822. For the next fifteen years, he painted mostly in New York and Boston, except for the years 1828–30 in Europe, where he made an extended tour of Italy. Rembrandt also numbered among the first American artists to work in lithography, which he employed to reproduce and publicize some of his paintings. In 1837 he reestablished his studio in Philadelphia. He published *Notes on Italy* (1831), based on the diary of his 1829–30 sojourn; *Graphics* (1834), an influential drawing manual; and *Portfolio of an Artist* (1839), an anthology that included samples of his own poetry. Rembrandt's second wife, **Harriet Cany Peale** (1800–1869), whom he married in 1840, also painted (she is known to have done still lifes, *genre subjects, and copies of her husband's works), as did his daughter **Rosalba Carriera Peale** (1799–1874), a painter and printmaker who produced portraits and landscapes. Of the other eight children who survived childhood, only son **Michael Angelo Peale** (1814–33) prepared to follow his father's profession, but he died too young to realize his ambition.

One of Rembrandt's most engaging portaits, *Rubens Peale with a Geranium* (National Gallery, 1801), depicts his teenage brother with the first specimen of that plant brought to the United States. As the painting suggests, **Rubens Peale** (1784–1865), painter and museum director, was drawn to scientific interests. Born in Philadelphia, he spent most of his adult life managing his father's museum (1810–22), the Baltimore museum established by Rembrandt (1822–25), and then a similar institution in New York. However, he is known also for still life paintings done during the ten years before his death. After quitting the museum business, he moved in the 1840s to a farm near Schuylkill Haven, Pennsylvania, about seventy miles from Philadelphia. There he pursued interests in natural history, dabbled in mesmerism and other pseudo-scientific fads, and about 1855 began to paint regularly. With their somewhat flattened forms, his highly detailed still lifes betray his lack of academic training, but they possess a naive vigor. Some of his best portray flowers, and he also painted landscapes. In an offbeat departure, he occasionally depicted groupings of game birds (taken from stuffed specimens) in their natural habitats. In less original moments, he copied works by other family members. In 1864 he returned to Philadelphia. His daughter, **Mary Jane Peale** (1827–1902) shared her father's affinity for still lifes. She also painted portraits and, on occasion, other themes. Born in New York, she studied with her uncle Rembrandt and with Thomas *Sully in Philadelphia. She lived at her parents' farm from the mid-1850s until 1864, spurring her father's interest in painting. Thereafter she resided in Philadelphia, specializing in fresh and delicate flower pieces.

A generation younger than his oldest brother Raphaelle, naturalist, explorer, and painter **Titian Ramsay Peale** (1799–1885) developed into the family's most committed and scholarly scientist. Devoted to renderings of natural history, his painstaking drawings and watercolors constitute his most recognized and skilled work, but he also used oil, primarily after about 1850, for more interpretive landscapes, a few portraits, and occasionally, other subjects. By the time he was seventeen, he was preparing color plates to appear in Thomas Say's prospectus volume for his *American Entomology* (1824–28). He soon accompanied Say on an 1817–18 working trip to Florida, the first of Titian's numerous scientific journeys. In 1819 he departed with Stephen H. Long's federally sponsored expedition to the Rockies, returning early in 1821. He made a second trip to Florida in 1824–25 to aid Charles Lucien Bonaparte in preparing his *American Ornithology* (first volume 1825). Additional collecting trips during ensuing years included a journey to South America from 1830 to 1832. Between 1838 and 1842 he crisscrossed the Pacific with another government expedition. When in Philadelphia, Titian worked as a naturalist at his father's museum and participated in the scientific life of the city. In 1846 he took a position in Washington at the federal patent office, where he remained until 1873. Upon retirement, he returned to Philadelphia. During all these years in Washington and afterward, he remained active as an artist and natural scientist, pursuing especially a long-standing devotion to North American butterflies. He also became an enthusiastic amateur photographer. At his death, he was Charles Willson's last surviving child. Extending for more than 120 years the artistic quest that his father had embarked upon in the 1760s, Titian's life also crowned the scientific endeavors that distinguished the family for a century. While a few younger Peales continued to paint, Titian's death effectively closed the era when the Peale name represented an important force in American culture.

Pearlstein, Philip (1924–). Painter and printmaker. A pioneer in the reinvigoration of figurative painting in the 1960s, he is known for studio compositions of nude, mostly female models. His matter-of-fact approach stresses physical actuality and formal organization. A Pittsburgh native, he served during World War II in the U.S. Army before earning a BFA from the Carnegie Institute of Technology (now Carnegie Mellon University) in 1949 and a master's degree in art history from New York University's Institute of Fine Arts in 1955. When he moved permanently to New York shortly after graduation from Carnegie, he lived briefly with his former classmate Andy *Warhol. Through the 1950s he painted representational works, mostly landscapes, in a vigorously brushed style related to *abstract expressionism. Around 1960 Pearlstein formulated his signature approach, stressing clinically dispassionate vision. Precisely delineated in sculptural detail, his affectless models inhabit believable space, but their poses conform to the formal demands of the two-dimensional picture surface. Treated, according to the artist, as still life elements, they often hold uncomfortable or awkward positions, while the framing edge frequently slices body parts with impersonal abruptness. Although his work bears some relationship to *photo-realism in its objectivity, Pearlstein has no interest in mechanical process and always works from a model. Many images incorporate furniture, antiques, patterned textiles, or other subsidiary decorative objects as visual foils to the pale human forms. Pearlstein has also been active as a graphic artist, in particular producing many color lithographs of subjects related to his paintings. From 1963 until he retired in 1988, he taught at Brooklyn College.

Peck, Sheldon (1797–1868). Painter. The generally dour, staring, and ill-proportioned sitters who populate his portraits nevertheless project a strong presence through Peck's willful simplification and emphatic design. Self-taught, he started painting in New England, relocated to western New York State, and finally settled permanently in Babcock Grove (now Lombard), Illinois. The three geographic areas correspond with three fairly distinct periods in the evolution of his work. Born and raised in Cornwall, Vermont, he probably began painting around 1820. Using wood panels as supports, he produced bust- and half-length likenesses, usually set against dark backgrounds. As he forged a distinctive style, he played harshly sculptured faces against flatter clothing, which he soon began to elaborate with decorative detail. In 1828 he settled in Jordan, just west of Syracuse, on the recently opened Erie Canal. There his colors became lighter, and he began to employ more elaborate settings, suggesting new familiarity with more sophisticated models. In 1836 he departed for Illinois. After a short period in Chicago, he purchased land about twenty miles west of the city. There he prospered as a farmer, while continuing his portrait business as well. Later he also took *daguerreotype portraits, but his paintings show no evidence that he wished to mimic photographic veracity. Perhaps he purposefully intended to differentiate his grander product from small, colorless daguerreotypes. Painting now on canvas, he often displayed his figures at full length, sometimes in groups of two or more. His colors brightened and settings took on more than incidental importance, as he amplified his sitters' circumstances with furniture, fruit and flowers, books and newspapers, and other accoutrements. Sometimes he edged his canvases with painted frames imitating wood. His son **Charles Peck** (1827–1900) painted landscapes, including some of the West, as well as portraits. Also a photographer, served in that capacity in the Union army during the Civil War. He worked in St. Louis as well as Chicago, where he died. The Sheldon Peck Homestead in Lombard is open to the public under the auspices of the local historical society.

Pelham, Peter (1697–1751). Printmaker and painter. A portrait specialist active chiefly in Boston, he ranks as the first mezzotint engraver to work in the American colonies. As stepfather to John Singleton *Copley, he played an important role in the nation's early art history. Born in London, Pelham learned his craft in the shop of a leading engraver, John Simon, and found some success before emigrating in 1727. In Boston he supplemented his income as an artist with several pursuits that indicate acquaintance with a range of polite accomplishments. In addition to teaching school, he offered instruction in music, dancing, needlework, and other decorative crafts. His first American mezzotint engraving, a portrait of clergyman Cotton Mather (1727), numbers among his finest. Based on Pelham's own painting (American Antiquarian Society, 1727), the bust-length image demonstrates his familiarity with Godfrey Kneller's late Baroque portrait mode, which dominated contemporary London taste. Pelham also made engravings after paintings by John *Smibert and John *Greenwood. He died in Boston.

His son, painter and printmaker **Henry Pelham** (1749–1806), owed much to Copley, for he was only a toddler when his father died. While training in his half brother's studio, he posed for Copley's *Boy with a Squirrel*. In a flagrant bit of plagiarism, Paul *Revere copied Pelham's drawing of the Boston Massacre for his own noted propaganda print of *The Bloody Massacre Perpetrated in King Street Boston on March 5th 1770* (1770). (Pelham soon issued his own version, but voiced outrage that Revere had stolen his design.) As he secured commissions in Boston and Philadelphia, Pelham's miniature and full-size portraits showed promise. However, his American career remained brief. A Loyalist, he sailed for Barbados in 1776 and soon joined Copley in London. For the rest of his life, he resided there and in Ireland, where he died.

Pelton, Agnes (1881–1961). Painter. Inspired particularly by Kandinsky's example and the teachings of Theosophy, she developed a personal and romantic form of nonrepresentational painting often featuring suggestions of landscape or other natural forms. Characteristically suffused with a glowing light, the space within her paintings hosts hard-edge, often levitating abstract and symbolic elements. Born to American parents in Stuttgart, Pelton spent her early childhood in Germany. From 1890 she lived in Brooklyn, where she studied for five years at the Pratt Institute. She continued her study with Arthur Wesley *Dow through the summer of 1900. In 1910 she departed for a year in Italy. Although she exhibited in the *Armory Show and pursued avant-garde ideas, her work remained rooted in representation until after she moved from New York to rural Long Island in 1921. Later, she sometimes painted realistic landscapes, which she sold in order to underwrite the more adventurous work that began to take shape in the mid-1920s. In 1931 she settled permanently in Cathedral City, California, near Palm Springs. Here, in relative seclusion, she often drew on her experience of the desert and its vast, empty spaces to create glowing, meditative images. In 1938 she joined with several other painters, notably Raymond *Jonson, to form the short-lived *Transcendental Painting Group.

Pène du Bois, Guy (1884–1958). Painter and art critic. In characteristic figurative works of the 1920s, he depicted the upper class with a cold eye. Smooth, simplified volumes sculpt his society figures, who seem to have little capacity for personal relationships. Although sometimes approaching social criticism, Pène du Bois's inherent satire generally yields to a fascination with chic and an apparent distaste for probing beyond appearances into the realm of character. As a writer, he championed the American realist tradition but also endeavored to explain modern currents. Born in Brooklyn, Pène du Bois trained at the New York School of Art (now Parsons, the New School for Design) with William Merritt *Chase, Robert *Henri, and Kenneth Hayes *Miller—the leading art teachers of the early twentieth century—before embarking for study in Paris in 1905–6. After his return to New York, his paintings reflected the painterly realism of the *Ashcan School. Although he helped to plan the *Armory Show and exhibited six works, he concentrated on writing for about fifteen years, working as a newspaper critic and from 1913 serving for most of seven years as editor of the magazine *Arts and Decoration*. Upon leaving his editorial post as his mature style emerged, he settled in Westport, Connecticut. He lived in France from 1924 to 1930 and again in the mid-1950s. After his work lost its acute edge during the 1930s, he eventually he became a studio painter of bland portraits, still lifes, and nudes. Continuing to write, he published books on John *Sloan, William *Glackens,

Edward *Hopper, and Ernest *Lawson. His autobiography, *Artists Say the Silliest Things*, appeared in 1940. He died in Boston following an extended illness.

Penn, Irving (1917–). Photographer. Known especially for portrait and fashion work, he has also addressed other subjects, always with unforced elegance, a flair for abstract design, and technical perfectionism. Although most of his best-known photographs are black-and-white, he has also worked effectively in color. Born in Plainfield, New Jersey, he trained as a commercial artist in Philadelphia. While subsequently working in New York, he also continued painting, as he has from time to time ever since. In 1943 he was hired by *Vogue*'s art director Alexander *Liberman as his assistant. Although Penn had taken personal photographs for several years, he became interested in using the medium professionally only after he had joined the magazine. For *Vogue*, Penn produced ravishing fashion photographs but also took on other diverse projects. For a celebrity portrait series begun in 1948, he positioned his sitters in a tight corner, specially constructed in his studio. This constricted space, limiting his options and the subject's, produced novel interpretations of their personalities. In the same year, while traveling in Peru, Penn for the first time photographed indigenous people against blank backgrounds. In subsequent years, he traveled widely, capturing the faces, body language, and adornment of those whom the modern world had barely touched, as well as tradesmen and other culturally overlooked urban dwellers. By turning ethnography into a fashion shoot, he responded at an early date to postmodern questions about cultural identity, imperialism, and construction of the ideal. In the 1970s Penn extended his quest for order and beauty to highly improbable subjects. A series of found objects from the streets included such detritus as discarded cigarette packages, a mud-crusted glove, and battered paper cups. By presenting these subjects unsentimentally in large, sharply detailed, impeccably crafted platinum prints, Penn gave them the dignity of expensive items. Reiterating the modern notion that aesthetic value is created by the artist, not the subject, Penn demonstrated in this series that he was up to the challenge. Collections of his work include *Moments Preserved* (1960), *Worlds in a Small Room* (1974), which presents his studies of international clothing and body adornment, and the career survey *Passage: A Work Record* (1991).

Pennell, Joseph (1857–1926). Printmaker, illustrator, and painter. A prolific and internationally known etcher and lithographer, he resided in London during most of his working life. Nearly always featuring recognizable places, his widely reproduced images evoke the era's cities, industries, and engineering triumphs, as well as picturesque historical sites. An admirer of James Abbott McNeill *Whistler, who became a personal friend, he eventually became the older artist's first biographer. As a tireless crusader for the appreciation of artistic printmaking, he wrote, lectured, and promoted exhibitions. A Philadelphia native, he studied at the Pennsylvania School of Industrial Art (now University of the Arts) and the *Pennsylvania Academy of the Fine Arts. Privately, Philadelphia painter and printmaker Stephen James Ferris (1835–1915) assisted his development as an etcher. From his early twenties, Pennell worked regularly for major magazines as an illustrator. In 1883 he departed for Europe, where he subsequently resided, primarily in London, for more than thirty years. However, he traveled ceaselessly in search of new subjects, augmenting his reputation as a printmaker with illustrated travel articles and books. After marriage in 1884, his wife usually coauthored his publications. In 1888 he was appointed art critic for a London newspaper, and during the 1890s he was associated with several important illustrated magazines. Also during the 1890s he began to work frequently in lithography and became active in promoting the medium. In 1917 he returned permanently to New York. Remaining active throughout his final years, in 1922 he took on the task of reinvigorating printmaking at the *Art Students League. Drawn to Whistler's work during his early days in Philadelphia, Pennell worked at first in a similarly delicate and impressionistic style. The two artists met in 1884 but became close only in 1893 while in Paris. By then, Pennell's style was becoming bolder, more atmospheric, and more forcefully descriptive. He increasingly preferred lithography or ink drawings to achieve dramatic tonal effects. Near the end of his life, Pennell published an autobiography, *Adventures of an Illustrator* (1925). *Lithography and Lithographers* (1898) pioneered for English-speaking audiences appreciation of the medium as a legitimate means of artistic expression. His other books include *The Life of James McNeill Whistler* (1908), *Etchers and Etching* (1919), and *The Graphic Arts: Modern Men and Modern Methods* (1921). *A Canterbury Pilgrimage* (1885) and *An Italian Pilgrimage* (1887) number among numerous travel publications. In addition, he illustrated scores of books by others, including many of the prominent names of his day.

Penniman, John Ritto. *See* FISHER, ALVAN.

Pennsylvania Academy of the Fine Arts. An art museum and school in Philadelphia. Founded in 1805, it is the oldest such institution in the United States. Architect Frank Furness designed its Victorian Gothic headquarters, completed in 1876 and today a National Historic Landmark. The origins of the academy date to 1791 when Charles Willson *Peale put into motion efforts to set up an art school. Envisioning regular exhibitions and organized instruction, by the end of 1794 Peale had enlisted about thirty artists, professional and amateur, to organize the Columbianum. However, it failed after presenting a single show, America's first significant exhibition of contemporary art, at the old statehouse (now Independence Hall) in 1795. Ten years later Peale and William *Rush convened about seventy local businessmen and art patrons to establish the academy. Chartered in 1806 and at first focused on establishing a collection, in that year it obtained more than fifty casts of classical sculpture from the Louvre. With the successful example of Peale's own museum of art and science in mind, exhibitions in the academy's newly completed original building began in 1807. Honorary academicians were first named in 1811, and life drawing classes soon followed. Also began in 1811, annual exhibitions showcasing recent work persisted until 1969. Still vital today, the school remained for more than a century unrivaled as a center of art instruction outside New York. Its substantial collection ranks in the forefront among museums of American art.

Pereira, I. Rice (1902–71). Painter. In innovative geometric abstractions layered on panes of glass or transparent plastic, she created unstable images that appear to change as the viewer moves. Incorporating light as an active element, these unusual works underline qualities of flux and contingency that emphasize her metaphysical intentions. Born in Chelsea, near Boston, Irene M. Rice lived during childhood in several Massachusetts localities and attended high school in Brooklyn. She received her professional training between 1927 and 1931 at the *Art Students League, where Jan *Matulka numbered among her teachers. Following marriage in 1929 to Humberto Pereira, she subsequently preferred the form I. Rice Pereira for her professional name. (After a separation, in 1938 this marriage ended in divorce. She was married to George Wellington Brown from 1942 until 1950, the year she married George Reavey, but they divorced in 1959.) In 1931 she studied briefly in Paris with Purist painter Amédée Ozenfant. Before her return in 1932, she traveled in Europe and North Africa. During the Depression, she worked for several years on *federal art projects and joined the *American Artists' Congress. *Machine Composition #2* (Smithsonian American Art Museum, 1937) reflects her dominant interest in mechanical imagery during this period. Around the beginning of 1938 she began to work with pure geometric abstraction and about a year later, first painted on glass. By the mid-1940s this technique had evolved into idiosyncratic arrangements of transparent planes fixed in shallow boxes in front of painted panels. Simple geometric shapes, along with lines and sometimes freely painted color areas, interact with those in front or in back as the viewer changes position. Abandoning this singular approach after 1952, she subsequently lavished much of her energy on writing art theory and poetry as she yielded to a romantic quest to bind her art with transcendental ideas. Her synthesis of neo-Platonic mysticism and alchemy with modern psychology, science, and philosophy first appeared in a 1951 article. In subsequent years, she published many books (and produced several unpublished manuscripts). *The Nature of Space: A Metaphysical and Aesthetic Inquiry* (1956) ranks as the most lucid of her dense and difficult treatises. Other books include *The Lapis* (1957) and *The Transcendental Formal Logic of the Infinite* (1966). Her art little recognized during the later years of her life, near the end of 1970 Pereira moved to Marbella, Spain, where she died.

Performance art. A type of interdisciplinary, time-bound expression focusing attention on the artist's body and psyche. Originating as a distinctive form around 1970 and peaking during the 1980s, it grew most immediately from *happenings, *fluxus, *conceptual art, and contemporary dance tendencies, as well as the period's countercultural individualism and anticommercialism. However, a related, longer history may be traced at least to early twentieth-century futurist and dada shenanigans aimed at smashing artistic conventions. Recent manifestations sometimes are known as performative art. Associated with galleries, art centers, cafes, and alternative spaces rather than theaters, performance art generally dispenses with the trappings of staged drama and usually makes little effort to entertain. Typically, it offers only limited visual appeal in terms of sets, costumes, lighting, and so forth. Performance artists commonly play themselves though they may assume character roles, most often as stereotypes useful for ironic comment. Frequently monologues, performance events tend to favor self-revelatory and often self-absorbed content. They may incorporate narrative but often remain discursive. Intentionally or not, performance events often display an unrehearsed quality that presumably lends authenticity to the material. Performance events usually take place before a live audience, but they may be taped, photographed, or recorded for wider distribution. Artists who have included performance pieces within multimedia careers include Vito *Acconci, Bruce *Nauman, and Dennis *Oppenheim, as well as Eleanor Antin (1935–), Janine Antoni (1964–), Chris Burden (1946–), Joan Jonas (1936–), Meredith Monk (1942–), Adrian Piper (1948–), Mierle Laderman Ukeles (1939–), and radical *feminist artist Carolee Schneeman (1939–). Performance art also has produced significant specialists, such as Laurie Anderson (1947–), who blends the form with original music, Karen Finley (1956–), and Martha Wilson (1947–).

Perry, Lila Cabot (1848–1933). Painter. Also a poet. An early exponent of impressionism in Boston, she painted landscapes, *genre scenes, and portraits. Through personal friendship with Monet, she helped to popularize his work in the United States. Born in Boston into the prominent Cabot family, in 1874 she married Thomas Sargeant Perry, a professor and literary historian. As their Boston home became a gathering place for the intellectual and social elite, she studied painting at the Cowles School of Art with Robert *Vonnoh and Dennis Miller *Bunker. In 1887 she went to Paris to work at the Académie Julian and Académie Colarossi. Two years later she met Monet during a summer in Giverny, where she spent about ten seasons over two decades, several as his next-door neighbor. There she also befriended Camille Pisarro, as well as other progressive French and American artists. From 1898 until 1901 she painted many Japanese subjects while residing in Tokyo, where her husband had accepted a teaching position. Between 1886 and 1923 she published four volumes of poetry. From 1903 she often recorded landscape views from the surroundings of a vacation home near Mount Monadnock in Hancock, New Hampshire, where she died. Perry's debt to Monet is particularly evident in landscapes, which closely adapt her mentor's brilliant colors, vigorous brushwork, and insubstantial form. *Lady with a Bowl of Violets* (National Museum of Women in the Arts, Washington, D.C., c. 1910) demonstrates a characteristically more structured approach to form in figure paintings, although the richly hued, broken brushwork and sensitive response to effects of light confirm the attraction of impressionist practice.

Persico, Luigi (1791–1860). Sculptor and painter. Known particularly for neoclassical embellishments to the U.S. Capitol, he also executed a number of important portrait busts. Born in Naples, he emigrated to the United States in 1818. In Philadelphia and elsewhere in Pennsylvania he painted portraits and taught drawing, while also pursuing sculptural commissions. In 1825 he settled in Washington, D.C., and began work on three over-life-size allegorical figures for the Capitol's east pediment. Symbolizing *Genius of America* (1825–28; original sandstone sculptures replaced with marble copies in 1959–60), classically robed females personify the nation flanked by Justice and Hope. In 1834 Persico's marble figures of *Peace* and *War* (U.S. Capitol, in storage, replaced by copies in the 1960s) were installed in niches on the east facade, while a decade later his marble *Discovery of America* (U.S. Capitol, in storage, 1837–44) was placed beside the east staircase. It depicts a triumphant Columbus dominating, both visually and thematically, a nearly naked Indian woman who turns to flee. Although the sculpture supported popular mid-nineteenth-century expansionist ideology, it led to no further federal commissions for the artist, in part because nationalistic interests by this time favored American artists. Persico worked again in Philadelphia and in Boston before leaving the United States in 1855. He died in Marseilles. His brother, painter **Gennaro Persico** (?–c. 1859), also born in Naples, worked principally as a portrait and miniature painter. After his arrival in the United States around 1820, he spent about a decade in Philadelphia and other Pennsylvania locations before settling in Richmond, Virginia. In the early 1840s he left for Naples but about ten years later was back in Richmond. He is thought to have died at sea.

Peterdi, Gabor (1915–2001). Printmaker and painter. Originally a painter, he had turned his attention to printmaking before he arrived in New York in 1939. Born near Budapest, he studied there and in Rome before continuing his training in Paris, where he worked for several years at *Atelier 17. After emigrating to the United States, he served during World War II in the U.S. Army; then he participated once again at Atelier 17, now relocated to New York. Primarily interested in intaglio work, he began to develop flexible and innovative techniques while working within that workshop's surrealist milieu. From the late 1940s, he sometimes incorporated color into his work. During the 1950s he gradually replaced irrational elements with naturalistic allusions, while retaining a linear vigor that often suggests *abstract expressionism's improvisational effects. Through references to organic life, rock surfaces, and other observed phenomena, he embraced nature's creative force as an antidote to human destructive impulses. He taught at Yale University from 1960 until his retirement in 1987. He died in a hospice near his home in Stamford, Connecticut. His *Printmaking: Methods Old and New* (1959) remains a classic text.

Peto, John Frederick (1854–1907). Painter. His trompe-l'oeil still lifes include tabletop or shelf compositions and arrangements of objects hung before vertical surfaces, as well as many rack pictures that feature letters, photographs, clippings, or other scraps tucked informally behind tapes on an early sort of bulletin board. Peto labored in relative obscurity during his lifetime and was completely forgotten later. Even before his death, some of his paintings were fraudulently passed off as William *Harnett's work. By the time Alfred *Frankenstein began his research into Harnett's career in the 1940s, Peto's artistic personality had been almost completely submerged in Harnett's. Upon visiting Peto's former studio, Frankenstein realized that many objects preserved there appeared in still lifes he was then able to attribute to Peto. His scholarship identified much of Peto's output and established the artist's modern reputation. Despite the confusion with Harnett's work, their approaches remain quite distinct stylistically, iconographically, and expressively. Peto was less technically accomplished, but also his aims diverged from Harnett's. While highly illusionistic, Peto's objects are less sharply rendered, less insistently three-dimensional, and texturally less differentiated. His lighting is more atmospheric and more considered for its own sake. His subjects are less glamorous than many of Harnett's, and the well-worn, humble objects he normally painted often emphasize decay and pessimism. His best work conveys an introspective poetry rather different from Harnett's grander and more dignified effects. Born in Philadelphia, Peto studied for a short time in the late 1870s at the *Pennsylvania Academy of the Fine Arts, where he met Harnett. He remained in Philadelphia until 1889, when he moved permanently to Island Heights, on the New Jersey shore at the mouth of the Toms River. He apparently always had difficulty making ends meet and is thought to have worked on occasion as a photographer, portrait painter, sculptor, and musician. After 1899 he no longer exhibited and apparently drifted out of contact with the art world. His later paintings, although increasingly introspective and even hermetic, demonstrate a continuing interest in abstract form, harmonious arrangement of shapes, pearly colors, and a unifying mellow light sometimes accompanied by shadowy contrasts of tone. Peto most commonly pictured old books on a shelf, often accompanied by other everyday household items, such as writing materials, candles, and pipes. *Old Time Card Rack* (Phillips Collection, 1900) exemplifies Peto's most distinctive specialty, which he pursued intermittently from 1879. In this late example, the dark background strikes a somber tone. A number of items, all battered and worn, are affixed to the wall itself or held in place by a simple arrangement of tapes that form a square crisscrossed by diagonals. The varied colors of these flat objects make a spare, asymmetrical pattern across the surface. The representation of a Lincoln photograph, which Peto included also in about a dozen other rack compositions, reinforces the artist's feeling for the passage of time, the brevity of life, and the tragic dimension of human experience. He died in New York, where he had gone for medical treatment.

Phillips, Ammi (1788–1865). Painter. Often dramatic, nearly always charming, his untutored work ranks at the top of American country portraiture. Adapting high-style prototypes to his abilities and preferences, he forged striking and distinctive effects from arresting patterns, elegant color combinations, closely observed detail, and convincingly rendered individual presence. During a prolific career of more than fifty years, he worked itinerantly in the region where Connecticut, New York, and Massachusetts adjoin. Phillips was born in the northwestern Connecticut town of Colebrook, where he grew up. By about 1811 he was working professionally in a manner probably most indebted to the example of Reuben *Moulthrop. Over time, as he encountered other artists or their work, his style responded. Before modern research had clarified his contribution, groups of his paintings were attributed to fictions known as the Border Limner (active along the Massachusetts-Connecticut border) and the Kent Limner (active in and around Kent, Connecticut). In the Border group, now known to date between about 1812 and 1819, strong outlines and pastel colors often create a pearly, dreamy atmosphere. Probably after contact with the work of Ezra *Ames, his work became darker and more naturalistic. During the masterful Kent period of the 1830s, strongly stylized patterns, inventive compositions, exquisite ornamentation, and bright colors prevailed. In succeeding decades, his work evolved toward a less idiosyncratic approach, and by the 1850s a greater interest in three-dimensional modeling suggests the influence of photographs. Over the years, Phillips made his home in the New York municipalities of Troy, Rhinebeck, Amenia, and Northeast. He died in the western Massachusetts town of Curtisville (now Interlaken), where he had resided during his last six years.

Phillips, Duncan (1886–1966). Collector, art writer, and museum director. In 1921 he established the first museum of modern art in the United States, the Phillips Memorial Gallery (now Phillips Collection) in Washington, D.C. Phillips steadfastly supported living American modernists during the many years when their art remained unfashionable. He also collected French impressionists and postimpressionists, as well as European modernists and select examples of earlier European art. As the result of his prescience, the Phillips Collection owns the largest collection anywhere of work by Arthur *Dove, along with major representations of paintings by John *Marin and Georgia *O'Keeffe. Other progressive Americans well represented in the museum's holdings include the *Eight, other artists of Alfred *Stieglitz's circle, *abstract expressionists, and independents such as Charles *Sheeler and Karl *Knaths. Earlier Americans such as Thomas *Eakins, George *Inness, Albert Pinkham *Ryder, and John *Twachtman also are included.

Duncan Clinch Phillips was born in Pittsburgh. Upon moving to Washington in 1896, his parents built the house that still serves as the more intimate part of the museum. In 1908 Phillips graduated from Yale University with a major in English. Subsequently he traveled, collected art, and wrote. Initially conservative in his taste, he was repelled by early contacts with modern art. In 1920, after his father and brother died in close succession, the family collection was incorporated as a memorial. The following year, part of the house was opened to visitors three afternoons a week. As Phillips's taste expanded, acquisitions increasingly reflected his engagement with modern art. In 1930 the family moved, making the entire house available to the public. A large adjoining annex was built in 1960, and a substantial further expansion opened in 2006. His wife, painter **Marjorie Acker Phillips** (1895–1985) studied in New York with Kenneth Hayes *Miller and her uncle, Gifford *Beal. After marriage in 1921, she continued to paint impressionist-influenced work while assisting her husband in development of the museum. She participated fully in selecting acquisitions, and her artist's eye helped to liberalize her husband's taste. Upon his death, Mrs. Phillips became director. She was succeeded in 1972 by their son, Yale-educated **Laughlin Phillips** (1924–), a former foreign service officer and editor, who served for twenty years. While the collection continues to expand and to encompass new interests, at the same time, it continues to favor cosmopolitan, richly visual, and contemplative work that extends the founder's taste. Phillips wrote several books, including *The Enchantment of Art* (1914; revised 1929), *Collection in the Making* (1926), revealing the author's change of heart about modernism, *The Artist Sees Differently* (2 vols., 1931), and *The Leadership of Giorgione* (1937). Marjorie Phillips published *Duncan Phillips and His Collection* in 1970.

Phillips, Helen. *See* ATELIER 17.

Photography, American. In the United States, as elsewhere, images fixed by chemical responses to light excited widespread interest as soon as the process became available. Although photography's "truth" to reality appealed to a large audience, from its earliest days sophisticated observers realized that the medium offered aesthetic as well as utilitarian potential. Europeans produced the first permanent images, but Americans quickly contributed to photography's technical and artistic development. Press reports of the photographic process initially appeared in the United States in the early months of 1839, shortly after the first successes abroad. Samuel F. B. *Morse proved instrumental to the introduction of the daguerreotype process to the United States later that year. Photographic portraits almost immediately caught the popular imagination, and in the 1840s daguerreotype studios dotted the nation. Outstanding practitioners included Albert *Southworth, working in partnership with Josiah Hawes, and Mathew B. *Brady. Because of the daguerreotype's limitations, few photographers attempted subjects other than portraits. However, some took their cameras into the street or even into the country to capture the earliest photographic views of cities and their rural environs.

Daguerreotypes are unique images on silver-plated copper. (There are no negatives from which copies can be made.) Because their image surfaces are delicate, they were fitted into cases, under glass, for hand viewing. Daguerreotypes recorded minute detail with extraordinary precision, but their dimensions remained small. The standard "sixth-plate" portrait measured 2.75 × 3.25 inches. Whole plates were 6.5 × 8.5 inches; few daguerreotypes were larger. To increase the effect of realism, subtle hand-tinting of flesh and perhaps a few details became common in portraits.

The time required for a sitting decreased rapidly, within a decade from several minutes in bright sunlight to less than thirty seconds in a studio interior. As the daguerreotype's circumstances imply, throughout the history of photography, technical factors have limited or stimulated aesthetic qualities. Although the best daguerreotypes are objects of great beauty and refinement, under pressure of faster and more flexible methods, the process virtually disappeared from American photographic practice after about twenty years. In England and France, where early photography also flourished, it fell from favor even earlier. There, a process for making photographic prints from paper negatives came into use during the 1840s, but this technique found little appeal in the United States. Indeed, American fondness for daguerreotype portraits sustained their popularity for at least a decade after the next decisive improvement appeared in England.

Introduced in 1851, the glass-plate technique offered exposure times of a second or two. Only the plate and its camera size limited dimensions, and duplicate prints were easily produced. In the early wet-plate method, glass negatives coated with a substance known as collodion had to be exposed while still damp. Practitioners therefore had to carry with them not only the heavy and fragile plates but also an instant darkroom. Despite these impediments, the method's documentary potential was firmly established during the Civil War. Although action shots still were not possible, this became the first major conflict in history to be extensively photographed. George *Barnard, Brady, Alexander *Gardner, and Timothy *O'Sullivan numbered among the most distinguished pioneers of this early photojournalism. After the war, the still little-known American West drew adventurous documentarians, including William Henry *Jackson, Eadweard *Muybridge, O'Sullivan, and Carleton *Watkins. From the 1860s, nearly all landscape and other reportorial photographers produced a sideline of mass-market stereographs. Widely popular in American drawing rooms into the early twentieth century, the paired images originated in cameras fitted with double lenses set about as far apart as a person's eyes. Mounted on cardboard, these twinned pictures produced remarkable three-dimensional effects when examined through a hand-held viewer. The collodion process also made possible several popular portrait types. In imitation of the daguerreotype, the ambrotype image on glass was backed with dark material and sealed in a daguerreotype case. Secured on black-enameled metal, tintypes appeared in vast quantities as inexpensive, small, and generally unpretentious portraits for ordinary Americans. Cartes-de-visite became a rage in the early 1860s, as these 4 × 2.5-inch paper photographs mounted on stiff cardboard came into use as calling cards. A 6.5 × 4.5-inch variation, the cabinet photograph, soon followed.

A dry-plate technique, using a gelatin emulsion on glass, became commercially available in the late 1870s. This method cut exposure time and was simpler to use in the field. Muybridge's motion studies of the 1880s notably demonstrated the utility of the nearly instantaneous photography now possible. Speed also permitted the development of hand cameras, not mounted on a tripod. In 1888 George Eastman (1854–1932) began marketing the Kodak hand camera, using roll film, a development that quickly democratized photography by making it possible for any amateur to produce snapshots. Serious photographers resisted. In the 1890s they supported an international movement that emphasized the artistic potential of the medium by stressing refined aesthetic taste and sensuous printing, often using complex methods. In Boston, F. Holland *Day achieved rarified literary expression. However, in New York his more straightforward rival Alfred *Stieglitz came to dominate the American movement by forming the *Photo-Secession in 1902. The group had its own New York gallery, known as *291, and published **Camera Work*. Stieglitz's associates included Alvan Langdon *Coburn, Gertrude *Kasebier, Edward *Steichen, and Clarence *White.

As the introduction of modern European art and the outbreak of World War I disrupted conventions, art photographers turned away from the languid poetry of most Photo-Secession work in favor of sharp-focus realism. Paul *Strand and Charles *Sheeler led the way. Preceded by the investigative reporting of Lewis *Hine and Jacob *Riis, enthusiasm for factual reporting attracted many of the best 1930s photographers, such as Walker *Evans and Dorothea *Lange. For the quarter century after the mid-1930s, photojournalism flourished in the hands of such photographers as Margaret *Bourke-White, Robert *Capa, and W. Eugene *Smith. Meanwhile, Ansel *Adams, Imogen *Cunningham, and Edward *Weston, among others, used sharp-focus techniques to explore the expressive potential of form. After World War II, Robert *Frank and Diane *Arbus portrayed American society with newly critical eyes. Their sensibilities reverberated through antiromantic street photography of the 1960s and 1970s, made feasible by smaller cameras and faster film. Bruce *Davidson, Lee *Friedlander, William *Klein, and Garry *Winogrand excelled at this approach. Eliot *Porter numbered among few serious photographers who preferred color film before the 1970s, when William *Eggleston spurred its use. Concurrent with these postwar developments, a strain of symbolic, mythic, or psychologically evocative photography found expression in the work of Aaron *Siskind, Jerry *Uelsman, and Minor *White, among others. In recent decades, the boundary between artist and photographer has often proved irrelevant, as both have taken advantage of technological advances and an eclectic artistic atmosphere. Andy *Warhol, Robert *Rauschenberg, Nan *Goldin, and Barbara *Kruger exemplify the use of varied photographic approaches within an art-world context. Today computer-assisted digital techniques not only record visual reality but also subvert objectivity by manipulating visual information.

Photo-realism. A form of representational art based directly on photographs, rather than the observation of nature. Acknowledging the role of photographic intermediaries as pathways to or substitutes for contemporary experience, the tendency became popular in the late 1960s and 1970s. Photo-realist paintings typically mimic vernacular photographs or snapshots, setting up tensions between casual composition, the relatively banal but highly veristic character of their imagery, and flawless, technically adroit execution. In its mundane subject matter and enthusiasm for commercial photography, *pop art helped set the stage for photo-realism. The term "super-realism" has sometimes been employed as an alternative name for the movement, although that designation may also include highly realistic work not derived from photography.

Chuck *Close ranks among the movement's principal artists. Among other leaders, painter and printmaker Richard Estes (1936–) concentrates on architectural subjects. Although he takes preliminary color slides of the generally nondescript urban settings that appear in his paintings, he adjusts and rearranges details to intensify the visual impact of forms and extract coherence from disorder. Reflective surfaces, particularly storefront display windows, often emphasize streetscape spectacle. By including in these mirrored illusions scenic elements that lay outside the field of vision, even behind the spectator, he manipulates space for dynamic effect. Although Estes was born in Kewanee, Illinois, site of the nearest hospital, his family lived in the central Illinois town of Sheffield, where he grew up. He studied at the School of the Art Institute of Chicago from 1952 to 1956. In the late 1950s he moved to New York, which has provided most of his subject matter, although he also has pictured other cities, as well as a few rural locations. The elements of his mature approach coalesced in the mid-1960s, as he began to demonstrate mature control of a crisp, virtuoso technique in the service of optical complexity. With time he gradually shifted his emphasis from reflections to odd angles of vision that continue to translate the city's actuality into a slightly disorienting experience. As a graphic artist, he has worked mainly with color screen printing and woodcut processes. He continues to live in New York, while also maintaining a residence in Maine.

Among other photo-realists, Robert Bechtle (1932–) specializes in scenes of Bay Area residential areas. Although cars have been central to his iconography, in his frozen views nothing moves. At a glance, his compositions often seem as trite as his subjects, with little of the intricacy that distinguishes Estes's work. Yet, a sensitive technique enhances their simplicity to evoke the warmth of California light and mitigate with affection his frankness in delineating the Golden State's materialism. Born in San Francisco, Bechtle graduated in 1954 from the California College of Arts and Crafts (now California College of the Arts) in Oakland. He served in the U.S. Army for two years before returning to the school to earn an MFA in 1958. As his earlier approach became more precise and literal, Bechtle's mature style emerged around the time he started teaching at San Francisco State University in 1968. He retired in 1999. Brooklyn-born painter and printmaker Robert Cottingham (1935–) generally features the alphabetical and numerical imagery of advertising, billboards, and neon signs. A graduate of Pratt Institute, he lives in Newtown, Connecticut. Ralph Goings (1928–) paints the mass-market vernacular of pickups, trailers, and especially diners and lunch counters—from the exterior and interior—as well as, more recently, still lifes of table furnishings from such establishments. Born in Corning, California, he received a BFA from the California College of Arts and Crafts in 1953 and an MFA from Sacramento State College (now University) in 1965. He moved to New York in the 1970s and today resides in upstate Charlotteville, New York, and Santa Cruz, California.

Photo-Secession. Loosely organized group of art photographers active between 1902 and 1910. Founded by Alfred *Stieglitz, the organization sought recognition for photography as an art form. Most of its adherents remained amateurs who disdained commercial, literal, and utilitarian purposes of professional photography, embracing instead the values of *pictorialism. Early in 1902 Stieglitz organized a large exhibition of "American Pictorial Photography" for New York's National Arts Club. Although the catalogue specified that it had been "arranged by the Photo-Secession," Stieglitz only later gathered others into a genuine organization. The name he coined, "Photo-Secession," derived from contemporary Secessionist movements founded by anti-academic artists in Europe. At the end of 1902 Stieglitz published the first issue of **Camera Work*, the Photo-Secession's sumptuous magazine. In 1905 he opened the Little Galleries of the Photo-Secession, soon better known by the nickname *291, taken from its Fifth Avenue address. Both initially served the photographic community but within a few years came to be dominated by the modern art that increasingly fascinated Stieglitz. Although he rationalized that the art provided a context for understanding and evaluating photography, many Photo-Secessionists became disgruntled by this deviation from their central interests. Stieglitz's landmark exhibition of six hundred photographs by Photo-Secessionists and related photographers at the Albright Art Gallery (now Albright-Knox Gallery) in Buffalo, New York, at the end of 1910 proved his last meaningful gesture of support for pictorialism, as well as the Photo-Secession's swan song. Organized as an historical celebration of photography's accomplishments, the exhibition testified to fulfillment of the group's objective, recognition for photography as a fine art. The show's success paradoxically undermined the Photo-Secession, however, for Stieglitz's autocratic handling of the event irreparably aggravated some leading members, especially those already offended by his changing aesthetic. The group quickly splintered and dissolved, but under Stieglitz's control, *Camera Work* and 291 soldiered on until 1917. In addition to playing an important part in the art politics of its day, during its brief existence the Photo-Secession brought together most of the period's finest American photographers. The original steering committee included Gertrude *Käsebier, Edward *Steichen, and Clarence *White, as well as Philadelphian John G. Bullock (1854–1939), known for graceful landscapes; New York native Frank Eugene (1865–1936), who worked from about 1901 in Germany; and Thomas *Eakins student Eva Watson-Schütze (1867–1935), who moved from Philadelphia to Chicago in 1901. In addition to Anne *Brigman, Alvin Langdon *Coburn and George *Seeley, the group included also among its more than one hundred members Alice Boughton (1865–1943), a New York artist who specialized in portraits and figure studies; San Francisco native Francis Bruguière (1879–1945), also a painter, who experimented at an early date with photographic abstraction; and Bostonian Sarah Choate Sears (1858–1935), known as a painter before she began her work as a photographer of figures and still lifes.

Pickett, Joseph (1848–1918). Painter. Self-taught, he is known for naive but charming landscapes and scenes from the American Revolution. He was born in *New Hope, Pennsylvania, which remained his home all his life, although as a young man he traveled with carnivals during summers. At age forty-five he opened a general store in New Hope and began to paint, at first with house paints but later with artists' colors. Often he incorporated sand or other substances in his paints in order to build up a textured surface. He worked slowly, and few surviving works are known. Depicting a steam train racing along a river through a small town, *Manchester Valley* (Museum of Modern Art, 1914–18) exemplifies his sure instincts in achieving lively, colorful effects with unperspectivized, shadowless forms and acutely rendered detail.

Picknell, William Lamb (1853–97). Painter. Interested primarily in landscapes, he also created figural images. He worked mostly in France and along the Massachusetts coast north of Boston. In scenes recording conditions of light ranging from glaring sunlight to silvery haze, he generally preferred solidly built pictorial structure and well-defined forms, often rendered with richly scumbled and textured paint. Limited passages in some late paintings suggest an interest in contemporary impressionists' broken-color technique. A Vermont native, he was born in Hinesburg but moved as a small child to North Springfield. In Boston from 1867, he worked in a frame shop before leaving for Europe in 1872. After two years in Rome with George *Inness, he studied in Paris with Jean-Léon Gérôme during the winter of 1874–75. The previous summer he had first visited Pont-Aven, where he then returned for several years. Here in Brittany, Robert *Wylie provided additional informal training. During the 1880s Picknell lived primarily in Waltham, Massachusetts, but traveled often. He spent two winters in England and also visited Florida and California. During summers he regularly painted at Cape Ann, in Annisquam, a seaside village that was beginning to attract artists in considerable numbers. Again abroad through most of the 1890s, he resided at Moret-sur-Loing, on the edge of the Forest of Fontainebleau, but often spent winters in the south of France. His health failing, he returned to Massachusetts during the summer of 1897 and died at Marblehead. *Road to Concarneau* (Corcoran Gallery, 1880), which made his reputation when shown at the Paris Salon, remains his best-known work. Constructed along the road's deep perspective into flat terrain, it exemplifies particularly well Picknell's interest in rendering the intense sun of mid-summer. Suggesting his versatility, *On the Borders of the Marsh* (Pennsylvania Academy), a very different painting of the same year, represents a mode much closer to *Barbizon intimacy. Here, a flattened screen of trees almost entirely constrains the eye to a shallow foreground. The painting's pearly light and subdued color harmonies effectively evoke the unglamorous damp chill of late winter or early spring. His brother, painter **George W. Picknell** (1864–1943), also specialized in landscapes. Born in North Springfield, Vermont, he studied in Paris and subsequently worked in France for a number of years. In 1912 he settled permanently in Silvermine, Connecticut, an artists' colony near New Canaan. His later work focused on local scenery.

Pictorialism. An international art photography movement cresting in the first decade of the twentieth century. Pictorialism aimed for artistic effects that imitate and rival those of traditional pictorial arts, particularly painting and graphic media. More specifically, the term in this period came to be particularly associated with gentle idealism, spiritual longing, and wistful retreat from the modernizing forces transforming Western societies. In the United States, with the exception of F. Holland *Day, the *Photo-Secession represented nearly all of the best pictorial photographers, including Alfred *Stieglitz, Edward *Steichen, and Clarence *White. Pictorialists often favored a soft-focus technique and nearly always fabricated photographic prints as luxury objects. In other respects, such as style and subject matter, their work varied considerably. Regarding themselves as artists, pictorialists held that their work transcended the mechanical origins of photography. Through their refined subjectivity, they sought to express inner truth, to evoke moods, or to provoke awareness of transcendental mysteries. Often highly attuned to the effects of light within their photographs, they preferred platinum prints for the warmth and subtle tonal range that method provided (as opposed primarily to harsher, sharper silver processes). In addition, pictorialists commonly manipulated photographic procedures to achieve effects they desired. Unconcerned with the purity of the medium and often believing that any intervention was justified if it served the artist-photographer's intentions, they willfully altered negatives by hand, employed double exposures, printed one negative over another, recorded staged scenes, and/or used substances in the printing process (gum bichromate was a favorite) that produced effects of oil paint, pastel, or other traditional media. Their subjects typically were drawn from landscape, domestic life, or allegory, although urban scenes also appeared. Shallow space, asymmetrical balance, and organizational simplicity stand among common elements of pictorialist composition. Much pictorial work shares the sensibility pervading *tonalism and other forms of late impressionism, especially those affected by symbolism. The work of James Abbott McNeill *Whistler was widely emulated, and ideas drawn from the *Arts and Crafts movement and from *japonisme also proved important. Initially an innovative and provocative practice, by the second decade of the century pictorialism came to seem enervated, mannered, and tied to an increasingly outmoded Victorian romanticism. Yet, as a movement, it survived into the 1920s. In 1916 White led adherents including Gertrude *Käsebier and Alvin Langdon *Coburn in forming the Pictorial Photographers of America. By enlarging the notion of pictorialism to include more objective and less sentimental approaches, the varied accomplishments of the group's progressive figures counteracted the aesthetic backwater into which the earlier phase of the movement had fallen.

Pictorial Photographers of America. *See* PICTORIALISM.

Pierce, Florence Miller. *See* TRANSCENDENTAL PAINTING GROUP.

Pierce, Horace Towner. *See* TRANSCENDENTAL PAINTING GROUP.

Pierce, Leona. *See* FRASCONI, ANTONIO.

Pine, Robert Edge (c. 1730–88). Painter. Known for portraits and narrative subjects, he was probably born in London and accomplished his best work in England during a successful career of some twenty-five years. He emigrated to Philadelphia in 1784, planning to produce a series of paintings portraying important events from the new nation's struggle for independence. He found little support for this goal, however, and at his death left only one unfinished canvas related to the project. During his short American career, he turned instead to portraiture. He painted George Washington on several occasions, as well as other leading figures of the Revolutionary era. A rendition of two well-dressed young boys playing with tops, *Charles and John Vaughn*

(Westmoreland Museum of American Art, Greensburg, Pennsylvania, c. 1785–88) demonstrates his technical fluency as well as the graceful ease that marks contemporary British portraiture.

Pinney, Eunice (1770–1849). Painter. A self-taught watercolorist, she painted a wide variety of subjects, including religious, literary, and *genre scenes as well as landscapes and allegories. Usually loosely adapting prior visual sources, such as prints or book illustrations, she composed original, lively, rhythmically patterned, and carefully balanced images that show little regard for perspectival accuracy or three-dimensional modeling. Many works seem to carry personal meaning related to the circumstances of her life. Born in Simsbury, Connecticut, near Hartford, Eunice Griswold grew up on a farm and lived in the area all her life. Married in 1789 to Oliver Holcomb, in 1797 she left her abusive husband, obtained a divorce, and married Butler Pinney. She apparently did not begin to paint until she was nearly forty, and most of her work seems to have been completed during the next fifteen years or so. She is thought to have died in Simsbury.

Pinto, Jody. *See* LAND ART.

Piper, Adrian. *See* PERFORMANCE ART.

Pippin, Horace (1888–1946). Painter. A self-taught African American, he produced works of great visual sophistication and emotional resonance. His large and consistent body of work, which includes many different types of subject, elevates his contribution beyond the level normally achieved by untrained artists. Drawing on observation, memory, and imagination, he painted *genre scenes, landscapes, and still lifes, as well as literary, religious, and historic themes. Pippin was born near Philadelphia, in West Chester, Pennsylvania, and lived there during his adult life, although he grew up in Goshen, New York. After his formal education ended with the eighth grade in a segregated one-room school, he worked at menial jobs, as he continued to do after moving to Paterson, New Jersey, in 1912. Sent to France with the U.S. Army in 1917, he fought at the front until wounded nearly a year later. He had drawn since childhood, but it was his World War I service that slowly transformed him into an artist after he returned to West Chester, his right arm now useless. By stubbornly trying to make art (he concentrated at first on burning designs into wood panels) as he reflected on his military experience, he not only found purpose for his life but also strengthened his arm. In 1928, when he was forty, he started his first important oil painting, *The End of the War: Starting Home* (Philadelphia Museum), an apocalyptic vision of trench warfare. After three years and dozens of paint layers, he completed this antiwar statement with a hand-carved frame depicting war materiel in relief. While gradually developing greater fluency, he painted in obscurity until 1937 when art critic Christian Brinton (1870–1942), a West Chester native who retained ties there, discovered his work and brought it to the attention of the New York art world. Only a year later, his paintings appeared in a show at the *Museum of Modern Art, and before his death several major museums hosted solo exhibitions of his work. In 1940 Pippin met collector Albert C. *Barnes. Through visits to the Barnes Foundation, where he became familiar with the works of Renoir and Matisse, he grew artistically. As his color brightened and he enhanced his facility for abstract design, Pippin nevertheless always retained a flat, somewhat awkward manner of drawing and a preference for two-dimensional, shadowless forms. Nearly all Pippin's works focus on African Americans, and many of the best connect intimately to his inner life. Most of these date from the 1940s, when he was in full control of his technique and confident of his vision. In *The Domino Players* (Phillips Collection, 1943), two women compete on a kitchen table as a youngster looks on. Behind them, near a glowing stove, a woman sews a bright quilt. As is usual among his many tranquil domestic scenes, the subject derives from idealized memory, although many details are acutely observed. *John Brown Going to His Hanging* (Pennsylvania Academy, 1942), the final scene from a series on the abolitionist, poignantly contemplates the tightly bound martyr's last moments on a horse-drawn cart as he passes an interracial crowd. Compositionally, a stark black-and-white pattern, relieved by blood-red accents, enhances the somber theme. An African-American woman, clad in the Civil War colors of blue and gray, faces the spectator at the side: she is the artist's grandmother, his witness and narrator, and his personal connection to this violence-drenched moment.

Pittman, Benn. *See* NOURSE, ADELAIDE.

Polk, Charles Peale. *See* PEALE, CHARLES WILLSON.

Pollock, Jackson (1912–56). Painter, printmaker, and occasional sculptor. The iconic *abstract expressionist, he forged a singular style of great expressive power. Skeins of dripped, poured, and flung paint dominate his key *all-over paintings of the late 1940s and early 1950s.

Using gestural motions while working over canvases spread on the floor, he created an untrammeled poetry that resonated with American traditions of individuality, grandiloquence, and ambition. His work meshed as well with the psychic bent of postwar society, reflecting fear of chaos and destruction as well as its opposite: hope for a world made new. Although often criticized for its supposed lack of skill, his technique required much discipline and creative control. Among imitators, no one came close to matching his achievement. Since his early and violent death, Pollock has also come to embody the myth of the tragic hero, tortured by the spiritual and psychic forces responsible for his art. However romanticized this view may be, he undeniably experienced much inner turmoil. An alcoholic troubled by lifelong insecurities about personal worth, sexuality, and human relationships, he believed that art came from the unconscious. Apparently his creative process provided some relief from psychic tensions. At the same time, the work itself and its critical reception provoked additional anxieties, as he suffered doubts about the value of his art and worried about his professional reputation. Pollock's inmost thoughts remain obscure, as he left few letters or other written records. He produced virtually all of his important work in a single decade, the period from his early thirties into his early forties. Nearly all the celebrated all-over canvases date from only four years, 1947 through 1950. A fallow period of some eighteen months, during which he hardly painted, preceded his death in an automobile accident. He was behind the wheel, drunk, and possibly suicidal.

Paul Jackson Pollock was born in Cody, Wyoming, but his impecunious farming and ranching family left there before he was a year old. During his youth, they moved nine times among various Arizona and California locations. Unlike many well-known artists, as a child Pollock showed little interest in drawing. Although passably well read as an adult, suspensions and expulsions marred his high school years, and he did not graduate. At the last school he attended, Manual Arts High School in Los Angeles, a teacher stimulated his interest in art and in philosophy. In particular, theosophical teachings that encouraged self-discovery made an important impression. There, too, he became a close friend of Philip *Guston. About the time he moved to New York in September 1930, he dropped the first name of Paul. He enrolled at the *Art Students League, where his mentor Thomas Hart *Benton imbued his pupil with antimodern prejudices, with his belief in the need to root art in native experience, and with his admiration for dynamic and muscular stylization, particularly as realized on the heroic scale of murals. Within a few years of leaving the league early in 1933, Pollock shed his antipathy for modern art, but aspects of Benton's teaching remained permanently relevant to Pollock's thinking. In the mid-1930s Pollock also admired the Mexican mural painters, particularly David Alfaro Siquieros. His experimental workshop, which Pollock attended in 1936, stimulated interest in unorthodox techniques. As well, he was drawn to the work of Albert Pinkham *Ryder. Pollock's paintings of the 1930s generally offer rhythmic interpretations of imaginary western scenes, often dark-toned and mysterious.

From August 1935 until 1942, Pollock was employed most of the time by a *federal art project. After a brief stint with the murals program, he worked subsequently as an easel painter. However, the strains of poverty and fear of failure as an artist exacerbated an alcoholic tendency that had been a problem since he was about fifteen. In 1937 he first sought treatment, and following a breakdown the following year, he was hospitalized for several months. From 1939 through 1941, he worked successively with two Jungian analysts who assisted his emergence as an individualistic creative personality. As part of his therapy, he produced drawings in which he reoriented his interests toward aspects of the period's fascination with primitivism and surrealism. Among models of accomplishment, Picasso and Mexican muralist José Clemente Orozco took on particularly important roles. At a deeper level, Pollock began to understand that both his art and his self-preservation depended upon his ability to transform psychic forces into aesthetically valid statements. Around 1940 John *Graham took on an important role in leading Pollock toward a more sophisticated understanding of New York's artistic milieu. Further, by inviting both to participate in an important January 1942 gallery show, he also was indirectly responsible for initiating the relationship between Pollock and Lee *Krasner. Better trained, more accomplished as an artist, more intellectually trenchant, and better acquainted among the people who counted in the New York art world, Krasner intuited Pollock's potential greatness and undertook to shape his success. Perhaps even most important than her professional encouragement and the order she brought to his life, Krasner offered Pollock, probably for the first time in his life, a stable emotional relationship. Theirs was not an easy partnership, but it provided essential nurturance for the artistic achievements of both, although Krasner's were largely deferred. In their years together, she put his career first. They started living together in late summer 1942 and were married in October 1945. The influence of Graham and Krasner was augmented in the early 1940s by new contacts with surrealist-oriented artists, including William *Baziotes and Gerome *Kamrowski, but most notably Roberto *Matta. He encouraged Pollock to experiment with automatist techniques, to incorporate accidental effects in his art, and to pursue risky aesthetic strategies. Miró's 1941–42 retrospective at the *Museum of Modern Art reinforced such tendencies. From 1942 Peggy *Guggenheim's interest in Pollock's work allowed him to relinquish the odd jobs that had been his support and to concentrate more fully on his painting. He staged his first one-person show at her gallery, *Art of This Century, in 1943 and exhibited there twice more before the gallery closed in 1947.

Characteristic paintings of the early 1940s incorporate within heavily painted, pulsing compositions representational fragments derived from primitivizing or mythic sources. Passages of splattered and dribbled paint in some of these works prefigure the gestural technique he fully embraced a few years later. *Male and Female* (Philadelphia Museum, c. 1942), *Guardians of the Secret* (San Francisco Museum of Modern Art, 1943), and *The She-Wolf* (Museum of Modern Art, 1943) numbered among such paintings included in his first solo show. Their audacious novelty startled the art public, and MoMA confirmed his stature as an important artist when it purchased *The She-Wolf* the following year. Even before this first Pollock painting entered a public collection, the artist had produced a work that surpassed anything he had achieved to date and forecast the all-over paintings yet to come. For the entrance hall of Guggenheim's apartment, Pollock painted the breakthrough *Mural* (University of Iowa Museum of Art, Iowa City, 1943–44; dated 1943), an internationally unprecedented work. Its twenty-foot length, covered with vigorous paint swirls that vaguely suggest a procession of abstracted figures, demands a new kind of relationship with the viewer it practically engulfs, especially when viewed as intended within a relatively shallow space. Its scale, aggressively interlocked solids and voids, muscular physicality, and crude assault on the intellect register with force even today. In the mid-1940s Pollock followed this achievement with densely painted works that gradually obliterate imagery, as exemplified by *Eyes in the Heat* (Peggy Guggenheim Collection, Venice, 1946), which retains only reminiscences of ocular forms embedded in the swirling materiality of paint. Despite Pollock's creative achievement, sales were few. Self-criticism tore at his fragile ego, in a familiar pattern that he relieved with drink.

To escape the milieu that exacerbated his alcoholism, a couple of weeks after their marriage, Pollock and Krasner moved to Springs, a village within the town of East Hampton, on the eastern end of Long Island. There, in relative isolation from day-to-day art-world pressures, Pollock reconnected with nature as he had not since leaving the West. Over the next year and a half, his painting lost its haggard belligerency to more relaxed and expansive rhythms, realized on a large scale. Imagery gradually evaporated as manipulation of paint became central. His direction at this point probably benefited from the emphasis on process, linear freedom, and intuition at *Atelier 17, which he had frequented in 1944. In 1947 he embarked on the all-over drip paintings that permanently sealed his reputation as a giant of twentieth-century art. Endeavoring to escape the limitations of brushwork, he applied thinned paints by pouring directly from a can or flinging the liquid from the end of a stick. Because they are less viscous than oil, he often used enamels and metallic paints, and he sometimes added texture by embedding sand or other non-art materials in the paint. Pollock's working process famously required complete psychic and physical involvement, as he seemed to dance his paintings into being. Often, at various stages in the process, Pollock put the canvases aside, sometimes for long consideration, before initiating the next working session. In a well-known 1947 statement for **Possibilities*, Pollock explained that tacking the canvas to the floor allowed him to work on it from all four sides, to "literally be *in* the painting," a process that he likened to Indian sand painting. He further explained, "When I am in my painting I'm not aware of what I'm doing. It is only after a sort of 'get acquainted' period that I see what I have been about."

In their public introduction at the Betty *Parsons Gallery in January 1948, the first group of signature paintings included such completely realized achievements as *Cathedral* (Dallas Museum of Art, 1947) and *Full Fathom Five* (Museum of Modern Art, 1947). The previous fall Clement *Greenberg had already deemed Pollock "the most powerful painter in contemporary America and the only one who promises to be a major one," and generally favorable critical opinion greeted the show. In the fall of 1948, Pollock began successful alcoholism treatment with a Long Island doctor. During the following two productive years, with the appearance of such masterpieces as *Number 1, 1950 (Lavender Mist)* (National Gallery, 1950) and *Autumn Rhythm (Number 30)* (Metropolitan

Museum, 1950), his reputation soared. In July 1950, Pollock met Hans Namuth (1915–90), a photographer becoming particularly known for insightful portraits of artists and other cultural figures. Pollock agreed to allow Namuth to photograph and film him at work. At the conclusion of the final session, held outdoors on a chilly late November afternoon, Pollock had his first drink in two years. His doctor had died some months previously, the artist had become a public figure although sales of his work were few, and performing for the camera may have been a stressful violation of his private relationship with his art. Moreover, his annual Parsons Gallery show was about to open, revealing to the public his finest and most ambitious work to date. Much was at stake. One drink led to too many, and before the evening was over he had staged a drunken scene before guests. Although important paintings followed, he never regained his equilibrium. Bouts of depression that he could relieve only with alcohol became increasingly common.

Unwilling to repeat himself by turning out additional works of the type now associated with his name, in 1951 he abandoned the format that had made him famous. Returning to fragmented imagery, he limited his means to black enamel on unprimed canvas. These paintings debuted to muted reception late that year in his last show at Parsons. In subsequent work, which appeared in three shows at the Sidney Janis Gallery, he sought renewal through erratic extension or synthesis of previous tendencies. His limited work from 1952–53 includes canvases featuring imagery as well as completely abstract works, some painted, some poured. More than eleven feet wide, the evocative but unresolved *Portrait and a Dream* (Dallas Museum of Art, 1953) pointed to the artist's current dilemma. A colorful, semiabstract, conventionally executed head on the right of the horizontal composition confronts a black, poured "dream" of intricate linearism suggesting the form of a woman. Yet, the same period produced the masterful abstraction, *Blue Poles: Number 11* (National Gallery of Australia, Canberra, 1952), a frenzied symphony of tangled hues organized around eight dark blue voids or "poles."

In 1954 he painted relatively few works, though the dense *White Light* (Museum of Modern Art, 1954) demonstrates continued power. Nevertheless, by early 1955, he had reached a creative impasse. Depressed, he perhaps questioned his own worth but, feeling that his art had been misunderstood, insisted that it had not received the recognition it deserved. Perhaps in defiance of his own best interests, which had always benefited from creative activity, he more or less stopped painting. On an August night the next year, only a few hundred yards along Fireplace Road from his home and studio, he ran his convertible off the road, catapulted from the car when it flipped over, collided with a tree, and died instantly. In his last months, he knew that he had achieved a measure of success among art-world elite, but he also felt that popular culture generally represented him as an artistic fraud. Not long before his death, *Time* magazine nailed him as "Jack the Dripper." He could not have known that his work would forever change what it means to be a painter, that within a few years his paintings would sell for prices unmatched by those of any American artist, and that he would be in large part responsible for relocating the art world's center of gravity from Paris to New York. The house and studio where Pollock and Krasner lived and worked in Springs have been preserved as the Pollock-Krasner House and Study Center, administered by the Stony Brook Foundation under the aegis of the State University of New York at Stony Brook.

Two brothers also became artists, though neither came close to matching Jackson's talent or reputation. Born in Denver, **Charles Cecil Pollock** (1902–88) was a painter and lithographer. At the end of 1921 he quit high school to move to Los Angeles, where he studied at the Otis Art Institute (now Otis College of Art and Design). He soon began regularly sending *The Dial* and art magazines home, where they intrigued and inspired his younger brothers. Continuing to embody for them the romance of the art life, in 1926 he moved to New York. He studied with Benton at the Art Students League, paving the way there for Jackson. In 1935 he relocated to Washington, D.C., to work for the Resettlement Administration but after less than two years moved on to Detroit, where he served as a federal art administrator until 1942. He then taught at Michigan State University in East Lansing until the mid-1960s. Within a few years, he moved permanently to Paris but continued to exhibit in New York. His early work reflects the regionalist interests of the time, while from the 1940s onward he produced abstractions. To escape Jackson's shadow, in the 1940s he showed his work in New York under the name Charles Pima. The family member emotionally closest to Jackson, as well as the closest in age, painter and printmaker Sanford McCoy (1909–63), known as Sande (or Sandy), worked in the early 1930s with Siqueiros in Los Angeles, where Jackson's friends Guston and Chicago-born surrealist painter and printmaker Reuben Kadish (1913–92) also assisted his development. (Kadish moved east in the mid-1940s, worked as an abstract expressionist, later took up sculpture, and taught at Cooper Union from 1960 until a few months before his death in Manhattan.) In 1935, the year after he arrived in New York, Sande changed his surname to McCoy, his father's birth name. (The father's name had been changed to Pollock when he was adopted at an early age.) With Jackson, he found work with a federal art project and resumed contact with Siquieros at the New York workshop. In 1942 he moved permanently to Deep River, Connecticut. He later ran a print shop in nearby Essex. He died of leukemia in a Boston hospital.

Pomarède, Léon de. *See* WIMAR, CHARLES.

Poons, Larry. *See* OP ART.

Poor, Henry Varnum (1887–1970). Painter and ceramist. A singular artist-craftsman, as a painter he focused on figural works but also executed landscapes and still lifes. In addition, he created murals, ceramics, and architectural designs. Born in the central Kansas town of Chapman, Poor grew up with a naturalist's love of the countryside. After graduating from Stanford University, in 1910–11 his artistic education proceeded at the Slade School of Art in London and the Académie Julian in Paris. He returned to teach at Stanford, but soon numbered among the founders of the California School of Fine Arts (now San Francisco Art Institute). Later, he helped to establish the Skowhegan (Maine) School of Painting and Sculpture. Following military service in World War I, in the 1920s he personally constructed a home to his own designs in New City, in the Hudson River Valley. Inspired by *Arts and Crafts precedents, Poor's stone house integrates extensive handmade detailing, including much ceramic ware. Self-taught in pottery, Poor often applied painted ornamentation to his pieces. He also designed residences for several friends. Poor's early painting shows a debt to Cézanne's example, but in the 1920s he began to work more expressionistically. With time, his painting became softly romantic and more directly realistic, as in the figure study *Pink Table Cloth* (Cleveland Museum of Art, 1933), although underlying structure and patterning suggest his continuing interest in modernism. His 1930s murals for a *federal art project led to other decorative commissions. During World War II, he headed the U.S. Army's Art Unit in Alaska, where he portrayed the landscape and resident Eskimos. This experience provided the basis for his illustrated book, *An Artist Sees Alaska* (1945). He also published *A Book of Pottery: From Mud into Immortality* (1958). He died at his New City home.

The artist's stepdaughter, painter **Anne Poor** (1918–2002), born in New York, studied at the *Art Students League and Bennington (Vermont) College. She is known for landscapes, flowers, and figure paintings, as well as scenes of World War II and murals. Long associated with Skowhegan, she also traveled widely. *Greece* (1964) reproduces her views of that country, along with text by Henry Miller. She died at Nyack, not far from her Hudson River Valley home in Haverstraw.

Pop art. Term describing art that draws imagery from popular or consumer culture, especially as represented in mass-media sources. It emerged in New York around 1960. The young artists who formulated the tendency generally rejected *abstract expressionism's passionate individualism, painterly technique, and what they saw as its philosophical pretensions. Instead, they adopted banal, ready-made forms from the urban environment as subject matter. Technically, they preferred the smooth execution of commercial art, with its clean edges and unmodulated color areas. In its negation of personal expression, lack of regard for originality, and embrace of vulgarity, it violated nearly all prevailing aesthetic standards. Initial viewers reacted not only with distaste but also with confusion, and pop art's meaning has never been entirely rescued from ambiguity. Simultaneously celebratory, sardonic, and indifferent, it stood above all as an affirmation of new possibilities in picture-making. In the late 1950s, work by Jasper *Johns and Robert *Rauschenberg provided early intimations of the pop art sensibility. During its heyday between then and the early 1970s, Roy *Lichtenstein, James *Rosenquist, and, above all, Andy *Warhol ranked among central figures. Other important artists associated with the tendency include Jim *Dine, Robert *Indiana, Claes *Oldenburg, Edward *Ruscha, and Tom *Wesselman. Pop art abroad showed particular strength in London, although its tone differed from the American version. Less radical, the British version remained more intellectually engaged with a critique of mass culture and visually more inflected by the standards of fine art. Lawrence *Alloway is generally credited with coining the name in the late 1950s. In New York, the movement initially was identified as neo-dadaism or the New Realism.

Pope, Alexander (1849–1924). Painter and sculptor. He specialized in animal subjects but is most admired today for grandiose trompe-l'oeil still life paintings. Most depict dead game and hunting paraphernalia, but some are devoted to military items. Born in Dorchester (now part of Boston), Pope remained in the area all his life. He probably studied briefly with William *Rimmer, but considered himself self-taught. Illustrations of animals for two lithographic portfolios (1878 and 1882) and carvings of both living animals and dead game launched a highly successful career. He began to paint in oils in 1883 and became popular for portraits of prizewinning livestock, racehorses, and pets. Particularly during the last two decades of his life, he also painted likenesses of people. Between 1887 and 1900 he produced large still lifes, evidently inspired by William *Harnett's example. These elaborate representations of sensitively arranged items, illusionistically deployed against vertical supports, emulate Harnett's deceptive actuality, rich old master coloration, and serious demeanor. Pope also painted several unconventional trompe-l'oeil works depicting chickens or dogs seemingly caged in wood crates behind wire mesh. From 1903 Pope resided in Hingham but retained his Boston studio.

Porter, Fairfield (1907–75). Painter, printmaker, and art writer. His calm, carefully structured, and somewhat decorative representational paintings look back through impressionism to the old masters but also respond to modernist abstraction. In addition to distinguished portraits, his subjects included figural studies, landscapes, and still lifes, mostly drawn from domestic life and intimately familiar surroundings. However, the dependably genial tone of Porter's work, an aesthetic device, masks misfortunes and psychological tensions within the very subjects of home and family that the artist celebrated so appealingly. An astute observer of contemporary and traditional art, he wrote art criticism for many years, served as an associate editor at *Art News*, wrote a regular weekly column for *The Nation*, and published a monograph on Thomas *Eakins (1959). A selection of his shorter pieces, edited by Rackstraw Downes, appeared as *Fairfield Porter: Art in Its Own Terms; Selected Criticism, 1935–1975* (1979). Born in the Chicago suburb of Winnetka, in 1928 Porter graduated from Harvard University with a major in fine arts, mainly art history. For the next two years, he worked at the *Art Students League, where Boardman *Robinson and Thomas Hart *Benton numbered among his teachers. He also made the acquaintance of John *Marin, whose work he admired, as well as Alfred *Stieglitz. He had already traveled rather widely in Europe on two prior occasions when he departed for a year in Italy in September 1931. There he met Bernard *Berenson and closely studied the Renaissance masters. Following his return to New York in 1932, he became active in left-wing politics, an interest he continued to pursue while again residing in Winnetka from 1936 to 1939. At the end of 1938, when their work appeared in an exhibition at the Art Institute of Chicago, he was greatly impressed by the stylized realism of Pierre Bonnard and Édouard Vuillard. Yet, his wide-ranging taste encompassed also the work of his friend Willem *de Kooning, whose friendship he renewed when he moved east again. In 1939 Porter took up residence in Peekskill, on the Hudson River above New York, but three years later moved back into the city. In 1949 he moved permanently to Southampton, on eastern Long Island. There and in Maine, on his family's privately owned Great Spruce Head Island in Penobscot Bay, where he had summered since childhood, his characteristic style flowered. Concentrating on effects of light and color, mostly in pastel tones, he flattened space to emphasize formal relationships and painterly surface. Once he had arrived at this distinctive expression of personal feeling, his style changed little, but bolder and less naturalistic colors appear in later paintings. Porter's color lithographs resemble his paintings, but he also used the medium to create black-and-white images.

His brother, photographer **Eliot Porter** (1901–90), an early master of the medium's chromatic technology, paved the way for nature photography in color. His delicate, high-resolution images capturing the moods and poetry of landscape promoted acceptance of color photography as a fine art. Also born in Winnetka, Eliot Furness Porter preceded his brother to Harvard, where he graduated in 1924 with a major in chemical engineering. He continued there in medical school and received his MD degree in 1929. For the next decade he remained at Harvard to teach and do research in bacteriology. As an amateur ornithologist, he had photographed birds since he was a teenager, gradually turning his camera to other nature subjects as well. In January 1939, at the end of a successful show at Stieglitz's American Place gallery, he opted for a career in photography. Within a few years he found general recognition as the country's foremost noncommercial color photographer. His compositions rely on the organization of hues rather than black-and-white pattern. Later, he traveled widely, recording scenery and its individual details with the aim of fostering environmental awareness by drawing attention to nature's beauty and its relationship to mankind's experience. The first of his several books published by the Sierra Club, *In Wildness Is the Preservation of the World* (1962), with the photographer's selection of texts by Henry David Thoreau, was also the organization's first color book in a long series of handsomely produced volumes for the general public. A double volume, *The African Experience* and *The Tree Where Man Was Born*, compiled with Peter Matthiessen, initiated projects focused on human culture. Porter's numerous other photographic collections include *The Place No One Knew: Glen Canyon on the Colorado* (1963), *Birds of North America: A Personal Selection* (1972), *Antarctica* (1978), *Eliot Porter's Southwest* (1985), *Maine* (1986), and, with Wilma Stern, *Monuments of Egypt* (1990). *Summer Island: Penobscot Country* (1966) includes autobiographical reminiscences of his experiences in Maine. A resident of the area since 1946, he died in Santa Fe, New Mexico.

Porter, James Amos (1905–70). Painter and art historian. Born in Baltimore, Porter was associated with Howard University in Washington, D.C., throughout his adult life. Following his graduation in 1927, he was appointed to its teaching faculty. In 1953 he became director of the school's art gallery, as well. He also studied in New York: painting at the *Art Students League, art education at Teachers' College, Columbia University, and art history at New York University, where he earned a master's degree in 1937. He also studied in Paris in 1935. An inspiring teacher, he was also the first scholar of African-American art history. With his grounding in the studio, his broad grasp of art history, and his tenacity as a researcher, he recovered much African-American work from oblivion and placed it within a historical context. Impatient with calls for a race-based African-American aesthetic, he resisted what he saw as uncritical enthusiasm for black art within the *Harlem Renaissance. On the other hand, his insistence on mastery of technique and tradition sometimes blinded his critical judgment to the accomplishments of more experimental artists. His pioneering *Modern Negro Art* (1943) introduced the evolution of African-American achievement in the arts. After World War II, he traveled to Cuba, Haiti, and Brazil to expand his knowledge of art from the African diaspora. As a painter, Porter generally adhered to a sober realism sometimes lightened by impressionist-influenced brushwork. Known especially as a portraitist, he recorded many notable African Americans. In such figure studies as the contemplative *Woman Holding a Jug* (Carl Van Vechten Gallery, Fisk University, Nashville, Tennessee, 1930), he depicted blacks with dignity and classic beauty. During a year-long visit to Africa in 1963–64, his style loosened, and he began to paint more expressionistically. He died in Washington.

Porter, Rufus (1792–1884). Painter. Also an inventor, editor, and writer. Known particularly for landscape murals, he also painted portraits, which he found he could produce rapidly and cheaply after he built a camera obscura to assist his hand. Virtually personifying Yankee ingenuity, he also founded *Scientific American* magazine and devised numerous mechanical inventions. Born into a farming family in the northeastern Massachusetts town of West Boxford, at nine he moved with his family to Maine. By about 1810 he worked as a house and sign painter in the Portland area. Around 1815 he began painting portraits and cutting paper silhouette profiles. For the next decade he worked itinerantly, ranging throughout New England and as far south as Virginia. His first known mural dates to 1824. Before he turned to other pursuits in the 1840s, he painted landscapes on the walls of scores of New England houses and taverns. Some are merely overmantel scenes, but others wrap around entire rooms. All depict idealized landscapes of the sort popularized by the *Hudson River School, although he sometimes included fanciful elements or details of local scenery. With time his work became more sophisticated, but he regularly used labor-saving devices such as generalized foliage and stenciled elements in creating his charming decorations. In the mid-1820s Porter assembled an instructional manual, *A Select Collection of Valuable and Curious Arts, and Interesting Experiments*. After five years of editing *American Mechanic* magazine in New York, in 1845 he founded *Scientific American*, originally a weekly devoted to new inventions. He sold it the following year, but by then had written nearly fifty columns for the periodical, describing his experiences as an artist and offering encouragement to amateurs. For the rest of his life he focused on inventions. In 1849 he published plans for a form of aerial transport. Applying his practical mind to religious matters, in 1852 he published *Essential Truth*, a compilation of several hundred biblical extracts. Frequently on the move throughout his life, he lived at numerous locations in New England, as well as in New York and Washington, D.C. While residing in Bristol, Connecticut, he died on a visit to West Haven.

Portraiture, American. From the early days of settlement, colonists demonstrated interest in sustaining the portrait traditions of their homelands. Until at least the middle of the nineteenth century, nearly all painters and sculptors produced likenesses, if only because willing patrons could be found. Beginning in the 1840s photography began to undercut this source of steady employment, and by the twentieth century the new medium commanded the portrait field. Throughout the colonial period, portraiture dominated the practice of painting and claimed the finest artists' attention. The first important artist to practice in the North American colonies, the anonymous *Freake Painter, painted portraits in an exquisite, late Elizabethan mode during the 1670s. John *Smibert brought an up-to-date Baroque style to New England in 1729. Robert *Feke, the most accomplished American painter of the 1740s, practiced in a lighter and more graceful mode, modeled on rococo precedents. From the 1760s until he left in 1774 for London, John Singleton *Copley painted portraits in a powerful, highly realistic style. Gilbert *Stuart dominated portraiture after the Revolution. His painterly style and romantic, individualistic concept of personality suited leading citizens of the new republic. Especially during the second quarter of the nineteenth century, Thomas *Sully provided Americans with glamorous, lively images of themselves, in a fluid style indebted to the great English portraitists of the period. The work of Chester *Harding reflected the same English precedents, but he preferred a blunter, down-to-earth realism. In the same period, widespread popular appreciation for portraiture encouraged many aspiring artists who had little or no academic training to make a career in art. Sometimes itinerant, they worked throughout the country but particularly in New England, practicing simplified forms of the high-style portraiture of urban centers. Among them, Ammi *Phillips developed a particularly cogent manner emphasizing pattern, color, and observed detail. In the same period, George *Catlin specialized in portraits of Indians from the West. Portrait sculpture was less common, but nevertheless formed an important component in the practice of most of the period's sculptors, such as Horatio *Greenough, Erastus Dow *Palmer, and Hiram *Powers.

In the 1840s photography began to attract sitters with an appeal to objectivity. Yet the traditional associations of the painted image and its idealizing or interpretive possibilities sustained painted portraiture throughout the century. The best portrait photographers combined factuality with compositions, poses, and other conventions learned from portrait painting. Albert *Southworth and Mathew *Brady rank among early masters. In mid-century, G. P. A. *Healy became the first American portrait painter acclaimed on both sides of the Atlantic. His later work, like that of many competitors after the Civil War, often displays a literalism attributable to the influence of photography. Yet, among others who resisted the look of the new technology, such painters as Thomas *Eakins and John Singer *Sargent extended the viability of the painted portrait until after 1900. In the years around the turn of the century, Alvin Langdon *Coburn, Alfred *Stieglitz, and other photographers associated with *pictorialism produced sensitive portrait work. Among realist painters of the early twentieth century, Robert *Henri made a specialty of the genre. Edward *Steichen's stylish, sharp-focus images of the 1920s and 1930s, often picturing celebrities of the day, promoted the authority of photography as the preferred medium for later portraiture. Richard *Avedon, Arnold *Newman, and Irving *Penn have numbered among notable practitioners. During the later twentieth century, Alice *Neel sustained the vitality of painted portraiture with expressionistic impressions, while Andy *Warhol brought to portraiture a *pop art gloss.

Possibilities. *See* ABSTRACT EXPRESSIONISM.

Postminimalism. *See* MINIMALISM.

Postmodernism. An elusive yet influential concept describing antimodern tendencies arising in the late twentieth century. As the name suggests, the key to understanding postmodernism lies in defining its difference from modernism. However, this effort has often foundered on simplistic overgeneralizations about modernism, in itself a contested concept, as are such other vast categories as *romanticism or the Renaissance. Postmodernism as a form of expression in art can be linked to contemporary developments in communications technology, popular culture, corporate practice, and governmental organization, as well as to intellectual debates over linguistics, Marxist theory, and post-Freudian psychology. Although the term occurred from time to time in earlier texts, it first achieved prominence in its contemporary sense with respect to architecture. Robert Venturi's *Complexity and Contradiction in Architecture* (1966) initiated the assault on International Style principles, while certain 1970s works of such designers as Philip Johnson, Charles Moore, Robert A. M. Stern, and Venturi himself mixed modernist forms with abstracted historicism. Although *pop art provided an impetus for these developments, particularly in Venturi's case, it was only in the late 1970s that artistic pluralism of the time came to be discussed as a manifestation of postmodernism.

Especially during the 1980s, academic writers, critics, and artists generated a huge literature on the nature and meaning of postmodernism. Despite lack of consensus, the discourse has clarified important characteristics of postmodern American art. Overwhelmingly, the formalist position upheld by Clement *Greenberg and others has been devalued by demands for "relevance" and greater creative freedom. The notion that art no longer exists in an autonomous aesthetic realm implies its entanglement with contemporary commodity culture. Without notions of purity to uphold, artists are free to engage in narrative or to make use of popular or commercial culture. Postmodern artists also reject the modern fixation on the essence of individual media, instead mixing traditional techniques of painting, sculpture, and photography at will or expanding into other media, such as *installation art, *video art, and *performance art. Many postmodern artists airily dispose of the modern search for personal authenticity by embracing superficiality, indifference, or destablized identities. The decentered, multivalent psyche resonates in a contemporary culture of spatial, temporal, and psychological discontinuities, as the individual increasingly experiences a world of rapid change, accelerated information growth, media fusillades, and intense commercialization. With no fixed self but only a flow of sensory experience provided by the prevailing technological culture, originality itself becomes impossible, and perhaps beside the point. Outright appropriation is authorized, even to plagiarizing the work of earlier artists. Postmodernists have borrowed from linguistics in asserting that meaning, if any exists, must be relational rather than intrinsic and therefore cannot be universal. Following Marxist-influenced philosophical trends, postmodernists often seek to reveal hidden agendas through processes of deconstruction that often intermix with sociological analysis. As this cluster of overlapping generalizations implies, postmodern art embraces related tendencies but cannot be strictly defined. As an international theoretical debate, postmodernism has figured centrally in writings of Jean Baudrillard, Hal Foster, Jürgen Habermas, Fredric Jameson, Rosalind, Krauss, Jean-François Lyotard, W. J. T. Mitchell, and Craig Owens, among others. With his passionless facade and creative mixing of high and low forms, Andy *Warhol led the way for artists.

As a practice, postmodernism has embraced several related but distinct tendencies. Jean-Michel *Basquiat and several other painters lionized in the 1980s stand out among those at the time labeled neo-expressionists. At the outset of the decade, painter, printmaker, and sculptor Julian Schnabel (1951–) set the pace for brash tastelessness with garish paintings on velvet, broken crockery glued to canvas, and other aggressively physical surfaces, sometimes embellished with three-dimensional objects. His frantic brushwork often roughly delineated figurative themes alluding to grand human aspirations and fears. Borrowing with abandon from sources from old masters to mass media, he denied that his intentions had anything to do with self-expression, despite their high-flown romantic air. Born in New York, Schnabel graduated from the University of Houston in the early 1970s and has in recent years worked primarily as a filmmaker. David Salle (1952–) juxtaposed and overlaid figural imagery culled from romance and pornography magazines, old master paintings, movies, and other sources. His provocative paintings seemed to exemplify individual subordination to a media-saturated environment and to reflect the absurd condition of contemporary consciousness as a ceaseless flow of responses to artificial visual stimuli. Born in Norman, Oklahoma, Salle grew up in Wichita. After receiving a BFA from Valencia's California Institute of the Arts in 1973 and an MFA two years later, he moved to New York. He has also designed sets and costumes for theatrical and dance performances, and has directed a film. Draftsman, painter, sculptor, and photographer Robert Longo (1953–) first came to attention in the early 1980s with his Men in the Cities series of black-and-white drawings. Adapted from photographs, these isolated, over-life-size men in suits twist or fall in apparent incidents of brutality. Although related to *photorealism, the works abstracted their subjects to achieve compelling grace combined with an air of menace as well as ambiguity with respect to meaning and artistic intention. Later paintings, often combined with sculptural components, continued Longo's fascination with violent, irrational forces at work in the culture. Born in Brooklyn, Longo graduated from the State University College at Buffalo in 1975 and returned to New York in 1977. He, too, later worked with film and designed sets and costumes. In the 1990s he returned his focus to drawing, gradually refining his technique and heading into more introspective territory.

Another aspect of 1980s postmodern art took its cues from consumer and popular culture. Early in the decade, Jeff Koons (1955–) exhibited ordinary household vacuum cleaners, resplendently displayed singly or in groups within Plexiglas vitrines. Since then, he has relentlessly probed the permeable interface between commodity culture and the art world. By inserting non-art items into an art context, he transforms the vulgar or kitsch object into saleable high art. Among his most sensational works have been painted ceramic sculptures suggesting blown-up souvenirs, some highly eroticized, and the huge *Puppy* (1992), a lovable "stuffed animal" framework more than forty feet tall, covered entirely with flowering plants. Since the mid-1990s he has created an Easyfun series of brightly colored oil paintings composed from photo-realistic fragments. As is the case with nearly all of his work, fabrication is left to assistants or craftspersons, suggesting a debt to *conceptual art. A native of York, Pennsylvania, in 1976 Koons graduated from the Maryland Institute College of Art in Baltimore. Painter, printmaker, and sculptor Keith Haring (1958–90) employed cartoonlike imagery to create what he hoped would be a genuinely popular art. Born in Reading, Pennsylvania, he grew up in nearby Kutztown. After moving to New York in 1978, he attended the School of Visual Arts, worked as a street artist, and participated in the era's frenetic club culture that bridged punk and hip-hop. In 1980 he began to develop a distinctive style of simple figures rendered in outline. Usually interlocking in vigorous, dynamic patterns, these childlike representations often addressed serious social issues. In 1986 he opened the Pop Shop boutique in SoHo to retail his work. It remained in operation until 2005. In addition to paintings, he created work in a grand variety of formats, mass-produced his designs on consumer items such as T-shirts and umbrellas, and often participated in public or educational projects. In the final years before his death from AIDS, Haring's increasingly ambitious work reached new levels of formal and thematic complexity. *Keith Haring Journals* (1996) presents his diary entries from 1977 to 1989. His Visual Arts classmate Kenny Scharf (1958–), a painter, printmaker, and sculptor, shares Haring's desire to reach a wide audience. He developed a wacky, high-spirited, eclectic style, blending television-cartoon imagery, mid-century *biomorphism, and the visionary spaces of surrealists such as Roberto *Matta and Yves *Tanguy. While continuing a long-standing interest in applying raucous psychedelic ornamentation to environments and individual objects, including cars, televisions, and a Pace Arrow motor home, he has more recently also tried his hand at cartoon animation. Born in Los Angeles, where he resides today, he received his BFA in 1980.

A leader in the postmodern assault on originality, Sherrie Levine (1949–) in the early 1980s photographed reproductions of prints by Walker *Evans and then other major modern photographers. Denying that artistic originality was possible, in these iconoclastic appropriations she also questioned the commodity status of master photographers' work, which had recently risen sharply in value. Later she made watercolor copies of illustrations of paintings by Matisse and other modern artists. Since these were miniaturized versions of well-known paintings, identical in size to the book-illustration "originals," they further complicated questions of authenticity, meaning, and market value. In the late 1980s, she painted flat-footed generic abstractions, hoping to hasten the death of modernism by depreciating its central feature. Born in Hazleton, Pennsylvania, Levine graduated from the University of Wisconsin at Madison in 1969 and four years later received an MFA there. She moved to New York in 1975. In more recent years, she has repudiated much of the academic theory that supported her insouciant deconstructive works, which she nevertheless continues to elaborate, as if plagiarizing her own work.

Post-painterly abstraction. *See* NEW YORK SCHOOL.

Potter, Edward Clark (1857–1923). Sculptor. Chiefly interested in animal imagery, he remains best known for the paired marble lions (1910–11) guarding the Fifth Avenue approach to the New York Public Library. Although initially criticized as insufficiently regal, they have come to be regarded with great affection among New York's most familiar landmarks. As a specialist in horses, Potter collaborated with Daniel Chester *French on three important equestrian monuments and executed five on his own. Besides animals, he produced portraits and other figural works. Potter was born in New London, Connecticut. He attended Amherst (Massachusetts) College for three semesters before heading to Boston in 1879 to study art. In 1883 he became French's studio assistant. After two years he moved to Vermont to work at a marble quarry and oversee cutting of his mentor's work. In 1886 he departed for Paris, where he studied with figure sculptor Antonin Mercié and animal specialist Emmanuel Frémiet. After his return to the United States in 1890, he settled in Enfield, north of Hartford, Connecticut. Soon he was at work with French on several major groups for the 1893 World's Columbian Exposition in Chicago. During the subsequent decade, as he and French produced their joint equestrian monuments, his independent career also flourished. In 1902 he moved permanently to Greenwich, Connecticut. He died at his summer home in New London.

Potthast, Edward Henry (1857–1927). Painter and illustrator. His reputation rests primarily on bright, freely brushed renditions of carefree leisure moments, particularly beach scenes, dating from the early twentieth century. He also painted landscapes observed under diverse conditions of illumination, including moonlight, as well as portraits, *genre scenes, and nudes. Indebted to impressionism's sparkle, his mature style accents loose, painterly application of clear, vivid hues. A Cincinnati native, from his teenage years Potthast worked as a lithographer and illustrator. He relinquished these pursuits in favor of painting full time only as he approached forty. Intermittently until 1887 he pursued formal art training at the McMicken School of Design (now the Art Academy of Cincinnati). In 1882 he departed for Europe, where he remained for about three years. After a sojourn in Antwerp, he settled in Munich, where he picked up the fluent, dark-toned approach popular there. During a second period abroad, from 1887 to 1889 or 1890, he worked in Paris and the nearby countryside. Depicting a barefoot peasant girl picking flowers, *Sunshine* (Cincinnati Art Museum, 1889) combines a solidly constructed figure with the feathery brushwork, light tonality, and broken colors of impressionism. In the mid-1890s Potthast left Cincinnati for New York, where he soon specialized in the more spontaneous effects and overtly modern subjects of his best-known work. Children playing at water's edge in *A Holiday* (Art Institute of Chicago, 1915) enact a tableau of joyous innocence. Despite the apparent informality of its composition, carefully arranged forms and hues discipline its sensuous brushwork and freshly appealing chromatic touches. Potthast often recorded activities observed in Central Park, but on the beaches of Long Island he found the relatively intimate scale and intense sunlight that particularly suited his interests. Less convincingly, during these years he also painted scenes of the West, particularly the Grand Canyon, and a few late figural allegories. He died in his New York studio.

Pousette-Dart, Richard (1916–92). Painter, sculptor, and photographer. Unique among significant *abstract expressionists in his overt embrace of a spiritual dimension within his art, he remained always somewhat apart from others in the movement. Born in St. Paul, Minnesota, he spent his early years in Valhalla, north of New York. Essentially self-taught as a painter, he attended Bard College in Annandale-on-Hudson, New York, for a year. His early mélange of cubist space with elements of organic surrealism had coalesced by the time he moved to New York. There, in 1937 he became an assistant to Paul *Manship, an old friend of his father's. Particularly attuned to sources in American Indian art, in thickly painted webs of symbols and abstract signs he shared the nascent abstract expressionists 1940s quest for universalizing allusions to the primal and the unconscious. Through the 1950s, forms submerged in layers of paint became increasingly indeterminate. By the 1960s he had purged representation entirely, activating his canvases with pulsing, radiantly hued surfaces that offer hovering materializations of mystical states. Employing a painstakingly meticulous technique, he typically assembled these transcendental works from a myriad of dotted brushstrokes. Yet his sensitively varied work always maintained a fresh poetry reflecting devotion to the solitary act of painting and indifference to art world opinion. In later years he also combined sculptural elements and found objects into painted reliefs. In addition, throughout his life, he used photography to portray his friends and probe patterns found in nature. He died in the New York apartment he had maintained while living principally in the Hudson River Valley, at Sloatsburg from 1951 to 1958 and then in nearby Suffern. His father, **Nathaniel Pousette-Dart** (1886–1965), an art writer and painter, was born Nathaniel Pousette in St. Paul but hyphenated his name upon marriage. Following early training in St. Paul, he studied in New York with Robert *Henri and at the *Pennsylvania Academy of the Fine Arts with Thomas *Anshutz. He had visited Europe twice before his return to St. Paul in 1912. Once again in New York three years later, he soon became a successful graphic designer, instrumental in the introduction of modern art into magazine advertising. His mildly expressionistic landscapes and figural works reveal an admiration for van Gogh, Cézanne, El Greco, and Albert Pinkham *Ryder. Besides *American Painting Today* (1956), his books include monographs on Childe *Hassam (1922), Robert *Henri (1922), Abbott H. *Thayer (1923), Winslow *Homer (1923), John Singer *Sargent (1924), and James Abbott McNeill *Whistler (1924). He died in Valhalla, New York, where he had made his home for some forty-five years. Richard's daughter, abstract painter **Joanna Pousette-Dart** (1947–), lives in New York. Born there, she graduated from Vermont's Bennington College in 1968. In the 1970s she investigated relationships between gridded structure and color but adopted a freer and more painterly approach during the following decade. In her recent buoyant work, flat color areas deployed on shaped canvases evoke luminous landscape spaces.

Powell, Earl Alexander, III. *See* NATIONAL GALLERY OF ART.

Powell, William Henry. *See* MURAL PAINTING.

Powers, Hiram (1805–73). Sculptor. The creator of works epitomizing the *neoclassicism of his day, he rose to international prominence. Stressing ideal form, silky modeling of white marble surfaces, and controlled emotion, his work evokes antique precedents but discloses also a taste for realism. Often he embellished his subjects with anecdotal detail. Supported by his Swedenborgian beliefs, Powers's faith that the human form reflected divine presence informed his nudes, including his most popular work, the *Greek Slave* (Raby Castle, Durham, England, 1845; Corcoran Gallery, 1846, and four later versions; modeled 1840–43). In much of Europe as well as the United States, this female captive ranked as the most widely known mid-nineteenth-century work of art. Praised also for other allegorical or narrative conceptions, Powers was highly regarded as well for some 150 portrait busts. Many of these seem strikingly natural. Powers was born in Vermont, near Woodstock, but moved in 1818 to Cincinnati. There as a young man with a knack for mechanical handiwork, he found work at Joseph Dorfeuille's Western Museum, where he produced wax figures, most notably for an animated simulation of Dante's *Inferno*. Beginning in 1828, he learned the rudiments of sculpture from Berlin-born Frederick Eckstein (c. 1775–1852), who had settled permanently in Cincinnati five years earlier. After attracting local attention with his portrait busts, in 1834–35 Powers modeled a likeness of Andrew Jackson (Metropolitan Museum, 1839), which made his reputation. Using a common device of the period, Powers swathed the president's shoulders in an illusionistic toga, but he rendered the aging man's visage with unsparing naturalism. Even so, Jackson projects an air of inner resolution and nobility, recalling the portraiture of Republican Rome.

In 1837 Powers departed for Italy. With the initial assistance of Horatio *Greenough, he settled permanently in Florence. Soon he aspired to make his mark with ideal subjects in marble, beginning with *Eve Tempted* (Smithsonian American Art Museum, 1839–42), his first nude. Before this was completed, he began *Fisher Boy* (Brookgreen Gardens, Murrells Inlet, South Carolina, 1846; modeled 1841–44), one of the earliest American male nudes, and the celebrated *Greek Slave*. Although loosely inspired in form by the classical *Medici Venus*, the *Slave* evokes a living model, while narrative details, such as a cross and the chain that binds her hands, deviate from classical generality. For the theme, Powers imagined an episode in Greece's 1820s war of independence. Contributing to a long history of the West's fascination with and repulsion for oriental civilizations, the young woman is displayed as if for sale in a market, following her capture by enemy Turks. For Powers and his Victorian audience, the demurely submissive figure's triumph of purity over evil evasively rationalized its overtly sexual appeal. Trumping objections to nudity, her sensuous body was on display against her will, according to the artist. Even her composure indicated inner grace and serenity. The *Greek Slave* appeared in London in 1845 before being shown in New York in 1847 and at later international expositions. As it toured the United States from 1847 to 1849, an accompanying pamphlet aided reception with shrewd commentary calculated to defuse its nudity, along with the approbation of a Christian minister. Besides its complex appeals to erotic, religious, and political meanings, the piece additionally resonated with the highly charged contemporary debate over slavery in the United States. Exemplifying an early instance of the intersection of high art and popular spectacle, the work inspired a virtual mania, becoming a cultural icon reproduced in varied sizes and materials for middle-class consumption, in addition to the replicas and variants that emerged from Powers's studio. By about 1850 Powers ranked as the most prominent American artist in Florence. While he continued to create ideal figures and portraits, his workshop also turned out replicas of his more sought-after pieces. His bust of *Proserpine* (1840), a mythological goddess, is known in more than one hundred examples in three sizes. Despite his continuing popularity in some quarters, Powers's most significant work dated to the 1840s. After the Civil War, his authority waned as more naturalistic taste supplanted neoclassicism.

Two sons who also became sculptors worked primarily as portraitists. **Preston Powers** (1843–1931), christened William Preston, was born in Florence. Employed as a young man at varied occupations in Florence and the United States, after serving in the U.S. Navy he returned to Florence to assist in his father's studio. Later he spent much of his time in the United States. *The Closing Era*, his monumental bronze of an Indian hunter standing over a buffalo (state capitol grounds, Denver, 1893), won praise at the World's Columbian Exposition in Chicago. He died in Florence. Also a professional photographer of portraits and views, **Longworth Powers** (1835–1904) was born in Cincinnati, worked primarily in Florence, and died there.

Pozzatti, Rudy (1925–). Printmaker, painter, and sculptor. A versatile and accomplished technician in both intaglio and relief processes, he is known particularly for prints that combine representational and abstract form in bold compositions. His images embrace a wide range of themes, including architecture, nature, the history of art, religion, and politics. Born in Telluride, Colorado, Rudy Otto Pozzatti served in the U.S. Army for three years before graduating in 1948 from the University of Colorado in Boulder and earning an MFA two years later. His teachers there included Max Beckmann and Ben *Shahn. During a visit to Italy in 1952, he first encountered the rich architectural and artistic legacy that has inspired many prints. From 1956 until retirement in 1991 he taught at Indiana University in Bloomington, where he continues to reside.

Pratt, Matthew (1734–1805). Painter. His best-known painting numbers among American artists' earliest pictorial responses to studio practice and its theoretical underpinnings. Fresh, direct, and pictorially complex, *The American School* (Metropolitan Museum, 1765) evokes the art life of Benjamin *West's circle in London. Although Pratt tried his hand at history painting and still life, his professional effort generally was limited to portraiture, reflecting the preference of the American market in his day. Even so, after twenty productive years before the Revolution, he eventually turned to other pursuits. A lifelong Philadelphian, Pratt learned his craft during an apprenticeship between 1749 and 1756 with his uncle, James Claypoole (1720–84), an artisan who also traded in art supplies and may have painted portraits (none conclusively identified). Until 1764 when he departed for London, Pratt worked primarily as a portrait painter in Philadelphia. Regarded as West's first American student, for the next two-and-a-half years Pratt worked informally with the slightly younger but better trained painter. Completed during this period, *The American School* depicts West, at left, and Pratt, seated before an easel at right, along with three unidentified young men. Their anonymity barely matters, for the painting subordinates individual identity to pictorial challenges and the absorbing pleasures of artistic creation. During the final year and a half of his stay in England, Pratt painted portraits in Bristol. After returning home in 1768, he portrayed clients in New York and Williamsburg, Virginia, as well as in Philadelphia. On a visit to Europe in 1770 he worked for some months in Ireland and England. From the mid-1770s, his activities in Philadelphia included teaching drawing, selling art supplies, and painting signs renowned for excellence in their day. Pratt's cousin James Claypoole Jr. (c. 1743–before 1815) became a more accomplished artist than his father, who presumably trained him also. Born, as his father had been, in Philadelphia, he was professionally active in that city from the early 1760s, primarily as a portraitist. Also a printmaker, he is known to have produced political cartoons. Intending to go to London for additional training, he left around 1769 but instead continued to practice his craft in Kingston, Jamaica and may never have returned.

Precisionism. A representational style emphasizing clean, clear, precise forms drawn from urban and industrial subjects but nearly always devoid of human presence. Widespread particularly in the 1920s and 1930s, precisionism promoted visual objectivity over self-expression. Although many of the period's most creative artists were drawn to precisionism, the tendency never yielded an organized group nor a coherent program. Like artists of the *American scene movement, precisionism's practitioners wished to create a modern though distinctly American art. In both cases, emphasis on a recognizably American iconography grew in part from this generation's disillusionment with Europe in the wake of World War I. Additionally, precisionism's structure and clarity contributed to a widespread return to classical order in arts of the West after the chaos of World War I. Although it developed independently in the United States, precisionism shares traits with the French work of the Purists and Fernand Léger and with analogous tendencies elsewhere in Europe. Precisonism expressed the period's optimistic faith in objective, scientific seeing and thinking as keys to better living conditions—and even to better spiritual conditions—for all Americans. An attraction to honesty, directness, and unconcealed functionalism led many precisionists and their admirers to pioneer appreciation of vernacular and folk art forms. In the 1920s, precisionists were often called "immaculates." The style has also been known by the terms machine abstraction and cubist-realism.

Precisionist sources include cubism, sharp-focus photography, machine imagery in the work of Marcel *Duchamp and other artists of *New York dada, and the detached and often ironic sensibility cultivated in Walter *Arensberg's circle. The work of Charles *Sheeler most clearly demonstrates the style's essential features. Other central figures include Ralston *Crawford, Preston *Dickinson, and Niles *Spencer. Much of the work of Charles *Demuth and *Georgia O'Keeffe relates to the precisionist aesthetic. Photographers who produced kindred images include Sheeler and Paul *Strand. Some precisionist paintings, such as Sheeler's *Bucks County Barn* (Museum of Modern Art, 1932), offer straightforward, almost photographically exact representation. In an alternative approach exemplified by Demuth's *My Egypt*, abstracted and rearranged forms evoke the spirit of modernity.

Prendergast, Maurice (1859–1924). Painter and printmaker. The first American to formulate a style based on European postimpressionism, he worked in a decorative, patterned manner well suited to the emotional tenor of his characteristically festive subjects. In developing this approach, he drew first on the work of James Abbott McNeill *Whistler and Manet. Later he admired the paintings of Pierre Bonnard and Édouard Vuillard. During a visit to Paris in 1907, he was impressed by Cézanne's innovations. Other important sources of his mature style include the work of Pierre Puvis de Chavannes, Georges Seurat, Paul Signac, and Matisse. In its subject matter, most of Prendergast's work sustained the impressionists' fascination with uncomplicated leisure pursuits. Although Prendergast worked in oil throughout his life, it was his preferred medium only in later years. He achieved particular distinction with luminous watercolors and produced more than two hundred works in the relatively unusual monoprint technique, which he abandoned around 1902. He also designed posters and book illustrations.

Born in St. John's, Newfoundland, Maurice Brazil Prendergast moved with his family to Boston in 1868. With little schooling and almost no art instruction but some experience as a commercial artist, in 1886–87 he went briefly to England, the first of several trips to Europe. By the late 1880s, he ranked as the only significant artist in the United States working in a style based on advanced European painting, a distinction he held for nearly twenty years. From 1891 through 1894 he lived in Paris, where he studied at the Académie Julian and the Atelier Colarossi. Nominally a shore view, the watercolor *Revere Beach* (Canajoharie [New York] Library and Art Gallery, c. 1896–97) functions as a meditation on color and pictorial structure. On a decisive eighteen-month trip to Italy in 1898–99, he worked mostly in Venice as his style became brighter and more fluid. He returned once to Venice and on two occasions to Paris before World War I. Stronger hues and greater attention to abstract form mark the paintings he chose to include in The *Eight's 1908 show. Prendergast had little in common with the stylistic aims of the other exhibitors, but he shared their desire to replace academic art with something fresher. After showing seven works in the 1913 *Armory Show, the following year Prendergast moved permanently to New York, although he regularly visited New England coastal resorts during summers. During this last decade of his life, tapestry-like friezes offer a refined and arcadian world of pleasurable activity, as in *The Swans* (Addison Gallery of American Art, Phillips Academy, Andover, Massachusetts, 1916–18), a shore scene intermingling white birds with graceful women.

His brother **Charles Prendergast** (1863–1948), also a painter, is better known for frames, decorative objects, and most of all, polychrome relief carvings, sometimes also gilded. Born, as was his brother, in St. John's, Newfoundland, Charles James Prendergast grew up in Boston and left school at an early age. As a young man, he drifted among occupations until turning to custom frame making in the mid-1890s. A longtime companion to his bachelor brother, he moved to New York with Maurice and married only after Maurice's death. He began to make his distinctive painted, low-relief panels shortly after a 1911 trip to Italy. Decorative and idyllic, these dreamlike scenes reflected his interests in ancient, medieval, and Renaissance art and in Persian miniatures. After about 1930 he increasingly turned to themes from contemporary life, rendered in a flattened, deliberately naïve manner.

Prentice, Levi Wells. *See* DECKER, JOSEPH.

Pre-Raphaelitism, American. Term designating a tendency inspired by the painters of the British Pre-Raphaelite Brotherhood, who admired the simplicity and purity they perceived in work of early Renaissance artists preceding Raphael. Following the English painters' devotion to exactingly illusionistic detail, glossy finish, and moral urgency, American Pre-Raphaelites generally applied these precepts to depiction of landscape or other natural subjects, such as still lifes set outdoors. Few Americans were drawn to the didactic and frequently sentimental narratives favored in England, and most rejected the high-keyed color and decorative elaboration associated with the style there. Although the number of Americans who identified themselves with the movement remained small, the Pre-Raphaelite ideal of truth to nature and the Brotherhood's conflation of art, nature, and ethical or spiritual goals resonated widely in the United States. As a spokesman for its ideals, the respected English aesthetician and art critic John Ruskin proved instrumental in disseminating such ideas. Broadly filtered throughout the artistic community, these affected a large swath of nineteenth-century American still life, *genre, and landscape, including the *Hudson River School.

During a sojourn in England, William James *Stillman developed an enthusiasm for the work of Dante Gabriel Rossetti, John Everett Millais, and other British Pre-Raphaelites. After his return, in 1855 he founded *The* **Crayon*, which introduced such work to Americans. Two years after it ceased publication in 1861, a small group of Pre-Raphaelite enthusiasts organized the Association for the Advancement of Truth in Art. From 1863 until 1865 this group put out another magazine, *The New Path*. Pre-Raphaelitism in the United States peaked in the late 1850s and 1860s, but its influence continued to reverberate. Leading American Pre-Raphaelites include Fidelia Bridges (1834–1923), John William *Hill, Charles Herbert *Moore, and William Trost *Richards. Although Henry Roderick Newman (1843–1917) spent most of his professional life abroad (from 1870 Florence was his permanent residence, although he often traveled elsewhere), he remained true to his Pre-Raphaelite roots. Thomas Charles Farrer (c. 1840–91), an English painter who came to New York about 1860 and stayed for more than a decade, played an instrumental role in organizing and promoting the movement. His brother, painter and etcher Henry Farrer (1843–1903), also born in London, stayed on in the United States, remaining attuned to the style, as did Hill's son, John Henry *Hill. Critic Clarence *Cook helped to found the Association and served, for a year, as *The New Path*'s first editor.

Primary Structures. *See* MINIMALISM.

Prior, William Matthew (1806–73). Painter. Primarily a portraitist, he also produced some landscapes. As he openly advertised, Prior worked in two distinguishable portrait styles. Only with the more expensive did he provide three-dimensional modeling, especially for facial features. Even his "flat picture(s) . . . without shade or shadow at one-quarter price" display strong pattern, careful design, and an aptitude for catching individual features, but the more finished works better measure his artistry. Often including a fairly elaborate setting, these demonstrate his desire to adapt sophisticated stylistic and iconographic models when he could find willing clients. A religious enthusiast, in the 1840s Prior developed the unusual specialty of painting dead children whose likenesses he received in communication with the spirit world. In the 1860s he published two books on religious subjects. When *daguerreotypes began to limit his market in mid-century, he achieved popular success with reverse paintings on glass of famous Americans, particularly George Washington. Mostly also dating from his later years, his romantic landscapes, often based on prints, include winter scenes, moonlit visions, and views of Washington's home or tomb. Born in Bath, Maine, he apparently remained self-taught as an artist. He continued throughout much of his career to supplement his income with artisanal work, such as sign painting and ornamental decoration, which he first undertook as a teenager. By 1824 he was painting portraits in Portland, where he settled in the early 1830s. There he worked along with his wife's brothers. Three (until one died in 1839) apparently limited themselves to applied art, but Sturtevant J. Hamblin (or Hamblen) (1817–84) developed into an independent portrait painter, active from 1837 until 1856, and became sufficiently skilled that some of his work from the 1840s and early 1850s may be confused with Prior's. In 1840 the entire extended family moved permanently to Boston, although Prior continued his established practice of also working itinerantly. These trips took him throughout New England and as far south as Baltimore, but he stayed primarily in Massachusetts and Maine.

Process art. A form of art that incorporates evidence of its own making into its aesthetic structure. The term dates to the mid-1960s, when many artists, conditioned by *abstract expressionism's gestural brushwork, began to integrate the creative procedure into other forms of art. Some also exploited the perishability of materials and their alteration over time. At first, process art often overlapped with *minimalism or *conceptual art, but since that time it has affected the procedures of artists pursuing other ends. Process art also reflected interest in experience for its own sake and, through its frequently unstable nature, often challenged the marketability of the art product. Leading artists associated with the tendency include Robert *Morris, Richard *Serra, and Eva *Hesse.

Proctor, Alexander Phimister (1862–1950). Sculptor. A specialist in depictions of animals, particularly the game of the American West, he also represented American Indians and other figural subjects. His finely detailed, tabletop bronzes intended for domestic interiors paralleled many monumental public commissions. Proctor was born in Bozanquit (or Bosanquet), in western Ontario, Canada, but grew up in Michigan, Iowa, and from 1871, Denver. There he developed a lifelong affection for outdoor life. In 1885 he left for New York, where he studied at the *National Academy of Design and the *Art Students League. Instruction from John *Rogers aided his progress as a sculptor. He also studied animal anatomy. Proctor first attracted national attention with more than thirty life-size wild animals, as well as equestrian figures of a cowboy and an Indian, created for Chicago's World's Columbian Exposition of 1893. That fall he departed for Paris, where he studied with animal sculptor Denys Peuch. He returned to the United States the following year at the invitation of Augustus *Saint-Gaudens to model the horse for the older sculptor's monument honoring *General John A. Logan* (Grant Park, Chicago, 1894–97). He soon repeated this task for Saint-Gaudens's even more splendid equestrian *General Sherman Led by Victory*. From 1895 to 1900 Proctor again studied and worked in Paris, where his work won praise at important exhibitions. Reestablished in New York, he completed many of his most important animal sculptures before leaving in 1914. He lived in Oregon and Idaho before settling four years later in Palo Alto, California. In subsequent years he received many commissions for public monuments, mostly located in western states. He lived in Europe again from 1925 to 1928, in Rome for two years, and then in Brussels. He died in Palo Alto. In their carefully detailed presentation of animal and human physiology and movement, his sculptures suggest the beauty, variety, and power of nature. His numerous buffalo, elks, panthers, and other large animals, as well as Indian themes, also celebrate the vanishing frontier West of his youth as a distinctive, vital, and particularly American locale. His autobiography appeared in 1971 as *Alexander Phimister Proctor, Sculptor in Buckskin*.

Provincetown, Massachusetts. *See* ARTISTS' COLONIES.

Public Works of Art Project (PWAP). *See* FEDERAL ART PROJECTS.

Puryear, Martin (1941–). Sculptor and printmaker. His laboriously hand-crafted, elegant, and idiosyncratic sculptures draw on diverse forms of cultural expression, as well as *minimalism, *process art, and the work of modern masters, particularly Brancusi but also including Arp, Alberto Giacometti, and Isamu *Noguchi. He most often works with wood, which he variously bends, joins, and polishes or paints, but has also used other materials, notably such nontraditional substances as wire mesh and tar. Complex, abstract, tactile, and generally organic forms allude to other natural and man-made objects but only indirectly. His contemplative works almost never reveal their formal integrity from any one viewpoint but demand inspection over time as the viewer circles around. Close examination of the means of their construction often contributes to their appeal. In 1989 Puryear received a MacArthur Foundation "genius" award. Born in Washington, D.C., he switched from the study of biology to art while studying there at Catholic University of America. Following graduation in 1963, he served for two years in the Peace Corps in Sierra Leone. One of few African Americans to experience immersion in African society, he has said that he felt like an outsider in that context, but he was drawn to craft traditions. His experience of working with local carpenters to learn their methods had long-term consequences for his artistic development, while the African artifacts more commonly admired in the West had little impact. In his mature career, while remaining sensitive to his African-American heritage, he has refrained from forcing his art into the service of identity politics. Rather, while open to metaphorical readings, his personal formalism foregrounds inherent qualities of material and shape with clarity, simplicity, and expressive reticence. From 1966 to 1968 Puryear studied printmaking and sculpture at the Swedish Royal Academy of Art. While residing in Stockholm, he also studied Scandinavian craft traditions and modern design. Between 1969 and 1971 he earned an MFA at Yale University. After teaching for two years at Fisk University in Nashville, he moved to New York. Following a 1977 studio fire that destroyed much of his work, he relocated in 1978 to Chicago, where he taught for a decade at the University of Illinois. During these years, he assimilated traditional boat-building techniques and worked with yurt-like forms, while also completing the earliest of his monumental outdoor and public art projects. On an extended visit to Japan in 1983, he observed traditional architecture and garden design. In 1990 he moved permanently to a new home in Accord, in the Catskills region some seventy-five miles north of New York. Each work that comes from his studio continues to achieve remarkable singularity, attesting to the artist's patience, ingenuity, and meticulous attention to detail.

Pyle, Howard. *See* WYETH, N. C.

q

Quidor, John (1801–81). Painter. The first native artist to specialize in narratives taken from American literature, he contributed to *romanticism's zest for emotionally charged subjects. Resisting contemporary taste for realism, his best-known images expand on fictional themes from Washington Irving and, on two occasions, James Fenimore Cooper. Quidor's idiosyncratic, exaggerated style suits his penchant for the fantastic, grotesque, and comical in his subjects. He also painted religious scenes and occasional landscapes. Born in Tappan, on the Hudson River, as a child he moved with his family to New York. There he trained in the studio of John Wesley *Jarvis. As a young man, he may have worked as a portraitist, but he apparently made his living fashioning signs, banners, and other decorative items. In paintings he synthesized a personal and painterly style from such sources as seventeenth-century Dutch *genre, the works of William Hogarth and other eighteenth-century English satirists, and the fluid French rococo. All of these he must have known primarily, if not exclusively, through engravings, from which he frequently adapted direct quotations. Quidor's reputation rests on relatively few surviving paintings, dating chiefly to the late 1820s and 1830s. Except for one small religious painting, no works survive from the years between 1839 and 1855, although he is known to have painted seven enormous biblical scenes during the 1840s. In 1836 he left for Illinois, where he lived in the Quincy area until returning to New York in 1849. Several paintings date to the period after 1855, but he apparently became inactive as an artist before the end of the 1860s. In 1868 he moved across the Hudson River to Jersey City, where he died, having achieved little recognition. In dramatic and moody works such as *Ichabod Crane Pursued by the Headless Horseman* (Yale University Art Gallery, 1828) and *Return of Rip van Winkle* (National Gallery, 1829), capacious compositions complement nervously energetic drawing. By subordinating anecdotal detail to pictorial values, his inventive constructions transcend the literary sources that inspired them. In work of the 1850s and 1860s, heavy glazing and limited color contribute to vaporous and generalized effects.

Quinn, John (1870–1924). Collector, patron, and crusader for free expression. Also a lawyer. Although he assembled one of the most adventurous American collections of all time, his holdings were dispersed after his death. His art collection included American, Irish, and British work, but its chief glories were French. He owned major works by Cézanne, Seurat, Picasso, and Brancusi, along with other post-impressionists and modernists. His last purchase, made on the advice of Picasso only months before his death from cancer at fifty-four, was Henri Rousseau's haunting *Sleeping Gypsy* (Museum of Modern Art, 1897). He owned paintings by most of the major American modernists, including Marsden *Hartley, John *Marin, and Charles *Sheeler, as well as an exceptionally large representation of the work of his friend Walt *Kuhn. Drawn to artists as well as art, Quinn served as the legal advisor for the *Armory Show and was instrumental in achieving repeal of the federal import tariff on contemporary art. Born in Tiffin, Ohio, southeast of Toledo, Quinn grew up there and in nearby Fostoria. He spent a year at the University of Michigan before going to work for a former Ohio governor. In 1891 when his mentor was appointed secretary of the treasury, the young man followed him to Washington, D.C. He earned a law degree from Georgetown University in 1893 and a second law degree from Harvard University in 1895. Subsequently he practiced in New York, where he enjoyed a lucrative career in banking law. Soon a supporter of Irish independence and the literary revival in that country, he began collecting books and manuscripts. Eventually he owned some 12,000 items encompassing British and American literature, as well as Irish. Among other courageous acts, he purchased the manuscript of James Joyce's *Ulysses*, defended its author in court against obscenity charges, and arranged for publication of T. S. Eliot's *The Waste Land*. Quinn sold his literary collection at auction in 1923 and 1924, shortly before he died. His will stipulated the same fate for his art. After some items were disposed of privately, the estate auctioned twenty-eight hundred works in Paris in 1926, followed by another eight hundred in New York the following year. The prices realized at these sales were important to American collectors and museums in validating the worth of modern art. The loss of Quinn's treasure set New York art lovers to wondering what might have happened if there had been a museum to welcome his collection, helping to set into motion the founding of the *Museum of Modern Art two years later.

r

RYDER

Ringgold

Rockwell

RAUSCHENBERG

Riis

Revere

Remington

Rothko

Rainer, Yvonne. *See* HELD, AL.

Ramírez, Martin (1885–1960). Mixed-media draftsman. Self-taught as an artist, he created unworldly fantasies suggesting the subconscious mind in action. Architectural forms, tunnels, and animals recur frequently in his private iconography. Born in the Los Altos region of Jalisco, Mexico, he moved to California when he was about thirty to work in mining and railroad construction. In the early 1930s he was diagnosed with paranoid schizophrenia. Soon permanently institutionalized, he spent his final fifteen years in a state mental hospital at Auburn, northeast of Sacramento. There, a psychologist recognized the quality of his obsessive, patterned works and encouraged his talent. Incorporating remembered and observed elements in unexpected combinations, Ramírez often added color in crayon or watercolor, and occasionally included collage elements cut from magazine illustrations. *Untitled (Church)* (Smithsonian American Art Museum, c. 1950) features elaborate architectural elements, probably remembered from the colonial baroque buildings of his childhood. Possibly stimulated by the memory of a sculpture, a horse within an arch above the tunnel-like entrance dominates a rudimentary facade with twin towers. On either side, tall, domed structures suggest other parts of the church, while a cloister loggia extends to one side. An elaborate foreground pattern apparently stands for brick stairs leading up to the entrance, and a cyclone-like form spins to one side in the background. As is the case with most of Ramírez's works, although meaning remains obscure, the energy and intricacy of the artist's handiwork convey the mind's robust ability to travel to its own destinations.

Ranger, Henry Ward (1858–1916). Painter. Known especially for richly painted, intimate woodlands, he ranked among the most popular American landscape painters in the years around the turn of the twentieth century. He also painted open pastorals, as well as city and shore views. Rooted in the *Barbizon method and indebted to the example of George *Inness's late style, his work contributed to the period's enthusiasm for *tonalism. Some works, particularly from the later part of his career, demonstrate admiration for impressionism's vivid chromatic effects and flickering light. Ranger rarely emphasized topographical accuracy, preferring instead to evoke poetic moods. Picturing a hazy Manhattan beyond the graceful arches of a bridge spanning the Harlem River, *High Bridge, New York* (Metropolitan Museum, 1905) skillfully deploys patterned forms, appealing colors, and lively brushwork. Even this scene of industrialized modernity submits to his characteristic decorative romanticism. Born in Syracuse, New York, Ranger studied for two years at Syracuse University. Mostly self-taught as an artist, he had begun painting in watercolor before he left the university in 1875. Two or three years later, he moved to New York. There, as he continued to specialize in watercolor, his detailed approach soon became more fluid and atmospheric. He spent most of the 1880s traveling and working in Europe, while developing his oil technique. He particularly admired the Barbizon masters' lyric images and the picturesque scenes of contemporary Dutch landscape and *genre painters, as well as the old masters. In 1888 he resettled in New York but continued to travel often in search of landscape subjects. Credited as the founder of its summer art colony, in 1899 he first visited *Old Lyme, Connecticut. From 1905 he spent summers at Noank, a little farther east along the Atlantic shore, while often wintering in the Caribbean. Illness curtailed his activity for about three years before his death in New York. His views on art appeared as *Art-Talks with Ranger* (1914) by Ralcy Husted Bell. In a notable gesture of support for American art, Ranger bequeathed his considerable estate to the *National Academy of Design for the purchase of paintings by living artists of the United States. In a day when few museums actively collected contemporary art, he stipulated that these works should be distributed to institutions throughout the nation. Since 1919, the fund has placed more than six hundred paintings.

Ranney, William (1813–57). Painter. Known particularly for scenes of western life, he also painted other *genre, sporting, and historical subjects, nearly all situated outdoors. Working in a studio filled with western props, such as guns, saddles, and other paraphernalia, as aids to verisimilitude in his popular specialty, he helped to crystallize American notions of frontier experience. A native of Middletown, Connecticut, William Tylee Ranney lived as a youth in North Carolina. By the time he was about twenty, he was studying drawing in Brooklyn. Although his formal art instruction remained limited, he developed a highly realistic painting style emphasizing minute detail and polished surfaces. In 1836 he traveled to Texas, but after his return the next year he continued to paint portraits, anecdotal scenes, and other narratives. About ten years later, as Charles *Deas gained acclaim for western subjects and the Mexican War intensified interest in the area Ranney had visited, he returned for inspiration to the drawings and memories of his only journey to the region. Some of his western scenes emphasize action and adventure, but many quietly idealize the daily life of frontiersmen and pioneers. *Old Scout's Tale* (Thomas Gilcrease Institute of American History and Art, Tulsa, Oklahoma, 1853) depicts several listeners, including a mother and three children, absorbed by a frontiersman's narrative as they camp beside a covered wagon, presumably during a break in their journey westward. Several carefully rendered horses and dogs provide the animal companions common in Ranney's images. After living for a few years in Weehawken, New Jersey, across the Hudson River from New York, about 1853—already suffering from the tuberculosis that took his life—he moved permanently to nearby West Hoboken.

Ransom, Alexander. *See* SHATTUCK, AARON DRAPER.

Rattner, Abraham (1895–1978). Painter and printmaker. Known for expressionist figural works and landscapes, he employed a modern vocabulary to address timeless themes of suffering, death, and spiritual joy. Born in Poughkeepsie, New York, he began his training in Washington, D.C., at George Washington University and the Corcoran School of Art (now Corcoran College of Art and Design). He then enrolled at the *Pennsylvania Academy of the Fine Arts, but his studies were soon interrupted by World War I service in the U.S. Army. He returned to the academy but left for Europe in 1920. He lived chiefly in Paris, where he pursued additional training and established his career as a masterful colorist and accomplished draftsman. By the time of his repatriation at the outbreak of World War II, he had thoroughly absorbed cubism, futurism, and other modern modes of figuration. Picasso and Georges Rouault numbered among particularly strong influences. Rattner lost most of his interwar painting when he left Paris. During ensuing years, the Bible provided an important source of themes, although even scenes of everyday life often speak with religious intensity. As a Jew, Rattner naturally turned to the Old Testament, but he also drew on universal meanings available in New Testament subjects. Commenting on man's inhumanity to man, *Transcendence* (Brooklyn Museum, 1943) depicts the body of Christ before the cross, with mourners and soldiers suggested to one side. A series of overlapping heads starts with Christ's visage of earthly suffering and ends with a youthful, spiritualized face. Rattner's characteristically rich colors and a skillful melding of representation and abstraction unify this strange but powerful visualization. Some later works moved close to *abstract expressionism. Strong and freely brushed colors dominate the figural structure in *Song of Esther* (Whitney Museum, 1958). Rattner also executed a number of decorative commissions, including tapestries, mosaics, and stained glass windows. He died in New York. In 1949 he married painter and printmaker Esther Gentle (1905–98), whose early representational work moved toward abstraction in the 1940s. She also maintained a New York gallery for a number of years.

Rauschenberg, Robert (1925–2008). Painter, sculptor, printmaker, photographer, and theater artist. His declared intention to "act" in the "gap" between art and life, as he put it in 1959, succinctly characterizes his contribution to art history. In the 1950s he broadened *abstract expressionism to include non-art elements. His recognition of the aesthetic potential of ordinary objects stimulated the development of *pop art, while his interest in incorporating in the art object signs of its own making opened the way for *process art. Other aspects of his work resonated in *minimal, *conceptual, and *performance art. However, his multifarious and inclusive approach always remained beyond the reach of any single art movement. He also facilitated the use of photography as an unremarked component of fine art and fostered acceptance of hybrid genres of all sorts. Over time, he increasingly became a sort of reporter, witnessing and assembling representations of the newsworthy events and ordinary minutiae of his time. As a generator of ideas, he numbered among indispensable figures of late twentieth-century art.

Born in Port Arthur, Texas, Milton Ernest Rauschenberg later officially changed his name to Robert. Not long after he enrolled at the University of Texas to study pharmacy, he was drafted. Trained in the U.S. Navy as a neuropsychiatric technician, he spent his tour of duty in California. In 1947 he began his professional art training at the Kansas City Art Institute. In March 1948 he arrived in Paris, where he studied without much enthusiasm at the Académie Julian. That fall he enrolled at *Black Mountain College to study with Josef *Albers. After a year, he moved to New York and until 1952 continued his studies at the *Art Students League, where Morris *Kantor and Vaclav *Vytlacil numbered among his teachers. In the spring of 1951 Betty *Parsons staged his first one-person show at her gallery, as simultaneously his work appeared in the abstract expressionists' *"Ninth Street Show." He also met John *Cage that season before returning in the summer to Black Mountain, as he did again the following year. During those sessions, Harry *Callahan and Aaron *Siskind stimulated his already growing interest in photography as an art form, while Franz *Kline, Robert *Motherwell, and Jack *Tworkov encouraged his painting. In 1952 he participated there in a Cage event that anticipated *happenings. That fall he departed for Europe with Cy *Twombly to travel and work until the next spring mostly in Italy but also in North Africa and Spain.

This rich mix of early experiences soon came to fruition as Rauschenberg embarked upon original and influential work in the mid-1950s. Until this time, he had worked on several series of monochrome paintings, as well as experiments in photography, collage, and *assemblage. In retrospect, it is apparent that one particularly provocative work not only deliberately challenged New York's advanced taste but also announced his intention to revamp the field. After persuading Willem *de Kooning to give him a drawing, Rauschenberg laboriously erased it and retitled the resulting spectral image *Erased de Kooning Drawing* (San Francisco Museum of Modern Art, 1953). At once a salute to the older artist's stature and an anti-art, dadaist provocation, it also alerted contemporaries to the potential of the conceptual gesture. Early in 1954 Rauschenberg met Jasper *Johns, who quickly became a close friend. For a while they worked together decorating department store display windows for the legendary designer Gene Moore, and off and on they were lovers, but most significantly they spurred each other to new levels of creative achievement during the next few years. In addition to each other's criticism, both responded to Cage's ideas particularly and, from a distance, to Marcel *Duchamp's. Rauschenberg had already demonstrated a sensuous attraction to materials in varied cobbled-together works, but in the mid-1950s he began to bring large objects into conjunction with painting to create what he called "combines." Neither painting nor sculpture exactly, most of them hang on the wall but incorporate all manner of accessories, generally commonplace objects or the sort of detritus that found its way into contemporary *junk sculpture. An early example, *Rebus* (Museum of Modern Art, 1955), collages together newspaper comic strips, a small reproduction of Botticelli's *Birth of Venus*, news photos, and children's art within a visual catalogue of recent painting techniques. In its messy juxtapositions of high and low culture, its unresolved visual and thematic tensions, and its reprise of art-making techniques, it prefigured much that would come in Rauschenberg's career. However, the most notorious combine approximates sculpture. *Monogram* (Moderna Museet, Stockholm, 1955–59) features on a painted canvas base a stuffed long-horned angora goat, with paint-daubed face and an automobile tire around its middle.

Although the combines failed to sell, they attracted considerable interest in March 1958 when Leo *Castelli featured them in his first show devoted to Rauschenberg's work. In 1959 the artist embarked on a suite of thirty-four drawings inspired by the cantos of Dante's *Inferno* (Museum of Modern Art, 1959–60). Using a novel transfer technique, he incorporated borrowed imagery from published illustrations along with his own painted and drawn elements. Free association governed his approach to narrative, giving the individual drawings a dreamlike ambiguity. In 1962, following Andy *Warhol's example, he began using screen prints to achieve similar effects on canvases. So congenial was this process that within a couple of years he altogether ceased making combines. Subsequently he employed the screen print technique, or variations on it, in thousands of paintings and in an extensive engagement with printmaking, primarily lithography, begun also in 1962. With the screen print process, he was able to embed in his paintings photographic images of all sorts, particularly news pictures that register the increasing importance of mass-media communication in contemporary life. In a leap to worldwide celebrity, in 1964 Rauschenberg won the top prize for painting at the Venice Biennale. However, in the immediate aftermath of this honor, he almost abandoned painting for several years. Also in 1964 he ended more than a decade of intense collaboration with choreographer Merce Cunningham and instead expanded his involvement with other sorts of staged theatrical events. He also made interactive works that responded to the viewers' presence and sometimes included sound elements. In 1966 he spearheaded the formation of *Experiments in Art and Technology to promote interaction between artists and scientists.

By the end of the 1960s, Rauschenberg had renewed his interest in two-dimensional media, to which he now brought a new elegance and breadth of vision. Among the most appealing works of the 1970s, the Hoarfrost series (1974–76) consists of gauzelike textiles imprinted with imagery and hung loosely in lyrical, layered arrangements. Extending and amplifying the artist's interest in the social purposes of art, the Rauschenberg Overseas Culture Interchange, initiated to stimulate world understanding through visual communication, consumed nearly all his time from 1984 until 1991, as well as millions of his own dollars. He traveled to ten countries for the express purpose of working with local artists, staged exhibitions in their home countries, and produced a huge, multireferential final display. Rauschenberg died at his longtime Captiva Island home, off the Florida Gulf Coast. Despite health problems during his final years, including a 2002 stroke that paralyzed his right side, with assistance he continues working productively. In 2005 he exhibited works from Scenarios, a new series of fresh and lucid digitized pigment transfers, emphasizing, as usual, his fascination with looking at the world.

Born in New York, his son **Christopher Rauschenberg** (1951–) is a photographer based in Portland, Oregon. He earned a B.A. in photography at Evergreen State College in Olympia, Washington. Since undertaking a 1997–98 project to re-photograph Eugène Atget's Paris, he has traveled the world, aiming his camera principally at architecture to capture formal qualities inflected by human milieus. He works mostly in subdued color and often combines two or more contiguous images to provide a wider angle of eloquent vision. His mother, painter and printmaker Susan Weil (1930–), was married to Rauschenberg from 1950 until 1952. She spent her early childhood in New Jersey but later lived in New York, where she studied with Rufino Tamayo and Vytlacil at a private high school. Better educated as an artist than Rauschenberg when they met in Paris during the summer of 1948, she studied along with him at Black Mountain and at the Art Students League. During their years together, they collaborated on a number of works, most notably a series of large blueprint "drawings" made by exposing the light-sensitive paper to record images, usually nude human bodies, placed on top of it. Since then, she has engaged relationships between literary and visual art in interpreting many challenging works, including writings of James Joyce. Recent paintings, some reassembled from fragments, suggest time passing within a context of daily life. She also creates books and design sets, particularly for dance preformances. She lives in New York.

Ray, Man. *See* MAN RAY.

Ream, Vinnie. *See* HOXIE, VINNIE REAM.

Rebay, Hilla. *See* GUGGENHEIM, SOLOMON R.

Redfield, Edward Willis (1869–1965). Painter. A landscapist often considered the leading figure among artists associated with *New Hope, Pennsylvania, Redfield produced vigorous, unsentimental views of the Delaware River Valley. He became particularly known for winter scenes, such as *Laurel Run* (Butler Institute of American Art, Youngstown, Ohio, 1916). The snow-covered ground catches blue-purple shadows from a diagonal screen of small trees along an unfrozen brook. Yellowish leaves lingering on the vegetation provide enlivening touches. Although contemporaries generally considered him an impressionist, Redfield practiced a painterly realism quite distinct from the fluttering touch, broken colors, and patterned, screenlike surfaces of that movement. Often delineated with a textured impasto, his crisp forms provide sharp contrasts of tone. In spirit and technique, he shared much with his friend Robert *Henri. Although he painted gentle terrain, he infused it with drama and grandeur, often amplified by relatively large scale. To preserve spontaneity and freshness, he normally painted out-of-doors and quickly, in front of his subject. Born in Bridgeville, Delaware, he grew up in Camden, New Jersey. He studied at the *Pennsylvania Academy of the Fine Arts before departing for Europe in August 1889. In Paris he studied at the Académie Julian and the École des Beaux-Arts, but he also admired impressionist painting. While abroad, he visited London and painted as well at other sites in the French countryside and in Venice. Following his return to the United States in 1892, he made his home in the Philadelphia area until 1898, when he settled permanently in Center Bridge, Pennsylvania, on the Delaware River just above New Hope. Again in France from 1898 until 1900, he resided in Alfort, not far from Paris. During this sojourn he painted dark-toned, snow-covered streetscapes comparable to Henri's contemporary Parisian cityscapes, as both found their way beyond the fashionable clichés of late impressionism. Subsequently Redfield occasionally painted views of American cities. Beginning in 1903 he also worked at Boothbay Harbor, Maine, for a number of summers. In 1947 he destroyed a great many canvases that did not satisfy his critical eye. He completed his last painting from nature in 1948. Troubled by failing sight, he subsequently painted occasionally for pleasure but no longer worked professionally.

Reed, Luman (1785–1836). Collector and patron. Also a merchant. A successful dry goods and grocery wholesaler, in the 1830s he assembled the most notable collection of contemporary American art in New York. A pioneer in supporting living artists, he befriended and encouraged several of those whose work he bought, including Thomas *Cole, Asher B. *Durand, and William Sidney *Mount. Reed was born near the Massachusetts border in Green River (now Austerlitz), New York, where his parents farmed. In 1792 the family moved to Coxsackie, a Hudson River town south of Albany. He received little formal education before entering the grocery trade there while still in his teens. He moved to New York about 1815 and by 1832 had amassed sufficient fortune to retire. His earliest art purchases were old master paintings (some of questionable authenticity), but when he retired he turned his full attention to living American artists. Notably, in 1833 he commissioned Cole's celebrated *Course of Empire* series. However, he did not live to see its anticipated installation in the art gallery designed by Alexander Jackson Davis for the top floor of his elegant lower Manhattan residence. In an unprecedented step, once a week Reed admitted the public to his two-room gallery, where he also displayed natural history specimens and permitted access to his large collections of art books and prints. Several years after his death, friends purchased Reed's paintings to serve as the central component of the New-York Gallery of the Fine Arts, the city's first museum devoted solely to art. Fiscally unstable, this organization never found a permanent home. In the late 1850s, its collection passed to the New-York Historical Society.

Refregier, Anton (1905–79). Painter and printmaker. Although remembered primarily as a muralist, he also produced easel paintings. His figural style of simplified forms modernized tradition to address contemporary realities. Often he presented representational elements within strong, abstractly organized compositions. Born in Moscow, as a teenager he moved with his family to Paris. There he worked as a studio assistant to Russian-born sculptor and painter Nicholas Vasilieff (1892–1970), later active in the United States. Refregier emigrated to the United States in 1920 and became a citizen ten years later. In 1925 he graduated from the Rhode Island School of Design in Providence. He also studied with Hans *Hofmann in Munich. In New York he worked with decorators and stage designers before the *federal art projects provided the initial opportunities for which he is best known. His government-sponsored murals included major projects at New York's Rikers Island penitentiary and the WPA Building at the 1939 World's Fair. His ambitious series of twenty-seven panels depicting California history (1946–48) for the Rincon Annex Post Office in San Francisco remains among the landmark achievements of the era. A left-wing idealist, Refregier championed noncommercial art cooperatively produced in the spirit of the Renaissance atelier. From the late 1920s, he lived in *Woodstock. He died in Moscow, where he had been invited to paint a mural. He published a textbook on figure drawing (1948), as well as *We Make Our Own Tomorrow—An Artist's Journey* (1965).

Regionalism. *See* AMERICAN SCENE MOVEMENT.

Reid, Robert (1862–1929). Painter. A decorative impressionist particularly fond of combining attractive young women with flowers, he also painted landscapes, nudes, and other figure subjects. Among the most active muralists of his day, in this pursuit he generally adopted the period's prevailing classical idealism. Numbering among founding members of The *Ten, he also taught for many years in Boston at the School of the Museum of Fine Arts, in New York at Cooper Union and the *Art Students League, and from 1920 to 1927 at the Broadmoor Art Academy in Colorado Springs. Born in Stockbridge, Massachusetts, Robert Lewis Reid enrolled in Boston's museum school in 1880. In the fall of 1885, after studying for several months at the Art Students League, he continued on to Paris. There he studied at the Académie Julian for three winters, while painting during summers in a Normandy fishing village. He also traveled in Italy during the winter of 1886–87. Only after returning to New York during the summer of 1889 did he begin to relinquish his academic training for more up-to-date impressionism. He did not fully embrace the new style until the mid-1890s, after completing his first murals at the 1893 World's Columbian Exposition in Chicago. Subsequently, for more than twenty years he alternated between easel and mural painting. In addition, he devoted the years between 1901 and 1905 largely to stained glass windows for the new Gothic-style Unitarian Memorial Church in Fairhaven, Massachusetts, near New Bedford. His murals decorated the walls and ceilings of numerous public venues, including the new Library of Congress (1897), the United States pavilion at the 1900 Exposition Universelle in Paris, the Massachusetts State House (1901), and the Palace of Fine Arts at the 1915 Panama-Pacific Exposition in San Francisco. In *The White Parasol* (Smithsonian American Art Museum, 1907), a young woman in white, her head framed by the parasol, stands before a bank of flowers and holds in one arm a large bouquet. The lush floral screen in a limited range of harmonious tones sets off the characteristically crisply drawn figure. By this time, Reid had become fascinated with Japanese art, which provided a number of his canvases with more overtly exotic motifs. From around 1915, he often employed a sketchy approach. After suffering a stroke, Reid lived for the final two years of his life in New York's Finger Lakes region, at a sanatorium in Clifton Springs.

Reinhardt, Ad (1913–67). Painter, collage artist, and printmaker. Although associated with *abstract expressionism, he practiced an unusually severe and reductive form of painting. Disdaining subjectivity, symbols, and personal expression, he aimed for a timeless and transcendental, purely visual experience. In his signature paintings, barely perceptible rectangles in varying shades of black or extremely dark color float on the surface of canvases that appear solid black at a glance or from a distance. His dictum "Art is art. Everything else is everything else" succinctly summarizes his notion of art's autonomy. Along with his austere work, his fierce, defiant, and rigorous intellectualism fostered the development of *minimalism. An effective writer and theorist, he also excelled as a cartoonist and often skewered the art world with mordant wit. His targets included insider blather as often as philistine obtuseness.

Adolph Dietrich Friedrich Reinhardt was born in Buffalo but grew up in New York. During four years at Columbia University, he studied art history with Meyer *Schapiro and became a lifelong friend of writer and Trappist monk Thomas Merton. After graduation in 1935, he studied at the *National Academy of Design and then, in 1936–37, at the American Artists School, where Carl *Holty numbered among his teachers. In 1937 he joined the *American Abstract Artists and soon also became a member of the *American Artists' Congress. Its leader, Stuart *Davis, influenced Reinhardt's early painting, which drew also on cubism and, importantly, Mondrian's abstraction. For several years until 1941 he worked for a *federal art project. Between 1943 and 1947, he also frequently commented on art in cartoons published in the liberal *PM* newspaper. (Later he produced humorous drawings for art publications.) Inducted into the U.S. Navy early in 1944, he spent about a year in military service in San Diego. Between 1946 and 1952 he continued his study of art history, with particular attention to Asian art, at New York University's Institute of Fine Arts. Betty *Parsons showed his work from 1946 onward. In 1947 he accepted a position, which he retained for the rest of his life, teaching art history at Brooklyn College. He first went to Europe in 1952, and six years later he spent about a year circling the world. In the early 1940s, he experimented with collage and then, as the decade progressed, with linear and gestural approaches to *all-over patterning. By the end of the decade he had devised a style of small, interlocking rectangular elements, usually brightly colored, flickering across the canvas. In the early 1950s Reinhardt's characteristic monochrome geometry coalesced, partly in response to the work of Josef *Albers. At first his paintings were red, then blue before becoming black in the late 1950s. From 1960 he used five-foot-square canvases, divided into nine-part grids by barely perceptible rectangles. Proud of his intentionally difficult art, he gleefully pointed out that his black paintings were unmarketable, unphotographable, inexplicable, and useless. Nevertheless, perhaps in spite of himself, perhaps not, Reinhardt created an individual style of considerable power and often, no little beauty. He died of a heart attack in his New York studio. Selected writings, edited by Barbara *Rose, appeared in 1975 as *Art-as-Art*.

Reiss, Winold. *See* DOUGLAS, AARON.

Remington, Frederic (1861–1909). Painter, sculptor, and illustrator. Also a writer. A foremost interpreter of the mythic Old West, he portrayed the intense, action-filled lifestyle of cowboys, Indians, soldiers, and other frontiersmen. On occasion, he addressed other narrative subjects, as well. Although topography does not play a central part in Remington's characteristic images, from time to time he created pure landscapes, especially in his later years. While he remained devoted to frontier imagery, around the turn of the century the tenor of his previously descriptive painting changed, as he became more absorbed with issues of mood and artistic expression. The retrospective melancholy of many later works parallels the urbanizing nation's unease about effects of modernization, including erosion of the uncomplicated way of life Remington idealized. Despite his identification with roughshod western subjects, personally he remained a worldly easterner, creating most of his work in or near New York, where he kept in touch with other artists and progressive aesthetic attitudes. As a mediator between two regions of the country, Remington may have been more responsible than any other individual for crystallizing a long-lived set of popular conceptions about the West. Born in the far northern New York town of Canton, when he was eleven Frederic Sackrider Remington moved with his family to Ogdensburg, not far away. After two years at a military boarding school in Massachusetts, in 1878 he entered Yale University, where he studied drawing at its new fine arts school. He left early in 1880 to work as an office clerk until August 1881, when he departed on his initial trip west. Early in 1882 he published the first of hundreds of illustrations in leading mass-market magazines, but from 1883 until mid-1885 he worked as a rancher in Kansas and then as a saloonkeeper in Kansas City. He traveled throughout the Southwest before returning to New York later that year to work full time as an illustrator for books and magazines. Within two or three years he had achieved an unrivaled reputation for western subjects. Meanwhile, studies at the *Art Students League in 1886 signaled his desire to become known as a serious artist. The following year he began exhibiting watercolors, soon followed by oils. Concurrently, he traveled regularly in the West, sketching, photographing, and collecting source material for his illustrations. Other trips took him to Europe and North Africa, while in 1898 he traveled to Cuba to witness the Spanish-American War, but these experiences found their way into relatively few drawings and paintings. In 1890 he moved to New Rochelle, a New York suburb. While building his reputation as a painter, in 1895 began to produce sculpture as well. In 1899 he purchased Ingleneuk Island in the St. Lawrence River as a summer residence. Only months before his death there following an appendectomy, he moved to a farm in Ridgefield, Connecticut. In addition to many short stories and nonfiction articles that appeared in magazines, Remington published a novel, *John Ermine of the Yellowstone* (1902), and seven collections of shorter pieces. His illustrations enhanced books by Theodore Roosevelt, Francis Parkman, Owen Wister, and other prominent authors.

The paintings that made Remington's reputation as an artist during the later 1880s and 1890s resembled his illustrations. Tightly focused on figural groups, sharply detailed, and filled with action, they illuminate a way of life devoted to manly virtues of strength, independence, bravery, and persistence. From the end of the 1890s, Remington increasingly pictured moments of solitude and introspection among his cast of male westerners. At the same time, as he engaged aesthetic issues that interested impressionist and *tonalist painters, unnaturalistic color, simplified and flattened compositions, and painterly brushwork supplanted his previous literalism. In its depiction of soldiers on their galloping steeds, *On the Southern Plains* (Metropolitan Museum, 1907) combines his longstanding attention to minute detail of costume and animal locomotion with newer interests in delicate brushwork and bright colors perceived in strong sunlight. Among late paintings, more than seventy night scenes number among his most evocative and original works. Like his illustrations and descriptive paintings, Remington's intricately detailed, lively bronzes emphasize rough-and-ready western themes. Except for *The Cowboy* (Fairmount Park, Philadelphia, 1905–8), his twenty-odd pieces suited domestic interiors as tabletop statuettes. Often modifying themes that had already appeared in his paintings or illustrations, they skillfully evoke movement, drama, and authenticity. With its swirling, interlocked forms, an audaciously conceived group of two cavalrymen, two Indians, and five horses, *The Old Dragoons of 1850* (Metropolitan Museum, 1907; modeled 1905) summarizes Remington's ingenuity, compositional control, fluid modeling, and technical finesse.

Resnick, Milton (1917–2004). Painter. An *abstract expressionist, he first created vigorous compositions of solid, heavily impastoed shapes. By the end of the 1950s, these evolved into sensuous but lyrical fields of small strokes, sometimes realized on an enormous scale. During the 1960s, his work became denser and nearly monochrome. With meticulous attention to nuance, he sustained this approach for the next three decades, often belaboring canvases until they staggered under massive amounts of paint. In the 1990s landscape and figural elements emerged in his work, as if from the painterly depths, suggesting poignant connections to memory and dreams. Rachmiel Resnick, nicknamed Milya, was born in the Ukrainian village of Bratslav. At the age of five he arrived with his family in New York. As a teenager, he studied commercial art at Pratt Institute but soon transferred to the fine art program at the American Artists' School. In 1934, at seventeen, he left home because his father refused to accommodate his wish to become an artist. This act of defiance presaged fierce and single-minded dedication to painting throughout his life. In the late 1930s he became a close friend of Willem *de Kooning and associated with the circle of artists who would become known as abstract expressionists. Drafted, he served in the U.S. Army through most of World War II and then studied in Paris on the GI Bill until 1948. Upon his return, he worked at Hans *Hofmann's school. Having missed most of the 1940s in New York, to his dismay he was frequently regarded in the 1950s as a newcomer, a disciple of de Kooning, and a second-generation abstract expressionist. Resnick did not have his first one-person show in New York until 1955. With his contemporaries reaching the height of their fame as he was only just getting started professionally, he came to feel excluded from his rightful place among the artists who had been friends since youth. His resentment fed an absolutist devotion to the process of driving paint toward pure aesthetic experience, uncontaminated by self-expression or social utility. Resnick's mature style of delicate brushstrokes forming a continuous screen of paint looks back to the example of Monet. Yet his encrusted surfaces produce a heavy materiality that hints obliquely at *minimalist emphasis on the physical presence of the object. Resnick maintained a second residence in Cragsmoor, New York, a longtime Shawangunk Mountains magnet for artists. In declining health during his final years, he committed suicide at his home in Manhattan. Geoffrey Dorfman's *Out of the Picture: Milton Resnick and the New York School* (2003) includes transcripts of his lectures and contributions to panel discussions.

In 1961 he married painter Patricia Passlof (1928–), known as Pat, his companion of nearly a decade. Born in Brunswick, Georgia, she studied at *Black Mountain College in 1948. There she encountered de Kooning and continued to study with him in New York. In 1951 she received her BFA from Cranbrook Academy of Art near Detroit. Her abstract expressionist origins, tempered by the greater discipline of 1970s modular forms, resulted in painterly abstraction of quiet power. In the 1990s individually rendered figures, horses, or centaurs inspired by classical Greece appeared across large fields activated with dense brushwork. Most recently, grids of crosshatched strokes provide armatures for sophisticated and passionate displays of brushwork in rich and often unexpected color combinations. She has taught for many years at the College of Staten Island, a division of the City University of New York.

Revere, Paul (1734–1818). Engraver and silversmith. Also a patriot and industrialist. Transformed into a folk hero in Henry Wadsworth Longfellow's 1861 poem "Paul Revere's Ride," Revere figured also among the most important early American artisans. As an engraver, he issued scenic and portrait prints, bookplates, trade cards, currency, and other ephemera, besides producing book and periodical illustrations. A lifelong Bostonian trained in his father's shop, he was already known his twenties as a distinguished silversmith. At the same time, he became active politically and before long was allied with Boston's Whig elite in their quarrels with the Crown. Not long after John Singleton *Copley painted his portrait, Revere thanklessly plagiarized the work of Copley's half brother, Henry *Pelham, for the composition of his inflammatory hand-colored engraving *The Bloody Massacre Perpetrated in King Street Boston on March 5th 1770* (1770), among the first visual images to be widely diffused in American popular culture. The relative crudeness of the figural drawing intensifies its anti-British sentiment, while a long inscription added below leaves no doubt as to its propagandistic purpose. During and after the Revolution, Revere extended his knowledge of metal into other enterprises, including a weapons foundry and copper-rolling mills, and also became engaged in other business enterprises. His federal-period silver reflects elegant *neoclassical taste.

Richards, William Trost (1833–1905). Painter. An expert draftsman who produced masterful watercolors as well as oils, he specialized in landscapes and maritime scenes. Influenced in his early development by prevailing *Hudson River School and *luminist tastes, in the 1860s he numbered among the most accomplished artists practicing the extremely detailed realism of American *Pre-Raphaelitism. Later his brushwork became somewhat looser, but he never relinquished his commitment to scrupulously accurate observation. Born in Philadelphia, Richards remained a resident of the area for most of his life. As a teenager he was employed as a designer and illustrator at an ornamental metalwork firm, while concurrently studying with Paul *Weber. He also may have attended classes at the *Pennsylvania Academy of the Fine Arts. In 1855 he departed for Europe. During a year abroad, he worked in Düsseldorf for several months and toured the Continent. He returned to Europe on several occasions. In 1866–67 in London he first observed at firsthand J. M. W. Turner's work, which he had long admired, while between 1878 and 1880 he produced vigorous renditions of the rocks and surf along the English coast, particularly in Cornwall. Prompted by exposure to British Victorian painting as well as by English critic John Ruskin's writings endorsing truth to nature, in the late 1850s Richards embarked on obsessively detailed yet still freshly vibrant botanical and geological studies in the spirit of Pre-Raphaelitism. In the mid-1860s he began to turn away from other scenic northeast locales to explore the coastal subjects in which he later specialized. At the same time, he increasingly employed watercolor to capture precise effects of atmosphere and sea. Around 1870, large, highly finished exhibition watercolors became a mainstay of his practice, and he was soon regarded among the foremost American specialists in the medium. Richards's coastal views record the Atlantic seaboard from New Jersey to Maine, but he was particularly partial to the vicinity of Newport, Rhode Island, and nearby Narragansett Bay. He first visited there in 1874. Following several subsequent sojourns, he built a summer house on Conanicut Island in 1882. After 1890 he lived permanently in Newport. Richards characteristically combined closely observed detail with an expansive sweep of space. In marine views, he unerringly registered the transient insubstantiality of the ever-changing sea and sky, usually in contrast with immutable, rocky shores. Although Richards commonly worked near popular seashore retreats, his paintings rarely convey the carefree gaiety associated with vacations. Usually devoid of human presence, his intimate yet majestic meditations suggest the ceaselessness of natural processes, the vastness of the universe, and the insignificance of individuals.

Richards's daughter, Anna Richards Brewster (1870–1952) painted landscapes, urban views, portraits, and other subjects in pastel and watercolor, as well as oil. Born in Philadelphia and trained in New York and Paris, she did much of her most appealing work during a subsequent ten-year residency in England. Her views of London and other localities abroad combine softly atmospheric effects with recognizable landmarks and other clearly delineated features. In 1905 she married William Tenney Brewster, an English professor. They settled in the New York suburb of Scarsdale, summered at the Rhode Island shore, and traveled to varied destinations that became subjects of her art.

Richardson, E. P. (1902–85). Art historian and museum director. His accessible overview, *Painting in America: The Story of 450 Years* (1956), kindled both scholarly and public interest in native art. To facilitate research on art in the United States, he co-founded the *Archives of American Art in 1954. Born in Glens Falls, New York, Edgar Preston Richardson graduated in 1925 from Williams College in Williamstown, Massachusetts. For the next three years, he studied painting at the *Pennsylvania Academy of the Fine Arts. In 1930 he took a position at the Detroit Institute of Arts, where he remained until 1962, serving during the last seventeen of those years as the museum's director. From 1962 until 1966 he headed the Winterthur (Delaware) Museum. His other books include *American Romantic Painting* (1944) and *Washington Allston: A Study of the Romantic Artist in America* (1948). He also served as editor of *Art Quarterly* from 1938 until 1967. He died in Philadelphia, where he resided during his final years. His wife, painter **Constance Coleman Richardson** (1905–2002), is known particularly for landscapes, especially views of the upper Midwest and Wyoming. Born in Indianapolis, she studied at Vassar College and at the Pennsylvania Academy before marriage in 1931. She, too, died in Philadelphia.

Richter, Gisela. *See* METROPOLITAN MUSEUM OF ART.

Richter, Hans (1888–1976). Painter, sculptor, and filmmaker. His interest in sequential transformation of abstract designs led to the creation of what was probably the first abstract film. Born in Berlin, he received his professional training in the art academies of Berlin and Weimar. In 1916 he joined the dada movement in Zurich. Although he shared the group's essential nihilism, he sought a more affirmative path for his art. Inspired by the rhythmic quality of music and its mutations of nonnaturalistic patterns through time, in 1918 he began to produce long, scroll-like paintings in which abstract forms develop in the manner of musical themes from one segment to another. In *Prelude* (Yale University Art Gallery, 1919) ten images of interlocking abstract elements evolve consecutively, each from the preceding arrangement. After returning to Germany in 1919, Richter applied the same idea in his first abstract film, *Rhythm 21* (1921). Two additional films based on the same technique appeared in color before Richter turned to representational cinema flavored with surrealism. After emigrating to the United States in 1941, he subsequently became a citizen. From 1942 to 1956 he taught filmmaking at City College of New York. The best-known of his later films, the feature-length *Dreams That Money Can Buy*, begun in 1944 includes surrealistic sequences by Alexander *Calder, Marcel *Duchamp, Max *Ernst, Fernand Léger, and *Man Ray, as well as his own. Richter gave renewed attention to painting in later years, again often employing the scroll format but frequently enriching his surfaces with collage elements including newsprint and photographs. He died in Locarno, Switzerland. Most of his writings appeared in German. *Dada: Kunst und Anti-Kunst* (1964), usually considered his most important publication, appeared as *Dada: Art and Anti-Art* in 1965. *Hans Richter by Hans Richter*, edited by Cleve Gray, was published in 1971.

Rickey, George (1907–2002). Sculptor, painter, and art historian. Depending for their full effect on movement, his unique metal abstractions feature freely rotating elements pivoting on mounts supported by fixed verticals. Surfaces are generally brushed or burnished to provide variety and sensuous appeal. Claiming that his art had more in common with clockwork than with sculpture, he employed precise engineering to transform the innovations of constructivism into elegant structures demanding the viewer's time as an element of aesthetic experience. Along with Alexander *Calder, he stands as a principal innovator of kinetic sculpture, and he remains the foremost practitioner of such sculpture intended for outdoor settings. Unlike Calder, he generally restricted his formal vocabulary to geometric shapes, at first creating slim, planar, sometimes needlelike elements to gyrate in the breeze, later working with complex combinations of open or closed geometric shapes, as well as boxy components. Occasionally deviating from normal practice, he also created motorized works, as well as completely or partially painted ones. George Warren Rickey, born in South Bend, Indiana, moved with his family to Scotland in 1913 and grew up near Glasgow. While studying modern history at Oxford University, he also took courses at the Ruskin School of Drawing in Oxford. After receiving his BA in 1929, he studied for a year in Paris with André Lhote and at the Académie Moderne with Fernand Léger and Amédée Ozenfant. He returned in 1933 to Paris for another year, but otherwise lived in the United States, producing paintings and murals indebted sometimes to Cézanne, sometimes to the socially oriented work popular in the 1930s. In the U.S. Army Air Corps during World War II, he learned welding and gained experience in a machine shop. After demobilization, he studied art history at New York University's Institute of Fine Arts and learned printmaking with Mauricio *Lasansky at the State University of Iowa (now University of Iowa) in Iowa City before moving to Chicago in 1948. There he studied for a year at the Illinois Institute of Technology's Bauhaus-oriented Institute of Design, which reinforced his interests in industrial materials, engineering, and abstraction. Interested also in Calder's work, he experimented with mobiles. These evolved toward the end of the 1950s into the simplified compositions that built his reputation. In 1960 he moved to a farm in East Chatham, New York, near the Massachusetts border. There his rural acreage accommodated development of increasingly large outdoor pieces. To facilitate production of the many public commissions that came his way, he later also maintained studios in Berlin and Santa Barbara, California. Rickey continued to work productively into his nineties. His last, and largest, sculpture, more than fifty-seven feet tall, was installed at the Hyogo Prefectural Museum of Art in Japan only months before his death in St. Paul, Minnesota, where he had lived for a brief period at the end of his life. In 1967 he published an authoritative study, *Constructivism: Origins and Evolution*, for some time widely recognized as the standard work on the movement.

Riis, Jacob August (1849–1914). Photographer. Also a social reformer. A pioneer of documentary photography, he used his craft to rouse the public about societal problems, especially conditions among the urban poor. Although his intentions were purely factual, his deftly composed and skillfully lighted images are as powerful as they are informative. Riis's well-known *How the Other Half Lives: Studies Among the Tenements* (1890), illustrated with halftones and line engravings taken from his photographs, inspired new building codes and measures to clean up slums. Born in Ribe, Denmark, and trained as a carpenter in Copenhagen, Riis arrived in the United States in 1870. While working as a journalist in New York, he became outraged at the cycle of poverty, crime, and despair that he witnessed in lower-class neighborhoods. The invention of the magnesium flash, which for the first time made short exposures possible in low light, spurred his determination to supplement his writing with visual evidence. At first he worked with amateur volunteers, but in 1888 he began taking his own photographs. Although his work as a photographer was limited to the next ten years, his impact was not. Among the first photographers to confront unpleasant realities without relying on picturesque sentimentalities, he produced unflinching records that advanced the course of documentary photography. Riis's most striking and original works are the photographs he took of people in their decrepit homes or back-alley hangouts. "Home of the Italian Rag Picker, Jersey Street" (c. 1888–89), a particularly stirring image, captures in the harsh light of Riis's flash a careworn woman holding an infant while seated among her rag bags within a cramped interior. Washtubs, a dustpan, a hat hung neatly on the wall, and a clear space in the room's center suggest her resistance to chaos. As is usual among his portraits of the downtrodden, Riis gives pictorial importance to the immediate environment, reinforcing his reformist message that the problems of the poor are embedded in their surroundings. Riis published more than a dozen books, including several promoting reform and a biography of his ally President Theodore Roosevelt (1903). The title of Riis's autobiography, *The Making of an American* (1901), hints at the patriotic and optimistic motivations for his crusade. He died in the central Massachusetts town of Barre, where he had moved only the previous year.

Rimmer, William (1816–79). Sculptor, painter, and draftsman. Among the most original American artists of the nineteenth century, he produced cosmopolitan, psychologically charged work in several media. Talented, highly motivated, successful as a teacher, and admired by other artists, he was also plagued by poverty, misfortune, and self-doubt. His art was not widely appreciated in his own time, and much of it has been lost. Born in Liverpool, Rimmer left England with his family for Nova Scotia when he was two years old. They continued on to Boston in 1825. Raised to believe that his father was the lost son of Louis XVI and Marie Antoinette, the artist apparently never questioned this claim. Although the father worked as a cobbler, he provided for his children a rich cultural environment to prepare them for their royal prerogatives. Responding to this upbringing, at the age of fifteen the gifted Rimmer carved a sophisticated gypsum statuette that prefigured major aspects of his later work. Perhaps the first American male nude sculpture, it suggests not only his originality in attempting such a representation but also his commitment to the human body as the touchstone of expressive meaning. It also reveals his awareness even as a youngster of the classical tradition (often, as here, filtered through Michelangelo) to which his sculpture consistently responded. Moreover, this *Seated Youth*, also known as *Despair* (Museum of Fine Arts, Boston, 1831) provides the earliest evidence of Rimmer's lifelong preoccupation with themes of alienation and psychological suffering. Despite the promise of this carving, Rimmer did not subsequently devote sustained attention to sculpture for nearly three decades. During the 1830s he worked at a variety of trades, including sign painting and lithography. Essentially self-taught in everything he undertook, he began painting portraits and by the early 1840s was working itinerantly. Soon he became interested in medicine and through self-directed study, as well as dissections at the Massachusetts Medical College, trained himself to become a physician. In the process he gained a superb knowledge of anatomy, which served him well in later artistic endeavors. From 1848 until 1863 he practiced medicine, but by 1860 he had begun to work productively as a sculptor. In the early months of 1861 he produced his first life-size work, *The Falling Gladiator* (original plaster, Smithsonian American Art Museum), a powerful, heroically struggling nude. Later that year he began lecturing on artistic anatomy, initiating an influential teaching career. Between 1864 and 1866 he headed a private art school in Boston. For the next four years he directed the women's division of Cooper Union in New York. Returning permanently to the Boston area, he later taught at the School of the Museum of Fine Arts. His methods appeared in two books, *The Elements of Design* (1864) and *Art Anatomy* (1877). For the latter he prepared hundreds of superb drawings, as expressive as they are informative. He died in South Milford, Massachusetts.

While in New York, Rimmer modeled one of his most poignant works, the small-scale *Dying Centaur* (original plaster, Museum of Fine Arts, Boston, 1869), both formally and conceptually a work of surpassing skill and intelligence. In this image of aspiration and defeat, the lower body in the form of a horse, still showing signs of struggle, lies on its side, as the nude man's upper body strains to rise. The work demonstrates Rimmer's continuing debt to classical sculpture and probably reflects also familiarity with work by French animal sculptor Antoine-Louis Barye. However, in its formal vitality and fluid surfaces, as well as its integration of physical and mental anguish, the work also anticipates Rodin's work, indebted to the same sources. Rimmer's surviving paintings are few, but among them the best known, *Flight and Pursuit* (Museum of Fine Arts, Boston, 1872), continues the emotional complexity that distinguishes his sculpture. Two men are seen running through a Moorish palace, creating a mood of mystery and terror. As with Rimmer's sculptures, meaning is indeterminate, free of specific literary ties. Although plausible personal and political interpretations have been offered, the image nevertheless creates emotional impact through visual means alone.

Rinehart, William Henry (1825–74). Sculptor. Known primarily for ideal figures representing classical themes, he occasionally treated other subjects and also produced many portraits. Grace, dignity, and formal simplicity infuse his calm approach to the ideals of *neoclassicism. The unaffected standing male and female figures of *Leander* (Newark [New Jersey] Museum, 1859) and *Clytie* (Metropolitan Museum, 1872; modeled 1869–70) number among the particularly classical in spirit. *Latona and Her Children, Apollo and Diana* (Metropolitan Museum, 1874; modeled 1870), a complex pyramidal group and Rinehart's last major classical endeavor, recapitulates his strengths, endowing the literary source with monumentality and meditative reserve. Appropriately, Rinehart's portraits display a greater naturalism, although he sometimes swathed the shoulders of his busts in generalizing togalike garments. Born on a Maryland farm near Union Bridge, Rinehart learned to handle his medium as a stonecutter. He continued to follow this trade after moving about thirty miles to Baltimore around 1844. Mostly self-taught as an artist, he attended evening classes at the Maryland Institute for the Promotion of the Mechanic Arts (now Maryland Institute College of Art) about 1850 and soon began to establish a local reputation as a sculptor. In 1855 he departed for Italy. During two years in Florence, he mastered the prevailing neoclassical style. After subsequently working in Baltimore for about a year, he sailed again in 1858 for Europe. At this time he settled in Rome, where he remained except for two visits to the United States. Despite declining enthusiasm for neoclassical sculpture by the time he reached his maturity as an artist, Rinehart nevertheless executed some of the style's benchmark works. Rinehart's public commissions include the bronze *Chief Justice Roger Brooke Taney* (State House grounds, Annapolis, Maryland, 1872; modeled 1867–71), and an unusually large number of funerary monuments. He designed the bronze *Love Reconciled with Death* (Greenmount Cemetery, Baltimore, 1866–67) as a memorial to the wife of William T. *Walters, his most important patron. Although not particularly characteristic, his most popular work (some twenty marble replicas exist), the sentimental 1859 *Sleeping Children* (original plaster, Peabody Institute, Johns Hopkins University, Baltimore), embellishes a tomb for the Hugh Sisson children in the same cemetery.

Ringgold, Faith (1934–). Painter, printmaker, mixed-media sculptor, and performance artist. Colorful, imaginative, and witty, her art focuses on subjects related to civil rights, feminism, or her relationship as an artist to history. Her singular narrative "story quilts" make innovative use of fabrics in combination with painting. Born in New York, Faith Jones grew up in Harlem. In 1950 she married classical and jazz pianist Robert Earl Wallace, but they later separated and were divorced in 1956. Following her graduation in 1955 from City College of New York, where Robert *Gwathmey and Yasuo *Kuniyoshi numbered among her teachers, she taught art in New York public schools for nearly twenty years. In 1959 she completed a master's degree at City University of New York, and in 1962 she married Burdette Ringgold. Until 1963 she worked primarily as a landscape painter. Inspired by the burgeoning civil rights campaign, she subsequently addressed political themes in a bold, posterlike style. As the women's movement gained strength in the early 1970s, she found the primary theme of her mature work, the struggles and joys of African-American women. Recruiting her mother, Willi Posey Jones—an accomplished seamstress—as a collaborator, Ringgold began producing soft sculptures and paintings on cloth, including some abstract works based on African designs. She often used these as props for lectures and performances. In 1983 she initiated her extended series of inimitable story quilts featuring painted pictorial elements, usually combined with border texts. A sequence of twelve, collectively titled The French Collection (1991–97), offers a whimsical rumination on race, gender, and cultural history through the story of a black American teenager who escapes to work in Paris during the 1920s as an artist and model. In 1984 Ringgold started teaching half of each year at the University of California at San Diego, while otherwise remaining in the New York area. Currently an emerita professor at UCSD, she makes her home in Englewood, New Jersey. Her memoir *We Flew over the Bridge* appeared in 1995. Since 1991 she has also published several illustrated children's books. Ringgold's daughter, critic and theorist Michele Wallace (1952–), a New York University PhD, often considers the visual arts within writings centered on gender and race.

Ritman, Louis. *See* GIVERNY GROUP.

Rivers, Larry (1923–2002). Painter, printmaker, and sculptor. Also a musician and poet. An unstable mix of passion, vulgarity, humor, ambition, and extravagance fueled his wide-ranging accomplishments. In the 1950s he introduced startlingly irreverent subjects into painting, prefiguring *pop art in their references to mass culture, the mediating role of photography, and banal or commonplace objects. At the same time, without losing sight of *abstract expressionism's accent on process, he anticipated the reinvigoration of figuration. Later he experimented widely with techniques and materials in restless and often contrarian responses to contemporary life and to the tradition of art. His works loosely respond in overlapping groups to themes related to autobiographical experience, history or politics, artistic tradition, and show business. Born in the Bronx, Yitzroch Loiza Grossberg changed his name in 1940, around the time he began working professionally as a jazz saxophone player. After service in 1942–43 in the U.S. Army Air Corps, he studied theory and composition at the Juilliard School of Music. Through musician friends he met Jane *Freilicher, who encouraged his interest in art. In 1947–48 he studied with Hans *Hofmann. He also studied in 1948 with William *Baziotes at New York University, where he completed his bachelor's degree in 1951. Although more or less self-taught as a draftsman, he developed virtuoso facility. Already dissatisfied with *abstract expressionism, he absorbed with interest the *Museum of Modern Art's 1948 exhibition of Pierre Bonnard's work. On a 1950 trip to Europe, at the Louvre and elsewhere he admired grand manner history painting.

In the early 1950s his personal combination of representation and loose, improvisational brushwork came together. *Washington Crossing the Delaware* (Museum of Modern Art, 1953), recalls in general terms Emanuel *Leutze's precedent, a painting well known but not highly esteemed among New York's art community. The figures in the Rivers painting loom from a painterly, abstracted pictorial surface at odds with the stateliness of the historical and patriotic subject. The combination, seeming to parody both gestural painting and the old master tradition, as well as patriotic Americanism, satisfied his intention to provoke, reinvigorated the use of irony as an aesthetic gambit, and initiated a vogue for mocking high art. The painting also introduced a long series of works paying sly homage to celebrated artists of the past, including Rembrandt, Jacques Louis David, Manet, and Matisse. Soon Rivers again startled his audience with *Double Portrait of Berdie* (Whitney Museum, 1955), showing two unidealized views, as if they inhabited the same room, of his naked, middle-aged mother-in-law. As pop art coalesced in the early 1960s, Rivers responded with distaste to its literalism. While often addressing subjects from popular culture, he retained the sensuous painted surface that signified uniqueness and authenticity, while also accommodating ambiguity as an element of meaning. Active also as a sculptor since the early 1950s, during the following decade he introduced three-dimensional components, sometimes including found objects, into his pictorial works. The multimedia *History of the Russian Revolution: From Marx to Mayakovsky* (Hirshhorn Museum, 1965) combines wood, canvas, glass, metal, and other materials, as well as several painting and drawing media. With its dimensions exceeding 13 × 33 feet, this work represents the apex of his ambitious but also tongue-in-cheek historicism. In the 1970s and later, he focused particularly on assembled, sometimes spray-painted reliefs that combine painted canvas with three-dimensional elements, most often sculpted foamboard. These typically comment humorously on celebrity culture, fashion, show business, or artistic forebears. Clever, high-spirited, and skillfully executed, they nevertheless lack the subversive subtleties of his more original earlier work.

The versatile Rivers worked professionally as a musician on a steady basis through the 1980s and played publicly on occasion into his last months. He produced a sustained stream of prints, including some that relate to poetry of friends, such as Kenneth Koch and, most particularly, his intimate acquaintance Frank O'Hara, whose fragmentary and autobiographical method paralleled Rivers's own distinctive approach. He also designed sets for theatrical performances and experimented with film and video. A sometime actor, he appeared in off-Broadway shows and in 1959 numbered among the characters in the legendary beat film *Pull My Daisy*, directed by Robert *Frank and Alfred *Leslie. Rivers's poetry appeared in literary magazines. Intellectually inquisitive and eager for new experiences, he traveled widely and worked for periods of time in London and Paris. He remained active until the final days before he died at his eastern Long Island home in Southampton, where he had resided for nearly fifty years. In 1979 he published *Drawings and Digressions*, compiled with the assistance of Carol Brightman. Written with playwright Arnold Weinstein, *What Did I Do? The Unauthorized Autobiography* (1992) charts the eccentric frenzy of his life while also reflecting on the history of his times.

Robinson, Boardman (1876–1952). Painter, printmaker, and illustrator. His accomplished murals contributed to enthusiasm for wall painting in the late 1920s and 1930s, while in the first two decades of the twentieth century he invigorated American drawing and illustration with a forceful, sketchy style derived from French precedents. Later he illustrated many classic literary works with bold designs. Born in Somerset, Nova Scotia, Robinson lived as a child in Wales. In the mid-1890s he arrived in Boston, where he studied art at the Normal Art School. He then went to Paris, where he imbibed the graphic style of Jean-Louis Forain and his antecedents in the work of Honoré Daumier and the impressionists. Upon settling in New York, he had difficulty selling his advanced work but eventually found full-time employment as a newspaper artist. His already leftist social views intensified in 1915 as he traveled in eastern Europe with the radical journalist John Reed. Robinson contributed regularly to *The* *Masses* and *The* *Liberator*. In 1919 he began teaching at the *Art Students League and redirected his energies chiefly to painting, drawing subjects from history as well as the contemporary world. In 1927, with his first mural commission—ten scenes depicting the history of commerce for a Pittsburgh department store—Robinson helped to initiate the revival of mural painting that proved central to art of the 1930s. After moving to Colorado in 1930, he often essayed heroic mountain scenes inspired by the dramatic surroundings. He died in Stamford, Connecticut, not far from the home of his final years in Darien.

Robinson, Theodore (1852–96). Painter. An impressionist, he numbers among the American movement's earliest, most knowledgeable, and most influential exponents. In forming his personal style, he augmented structured compositions reflecting academic training with French impressionism's spontaneous brushwork and atmospheric concerns. Robinson preferred subtle and muted color harmonies, which lend to some canvases a pensive mood suggestive of *tonalism. Monet's impact on his work was particularly strong during the several years that Robinson resided during warmer months next door to the French painter's home in Giverny. There Robinson often recorded the local landscape, but after his permanent return to the United States in December 1892 he determined to emphasize the particularity of American subjects. Many of these later paintings depict individually recognizable rural views, but he addressed urban scenes as well. Throughout his career, he also painted figure studies, as well as a few portraits. He shared in the late nineteenth century's general enthusiasm for Japanese art but differed from most contemporary painters by regularly taking photographs as "sketches" for figure paintings. Three years after Theodore Pierson Robinson's birth in Irasburg, Vermont, his family left for Illinois. In 1856 they moved to southern Wisconsin, where he grew up in Evansville. After brief initial studies in Chicago, in 1874 Robinson continued his training during two years at the *National Academy of Design, where Lemuel Everett *Wilmarth numbered among his principal instructors. In 1875, while still enrolled at the academy, Robinson helped to organize the *Art Students League. The following year, he began studies in Paris, where he worked with Émile-Auguste Carolus-Duran and Jean-Léon Gérôme. During an 1877 summer visit to Grez-sur-Loing, a popular artists' destination in the *Barbizon region, he began painting outdoors. Following an extended stay in Venice, where he spent some weeks in the company of James Abbott McNeill *Whistler, he returned to the United States toward the end of 1879. Soon resettled in New York to continue painting, during the next several years he also wrote art criticism and worked on decorative projects with John *La Farge and others. In the spring of 1884 he again left for Paris. During the following eight years, broken by several visits to the United States, he spent more and more time in the French countryside. At first returning to the Barbizon area, he combined figures, often peasants or craftsmen, and landscape in increasingly fluid and painterly scenes. Evidence suggests that he may have first met Monet, later a lifelong friend, in Giverny in 1885. As he sojourned for several months in the village in 1887 and returned each year through 1892, his brushwork responded to Monet's approach. Among several Seine valley overviews from a site above Giverny, *A Bird's Eye View* (Metropolitan Museum, 1889) characteristically combines architectonic design with broken colors, here applied in a pearly scheme dominated by lavenders and pale greens. Robinson's attention to the geometry of the village houses suggests Cézanne's more inherently structural approach, but the work's decorative serenity typifies his own sensibility. During his final years in New York, Robinson continued his practice of finding most subjects outside the metropolis, primarily at locations in New York State and New England. An 1894 visit to *Cos Cob, Connecticut, produced a notable series of shore scenes, including some of his most brilliantly colored and abstractly composed images. Never in robust health, Robinson died in New York before his forty-fourth birthday.

Robus, Hugo (1885–1964). Sculptor and painter. Initially a painter, he is remembered particularly for sleekly stylized figural sculpture produced after 1920. Born in Cleveland, he graduated from the Cleveland School (now Institute) of Art before moving to New York. At the *National Academy of Design his teachers included Emil *Carlsen and Edgar Melville *Ward. In 1912 he left for two years in Europe, where he lived mainly in Paris but also traveled widely and painted for several months in the French countryside. One winter, he took a sculpture class with Antoine Bourdelle. Through these years he painted mostly in an impressionist style, but after returning permanently to New York he experimented with modern approaches influenced by cubism and futurism. Around 1920 Robus started modeling sculpture (he rarely carved), soon adopting the smooth, generalized manner of his mature output. Interested in suggesting movement and kinaesthetic rather than optical truth, he often lengthened or distorted shapes, always with a feel for flowing line and graceful contours. His marble *Girl Washing Her Hair* (Museum of Modern Art, 1940; original plaster, 1933), a slender nude reduced to an arch from waist to downward-streaming hair, demonstrates his capacity for refining moments of everyday life into eye-catching modernist forms. He died at his Hudson River Valley home in New City, where he had maintained a residence since 1918.

Rockburne, Dorothea (1934–). Painter, printmaker, and installation artist. Known particularly for conceptually based, often spatially complex, geometric compositions from the 1970s and 1980s, she employed mathematical principles to determine rigorous relationships among shapes. Many of her signature works incorporate innovative folded elements. Born in Montreal, she was naturalized as an American citizen in 1991. She moved to the United States in 1950 to enroll at *Black Mountain College, where she studied with Franz *Kline, Philip *Guston, Jack *Tworkov, Esteban *Vicente, and John *Cage. In 1955 she relocated permanently to New York. Becoming dissatisfied with painting around 1960, Rockburne instead participated in dance events and *happenings for several years. From 1963 until 1968 she also worked as an assistant to Robert *Rauschenberg. As she returned to studio work in the late 1960s, she contributed to the prevailing *minimalist aesthetic with spare, yet often materially sensuous paintings, drawings, and *installations. Demonstrating also an affinity for *process art, many of these incorporated industrial materials, such as tar and crude oil. In 1971 she began the series Drawing Which Makes Itself, using folds to define shapes and planes. She soon elaborated these in drawings and paintings incorporating color, along with creasing and shaped contours. In the late 1980s her work began to lose its constructivist tone as she accommodated more expansive, lyrical, and contingent formal relationships. In 1991 while residing in Rome, she embarked on a new direction, inspired by an interest in astronomy. For the most part abandoning geometric form, she brought color to the forefront. In the mid-1990s, she showed mural-sized paintings that engulf the viewer in celestial spaces, but many subsequent paintings and drawings revel, often on a fairly small scale, in materials and sensuous surfaces that need no justification in scientific theories.

Rockefeller, John D., Jr. (1874–1960). Art collector and patron. Also a businessman. Son of the enormously wealthy founder of Standard Oil, he continued his father's business interests and philanthropy, while in addition becoming an art enthusiast. Born in Cleveland, John Davison Rockefeller graduated from Brown University in 1897. By 1910 he had almost completely retired from business to pursue philanthropic interests. His power and money exerted lasting effects on American culture. Among many other notable projects, in 1929 he commissioned the construction of New York's Rockefeller Center, a unique ensemble of modern skyscrapers enriched with numerous contemporary paintings and sculptures. When that undertaking began, he was already involved in a philanthropic passion of many years: the Cloisters, an upper Manhattan venue opened to the public in 1938 as a showcase for the medieval collection of the *Metropolitan Museum of Art. He died in Tucson, Arizona. **Abby Aldrich Rockefeller** (1874–1948) became his wife in 1901. Born in Providence, Rhode Island, Abby Greene Aldrich was active in charitable work before their marriage. In the 1920s she became a major collector of modern and contemporary European and American art. At the end of the decade, along with Lillie P. *Bliss and Mary Quinn (Mrs. Cornelius J.) *Sullivan, she founded the *Museum of Modern Art. She and her husband made significant gifts to that institution—although he never appreciated the work it sponsored. They also provided funding for the restoration of colonial Williamsburg, Virginia, where her collection of American folk art is housed in a separate museum. She died in New York.

Their eldest son, philanthropist and collector **John D. Rockefeller III** (1906–78), was born in New York and graduated from Princeton University in 1929. Drawn principally to Asian art, he amassed a major collection that he bequeathed to the Asia Society, which he had founded in 1956. An automobile accident north of New York, near his Pocantico Hills estate, took his life. His wife, **Blanchette Rockefeller** (1909–92) collected mainly contemporary work and continued her mother-in-law's enthusiastic backing for MoMA. Born in New York, Blanchette Ferry Hooker graduated from Vassar College in 1931. She died at her home in suburban Briarcliff Manor, New York. A second son, **Nelson Aldrich Rockefeller** (1908–79), was born in Bar Harbor, Maine, and graduated from Dartmouth College in 1930. A longtime leader in the Republican party, he served as governor of New York State for four terms and as vice president in Gerald Ford's administration. Besides forming major collections of modern and tribal art, in 1954 he founded New York's Museum of Primitive Art. (Later he donated these holdings to the Metropolitan Museum). He also continued his mother's support of MoMA. He died in his New York office. Another brother, collector and international banker **David Rockefeller** (1915–), chiefly prefers late-nineteenth- and twentieth-century art. Born in New York, he graduated from Harvard University in 1936 and earned a PhD from the University of Chicago four years later. He, too, numbers among longtime MoMA supporters.

Rockwell, Norman (1894–1978). Painter and illustrator. Known to millions for illustrations based on his technically accomplished oils and watercolors, he established his name with images of small-town family life. Anecdotal, detailed, tolerant, and affectionate, they present commonplace experiences with a variable mix of humor, nostalgia, and sentimentality but little inquiry into the life of mind and emotions. Some images address serious subjects related to the social history of his times, including World War II, the civil rights movement, and space exploration. His work as a whole provides an exceptionally rich panorama of the concerns of ordinary Americans over a period of more than half a century. He also painted a number of portraits. Because Rockwell's name has become synonymous with an idealized vision of American life, it may be futile to try to disentangle observation from mythmaking in his work. Although he is known as an illustrator because, as he intended, his images first appeared in the mass media rather than fine art environment, his images nevertheless rarely function as illustrations. Rather than interpreting preexisting texts, they present original narratives in the tradition of nineteenth-century *genre painting.

Norman Percevel Rockwell was born in New York and grew up in the area. His early love of Charles Dickens's fiction whetted his taste for abundant narrative detail and intriguing characters. Having decided to become an illustrator, he left school at fourteen to study at William Merritt *Chase's school and two years later entered the *National Academy of Design. Subsequently, he also studied at the *Art Students League. In 1917–18 he served for about a year in the U.S. Navy. Coming of age in an era of flourishing illustration, he learned much from its leading practitioners, including Maxfield *Parrish and Howard *Pyle. Additionally, he admired the old masters, but also found much of interest in modern art. From the 1920s he traveled often to Europe, where he enlarged his understanding of both. An obsessive worker, Rockwell developed great dexterity in his craft. Moreover, he approached each illustration as a research project, working out details with anthropological precision as he progressed through sketches and studies toward the final product. Already receiving commissions as a teenager, Rockwell landed his first cover assignment for *Boy's Life* in 1913, initiating a series of more than 250 illustrations for that magazine, as well as a long association with Scouting. About a year later he moved to suburban New Rochelle, where several other important illustrators lived. Fame arrived via the *Saturday Evening Post*, which ran approximately 320 of his covers between 1916 and 1963. By the 1930s he was widely in demand among magazines, book publishers, and commercial enterprises. From 1939 until 1953 he lived north of Bennington, Vermont, in the vicinity of Arlington, also a haven for illustrators. He then moved permanently to Stockbridge, in western Massachusetts, where he continued to work productively into his eighties. Founded with the artist's help in 1969, the Norman Rockwell Museum there houses a large collection of his work, along with archives and memorabilia. Autobiographical reminiscences, as told to his son Thomas Rockwell, appear in *My Adventures as an Illustrator* (1960).

Rodia, Simon (1879–1965). Creator of an architectural sculpture, known as the Watts Towers, in the Watts district of southern Los Angeles. Born in Ribottoli, not far from Naples, Sabato Rodia later called himself Sam, but the incorrect name of Simon has remained in general use since it appeared in a 1937 newspaper article. He emigrated with his family to Pennsylvania as a teenager and within a few years continued on to California. Working as a laborer and tile setter, he lived in Los Angeles most of his adult life. In 1921 he began working alone on a street corner near his home in a nondescript urban area, bringing to life a visionary monument to ornamental beauty. Walls, benches, and terraces at ground level, as well as subsidiary spires, surround the ensemble's centerpiece, an airy, ten-story tower of concrete on scaffolding of metal rods and mesh. Glass, ceramic fragments, seashells, and other found materials, along with incised patterns, richly embellish nearly all surfaces. Substantially complete by 1948, the extravagant whole testifies to the power of Rodia's persistence, ambition, and imagination. In the mid-1950s Rodia retired to the San Francisco Bay Area, where he lived in Martinez until his death. Subsequently threatened with destruction, his eccentric creation eventually was restored with public funding and granted

National Historic Landmark status. Today the monument is a state park. The city administers the site and provides cultural programming there.

Roesen, Severin (probably 1815 or 1816–72 or later). Painter. A still life specialist, he is known for opulent displays of flowers and fruit. Wine glasses, pitchers, and additional tableware frequently also appear, and occasionally landscape is visible in the background. Spearheading the American taste for luxuriant still lifes based on Baroque precedents, these works celebrate the earth's abundance and the nation's increasingly comfortable standard of living. However, Roesen's habit of combining perfectly ripe fruits and mature flowers, regardless of the season to which they actually belong produces a whiff of unreality. A native of Germany, where he may have been trained as a porcelain painter, he apparently worked in Cologne. The style he imported updates seventeenth-century Dutch still life tradition for a Victorian audience, probably at least in part through the example of nineteenth-century Düsseldorf intermediaries. Around 1848 he arrived in New York, where he resided until relocating to central Pennsylvania in 1857 or early the following year. He worked in Huntington, and perhaps elsewhere, before settling a few years later in Williamsport. He disappeared from the historical record in 1872. In the intricate and unusually large but nevertheless representative *Still Life: Flowers and Fruit* (Metropolitan Museum, c. 1850–55), blossoms and fruits establish a lively, colorful pattern across the canvas. At the same time, each specimen captures with utmost fidelity the coloring, texture, and three-dimensional form of its botanical species. Exemplifying a device common to many of his works, natural elements hang over the front edge of the table, enhancing the illusion of spatial volume by seeming to push into the spectator's space. The bird's nest with eggs and the glinting reflection of a window in the glass vase number among a repertoire of virtuoso devices that Roesen often repeated.

Rogers, John (1829–1904). Sculptor. Known principally for small figural groups illustrating everyday life, he also produced a few ideal subjects, as well as life-size portraits. In characteristic tabletop pieces, inexpensively reproduced in plaster, he disregarded the fashion for *neoclassicism in sculpture. Instead, he combined realistic observation and anecdotal narrative to please a burgeoning middle class. Unrivaled in his specialty, he addressed the mid-century audience that also admired *Currier & Ives prints, *genre paintings by such artists as William Sidney *Mount and George Caleb *Bingham, and the self-consciously realistic literature of mid-century. Born in Salem, Massachusetts, he lived as a child in Northampton and in Roxbury, a Boston suburb. After leaving school at sixteen, he worked for a decade at varied trades, mostly requiring some form of mechanical skill, first in Boston and later in Manchester, New Hampshire (interrupted by nearly a year in New York), and Hannibal, Missouri. In 1849 he began modeling in clay during his spare time. The loss of his job in the economic slump of 1857 apparently spurred thoughts of becoming a professional sculptor. In the fall of 1858 he departed for Europe, intending to stay for several years. Unhappy with the academic training he encountered in Paris and Rome, he returned to Roxbury after seven months. While subsequently employed in Chicago, he continued to model in his leisure time.

Finding that his work was admired in Chicago, he moved in November 1859 to New York. There he quickly attracted critical praise and within a few years headed a large workshop that turned out replicas in great numbers. Rogers modeled all the originals, producing almost ninety during the course of some thirty-five years. His assistants, who sometimes numbered as many as sixty, turned out tens of thousands of reproductions, using molds made from bronze originals to form the plaster, which was painted in a monochrome gray or brownish tone to simulate stone or bronze. Sold through mail-order catalogues as well as retail stores, his work reached the height of its popularity during the 1870s. By the late 1880s, changing tastes had eroded its appeal. Suffering from health problems, Rogers retired from artistic activity and sold the business in 1893. In 1895 he moved permanently to New Canaan, Connecticut, where he had previously summered. Among the pieces that made his reputation, several addressed topics related to the Civil War. One of the first, *The Slave Auction* (1859), dramatized his abolitionist views. The most popular and most numerous of his groups illustrate everyday moments with humor and sympathy. He also produced a number of subjects based on literary or historical themes. Intended for a mass market, the finely detailed Rogers Groups, as they came to be called, achieve easily legible meaning through simple, well-constructed compositions. Although often sentimental, they nonetheless present characters with dignity and affection. Today Rogers's small sculptures provide a glimpse of an idealized American past, but in their day they enabled large numbers of people to enjoy a previously somewhat inaccessible art form.

Rogers, Randolph (1825–92). Sculptor. Residing in Rome throughout his professional life, he ranked among the most popular and productive sculptors of his day. His work extended mid-nineteenth-century *neoclassicism toward formal complexity, the suggestion of movement, and eloquent emotion. In addition, he frequently embellished his work with the realistic narrative detail popular during the Victorian era. One of the nineteenth century's best-known sculptures, *Nydia, the Blind Flower Girl of Pompeii* (National Gallery, 1860; modeled c. 1853–54) depicts a character from Edward Bulwer-Lytton's enormously popular 1834 novel, *The Last Days of Pompeii*. The unseeing young woman flees as she strains to hear, her swirling garments threatening to entangle her legs and walking staff. But the classical serenity of her face and the grace of her posture speak of innocent virtue and heart-wrenching vulnerability to her predicament. Rogers found buyers for several dozen replicas in two sizes. Many of his other ideal compositions also illustrate literary or *genre themes, rather than classical subjects. His civic monuments and numerous portrait busts display a sensitive naturalism. Born in upstate Waterloo, New York, Rogers grew up in Ann Arbor, Michigan. After about a year in New York, where he took up sculpture in his spare time, in 1848 he departed for Italy. He subsequently resided there, with occasional visits to the United States. In Florence he studied under neoclassical sculptor Lorenzo Bartolini. During the three years before he left to establish his own studio in Rome, he became an accomplished modeler. However, he never learned to carve marble, leaving him even more dependent than most sculptors of his day on Italian workmen. Nevertheless, his career soon flourished. His first ambitious ideal work, the classically restrained but realistically detailed *Ruth Gleaning* (Metropolitan Museum, 1855 or 1856; modeled 1850), which he had begun in Florence, secured his reputation and eventually spawned some twenty life-size replicas and many additional smaller ones. His last important literary work, *The Lost Pleiad* (Art Institute of Chicago, 1874–75), elicited more than one hundred orders for replicas in two sizes. Demonstrating his evolution toward baroque form, this semi-nude, female personification dramatizes a myth as she twists sharply while floating in billowing drapery, marble clouds at her feet. In 1854 Rogers accepted his first public commission, a life-size *John Adams* (Memorial Hall, Harvard University, Cambridge, Massachusetts, 1854–59). Subsequently, he remained almost continuously at work on embellishments for public spaces. In 1855 he began a pair of bronze doors for the U.S. Capitol (central portico, east facade; installed 1863; cast 1859). Illustrating the life of Christopher Columbus, the doors mimic Lorenzo Ghiberti's fifteenth-century *Gates of Paradise* in format and style. After Thomas *Crawford's death in 1857, Rogers completed his friend's monument to George Washington (state capitol grounds, Richmond, Virginia, 1869). For this grand ensemble he provided three large portrait figures and six allegories. During the 1860s and 1870s his flair for combining patriotic idealism with convincing realism kept him in demand for commemorative monuments, usually in bronze. Often memorializing the Civil War or its heroes, these civic commissions can be found in Cincinnati, Detroit, Philadelphia, New York, and other locations. In the early 1880s a stroke ended his artistic career. He died in Rome.

Romanticism, American. An expression of the unruly international sensibility embracing emotion, intuition, imagination, rapturous response to nature, and social and political freedom, while disdaining classical rationalism, order, and respect for principles. Romanticism implied that reality cannot be fully comprehended by the intellect alone. This idea underlay romanticism's unifying theme: individual experience as a source of truth. The quest for nonrational paths to understanding glorified extreme forms of human behavior, as well as bizarre, mysterious, and visionary activities. The genius, the hero, the mystic, and the outlaw became glamorous types, whereas religion, drugs, travel, and art itself were seen as means of achieving heightened consciousness. Emphasis on the individual also elevated appreciation for the daily lives of ordinary people and for mundane reality as a source of beauty and wonder. Developing in the later eighteenth century, romanticism transformed the intellectual, artistic, and social life of the Western world. Although it crested in the first decades of the nineteenth century, many aspects of romanticism persist even today. Romanticism is commonly characterized as the antithesis of classicism, but in the visual arts *neoclassicism can be seen as the first important portent of full-blown romanticism. Although neoclassical artists professed devotion to order, harmony, balance, and ideal form, their attachment to these qualities often betrayed an irrational passion characteristic of the romantic temperament. In addition, neoclassicism's inherent nostalgia and yearning for the exoticism of the past suggest romantic inclinations. An early neoclassicist, Benjamin *West played an important role in the formation of Anglo-American romanticism. In the United States, landscape painting predominated among expressions of the romantic temper. In this, Thomas *Cole led the way, followed by such practitioners as Asher B. *Durand and Fitz Hugh *Lane. *Genre painting, stressing the diversity of experience embedded in unexceptional lives, also flourished. William Sidney *Mount and George Caleb *Bingham number among leaders in this specialty. Portraiture in the romantic era often emphasized the emotional warmth of sitters, their spiritual purity, or their alertness to life, in lieu of the self-control and social distinction that had been more prominent in the eighteenth century. Gilbert *Stuart, especially in his later work, set an influential standard in rendering this conception of personality. Washington *Allston, John *Quidor, Daniel *Huntington, and many others addressed romantic literary or imaginative topics.

Rondel, Frédéric. *See* HOMER, WINSLOW.

Rose, Barbara. *See* STELLA, FRANK.

Rose, Guy. *See* GIVERNY GROUP.

Rosenberg, Harold (1906–78). Art critic. Also an essayist and poet. Known especially as a leading supporter of *abstract expressionism, he brought to his criticism a humanistic, literary background. He endeavored to understand the artist's intentions and the intellectual complexity of the art work's ethical and political context, rather make judgments solely on the basis of formal values. Although he and Clement *Greenberg played key roles in articulating the nature and importance of abstract expressionism before the style was widely accepted, Greenberg's more reductive approach came to dominate art world opinion during the 1960s. Born in New York, Rosenberg studied for a year at City College of New York before enrolling in 1924 at Brooklyn Law School. Three years later, he received a degree but was stricken with osteomyelitis, a serious bone malady that permanently disabled him. While recuperating, he reoriented his ambitions toward writing. In 1930 he began publishing poetry and fiction in such well-regarded literary journals as *transition* and *Poetry*. Becoming interested during the early 1930s in Marxism, he also published essays and politically inspired creative pieces in leading left-wing magazines, including *Partisan Review* and *New Masses*. As well, he found employment as an assistant on the mural program of a *federal art project and became editor of *Art Front*. This immersion in the artistic, political, and literary culture of 1930s New York formed his mature outlook, but by the late 1930s he had decisively rejected Communism. As a public intellectual, he unflinchingly favored democratic society and artistic freedom, while also vigorously opposing middle-class conventionality.

Between 1938 and 1942 Rosenberg worked in Washington, D.C., where he served as art editor of the WPA's American Guide series. Subsequently, while working for the Office of War Information in New York, in 1943 he purchased a residence on eastern Long Island, where artists were beginning to congregate in substantial numbers. Through his contacts there as well as in New York, he developed personal relationships with artists and by 1947 had begun to write informed essays about their work. In 1952 Rosenberg achieved prominence internationally with the publication in *Art News* of his essay "The American Action Painters," offering a new aesthetic rooted in existential process and undermining the disparity between art and life. His catchy phrase provided an easily grasped creative identity for such abstract expressionists as Jackson *Pollock, Willem *de Kooning, and Franz *Kline. Rosenberg continued to write regularly for *Art News* and from 1967 until his death, served as the *New Yorker's* art critic. While specializing in contemporary art, Rosenberg also wrote regularly on topics of political and cultural interest for publications such as *Dissent* and *Les Temps modernes*. From 1966 until 1978 he taught at the University of Chicago. He died in at his summer home in Springs, an area of East Hampton. *The Tradition of the New* (1959), an essay collection examining the urge to novelty during the previous century, remains Rosenberg's best-known publication. His other books on art and its milieu include *Arshile *Gorky: The Man, the Time, the Idea* (1962), *The Anxious Object: Art Today and Its Audience* (1964), *Artworks and Packages* (1969), *The De-Definition of Art: Action Art to Pop to Earthworks* (1972), *Discovering the Present: Three Decades in Art, Culture, and Politics* (1973), *Willem *de Kooning* (1974), *Art on the Edge: Creators and Situations* (1975), *Barnett *Newman* (1978), and the posthumous 1985 *Art and Other Serious Matters* and *The Case of the Baffled Radical*. *Trance Above the Streets* (1942) is a collection of poetry.

Rosenquist, James (1933–). Painter, printmaker, and occasional sculptor. A major contributor to *pop art, he specialized during the 1960s in monumental paintings juxtaposing extreme close-ups of unrelated subjects from popular culture. Rosenquist's experience as a billboard painter drove the formation of his personal style of immediately readable forms, garish colors, and distorted scale. The pessimistic, unsettling, and irrational tone of his work contrasts markedly with the easy-going banality of much pop art. Rosenquist's best known work, *F-111* (Museum of Modern Art, 1964–65), bears the name of the U.S. Air Force bomber it represents, interrupted by a number of unrelated vignettes. These include a little girl grinning under a hairdryer, a mushroom cloud, a tangle of canned spaghetti, a birthday cake, and a heavily treaded tire. With its implicit criticism of gluttonous consumer culture, defense spending, and the Vietnam War, the work prefigures many that carry a socially critical outlook. Much of his later art stresses decorative resolution, but disturbing overtones remain common. Born in Grand Forks, North Dakota, in 1942 James Albert Rosenquist moved with his family to Minneapolis. In 1952 he enrolled at the University of Minnesota, where he studied with Cameron Booth (1892–1980), a painter whose work evolved from modernist-inflected regionalism to pure abstraction. Rosenquist also gained initial experience as a commercial billboard painter before leaving for New York in 1954. During a year at the *Art Students League, his teachers included Edwin *Dickinson, George *Grosz, and Morris *Kantor. In the late 1950s he again worked as a billboard artist. In 1960 he decided to paint full time, abandoned his abstract style, and soon completed his first studio painting to employ commercial techniques and imagery related to advertising. In 1965 *F-111* created a sensation when it appeared at Leo *Castelli's gallery. Ten feet high and eighty-six feet in length, the multipanel work wrapped around the gallery's walls, enveloping the spectator in a surrealistic visual and psychological collage. In later decades, overt political critiques diminished as he addressed varied subjects with great technical skill and no loss of formal power. An uneasy atmosphere emanating from their peculiar subject matter, an early 1990s series of overscaled Gift-Wrapped Dolls focuses on prettified faces, partially concealed by wrinkled cellophane. The radiant, abstracted forms in the bravura Speed of Light series from about ten years later evoke, as the artist intended, the dizzying collapse of time in an Einsteinian universe. Active as a printmaker since the 1960s, he has worked primarily with lithography. Rosenquist divides his time between Manhattan, the rural suburb of Bedford, New York, and Aripeka, on Florida's Gulf Coast north of Tampa Bay, where he has maintained a residence and studio for some thirty years.

Rosler, Martha (1943–). Photographer, performance artist, video artist, and mixed-media artist. Employing photography along with techniques related to *conceptual art, *performance art, and *installation art, she seeks to elicit critical thought on social and political issues. While questioning the ideological nature of all representation, she aims her aesthetic and ethical drive at apperception of lived social experience and its sometimes hidden meanings. Born in New York, in 1965 she graduated from Brooklyn College, where she majored in English and studied with Ad *Reinhardt. In her early years as an artist, she painted but also took street photographs and began to experiment with montage. She credits Jean-Luc Godard's stringent yet powerful films of the early 1960s as a formative influence on her sensibility. In 1968 she moved to San Diego, where she earned an MFA from the University of California in 1974. Rosler first came to public attention with a series of photomontages collectively titled Bringing the War Home (1967–72). In these, she combined images from the Vietnam War with representations of suburban interiors gleaned from popular magazines, shockingly resituating the televised war into the homes where it could be viewed on a nightly basis. In the 1970s she produced work related to *feminist art, often stressing the relationships between food and women's lives, as in the 1975 video *Semiotics of the Kitchen*. In 1980 Rosler returned to the New York area. Since then, while teaching at Rutgers University in New Brunswick, New Jersey, she has continued to probe social problems, such as homelessness and social alienation. Her 2004 anthology, *Decoys and Disruptions: Selected Writings, 1975–2001*, comprises thirteen critical essays, along with illustrations from her work.

Rosofsky, Seymour. *See* CHICAGO IMAGISM.

Ross, Charles. *See* EARTH ART.

Ross, Denman (1853–1935). Art theorist and collector. His writings advocating scientific principles as the basis for art interested many artists during the early twentieth century. Although Ross had no use for modern art, which he saw as idiosyncratic and irrational, he believed that identification of design universals would advance the progress of art by enabling artists to transcend the limits of traditional practice. Ross's interest in reconciling art and science was widespread at the time, and other popular theorists shared his goals. Ross's own thinking was influenced by the ideas of Hardesty Gillmore Maratta (1864–1924), who devised an influential color system, and Jay (born Edward John) Hambidge (1867–1924), who attracted a following for his method of mathematically based design known as "dynamic symmetry." Born in Cincinnati, Denman Waldo Ross graduated from Harvard University in 1875 and five years later received a PhD in history. Attracted to *Pre-Raphaelitism through Charles Eliot *Norton's Harvard lectures, he studied privately in Italy with Henry

Roderick *Newman. In 1899 he returned to Harvard, where he remained on the faculty for the rest of life. In addition to European and Asian paintings and sculptures, his wide-ranging collection of some 16,000 objects included decorative arts from around the world. *A Theory of Pure Design* (1907) remains his most important book. Other significant publications include *On Drawing and Painting* (1912) and *The Painter's Palette* (1919). He died during a visit to London.

Rossiter, Thomas Pritchard (1818–71). Painter. Known especially for historical subjects, he also painted religious works, portraits, and relatively fewer *genre subjects. He was born in New Haven, Connecticut, where he studied with Nathaniel *Jocelyn before opening a portrait studio in 1838. He also worked in Troy, New York, and in New York City prior to departing for Europe in 1840, along with Asher B. *Durand, John *Casilear, and his longtime friend John *Kensett. After visiting London, he settled in Paris for a year, then moved on to Rome. There he made his home for four and a half years, while also traveling throughout Italy as well as into Switzerland and Germany. From 1846 until 1853 he worked in New York. During a subsequent sojourn in Paris, he won a gold medal at the 1855 Exposition Universelle. He returned in 1856 to New York, but in 1860, while retaining his New York studio, he moved to Cold Spring, New York, on the Hudson River. During his years abroad, Rossiter mastered an easily readable realism, which he employed to create the stagy, historically plausible, morally didactic canvases that are his major legacy. Although some depict events of enduring consequence, such as *Signing the Constitution of the United States* (Fraunces Tavern Museum, New York, 1867), his historical narratives more frequently hinge on anecdote. Such works, including several depicting the domestic life of George Washington, appealed to mid-century interest in the personal virtues of heroic individuals. He died at his Cold Spring home.

Roszak, Theodore (1907–81). Sculptor, draftsman, painter, and printmaker. Best known for welded and brazed sculptures that embody *abstract expressionist aims, he had earlier numbered among the most innovative and perceptive American practitioners of constructivist art. However, disillusioned by the savagery of World War II, he lost faith in the power of reason to generate aesthetic principles. Like others of his generation, in his mature works Roszak attempted to create expressionistic visual analogues for universal truths and moral values. Spikey, agitated forms predominate, but some works from the 1950s and later incorporate figural or animal imagery. Born in Poznań, as a toddler he left Poland with his family to settle in Chicago. He later was naturalized as a U.S. citizen. He started his professional training at the School of the Art Institute of Chicago but in 1926 left for New York to study painting at the *National Academy of Design with Charles *Hawthorne. He also studied privately with George *Luks and attended philosophy classes at Columbia University. In 1927 he returned to the Art Institute for another year before once again heading east to visit museums and work for a time at *Woodstock. In 1929 he departed for Europe, where he lived in Prague during most of an eighteen-month sojourn but also traveled to Paris and other cities. During this time, he acquired a more profound understanding of cubism, surrealism, and other aspects of modern art, while also becoming familiar with Bauhaus teachings. Upon his permanent return to New York in 1931, the romantic realism of his earlier paintings gave way to work suggesting the influence of Giorgio de Chirico and other European artists he admired. By the following year, he was working also as a sculptor. Except for a few reliefs in painted plaster or other material, he specialized in constructions that combine machinelike geometric components into tight, clean compositions. These often feature painted elements, as well as industrial and other unconventional art materials. He also made photograms, registering on photosensitive paper the poetry of shadows cast by combinations of geometric and *biomorphic elements. Employed for several years by *federal art projects, in 1938 he joined the faculty of the government-sponsored Laboratory School of Industrial Design, where László *Moholy-Nagy was the presiding spirit. While working from 1940 through World War II as an aircraft designer, he sometimes softened the rigidity of his sculptural constructions with organic elements suggesting a continuing attraction to surrealism. After the middle of that decade, such biomorphic tendencies overwhelmed geometric precision. From then on, his generally rough-surfaced forms manifest a spontaneous and gestural aesthetic. The subjects of these works typically relate to psychological and historical themes that acknowledge a darker side to human experience than could be conveyed through the confident rationality of constructivism. Pushing farther in this direction, from the 1960s Roszak produced visionary drawings that became a primary medium of expression as illness in later years limited his ability to manipulate heavy materials.

Rothenberg, Susan (1945–). Painter and printmaker. A leader in the 1970s rehabilitation of large-scale, image-based, nonironic, gestural painting, in 1975 she first came to national attention with generalized horse silhouettes anchored with diagonal lines on otherwise image-free canvases. She has subsequently complicated her repertoire with other subjects, including the human form, and more intricate compositions, but she continues to explore figure-ground pictorial tensions. Rooted in personal experience, her imagery incorporates issues of perception, memory, and imagination. Born in Buffalo, New York, she received a BFA in 1966 from Cornell University in Ithaca. She then pursued additional training in Washington, D.C., at George Washington University and the Corcoran School of Art (now Corcoran College of Art and Design). After moving to New York in 1969, she experimented with varied painting formats as well as *process art and *performance art until her signature approach coalesced. Also an active and original printmaker, she has worked in several media, including woodcut, etching, mezzotint, and lithography. Her 1971 marriage to Canadian-born New York sculptor George Trakas (1944–) ended in divorce five years later. In 1989 she married Bruce *Nauman and moved to Galisteo, New Mexico.

Rothenberg played a central role in the development of what came to be known as New Image painting, a tendency combining representation and abstraction. The sensibility took its name from a prescient 1978 exhibition curated by Richard Marshall (1947–) at the *Whitney Museum of American Art. Philip *Guston provided an important impetus for the development of New Image work, which generally sought to maintain *abstract expressionism's personal brushwork, large scale, and serious aesthetic demeanor while at the same time acknowledging the visual and metaphorical appeal of representation. Besides Rothenberg, the Whitney Museum show's nine other painters included Nicholas Africano (1948–), Jennifer Bartlett (1941–), Robert Moskowitz (1935–), and Joe Zucker (1941–).

Rothko, Mark (1903–70). Painter. A leading *abstract expressionist, he originated a distinct form of expression featuring grand and sonorous, nebulous rectangles seemingly floating on the surface of the canvas or just behind it. Although transcendental in tone, his works nevertheless remain securely grounded in sensuous materiality and in human experience. Their magisterial presence, achieved almost entirely with color, and their vast, sublime spaces provided compelling precedents for the development of *color field painting. Although he played down mystical readings of his work, perhaps more clearly than any other abstract expressionist, Rothko demonstrated that the new art was up to the task of encoding spiritual resonance for the modern viewer. Born Marcus Rothkovitch in Dvinsk, Russia (now Daugavpils in southeastern Latvia), in 1940 he first used the shortened name by which he became known, but he did not legally adopt it until nearly two decades later. As a boy, he settled in 1913 with his family in Portland, Oregon. After two years at Yale University, he left in 1923 to study at the *Art Students League for a few months before returning to Portland. In 1925 he settled permanently in New York, again briefly enrolling at the Art Students League. These two periods of instruction, which included a painting class with Max *Weber, constituted his only formal study of art. He did not visit the art capitals of Europe until 1950, after he had formulated his distinctive approach. His expressionist work of the late 1920s includes figure paintings, landscapes, and still lifes. Around 1929 he befriended Milton *Avery, whose approach contributed to a redirection of Rothko's interests, as he gradually responded to the older painter's simplified forms and broad color areas.

In 1935 Rothko helped to found The *Ten, between 1936 and 1939 he was employed by *federal art projects as a muralist and easel painter, and in 1938 he became an American citizen. The figural work of the 1930s, stressing lonely and alienated individuals in enigmatic settings, began to give way late in the decade to the period's growing interest in *automatism. This was abetted in the early 1940s by fascination with the psychological investigations of Freud and Jung, as well as with universal human experiences encoded in myths, symbols, and archaic art. Soon, he developed a personal variant of surrealism, picturing mostly abstract, *biomorphic forms floating in space. During the mid-1940s, Rothko often realized such works in fluent watercolor, or subsequently in thinned-out oils, sometimes incorporating unpremeditated or technically unconventional elements. In a final reevaluation of his practice, during the late 1940s Rothko boldly claimed new ground with signature paintings based on hovering rectangles. His 1949 exhibition at Betty *Parsons's gallery was the first devoted entirely to such works.

Once he found his preferred format, Rothko spent the remainder of his life refining it. The relatively lyrical colors of many early examples darkened from the late 1950s, as the paintings, large to begin with, often took on gargantuan proportions. The contemplative aspect of his work correspondingly came to invoke disquieting states. As early as 1943, in a letter to the *New York Times* composed with Adolph *Gottlieb and Barnett *Newman, Rothko had expressed his preference for an art that was "tragic and timeless." The letter also emphasized the priority of subject matter, a position that Rothko never relinquished. Disliking formal responses to his art, he disavowed even the notion that he was an abstract painter, countering with the assertion that he sought pure expression of human emotion, but not his own. Denying that his art reflected inner states, he insisted that his interest lay in the human condition. To enhance the contemplative impact of his work and avoid competing distractions, Rothko took an intense interest in the public presentation of his paintings, coming to prefer that they be shown only in carefully arranged ensembles that preserved the integrity of his vision. Duncan *Phillips conceived the earliest such permanent museum space, devoting a small room in his museum to Rothko's paintings of the mid-1950s. (Relocated during a subsequent renovation, the room remains intact within the Phillips Collection.) Although not conceived as a unit, the Phillips paintings present a coordinated ensemble, and the artist provided advice concerning their installation. In 1958 Rothko received the first of three major commissions for particular spaces, allowing the most complete realization of his intentions in somber ensembles of reds, browns, blacks, and/or purples. Completed in 1959 for Ludwig Mies van der Rohe's new Seagram skyscraper on Park Avenue, the series intended for the Four Seasons restaurant ranked as the most prestigious commission yet given to an abstract expressionist. It was never installed. Fearing that his work would be interpreted as decoration, Rothko later donated nine of these canvases to London's Tate Gallery (now Tate Modern), with the proviso that they be shown in a room by themselves. In 1962–64 he painted several works for a single, smaller room at Harvard University's Holyoke Center. (They were removed from permanent display in 1979.) In 1964 he received a commission for what has often been considered his masterwork, a suite of fourteen nearly monochrome works (1964–67; installed 1971) for Philip Johnson's interdenominational chapel in Houston. Illness in the spring of 1968 restricted Rothko's creative activity. After his health improved somewhat, a few particularly profound and radiantly hued paintings preceded a final interrelated sequence of melancholy pairings featuring black or brown rectangles surmounting gray ones, usually subtly inflected with color. A narrow white edge, more clearly defined than is usual in Rothko's work, sets up complicated spatial relationships between real and painted space, between image and viewer. At the height of his creative powers, having achieved public acclaim and financial security, he died a suicide in his New York studio. The painter's early 1940s views on aesthetic and philosophical topics appear in *The Artist's Reality: Philosophies of Art* (2004), edited by his son Christopher Rothko.

Rothstein, Arthur (1915–85). Photographer. Known for Depression-era documentary work, he created an icon of Dust Bowl devastation, "Farmer and Sons Walking in Dust Storm, Cimarron County, Oklahoma" (1936), depicting a man and two little boys trudging into the wind toward a weather-beaten hovel in a desolate landscape. Rothstein also numbered among leaders in developing magazine photojournalism. Shortly after graduation from Columbia University in 1935, the native New Yorker accepted the invitation of Roy Stryker, formerly a professor there, to set up the photography laboratory in Washington, D.C., for a new documentary project of the Resettlement Administration, later the *Farm Security Administration. Rothstein had pursued photography only as a hobby, but within months he joined the photographic team, learning on the job from more experienced members, including Walker *Evans and Ben *Shahn. With the agency he traveled from Vermont to New Mexico, recording lives of ordinary citizens. In 1940 Rothstein joined the staff of *Look* magazine, where he remained, except for World War II service, until it folded in 1971. From 1972 until his death, he served as an editor at *Parade*. He published many articles and books, including an influential textbook, *Photojournalism* (1956). Other publications include *Color Photography Now* (1970), *Words and Pictures* (1979), *Arthur Rothstein's America in Photographs, 1930–1980* (1984), and the posthumously published *Documentary Photography* (1986). He died in the New York suburb of New Rochelle, where he had made his home since the early 1950s.

Rourke, Constance (1885–1941). Historian of American culture. Widely interested in native expression in its literary, visual, and popular forms, she conceived a broadly democratic purpose for the arts. Responsive to the value of vernacular and regional forms, she pioneered in discerning an American tradition that encompassed both established arts and popular culture. Her best-known work remains *American Humor: A Study of the National Character* (1931). Among other books are two on artists: **Audubon* (1936) and *Charles *Sheeler: Artist in the American Tradition* (1938). Edited by Van Wyck Brooks from an unfinished manuscript, the posthumously published *Roots of American Culture* (1942) particularly stimulated scholarship in the nascent field of American Studies. Born in Cleveland, Constance Mayfield Rourke grew up in Grand Rapids, Michigan. After graduating in 1907 from Vassar College in Poughkeepsie, New York, she taught elementary school for a year before continuing her studies in Paris and London. From 1910 to 1915 she taught English at Vassar. Thereafter she supported herself principally as a freelance writer. During these years she again made her home in Grand Rapids, where she died.

Ruscha, Ed (1937–). Painter, draftsman, photographer, and printmaker. Since the 1970s a central contributor to recent interest in relationships between art, language, and meaning, he came to attention in the early 1960s with paintings related to *pop art and photographs of banal subjects. The bright, cleanly executed, and sardonically witty paintings of this time, generally depicting gas stations, advertising billboards, or other aspects of commercial culture, celebrated their subjects' visual allure. Although also wryly conceived, the photographs drew attention to the monotony and conformity of mid-twentieth-century American life. Born in Omaha, Nebraska, Edward Joseph Ruscha grew up in Oklahoma City. In 1956 he left for Los Angeles and has since remained in the area. (Today he also maintains a residence in the eastern California desert.) Upon arrival, he enrolled at the Chouinard Art Institute (now the California Institute of the Arts). At the beginning of the 1960s, he developed his eye for precise layout while working as a graphic designer, initiated a serious engagement with photography during seven months of European travel, and abandoned his earlier *abstract expressionist form of painting in favor of small collages demonstrating interest in the work of Jasper *Johns and Robert *Rauschenberg. In 1963 he published the first of sixteen unpretentious, mostly text-free, photographic books, each devoted to a single subject, such as gasoline stations, parking lots, or swimming pools. The fifty-some accordion foldout panels of *Every Building on the Sunset Strip* (1966) remains among the best known. Indebted to his admiration for Walker *Evans, individual photographs recall casual snapshots, but the series format enhances their impact. Recording predetermined sequences of items, his *conceptual approach shunned choices based on aesthetic or personal meaning. On the other hand, although they present similar subjects, his boldly designed paintings of the time emphasize artistic decision-making in their abstraction of observed forms. By the late 1960s calligraphy, along with the typography of signage that appeared in his paintings and photographs, stimulated creative approaches to representing words or phrases in exquisitely crafted drawings, often in unconventional media such as gunpowder, coffee, or Pepto-Bismol. For the Venice Biennale in 1970 he produced his only *installation, *Chocolate Room* (Museum of Contemporary Art, Los Angeles), featuring shinglelike—and fragrant—chocolate silkscreens completely covering the walls of a room. Later paintings and drawings investigate varied formal and thematic concerns but nearly always focus on language or its exclusion. In the 1970s he also made films, and he has editioned prints throughout his career. His mural for the Miami-Dade County Public Library (1985) aptly foregrounds a line from Shakespeare's *Hamlet*: "Words without thoughts never to Heaven go." In 2005 his work alone represented the United States at the Venice Biennale. Edited by Alexandra Schwartz, *Leave Any Information at the Signal: Writings, Interviews, Bits, Pages* (2002) constructs an autobiography from fragments.

Rush, William (1756–1833). Sculptor. The first native-born sculptor of note, he remained primarily a woodcarver but also modeled terra cottas. Rising from artisanal beginnings, eventually he forged a fresh and ambitious original synthesis of the woodcarver's craft with sophisticated imported traditions. A lifelong Philadelphian, he established that city's preeminence in sculpture in the first decades of the nineteenth century. In partnership with leading architects, he executed a number of important commissions for public places. Active in civic life, he served on the city's council for more than twenty-five years. Also a leader in the Philadelphia art community, in late December 1794 he joined his friend Charles Willson *Peale and others in founding a short-lived artists' society, and in 1805 he participated in establishing the *Pennsylvania Academy of the Fine Arts. He later served as a director for more than twenty years. A ship carpenter's son, in 1771 Rush was apprenticed for three years to woodcarver Edward Cutbush, an emigrant from London. After serving in the Revolutionary War, Rush became renowned for ship figureheads, which enhanced the city's international preeminence in that craft. His first important extant sculptures, over-life-size female figures symbolizing *Comedy* and *Tragedy* (on loan to Pennsylvania Academy, 1808), were commissioned by architect Benjamin Henry Latrobe for niches on the facade of his remodeled Chestnut Street Theater. Like most of Rush's wood sculptures (as well as some terra cottas), these were originally painted to simulate stone. Despite their fussily ornate drapery, the pieces demonstrate strengths then rarely visible in American sculpture, including control of anatomical substance and classical contrapposto, a sense of movement, rich patterns of light and shade, and knowledge of prototypes in old master sculpture and painting. Rush's artistic development benefited from antique sculpture casts recently acquired by the Pennsylvania Academy and from a small number of locally available works by Jean-Antoine Houdon, Giuseppe *Ceracchi, and other foreign-born visitors or residents. In addition, during the early 1790s Rush had received some instruction in clay and wax modeling from Joseph *Wright. The success of the theater sculptures led almost immediately to Rush's commission for the *Water Nymph and Bittern* (also known as *Allegory of the Schuylkill River*; now destroyed, 1809; bronze cast, Fairmount Park, Philadelphia, 1854) that splashed water into a prominent landmark, the fountain in Center Square in front of Latrobe's pump house. The monumental water nymph demonstrates Rush's rapid progress in creating more unified visual experience. His simplified drapery now appropriately clings wetly to the full-bodied female figure. Although Rush never lost a fondness for decorative embellishment, he nevertheless admired the early nineteenth century's *neoclassicism. His allegorical figures of the *Schuylkill Chained* and the *Schuylkill Freed* (both Philadelphia Museum, c. 1828), made to adorn Latrobe's Fairmount Waterworks on the Schuylkill River, adapt classical river gods to an American iconography. Although nearly all of Rush's large figural sculptures portray allegorical subjects, he also carved a life-size standing *George Washington* (Independence Hall, Philadelphia, 1814), melding realism with classical elements. Most of Rush's other portraits are terra cotta busts. Combining naturalistic features and vivid characterization with delicacy of form and surface, the best recall Houdon's precedents.

Russell, Andrew Joseph (1830–1902). Photographer. He remains particularly associated with railroads, which he photographed during the Civil War and, afterward, in the West. Born in Nunda, in western New York State, Russell worked as a young man as a photographer in New York. During these early years of his career, he also painted landscapes and occasionally other subjects. During the Civil War he served as a captain in the U.S. Military Railroad Construction Corps, and in that capacity photographed the technological underpinnings of the conflict. In 1868 Russell was hired by the Union Pacific Railroad to document its progress in laying rails across the West. That year and the next, Russell produced a stunning record of the work that united the continent, a feat with both practical and symbolic implications. Russell organized the vacant landscapes into large, abstract patterns, with the rail bed frequently leading the eye into the distance. The splendor and vastness of the region's natural phenomena play against human will and the seemingly relentless progress of technology. As counterpoint, he often included tiny, faraway figures that serve as spatial markers or meditative reminders of human frailty. Russell was there, at Promontory Point, Utah, to record the celebration on 10 May 1869, when teams working from east and west met to unite their efforts. Later that year the railroad published *The Great West Illustrated in a Series of Photographic Views across the Continent*, including fifty of his prints. Russell subsequently returned permanently to New York, where he photographed for newspapers and other periodicals.

Russell, Charles Marion (1864–1926). Sculptor, painter, and illustrator. Also a writer. A resident of Montana throughout his adult life, he specialized in western subjects. His cowboys, Indians, and hunters personified the romance of frontier and wilderness. Russell's embrace of individualism, adventure, and courage appealed to an increasingly urbanized population around the turn of the century, when the action-packed, outdoor life he depicted was vanishing. Born in the Oak Hill neighborhood of St. Louis, Russell departed as a teenager for Montana, where he worked as a trapper and cowboy while pursuing his interests in sketching and modeling. The experience of living for six months in 1888 among Canadian Indians provided insights into their way of life. Without formal artistic training, Russell endeavored to record the activities he observed. He further enhanced the authenticity of his work by collecting for reference artifacts of the Old West. He published his first magazine illustration in 1888 and subsequently regularly provided drawings for magazines and books. In 1893 he began working as a full-time artist in the area of Great Falls, where he settled in 1897. After years of modeling in wax, he had his first bronze cast in 1904. Buoyed in part by Frederick *Remington's previous success with western subjects, around this time Russell also began to enjoy a national reputation, which only increased with Remington's death in 1909. In 1912 his mural depicting Lewis and Clark's encounter with the Flathead Indians was installed in the state capitol at Helena.

Eventually he achieved particular popularity among Hollywood celebrities and had begun to build a house in Pasadena before he died in Great Falls. For the last two decades of his life, he summered at a cabin on Lake McDonald in Glacier National Park, often in the company of other artists and writers. His Great Falls home and adjacent log cabin studio are National Historic Landmarks, administered by the nearby C. M. Russell Museum, which presents his work in the context of other regional artists. He began publishing short stories in 1897. Collections of these, along with essays, appeared as *Rawhide Rawlins Stories* (1921), *More Rawhides* (1925), and *Trails Plowed Under* (1927).

Russell, Morgan (1886–1953). Painter and sculptor. An originator of *synchromism, he numbered among leaders of an international avant-garde for a few years in the 1910s. Born in New York, he studied architecture for two years before turning to sculpture. Between 1906 and 1908 he worked at the *Art Students League and the New York School of Art (now Parsons, the New School for Design). James Earle *Fraser and Robert *Henri numbered among his teachers. He had already visited Europe twice when he settled in Paris in 1909. There he studied briefly with Matisse, became enamored of Cézanne, and gradually abandoned sculpture for painting. In 1911, in a color theory class taught by Canadian painter Ernest Percyval Tudor-Hart, he met Stanton *Macdonald-Wright. Together, the next year they formulated synchromism. Russell's 1913 *Synchromy in Green* (destroyed), the first exhibited synchromist work, included representational elements, but within months Russell's work approached pure abstraction. Starting with drawings of Michelangelo's sculpture, particularly the torqued *Dying Slave*, he abstracted the forms into planes of solid color. The resulting nonobjective paintings convey in forceful color patterns something of the muscular energy inherent in Michelangelo's work. Russell moved on to abstractions that did not originate in figure studies, but he continued to prefer thickly painted wedges and shafts of strong color. Circular forms occasionally appear, as in *Cosmic Synchromy* (Museum of Art, Munson-Williams-Proctor Arts Institute, Utica, New York, 1913–14). In 1915 he returned temporarily to sculpture. By 1920 he had isolated himself in a small French town, which remained his home for many years. During the 1920s he titled some of his paintings with the synchromist label, but in later years he returned to the figure. After about 1930, he devoted much of his work to Catholic religious themes. In 1946 he returned to the United States to settle in the Philadelphia suburb of Ardmore. He died in a nursing home in nearby Broomall, five years after a stroke limited his ability to paint.

Ryan, Anne (1889–1954). Collage artist, painter, and printmaker. Also a writer. Known principally for small collages, Ryan found inspiration in the work of the German artist Kurt Schwitters, whose work she first encountered in 1948. Born in Hoboken, New Jersey, Ryan enrolled at the College of St. Elizabeth in nearby Morristown but left during her junior year to marry William J. McFadden. She initially directed her creativity toward fiction and poetry. After her marriage ended in the 1920s, she worked for two years in Europe as a freelance writer. During this time, she lived primarily on the island of Majorca but also traveled to Paris and other cities. Upon her return in 1933 she settled permanently in Greenwich Village. With the encouragement of artist friends who shortly became known as *abstract expressionists, in the late 1930s Ryan began to paint. After turning to printmaking in 1941 at *Atelier 17, she soon specialized in color wood engravings. The intimate collages she produced during her last six years combine a fine sense of unregimented abstract design with colors, textures, and emotional associations she found in papers and fabrics. *Collage, 256* (Museum of Modern Art, 1949) combines linear elements of string with shapes from cloth and papers, both colored and printed. She suffered a stroke while working in her studio and died less than a month later at a son's home in Morristown. Ryan brought out a book of poetry, *Lost Hills*, in 1925 and continued to publish short fiction throughout her life.

Ryder, Albert Pinkham (1847–1917). Painter. Also a poet. Lustrous, visionary, and unprecedented, his paintings beckon to a reality beyond appearances. Nature's elemental forces provide a constant reference point, with images of the sea, often moonlit, among his most powerful creations. Without illustrating them directly, he often drew themes from literary or biblical sources. While revitalizing the romantic tradition, he also heralded aspects of modernism in his simplified and abstracted forms, his self-willed individualism, his preference for expression over technical proficiency, and his psychologically perceptive embrace of memory and imagination. Despite reclusive habits and indifference to material success, he found admiration from other artists and a few collectors who assured a modest income. Even during his lifetime the forgeries that outnumber his securely documented works began to appear. He exhibited in the *Armory

Show and directly inspired such later painters as Marsden *Hartley and Jackson *Pollock. Born in New Bedford, Massachusetts, then the world's most active whaling center, Ryder was troubled from childhood with eye problems. He ended his formal education with grammar school but nevertheless acquired an extensive knowledge of literature. A pious family background presumably stimulated his nondoctrinal and mystical religious sensibility. Ryder apparently began painting on his own. After moving with his family to New York between 1868 and 1870, he turned for his earliest professional training to painter and engraver William Edgar Marshall (1837–1906), who had studied with Asher B. *Durand in New York and with Thomas Couture in Paris. Although primarily a portrait painter, Marshall must have impressed his pupil with his own deep-seated belief in art as a repository of spiritual meaning. In 1871 Ryder gained admission to the *National Academy of Design, where he intermittently studied drawing for four years with Lemuel Everett Wilmarth (1835–1918), a still life and *genre specialist who had trained in Munich and Paris. During his academy years, Ryder established lasting friendships with a number of fellow students who went on to major careers, notably J. Alden *Weir. In the mid-1870s, Ryder's maturing style owed much to the example of such French-oriented contemporaries as William Morris *Hunt, John *La Farge, and Louis Comfort *Tiffany, with their interests in painterly colorism, exotic subjects, *japonisme, and the *aesthetic movement. Some months after it was organized in 1877, Ryder joined other vanguard artists in the *Society of American Artists. In 1877 Ryder's first trip abroad took him to London and briefly to Amsterdam. During a second, five-month trip in 1882 he toured the Continent and visited North Africa. Unlike most of his successful late-nineteenth-century American contemporaries, Ryder never studied in Europe, but he found there what he needed in old master painting and an expanded acquaintance with the work of congenial living or recently deceased artists, especially Jean-Baptiste-Camille Corot, Jean-François Millet, Adolphe Monticelli, and Matthijs Maris. The next two decades proved Ryder's most productive, and most of his best-known works come from this period. Their precise chronology is impossible to establish, however, as scholars remain uncertain about the dating of individual works. Ryder typically worked on paintings over long periods of time, he did not date them, and he kept no records.

As his creative powers flourished, he increasingly withdrew into a solitary existence dedicated to his art. In the late 1880s he stopped exhibiting. He deviated from a secluded life in Greenwich Village only twice, in 1887 and 1896, each time to spend a few weeks in London. From the early 1880s he relied increasingly less on observation. Turning away from the *Barbizon-inspired landscapes and animal scenes that had been his primary interest, he began to concentrate on invented subjects. He regularly adopted themes derived from conventionally admired literature, including Shakespeare's plays, English pastoral poetry, earlier nineteenth-century British romanticism, the Bible, and other disparate sources including the works of Henry Wadsworth Longfellow, Edgar Allen Poe, and Chaucer. However, reflecting contemporary international symbolist tendencies, Ryder's suggestive paintings center on atmosphere and mood, rather than dramatic incident or narrative plausibility. As he pushed the technique of oil painting almost to its limits of glazing and scumbling (and sometimes beyond, as subsequent deterioration has revealed), he gave to the multilayered, glowing paint surface a role in the emotive content of his generalized and patterned forms. Whether pastoral or violent, distilled nature plays a central part in amplifying human content. Many paintings emphasize emotional tenderness, as in the transitional *Spring* (Toledo [Ohio] Museum of Art, late 1870s). Mediating between perceived reality and ecstatic dream, its glowing landscape forecasts a large number of idylls that fuse figures (in this case a woman holding a small child) and outdoor settings. In an especially heartbreaking vision, the tiny *Dead Bird* (Phillips Collection, date uncertain) stands among Ryder's most poignant creations. Combining empathetic scrutiny with allusive overtones to literary and religious symbolism, the life-size, isolated, and tenderly studied bird points to the vulnerability of all life as it translates particular experience into universal motif. Other paintings invoke the fury of nature to emphasize mankind's helplessness in the face of fate. A particularly effective example, *Jonah* (Smithsonian American Art Museum, begun in the mid-1880s) draws on precedents in the work of Rembrandt, Delacroix, and J. M. W. Turner to illustrate the Old Testament parable. Jonah flounders in terror among huge waves that threaten to overturn his boat and overwhelm his mariner companions. Below the figure of God presiding in the sky, a whale bears down on the doomed prophet. Melodramatic, the image nevertheless connotes spiritual adversities and the possibility of redemption. Less tumultuous but thematically related, *Toilers of the Sea* (Metropolitan Museum, early 1880s) pictures a small sailboat about to crest a wave under a moonlit sky. Its title echoing a Victor Hugo novel, the painting emblematizes in reduced but richly painted forms the human journey through the unknown. When he exhibited the painting in 1884, Ryder accompanied it with a short original poem, one of numerous examples expanding upon the spirit of particular works. He also produced independent verses and published a few during his lifetime. As he aged Ryder's health declined, and little new work appeared after about 1900. Following a collapse in 1915, friends took him into their home in Elmhurst, on Long Island, where he died. The *Metropolitan Museum of Art hosted a memorial exhibition in 1918, and Ryder soon joined Thomas *Eakins and Winslow *Homer as the iconic American artists of their generation.

Ryman, Robert (1930–). Painter and printmaker. His personal variation on *minimalism features painterly, expressive brushwork within a format limited to square supports and white paint. Although he occasionally deviates from this approach, for the most part he has honored these restrictions for more than forty years. His subtle variations in hue, texture, scale, along with relationships of edges to brush marks, suffice to create meditations on the traditional concerns of painting and on the conceptual underpinnings of contemporary abstraction. Born in Nashville and almost entirely self-taught as an artist, in 1948 Robert Tracy Ryman entered Tennessee Polytechnic Institute in Cookeville, about fifty miles to the east. He returned the following academic year to Nashville to study music at the George Peabody College for Teachers (now part of Vanderbilt University). In late 1950 he enlisted in the U.S. Army (he was assigned to a band) and after discharge early in 1952, settled permanently in New York to pursue his desire to become a jazz musician. From his earliest paintings, made in 1953, he concentrated on examining the fundamentals of his craft, soon creating monochrome works that extended *abstract expressionism's intuitive gesturalism, while also reacting against its lack of discipline and its psychological content. Characteristic all-white works made his reputation in the mid-1960s. In 1961 Ryman married Lucy *Lippard, but they divorced several years later. In 1969 he married abstract painter Merrill Wagner (1935–). Born in Seattle, in 1957 she received a BA from Sarah Lawrence College in Bronxville, New York, before continuing her studies at the *Art Students League.

Ryther, Martha. *See* KANTOR, MORRIS.

S

Sargent Shahn Stuart Smithsonian Institution Saint-Gaudens Stella Stieglitz Saul Steinberg

Saar, Alison. *See* AFRICAN-AMERICAN ART.

Saar, Betye. *See* AFRICAN-AMERICAN ART.

Saar, Lezley. *See* AFRICAN-AMERICAN ART.

Sage, Hetty. *See* BENBRIDGE, HENRY.

Sage, Kay (1898–1963). Painter. Also a poet. A surrealist, she realized hallucinatory visions in a crisp, severe style. Born in Albany, New York, Katherine Linn Sage spent most of her childhood and young adulthood in Europe, except for the World War I years, when she took classes at the Corcoran School of Art (now Corcoran College of Art and Design) in Washington, D.C. Although she also had some instruction in Rome in 1920, she otherwise remained largely self-taught as an artist. While married to an Italian prince from 1925 to 1935, she lived in Rome and Rapallo, published poetry, and made the transition in her painting from a representational style to one influenced by Giorgio de Chirico's metaphysical voids. In 1937 she moved to Paris. Soon accepted into surrealism's inner circle, she particularly admired Yves *Tanguy's enigmatic works. Her mature paintings reverberate with Tanguy's vast and melancholy spaces, but she pursued her own eerie iconography. Typically, she measured out her landscapes with incoherent, often damaged architectural elements. These sometimes combine with geometrically precise natural forms, such as rocks, or with fragments of drapery. A strong, clear light usually illuminates her desolate vistas drained of all but the most subdued color. The foreboding *No Passing* (Whitney Museum, 1954) depicts a line of slablike towers receding to the horizon, in combination with a few wisps of drapery and numerous menacingly sharp sticks and other fragments. As World War II broke out, Tanguy followed her to New York, and they married in 1940. The following year, they settled permanently in rural Woodbury, Connecticut. After Tanguy died in 1955 and cataracts began to impair her eyesight soon afterward, Sage lived reclusively. In these later years she experimented with assemblages but turned much of her creative energy to poetry, publishing four volumes between 1957 and 1962. Weighed down nevertheless by depression and alcoholism, she took her own life. An autobiographical account of her early life appeared in a 1996 bilingual edition as *China Eggs/Les Oeufs de porcelaine*.

Saint-Gaudens, Augustus (1848–1907). Sculptor. The foremost American sculptor by the time he was about thirty, he created several of the period's most imposing public monuments. He also produced many small-scale works, including several dozen noteworthy relief portraits. Usually cast in bronze, his naturalistic yet elegant, technically adroit pieces seamlessly fuse real and ideal in refined detail, fluid contours, texturally variegated surfaces, and shadows contrasting with highlights. Born in Dublin, Saint-Gaudens (sometimes spelled without the hyphen) arrived about six months later with his parents in the United States. He grew up in New York, where in 1861 he began his training as a cameo cutter. During evenings he took classes at Cooper Union and then at the *National Academy of Design. The first American sculptor to train in Paris, he departed in February 1867 and was admitted to the École des Beaux-Arts just over a year later. In September 1870 he left Paris for a sojourn in Limoges before continuing on to Rome. Except for about a year in New York in 1872–73, he resided there until 1875. While in Rome, he tried his hand at painting and in 1872 modeled his first life-size work, a pensive, seated marble *Hiawatha* (private collection, on loan to the Metropolitan Museum, 1874–75), reflecting Rome's prevailing *neoclassicism.

After returning to New York, he worked on decorative projects for the studio of Louis Comfort *Tiffany and assisted John *La Farge on several projects, including the murals for Trinity Church in Boston. In association with other progressive artists, in 1877 he helped to found the *Society of American Artists. Awarded in 1876, his first important commission, the *Farragut Monument* (Madison Square Park, New York, 1881) was modeled during another sojourn in Paris from 1877 to 1880. Initiating his practice of collaborating with architects on the settings for his public monuments, in Paris he worked with architect Stanford White on design of the pedestal as well as a landscaped enclosure (later destroyed). The monument features a bronze portrait of the Civil War admiral standing on a curved bluestone base carved with female personifications of Loyalty and Courage in flowing low relief. Its unveiling in 1881 established Saint-Gaudens among the most significant artists of the era and its outstanding sculptor. By this time, he had synthesized his varied early experiences into a distinctive personal style. Cameo cutting trained him for finely detailed work, especially in relief. Paris provided technical expertise and the Beaux-Arts taste for dramatic form, graceful realism, and the appearance of spontaneity. In Italy he came to appreciate early Renaissance sculpture, as well as classical precedents, positioning him to become a major contributor to the *American Renaissance. His collaborations with other creative young artists strengthened a predilection for the opulence and refinement of the *aesthetic movement. Applied to his American subjects, Saint-Gaudens's fusion of these disparate sources won accolades as an independent, native sculptural expression. His work eventually received warm recognition in France as well.

The success of the Farragut memorial stimulated commissions for a succession of public monuments. The next year he was already at work on preliminary studies for the monumental *Shaw Memorial* (Boston Common; officially commissioned 1884), although it was not completed until 1897. Framed in a classicizing stone setting by architect Charles Follen McKim, the bronze monument presents an almost completely three-dimensional equestrian portrait of Civil War colonel Robert Gould Shaw against a lower-relief depiction of sixteen individualized marching soldiers. These represent the Union's first African-American volunteer regiment, which Shaw commanded until his death in battle. An unprecedented amalgam of equestrian monument and narrative relief, the image includes also an allegorical Victory floating above. A timeless counterpoint to the realism of the troops, the apparition invokes peace and remembrance. The Civil War and martyrdom similarly provided subtexts for Saint-Gaudens's bronze *Abraham Lincoln* (Lincoln Park, Chicago, 1884–87). The standing president, head bowed, redefined the ungainly war commander into a brooding tragic hero. Behind him, a vacant chair, designed by White (along with the granite base), provides dynamism to the composition, suggesting that Lincoln has just risen, but its emptiness also reinforces the idea of loss. Sorrow also informs another important collaboration with White, the *Adams Memorial* (Rock Creek Cemetery, Washington, D.C., 1886–91). Commissioned by writer and historian Henry Adams for his wife's grave, it features a hooded, seated figure, poignantly embodying grief. In 1891 White commissioned one of Saint-Gaudens's landmark sculptures, the gilded nude *Diana*, for the tower of his Madison Square Garden, then the tallest structure in Manhattan. The original eighteen-foot version (lost; 1891) was replaced two years later by a thirteen-foot reduction (Philadelphia Museum, 1893), better scaled to the architecture and light enough to turn in the wind. His only important nude and a signal work of the American Renaissance, it reinterprets the classical ideal in lithe, lively form. Saint-Gaudens's last major public monument brilliantly recapitulates his technical and conceptual strengths. Set high upon a pink granite base designed with McKim, the gilded *General Sherman Led by Victory* (Fifth Avenue and Fifty-ninth Street, New York, 1903; modeled 1891–1900) depicts the Civil War leader on horseback, preceded by a winged Victory. As draperies swirl about both figures, she propels the group forward in the direction of her uplifted right arm. In the other hand she holds the palm of victory. Exalted by the dynamic beauty of Saint-Gaudens's imagery and formal structure, the honored hero moves from the realm of earthly battles to his place within the sweep of history.

Concurrently with highly visible projects, Saint-Gaudens produced more intimate pieces as well. In numerous innovative relief portraits, he drew on early Renaissance precedents, perfecting a painterly approach that employed subtle gradations in depth to create atmospheric illusions. One of the best known, the circular *Robert Louis Stevenson* (Metropolitan Museum, 1910; modeled 1887–88), depicts the author propped on pillows while writing in bed, as he often did after contracting tuberculosis. The finely detailed profile head to the right of center balances lines of poetry inscribed in the vacant space above his bent knees. Saint-Gaudens's private work also included decorative projects, notably for the Henry Villard Houses (1881–83) on Madison Avenue and for Cornelius Vanderbilt II's Fifth Avenue mansion, where his friend La Farge was in charge of interior embellishment. There, the central feature of Saint-Gaudens's entrance hall, a huge fireplace mantel (Metropolitan Museum, 1881–83) in marble, oak, and mosaic, employs a decorative classicism to lavish effect. Paired, nearly life-size female caryatids in Greek-inspired dress support either side of an architectural arrangement of pilasters and friezes, with a mosaic of Saint-Gaudens's design in the center. Despite prodigious creative output, Saint-Gaudens taught at the *Art Students League and in his own studio, becoming one of the era's most important art instructors and mentors. He traveled to Paris in 1889 and again resided there from 1897 to 1900. By the time of his final return to the United States, Saint-Gaudens already knew that he had cancer, but he continued working until the last year or so of his life. In 1885 the sculptor had purchased a summer home in Cornish, New Hampshire. In 1900 this became his principal residence, and he died there. Today it honors his memory as the Saint-Gaudens National Historic Site.

A little more than a year before he died, Saint-Gaudens began compiling *The Reminiscences of Augustus Saint-Gaudens.* Edited and augmented after his death by his son **Homer Saint-Gaudens** (1880–1958), with the assistance of Royal *Cortissoz, it appeared in two volumes in 1913. Born in Roxbury, near Boston, Homer graduated from Harvard in 1903. After working in journalism and in the theater, from 1922 until 1950 he headed the fine art division of the Carnegie Institute (now Carnegie Museum of Art) in Pittsburgh. In 1941 he published *The American Artist and His Times.* Augustus's brother, sculptor **Louis St. Gaudens** (1854–1913), preferred a variant form of the family name. Born in New York, he took drawing classes at the National Academy of Design before learning the technique of cameo cutting from Augustus during his elder brother's return visit to New York in 1872–73. He accompanied Augustus back to Rome and subsequently, while Augustus resided in Paris, he studied at the École des Beaux-Arts from 1878 to 1880. Following their return to New York, Louis worked under Augustus's direction on important commissions, but on his own also produced architectural decorations, a few freestanding public sculptures, and other works. After marrying in 1898, he lived in Flint, Ohio, his wife's hometown until 1900, when he settled permanently in Cornish. Louis's wife, sculptor **Annetta Johnson St. Gaudens** (1869–1943), born and raised on a farm, studied art in Columbus before enrolling for two years at the *Art Students League. There her future brother-in-law numbered among her instructors, and she became his assistant in 1894. After she and Louis moved to Cornish, she again assisted Augustus, as well as her husband, and only after their deaths turned full attention to her own art. Working in marble and bronze, as well as terra cotta, she executed portraits, monuments, and garden sculpture. Active in conservationist, temperance, and suffragist movements, she often incorporated themes related to her convictions into her work. In later years, she lived in Denver and then in Pomona, California, where she died.

Saint-Mémin, Charles Balthazar Julien Févret de (1770–1852). Painter, draftsman, engraver, and museum director. Almost exclusively a portraitist, he is known for detailed profile likenesses set against blank backgrounds. For accuracy, he used a French mechanical invention known as a physiognotrace to establish the contours of the sitter's face at nearly life size. He then modeled interior details using black and white chalks to achieve delicate sculptural effects on the tinted paper he favored. For many of his customers, he also produced supplementary mementos by engraving two-inch circular copies, reduced with another mechanical aid, the pantograph. Saint-Mémin's hundreds of clients included such notables as George Washington, Thomas Jefferson, John Adams, Charles Willson *Peale, and the explorers Meriwether Lewis and William Clark. Between 1804 and 1807 he also produced valuable records of eight American Indians, who visited Washington as delegates from western tribes. A few watercolor portraits and landscapes from his hand also survive. Born in Dijon, in 1790 Saint-Mémin fled France's Revolutionary turmoil. Following a period in Switzerland, he arrived in New York in 1793. At first he engraved city views and maps, but in 1796 went into the portrait business with another Frenchman, Thomas Bluget de Valdenuit (1763–1846), who introduced Saint-Mémin to the use of the physiognotrace. After his partner returned to France about a year later, Saint-Mémin was assisted for several years by another French emigré, Louis Lemet (c. 1779–1832), who later worked on his own. From 1798 until 1810 Saint-Mémin made his home in Burlington, New Jersey. Until 1803 he worked primarily in nearby Philadelphia but later journeyed also to Baltimore, Washington, Richmond, and Charleston, South Carolina. After a visit to France from 1810 until 1812, he lived in New York, working as an artist but no longer employing the physiognotrace. In 1814 Saint-Mémin returned permanently to his family home, renounced his American citizenship, and put an end to his professional artistic career. From 1817 until his death in Dijon, except for a brief period during the 1848 political upheavals, he headed the fine arts museum there.

Salle, David. *See* POSTMODERNISM.

Salmon, Robert (c. 1775–c. 1848/51). Painter. Known primarily for marine and shore scenes, he had already reached middle age when he arrived in the United States. Nevertheless, he contributed influentially for about fourteen years to the art life of Boston, where he lived in a shanty near the shore. There he cultivated a mode of vision that fed development of *luminism, as he variously documented the bustling commercial waterfront, recalled the coast of

Great Britain, or appealed to poetic fancy. Salmon was born near Whitehaven, Cumberland (now Cumbria), on England's northwest coast. His earliest known works date to about 1800. Before departing in 1828 for the United States, he worked primarily in Liverpool and in Greenock, on the Clyde, west of Glasgow. In Boston he created stage sets and large panoramic canvases, yet many of his paintings are tiny, often on panel. He is believed to have returned permanently to England in later years, but the circumstances of his death are not known. *Boston Harbor from Constitution Wharf* (United States Naval Academy Museum, Annapolis, Maryland, 1833) captures in meticulous detail sailing vessels, rowboats, and quayside activity at an early morning hour. As the sun rises above a hazy horizon, the glowing, Claudian sky and still, reflective water produce a transfixing mood. As in many of his works, Salmon's imported style, based on popular models in English and Dutch marine painting, seamlessly accommodates a local and recognizably American subject.

Samaras, Lucas (1936–). Painter, sculptor, photographer, and installation artist. Employing a wide range of materials and techniques, he follows the imagination where it takes him. Usually it follows a narcissistic route back to the self. His own body, experiences, and psychological tensions supply major themes. Often bizarre, frequently obsessive, his disturbing art extends the surrealist spirit, while also acknowledging the 1960s impulse to conflate art and life. Born in Kastoria, Greece, in 1944 he settled with his family in West New York, New Jersey, across the Hudson River from Manhattan. He was naturalized as a citizen in 1955. In 1959 he graduated from New Brunswick's Rutgers University, where he studied with Allan *Kaprow. There he also made the acquaintance of George *Segal, Robert *Whitman, and others he joined in *happenings. Until 1962 he continued his education with classes in art history at Columbia University, where Meyer *Schapiro numbered among his teachers. He also studied acting. From around 1960 he began to develop the constructions and *assemblages that first brought him recognition as an artist. Of particular importance, a series of boxes, variously altered, produce a range of effects. Some, like reliquaries, are covered in opulent materials, while pins, razor blades, or other menacing materials transform others into objects of terror. Interiors often reveal mirrors, photographs, texts, or intriguing finishes. In the late 1960s, he applied similar alterations to other ordinary items, such as chairs. When he moved into the city in 1964, he created *Room*, a gallery *installation evoking his prior boxlike bedroom studio in his parents' apartment. An 8 × 8 × 10-foot variation on enclosed spaces, *Mirrored Room* (Albright-Knox Art Gallery, Buffalo, New York, 1966), covered inside and out with mirrors, disrupts the approaching spectator's spatial orientation, and then, upon his entry, infinitely reflects the viewer's body in all directions. In 1969 Samaras began using a Polaroid camera to photograph himself, accenting unsettling effects. These Autopolaroids anticipated a more startling series of Phototransformations, which were Polaroids manipulated before the emulsion set, causing the image to distort, often grotesquely. Besides additional photographic experiments, later work continues to indulge the fantastic as it ranges from bronze sculpture through jewelry and sewn patchwork "quilts" to pastel drawings and most recently, digital movies.

Sample, Paul (1896–1974). Painter. While many of his earlier paintings include *genre elements, he became increasingly devoted to landscape, drawing on long familiarity with the hilly topography of New Hampshire and neighboring Vermont for many of his best-known, somewhat idealized scenes. His mature style features formal simplification and careful attention to compositional structure. Born in Louisville, Kentucky, during childhood Paul Starrett Sample moved frequently with his family. Before his graduation in 1921, he interrupted his education at Dartmouth College in Hanover, New Hampshire, to serve during World War I in the U.S. Merchant Marine. Subsequently, he studied painting privately with Jonas *Lie. In 1925 he moved to Los Angeles, where he worked for a year at the Otis Art Institute (now Otis College of Art and Design) before accepting a teaching position at the University of Southern California. In 1938 he returned to Dartmouth as artist-in-residence. During World War II, he served as an artist-correspondent for *Life* magazine, and afterward he was able to draw on his Depression-era experience as a *federal art project muralist when he received a number of private decorative commissions. Throughout these years he resided in Norwich, Vermont, where he remained after retirement from nearby Dartmouth in 1962. He died in a Hanover hospital. Among his finest evocations of the wintry season in that region, *Lamentations V:18 (The Fox Hunt)* (Addison Gallery of American Art, Phillips Academy, Andover, Massachusetts, 1938) offers a crisp depiction of hunters and dogs on a snowy hillside, almost certainly inspired by Pieter Brueghel the Elder's renowned *Hunters in the Snow* (Kunsthistorisches Museum, Vienna, 1565). Depicting figures in a rolling farm landscape, *Janitor's Holiday* (Metropolitan Museum, 1936) more clearly shares interests with regionalists among *American Scene painters. Although such paintings suggest nostalgic fondness for rural life, Sample's dignified work generally avoids the overt moralizing and false cheerfulness associated with much regionalism. He also painted industrial landscapes, factory workers, marine views, and portraits.

Sandback, Fred. *See* MINIMALISM.

Sandler, Irving (1925–). Art historian and critic. The primary chronicler of the unfolding history of art in New York since the 1950s, he has maintained an open-minded approach to the ebb and flow of forms and ideas over several decades. Particularly astute in his assessments of the *abstract expressionists and artists of the *New York school, he has maintained personal relationships with an extraordinary number of artists. His studio-based understanding of their goals and styles provides freshness and insight to his large-scale narratives. He has also worked on behalf of artists' organizations and public art, while teaching for many years, most notably for some three decades at the State University of New York at Purchase, where he remains an emeritus professor. A lifelong New Yorker, Irving Harry Sandler received his BA from Philadelphia's Temple University in 1948 and a master's degree in American history from the University of Pennsylvania in 1950. In 1976 he earned a PhD in art history from New York University. Fascination with contemporary New York art led to his first art world job in 1956, when he was appointed (in the words of one artist) as "manager of the Tanager," a cooperative gallery on Tenth Street, in the heart of New York's avant-garde community. In the same year he volunteered to look after affairs of the legendary abstract expressionist hangout known simply as The *Club, a position he retained until the organization disbanded in 1962. In the late 1950s and early 1960s, he regularly wrote art criticism for *Art News* and the *New York Post*. In 1972 he was instrumental in founding Artists' Space, an early alternative gallery. Since 1958 he has been married to **Lucy Freeman Sandler** (1930–), a prominent historian of medieval art. In addition to numerous essays in periodicals and exhibition catalogues, his publications include *The Triumph of American Painting: A History of Abstract Expressionism* (1970), *The New York School: Painters and Sculptors of the Fifties* (1978), *American Art of the 1960s* (1988), and *Art of Postmodern Era: From Late 1960s to Early 1990s* (1996), as well as monographs on Alex *Katz, Al *Held, Mark *di Suvero, neon light sculptor Stephen Antonakos (1926–), and others. In 2003 he published the memoir *A Sweeper-Up After Artists*.

Sargent, Henry (1770–1845). Painter. Reflecting the gracious lifestyle of Boston's early-nineteenth-century elite, his two best-known works number among early examples of American *genre painting. Sensitively handled light and space lend a meditative poetry to *The Dinner Party* (Museum of Fine Arts, Boston, c. 1821) and *The Tea Party* (Museum of Fine Arts, Boston, c. 1821–25). Depicting social gatherings in elegant federal-era interiors, these amply proportioned paintings demonstrate Sargent's awareness of French *neoclassical painting in their clearly articulated, illusionistic spaces and crisp definition of forms. At the same time, the paintings' warm tonalities and their air of comfortable domesticity suggest the seventeenth-century Dutch paintings he admired. Sargent also painted portraits as well as historical and religious subjects. Born in Gloucester, Massachusetts, he lived in Boston as a child. In 1793 he departed for London, where he studied for four years with Benjamin *West and received encouragement from John Singleton *Copley. After returning to Boston, he served in the military from 1799 until 1815 as well as in the Massachusetts legislature in 1812 and from 1815 until 1817. An advocate of American art, he actively contributed to the development of Boston's art life through personal and institutional initiatives.

Sargent, John Singer (1856–1925). Painter. A cosmopolitan expatriate, internationally celebrated, he exploited remarkable technical facility in an extraordinarily large body of varied work. Although famed for grand-manner portraits, he also painted notable landscapes and *genre scenes. Surpassed as a watercolorist by few artists, he brilliantly registered fresh visual experience in an audaciously free and coloristic style related to contemporary impressionism. In his mid-thirties he first tackled the mural commissions that subsequently absorbed much of his creative effort. These center on invented, allegorical subjects featuring ideal figures. Born to American parents in Florence, Sargent was educated by tutors, with occasional stints in private schools, as his parents restlessly moved around Europe. His mother, an amateur but avid watercolorist, provided his earliest artistic instruction. He studied for a year at the Accademia delle Belle Arti in Florence before enrolling in 1874 at Paris's École des Beaux Arts, where for three years he absorbed the academic tradition. Concurrently and more importantly, he worked with Émile-Auguste Carolus-Duran, a fashionable portraitist and muralist who encouraged him to paint from observation in a fluent and unfussy style. At the age of twenty, Sargent made the first of many Atlantic crossings. He spent more than four months taking in Philadelphia's Centennial Exhibition, traveling in the Northeast, and visiting Montreal, Niagara Falls, and Chicago. By 1878, when he exhibited the vivid *Oyster Gatherers of Cancale* (Corcoran Gallery) in Paris, he had mastered a fluid naturalism that captures effects of summer sunlight on the Breton shore. Although already indebted to impressionism, Sargent continued to find in the old masters, particularly Velázquez and Frans Hals, inspiration for his painterly approach. An atmospheric rendering of a dancer in a Spanish cafe, *El Jaleo* (Isabella Stewart Gardner Museum, Boston, 1882) captures effects of light and movement within a darkened interior. In addition to painting such subject pictures, during these years Sargent also began his career as a portraitist, demonstrating an extraordinary ability to capture individual likeness with lively flair and insight into personality. *Four Daughters of Edward Darley Boit* (Museum of Fine Arts, Boston, 1882) depicts the little girls in a family interior dominated by two enormous Chinese vases. In its asymmetrical design, attentiveness to Asian decor, and optical directness, it signals his interests in *japonisme, as well as the work of James Abbott McNeill *Whistler, Manet, and Degas. A flamboyant portrait exhibited in 1884 negatively affected Sargent's rising reputation in Paris. Depicting Madame Pierre Gautreau but exhibited as *Madame X* (Metropolitan Museum, 1883–84), the provocative image stimulated intense criticism. The subject's haughty demeanor, her unconventional pose with face in profile, the unnatural pallor of her dramatically bared arms and shoulders, and the composition's uningratiating spareness offended many viewers.

Career in jeopardy, Sargent heeded the encouragement of his friend Henry James to move to England. During the second of two extended visits to England in 1884 and 1885, preceding his permanent relocation in 1886, Sargent worked at Broadway, in the Cotswolds, at the invitation of Edward Austin *Abbey, one of a number of Americans who congregated in the village. Painted there, *Carnation, Lily, Lily, Rose* (Tate Britain, London, 1885–86) established Sargent's success in England. A large work picturing two white-frocked girls lighting Japanese lanterns as dusk falls on a flower-filled garden, it remains among Sargent's most decorative and appealing works. Like most of the artist's major works, although fresh and informal it represents a highly premeditated performance, extensively reworked during two seasons. Nevertheless, because it seemed "unfinished," English contemporaries regarded the work as impressionist. In fact, however, his work moved decisively toward impressionism's broken colors and fleeting effects only in the later 1880s, and he never fully adopted the French group's methods. He had known Monet for several years before they spent time together in Paris and Giverny in 1887. Painted in a style deeply responsive to the French artist's, Sargent's *Claude Monet Painting at the Edge of a Wood* (Tate Britain, London, 1887–89) documents their shared plein air activity and anticipates Sargent's extensive engagement with outdoor work. Concurrently, during the 1880s, in the United States as in England, Sargent continued to develop as a portrait painter. By the time he withdrew from this activity in 1907 (though he continued to produce occasional examples), he had entirely dominated the practice in both countries for more than a decade. Unsympathetic observers have accused Sargent of squandering his talent on the vanities of the rich. In his society portraits he was not above flattery, but he almost single-handedly modernized a stagnating genre. In his hands, the painterly tradition of van Dyke, Gainsborough, and Joshua Reynolds received a fresh infusion of vitality, freedom, and up-to-date glamour. The compelling originality of many individual likenesses, their striking evocation of personality, and his unfailingly nimble brushwork demonstrate the artist's serious intentions and his grasp of individuality in a new age. For more than thirty years, Sargent rendered such penetrating characterizations as the wistfully intelligent *Mrs. Charles Gifford Dyer* (Art Institute of Chicago, 1880) or wry and worldly *Henry James* (National Portrait Gallery, London, 1913). In other works, aristocratic style competes with character. In one of a series of complex group portraits completed around the turn of the century, the attractive, wealthy, married, and titled *Wyndham Sisters* (Metropolitan Museum, 1900) revel in opulence, but they nevertheless embody in their sensuality and alertness the spirited modernity of their cultured social milieu. While portraits absorbed most of his studio time, Sargent took advantage of his itinerant ways to paint landscapes and other picturesque subjects during summer excursions from London. Until World War I permanently interrupted his habits, he regularly visited the Continent, particularly the Alps and Italy, but also explored North Africa, the Near East, and the United States. After about 1900 he usually employed watercolor for his travel scenes, recording lush scenery, Venetian architecture, traveling companions at leisure, sometimes posed in exotic costumes, and other visually stimulating imagery. Seemingly holiday pictures that might have been painted as a form of relaxation, in fact the artist exhibited and sold these watercolors with care, creating a market for them and evidently considering them an important part of his artistic legacy. His fluid and lyrical technique, at once gorgeous and economical, often flourishes passages of nearly abstract brushwork.

Beginning in 1890, Sargent took on challenges of an entirely new sort. Responding to the enthusiasm for murals characteristic of the *American Renaissance, he subsequently devoted much energy to epic public art, in the process inverting his normal priorities. In smaller paintings, Sargent worked directly from perceptual experience, rarely accommodating literary or metaphorical overtones. However, ideas drove his ambitious mural schemes. The Boston Public Library cycle, commissioned in 1890 and serially installed in 1895, 1903, 1916, and 1919, examines the philosophical basis of Western religious thought. He also provided allegorical mural decorations for Boston's Museum of Fine Arts (1916–25) and for Harvard University's Widener Memorial Library (1922). While these architectural embellishments lack the panache of his easel work, they provide effective multifigure decoration of considerable intellectual sophistication. Stylistically, he drew eclectically from traditional and modern sources, including Baroque classicism, major currents in contemporary mural painting, particularly the widely admired work of French artist Pierre Puvis de Chavannes, and his own responses to contemporary theater and dance. In his only significant foray into history painting, *Gassed* (Imperial War Museum, London, 1919), he pictured nearly life-size British soldiers clinging one to another after being blinded in a World War I assault. To prepare for this commission from the British government, at age sixty-two he tolerated four months of hardship at the western front. Following Sargent's death in London, the art community gathered in force for a memorial service at Westminster Abbey. The next year large exhibitions honoring his achievement appeared on both sides of the Atlantic, at London's Royal Academy and New York's *Metropolitan Museum of Art.

Sarony, Napoleon. *See* TILE CLUB.

Sartain, John (1808–97). Printmaker and painter. Also a publisher. Among the finest print technicians of his day, he produced numerous illustrations for periodicals, as well as individual reproductions of many well-known paintings. As a painter, he specialized in portraits and miniatures. Born in London, he gained proficiency in mezzotint engraving and miniature painting before settling in Philadelphia in 1830. Active for decades in the cultural life of the city, he established the prominence of the Sartain name, which remained conspicuous there into the twentieth century. From 1848 to 1852 he published *Sartain's Union Magazine of Literature and Art*, where many of his own illustrations appeared, along with his commentary, as well as poetry, fiction, and essays from leading literary figures of the day. In 1886 Sartain published *Annals of the Sartain Tribe, 1557 to 1886*, while his memoir, *The Reminiscences of a Very Old Man* (1899), appeared posthumously. Four of Sartain's children followed him into artistic careers. **Henry Sartain** (1833–95), primarily a printer, worked largely in association with his father's enterprises. **Samuel Sartain** (1830–1906), who studied painting in France and Italy, exhibited portraits and *genre scenes but eventually turned primarily to engraving and printing. **William Sartain** (1843–1924) served in the Civil War and worked as engraver before an 1867 visit to Paris ignited his determination to become a painter. After study at the *Pennsylvania Academy of the Fine Arts and with Christian *Schussele, he followed Thomas *Eakins to Paris in 1869. In addition to visiting a number of other locations as well, the two friends spent nearly the entire first half of 1870 together in Spain. In Paris he studied with Léon Bonnat, while a four-month sojourn in Algeria fueled a long-term interest in Arab subjects. After returning to the United States in 1877, he settled permanently in New York, although for some time he commuted to Philadelphia to teach. Besides figural works, particularly orientalist scenes, he painted landscapes, often in a *tonalist mode. These frequently depicted the marshlands around Nonquitt, Massachusetts, where he regularly summered, or along the Manasquan River in New Jersey. The most prominent of the siblings, **Emily Sartain** (1841–1927), an accomplished painter and engraver, played a leading role in promoting artistic education and opportunities for women. Friend of Mary *Cassatt, Louisine *Havemeyer, and Eakins, she studied at the Pennsylvania Academy before traveling to Europe with Cassatt in 1871. After a winter in Italy, she worked principally in Paris until 1875, when she returned to Philadelphia. Progressive in her views regarding art education, from 1886 until 1919 she headed the Philadelphia School of Design for Women (now Moore College of Art and Design), while spending nearly every summer in Europe. Upon retirement, she relocated to San Diego, California, but continued regular sojourns abroad. She died on a visit to Philadelphia. Her niece, **Harriet Sartain** (1873–1957), Henry's daughter, succeeded Emily as leader of the Philadelphia School of Design for Women, where she herself had previously studied and taught. Remaining in the position until she retired in 1946, she became known as a spokesperson for broader and more democratic art education.

Satterlee, Walter. *See* DAINGERFIELD, ELLIOTT.

Saul, Peter (1934–). Painter and printmaker. His violent, vulgar, and abjectly sexual blend of *pop art and surrealism often acidly satirizes social conditions or political events. Born in San Francisco, he studied for two years at the California School of Fine Arts (now San Francisco Art Institute) before transferring in 1952 to Washington University in St. Louis. Following his graduation in 1956, he spent several years in Europe. In Paris he received encouragement from Roberto *Matta, whose work he admired. Abroad, he began to merge representation with styles of the modern masters, achieving a mischievous originality lacking the toxic goofiness of the characteristic work that emerged in the mid-1960s. Related to underground comic books of the period, as well as the spirit of California *funk art, this personal style features grotesque exaggeration, manic activity, and jarring colors. In the 1980s and 1990s he concentrated on an extended series of distorted portrait heads, some accompanied by texts in speech bubbles. Anticipating important aspects of Philip Guston's late figural work, his paintings also prefigure a taste among younger artists of recent years for unconstrained formal invention in combination with mass media imagery. After twenty years in Austin, where he taught at the University of Texas, he moved in 2000 to Germantown, New York, in the Hudson River Valley.

Saunders, Raymond. *See* AFRICAN-AMERICAN ART.

Savage, Augusta (1892–1962). Sculptor. Largely because much of her work was lost or destroyed, she is more remembered today for her community activism during the *Harlem Renaissance than for her art. During a difficult life, racism and persistent poverty limited artistic achievement, and many of her sculptures were never cast in permanent material. Born in Green Cove Springs, south of Jacksonville, Florida, Augusta Christine Fells graduated from high school in West Palm Beach and attended Tallahassee State Normal School (now Florida A&M University) for a year. After moving to New York, in 1921 she enrolled at Cooper Union, where she completed the four-year course of training in three years. Subsequently, she worked with Hermon *MacNeil and achieved some success in modeling likenesses of African Americans, including such leaders as W. E. B. Du Bois and Marcus Garvey. In 1923 she married attorney Robert L. Poston, a Garvey deputy in the Universal Negro Improvement Association, but he died at sea four months later, as he returned from work in Liberia. (First married at fifteen, she was soon left a widow with a child. Around 1915 she married carpenter James Savage, but they divorced after a short time.) Her best-known work, the 1929 *Gamin* (original plaster, Smithsonian American Art Museum), a realistic bust of an African-American youngster, won for its creator a fellowship that financed a trip to Europe. There, until the end of 1931, besides traveling, she studied in Paris with sculptor Charles Despiau, among others. Returning to New York during the Depression, she turned primarily to teaching. When the Harlem Community Art Center was organized in 1937 under her leadership, Savage was named to direct this workshop supported by a *federal art project. Adept at identifying talent as well as nurturing and promoting it, she was an important figure in the lives of a younger generation of artists, including Jacob *Lawrence and Norman *Lewis. In 1939 Savage left the art center to concentrate on a commission for the New York World's Fair. Her sixteen-foot-high *Lift Every Voice and Sing*, a tribute to the African-American musical heritage, featured the form of a harp melded with bodies of black choristers. Realized only in plaster (painted for the exposition to resemble dark stone), it was destroyed when the fair ended. Disillusioned by her own lack of critical success and the loss of federal support for the arts, in the mid-1940s she abandoned her art career and moved to the Hudson River Valley. There she taught art to children and worked on a mushroom farm in Saugerties. Near the end of her life, she returned to New York, where she died.

Savage, Edward (1761–1817). Painter, engraver, and museum proprietor. Born west of Boston, in Princeton, he apparently remained self-taught as an artist. His earliest efforts demonstrate admiration for John Singleton *Copley's work. Primarily a portrait painter, Savage worked in Boston between 1785 and 1789 and then in New York for two years. Drawn to London, presumably by the presence of Benjamin *West as well as the opportunity to learn printmaking skills, he remained abroad for approximately three years. Upon his return to the United States in 1794, he again resided in Boston for about a year before moving to Philadelphia, where he exhibited an early *panorama, a 130-foot depiction of London. In addition to resuming his portrait career, he also issued engravings and opened a gallery to display "ancient and modern paintings," including his own, as well as curiosities and inventions. In Philadelphia he also completed his best-known work, *The Washington Family* (National Gallery, 1789–96), a monumental group portrait of the first president, his wife, her two grandchildren, and Washington's slave William Lee. A bit stiff, the figures nevertheless suggest gracious informality as they pose within a grand interior overlooking a landscape vista. Issued later as an engraving that remained popular for several decades, the image numbers among the earliest attempts to domesticate the remote and iconic general. In 1801 Savage moved to New York but later returned to Boston, probably in 1810. In both locations, he reopened his gallery, to which he added natural history displays. He died at his farm in Princeton.

Saÿen, H. Lyman (1875–1918). Painter. Born in Philadelphia and trained as a scientist, as a young man Henry Lyman Saÿen excelled in electrical engineering and early X-ray technology. He began his study of art in 1899 at the *Pennsylvania Academy of the Fine Arts, where Charles *Grafly and Thomas *Anshutz numbered among his teachers. In 1906 when he left for eight years in Paris, he was a well-trained academic artist and illustrator. While studying with Matisse in 1908, he developed a bright fauve style. Composing with broad strokes of color, he painted Parisian street scenes. Returning to Philadelphia, he focused on landscapes of vividly colored, flattened patterns. In *Scheherazade* (Smithsonian American Art Museum, 1915), elements of a house and garden are barely distinguishable within a riot of energetically interacting colors. In his last two years, Saÿen moved toward a more complex and intellectually ordered manner of working. Compositions became flatter and color areas, more precisely bounded. He experimented with collage elements and trompe l'oeil patterns suggesting such materials as wallpaper. With their flat, interlocking compositions and sophisticated interaction of reality and illusion, these paintings paralleled French developments in Synthetic cubism. Within these works, unique in American practice of that time, Saÿen sometimes included motifs that related to his developing interest in American Indian art. His life cut short at the age of forty-three, Saÿen remained little known for the next half century.

Scanga, Italo. *See* NAUMAN, BRUCE.

Scaravaglione, Concetta Maria (1900–1975). Sculptor. A figurative artist specializing in depictions of women, she worked in many media, including stone, wood, and welded copper. Born in New York, she trained at the *National Academy of Design, the *Art Students League, and elsewhere before studying direct carving in 1924 with Robert *Laurent. In the 1930s she executed several pieces for the *federal art projects, and in 1947 she was the first woman to win the Prix de Rome, which allowed her to spend three years abroad. Her teaching career at several institutions culminated in a fifteen-year period at Vassar College in Poughkeepsie, New York. Upon her retirement 1967, she settled permanently in New York. Characteristically life-size or larger, Scaravaglione's sculptured women often are accompanied by children or animals. Forms are generalized into simple volumes that modernize traditional concerns for composition and structure. The dignified tenor of her work reflects an unsentimental appreciation for varied human experience.

Schamberg, Morton Livingston (1881–1918). Painter and photographer. The death of this versatile modernist in the 1918 influenza pandemic foreclosed one of the most promising careers of his generation. In less than a decade, he painted advanced color abstractions, pioneered in using mechanical imagery, helped to initiate sharp-focus modern photography, and contributed to *New York dada. His name is perhaps best known in connection with a notorious dada artifact, a small found-object sculpture sardonically titled *God* (Philadelphia Museum, c. 1916–18). Although he has traditionally been given credit as the fabricator, he may have collaborated on, or possibly he only photographed, this kitchen-sink plumbing trap mounted on wood. In any event, Schamberg had a hand in bringing it to life as a work of art. A Philadelphian, Schamberg trained as an architect at the University of Pennsylvania. Before receiving his degree in 1903, he had already taken up the study of painting with William Merritt *Chase, and in the fall of that year he entered the *Pennsylvania Academy of the Fine Arts. After graduating in 1906, he left for a year in Paris. (He had already spent three summers in Europe.) Upon his return, he shared a studio in Philadelphia with academy classmate Charles *Sheeler. Late in 1908, he again departed for Europe. Sheeler soon joined him for a few months, and together they experienced a decisive confrontation with modern art. After Schamberg's return in 1910 to Philadelphia, he shared a weekend house with Sheeler in Doylestown. To support themselves, in 1912 both took up photography (Schamberg specialized in portraits), and the following year both exhibited paintings in the *Armory Show. By this time Schamberg had already worked through a fauve-inspired period and had begun to develop a brightly colored form of cubist painting, which sometimes amounted to complete abstraction. (These works bear similarities to *synchromism, but Schamberg probably developed his style independently.) While continuing to live in Philadelphia but regularly visiting New York, around 1916 his painting took a revolutionary new tack. He was probably the first American to produce simplified and stylized images of machines, or mechanical-looking objects. Such works as *Mechanical Abstraction* (Philadelphia Museum, 1916) prefigure aspects of *precisionism. By this time, he had come to know the dada circle that gathered at Walter *Arensberg's New York apartment. *God*, which was acquired by the Arensbergs, represents his thorough understanding of the ironic tone that flourished in their circle. Schamberg's thinking about the machine as a metaphor for modern life may have been stimulated there by the work of Marcel *Duchamp and French artist Francis Picabia. Concurrently, along with Sheeler, he investigated photography's ability to capture structurally vigorous but emotionally cool images. He died in Philadelphia, two days before his thirty-seventh birthday.

Schapiro, Meyer (1904–96). Art historian, critic, and painter. Among the outstanding art historians of the twentieth century, he surpassed nearly all his colleagues in originality of thought and influence in the field. He also painted for pleasure throughout his career and often exhibited landscapes and figure studies. As well, he numbers among few scholars of his era who maintained strong and intimate connections to the New York art community. Variously teacher, mentor, and friend to artists and critics, he also counted many literary and intellectual figures among his acquaintances. Born in Siauliai, Russia (now Lithuania), Meir Schapiro arrived with his family at Ellis Island in 1907. He grew up in Brooklyn and remained permanently in New York. Interested in art even as a child, at an early age he took a class with John *Sloan. After graduating from Columbia University in 1924, he began graduate study in anthropology with his undergraduate mentor Franz Boas, but he soon switched to art history. In France in 1926 and 1927, he pursued groundbreaking research on the twelfth-century sculpture of the abbey church and cloister at Moissac. This work, the basis of his doctoral dissertation, established his professional credentials and elevated the Romanesque as a subject of art historical inquiry. He began teaching at Columbia in 1928, the year before receiving his PhD, and remained on the faculty until he retired in 1973. Despite his eminence as a medievalist, he remained interested in the art of all periods, particularly the modern era. In the 1930s, he participated in the left-wing *American Artists' Congress and was instrumental in the early 1940s in forming a nonpolitical alternative, the Federation of Modern Painters and Sculptors. As émigré European artists gathered in New York during World War II, he acted as an important conduit between them and their American counterparts. Arshile *Gorky, Allan *Kaprow, Roberto *Matta, Robert *Motherwell, Ad *Reinhardt, Lucas *Samaras, Irving *Sandler, Kurt *Seligmann, and Minor *White, as well as André Breton and Fernand Léger, number among those whose lives he directly touched. Besides slender monographs on van Gogh (1950) and Cézanne (1952), his publications include *Words and Pictures* (1973), treating illuminated manuscripts; *The Romanesque Sculpture of Moissac* (1985); and several volumes of collected essays and lectures, including compilations related to impressionism and to Picasso.

Schapiro, Miriam (1923–). Painter, printmaker, and collage artist. As an innovator in the *feminist art and *pattern and decoration movements, she holds a central place in the history of 1970s art. Her leadership in promoting women's neglected contributions and in championing ornament contributed to reorienting American art's priorities toward more pluralistic and aesthetically tolerant standards. Born in Toronto, she later lived in New York. There she enrolled in 1941 at Hunter College but after two years transferred to the State University of Iowa (now University of Iowa) in Iowa City. Following graduation in 1945, she stayed on to earn an MA in printmaking the following year and an MFA in painting in 1949. At Iowa she served as Mauricio *Lasansky's first studio assistant. Subsequently, she lived for two years in Columbia, Missouri, before returning in 1952 to New York. During the 1950s she painted in an *abstract expressionist style, which gave way in the 1960s to *hard-edge geometric work. In 1967 she moved to Southern California, where the period's nascent feminism affected her thinking. With Judy *Chicago, in 1971 she founded the Feminist Art Program at the California Institute of the Arts in Valencia. This program, the first of its kind, soon became a hotbed of revisionist thought and woman-centered artistic creativity. Schapiro's reevaluation of women's traditional crafts opened her eyes to decorative expression, leading to her first works of "femmage," a form of collage incorporating such common domestic materials as lace, buttons, embroidery, and sequins. In 1975 she returned to New York, where she participated enthusiastically in the pattern and decoration movement, while also continuing to promote women's art. She numbered among leaders of the collective that founded the feminist journal *Heresies*, first published in 1977. Since the late 1970s she has casually mixed elements of stylized representation, abstract decoration, and mixed-media fabrication in generally brightly colored, exuberant works combining the discipline of structure with the pleasure of opulent detail.

In 1946 Schapiro married painter, printmaker, and art critic Paul Brach (1924–2007), then also a student at Iowa. Born in New York, Paul Henry Brach served in the military during World War II and graduated from Iowa in 1948. He received his MFA there two years later. He, too, participated in the abstract expressionist milieu during the 1950s and later gradually simplified his painting toward poetic geometry. In the mid-1970s he initiated an extended series of Southwestern scenes. Subsequently he produced intellectually controlled, masterfully chromatic abstract works that sometimes allude to landscape. Throughout his career he published astute evaluations of fellow artists' work, in later years primarily in *Art in America*. Also a teacher throughout his career, he served on the faculty of several institutions before retirement in 1995. At the time of his death, Brach and Schapiro made their home near the eastern end of Long Island, in the Hamptons, where they had previously summered since the 1950s.

Scharf, Kenny. *See* POSTMODERNISM.

Schmidt, Katherine. *See* KUNIYOSHI, YASUO.

Schnabel, Julian. *See* POSTMODERNISM.

Schneeman, Carolee. *See* PERFORMANCE ART.

Schofield, Walter Elmer (1867–1944). Painter. An expatriate during most of his career as a landscape specialist, during frequent sojourns in the United States he painted American scenes, especially in the Delaware River Valley around *New Hope. Although contemporaries often identified him as an impressionist, he employed a vigorous, painterly realism to convey a sense of outdoor light and space. Like his friend Edward *Redfield, who worked in a similar style, he routinely painted outdoors, favored large canvases, and became known for winter scenes. As well, he painted marines, harbor views, and picturesque villages, particularly along the coasts of France and England. Characteristically sharp tonal contrasts energize the intimate woodland *Winter* (Pennsylvania Academy, c. 1899). Its snowy banks border a stream that reflects the season's pale light. Although the water here is placid, in many of Schofield's views, dashing brushwork mimics turbulent movement. A Philadelphia native, he studied at Swarthmore College but left before graduating to enroll at the *Pennsylvania Academy of the Fine Arts. During three years there, he encountered Robert *Henri and other realists whose interests went beyond the established conventions of impressionism. In 1892 he arrived in Paris, where he studied at the Académie Julian but soon also painted landscapes in the nearby countryside. From about 1895 he worked in Normandy and Brittany but in 1903 settled in the art colony of St. Ives in Cornwall, England, where he died.

Schrag, Karl (1912–95). Printmaker and painter. Known especially for semi-abstract, expressionistic landscapes, he also produced portraits and other figural subjects. Born in Karlsruhe, Germany, he studied art in Geneva and Paris before spending two years in Belgium. After moving to New York in 1938, he studied printmaking at the *Art Students League. In the 1940s he worked with Stanley William Hayter at *Atelier 17, then took over direction of the workshop when Hayter left the country in 1950. During his early years in New York, his work sometimes reflected the prevailing *American Scene interest in reporting on contemporary American life. His etching and aquatint *Madonna of the Subway* (1939) depicts a sweet young woman and her child, surrounded by the urban throng. Later, in both prints and paintings, he deployed energetic forms and lines to create exuberant landscapes, often specifically related to Maine where he summered for more than forty years on Deer Isle. As in *First Sunlight After Rain, No. 2* (1955), an etching, he employed color, often in brilliant tones, as a major expressive element. Schrag taught at Cooper Union from 1954 to 1968. He died at his home in Manhattan.

Schulze, Franz. *See* CHICAGO IMAGISM.

Schussele, Christian. *See* EAKINS, THOMAS.

Schütze, Eva Watson. *See* WATSON-SCHÜTZE, EVA.

Scudder, Janet (1869–1940). Sculptor. Notable for its lively naturalism, playful spirit, fine detail, and graceful forms, Scudder's best work dates from the period before the 1920s. Her *Young Diana* (1910), a charmingly lithe nude child, poses as the classical goddess with bow.

Like most of her popular works, it exists in multiple bronze copies, which were in demand as garden ornaments. Born in Terre Haute, Indiana, Netta Deweze Frazee Scudder adopted the first name of Janet while studying for three years at the Art Academy of Cincinnati. In 1891 she moved to Chicago, where she took classes at the School of the Art Institute of Chicago and soon was hired to assist Lorado *Taft. In the fall of 1893 she moved to Paris, where some months in the studio of Frederick *MacMonnies proved decisive to her development. In the summer of 1894 she left for New York but in 1896 returned to Paris and reinstated her connection with MacMonnies. Before she once more settled in New York in 1899, a trip to Italy brought her in touch with the Renaissance and antique sculpture that inspired her mature work. Collaborating in New York with architect Stanford White, she won favor among wealthy homeowners for her decorations. After 1913 she worked primarily at her villa near Paris, although she kept an apartment in New York for frequent visits and traveled elsewhere, as well. In later years, her sculpture became more static and stylized, and she also took up painting. She relocated to New York in 1939 and died the next summer while vacationing in Rockport, Massachusetts. Her autobiography, *Modeling My Life*, written with the assistance of Norval Richardson, appeared in 1925.

Sears, Sarah. *See* PHOTO-SECESSION.

Seeley, George (1880–1955). Photographer. A *pictorialist, he created exquisitely refined, luminous, soft-focus visions, suggesting moods and dreams. Enigmatic and indeterminate, they transport the viewer into an aestheticized realm belonging to history or to a timeless present. George Henry Seeley made his home all his life in his native town of Stockbridge, Massachusetts. He studied at the Massachusetts Normal Art School (now Massachusetts College of Art) in Boston between 1897 and 1902. Toward the end of this period, F. Holland *Day encouraged his interest in photography. For two years after his return to Stockbridge, he served as an art supervisor for local public schools. Later he worked as a correspondent for the Springfield, Massachusetts, newspaper, but for most of his life he had no regular job. Relatively isolated and disengaged, he devoted his life to photography, gardening, ornithology, oil painting, and other avocations. Seeley probably came to Alfred *Stieglitz's attention when his work was widely admired in a New York group exhibition in 1904. Stieglitz recruited him for the *Photo-Secession, showed his work at *291, and published his photographs in *Camera Work*. Much of Seeley's best work was done between about 1905 and 1910. After 1920 he curtailed his photographic activity. Compared to the work of many art photographers of his day, Seeley's is relatively straightforward. Although he posed his figural scenes and avoided sharp focus, his photographs are otherwise free of manipulation, as well as gimmicky printing. Most works depict people in repose, usually serene women, in domestic or, more often, landscape settings. They are frequently garbed in flowing gowns, vaguely classical in feel but not in detail. Subtly illuminated and organized in large tonal areas, "The Burning of Rome" (1906) presents two of his sisters in long, white dresses, seated in dappled sunlight, caught in a dual reverie of great loveliness. (The title presumably should be interpreted metaphorically.) Seeley also experimented with color photography within a year or so of the first public demonstration of the Autochrome process, in 1907. The delicately tinted "Still Life with Grapes" (c. 1908) confirms his skill in composition and lighting. Besides his figural works and such occasional still lifes, Seeley also made pure landscapes. In some, including the 1909 "Winter Landscape," patterns he found in nature approach abstraction.

Segal, George (1924–2000). Sculptor, painter, draftsman, and photographer. Known for plaster figurative sculptures usually depicting routine activities, he also was an early participant in *happenings. Most of his works combine one or more figures with other objects to create life-size tableaux. Cast from living models, his figures display an actuality made unsettling by their immobilized poses and introspective countenances. Although his work relates to *pop art's commonplace subjects and disrespect for distinctions between art and reality, Segal's fundamental concerns lay elsewhere. Thematically, psychologically, and formally, his work continues humanistic traditions. Metaphor and the poetry of form anchor his enterprise. He gave scant attention to consumer culture, except as it impacted his subjects' mental states. The tone of contemplation and individual isolation suggests his admiration for Edward *Hopper's paintings, while the additive nature of his works connects them to contemporary *assemblages. Segal also on occasion addressed social, historic, or political concerns, or created still-life arrangements. From the late 1960s he sometimes painted his figures, nearly always in a single color, and about a decade later began casting some work in bronze for outdoor settings. Born in the Bronx, he moved with his family in 1940 to a chicken farm near New Brunswick, New

Jersey, and lived nearby for the rest of his life. As a young adult, he developed his own adjacent farm. Segal's education extended over a period of more than twenty years, and his development as an artist was correspondingly slow, as he raised chickens, taught school, and painted expressionist canvases. He studied at Cooper Union in Manhattan, Rutgers University in New Brunswick, and Pratt Institute in Brooklyn before receiving his art education degree in 1950 from New York University, where Tony *Smith and William *Baziotes numbered among his teachers. In 1953 he befriended newly appointed Rutgers professor Allan *Kaprow, who put him in touch with John *Cage, Marcel *Duchamp, Meyer *Schapiro, and young artists moving beyond *abstract expressionism. In 1963 Segal completed an MFA at Rutgers.

In 1958, the year Kaprow staged his initial happening on Segal's chicken farm, Segal made his first sculptures out of chicken wire. A couple of years later, he had the idea of using newly available plaster-impregnated gauze bandages to wrap a figure and so obtain a cast. He used himself as the model for the first characteristic work, *Man at a Table* (Städtisches Museum Abteiberg, Mönchengladbach, Germany, 1961), a ghostly white figure seated at a real table before a window framework. Although the wrapping process might seem mechanical, to achieve the effects he desired Segal worked on the cast as it was drying and afterward. By the late 1960s he had complicated the procedure further by using the plaster shells as molds to achieve a subtler realism. Besides freestanding full figures, Segal also made evocative body fragments and relief sculptures. Well received when first exhibited in the early 1960s, Segal's signature approach remained relatively consistent, but variety in techniques and themes kept it fresh. The 1960s produced many of his most evocative works, generally occupational or domestic subjects. Later, for public venues, he addressed historic events, such as the Kent State massacre, the Stonewall riots, and the Holocaust. In 1997 he completed three ambitious groupings for the Franklin Delano Roosevelt Memorial near the Washington Mall. He also portrayed several biblical events, such as *Abraham's Farewell to Ishmael* (Miami Art Museum, 1987). A late portrait series indebted to the example of Rembrandt crowns his achievement as a draftsman. The subjects of his evocative photographs generally parallel his sculptural interests, picturing people in their environments. His daughter, painter and photographer **Rena Segal**, continues to live in the New Brunswick area. She graduated from New Jersey's Montclair State University in 1975 and earned an MFA at Rutgers two years later. Rarely encompassing figures, her paintings in recent years have centered on abstracted landscape motifs rendered with an impressionist touch.

Seitz, William C. *See* OP ART.

Seliger, Charles (1926–). Painter, printmaker, and draftsman. Born Charles Zekowski in New York, he grew up across the Hudson River, in Jersey City. Seliger left high school in the tenth grade and started painting on his own. He never received any formal art training but began to work under the influence of Kandinsky's early free-form abstractions. Through Jimmy *Ernst, who included Seliger's work in a 1943 gallery exhibition he organized, Seliger met the major surrealists and soon developed a personal variation on their approach. Two years later, he mounted his first one-person exhibition at Peggy *Guggenheim's *Art of This Century. Seliger's *biomorphic forms originally derived from plants and insects, but soon became more abstract as their visual complexity suggested metamorphic processes. With their intricate, jewel-like surfaces and mysterious forms floating in a shallow but indeterminate space, his paintings related to those of the emerging *abstract expressionists as well as those of committed surrealists. He has continued to refine this approach in paintings generally confined to small dimensions. As a printmaker, he is particularly known for monotypes.

Seligmann, Kurt (1900–1962). Painter, printmaker, and set designer. Born in Basel, Switzerland, he studied at art schools in Geneva and Florence before moving to Paris in 1929. After painting hard-edge abstractions early in his career, in the mid-1930s he gravitated toward surrealism. At this time he developed his characteristic, partially abstract figural style, often featuring wildly gyrating draperies. Creating effects of instability, fear, and pessimism, these works reflect disgust with the interwar political and military situation in Europe. He also made generally more serene sculptural objects. Particularly effective among these is a series of large bottlelike forms that sprout graceful human appendages. For several months in the summer of 1938, he lived in British Columbia in order to pursue ethnographic study of North American Indian art and life. After emigrating to the United States in 1939, he was naturalized as a citizen. In New York his controlled, image-based approach had little direct effect on the emerging *abstract expressionist vanguard, but he established a significant presence as an accomplished artist and teacher, active in affairs of the progressive art community. Sharing his scholarly temperament, he became a close friend of Meyer *Schapiro. In the early 1940s Seligmann's art became more cryptic, but no more optimistic, as it sometimes incorporated tornado-like forms moving through indeterminate landscapes. In his last years, he painted somber abstractions filled with stringy forms. A longtime student of the occult, in 1948 he published a classic study, *The Mirror of Magic*. In diminished health during his final years, he moved from New York to a farm at Sugar Loaf in the Catskills Mountains. He died outside his home there of a self-inflicted gunshot wound, which was officially ruled accidental.

Sellers, Anna. *See* PEALE, CHARLES WILLSON.

Selz, Peter. *See* FUNK ART.

Sepeshy, Zoltan L. (1898–1974). Painter. Best known for cityscapes and industrial landscapes, he sometimes recorded these subjects with straightforward, energetic realism, while in other cases he drew on cubist fragmentation to rearrange elements of the visual setting. One such painting, *Scranton Coal Chute* (Cranbrook Art Museum, Bloomfield Hills, Michigan, 1935), dynamically interprets a mining operation. As well, he created landscapes and figural compositions of energetic, interlocking forms depicting people in the activities of modern life. His late work included religious themes, and he also painted murals. Born in Kassa, Hungary (now Kosice, Slovakia), he trained as an artist in Budapest and Vienna. He emigrated to the United States in 1921, settling in Detroit after a short period in New York. For thirty-five years before his retirement in 1966, Sepeshy taught or served as an administrator at the Cranbrook Academy of Art in Bloomfield Hills, Michigan. In the thirteen years after 1946, he served as director, succeeding the founder Eliel Saarinen. He died in nearby Royal Oak.

Serra, Richard (1939–). Sculptor, draftsman, printmaker, and film and video artist. Best known for monumental steel abstractions, throughout his career he has emphasized the weight of materials and their interaction with specific spaces. While his work originated in the context of *minimalism, he also made important contributions to *process art. Born in San Francisco, in 1961 Serra received a BA in English from the University of California after study at the Berkeley and Santa Barbara campuses. From that fall until 1964, he studied at Yale University, earning BFA and MFA degrees. For the following two years he lived in Europe with Nancy *Graves (they married in 1965 but divorced five years later) before settling in New York. Upon his return, he started experimenting with the physical properties of nontraditional materials, such as rubber and fiberglass. In a group of Splash pieces executed between 1968 and 1970, he cast molten lead by sloshing it into corners or intersections of wall and floor. In 1969 he embarked on a series of large sculptures made from detached, weighty metal elements balanced to remain in place through gravity alone. In the same period, he also began experimenting with film and video. Before the mid-1960s Serra had worked primarily as a painter, and he has continued to pursue two-dimensional concerns in drawings and prints, primarily lithographs, defining simple images with aggressive draftsmanship. Serra became the object of public attention after his *Tilted Arc* (1981) was installed in lower Manhattan's Federal Plaza (also known as Foley Square), dividing the space it occupied. Many plaza-users found this rusty metal wall objectionable. After much controversy, in 1989 it was removed to storage, despite Serra's contention that the work's integrity depended upon its placement in the particular space for which it had been designed. Undeterred, Serra has continued to pursue ever-larger projects. As they have grown in ambition, they have also increasingly attained poetic force on an epic scale. First shown in 1997, a series of Torqued Ellipses (followed by Torqued Spirals) present curved sheets of two-inch-thick rolled steel in dynamic configurations. Inspired by an early 1990s visit to Francesco Borromini's Baroque masterpiece, the church of San Carlo alle Quattro Fontane in Rome, the sculptures bend and twist, encouraging the moving viewer to engage questions of perception and its links to time. Building on the success of these works, in 2004–5 Serra arranged a vigorously interrelated sequence of eight pieces, each some thirteen or fourteen feet in height, in a 430-foot gallery within the *Guggenheim Museum's Frank Gehry-designed Bilbao satellite. Claiming the entire space as a sculptural field, this singular theatrical installation titled *The Matter of Time* may long remain unmatched for ambition and impact.

Seymour, David. *See* CAPA, ROBERT.

Shahn, Ben (1898–1969). Painter, printmaker, photographer, book illustrator, and graphic designer. A close observer of modern life, in paintings and graphic works Shahn forged an ornamental yet directly expressive style combining description, formal abstraction, and linear eloquence. His photographs, nearly all from the 1930s, capture spontaneous human moments. Compositionally influenced by his training as an artist, his photographs in turn affected his painted imagery. Originating in left-wing political and social views, many of Shahn's most significant early works evoke empathy for victims of injustice. Around 1940 the artist began to think in more universal terms, emphasizing common human experiences over social meanings. As his art continued to deepen psychologically during World War II, he subsequently often found melancholy poetry in mythic or allegorical themes. Religious subjects, usually related to his Jewish heritage, also occur in his late work. Born in Kovno, Russia (now Kaunas, Lithuania), Benjamin Shahn grew up in Brooklyn after emigrating with his family in 1906. In 1913 he was apprenticed to a commercial lithographer, receiving training that would finance his studies and travel through the 1920s. He took evening classes to prepare for college, and studied during the academic year 1916–17 at the *Art Students League with Paris-trained painter George Bridgman (1865–1943), best known as a teacher of artistic anatomy. Between 1919 and his 1924 departure for Europe, Shahn studied at New York University, the City College of New York, and the *National Academy of Design. Subsequently, for seven months, he worked in Paris and traveled in Europe and North Africa. Abroad again in 1928–29, he remained for more than a year on the Tunisian island of Djerba and then traveled to Paris and Spain. Following his return, he sought to engage socially relevant content and soon formulated his distinctive style of expressive line, flattened shapes, and interplay of recognizable detail with abstract form. When they were exhibited in 1932, Shahn secured his reputation with twenty-three gouaches devoted to The Passion of Sacco and Vanzetti, a series that remains among his most enduring accomplishments. Organized into three sections, the paintings narrate the arrest, trial, and 1927 execution of two Italian immigrants accused of murder. Many, including Shahn, thought that the pair had been unjustly treated because they were foreigners and political radicals. The adversarial content of the Passion series placed Shahn in the company of other 1930s artists active as social realists in the *American Scene movement. Like many of them, Shahn participated eagerly in New York art politics. He joined the Artists' Union, worked for **Art Front*, enrolled in the *American Artists' Congress, assisted Mexican muralist Diego Rivera for nearly a year, and participated in *federal art projects. In 1937–38, with Bernarda Bryson, he executed a major mural under federal auspices for the school and community center of the newly established town of Jersey Homesteads (now Roosevelt), New Jersey. His other mural projects include large-scale publicly funded works at the Bronx Central Post Office (1938–39, also with the assistance of Bryson) and at the new Social Security Building in Washington (1940–42).

In the early 1930s, about the time he developed a recognizable personal style of painting, Shahn became interested in photography. Although he probably intended at first to use the medium to record "sketches" for his paintings, he soon recognized its artistic possibilities. His close friend Walker *Evans encouraged his interest and provided technical advice. In the early 1930s, as he photographed the streets of New York, Shahn developed a personal photographic style in many ways analogous to his manner of painting. His photographs generally feature close-up images of people, compressed space, and asymmetrical composition. In the mid-1930s, under the auspices of the *Farm Security Administration, he undertook two photographic surveys of the South and spent the summer of 1938 recording rural and small-town life in Ohio. Following completion of that project, he abruptly abandoned photography except for occasional instances. Nevertheless, he continued to draw imagery from his backlog of photographs for paintings, including some of the best known. *Handball* (Museum of Modern Art, 1939), depicting youths competing against a blank wall, derives from a New York photograph of the early 1930s. As here, Shahn's experience as a photographer affected the compositions of many paintings that make use of photographic devices such as abrupt cropping and oddly foreshortened angles of vision. In 1939 Shahn moved permanently to Jersey Homesteads. There he gave renewed attention to easel painting, although other projects, such as the social security mural, intervened in the 1940s. Among other activist undertakings of the period, in 1942–43 Shahn designed posters for the federal government's Office of War Information (only two of these were printed, the others being rejected for reasons that were never made public) and between 1944 and 1946 worked for a CIO political action committee. In paintings of the early 1940s Shahn began to turn toward the recurrent philosophical themes of his later art. In *The Red Stairway* (Saint Louis Art Museum, 1944), a man on crutches labors to ascend a staircase that rises intact along the exterior of a partially ruined building. The structure is situated in the midst of rubble, which another man strives to clear. Obviously referring to World War II destruction, Shahn meant for the painting to comment on the bittersweet human capacity for hope in the midst of devastating circumstances. Later, many of his paintings referred even more allegorically to the human condition. Shahn perhaps most successfully realized the symbolic possibilities of specific events in his sequence, The Voyage of the Lucky Dragon. Originating in a 1957 commission to illustrate a three-part series in *Harper's* magazine, the eleven subsequent paintings, first shown in 1961, portray the fate of a doomed crewman from a Japanese fishing boat contaminated by fallout from an American hydrogen bomb test in the Pacific. Shahn's many illustrated books share with certain paintings and graphics, especially from the later part of his career, a creative sensitivity to the relationship between images and words. At the time of his 1947 retrospective exhibition at the *Museum of Modern Art, at forty-nine Shahn ranked as the youngest painter ever accorded this honor. Before long, however, *abstract expressionism dominated the art conversation in New York and diminished his critical position. However, he remained a public figure, appreciated and honored by a large audience. He articulated his humanistic ideas about art in *The Shape of Content* (1957). Shahn died in a New York hospital.

Shahn's widow, painter, printmaker, and illustrator Bernarda Bryson (1903–2004), continued to live in Roosevelt, New Jersey, until her death there. She was educated at Ohio University in Athens, Ohio, her birthplace, at Ohio State University in Columbus, and at the Cleveland School (now Institute) of Art. Although she and Shahn lived together from 1935, they did not marry until 1967. Her stylistically and thematically varied art often displays a surrealistic sense of mystery. Two of their children, **Jonathan Shahn** (1938–) and **Abigail Shahn** (1940–), known as Abby, also are artists. Jonathan, a figurative sculptor, lives in Roosevelt. Abby, a painter and ceramist who works with brightly colored, partially abstract imagery, has resided in Maine for more than three decades. Shahn's daughter **Judith Hermine Shahn** (1929–), from an earlier marriage, also is a painter who has worked in many locations but today makes her home on Cape Cod in Truro, where her father had spent many summers.

Sharples, James (1751/52–1811). Painter. He headed a family of portrait artists who worked in nearly indistinguishable styles, together producing the finest American pastels of the period. These are generally three-quarter or profile portrait busts, small in format (typically 9 × 7 inches) on lightly textured gray paper. A native of Lancashire, Sharples studied painting in London. He worked there and in other English cities before traveling to America in the mid-1790s. Within a few months, he settled in Philadelphia, but in the later 1790s moved to New York. He apparently worked itinerantly prior to sailing for England in 1801. Until once again relocating in New York in 1809, he lived at Bath, where he exhibited portions of his large inventory of American likenesses. During his American sojourns, he portrayed many prominent persons, including George Washington and John Adams. He may have employed a mechanical aid, the physiognotrace, to achieve a high degree of accuracy in rendering profiles. Sharples's third wife, **Ellen Wallace Sharples** (1769–1849), accompanied him on his journeys. She seems to have been employed primarily in making copies of his originals. **Felix Thomas Sharples** (c. 1786–after 1823), a son of Sharples's second marriage, returned with his half brother **James Sharples Jr.** (c. 1788–1839), Ellen's son, to the United States in 1806. Felix then worked in Virginia, while James Jr. was active in Albany, New York. The daughter of James and Ellen, **Rolinda Sharples** (1793/94–1838), also worked in the family tradition but often employed oils. She accompanied her parents back to the United States on the 1809 voyage. When the rest of the family settled in Bristol, England, after James's death in New York, Felix remained in the United States. He continued to work, probably itinerantly, in eastern Virginia for some years, but in the mid-1820s he disappeared from the historical record.

Sharrer, Honoré (1920–). Painter. In recent decades known for quirky, often dreamlike, surrealistic images, Sharrer earlier employed her tight, highly detailed but imaginative approach to focus on the lives of ordinary Americans, often within self-consciously posed tableaux. A cultivated ingenuousness and patterned colors contribute to a charmingly naive spirit that accommodates unsettling notes. *Tribute to the American Working People* (Smithsonian American Art Museum, 1946–51), modeled on the form of an early Renaissance altarpiece, pays homage to blue-collar dignity. In the central panel, replacing the saint's image of earlier centuries, a workman stands before a gabled building. From its windows, varied individuals look out or, oddly, turn their backs. Similarly leavened with peculiarities, four smaller *genre scenes flank the central panel. The focus on working-class experience suggests ties to the *American Scene movement popular in her youth, but the characteristic combination of fact and fancy establishes an affinity with *magic realism. Honoré Desmond Sharrer was born in West Point, New York, but moved often during her youth. At the age of fourteen she was already studying art in Paris, where her family lived for a time. After they moved to San Diego in 1935, she graduated from high school in nearby La Jolla in 1938, studied art at Yale University for a year, and continued her training at the California School of Fine Arts (now San Francisco Art Institute) in 1940–41. During World War II she became interested in leftist politics and worked in the defense industry, first on the West Coast and after 1943 near New York. In 1947 she married history professor Perez Zagorin and left New York for Amherst, Massachusetts. After two years, the couple departed for England, then lived in Poughkeepsie, New York, in Montreal, and in Europe. From 1965 until 1994 they remained in the Rochester, New York, area. She currently resides in Charlottesville, Virginia. Her mother, painter **Madeleine Ellen Sachs Sharrer** (1898–1988), born in Colorado Springs, Colorado, studied in New York with George *Luks and Charles *Hawthorne and in Paris. She exhibited portraits and still lifes. Following the death of her first husband, she married Reginald Poland (1893–1975), director of the San Diego Museum of Art. She died in Guilford, Connecticut, where she had lived since the early 1950s.

Shattuck, Aaron Draper (1832–1928). Painter. Primarily a landscapist, he is known particularly for views of New Hampshire's White Mountains, but he also painted the Atlantic coast and other locales. In addition, he produced occasional portraits or other figural works. Born in Francestown, New Hampshire, in 1851 he studied portrait painting in Boston with Alexander Ransom (active 1840s–1860s). He and his teacher departed the following year for New York, where Shattuck also worked at the *National Academy of Design. By 1855 landscape in the *Hudson River School mode figured as his primary interest. Some works also demonstrate his affinity for the clarity, serenity, and attention to atmospheric effects characteristic of *luminism. With its detailed trees and foreground rocks, carefully observed light effects, and intimate tone, *Stream in a Rocky Gorge* (New Britain [Connecticut] Museum of American Art, c. 1860) recalls the contemporary woodland interiors of his friend John *Kensett. A number of paintings from the late 1850s and early 1860s demonstrate an interest in *Pre-Raphaelite hyperrealism. During the 1870s Shattuck's brushwork became somewhat looser, while his subjects took on a more pastoral cast, reflecting his move to a farm in Granby, Connecticut, north of Hartford. The alterations in his approach also suggest the period's shift in taste toward *Barbizon painting. In the late 1880s, beset by illness and dissatisfaction with art, he ceased painting. For the next forty years, he devoted his time to farming and devising inventions.

Shaw, Joshua (c. 1777–1860). Painter. Known particularly for landscapes, he also produced *genre scenes, allegorical and imaginative images, and views of Indian life. His early enthusiasm for American landscape prefigured the development of the *Hudson River School. In the first major publication devoted to American landscape, *Picturesque Views of American Scenery* (serially issued, 1819–21), he lamented a general inattention to the varied and beautiful forms of nature found in the United States. John *Hill engraved its hand-colored aquatint illustrations from Shaw's originals. Shaw also contributed to the establishment of an art community in Philadelphia, worked on mechanical inventions, and published a popular manual, *A New and Original Drawing Book* (1819). Born in Bellingborough, Lincolnshire, he remained mostly self-trained as a painter. He worked successfully in Bath and in London before relocating to Philadelphia in 1817. He soon began traveling to record American landscapes, making use of his English technique and style to emphasize the idyllic qualities of scenery he encountered. He traveled so much, in fact, that in 1822 he published an early guidebook, *United States Directory for the Use of Travellers and Merchants, Giving an Account of the Principal Establishments, of Business and Pleasure, Throughout the Union*. Around 1843 he moved to Bordentown, New Jersey, just south of Trenton on the Delaware River. He worked there for another decade before a stroke forced him to cease painting. He died in nearby Burlington. Despite his advocacy for American landscape, Shaw painted many identifiably British scenes, perhaps responding to the taste of collectors in the period before native landscape found a wide audience. A representative American subject, *On the Susquehanna* (Museum of Fine Arts, Boston, 1839), depicts with characteristically lyric feeling a wide, tree-framed expanse of languid river. Always particularly attentive to light, Shaw here skillfully observes its effects to unify the composition and suggest precise qualities of atmosphere.

Sheeler, Charles (1883–1965). Painter and photographer. The central figure in *precisionism, he ranks also among leaders in the early development of sharp-focus photography. A native of Philadelphia, Charles Rettew Sheeler Jr. began his art training between 1900 and 1903 at the Philadelphia School of Industrial Art (now University of the Arts). At the *Pennsylvania Academy of the Fine Arts, where he studied for the following three years, William Merritt *Chase influenced his early painterly style. Although he had made previous summer trips to Europe, it was only during an extended stay in the company of his academy classmate and studio partner Morton *Schamberg in late 1908 and 1909 that Sheeler became interested in modern art. The 1913 *Armory Show, in which he showed Cézanne-influenced work, also contributed to his education in recent tendencies. By this time working as a commercial photographer in Philadelphia, at the weekend home he shared with Schamberg in nearby Doylestown, he pursued both painting and noncommercial photography. During these years, he also began to appreciate the refined clarity of Shaker artifacts and the unassuming strength of rural architecture. In photography, he experimented with a sharp-focus technique, which placed him in the forefront of a new sensibility, as is evident in "Side of a White Barn" (c. 1916–17). In painting, his color-saturated cubist style positioned him among the most experimental artists of the decade and won his work a place in the 1916 *Forum Exhibition.

After the untimely deaths in 1918 of his friends Schamberg and H. Lyman *Saÿen, the next year Sheeler moved to New York. There he had already come to know photographer Alfred *Stieglitz, as well as the creative and intellectual circle that gathered at Walter *Arensberg's apartment. In 1920 he collaborated with Paul *Strand on an innovative short film, *Manhatta* (inspired by a Walt Whitman's poetry), interpreting the built environment as a manifestation of human vigor and creativity. Through the following decade, Sheeler continued to work from his Manhattan studio as a freelance industrial and advertising photographer, but from 1926 he lived in South Salem, north of the city near the Connecticut border. Commissioned in 1927 to photograph the Ford Motor Company's unprecedented new River Rouge plant close to Detroit, he produced dramatic photographs, such as "Criss-Crossed Conveyors, Ford Plant" (1927), powerfully evoking an industrial sublime manifest in the factory's architectural and mechanical features. Two years later, in France he photographed Chartres Cathedral with equally stunning results. Despite his prowess in the medium, Sheeler came to have increasing doubts about the role of creativity in photography. In 1931 he temporarily relinquished the medium for several years in order to focus single-mindedly on painting, and the following year he moved across the state line to Ridgefield, Connecticut.

Meanwhile, in his 1920s paintings Sheeler gradually abandoned the abstracting tendencies of his earlier work in favor of an increasingly intense engagement with representational exactitude. At first, he simplified urban architectural forms, as in *Church Street El*, (Cleveland Museum of Art, 1920). With time, as he introduced increasingly photographic detail, sharply focused and deftly composed still lifes and domestic spaces gained importance as subjects. Picturing his Ridgefield house and furnishings, *American Interior* (Yale University Art Gallery, 1934), crisply and unsentimentally documents his affection for vernacular artifacts, including a Shaker box, a rag rug, a ladder-back side chair, and other examples of Americana. From the early 1930s onward, many Sheeler paintings so closely resemble the photographs that stimulated them that they are difficult to differentiate when both are seen in black-and-white reproduction. A photograph made for *Fortune* magazine served as the "sketch" for *Rolling Power* (Smith College Museum of Art, Northampton, Massachusetts, 1939), an intensely detailed painting of train wheels seen at close range. Yet close analysis always reveals myriad alterations in Sheeler's translation from the mechanical medium to the handmade. Many such paintings also betray the artist's underlying ambivalence about industrial progress. For example, although *American Landscape* (Museum of Modern Art, 1930) envisions a stunning technological utopia based on the River Rouge industrial site, disquieting undertones emanate from its ruthless coldness and the absence of human participants. Similarly his fondness for the pre-industrial vernacular undercut his idealization of modern technology's most advanced products. However, united by functional and formal rigor, these dual interests emphasize the New World, remaining independent of Europe for their meaning. At its best, transcending the literal physicality of objects, Sheeler's vision summons the enigmas in human perceptions of reality. In the mid-1940s his painting style changed dramatically. He abandoned detailed realism in favor of more abstract compositions. These he synthesized mostly from images of architecture, seen as overlapping and sometimes transparent forms that often suggest the effect of photographic double exposures. A 1959 stroke ended the artist's career. He died in a Dobbs Ferry hospital, not far from his home in Irvington-on-Hudson, where he had resided since 1942.

Shelburne Museum. *See* HAVEMEYER, LOUISINE.

Sherman, Cindy (1954–). Photographer and filmmaker. Photographing herself in varied guises, she regularly invokes female stereotypes to undermine appearance as the measure of selfhood, while also highlighting the role of commercial mass media in forming contemporary values. Born in the New York suburb of Glen Ridge, New Jersey, Cynthia Sherman grew up on Long Island, in the north shore town of Huntington. After graduating from the State University College at Buffalo in 1976, she moved to New York the following year with her boyfriend, Robert *Longo. In 1978 she embarked on the project that first brought her name to widespread attention. The black-and-white Untitled Film Stills picture the artist impersonating recognizable types from earlier mainstream movies. Her characters range from sultry to domestic, from career girl to bad girl. In 1980 she began working in color most of the time, and the size of her prints gradually expanded during that decade. Initiating an increasingly provocative and even offensive approach, the sequences of Disasters and Fairy Tales stress the morbid and grotesque. After concentrating for a time on models other than herself, in 1989 she showed up again in the imaginary History Portraits. In the 1990s she used mannequins and prosthetic body parts for works stressing sex, mutilation, and abasement. Sherman made her debut as a film director in 1997, with the release of *Office Killer*, a horror comedy. In 2000 she returned to her early straightforward approach in fictional personas mostly parodying the milieu of Hollywood glamour. More recently, clowns have entered her repertoire. In 1984 she married French-born *video artist Michael Auder (1944–), but they divorced nearly fifteen years later.

Shinn, Everett (1876–1953). Painter. As a participant in the *Ashcan School, Shinn recorded New York street life, but the glamour of the theater and high society also appealed to him. A facile stylist, he was always drawn more to appearances than to social or psychological analysis. Born in Woodstown, New Jersey, below Philadelphia, Shinn worked as an industrial designer in Philadelphia before enrolling in 1893 at the *Pennsylvania Academy of the Fine Arts, where Thomas *Anshutz numbered among his teachers. During four years there, he worked part time as a newspaper illustrator, which brought him into contact with William *Glackens, George *Luks, and John *Sloan, as well as Robert *Henri. In 1897 he moved to New York, where he embarked on a successful career as an illustrator for newspapers, books, and magazines. He also gained favor for pastels and drawings representing the city's quick-paced drama. Inspired by art he saw in 1900 on his first trip abroad, particularly Degas's work, he enlarged his subject range to include many examples of cafe and theater life, as in *London Hippodrome* (Art Institute of Chicago, 1902). After he participated with his Philadelphia friends in the 1908 exhibition of The *Eight, Shinn gradually drifted away from them. In a significant departure from his later interests, a 1911 mural of industrial imagery in the Trenton, New Jersey, city hall ranks among the earliest to depict *social realist subject matter in decoration of a public venue. More often, the incisive reality Shinn had strikingly captured earlier gave way to a decorative flair that served him well as a celebrity portraitist and muralist for private homes and public buildings. A love of theater led him from amateur productions to professional set design and to art direction of several early films. In poor health during the final two years of his life, he died in New York. His first wife, painter and illustrator **Florence Scovel Shinn** (1869–1940), born in Camden, New Jersey, studied at the *Pennsylvania Academy of the Fine Arts before marriage in 1898. The couple divorced in 1913. In the 1920s she became a well-known lecturer and writer of spiritually oriented self-help books. She died in New York.

Shirlaw, Walter (1838–1909). Painter and illustrator. His varied subjects, including *genre scenes, portraits, landscapes, nudes, and still lifes, evidence the rich brushwork and warm coloration of his training in Munich. Also active as a mural painter, he served as the first president of the *Society of American Artists and taught at the *Art Students League. Born in Paisley, as a toddler Shirlaw emigrated from Scotland with his family. In New York he learned engraving and began to paint on his own. He worked for several years in Chicago and journeyed to the West before departing in 1870 for Munich, where he knew Frank *Duveneck and William Merritt *Chase. Settling in New York in 1877, he numbered among the first to introduce the painterly approach to oil painting then fashionable in Europe and soon widely adopted among forward-looking Americans. Subsequently he also worked in watercolor, produced drawings that appeared as illustrations in leading magazines, designed stained glass windows, and executed murals in the 1890s for the World's Columbian Exposition in Chicago and for the new Library of Congress in Washington, D.C. In 1889 he again journeyed west to record Indian life in fluid, vigorous drawings and oil studies. Especially after about 1900, he traveled extensively in Europe. He died in Madrid.

Shore, Stephen. *See* NEW TOPOGRAPHICS.

Siegel, Arthur. *See* CALLAHAN, HARRY.

Siegriest, Louis. *See* SOCIETY OF SIX.

Simmons, Edward. *See* TEN, THE.

Siporin, Mitchell (1910–76). Painter and printmaker. His expressionistic realism, inspired by the Mexican mural movement of the 1930s, harnesses the formal experimentation of modernism to socially meaningful, often leftist content. Born in New York, he grew up in Chicago, where he studied at the School of the Art Institute of Chicago and with Ukrainian-born printmaker and painter Todros Geller (1889–1949). In the 1930s he worked in Chicago on *federal art projects, painting murals such as the multipanel *Teaching of the Arts* (1938) at Lane Technical High School. Generally, as here, his figural compositions rely on simple, ample forms, but he sometimes used a more agitated style, lending support to content that revealed human suffering and drama. In easel paintings, Siporin often modified his *social realism to work somewhat more imaginatively, fabricating elements that enhance the impact of his themes, as in *The Refugees* (Museum of Modern Art, 1939). During World War II he served as an artist with the U.S. Army. For more than twenty years before his death, he taught at Brandeis University in Waltham, Massachusetts. He lived in nearby Newton and died in Boston.

Siskind, Aaron (1903–91). Photographer. His bold, graphic, nearly abstract images from the 1940s and 1950s rank as the most important photographic equivalents of *abstract expressionism. Although he remained committed to the basic processes of straight black-and-white photography, in these works emphasizing archetypal representation, self-sufficient imagery, flattened perspective, and ambiguous meanings, he entered into an artistic dialogue with avant-garde painting. A New York native, Siskind studied literature at City College of New York. Following graduation in 1926, he taught English in local public schools until 1947. Concurrently he probed social realities as a documentary photographer, notably in Harlem, from about 1930 through the early 1940s. With time, however, he came to believe that the full truth of his subjects could not be communicated objectively. With this in mind, in Gloucester, Massachusetts, during the summer of 1944, he consciously set out to retrain his eye. By focusing on mundane subjects and emphasizing nongeometric formal elements, he transferred meaning from the subject to the photograph as a work of art. After this time, he infrequently photographed people, but often chose subjects that disclose human activity and sometimes comment indirectly on issues related to communication. His themes included stone walls, peeling paint, corroded statues, and weather-beaten billboards, reconceived as forceful abstract compositions. Usually seen at close range, their constituent elements, pried loose from original meanings, suggest emotional and psychological relationships. By the late 1940s, Siskind had become acquainted with abstract expressionist leaders, including Barnett *Newman and Mark *Rothko. In 1951 he ranked as the sole photographer to participate in the group's landmark *"Ninth Street Show." "Martha's Vineyard 124" (1954), an arrangement of gritty megaliths, recalls the structural tensions, dramatic scale, and brooding heroism of paintings by his friend Franz *Kline. Other works suggest the *all-over compositions and spontaneous effects of work by Jackson *Pollock. In 1951 Siskind began teaching at Chicago's Institute of Design (now part of Illinois Institute of Technology), where he soon numbered among the nation's leading photography instructors. When Harry *Callahan left in 1961, Siskind replaced him, heading the photography department until 1970. He then followed Callahan to Providence, where he taught until 1976 at the Rhode Island School of Design and remained in retirement. He died there. Collections of his photographs include *Aaron Siskind: Photographs* (1959) and *Places: Aaron Siskind Photographs* (1976). His will established the Aaron Siskind Foundation, which awards grants to individual photographers.

Skillin, Simeon, Jr. (1756–1806). Sculptor. The most proficient member of a Boston family enterprise, he enlarged the artisanal woodworking tradition to reflect fine art practice. By the 1790s he often relied on books or prints to devise a provincial response to *neoclassicism. Despite his accomplishments, Skillin never achieved the expertise of his exact contemporary William *Rush in handling three-dimensional form, nor his cultural sophistication. His father, **Simeon Skillin** (1716–78), established the workshop that trained Simeon Jr. and his brother **John Skillin** (1745/46–1800). Although the founder was well known as a carver of ship figureheads, none of his work can be specifically identified today. The great bulk of the sons' work also has perished, and few attributions can be documented. Of those, the allegorical *Plenty* (Peabody Essex Museum, Salem, Massachusetts), known to have come from the workshop in 1793, represents a capability in presenting human form and a familiarity with classical symbolism. In addition to continuing the elder Samuel's marine specialty, the shop produced architectural decorations, including important elements of Charles Bullfinch's designs, as well as furniture embellishments and garden ornaments. A third brother, **Samuel Skillin** (1742–93) worked also in Philadelphia before the Revolution. Although subsequently in Boston, generally he did not participate in the workshop and seems not to have found much success. His son **Simeon Skillin III** (1766–1830) later worked in New York.

Sleigh, Sylvia (1916–). Painter. Known for figural images, landscapes, and still lifes, Sleigh gained prominence in the 1970s for her contributions to *feminist art. Her subjects at that time included portraits of other women artists, sometimes sporting tongue-in-cheek mythological guises, and more notoriously, sensuous male nudes. Born in Llandudno, North Wales, she received her training at the Brighton School of Art in Sussex, studied art history at the University of London, and held her first one-person show in London in 1954. She moved to New York in 1961. Active in the feminist movement from an early date, in the 1970s she put her delicately detailed realism to its service. In a complex 1977 group portrait, the twenty-one current members (including Sleigh) of A.I.R., a pioneering, artist-run women's gallery, form a spirited cohort. Sleigh's satirical role-reversal images of men in voluptuous poses draw on the tradition of Titian and Velázquez to subvert the male gaze. Among later works, the seventy-foot-long *Invitation to a Voyage: The Hudson River at Fishkill* (1979–99) ranks as the most notable. With a nod to French rococo painter Jean-Antoine Watteau, she delivers a modern pastorale inhabited by city friends enjoying a summer day at water's edge.

In 1943 Sleigh met Lawrence Alloway (1926–90), later a prominent critic, who was also taking art history classes at the University of London. They married in 1954, after she was divorced from painter Michael Greenwood. A London-area native, in the mid-1950s Alloway figured prominently in the progressive circle that spawned the development of British *pop art, which he christened in a 1958 essay. After the couple moved to the United States, he taught for a year at Bennington (Vermont) College before they settled permanently in New York. Both were later naturalized as American citizens. He worked as a curator and teacher, in addition to writing wide-ranging art criticism that demonstrated an unusually acute attentiveness to forms of popular culture. His books include *The Venice Biennale, 1895–1968: From Salon to Goldfish Bowl* (1969), *Violent America: The Movies, 1946–1964* (1971), *American Pop Art* (1974), *Topics in American Art Since 1945* (1975), and monographs on American artists.

Sloan, John (1871–1951). Painter and printmaker. Remembered especially for sympathetic portrayals of urban life executed in a rich, painterly style during his early career, he remained an important force in the art life of New York for many years. He exhibited with The *Eight, participated for decades in organizing and promoting *independent exhibitions, taught for more than twenty years at the *Art Students League, and demonstrated a commitment to social justice and pacifism in drawings and cartoons for politically motivated publications. Born in the central Pennsylvania town of Lock Haven, John French Sloan moved with his family to Philadelphia in 1877. He left high school at sixteen to take varied jobs for several years. In 1892 he began working as a newspaper illustrator, while also taking classes for a year with Thomas *Anshutz at the *Pennsylvania Academy of the Fine Arts. Soon he was mixing with other artist-illustrators, including William *Glackens (a high school friend), George *Luks, and Everett *Shinn, while also finding encouragement from Robert *Henri. In these years, Sloan expanded his practice to include poster design, as well as both book and magazine illustration. Through his mastery of the compositional principles of Japanese prints and art nouveau ornamentation, he gained national recognition as a graphic artist. He also began to work with etching, a technique he later exploited in an extended series of urban scenes. Meanwhile, Sloan began to paint the urban environment in a style derived from old masters. By 1900 his work—as in *East Entrance, City Hall, Philadelphia* (Columbus [Ohio] Museum of Art, 1901)—displayed the painterly handling, strong compositions, sensitivity to light effects, and eye for the telling detail that characterize his best work. Sloan also brought warm humanity and democratic dignity to all his subjects.

In 1904 Sloan moved permanently to New York, where his Philadelphia *Ashcan School friends were gravitating. After The Eight's 1908 exhibition, Sloan continued for several more years to paint appealing visions of New York life, such as *McSorley's Bar* (Detroit Institute of Arts, 1912). However, even before he showed several works in the 1913 *Armory Show, he had begun to search for a more systematic method of painting, studying in particular the theories of Hardesty *Maratta, in addition to examples of European postimpressionism. Beginning in 1914, Sloan expanded his subjects to include views of locales where he regularly summered, first in Gloucester, Massachusetts, and from 1919, in Santa Fe, New Mexico. In later years, he produced many studio figures, emphasizing plasticity with an uningratiating technique of contour lines and hatching, as in *Nude and Nine Apples* (Whitney Museum, 1937). Important through most of his career as a teacher and promoter of artistic liberalism, Sloan served as art director from 1912 to 1916 for *The* *Masses. From 1916 until 1938 he taught regularly at the Art Students League. In 1939 he published *Gist of Art*, a combination memoir and aesthetic treatise. Because of health concerns in his final year, Sloan canceled his usual summer trip to Santa Fe, where he had owned a home since 1920. While vacationing in Hanover, New Hampshire, he died. Edited by Bruce St. John, his informal writings appeared posthumously as *New York Scene: From the Diaries, Notes and Correspondence 1906–1913* (1965).

His wife, painter and printmaker **Helen Farr Sloan** (1911–2005), numbered among his pupils at the Art Students League in the 1920s and assisted in preparation of *Gist of Art*. They married in 1944. Born in New York, she, too, produced scenes of everyday life, as well as landscapes. During the final years before her death in Wilmington, she lived in Delaware. John Sloan's sister, painter **Marianna Sloan** (1875–1954), also born in Lock Haven, studied with Henri at the Philadelphia College of Design for Women (now the Moore College of Art and Design) and in Europe. Known particularly for landscapes, often watercolors, mostly in a slightly hazy, romantic style, she also painted murals. She continued to reside in the Philadelphia area.

Slobodkina, Esphyr (1908–2002). *See* BOLOTOWSKY, ILYA.

Smibert, John (1688–1751). Painter. The first professionally trained artist to work in the American colonies, he limited his practice almost exclusively to the portraits his market demanded. Boston patrons and visitors to that city commissioned some 250 likenesses. (He painted also in Philadelphia and New York during a single working trip, in 1740.) As a role model to painters, he was important for the quality of his work, his collection of European originals and copies, and the example of his professional ambitions. A native of Edinburgh, Smibert was apprenticed there from 1702 to 1709 to a house painter and plasterer. Subsequently, in London he painted coaches and copied paintings for dealers before entering an art school. During two years there, he came under the tutelage of Godfrey Kneller, the reigning British portraitist, whose manner formed Smibert's technique and taste. In 1716 he returned to Edinburgh to set up his own portrait practice. After three years, to complete his education as an artist in the grand tradition, he set off to travel and study in Italy. There he also copied old masters and collected paintings, prints, and sculpture casts. As well, he painted portraits, including one of Dean George Berkeley, the Irish-born clergyman and Idealist philosopher whose friendship would change Smibert's life.

Smibert returned to London in 1722 to participate in the competitive market for likenesses. After Berkeley appeared there in 1726, he convinced Smibert to assist him in establishing a college in Bermuda, where the artist would instruct students in painting, drawing, and architecture. With others, they departed late in 1728 but in January 1729 landed at Newport, Rhode Island, to await arrival of additional funds (which never came). Well received on a visit to Boston, Smibert soon settled there permanently. In May of that year he received his first known American commission, a prestigious opportunity to paint Elizabeth Brinley Hutchinson (Virginia Museum of Fine Arts, Richmond), the governor's wife. In his early Boston work, Smibert replicated the style and formats that had brought him modest success in London, but after the mid-1730s, his work sometimes showed greater technical and conceptual simplicity. Nevertheless, at his best he never lost his painterly touch, his interest in lively composition, and his ability to evoke both appearance and personality. Late in 1729 or early the following year, he resumed work on the most impressive and influential painting of his career. Signed and dated with the presumably commemorative year of 1729, the work was conceived in England but could not have been finished before late 1730 or, more likely, 1731. *The Bermuda Group* (Yale University Art Gallery) vividly portrays Berkeley, the painter himself, and a Berkeley admirer who had commissioned the work in 1728, before the group departed London. It includes also two other associates, Berkeley's wife and their infant son, and her traveling companion. At approximately 6 × 8 feet, it remained the largest painting executed in the colonies before the middle of the eighteenth century, as well as the most sophisticated and complex. Arrayed in varied poses around a table covered with a fashionable turkey-work rug, the figures form an intimate and lively group, despite residual stiffness in some of their poses and a tendency to generalize faces toward the Knelleresque ideal. (The painter and the patron, shown without the formal wigs the other three men wear, are also the most individualized.) Behind them, stately columns rise beyond the frame. In the distance, an idealized landscape may commemorate New England's shoreline.

Through other activities besides painting, Smibert contributed immeasurably to Boston's cultural life. By early 1730 he had staged what may have been the first colonial art exhibition, a display of his own recent paintings along with copies of old masters. After that, his collection of copies, prints, casts, and examples of his own work (including *The Bermuda Group*) remained continuously on view in his studio until long after his death, in effect constituting the first American art gallery. While educating his public, Smibert, like many colonial artists, maintained a sideline occupation. From about 1734, his retail business in a shop below his studio sold imported artists' supplies, prints, frames, and other art-related materials. In addition, he designed Boston's Faneuil Hall (1740–42), the city's first market (after two and a half centuries of modifications and renovations, a thriving shopping mall today), and painted donor Peter Faneuil's portrait (now lost) for display there. He may have designed other structures, as well. In later years (and possibly earlier as well), he occasionally painted landscapes, but only one survives. By the 1740s, his ponderous late Baroque style was out of fashion in London and soon would be eclipsed in the colonies. Facing changing taste, as well as failing health and eyesight, Smibert slowed his artistic activity and stopped painting professionally about 1746. His talented son **Nathaniel Smibert** (1735–56) continued the portrait business but died too young to leave a major artistic legacy.

Smillie, James (1807–85). Printmaker. His engraved reproductions of major mid-nineteenth-century paintings interpret the originals with such sensitivity and technical finesse that they have been considered works of art in their own right. His prints included numerous landscapes after *Hudson River School artists, including Asher B. *Durand and John *Kensett, as well as Thomas *Cole's *Voyage of Life*. Smillie's perfectionism culminated in a masterful rendition (1863–66) of Albert *Bierstadt's celebrated *The Rocky Mountains, Lander's Peak*. Here, he combined etching, engraving, and aquatint to convey the original's tonal and atmospheric effects, no less than its extensive detail. Smillie was born in Edinburgh and received his first artistic instruction during an apprenticeship to a silver engraver. In 1821 he moved with his family to Quebec. Largely on his own, there and on a subsequent sojourn in London and Edinburgh he developed his abilities as a draftsman and engraver. After returning to Quebec in 1828, he relocated to New York about two years later. Although artists admired his skill, financially Smillie found it necessary throughout his career to pursue more lucrative aspects of his profession, engraving bank notes and illustrations for books and periodicals. Smillie visited Europe for some months in 1862. Two or three years later he began spending periods of time in Poughkeepsie, New York, where he subsequently made his home and eventually died.

As painters, two sons extended their father's artistic legacy. Born in New York, both are remembered chiefly as landscapists, rooted in a pastoral Hudson River School approach. By the 1880s their styles accommodated the shifting taste toward more personally expressive and less detailed views. After beginning his career as an assistant to his father, **James David Smillie** (1833–1909) remained active also as a printmaker. In the wake of their trip together to Europe in 1862, he turned his attention primarily to fine art, continuing as a commercial engraver only as financial necessity demanded. Trips to the West in 1871 and to Europe in 1884 and on later occasions provided subjects for his art, as did travels in New England and the mid-Atlantic states. In the 1870s he began regularly visiting Montrose, Pennsylvania, about fifty miles northwest of Philadelphia. There in 1881–82 he built a substantial vacation house of his own design, while he later summered at an Adirondack cabin. An active participant in the *watercolor movement and the *etching revival, he died in New York. **George Henry Smillie** (1840–1921) picked up the rudiments of art in his father's studio before studying painting with James MacDougal *Hart. He subsequently worked in tandem with his older brother and, like him, became an accomplished watercolorist. They regularly worked in adjacent studios and sketched together during summer trips, including the 1871 excursion through the West and the 1884 trip to France and England. He lived in Ridgefield, Connecticut, for a time before moving to Bronxville, New York, where he died. His wife, **Helen Sheldon Jacobs Smillie** (1854–1926), known as Nellie, also a painter, was known especially for floral still lifes. Trained at the *National Academy of Design and Cooper Union, she studied privately with her husband's brother before her 1881 marriage.

Smith, David (1906–65). Sculptor, painter, draftsman, and photographer. Among the most significant American sculptors of the twentieth century, he ranked as the first to grasp the potential of welded metal as a sculptural medium. Nonrepresentational despite lingering attachments to figure and landscape, often indebted to surrealism as well as cubism and constructivism, sophisticated but not arty, bold, grandly scaled, and attentive to materials, his varied and unprecedented works embody the spirit of *abstract expressionism. He began using the welded metal technique only a few years after Picasso and fellow Spaniard Julio González introduced the method. Only Alexander *Calder rivaled Smith's radical disregard for the structural logic of traditional sculpture and his demonstration that sculpture could be conceived as a kind of drawing in space. Moreover, Smith's additive method fostered the flowering of *assemblage, his most radically simplified pieces afforded exemplars to *minimalist artists, and his casual incorporation of detritus provided an important precedent for the development of *junk sculpture. Trained as a painter, Smith continued to paint after he turned to sculpture. Throughout his life, he also drew more or less every day, working out ideas for sculpture but also exploring unrelated territory. With almost no professional instruction in sculpture, he improvised techniques from those learned on the job as a metalworker. At the same time, his background in painting facilitated innovative use of color in some sculpture, particularly after 1960.

David Roland Smith was born in Decatur, Indiana, about forty miles from Indianapolis. He moved with his family in 1921 to the western Ohio town of Paulding, where he finished high school in 1924. After a year at Ohio University in Athens, he worked at the Studebaker automobile plant in South Bend, Indiana. In the fall of 1925 he enrolled at Notre Dame University there but soon left to accept a white-collar job at Studebaker. In 1926 he was transferred to Washington, D.C., and then to New York that autumn. At the end of 1926 he enrolled part-time at the *Art Students League. The following fall he left his job to study painting and drawing full time but later interrupted his training at intervals to take other employment, including several months as a seaman on an oil tanker. During the next four years, his teachers at the league included John *Sloan, the celebrated drawing instructor Kimon Nicolaides (1892–1938), and most importantly, Jan *Matulka, who inspired enthusiasm for European modernism, including the nonobjective work of Kandinsky and Mondrian. By around 1930 Smith had also become acquainted with John *Graham, an essential conduit for the latest in European art, including welded sculpture. Soon Smith also befriended Stuart *Davis, Willem *de Kooning, and Arshile *Gorky, who reinforced his interests in modern developments.

During an eight-month visit to the Virgin Islands, he began to experiment with constructions of found materials. Not long after his return in June 1932, he acquired the equipment for soldering and then welding metals. In 1933 he produced his first metal objects and rented a space at a Brooklyn machine shop, the Terminal Iron Works, to facilitate this direction in his work. In October 1935 he left on his first trip to Europe, where he visited Paris, Athens, and London, among other cities, and then traveled on to Leningrad (now St. Petersburg) and Moscow before returning to New York the following summer. In 1937 he found employment for two years with a *federal art project. The following year he joined the *American Abstract Artists. While exhibiting nonrepresentational work with that group, he embarked on his best-known early works, fifteen *Medals of Dishonor* (1938–40). Crowded with expressionistic imagery, these cast bronze reliefs contributed to the left-wing social consciousness prominent among New York artists. Recording Smith's dismay over the Spanish Civil War and Nazi Germany's increasing aggression, they disparage violence and brutality while also making pointed reference to recent political events.

In 1940 Smith moved permanently to an upstate New York farm he had purchased in 1929 as a summer residence. Located in the Adirondack Mountains at Bolton Landing on Lake George, it provided a bucolic setting for his workshop, also called the Terminal Iron Works in acknowledgment of his Brooklyn experience. However, during World War II he produced little sculpture. As an alternative to military service, he worked in Schenectady assembling tanks and locomotives. At the same time, because metal for sculpture was virtually unobtainable, he learned to work with marble at a cemetery monument firm. From 1944, when he returned to his art full time, until the end of the decade, he experimented widely with the possibilities of welded metal. His interests included, in varying combinations, symbolic imagery, expressionistic and surrealistic form, found objects, reliefs, and centralized, totemlike structures encrusted with varied objects. However, most fruitful for the immediate future, linear, open-form compositions resulted by the early 1950s in his first masterworks. The best known, *Hudson River Landscape* (Whitney Museum, 1951), mimics with wandering lines derived from *biomorphic surrealism the rolling contours of the Hudson River Valley. Points of interest punctuate the looping forms, as in a landscape particular features catch the eye. From the early 1950s, as his pieces took on increased scale, he placed examples of his sculpture around his rural acreage, so they could be seen outdoors as he preferred. Despite their industrial origins, Smith's pieces commune with nature, exemplifying a quintessentially American fusion of the romance of technological progress with the rhapsody of human immersion in landscape. Rhythmic disposition of their component parts and surfaces made responsive to natural light connect even his geometric works to this unified duality.

Much of Smith's mature work belongs to overlapping series, each playing out ramifications of a single idea in multiple variations. In the first of these, the Agricola series of twenty-two sculptures produced between 1951 and 1957, he incorporated farm tools and machinery parts that allude to agricultural life, revealing an unexpected fantasy even as they also accent formal interests. In this pathbreaking series, Smith explored the realization that he could create highly original structural disjunctions by so radically disassociating side and front views that it is not possible to anticipate the appearance of the second aspect when only one is seen. Different in their approach to form but continuing the highly abstracted figuration of the Agricola works, the Tanktotem sculptures begun in 1953 incorporate commercial boiler tops, while the Sentinels begun in 1957 comprise lanky vertical pieces. Around 1960 Smith began to simplify, clarify, and emphasize structure. As in the Zig sculptures and his most famous group, the Cubi series, the work of his later years presents an emphatic stress on abstraction, with a concomitant decline in surrealistic or allusive references. The twenty-eight large Cubis combine severe, geometric, mostly boxlike forms in dynamic, often impishly unbalanced compositions. While introducing an emphasis on volume, they nevertheless avoid weightiness. Their stainless steel surfaces are burnished in circular patterns that soften forms and enliven visual appeal. While working for several months in Voltri, Italy, in 1962, he embarked on the more irregular Voltri series, continued in the Voltri-Bolton pieces made after he returned home. Both feature spontaneous compositions of used tools and machine parts from Italy. Concurrently, beginning in 1957 Smith produced an extensive series of spatter-paintings. For these, he placed on paper or canvas forms related to those of his sculpture, using them as stencils as he sprayed enamel paint. Throughout his career, he also produced photographs. Some, especially earlier, reflect his interest in imaginative, even surreal imagery, while another large group documents his sculptures with particular sensitivity to their visual qualities. At the height of his powers as an artist, Smith died from injuries suffered when his truck flipped over on a road near Bennington, Vermont. He left a powerful legacy. Like de Kooning, who was just two years older and drew on similar sources, Smith created a body of work so rich in meaning and so varied in effect that its potential interested artists who pursued quite different aesthetic projects. Edited by Cleve Gray, *David Smith by David Smith* (1968) collects his reflections and ideas.

From 1927 until 1952, Smith was married to sculptor, printmaker, and painter Dorothy Dehner (1901–94). During these years, she focused on painting and drawing, but after the divorce her career as a sculptor flourished. Born in Cleveland, she moved with her family in 1915 to Pasadena, California. She studied for a year at UCLA before relocating to New York in 1922 to work in theatre. In 1925 she traveled extensively in Europe, where she so admired the modern art she encountered that she enrolled at the Art Students League on her return that fall. There she studied with Kenneth Hayes *Miller, as well as with Nicolaides and Matulka. Through the 1940s she employed both biomorphic abstraction and representation in her paintings and drawings. After she separated from Smith late in 1950 (they divorced in 1952), she completed her education at Skidmore College in Saratoga Springs, New York. Upon receiving her art degree in 1952, she settled permanently in New York. That year she mounted her first New York gallery show and also learned engraving at *Atelier 17. She married Ferdinand Mann in 1955 and subsequently often sojourned at their country house in Croton-on-Hudson, New York. She remained active for nearly another four decades as a sculptor and printmaker, only rarely as a painter. Her three-dimensional, cast metal work centers on abstract, organic forms, often invoking landscape. In the mid-1970s she worked for a time with wood, combining attractively grained elements into small constructions. Later, she returned to the larger metal creations that she continued to produce until the final years of her life.

Smith, Henry Holmes. *See* UELSMANN, JERRY.

Smith, John Rubens. *See* GIFFORD, SANFORD.

Smith, Leon Polk. *See* HARD-EDGE PAINTING.

Smith, Pamela Colman. *See* STIEGLITZ, ALFRED.

Smith, Thomas (active c. 1650–c. 1691). Painter. The first resident painter whose name can be linked to specific works, he numbered among the earliest colonial artists to work in a style derived from naturalistic Renaissance-Baroque practice. His most important work, the first American self-portrait (Worcester [Massachusetts] Art Museum; probably c. 1690), stands among only five generally accepted attributions. Probably born in England, he is thought to have arrived around 1650 in Boston, presumably as a trained painter. Possibly also a sea captain, he has traditionally been known as Captain Thomas Smith. One datable work, *Major Thomas Savage* (Museum of Fine Arts, Boston, 1679), and one documentary reference from 1680 provide the only solid evidence concerning the period of his activity in Boston. In the half-length self-portrait, Smith wears somber black attire. Strong three-dimensional facial modeling emulates the distant sophistications of Baroque style, as does an emphatically rendered triangle of lace below the throat. A curtain drawn back with a tasseled cord and a glimpse into the distance (here, through a window) demonstrate Smith's familiarity with current international portrait conventions. Intriguingly, the remote view encompasses a naval battle, although its significance to the painter's life remains unknown. On the table before him, Smith's right hand rests on a human skull weighting a piece of paper displaying a poem. Long employed as reminders of death, skulls appeared often in European seventeenth-century still lifes. Smith's initials appended to the legible verses suggest that he wrote the poetry. Also a meditation on death, in style and theme it reflects the slightly earlier, ornate Metaphysical poetry of England. In the absence of additional biographical information about the artist, interpretation of this painting remains conjectural. Yet nothing comparable to its complex ambitions appeared in the colonies for another generation.

Smith, Tony (1912–80). Sculptor, painter, and architect. His monumental, nonrepresentational sculptures continued into the 1960s and 1970s the *abstract expressionists' romantic quest for a transcendent and heroic art. At the same time, his work relates to the *minimalism of younger artists, who valued his simplified, geometrically determined form and a cool demeanor. In paintings and architectural projects as well, Smith's manipulation of structure and space communicated his yearning to discover an underlying order to existence. Anthony Peter Smith was born in South Orange, New Jersey. He took classes at Fordham University in New York and spent a year at Georgetown University in Washington, D.C., before studying part-time at the *Art Students League in New York from 1933 to 1936 and at the New Bauhaus (now the Illinois Institute of Technology's Institute of Design) in Chicago in 1937–38. Subsequently, he worked for two years with architect Frank Lloyd Wright. In the 1940s and 1950s, Smith designed a number of residences, but only a few were built. After moving to New York in 1945, he soon became friendly with abstract expressionists. He had been painting since the 1930s, working through various modernist styles. In the 1950s he produced a series of large field paintings featuring flat, *biomorphic abstract forms floating within carefully ordered spaces. Later, he worked with simplified geometric elements.

Although his experiments with three-dimensional form went back to childhood, Smith's mature sculpture emerged only in the early 1960s. *Die* (National Gallery, 1968; originated 1962) at a glance exemplifies his connection to minimalism, but upon closer inspection its refinements reveal interests at odds with those of that literalist movement. A six-foot black cube, *Die* could not be simpler in form. However, it mysteriously "floats" about an inch off the floor, supported by a hidden base. Its scale is classical, related to the spectator by dimensions derived from Leonard da Vinci's famous drawing of a man set inside a circle and a square. The surface of the cube, steel with an oiled finish, lends a slightly irregular and sensuous vibrancy. Even the name of the work is suggestive. In the end, *Die* is more a contemplative metaphor than a minimalist object. Smith's interest in the tensions between forms and meanings pervades his later work as well. As in the monumental *Gracehopper* (Detroit Institute of Arts, 1972), measuring twenty-three feet high and forty-six wide, his distinctive sculptural idiom plays orderliness and stability against contingency and organic fluidity. Often achieving a lively, even baroque, sense of movement, geometric elements form unanticipated patterns that can be fully discovered only by moving around (and sometimes through) the sculpture. The works are usually painted in a matte black, though a few reverberate with bright color. Many seem to create their own environments through their large scale and complex relationships to the spaces around them. They function well in relation to architecture, as mediating elements between the implacable urban fabric and the human observer. Smith died in a New York hospital.

Two daughters also are artists. Chiara, a figurative sculptor known as **Kiki Smith** (1954–), frequently treats the female body, often in relationship to political and social questions. Although they sidestep overt polemic, these works acknowledge pain, humiliation, and vulnerability. She also works with themes drawn from nature. Born in Nuremberg while her parents were abroad for two years, she grew up in South Orange, where the family settled permanently in the mid-1950s. Before moving to New York in 1976, she studied in San Francisco and Hartford but remains largely self-taught as an artist. She also exhibits drawings, collages, prints, and work in other media. New York photographer **Seton Smith** (1955–) produces meditative, often partially unfocused images of architecture or landscape to suggest interaction of memory and cognition.

Smith, W. Eugene (1918–78). Photographer. A leading photojournalist, Smith is remembered particularly for humanistic photo-essays that locate universal values in the experience of individuals. Many of his best series first appeared in *Life* magazine. Convinced that photography is a narrative medium, Smith harbored grandiose dreams of encompassing in his images the total reality of situations he investigated. Driven to transcend the objectivity of documentary photography, he immersed himself before photographing in his subjects' physical and psychological circumstances. Sometimes he even rearranged events before his camera in order to produce an intensified experience for the viewer. A native of Wichita, Kansas, William Eugene Smith began to photograph for local newspapers while still in high school. Before the end of his first year at Notre Dame University, he left for New York to freelance for several magazines. In 1942 he went to the Pacific to cover World War II, primarily for *Life*. He accompanied the troops through numerous dangerous battles and was gravely wounded during the invasion of Okinawa in May 1945. A long convalescence and dozens of surgeries ensued before he returned to photography in 1947. Reportedly, the first picture he then took numbers among the twentieth century's most cherished images. "Walk to the Paradise Garden" pictures two small children (his own), walking away from the viewer into a forest clearing. When the photograph appeared as the final image in Edward *Steichen's celebrated 1955 "Family of Man" exhibition, these innocent beings moving into the light symbolized postwar optimism about the future. After the war, Smith produced his best-known *Life* essays, including "Country Doctor" (1948), "Spanish Village" (1951), and "Man of Mercy" (1954), profiling Dr. Albert Schweitzer. However, the years at *Life* were marred by constant battles between Smith and the editorial staff over control of his prints and their presentation. He gradually withdrew from the magazine and left altogether in 1954. In 1956 he accepted a commission to produce a photo-essay on the city of Pittsburgh. Ignoring the limitations of the project, he spent most of a year making some ten thousand photographs and another three years printing his negatives and working on layouts. Although small selections of his Pittsburgh prints appeared, he never was able to publish the epic masterwork he had in mind. Smith won international acclaim for his environmentally oriented final major photo-essay, "Minamata" (1975). The product of several years' work, it treats a Japanese fishing village stricken with the effects of industrial pollution. He died in Tucson, Arizona.

Smithson, Robert (1938–73). Sculptor, draftsman, and experimental artist. Remembered particularly for *Spiral Jetty* (Dia Foundation, 1970), he ranked as a leading figure in the genesis of *earth art but also contributed to *minimalism, *process art, and *conceptualism. Blending environmental and apocalyptic thought, his writings affected many artists of the late 1960s and early 1970s. A New Jersey native, Robert Irving Smithson was born in Passaic and grew up in Rutherford and Clifton. While still in high school, he studied at the *Art Students League, briefly at the Brooklyn Museum's school, and privately with Isaac *Soyer. His *abstract expressionist-inflected painting of the late 1950s, when he settled in New York, frequently incorporated figural imagery related to his wide-ranging reading in classical and science fiction literature or drawn from religious art, particularly of the Byzantine period. By 1964 he had turned his attention primarily to minimal sculpture. Besides experimenting with the dematerializing effects of mirrors, he produced modular, geometric works that emphasize mathematical relationships. Avidly interested since childhood in natural science, in the same period he began to seek ways to combine this form of knowledge with his evolving critique of modernity. Smithson's New Jersey childhood had sensitized him to the disruptive effects of industrialization on the landscape. After the mid-1960s he frequently drew on locations in his home state in formulating art works. His first important article, "Entropy and the New Monuments," which appeared in *Artforum* in 1966, announced his preoccupation with the Second Law of Thermodynamics and its implication that the universe is winding down. A series of Nonsites from the late 1960s incorporated earth, rocks, and detritus from ravaged locations into gallery *installations juxtaposing the natural material—in bins or on the floor, sometimes divided by mirrors—with photographs and maps of the collection areas. For his most explicit homage to entropy, *Partially Buried Woodshed* (Kent [Ohio] State University, 1970), he heaped dirt upon an unused shack until its main supporting beam began to crack. Left to natural consequences, it eventually collapsed but has been preserved as an art work as the artist intended. After several years of contemplating large-scale earthworks,

Smithson executed the well-known *Spiral Jetty* in Utah's Great Salt Lake. Made from bulldozed rock and dirt, this fifteen-hundred-foot whorl reaches from shore into the dark, pinkish water, following a pattern chosen for symbolic resonance, as well as its association with natural growth. For much of its history, the work has been under water, but from time to time it emerges into view, coated with salt crystals. Following completion of *Broken Circle/Spiral Hill* (1971) near Emmen, Holland, Smithson was engaged in executing *Amarillo Ramp* (1973) near Amarillo, Texas, when he died in a plane crash while inspecting the site. With the help of his friends, his widow, sculptor Nancy Holt (1938–), completed the piece. She also edited *The Writings of Robert Smithson* (1979).

Born in Worcester, Massachusetts, in 1960 Nancy Louise Holt graduated from Tufts University in nearby Medford and moved to New York. She and Smithson married in 1963. In her best-known work, *Sun Tunnels* (in the desert near Lucin, Utah, 1973–76), four enormous concrete tubes, each more than nine feet in diameter, lie in a rough X-formation that draws attention to eternal natural phenomena. Aligned with the winter and summer solstices, the tubes frame the rising and setting sun on those days, while holes cut in their upper surfaces provide views of particular constellations. She has continued to specialize in site-specific outdoor works that emphasize the historical continuities and perceptual possibilities of their locations. Earlier in her career, mostly during the 1970s, she also worked with film and video. She lives in Galisteo, New Mexico.

Smithsonian Institution. A federal institution devoted to research and education in art, science, and history. Celebrated for its museums, it encompasses also libraries, archives, scholarly research facilities, and the National Zoological Park. Except for the Cooper-Hewitt, National Design Museum in New York, its constituents enhance Washington, D.C., mostly around the Mall. Smithsonian museums include several important to the study of American art, namely the Smithsonian American Art Museum (previously known successively as the National Gallery of Art, the National Collection of Fine Arts, and the National Museum of American Art) with its satellite Renwick Gallery, the National Portrait Gallery, the *Hirshhorn Museum and Sculpture Garden, and the *Freer Gallery of Art. Supplementing these with related material are the National Museum of the American Indian, which operates a lower Manhattan outpost known as the George Gustav Heye Center, the National Museum of American History, and the Anacostia Community Museum, a repository of material related to African-American history and culture. The Smithsonian also comprises the Archives of American Art, an unrivaled compendium of primary documents related to art and artists of the United States. Headquartered in Washington, it maintains ancillary research centers elsewhere. Other components of the Smithsonian include the National Air and Space Museum, the National Museum of African Art, the Arthur M. Sackler Gallery (devoted to Asian art), the National Museum of Natural History, and the National Postal Museum. A quirk of history led to the Smithsonian's founding. At his death in 1829, British scientist James Smithson, who had never visited North America, left his estate to a nephew. For unknown reasons, he additionally stipulated that if this relative should die without heirs, as he did in 1835, the estate should then accrue to the United States "to found at Washington, under the name of the Smithsonian Institution, an Establishment for the increase and diffusion of knowledge." In 1836 Congress accepted the gift, which amounted to more than half a million dollars, and ten years later finally chartered the institution as a trust governed by a board of regents. Designed by architect James Renwick and completed in 1855, the original red sandstone Smithsonian building, popularly known because of its medieval architectural style as the Castle, remained in use as an exhibition space for more than a century. Today it houses administrative offices and an information center.

Snelson, Kenneth (1927–). Sculptor and photographer. Known primarily for elegant abstract structures of apparently free-floating tubular elements, he also takes extreme wide-angle photographs of gardens and urban infrastructure. The sculptures, which employ wires or cables to hold the tubes in position, depend for their effect on forces of tension and compression. Shiny stainless steel and aluminum have been favored materials, although he has on occasion worked with other metals or with such combinations as bamboo and rope or string. Many of his finest works reach monumental scale and are intended for outdoor locations. Although the success of Snelson's method depends upon his considerable analytical skills, he designs individual pieces intuitively. Generally asymmetrical, they often suggest organic growth in their complex, muscular organization. Born in Pendleton, Oregon, Kenneth Duane Snelson studied at the University of Oregon in Eugene for two years before heading to *Black Mountain College in 1948. Then a painter intending to study with Josef

*Albers, he changed direction upon encountering architect Buckminster Fuller, who set him on a course of discovery concerning natural forces that shape the visible world. Within months, he began making delicate structures that initiated the evolution of his characteristic work. Although Fuller's inspiration was decisive to the young artist, Snelson claims with plausible justification that his innovations proved critical to Fuller in conceptualizing the theoretical basis of his famous geodesic domes. After leaving Black Mountain in 1949, Snelson continued his studies at the Illinois Institute of Technology's Bauhaus-oriented Institute of Design in Chicago and then in Paris, where he studied with Fernand Léger. He later also took engineering courses to sharpen his understanding of structure. In 1952 Snelson moved to New York, where he supported himself for about fifteen years by working as a cinematographer. Until the middle of the minimalist 1960s, Snelson was regarded more as a quirky engineer than as a sculptor, although he had achieved his mature, airy style by around 1960. However, before the end of the decade, his unique formal purity began to attract numerous clients. A futuristic blend of Brancusi's *Endless Column* (Târgu-Jiu, Romania, 1937–38) and constructivism, *Needle Tower* (Hirshhorn Museum, 1968) rises sixty feet above its base, presenting a gravity-defying arrangement of interrelated tubes that appear to be independently suspended in space. They diminish in size as they ascend, enhancing the effect of height. Also integrating perceptions of space and mass, Snelson's emphatically horizontal photographs are taken with a special camera that can accommodate as much as 360 degrees of vision. Since around 1990, he has also explored space and form with computer-generated images.

Sobel, Janet (1894–1968). Painter. She achieved brief acclaim for her *abstract expressionist work in the mid-1940s but soon faded into obscurity. Born Jennie Lechovsky in Ekaterinoslav, Russia (now Dnipropetrovsk in central Ukraine), in 1908 she arrived with her family in New York. Two years later she married Max Sobel, who ran a jewelry business. For the next twenty-seven years, she lived as a mother and housewife in Brooklyn but took up painting in her early forties. Remaining self-taught, she produced colorful figurative works in an imaginative, unacademic, and decorative style. By 1944 she was dripping and pouring paint while employing automatist methods to create dynamic *all-over paintings. Traces of figuration remain in early examples, but by the time she described herself as a surrealist in 1946, much of her work was entirely abstract. In 1947 she moved permanently to the northern New Jersey suburb of Plainfield, where she continued to work in seclusion for some time, reverting again to figural fantasies.

Social realism. *See* AMERICAN SCENE MOVEMENT.

Société Anonyme, Inc. An association founded in 1920 by Katherine *Dreier, Marcel *Duchamp, and *Man Ray as an "International Organization for the Promotion of the Study in America of the Progressive in Art." Man Ray came up with the name Société Anonyme, although Duchamp had to explain to him that the French phrase meant "corporation." When a lawyer added "Inc." on the incorporation papers, thus making the full name "incorporated corporation," it took on a charmingly absurd, dada-inflected tone. Dreier conceived the organization and remained its driving force. Duchamp continued to provide assistance through many years, but Man Ray played little part after he left for Paris in 1921. The Société Anonyme organized exhibitions, sponsored lectures and publications, and bought works for a permanent collection, often referred to as a museum. In actuality, for only a few years the group staged temporary exhibitions from a tiny gallery, which opened in New York in 1920 with a survey of sixteen modern works. It was thus the first institution in the country to put forth a program supporting modern art. The Société Anonyme gallery presented work by important European modernists, as well Americans such as Man Ray, Marsden *Hartley, and Joseph *Stella. Kandinsky's first one-person exhibition in the United States was held there in 1923. Other Europeans introduced at the Société's gallery include Paul Klee, Joan Miró, and Kurt Schwitters. The most important of the group's more than eighty exhibitions was the "International Exhibition of Modern Art" held at the Brooklyn Museum in 1926. Including more than three hundred works, this ranked as the first American show to present a systematic survey of recent advanced international art. Through the 1920s, the Société played an important role in making modern art available in New York. After 1929, the newly founded and much better funded *Museum of Modern Art made it redundant. Its collection of more than six hundred items went to Yale University in 1941, and the organization officially disbanded in 1950.

Society of American Artists. Organization of late-nineteenth-century progressive artists, established primarily to present members' work to the public through exhibitions. Founded as the American Art Association in 1877 by cosmopolitan, generally younger artists, it was renamed the following year. Most original members had trained in Europe, where they typically embraced the era's new anti-academic spirit in Paris or Munich. More interested in form and technique than in moralistic or didactic content, they generally valued painterliness (or, in the case of sculpture, richly modeled surfaces), spontaneity, and personal expression. Although the group formed in dissatisfaction with the *National Academy of Design, differences between the two organizations narrowed by the end of the century, and in 1906 they merged. The association came together during a meeting at the home of cultural lions Richard Watson Gilder, a prominent editor and writer, and his wife Helena de Kay Gilder (1846–1916), a painter and activist in the cause of up-to-date art. Other early members included Walter *Shirlaw, who was elected the first president, Augustus *Saint-Gaudens, John *La Farge, Will H. *Low, and Olin Levi *Warner.

Society of American Wood-Engravers. *See* KINGSLEY, ELBRIDGE.

Society of Independent Artists. *See* INDEPENDENT EXHIBITIONS.

Society of Six. *See* GILE, SELDEN.

Sommer, Frederick (1905–99). Photographer and painter. His understated but disquieting photographs often treat decay, disintegration, and desolation. Among his most original works, horizonless desert landscapes are filled with crisp detail and yet devoid of incident. Sommer also employed varied photographic and mixed-media techniques to produce abstract prints. Most notably, he developed a method of capturing patterns of smoke on glass and then printing from these "negatives," which he sometimes altered by hand. Born Fritz Carlos Sommer in Angri, Italy, he moved in 1913 with his family to Brazil. As a young man, he trained as an architect in Rio de Janeiro before moving to the United States in 1925. After earning a master's degree two years later in landscape architecture at Cornell University, he returned to Brazil to practice. Seeking a cure for tuberculosis, he moved to Switzerland in 1930 and the following year to Tucson, Arizona. In 1939 he was naturalized as a United States citizen. During convalescence, he turned to painting and drawing, while also expanding the broad grasp of philosophy, science, and art that characterized his intellect. In the mid-1930s, after meeting Alfred *Stieglitz and Edward *Weston, photography became his principal interest. By the late 1930s, he was producing elegant but disturbing compositions that often included such unanticipated subjects as dead animals or chicken entrails. To many observers, a 1939 image of an amputated leg and foot proved particularly challenging. In 1941 he began to photograph the harsh desert landscape with a directness that contrasted startlingly with conventional interests in revealing the beauty of nature. In these, he often directed his view so that the ground extends in all directions beyond the edge of the frame, forming an unremitting vista of impeccably printed rubble. Some of these precede, and may even have influenced, the *abstract expressionists' *all-over compositions. In the same year, he also established a friendship with Max *Ernst, who recognized and encouraged inherently surrealistic tendencies in his work. In the late 1940s Sommer began to experiment with varied photographic processes, including photograms, montages, and paint-on-cellophane, as well as the smoked glass technique. In 1962 he started photographing cut paper abstractions, which he hung and lighted to enhance their spatial drama. Anticipating postmodern appropriation, he also created new works of art by altering and photographing works by other artists. His two-volume *Sommer: Words and Pictures* appeared in 1984. Active as an artist into his nineties, he died at his home in Prescott, Arizona, where he had lived since 1935.

Sonnabend, Ileana. *See* CASTELLI, LEO.

Southworth, Albert Sands (1811–94). Photographer. An early practitioner of the medium, he worked in Boston in partnership with Josiah Johnson Hawes (1808–1901). Responsible for some of the finest portrait *daguerreotypes, their studio pioneered in representing other subjects as well. A native of Fairlee, Vermont, Southworth was educated at Phillips Academy in Andover, Massachusetts, and became a pharmacist. Born in East Sudbury (now Wayland), Massachusetts, Hawes trained as a carpenter but worked as a self-taught portrait painter. Independently, both men were inspired to become photographers in 1840, when a French visitor to Boston demonstrated the daguerreotype technique. Southworth soon opened a studio, and Hawes joined him in 1843. Together they devised improvements to their craft and aspired to the highest standards of artistic accomplishment. Intent on capturing character as well as physical likeness, they employed dramatic lighting, skillfully arranged poses, and simple settings that concentrate attention on the sitter. Besides ordinary citizens, their clients included numerous contemporary luminaries, including well-known Bostonians as well as passing celebrities. Sensitive but powerful likenesses of Massachusetts chief justice Lemuel Shaw, entertainer Lola Montez, and writer Harriet Beecher Stowe number among their best-known images. Outside the studio, they trained their cameras on unusual subjects, including a hospital operating room, Niagara Falls, and celestial eclipses. In 1849 Southworth departed for two years in California, where he hoped to find gold but did not. Subsequently he suffered health problems and consequently withdrew in the early 1860s from active participation in the studio. In 1872 he published *Twenty-three Years under a Skylight, or Life and Experiences of a Photographer*. He died in Boston. After Southworth's retirement, Hawes continued the business on his own, sustaining the partnership's high-quality reputation with paper prints after the daguerreotype's popularity faded. He died in Crawford Notch, in New Hampshire's White Mountains.

Soyer, Raphael (1899–1987). Painter and printmaker. A committed humanist, he specialized in portraits and sympathetically observed scenes of New York life. Born Raphael Schoar in Borisoglebsk, Russia, along with others in his family he assumed a new surname upon arrival in the United States in 1912. They soon settled permanently in New York, and Soyer trained primarily at the *National Academy of Design between 1918 and 1922. He also studied more briefly at Cooper Union and at the *Art Students League, where Guy *Pène du Bois ranked as his most important teacher. At the outset, Soyer was attracted to the *Ashcan School's earlier urban realism. In the 1920s, becoming enamored of Degas's art, he often adapted the French artist's compositional strategies and intimate tone in rendering pensive individuals, seemingly caught unaware. During the 1930s, like other social realists among the *American Scene painters, Soyer identified with the exploited lower classes and tried to convey their helplessness in the face of forces beyond their control. However, his work almost never incorporated overtly political messages, and many paintings of the period speak more generally. *Railroad Station Waiting Room* (Corcoran Gallery, c. 1938–40) conveys the loneliness of urban life and the boredom of idleness. In later years, he specialized in studio work, observing human experience through visiting sitters. Although on good terms with leading avant-garde artists and writers, he remained unmoved by mid-century enthusiasm for abstraction and eloquently defended the purposes of a representational alternative. He published *A Painter's Pilgrimage* (1962), *Self-Revealment: A Memoir* (1969), and *Diary of an Artist* (1977), as well as a study of Thomas *Eakins (1966). He continued to paint until shortly before his death.

His twin **Moses Soyer** (1899–1974) enjoyed a parallel career, although the two tried to avoid influencing each other. He studied at several schools, including Cooper Union and the National Academy, and was attracted to the work of Robert *Henri and George *Bellows before developing his own affinity for Degas's work, along with a deep admiration for Rembrandt. He, too, adopted a humanitarian and tolerant point of view. His most politically charged work dated from the 1930s, but he continued even then also to paint more neutral scenes. *Artists on the WPA* (Smithsonian American Art Museum, 1935–36) vividly evokes the artistic activity of a communal studio. His articles defending social realism and attacking regionalism contributed to a vigorous 1930s discussion about the purposes of art. From the 1940s, as his art became less socially engaged he often painted ballet dancers as well as portraits. He died while working in his studio.

Their brother **Isaac Soyer** (1907–81), born in Tombov, Russia, shared his brothers' serious, often melancholy tone in quietly introspective scenes taken from everyday life in New York. He arrived in the United States in 1914, two years later than the twins who would become more accomplished artists. He followed his brothers' example in studying at Cooper Union and the National Academy, as well as other schools, and in treating modern life with techniques derived from traditional painting. The man and a woman sharing a space but oblivious to each other in *Cafeteria* (Memphis Brooks Museum of Art, 1930) suggest the isolation of modern life. A more politically conscious work, *Employment Agency* (Whitney Museum, 1937), portrays individuals not only emotionally cut off from each other but also discouraged by lack of economic opportunity. All three brothers became American citizens, found support in the *federal art projects, and participated in the *American Artists' Congress.

Speicher, Eugene (1883–1962). Painter. Known especially for portraits of women, he also painted landscapes and still lifes. Born in Buffalo, Eugene Edward Speicher studied at the school of the Buffalo Fine Arts Academy (now a division of the State University of New York at Buffalo) for four years before moving to New York in 1906. At the *Art Students League during the next two years, William Merritt *Chase and Robert *Henri ranked as his most important teachers. In 1910 he traveled abroad on the first of several trips to visit European museums. An early arrival at *Woodstock, he remained associated with that artists' retreat until he died at his home there. He also maintained a New York residence. Speicher's early work showed an interest in *Ashcan School directness and vitality, but he soon turned to painting the figure with a solid, volumetric approach derived from traditional European painting. After exposure to the work of Cézanne and other modern artists, he generalized, simplified, and slightly flattened forms to produce dignified renditions of individuals usually lost in dreamy inwardness, as in *Lilya* (Cincinnati Art Museum, 1930). Nonfigural subjects often show a freer application of paint and looser definition of form. Speicher's blend of modern and traditional elements remained highly respected into the 1940s but fell out of favor when critical attention turned to abstraction.

Spencer, Lilly Martin (1822–1902). Painter. The most successful woman painter of the mid-nineteenth century, she is known for domestic *genre scenes. Her engrossingly detailed and brightly colored images usually focus on the lives of women and children. Nearly always cheerful and sometimes gently humorous, they nevertheless offer nuanced responses to complexities of nineteenth-century gender politics and family relations. Most reflect mid-century notions idealizing woman's virtue. They emphasize the mother's role in providing for her family a safe and happy home ruled by Christian values, a point of view that reflected liberal thinking in the 1840s but later hardened into dogma. At the same time, some of Spencer's work responds, if only obliquely, to voices of early feminists (such as her own mother). Occasionally, she strikes an ironic note, at least for the viewer predisposed to observe it. Concurrently, Spencer also painted romantic scenes inspired by literature or history. Her broader interests suggest that the focus on domestic genre during the years when her work was most popular reflects expectations of critics and patrons for a woman artist. The development of her reputation profited from the *American Art-Union's sponsorship, and she found a wide audience for prints of her work.

Born Angélique Marie Martin to French parents in Exeter, England, she emigrated with her family to New York in 1830, but after three years they moved to Marietta, Ohio. In Cincinnati during the early 1840s she benefited from James Henry *Beard's assistance and encouragement. Declining Nicholas *Longworth's offer to finance art studies elsewhere, she remained essentially self-taught and never thoroughly mastered figure drawing or perspective. (Recognizing her deficiency even after she had attained success, she later attended evening classes at the *National Academy of Design.) In 1844 she married Englishman Benjamin Rush Spencer, and they decamped for New York four years later. The Spencers probably had thirteen children (records are unclear), with seven surviving to maturity. The artist not only tended her brood but also acted as the family's primary breadwinner. (Her husband served as her business manager and helped out in the studio. Although he was sometimes listed in city directories as a painter, no independent works have been located.) In 1858 the family moved to Newark, New Jersey, and in 1879 to Highland, New York, on the Hudson River. In 1900, following her husband's death ten years earlier, she returned permanently to New York City. One of Spencer's most widely popular images, *Shake Hands?* (Ohio Historical Society, Columbus, 1854) suggests her ability to manipulate unstable meanings. A broadly smiling, confident woman works in a well-stocked kitchen elaborated with numerous still life vignettes of food and utensils. To the viewer she extends her flour-dusted right hand in an offer of acquaintance. While apparently delighted with her conventional domestic duties, she also radiates a sense of healthy self-reliance and competence. Moreover, the proffered hand itself signals her independence, for the handshake remained at this time primarily a male gesture related to the affirmation of equality. As the market for genre in general declined in the late 1850s, Spencer's art began to go out of fashion. Following the cost-cutting move across the Hudson River, she was reduced for several years to making a living by coloring photographs and drawing ladies' magazine illustrations. After the Civil War she responded to changing taste by enlarging her repertoire of subjects to include allegory, portraits, miniatures, and still lifes. Her technique broadened in the 1880s, as she tried to accommodate fashionable styles, but she never recovered preeminence as a popular interpreter of middle-class urban family life. Nevertheless, she continued painting until the last day of her life.

Spencer, Niles (1893–1952). Painter. Associated with *precisionism, he specialized in subtly modulated architectural landscapes but also painted still lifes. Born in Pawtucket, he graduated in 1915 from the Rhode Island School of Design in nearby Providence. Subsequently he studied at the Ferrer School in New York with Robert *Henri and George *Bellows. While continuing to live in New York, he sojourned frequently along the New England coast in such favored locales as Ogunquit, Maine, and *Provincetown, on Cape Cod. Spencer's personal style emerged in 1921–22 in response to his first direct encounter with European art. Drawn to Cézanne and cubism, he also appreciated the architectonic frescoes of the early Italian Renaissance. In characteristic works, tonally adjusted planes define the forms of buildings, while spaces are often compressed or distorted to suit the painting's structural demands. Typically reserved in tone, *Buildings* (Columbus [Ohio] Museum of Art, c. 1924) offers an analytical view of a space hemmed in across rooftops. Spencer's still lifes usually offer more directly realistic description than his architectural scenes. *The Green Table* (Whitney Museum, 1930) includes three sensuous lemons and a brimmed hat arranged on a reflective tabletop set in a corner defined by plain surfaces. From the mid-1940s, with paintings such as *In Fairmont* (Museum of Modern Art, 1951), his work became more abstract and frequently more dynamic without abandoning its architectural basis. In later years he made his home in the Delaware River town of Dingman's Ferry, Pennsylvania, where he died.

Spero, Nancy. *See* GOLUB, LEON.

Spiral group. *See* AFRICAN-AMERICAN ART.

Stamos, Theodoros (1922–97). Painter. An *abstract expressionist, in early paintings he favored *biomorphic shapes floating through mysterious primeval spaces. Often resembling the work of William *Baziotes, these works grew also from the artist's admiration for aspects of surrealism and for the work of Arthur *Dove. In addition, they incorporated interests in natural history, ancient myth, and the power of primitive forms. During the 1950s feathery brushstrokes created limited but energized color areas. Continuing to simplify and condense, in the 1960s he completed his most reductive canvases, based on rectangular elements. Later, under the general rubric of the Infinity Field series, he arrived at serene and poetic color abstractions, sometimes traversed by linear elements. Reflecting his appreciation for the spiritual dimension of nature and for eastern philosophies, these generally allude to nature, often suggesting atmospheric landscapes or seascapes. Born in New York, Stamos began to study sculpture in evening classes at the American Artists School while still in high school, which he abandoned in 1939, a few months short of graduation. As he learned to paint on his own, from 1941 until 1948 he ran a framing shop, which brought him into contact with artists and their work. He had his first one-person show in 1943 at a gallery directed by Betty *Parsons, who included him among her artists after she opened her own space. In 1947 he traveled to the West Coast, where he visited Mark *Tobey. On a trip to France, Italy, and Greece the following year, he made the acquaintance of a number of leading European artists. During the several years after the death of his good friend Mark *Rothko in 1970, Stamos's artistic accomplishments were overshadowed in the public mind by a lengthy court battle concerning his role in administering Rothko's estate. Stamos and two other executors charged with overseeing disposition of Rothko's paintings were accused of impropriety in their transactions with the Marlborough Gallery. They had allowed the gallery to reap enormous profits from the sale of Rothko's work without realizing commensurate benefits to the estate, while at the same time Stamos joined the gallery's prestigious stable in 1971 and had his first show there the following year. As part of the settlement, his house in Manhattan was taken from him, although he was allowed life tenancy. Meanwhile, in 1970 Stamos visited Greece, his parents' homeland, for only the second time. He subsequently summered regularly on the Ionian island of Lefkada (or Levkás) and died an honored son of Greece in a hospital in Yiannina (or Ioánnina) in the northwestern part of the country.

Stanczak, Julian. *See* OP ART.

Stankiewicz, Richard (1922–83). Sculptor. Known for welded *assemblages of scrap metal, in the 1950s he pioneered the use of found materials in sculpture. At first, his inventions made witty use of visual analogies between mechanical and anthropomorphic shapes. By the early 1960s, he more frequently emphasized purely formal qualities of his materials. Combining precedents in the sculpture of Picasso, Alexander *Calder, and David *Smith with the spirit of dada interventions and surrealist fantasies, his innovative work figured prominently in establishing the legitimacy of *junk art. Born in Philadelphia, Richard Peter Stankiewicz moved with his family to Detroit. After working in the Civilian Conservation Corps, a federal depression-relief project, he served in the U.S. Navy from 1941 until 1947. He then moved to New York to study painting with Hans *Hofmann. In 1950 he left for a year in Paris, where he studied briefly with painter Fernand Léger and then with sculptor Ossip Zadkine. While abroad he began producing abstract terra cottas, which evolved into linear, plaster-covered wire sculptures. The characteristic junk sculptures emerged not long after his return to New York in June 1951. Sometime during the following winter, while digging a garden space outside his studio building, he unearthed pieces of industrial detritus. After initially tossing them aside, he observed their aesthetic potential and bought a do-it-yourself book to learn welding. In 1953 he first showed the new work, which was almost immediately recognized for its originality but also, in the minds of many observers, for its shocking lack of taste and serious purpose. With time, his work gained appreciation for its formal logic, homage to urban civilization, psychological acuteness, and contribution to the period's rethinking of the intersection between art and life. Stankiewicz's popularity waned after the early 1960s, at least partly because the artist abandoned New York. In 1962 he moved permanently to rural Worthington in western Massachusetts. From 1967 until retirement in 1981, he taught at the State University of New York at Albany. On a 1969 visit to Australia, he adopted a cleaner and more structural approach in fifteen large sculptures made of steel. During the 1970s and early 1980s he used found and fabricated elements in sculptures that variously incorporate allusion and abstraction. He died at his home in Worthington.

Stanley, John Mix (1814–72). Painter. Known primarily for views of the American West and its Indian tribes, he also painted portraits and occasionally other subjects. Stanley probably spent more time in the West than any other professional artist of the mid-nineteenth century, and he ranged more widely, from territorial New Mexico to Puget Sound. In 1848 he even traveled to Hawaii, where he painted portraits of the royal family. Fires at the *Smithsonian Institution and at P. T. Barnum's American Museum destroyed much of his most important work in 1865. Born in the Finger Lakes region of New York State, in or near Canandaigua, Stanley soon moved with his family to Buffalo. He was apprenticed to a wagon maker in Naples, in the area of his birthplace, in 1828 but by 1832 was working as a sign and house painter in Buffalo. Largely self-taught as an artist, he moved to Detroit in 1834 and set up a portrait business. Between 1836 and 1842, he traveled widely throughout the Midwest and East seeking commissions. He apparently first painted Indian subjects in Minnesota in 1839 and by 1842 had decided to dedicate his artistic skills to documenting tribal individuals and customs. While continuing to travel and add new paintings, in 1846 he began exhibiting his Indian Gallery, which visited a number of cities before 1852, when he deposited it on loan to the Smithsonian (where most of it perished in the 1865 fire). Following his final trip West in 1853, he made his home in Washington, D.C. There he completed his Western Wilds *panorama, followed by a Civil War panorama during the early 1860s. In 1863 he settled permanently in Detroit. During the remainder of his career he worked mainly as a portraitist but also continued to draw on his Indian material to produce new images. Although he worked in a clear, descriptive style, Stanley was less of a documentarian than such scientifically motivated predecessors as George *Catlin and Karl *Bodmer. Most of his western paintings portray subjects posing in orderly, easily legible compositions. Slightly generalized form and luminous light contribute to an idealized tone. Although some works perpetuate stereotypical views of Indian character and way of life, Stanley's pictures effectively convey the grandeur of the western landscape and the essential dignity of the varied peoples who lived there.

Stebbins, Emma (1815–82). Sculptor and painter. Although she worked primarily as a painter until she was over forty, she is remembered for her sculpture, mostly dating to the 1860s. Her bronze *Angel of the Waters* (1870; installed 1873; modeled 1862) atop Bethesda Fountain in Central Park remains her most significant achievement. She generally worked in marble, often on a small, tabletop scale. Unlike most sculptors of her day, Stebbins insisted on carving the stone herself instead of hiring professional workmen. Born in New York, Stebbins studied with Henry *Inman and Edward *Brackett. Although she did not work professionally, she achieved some recognition as a painter, while also experimenting with sculpture. In 1856 she sailed for Europe and within months settled in Rome, where she studied sculpture with Maine-born Benjamin Paul Akers (1825–61), whose few surviving marbles accentuate romantic sentiment and technical delicacy. She also soon became acquainted with Harriet *Hosmer and her circle of independently minded women, including the American actress Charlotte Cushman, who became Stebbins's long-term companion. With the support of such friends, she established herself professionally within the prevailing *neoclassical style. Among the earliest American women sculptors to win commissions for public monuments, in 1860 she received the first of these, a contract for a bronze *Horace Mann* (State House grounds, Boston; cast 1867). Upon moving in 1870 to Newport, Rhode Island, with Cushman, she abandoned her artistic career to attend to her friend's declining health. In 1878, two years after Cushman's death in Boston, Stebbins published *Charlotte Cushman: Her Letters and Memories of Her Life*. She died in New York.

Steichen, Edward J. (1879–1973). Photographer, painter, and curator. A leader in photography for more than half a century, as a young man he numbered among stars of *pictorialism. During the same years, he also painted *tonalist landscapes that share the intimate, poetic sensibility of his contemporary photographic prints. Championed by Alfred *Stieglitz, he participated actively in the *Photo-Secession. While living in Paris, he identified much of the modern art that Stieglitz introduced to America at *291. During World War I, he worked in aerial reconnaissance, which precipitated redirection of his expressive goals toward sharper realism. By fusing naturalism and artifice into stylish images, he became the leading American commercial photographer of the 1920s and 1930s. Later, as a curator at the *Museum of Modern Art, he assembled important shows, including the landmark 1955 "Family of Man" exhibition. His crisp nature studies of later years recapitulated, with different means, the poetry of his early work. Born in Luxembourg, Edouard Jean Steichen later Americanized his name. In 1881 he moved with his parents to Hancock, on Michigan's upper peninsula. Eight years later, the family settled in Milwaukee. There, at fifteen, he began a four-year apprenticeship at a lithography company, while also beginning to paint. After buying his first camera in 1895, he quickly mastered advanced artistic taste. The asymmetrical formal harmonies of his full-length 1898 "Self-Portrait" derive from Whistlerian precedents, while its introspective mood and sensuous beauty reveal his sympathy for contemporary pictorialist ideals. After achieving recognition in photography shows, like most ambitious artists of his generation he headed for Paris. On the way, in the spring of 1900, he stopped in New York to meet Stieglitz, who bought three of the young man's landscape prints. In Paris Steichen briefly studied painting, absorbed both traditional and contemporary art, and began a serious engagement with portrait photography. He particularly singled out artists and writers, such as Rodin and Maurice Maeterlinck, whose impressionist and symbolist aesthetic goals paralleled his own.

Between 1902 and 1906 Steichen lived in New York, where his portrait career flourished among the city's elite. In 1903 he captured a quintessential J. P. *Morgan in a powerful image of the scowling titan gripping his chair arm like a weapon. During this period, he also worked closely with Stieglitz in defining and establishing the Photo-Secession. In 1902 he designed its magazine, **Camera Work*, and his work appeared in several subsequent issues. Working with Stieglitz to establish 291 in 1905, Steichen designed the premises as well as early exhibitions. After his return to Paris in 1906, he acted as Stieglitz's representative in lining up art to be shown in New York. After a short residency in Paris, Steichen moved to nearby Voulangis, where he made his home until World War I forced his repatriation in 1914. During these years, in seeking to infuse the photographic experience with the richness of painting, Steichen expertly used gum bichromate and other complex printing techniques, as well as platinum, and in 1907 he numbered among the first to learn the Autochrome process, with which he soon achieved luminous color photographs.

Between 1917 and 1919, while serving in the U.S. Army, Steichen pioneered in techniques of aviation photography. This work, which required clarity of detail, stimulated a transition from the poetic vagueness of his pictorial work to a cleaner vision. After 1919, again residing at Voulangis in relative isolation, he undertook a rigorous technical examination of the photographic process and around 1922 gave up painting. From 1923 until 1938, he served as a photographer for Condé Nast publications in New York. He also accepted assignments from other mass-circulation publications and worked in advertising. During these years, his originality, design skill, and flair for glamour transformed commercial photography and raised the status of the profession. Relying now on sharp-focus technique and direct printing, he brought a fresh modernity to his subjects. Continuing to demonstrate that portraiture is an art of interpretation, he also produced stunning and often unexpected images of arts and entertainment luminaries. The most memorable include Gloria Swanson (1924), Greta Garbo (1928), Maurice Chevalier (1921), Charlie Chaplin (1931), Martha Graham (1931), Paul Robeson (1933), and Lillian Gish as Ophelia (1936).

Following a year in Mexico in 1938–39, he again put his talents to patriotic use, working from 1942 to 1946 for the U.S. Navy. In addition to taking pictures in the Pacific theater, he supervised a unit that produced some of the war's best-known combat images. *The Blue Ghost: A Photographic Log and Personal Narrative of the Aircraft Carrier U.S.S. Lexington in Combat Operation* (1947) describes his experiences. After arranging two war-related photography exhibitions at MoMA, in 1947 he became director of its photography department. During fifteen years there, he arranged more than fifty exhibitions, including "The Family of Man." The most popular photography exhibition ever staged, this group of more than five hundred photographs was seen by some nine million visitors as it traveled the globe during the next several years. It promoted Steichen's humanistic ideal of advancing universal understanding through a medium that he believed to be accessible to all. Much of Steichen's late work centered on his estate in West Redding, Connecticut, which he purchased in the late 1920s. Indulging his love of nature (he bred prize-winning delphiniums), he circled back to his early successes by finding lush and spiritual beauty in landscape photographs. These sharply detailed transformations of nature into art often centered on a favorite shadblow tree, which doubled as fact and metaphor. In 1963 Steichen published *A Life in Photography*, copiously illustrated with his work. Active until the final months of his life, he died at his home in West Redding the day before his ninety-fourth birthday.

Stein, Gertrude (1874–1946). Writer and collector. A discerning connoisseur of modern art, she amassed a highly significant collection at an early date. Although it included only isolated examples of American art, her acquisitions provided for many artists who visited her legendary Paris salon an education in new ways of seeing. In part inspired by sharp observation of the structure and meaning of the avant-garde art she purchased, her experimental prose style exerted a formative influence on modern literature and provided to young American artists a suggestive model of abstract form. The cubist approach of her friend Picasso was particularly significant to Stein's thinking. After he completed her famous portrait (Metropolitan Museum, 1906) that proved central to his own development, she in turn wrote appreciatively about the artist and his work in essays and a short book, *Picasso* (1938). Stein also purchased the work of Cézanne, Juan Gris, Matisse, and other leading modernists. She was born in Allegheny, Pennsylvania (now part of Pittsburgh), but spent her early years in Vienna and Paris. When she was six, the family settled in Oakland, California. She lived briefly in San Francisco and in Baltimore before enrolling at the precursor to Radcliffe College (now a division of Harvard University). Following her graduation, in 1897 she began medical studies at Johns Hopkins University but left without completing a degree. In 1903 she settled in Paris. Following a visit in 1904, she subsequently returned only once to the United States, for a celebrated lecture tour in 1934. Most of her collection was formed in the decade before World War I. In 1933 she published *The Autobiography of Alice B. Toklas*, a narrative of her life, slyly cast in the voice of her companion of many years. Stein died in Paris.

Collector, critic, and aesthetician **Leo Stein** (1872–1947) collaborated for a few years with his sister Gertrude on purchases, sometimes agreeing to own the work jointly, after they took up residence together in Paris in 1903. However, by 1908 Leo was beginning to have second thoughts about the extreme forms of modernism that Gertrude continued to support. After a short period in the United States, in 1913 he moved permanently to Settignano, near Florence. He continued to write about art from a conservative point of view. Their brother **Michael Stein** (1865–1938), along with his wife, **Sarah Samuels Stein** (1870–1953), also collected modern art, with particular emphasis on Matisse's work. They, too, moved to Paris in 1903. Like his younger brother and sister, Michael was born in metropolitan Pittsburgh, later lived in the San Francisco Bay Area, and studied at Johns Hopkins. In 1935 Michael and Sarah returned permanently to California. None of the Stein family collections remained intact after their deaths.

Steinberg, Saul (1914–99). Painter, draftsman, and sculptor. Best known for works published as cartoons, primarily in the *New Yorker* magazine, he commented broadly, if humorously, on modern life, its follies, and its discontents. An extensive knowledge of modern and traditional art fed his imaginative, witty, economical, and psychologically perceptive style. Notions of identity, masquerade, and cultural displacement pervade his work. Among his most original conceptions, a long series of drawings elaborate visually upon the meaning of words. In addition to his published drawings, he created paintings, murals, *assemblages, collages, and illustrated books. Born in Râmincul-Sarat, he graduated from high school in nearby Bucharest and studied philosophy for a year at the city's university prior to leaving Romania in 1933. In Milan he studied architecture and earned his doctorate in 1940, although he never worked professionally as an architect. His first cartoons appeared in Italian publications in the mid-1930s and his first *New Yorker* drawing in 1941. In 1942 he arrived in New York. The following year he mounted his first solo gallery show, arranged under the auspices of Betty *Parsons, became an American citizen, and began three years of service in the U.S. Navy. Afterward, he made his home in New York but traveled extensively in the United States and abroad. During the war and afterward at the Nuremberg Trials, he made drawings, many published in the *New Yorker*, with a reporter's eye for observed detail. In the 1950s he developed the more abstracted and philosophical point of view associated with his mature drawing style. In Steinberg's classic 1976 *New Yorker* cover, a Manhattanite's overview of the United States, only a flat and unappealing sliver of land separates the Pacific Ocean from the Hudson River. It numbers among the many images that place the artist as a bemused outsider in the adopted country that he affectionately found exhilarating but flawed. Steinberg died at his home in Manhattan. His books, each devoted to a different theme, include *All in Line* (1945), *The Art of Living* (1949), *Passport* (1954), *The Labyrinth* (1960), *The New World* (1965), *Le Masque* (1966), *The Inspector* (1973), *Documents* (1979), and *The Discovery of America* (1992). Memoirs appear in *Reflections and Shadows* (2002), based on tape-recorded interviews conducted by Aldo Buzzi in 1974 and 1977.

In 1943 he married recently divorced painter, collage artist, printmaker, and occasional sculptor Hedda Sterne (1916–). They separated some years later but did not divorce. Hedwig Lindenberg studied for two years at the University of Bucharest, in the city of her birth, before moving to Paris in 1930. She married a Romanian, Frederick Sterne, in 1932 and in 1941 arrived in New York, where she quickly became acquainted with émigré artists, as well as young Americans who would soon be known as *abstract expressionists. She is particularly remembered among them as the only woman in the celebrated photograph of the *Irascibles, published in *Life* magazine in 1951. For nearly four decades from the mid-1940s, Parsons also showed Sterne's work. During the 1940s it varied from expressionistic representation to near abstraction, often incorporating *biomorphic forms that carry surrealist overtones. She also made small abstract sculptures assembled from evocative found materials. Somewhat later she favored machine-based imagery, while during the 1970s she produced diaristic works incorporating handwriting. Ever flexible in her approach to art, she continued working experimentally until late 2004 when she suffered a stroke. Throughout her career, she also painted portraits.

Steiner, Ralph (1899–1986). Photographer and filmmaker. His crisp, witty, and formally inventive approach to photography complemented the mechanical, architectural, and mass-produced subjects he particularly favored. Born in Cleveland, he graduated in 1921 from Dartmouth College. Before working as an advertising and magazine photographer, he studied for a year at Clarence *White's New York photography school, where he sharpened his eye for design. In its unexpected angle of view, extreme close-up treatment, and insistent, rhythmic patterning, "Typewriter Keys" of 1921–22 anticipates that decade's subsequent fascination with the expressive possibilities of objectivity. His work of the later 1920s and 1930s often parallels the spirit of Charles *Sheeler's machine-oriented *precisionist work. "Ford Model T" (c. 1929) displays a bold, clean composition found in the fender area over a front wheel. For "Portrait of Louis *Lozowick" (1930), he posed his artist-friend before a pattern of cogged wheels, part of a large machine of undisclosed function. The bold, abstract composition testifies to the photographer's (and the sitter's) attraction to the romance of technology. Steiner also appreciated the eloquence of the mundane, from urban billboards to rural porches. His work in this vein parallels, and sometimes prefigures, Walker *Evans's imagery. Steiner began making documentary films in the late 1920s. He worked in the mid-1930s with Paul *Strand, Willard *Van Dyke, and others on the Pare Lorentz documentaries, *The Plow That Broke the Plains* (1936) and *The River* (1937), and with Van Dyke to make *The City* for the 1939 World's Fair in New York. In the late 1940s he worked in Hollywood, mostly on short subjects. Steiner published *A Point of View* (1978) and *In Pursuit of Clouds: Images and Metaphors* (1985). He died in a hospital in Hanover, New Hampshire, not far from his final home in Thetford Hill, Vermont.

Stella, Frank (1936–). Painter, printmaker, and sculptor. At twenty-three, he made his name with severely reductive, black "pinstripe" paintings that heralded the approach of *minimalism. A few years later, he began painting bright, geometrically organized, *hard-edge works that continued the use of shaped canvases begun with the earlier series in 1960. Eventually, these paintings reached out from the wall to approximate relief sculptures (although the artist insisted on their pictorial nature). Later he turned primarily to sculpture, producing large-scale, flamboyant works, often intended for display in public places. He has also tried his hand at architecture. The trajectory of his interests from extreme simplicity to extreme complexity, from two dimensions to three, and from reticence to rhetorical excess attends a restless aesthetic in action. Born in the Boston suburb of Malden, Frank Philip Stella began his study of art during four years at Phillips Academy in Andover. There he became interested in abstraction through painter and teacher Patrick Morgan (1904–82) and his wife, painter Maud Morgan (1903–99). As an artist committed to abstract art from his high school years, Stella ranks among the earliest major artists to be trained entirely in that tradition. In 1954 he enrolled at Princeton University. While studying with Stephen Greene (1918–99), then a figurative painter whose interests were evolving toward abstraction, and with William C. *Seitz, Stella also became conversant with the latest developments shown in New York galleries. Early in 1958, the flags and targets in Jasper *Johns's first one-person show particularly caught his attention. Shortly before graduating with a degree in history that spring, Stella renounced his *abstract expressionist approach to combine brushy stripes and isolated rectangles in simple formats. Within months after subsequently moving to New York, he started his flat, nonrelational black series, which quickly made an impression. The next summer he joined the Leo *Castelli gallery, and at the end of 1959 a landmark *Museum of Modern Art show, "Sixteen Americans," organized by Dorothy C. *Miller, included four of his recent paintings (one bought by the museum). Executed in black house paint, the 1959 paintings consist of bands about three inches wide in regular, extremely simple patterns of verticals and horizontals. (In a later group from 1959–60, the parallel stripes work on the diagonal.) Although personal touch is suppressed, the paintings retain a handmade appearance, as slight irregularities appear along the edges of the narrow, unprimed canvas interstices that separate the stripes. Despite their reference to abstract expressionism in scale, ambition, and *all-over compositional strategy, they offended most observers of the time. Particularly distressing were the paintings' emotional inertness, their lack of visual incident, and their refusal to engage questions of meaning. "What you see is what you see," Stella later rejoined. Young minimalists were listening.

The black paintings as a group foretold Stella's subsequent method of working through a single idea in a sequence of preconceived paintings. In 1960 he deviated from black to work with metallic paints in a series that appeared in his first solo show at Castelli's that year. These were followed by colors, as he began to alter the outlines of his canvases, at first with simple notches, later with more complex configurations. In these shaped canvases, stripes paralleling the edges appear to be determined by them, further emphasizing the objectlike nature of his work. Around this time, he worked toward elimination of nearly all visible brushwork in favor of smooth, unmodulated hues. In a 1966 series, limited numbers of ample geometric elements appear within irregular polygons or other oddly shaped formats. In 1967 he embarked on an extended Protractor series (completed in 1971), based on circles and semicircles. In these, wide bands of hot, even fluorescent color follow the edges of his shaped canvases but seem to intersect, passing over and under each other in complex visual displays. (In a variant set, he deployed the same sort of curved stripes within rectangular formats.) This series introduced a marked decorative element, related particularly to his admiration for Matisse and for Celtic and Islamic ornamental schemes, while playing into a taste that came to fruition in the *pattern and decoration movement. During these same years, Stella enlarged his artistic practice by turning to printmaking, lithography particularly, but also several other processes, which he often freely combines. In the mid-1970s he also produced small editions of hand-painted multiples made from cast paper. By about 1975, all sense of restraint had disappeared from his art. His previously disciplined, rationally ordered designs gave way to manic conglomerations of two- and three-dimensional elements, filled with whiplash curves and adorned with feverish brushwork, glitter, and metallic sheen. Just as he had played a central role in formulating a minimalist aesthetic, he now contributed to an emerging *postmodern taste for vulgarity, excessiveness, and the showmanship of commercial culture. A residency at the American Academy in Rome in 1982–83 allowed Stella to reflect on the relationship of his art to old masters. In six lectures delivered at Harvard in 1983 and published in 1986 as *Working Space*, he codified his thoughts about the revitalizing effects of manipulating pictorial and actual space for dramatic effect, as prefigured in Baroque art. His ruminations on such matters provided a theoretical base for subsequent forays into high-relief wall pieces, as well as dizzying three-dimensional works, often sited in public spaces, although he continued to paint, as well. Since the 1990s a long-standing attraction to architecture has generated a number of projects emphasizing swooping, torqued, sculptural forms. Most remain unbuilt.

While on his first trip abroad, including visits to several European countries and Morocco, in London at the end of 1961 Stella married art historian and critic Barbara Rose (1937–). They divorced in the mid-1970s. Born in Washington, D.C., and educated at Smith College in Northampton, Massachusetts, New York's Barnard College, and Columbia University, she has written widely on twentieth-century American art. Her publications include *American Art since 1900* (1967), an anthology of readings on American art from 1900 to 1975, and monographs on Helen *Frankenthaler, Alexander *Liberman, Claes *Oldenburg, and Robert *Rauschenberg, among others.

Stella, Joseph (1877–1946). Painter and draftsman. Best known for radiant, futurist-influenced images of New York's architecture and bridges, he later replaced this vibrant modernist style with a precise realism often tinged with mystical overtones. A consummate draftsman, he produced exquisite silverpoint studies from nature. Born in Muro Lucano, near Naples, Giuseppe Stella moved to New York in 1896 and the next year began his training at the *Art Students League. Less than a year later he transferred to the New York School of Art (now Parsons, the New School for Design), where he studied until 1901 with William Merritt *Chase. He then worked as an illustrator while painting somberly realistic city scenes. In 1909 he left for Italy and two years later moved on to Paris, where he was first drawn to cubism and other forms of modern art. Late in 1912 he returned to New York, in time to exhibit in the 1913 *Armory Show. Soon afterward, his initial futurist work, *Battle of Lights, Coney Island* (Yale University Art Gallery, 1913–14) numbered among the first, and one of relatively few, American paintings to demonstrate an understanding of that Italian modernist style. His colorful, swirling interpretation of the famous amusement park remains among his signal accomplishments. Throughout the following decade Stella produced romantic, semi-abstract interpretations of New York highlights, particularly the Brooklyn Bridge, which he treated metaphorically as an embodiment of American civilization. He also painted some colorful, purely abstract works. By 1916 he had begun to produce nature studies and symbolic abstractions, such as the pastel *Nativity* (Whitney Museum, 1917–18). Presaging his subsequent eclecticism, his work of the early 1920s ranged from industrial and urban subjects in a style related to *precisionism to hard-edged, decorative nature studies suggesting surrealism. In 1923 he was naturalized as a United States citizen. After several years of moving frequently between the United States and Europe, from 1934 he resided permanently in New York, where he was soon employed by a *federal art project. Valuing both tradition and the innovations of modernism, during these years he used whatever means seemed appropriate to his fundamentally poetic and symbolic objectives. At times, his work combined tropical subject matter (inspired by a 1938 visit to Barbados) with a sensuous ornamental style, while at others it reflects an admiration for classical art. His varied output also includes figural studies imbued with religious meaning. In addition, he produced formally sophisticated collages incorporating detritus and other non-art materials. Declining health ended his career in 1942.

Stephan, John. *See* ABSTRACT EXPRESSIONISM.

Stephenson, Peter. *See* HOSMER, HARRIET.

Sterne, Hedda. *See* STEINBERG, SAUL.

Sterne, Maurice (1878–1957). Painter, printmaker, and sculptor. Remembered particularly for semi-abstract paintings of exotic and "primitive" subjects, he found potent inspiration in a two-year residence on Bali. The best of these works combine a seductive and sensual vision of life on that distinctive island with cubist-derived forms arranged in shallow space, as in *Bali Bazaar* (Whitney Museum, 1913–14). Like Gauguin and many subsequent modern artists, Sterne deeply admired the arts and lifestyles of cultures untouched by Western rationalism and capitalism. Born in Liepāja, Russia (now Latvia), he lived for a time in Moscow before arriving in New York. At a young age, he worked for an engraving firm and studied drawing at Cooper Union. After training from 1894 until 1899 at the *National Academy of Design, in 1904 he embarked on a decade of global travel. Following several years in Europe, where he absorbed Cézanne's work, early Renaissance painting, and classical sculpture, he traveled on to Egypt, India, Burma, and, finally, to Bali. Following his return to New York in 1915, his Balinese paintings made his reputation and attracted the attention of Mabel Dodge (later *Luhan), to whom he found himself uneasily married in 1917. Soon Sterne moved (alone) to Santa Fe, New Mexico, to paint indigenous Indians. After Dodge arrived at the end of that year to colonize New Mexico with her bohemian friends, she and Sterne quickly parted ways. (They divorced a few years later.) Later Sterne worked for long periods in Anticoli Corrado, not far from Rome, attempting to capture ideal beauty in depictions of peasants rendered in a purified, linear style, as in *Breadmakers* (Museum of Fine Arts, Boston, 1923). His still lifes of this time retain closer ties to Cézanne. In 1933 the highly regarded Sterne numbered among the first American artists to be accorded a one-person show at the *Museum of Modern Art. Subsequently, he secured one of the most prestigious mural commissions of the *federal art projects, a series of twenty scenes on the subject of Man's Struggle for Justice (installed in 1941), for the Justice Department building in Washington, D.C. From the mid-1940s Sterne summered in *Provincetown, on Cape Cod, where he painted fresh seascapes that are less intellectually restrained than much of his previous work. He died at his primary residence in Mount Kisco, north of New York City. Sterne's autobiographical writings appear in *Shadow and Light: The Life, Friends, and Opinions of Maurice Sterne* (1965), edited by Charlotte L. Mayerson.

Stettheimer, Florine (1871–1944). Painter. Sophisticated, witty, and eloquent, her idiosyncratic figurative paintings stand alone in the history of modernism. Working in a faux-naive style, she incorporated narratives and symbols into complex tableaux reflecting astute comprehension of art history, contemporary art, literature, and modern thought. Financially independent, Stettheimer did not need to sell her art, so she did not. Although she socialized with art world luminaries, she had no taste for publicity and rarely exhibited. She took her art very seriously and worked assiduously for an audience largely restricted to a tiny group of other art professionals. Born in Rochester, New York, she spent most of her childhood in Europe. Between 1892 and 1895 she studied at the *Art Students League, where her teachers included H. Siddons *Mowbray and Kenyon *Cox. Subsequently, except for visits to New York, until 1914 she lived in Europe with her mother and two sisters, while steadfastly continuing to pursue her calling. Yet only after her repatriation, when she was forty-three, did she begin to resist her conventional training and formulate a personal style. For the next two years, she painted in a high-keyed manner indebted to Matisse. However, when she showed these works in 1916, nothing sold. Disappointed, she never again mounted a one-person exhibition. As she subsequently persevered in synthesizing her individual artistic approach, the Stettheimer ladies also consolidated their legendary lifestyle. While *maman* Rosetta presided at their capacious Upper West Side apartment, Caroline, known as Carrie, spent twenty-five years decorating an enormous dollhouse (Museum of the City of New York) that featured tiny modern art works by the sisters' acquaintances. Henrietta, or Ettie, who held a doctorate in philosophy from the University of Freiburg, wrote fiction. Together, the "Stetties" often lavishly entertained their friends, drawn largely from the cream of New York's artistic community.

Characteristic subjects of Stettheimer's mature work derive from this social world. Many paintings portray individuals or groups, often participating in leisure activities. Other paintings present fantasies, social commentaries, or flower arrangements. Reflecting the artist's interest in such precedents as Japanese prints, early Renaissance painting, and Persian miniatures, color, pattern, and rhythm organize her decorative and playful compositions. Figures have neither physical bulk nor psychological presence, even when they are clearly recognizable individuals. Because many works seem to visualize the very experience of remembering, it is perhaps not surprising that Marcel Proust ranked as her favorite author. The quality of her work also was indebted to Freud, Henri Bergson, and surrealism. Based on remembered afternoons at a country home where the Stettheimers entertained in summer, *Sunday Afternoon in the Country* (Cleveland Museum of Art, 1917) portrays numerous friends in a lush, frilly garden overlooking the Hudson River. Pale reds and yellows predominate, suggesting atmospheric warmth, psychological intensity, and disregard for literalism. Space recedes upward on the canvas and few of the design elements overlap, giving a tapestry-like effect of detailed pictorial moments arrayed for the viewer's delectation. Among the twenty figures inhabiting this momentary paradise appear Edward *Steichen who photographs Marcel *Duchamp, Jo *Davidson, the *pictorialist portrait and society photographer Baron Adolf de Meyer (1868–1946), Indian musician Ratan Devi in traditional garb, a Ballets Russes dancer, and other figures from the arts, along with her mother and sisters. Stettheimer herself, seated before an easel, records the charming antics of her friends. In 1934 Stettheimer achieved public acclaim as designer of costumes and sets for the opera *Four Saints in Three Acts*, with libretto by Gertrude *Stein and music by Virgil Thomson. Stettheimer clothed an all-black cast in white and draped the stage with a cellophane backdrop to produce quivering, insubstantial reflections. Her participation in this quintessential product of American modernism validates her acute understanding of the movement's essential qualities. In the following year, Stettheimer's mother died, and the glamorous, pleasure-loving household broke up. Thereafter, Stettheimer lived alone for the first time and was able to devote herself more wholly than ever to her art. In these last years she completed her most popular group of works, four high-spiritedly ironic *Cathedrals* (all Metropolitan Museum) presenting elaborate testimonials to the bedrock elements of Manhattan culture: entertainment in *Cathedrals of Broadway* (1929), society in *Cathedrals of Fifth Avenue* (1931), finance in *Cathedrals of Wall Street* (1939), and art in *Cathedrals of Art* (1942–44, possibly unfinished). Stettheimer also wrote accomplished, unaffected poetry, which extends into another medium the wry charm, keen perception, and controlled passion of her paintings. In the finest of her poems and paintings, like a worldlier Emily Dickinson, she shares fragmented glimpses of a richly imaginative inner solitude.

Steward, Joseph. *See* WALDO, SAMUEL LOVETT.

Stieglitz, Alfred (1864–1946). Photographer, gallery director, collector, and crusader for modernism. Indispensable for half a century to the visual arts in America, during the 1880s he achieved international recognition for his photography. Wishing to liberate the medium from both scientific literalism and mindless sentimentality, he understood at an early date that despite its mechanical origins, photography could be an art form. He spearheaded the movement for *pictorialism in the United States and eventually paved the way for American museums' acceptance of the new medium. As an editor, exhibition organizer, and director of the 291 gallery, he worked tirelessly to advance technical and aesthetic excellence. Although he only gradually accepted modern art, even before 1910 radical forms of European expression had begun to interest him more than most current photography. Before the *Armory Show of 1913, his 291 provided the only American venue where modern art could regularly be seen. Because interest in European modernism exploded in the wake of that huge and sensational exhibition, Stieglitz then preferred to show American artists. In the last years of 291 and at his successive showplaces, The Intimate Gallery (1925–29) and An American Place (1929–46), he showed native modernists almost exclusively.

Born in Hoboken, New Jersey, in 1871 Stieglitz moved with his family into Manhattan. He enrolled, at the age of fifteen, at City College of New York in 1879. After his father retired from business, in June 1881 the entire family embarked for Europe. After a year at a *Gymnasium* in Karlsruhe, in the fall of 1882 he began engineering studies at Berlin's Polytechnikum, while also auditing university courses. In January Stieglitz bought his first camera and began his study of photographic chemistry with its leading expert, Professor Hermann Wilhelm Vogel. By the spring of 1885, it was clear to the young man that his future lay in photography rather than engineering, and he abandoned scientific training. Two years later he won his first important photographic competition and began to publish his work in specialized journals. During this early period he photographed rural scenes, peasants, churches and castles, views of Venice, and other picturesque subjects. Although he occasionally cropped negatives to improve the structure of his images, except for a few youthful experiments he did not otherwise alter his work, which he printed with perfectionist care. Through the years, his photographs became technically and expressively more refined, but this basic approach remained constant as he concentrated on finding the perfect vantage point and moment to invest an image with his inner apprehension of its significance. However, as an activist in the turn-of-the-century photography community, he supported many art photographers who imitated effects of painting in their prints, often by manipulating processes and sometimes by staging images.

After his return to New York in 1890, he began to photograph street life, as his interest shifted from the picturesque toward the vitality of the emerging modern city. In the simple but masterfully composed "The Terminal, New York" (1892), a driver tends to streetcar horses in a snowy cityscape, as steam rises from the animals' flanks. Stieglitz's attraction to the vibrancy of ordinary life paralleled a cultural shift toward realism among contemporary progressive thinkers. His street photographs also prefigure similar subjects in paintings by Robert *Henri and the *Ashcan School a few years later. Becoming a leader during the 1890s of the New York art photography community, Stieglitz served as an editor for *American Amateur Photographer* and then for *Camera Notes*, the quarterly of the Camera Club of New York, which he also served as an officer. He continued to win prizes abroad, was elected to London's prestigious Linked Ring (the first American to be so honored), and in 1899 mounted a major retrospective exhibition at the Camera Club. After relations with his fellow photographers became strained, in 1902 Stieglitz took steps to exert his control over the art photography movement. In the spring he mounted a show at the National Arts Club and dubbed its participants the *Photo-Secession. By the end of the year, the first issue (dated January 1903) of his luxurious magazine **Camera Work* was ready for distribution. For some years the premier American organ of modern creative expression, the magazine's identity nevertheless gradually suffered as Stieglitz's growing attention to art and contemporary culture drew its contents away from photographic topics. After the Armory Show, interest declined, and the publication folded in 1917.

In November 1905, Stieglitz expanded his duties—and power—by opening a gallery. Officially the outpost of his amorphous photography group, the Little Galleries of the Photo-Secession soon became known as 291 from the number of its address on Fifth Avenue. Along with Edward *Steichen, his junior partner in the endeavor, almost from the beginning he entertained notions of showing other art forms in addition to photography. In January 1907, the symbolist drawings of

Pamela Colman Smith (1877–1925) appeared as the first nonphotographic exhibition. The following summer, Stieglitz sailed for Europe, on one of the periodic voyages that he continued to make until 1911. En route, he took what remains his single most famous photograph, "The Steerage," a formally and psychologically complex image of passengers from the ship's lowest class. Cut by decisive diagonals, eccentrically balanced, spatially intricate, and sociologically problematic, this image demonstrates Stieglitz's newfound appreciation for a more modern sensibility than had previously interested him. In January 1908, 291 showed drawings by Rodin, the first truly modern work to appear in the gallery, followed by Matisse in April. After that, a steady influx of new art came from Paris (usually sent by Steichen, who lived there). As well, between 1909 and 1912, 291 introduced Arthur B. *Carles, Arthur *Dove, Marsden *Hartley, John *Marin, Alfred *Maurer, Abraham *Walkowitz, and Max *Weber. Forming a loose circle of like-minded artists, these and a few others made the gallery a center for networking, debate, and instruction in the finer points of modern art. Although their styles varied widely, Stieglitz and the artists in his group generally agreed on their admiration for recent European developments, their belief that a distinctly American modernism of equivalent quality was possible, and their attraction to an art of individualized, intuitive personal response. To varying degrees, they also tended to regard nature as a starting point for their art.

Although the Armory Show marked a watershed in general awareness of modern art, Stieglitz, who claimed to care little for public opinion, played only a marginal part. Listed among the organizers, he distanced himself from the practical tasks, and only a few of his artists participated. However, he lent works from his own collection and bought the only Kandinsky painting in the exhibition. Capitalizing on the brouhaha around the show, at 291 he mounted an enormous concurrent retrospective of his own photography. After this event, Americans who made their New York debuts at 291 included Oscar *Bluemner, Elie *Nadelman, Paul *Strand (one of few photographers to appear in these years), and, most significantly for Stieglitz, Georgia *O'Keeffe. Her first one-person show there in the spring of 1917 closed 291. About a year later Stieglitz left his wife, who had little interest in any kind of art or artists, to begin a life with O'Keeffe. They married in 1924, as soon as he was able to divorce. From the summer of 1917 Stieglitz found himself free of gallery and publication responsibilities for the first time in years, and about a year later, reinvigorated by O'Keeffe's presence, he began once more to flourish as a creative artist. Soon he initiated a major project of succeeding years, his panoramic composite portrait of O'Keeffe herself. With his lover as co-conspirator, in hundreds of photographs Stieglitz investigated every facet of her physical body, her emotional makeup, and her personal identity. During the same years, while photographing around his family home at Lake George, a summer refuge throughout his adult life, he extracted intimations of transcendent perfection from the familiar rural environment. In 1922 he began to point his camera at the sky. What he first called a cloud series grew into his innovative Equivalents, tiny images of abstract cloud forms corresponding to feelings or psychological states. In the 1930s he produced a starkly geometric series of New York buildings and construction sites viewed from his windows. Failing health forced him to stop photographing in 1938.

In 1925 Stieglitz borrowed the Anderson Galleries for a major show, "Seven Americans," which amounted to mini-retrospectives for six of his artists plus himself. At the end of that year, he inaugurated The Intimate Gallery, his own space within the Anderson establishment. Four years later, in mid-December 1929, he opened An American Place. At these two galleries, he focused on Marin, O'Keeffe, and Dove, although he showed others as well until the last few years. Newcomers included Ansel *Adams and Eliot *Porter. Stieglitz remained "on deck," as he described his routine, at his gallery until the final days of his life. By then, the one-time champion of aesthetic revolution had fallen out of touch with new ideas and styles. Yet, the wisdom of his attachment to his three favorite artists has been confirmed by their continuing reputations. Throughout his career, Stieglitz purchased the work of other photographers and artists. In 1933 he placed a comprehensive selection of several hundred superior prints by other photographers at the *Metropolitan Museum of Art. After his death in New York, O'Keeffe donated the single finest example of some 1,550 prints of Stieglitz's own work to the *National Gallery of Art. She gave the Metropolitan nearly six hundred works of art and distributed the remainder of about 250 items to several institutions, with Fisk University in Nashville receiving the largest group.

Still, Clyfford (1904–80). Painter. An *abstract expressionist, he made his mark with looming, jagged, heavily impastoed compositions of enormous size. Frequently, a single hue, usually dark and often black, covers much of the canvas, while bursts of bright color shine from irregular interstices. At their best, his dramatic paintings echo vast spaces, suggest the power of natural forces, and imply metaphysical grandeur. But in his quest to "achieve a purpose beyond vanity, ambition, or remembrance," Still sometimes skirted bombastic melodrama. Despite his early contribution to abstract expressionism, Still loathed the New York art world, dismissed the entire heritage of European painting as worthless, and haughtily denied any influences on his work. At heart an extreme romantic, he cast his role in Nietzschean terms, seeing himself as a misunderstood visionary whose art constituted a spiritual bulwark against the corruptions of society. Born in Grandin, North Dakota, he moved with his family to Spokane, Washington, the following year but spent much of his youth on a homestead near Bow Island in eastern Alberta. Life in the West acquainted him with the incalculable spaces of the region's landscape and with the harshness of the elements. His account of a visit to New York in 1925 provides a preview of his notoriously cantankerous nature. He enrolled in the *Art Students League but left before the end of the first day (some accounts say after an hour), claiming that what he had encountered was a waste of time. In the end, he remained largely self-taught as a painter. Returning west, he graduated in 1933 from Spokane University (later Spokane Junior College). He earned a master's degree at Washington State College (now University) in Pullman and remained on the fine arts teaching staff until 1941. During these years, his painting evolved from an expressionistic treatment of regionalist themes to abstraction derived from figuration. Between 1941 and the fall of 1943 Still worked in wartime ship-building and aircraft industries in the San Francisco area but continued painting in his spare time. He then spent two years teaching at the Richmond Professional Institute (now part of Virginia Commonwealth University). In 1945 he moved to New York, where Peggy *Guggenheim gave him a show at her *Art of This Century Gallery early the next year. Around this time, his painting took on its mature characteristics of large scale and thickly painted forms with flamelike edges. In the fall of 1946 he began teaching at the California School of Fine Arts (now San Francisco Art Institute). There he exerted an important influence on the development of abstract expressionism in the Bay Area. At the same time, he remained in touch with New York artists and in 1947 had the first of three shows at the Betty *Parsons Gallery.

By 1950, when Still returned to New York, he was pushing against the limits of his style's premises, as well as the limits of what might be considered art at that time. Named for the period of its execution, 1951–52 (Art Institute of Chicago) presents an almost uninterrupted wall of black paint, slathered with a palette knife across thirteen feet of canvas almost ten feet tall. Only a small area of smoother black at the lower right corner, a slash of reddish brown near the left edge, and an irregular vertical white line to the right of center hold out against the darkness. (Still did not provide titles, other than dates and sequence numbers or letters, believing that language interfered with the paintings' visual autonomy.) After 1952 Still refused to show his art publicly until 1959, when Buffalo's Albright Art Gallery (now Albright-Knox Art Gallery) staged a retrospective exhibition of work produced between 1937 and 1957. From the early 1960s Still lived in near seclusion in rural Maryland. Here his painting shed some of its forbidding massiveness to take on a more lyrical tone. Incorporating a device he first investigated in the late 1950s, some works present areas of unprimed canvas in tension with painted shapes.

Still rewarded two museums that had shown his work—the Albright-Knox Art Gallery and the San Francisco Museum of Modern Art—with substantial groups of work covering various periods of his career but otherwise kept most of his work from public view. (His widow later gave another group to the *Metropolitan Museum of Art, which had staged a huge retrospective during the artist's final year.) At the time of his death in a Baltimore hospital, he left some two thousand works, including approximately 750 paintings (about five times the number in all public or private collections today), most of which have not yet been exhibited. Reflecting his belief that his paintings must be seen together, never with the work of other artists, his will specified that these holdings should be given to a city that would construct a museum for his work alone. In addition, he particularized precise conditions about the museum's size and display of the work. In 2004 the Still estate entered into such an agreement with the city of Denver, which has been allotted ten years to fulfill the artist's conditions. Because the work of Still's final twenty years remains so little known, the full measure of his contribution to art history will be possible only when—and if—the museum finally opens.

Stillman, William James. *See* CRAYON, THE.

Stock, Joseph Whiting (1815–55). Painter. Known chiefly for portraits, he created an unusually large number depicting children, who generally are shown standing in full length, often with their pets or toys. He also painted miniatures, landscapes, and other subjects, but of these only a few miniatures survive. For a self-taught country painter, his career is unusually well documented. His journal, painting records, will, and estate inventory together provide many insights into his circumstances and aspirations. By extension, the written record also sheds light upon the numerous untrained professionals who roamed the country in his day. Stock was born in Springfield, Massachusetts, which remained his home base until he died there of tuberculosis. Paralyzed from the waist down in an accident when he was eleven, he began painting in 1832. A local artist explained technical rudiments of the craft, and Stock turned for models of achievement to prints and illustrations, which he assiduously copied. Already beginning to receive commissions, in 1834 he achieved freedom from home confinement. A sympathetic doctor designed a wheelchair that even allowed him to travel by train to the East Coast and into New York State. In his prolific mature work, Stock employed strong outlines, bright colors, and decorative patterning to create genial likenesses. Faces usually show greater modeling than other elements, and his frequently ambitious compositions include accessories related to the sitter, as well as interior furnishings and occasional background landscapes.

Stone, Sylvia. *See* HELD, AL.

Storrs, John (1885–1956). Sculptor, printmaker, and painter. Among American sculptors, he remains conspicuous for early experiments in abstraction. Attracted to the fragmented planes and structural tensions of cubism, he became particularly known for architectural sculpture featuring stylized imagery. In this context, his work anticipated and then contributed to art deco's streamlining, geometric ornamentation, and chic contemporaneity. A Chicago native, John Henry Bradley Storrs studied and traveled abroad for a year before enrolling in 1908 in the School of the Art Institute of Chicago, where he studied with Lorado *Taft. He continued his training at Boston's School of Museum of Fine Arts and at the *Pennsylvania Academy of the Fine Arts, notably under Charles *Grafly. Subsequently in Paris he studied with Paul *Bartlett and in 1912 entered Rodin's studio, where his style emulated the master's and he became a favorite. At the same time, on his European travels, Storrs admired the clarity of Greek and Egyptian sculpture, which continued to inform his work for many years. With continued exposure to new art, over time he began to absorb the cubist idiom and before 1920 had developed the fundamentals of his mature style. His best-known architectural decoration, the thirty-three-foot aluminum figure of the goddess *Ceres* (1930) adorning the apex of Chicago's Board of Trade, synthesizes Storrs's interests in harmonious form and the machine age. Many of his freestanding abstract sculptures display an architectonic approach, presenting geometric blocks enlivened with restricted surface decoration. The marble *Forms in Space #1* (Whitney Museum, 1924), which rises more than seven feet tall, austerely communes with both International Style skyscrapers and *minimalist sculpture. He also experimented with constructivist-inspired welded fabrication and with space as a dynamic compositional element. Some of his industrially inspired pieces bear resemblances to *precisionism. Although he maintained an artistic presence in the United States through exhibitions, commissions, and frequent sojourns in Chicago (during his most productive years, he resided there for part of each year), Storrs retained his residency in France, where he died. While volunteering during World War II as a driver for the Red Cross, he was arrested by German forces. Exhausted by the experience of being held prisoner of war, although he eventually returned to his art, his best work had already been accomplished.

Story, William Wetmore (1819–95). Sculptor. Also a lawyer and writer. As an artist, he is known especially for interpretations of literary themes, usually drawn from antiquity or the Bible. He also produced portraits, mostly of friends or family, as well as narratives based on other sources. Although shaped by the prevailing *neoclassicism of his day, he achieved a personal variant emphasizing monumentality, restraint, and archeological or ethnographic exactitude. He also accommodated late-nineteenth-century interests in narrative and psychology. In Rome, where he lived for more than forty years, he numbered among celebrated members of the Anglo-American community. His many friends included such literary notables as Robert and Elizabeth Barrett Browning and Henry James, who wrote a two-volume biography, *William Wetmore Story and His Friends* (1903). In *The Marble Faun*, Nathaniel Hawthorne based his description of a sculpture by his fictional hero on one of Story's celebrated works. Born in Salem, Massachusetts, Story moved with his family when he was ten to Cambridge, where his father, a United States Supreme Court justice, served on the faculty at Harvard University. After graduating from Harvard in 1838 and from the university's law school two years later, Story worked as an attorney in Boston while also pursuing an amateur interest in the arts. Despite his lack of formal artistic training, after the elder Story died, his son agreed to provide a memorial sculpture (Memorial Hall, Harvard University, 1855; originally, Mount Auburn Cemetery, Cambridge) and departed in 1847 for Europe to develop the necessary skills. He soon settled in Rome, where for nearly a decade he vacillated between legal and artistic careers. Despite return visits to Boston, he never again lived in the United States for an extended period. In 1856 he closed his law practice to settle permanently in Rome. There his apartments in the Palazzo Barberini became a gathering place for English and American luminaries.

Story established his international reputation in 1862, when his marble *Cleopatra* (Los Angeles County Museum of Art, 1860; modeled 1858) and *Libyan Sibyl* (Metropolitan Museum, 1861) were exhibited at an international exhibition in London. These massive, brooding figures number among the most significant pieces of his career. Several other over-life-size figures, generally seated and draped (though sometimes partially nude), also picture powerful women, including *Sappho* (Museum of Fine Arts, Boston, 1863) and *Medea* (Metropolitan Museum, 1868; modeled 1865). Their passions are submerged in thoughtful reflection, as their grandly conceived, static forms play against detail establishing historical authenticity. Devoted to imaginative goals and financially independent, Story only occasionally accepted the portrait commissions that provided security for most of his contemporaries. However, he produced about a dozen prestigious public monuments, including *Chief Justice John Marshall* for the U.S. Capitol grounds (now United States Supreme Court; 1883–84) and *Francis Scott Key* (1886) in San Francisco's Golden Gate Park. In the final decade of his life, Story became less active as a sculptor but continued to travel and write. Devastated in 1894 by the death of his wife of fifty years, he produced a touching memorial for her grave. (The following year he was buried by her side.) Its face hidden as it collapses in misery, *Angel of Grief Weeping Bitterly over the Dismantled Altar of His Life* (Protestant Cemetery, Rome, 1895; modeled 1894) also concluded Story's sculptural work. During his final months, he lived with his daughter at Vallombrosa in Tuscany. Story's extensive and wide-ranging writings include poetry, fiction, art theory, essays, volumes of legal scholarship, and a tribute to his father, *The Life and Letters of Joseph Story* (1851). A two-volume travelers' companion to the Eternal City, *Roba di Roma* (1862), found the widest audience. The novel *Fiammetta* (1886) is often regarded as his most successful fiction. "Cleopatra," conceived as an accompaniment to the sculpture of that subject, is included in the poetry collection *Graffiti d'Italia* (1868). Collected essays appeared as *Conversations in a Studio* (1890) and *Excursions in Arts and Letters* (1891).

Two sons became artists. Born in Rome, Thomas Waldo, known professionally as **Waldo Story** (1855–1915), gradually took over his father's studio during the 1880s and became a well-known sculptor, particularly esteemed for portraits. His tiered *Fountain of Love* (Cliveden, Buckinghamshire, 1894–96) numbers among the best known of a number of commissions he executed in England. He died in New York. **Julian Russell Story** (1857–1919), who studied in Paris and for a time with Frank *Duveneck in Florence, painted portraits and romantic historical scenes. He died in Walton-on-Thames, England. Particularly during the 1880s, both brothers were friendly with James Abbott McNeill *Whistler in London.

Stout, Myron. *See* HARD-EDGE PAINTING.

Strand, Paul (1890–1976). Photographer and filmmaker. His compelling fusion of real and ideal pioneered a modern aesthetic of straight photography. He combined the camera's objective description with formal principles derived from cubism and other forms of modern art. Born in New York, Strand studied photography at the Ethical Culture School with Lewis *Hine, who introduced him to Alfred *Stieglitz's *291 gallery. Strand's earliest work reflected current *pictorialism, but about 1914 he began to produce original work that forecast both the formal and humanitarian concerns of his mature career. In a series of unsentimental but moving urban scenes, he combined visual patterns perceived in New York's architecture with the movement of passersby, suggesting not only the rhythms and energies of modern life but also its psychology. Stieglitz showed the photographs at 291 early in 1916 and published them in **Camera Work*. Additional Strand works constituted all the illustrations in the following year's final issue of the magazine. While experimenting with pure form during the summer of 1916, in radically original images Strand subordinated recognizable still life objects to compositional structure. "Abstraction, Porch Shadows, Twin Lakes, Connecticut" (1916) makes a bold and satisfying design from an arc of round table and shadows of a railing. Back in New York that fall, Strand turned to street portraits of anonymous subjects, often surreptitiously captured with a hand-held camera fitted with a right-angle lens. Dignified by their monumental presence in these images, the figures also highlight distinctively contemporary types. The following year, as one of the first artists to find formal beauty in machinery, the premier emblem of modernity, Strand helped to open an area of aesthetic investigation that interested *precisionists and others throughout the 1920s and 1930s. Moreover, as changing ideals entered photographic expression in the mid-1910s, Strand's example proved prophetic. Within a few years, nearly all serious photographers had abandoned pictorialism's romantic aspirations, its characteristic soft focus, and its painterly printing techniques. Following his discharge in 1919 from a year's service in the Army Medical Corps, Strand visited Nova Scotia, where he first tried landscape photography. He also experimented there with near abstractions from natural forms, such as rocks, prefiguring not only an important aspect of his own later work but also an interest of many later photographers. Strand collaborated in 1920 with Charles *Sheeler on the brief silent film *Manhatta*, a tribute to New York as a modern city, with texts by Walt Whitman. Continuing his interest in filmmaking until the mid-1940s, for a decade after 1922 he worked as a freelance cinematographer. He then worked as a documentary filmmaker in Mexico until 1935 and in the United States through World War II. Achieved in collaboration with Ralph *Steiner and Willard *Van Dyke, among others, the most notable of his films remains *The Plow That Broke the Plains* (1936), written and directed by Pare Lorentz.

Largely because he found the postwar American political atmosphere uncongenial to his left-wing convictions, Strand moved to France in 1950. During later years, he traveled widely, extending the ethnographic spirit of his last major project in the United States, a detailed investigation of New England. Continuing for the most part to employ view cameras and create finely crafted prints, he focused on rural and village life of traditional societies throughout Europe and North Africa. His photographs interpret landscapes and their inhabitants with crystalline intensity but also with appreciation for his subjects' moral dignity. Strand published a number of books that reflect his travels and his vision of community. *Time in New England* (1950), with text by Nancy *Newhall, was followed by *La France de profil* (1954), with text by Claude Roy; *Un paese* (1955), on Italy with text by Cesare Zavattini; *Tir a' Mhurain* (1962), on the Outer Hebrides with text by Basil Davidson; and others. He died near Paris, at his Orgeval home where he often photographed the garden after moving there in the mid-1950s. His first wife, painter **Rebecca Salsbury Strand** (1891–1968), later Rebecca James, posed for an emotionally intimate 1920s portrait series. They married in 1922 and separated eleven years later.

Struss, Karl (1886–1981). Photographer and cinematographer. Bold compositions and predominately urban subjects endow his soft, romantic images with an urgent modernity missing from the work of *pictorialist colleagues. Among the youngest major talents of the movement, Karl Fischer Struss was born in New York and began his study of photography in 1908 with Clarence *White at Columbia University. In the summer of the following year he photographed in Europe. The pictures from this trip caught the attention of Alfred *Stieglitz, who published some in **Camera Work*. Struss's 1911 "Pennsylvania Station" captures the magnificent, light-filled space of the terminal, which dwarfs anonymous figures crossing its expanse. Among pictorialists, only Alvin Langdon *Coburn, whose work Struss admired, approached this richly romantic apprehension of the modern metropolis. In achieving his effects Struss made use of virtuoso printing techniques, as well as a soft-focus lens of his own invention. In 1916 he numbered among founders of the *Pictorial Photographers of America. Following his discharge from World War I army service in 1919, Struss moved to Hollywood where he became a noted cinematographer, with well over a hundred films to his credit. He won (with Charles Rosher) the first Academy Award given in that category, for F. W. Murnau's *Sunrise* (1927). However, Struss continued to exhibit still photographs through the 1930s. He died in Santa Monica.

Stryker, Roy Emerson. *See* FARM SECURITY ADMINISTRATION (FSA) PHOTOGRAPHS.

Stuart, Gilbert (1755–1828). Painter. Today popularly known for likenesses of George Washington, Stuart dominated American portraiture of his day. Acutely rendered features enlivened by sensations of the sitter's psychology mark his natural yet elegant portraits combining virtuoso brushwork and radiant color. No other type of painting interested him. Most of his portraits are life-size half-lengths that focus attention on faces. Stuart's painted visages suited the increasingly romantic conception of character that emerged at the end of the eighteenth century. The newer point of view supplanted colonial standards of good taste and self-discipline with more unconstrained, individualistic, and imaginative self-definition. Born in North Kingston, Rhode Island, Stuart moved with his family in 1761 to Newport. In 1769 the recently arrived Cosmo Alexander (1724–72) accepted him as a pupil. Born in Scotland, Alexander had worked, primarily as a portraitist, in several colonial cities since 1766, following two decades of activity in Italy and The Hague as well as in London. Although Alexander's figures seem stiff and faces are somewhat generalized, he nevertheless captured agreeable expressions and attentively rendered his sitters' finery. Stuart accompanied Alexander to Philadelphia and other locales before they sailed abroad together in 1771. However, Alexander died in Edinburgh the next summer, leaving the young artist without resources. Stuart eventually worked his way back to Newport, where he returned to his fledgling career and soon supplemented what he had learned from Alexander with an appreciation of John Singleton *Copley's magisterial style.

In 1775 Stuart departed for London. There his provincial, linear style soon gave way to the sophisticated English portrait mode established by Joshua Reynolds and Thomas Gainsborough. In 1777 Benjamin *West took him on as a studio assistant. For several years, while also honing his technical skills, Stuart worked on West's large historical canvases and state portraits. Not long after commencing an independent career, at the Royal Academy in 1782 Stuart exhibited *The Skater* (National Gallery, 1782), depicting at full length William Grant of Congalton poised on Hyde Park's frozen Serpentine. Capturing a fleeting moment with verve and grace, this novel image made Stuart's reputation. Immediately numbering among London's best-paid portraitists, he successfully competed against such painters as George Romney and Henry Raeburn, whose work had informed his own development. In 1787 he departed for Dublin, probably to escape debts and obligations. There the charming and witty painter once again triumphed, lived lavishly, and left under a cloud. Upon establishing a studio in New York in the spring of 1793, Stuart was acknowledged as the premier portraitist working in the United States. Some of the work postdating his return accommodates the affection lingering in America for Copley's clear and exacting transcriptions of physical reality. *Mrs. Richard Yates* (National Gallery, 1793–94) is much more highly finished than Stuart's English and Irish work had been. As always, the face is Stuart's center of interest, but much tighter brushwork provides greater volume and more descriptive textures than is characteristic of most of Stuart's work. However, the expressive gesture of Mrs. Yates's hands, caught in a pause while sewing, is scarcely less important than her face to the characterization, and the portrayal radiates an inner animation markedly different in spirit from Copley's sober objectivity. On the other hand, for a more worldly client, at nearly the same time Stuart painted *Matilda Stoughton de Jáudenes* (Metropolitan Museum, 1794) in the style he had refined abroad. Depicting the subject arrayed in the most elaborate fashion of the day, the painting numbers among the most elegant performances of Stuart's American years.

Late in 1794 Stuart moved to Philadelphia, then the federal capital. There and in Washington, D.C., between 1803 and 1805, Stuart completed an extended series portraying leaders of the new nation. They included such notables as Thomas Jefferson, James Monroe, Albert Gallatin, Stephen Decatur, and, most importantly, George Washington. For the rest of the painter's life, the first president provided a profitable subject. Although Stuart produced numerous replicas and variants, Washington apparently sat for him on only two or three occasions. The first of these, in 1795, provided the basis for the Vaughan-type portrait, a half-length image of a reserved national leader. At a sitting the following year, Stuart rendered the president's personality more vividly in what has remained the iconic likeness. The Athenaeum portrait (jointly owned by the Museum of Fine Arts, Boston, and National Portrait Gallery, Washington, D.C., 1796) captures in an unfinished bust Washington's dignified demeanor and shrewd glance. Its composition, featuring the head positioned against a blank background at the apex of a pyramid formed by the upper body, represents the preferred format of Stuart's later career. The Athenaeum portrait remained in Stuart's hands, serving as the model for dozens of replicas. It may also have provided the model for the head in the Lansdowne-type portrait, Stuart's most ambitious treatment of Washington. This full-length standing figure based on continental grand manner precedents (most directly, a well-known engraving after a Hyacinthe Rigaud portrait) conveys the subject's authority and historical importance, but its grandiloquent manner conflicts with Stuart's strength—presentation of individuality. (Besides nearly identical versions of this work, Stuart also produced at least two variants based on this pose.) In the summer of 1805 Stuart moved permanently to Boston, where he continued to paint until the final weeks of his life. His popularity remained high as he generally simplified compositions to concentrate more intently on heads. Among the masterpieces of this approach, his likeness of John Adams (private collection, 1824; replica, Smithsonian American Art Museum) renders a vivid sense of the intelligent personality enduring within the eighty-nine-year-old's ailing body. Although he did not take students, many younger painters sought Stuart out and received generous advice. More generally, his work set a widely emulated standard for portraiture through much of the nineteenth-century. Without his flair or insight, painter **Jane Stuart** (1812–88) extended her father's portrait manner in replicas and independent works. She learned her craft in his studio and occasionally also painted *genre and religious subjects. Although she moved permanently to Newport, Rhode Island, she maintained a Boston studio until it burned in the 1850s and destroyed much of her work.

Stuart, Michelle. *See* LAND ART.

Sturges, Jonathan. *See* DURAND, ASHER BROWN.

Subjects of the Artist school. *See* ABSTRACT EXPRESSIONISM.

Sugarman, George (1912–99). Sculptor, painter, printmaker, and collage artist. His unprecedented polychrome sculptures join geometric and organic components into meandering or discontinuous compositions. These eye-catching constructions draw on the informality of *abstract expressionism, the colors of Matisse's work, the spatial freedom of Alexander *Calder's sculptures, the freewheeling exuberance of the Baroque, and the jazzy irreverence of popular culture. Despite their lighthearted demeanor, Sugarman's works challenged prevailing notions. With their vigorous intrusion into the viewer's own space, his sculptures from the early 1960s rank among the earliest to disdain even an implied pedestal. Sugarman also numbers among the first sculptors of that time to dissociate from the angst-laden forms of surrealist and symbolic art characteristic of the 1940s and 1950s. Like painters who also emphasized structure, such as Ellsworth *Kelly, Kenneth *Noland, and his friend Al *Held, he abandoned abstract expressionism's transcendental aims while relishing a more complicated aesthetic than would soon come to the fore in *minimalism. A lifelong New Yorker, Sugarman received his BA from City College of New York in 1935 and served in the U.S. Navy between 1941 and 1945. He did not begin serious practice of art until 1951, when he left for Paris. There he received his only formal training while studying sculpture with Ossip Zadkine for less than a year. Subsequently he worked in Paris and traveled throughout Europe, taking particular note of Gianlorenzo Bernini's seventeenth-century work. After returning to New York in 1955, he carved unpainted, roughly textured, *biomorphic wood sculptures. Modernist notions of truth to materials went out the window in 1959, as he initiated his signature approach. Smoothing wood surfaces and coating them with paint, he generally differentiated the constituent parts of a work with varied hues. For an early brightly colored work, *Yellow Top* (Walker Art Center, Minneapolis, 1960), he stacked seemingly haphazardly shaped, though generally more or less planar forms into a buoyant construction. Other typical works drifted across the floor, or were sometimes attached to a wall. In 1969 he completed the first of more than thirty commissions for outdoor public sculptures, generally fabricated in aluminum and also vibrantly colored. Sugarman maintained as well an interest in color-based, two-dimensional art. Besides painting intermittently, in the mid-1960s he started working with lithography, and during the 1980s he made many collages combining colored scraps of paper. He worked productively until the last year or two of his life. His will established the George Sugarman Foundation to provide financial assistance to promising painters and sculptors in need.

Sullivan, Mary Quinn. *See* MUSEUM OF MODERN ART.

Sully, Thomas (1783–1872). Painter. At the height of his career, from the late 1820s through the mid-1840s, he ranked as the nation's preeminent portrait painter. A prolific worker, he completed more than two thousand portraits as well as hundreds of history paintings, anecdotal subjects, and landscapes. His fluid and polished likenesses typically emphasize physical beauty and personal charm. Especially in later work, Sully's inherent romanticism sometimes acceded to mid-nineteenth-century sentimentality. Born in Horncastle, Lincolnshire, he emigrated with his parents from England in 1792. (He became an American citizen in 1809.) He lived in New York and Richmond, Virginia, before settling with the family in Charleston, South Carolina. There Sully's lifelong friend Charles *Fraser, a schoolmate, probably provided some early assistance as did a French-born miniaturist who married Sully's sister. In 1799 he departed for Richmond, where he worked with his brother **Lawrence Sully** (1769–1804), a portraitist who specialized in miniatures. Together in 1801 they moved to Norfolk, where Thomas found his first professional portrait commissions, but returned to Richmond within two years. In 1806 Sully relocated to New York for just over a year before continuing on to Hartford, Connecticut, for a few months. During this time, he visited Boston to seek instruction from Gilbert *Stuart. At the end of 1807 Sully settled permanently in Philadelphia. Although he found clients there, a year and a half later he sailed for London to improve his skills. He worked with Benjamin *West but was more impressed with the portrait style of younger British artists, most notably Thomas Lawrence, who befriended him.

Samuel Coates (Pennsylvania Hospital, Philadelphia, 1812–13) demonstrates the mastery he had achieved at the time of his return in 1810. The standing client stands at ease within a fully realized pictorial space, which innovatively features sunlight streaming through a background window. The fluent brushwork captures transient effects but also constructs a solid figure, presenting a sophisticated combination of seriousness and glamour. The artist's son posed for *The Torn Hat* (Museum of Fine Arts, Boston, 1820), but the painting is less a portrait than a generic image of youth. Dappled sun plays over the trusting face and thin shoulders of the bust-length subject, who embodies the romantic ideal of innocent and attractive childhood. At his best, Sully's narrative paintings also exemplify the stylish flair and emotional energy of his portraits. *Washington Crossing the Delaware* (Museum of Fine Arts, Boston, 1818) presents the Revolutionary general mounted on his white steed at the crest of a hill, dramatically turning to look back at the fateful river scene below. Although most of Sully's portrait work was done for the burgeoning, often socially ambitious middle class of his day, he also took on numerous official commissions. On his only other trip abroad, in 1837–38, Sully attained the privilege of painting the newly crowned *Queen Victoria* (full-length, on loan to the National Gallery; three-quarter figure, Wallace Collection, London, both 1838), while at home he was frequently called upon to portray the nation's leaders. These ranged across several decades from Thomas Jefferson to Abraham Lincoln. Although it did not appear in print until after his death, in 1851 he wrote *Hints to Young Painters* (1873). As the 1850s advanced and his health began to decline, Sully's popularity as a portraitist diminished, and he increasingly turned to emotionally appealing subjects that he, like others of the day, called "fancy pictures." With his encouragement and instruction, all six of Sully's children who survived to adulthood painted. Most notably, **Jane Cooper Sully** (1807–77), known after 1833 by her married name of Darley (her husband was the brother of F. O. C. *Darley), was active primarily as a portraitist for more than four decades, beginning about 1825. **Thomas Wilcocks Sully** (1811–47), a professional portraitist and miniaturist in a style similar to his father's, and **Rosalie Kemble Sully** (1818–47), who painted landscapes as well as portraits, both died too young to have established significant reputations.

Superrealism. *See* PHOTO-REALISM.

Sweeney, James Johnson. *See* GUGGENHEIM, SOLOMON R.

Swift, Henry. *See* F/64 GROUP.

Synchromism. A short-lived form of color abstraction, launched by Stanton *Macdonald-Wright and Morgan *Russell in 1913 while they lived in Paris. Very much in the contentious spirit of the time in Europe, they provided their "ism" with aggressive theoretical polemics. They did not intend to found a synchromist school, however, but only to differentiate their work from other movements of the day. "Synchromy," coined by Russell in 1912 to mean "with color," intentionally paralleled "symphony" in order to suggest an analogy between musical and visual rhythms. Although only the two founders exhibited under the synchromist banner, their work exemplifies an important early form of abstraction based on color, and it contributed to a brief enthusiasm for color abstraction on both sides of the Atlantic. Many American artists were at least briefly inspired to work in this manner during the second decade of the twentieth century, although some probably relied also on other models of color abstraction. The closest such source, known as orphism, practiced by Robert and Sonia Delaunay between about 1911 and 1914, might have contributed to the genesis of synchromism as well, although the two styles originated in different interests.

Macdonald-Wright and Russell developed synchromism by working from studies of the figure broken into planes of color. From this basis, they evolved abstractions in which no figural basis is discernible. Their ideas were driven by recent scientific investigations into color, as well as the widespread early modern interest in the relationships between music, emotion, and abstract art. In a 1913 exhibition in Paris, Russell exhibited *Synchromy in Green* (destroyed), the first painting titled a synchromist work. When he and Macdonald-Wright appeared in two subsequent exhibitions that year, they issued a manifesto claiming that because their work expressed volume and space, it was superior to the flat and weightless forms of orphism, which they found too decorative. This subtle distinction was lost on most observers, but it fueled their rhetoric for several years. The sole New York exhibition of synchromist work took place in 1914. During the next few years, American painters who produced related work included Thomas Hart *Benton, Patrick Henry *Bruce, and Andrew *Dasburg. In his book *Modern Painting: Its Tendency and Meaning* (1915), Macdonald-Wright's brother, Willard Huntington *Wright, made large claims for synchromism, insisting that it represented the culmination of Western art since the Renaissance. Nevertheless, by the end of the decade the originators and nearly all of their followers had moved on to other modes of expression.

Szarkowski, John (1925–). Curator, critic, and photographer. At the *Museum of Modern Art, he served as director of the photography department for nearly thirty years. His program there set the pace in the field at a time when few institutions were interested. In more than a hundred exhibitions, he featured established or previously unrecognized photographers, as well as thematic groupings. His shows included landmark presentations of work by Diane *Arbus, William *Eggleston, Walker *Evans, and Garry *Winogrand. An elegant and perceptive writer, Szarkowski has exerted unparalleled influence on how photography is understood and discussed. His presentation of photography as an independent medium with inherent characteristics and meanings has become widely accepted. He also demonstrated that while photographs have a special and intimate relation with the world, their significance depends equally on formal qualities. A native of Ashland, Wisconsin, Thaddeus John Szarkowski began taking photographs as a child. His study of art history at the University of Wisconsin was interrupted by service in the U.S. Army in 1945–46. Upon his graduation in 1948, took a position at the Walker Art Center in Minneapolis. In 1951 he began teaching art history at the Albright Art School (now merged with the art department of the State University of New York at Buffalo), while exploring the theory and practice of photography. *The Idea of Louis Sullivan* (1956), his first book, combines his admiring and revealing photographs of Sullivan's architecture with texts by and about the architect. In 1962 he succeeded Edward *Steichen at MoMA. Since his retirement from the museum in 1991, Szarkowski has returned to his own photography. His images of a favored subject, his upstate New York farm, appear in *Mr. Bristol's Barn* (1997). Earlier, he had published his own work in *The Face of Minnesota* (1958). Szarkowski's *Looking at Photographs: 100 Pictures from the Collection of the Museum of Modern Art* (1973) remains a model introduction to the principles and meanings of photography. His other books, some of which served also as exhibition catalogues, include *The Photographer and the American Landscape* (1963), *The Photographer's Eye* (1966), *New Documents* (1967), *Mirrors and Windows: American Photography since 1960* (1978), and **Stieglitz at Lake George* (1995).

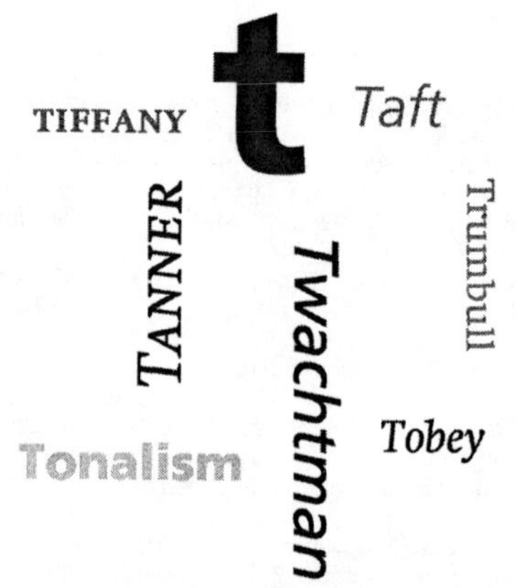

Taft, Lorado (1860–1936). Sculptor, art historian, and critic. A specialist in large-scale, powerful sculptural representations of abstract or symbolic themes, he also produced portraits. Romantic emotion often tinges his idealistic and humanitarian approach. He worked throughout his career in Chicago and ranked in his day as the Midwest's most prominent artistic personality. Regarding education as integral to his artistic mission, he served for many years on the faculty of the School of the Art Institute of Chicago. Later he taught also at the University of Chicago and, as a nonresident professor, at the University of Illinois. Lorado Zadoc Taft was born in the central Illinois town of Elmwood but moved as a child with his family to Champaign-Urbana. There he graduated from Illinois Industrial University (now the University of Illinois) in 1879. After earning a master's degree the following year, he departed for Paris, where he studied for three years at the École des Beaux-Arts. He returned home in 1885 and settled in Chicago the following year.

To adorn the Horticulture Building at the 1893 World's Columbian Exposition in Chicago, Taft produced two well-received figurative groups that established his reputation. During the next twenty years, before modernism began to make his approach seem old-fashioned, he conceived the greater part of his most impressive work, although some did not reach final form until much later. In 1898 he helped to found the Eagle's Nest summer art colony, on the Rock River near Oregon, Illinois. For many years there he enjoyed the company of Chicago artists and writers, including his brother-in-law Hamlin Garland. In 1906 on the Midway Plaisance, an open area remaining from the exposition grounds, he established Midway Studios (now a National Historic Landmark owned by the University of Chicago), where he subsequently worked, along with invited artists, students, and assistants. Taft's sculptural projects rely on the human form to explore ideas or to honor leading individuals. *Fountain of the Great Lakes* (outside the south wing of the Art Institute of Chicago, 1913), representing the five interconnected lakes as female figures who pass the waters of the fountain from one to the next, and *Alma Mater* (campus of the University of Illinois at Urbana-Champaign, 1929), a personification of the welcoming university flanked by Learning and Labor, number among many straightforwardly metaphorical formulations. Others seek to invoke a spirit of mystery or obscurity. Created in 1907–8 but not put into bronze until eighty years later, *The Blind* (Krannert Art Museum and Kinkead Pavilion, University of Illinois, Urbana-Champaign) demonstrates a debt to Rodin in its expressionistic forms and sense of movement. Thematically inspired by Belgian symbolist Maurice Maeterlinck's 1890 play of that name, it demonstrates Taft's ability to grapple with cryptic subjects, as well as his willingness to deviate from a naturalistic aesthetic. Taft continued in this vein with his ambitious 110-foot-long, concrete *Fountain of Time* (Washington Park, Chicago, 1922), which incorporates some one hundred figures, and the similarly grandiose, uncompleted *Fountain of Creation*. These developed in response to Taft's 1910 commission from the University of Chicago for a comprehensive design of the Midway Plaisance, where they were envisioned as bookends for his unrealized parklike venue honoring humanity. Although such works embraced antimaterialistic concerns associated with advanced aesthetic tendencies, Taft rejected the abstraction and distortion associated with modernism. Nevertheless, several of his last works accommodate a taste for formal simplification and sleek surfaces, suggesting continuing reappraisal of his artistic premises. The granite *Crusader*, a medieval knight (Graceland Cemetery, 1931) marking the grave of newspaper publisher Victor Lawson, stands in watchful repose, his monumental form uninterrupted by extraneous detail or intricate surface modeling. As well, Taft was the only sculptor of his generation to participate in designing Chicago's 1933 Century of Progress exhibition, where his contribution conformed to the fair's art deco ambience. Although troubled by health problems in his last few years, Taft continued to work until a week before he died at his Midway Studios home. Taft's readable and astute *History of American Sculpture* (1903) remained the standard reference on the subject for more than sixty years. He also published *Modern Tendencies in Sculpture* (1921), based on 1917 lectures defending tradition.

Tait, Arthur Fitzwilliam (1819–1905). Painter and lithographer. Although he never traveled beyond Chicago, he is best known today for dramatic images of western life, usually scenes of struggle between frontiersmen and Indians or wild animals. However, these number only about a dozen different images (some known in several variants), painted during the 1850s and early 1860s. In addition, he painted popular *genre scenes of outdoor leisure activity, such as hunting and camping, as well as birds and animals set in natural surroundings. He also helped to initiate the nineteenth-century vogue for still lifes featuring dead game birds or fish. Many of his works became known to a wide public through prints issued by *Currier & Ives or other firms. Tait was indebted to *Pre-Raphaelitism for the precise realism of his style and to the traditions of English sporting prints and animal paintings for his subjects. For western scenes, he borrowed particularly from the work of William *Ranney, but he also knew the art of George *Catlin and other artist-explorers. Born in Livesey Hall, near Liverpool, Tait went to work at fifteen for an art dealer in Manchester. There he taught himself to paint by studying art books and works on display at the city's Royal Institution. During the 1840s he worked as a teacher and lithographer before emigrating to the United States in 1850. He subsequently lived in New York or its suburbs. Within a year or two, he first visited the Adirondack Mountains, where until the 1880s he summered regularly and occasionally stayed through the winter. His images helped to popularize the region as a tourist and sporting destination. Later Tait spent summers in rural areas closer to the city, and some works of this period reflect the bucolic environment he observed there. He died at the residence of his final years, in Yonkers.

Tamarind Lithography Workshop. A print studio dedicated to all aspects of fine art lithography and its dissemination. Founded in Los Angeles in 1960, Tamarind quickly became a leading force in the transformation of American printmaking. While contributing to a general revival in creative printmaking and to initiation of a flourishing print market, it more specifically spurred a renewal of fine art lithography, which had then languished for some time. At the end of its first decade, with a solid record of achievement in place and a new recognition of lithography's potential by then widespread, the workshop relocated to Albuquerque, where it continues to function as the Tamarind Institute under the auspices of the University of New Mexico. Tamarind's founder and guiding spirit, June Wayne (1918–), persuaded the Ford Foundation to underwrite establishment of the workshop as a facility for technical research and creative development in lithography. To promote the medium's potential, Tamarind awarded fellowships to well-known printmakers and painters while also welcoming other guest artists. Along with several other printmaking ventures, it facilitated a significant shift from studio-based, hands-on practice among technically proficient intaglio or woodcut specialists to a system that allowed artists with little or no previous experience to produce prints with the assistance of in-house master printers. This development went hand in hand with an explosion in the demand for fine art prints. The lithographic technique, congenial to bold forms, bright colors, and relatively large scale, allowed *abstract expressionist, *color field, and *pop artists to translate their styles into saleable printed form. Since the 1960s, it has become standard practice for nearly all major painters, as well as many sculptors, to include printmaking among their activities. To name only a few, the workshop's early artist-participants included Josef *Albers, Richard *Diebenkorn, Sam *Francis, Antonio *Frasconi, Misch *Kohn, Reuben *Nakian, Louise *Nevelson, Nathan *Oliveira, and Karl *Schrag. Tamarind's success in nurturing a substantial body of high-quality work validated the Ford Foundation's decade of support and has allowed the successor Institute to continue an educational mission through university support, a patchwork of grants, and sales of lithographs.

A Chicago-born painter and tapestry designer, as well as printmaker, June Wayne left school at fifteen to become a painter. Remaining mostly self-taught as an artist, she nevertheless was exhibiting her work before she reached the age of twenty, when she was hired by a *federal art project. In the late 1940s, while living in Los Angeles, she took up lithography with great enthusiasm, eventually becoming an expert technician. Her generally symbolic work, combining abstract and figurative elements as the occasion demands, draws inspiration from varied subjects, including perceptual effects, scientific knowledge, and many literary texts. She is also remembered for a classic feminist-era essay, "The Male Artist as Stereotypical Female," published in 1973 in the *Art Journal*.

Painter and printmaker Clinton Adams (1918–2002) assisted Wayne in planning and implementing the Tamarind Workshop and remained closely involved with its progress, even after becoming a dean at the University of New Mexico in 1961. He served as the Tamarind Institute's director from 1970 until 1985, when he retired from the university. A native of Glendale, he graduated from nearby UCLA in 1940 and received a master's degree two years later. Following military service until 1946, he then taught at UCLA, the University of Kentucky in Lexington, and the University of Florida in Gainesville. His paintings and prints range from stylized representation to complete abstraction. In 1974 he founded a scholarly journal, *The Tamarind Papers*, which he continued to edit for many years. In addition, he published several books on topics related to printmaking, including two of particularly lasting importance, the authoritative *Tamarind Book of Lithography: Art and Techniques* (1971; with Garo Antreasian) and *American Lithographers, 1900–1960: The Artists and Their Printers* (1983).

Garo Antreasian (1922–) served as the initial technical director at Tamarind. Born in Indianapolis, Garo Zareh Antreasian served as a combat artist during World War II, after earning his BFA at the Herron School of Art (now Herron School of Art and Design of Indiana University-Purdue University at Indianapolis). Following additional training at the *Art Students League, he returned to Indiana to teach. He took a leave of absence to assist in the early days at Tamarind, and in 1964 he followed Adams to the University of New Mexico, where he taught until 1987. Predominately abstract, Antreasian's work shows great variety in visual and technical characteristics.

Among other centers that boosted lithography during the 1960s and 1970s, Universal Limited Art Editions in West Islip, on the south shore of Long Island, played a particularly important role. Founded in 1957 by another visionary woman, Russian émigré Tatyana Grosman (1904–82), it attracted such major talents as Jasper *Johns and Robert *Rauschenberg, who made their first lithographs at the workshop, as well as Jim *Dine, Helen *Frankenthaler, Grace *Hartigan, Robert *Motherwell, Barnett *Newman, and Claes *Oldenburg, among many others. Tatyana Aguschewitsch studied art in Dresden, where she met painter and printmaker Maurice Grosman (1900–1976). They married in 1931 and lived in Paris before World War II. She died in a New York hospital. Although she had no direct printing experience, at ULAE she emulated the great print ateliers of Europe in her desire to attract the finest artists to printmaking in order to publish artists' books and portfolios of the highest quality. In the late 1960s she added an intaglio workshop and before long, offset and woodcut facilities to the ongoing lithography venture. ULAE's first major portfolio publication, *Stones* (1957–59), combined images by Larry *Rivers with the poetry of Frank O'Hara. She enticed printmaker and fabled printer Robert Blackburn (1920–2003) from New York, his lifelong home, to work as ULAE's first technician on this and subsequent projects. After six years, he returned to his own open-access Printmaking Workshop, established in 1948 to provide particular welcome to fellow African Americans at a time when their opportunities remained limited. In 1992 Blackburn was awarded a MacArthur Foundation "genius" grant. ULAE continues under the leadership of Bill Goldston, a graduate of the University of Minnesota.

Pathbreakers Tamarind and ULAE stimulated the development of scores of collaborative workshops, partly by example and partly by training a technically competent new generation of artists and master-printers who established their own premises. Technical wizard Kenneth Tyler (1931–) worked at Tamarind before establishing Gemini G. E. L. (Graphics Editions Limited) in 1965 (known until 1967 as Gemini Ltd.) in Los Angeles. After a few years, this studio also expanded beyond lithography into other media, including intaglio, screen printing, and even sculptural multiples. In 1974 Tyler opened a new venture, Tyler Graphics, in the northern suburbs of New York. This operation gained renown for complex, multimedia printing ventures for such artists as David *Hockney, James *Rosenquist, and Frank *Stella. Tyler retired in 2002.

Upon receiving her MFA in 1962 from the California College of Arts and Crafts (now California College of the Arts) in Oakland, Kathan Brown (1935–) started a community-based intaglio studio that soon became Crown Point Press, since 1986 headquartered in San Francisco. She introduced etching techniques she had learned in London, promoted other intaglio approaches, and in the 1980s added woodcuts. Crown Point's roster of published artists, initiated in 1965 with portfolios by Richard *Diebenkorn and Wayne *Thiebaud, has particularly favored *minimalists and *conceptualists, including Sol *LeWitt and John *Cage. *Ink, Paper, Metal, Wood: Painters and Sculptors at Crown Point Press* (1996) chronicles her experiences. Subjects of other books include aspects of printmaking and the creative process.

Tanager Gallery. *See* SANDLER, IRVING.

Tanguy, Yves (1900–1955). Painter. During World War II and after, in company with other displaced surrealists in New York, this

Paris native contributed to the internationalization and creative growth of American art. Arshile *Gorky and Boris *Margo numbered among those who profited directly from his example. He emigrated to the United States in the fall of 1939 and became a citizen in 1948. During the late 1930s in Paris, his work provided an important formative influence on the artistic development of Gordon *Onslow Ford and Roberto *Matta, as well as Kay *Sage, whom he married in 1940. From 1941 they lived in Woodbury, Connecticut. He died in a hospital in nearby Waterbury. As a young man, Tanguy traveled with the merchant marine from 1918 to 1920 and served in the army during the following two years. With no formal art training, he began sketching after his return to Paris. A chance encounter in 1923 with a painting by Giorgio de Chirico inspired him to become a serious artist. Two years later he met surrealist leader André Breton and soon became identified with that group. By 1927 he had developed the fundamental characteristics of his mature style, which featured precisely painted but unidentifiable *biomorphic and geological objects arrayed in limitless space, usually with no discernable horizon. Over time, these haunted and somber landscapes became more measured, more strongly lit, more intricate, and more sharply colored. In a late work, *The Mirage of Time* (Metropolitan Museum, 1954), the foreground features a complex array of brittle, organic forms, accompanied by some menacingly sharp-edged, warped rectangles. Beyond is a desolate terrain, which merges through a vaporous area into hazy, atmospheric sky.

Tanner, Henry Ossawa (1859–1937). Painter and printmaker. The preeminent African-American artist of his day, Tanner specialized in visionary biblical subjects. He also painted *genre scenes, portraits, landscapes, and animal pictures. Internationally recognized, he lived in France during most of his career. The first black elected to the *National Academy of Design, he engaged sophisticated post-impressionist and symbolist currents. Yet his expression remained independent, unpretentious, and accessible to a nonspecialist audience. Tanner was born into an accomplished, intellectually oriented family in Pittsburgh. Reflecting his parents' dedication to civil rights, his unique middle name derives from the Kansas Territory town of Osawatomie, home of radical abolitionist John Brown in the mid-1850s. As a child Tanner moved with his family to Philadelphia, where he trained in the early 1880s under Thomas *Eakins and Thomas *Hovenden at the *Pennsylvania Academy of the Fine Arts. He painted seascapes and animal subjects before leaving in 1889 for Atlanta. There he opened an unsuccessful photography studio and taught at Clark College (now part of Clark Atlanta University). Early in 1891 he departed for Europe, where he subsequently made his home. In Paris he studied at the Académie Julian with Jean-Paul Laurens and Jean-Joseph Benjamin-Constant. During the summer of 1891 in Brittany, he became familiar with the work of Gauguin and other post-impressionists. In the early 1890s he painted both French and American genre subjects, including one of his best-known works, *The Banjo Lesson* (Hampton [Virginia] University Museum, 1893). Transforming the stereotypical black banjo player into a figure of dignified humanity, it pictures an old man instructing the small boy on his lap. With its uncomplicated composition, richly worked paint surface, and glowing, almost transcendental light, the painting creates a mood of detachment from worldly concerns. Art unites the two in psychological intimacy, sensuous pleasure, and purpose.

Within a few years, Tanner turned chiefly to religious subjects, which he interpreted with increasing attention to the abstract elements of form and color as carriers of mood and spirituality. From his visits to the Holy Land in 1897 and 1898–99 and to North Africa in 1908 and 1912, he brought back ethnographic and archeological detail. More importantly, he employed his observations of light, vernacular architecture, and flowing costume to re-imagine sanctified themes, often allegories of justice and compassion. In the *Miraculous Haul of Fishes* (National Academy Museum, New York, 1927 or earlier), Christ and the fishermen appear as frail laborers within the ample, listing, lozengelike shape of their heavy boat. Streaming, golden light and resplendent colors suggest the potential of mundane activity to yield events of wondrous import. From 1904 Tanner made his home for some time in Sceaux, a Paris suburb, but also frequently visited his country house in the artists' colony of Trépied, near Étaples on the English Channel. Menaced there in 1914 by the advancing German army, Tanner fled temporarily to England. Even after his return, he found creative activity impossible during World War I. He worked with the Red Cross and at the war's conclusion immediately traveled to the front to record American soldiers, particularly African Americans. He continued to paint almost until his death in Paris.

Tanning, Dorothea (1910–). Painter, sculptor, and printmaker. Also a writer. With almost no formal training in art, she made a place for herself among the surrealists who congregated in New York during the early 1940s. As the wife of Max *Ernst from 1946 until his death in 1976, she lived mostly in Europe. Since her return to New York a few years later, she has continued to work productively, although she turned from art to poetry in the late 1990s. In addition, she has established a foundation to support the study of surrealism and has endowed an annual poetry prize (among the most remunerative literary awards offered) through the Academy of American Poets. Born in Galesburg, Illinois, she attended Knox College there for two years before moving to Chicago. She enrolled in the School of the Art Institute of Chicago but left after a few weeks, finding its curriculum dull. In 1935 she departed for New York, where she was fascinated by the following year's landmark "Fantastic Art, Dada, Surrealism" at the *Museum of Modern Art. Realizing that surrealism encompassed her own imaginative objectives, she quickly began to develop a distinctive approach. Through Julien *Levy's gallery, where she showed her work in 1942, she became personally acquainted with surrealists, including Ernst. Their marriage followed her divorce from journalist Homer Shannon. She and Ernst built a house near Sedona, Arizona, where they lived much of the time for six years before moving to Paris. From the mid-1960s they resided in Seillans, in the south of France. Literature and book illustrations had first captured Tanning's dreams as a child. From the beginning her own work drew on such sources as she portrayed invented, enigmatic subjects with a minutely realistic technique. Frequently harboring sexual overtones, these most often focus on girls and young women seemingly caught by external forces. During the 1950s she abandoned sharp-focus representation, and some of her work became almost abstract, suggesting ineffable presences within billowing colors, as in *Paris and Vicinity* (Whitney Museum, 1962). In the late 1960s and 1970s she created soft sculpture, sewn creations that continue her interest in the expression of mystery through the human body. Her last major series of paintings, completed in 1997, featured enlarged, sexually inflected flowers. Tanning has also worked as a designer for theater and ballet. In 1986 she published *Birthday*, an autobiographical memoir. A fuller account, *Between Lives: An Artist and Her World*, appeared in 2001. A volume of poetry, *A Table of Content*, was issued in 2004, as was her novel, *Chasm*.

Taos, New Mexico. *See* ARTISTS' COLONIES.

Tarbell, Edmund (1862–1938). Painter. A leading Boston artist, in the 1890s he spearheaded the impressionist movement there. Later he specialized in softly finished, elegant, and pearly interiors inhabited by women of cultivated leisure. They characteristically pursue quiet activities, such as reading or sewing, amid tastefully selected decorative objects suggesting antiquarian and orientalist interests. Tarbell also painted portraits and still lifes. A popular and influential teacher, he served on the faculty of Boston's School of the Museum of Fine Arts from 1889 until 1913. Born in West Groton, northwest of Boston, Edmund Charles Tarbell spent most of his youth in Dorchester (now part of Boston). He worked at a lithographic company and took drawing classes before entering the Museum school in 1879. In the fall of 1884 he left for Europe, where he remained for nearly two years, broken only by a visit home in 1885. In addition to visiting other European art centers, in Paris he absorbed the academic tradition at the Académie Julian and studied also with New York-born expatriate figure and portrait painter William Turner Dannat (1853–1929). Around 1890 Tarbell abandoned the rather dark and academic style he had mastered in Paris in favor of a colorful, feathery, impressionist treatment of mostly outdoor scenes. However, the figures, predominately women, who inhabit these works continue the solid draftsmanship of his French training. The paintings secured his national reputation, and in 1898 he numbered among the founding exhibitors in *The Ten. As the 1890s drew to a close, he turned more frequently to light-filled indoor scenes that suggest his appreciation for Degas's innovative compositions and for Japanese prints. Early in the 1900s, he closely studied the work of seventeenth-century Delft painter Jan Vermeer, whose international reputation had been enthusiastically rehabilitated in recent decades. Tarbell's exquisitely crafted signature style draws on the Dutch painter's taste for the abstract beauty of serene domesticity, but also continues to acknowledge impressionism's interests in light and informal structure. Although technically conservative and retrospective in tone, his work in this mode generated such popularity among local painters that he is often identified as the leader of a Boston School. Remaining in great demand nationally as a portraitist, his commissions included likenesses of three presidents, as well as international figures and leading businessmen. In 1918 Tarbell became head of the Corcoran School of Art (now Corcoran College of Art and Design) in Washington, D.C., but continued to spend much of his time in Boston, where he retained a studio until the end of his life. When he left this position in 1926, he retired to his New Hampshire vacation home in the village of

New Castle, on an island just east of Portsmouth. He died there, forty-five years after his first summer visit.

Tawney, Lenore (1907–). Fiber and assemblage artist. In the 1950s and 1960s, along with a few others, she liberated fiber from the flat, rectangular format imposed by the loom and demonstrated that her material could participate in the artistic dialogue then normally reserved for painting and sculpture. During the same period, she also began making collages and surrealistically flavored *assemblages of poetically related objects and texts, usually arranged within boxlike containers. This approach flowered in the 1990s with a series of transparent Plexiglas boxes supporting delicate webs of threads entangled with small, imaginatively charged objects. Whatever her means, Tawney's individualistic trajectory has engaged a personal and somewhat mystical interest in achieving transcendence through visual experience. In this, she has been influenced by Eastern philosophies and travels in Asia. Leonora Agnes Gallagher as a child shortened her first name. She grew up in her birthplace, Lorain, Ohio, not far from Cleveland. After 1927, evening classes at the School of the Art Institute of Chicago initiated her professional training. In 1941 she married George Tawney, a psychologist, who died a year and a half later. Drawn to sculpture, she studied from 1943 until 1945 at the University of Illinois in Urbana-Champaign. Following six months in Mexico, she returned to Chicago. In 1946 she enrolled for a year at the Institute of Design (now part of the Illinois Institute of Technology), where Alexander *Archipenko became her mentor, while other instructors included László *Moholy-Nagy and Chicago-born abstract painter Emerson Woelffer (1914–2003), later a fixture of Los Angeles modernism. After continuing to work privately with Archipenko in Chicago and *Woodstock, she left for Europe. While living in Paris from 1949 until 1951, she also traveled in Europe and North Africa. After additional study for a brief period in 1954 at the Penland (North Carolina) School of Crafts, in the mid-1950s, she began to focus on fiber art. Within a few years, she used innovative techniques to produce free-hanging, often monumental works that produce striking effects through knotting, braiding, and other unconventional means in combination with more traditional weaving. In 1957 she settled permanently in New York, where she soon befriended Agnes *Martin, as well as Ellsworth *Kelly, Jack *Youngerman, and others interested in a more formal and reticent alternative to the prevailing *abstract expressionist aesthetic. In perhaps her best-known series, begun in the late 1970s, thousands of threads hang suspended from blue canvases, to provide quivering and diaphanous Clouds.

Taylor, Henry Fitch (1853–1925). Painter. After seeing the *Armory Show only months before his sixtieth birthday, he abandoned an impressionist style for one based on cubism. Born in Cincinnati, he worked in the theater as a young man. In the 1880s he spent several years in France, studying in Paris and painting at Giverny, as well as elsewhere in the countryside. After his return to the United States in 1888, he lived much of the time in *Cos Cob, where he numbered among the early arrivals and longtime visitors. From 1908 he managed New York's Madison Gallery in partnership with his future wife, artist and interior decorator Clara Potter Davidge (1858–1921). (They married in 1913). Widely acquainted among artists, he hosted the initial planning meeting for the Armory Show at this gallery and continued to assist in its realization. In the aftermath of the exhibition, he combined his longstanding interest in color with a new attraction to the work of Cézanne and the cubists. Originating a system of harmony based on psychological effects of color, which he also correlated with the musical scale, Taylor was drawn particularly to the work of French cubist Albert Gleizes. Taylor's work also reflects knowledge of orphism and *synchromism. His pastel-toned gouache *The Parade—Abstracted Figures* (Whitney Museum, c. 1913) presents generalized figures and horses in a composition of interlocking and overlapping planes. He died in Plainfield, New Hampshire.

Tchelitchew, Pavel (1898–1957). Painter and stage designer. Laced with metaphysics and mysticism, his refined, complex, and sometimes extravagant figurative paintings hover at the edge of surrealism. He remains best known for *Hide and Seek* (Museum of Modern Art, 1940–42), a phantasmagoric allegory of childhood. In the center, a girl followed by a butterfly walks away from the viewer, into the middle of what appears to be an uprooted tree, possibly symbolizing the tree of life. Around its perimeter appear partial representations of other children and infants, most prominently two flanking heads regarding in apparent alarm the disappearing girl. Lurid, unnaturalistic colors enhance the work's strangeness as does the artist's subsequently favored strategy of revealing blood vessels, bones, and muscles. Although his esotericism and elegant draftsmanship fell out of fashion after mid-century, more recently Tchelitchew's restless and experimental art seems newly relevant to current interests in the body, in homoerotic desire, and in layered meanings. Born in Kaluga, Russia, he studied for two years at Moscow University and at the art academy there before fleeing from the Russian Revolution to Kiev in 1918. There he continued his studies at the academy, where Alexandra Exter numbered among his principal instructors. In 1921 he went to Berlin, where he worked mostly as a stage designer for two years before proceeding on to Paris. Turning his attention chiefly to painting, he accelerated his evolution, begun in Kiev, away from the cubist- and constructivist-influenced approach of his early years. He became known for portraits and painted a variety of other subjects, including landscapes and entertainment themes, drawn often from the circus or bullfight. Stylistically, these ranged from fairly direct realism to distortion that allied his work peripherally with a short-lived Parisian tendency known as neo-Romanticism. After they met in 1931, he remained the lifelong companion of Mississippi-born American writer and film enthusiast Charles Henri Ford (1908–2002), founder in 1940 of the surrealist *View* magazine, an important voice of the New York avant-garde until 1947. While living in New York from 1934, Tchelitchew continued stage work until 1942. In 1952 he became an American citizen, but by then he was already spending much of his time in Italy. In the last years before his death in Rome, he lived in nearby Frascati, where he practiced an individualistic form of abstraction that grew from his interest in the body's inner systems of circulation and neural communication.

Ten, The. Group of painters who showed their work together for twenty years, beginning in 1898. Particularly associated with impressionism, the group nevertheless embraced other practices, including *tonalism and *mural painting. Sometimes the group is identified as Ten American Painters, from a sign announcing their first exhibition, which took place in New York. The painters themselves never officially adopted a collective name. The small, informal association represents an early instance of American artists organizing to oversee the exhibition and reception of aesthetically congenial work. Its members, who resided in Boston or New York, resigned from the *Society of American Artists in order to show together in circumstances where they could jointly control the quality, coherence, and tastefulness of their exhibitions. They exhibited their work annually, mostly in New York. No officers, juries, or prizes were involved. All were mature, established artists by the time they came together, and all enjoyed successful careers. Initiated by Childe *Hassam, John *Twachtman, and J. Alden *Weir, the group included also Frank *Benson, Joseph *DeCamp, Thomas Wilmer *Dewing, Willard *Metcalf, Robert *Reid, Edward Emerson Simmons (1852–1931), and Edmund *Tarbell. Abbott *Thayer and Winslow *Homer declined invitations to join. William Merritt *Chase replaced Twachtman after his death.

A later group known also as The Ten exhibited in New York between 1935 and 1939. Concerned primarily with issues of formal structure in painting, it comprised nine artists, reserving a tenth exhibition slot for guests. Its leading founders included Adolph *Gottlieb, Mark *Rothko, and Ilya *Bolotowsky. Others who participated at some point include Lee *Gatch and John *Graham.

Thayer, Abbott Handerson (1849–1921). Painter. Also a naturalist. An important contributor to the *American Renaissance, he is known primarily for idealized figure compositions. He also painted portraits, landscapes, and occasional still lifes. His images of classically garbed women epitomize late nineteenth-century romantic exaltation of feminine virtue and beauty. Often outfitted with angelic wings, they are sometimes accompanied by children. Thayer brought to his landscapes a parallel yearning for spiritual escape from modern banality, as is especially evident in his depictions of New Hampshire's Mount Monadnock. Interested from childhood in wildlife, during the 1890s he gravitated once again toward this subject and in the last two decades of his life devoted much attention to artistic and scientific investigations of nature. This work resulted in notable observations on protective coloration in birds and animals. Born in Boston, as a small child he moved with his family to Woodstock, Vermont, and then to Keene, in southwest New Hampshire. There, in the nearby countryside, he developed affection for the wild creatures that provided his earliest painted subjects. Upon graduation from Boston's Chauncy Hall School in 1867, he rejoined his family in Brooklyn. There he began his professional training at the Brooklyn Academy of Design but switched in 1870 to the *National Academy of Design. On the first and longest of several European sojourns, from 1875 to 1879 he lived in Paris, where he studied at the École des Beaux-Arts. Although Jean-Léon Gérôme ranked as his most important teacher, Thayer resisted the highly polished realism of his mentor, developing instead a painterly manner that became richer and looser with time. Following his return, he at first found success in New York as a portraitist but gradually turned his interest toward more generalized, symbolic figures, often relying on his family as models. His wife's protracted illness and eventual death in 1891 intensified Thayer's production of allegorical images, often based on High Renaissance prototypes. In 1901 Thayer returned permanently to the Keene area. He lived at Dublin, where he had previously maintained a studio, within view of Mount Monadnock. There he adopted a roughhewn way of life and poured much of his energy into wildlife studies. However, his interest in landscape painting also flourished. His images of Monadnock particularly reflect his intensely spiritual regard for nature, formed under the influence of Ralph Waldo Emerson's Transcendentalist writings. In these his brushwork became richly expressive, with passages of nearly abstract color, while compositions reflect the simplicity he admired in Japanese prints. With his son, in 1909 he published *Concealing Coloration in the Animal Kingdom*, summarizing the results of many years of investigation. Although challenged by some, Thayer's theories influenced the later development of military camouflage. An authority on birds, his son, **Gerald Handerson Thayer** (1883–1935), born at Cornwall-on-Hudson, New York, was a painter and illustrator known for wildlife subjects. Thayer's second wife, painter Emmeline Buckingham Beach (1849/50–1924), known as Emma, specialized in flower still lifes and nature studies. They married in 1891.

Theus, Jeremiah (1716–74). Painter. Known to have painted close to two hundred portraits in the region, he dominated mid-eighteenth-century portrait painting in Charleston, South Carolina, and the surrounding area. As was the usual practice for colonial artists, he sought commissions for other types of decorative painting as well, and early in his career he gave drawing lessons. A native of Chur, Switzerland, in 1735 he emigrated to South Carolina with his parents, who settled in Orangeburgh Township; within about five years Theus had moved permanently to Charleston. His portraits rely on fashionable formulas he must have known from prints, and his sitters generally pose stiffly and formally. His clients' features tend to conform to an ideal modish type, and there is much emphasis on the glamour of their clothing. Nevertheless, he was able to impart appealing rococo lightness in color and detail, and at their best his faces posses an alert charm. Although most of his portraits are modestly scaled bust- or waist-lengths, frequently set in ovals, a particularly ambitious work, *Elizabeth Wragg Manigault (Mrs. Peter Manigault)* (Charleston [South Carolina] Museum, 1757), shows a three-quarter figure caught in forward motion, indicated by billowing drapery. The gesture of Mrs. Manigault's left hand leads the viewer's eye to an atmospheric, parklike vista. This slice of nature, leading into distant space on the right, balances the shallow depth at left and provides a counterpoint to the artificialities of costume and setting. In a similar contrast, the woman's plain face suggests withdrawn reflection, as well as colonial esteem for straightforward representation, but her sumptuous apparel bespeaks style-conscious social ambition.

Thiebaud, Wayne (1920–). Painter and printmaker. His bright, lusciously painted 1960s consumer items, particularly edible ones, resonated with *pop art. He often used repetition and uniformity to lampoon, but only gently, the mass-produced perfection of standardized favorites, especially rich desserts. By minimizing depth in regular arrays across his canvases, he called to mind cafeteria or shop window displays. Since the 1970s he has particularly focused on landscapes and urban streetscapes, abstracted into patterns and sensuously rendered in rich colors. In many, the stark illumination of the food paintings gives way to evocative light effects. Born in Mesa, Arizona, Wayne Morton Thiebaud grew up in Southern California. After graduating from high school in Long Beach, he worked for more than a decade as a cartoonist and graphic designer, except for the period between 1942 and 1945, when he served in the U.S. Army Air Force. He subsequently studied at San Jose State University and Sacramento State College (now California State University, Sacramento), where he earned bachelor's and master's degrees. Before completing his studies, in 1951 he began teaching at a Sacramento junior college, where he remained through the decade while painting works related to *abstract expressionism. Since 1960 he has taught at the University of California at Davis. In the 1970s he established a residence in San Francisco as well. Also in 1960 he began to make his reputation with opulent paeans to the American appetite. Within a few years, he painted figural works in a similarly poker-faced style but by the late 1960s had begun to grapple with outdoor views. Many of these picture hilly San Francisco, often in vertiginous perspectives, or the flat agricultural terrain around Davis. Some represent other areas of the West or borrow from imagination and memory. As a printmaker, he has worked in both intaglio and relief techniques.

Thomas, Alma. *See* WASHINGTON COLOR SCHOOL.

Thompson, Jerome (1814–86). Painter. Although he successfully pursued nearly every type of subject popular in his day, he is remembered especially for charming rural idylls depicting scenes of labor or leisure set within luminous, hilly New England landscapes. Dating to the 1850s, these distinctive views integrating *genre and landscape give visual form to the psychological and spiritual benefits of human harmony with nature. His father, **Cephas Thompson** (1775–1856), a self-taught portrait painter, made his home in his native Middleborough, Massachusetts, south of Boston. Jerome was born there during the years when his father traveled extensively in search of portrait commissions, as he did until 1825. After picking up the fundamentals of painting in the family shop, at seventeen Jerome started practicing professionally in Barnstable, on Cape Cod. By 1835 he was painting portraits in New York. Between 1842 and 1844 he traveled as a portraitist through the South, as had his father. Upon his return to New York, he began to specialize in genre subjects, drawing on precedents in English prints and the work of William Sidney *Mount. Between 1852 and 1854 Thompson lived in England, where he augmented his knowledge of both old master and contemporary painting; he seems to have been particularly impressed with current *Pre-Raphaelite work. During the next few years, he brought to fruition his original blend of genre and landscape, most often nostalgic scenes of harvest or picnicking. These incorporate his varied interests in the detail of Pre-Raphaelitism, the sentiment of Victorian narrative, and the limpid idealism of *Hudson River School views. An extended visit to the Midwest during the early 1860s provided inspiration for later scenes of the region and Indian life. These new interests accompanied a general expansion of Thompson's practice, as his work became more varied, eclectic, and imaginative but also more removed from everyday experience. During the final decades of his career, he produced numerous romantic narratives, allegories, and nudes in a generally looser style than his earlier tightly descriptive technique. His "pencil ballads" illustrating popular songs or poems, such as "The Old Oaken Bucket," numbered among his works distributed as steel engravings or chromolithographs to an appreciative mass audience. In 1884 Thompson bought an estate in northern New Jersey's Glen Gardner, where he died. His wife, painter **Marie May Tupper Thompson** (?–1926), nicknamed Minnie, worked primarily as a portraitist. After they married in 1876, she collaborated with him on some likenesses. Following his death she continued to work professionally under his name, even though she remarried.

A brother and a sister also became artists. **Cephas Giovanni Thompson** (1809–88) was known particularly for portraits and Italian scenes, but he also painted genre and historical subjects. Like Jerome, he was born in Middleborough and initially trained by his father. At eighteen he established a portrait practice in Plymouth, Massachusetts. He subsequently worked in Boston, where he studied with David Claypoole *Johnston, in Philadelphia, and elsewhere before arriving in New York in 1837. There he flourished for a decade as a fashionable portrait painter. *Spring* (Metropolitan Museum, 1838), a softly romantic, idealized portrait of a young woman, exemplifies his most appealing strengths. In 1847 he moved to New Bedford for two years and then lived in Boston before sailing to Europe. He resided for most of the 1850s in Rome. In 1859 he returned permanently to New York but continued to produce Italian subjects during the remainder of his career. Also born in Middleborough and trained by her father, **Marietta Tintoretto Thompson** (1803–92) became a portraitist who specialized in miniatures. Along with her brothers, she settled in New York in the mid-1830s. She died in Raynham, not far from her birthplace.

Thompson, Launt (1833–94). Sculptor. Known chiefly for portraits, he also produced ideal works. Although his art was rooted in the nineteenth-century taste for *neoclassicism, his notable portrait sculpture displays a dignified naturalism. Born in Abbeyleix, Queens County, Ireland, in 1847 Thompson arrived in Albany, New York. There within a year or two he began working in *Erastus Dow Palmer's studio. In the late autumn of 1858 he moved to New York, where he pursued additional instruction at the *National Academy of Design. At first he specialized in cameos and reliefs but soon moved on to more ambitious portraits and figural sculptures. Thompson first returned to Europe only after establishing his proficiency as a sculptor. Praise for two works in the 1867 international exposition in Paris drew him abroad. While living mostly in Rome before returning in 1869, his style moved toward greater realism. Thompson remained busy with portrait commissions until again sailing for Europe in 1875. Among his likenesses of this period, *Charles Loring *Elliott* (Metropolitan Museum, 1870), in marble, and *Sanford *Gifford* (Metropolitan Museum, 1871), in bronze, exemplify his characteristically vigorous modeling, refined surfaces, and vivid individuality. The second sojourn abroad proved his undoing.

After visiting England and Paris, he lived in Italy, mostly in Florence, but mental instability and alcoholism derailed his career. He accomplished little after his return to New York in 1881. In 1890 he was permanently committed to a mental institution in Middletown, New York, where he died.

Tiffany, Louis Comfort (1848–1933). Designer and painter. Known to a wide audience for spectacular work in glass, he excelled in virtually all decorative media, including ceramics, jewelry, enamelwork, metalwork, and mosaic. He also designed entire interiors integrating numerous media into harmonious relationships. In the 1880s he was central to reviving stained glass as an artistic medium, as he developed new production techniques and popularized its use in both private and public buildings. In the mid-1890s he devised the "Tiffany lamp," a form he created by wrapping a modern invention, the electric light bulb, with a shade fabricated from stained glass. Tiffany also pioneered new forms and techniques in the making of glass vases. For these, in 1894 he patented his *favrile* technique, deriving the name from an Old English word meaning "handmade." (The word later came to be applied as well to other products of his workshops.) In all media, Tiffany combined lush sensuousness with impeccable craftsmanship. Derived largely from the natural world, his formal vocabulary most often depicted or evoked the shapes of flowers, leaves, vines, and other eye-catching phenomena, such as peacock feathers. But he was a student of history, too, and often found inspiration in other historical or geographical cultures, including Byzantine, Islamic, and Celtic. As these sources suggest, although Tiffany was often daringly original, he remained also a master of synthesis. His work dovetails with nineteenth-century tastes for romantic revivals, exoticism, and orientalism. In addition, his sense of abstract pattern and asymmetrical balance connects to contemporary *japonisme. By combining these design elements with flowing, sinuous line, he became a leading exemplar of art nouveau. His attitudes toward the value of fine craftsmanship and the unity of design derive from the *Arts and Crafts movement, while his ability to inspire belief that life can be lived as a work of art places him squarely at the center of the *aesthetic movement.

Born in New York and educated in boarding schools, Tiffany was the son of the founder of the New York jewelry and silver company that still caters to the luxury trade. At eighteen, after a trip to Europe, he set his sights on becoming a painter. He studied for a year at the *National Academy of Design and with George *Inness before pursuing further training in Paris in 1868. During this sojourn abroad, he also traveled in Spain, North Africa, and Egypt. Following his return to New York he worked as a painter, often choosing subjects from scenes he had observed on his travels. After developing an interest in stained glass, in 1879 Tiffany joined together with Samuel *Colman and two other artists to pursue interior design projects under the name Louis C. Tiffany and Associated Artists (often shortened to Associated Artists). Although the alliance was successful (even fulfilling a commission to redecorate several rooms in the White House), it was terminated in 1883, and Tiffany transferred his projects to his own workshops. A large corps of artist-designers worked under his direction, eventually producing luxury ware not only for the wealthiest Americans but also for the upper middle class. When his father died in 1902, Tiffany became artistic director of Tiffany and Company. After this, much of his time was devoted to management of the company as well as his own studios. However, his artistic achievements in these years include his most important jewelry and the construction of Laurelton Hall (completed 1904, destroyed by fire in 1957), his magnificent home, with adjacent studio facilities, in Cold Spring Harbor on Long Island. By the time Tiffany died in New York, modernism had made his taste seem old-fashioned, but an enthusiastic revival of his reputation began in the 1950s. Mostly written by the artist himself, Charles de Kay's *The Art Work of Louis C. Tiffany* (1914) in effect serves as an autobiography.

Tiger's Eye. *See* ABSTRACT EXPRESSIONISM.

Tile Club. An informal New York artists' group. Founded in the fall of 1877, it provided camaraderie and a venue for discussion of artistic matters. At first, members gathered weekly to paint tiles, a decorative activity reflecting *aesthetic movement interests. However, after a year or two the commitment to "tiling" dwindled, and other artistic activities, such as sketching, eventually supplanted the original purpose. The group also organized summer outings, which generally included the newly fashionable pursuit of plein air drawing or painting. The club apparently disbanded within a year after publishing *A Book of the Tile Club* (1886), a lavish compendium featuring illustrations of members' work (but only one tile design) and light-hearted accounts of the group's activities. Intentionally exclusive as well as somewhat secretive, the club was by agreement (there were no bylaws) limited to twelve men. However, membership was somewhat fluid as participants sojourned intermittently in Europe or drifted away. In addition, there were at times honorary members. Generally limited to professional artists or illustrators, the group permitted exceptions, including lithographer-turned-society photographer, Napoleon Sarony (1821–96), and architect Stanford White, as well as a few musicians and writers. Major artists on the roster at one time or another included Edwin Austin *Abbey, William Merritt *Chase, Winslow *Homer, Augustus *Saint-Gaudens, John *Twachtman, and Elihu *Vedder.

Tintype. *See* PHOTOGRAPHY, AMERICAN.

Tobey, Mark (1890–1976). Painter and printmaker. Noted for calligraphic "white writing," he developed this specialty in response to East Asian art, especially Zen Buddhist painting. Appearing first in the mid-1930s, the pale markings originally overlay representational subjects. Within a few years, as recognizable forms almost entirely disappeared, his work presaged the *all-over canvases of such *abstract expressionists as Jackson *Pollock. However, Tobey's relatively small, elegant, and meditative works shun the reckless élan associated with that movement. An adherent of the Baha'i faith, he investigated space, light, and movement as elements in the construction of a mystical aesthetic universe. Mostly self-taught, Tobey spent many years finding himself as an artist. He explored numerous avenues of expression, traveled widely, and ultimately drifted farther from the conventions of European tradition than any of his contemporaries. A Wisconsin native, Mark George Tobey was born in Centerville, about fifty miles west of Madison, and lived as a child in Trempealeau, along the Mississippi River. He attended high school in Hammond, Indiana, where his family relocated in 1906. Saturday classes during these years at the School of the Art Institute of Chicago constituted his entire professional training. After the family moved again, to Chicago in 1909, he became a fashion illustrator and in 1911 went to New York to pursue a career in illustration. While moving back and forth through much of the 1910s between New York and Chicago, he added portraiture and interior design to his skills. For years, while retaining ties to representation, his painting inquired erratically into expressionism, cubism, and other modern modes as he attempted to work out an aesthetic position for himself. In 1918 he converted to the Baha'i religion, which reinforced the feeling for nature developed during his small-town childhood.

In 1922 he moved to Seattle, where he became a teacher and began to study brush painting with a Chinese artist. In 1925 he went to Paris for two years. While living there, he traveled widely in Europe and the Middle East. Subsequently, he bounced around between New York, Chicago, and Seattle, before taking a position in 1931 at Dartington Hall, a progressive arts center and school, in Devon, England. He remained there until 1938 but continued to travel incessantly. A trip to the Far East in 1934–35 proved decisive. He immersed himself in Chinese culture and lived for a month in a Zen monastery in Kyoto. Upon his return to England, he began to produce works heralding his distinctive style. Drawing upon aspects of Asian thought, as well as his deeply felt Baha'i convictions, he hoped to reconcile opposites, symbolize the oneness of being, advance self-knowledge among viewers, and promote universal brotherhood. As war loomed in Europe, Tobey returned to Seattle. There he befriended John *Cage, began an intensive study of music—which affected his notions of formal expression and the relationships of time and space—and sketched often at the teeming Pike Place Market, where incessant activity provided vibrant energy that remained as he detached line from representation. His earliest mature, completely resolved works in his personal style date to the early 1940s, when he already had passed the age of fifty. White lines (accompanied by a few black ones) whiz across the darker, mottled surface of *Universal Field* (Whitney Museum, 1949), creating a unified visual experience that integrates individually unstable elements into an evocation of cosmic wholeness. Executed in tempera and pastel on cardboard, it illustrates the artist's penchant for working with water-based paint and/or pastel on paper surfaces, even for his most ambitious paintings. Although his singular style won international recognition, he nevertheless modified or even temporarily abandoned it as his evolving ideas demanded different approaches. Notable deviations include a number of paintings and prints based on the Japanese "flung ink" technique. Throughout his mature career, Tobey remained loyal to the philosophically humanistic and spiritually didactic underpinnings of his art. Even more appreciated in Europe than in the United States, in the mid-1950s he again lived for about a year in Paris. In 1958 he won the international grand prize at the Venice Biennale, following only James Abbott McNeill *Whistler in 1895 among Americans so honored. In 1960 he moved to Basel. Despite failing health in his final years, he worked almost until his death there.

Tomlin, Bradley Walker (1899–1953). Painter. Known for lyrical, calligraphic *abstract expressionist paintings, he had earlier produced accomplished representational and cubist-influenced works. His signature abstract paintings feature floating bands, often tangled in rhythmic patterns, superimposed over delicately harmonized areas of muted color. A native of Syracuse, New York, Tomlin graduated in 1921 from Syracuse University with a degree in painting. Already a published illustrator, he moved permanently to New York, where he worked as a commercial artist and then as an art teacher for some two decades while at the same time pursuing his development as a painter. He also traveled to Europe four times between 1923 and 1934. On the first trip he studied for several months in Paris. For many years, he summered in *Woodstock. After engaging a range of subjects and styles in his earlier work, from the late 1930s he more consistently employed cubist compositional techniques, although the tenor of his images hints at surrealist leanings. The masterful *Still Life (Inward Preoccupation)* (Whitney Museum, 1939) combines enigmatic representational elements with sonorous planes of color dominated by favored browns and greens. His typical whites and an unexpected patch of blue enliven the composition. Through friends Robert *Motherwell and Adolph *Gottlieb, he moved into the abstract expressionist circle in the mid-1940s and formulated an individual style before the end of the decade. His contribution to the movement remained tethered to the discipline acquired during long immersion in traditional and early modern art. Despite his methodical approach, in generally modestly proportioned canvases he nevertheless achieved spontaneous and animated effects, often suggesting arrested movement. Crowded with suspended brush marks, his larger final paintings integrate with assured eagerness his longtime aesthetic preoccupations. Pictorial logic and expressive feeling find equilibrium.

Tonalism. Term describing late-nineteenth- and early-twentieth-century American painting and photography characterized by harmonious colors, vaguely defined forms, introspective moods, and romantic appreciation for nature. Generally rejecting scientific and materialist approaches to reality, tonalists adopted an intuitive and sometimes spiritual point of view. Specializing in evocative, intimate pastoral views, they rarely engaged the urbanizing, industrializing world they inhabited. Not an organized movement, tonalism represented a sensibility rather than a style. Among painters, George *Inness and James Abbott McNeill *Whistler spearheaded its development. Other prominent adherents included Ralph *Blakelock, Thomas Wilmer *Dewing, Dwight *Tryon, and John *Twachtman. Photographers associated with *pictorialism often worked in a similar spirit. They included Gertrude *Kasebier, Edward *Steichen, Alfred *Stieglitz, and Clarence *White. Widespread from the 1880s into the early 1900s, tonalism prevails in the work of many who—earlier, later, or concurrently—worked also in other modes, partly because, with its roots in *Barbizon and *luminist painting, tonalism overlapped other contemporary tendencies. Tonalists studied effects of color and light in nature, but they avoided impressionism's colorful sparkle and exuberant temperament. They cultivated the unknowable, but they preferred meditative serenity to symbolist drama. *Japonisme influenced their taste for simplicity, patterning, and asymmetry. Acknowledging tonalism's prevailingly muted color schemes, the term appeared occasionally in critical writing of the early twentieth century. However, it came into general use only after 1972, when art historian Wanda Corn (1940–) published *The Color of Mood: American Tonalism 1880–1910*, which served as the catalogue for an exhibition of the same name.

Tooker, George (1920–). Painter. Painstakingly crafted, his eerie depictions of modern life emphasize alienation, grief, and existential anxiety. Minutely realistic detail lends believability to imaginary settings, while immobilized figures embody states of psychological unease. His best known painting, *The Subway* (Whitney Museum, 1950) depicts self-absorbed individuals trapped in a claustrophobic, geometricized space suggesting a New York subway station. The most prominent figure, a woman who treads hesitantly forward, betrays in her facial expression and body language an inner dread that echoes among other travelers. Tooker's settings often suggest the dehumanizing aspects of modern life, a point emphasized by the lack of individuality among his characters, who seem deadened by routine, stultified by bureaucracy, or enervated by loss of faith. Some works of more recent years accentuate the spiritual life of his figures, in some cases reflecting the Catholicism to which he converted in the early 1970s. Born in Brooklyn, Tooker studied at Phillips Academy in Andover, Massachusetts, from 1936 to 1938 and graduated in 1942 with a major in English literature from Harvard University. Subsequently, at the *Art Students League his teachers included Kenneth Hayes *Miller and his mentor Reginald *Marsh. While studying privately in the mid-1940s with Paul *Cadmus, Tooker switched from oil painting to egg tempera, a laborious technique suitable to small-scale detail. Early Italian Renaissance painting and the work of J.-A.-D. Ingres numbered among important influences on the formation of his style. Because his paintings present believable elements within unreal images, Tooker is often grouped with the practitioners of *magic realism. At the same time, in his close observation of American life, Tooker extends and subverts the interests of the *American Scene movement. Since 1960 he has resided in Hartland, Vermont, although between 1968 and 1974 he regularly wintered in Malaga, Spain. African-American figurative painter William Christopher (1924–73), Tooker's partner of more than twenty years at the time of his death in Spain, was born in Columbus, Georgia, and studied in Paris before working in New York with Amédée Ozenfant and Hans *Hofmann.

Torr, Helen. *See* DOVE, ARTHUR.

Transcendental Painting Group. *See* JONSON, RAYMOND.

Traylor, Bill (1854–1949). Draftsman. Illiterate, untrained as an artist, born into slavery, and indigent in old age, he focused on his art only after he had reached his eighties. Mostly between 1939 and 1942 he turned out a striking body of energetic, whimsical drawings in pencil and poster paints on paper or cardboard. Born on a plantation near Benton, Alabama, he remained a sharecropper there until the late 1930s when he moved to Montgomery. A lack of technical sophistication suited his offbeat imagination. Blithely ignoring anatomy, perspective, and other conventions, Traylor represented people and animals, together with occasional objects, as flat patterns. Often sporting hats or other distinctive accoutrements, his lively, pictographic characters flicker vigorously across the surfaces of such works as the typically whimsical *Dancing Man, Woman and Dog* (Smithsonian American Art Museum, 1939–42). Two figures with cartoony faces and big hair, along with an excited pet, animatedly jitterbug with animal abandon. No work is known from the four years after he moved to Washington, D.C., in 1942. There he soon lost a leg to amputation. After visiting children in other northern cities, he returned permanently to Montgomery. Although he resumed art making, his health was deteriorating. The work of these last years was of diminished quality and little survives.

Trubetskoy, Paul. *See* VONNOH, BESSIE POTTER.

Truitt, Anne. *See* WASHINGTON COLOR SCHOOL.

Trumbull, John (1756–1843). Painter. The first significant painter of subjects from American history, he is known also for portraits and landscapes. His four representations of events from the Revolutionary era number among eight large paintings embellishing the U.S. Capitol rotunda. Trumbull was born into a prominent family in Lebanon, Connecticut. Before he graduated from Harvard College in 1773, he had decided to become a painter. His progress was slowed by the Revolution, in which he served for more than two years, part of the time as an aide to General George Washington. After resigning his commission (he nevertheless always remained attached to the honorific title of colonel), he settled in Boston in 1778. With its strongly modeled figures and shiny table top, the *Family of Jonathan Trumbull* (Yale University Art Gallery, 1777) demonstrates his admiration for the work of John Singleton *Copley, who had earlier given advice to the young artist. Trumbull departed in 1780 for Europe. After a brief stay in France, he continued on to London, where Benjamin *West agreed to take him as a student. Within a few months, Trumbull was arrested as a spy, convicted, jailed for more than half a year, and expelled from the country. He returned home, by way of Holland, but in 1783 departed again for London, where he worked at the Royal Academy as well as in West's studio. Soon he determined to make his reputation with a series devoted to the history-making events that had recently occurred in America. Inspired by West's and Copley's successes, he followed their lead in depicting subjects with narrative vigor, moral seriousness, and accurate detail. Although he had initially envisaged fourteen subjects, he completed eight modestly sized oil paintings (all Yale University Art Gallery) that were intended both as models for engravings and as source material for the enlargements he hoped to produce. Before August 1786, he had completed the first two, *The Death of General Warren at the Battle of Bunker's Hill* and *The Death of General Montgomery in the Attack on Quebec*. These accompanied him to Paris, where he sojourned for several months at the invitation of Thomas Jefferson, then the American minister to France. There, with its author's assistance, he began *The Declaration of Independence*, which shows Jefferson presenting a draft to John Hancock before a large gathering of participants. Trumbull returned to Paris the following year to add to this work life portraits of Jefferson, John Adams, and Benjamin Franklin, as well as likenesses of French officers in his rendition of *The Surrender of Lord Cornwallis at Yorktown*. The eight Revolution paintings, along with the portrait studies made in preparation for them, are regarded as Trumbull's finest and most original achievement.

Demonstrating the fluent, painterly style he had mastered in London, the richly hued, carefully composed narratives convey his patriotic themes with romantic intensity.

Trumbull returned to America late in 1789, planning to arrange for engravings of his paintings and to continue his visual research. While also accepting independent portrait commissions, during the next few years he visited Revolutionary sites and made many small, often miniature-sized, oil likenesses of participants in the events he wished to paint. These tiny, sparklingly animated busts number among the most appealing portraits of his career. However, he was able to attract little support for his historical project. Discouraged, he virtually ceased painting after accepting an appointment in 1793 as secretary to Supreme Court justice John Jay, whom he accompanied to London in the following year. For some years Trumbull remained active in Europe as a diplomat and businessman. After 1800 he gradually resumed painting but rarely recaptured his prior technical facility and fervent sentiment. In 1804 he moved to New York, where he found considerable success as a portraitist, although many of these later works seem dry and conventional, especially in comparison to the contemporary work of Gilbert *Stuart. A few landscapes from this period prefigure *Hudson River School accomplishments. Trumbull spent the years from 1808 to 1815 once again in England.

After his final return to the United States, briefly his fortunes appeared to brighten. In 1817 Congress awarded him the first important federal commission, authorizing him to undertake the four monumental murals for the Capitol. In the same year, he was elected president of the *American Academy of the Fine Arts, a position he retained until 1836. However, both these undertakings ended in partial disappointment. For the Washington project, he produced life-size versions of his studies picturing the writing of the Declaration of Independence and the surrenders at Yorktown and Saratoga, as well as *The Resignation of General Washington*. When they were installed in 1826, the works were widely criticized for their failure to achieve the painterly and emotional qualities that had energized his earlier work. Meanwhile, his authoritarian rule at the academy led to such dissatisfaction that a large bloc of dissident artists resigned in 1825 to form the *National Academy of Design, in some respects a rival institution. Despite animosities, Trumbull nevertheless afterward remained for more than a decade the most powerful individual in the New York art world. At the same time, he suffered failing eyesight, ill health, and financial problems. In 1831 he transferred his unsold paintings to Yale University in return for a lifelong annuity and establishment of a gallery. Trumbull assisted in designing the gallery, the country's first college art museum, which opened in 1832, but was demolished in 1901. Among other architectural projects, his only surviving work is the *neoclassical Meeting House (1804–6) in his Connecticut hometown. The first college-educated American artist, he was also the first to publish a personal history, which appeared in 1841 as the *Autobiography, Reminiscences, and Letters of John Trumbull from 1756 to 1841*. After his death in New York, he was buried, as he wished, in the Trumbull Gallery at Yale.

Tryon, Dwight (1849–1925). Painter. A landscape specialist, he is known particularly for intimate, uninhabited woodlands but also painted sea and shore views, as well as a few cityscapes. Occasionally *genre elements animate his rural images. A leading contributor to *tonalism, he made a specialty of lyric, atmospheric scenes, often featuring trees that form a flattened screen linking foreground and sky. Rooted in the *Barbizon approach and the example of George *Inness, his painting style also responded to the work of James Abbott McNeill *Whistler and to aspects of impressionism. Born in Hartford, Connecticut, and initially self-taught, Dwight William Tryon painted New England landscapes and shore scenes indebted to *Hudson River School principles before going abroad in 1876. In Paris he studied with a student of the romantic neoclassicist J.-A.-D. Ingres. He also benefited from acquaintance with several Barbizon painters, most notably Charles-François Daubigny, and closely studied the work of the recently deceased Jean-Baptiste-Camille Corot. During summers he painted in rural locations in France and elsewhere, and in 1879 worked in Venice. He returned to New York in 1881 with a dark, moody approach that soon mellowed toward impressionism's lighter hues and shimmering brushwork. Within a year or two he established a summer studio in South Dartmouth, Massachusetts, on the shore near New Bedford. He continued to vacation there regularly after accepting a teaching position in 1886 at Smith College in Northampton, Massachusetts. While remaining on the faculty for thirty-seven years, he also assisted the institution in developing its notable art collection. At his death, he bequeathed funds for the construction of a college art gallery, demolished in 1970 but replaced with Tryon Hall, the core of the Smith College Museum of Art. An important patron from 1889, Charles Lang *Freer purchased many of Tryon's finest works, which peaked in number during the artist's most productive period, approximately two decades beginning in the late 1880s. As in the typically sensitive meditation *Sunrise: April* (Freer Gallery of Art, Washington, D.C., 1897–99), these crowning achievements delight in delicate color harmonies, muted natural light, and indistinct forms arranged in ornamental patterns. Little interested to achieve representational accuracy in such works, Tryon sought rather to evoke the sentiment of nature through ideal compositions constructed from memory. He also began working frequently in pastel around 1890. After about 1910, he painted relatively little and because of illness ceased working altogether during the year before his death in South Dartmouth.

Tuckerman, Henry Theodore (1813–71). Critic. A leading American mid-nineteenth-century writer on art, he is remembered today chiefly for his *Book of the Artists: American Artist Life* (1867). Profiling artists from colonial days to his own time, the work reflects his personal acquaintance with the New York art world. He also wrote literary criticism, poetry, travel essays, and biographies. Tuckerman was born in Boston, where he was educated at Boston Latin School and Harvard. Because of poor health, in 1833 he left college after two years to depart for about a year in Italy, which ignited his interest in art and literature. After his return, he served as a magazine editor and began a prolific writing career. He again sojourned in Italy between 1836 and 1838, and later spent about a year in England. In 1845 he moved to New York, where for many years he wrote on art and other subjects for periodicals and continued to turn out a steady stream of books. His first book on art, *Artist-Life, or Sketches of American Painters* appeared in 1847. Tuckerman's art criticism reflects both a cosmopolitan appreciation of European culture and an enthusiasm for the development of a native school of American art, which he identified primarily with landscape painting. He died in New York.

Turrell, James (1943–). Sculptor and designer. Known for ethereal museum installations using light as a medium, he has also been engaged for more than thirty years with the transformation of Arizona's Roden Crater into an enormous celestial observatory. The completed project will use light from the sky to pursue on a vast scale his foremost project, elucidating the nature and effects of the visual experience itself. Born in Los Angeles, in 1965 James Archie Turrell received a bachelor's degree in mathematics and psychology from Pomona College in nearby Claremont. That fall he enrolled in graduate school to study art at the University of California at Irvine, where his teachers included John *McCracken and British-born artist, writer, and *Artforum* staffer John Coplans (1920–2003), later also a photographer. In 1966 Turrell realized his first light piece with a high-intensity beam projected across the corner of a room to create the illusion of a shining, three-dimensional cube. Before the end of the academic year Turrell left Irvine, although in 1974 he earned a master's degree from Claremont Graduate School. Working on his own in the Ocean Park neighborhood of Santa Monica, where he maintained a studio until 1974, he experimented with effects that could be achieved on a flat wall with projection techniques. In its simplicity this work related to *minimalism, and its dematerialization suggested *conceptual art. But the seductive, almost magical effects of the projected light pieces provided an altogether different expressive tenor from that of the cerebral and austere New York-based movements. In 1968 Turrell met Robert *Irwin, who soon involved him in the Los Angeles County Museum of Art's Art and Technology Program. This project paired the two artists with physiological psychologist Edward Wortz, giving them access to scientific input into their study of visual fields. Turrell participated for about eighteen months. He then developed a succession of mechanisms for creating illusions of space, by employing colored light, or for enhancing perception of real space, by cutting unexpected apertures, usually in ceilings, to permit views of the heavens from interior "skyspaces," as he calls them.

Searching for a symmetrical, truncated, extinct volcano, in 1974 Turrell discovered the isolated Roden Crater, his subsequent obsession. Its bowl, today smoothed out but not much altered, physically completes what visitors to its center will perceive as the interior of a perfect sphere above. Viewers will be able to lie on their backs for a glimpse into space as never quite before seen. A hole in the base of the bowl allows light into the interior, which contains passageways and other rooms, some lighted by apertures aligned with the movements of the sun and moon. Although Turrell's effects have often been interpreted in mystical terms, he refutes such claims with the assertion that "My art is about your seeing." The Quaker childhood that may have predisposed his fascination with outer as well as inner light resurfaced in the late 1990s, when he designed a Quaker meetinghouse in Houston. This experience generated a new interest in simplified domestic furnishings. In recent years, he has split his time between his home near Flagstaff and Ireland, where he has worked with a potter and a cabinetmaker, developing a line of Wedgwood-inflected black basalt tableware that enhances the design of his crisply elegant cherry wood furniture.

Tuttle, Richard (1941–). Sculptor, printmaker, draftsman, painter, and installation artist. His intimate, unassuming abstract sculptures focus attention on materials, spatial relationships, and subtleties of scale. Generally *assemblages of commonplace, usually domestic materials, these understated pieces set the reticent aesthetic seen also in his prints and other endeavors. Rooted in *minimal art, since the late 1970s his work has grown richer with no loss of delicacy. Born in Rahway, New Jersey, Tuttle grew up in nearby Roselle. In 1963 he graduated from Trinity College in Hartford, Connecticut. He then moved to New York and enrolled in graduate school at Cooper Union but stayed only for one semester. Around the time he entered brief military service, he befriended Agnes *Martin, who remained a mentor throughout her life. Subsequently he worked as a gallery assistant to Betty *Parsons, who gave him his first one-person show in 1965 and continued to represent his work until her death. Tuttle's earliest notable achievement, a mid-1960s series of tiny folded-paper cubes cut with slits, seemed to chide the current vogue for large, physically muscular sculpture. Instead, he proposed a modest, wistful art that wandered toward dematerialization, while drawing attention to properties of materials and to the way the art activates the space around it. The drape of a fabric, the twist of a wire, or faint pencil marks on a wall served his purposes. Since the late 1970s, he has elaborated this humble approach with more complex assemblages in combination with richly brushed surfaces, often boasting offbeat colors. He divides his time between New York and Abiquiu, New Mexico.

Twachtman, John (1853–1902). Painter and etcher. Primarily a landscape artist, he ranks among the finest American impressionists. However, in his most distinctive work, he abandoned the movement's analytical approach to color and light. Instead, he emphasized decorative color and form as keys to the inner meaning of nature. Much of his work suggests the meditative hush of *tonalism. Preferring subtle color harmonies perceived under even illumination, he often painted winter scenes that capture delicate effects of light reflected on snow and ice. Indebted as were so many of his contemporaries to the example of Japanese art, he often devised flattened patterns that sometimes undermine representational veracity. In this, as in his interest in art's spiritual and psychological dimensions, he anticipated goals of the modernist generation that followed. A Cincinnati native, John Henry Twachtman began his training at the McMicken School of Design (now the Art Academy of Cincinnati). There he encountered Frank *Duveneck, who took his talented pupil with him when he returned to Munich in the summer of 1875. Twachtman studied at the Royal Academy and adopted the rich, painterly style associated with Munich's realist painters. In the spring of 1877 he traveled to Venice with Duveneck and William Merritt *Chase for an extended stay. About a year later, he returned to Cincinnati but moved to New York that autumn. There he associated with other progressive artists, soon becoming a member of the *Society of American Artists and the *Tile Club. During another year in Cincinnati, in the winter of 1879 he made the first of some twenty etchings, indebted in their approach to the example of James Abbott McNeill *Whistler's popular work. Except for a trip home in the spring of 1881, from the fall of 1880 until December of the following year, he traveled and worked in Europe, with extended periods in Italy and, with J. Alden *Weir, in Holland. Following another Cincinnati sojourn, in 1883 he departed to study in Paris at the Académie Julian with Gustave Boulanger and Jules-Joseph Lefebvre. He also painted in rural locations during this European visit, which proved decisive to his artistic development. Extending an emphasis on drawing and simplified composition, which had begun in the months before his departure, he forged a personal synthesis from varied contemporary sources, including the work of Whistler and French painter Jules Bastien-Lepage as well as impressionism. He also began working extensively in pastel, a medium congenial for its synthesis of line and color.

Following an autumn in Venice with Robert *Blum, he returned permanently to the United States in January 1886. In 1889 he settled in a Greenwich, Connecticut, farmhouse on about seventeen acres and began commuting to New York to teach at the *Art Students League. He taught also during summers in *Cos Cob. During the 1890s Twachtman occasionally traveled to paint at other scenic locations but mostly drew subjects from his rural acreage. As he returned repeatedly to motifs found there, his distinctive personal style came to fruition. Austere but intimate, sensuous yet ethereal, *Icebound* or *Snowbound* (Art Institute of Chicago, 1889) pictures the pond he called Hemlock Pool. The screenlike painting's grays and whites, enlivened by the orange-red of a few clinging leaves, surround the arabesque edge of dark, greenish water. Although it demonstrates the artist's commitment to the impressionist bedrock of visual sensation, the work deviates from the broken colors associated with the French movement, instead building the image from thickly applied layers of paint. In 1898 he exhibited as a founding member of *The Ten. During the final three summers of his life he worked at Gloucester, Massachusetts, where he adopted a more spontaneous approach, incorporating brighter colors and more gestural brushwork. Brilliantly transcribing ephemeral effects, these included the last works he completed before his death there.

His wife, **Martha Scudder Twachtman** (1858–1936), exhibited etchings for some years after marriage in 1881 but later relinquished professional achievement to domestic responsibilities. Known as Mattie, Martha Scudder was born in Cincinnati and studied there at the School of Design and in Europe. She died in Greenwich. Also born in Cincinnati, their son **J. Alden Twachtman** (1882–1974), a painter, illustrator, and architect, studied in Paris. He lived for most of his life in Greenwich but died in Middletown, Connecticut.

Twombly, Cy (1928–). Painter, sculptor, printmaker, and draftsman. His undemonstrative, elegant, and private art grows out of surrealism and *abstract expressionism but also pays homage to the classical past. Meditating on themes related to memory, loss and recuperation, and the relevance of history, he has resided in Italy for half a century. Born in Lexington, Virginia, where since the mid-1990s he has maintained a second residence, Edwin Parker Twombly Jr. enrolled in 1947 at Boston's School of the Museum of Fine Arts, but in 1949 transferred to Washington and Lee University in his hometown. In 1950 he took up studies at the *Art Students League, where he worked with Will *Barnet, Morris *Kantor, and Vaclav *Vytlacil. At *Black Mountain College in the summer of 1951 and following winter, Franz *Kline and Robert *Motherwell numbered among his teachers. In his artistic maturation, a 1952–53 voyage of discovery may have exerted more weight than schooling. Traveling through Italy, Morocco, and Spain with Robert *Rauschenberg, he experienced at first hand the Mediterranean culture and traditional arts foundational to his artistic individuality. Military service followed in 1953–54. Subsequently adapting abstract expressionism's scale, gestural brushwork, *all-over compositions, and heroic thematics to his penchant for calligraphic tangles rooted in surrealism, he worked out the major characteristics of his painting style before he departed more or less permanently for Rome in 1957. There, ancient references became more pointed as he sometimes included written or symbolic allusions to literature and myth, and even more often drew attention to his Mediterranean inspiration in the titles of his paintings. Especially since the mid-1970s, his work has often alluded in its coloration and spatial dynamics to classical landscape. Although he tried his hand at *assemblages in the 1950s, sculpture emerged as an important aspect of his work only in 1978. Generally, its pale forms, freely constructed from plaster and/or found objects, refer back to classical themes while playing off quirky, surrealistic elements. His son, painter and sculptor **Alessandro Twombly** (1959–), was born in Rome, where he continues to reside.

291 gallery. *See* STIEGLITZ, ALFRED.

Tworkov, Jack (1900–1982). Painter and printmaker. After making his reputation with *abstract expressionist canvases featuring boldly slashing brushstrokes, in the 1970s he imposed a discipline of geometric shapes on clouds of tiny, flickering marks. Born in Biala, now in Poland near the Russian border, Jacob Tworkovsky moved with his family to New York in 1913 and was naturalized as a U.S. citizen in 1928. Intending to become a writer, he studied literature from 1920 until 1923 at Columbia University, but also took art courses. During this period the work of Cézanne became a long-standing interest. In 1923 he enrolled at the *National Academy of Design, where Charles *Hawthorne ranked as his most important teacher. Around this time he also began regularly summering in *Provincetown. In 1925–26 he studied at the *Art Students League with Guy Pène *du Bois and Boardman *Robinson, among other instructors. Karl *Knaths and Lee *Gatch also proved important to his development. During the 1930s, the social realist approach of the *American Scene movement claimed his attention. From 1934 until 1941 he worked for a *federal art project. Subsequently, he ceased painting while employed as a tool designer for the World War II effort. By 1945 he had returned to his art, soon moving away from representation toward an abstract approach suggesting the influence of his friend Willem *de Kooning. While teaching during the summer of 1952 at *Black Mountain College, he formulated the signature style that characterized his work through the 1960s. In the large and forthright *Crest* (Cleveland Museum of Art, 1958), extended, gestural brushstrokes in darkly sonorous colors seem to resist a grid in their placement along roughly vertical or horizontal coordinates. From the late 1940s Tworkov pursued an active teaching career, culminating in his appointment as head of the School of Art and Architecture at Yale University from 1963 until 1969. Around the time he retired, he more pointedly emphasized structure over spontaneity. Yearning for a more transcendent form of expression, he soon achieved lyrical effects with precisely organized compositions, most often based on triangles. Although color effects also became subdued, often nearly monochrome, he animated the surface of his work with quivering strokes of sensitively calibrated hues. He died in Provincetown.

Tworkov's sister, Janice Brustlein (1903–2000), painted professionally as Biala. In the tradition of Matisse or Milton *Avery, her landscapes, interiors, and still lifes balance representation with abstraction. Sharing her brother's birthplace, she, too, arrived in New York in 1913 and later became a U.S. citizen. She studied briefly at the National Academy of Design and worked with Edwin *Dickinson in Provincetown. Following a brief marriage in the mid-1920s to Gatch, she left for Paris, which thereafter remained her principal residence. She sojourned often in New York and regularly showed her work there for more than sixty years. While living with the English writer Ford Maddox Ford for about ten years before his death in 1939, she illustrated several of his novels. In New York in 1943 she married Alsatian-born painter Daniel Brustlein (1904–96), who signed his *New Yorker* cartoons Alain. She died in Paris. Tworkov's daughter, painter Hermine Ford, is known for lively abstractions. She is married to New York painter Robert *Moskowitz.

Tyler, Kenneth. *See* TAMARIND LITHOGRAPHY WORKSHOP.

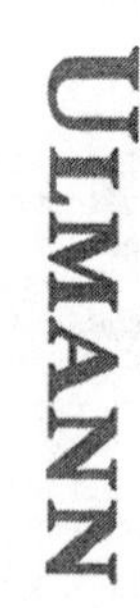

Uelsmann, Jerry (1934–). Photographer. Known for complex and richly metaphoric fictional works, he states his goal simply: "Ultimately," he has said, "my hope is to amaze myself." Combining several negatives into individual images, he produces what appear to be fantastic or hallucinatory documents. Born in Detroit, Jerry Norman Uelsmann studied at the Rochester (New York) Institute of Technology with Minor *White. After receiving his BFA in 1957, he worked at Indiana University with Henry Holmes Smith (1909–86), an early advocate of abstraction in photography. By the time Uelsmann was awarded an MFA degree in 1960, he was already engaged in the synthetic process that coalesced into a mature style in the mid-1960s. Both technically and philosophically, Uelsmann's work derives largely from White's example. He never lost his admiration for the tradition of fine printing that White exemplified. Tonal subtlety and sharp detail remained basic to his work. In addition, Uelsmann enlarged upon White's belief that a photograph should transcend literal representation. Although he creates dreamlike scenes, Uelsmann does not tell stories or concoct overt symbols. Rather, his enigmas reflect twentieth-century philosophical, aesthetic, and psychological thought about the instability of meaning. In 1960 Uelsmann began teaching at the University of Florida and since retirement has remained in Gainesville. His publications include *Jerry N. Uelsmann* (1970), *Jerry Uelsmann: Silver Meditations* (1975), *Jerry Uelsmann: Photo Synthesis* (1992), and *Uelsmann/Yosemite* (1996).

Ufer, Walter. *See* TAOS ARTISTS' COLONY.

Ukeles, Mierle Laderman. *See* PERFORMANCE ART.

Ulmann, Doris. (1882–1934). Photographer. In records of vanishing rural subcultures, she achieved a unique synthesis of *pictorialist poetry, modern formal rigor, and social documentation. Throughout her career, she treated portraits as the index of human experience. Born in New York, after graduating from high school in 1900, she continued her education at the progressive Ethical Culture School, where she worked with Lewis *Hine. Later she took classes at Columbia University and elsewhere, while also beginning to photograph friends and family. Following marriage in 1914 to Charles Jaeger, a medical doctor and amateur photographer who had studied with Clarence *White, she too studied with White and soon became absorbed in portrait photography. Along with her husband, she participated in establishing the *Pictorial Photographers of America in 1916. Divorced by late 1921, within a few years she turned her attention to documenting lifestyles of traditional communities. She normally traveled for half or more of each year, visiting out-of-the-way places where premodern patterns prevailed. She ranged from New England to New Orleans but specialized in Appalachia and the South. Ulmann worked with a cumbersome, old-fashioned view camera, which required long exposures and motionless subjects. Posed in natural light and often monumentalized, her sitters, generally seen individually or in small groups, evince great solemnity, while the soft-focus lens she favored slightly generalizes and universalizes their individuality. The resulting character studies emphasize dignity, strength, resilience, and the sitters' emotional ties to each other. Ulmann's best-known series records life among some four hundred Gullah African Americans in South Carolina. Collected as *Roll, Jordan, Roll* (1933; reissued the following year in a deluxe edition with additional plates), with text by novelist Julia Peterkin, Ulmann's images romanticize a way of life barely touched by the Civil War and realize her intention to honor the human values embodied in an agricultural, deeply religious way of life. She shared a desire to recuperate a "true" America with many of the period's artists and intellectuals who promoted appreciation of early American art, architecture, and crafts. The fascination with American origins also flowered among regionalists in the *American Scene movement and among other documentarians, notably several of the *Farm Security Administration photographers. Ulmann's photographs also appeared after her death in *Handicrafts of the Southern Highlands* (1937), with text by Allen Eaton. She died at her home in New York.

Universal Limited Art Editions. *See* TAMARIND LITHOGRAPHY WORKSHOP.

V

Vanderlyn

Von Wiegand

VIDEO ART

Vedder

Voulkos

Van Der Zee

Vachon, John. *See* FARM SECURITY ADMINISTRATION (FSA) PHOTOGRAPHS.

Vail, Laurence. *See* GUGGENHEIM, PEGGY.

Valdenuit, Thomas Bluget de. *See* SAINT-MEMIN, CHARLES B. J. F. DE.

Van Beest, Albert. *See* BRADFORD, WILLIAM.

Van Bruggen, Coosje. *See* OLDENBURG, CLAES.

Vanderlyn, John (1775–1852). Painter. His relatively few but nevertheless distinguished literary and historical works were admired abroad but found little appreciation in the United States. American patrons preferred his portraits. He also painted landscapes, a *panorama of Versailles, and one of the eight huge narratives adorning the Capitol rotunda in Washington, D.C. The grandson of Pieter *Vanderlyn, he was born in the Hudson River town of Kingston. In 1792 he went to New York, where he pursued instruction in drawing and painting while employed by a dealer in art supplies. After some months in 1795–96 with Gilbert *Stuart in Philadelphia, Vanderlyn departed for Paris. The first major American artist to study there, during five years abroad he worked under François-André Vincent at the École des Beaux-Arts, assimilated the history of art at the Louvre, and absorbed the *neoclassicism of premier French painter Jacques-Louis David. Before he returned to New York in 1801, fired with ambition for his art, his forcefully conceived but delicately executed *Self-Portrait* (Metropolitan Museum, 1800) had been accepted for exhibition in the Salon. The first American-born artist to establish a career within that prestigious venue, he demonstrated in his initial appearance there that he had mastered a sound technique and the fashionable elegance of the French capital.

After two years in New York, he returned to Europe. There he burnished his reputation with his three most important subject paintings and some of his finest portraits. The first of the narratives, *The Death of Jane McCrea* (Wadsworth Atheneum, Hartford, Connecticut, 1804) interprets recent history with an anti-British slant, perhaps calculated to win favor in France. The work depicts two American Indians, believed to be Revolutionary War agents of an English general, about to slay a young American. Vanderlyn found his literary inspiration in American poet Joel Barlow's *Columbiad*, but he derived the figures from antique sculpture. Like some young French contemporaries, Vanderlyn tended to push neoclassicism's stern and high-minded didacticism toward romantic objectives. A subsequent two-year sojourn in Rome produced Vanderlyn's first major work on a classical theme, *Caius Marius Amid the Ruins of Carthage* (Fine Arts Museums of San Francisco, 1807). Here the drama is internal. A resplendent red cape exposing his bare upper torso, the virile Roman general in exile broods on wrongs he believes he has suffered and ponders his future course. Some months after Vanderlyn departed Rome at the end of 1807 to return to Paris, he accepted a medal for this painting from Napoleon at the Salon. At thirty-two, the artist stood at the height of his career and for the rest of his life would cherish the award, although he pawned it on occasion when times were lean. Soon he followed this success with a third major work, also a classical subject, *Ariadne Asleep on the Isle of Naxos* (Pennsylvania Academy, 1809–12), inspired in part by Correggio's *Antiope*. Both formally and thematically a feminine counterpart to his ruggedly masculine *Marius*, *Ariadne* features a life-size sleeping nude (the first in American art) in an idyllic landscape. With her faithless lover Theseus about to sail away in the distant background, when she wakes Ariadne too will confront an uncertain future in the aftermath of betrayal. Again the narrative hinges on psychological aspects of memory, desire, and destiny.

Following his return to the United States in 1815, Vanderlyn's career languished. His American audience remained largely indifferent to neoclassical history painting (*Ariadne* provoked outright hostility), and he was unable to secure commissions for the public monuments he had envisioned. In an attempt to capitalize on interest in panoramas, he went into debt to build a circular gallery to show his *Palace and Gardens of Versailles* (Metropolitan Museum, 1818–19). However, financial success eluded him despite the superior execution of his vast painting (18′ × 165′), his entrepreneurial willingness to show other panoramas in the little neoclassical building, and his temporary presentations of the Versailles painting elsewhere. (He continued nearly until the end of his life to arrange showings of this panorama around the country.) When the city took over the building in 1829, Vanderlyn moved to Kingston. There he mostly painted portraits of little distinction. From the same period, his several views of Niagara (which he had first recorded in 1801) and a few other landscapes demonstrate greater freshness. After finally receiving a commission in 1836 for a monumental history painting to decorate the U.S. Capitol, he spent the years from 1839 to 1846 working on it in Paris. However, the crowded, inert *Landing of Columbus*, installed in 1847, barely hints at strengths he had demonstrated during his earlier residence abroad. He died in Kingston.

Vanderlyn, Pieter. *See* PATROON PAINTERS.

Van Der Zee, James (1886–1983). Photographer. Known during his active years only in New York's African-American community, he preserved an intimate record of the *Harlem Renaissance era. His work came to the attention of a wider audience in 1969 when many prints appeared in a major and controversial exhibition, "Harlem on My Mind," at the *Metropolitan Museum of Art. Music was his first love, although he had begun as a youngster to experiment with photography. Born in Lenox, Massachusetts, in 1906 he moved to Harlem. A year or two later he left for Virginia but soon returned to found the Harlem Orchestra and play the piano at parties and other social functions. During these years, he continued to photograph family and friends, mainly on visits to Lenox. With his performance career threatened by the advent of recorded music, in 1916 he opened a portrait studio, soon a successful business that brought numerous commissions from well-known African Americans of the 1920s and 1930s. Even more engagingly, he recorded middle-class Harlem residents in their homes, capturing their genteel aspirations as well as their personal ties to each other. In addition, he was known for his success at group portraits (for school classes, clubs, funerals, and the like), and he photographed the daily life of Harlem, including scenes of work and recreation. During the 1920s he served as the official photographer of Marcus Garvey's Universal Negro Improvement Association. Van Der Zee's photographs remain important as records of his African-American community, as he intended, but his desire to achieve artistic effects lends distinction to his achievement. Careful attention to composition, lighting, and textures, together with his feel for classic structure, bring warmth and dignity to his subjects and provide his best works with a visual appeal that transcends documentation. He died during a visit to Washington, D.C.

Van Dyke, Willard. *See* F/64 GROUP.

Van Vechten, Carl (1880–1964). Photographer. Also a writer. Born in Cedar Rapids, Iowa, he graduated in 1903 from the University of Chicago. He then worked for a Chicago newspaper until 1906, when he moved to New York. As a correspondent for the *New York Times*, in 1908–9 he lived in Paris, where he socialized with Gertrude *Stein and her circle. After his return he was friendly with Walter *Arensberg, Mabel Dodge *Luhan, Florine *Stettheimer, and numerous other key players in the early history of modernism. Among the vanguard of whites who discovered the vitality of black culture, Van Vechten kindled interest in the *Harlem Renaissance with his novel *Nigger Heaven* (1926). After taking up photography in the 1930s, he documented the fabric of New York and, in the portraits that are his major contribution to the medium, its cultural leaders, especially African Americans. As a leading music critic of the 1920s, he championed modern innovators and numbered among early voices to give serious attention to popular forms, such as blues, ragtime, and musical theater. He died at his home in New York. His numerous books include several novels, seven volumes on musical topics, a collection of essays on literature, and two memoirs, *Sacred and Profane Memories* (1932) and *Fragments from an Unwritten Autobiography* (1955).

Vasilieff, Nicholas. *See* REFREGIER, ANTON.

Vedder, Elihu (1836–1923). Painter, illustrator, designer, and occasional sculptor. Recognized particularly for imaginative, enigmatic paintings, he worked also as a muralist and participated in the multimedia *aesthetic movement. His lavish 1884 edition of the *Rubáiyát of Omar Khayyám* remains a touchstone of fine book publishing. Vedder reorganized the discontinuous text to suit his interpretation, drew more than fifty spiritually charged illustrations, and designed all physical aspects of the book, including the cover. Eight years after Vedder's birth in New York, the boy moved with his parents to Cuba. Subsequently, he attended boarding schools in New York and frequently summered at his grandparents' farm in upstate Schenectady. Briefly an apprentice in a New York architectural office, Vedder afterward worked in Sherburne, New York, with Tompkins Harrison Matteson (1813–84), a painter and illustrator known for *genre and historical scenes. In March 1856 Vedder departed to study in Paris. The following summer, after touring Italy, he settled in Florence, where he met anti-academic young Italian painters known as Macchiaioli (from their use of *macchie*, spots or patches of color). Inspired by their plein air approach to landscape, he explored the Italian peninsula, producing picturesque village scenes and romantic country views that suggest *Barbizon precedents. During the same period, he came to share with James Jackson *Jarves an enthusiasm for early Renaissance painting. Vedder left for Cuba in 1860 and the following year settled in New York. There he became acquainted with writers who reinforced his literary bent and his attraction to a bohemian lifestyle—probably laced with drugs. Anticipating European symbolism and even surrealism, during the next four years he created his most visionary works. The enigmatic *Questioner of the Sphinx* (Museum of Fine Arts, Boston, 1863) shows an African man crouching before the mouth of the largely buried Egyptian monument, as if to hear it speak.

Following a sojourn in Boston, at the end of 1865 Vedder returned to Europe, where he subsequently resided, although he made frequent and sometimes extended visits to the United States until around 1900. After about a year in Paris, Vedder moved to Rome, which remained his home base. The presence of antique and Renaissance examples in Italy, particularly the works of Botticelli and Michelangelo, provided continuing inspiration. His development benefited also from contact with English artists during his visits to London in 1870 and 1876, and during their excursions to Italy. The idiosyncratic style evident in his later work owed a substantial debt to *Pre-Raphaelitism and the classicizing ornamentalism of such painters as Edward Burne-Jones and Lawrence Alma-Tadema, as well as to William Blake's book illustrations, William Morris's designs, and emergent art nouveau. As seen in the *Rubáiyát* illustrations, as well as easel paintings, murals, and other interior embellishments, this distinctive approach emphasized classical idealization, compressed space, limited color, and most notably, heavy, swirling line. Generally he chose allegorical subjects, as in his Library of Congress murals (1895) and *Minerva* mosaic (1897), which rank among his significant public commissions. After 1900 he was less active artistically. He summered regularly on Capri and devoted more time to writing. His reminiscences, *Digressions of V.*, appeared in 1910. He later published two collections of poetry, *Miscellaneous Moods in Verse* (1914) and *Doubt and Other Things* (1923). He died in Rome.

Vicente, Esteban (1903–2001). Painter, collage artist, printmaker, and sculptor. A participant in the first wave of *abstract expressionism, he remained dedicated to abstract painting for half a century and outlived all important colleagues in the movement. Over the years, the vigorous gesturalism of his early mature abstraction gave way to more lyrical chromaticism related to *color field painting. Born in Turégano, near Segovia, he grew up in Madrid and trained there for three years at the Royal Academy of Fine Art of San Fernando. Initially drawn to sculpture, by 1928 he had turned to painting, but his artistic personality emerged slowly. While painting from nature, often recapitulating aspects of postimpressionism, from 1929 he divided his time mostly between Paris and Barcelona, but also spent a year on the island of Ibiza. In 1936 he moved to New York, becoming a U.S. citizen in 1940. He worked first as a portrait painter. Not until the 1940s did he begin a serious engagement with modern tendencies, but by the end of the decade he had achieved an abstract style related to the work of such friends as Willem *de Kooning and Hans *Hofmann. Never an innovator, he nevertheless numbered among the earliest and most consistent abstract expressionists, synthesizing avant-garde notions of form, color, and composition with skill and eloquence. Continuing to evolve incrementally, his career displayed no major stylistic shifts, yet his approach never became formulaic. He achieved some of his most convincing results in luminous arrangements of flat shapes elegantly balanced on the surface of the canvas. From the 1960s on, some incorporate collage elements. During the same years, he also made a limited number of small, often whimsical, abstract sculptures assembled from disparate, usually painted elements. Vicente taught at several leading art schools, including *Black Mountain College and Yale University. He helped to found the New York Studio School in 1964 and taught there for thirty-five years. He continued working productively nearly until the end of his life. For a number of years he divided his time between New York and an eastern Long Island home in Bridgehampton, where he died. Opened in 1998, the Esteban Vicente Museum of Contemporary Art in Segovia highlights his career within a context of Spanish modernism.

Video art. Term referring to art employing videotape as its medium. As a flexible technique, it encompasses a considerable range of styles, approaches, and intentions, as well as varied presentation formats. Like *performance art, video art gives its practitioners the opportunity to exploit duration in combination with the spatial concerns that have always been at the heart of visual arts. Just as performance art for the most part has shunned traditional theatrical practices, video art evolved in ways that avoided established conventions of filmmaking. Many artists look to video as one among varied multimedia possibilities that might open up previously unknown forms of perception and expression. In its frequent association with forms of *conceptual art or performance art, video has documented or extended the audience for original works, as in tapes by Vito *Acconci, Bruce *Nauman, Martha *Rosler, and William *Wegman. Artists also make freestanding videos with the express intention of presenting the results on television, either broadcast or cable, or on monitors in a gallery. Some of these engage the creation of new forms of visual imagery, most often in one way or another computer-generated. In recent decades, video art has developed into an elaborate form of *installation art, sometimes in combination with other media. Video art was made possible by the advent of portable home video recorders in 1965, when Nam June *Paik led the way. About a year later, video art benefited from the enthusiastic idealism surrounding the formation of *Experiments in Art and Technology.

Bill Viola (1951–) ranks as the best known among American artists who have specialized in autonomous video installations. He generally uses the new technology to explore traditional humanistic concerns. Born in New York, he graduated in 1973 from Syracuse University, where he worked in a new media program. Viola has traveled widely, studying artistic and spiritual traditions that inform his quest for self-knowledge and for insights into existential meaning. His characteristically meditative installations approach universal human themes with stately movement, resplendent imagery, and intriguing visual effects. Since the early 1980s, he has resided in Long Beach, California. *Reasons for Knocking at an Empty House: Writings, 1973–1994* (1995) brings together a selection of essays, project descriptions, and other written and illustrative material.

Among other important contributors to video art, few have achieved Viola's theatrical effects and his appeal to relatively large audiences, but their work nonetheless demonstrates varied creative responses to the medium. For his distinctive, complex video installations, Gary Hill (1951–) often proceeds from literary texts to create sensuous, fluid visual analogues dwelling on issues of language, communication, perception, and thought processes. Born in Santa Monica, he grew up in the Los Angeles area. Originally interested in sculpture, he moved in the late 1960s to *Woodstock, where he worked briefly at the local *Art Students League outpost, studied painting privately, and participated in a community video project. While continuing through the 1970s to obtain practical experience with the video medium at various upstate New York operations, he developed his own conceptually based form of video art. In 1985 he moved to Seattle, where he continues to reside. New York-based Mary Lucier (1944–) remains best known for a painterly, seven-screen installation, *Ohio in Giverny* (1983), juxtaposing her childhood home in Bucyrus with the lush garden where Monet so often painted. After receiving a BA in English in 1965 from Brandeis University in Waltham, Massachusetts, she pursued art training there and at Boston's School of the Museum of Fine Arts. Initially drawn to performance, sculpture, and photography, in 1973 she turned to video, which she has employed most often to celebrate natural beauty and its interaction with memory and metaphor. Her poetic installations sometimes include objects that expand upon the videos' themes. Dara Birnbaum (1946–) pursues a very different sensibility in her fast-paced videos collaged together from fragments of broadcast television advertisements or shows, often variously altered electronically. Born in New York, where she continues to reside, in 1969 she graduated from Pittsburgh's Carnegie-Mellon University with a degree in architecture. She earned a BFA from the San Francisco Art Institute and received additional training in New York at the New School for Social Research (now New School). After turning to video in 1978, she soon became an early practitioner of *postmodern appropriation, which she often approaches from a feminist perspective. Her videos particularly investigate relationships among technology, culture, and media.

View. *See* FORD, CHARLES HENRI.

Viola, Bill. *See* VIDEO ART.

Volk, Douglas. *See* MURPHY, ADAH CLIFFORD.

Von Eichman, Bernard James. *See* SOCIETY OF SIX.

Vonnoh, Robert (1858–1933). Painter. Known for portraits, figure studies, and outdoor views, he numbered among the first to introduce to the United States a style strongly indebted to French impressionism. Born in Hartford, Connecticut, as a small child Robert William Vonnoh moved to Roxbury (now part of Boston). He completed four years of training at Boston's Massachusetts Normal Art School (now Massachusetts College of Art) in 1879 and two years later departed to study in Paris. He returned to Boston in 1883 but after four years embarked on a decisive sojourn in France. While residing in the artists' colony of Grèz-sur-Loing, south of Fontainebleau, he came to value immediate sensations and adopted the impressionists' colorful, broken brushwork. His close-up 1888 studies of a poppy field rival the optical intensity, casual organization, and uninhibited brushwork of Monet's Giverny flowerbeds. Yet, in many other works Vonnoh retained the disciplined compositional structure and solid masses of his traditional training. In a characteristic compromise, his large and joyous showpiece *Coquelicots (Poppies), "In Flanders Field"* (Butler Institute of American Art, Youngstown, Ohio, c. 1890) juxtaposes clearly delineated figures with the more loosely rendered meadow they inhabit. Vonnoh returned to Boston in 1891 but soon accepted a teaching position at Philadelphia's *Pennsylvania Academy of the Fine Arts, where he served as an influential teacher until the mid-1890s. (After 1918 he again taught there for several years.) Subsequently he resided primarily in New York but also spent periods elsewhere, particularly in France and in *Old Lyme, Connecticut. He continued during summer escapes to paint landscapes, while during winters he specialized increasingly in portraits. His late landscapes, mostly painted in France, show greater restraint in color and brushwork. From the mid-1920s diminished eyesight curtailed his artistic activity. Vonnoh died in Nice, France.

In 1899 he married sculptor **Bessie Potter Vonnoh** (1872–1955). Known especially for graceful, intimate, small-scale bronzes, she specialized in themes of genteel domesticity centered on women and children. Born in St. Louis and raised in Chicago, Bessie Onahotema Potter began to study in 1886 with Lorado *Taft, even before she entered the School of the Art Institute of Chicago, where he taught. She also assisted with his decorations for the 1893 World's Columbian Exposition. In Paris in 1895, contact with Rodin reinforced the impressionistic approach to modeling she had already developed after seeing the Rodin-inspired bronzes of Italian-born Russian-American Paul Trubetskoy (1866–1938) at the Chicago World's Fair. She journeyed to Europe again in 1897 and after marriage accompanied her husband on his travels. Following his death, her activity as a sculptor tapered off. Remarried in 1948 to urologist Edward Keyes, she was again widowed the following year. After suffering a stroke, she was inactive in the three years before she died in New York. In *Daydreams* (1903), a characteristic bronze, two young ladies in flowing gowns suggesting Greek costume lounge on an Empire-style sofa, easily recognizable to contemporaries as a valuable antique. As they relax and perhaps dream together, one holds on her lap an open book, which presumably has sparked their reverie. Although the moment is static, Vonnoh's modeling provides life and warmth. In its depiction of a cultured lifestyle, her vision partakes of the *American Renaissance. She also produced portraits, occasionally in marble. During the 1920s she worked frequently on a larger scale, producing life-size nude and draped figures that often figure as fountain or garden ornaments.

Von Wicht, John (1888–1970). Painter and printmaker. An abstract artist, in his student years he was attracted to Kandinsky's work, which remained the touchstone of his career for many years. Born in Malente, in the Holstein region of Germany, Hans von Wicht studied in the art schools of Darmstadt and Berlin. While serving in the German army during World War I, he was severely wounded. After traveling through Europe, he came to the United States in 1923 and became a citizen in 1936. Von Wicht exhibited with the *American Abstract Artists, and during the 1920s and 1930s executed a number of murals and other architectural commissions in mosaic or stained glass. In 1939, under the sponsorship of a *federal art project, he completed a mural of tightly drawn, floating geometric shapes for WNYC radio station in New York. Like some of his other 1930s work, this openly emulates the disciplined style of Kandinsky's contemporaneous Bauhaus years. Other paintings are somewhat freer and more painterly, although echoes of Kandinsky's vocabulary reverberate. In the 1950s he adopted a less analytical approach, related to *abstract expressionism. These later paintings feature colorful bursts of brushstrokes soaring on their own. He died at his home in Brooklyn.

Von Wiegand, Charmion (1899?–1983). Painter, collage artist, and art writer. Born in Chicago, she lived during childhood in San Francisco and went to high school in Berlin. Self-taught as an artist, after graduating from Barnard College in New York, she enrolled in the journalism school at Columbia University. She also studied art history there and at New York University. In the mid-1920s, while working as a newspaper reporter, she began to paint, at first mostly landscapes in a somewhat expressionist style. In 1929 she went to Moscow for three years, as correspondent for the Hearst newspapers. After her 1932 marriage in New York to leftist writer Joseph Freeman, a founder of **New Masses* and later, *Partisan Review*, she soon turned to painting and writing about art on a full-time basis. She contributed regularly to his magazines, as well as others, including *Art Front, for which she also served as an editor. After meeting Mondrian in 1941, she wrote the first article explaining the principles of his neoplasticism to an American audience. The Dutch expatriate's art and philosophy convinced her to work abstractly, and through his encouragement she joined the *American Abstract Artists, later serving a term as the organization's president. In the early 1940s von Wiegand worked with Mondrian's restricted vocabulary of horizontal and vertical lines combined with primary colors. Soon she relaxed her means to accommodate a subtly contemplative and mystically tinged sensibility, enriched by her study of Asian—particularly Tibetan Buddhist—art and philosophy. Although her rhythmic, harmonious, and delicate paintings continued generally to rely on simple geometric structures, she sometimes enlivened them with offbeat shapes and consistently enriched their effects with exquisitely chosen color. Executed in yellow with black, white, and shades of gray, the intricate, twinkling *City Lights* (Whitney Museum, 1947) consists mostly of small rectangles, but here and there raylike shapes occur, and at the center top a black line supporting a tiny white circle whimsically suggests a globular street light. In the late 1940s, impressed by Kurt Schwitters's work, she began to make collages. Although these, too, usually depend on underlying grid structures, they often are compositionally less stringent than her paintings. Frequently they include illustrations, decorative materials such as lace, and elements referring to Tibetan or other exotic cultures. During her final two decades, she painted iconic, patterned works that overtly incorporate her spiritual interests in Buddhist traditions and her travel experiences in India and Tibet. She died in New York.

Voulkos, Peter (1924–2002). Sculptor, ceramist, painter, and printmaker. An unequaled force in legitimizing clay as a fine art medium, he created powerful works in the spirit of *abstract expressionism. With his magnetic personality, skillful technique, and uninhibited ethos, he earned nearly mythic stature as he transformed a craft tradition into one of personal expression and abstract form. Besides contemporary American painting and sculpture, the sources of his individualistic work include ceramics by Picasso and Miró, Japanese pottery, and Zen Buddhist thought, as well other philosophies and forms of mystical experience. Fearless in appropriating processes from other media, he drew on an eclectic array of methods, ranging from fine arts to industry. He also worked in cast metal, mostly during the 1960s, and intermittently produced paintings and prints. Born in Bozeman, Montana, he worked in a Portland, Oregon, foundry before he was drafted into military service in 1943. He then studied painting at Montana State University in his hometown, but a ceramics course in his final year changed his life. After graduating in 1951, he headed for Oakland to earn an MFA degree the following year from the California College of Arts and Crafts (now California College of the Arts). Returning to Montana, he worked and taught in Bozeman and Helena. During the summer of 1953 he taught at *Black Mountain College and then visited New York, making the acquaintance of abstract expressionist painters and other avant-garde figures. Their work prompted dissatisfaction with his refined wheel-thrown work, and he began treating clay with freedom and spontaneity, slab-building pieces of great gestural vigor and little practical use. In 1954 he accepted a faculty position at the Los Angeles County Art Institute (now Otis College of Art and Design), where the ceramics department he founded soon became known as the most adventurous clay milieu in the country. While subsequently teaching from 1959 at the University of California at Berkeley, he soon added bronze casting to his repertoire. Initially sharing the rough-hewn look of his clay pieces, the metal sculptures later displayed smooth, elegant shapes often fabricated on a monumental scale and daringly cantilevered together. After the late 1960s he rarely worked in bronze until initiating a new round of experiments in the final years of his life. Following his retirement from the university in 1985, he continued to reside in the East Bay. He died suddenly in Bowling Green, Ohio, after conducting a workshop there.

Vroman, Adam Clark (1856–1916). Photographer and collector. On eight trips to Arizona and New Mexico between 1895 and 1904, he created his best-known works, images of Hopi and Zuni Indians, their villages, and their landscape. He also photographed throughout California, with special attention to Spanish colonial architecture, and in the Midwest. Born in La Salle, Illinois, as a young man Vroman lived in Rockford, where for seventeen years he worked for the railroad. In 1894 he opened a bookstore (still in business) in Pasadena, California. Vroman counted history and archeology among his wide-ranging interests. A fastidious photographer, he nearly always used a view camera to make glass-plate negatives, which he printed on platinum paper. Vroman's carefully crafted compositions provide a wealth of visual information about individual Indians, their lifestyles, ceremonies, and dwellings. He numbered among the most consistently respectful and direct of the photographers drawn to tribal subjects during a period when such material was widely popular. He did not idealize his subjects into mythic icons, nor did he historicize them by excluding traces of the present from his images. Rather, he individualized them as personalities. Some of his photographs even acknowledge the presence of outsiders, including tourists, who were by this time regularly encountered on tribal lands. In 1909 Vroman traveled to Japan and elsewhere in Asia. He took along a small camera, but his photographs from this trip do not match the quality of his earlier work. In any event, his main purpose was to acquire Asian art, extending his discriminating achievements in collecting American Indian art and books about the Southwest. He died in Altadena, not far from Pasadena, while visiting a friend.

VVV. *See* HARE, DAVID.

Vytlacil, Vaclav (1892–1984). Painter and sculptor. As a teacher, he played an important role in transmitting European modernism to younger Americans, especially during the 1930s and 1940s. Born in New York, Vytlacil took classes at the School of the Art Institute of Chicago before entering the *Art Students League in 1913. He taught in Minneapolis between 1916 and his departure in 1921 for Europe. Between 1922 and 1926 he studied in Munich with Hans *Hofmann. His early achievements reflect a range of interests from Cézanne through Picasso and Matisse, whose styles he absorbed while living in Paris. He began teaching at the Art Students League in 1928 but returned the next year to Europe, where he worked in Paris and Italy until 1935. Subsequently he taught at several schools in New York and elsewhere, as well as at *Black Mountain College, until 1946 when he returned to the Art Students League, remaining until retirement in 1978. He died in New York. Although he never entirely repudiated representational elements, by the 1930s his work was generally abstract, and he signed on as a founding member of the *American Abstract Artists. His vigorous paintings of the late 1930s and 1940s combine geometric and *biomorphic forms. The rough-hewn *Construction 2* (Hirshhorn Museum, 1935), a painted wood relief sculpture with metal elements, reveals the expressionist tenor of his sensibility. Its informality, unusual in prewar American abstract art, mediates between the aesthetic of Kurt Schwitters and the junk *assemblages of two or three decades later. With abstract painter and former student Rupert Turnbull (1899–1940s?), he published a technical manual on egg tempera painting in 1935.

W

Warhol Whitney Weegee Weston West Washington Color School Wyeth Wood Whistler

Wagner, Merrill. *See* RYMAN, ROBERT.

Waldo, Samuel Lovett (1783–1861). Painter. A portrait specialist, he also executed occasional landscapes and imaginative subjects. During most of his career, he collaborated on portraits with William Jewett (1792–1874). A native of Windham, Connecticut, Waldo grew up on a farm and as a teenager received his first training in nearby Hartford from self-taught minister-turned-portrait painter Joseph Steward (1753–1822), who also operated a museum of art and natural history. Subsequently, Waldo worked professionally for a few years in Hartford, Litchfield (about twenty-five miles west), and Charleston, South Carolina, before sailing to London in 1806. There he met John Singleton *Copley, worked with Benjamin *West, and studied at the Royal Academy. Upon his return in January 1809, he settled permanently in New York. His self-portrait of a few years later (Metropolitan Museum, c. 1815) demonstrates technical mastery of a fluent, painterly approach and an imaginative capacity to realize vivid characterization charged with romantic fervor. Not long after Waldo established his New York studio, Jewett began work there as an apprentice and then assistant. Born in East Haddam, Connecticut, and like his mentor a farm boy, Jewett had previously painted carriages in a New London coach maker's shop. Although he never equaled Waldo's painterly facility, the two participated in a prolific and lucrative partnership from 1818 until 1854, when Jewett retired to a farm in Bergen Hill, New Jersey. He died in nearby Jersey City. Jewett's independent works are few, although they include some *genre and still life paintings as well as portraits. He and Waldo worked together so seamlessly that it is fruitless to attempt to distinguish individual contributions to their joint commissions. Much of their studio output became somewhat formulaic, characterized by simple half-length poses, highly finished facial modeling, and strong contrasts of light and dark. However, the partners' reputation for individual likenesses rendered with directness, animation, and dignity attracted a large and fashionable clientele.

Walker, John. *See* NATIONAL GALLERY OF ART.

Walker, Kara. *See* AFRICAN-AMERICAN ART.

Walker, William Aiken (1838–1921). Painter. Known particularly for Southern *genre scenes, often portraying African Americans, he also painted landscapes and still lifes. A native of Charleston, South Carolina, he was mostly self-taught as an artist. Wounded in a Civil War battle while serving in the Confederate military, he was subsequently stationed primarily in Charleston and Richmond. During this period he produced maps, drawings for defensive fortifications, and records of destruction. Later, he ranged widely through the rural South, illustrating the daily lives of its mostly black inhabitants, usually sharecropping ex-slaves. However, some urban scenes depict activities in Charleston and other centers, including Baltimore and New Orleans. Following a two-month sojourn in Cuba during the winter of 1869–70, he departed a few months later for his only visit to Europe. Despite their reportorial detail, his paintings generally disregard the problematic issues of Reconstruction and its aftermath, and only rarely do they provide insight into their subjects' psychology or social conditions. To advance his documentary intentions, he often relied on photographs as studies. A pair of lithographed scenes of the cotton trade issued by *Currier & Ives in 1884 solidified his reputation as an interpreter of the South. After 1890 he turned often to pure landscape. He died in Charleston.

Walkowitz, Abraham (1878–1965). Painter, draftsman, and printmaker. Known especially for fluid, evocations of dancers in motion, he also created dynamic responses to urban skyscrapers, as well as abstract works that number among early American examples. Born in Tyumen, in the Siberian Urals, as a youngster he arrived with his family in New York. Trained between 1898 and 1900 at the *National Academy of Design and other schools, he worked in a precise representational style until leaving for Europe in 1906. During a year spent mostly in Paris, he studied briefly at the Académie Julian and encountered modern art at first-hand, but also traveled in Italy. After his return, he painted New York life in vivid scenes that reflect his enthusiasm for the writings of Walt Whitman, as well as his interests in post-impressionism and fauvism. In 1909, he shared quarters with Max *Weber, whom he had met in Paris, and by 1912 he was acquainted with Alfred *Stieglitz. For several years he served as a devoted acolyte at the *291 gallery, where he had four exhibitions. He also exhibited in the *Armory Show and the *Forum Exhibition. Inspired by Kandinsky's example and writings, beginning about 1913 he created works that are among the early examples of nonobjective art. *Creation* (Metropolitan Museum, 1914), a composite of eight pastels, relies on bright colors and flat, predominately *biomorphic shapes. Also during these years, in hundreds of drawings inspired by modern dancer Isadora Duncan, he expanded upon the linear approach to the human body seen in Rodin's drawings. Smitten upon seeing Duncan perform in Paris, Walkowitz continued for years to regard her as an embodiment of spontaneity and liberation. He also did paintings and drawings of New York architecture, ranging from angular compositions reflecting his knowledge of cubism and futurism to linear swirls capturing the city's energy in abstract form. *New York* (Whitney Museum, 1917), a tangle of lines held in a shallow space, prefigures certain works of *abstract expressionism. After 1920 he turned mostly to simplified figural works and still lifes, painted in oils. Reflecting the leftist politics he had long espoused, in the 1930s social concerns appeared among his subjects. Claiming he was engaged in a scientific experiment, in 1944 at the Brooklyn Museum he mounted a show of his own likeness by a more than one hundred other artists. *Time* called him "the world's most prolific portrait sitter." Shortly before, he had stopped painting because of failing eyesight, which had slowed his output for some time. He died at his home in Brooklyn.

Wall, William Guy (1792–c. 1864). Painter. A landscape specialist, he is known chiefly for watercolors of the Hudson River Valley and nearby areas. Combining topographical accuracy with poetic feeling, these anticipate *Hudson River School work. His *Hudson River Portfolio* (1821–25) ranks as the finest early publication featuring American landscape. Born in Dublin, Wall trained as an artist before sailing to New York in 1818. Two years later he set off to explore the Hudson River. The resulting watercolors made his reputation when they appeared in the *Portfolio* as hand-colored aquatint engravings by John *Hill. For several years after 1828, Wall lived in Newport, Rhode Island, and New Haven, Connecticut. From 1835 he resided in Ireland, except for the period between 1856 and about 1860, when he returned to the Hudson River Valley. In these later years, he worked primarily in oil. His final years remain obscure, and nothing is known about the circumstances of his death. Perhaps the most proficient watercolorist working in the United States during the early nineteenth century, Wall employed a technique grounded in British practice. The large (almost three feet wide) *New York from the Heights near Brooklyn* (Metropolitan Museum, 1823) demonstrates his skill in rendering a particular scene with delicacy, tonal unity, and respect for traditional principles of landscape composition. Characteristically, a luminous atmosphere hovers above still waters that reflect nearby objects, creating a vision of exceptional tranquility.

Wallace, Michele. *See* RINGGOLD, FAITH.

Walters, William Thompson (1819–94). Art collector. Also a businessman. His acquisitions, augmented by those of his son **Henry Walters** (1848–1931), provided the original holdings of Baltimore's Walters Art Museum. Born in Liverpool, not far from Harrisburg, Pennsylvania, Walters studied engineering in Philadelphia before settling permanently in Baltimore in 1841. Although he later sold many American works, during the 1850s he counted as an important early patron of American artists, including local residents William Henry *Rinehart and Alfred Jacob *Miller, as well as *Hudson River School painters. In Paris from 1861 to 1865, he turned his attention to living Europeans and to old masters. He also during the same years became an enthusiast for Asian art, and in the following decade numbered among the first Americans to acquire an extensive selection, purchased mostly during later trips to Europe. From 1874 he opened his collection to the public on a limited basis. Born in Baltimore, his son Henry Walters, also a businessman, resided permanently in New York. He acquired art on a grander scale than his father and expanded the collection's scope to include European and Asian fine and decorative art of all periods until the early twentieth century. Opened to the public in 1909, the Renaissance-style building he commissioned was bequeathed along with the entire collection to the city of Baltimore. Known as the Walters Art Gallery and subsequently much enlarged, it assumed its present name in 2000. Its medieval, nineteenth-century, and European decorative art collections, along with a large inventory of manuscripts and rare books, rank among its outstanding features.

Ward, John Quincy Adams (1830–1910). Sculptor. A straightforward realist, he played an important part in redirecting American sculpture away from *neoclassicism. A principal figure in the post–Civil War art establishment, he executed numerous public monuments and privately commissioned portraits as well as a number of ideal subjects, primarily architectural embellishments. Atypically for a nineteenth-century American sculptor, Ward traveled to Europe only after he had matured as an artist and established his reputation. Although he worked directly from nature, his work reveals also a thoughtful understanding of sculptural tradition. Born in Urbana, Ohio, in 1849 Ward entered the studio of Henry Kirke *Brown, where he remained for seven years. After subsequently working on his own for about two years, mostly in Washington, D.C., he settled permanently in New York. By this time, he had already modeled *The Indian Hunter* (1859), which securely established his position as a leading sculptor. In preparation for this work, Ward traveled to Dakota Territory to research Indian life. The pose of his young tribesman with a dog reflects the artist's awareness of antique sculpture, but in anatomy and incidental details he achieved a high degree of observational realism. In 1869 a revised and enlarged bronze version became the first American sculpture to be placed in Central Park. Thereafter, he enjoyed constant demand for portraits and civic monuments. Particularly on the first of two trips to Europe, in 1872 and 1887, contemporary French sculpture impressed Ward. Although he did not adopt the extravagant neo-Baroque effects and surface impressionism of some in the French school, his work veered closer to Beaux-Arts taste, as in many later ensembles combining bronze statuary with stone supports. His supple naturalism satisfied contemporary taste for factualism combined with vigorous expression. Such ensembles as the *James Abram Garfield Monument* (The Mall, Washington, D.C., 1887) and the powerful *Henry Ward Beecher Monument* (Cadman Plaza, Brooklyn, 1891), both on granite bases designed by Paris-trained architect Richard Morris Hunt, number among the era's most impressive civic monuments. By the 1870s Ward had become a mainstay of the New York art world and a habitué of distinguished social circles. At his country house in the Catskills, where he enjoyed outdoor pursuits, he also frequently entertained influential friends. In the 1890s gradually declining health began to limit his output, although not the quality of his work, and he finally became inactive about a year and a half before his death.

His brother, painter **Edgar Melville Ward** (1839–1915), remains best known for *genre subjects. *The Coppersmith* (Metropolitan Museum, 1898) numbers among a distinctive series portraying artisans or other workingmen. He painted landscapes, as well. Also born in Urbana, Ohio, he graduated from Miami University in Oxford, Ohio, before beginning his artistic training at the *National Academy of Design in 1865. In 1872 he departed for additional study in Paris, where he remained for several years before returning permanently to New York. By the time of his retirement in 1909, he had taught at the National Academy for more than twenty-five years.

Ward, Nina de Creeft. *See* DE CREEFT, JOSE.

Warhol, Andy (1928–87). Painter, printmaker, sculptor, and filmmaker. The central figure in *pop art, he combined the forms of consumer culture, the technologies of mass production, and a taste for notoriety into a freewheeling career in several media. Pursuing fame while remaining an enigma, he played a major role in creating the contemporary overlap of high art, fashion, commercialism, and celebrity. He discerned within the superficial products of contemporary American civilization the materials for optically and philosophically provocative art. His work helped to blur traditional distinctions among visual arts media, narrow the divide between fine and commercial art, and erase controversy over the use of photography as a creative tool. In sum, as Robert *Rauschenberg wrote after Warhol's death, "he befuddles critical history."

Born Andrew Warhola in Pittsburgh, he began using the shortened form of his name when he moved to New York. He studied art at the Carnegie Institute of Technology (now Carnegie Mellon University), where Balcomb *Greene numbered among his teachers. Following graduation in 1949, he moved to New York with classmate Philip *Pearlstein. There as a commercial illustrator and department store window designer for some thirteen years, he honed his considerable skills as a draftsman, worked with the best professionals in the field, won important awards, and received generous financial compensation from prestigious clients. At the same time, with his eye on success in the fine arts, he continued to draw, make collages, and paint, sometimes incorporating commercial techniques into his processes. He mounted his first solo gallery show in New York in 1952. Titled "Fifteen Drawings Based on the Writings of Truman Capote," it forecast his contribution to gay culture. Intrigued by the early work of Rauschenberg, Jasper *Johns, and others moving away from the prevailing *abstract expressionism, in 1960 he began adapting comic book and advertising images as subjects for painting. At first he used painterly brushwork but quickly moved toward more mechanical execution. In mid-1962 he virtually abandoned painting by hand, instead adapting the commercial silkscreen process to his fine art production. Subsequently, aided by assistants, he typically combined painted canvas and printed photographic images. Emphasizing the impersonal nature of his art, he called his studio the Factory.

Warhol entered the limelight with landmark 1962 exhibitions in Los Angeles and New York. These featured silkscreen paintings based on such subjects as Campbell's soup cans, Coca-Cola bottles, and publicity photographs of celebrities including Elvis Presley, all remarking on consumerism. Using the same technique to somewhat different effect, sobering meditations on violence also originated in 1962. Recycling disturbing news photographs, he presented car crashes, race riots, suicides, electric chairs, and other unsettling images, as well as a memorable Jackie group, depicting the widowed Jacqueline Kennedy shortly after the president's assassination in 1963. In his Marilyn Monroe series, begun shortly after her suicide in 1962, associations with mortality undermine the beauty of her smiling face. Repetition of identical images across many canvases reinforces their connection to the mindless yet insistent claims of advertising on modern consciousness. In 1964 ersatz cartons of Brillo and other grocery store items extended his method into three dimensions. These screen-printed wood boxes virtually reproduced, rather than pictured, commonplace contemporary products. In 1963 the enormously prolific artist initiated an involvement with filmmaking that dominated his time for several years. Like his visual art, the films explore technical and conceptual fundamentals of the medium. The eight-hour *Empire* (1964), a continuous, stationary shot of the Empire State Building, explores boredom as an aesthetic device and emphasizes medium over subject. In 1968 he almost died from wounds inflicted by a disgruntled would-be actress, Valerie Solanas, who shot him several times in the abdomen.

Upon recovery, in 1969 he inaugurated *Interview* magazine, which fed on celebrity culture, as did several subsequent videotaped shows distributed on cable television. Begun in 1972, his portraits of Mao Zhedong, subverting the communist strongman with the trappings of capitalist glamour, reinvigorated his painting career. Subsequently in great demand among moneyed and famous clients, he concentrated for the rest of the decade on commissioned portraiture. Working from Polaroid snapshots, he treated his subjects in the style of his 1960s images based on film stills of movie stars. A preoccupation throughout his career, his self-portraits endlessly toyed with variants of a mask concealing his inner life but becoming more haunting with the passage of time. In his widely quoted prediction that "in the future everybody will be world-famous for fifteen minutes," he offered his slant on the media saturation he often addressed, noting its destabilizing effects on personal identity. In the 1980s he interacted and occasionally collaborated with several younger artists, most notably Jean-Michel *Basquiat. At the same time, his screen-printed works gained complexity, with virtuoso brushwork sometimes elaborating images underneath. Among his final works, many address old master precedents, particularly religious subjects. A group based on the imagery of Leonardo's *Last Supper* number among the strongest, perhaps in response to unspecified inner convictions related to his Catholic faith and his regular participation in serving dinners to the needy at a Manhattan church. Warhol died in New York from unexpected complications of routine gall-bladder surgery. His published writings include *Andy Warhol's Index* (1967), *A: A Novel* (1968), *The Philosophy of Andy Warhol (From A to B and Back Again)* (1975), *Andy Warhol's Exposures* (1979; with Bob Colacello), *POPism: The Warhol '60s* (1980; with Pat Hackett), and *America* (1985). Edited by Pat Hackett, *The Andy Warhol Diaries* (1989) appeared posthumously, as did *I'll Be Your Mirror: The Selected Andy Warhol Interviews, 1962–1987* (2004), edited by Kenneth Goldsmith. As Warhol directed, the artist's multimillion-dollar estate funded the Andy Warhol Foundation for the Visual Arts, which in 1994 opened the Andy Warhol Museum in Pittsburgh to house the single largest collection of his work, present related exhibitions, and maintain research archives. The foundation also makes grants in support of innovative programming at cultural institutions. As well, it underwrote the Warhol Family Museum of Modern Art, founded in 1991 in Medzilaborce, Slovakia, near the home village of the artist's parents.

Warner, Olin Levi (1844–96). Sculptor. A specialist in portrait busts and medallions, he also created ideal subjects. Born in West Suffield, north of Hartford, Connecticut, he spent his early years in upstate Amsterdam, New York, and in Vermont. Aspiring to become a sculptor, he drew in his spare time while working for six years as a telegrapher at several locations in New York and Georgia. In 1869 he departed for Paris, where he studied at the École des Beaux-Arts and worked briefly as an assistant to Jean-Baptiste Carpeaux. Among the first sculptors from the United States to train in Paris, he helped to redirect American taste away from the dominant *neoclassicism of mid-century toward the livelier, more spontaneous, and more natural Beaux-Arts approach that supplanted it. Upon his return in 1872 he settled permanently in New York. An early member of the progressive *Society of American Artists, he had begun by about 1880 to win attention for sensitive portraiture, followed by recognition for several imaginative works. He also received commissions for public monuments and architectural embellishments. At the time of his death following a bicycling accident, he had embarked on the most significant commission of his career: two pairs of bronze doors for the new Library of Congress. The bronze portrait bust of his colleague *J. Alden *Weir* (Metropolitan Museum, 1897–98; modeled 1880) characterizes Warner's French-derived style, an idealizing combination of subtle modeling, lively expression, technical expertise, and individuality. Similarly indebted to contemporary French practice, Warner's seated bronze *Diana* (Metropolitan Museum, 1897–98; modeled c. 1885–87) ranks among the first American nudes to present the beauty of the unclothed body for its own sake. Despite the classical allusion, only the arrow she absently holds on the ground identifies the literary theme. Warner set up a temporary studio in Portland, Oregon, in the fall of 1889, after receiving a commission for the Skidmore Fountain there and for several portraits. He returned to the Columbia River area in 1891 to complete a distinctive set of eight profile medallions of Northwest American Indian leaders. For the World's Columbian Exposition of 1893 he served as a juror, created a number of architectural sculptures, and designed the fair's commemorative half-dollar.

Washington Color School. A loosely associated group of Washington, D.C., artists who initiated important developments in chromatic abstraction, particularly during the late 1950s and 1960s. They moved away from *abstract expressionism's' gestural and subjective approaches to concentrate on color's optical properties and its role in organizing pictorial experience. Their large works, generally executed in acrylic paint on raw canvas, contributed to the *color field and *hard-edge tendencies in 1960s painting and deeply affected subsequent artistic developments in the capital. The high regard among Washington painters for chromatic subtlety and fine craftsmanship owes a debt to the nature of the modern art collection Duncan *Phillips showed in his public gallery there. A 1965 exhibition "The Washington Color Painters," mounted at the Washington Gallery of Modern Art, crystallized the group's identity.

Morris *Louis and Kenneth *Noland rank as principal figures. The best-known of other participants in the defining 1965 show, painter and printmaker Gene Davis (1920–85) specialized in broadly horizontal compositions of vertical stripes. Born in Washington, Gene Bernard Davis studied for a year at the University of Maryland before transferring in 1939 to Wilson Teachers College (now part of the University of the District of Columbia). After leaving in 1941, he was employed as a journalist and writer until 1968. Following a stint in Jacksonville, Florida, he worked in New York until 1945, when he returned to Washington. Self-taught in art except for a high school drawing class, he took up painting seriously around 1950. For several years he experimented with varied approaches, indebted particularly to abstract expressionism and to the work of Paul Klee before he noted the early work of Jasper *Johns and Frank *Stella. Around 1958 he began to work out his standard formula, limited to hard-edge, unmodulated, contiguous bands of a single width within each painting. He believed that this elementary method of dividing the canvas allowed the viewer to disregard structure in order to concentrate on color and interval. Often as much as twenty feet wide, his paintings reverberate with intuitively arranged, rippling chromatic rhythms. He died in Washington.

Thomas Downing (1928–85) painted geometric forms, usually circles, distributed across each canvas in regular, two-dimensional patterns. Born in Suffolk, Virginia, he graduated in 1948 from Randolph-Macon College in Ashland. For the next two years he studied at Pratt Institute in Brooklyn. From late 1950 until the summer of 1951, he traveled in Europe and worked in Paris. Following military service, in 1953 he settled in Washington, where he briefly studied with Noland. Around 1960 he adopted the circle as his principal motif. Unlike Noland, who strove at that time to negate suggestions of depth, Downing encouraged a flickering spatial dimension. Probably reflecting familiarity with Josef *Albers's chromatic experiments, his circles of varied size and hue force the illusion that the disks float at slightly different depths. In some cases, his optical trickery suggests the diversions of *op art. Downing moved to New York in 1971, lived briefly in Houston in 1975, and then settled permanently on Cape Cod, in *Provincetown.

A lifelong Washingtonian, Howard Mehring (1931–78) shared Downing's studio in the late 1950s. At that time, he painted unconventional monochrome works, but around 1960 he initiated his characteristic approach featuring colorful, geometric arrangements of large, classically disposed shapes. Most of his paintings belong to one of several distinct series, some based on the formal characteristics of individual letters of the alphabet. Paint is customarily flatly applied, but he sometimes used a spatter technique for variety. He graduated in 1953 from Wilson Teachers College and studied with Noland at Catholic University, where he received his MFA in 1955. From the early 1960s, he traveled often to Europe, particularly to Venice, where he found inspiration in the rich color harmonies of Renaissance paintings. In the late 1960s, while engaged on a series featuring colored bands in the shape of the letter Z, he inexplicably stopped painting, although he continued to draw. He died while on an excursion to Annapolis, Maryland.

Although he did not appear in the "Color Painters" exhibition and his color-based art departed from theirs in important ways, Leon Berkowitz (1911–87) nevertheless ranks as a central player in the Washington color milieu. Born in Philadelphia, he earned a BFA degree at the University of Pennsylvania in 1942, served in the military from 1943 to 1945, and received an MA from George Washington University in 1948. A teacher throughout most of his career, from 1969 until his death he served on the faculty of the Corcoran School of Art (now Corcoran College of Art and Design). With his poet-wife Ida Fox, in 1945 he founded and subsequently directed the interdisciplinary Washington Workshop Center for the Arts, an important nexus of personal acquaintance among Color School participants. After the center closed in 1956, he traveled widely in Europe for several years. As a painter, Berkowitz began as a landscape artist who paid particular attention to skies. In the mature work that emerged in the 1970s, he glazed numerous layers of oil paint to produce luminous presences devoid of variation other than slight color modulations. His best paintings achieve a mystical radiance quite at odds with the more objective work of core Color School painters.

The Washington Color School context provided aesthetic grounding for other local artists who developed their individual styles in the 1960s. Notable among them, painter Sam Gilliam (1933–), born in Tupelo, Mississippi, graduated from the University of Louisville in 1955 and received his master's degree there in 1961. By that time he was already teaching in Washington's public school system. In the mid-1960s he made his mark with large stained abstractions, at first mounted on stretchers but from 1968 left to hang loose in sculptural folds. Later, such drape paintings grew to huge dimensions, sometimes as site-specific *installations. He has also made use of adjunct materials to create mixed-media three-dimensional objects as well as collages and *assemblages. Remaining a Washington resident, he continues to produce richly colored abstractions of widely varying media and scale.

A Washington resident most of her life, late-bloomer Alma Thomas (1891–1978) evolved an individual style only after retiring from her career as a public school art teacher. Alma Woodsey Thomas, born in Columbus, Georgia, moved with her family in 1907 into the Washington house where she lived for the rest of her life. She studied at Miner Normal School (now part of the University of the District of Columbia) and taught for six years in Wilmington, Delaware, before enrolling at Howard University. After graduating in 1924, she taught art in a Washington junior high school until her retirement in 1960. In the mid-1930s she completed a master's degree in art education from Columbia University. For some twenty-five years, she painted in a representational style indebted to Cézanne and Matisse, participated actively in the local art community, and found encouragement from friends such as Lois Mailou *Jones. In 1950 she began taking painting classes at American University, where Jacob *Kainen numbered among her instructors. There she began to explore color and pattern as independent compositional elements. After becoming personally acquainted with major Washington Color School artists, in her mid-seventies she developed a personal abstract style, featuring joyous, striped arrangements of mosaic-like brush marks. Inspired by nature as well as art, Thomas sometimes placed the dominant vertical bands of color on top of varied "background" hues to give the effect of looking through a screen of flowers or vegetation into a garden. Later works often feature patterns that depart from stripes to incorporate other *all-over effects. By the early 1970s, she had established a national reputation, solidified in 1972 by one-person shows of her work at the *Corcoran Gallery of Art and the *Whitney Museum of American Art.

Anne Truitt (1921–2004) carried Washington Color School sensibilities into three dimensions. Her impeccably crafted, smoothly painted geometric volumes merge painting and sculpture. Although *minimalist in form, they are more personal, more psychologically charged, and more concerned with optical response than most products of that movement. Born in Baltimore, Anne Dean grew up in Easton, on Maryland's rural eastern shore. A psychology major at Bryn Mawr College in suburban

Philadelphia, she graduated in 1943. Four years later she married James Truitt, a journalist, whose professional responsibilities demanded frequent moves to locations in the United States and abroad. (They separated in 1969 and divorced two years later.) She began working seriously as an artist toward the end of the 1940s. In 1948 she enrolled at Washington's Institute of Contemporary Art and soon befriended Noland. In 1950 she studied at Dallas's art museum school and for the rest of the decade experimented with varied media in expressionistic forms. While again residing in Washington between 1960 and 1964, stimulated in part by the work of Ad *Reinhardt and Barnett *Newman, in 1961 she began to create the classically calm works of her mature style. Most are wood, built by cabinetmakers. Truitt returned permanently to Washington in the late 1960s, and from 1975 she taught for more than twenty years at the nearby University of Maryland. With time, she specialized in squared columns of some five to eight feet in height. These are usually lightened visually by quarter-inch "pedestals" that lift the pieces just off the floor. Many are painted in monochrome hues, but others display inventive juxtapositions of color and shape. She also produced paintings that share the formal and expressive concerns of her sculptures. Truitt published three autobiographical memoirs, *Daybook* (1982), *Turn* (1986), and *Prospect* (1996), each subtitled *The Journal of an Artist*.

Watercolor movement, American. Designation for a surge of interest in watercolors among serious artists and collectors during a period from the mid-1860s through the mid-1880s. Previously, watercolor had been widely considered a minor medium, suitable for sketches, amateur work, and documentary purposes, such as scientific illustrations, topographical records, and architectural renderings. Anticipated by increasingly frequent harbingers in the previous two decades or so, around 1860 attitudes toward watercolor shifted for several reasons. The popular writings of English aesthetician John Ruskin promoted the medium and drew attention to J. M. W. Turner's brilliant achievements. After the Civil War, American artists traveled abroad in greater numbers than previously, encountering Continental and English watercolor practice. More important, many absorbed a new, anti-academic aesthetic that promoted qualities well served by watercolor, including greater intimacy, technical freedom, fleeting perceptions, and personal expression. In addition, many approved of watercolor's presumably democratic character. Because it was already well established as a polite accomplishment, watercolor painting was often regarded as an unspecialized activity open to all. Moreover, the expansion of taste for watercolors opened new markets, appealing to middle-class audiences with a less expensive product. In 1866 Samuel *Colman, the organization's first president, along with three others founded the American Society of Painters in Water-Colors (renamed in 1877 the American Watercolor Society and still in existence). The most prominent of many organizations devoted to watercolor nationwide, it sponsored an energetic exhibition program that validated watercolors as finished works of art. William Trost *Richards and Thomas *Moran numbered among artists who enthusiastically and expertly embraced the medium. After the mid-1880s, interest in watercolor as such diminished somewhat. Yet, the movement left an important legacy of taste among artists and collectors alike. Winslow *Homer and John Singer *Sargent, for instance, produced great numbers of technically and conceptually distinguished examples.

Watkins, Carleton (1829–1916). Photographer. The first significant photographer to record the American West, he produced commensurately large and stately views of its scenic grandeur. Characteristically organizing form into simple masses that shape intervening voids, he heightened straightforward factuality with nature's mysterious drama. Watkins's revelatory photographs of the Yosemite Valley spurred Congress, in the first such federal act, to preserve this scenic wilderness as a public trust in 1864. (The area became a National Park in 1890.) Although much of his later work pictures the evidence of human impact on the landscape, in the early 1860s Watkins deliberately stressed the untouched purity of wilderness. Besides such landscapes, other subjects included San Francisco streetscapes, estates of wealthy friends and patrons, California missions, and close-up studies of fruit and other regional produce. Born in Oneonta, New York, Carleton Emmons Watkins arrived in California in the early 1850s. After settling in 1853 in San Francisco, he learned the *daguerreotype process but around 1857 switched to the new wet-plate technology. In 1858 he opened his own studio and began to photograph the landscape, as he developed the technical mastery that soon distinguished his prints. Three years later he made the first of many forays into Yosemite, lugging a camera custom-made to hold plates measuring 18 × 22 inches. The grandiose scale and intimate detail of his resulting prints made his reputation. Subsequently he worked frequently for commercial clients, including railroad, mining, and timber interests. On assignment and in search of new inventory, he traveled throughout the western United States. An 1867 voyage up the Willamette and Columbia Rivers produced a particularly impressive series. Hired by the Oregon Steam Navigation Company, he recorded its transport operations while also capturing majestic panoramas and intimate glimpses of the stunning river scenery. At the height of his career, from the mid-1860s through the early 1870s, he enjoyed international acclaim, financial security, and the friendship of San Francisco's social and artistic elites. Economic setbacks, family problems, and deteriorating health, including failing eyesight, plagued his later years. Already in near poverty by the mid-1890s, he lost his studio, his inventory, and his negatives in the 1906 San Francisco earthquake and fire. Disheartened and almost completely blind, he withdrew to Yolo County in the Sacramento Valley. Declared legally incompetent in 1909, in 1910 he was committed permanently to the Napa State Hospital for the Insane.

Watkins, Franklin C. (1894–1972). Painter. Known for imaginative subjects and for portraits, Watkins remained an individualist whose work resists easy classification. Although born in New York, Franklin Chenault Watkins lived in Kentucky and North Carolina during his early years and spent most of his adult life in Philadelphia. After two years at the Groton (Massachusetts) School, he studied at the University of Virginia in Charlottesville during the 1910–11 academic year and at the University of Pennsylvania the following year. At that time, he took his first classes at the *Pennsylvania Academy of the Fine Arts, where he subsequently studied full time and later taught. During World War I he served in the U.S. Navy. In the 1920s he developed an emotional, expressionistic style of distorted forms and vigorous brushwork. *Suicide in Costume* (Philadelphia Museum, 1931) earned his first critical acclaim. In a rough, sketchy technique, it presents a reveler who has toppled backward onto a table, smoking gun in hand. With time, employing a more subdued approach, he became known as one of the finest portraitists of the day. At their best, his likenesses recall the insight and dignity of Thomas *Eakins's work. In later decades he also painted still lifes and occasional religious subjects. He died in Bologna, during a visit to Italy.

Watson-Schütze, Eva. *See* PHOTO-SECESSION.

Watts, Robert. *See* FLUXUS.

Waugh, Frederick Judd (1861–1940). Painter. Remembered almost exclusively for magisterial marine paintings from the later part of his career, he also painted *genre scenes, landscapes, and portraits. Waugh first drew widespread acclaim for *The Roaring Forties* (Metropolitan Museum, 1908), a large canvas devoted exclusively to the turbulent sea. (The title refers to stormy latitudes of the North and South Atlantic.) The awesome force of nature continued as the major theme of his numerous coastal views. Depicted with close attention to effects of light, convincingly rendered waves typically surge and froth along desolate and often craggy shores. Born in the Delaware River town of Bordentown, New Jersey, Waugh grew up in Philadelphia and studied there from 1880 until 1883 at the *Pennsylvania Academy of the Fine Arts with Thomas *Eakins and Thomas *Anshutz. In 1882 he spent a summer in Europe. The following year he moved to Paris to continue his training at the Académie Julian, where Adolphe-William Bouguereau numbered among his teachers. During summers he painted in Grez-sur-Loing, near Fontainebleau, and in Brittany. His plein air scenes from this time suggest the influence of Jules Bastien-Lepage in their firmly drawn figures, often peasants, set against atmospheric landscapes. In 1885 he returned to Philadelphia to concentrate on portraits and commercial illustrations. Seven years later he again left for Europe, on a sojourn that lasted fifteen years. He lived in Paris at first, then in the Channel Islands from 1893 until 1895. Subsequently he resided in England, primarily in the London area, but also kept a studio in Cornwall, at the artists' colony of St. Ives. During this period he began specializing in seascapes but also continued working as an illustrator until his return to the United States in 1907. He lived in Montclair, New Jersey, until 1915, when he relocated to Kent, Connecticut. He usually summered near the sea in New England and occasionally traveled to other locations to observe the ocean. His illustrated children's fantasy *The Clan of Munes* (1916) reflects the artist's appreciation for Monhegan Island, Maine, a frequent summer destination. In 1927 he moved permanently to *Provincetown, at the tip of Cape Cod.

Several members of Waugh's family also were painters. His father, **Samuel Bell Waugh** (1814–85), a leading Philadelphia portraitist, also painted landscapes and other subjects. Born in the western Pennsylvania town of Mercer, he studied in Philadelphia before traveling in Europe for eight years, perusing the old masters on his own. He died in Janesville, Wisconsin. Frederick Waugh's mother, **Mary Eliza Young Waugh**, painted miniatures. A half sister, **Ida Waugh** (?–1919), painted portraits, religious or allegorical subjects, and genre scenes, often featuring Dutch subjects.

Known for her depictions of children, she also worked as an illustrator, particularly of children's books. She was born in Philadelphia and studied at the Pennsylvania Academy before going to Paris for additional training at the Académie Julian. Frederick Waugh's son, **Coulton Waugh** (1896–1973), born in England, became best known as a comic strip artist, although he worked also as a painter. He lived in Provincetown for many years. His history, *The Comics* (1947), numbered among the first serious works on the subject.

Wayne, June. *See* TAMARIND LITHOGRAPHY WORKSHOP.

Webb, Electra Havemeyer. *See* HAVEMEYER, LOUISINE.

Webb, Todd (1905–2000). Photographer. Known especially for scenes of postwar New York, he combined a documentary interest in the life of his times with dignified artistry in composing images. Born in Detroit, Charles Clayton Webb grew up there and in Ontario, Canada. As a young man he worked in Detroit and California before leaving on a trip to Panama, where he turned his attention to photography. After he returned to Detroit, he found encouragement from Harry *Callahan and Arthur *Siegel, but was also influenced by Ansel *Adams, Walker *Evans, and Helen *Levitt. After service as a navy photographer during World War II, he moved to New York. There he used a large view camera, which allowed him to construct stately compositions with delicate tonal range. He particularly photographed the architecture and commercial culture of the city, appreciating their relationship to the emotional lives of ordinary people. In the mid-1950s he photographed along the Santa Fe and Oregon trails. For other projects, he recorded the streets of Paris and created a notable twenty-five-year series devoted to his friend Georgia *O'Keeffe and the New Mexico landscape she painted. At various times he lived in Santa Fe, in the south of France, and in Bath, England, before settling permanently in Maine. He died in a hospital in Lewiston, not far from his final home in Auburn.

Weber, Max (1881–1961). Painter, printmaker, and sculptor. Also a poet. While assimilating European modern styles more eagerly than any other American, especially in the decade before 1917, he achieved in his finest works original interpretations of these approaches. His writings of this time demonstrate a well-informed grasp of modern theories of art and expression. During the 1920s and 1930s, his work shifted toward figurative expressionism. His Jewish faith and its heritage became increasingly important thematically from the 1920s. Born in Bialystok, Russia (now Poland), he moved with his family to Brooklyn when he was ten. He graduated from Pratt Institute in 1900, but then worked for another year with his Pratt mentor Arthur Wesley *Dow. After teaching in Virginia and Minnesota, Weber left for Paris in 1905. During his first two years there, he studied at the Académie Julian and elsewhere, but his artistic development soon responded to the experimental modernism of artists with whom he became acquainted. He shared his generation's widespread adulation of Cézanne, studied under Matisse, and knew Picasso, Georges Braque, Gertrude *Stein, and the elderly self-taught original, Henri Rousseau, whom he greatly admired. Weber also traveled in Europe and became familiar with African art on view in Paris. In 1909 he returned to New York and soon made contact with Alfred *Stieglitz, who mounted his only solo show at *291 in 1911. He also found support at the Newark (New Jersey) Museum, where his 1913 show ranks as the first American museum show devoted to a modern artist.

After Weber returned from Europe, he tried his hand at several styles drawn from European models, often with sophisticated results. He also embarked on the study of American Indian and pre-Columbian art, championing the virtues of "primitive" expression in an article as early as 1910. For several years, he often worked in a bright fauve idiom, sometimes including figures that already suggest his interest in tribal art. *Fleeing Mother and Child* (New Jersey State Museum, Trenton, 1913) offers a powerfully reduced image of a blocky, stylized woman carrying her child. Behind them are a starkly barren blue tree and three birds. The entire remaining surface is painted bright red, recalling Matisse's audacious *Red Studio* (Museum of Modern Art, 1911). In the same period, some of his work took on cubist characteristics. As early as 1911, *Figure Study* (Albright-Knox Art Gallery, Buffalo, New York) directly adapts Picasso's early cubism to the depiction of a nude woman. Around 1912 he produced virtually abstract pastel studies of organic forms. Between 1912 and 1916 he addressed the theme of the modern city with a series of paintings related to New York. *Chinese Restaurant* (Whitney Museum, 1915) adapts the spread-out forms of synthetic cubism, along with futurist force lines, to evoke a particular establishment. During the following two years he painted semi-abstracted, often paired figures in odd amalgams, as in *Two Musicians* (Museum of Modern Art, 1917), which combines a decorative cubism with stylization drawn from African art. Weber was particularly active as a sculptor during the few years after 1910, although he returned to it from time to time throughout his career. He numbered among the first Americans to produce abstract sculpture, as in the bronze *Spiral Rhythm* (Hirshhorn Museum, 1915), an accomplished cubist invention. As early as 1910, Weber also made relief prints. The most original of these are tiny, crudely carved woodblocks, which he sometimes printed in multiple colors from a single block, as in *Mother and Child* (c. 1919). Mostly between 1928 and 1933 he also made lithographs, often based on prior paintings.

In 1921 Weber left Manhattan for suburban Long Island where his work continued the evolution begun a few years previously toward a more directly representational character than had earlier been common. Figural works, landscapes, and still lifes appeared. His 1930 retrospective at the *Museum of Modern Art ranks as the first at that institution to honor an American contemporary. During the Depression years, Weber's art often demonstrated empathy for the plight of the unfortunate. In somber tones, *At the Mill* (Newark Museum, 1939) depicts impoverished workers outside a factory. While actively participating in the *American Artists' Congress, Weber argued in an important speech before the group for reciprocity between modern art and social transformation. Beginning around 1940 he forged a consistent personal style featuring fluttering line within colorful compositions, often fanciful in mood. These emotionally charged, often lyrical figural works from the remainder of his career most often picture Jewish themes, but music provided another particular interest, as in *Flute Soloist* (University of Iowa Museum, Iowa City, 1955). He died at his home on Long Island, in Great Neck, where he had resided for some years. Weber's publications include *Cubist Poems* (1914) and *Primitives* (1926), a poetry collection illustrated with his own prints, as well as *Essays on Art* (1916), and an autobiographical work titled *Max Weber* (1945).

Weber, Paul. *See* HASELTINE, WILLIAM STANLEY.

Weegee (1899–1968). Photographer. As a brash press photographer in New York, he took sensational pictures of crime scenes, accidents, fires, and other disasters, mostly during the decade after 1935. He also captured startling, sometimes surrealistic, and often satirical moments in the flow of urban experience. Contrasting high and low culture, a celebrated image, "The Critic" (1943), shows two heavily jeweled, middle-aged women arriving for opening night at the Metropolitan Opera House, apparently oblivious to the presence of a disheveled, destitute woman who throws them a caustic glare. Despite artistic aspirations, Weegee cared little for the rules of composition or for fine printing. Using glossy paper, he accentuated the bold contrasts of light and dark that naturally occurred in his typical flash-lit night scenes. Odd perspectives, unconventional angles, and figures cut by the frame only intensified the violence, mayhem, and boorishness of his subjects. Despite the immediacy and seeming casualness of his views, he nevertheless intensified their impact through strong, well-organized tonal patterns. Born Usher Fellig in Zloczew, Austria (later Poland; now Zolochev, east of Lviv, Ukraine), he became Arthur Fellig in 1910, upon arriving at Ellis Island with his family. They settled in New York. Three years later, he left school to work in various jobs, mostly photography-related, including stints in the darkrooms of the *New York Times* and Acme Newspictures (later absorbed by United Press). With time, he also received news assignments, and in 1935 he began to freelance, peddling his work to several newspapers. Soon he took the professional name Weegee, which he often expanded to Weegee the Famous. He liked to claim that the name was derived from the popular Ouija board because he had mystical power in ascertaining where news was happening. In actuality, in order to shadow nocturnal law enforcement personnel, he lived across the street from police headquarters and had a radio scanner in his car. After experimenting with a handheld movie camera for several years, in 1947 he moved to Hollywood, where he entered the filmmaking business and even acted in some minor roles. In 1948 he completed *Weegee's New York*, the first of several short feature films. In California, with the aid of special lenses he also made distorted and sometimes disfiguring portraits and nude studies. Considering these more artistic than his reportorial work, he extended the series after his permanent return to New York in 1952, and by the 1960s they constituted his major interest. His first book of photographs, *Naked City* (1945) became a best seller and inspired a movie of the same name. His other collections include *Weegee's People* (1946), *Naked Hollywood* (1953), *Weegee's Creative Camera* (1959), *Weegee's Creative Photography* (1964), and a posthumous book, *The Village* (1989), based on his dummy for a study of Greenwich Village. His autobiography, *Weegee by Weegee*, appeared in 1961.

Weeks, Edwin Lord (1849–1903). Painter and illustrator. A leading American orientalist, he specialized in detailed scenes of life in exotic locales, particularly India. He traveled extensively, often under adventurous circumstances, and spent most of his adult life abroad. Born in the Boston suburb of Newtonville, he embarked on a life of travel in 1869 when he visited Florida and South America. He worked in Paris for a year or two with academic realists Jean-Léon Gérôme and Léon Bonnat. On their example, he also traveled to North Africa, the Middle East, and Spain before returning to Newtonville in 1871. Between 1872 and 1878 he seems to have divided his time mostly between Boston and Morocco, and by 1880 he had settled permanently in Paris. In 1882–83 he lived for a year in India, where he returned on subsequent occasions. He also continued to travel elsewhere. An 1892 journey furnished material for *From the Black Sea through Persia and India* (1896), for which he also provided numerous illustrations. Weeks's characteristic paintings record with romantic flair the daily life he observed in far-flung lands. However, he also constructed historical scenes imagining the past with concrete verisimilitude. His work generally shows a painterly touch, but from the 1880s he sometimes preferred a more literal approach, probably influenced by photography. A large historical work depicting the seventeenth-century ruler Shah Jehan, *The Great Mogul and His Court Returning from the Great Mosque at Delhi, India* (Portland [Maine] Museum of Art, c. 1886) typically combines historical and ethnographic factualism, brilliant sunlight, and crisp detail.

Weeks, James. *See* BAY AREA FIGURATIVE PAINTERS.

Weems, Carrie Mae. *See* AFRICAN-AMERICAN ART.

Wegman, William (1943–). Photographer, painter, draftsman, sculptor, video artist, and conceptual artist. Although he has ranged freely across media in presenting idiosyncratic, inventive, and laid-back responses to contemporary American experience, he remains best known for slyly hilarious photographs of seemingly self-conscious Weimaraner dogs playing human roles. Punning titles often enhance the works' amiable *conceptualism. Born in Holyoke, Massachusetts, William George Wegman received a BFA degree from Boston's Massachusetts College of Art in 1965 and two years later an MFA from the University of Illinois in Urbana-Champaign. In the late 1960s he abandoned his early *minimalist approach to painting and sculpture to concentrate instead on conceptual works, often incorporating photography or the techniques of *video art. From the early 1970s, his dog Man Ray provided a willing, inexpensive, and photogenic accomplice. In 1979 Wegman began using large-format Polaroid film to create elegant, highly detailed, one-of-a-kind works of art. Their rarified appearance sharpened the fetching silliness of his canine subject, usually posed with costume and/or accessories. After Man Ray's death in 1982, Fay Ray, and later her children and grandchildren, took his place as actors. Concurrently, in 1972 Wegman began to create spare and generally sardonic drawings, often including texts. Later these became more illustrative and richer, and in 1985 he returned to painting, creating diaphanous fields overlaid with small, personally symbolic images, more recently often built around collaged postcards. After graduate school, Wegman taught in Wisconsin and Long Beach, California, but has made his home in New York since 1972. He also maintains a summer residence on a lake in Maine. He has published numerous collections of dog photographs.

Weil, Susan. *See* RAUSCHENBERG, ROBERT.

Weiner, Lawrence. *See* CONCEPTUAL ART.

Weir, Julian Alden (1852–1919) Painter and printmaker. A leading impressionist, he is known particularly for lyric landscapes and figure studies postdating his embrace of the new style around 1890. Earlier, Weir had established his reputation with sensuous, richly painted canvases, most notably still lifes that often incorporate lush floral elements. Responding to the *etching revival, during the late 1880s and early 1890s he produced approximately 140 etchings and drypoints in the prevailing loose, suggestive style inspired by James Abbott McNeill *Whistler. An active participant in the art life of his day, he taught at Cooper Union and the *Art Students League, numbered among the founding members of the *Society of American Artists and The *Ten, shared in *Tile Club pursuits, painted allegorical murals (his only large-scale works) for the 1893 World's Columbian Exposition in Chicago, and served as president of the *National Academy of Design from 1915 to 1917. Additionally, he assiduously promoted exhibition opportunities for American artists, while also advising Duncan *Phillips and other collectors on purchases. A native of West Point, on the Hudson River north of New York, he began his professional training at the National Academy in 1869. In the fall of 1873 he arrived in Paris, where he studied principally with Jean-Léon Gérôme but responded also to the art of a new friend, Jules Bastien-Lepage. He studied old master paintings during travels on the Continent and spent summers painting French peasant life in the countryside. Although he admired the work of Manet and Whistler, he at this time found impressionist painting unappealing. After returning to New York in the fall of 1877, he visited Europe on several subsequent occasions. From 1882 the area around his country home on a farm in the Branchville area of Ridgefield, Connecticut, provided landscape subjects and attracted as visitors such friends as Childe *Hassam, Theodore *Robinson, Albert *Ryder, John Singer *Sargent, and John *Twachtman. Weir also sometimes painted at his wife's family home at Windham, in east-central Connecticut, and during the summers of 1892 and 1893 worked closely with Twachtman in *Cos Cob, where he also visited at other times.

Although his 1880s etchings, watercolors, and pastels show experimental tendencies, through most of the decade Weir's canvases remained carefully finished, solidly designed, and somberly toned in rich, dark hues. *Roses* (Phillips Collection, 1883–84) contrasts heavy, pale blooms in two vases with the hard surface of a polished table top. A Renaissance Madonna relief in the rear shadows augments the mood of hushed solemnity. By 1890 Weir had altered his opinion of impressionism, soon becoming an early advocate of its light palette, feathery brushwork, and outdoor subjects. *The Red Bridge* (Metropolitan Museum, 1895) sets the freshly painted, orange-red iron structure of a new bridge, along with its watery reflection below, against organic forms of predominately green natural elements. Like many works of the mid-1890s, its combination of compositional drama and decorative pattern owes much to Weir's enthusiasm in this period for Japanese prints. After 1900 his characteristically delicate and romantic temper deepened, often leading his expression toward the evocative effects of *tonalism. He died in New York. The core of the Branchville farm, including Weir's house and studio, is now a National Historic Site administered by the National Park Service. It comprises also a studio built there by Mahonri *Young following his marriage to Weir's daughter, **Dorothy Weir** (1890–1947), a painter as well as the author (as Dorothy Weir Young) of the posthumously published *Life and Letters of J. Alden Weir* (1960).

His father, painter **Robert Walter Weir** (1803–89), taught drawing at West Point's United States Military Academy from 1834 until 1876. Interested primarily in romantic historical and literary subjects, he also rendered landscapes and portraits. Born in New York, he was mostly self-taught as an artist before leaving for Italy in December 1824. In Florence he studied for a few months with the neoclassical history painter Pietro Benvenuti. Toward the end of 1825 he moved to Rome, where he roomed with Horatio *Greenough. He visited Naples before sailing for the United States in March 1827. Although he never again went abroad, he continued for decades to paint occasional subjects inspired by his Italian experience, such as *Taking the Veil* (Yale University Art Gallery, 1863). Based ultimately on a ceremony the artist had witnessed in Rome, the event takes place in an invented Gothic interior but nevertheless demonstrates the artist's characteristic use of carefully painted detail and clearly constructed space to foster credibility. During seven years in New York after his return from Europe, Weir established a reputation among leading younger painters. Three years after he moved to West Point, the award of his most significant commission demonstrated his standing. Installed in the U.S. Capitol rotunda, this monumental work presents, with his usual concern for historical accuracy, the *Embarkation of the Pilgrims at Delft, Holland, July 22nd, 1620* (1837–43). After retiring from the academy, he lived for about four years in Hoboken, New Jersey, across the Hudson River from Manhattan, before moving permanently into New York.

Like his father and more original half brother Julian, **John Ferguson Weir** (1841–1926) was a painter. He also occasionally worked as a sculptor. Following his father's example as an educator, he headed the Yale University School of the Fine Arts (now School of Art) from 1869 until 1913. Although he painted landscapes, still lifes, portraits, figure studies, and a few literary narrative scenes, he is remembered particularly for several depictions from the 1860s and 1870s of working-class labor, a rare subject at the time. Born at West Point, Weir studied art only with his father. In the fall of 1862 he moved to New York, where four years later *The Gun Foundry* (Putnam Country Historical Society, Cold Spring, New York, 1864–66) established his reputation. Celebrating the heroism of industrial labor, it depicts the dramatically lit interior of a major Civil War–era industrial enterprise at Cold Spring, across the Hudson River from West Point. In September 1869, after touring Europe for eight months, Weir moved to New Haven to assume his duties at Yale. While serving as the first director of the nation's first collegiate art school (it offered professional training but was not yet integrated with the regular curriculum), he was responsible also for acquiring James Jackson *Jarves's important collection for the university. During four and a half decades at the university, time-consuming responsibilities diminished his creative output. Nevertheless, he continued to produce a range of painted subjects, especially landscapes and floral still lifes, as well as a few sculptures. Over time, his style evolved from the tight drawing associated with the *Hudson River School toward an atmospheric romanticism influenced by impressionism. He again visited Europe in 1881, 1901, and upon retirement. Subsequently he resided in Providence, Rhode Island, where he died. Edited by Theodore Sizer, his autobiography, *The Recollections of John Ferguson Weir*, appeared in 1957. Weir also wrote numerous periodical articles, as well as critical essays for the catalogue of Sanford *Gifford's memorial exhibition at the Metropolitan Museum of Art (1881) and for a Yale catalogue of John *Trumbull's work (1901). In addition, his spiritual inclinations found expression in *The Way: The Nature and Means of Revelation* (1889) and *Human Destiny in the Light of Revelation* (1903).

Wells, James Lesesne. *See* AFRICAN-AMERICAN ART.

Wendt, William (1865–1946). Painter. Among the best-known Southern California artists of his day, he celebrated the state's scenic grandeur in lush landscapes infused with the spirituality he ascribed to nature. Born in Bentzen, Germany, he moved to Chicago in 1880. There he briefly attended classes but remained mostly self-taught as an artist. In the mid-1890s he began visiting California. In 1898 he sojourned at the artists' colony of St. Ives in Cornwall, England. He again visited Europe in 1903 and on subsequent occasions until 1927. From 1906 until 1912 he lived in Los Angeles, but then permanently relocated to the coastal suburb of Laguna Beach. Around this time, his impressionist approach gave way to a broader method that accommodated interests in light and color while providing stability and order through graphic patterning related to the *California decorative style. Suggesting nature's majesty and the solace it offers, his work reflected Wendt's desire to reveal divine immanence in the landscape. His wife, sculptor **Julia Bracken Wendt** (1871–1942), known for portraits and allegorical subjects, was born in Apple River, Illinois, and spent most of her childhood about twenty miles from there, in Galena. She began her studies at the School of the Art Institute of Chicago in 1887. In 1893 in addition to executing her own commissions, she assisted her mentor Lorado *Taft in creating sculptural decoration for Chicago's World's Columbian Exposition. She maintained her own studio in Chicago before marrying in 1906 and moving with her husband to California. There she numbered among the Los Angeles area's leading sculptors. She died in Laguna Beach.

Wengenroth, Stow (1906–78). Printmaker and draftsman. Known particularly for sharply focused, detailed lithographs of New England's landscape and architecture, he numbered among his generation's finest craftsmen in black-and-white media. His technical expertise produced a wide range of tones and effects. Born in Brooklyn, he trained at the *Art Students League and the Grand Central School of Art between 1923 and 1927. He lived for most of his life on Long Island, but after twenty years in Greenport moved permanently in 1974 to Rockport, on the Massachusetts shore north of Boston. His devotion to the natural and manmade landscapes of the picturesque New England coast paralleled 1930s interests in regional description among the artists of the *American Scene movement. In *Moonlight* (1937), a view of two boats beached at low tide in the Rockport inner harbor, a lambent light suffuses the nocturnal scene. With its velvety surfaces, deep shadows, and sharply edged details, the prosaic view takes on a gently mysterious aura. The more dramatic *Untamed* (1947) shows several crows flying through an atmospherically rendered rainstorm above a forest clearing filled with minutely delineated vegetation and dead trees. He died in a hospital in Gloucester, not far from his home. In 1936 he published *Making a Lithograph*.

Wertmüller, Adolph (1751–1811). Painter. During his American years, he worked principally as a portraitist, but his career encompassed narrative painting as well. In Philadelphia he gained notoriety in 1806 by exhibiting his most famous painting, the titillating *Danae and the Shower of Gold* (National Museum of Fine Art, Stockholm, 1787). The incident resonates in American art history as one of the earliest instances of public outrage over the moral content of a painting. Adolph Ulrich (sometimes spelled Adolf and Ulric or Ulrik) Wertmüller was born in Stockholm. He trained as an artist there and in Paris prior to working in Rome and traveling through Italy between 1775 and 1779. Before returning to Paris in 1781, he worked in Lyon. Remaining in the capital until 1788, he was admitted to the French Academy and painted portraits of notables including members of the royal family. As the foremost Swedish painter of the day, he was appointed first painter to his native country's king. Wertmüller painted portraits in Bordeaux and Spain before traveling to the United States in 1794 to pursue his career in Philadelphia, New York, and Annapolis, Maryland. His 1794 portrait of *George Washington* (whereabouts unknown; replica, Metropolitan Museum, 1795) characteristically combines decorative, late rococo taste and glassy neoclassical polish. In 1797 he took up residence in Sweden once again, but returned to Philadelphia in 1800. After 1803 he painted little. He lived for the rest of his life on a farm along the Delaware River about twenty miles from Philadelphia.

Wesselmann, Tom (1931–2004). Painter, printmaker, and sculptor. An important contributor to *pop art, he is best known for 1960s compositions featuring nude females together with still life elements or, less often, landscapes. This series of Great American Nudes portrays erotic desire as an unremarkable aspect of consumer culture. In the style of billboard advertisements, the nudes and their faces are generally flatly painted, with only lips, nipples, and/or genitals given conspicuous definition. By oddly cropping the bodies, Wesselmann further dehumanized his voluptuous, bourgeois odalisques, who usually repose in brightly rendered middle-class interiors. Attentively depicted home appliances and processed food items contribute to an atmosphere of modern convenience and abundance. Some of the Nudes combine painted surfaces with actual products, such as radios or soft-drink bottles. At once celebratory and sardonic, his signature works reflect the increasing affluence of mid-twentieth-century American homes while also registering commercialism's assault on individual psychology. In the 1970s the sexual content of his work became more pointed, as he gave large-scale, decorative presence to isolated body parts, especially mouths, as in the Smoker series. His nudes and figural fragments, as well as their still life and landscape accompaniments, eventually inhabited sculptural space in an extended and sometimes highly abstracted series of inventive freestanding and wall-mounted cutouts. He also worked prolifically in several print media. Born in Cincinnati, he studied for two years at Hiram (Ohio) College before transferring to the University of Cincinnati. Service in the U.S. Army interrupted his progress for two years. Subsequently, he finished his BA in psychology and also studied at the Art Academy of Cincinnati. In 1956 he moved permanently to New York, where he continued his training for the next three years at Cooper Union. Although impressed in the late 1950s by the aggressive visual impact of *abstract expressionism, around 1960 he began to make figural collage paintings. These soon developed into the characteristic, sleekly painted images acknowledging the moment's raucous visual culture but also incorporating the spatial control, patterning, and chromatic authority observed in the work of Matisse and other modern masters. Under the pseudonym of Slim Stealingworth, he published *Tom Wesselmann* (1980), a third-person account of his career.

West, Benjamin (1738–1820). Painter, draftsman, and printmaker. Known especially for narratives based on history and literature, he also painted portraits. His many surviving drawings represent interests in subjects ranging from classical sculpture to landscape. The first American to gain international stature as an artist, he resided most of his life in London. Widely regarded in both England and America as the most important painter of his day, he enjoyed a sustained level of international celebrity perhaps never since equaled by a living American artist. Although West lived at the pinnacle of artistic success for many years, many modern viewers find his painting literary and too often shallowly conceived. His compositions endlessly combine and recombine standard poses and formats derived from the great masters of the Renaissance-Baroque tradition. But West's eclectic approach was precisely the source of his appeal to the audience of his time, especially when he tweaked expectation by introducing novelties. His paintings seemed at once learned, tasteful, and innovative. Although at its best his work excels within the academic tradition, some paintings suffer from flaccid draftsmanship, uninspired color, and little feeling for the sensuous quality of paint.

West was born in Springfield (now Swarthmore), Pennsylvania, close to Philadelphia, and started painting portraits when barely into his teens. After spending a year in Lancaster, where he came into contact with classical learning and attempted his first history painting, he moved to Philadelphia in 1756. There he made the acquaintance of artists who could offer useful instruction, such as German-trained painter John Valentine Haidt (1700–1780), who probably guided West's early development. Born in independent Danzig (now Gdańsk, Poland) and also a Moravian pastor, Haidt painted portraits and some of the earliest religious art known in the colonies. He had worked in London before emigrating to Pennsylvania in 1754 to reside primarily in Bethlehem, where he died. West's most inspiring mentor, William *Williams familiarized the young artist with some of the standard literature of European art theory, in addition to providing the example of his own accomplishment. West's American portraits also demonstrate his attraction to the work of John *Wollaston. West painted portraits in New York for a year before sailing to Italy in April 1760. There he remained primarily in Rome, where he developed into the history painter he had wished to become. From German painter Anton Raffael Mengs, friend and disciple of *neoclassical theorist Johann Joachim Winckelmann, West imbibed what he took to be the eternal rules of art. He also befriended Scottish painter and archeologist Gavin Hamilton and studied major monuments of the Renaissance-Baroque tradition throughout northern Italy. Despite his youth and inexperience as an artist, West quickly won favor in Roman art circles, partly by astutely trading on his exotic New World origins. Although he subsequently lived as an expatriate, West never relinquished his American identity, which offered a mark of distinction, and sometimes the latitude afforded to outsiders.

In 1763 West traveled to London and within a year decided to stay. By 1766 he enjoyed widespread acclaim for neoclassical paintings treating ancient themes with an austere and archeologically correct formal vocabulary derived from classical sculpture. The culmination of this tendency in his work, *Agrippina Landing at Brindisium with the Ashes of Germanicus* (Yale University Art Gallery, 1768), appealed to contemporary taste with a theme both sentimental and heroic. Situated within a pastiche of elements, the central figure group recalls a frieze from the Roman *Ara Pacis Augustae*. An early example of the taste that swept Europe and America before the end of the century, it propelled West to leadership of British history painting. In its stoic but emotionally charged interpretation of ancient history, its emphasis on the realistic rendering of every detail, and its cold, sculptural definition of form, it anticipates the later albeit more authoritative work of French neoclassicist Jacques Louis David. The painting also attracted the king's admiration, thus enhancing its prestige and initiating West's friendly personal relationship with George III. While completing more than fifty royal commissions, for more than three decades he received from the crown a generous annual salary, and in 1773 he assumed the office of historical painter to the monarch. In 1771 he exhibited another sensation, *The Death of General Wolfe* (National Gallery of Canada, Ottawa, 1770), among his most compelling and influential paintings. Representing a 1759 episode in England's war with France, this scene again mixes sentiment and morally edifying heroism but with a new twist. By re-creating the setting of a recent event, clothing participants in contemporary dress, and incorporating portraits, West provided the first important example of the modern, veristic history painting that became widely popular internationally in subsequent decades. For all its realism of detail, however, West adhered to standard academic practice in conceptualizing the scene. The composition echoes the format of the traditional pietà, and poses of major figures reflect grand manner conventions. Innovating again, within a few years West signaled the advent of *romanticism by turning from themes of restraint and personal rectitude to emotionally charged subjects, often evoking fear or astonishment, as in *Saul and the Witch of Endor* (Wadsworth Atheneum, Hartford, Connecticut, 1777). Abandoning the sobriety of his neoclassical forms, West gave imaginative realization to an emotionally charged Old Testament tale of doom. Its tone resembles such other early manifestations of romanticism as Henry Fuseli's bizarre paintings and Edmund Burke's theoretical ruminations on the Sublime. After 1800 West's major works increasingly addressed psychologically potent religious themes. Known in several versions attesting to his interest in the subject for nearly forty years, the visionary *Death on a Pale Horse* pictures the four horsemen of the Apocalypse as they wreak destruction. In its swirling forms, the oil sketch (Detroit Institute of Art, 1796) ranks as the most unified and compelling. Dominated by life-size figures on horseback, the enormous final version (Pennsylvania Academy, 1817) overwhelms with scale alone.

As a dominant figure in the London art world, in 1792 West followed Joshua Reynolds as president of the Royal Academy, which he had helped to found in 1768. He continued to exert the unparalleled influence of that post, except for one year, until his death. Although his career occasioned intermittent controversy and criticism, even in later years he remained productive and honored. At his death he was laid to rest beside Reynolds in St. Paul's Cathedral. West's impact on the history of art depended in no small part on his kindness to younger artists, both British and American. For his compatriots, far from home and often from sources of both emotional and financial support, he was of inestimable significance as a reliable mentor. He encouraged them, offered instruction, employed them in his studio, and introduced them to sophisticated London circles. Matthew *Pratt and Henry *Benbridge numbered among the first, in the mid-1760s. Around the same time, West began dispensing advice by mail to John Singleton *Copley in Boston. Other distinguished pupils include Charles Willson *Peale, Gilbert *Stuart, and John *Trumbull, as well as a later generation that encompassed Washington *Allston, Samuel F. B. *Morse, and Thomas *Sully. More than any other individual, West deserves credit for drawing American art into the mainstream of Western culture. His son, painter, draftsman, and printmaker **Raphael Lamar West** (1766–1850), continued to live in England but visited the United States between 1799 and 1802. Trained by his father, he also produced history paintings. Although he found modest success early in life, relatively little of his work has been identified, and he evidently had a limited artistic reputation at the time of his death in Bushey Heath, Hertfordshire.

Westermann, H. C. *See* CHICAGO IMAGISM.

Western Art-Union. *See* AMERICAN ART-UNION.

Weston, Edward (1886–1958). Photographer. His intense realism, formal purity, and impeccable printing played crucial roles in reorienting photographic practice toward a modern form of expression. Inspiring artistic heirs even today, he extended long-standing American artistic and philosophical traditions into the late twentieth century. Like such painters as John Singleton *Copley and Asher B. *Durand, he embodied the ideal in closely observed reality. Following in the path of Ralph Waldo Emerson and the Transcendentalists, he aspired to a personal and mystical relationship with universal life rhythms manifest in nature. Born in Highland Park, Illinois, Edward Henry Weston spent much of his childhood in nearby Chicago and developed an enthusiasm for photography as a teenager. He dropped out of high school in 1903 and moved to the Los Angeles suburb of Tropico (now part of Glendale) about three years later. He returned to Illinois in 1908 to attend a photography school in Effingham for a short time. In 1911 he opened his own portrait studio in Tropico. While working as a commercial photographer, he won many honors for his early creative work, which reflected the prevailing aesthetic of *pictorialism. In the 1910s, his growth as an artist was stimulated by his appreciation for modern forms of visual expression and by a friendship from about 1913 with photographer Margrethe Mather (1886–1952), who outpaced his grasp of contemporary art and thought. In her own pictorialist work, which peaked in the 1920s, she achieved a concentrated modern vision often emphasizing patterns in playful and delicate arrangements of objects.

During a visit to Middletown, Ohio, in 1922 Weston photographed the Armco Steel plant with a newly direct, unsentimental, and formally inventive approach. His dramatic interpretations of industry suggest the *precisionist romance with technology, seen also in photographs by Charles *Sheeler and Paul *Strand. Although he rarely returned to such subjects, the Armco series represents a decisive moment in his gradual, logical progression toward a personal style. A visit to New York, where he met Alfred *Stieglitz as well as Sheeler, Strand, and other leading photographers, reinforced his new direction. In 1923 Weston moved to Mexico City, accompanied by Tina *Modotti. There, mingling with a vital modernist community, he refined his vision by striving for simplicity and objectivity in aestheticized images of prosaic objects, perhaps most famously the toilet in his apartment. These works ratified his mature practice of operating with the most basic photographic equipment and techniques: large-format view cameras, small apertures, and long exposure times for maximum detail and depth of field. He used only natural light and produced only contact prints, which provided extreme clarity and allowed a wide range of subtly modulated tones. He returned to California late in 1926 and moved to San Francisco the following year. For about three years he emphasized uncanny realism in objective studies, often in extreme close-up, of isolated, usually natural objects, such as peppers or halved artichokes. Suggesting a Brancusian sculpture, "Shell" (1927) presents a pearly nautilus balanced so that its opening flares upward, as its outline provides a sinuous border. Against an entirely black background, it glows, an icon of art and nature. After Weston settled in Carmel in 1929, in a similar spirit he also photographed nudes, generally sliced by the picture frame, as well as rocks or vegetation he observed along the coast at Point Lobos. Throughout, formal elegance accompanies an unnaturally intense realism that seems to penetrate the essence of his subjects.

In 1932 Weston joined forces with six other photographers dedicated to straight photography to form the *f/64 group. Four years later he began photographing sand dunes near Oceano, sometimes in combination with nudes, with particular sensitivity to the rhythms of their formal structure. In 1937 he became the first photographer to win a Guggenheim fellowship, which he used to travel for two years, producing the photographs that appeared in *California and the West* (1940), along with text by his wife, Charis Wilson. By this time, he was moving away from his concentration on individual items or fragments, toward more expansive views that stress relationships within natural systems. His magisterial late landscape photographs demonstrate profound feeling for California's unique topography and vegetation. In 1948 he made his last photographs, at Point Lobos, in the knowledge that Parkinson's disease would soon end his career. During the final years before he died at his home in Carmel, he supervised the printing of his legacy. Weston's first book, *The Art of Edward Weston*, appeared in 1932. His daily journal from 1923 (he destroyed records from several earlier years) to 1944 was published in two volumes as *The Daybooks of Edward Weston* (1961–66), edited by Nancy *Newhall. Peter Bunnell edited *Edward Weston on Photography* (1983).

Two of Weston's sons, both born in Los Angeles, also were photographers. At thirteen **Brett Weston** (1911–93) abandoned formal education to travel to Mexico with his father. Enthusiastically taking up photography, he absorbed his father's style and later was invited to exhibit with the f/64 group. However, he often consciously turned to subjects that rarely interested Edward, such as industrial sites and the products of modern technology, and he tended to push closer to abstraction in graphic patterns of light and dark. In its irregular dynamism, "Broken Window, San Francisco" (1937), picturing only a void surrounded by jagged shards of glass and part of the window frame, anticipates the explosive forms of *abstract expressionism. Also a sculptor, Theodore Brett Weston worked for a *federal art project during the Depression. From 1943 to 1946 served in the U.S. Army. Although he traveled often, during most of his career he resided in California. He died in Kona, Hawaii, where he had maintained a home since the 1980s. **Cole Weston** (1919–2003) served in the U.S. Army during World War II and spent a year in New York on the staff of *Life* magazine, before returning in 1946 to Carmel to assist his father in printing negatives. In Edward's will, Cole was given sole authority to make additional prints and did so until 1988, when he turned exclusively to his own photography. While following his father's lead in choice of subjects from nature, he worked primarily in color. He died in Monterey.

Wheeler, Monroe. *See* LYNES, GEORGE PLATT.

Wheeler, Steve. *See* INDIAN SPACE PAINTING.

Whistler, James Abbott McNeill (1834–1903). Painter and printmaker. An artist of international renown, known for views and figural works, including many portraits, he spearheaded late-nineteenth-century interest in art for art's sake. Although he lived abroad throughout his career, his nuanced, delicate, transitory impressions held extraordinary fascination for American artists. In a notorious trial, he won a libel suit against the prominent English critic John Ruskin for defaming his work. Awarded only insignificant damages by the court, widely reviled in the press, and driven to bankruptcy, he had nevertheless articulately defended the proposition that the formal qualities of a work of art determine its aesthetic value. Characteristically titled to undermine the importance of subject, his *Arrangement in Gray and Black, No. 1* (Musée d'Orsay, Paris, 1871) remains popularly known as "Whistler's Mother." In his day, the artist's temperament augmented his fame. By turns contentious and charming, something of a dandy and famously witty, he cultivated a reputation as an eccentric bohemian. His sometimes impetuous and irresponsible personality contrasted with perfectionism in the studio.

Christened James Abbott at birth in Lowell, Massachusetts, as a young adult he added McNeill, his mother's maiden name, to his own. In childhood he lived in Stonington, Connecticut, and Springfield, Massachusetts, before leaving with his family in 1843 for Russia. After five years in St. Petersburg, he was sent to boarding school in England. His artistic aptitude was stimulated during vacations at the home of his stepsister, whose husband, Francis Seymour Haden, collected art and later became known as an etcher. After Whistler's father died in 1849, the youngster returned with his family to Pomfret in northeastern Connecticut. In 1851 he entered the United States Military Academy at West Point, where he studied drawing with Robert W. *Weir. Dismissed from the academy in 1854, he learned etching while working as a draftsman for the United States Coast and Geodetic Survey. In the fall of 1855, shortly after his twenty-first birthday, Whistler sailed for Europe, never to return, although he remained an American citizen. After a brief stop in London, he continued on to Paris. There he pursued conventional instruction at first, but his contacts with other progressive artists proved of more lasting importance to his development. He came to know and exchange ideas with a large and unusually diverse number of French and English artistic leaders. Eventually, with his cosmopolitan outlook and varied talents, he contributed substantially to several important tendencies of the late nineteenth century, including the *aesthetic movement, *japonisme, the *etching revival, *tonalism, and art nouveau, as well as the impressionist and symbolist sensibilities. These interconnections speak to the power of his example and of the theory he developed to support it, for his mature art remained stylistically independent of any group.

In Paris during the late 1850s, he befriended Gustave Courbet, whose work he greatly admired, as well as other realists. Like them, he also revered the great Dutch and Spanish painters of the seventeenth century. His first major painting, *At the Piano* (Taft Museum of Art,

Cincinnati, 1858–59), interprets these interests in terms of a predisposition to tranquility and decorative appeal. With the mid-century revival of etching already under way in Paris, in 1858 Whistler published his first print series there, a dozen etched views that came to be known as the French Set. In 1859 he moved to London, although he remained a frequent visitor on the Continent. In Paris during the next few years he met Manet, Monet, and other gifted contemporaries. Concurrently, in London he became familiar with *Pre-Raphaelite painting and befriended Dante Gabriel Rossetti. Painted in Paris, *The White Girl* (National Gallery, 1861–62), later retitled *Symphony in White, No. 1*, consolidates elements he admired in English and French precedents. The model's figural type, her psychic disengagement, and the richness of detail point to Pre-Raphaelitism, although Whistler avoided the melodrama and clutter common in that movement's work. On the other hand, as a tour de force in its presentation of a model clothed in white against a white ground, it suggests Courbet's or Manet's insistent physicality while deviating from their approach in its enigmatic mood. The painting's originality placed it among sensations of the notorious 1863 Salon des Refusés in Paris. Around the same time, Whistler began to incorporate into some compositions Japanese and Chinese costumes and decorative objects, responding to growing interest on both sides of the Channel in East Asian culture. Embellished with decorative objects including fans and a large ceramic vase, *The Princess of the Land of Porcelain* (Freer Gallery of Art, Washington, D.C., 1863–64) presents a woman clothed in flowing Japanese robes standing before a painted screen. By 1865 he was reaching beyond these superficial exoticisms to adapt the formal and spatial devices of Chinese and Japanese paintings into the structure of his work. This development, of primary importance for his personal aesthetic, complemented his lifelong quest to define the nature of beauty in terms of essentials. On a trip to South America in 1866, Whistler lingered in Valparaiso, where he painted ethereal seascapes as well as his earliest night scenes.

By the time he adopted the butterfly emblem (derived from his initials) as his artistic signature in 1869, he had embarked upon his most significant accomplishments. During subsequent decades he completed prodigious numbers of paintings, watercolors, etchings, lithographs, and pastels. Concurrently he expounded novel theories of art and participated in institutional and informal professional activities, such as teaching and organizing exhibitions. In portraiture his preferred format came to be the life-size, standing figure shown without accessories in a limited, sometimes indeterminate environment. Although individualized in features, clothing, and stance, these likenesses usually accommodate his typically introspective tone, bolstered by serene compositions and exquisite color harmonies. From the early 1860s, in titling his paintings Whistler often invoked musical modes, thus undercutting description and linking beauty to abstract sensations. A spare, banded study of sand, sea, and sky, *Harmony in Blue and Silver: Trouville* (Isabella Stewart Gardner Museum, Boston, 1865) includes his friend Courbet as a wispy figure contemplating the horizon. Perhaps ironically, the painting marks Whistler's departure from the more naturalistic sensibility of Courbet and the old masters. In this and other notable landscapes, particularly his night or evening scenes, from 1872 called *Nocturnes*, he pursued pure color and form, purged of narrative content and occasionally bordering on abstraction. Among many studies of the Thames River and its banks, *Nocturne in Blue and Gold: Old Battersea Bridge* (Tate Britain, London, 1872–73) memorably pictures the bridge from an unexpected, low viewpoint. In a particularly clear example of Whistler's use of Japanese sources, it echoes a Hokusai print. At the same time, its urban subject matter and evocation of a transient moment suggest parallels to the goals of French impressionism, although it differs in means and mood. In printmaking, Whistler's practice evolved along lines parallel to his painting. The masterful early Thames Set (1859), a group of London views, employs vigorous realism tempered by taste for the beautiful detail. Later this approach gave way to economy of means and emphasis on suggestion, with figures and architectural elements providing structure for ethereal and transient effects. As with many of his pure landscape paintings, their impact relies on finely rendered perceptions, produced with the slightest of means. Technically among the period's most proficient etchers, after the late 1880s Whistler also produced many equally accomplished lithographs. A transfer process developed in the 1870s enabled him to reproduce his delicate drawings. He also pioneered in artistic use of color lithography.

Two controversial events marked the late 1870s. At the request of shipping magnate F. R. Leyland, in 1876–77 Whistler redecorated a dining room to provide a suitable environment for *The Princess of the Land of Porcelain*, which Leyland had owned for several years. In Leyland's absence, he went far beyond their original understanding to transform the entire room into a dazzlingly rich work of art,

Harmony in Blue and Gold, the so-called Peacock Room. (Purchased in 1904 by Charles Lang *Freer, the room remains intact within the Freer Gallery of Art.) Inspired by peacocks' iridescent splendor, the artist painted the leather walls a deep blue-green, decorated the ceiling with a feather motif on a golden ground, gilded the finely detailed shelves already installed to showcase Chinese porcelains, and in golds and blue-greens rendered fighting and resting peacocks with exaggeratedly decorative tails. In creating a key work of the aesthetic movement, however, he lost a patron. On the heels of this debacle, during the summer of 1877 Ruskin responded to Whistler's nearly abstract *Nocturne in Black and Gold: The Falling Rocket* (Detroit Institute of Art, 1875) by naming him a "coxcomb" and accusing him of "flinging a pot of paint in the public's face." Whistler filed a successful libel lawsuit the next year, but his possessions were nevertheless auctioned to pay debts occasioned by the court action as well as other prodigal expenditures. To recuperate financially, he departed in September 1879 with a cash advance from a London gallery, the Fine Art Society, to produce twelve etchings of Venice before Christmas.

Venice absorbed him beyond all expectation. He stayed for fourteen months, producing about fifty etchings, close to a hundred pastels, and a dozen paintings as well as watercolors and drawings. For the most part ignoring the major tourist sites, he sought out the city's byways and unknown corners, recorded its watery panoramas and venerable architecture, and found appeal in its ordinary inhabitants glimpsed in everyday, if often picturesque, activities. While the etchings extended years of successful practice in this medium, his attention to pastel indicated a new interest in using colored chalks to produce completed works of art. Nearly always working on a dark ground, usually brown, he created understated but often jewel-like scenes. Following his return to London in November 1880, a generally positive reception for the Venice subjects set the stage for artistic fulfillment during the 1880s and 1890s. At the height of his fame, while working productively in several media, he nevertheless assimilated important aftereffects of the Venice sojourn. The Venice material provided an opportunity to devise new methods of display, which he amplified on later occasions. His simple, modern approach helped to revolutionize exhibition design. Moreover, his exclusive concentration in Venice on small works apparently stimulated interest in the question of scale. Subsequently, he painted many tiny and intimate works, reinforcing his contention that size and quality are unrelated. In 1888 Whistler married the widow of architect and designer E. L. Godwin, who had been a friend and collaborator. Also an artist, Beatrice died at thirty-eight in 1896. After their marriage, Whistler compiled *The Gentle Art of Making Enemies* (1890). A collection of thoughts and writings, it included his famous anti-Ruskinian "Ten O'Clock Lecture" (1885), in which he defended the independence of art from nature. From 1892 until late 1894 the couple lived in Paris, and after her death Whistler maintained a residence there until his health began to deteriorate in 1901. Subsequently he made his home in London, where he died, having done much to transform not only the appearance of art but also how people thought about it.

White, Charles. *See* AFRICAN-AMERICAN ART.

White, Clarence (1871–1925). Photographer. His serene, evocative images rank among the finest accomplishments of *pictorialism. Living in central Ohio and relying exclusively on his family and a few friends to pose for his idylls, White created a distinctive and coherent body of work between about 1898 and 1906. His softly focused, graceful platinum prints display fresh compositions, sensitive renderings of light, and an unaffected devotion to beauty. Born in the tiny village of West Carlisle, Ohio, Clarence Hudson White moved in 1887 with his family to the nearby county seat, Newark, where he graduated from high school three years later. He worked as a bookkeeper until 1904, when he left salaried employment in order to pursue full time the photography that had been an avocation since the early 1890s. By 1898, when his work in an important Philadelphia show came to the attention of the photographic community's national leaders, he had already formed an individual style, although he remained entirely without training in either art or photography. Based largely on the examples of Japanese prints and progressive painting styles of the day, particularly James Abbott McNeill *Whistler's, his highly original photographs demonstrate an understanding of asymmetrical balance, two-dimensional patterning, and composition based on tone. Many of White's photographs present staged poetic fantasies. In "Morning" (1905), a woman in white holding a glass ball drifts through a landscape suffused with the pearly illumination of dawn. Others draw on domestic life. "Ring Toss" (1899) depicts three preadolescent girls at play indoors, although their identities and activity are less important than issues of composition and lighting. With such works, White won numerous prizes and honors, and in 1902 Alfred *Stieglitz included him among the founding members of the *Photo-Secession.

In 1906 White moved to New York. Although this step put him at the center of the art photography movement, the city did not nourish his vision. Instead, the relocation ended the most creative phase of his life. Driven by the need to support his family and temperamentally unsuited to commercial work, he turned to teaching, eventually becoming the leading mentor to the next generation of photographers. In 1907 Arthur Wesley *Dow invited him to conduct classes at Teachers College, Columbia University, where he remained for many years while also teaching elsewhere. In 1910 he and painter Max *Weber founded a summer school in Maine, and four years later he established a New York photography school. Although White had distanced himself from Stieglitz since 1910, he remained active in art photography circles. In 1916, along with other disaffected Secessionists, he founded the *Pictorial Photographers of America and served as its first president. White's undogmatic approach to photography served him well as a teacher. At the same time, although he photographed very little, his own practice evolved, becoming more straightforward and modern. The landscape "Croton Reservoir" (1925) exemplifies the strengths of his emerging late aesthetic. Taken from a high vantage point, it captures a dynamic pattern of forms. White's sudden death in Mexico City while on a photography trip with students prevented him from fully realizing a new stylistic phase in his career. White's widow and students maintained his school until 1943.

White, John (probably before 1550–1593 or later). Painter and draftsman. Among the earliest Europeans to produce visual records of the New World, he worked primarily in watercolor. When they were published in England, his careful depictions of the Atlantic shore, its plants and animals, and its native inhabitants promoted new understandings of the previously unknown region. Although he had been preceded by Jacques Le Moyne de Morgues (c. 1533–85), who recorded similar subjects in Florida in the 1560s, White's work forms the earliest surviving pictorial record of North America. Except for one watercolor, the Frenchman's work is known only in engraved reproductions. White served as the official artist on a 1585–86 expedition sponsored by Sir Walter Raleigh to attempt settlement at Roanoke, Virginia. (Roanoke Island, sheltered inside the Outer Banks, now lies in North Carolina. Today's Roanoke, Virginia, is situated in the western part of the state.) During this sojourn, White also traveled in the region and may have reached Chesapeake Bay. Twenty-three of his watercolors, somewhat inaccurately engraved by Flemish artist and publisher Theodore de Bry in London, appeared in 1590 along with text by the expedition's scientist, Thomas Harriot. (Titled *A Briefe and True Report of the New Found Land of Virginia*, the Harriot text had first appeared without illustrations in 1588.) In 1591 de Bry also engraved and published Le Moyne's work.

White's origins, early life, and later years are obscure. He probably accompanied a 1577 exploratory expedition to the northwest Atlantic. In 1587 White sailed again for Roanoke with another group of settlers, this time as governor of the colony. He stayed only a short time before returning to England for supplies. Conflict between England and Spain prevented White from leaving once more for Roanoke until 1590. During a brief visit, he found that the settlement had disappeared, and no trace was ever found of the "Lost Colony." A 1593 letter written from his home in Ireland provides the latest sure evidence of White's existence, but he may have been the seagoing John White who died in 1606. Presumably a trained artist, White produced fresh and direct colored drawings. Although interested in scientific documentation, he conveyed in many of his observations of Indian life an idyllic tone of peace, order, and harmony with nature. One such watercolor (British Museum, London), inscribed "The manner of their fishing," depicts Indian techniques of catching fish, including spearing and trapping. Near the shore, four men in a "cannow" pass with a catch of large fish nearly filling their boat. In unnaturalistic perspective, fish swimming in the water suggest a range of species. A luminous sky and passing birds contribute to the tranquility of the scene.

White, Minor (1908–76). Photographer. A student of Zen Buddhism and other mystically oriented philosophies, he often chose points of view and conditions of light that pushed his impeccably crafted, sharp-focus works close to abstraction. In conscious emulation of Alfred *Stieglitz, he pursued the notion that a photograph should convey its maker's inner emotion, aroused by the subject before his camera. As editor for many years of the discriminating photography magazine *Aperture*, White published a wide range of artistic approaches and promoted a searching discourse about the medium. As well, he arranged many important photography shows that enlarged the discussion of images, often with an emphasis on metaphysical interpretation, and he served as an important mentor during a long teaching career. Born in Minneapolis, Minor Martin White graduated in 1933 from the University of Minnesota with a degree in botany. About the time he turned seriously to photography in 1937, he moved to Portland, Oregon, where the following year he joined a *federal art project to work as a documentary photographer. Drafted into the U.S. Army in 1942, he fought in the Pacific. Upon discharge in 1945, he moved to New York, where he studied art history at Columbia University under Meyer *Schapiro and worked with Beaumont *Newhall at the *Museum of Modern Art. As he developed a personal photographic style, he adopted Stieglitz's passion for the expressive equivalent, as well as his interest in sequencing, or arranging photographs in a particular order for aesthetic effect, later a key method in White's practice. After moving to San Francisco in 1946, he was attracted to Edward *Weston's purism and Ansel *Adams's dedication to nature. Both men also strengthened his commitment to flawless printing emphasizing tonal beauty. In 1952 he returned to New York, where, with others, he founded *Aperture* before moving the next year to Rochester, New York. Soon becoming the magazine's sole editor, he continued as the publication's guiding spirit until his death. With Stieglitz's **Camera Work* as his model, he produced an elegant, informative journal that upheld rigorous artistic standards and appealed only to a comparatively small audience of art photography enthusiasts. White was appointed to head the photography department at the Massachusetts Institute of Technology in 1965. He retired in 1974 and died in a Boston hospital, not far from his home in Arlington.

Characteristically clear, close-up views of nature fragments, White's photographs typically employ spatial and formal ambiguities to prevent precise identification of the subject and thus to encourage multiple meanings. "Moencopi Strata, Capitol Reef, Utah" (1962) pictures crisply edged geologic formations, but viewpoint, lighting, and lack of scale undercut representational readings. "Moon and Wall Encrustations"(1964) suggests a rolling landscape seen by ghostly light under a slightly misshapen moon. The title reveals that we are looking at something else entirely but does not permit the viewer to understand the subject completely. Other, more comprehensible views often suggest spiritual connotations. In 1956, he published *Exposure with the Zone System* (revised in 1963 as *Zone System Manual*), adapting Adams's system to intuitive photography. The autobiographical *Mirrors, Messages, Manifestations* (1969) supplements his photographs with poetic text. The posthumous *Minor White: Rites and Passages* (1978) accompanies a selection of his photographs with excerpts from letters and diaries.

Whitehead, Ralph Radcliffe. *See* WOODSTOCK ARTISTS' COLONY.

Whitman, Robert. *See* EXPERIMENTS IN ART AND TECHNOLOGY.

Whitney, Anne (1821–1915). Sculptor and illustrator. Also a writer. In her mid-thirties before she took up sculpture, she combined realism and *neoclassicism in works executed in both marble and bronze. Concerned throughout her life with issues of social justice, she infused many works with feminist or antislavery overtones. Her numerous portraits center on friends and acquaintances from New England's intellectual elite, including abolitionists, suffragists, and educators. Born in Watertown, Massachusetts, and for the most part privately educated, as a young woman she taught school for two years. From the late 1840s her writing earned a place within New England literary culture, and in 1859 she published her only book, *Poems*. A few years earlier, she had begun to model in clay. Determining to make a career as a sculptor, she studied anatomy and attended the *Pennsylvania Academy of the Fine Arts in 1860. After returning to Boston she received further assistance from William *Rimmer. Her desire to leave for Europe was checked by the Civil War, but she embarked on several major pieces. Among them, the 1864 *Africa* (destroyed) depicted the continent as a sleeping woman roused by the end of slavery. In 1867 she embarked on the first of three trips to Europe, where until 1876 she resided much of the time, mostly in Italy. In Rome she stirred controversy with the bronze *Roma* (Wellesley [Massachusetts] College, 1890; modeled 1869), a symbolic representation of the city as an old beggar woman, denoting the decay the artist observed in social conditions. Travels in Europe reinforced her interest in naturalistic, dynamically modeled form before this French aesthetic was widely accepted among American sculptors. In 1875 she won a competition for a public monument to Massachusetts's abolitionist senator, Charles Sumner. When her gender became known, the commission was withheld. Twenty-seven years later she reworked the piece for casting in bronze, financed by private donations (Harvard Square, Cambridge, Massachusetts, 1902). After settling permanently in Boston upon her final return from Europe, in the early 1880s Whitney bought 225 acres of scenic farm and forest land near Shelburne in northern New Hampshire, close to the Maine border and not far from Mount Washington. Passing her summers there, she added conservation to the list of charitable and reformist causes she continued actively to support into her later years.

Whitney, Gertrude Vanderbilt (1875–1942). Sculptor, collector, and museum founder. Although she was a serious, respected, and productive artist, Whitney's efforts on behalf of other artists, and of American art in general, dominate her historical reputation. In 1930 earlier efforts evolved into the Whitney Museum of American Art, her greatest legacy. It remains the premier museum devoted to the preservation, display, and encouragement of American art produced since the early twentieth century. A lifelong New Yorker born into one of the city's wealthiest families, she began her art training after a society marriage in 1896 to financier, horse breeder, and sportsman Harry Payne Whitney. She studied at the *Art Students League with James Earle *Fraser, among others, and in Paris, where Rodin offered encouragement. Her work, based in traditional figuration, was not stylistically adventurous but suited the public monuments that were her specialty. These ranged from realistic scenes of World War I (which she had witnessed as a volunteer in the hospital she established in France at its outset) to the idealism of the *Titanic Memorial* (commissioned in 1914, unveiled in 1931) in Washington's Potomac Park. Here, the tragic fate of hundreds is symbolized in a monumental granite figure that faces the void like a figurehead, arms outstretched, in possible allusion to the Crucifixion, and garments swirling. (Actress Kate Winslett echoed the pose in her rapturous stance at the liner's prow in the 1997 movie *Titanic*.)

While pursuing her own studies, Whitney began purchasing the works of other artists and giving financial assistance to needy comrades. After establishing a studio on MacDougal Alley in 1907, she often invited other artists to show their work on her premises. In 1914 she initiated a gallery, the Whitney Studio, on West Eighth Street, adjacent to her workplace, formalizing her financial and psychological support for American artists at a time when there were few alternatives. (Whitney also maintained a studio on her Long Island estate.) To manage this venture she hired Juliana Force (1876–1948), who continued to work closely with Whitney throughout her employer's life on a series of philanthropic activities aimed at assisting artists' careers. In 1918 they opened larger quarters nearby, known as the Whitney Studio Club. (In 1928 it became the Whitney Studio Galleries.) When the *Metropolitan Museum of Art refused Whitney's 1929 offer to donate her collection of some five hundred items, she decided to start her own museum. Chartered the following year, the Whitney Museum of American Art opened in 1931 on West Eighth Street, with Force as its first director. In 1954 it moved to Fifty-fourth Street, and in 1966, to its present Madison Avenue home, designed by Marcel Breuer.

A financial contributor to the *Armory Show and other *independent exhibitions, Whitney was sympathetic to progressive tendencies in art, but she had little affection for modernist abstraction. Consequently, the Whitney Museum's strength in the early years lay in its holdings of early twentieth-century representational art, including work by such friends as Jo *Davidson, Robert *Henri, and Ernest *Lawson. The museum also assembled the largest collection anywhere of Edward *Hopper's art, numbering about two thousand works (including those later donated by his widow). Since the founder's death, the collection has grown to encompass the full scope of American art since the early twentieth century. The museum's ongoing commitment to contemporary art is signaled by the well-established Biennial (originally, beginning in 1932, an annual exhibition), which showcases recent American art on a regular basis.

Whittredge, Worthington (1820–1910). Painter. A leading nineteenth-century interpreter of American landscape, he also produced portraits, *genre scenes, and a few still lifes. Born near Springfield, Ohio, at seventeen Thomas Worthington Whittredge moved about sixty miles to Cincinnati, where he learned sign and house painting. By the time he turned seriously to landscapes in the mid-1840s, he had also worked as a *daguerreotypist and portrait painter. As he absorbed *Hudson River School principles and apparently familiarized himself with the work of George Caleb *Bingham and other specialists in outdoor genre, he gained some success with views, but in 1849 he departed for Europe in search of instruction. He settled in Düsseldorf, where for a time he worked informally with the German romantic realist Karl Friedrich Lessing. He also soon befriended Emanuel *Leutze and posed for the general's figure in Leutze's celebrated *Washington Crossing the Delaware*. After sketching in Switzerland with Albert *Bierstadt and William Stanley *Haseltine during the summer of 1856, he continued on with them to Rome, where he remained for nearly three years. In Europe he consolidated his technique, refined his draftsmanship, and gained sophistication in current and traditional methods of constructing landscape. After his return, he lived in New York. Deeply impressed with Asher B. *Durand's achievements during his ten-year absence, he also was attracted to the work of younger landscape painters, such as John *Kensett and Sanford *Gifford, a friend from his days in Rome. To his clear drawing and compositional assurance, Whittredge added an intensified exploration of light and atmosphere, allying some of his work with *luminism. In subsequent years, he produced varied landscape types, including wilderness vistas and shore scenes, but his devotion to the woodland interior was particularly distinctive. Building on the example of Durand particularly, Whittredge on numerous occasions depicted enclosed forest spaces illuminated by subtle, flickering lights or radiant shafts. The experience of traversing what is now Colorado and New Mexico during the summer of 1866 proved a revelation to Whittredge. Relatively unmoved by the Rocky Mountains, he was instead overwhelmed by the silent immensity of the plains, by the effects of light and atmosphere that could be observed through great distances, and by elegiac traces of human experience. Two subsequent trips west in the 1870s reinforced his enthusiasm for this resolutely horizontal "Arcadia" (as he called it). In response, he produced numerous closely observed, understated plein air oil studies, as well as finished views. Much later, in the 1890s, he also traveled to Mexico. During the last quarter of the nineteenth century, as enthusiasm for *Barbizon and then impressionist painting affected American practice, Whittredge modified his style to accommodate new interests. In *A Breezy Day—Sakonnet Point, Rhode Island* (Amon Carter Museum, Fort Worth, Texas, c. 1880), a spit of land just breaks the long, low, and distant horizon. The fresh and inventive composition, the delicate but scintillating illumination, and the free handling of paint logically extend his previous concerns but also hint at impressionism. After he moved permanently to Summit, New Jersey, in 1880, his work sometimes responded to the broadly conceived, evocative landscapes of George *Inness, who lived in the area. Whittredge continued to paint into his eighties and in 1905 wrote an autobiography, first published in 1942 in the *Brooklyn Museum Journal*.

Wiggins, Guy Carleton (1883–1962). Painter. Extending impressionism well into the twentieth century, he specialized in New York cityscapes, particularly as seen during snowstorms. During summers in Connecticut, he painted landscapes. For some years associated with *Old Lyme, in 1937 he established his own art school nearby Essex. As well, he painted on travels throughout the United States and Canada. Although indebted to Childe *Hassam's example, Wiggins's softly romantic work indicates a milder sensibility. His wintry urban views domesticate urban bustle and tame the hostile weather. Born in Brooklyn, he spent part of his childhood in Europe and went to school in England. He enrolled at the Polytechnic Institute in Brooklyn to study architecture but left to train at the *National Academy of Design. Although he gleaned his knowledge of impressionism primarily from American artists, in his best work he achieved a free and convincing variant of the style. Before World War I he painted in England. He died in St. Augustine, Florida, while on vacation.

Wiggins received his earliest training from his father, **Carleton Wiggins** (1848–1932), a popular painter of *Barbizon-style landscapes, often featuring farm animals. Born in Turners (now Harriman), west of the Hudson River near Bear Mountain, John Carleton Wiggins moved as a youth to Brooklyn. He studied at the National Academy and with George *Inness. Later he worked and exhibited in England and France. He also traveled elsewhere on the Continent. While living in New York, from 1902 he spent his summers at Old Lyme, where he moved permanently in 1915. Guy's son, **Guy Arthur Wiggins** (1920–   ), paints landscapes, city views, and still lifes. Born in New London, he began painting under his father's instruction. After graduating from Stanford University in 1940, he earned master's degrees at Harvard University and the London School of Economics. Although he became a foreign service officer, he maintained his interest in art, studying at the Corcoran School of Art (now Corcoran College of Art and Design) in Washington, D.C., and elsewhere. In 1975 he turned to painting full time, pursuing additional training at the *Art Students League and traveling abroad. He lives in New York. From 1985 until 1999 he maintained a second home near Lambertville, New Jersey, across the Delaware River from *New Hope.

Wiles, Irving Ramsay (1861–1948). Painter. Among the most popular American portrait painters of his day, he also painted landscapes, marine subjects, and *genre scenes. Born in upstate Utica, he grew up in New York City. In 1879 he enrolled at the *Art Students League, where he developed a lasting friendship with his most influential teacher, William Merritt *Chase. In Paris between 1882 and 1884, Wiles studied at the Académie Julian and in the atelier of Émile-Auguste Carolus-Duran. Upon his return to New York, he supplemented painting with illustration for at least a decade. He also worked in watercolor and pastel. As his reputation grew, he increasingly turned his attention to portraiture, rendering sitters in a fluid, yet solidly constructed style. He also won praise for such genre paintings as *The Sonata* (Fine Arts Museums of San Francisco, 1889), picturing two attractive young ladies making music. The darkened interior sets off shimmering dresses painted with a fluency suggestive of John Singer *Sargent's portraits. During summers particularly, he also painted freer landscapes indebted to impressionist technique and vision. After 1900 he traveled often, both to Europe and within the United States.

Wiles died at Peconic, on eastern Long Island's North Fork. Originally drawn to the area in the mid-1890s to establish a summer painting school, he had lived there year-round for some years. The school replaced the Silver Lake Art School, where he had taught during the previous decade, west of New York's Finger Lakes region. His father had founded the school near Perry, his birthplace, in the late 1870s, and the two continued to teach together at Peconic. **Lemuel Maynard Wiles** (1826–1905), known principally as a landscape painter, worked in a style indebted to the *Hudson River School. He graduated from the New York State Normal School (now the State University of New York at Albany) in 1847. Largely self-taught as a painter, he worked with William MacDougal *Hart in Albany and in the early 1850s received some assistance from Jasper *Cropsey in New York. He moved there permanently shortly after Irving's birth but subsequently accepted teaching positions outside the city. Travels to the West and to Panama in the 1870s provided many subjects, but he was best known for views of rural New York State. Irving's daughter **Gladys Lee Wiles** (1890–1984), also known as Mrs. W. R. Jepson, a painter mainly of portraits but also other subjects, studied with Chase and Kenyon *Cox.

Wiley, William T. *See* FUNK ART.

Wilfred, Thomas (1889–1968). Artist who worked with light. His keyboard instrument, the Clavilux, or color organ, used painted glass, mirrors, colored lights, and polarizers to create diaphanous, ever-changing veils of color on a screen. He numbers among early visual artists to incorporate movement and duration into his artistic expression. Through his work, Wilfred aspired to connect human consciousness with universal, transcendental rhythms. His "lumia" art form (as he called it) attracted attention in the popular press and among avant-garde artists and photographers, including Roberto *Matta, László *Moholy-Nagy, and Francis *Bruguière. Born Richard Edgar Løvstrøm in Naestved, Denmark, he studied music and art in Copenhagen, London, and Paris. In 1905 he began to experiment with light as an abstract artistic medium, probably the first to do so. In 1916 he emigrated to the United States and by 1919 had built a Clavilux. He gave the first public performance of his visual music in New York in 1922. From 1930 until 1943 he headed the Art Institute of Light, devoted to scientific investigation of the aesthetic possibilities of light. He gave regular weekly concerts in its New York quarters, where his Clavilux was installed. He also built about two dozen additional versions of his instrument (later examples included electronic programming), as well as other related devices. He died in a Nyack, New York hospital near his home in West Nyack.

Williams, Emmett. *See* FLUXUS.

Williams, William (1727–91). Painter. Chiefly a portraitist, he adapted rococo style for an American audience. His paintings display precise detail, delicate coloring, and imaginative charm. Williams's wide range of pursuits and his colorful life suggest an inventive, adventurous personality. Like many colonial artists, he engaged in a range of income-producing activities besides painting. Offering instruction in music and drawing, he was ready also to paint signs and ships as well as undertake other forms of decoration, restoration, and framing. In 1759 he received handsome pay for stage sets, probably the first professionally executed in the colonies. His novel, *The Journal of Llewellin Penrose, A Seaman*, may have been the first written in North America, although it was not published until 1815 and then only in altered form in England. (An accurate text appeared in the United States in 1969.) As well as conversation pieces adapted from an English fashion, he also apparently painted a few independent landscapes. His personal library of imported books and prints further contributed to his impact on American art. Williams was born in Bristol, England. Apprenticed as a mariner, he abandoned his ship to live for two or three years in the Caribbean before arriving in Philadelphia in 1747. Except for a sojourn in the West Indies between 1760 and 1763, he remained in that city until 1769, when he moved to New York. In 1776 he resettled in London, but several years later moved to Bristol, where he died. Among relatively few surviving works, his full-length representation of fifteen-year-old Philadelphian *Deborah Hall* (Brooklyn Museum, 1766) numbers among the most imposing. Fashionably attired, she appears in an elaborate outdoor garden setting that provides a dignified ambience of wealth and privilege. Additionally, the surroundings probably allude to her personal attributes through symbolic elements derived from current emblem books.

Wilmarth, Lemuel. *See* RYDER, ALBERT PINKHAM.

Wilmerding, John. *See* HAVEMEYER, LOUISINE.

Wilson, Alexander (1766–1813). Draftsman. Also a naturalist and poet. Known for the precise, elegant hand-colored images in his nine-volume *American Ornithology* (1808–14), he also wrote the accompanying descriptive texts for this first comprehensive register of American birds. Born in Paisley, Scotland, Wilson left school at the age of ten. In 1779 he began work as a weaver, but later traveled itinerantly as a peddler and published poetry before emigrating in 1794 to the United States. While residing in several communities in eastern Pennsylvania and New Jersey, he worked at varied jobs and taught school. With the encouragement of William *Bartram, in 1804 he began to work in earnest on the survey of American birds to which he devoted the rest of his life. He also became an American citizen in 1804. Between journeys to record new species and solicit subscriptions for his serially issued project, he returned to Philadelphia to oversee printing of the *Ornithology*. A leading engraver of the period, fellow Scotsman Alexander Lawson (1772–1846) produced the illustrations. He had settled in Philadelphia in 1794 and later assisted Wilson in improving his drawing skills. While traveling in Kentucky in 1810, Wilson encountered John James *Audubon, who was inspired to embark on a similarly conceived project. Wilson recorded birds with scientific veracity in a fresh and clear style, but he lacked Audubon's flair for dramatic presentation and his more scientifically and aesthetically sophisticated interest in contextual habitats. Beginning to appear serially only fourteen years after Wilson's death in Philadelphia, Audubon's more powerful *Birds of America* soon eclipsed the reputation of *American Ornithology*. However, many in the scientific community continued to respect the accuracy of Wilson's illustrations. He also published *Poems* (1790).

Wilson, Fred. *See* AFRICAN-AMERICAN ART.

Wilson, Martha. *See* PERFORMANCE ART.

Wimar, Charles (1828–62). Painter. Known particularly for depictions of the West and its Indian inhabitants, he also painted portraits. Born in Siegburg, near Bonn, Karl (or Carl) Ferdinand Wimar lived in Cologne before emigrating with his family in 1843 to St. Louis, which remained his permanent home. There he worked for about four years with French-born artist Léon de Pomarède (1807–92). After traveling with him up the Mississippi River in 1849, Wimar assisted in painting a *panorama depicting the river. The trip encouraged Wimar's interest in wilderness and frontier subjects, as did the Indians he met when they visited St. Louis. Early in 1852 he arrived in Düsseldorf to study at the art academy, where Emanuel *Leutze numbered among his teachers. He absorbed the polished, highly realistic style popular there and began to paint dramatic narratives of Indian life, based on his own studies or the published work of others. After his return in 1856, he made several forays west, sketching and collecting Indian artifacts. He also numbered among the first to photograph indigenous western peoples. Characteristically portraying action, such as hunting or warfare (sometimes directed against whites), his tribal paintings nevertheless incorporate exacting details of costume, equipment, and behavior. During these years he also experimented with a softer technique, as in *Indians Approaching Fort Union* (Washington University Gallery of Art, St. Louis, 1859). Here a majestic, atmospherically rendered sweep of sky and earth envelops the aboriginal travelers, achieving a poetic integration of man and landscape. The year before his death from tuberculosis, he completed the first murals (now largely destroyed) to appear west of the Mississippi, in the dome of the St. Louis courthouse.

Winogrand, Garry (1928–84). Photographer. A leader in the development of street photography, he remains known for candid, naturalistic pictures of people, but also possessed an unusual knack for portraying animals. Like Walker *Evans and Robert *Frank, whose work he admired, he merged documentary photography with a personal artistic sensibility. His odd angles of vision, dramatic juxtapositions, subjects in action, and multiple centers of interest produce tense images embodying anxieties and psychological ruptures of modern life. At the same time, a cooler, more neutral tone than Frank's suggests the work of social landscape photographers such as Lee *Friedlander. Winogrand famously summarized his purpose in a wryly disingenuous remark: "I photograph to find out what something will look like photographed." What his subjects "look like" is frequently remarkably complex, and his apparently straightforward content often carries a surrealistic or comic edge.

Born in New York, Winogrand studied painting for a year at City College of New York, following a two-year stint in the U.S. Army Air Force. In 1948 he enrolled at Columbia University, but left to attend Alexey *Brodovitch's photojournalism classes at the New School for Social Research (now New School). After quickly finding success as a magazine photographer, in 1955 he set out across the country in search of a more personal form of expression. Eventually he financed his art with teaching rather than commercial work, as he continued to survey the nation's physical and psychological tenor in travels around the country. Winogrand moved from New York to Austin, Texas, in 1973, then settled in Los Angeles in 1978. He died in Tijuana, Mexico, while undergoing treatment for cancer. Among Winogrand's publications, two focus on relationships between people and animals: *The Animals* (1969), a charming survey of zoo life inside and outside the cages, and *Stock Photographs: The Fort Worth Fat Stock Show and Rodeo* (1980). Winogrand sought to show "the effect of media on events" in *Public Relations* (1977), a collection of pictures taken between 1969 and 1976. Surpassing this goal, in actuality he recorded the climate of moral and political extravagance that marked American society in the early 1970s.

Winstanley, William. *See* PANORAMA.

Wirsum, Karl. *See* CHICAGO IMAGISM.

Woelffer, Emerson. *See* TAWNEY, LENORE.

Wolcott, Marion Post (1910–90). Photographer. Remembered almost entirely for direct, unsentimental, and perceptive Depression-era documentary work from the South and New England, she hoped to relieve the distress of the rural poor by drawing attention to their predicament. However, on occasion her camera captured the persistence of middle-class standards or, less often, the continuity of privilege. In Florida she investigated downtrodden African-American migrant workers but also photographed "Two Young Couples in a Juke Joint, near Moorehaven, Florida" (1939), depicting nicely dressed white sweethearts in a booth at a bare-bones roadhouse. In New England, where she captured direct democracy in action at town meetings, she also documented wealthy skiers descending on the region. Born in Bloomfield, New Jersey, Marion Post grew up in nearby Montclair. As a young woman she studied modern dance in New York with Ruth St. Denis and Doris Humphrey before becoming a teacher. While traveling and studying from 1932 to 1934 in Europe, she began taking photographs. After her return, she taught for another year before turning full time to freelance photography. In 1938 she accepted a position with the *Farm Security Administration. While maintaining a residence in Washington, D.C., she traveled extensively until 1941, when marriage to Agriculture Department official Leon Oliver Wolcott effectively ended her career. They lived in rural Virginia, where she raised a family and again returned to teaching. Later, when her husband was assigned to foreign postings for the State Department, she traveled with him. During these years, she did not work professionally but continued to photograph her family, the landscape, and her journeys. After 1975, when she returned to photographing more regularly, she usually employed color film. In the late 1970s she settled in California, where she died at her home in Santa Barbara. *FSA Photographs/Marion Post Wolcott* (1983) surveys her work for the federal agency.

Wollaston, John (probably before 1720–75 or later). Painter. His style of portraiture, offering a new level of chic, took New York by storm after he arrived from London in 1749. At least until Joseph *Blackburn started working in New England a few years later, he was North America's best-trained painter. Only Jeremiah *Theus, working in distant Charleston, South Carolina, could offer a version of the newly fashionable rococo that Wollaston dispensed. After three years in New York, Wollaston worked for about a year and a half in the mid-Atlantic region. In Virginia from 1755 through most of 1757 (or possibly into 1758), he then moved on to Philadelphia. Between mid-1759 and the fall of 1765, when he appeared in Charleston, his whereabouts are undocumented, but evidence suggests he remained abroad, very likely in the West Indies. In 1767 he repatriated permanently to England, where he was last recorded in 1775. Born in London, Wollaston was probably the son of a portrait painter also named John. (His surname is sometimes spelled Woolaston or Woolston.) The younger Wollaston's first documented work dates to 1742, although several attributed pieces were completed earlier. As he achieved moderate success in the English capital, Wollaston's style evolved from the heavy, Knelleresque, late Baroque style of his father's generation to the lighter rococo that he imported to America. A pronounced mannerism, the tendency to slant eyes toward an almond shape, derives from English fashion of the 1740s. This affectation must have appealed to style-conscious colonists, for a number of native artists imitated the effect. Although stiffness in composition and poses marks much of Wollaston's formulaic work, colonists were apparently dazzled by his ability to confirm their social standing with glamorous costumes and a mood of festive nonchalance. After he left New York, Wollaston's paintings became more ambitious. Larger in size, more monumental, and usually including landscape backgrounds or other elaborate settings and props, they may reflect the greater wealth and more grandiose ambitions of mid-Atlantic and Southern colonists.

Wood, Beatrice (1893–1998). Painter, collage artist, draftswoman, printmaker, and ceramist. Leading lady of *New York dada, she remained active almost to the end of her 105 years, working in later years primarily with ceramics. Born in San Francisco, she spent much of her childhood in New York and was educated at a private boarding school in Bryn Mawr, Pennsylvania. Off to Paris while still in her teens, she studied art and acting until returning to New York in 1914. There, her career in modern art began after a chance meeting in 1916 with Marcel *Duchamp, who invited her to share his studio. Through him, she met Walter *Arensberg and became a regular guest at the avant-garde gatherings in his apartment. With the French writer Henri-Pierre Roché, she and Duchamp founded the dada magazine *The Blind Man* in 1917. (In its two issues, it created a stir, then expired.) During these years she began to create whimsical, often autobiographical drawings, watercolors, and collages. In 1918 she moved to Montreal to work in the theater but two years later returned to New York. In 1928 she relocated to the Los Angeles area. There, at the age of forty, she began an intensive involvement with clay, studying with several ceramic masters. She at first focused on humorous figurines, but her true accomplishment as an artist began only after she moved permanently to Ojai, northwest of the city, in 1948. She developed an unparalleled mastery of luster glazes, which she applied to simple, often unrefined bowls, chalices, and other traditional shapes. Attaining her finest artistic expression in her eighties and nineties, Wood continued to work at her potter's wheel every day until two years before her death. She published several books, including *I Shock Myself: The Autobiography of Beatrice Wood* (1985) and an account of her travels in India, *The Thirty-Third Wife of the Maharajah* (1992). Her personality partially inspired the female character at the center of Roché's novel *Jules and Jim* (later a François Truffaut film), as well as the centenarian who framed the narrative in the 1997 movie *Titanic*, directed by her Ojai neighbor James Cameron.

Wood, Grant (1891–1942). Painter and printmaker. Meticulously detailed scenes of American life and history brought him fame in the 1930s as a leader of the regionalist tendency within the *American Scene movement. Although he sought a distinctly American art rooted in the land and its citizenry, wry satirical elements contribute pungent overtones. Among the country's best-known paintings, Wood's *American Gothic* (Art Institute of Chicago, 1930), depicts a stone-faced, small-town patriarch and his dutiful spinster daughter (actually, the artist's dentist and sister) dressed in old-fashioned clothing and posed before a prim, white frame house featuring a Gothic-style window below its gabled roofline. Do they represent admirable American virtues of hard work, clean living, and Christian piety? Or is the artist poking fun at his subjects for their rigid, provincial way of life? The ambiguous painting's long-lived popularity reflects the range of interpretations that viewers of different backgrounds can bring to it. Moreover, informed viewers can savor its sophisticated composition and impeccable technique, while the painting's clear realism and decorative surface appeal to those with little knowledge of art history.

Born on a farm near Anamosa, Iowa, Grant DeVolson Wood moved with his family when he was ten to nearby Cedar Rapids, where he graduated from high school. He first studied art during summer sessions of 1910 and 1911 at the Minneapolis School of Design, Handicraft, and Normal Art, where he worked under a leading *Arts and Crafts advocate. Remaining essentially self-educated as an artist, for the next seventeen years his development proceeded slowly and irregularly, as he produced unexceptional impressionist portraits, landscapes, and still lifes. He attended some classes at the State University of Iowa (now University of Iowa) in Iowa City and at the School of the Art Institute of Chicago. Between 1920 and 1926 he made three trips to Europe, principally to Paris, where he again studied briefly, although he also painted in the French countryside and traveled to Italy. During these years, he also taught in public schools, designed jewelry and fine metalwork, and served in the U.S. Army as a camouflage specialist for about a year starting in late 1917. A fourth trip to Europe finally catalyzed his mature style in 1928. After designing a stained glass window for the Veterans Memorial Building in Cedar Rapids, Wood spent the autumn months supervising its fabrication in Munich. There, he renewed his appreciation of fifteenth- and sixteenth-century Northern Renaissance painting and probably saw examples of the latest German art movement, *Neue Sachlichkeit* (New Objectivity), which also featured a form of hard realism.

Among the first works in his mature personal style, *Woman with Plants* (Cedar Rapids [Iowa] Museum of Art, 1929) continues in the landscape background his prior loose technique, but the three-quarter length seated image of his mother reflects Flemish prototypes, such as the work of Hans Memling. The next year, Wood painted the first of his landscapes in the new style, *Stone City* (Joslyn Art Museum, Omaha, Nebraska), which reveals more clearly his developing penchant for decorative simplification of form.

In 1931 Wood applied his new manner to a historical theme, the *Midnight Ride of Paul Revere* (Metropolitan Museum), giving both drama and charm to the well-known fable seen from a bird's-eye view. Wood's painstaking technique of oil glazes restricted his output, but together his relatively few finished paintings catalogue an affectionately observed view of American life, spiced with satire directed at pretension, conceit, and other common foibles. The calculatedly naive effect of his approach, particularly visible in stylized, rolling landscapes, serves to heighten the uncertainty of Wood's meanings, for it can be seen as underlining the innocence of American life or mocking its narrowness. In the 1930s art critics and the popular press propelled Wood to national prominence by assigning him to a triumvirate of leading regionalists, along with Thomas Hart *Benton and John Steuart *Curry. Amid boosterism for a uniquely American art, the complexity of his vision often was lost. Recent scholarship has further suggested that the equivocation evident in the meaning of many works may reflect a mode of self-concealment necessary to a gay man living in an unsympathetic era and region. With two other artists, in the early 1930s Wood founded an art colony and school in Stone City, near Cedar Rapids, and for some months in 1934 he served as an administrator for a *federal art project in Iowa. After taking up lithography in 1937, over the next few years he produced a substantial number of prints. Wood died in Iowa City where he had served on the university faculty (except for a leave during the 1940–41 academic year) since 1934. Owned and administered by the Cedar Rapids Museum of Art, Wood's Cedar Rapids studio is open for public tours on a limited schedule.

Wood, Joseph. *See* JARVIS, JOHN WESLEY.

Wood, Thomas Waterman (1823–1903). Painter and etcher. Known particularly for *genre scenes, he painted portraits as well. The detailed settings of some portraits give these the air of independent genre subjects. Wood played a conspicuous part in the institutional art life of New York. He belonged to several important organizations and served as president of the American Water Color Society (1878–87) and of the *National Academy of Design (1891–99). In addition, in 1895 he founded a museum in Montpelier, Vermont, his birthplace and longtime summer home. His donation to what is now the T. W. Wood Gallery at Vermont College included several dozen of his own paintings, as well his copies of European specimens and works by contemporary American artists. Largely self-taught as an artist, while living in Boston during the mid-1840s Wood profited from the example of Chester *Harding's work and may have received instruction from him. By 1852 Wood had established a portrait studio in New York, but he also worked itinerantly during the next several years. He had begun to produce genre works by 1858, before he departed to travel and study in Europe. There he may have spent some time at the Düsseldorf Academy, but he traveled widely, investigating contemporary art and copying old masters. Following his return to the United States in 1859, he lived in Nashville, Tennessee, and Louisville, Kentucky, before settling permanently in New York in 1866. Wood employed a hard, detailed realism that enhanced the clarity of his anecdotal dramas of middle-class life. In a departure from conventional genre subjects of the period, Wood sympathetically recorded African Americans and their circumstances in a number of paintings. He generally offered a sweetened, unproblematic view of a vanishing way of life, which, together with his conservative style, gave his work an old-fashioned tone before the end of his career.

Woodman, Donald. *See* CHICAGO, JUDY.

Woodruff, Hale (1900–1980). Painter and printmaker. Known first for expressionistic interpretations of African-American life and history, he later contributed to *abstract expressionism. He also painted portraits, still lifes, and landscapes. Born in Cairo, Illinois, Hale Aspacio Woodruff grew up in Nashville and began his training at the Herron School of Art (now Herron School of Art and Design of Indiana University-Purdue University Indianapolis). He left in 1927 for Paris, where he took classes and sharpened his appreciation of modernism. He also sought out Henry Ossawa *Tanner at his home in Normandy. Upon his return in 1931 Woodruff took a teaching job in Atlanta, where he became an active participant in the city's cultural life. In 1936 he traveled to Mexico to study mural painting with Diego Rivera. This experience prepared him for several commissions from *federal art projects and educational institutions, notably three murals recounting the narrative of the *Amistad* mutiny in a vigorously descriptive style (Talladega [Alabama] College, 1938–39). Here and in many works of the 1930s he demonstrated the racial pride encouraged by the *Harlem Renaissance, as well as the *American Scene movement's interest in particulars of the nation's daily life and history. In 1946 Woodruff moved to New York, where he taught at New York University while developing an abstract expressionist style. Although he often incorporated African motifs into abstract compositions, he came to believe that it was foolhardy for African-American artists to emphasize racial difference. *Carnival* (Wadsworth Atheneum, Hartford, Connecticut, 1950), an abstract arrangement of colorful, angular forms, bears no direct relationship to black life, but *Celestial Gate* (Spelman College, Atlanta, 1969), a glowing and freely brushed invention, includes forms from Ashanti gold weights and Dogon carved doors. In the early 1960s Woodruff numbered among the major participants in the African-American *Spiral group. Following retirement from NYU in 1968, he continued to reside in New York, where he died.

Woodstock, New York. *See* ARTISTS' COLONIES.

Woodville, Richard Caton (1825–55). Painter. A *genre specialist, he spent most of his career painting American subjects while living in Europe. Though they are relatively few, he also executed portraits and historical or literary anecdotes. A Baltimore native, Woodville entered the University of Maryland medical school there in 1842 but left after a year. His tastes in art were formed in part by Robert *Gilmor's collection, which included genre paintings by William Sidney *Mount and others, as well as seventeenth-century Dutch examples. In 1845 Woodville went to Düsseldorf. There he acquired sophisticated technical skills while studying at the academy for a year and then privately with Carl Ferdinand Sohn. Düsseldorf's predilection for precise realism, smooth finish, and anecdotal subject matter reinforced prior interests. Woodville had brought to Europe sketches of American scenes, which he soon began to use as the basis for meticulous small paintings of middle-class life. In the spring of 1851 Woodville moved to Paris but two years later relocated to London, where he spent most of his few remaining years. At least twice during his European sojourn, he returned to the United States to seek additional material for paintings, which he regularly dispatched to American venues instead of showing them in Europe. Woodville died in London of a morphine overdose, perhaps accidentally ingested. Among his best-known paintings, *War News from Mexico* (Manoogian Foundation, on loan to National Gallery, 1848) characterizes the qualities that brought him acclaim. Along with a complex but well-defined composition and wealth of miniaturistically scaled, subordinate detail, his clear colors, able draftsmanship, and deftly handled light provide visual appeal and narrative associations. In this dramatically charged moment, set within a shallow box of space, representative American types cluster around a newspaper reader. Augmenting the impact of the work, certain details acknowledge the war's potential effect on such important issues as slavery and territorial expansion. Widely praised when it was shown for several months in 1849 at the *American Art-Union, the painting became one of the best-known mid-century images when the organization subsequently distributed fourteen thousand prints of it. Like other subsequent works, his depiction of three men in a tavern interior, *Waiting for the Stage* (Corcoran Gallery, 1851), employs similar elements to create a more intimate, psychologically nuanced image. His son, also Richard Caton Woodville, a painter and illustrator usually known professionally as **Caton Woodville** (1856–1927), was born in London after the death of his father. In his youth he lived in St. Petersburg. Later he, too, studied in Düsseldorf and resided for a time in Paris before settling permanently in London. He became widely known for battle scenes. His *Random Recollections* appeared in 1914.

Works Progress Administration-Federal Art Project (WPA-FAP). *See* FEDERAL ART PROJECTS.

Wright, Patience Lovell (1725–86). Sculptor. The first professional sculptor active in the American colonies, she fashioned wax heads in the round or in relief. Because her medium was so perishable, only a single known work survives, but she was acclaimed in her own time in Europe as well as in America. Born in Bordentown, New Jersey, Patience Lovell grew up on a farm and was self-taught as an artist. Widowed with five children in 1769, she used her artistic talent to support her family. Wright specialized in highly lifelike wax images, which she colored and supplied with eyelashes, eyebrows, and other features to enhance their realism. Anticipating the techniques of the French-born Londoner Marie Tussaud, she supplied some of the three-dimensional heads with clothed bodies and exhibited them on tour, with much success. She lived in New York before departing in 1772 for London, where her exhibition of celebrity figures drew numerous viewers. She soon received many portrait commissions, primarily for profile reliefs. From abroad she continued to contribute to a Philadelphia waxworks run by her sister Rachel Lovell Wells (1735–96), also a wax modeler. An ardent patriot, Wright may have gathered intelligence (supposedly from chattering clients) during the American Revolution. It is more firmly documented that she opened her house to Americans and corresponded with leaders of the nascent nation.

She later also worked in Paris but died in London. The intense realism of Wright's approach foreshadowed late-eighteenth- and nineteenth-century aesthetic interests, while her showmanship contributed to the early development of mass commercial entertainment.

Joseph Wright (1756/57–93), a son named for his father, worked as a portrait painter, sculptor, printmaker, and medallist. Also born at Bordentown, he studied at the Academy of Philadelphia (now University of Pennsylvania) from 1769 until 1772 before following his mother to London. In 1775 he became the first American-born student admitted to the Royal Academy Schools, where he studied until 1781. Benjamin *West numbered among his teachers. His likenesses earned some success in London and in Paris before he returned to America in 1782 to continue his career as a portrait painter. He lived in Philadelphia until 1786, when he moved to New York for about four years before returning permanently to Philadelphia. His 1783 clay bust (unlocated) ranks as the first known portrait sculpture of George Washington. During the final two years before his premature death during a yellow fever epidemic, he ranked as the foremost designer of coins and medals for the new United States Mint.

Wright, Willard Huntington. *See* MACDONALD-WRIGHT, STANTON.

Wyant, Alexander Helwig (1836–92). Painter. Devoted to landscape, in early work he reflected prevailing *Hudson River School standards but later, while retaining an affection for closely observed detail, preferred a richly worked, moody form of expression, more consonant with the growing taste for *Barbizon-inspired work. His subtle color harmonies, controlled luminosity, and predilection for meditative understatement ally his mature style with *tonalism. Throughout, his work suggests a melancholy subjectivity. Born in Evans Creek, Ohio, south of Cleveland, he soon moved across the state to Defiance, where he grew up. As a young man he began painting landscapes while working as a sign painter. After encountering George *Inness's work in Cincinnati in 1857, Wyant soon visited New York to meet him and in 1860 returned there for a year of study. After additional preparation in Cincinnati, in 1863 he moved permanently to New York. Impressed by the hyperrealistic landscapes of Hans Friedrich Gude, a Norwegian painter associated with the Düsseldorf School, in 1865 Wyant journeyed to Karlsruhe to study with him but remained only a few months. While abroad, he completed his most important Hudson River-style work, the meticulously rendered *Tennessee* (formerly, *Mohawk Valley;* Metropolitan Museum, 1866), a large and somber panorama. After resettling in New York in 1867, he gradually began to assimilate more atmospheric and painterly tendencies into his realistic vocabulary, reflecting Inness's continued influence and the enthusiasm he had developed on a visit to London for John Constable's work. Fond of watercolor, he regularly exhibited works in this medium. An arduous 1873 journey through New Mexico and Arizona with a federal geological survey team precipitated a breakdown in his health. Incapacitated on his right side by a stroke, he trained himself to paint with his left hand. Although this practice may have contributed to the more generalized approach of his later work, finely detailed passages also occur. Drawn for summer visits from the mid-1870s to the Adirondack village of Keene Valley, after marriage in 1880 to a student, painter **Arabella Locke Wyant** (?–1919), he resided there much of the time through the subsequent decade. Although he continued to maintain a New York studio, from 1889 he resided chiefly in the Catskills art colony of Arkville, where his home overlooked the Delaware River. Restricted by increased paralysis during these final years, he painted intimate, evocative works commingling memory with observation. At his death in New York, he numbered among the most highly regarded landscapists of his day.

Wyeth, Andrew (1917–). Painter. A hugely popular realist of great technical dexterity but little conceptual originality, he specializes in contemplative figural works, nature studies, and domestic interiors. Tempering painstaking detail with a grayed palette, differentially focused areas of indistinct softness, unusual light effects, and cleverly manipulated spaces, he develops a slightly melancholy aura of expectation, mystery, and spirituality around otherwise commonplace subjects. For the most part, his work bypasses the modern world in its subjects and grapples with few intellectual issues. Nearly all of Wyeth's work has been executed in water-based paints, either watercolor (typically in a dry brush technique) or tempera. A lifelong resident of Chadds Ford, Pennsylvania, Andrew Newell Wyeth has based his vision largely on his experience of that area of the Brandywine River valley west of Philadelphia. The vicinity of his longtime summer home on the Maine coast in Cushing, south of Rockland, has also been important. A frail child, he was tutored at home and never attended college or art school. At twenty, he mounted his first one-person show in New York. It quickly sold out, setting him on the road to commercial success. His characteristic fusion of style and subject has changed little since it definitively coalesced in the early 1940s. In *Christina's World* (Museum of Modern Art, 1948), Wyeth's most famous painting and more genuinely affecting than most, crisp technique and haunting atmosphere suggest the *magic realism popular during the 1930s and 1940s. Sitting on the ground in an expansive field, the artist's Cushing neighbor Christina Olson twists in apparent yearning toward a remote farmhouse that mirrors her own isolated and vulnerable condition. Whether or not the viewer knows that the subject had been crippled by polio, the image summons an ambiguous mélange of emotions and has been called a symbol of the human condition. (Made famous by the painting and today a property of the Farnsworth Art Museum in nearby Rockland, the Olson house is open for public tours.)

In 1976 the *Metropolitan Museum of Art staged an enormous retrospective of Wyeth's work, the first ever devoted to a living, American-born artist. Ten years later media attention swirled around Wyeth (his work appeared on the covers of both *Time* and *Newsweek*) when a sizeable group of works known as the Helga paintings (1971–85) first became publicly known. Picturing a solidly built, blonde neighbor in various states of dress and nudity, they fueled speculation about the artist's private life. About one hundred of the works appeared in a touring exhibition that originated the following year at the *National Gallery of Art. Around the same time, the artist purchased a decommissioned lighthouse on an island not far from his Maine home for use as a studio and part-time residence. Although he commutes by private plane between his Maine and Pennsylvania residences, his tasteful images generally continue to romanticize rustic dilapidation and an alienated psychology.

His father and early artistic mentor, **N. C. Wyeth** (1882–1945), was a leading illustrator of adventure narratives and children's books during an era when that art flourished. Wishing to be taken seriously as a painter, he also produced landscapes and figural works, but these generally demonstrate less originality than his illustrations. Born on a farm near Needham, Newell Convers Wyeth received early training in nearby Boston before departing in 1902 for the Brandywine Valley. There he studied in Wilmington, Delaware, for several years with one of the period's foremost graphic artists, book and magazine illustrator Howard Pyle (1835–1911), a specialist in historical subjects and action stories. Wyeth soon established his permanent home in Chadds Ford and in the early 1920s, bought a residence at Port Clyde, not far from Cushing, initiating the family tradition of summering in Maine. He excelled at representing motion and characterizing emotionally gripping fictional moments. Slightly flattened space, patterned forms, and brilliant, sometimes unnaturalistic colors generate vivacious and forceful images. He died when a railroad train slammed into his car near Chadds Ford. Under the aegis of the Brandywine River Museum in Chadds Ford, his house and studio are open for public tours.

Andrew's son **Jamie Wyeth** (1946–), also a painter, has extended his father's exacting realism into more psychologically fraught territory. Born in Wilmington, James Browning Wyeth, like his father, grew up in Chadds Ford, was educated at home (after sixth grade), and mounted his first one-person New York show at the age of twenty. He has devoted much attention to portraiture, notably including an unsettling likeness of Andy *Warhol (Cheekwood Museum of Art, Nashville, Tennessee, 1976) and a Rudolf Nureyev series, as well as to careful depictions of individual animals, such as *Portrait of a Pig* (Brandywine River Museum, 1970). Other works present conundrums with surrealistic overtones. After purchasing Rockwell *Kent's Monhegan Island residence directly from the older artist in the late 1960s, he subsequently painted many local subjects. In the early 1990s he added his father's lighthouse studio to his properties, which include also a farm on the Brandywine near Chadds Ford. At the Farnsworth Art Museum, the Wyeth Center provides a venue for the study of regional work by three generations.

Two of Andrew's sisters also became painters who shared his penchant for detailed realism. **Henriette Wyeth** (1907–97) and **Caroline Wyeth** (1909–94) were educated at Quaker Friends' schools and learned to paint as Andrew did, in their father's studio. In 1929 Henriette married Peter *Hurd, who assisted Andrew in mastering tempera technique. From 1938 they lived on a ranch in the New Mexico hills near San Patricio, west of Roswell. She specialized in portraits, but also painted still lifes and, occasionally, other subjects. Caroline remained all her life in the family home and played a significant role in training Jamie. She painted still lifes and other subjects related to the Brandywine area.

Wylie, Robert (1839–77). Painter. A specialist in scenes of French peasant life, he also painted landscapes. Regarded as the founder of the art colony in Pont-Aven, he resided in Brittany for most of his short career and came to be as highly respected in France as he was in the United States. His picturesque Breton interiors explore details of costume and setting with painterly brushwork and rich chiaroscuro that underscore the solemn dignity of his rural subjects. Born at Douglas on the British Isle of Man and orphaned as a child, he lived in Philadelphia under the care of an uncle. He trained as a carver of ivory umbrella handles before becoming an expert draftsman at the *Pennsylvania Academy of the Fine Arts. He had begun sculpting before he visited London in 1859 or 1860. To continue his studies, he arrived in Paris at the end of 1863 and soon turned entirely to painting. During the summer of 1864 he first visited Pont-Aven and a year or two later became the first artist to settle in the village. He fully adopted its way of life and eventually died there of tuberculosis. As an enthusiast for the locale and the only American artist known to have learned the Celtic Breton language, the personable young man spearheaded the village's development as an art colony. Other Americans soon attracted there included Frederick *Bridgman, Thomas *Hovenden, and William Lamb *Picknell. Wylie's closely observed and sympathetic studies of his unsophisticated neighbors appealed to romantic fascination with the supposed strength and virtue of "primitive" country people, thought to be uncorrupted by industrialization and secular materialism. As the artist recognized, however, their isolation and ignorance sometimes had unhealthy consequences. *A Fortune Teller of Brittany* (Corcoran Gallery, c. 1872) highlights an elderly sorceress who frightens a young woman as others look on in consternation. Reflecting Wylie's characteristically intimate grasp of local customs, it also recalls Baroque and nineteenth-century realist precedents in its deft composition and dramatic illumination.

y

Youngerman Yunkers YOUNG

Yoshida, Ray. *See* CHICAGO IMAGISM.

Young, Mahonri (1877–1957). Sculptor, painter, and printmaker. Known particularly for tabletop bronzes of laborers and athletes, he also modeled American Indian subjects and completed several works related to his Mormon heritage. In forming his naturalistic approach, he rejected modern innovation and academic tradition while learning from both. Born in Salt Lake City, a grandson of founder Brigham Young, Mahonri Mackintosh Young lived on a farm in early childhood but from 1884 resided in the city. Without finishing high school, he began his art studies in his hometown before moving in 1899 New York, where he worked at the *Art Students League with Kenyon *Cox. In 1901 he continued on to Paris for additional study. Following his return in 1905, he lived in Salt Lake City for five years before settling in New York. Inspired in Paris by depictions of workers in Jean-François Millet's paintings and in Constantin Meunier's sculptures, he soon produced small bronzes depicting physical labor. *Man with a Wheelbarrow* (Whitney Museum, 1915) dignifies an unglamorous worker whose lower-class origins find parallels in the subjects of *Ashcan School paintings and Abastenia St. Leger *Eberle's sculptures. However, socially conscious sculpture found little public appeal, and after the *Armory Show—which he helped to organize—Young turned increasingly to other themes. Three trips to the Southwest between 1912 and 1918 provided material for works devoted to American Indians. In the 1920s he lived again in Paris for two and a half years, during which he produced many of his popular prizefighter sculptures, such as *Groggy* (Whitney Museum, 1926). While teaching frequently from 1916 until 1943 at the Art Students League, in 1931 he married painter Dorothy *Weir. For Salt Lake City, in 1947 he completed a vast monument, *This Is the Place*, commemorating his ancestors' arrival in the area. A monumental marble portrait of Brigham Young, installed in Statuary Hall of the U.S. Capitol in 1950, was his last major work. In addition to paintings, he also produced a body of prints, mostly etchings. In poor health during his final years, he died in a Norwalk, Connecticut, hospital, not far from his long-time summer residence. His son, art historian **Mahonri Sharp Young** (1911–96), published several books about American art, including *The Eight: Realist Revolt in American Painting* (1973), *Early American Moderns: Painters of the Stieglitz Group* (1974), and *American Realists: Homer to Hopper* (1977), as well as a monograph on George *Bellows (1973). Born in New York, he graduated in 1933 from Dartmouth College in Hanover, New Hampshire, and earned a master's degree at New York University in 1951. From 1942 until 1946 he served in the U.S. military. In 1953 he became director of the Columbus (Ohio) Gallery of Fine Arts (now Columbus Museum of Art). After retiring in 1976, he lived on eastern Long Island, where he died at Bridgehampton.

Youngerman, Jack (1926–). Painter, sculptor, and printmaker. He made his reputation in the 1960s with large, brightly colored abstractions, generally focused on a few cleanly defined, jagged-edged shapes, tightly locked into the picture plane. Related to the generally less agitated work of his friend Ellsworth *Kelly, these canvases contributed to the popularity of 1960s *hard-edge painting. Born in St. Louis, Youngerman studied at the University of North Carolina before entering military service in 1944. Two years later he resumed his education at the University of Missouri. After receiving a BA in 1947, he left for Europe. In Paris, where he befriended Kelly, he studied in 1947–48 at the École des Beaux-Arts. Before settling in New York in 1956, he traveled extensively in Europe and worked on projects in Lebanon and Iraq with French architect and urban planner Michel Ecochard. Drawn to Matisse, Mondrian, and other masters of simplified form, while still in Europe he began painting the bold shapes that characterize his mature work. In New York, he gradually abandoned an impasto technique in favor of smooth paint application, showing little trace of brushwork. By the late 1960s, he often employed less expressionistic, sensuous forms abstracted from nature and set within ambiguous figure-ground relationships. Since the 1970s, he has turned increasingly to sculpture. In the 1990s and after, his three-dimensional work culminated in large, spiraling, columnar works indebted to Brancusi (whose studio he visited during his formative years) and in painted plywood reliefs that recall works by Arp. Crafted from laminated layers and featuring sensuously polished wood surfaces, the columns reengage the modern search for ideal form, while the wall pieces jump with quirky energy. As a printmaker, Youngerman has worked in several media but primarily lithography. He lives in Bridgehampton, near the eastern end of Long Island.

Yunkers, Adja (1900–1983). Printmaker and painter. Associated with *abstract expressionism during the 1950s and 1960s, he subsequently simplified his approach without relinquishing its emphasis on the poetic and painterly. Noted for complex color woodcuts, he worked as well in other print media, including intaglio, lithography, and screen print. He also favored pastel. Born in Riga, Russia (now Latvia), from 1914 he studied art in St. Petersburg. Three years later he embarked on a peripatetic existence of three decades, working and continuing to study in Paris and elsewhere in Europe, as well as in Latin America. In 1939 he settled in Stockholm, where he edited and published two art magazines, *Ars* and *Creation*. In 1947 he moved to the United States and was naturalized as a citizen six years later. A celebrated woodcut polyptych numbered among works that positioned Yunkers as a leader of the 1950s woodcut resurgence. Comprising twenty-eight blocks, each printed in multiple colors, the abstract *Magnificat* (1953) measures fourteen feet wide. After 1960 he became more interested in lithography. Although he worked in New Mexico shortly after his arrival in the United States and later taught occasionally elsewhere, he resided primarily in New York, where he died.

In 1952 he married art critic and historian Dore Ashton (1928–), noted particularly for writings on abstract expressionism and the *New York School. She brings to her consideration of these artists a rich philosophical, literary, and historical context. Born in Newark, New Jersey, she earned a bachelor's degree at the University of Wisconsin in 1949 and a master's degree from Harvard University the following year. After serving for three years as an editor at *Art Digest*, she wrote art criticism for the *New York Times* from 1955 until 1960. Since 1968 she has been a professor at Cooper Union. She has also lectured widely and curated a number of exhibitions. *The Unknown Shore: A View of Contemporary Art* (1962) provides an informed and personal response to abstract expressionism and related European work. *The New York School: A Cultural Reckoning* (1973; published the previous year in England as *The Life and Times of the New York School: American Painting in the Twentieth Century*) scrutinizes cultural conditions sustaining mid-twentieth-century American art. Her other books include *Modern American Sculpture* (1968), *A Reading of Modern Art* (1969), and *A Fable of Modern Art* (1980). In addition, she has published monographs on Joseph *Cornell, Philip *Guston, Richard *Lindner, Isamu *Noguchi, and Mark *Rothko, among others, and has compiled anthologies of artists' writing. She and Yunkers separated before his death, and in 1985 she married critic and writer Matti Megged. She lives in New York.

Z

ZERBE

Zorach

Zakanitch, Robert Rahway. *See* PATTERN AND DECORATION.

Zerbe, Karl (1903–72). Painter. Although much of his work employs the traditional oil medium, he was known for reviving the ancient technique of encaustic, or wax painting. However, because of its negative effect on his health after about a decade of exposure, in 1949 he turned instead to polymer tempera and then, several years later, to acrylic. Stylistically, Zerbe's predominately figurative work reflects broad acquaintance with modern art, including the work of Picasso, Max Beckmann, and the Mexican muralists. Expressionism proved a significant source, but he sometimes incorporated imaginative elements suggesting surrealism. He often painted clowns whose melancholy demeanor suggests their human plight. Zerbe also produced more abstract work, which draws on cubism and other modern traditions. Born in Berlin, he moved with his family as an infant to Paris, then to Frankfurt in 1914. In 1921 he began training in Munich, where he continued to live, except for a sojourn in Italy from 1924 to 1926 and an extended visit to Paris in 1930–31. Recognized as a leading young painter in his native country, as a Jew he fled the Nazi takeover. Following a visit to the United States in 1934 and subsequent return to Paris, in 1935 he settled in Boston. There he soon accepted an invitation to head the painting department at the School of the Museum of Fine Arts. He was naturalized as a citizen in 1939. After 1955 he taught at Florida State University in Tallahassee but continued to summer on Cape Cod. He died in Tallahassee.

Zorach, William (1889–1966). Sculptor and painter. Although an accomplished painter, after 1922 he specialized in carved wood or stone renderings of simplified, often chunky human figures and animals. Born Zorach Samovich in Eurberich, Russia (now Jurbarkas, Lithuania), in 1893 he moved with his family to Port Clinton, Ohio, before settling in Cleveland three years later. Without finishing grade school, he left to work for a commercial lithographer. In 1905 he began his professional training in evening classes at the Cleveland School (now Institute) of Art and in 1908 enrolled at the *National Academy of Design. More briefly, he also studied at the *Art Students League before leaving at the end of 1910 for a year in Europe. In Paris he encountered modern art, as well as his future wife, painter and printmaker Marguerite Thompson, his guide to the new tendencies. Almost immediately, his painting responded to fauvism's bright colors, exaggerated forms, and spontaneous brushwork. After returning for a year to Cleveland, late in 1912 he married Marguerite in New York. Known since grade school as William Finkelstein, at this time he changed his surname to Zorach. The couple lived in Greenwich Village, summered at various country locations, exhibited in the 1913 *Armory Show and the 1916 *Forum Exhibition, and around 1915 together came under the spell of cubism, which they integrated with studies from nature. His *Mirage—Ships at Night* (Smithsonian American Art Museum, 1919) combines aspects of both into a visionary image of boats on a moonlit sea.

In 1917 he first tried his hand at sculpture and by 1922, had decided to devote himself to this medium, although he continued throughout his career to work actively in watercolor. Zorach numbers among the first American sculptors to respond to African tribal work. He also was drawn to other premodern traditions, including archaic Greek, Mesopotamian, and Egyptian sculpture, as well as the refined, reductive formalism of Brancusi, whom he had met in Paris. From these sources he forged a personal style of blocky solemnity, simplified shapes, and distortion for emotional power. While also emphasizing inherent qualities of his materials, he enhanced these "primitive" qualities with direct carving, which was uncommon in American sculpture of the early 1920s. The half-length marble *Child with Cat* (Museum of Modern Art, 1926) exemplifies his compact approach to form, effective use of unpolished surfaces, and dignified expression. Later he also modeled with clay. Through his studio creations and public commissions, his articulate commentaries, and his many years of teaching, Zorach exerted a major influence on the development of American sculpture.

Beginning in 1929, he taught at the *Art Students League for three decades. He died in a hospital in Bath, Maine, near the waterside village of Robinhood on Georgetown Island, where the Zorachs had owned a summer home since 1923. In 1945 two articles about his own work appeared as a volume titled *William Zorach*. He also published *Zorach Explains Sculpture: What It Means and How It Is Made* (1947) and *Art Is My Life: The Autobiography of William Zorach* (1967).

Marguerite Thompson Zorach (1887–1968), born in Santa Rosa, California, and raised in Fresno, sailed in 1908 to Paris, where she admired the art of the Matisse and the fauves. In 1911 she traveled around the world, via Venice, the Near East, Asia, and back to California. She spent the summer of 1912 painting and writing poetry in the Sierra Nevada Mountains, responding to the grandeur and emotional power of nature. Following her first one-person exhibition later that year in Los Angeles, she left for New York and married William the day after her arrival. Although the influence of cubism after about 1915 made her paintings more somber and less spontaneous, she continued in her best work to convey a deeply felt response to nature. *Half Dome, Yosemite Valley, California* (Brooklyn Museum), a watercolor done on a trip the Zorachs took in 1920, depicts the landmark mountain in a composition of flattened, somewhat angular forms realized in shades of tan, brown, and leaden blues and greens. The patterning of this work relates to the embroidered "tapestry paintings" that she had already begun to make. Although she continued to paint, needlework became the dominant medium of her art, especially in the 1920s. Often she used an intentionally naive style for these decorative works. Mostly dating before the mid-1930s, her prints, including etchings, linocuts, and lithographs, augment her reputation as a skillful and spirited designer. Her late paintings are predominately landscapes. The Zorachs collaborated on many projects, and she also proved instrumental to her husband's success as a sculptor. He often relied upon her preliminary drawings, which sometimes included the original sketches of an idea. Because of her unselfish devotion to his career and her own attraction to embroidery, a medium not frequently accorded the same respect as painting, her reputation as an artist failed to fulfill the promise of her highly original early work. She died in a hospital near her home in Brooklyn, where she and her husband had resided since 1935. The Zorachs' daughter, Dahlov Ipcar (1917–), a painter, printmaker, illustrator, and muralist, is best known for expressionistic, semi-abstract paintings of animals. Born in Windsor, Vermont, she grew up in New York. Encouraged as an artist by her parents, she did not pursue formal training. Since shortly after her marriage in 1936 to Adolph Ipcar, she has resided in Georgetown, near her parents' summer residence. As an author and illustrator, she is known for numerous children's books. The Zorachs' son, **Tessim Zorach** (1915–95), was a collector who specialized in pre-Columbian work from Ecuador.

Zucker, Joe. *See* NEW IMAGE PAINTING.

LaVergne, TN USA
19 November 2010

205486LV00001B/1/P